3 1994 01528 7086
FEB 19 2015
SANTA ANA PUBLIC LIBRARY
D0034747

lonely planet

Argentina

918.20473 BAO
Bao, Sandra
Argentina

$27.99
CENTRAL 31994015287086

THIS EDITION WRITTEN AND RESEARCHED BY

Sandra Bao,
Gregor Clark, Carolyn McCarthy, Andy Symington, Lucas Vidgen

PLAN YOUR TRIP

OBELISCO, BUENOS AIRES P66

MICHAEL TAYLOR /GETTY IMAGES ©

TOUCAN, IGUAZÚ FALLS P195

JOHN W BANAGAN /GETTY IMAGES ©

ON THE ROAD

Contents

MONTEVIDEO, URUGUAY
P514

ON THE ROAD

LONELY PLANET /GETTY IMAGES ©

Contents

FÚTBOL (SOCCER) SPECTATORS P80

UNDERSTAND

SURVIVAL GUIDE

SPECIAL FEATURES

Welcome to Argentina

It's apparent why Argentina has long held travelers in awe: tango, beef, gauchos, fútbol, Patagonia, the Andes. The classics alone make a formidable wanderlust cocktail.

City Life

Arriving in Buenos Aires is like jumping aboard a moving train. Outside the taxi window, a blurred mosaic of a modern metropolis whizzes by, and then the street life appears – the cafes, the purple jacaranda flowers draped over the sidewalks (in spring!) and *porteños* (residents of Buenos Aires) in stylish clothing purposefully walking past handsome early-20th-century stone facades. And it's not just Buenos Aires that's a stunner – Córdoba, Salta, Mendoza and Bariloche each have their unique personalities and unforgettable attractions, so don't miss them.

Natural Wonders

From mighty Iguazú Falls in the subtropical north to the thunderous, crackling advance of the Glaciar Perito Moreno in the south, Argentina is a vast natural wonderland. The country boasts some of the Andes' highest peaks. It's home to rich wetlands that rival Brazil's famous Pantanal, mountains painted in rustic colors, deserts dotted with cacti, massive ice fields and arid steppes in Patagonia, cool lichen-clad Valdivian forests, Andean salt flats, a spectacular Lake District, penguins, flamingos, capybaras and more. All are stunning sights and adventures just waiting to be experienced.

The Cuisine

Satisfying that carnal craving for juicy steak isn't hard to do in the land that has perfected grilling wonderfully flavorful sides of beef. *Parrillas* (steak restaurants) are everywhere and will offer up any cut you can imagine. And if you're a fan of pizza and pasta, these Italian staples are ubiquitous as well. But there's more – in Buenos Aires you can experience a huge variety of ethnic cuisine, from Southeast Asian to Middle Eastern to Scandinavian. Down it all with that famous Argentine wine, and you'll be struggling to maintain your waistline.

Argentine Culture

Tango is possibly Argentina's greatest contribution to the outside world, a steamy dance that's been described as 'making love in the vertical position.' And what about *fútbol* (soccer)? Argentines are passionately devoted to this sport and, if you're a fan, experiencing a live match should definitely be on your itinerary. Add a distinctive Argentine take on literature, cinema, music and arts, and you have a rich edgy culture – part Latin American and part European – that you can't help but fall in love with.

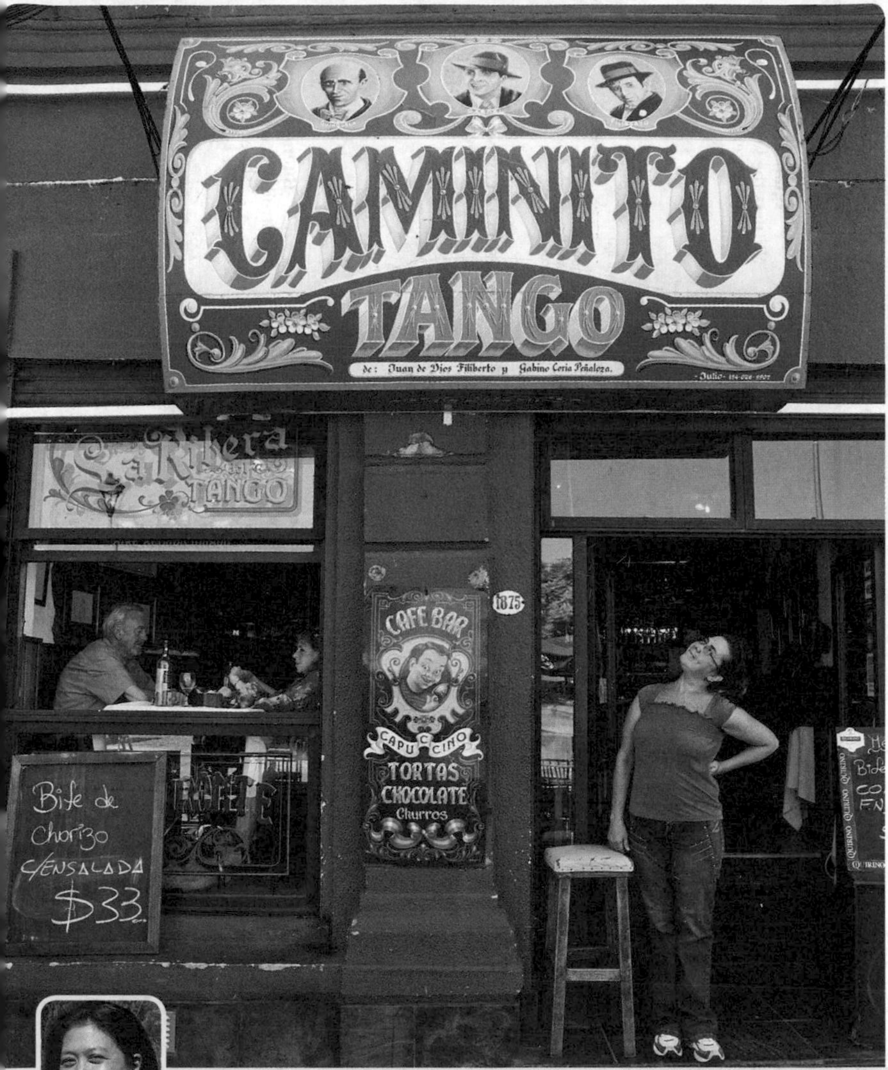

Why I Love Argentina

By Sandra Bao, Author

Argentina is my country – this is where I was born and raised, where I lived until my family emigrated to the USA. It's changed drastically since I was a little girl, but what I love most about Argentina is its people. They've nurtured their creativity, adaptability and perseverance, through good and very bad times, all while maintaining their traditions, humor and pride. I'm always happy to go back to this amazing place and its inhabitants – it's been a real privilege.

For more about our authors, see p640

Above: Bar on El Caminito (p69), Buenos Aires

Argentina & Uruguay

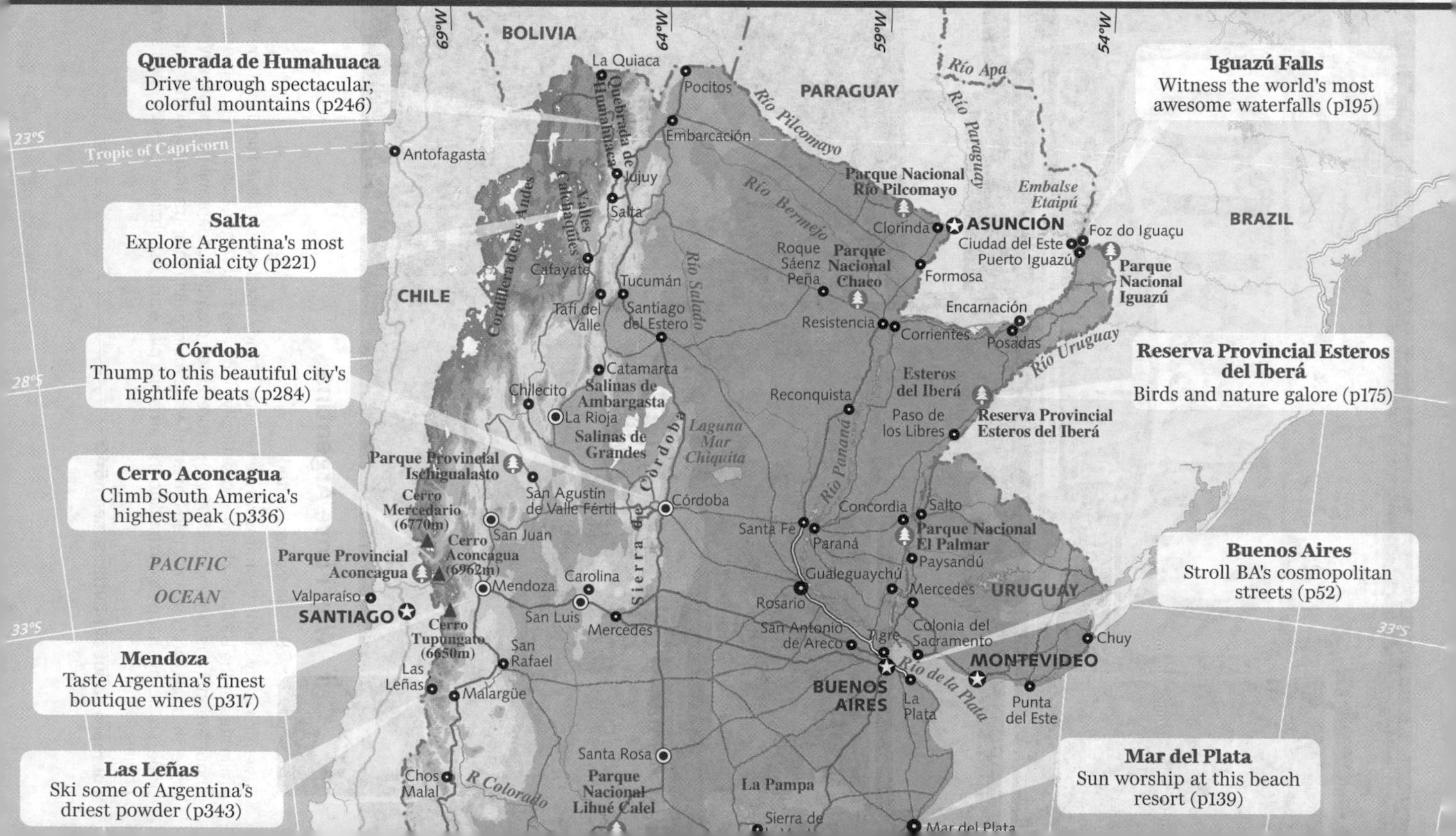

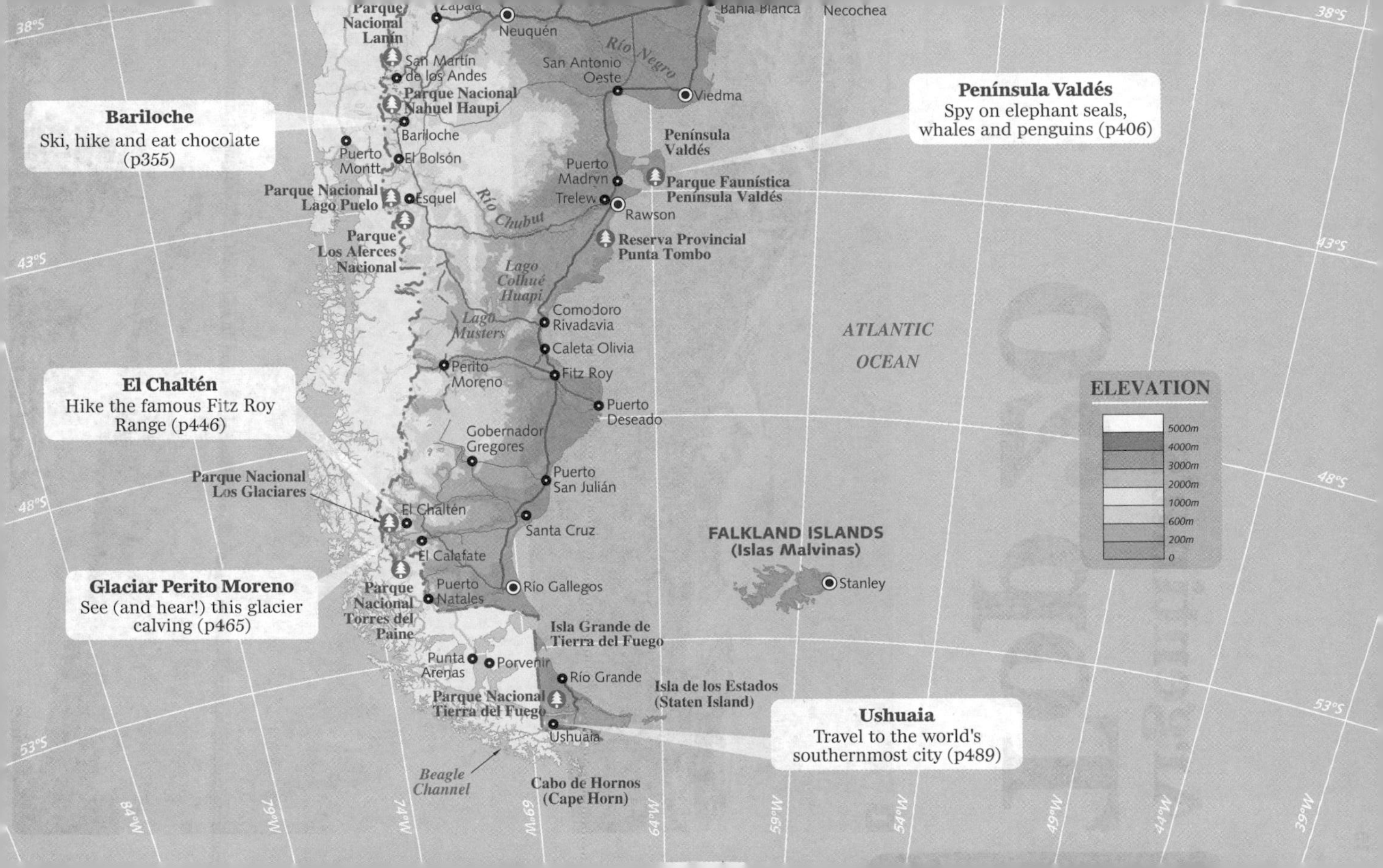
Bariloche
Ski, hike and eat chocolate (p355)
El Chaltén
Hike the famous Fitz Roy Range (p446)
Glaciar Perito Moreno
See (and hear!) this glacier calving (p465)
Península Valdés
Spy on elephant seals, whales and penguins (p406)
Ushuaia
Travel to the world's southernmost city (p489)
ATLANTIC OCEAN
ELEVATION
5000m
4000m
3000m
2000m
1000m
600m
200m
0
FALKLAND ISLANDS
(Islas Malvinas)
Stanley
Parque Nacional Lanín
Zapala
Neuquén
Bahía Blanca
Necochea
San Martín de los Andes
Parque Nacional Nahuel Haupi
Bariloche
Puerto Montt
El Bolsón
Parque Nacional Lago Puelo
Esquel
Parque Los Alerces Nacional
Río Negro
San Antonio Oeste
Viedma
Península Valdés
Puerto Madryn
Trelew
Rawson
Parque Faunística Península Valdés
Reserva Provincial Punta Tombo
Río Chubut
Lago Colhué Huapi
Lago Musters
Comodoro Rivadavia
Caleta Olivia
Fitz Roy
Perito Moreno
Puerto Deseado
Gobernador Gregores
Puerto San Julián
Parque Nacional Los Glaciares
El Chaltén
Santa Cruz
El Calafate
Parque Nacional Torres del Paine
Puerto Natales
Río Gallegos
Isla Grande de Tierra del Fuego
Punta Arenas
Porvenir
Río Grande
Isla de los Estados (Staten Island)
Parque Nacional Tierra del Fuego
Ushuaia
Beagle Channel
Cabo de Hornos (Cape Horn)
38°S
43°S
48°S
53°S
84°W
79°W
74°W
69°W
64°W
59°W
54°W
49°W
44°W
39°W

Argentina's Top 20

1

Glacier Perito Moreno

1 As glaciers go, Perito Moreno (p464) is one of the most dynamic and accessible on the planet. But what makes it exceptional is its constant advance – up to 2m per day. Its slow but constant motion creates incredible suspense as building-sized icebergs calve from the face and spectacularly crash into Lago Argentino. You can get very close to the action via an extended network of steel catwalks and platforms. A typical way to cap the day is with a huge steak dinner back in El Calafate.

Iguazú Falls

2 The peaceful Río Iguazú, flowing through the jungle between Argentina and Brazil, plunges suddenly over a basalt cliff in a spectacular display of sound and fury that is truly one of the planet's most awe-inspiring sights. Iguazú Falls (p195) is a primal experience for the senses: the roar, the spray and the sheer volume of water will live forever in your memory. But it's not just the waterfalls; the jungely national parks that contain them offer a romantic backdrop and fine wildlife-watching opportunities.

DAMIEN SIMONIS/GETTY IMAGES ©

MICHAEL RUNKEL/GETTY IMAGES ©

Quebrada de Humahuaca

3 You're a long way from Buenos Aires up here in Argentina's northwestern corner, and it feels a whole world away. This spectacular valley of scoured rock (p246) in Jujuy province impresses visually with its tortured formations and artist's palette of mineral colors, but it is also of great cultural interest. The Quebrada's settlements are traditional and indigenous in character, with typical Andean dishes supplanting steaks on the restaurant menus, and llamas, not herds of cattle, grazing the highland grass. Below: Cerro de los Siete Colores (Hill of Seven Colors, p247)

Cementerio de la Recoleta

4 A veritable city of the dead, Buenos Aires' top tourist attraction (p71) is not to be missed. Lined up along small 'streets' are hundreds of old crypts, each uniquely carved from marble, granite and concrete, and decorated with stained glass, stone angels and religious icons. Small plants and trees grow in fissures while feral cats slink between tombs, some of which lie in various stages of decay. It's a photogenic wonderland, and if there's a strange beauty in death you'll find it in spades here.

3

REPORTAGE/GETTY IMAGES ©

4

Hiking the Fitz Roy Range

5 With rugged wilderness and shark-tooth summits, the Fitz Roy Range (p452) is the trekking capital of Argentina. Experienced mountain climbers may suffer on its windswept and tough world-class routes, but the beautiful hiking trails are surprisingly easy and accessible – and park rangers help orient every traveler who comes into the area. Once on the trail, the most stunning views are just a day hike from town. Not bad for those who want to reward their hard work with a craft beer at El Chaltén's nearby La Cervecería brewpub.

Wine Tasting around Mendoza

6 With so much fantastic wine on offer, it's tempting just to pull up a bar stool and work your way through a list – but getting out there and seeing how the grapes are grown and processed is almost as enjoyable as sampling the finished product. The best news is that wine tasting in Argentina isn't just for the wine snobs – there's a tour (p321) to meet every budget, from DIY bike tours for the backpackers to tasting-and-accommodation packages at exclusive wineries.

Ushuaia, the End of the Earth

7 Location, location, location. Shimmed between the Beagle Channel and the snowcapped Martial Range, this bustling port (p489) is the final scrap of civilization seen by Antarctica-bound boats. Snow sports brighten the frozen winters and long summer days mean hiking and biking until the wee hours. Happening restaurants, boisterous bars and welcoming B&Bs mean you'll want to tuck in and call this port home for a few days.

Buenos Aires' Food Scene

8 Believe the hype: Argentine beef is some of the best in the world. Eat, drink and be merry at one of the country's thousands of *parrillas* (steak restaurants), where a leisurely meal can include waiters pouring Malbec and serving up slabs of tasty steaks. But there's so much more in Buenos Aires (p88) – closed-door restaurants, pop-up restaurants and molecular gastronomy have all become buzzwords in Argentina's capital city, where you can also find nearly any kind of exotic ethnic cuisine.

7

8

CHRISTIAN HEINRICH/GETTY IMAGES ©

SHAUN LOMBARD/GETTY IMAGES ©

Gaucho Culture

9 One of Argentina's most-enduring icons is the intrepid gaucho, who came to life after Spaniards let loose their cattle on the grassy pampas so many centuries ago. These nomadic cowboys lived by taming wild horses (also left by the Spaniards), hunting cows and drinking *mate* (a bitter ritual tea). Today the best place to experience gaucho culture is during November's Día de la Tradición (p123) in San Antonio de Areco. Otherwise check out folkloric shows at *estancias* (ranches) or at the Feria de Mataderos in Buenos Aires.

Ruta de los Siete Lagos

10 A journey of extraordinary beauty, the Ruta de los Siete Lagos (p373; Seven Lakes Route) is a not-to-be-missed road trip. Your vehicular adventure winds through lush forests, past waterfalls and dramatic mountain scenery, and skirts the various crystal-blue lakes that give it its name. Stop for a picnic and go swimming, fishing and camping. You can also bus it in a couple of hours or bike it in four days – but experiencing this gorgeous route is a decision you won't regret.

Top right: Lago Falkner

Nightlife in Córdoba

11 Boasting seven universities (and counting), it's no surprise that Argentina's second city (p284) is one of the best places for night owls in the entire country. The wide variety of cute sidewalk bars, thumping megadiscos and live-music venues (all more or less within walking distance) could keep you occupied for months. While you're in town, try to catch a *cuarteto* show – popular all over the country, this music style was invented in Córdoba and all the best acts regularly play here.

DAN HERRICK/GETTY IMAGES ©

San Telmo

12 One of Buenos Aires' most charming and interesting neighborhoods is San Telmo (p66), lined with cobblestone streets, colonial buildings and a classic atmosphere that will transport you back to the mid-19th century. Be sure to take in the Sunday *feria* (street fair), where dozens of booths sell handicrafts, antiques and knickknacks, while buskers perform for loose change. Tango is big here, and you can watch a fancy, spectacular show or catch a casual street performance – both will wow you with amazing feats of athleticism. Above: Feria de San Telmo (p108)

Bariloche

13 A gorgeous lakeside setting, adjacent to one of the country's more spectacular and accessible national parks, makes Bariloche (p355) a winning destination year-round. During winter you can strap on the skis and take in the magnificent panoramas from on top of Cerro Catedral. Once the snow melts, get your hiking boots out and hit the trails in the Parque Nacional Nahuel Huapi, where a well-organized network of mountain refuges means you can keep walking as long as your legs will take it. Top right: Parque Nacional Nahuel Huapi (p362)

Reserva Faunística Península Valdés

14 Once a tawny, dusty peninsula with remote sheep ranches, today Península Valdés (p406) is a hub for some of the best wildlife-watching on the continent. The main attraction is seeing endangered southern right whales get acrobatic and up close. But the cast of wild characters also includes killer whales (orcas), Magellanic penguins, sea lions, elephant seals, rheas, guanaco and numerous sea birds. There's a ton to be seen on shore walks, but diving and kayak tours take you even deeper into the ambience. Above: Southern elephant seal

Skiing at Las Leñas

15 Hitting the slopes at Las Leñas (p343) isn't just about making the scene, although there is that; this mountain has the most varied terrain, the most days of powder per year and some of the fastest and most modern lift equipment in the country. Splash out for some on-mountain accommodation or choose from a variety of more reasonably priced options just down the road, but whatever you do, if you're a snow bunny and you're here in season, mark this one on your itinerary in big red letters.

Colonial Salta

16 Argentina's northwest holds its most venerable colonial settlements, and none is more lovely than Salta (p221). This beautiful city is set in a fertile valley that acts as a gateway to the impressive Andean cordillera not far beyond. Postcard-pretty churches, a sociable plaza and noble buildings give it a laid-back historic ambience that endears it to all. Add in great museums, a lively folkloric music scene, some of the country's most appealing lodging and a fistful of attractions within easy reach: that's one impressive place. Bottom: Basilica de Salta

17

IAN TROWER/GETTY IMAGES ©

18

Jesuit Missions & Estancias

17 The Jesuits brought some fine things to Argentina – wine making and universities just to name two. They also constructed some gorgeous missions and *estancias*. Many are wonderfully preserved, listed as Unesco World Heritage sites and open to the public, often featuring fascinating museums. The crowds can't detract from the palpable sense of history in Alta Gracia, but if you'd like to have one to yourself (and maybe even sleep in the old slave quarters), head for the *estancia* Santa Catalina (p302). Top left: San Ignacio Miní (p191)

Reserva Provincial Esteros del Iberá

18 These protected wetlands (p175) offer astonishing wildlife-watching opportunities around shallow vegetation-rich lagoons. Head out in a boat and you'll spot numerous alligators, exotic bird species, monkeys, swamp deer, and possibly the world's cutest rodent, the capybara – but no, you can't take one home. It's an out-of-the-way location, and a wealth of stylish, comfortable lodges make this a top spot to book yourself in for a few days of relaxation amid an abundance of flora and fauna. Top right: White-necked heron

Cerro Aconcagua

19 The tallest peak in the western hemisphere, Aconcagua (p336) is an awe-inspiring sight, even if you're not planning on climbing it. People come from all over the world to do so, though it's not a task to be taken lightly. But if you can take the time to train and acclimatize and you're good enough to reach the top, you'll be granted the bragging rights as one of a select group that has touched the 'roof of the Americas.' Otherwise, just get a peek at it from the nearest vantage point and save your energy for wine tasting in Mendoza.

Mar del Plata

20 Argentina's premier beach resort (p139) is a heaving zoo in summer – but that's what makes it such fun. Compete with *porteños* (Buenos Aires residents) for a patch of open sand, then lie back and enjoy watching thousands of near-naked bodies worship the sun, play sand games or splash around in the surf. Outdoor activities such as surfing, fishing, horseback riding and even skydiving are also on deck. When the sun goes down it's time for steak or seafood dinners, followed by late-night entertainment from theater shows to nightclubs.

CRAIG PERSHOUSE/GETTY IMAGES ©

Need to Know

For more information, see Survival Guide (p597)

Currency
Argentine peso (AR$)

Language
Spanish

Visas
Generally not required for stays of up to 90 days. Americans, Australians and Canadians must pay a 'reciprocity fee' before arriving.

Money
ATMs widely available. Credit cards accepted at most midrange to top-end hotels, restaurants and shops, and some budget places. Black market for US dollars exists in Buenos Aires and some other cities around Argentina.

Cell Phones
Local SIM cards (and top-up credits) are cheap and widely available, and can be used on unlocked GSM 850/1900-compatible phones.

Time
Argentina Standard Time (GMT/UTC minus three hours).

When to Go

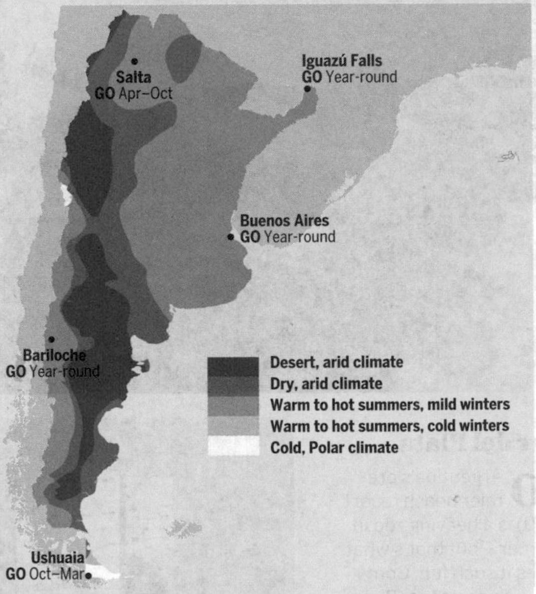

High Season (Nov–Feb & Jul)

- Patagonia is best (and most expensive) December to February.
- Crowds throng to the beaches from late December through January.
- For ski resorts, busiest times are June to August.

Shoulder (Sep–Nov & Mar–May)

- Temperature-wise the best times to visit Buenos Aires.
- The Lake District is pleasant; leaves are spectacular in March.
- The Mendoza region has its grape harvests and wine festival.

Low Season (Jun–Aug)

- Good time to visit the North.
- Many services close at beach resorts, and mountain passes can be blocked by snow.
- July is a winter vacation month, so things can get busy at some popular destinations.

Websites

Argentina Independent (www.argentinaindependent.com) Current affairs and culture, plus much more.

Argentine Post (www.argentinepost.com) Useful wide-ranging articles on BA and Argentina.

Lonely Planet (www.lonelyplanet.com/argentina) Destination info, hotel bookings, forums and more.

Important Numbers

Argentina country code	☎54
Directory assistance	☎110
International access code	☎00
National Tourist Information (in BA)	☎11-4312-2232
Police	☎101; ☎911 in some large cities

Exchange Rates

Australia	A$1	AR$7.04
Brazil	R$1	AR$3.32
Canada	C$1	AR$7.02
Chile	CH$100	AR$1.36
Euro zone	€1	AR$10.85
Japan	¥100	AR$7.70
NZ	NZ$1	AR$6.65
UK	UK£1	AR$12.99
Uruguay	UR$1	AR$0.35
USA	US$1	AR$7.80

For current exchange rates see www.xe.com.

Rates on the Rise

Lonely Planet aims to give its readers as precise an idea as possible of what things cost. Rather than slapping hotels or restaurants into vague budget categories, we publish the actual rates and prices that businesses quote to us during research. The problem is that prices change, especially in Argentina, where inflation runs rampant. But we've found that readers prefer to have real numbers in their hands.

Argentina remains a decent-value destination. Although we anticipate prices will continue to rise, we provide the prices given to us at the time of research. Call or check a few hotel or tour-operator websites before budgeting for your trip.

Daily Costs

Budget: Less than US$60

- ➡ Dorm bed: US$15–20
- ➡ Double room in good budget hotel: US$70
- ➡ Cheap main dish: under US$12

Midrange: US$60–120

- ➡ Three star–hotel room: US$90–175
- ➡ Average main dish: US$12–16
- ➡ Four-hour bus ticket: US$25

Top End: US$120 and up

- ➡ Five-star hotel room: US$200
- ➡ Fine main dish: over US$17
- ➡ Taxi trip across town: US$13

Opening Hours

There are always exceptions, but the following are general opening hours. Note that some towns may take an afternoon siesta break.

Banks 8am–3pm or 4pm Monday to Friday; some open till 1pm Saturday

Bars 8pm or 9pm–4am or 6am nightly (downtown, some open and close earlier)

Cafes 6am–midnight or much later; open daily

Restaurants noon–3:30pm and 8pm–midnight or 1am (later on weekends)

Shops 9am or 10am–8pm or 9pm Monday to Saturday

Arriving in Argentina

Aeropuerto Internacional Ministro Pistarini ('Ezeiza'; Buenos Aires) Shuttle buses (AR$90) travel frequently to downtown BA in 40 to 60 minutes; local buses (AR$6) take two hours to reach downtown. Use official city taxi services (AR$270); avoid touts.

Aeroparque Jorge Newberry ('Aeroparque', airport with domestic flights; Buenos Aires) Shuttle buses (AR$34) go frequently to downtown in 10 to 15 minutes, or take bus 33 or 45 (AR$5.50). Taxis cost around AR$50 to downtown or Palermo.

Getting Around

Air Argentina is a huge country, so flights are a good time saver.

Bus The best way to get around Argentina; fast, frequent, comfortable, reasonably priced and cover the country extensively.

Car Renting a car is useful for those who want independence in remote regions like Patagonia.

Train A few train lines can be useful for travelers but generally this is not the most efficient method of transportation.

For much more on **getting around**, see p612

What's New

Mercado Azul

Argentina's *mercado azul* (literally 'blue market', see p604) for US dollars offers significantly more than the official rate, especially in Buenos Aires. The downsides are scams, fakes bills and fly-by-night *cuevas* (unofficial exchange houses). Some hotels, restaurants and shops will give discounts for US-dollar transactions and sometimes change the dollars themselves.

Bike Lanes in Big Cities

Buenos Aires keeps expanding its bike-lane system and even created a free bike-share program – but bike friendliness is spreading to cities such as Córdoba and Mendoza, which boast new bike lanes as well.

Usina del Arte

Buenos Aires' La Boca neighborhood isn't known for upscale buildings, but this gorgeous new music venue – located in a remodeled electricity factory – bucks the trend. (p105)

Faena Arts Center

One of Buenos Aires' newest art spaces is housed in an old Puerto Madero flour mill with the aim of highlighting gigantic, larger-than-life installations. (p62)

Huella Andina

This new long-distance trail stretches 430km from Neuquén to Chubut provinces and through a national park. One day it's expected to link more than 600km of trails. (p432)

La Casona de Odile Hostel

Just outside El Bolsón, set on 2 hectares in the countryside, is one of Argentina's best hostels. The peaceful vibe and amenities – including an on-site microbrewery – can't be beat. (p367)

Museo de la Ciudad

La Rioja's new art gallery is a beautifully restored old building, offering temporary exhibits and historical items. (p61)

Ecoposada del Estero

Great for visiting Los Esteros del Iberá, this ecolodge provides not only comfortable beds but also great bird-watching – it's at the edge of a marshland. (p177)

Cristo del Portezuelo

While passing through scenic Chilecito, don't miss the great views from this huge Christ statue, accessed via 200 steps along terraced cactus gardens. (p278)

Museo de los Andes

This new Montevideo museum focuses on the famous 1972 Andean plane crash after which 16 survivors battled harrowing conditions for 72 days before being rescued. (p518)

Mercado Agrícola de Montevideo

Montevideo's newest foodie attraction is in a renovated early-20th-century market building. It has more than 100 merchants, including fruit and veggie vendors, cafes, restaurants and food shops. (p525)

For more recommendations and reviews, see lonelyplanet.com/argentina

If You Like...

Cities

Gourmet restaurants, world-class museums, fine shopping, cutting-edge music and rocking nightlife all contribute towards satisfying your needed dose of big-city culture.

Buenos Aires The mother of all Argentine cities. Plan to spend several days exploring the world-class offerings of this unique and astounding metropolis. (p52)

Córdoba From Jesuit ruins to modern art to *cuarteto* music, you'll experience it in this historic city. (p284)

Salta Argentina's most colonial city offers plenty of culture, from exceptional museums to famous *peñas* where you can experience authentic folk music. (p221)

Bariloche Ski, hike or go whitewater rafting during the day, then munch on chocolate and Patagonian lamb at night. (p355)

Ushuaia Stunningly located at the foothills of the Andes' southernmost reaches, Ushuaia is the world's main departure point for Antarctica. (p489)

Hiking & Mountaineering

Lining Argentina's western edge like a bumpy spine, the Andes rise to nearly 7000m at Aconcagua's peak and offer some of the continent's finest hiking and mountaineering.

Bariloche Set on the shores of Lago Nahuel Huapi, Bariloche is surrounded by snowy peaks that beckon climbers. (p355)

El Bolsón Drawing in hippies like patchouli is this laid-back town with hikes to forests, waterfalls and scenic ridges. (p366)

El Chaltén Argentina's ground zero for premier hiking, boasting gorgeous glaciers, pristine lakes and unparalleled mountain landscapes. (p446)

Mendoza Mountaineers flock here to summit Cerro Aconcagua, South America's highest peak. (p317)

Parque Nacional Torres del Paine This national park is in Chile, but very close to the Argentine border, and has some of the world's best hiking. (p479)

Beaches

Ah, those waves lapping on the shore, salty wind on your face and warm sand between your toes. What says 'vacation' more than a day at the beach? Whether you're looking for a party, adventure sport or isolation, Argentina has it.

Mar del Plata Popular with Argentina's middle class, 'Mardel' turns into the country's biggest summertime party. (p139)

Necochea Miles of beachcombing, decent surf breakers and a pine forest to explore. (p146)

Pinamar Popular destination with variety nearby – from affordable neighborhoods to one of Argentina's most exclusive beach resorts, Cariló. (p135)

Puerto Madryn Whether you like windsurfing, whale-watching or diving, Puerto Madryn caters to your desires. (p400)

Punta del Este Sure, it's in Uruguay, but in summer this famous beach is full of rich Argentines and celebrities, all here to party. (p549)

Food

Argentina is known for its steak, but in Buenos Aires ethnic restaurants abound, and around the country there are tasty regional cuisines.

Buenos Aires Closed-door and other specialty restaurants make this capital city a gourmet's delight. (p88)

Andean Northwest If you make it up north, be sure to try *locro* (a hearty corn-and-meat stew), *humitas* (sweet tamales) and empanadas. (p217)

Atlantic Coast Despite a huge coastline, Argentina isn't known for its seafood. If you're near the sea, however, there are places to sample fish, shrimp, oysters and king crab. (p134)

Lake District The area around Bariloche is known for its wild boar, venison and trout – plus locally made chocolates. (p353)

Patagonia If you like lamb, you'll like Patagonia. Here, *cordero* is on every menu and sheep ranches reign supreme. (p397)

Memorable Landscapes

Argentina is made up of amazing landscapes, from cactus-filled deserts to lofty Andean peaks to deep-blue lakes and verdant forests. Throw in the wonders of Iguazú Falls and Patagonia, and the word 'unforgettable' comes to mind.

Andean Northwest Undulating desert landscapes are punctuated by sentinel-like cacti, alien rock formations and whole mountainsides sporting palettes of colors. (p217)

Iguazú Falls Spanning more than 2.5km, these are the most incredible waterfalls you will ever see, bar none. (p195)

Lake District Argentina's 'little Switzerland' is just that – snow-dusted mountains looming over lakes edged by forest. (p353)

Andes Mountains Strung along the whole of South America, this spectacular mountain range is stunningly beautiful. (p336)

Patagonia Not many regions in the world can evoke the mysticism, wonderment and yearning of Argentina's last frontier – even if most of it is barren, windy nothingness. (p397)

(Top) Magellanic penguin (p434)

(Bottom) Parque Nacional Los Glaciares (North; p452)

Wildlife

Argentina's environments translate into homes for many creatures, from the flightless, grasslands-loving ñandú (rheas) to the majestic Andean condors and pumas, to the desert-dwelling camelids such as llamas, guanacos and vicuñas.

Península Valdés This bleak, oddly shaped peninsula attracts a plethora of wildlife such as southern right whales, elephant seals, Magellanic penguins and orcas. (p406)

Los Esteros del Iberá Rich and amazing wetlands that harbor a wide range of interesting critters, from comical capybaras, black caimans and howler monkeys to countless bird species. (p175)

Iguazú Falls These spectacular falls are located in tropical rainforest that is also home to several kinds of monkey, lizard and bird (including toucans!). Also watch for begging coatis. (p195)

Ushuaia The southernmost city in the world has a few colonies of cormorants, sea lions and even penguins. It's also the stepping-off point to Antarctica, a fantastic wildlife wonderland. (p489)

Wine Tasting

Malbec is the dark, robust plum-flavored wine that has solidly stamped the region of Mendoza on every oenophile's map. But Argentina has other worthy varietals – try a fresh torrontés, fruity bonarda or earthy pinot noir.

Mendoza Argentina's powerhouse wine region, which produces the majority of the country's grapes and boasts countless wineries. (p331)

San Juan Much less famous than its Mendoza neighbor, but well known for its syrah and bonarda; it also boasts a winery located in a cave. (p344)

Cafayate Just south of Salta, this smaller town – second only to Mendoza for its quality wine production – is famed for the torrontés grape, among others. (p236)

Neuquén You don't think of wine when you think of this unremarkable city in the Lake District, but there are a few great wineries nearby. (p393)

Colonial Architecture

While Argentina isn't world-renowned for its unique buildings, its status as an ex-Spanish colony means there are some fine examples of colonial architecture to be found – especially to the north of the country.

Córdoba Argentina's second-largest city boasts a beautiful center dotted with dozens of colonial buildings. (p284)

Salta Don't miss this city's most striking landmark, the colorful and intricate Iglesia San Francisco. (p221)

Tucumán This northern city – Argentina's fifth-largest – has more than its share of beautiful old architecture. (p257)

Buenos Aires It's mostly French- or Italian-styled buildings downtown, but head south to San Telmo for colonial buildings and cobblestone streets. (p52)

Colonia del Sacramento An easy boat ride away from BA lies Uruguay's architectural gem of a town, more popularly called simply 'Colonia.' (p535)

Adventure Sports

As the eighth-largest country in the world, Argentina covers a lot of ground and offers plenty of adventurous sports. Wild rivers, bare cliffs, snowy mountains and high thermals abound, so if you're looking for some adrenaline – you've found it.

Skiing & snowboarding The best ski resorts are Mendoza's Las Leñas & Los Penitentes, Bariloche's Cerro Catedral and San Martín de los Andes' Cerro Chapelco. (p36)

Rafting & kayaking Hit the pristine white waters rushing through the mountains around Mendoza, Bariloche and Esquel. (p38)

Mountain biking The mountains around Bariloche are great for adventurous trails, especially at Cerro Catedral in summer. (p38)

Rock climbing Try Cerro Catedral just outside Bariloche, the rocky walls around El Chaltén and the granite boulders of Los Gigantes, 80km west of Córdoba. Mendoza province also has some hot spots. (p35)

Paragliding Some of the loftiest spots are around La Cumbre, Bariloche and Tucumán. (p38)

Month by Month

TOP EVENTS

Fiesta Nacional de la Vendimia, March

Festival y Mundial de Tango, August

Carnaval, February

Día de la Tradición, November

Vinos y Bodegas, September

January

January is peak summer in Argentina. *Porteños* (residents of Buenos Aires) who can afford it leave their sweltering city and head to the beach resorts, which are very crowded and expensive. It's also high season in Patagonia, so expect top prices there too.

Festival Nacional del Folklore

Near the city of Córdoba, the town of Cosquín hosts the National Festival of Folk Music during the last week of January. It's the country's largest and best known *folklórico* (folk music) festival. (p296)

February

It's still summertime, but crowds at the beaches and in Patagonia start to thin later in the month. The Andean deserts and the Iguazú region continue to be very hot, but it's a great time to visit the Lake District. Mendoza's grape harvest begins.

Carnaval

Though not as rockin' as it is in Brazil, this celebration is very rowdy in the northeast, especially in Gualeguaychú and Corrientes. Montevideo, the capital of Uruguay, is another party spot. Dates vary depending on the city.

Fiesta Nacional del Mar

Celebrate the sea and its riches with Mar del Plata's marine-themed festival, which includes the coronation of a 'sea queen.'

March

Autumn is starting in Argentina and temperatures are more pleasant in Buenos Aires (though it's rainy). Prices fall at the beaches and in Patagonia, but the weather remains warm. The north starts to cool, and Iguazú Falls isn't quite so hot and humid.

Fiesta Nacional de la Vendimia

Mendoza city's nearly week-long Fiesta Nacional de la Vendimia kicks off with parades, *folklórico* events and a royal coronation – all in honor of Mendoza's wines. (p326)

April

The forests of the Lake District start changing from verdant green to fiery reds, yellows and oranges.

DÍA DE LA MEMORIA

Held on March 24 (the date a military coup took over the Argentine government in 1976), this public holiday commemorates the victims of Argentina's Dirty War. Over seven years, tens of thousands of people 'disappeared' and were never heard from again. See p579 for more on this tragedy.

JOHN W BANAGAN/GETTY IMAGES ©

RICHARD I'ANSON/GETTY IMAGES ©

(Top) Tango dancers, La Boca (p67), Buenos Aires
(Bottom) Parade participants, Montevideo Carnaval (p531)

Patagonia is clearing out but you might get lucky with decent hiking weather. Buenos Aires heads into low season, with still-pleasant temperatures.

Festival Internacional de Cine Independiente

Independent film buffs shouldn't miss this festival in BA, which screens more than 100 films from Argentina and Uruguay.

May

It's late autumn and Buenos Aires is cool as the rains die back. It's a good time to visit Iguazú Falls. The crowds also leave Mendoza – though its vineyards are still a gorgeous red from autumn leaves.

Día de Virgen de Luján

On May 8 thousands of devout believers make a 65km pilgrimage to the pampas town of Luján in honor of the Virgin Mary. Other pilgrimages take place in early October, early August, late September and on December 8.

June

Winter begins in Argentina. Services at the beach resorts and in Patagonia begin to dwindle, but it's an ideal time to visit the deserts of the Andean Northwest and the Iguazú Falls, which have less rain and heat at this time of year.

Fiesta de la Noche Más Larga

Ushuaia celebrates the longest night of the year with two weeks' worth of music and shows.

Anniversary of Carlos Gardel's death

On June 24, 1935, tango legend Carlos Gardel died in a plane crash in Colombia. Head to Buenos Aires' Chacarita cemetery to see fans pay their respects at his grave and statue.

July

Ski season is at its peak, so make sure your wallet is packed full and head off to the resorts around Bariloche, San Martín de los Andes and Mendoza. Whale-watching season starts heating up in the Península Valdés area.

Semana de Artesanía Aborígen

In the Lake District's Junín de los Andes, up to 20 surrounding native Mapuche communities get together to show off and sell their traditional arts and crafts.

August

Beach resort towns are dead and Patagonia is desolate and cold. Buenos Aires is still cool, but it's a great time to explore theaters, museums and art galleries.

Festival y Mundial de Tango

World-class national and international tango dancers perform throughout Buenos Aires during this two-week festival. It's a great way to see some of the country's best tango dancers and musicians do their thing.

September

Spring has sprung, and it's peak season for whale-watching (both southern right whales and orcas) around Península Valdés. Polo season begins in Buenos Aires and the ski slopes wind down.

Vinos y Bodegas

Lovers of the grape shouldn't miss this huge Buenos Aires event, which highlights vintages from dozens of bodegas (wineries) all over Argentina.

October

It's a fine time to visit Buenos Aires and Central Argentina. The season is just starting in Patagonia, but the crowds haven't quite descended. Flowers bloom in the Lake District.

Fiesta Nacional de la Cerveza/ Oktoberfest

Join the swillers and oompah bands at Argentina's National Beer Festival, Villa General Belgrano's Oktoberfest in the Central Sierras. (p303)

Eisteddfod

This lively Welsh festival, featuring plentiful grub and choral singing, takes place in the Patagonian towns of Trelew and Trevelin. It's great for one of those wait-am-I-really-in-South-America? moments.

November

In Buenos Aires the weather is perfect and the jacaranda trees show off their blooms. It's a good time to visit the beach resorts and Patagonia; the crowds and high prices are still a month or so away.

Día de la Tradición

This festival salutes the gaucho and is especially significant in San Antonio de Areco, the most classically gaucho of towns. It is also important in the mountain town of San José de Jáchal.

December

Summer begins and it's great beach weather at the resorts (before the January peak). It's also ideal weather for outdoor activities in the Lake District; penguin and hiking season starts in Patagonia.

Buenos Aires Jazz

This big jazz festival takes place over five days in venues all over the city, attracting tens of thousands of spectators. Sometimes takes place in November.

El Tinkunaco

This ceremony takes place on December 31 in the northern city of La Rioja, symbolizing the resolution of a cultural clash between colonizing Spaniards and the Diaguita (an indigenous people).

Itineraries

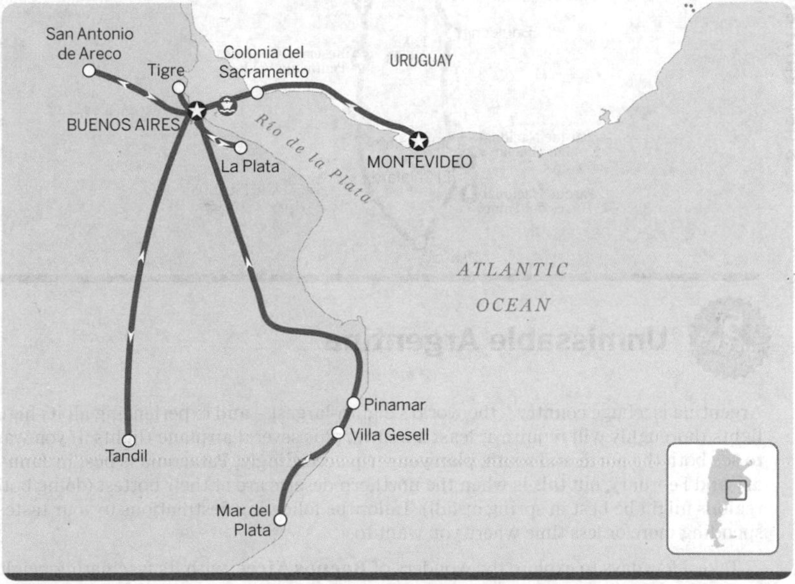

1 WEEK A Week Around Buenos Aires

Seen the capital city from top to bottom and wondering what else to do? Well, if you like water, **Tigre** is a great nearby choice – a bustling delta and popular *porteño* (Buenos Aires resident) getaway. And not far away is peaceful **San Antonio de Areco**, with a history of gaucho culture and surrounded by *estancias* (ranches) – or tidy **La Plata**, with its huge cathedral.

Perhaps you'd prefer the beach? **Pinamar** and **Villa Gesell** make a great summer weekend trip, as does **Mar del Plata** – the biggest Argentine beach destination of them all. Or head inland to **Tandil**, a pretty town near scenic hills and a large recreational reservoir.

And then there's Uruguay – just a (relatively) short boat ride away. **Colonia del Sacramento** is truly charming, filled with cobbled streets and atmospheric colonial buildings, while **Montevideo** is kind of like BA's little sister – smaller and less frantic, but still offering big-city delights such as a beautiful theater, historic downtown and eclectic architecture.

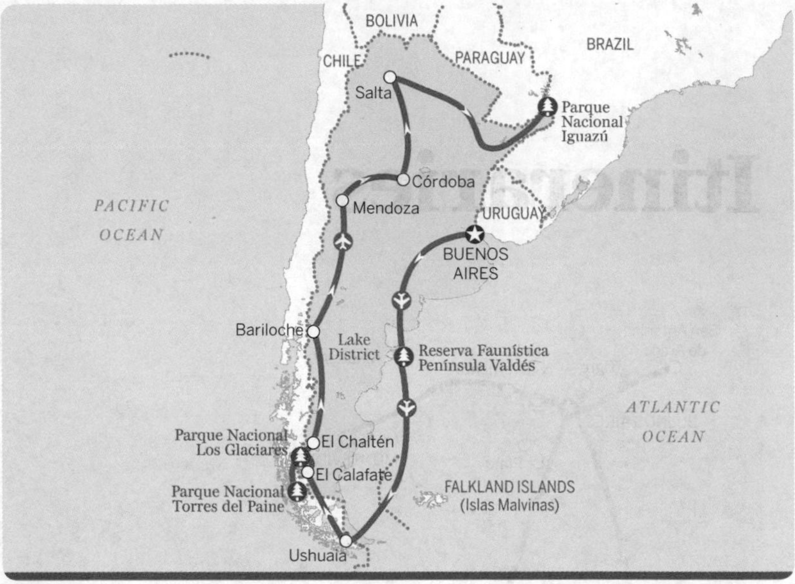

5 WEEKS Unmissable Argentina

Argentina is a huge country – the world's eighth-largest – and experiencing all its highlights thoroughly will require at least a month, plus several airplane flights. If you want to see both the north and south, plan your trip accordingly: Patagonia is best in January and February, but this is when the northern deserts are at their hottest (doing both regions might be best in spring or fall). Tailor the following destinations to your tastes, spending more or less time where you want to.

Take a few days to explore the wonders of **Buenos Aires**, with its fascinating neighborhoods and big-city sights. If it's the right season, fly south for wildlife viewing at **Reserva Faunística Península Valdés** – the whales, elephant seals and penguins are especially popular. From here hop another flight to **Ushuaia**, the southernmost city in the world and prime jumping-off point to Antarctica (add another two weeks and *minimum* US$5000 for this trip!).

Now you'll head north to **El Calafate**, where the stunning Glaciar Perito Moreno is one of the world's most unique sights. If you love the outdoors, cross the border to Chile's **Parque Nacional Torres del Paine**, an awe-inspiring cluster of mountains boasting some of the earth's most beautiful landscapes. Back in Argentina is **El Chaltén**, another world-class climbing, trekking and camping destination.

Further up the Andes is Argentina's **Lake District**, where a chocolate stop in **Bariloche** is a must. Gorgeous scenery, outdoor activities and lovely nearby towns can easily add days to your itinerary. Your next destination is now **Mendoza**, Argentina's wine mecca, which also offers great outdoor adventures and mind-blowing Andean scenery. A 10-hour bus ride lands you in **Córdoba**, the country's second-largest city with amazing colonial architecture and cutting-edge culture. From here go north to pretty **Salta**, where you can explore colorful canyons, charming villages and desert panoramas.

Pack up your bags again and head east to **Parque Nacional Iguazú**, where the world's most massive falls will astound you. Now fly back to Buenos Aires and party till your plane leaves.

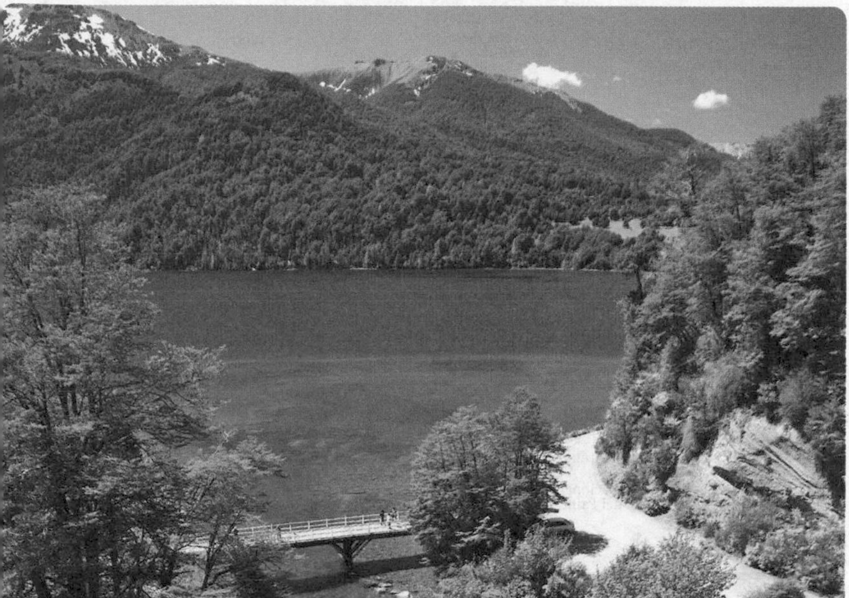

Above: Lago Nahuel Huapi (p362), near Bariloche

Right: Buildings on El Caminito (p69), Buenos Aires

JOHN W BANAGAN/GETTY IMAGES ©

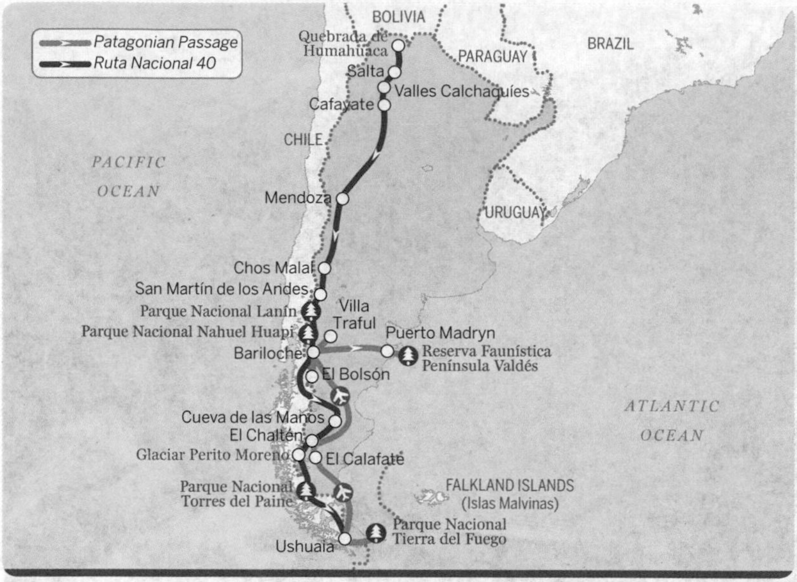

30 DAYS Ruta Nacional 40

Argentina's quintessential road trip, RN40 travels the length of the country. To do this adventure independently you'll need to rent a vehicle, ideally a 4WD as some sections are still unpaved.

Start near the amazingly colorful mountainsides of **Quebrada de Humahuaca** before hitting **Salta** and the wildly scenic villages of **Valles Calchaquíes**. Pause at lovely **Cafayate** before the long trip down to **Mendoza** to suss out the wine scene.

Continue south, stopping to check out the lagoons and hot springs around **Chos Malal**. Explore the national parks of **Lanín** and **Nahuel Huapi** or epic hiking before hitting **San Martín de los Andes** and **Bariloche**. Further on, sidetrack to **Cueva de las Manos** for indigenous art.

Stop at **El Chaltén** for top-drawer hiking, then experience the **Glaciar Perito Moreno**. Cross the border to Chile and explore stunning **Parque Nacional Torres del Paine** before your last stop, **Ushuaia**; it's as far south as any highway in the world goes.

18 DAYS Patagonian Passage

Begin in **Ushuaia**, where you can kayak or hop on a boat to cruise around the Beagle Channel and possibly see penguins. Nearby **Parque Nacional Tierra del Fuego** offers a few end-of-the-world hikes (literally).

Now fly to **El Calafate** and lay your eyes on the spectacular and unforgettable **Glaciar Perito Moreno**. Outdoors-lovers will want to cross the border and trek in Chile's famous **Parque Nacional Torres del Paine**. Head north again to **El Chaltén** for world-class hiking and camping.

Fly to **Bariloche**, where you can hike (or fish, or raft, or bike) for days on end in the gorgeous national parks of **Nahuel Huapi** and **Lanín**. If you have an extra day or two, take a day trip to the hippie enclave of **El Bolsón** or the cute village of **Villa Traful**.

Finally, stop in **Puerto Madryn** to see the whales, elephant seals and penguins at **Reserva Faunística Península Valdés** – just make sure it's the right season.

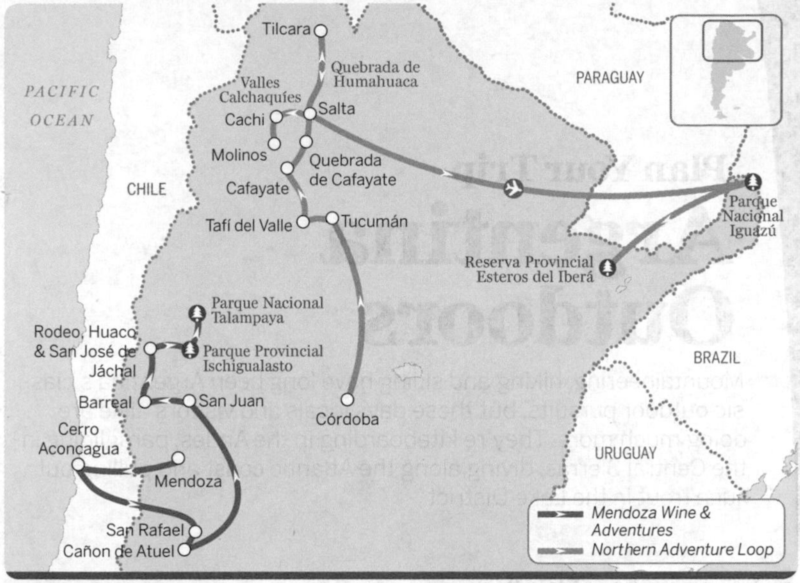

3 WEEKS Northern Adventure Loop

Start in **Córdoba**, Argentina's second-largest city, to explore one of the country's finest colonial centers.

Now head north to historic **Tucumán** for some eclectic architecture and a lively street scene. Over to the west is pretty **Tafí del Valle**, and getting there via a gorgeous mountain road is half the fun. A bit further north is beautiful **Cafayate**, the place to knock back some aromatic torrontés wine. Sober up and travel through the epic **Quebrada de Cafayate** to the otherworldly region of **Valles Calchaquíes** and the adobe villages of **Cachi** and **Molinos**.

Salta's central plaza is one of Argentina's best preserved; this is also where the famous 'Train to the Clouds' begins. Now journey north through the magnificently eroded valley of **Quebrada de Humahuaca**, where you can overnight in lively little **Tilcara**.

Return to Salta and fly to the incredible **Parque Nacional Iguazú**, home to unbelievable waterfalls. Another worthy destination is **Reserva Provincial Esteros del Iberá**, an amazing wetlands preserve full of capybaras, caimans and birds.

2 WEEKS Mendoza Wine & Adventures

Uncork your trip in beautiful **Mendoza**, located on the flanks of the Andes. Not only are there world-class vineyards surrounding the city, but outdoor enthusiasts will be in heaven. White-water rafting and skiing are awesome in the area, and **Cerro Aconcagua** (the western hemisphere's highest peak) isn't too far away.

Now take a crack-of-dawn bus to **San Rafael**, where you can rent a bike and ride out to the city's wineries – some of which specialize in sparkling wine. The area is also home to scenic **Cañon de Atuel**, a colorful mini Grand Canyon. Then backtrack up north to **San Juan** to try the excellent syrah and other regional whites. You can also rent a car and head west to ethereal **Barreal** for rafting, mountaineering and land sailing, then go further north to explore the remote and traditional villages of **San José de Jáchal**, **Rodeo** and **Huaco**.

Finally, be sure to visit the amazing landscapes of **Parque Provincial Ischigualasto** and **Parque Nacional Talampaya**, both boasting spectacular rock formations – along with petroglyphs and dinosaur fossils.

Plan Your Trip

Argentina Outdoors

Mountaineering, hiking and skiing have long been Argentina's classic outdoor pursuits, but these days locals and visitors alike are doing much more. They're kiteboarding in the Andes, paragliding in the Central Sierras, diving along the Atlantic coast and pulling out huge trout in the Lake District.

Best Bases for Thrill Seekers

Bariloche

One of Argentina's premier outdoor cities, with fine hiking, skiing, biking, fishing, rafting and even paragliding.

Mendoza

One word: Aconcagua. Plus great skiing, rafting, rock climbing and more.

El Chaltén

World-class hiking, trekking, rock climbing, kayaking and fishing.

Puerto Madryn

Dive with sea lions, or go windsurfing and kayaking.

Junín de los Andes

Gorgeous rivers offer some of the world's best fly-fishing (for huge trout!).

Córdoba

The closest city to Los Gigantes, Argentina's rock-climbing mecca (80km away).

Hiking & Trekking

Argentina is home to some superb stomping. The Lake District is probably the country's most popular hiking destination, with outstanding day and multiday hikes in several national parks, including Nahuel Huapi and Lanín. Bariloche is the best base for exploring the former, San Martín de los Andes the latter.

Patagonia, needless to say, has out-of-this-world hiking. South of Bariloche, El Bolsón is an excellent base for hiking both in the forests outside of town and in nearby Parque Nacional Lago Puelo. Parque Nacional Los Glaciares offers wonderful hiking in and around the Fitz Roy Range; base yourself in El Chaltén and wait out the storms (in the brewery, of course).

Head to Parque Nacional Torres del Paine, in Chile, for epic hiking. Tierra del Fuego also has some good walks, conveniently in Parque Nacional Tierra del Fuego.

Then there are the high Andean peaks west of Mendoza. Although these areas are more popular for mountaineering, there's some great trekking here as well. The northern Andes around Quebrada de Humahuaca are also good.

Most sizable towns in the Lake District and Patagonia have a hiking and mountaineering club called Club Andino. These are good places to get information, maps and current conditions. Bariloche, Junín de los Andes, El Bolsón and Ushuaia all have one.

Lonely Planet's *Trekking in the Patagonian Andes* is a great resource to have if you're planning some serious trekking.

Mountaineering

The Andes are a mountaineer's dream, especially in the San Juan and Mendoza provinces, where some of the highest peaks in the western hemisphere are found. While the most famous climb is Aconcagua, the highest peak in the Americas, there are plenty of others in the Andes – many of them more interesting and far more technical. Near Barreal, the Cordón de la Ramada boasts five peaks more than 6000m, including the mammoth Cerro Mercedario, which tops out at 6770m. The region is less congested than Aconcagua, offers more technical climbs and is preferred by many climbers. Also near here is the majestic Cordillera de Ansilta, with seven peaks scraping the sky at between 5130m and 5885m.

The magnificent and challenging Fitz Roy Range, in southern Patagonia near El Chaltén, is one of the world's top mountaineering destinations, while the mountains of Parque Nacional Nahuel Huapi offer fun for all levels.

Rock Climbing

Patagonia's Parque Nacional Los Glaciares, home to Cerro Torre and Cerro Fitz Roy, is one of the world's most important rock-climbing destinations. Cerro Torre is considered one of the five toughest climbs on the planet. The nearby town of El Chaltén is a climber's haven, and several shops offer lessons and rent equipment. If you don't have the time or talent for climbs of the Cerro Torre magnitude, there are plenty of other options.

Los Gigantes, in the Central Sierras, is fast becoming the country's de facto rock-climbing capital and has lots of high-quality granite. There's also climbing around Carolina.

In Mendoza province, Los Molles is a small, friendly hub for rock climbing, and there's more nearby at Chigüido (near Malargüe). Around Mendoza city are the draws of Los Arenales and El Salto.

Cerro Catedral, in Parque Nacional Nahuel Huapi, has popular climbing routes. There are also good routes in Torres del Paine, Chile. Finally, in the Pampas, there's some climbing in Tandil and Mar del Plata.

LAND SAILING

In San Juan province's Parque Nacional El Leoncito, the lake bed of Pampa El Leoncito has become the epicenter of *carrovelismo* (land sailing). Here, people zip across the dry lake bed beneath Andean peaks in so-called sail cars. If you're interested, head straight to Barreal.

Fishing

Together, Patagonia and the Lake District constitute one of the world's premier fly-fishing destinations, where introduced trout species (brown, brook, lake and rainbow) and landlocked Atlantic salmon reach massive sizes in cold rivers surrounded by spectacular scenery. It's an angler's paradise.

In the Lake District, Junín de los Andes is the self-proclaimed trout capital of Argentina, and lining up a guide to take you to Parque Nacional Lanín's superb trout streams is easy. Nearby Aluminé sits on the banks of Río Aluminé, one of the country's most highly regarded trout streams. Bariloche and Villa la Angostura are other excellent bases.

Further south, Parque Nacional Los Alerces (near Esquel) has outstanding lakes and rivers. From El Chaltén you can do day trips to Lago del Desierto or Laguna Larga. Río Gallegos is a superb fly-fishing destination. Other important Patagonian rivers include Río Negro and Río Santa Cruz.

The city of Río Grande, on Tierra del Fuego, is world famous for fly-fishing. Its Río Grande river holds some of the largest sea-run brown trout in the world.

Deep-sea fishing is possible in Camarones and Puerto Deseado; near Gobernador Gregores there's a lake with salmon and rainbow trout.

DOG SLEDDING

You can't say you've done it all until you've tried dog sledding. Argentina's a great place to start. Operators near Caviahue offer dog sledding, as do operators in San Martín de los Andes. And how about dog sledding at the end of the world, in Ushuaia? Obviously, this activity is possible only when there's snow, during the winter months of June to October (though in Ushuaia the season might be longer).

In subtropical northeast Argentina, the wide Río Paraná attracts fly-fishers, spin fishers and trollers from around the world, who pull in huge river species, such as surubí (a massive catfish) and dorado (a troutlike freshwater game fish). The dorado, not to be confused with the saltwater mahi-mahi, is a powerful swimmer and is one of the most exciting fish to catch on a fly.

Guides & Services

In smaller towns such as Junín de los Andes, you can usually go to the local tourist office and request a list of local fishing guides or operators. Another good option for independent anglers heading to the Lake District is the **Asociación de Guías Profesionales de Pesca Parque Nacional Nahuel Huapi y Patagonia Norte** (www.guiaspatagonicos.com.ar), which maintains a list and contact details of licensed guides for northern Patagonia and the Lake District. For information about fly-fishing, contact **Asociación Argentina de Pesca con Mosca** (☎in Buenos Aires 011-4773-0821; www.aapm.org.ar).

Many anglers use a tour agency based outside Argentina for guided excursions.

Rules & Regulations

In the Lake District and Patagonia the season runs from November to between mid- and late April. In the northeast the season runs from February to October. Certain lakes and streams on private land may stay open longer.

Trout fishing is almost always mandatory catch and release. Throughout Patagonia (including the Lake District), native species should *always* be thrown back. These are usually smaller than trout and include perca (perch), puyen (common galaxias, a narrow fish native to the southern hemisphere), Patagonian pejerrey and the rare peladilla.

Fishing licenses are required and available at tackle shops, *clubs de caza y pesca* (hunting and fishing clubs), and sometimes at tourist offices and YPF gas stations.

Skiing & Snowboarding

Argentina's mountains have outstanding skiing, offering superb powder and plenty of sunny days. Many resorts have large ski schools with instructors from all over the world, so language is not a problem. At some of the older resorts equipment can be a little antiquated, but in general the quality of skiing more than compensates.

There are three main snow-sport areas: Mendoza, the Lake District and Ushuaia. Mendoza is near Argentina's premier resort, Las Leñas, which has the best snow and longest runs; the resort Los Penitentes is also nearby. The Lake District is home to several low-key resorts, including Cerro Catedral, near Bariloche, and Cerro Chapelco, near San Martín de los Andes. Although the snow doesn't get as powdery here, the views are superior to Las Leñas. And Esquel, further south in Patagonia, has great powder at La Hoya.

The world's most southerly commercial skiing is near Ushuaia. The ski season everywhere generally runs from mid-June to mid-October.

Cycling

Cycling is a popular activity among Argentines, and spandex-clad cyclists are a common sight along many roads (despite a decided lack of bike lanes in the country). There are some outstanding paved routes, especially in the Lake District and, to a lesser extent, in the Andean northwest.

In the northwest there are several excellent road routes, including the highway from Tucumán to Tafí del Valle, the direct road from Salta to Jujuy and, arguably most spectacular of all, RN68, which takes you through the Quebrada de Cafayate. The Central Sierras are also great candidates for cycling, and the mostly paved

Above: Snowboarding, Patagonia

Right: Mountain biking, Río Negro region

MARCOS FERRO/GETTY IMAGES ©

WINDSURFING & KITEBOARDING

From around the world, windsurfing and kiteboarding fanatics drag an insane amount of gear to an isolated spot in the central Andes: Dique Cuesta del Viento, literally 'slope of the wind reservoir.' The reservoir, near the small village of Rodeo in San Juan province, is one of the best wind-sports destinations on the planet. Its consistent and extremely powerful wind blows every afternoon, without fail, from October to early May. We checked it out and it blew us away!

network of roads rolls past a countryside that is at times reminiscent of Scotland. Mendoza boasts some epic routes through the Andes, but most are doable only for the seasoned cyclist – those lacking thighs of glory can entertain themselves by pedaling between wineries in Maipú.

In the Lake District's Parque Nacional Nahuel Huapi there are several excellent loops (including the Circuito Chico) that skirt gorgeous lakes and take in some of Patagonia's most spectacular scenery. Cyclists often take their bikes on the Cruce de Lagos, a famous two-day boat/bus journey across the Andes to Chile.

Patagonia is a popular and mythical destination, with its desolate, beautiful landscapes and wide-open skies. However, be ready for fierce multidirectional winds and rough gravel roads. Take four-season gear even in summer, when long days and relatively warm weather make for the best touring. The classic road down here is RN40, but cycling is tough because of the winds and lack of water; most cyclists alternate sections with Chile's Carretera Austral.

In recent years Buenos Aires has become a more bike-friendly destination, with an expanding system of dedicated bike lanes, along with a free bike-share program. Mendoza and Córdoba also have some dedicated bike lanes.

Mountain Biking

Mountain biking is fairly undeveloped in Argentina and you'll find few places have true single tracks for mountain bikers. However, at most outdoor hubs (such as Bariloche) you can rent a mountain bike for a day of independent pedaling or for guided mountain-bike rides – a fantastic way to see parts of an area you wouldn't otherwise explore.

Good places with mountain-bike rentals include: San Martín de los Andes, Villa la Angostura, Bariloche and El Bolsón in the Lake District; Esquel in Patagonia; Mendoza and Uspallata in Mendoza province; Barreal in San Juan province; Tilcara in the Andean Northwest; and Tandil in La Pampa province.

White-Water Rafting & Kayaking

Currently, Río Mendoza and Río Diamante in Mendoza province are the reigning white-water destinations, while Río Juramento near Salta is an exciting alternative.

If you want great scenery, however, it's all about Patagonia. The Río Hua Hum and Río Meliquina, near San Martín de los Andes, and Río Limay and Río Manso, near Bariloche, are both spectacular. So is Río Aluminé, near wee Aluminé. From the Patagonian town of Esquel you can join a rafting trip on the incredibly scenic, glacial-fed Río Corcovado. A relatively unknown rafting destination is Barreal, but it's more about the epic Andean scenery than the rapids. Scenic Class II to III floats are possible on most of these rivers, while Class IV runs are possible on the Ríos Mendoza, Diamante, Meliquina, Hua Hum and Corcovado. Experience is generally unnecessary for guided runs.

Kayaking is possible on many of the rivers mentioned, and also around Ushuaia, El Chaltén, Viedma, Puerto Madryn, Paraná, Rosario and Salta. Sea kayakers have options at Río Deseado and the *estancia* (ranch) at Bahía Bustamante.

Paragliding & Skydiving

Paragliding is popular in Argentina and it's a great place to take tandem flights or classes. Many agencies in Bariloche offer paragliding. Tucumán, Salta, La Rioja and Merlo have options in the Andean Northwest. Perhaps the best place is La Cumbre, in Córdoba's Central Sierras – it's also a thrilling place to try skydiving.

Plan Your Trip
Eat & Drink Like a Local

Argentines take barbecuing to heights you cannot imagine. Their best pizzas vie with those of New York and Naples. They make fabulous wines. *Mate*, that iconic tea, doubles as a social bond between family and friends. And your taste buds will sing as they sample Argentina's delectable ice cream.

Staples & Specialties

Beef

When the first Spaniards came to Argentina, they brought cattle. But efforts to establish a colony proved unfruitful, and the herds were abandoned in the pampas. Here the cows found the bovine equivalent of heaven: plenty of lush, fertile grasses on which to feed, with few natural predators. After the Europeans recolonized, they bred these cattle with other bovine breeds.

Traditionally, free-range Argentine cows ate nutritious pampas grass and were raised without antibiotics and growth hormones. But this culture is being lost, and today nearly all beef in restaurants come from feedlots.

Average beef consumption in Argentina is around 58kg per person per year – though in the past, they ate much more.

Italian & Spanish

Thanks to Argentina's Italian heritage, the national cuisine has been highly influenced by Italian immigrants who entered the country during the late 19th century. Along with an animated set of speaking gestures, they brought their love of pasta, pizza, gelato and more.

Tips for Eating Out

Reservations

Only necessary on weekends at better restaurants (or high season at Mar del Plata or Bariloche, for example).

Budgeting

To save a few bucks at lunch, opt for the *menú del día* or *menú ejecutivo*. These 'set menus' usually include a main dish, dessert and drink.

Large, modern supermarkets are common, and they'll have whatever you need for self-catering, including (usually) a takeout counter.

Paying the Bill

Ask for your bill by saying, '*la cuenta, por favor*' ('the bill, please') or making the 'writing in air' gesture. Many restaurants accept credit cards, but some (usually smaller ones) only take cash.

At fancier restaurants, your final bill may arrive with a *cubierto* (small cover charge for bread and use of utensils). This is not a tip, which is usually around 10% and a separate charge.

MAGAIZA/GETTY IMAGES ©

Above: Woman drinking *mate* (p44)

Left: Chorizos

Many restaurants make their own pasta – look for *pasta casera* (handmade pasta). Some of the varieties of pasta you'll encounter are *ravioles, sorrentinos* (large, round pasta parcels similar to ravioli), *ñoquis* (gnocchi) and *tallerines* (fettuccine). Standard sauces include *tuco* (tomato sauce), *estofado* (beef stew, popular with ravioli) and *salsa blanca* (béchamel). Be aware that occasionally the sauce is *not* included in the price of the pasta – you choose and pay for it separately.

Pizza is sold at pizzerias throughout the country, though many regular restaurants offer it as well. It's generally excellent, so go ahead and order a slice or two.

Spanish cooking is less popular than Italian, but forms another bedrock of Argentine food. In Spanish restaurants here you'll find paella, as well as other typically Spanish seafood preparations. Most of the country's *guisos* and *pucheros* (types of stew) are descendants of Spain.

Local Specialties

Although *comida típica* can refer to any of Argentina's regional dishes, it often refers to food from the Andean Northwest. Food from this region, which has roots in pre-Columbian times, has more in common with the cuisines of Bolivia and Peru than with the Europeanized food of the rest of Argentina. It's frequently spicy and hard to find elsewhere (most Argentines can't tolerate anything spicy). Typical dishes can include everything from *locro* (a hearty corn or mixed-grain stew with meat), to tamales, *humitas* (sweet tamales) and fried empanadas.

In Patagonia, lamb is as common as beef. Along the coast, seafood is a popular choice and includes fish, oysters and king crab. In the Lake District, game meats such as venison, wild boar and trout are popular. In the west, the provinces of Mendoza, San Juan and La Rioja pride themselves on *chivito* (young goat). River fish, such as the dorado, pacú (a relative of the

THE BEEF ON BEEF

You walk into a traditional *parrilla* (steak restaurant), breeze past the sizzling grill at the entrance and sit down. You've never had to choose between more than two or three cuts of steak in your life, but the menu has at least 10 choices. What to do?

If you want to try a bit of everything, go for the *parrillada* (mixed grill). It often includes chorizo (beef or pork sausage), *costillas* (ribs) and *carne* (beef). It can also come with more exotic items such as *chinchulines* (small intestines), *molleja* (sweetbreads) and *morcilla* (blood sausage). Order a *parrillada* for as many people as you want and the *parrilla* will adjust servings accordingly.

Prime beef cuts include the following:

Bife de chorizo Sirloin; a thick and juicy cut

Bife de costilla T-bone or Porterhouse steak

Bife de lomo Tenderloin; a tender though less flavorful piece

Cuadril Rump steak; often a thin cut

Ojo de bife Rib eye; a choice smaller morsel

Tira de asado Short ribs; thin crispy strips of ribs

Vacío Flank steak; textured, chewy and tasty

If you don't specify, your steak will be cooked *a punto* (medium to well done). Getting a steak medium rare or rare is more difficult than you'd imagine. If you want a little pink in the center, order it *jugoso*; if you like it truly rare, try *vuelta y vuelta* and hope for the best. Don't miss *chimichurri,* a tasty sauce often made of olive oil, garlic and parsley. Occasionally you can get *salsa criolla*, a condiment made of diced tomatoes, onion and parsley.

If you're lucky enough to be invited to an *asado* (family or friends' barbecue), do attend – here the art of grilling beef has been perfected, and the social bonding is priceless.

piranha) and surubí (a type of catfish), are staples in the northeast.

Snacks

Kioscos (kiosks) are all over town and provide sweets, cookies, ice cream and packaged sandwiches. On many streets, *pancho* (hot dog) and *garapiñadas* (sugar-roasted peanuts) sellers prepare and sell their treats from carts.

Sandwiches de miga (thin, crustless sandwiches, usually with cheese and ham) are very popular tea-time snacks. *Lomitos* (steak sandwiches) are the pinnacle of Argentine sandwiches, while the *choripán* is a classic barbecue sausage sandwich.

Empanadas – small, stuffed turnovers ubiquitous in Argentina – are prepared differently throughout the country (for example, you'll find spicy ground-beef empanadas in the Andean Northwest, and in Patagonia lamb is a common filling). They make for a tasty, quick meal and are especially good for bus travel.

Desserts & Sweets

Two of Argentina's most definitive treats are *dulce de leche* (a creamy milk caramel) and *alfajores* (round, cookie-type sandwiches often covered in chocolate). Each region of Argentina has its own version of the *alfajor*.

Because of Argentina's Italian heritage, Argentine *helado* is comparable to the best ice cream anywhere in the world. There are *heladerías* (ice-cream stores) in every town, where the luscious concoctions will be swirled into a peaked mountain and handed over with a plastic spoon stuck in the side. Don't miss this special treat.

In restaurants, fruit salad and ice cream are almost always on the menu, while *flan* is a baked custard that comes with either cream or *dulce de leche* topping.

Drinks

Nonalcoholic Drinks

Argentines love their coffee, and you can order several versions. A *café con leche* is a latte (half coffee and half milk), while a *cortado* is an espresso with a little milk. A *café chico* is an espresso and a *lagrima* is mostly milk with a few drops of coffee.

Té negro or *té común* is black tea; herbal tea is usually *manzanilla* (chamomile). Chocolate lovers should try a *submarino*, a bar of chocolate melted in hot milk. Fresh-squeezed orange juice is *jugo de naranja exprimido*. A *licuado* is fruit blended with milk or water.

Even in big cities like Buenos Aires, the *agua de canilla* (tap water) is drinkable. In restaurants, however, most people order bottled mineral water – ask for *agua con gas* (with bubbles) or *agua sin gas* (without). In older, more traditional restaurants, carbonated water in a spritzer bottle (*un sifón de soda*) is a great for drinking. *Gaseosas* (soft drinks) are very popular in Argentina.

Alcoholic Drinks

Mendoza is Argentina's premier wine region and well known for its robust malbec, but other provinces also produce excellent wines. San Juan is famous for its succulent syrah and Cafayate for its torrontés, a crisp, dry white wine. Meanwhile, the Patagonia region is becoming a stronghouse for pinot noir.

If Argentina has a national beer, it's Quilmes. Order a *porrón* and you'll get a half-liter bottle; a *chopp* is a frosty mug of draft. Unless you order it with a meal, beer is usually served with a free snack.

Most fine restaurants have a wine list, called *la carta de vinos*. Sommeliers are scarce. For more on wine, see p322.

At the harder end of the spectrum, it's all about Fernet Branca, a bitter, herbed Italian digestif originally intended as medicine. Fernet con Coke is Argentina's favorite cocktail and, despite many claims that it won't give you a hangover, it will (trust us).

Where to Eat & Drink

Restaurants are generally open from noon to 3pm for lunch and 9pm to midnight for dinner, though exact hours will vary depending on the restaurant.

For the best meats, head to a *parrilla* (steak restaurant). Pizzerias bake pizzas and *panaderías* are bakeries. *Confiterías* (cafes serving light meals) are open all

Above: *Alfajores*
Right: Restaurant in La Boca (p91), Buenos Aires

GRANT FAINT/GETTY IMAGES ©

MATE & ITS RITUAL

The preparation and consumption of *mate* (pronounced *mah*-tay) is more than a simple drink. It's an elaborate ritual shared among family, friends and co-workers.

Yerba mate is the dried, chopped leaf of *Ilex paraguayensis*, a relative of the common holly. Argentina is one of the world's largest producers and consumers of the stuff, and its citizens down an average of 5kg per person per year.

Preparing and drinking *mate* is a ritual in itself. One person, the *cebador* (server), fills the *mate* gourd almost to the top with *yerba*, and then slowly pours hot water as he or she fills the gourd. The *cebador* then passes the *mate* to each drinker, who sips the liquid through the *bombilla*, a silver straw with a filter at the end. Each participant drinks the gourd dry each time. Remember it's bad form to touch the *bombilla*, and don't hold the *mate* too long before passing it on! A simple '*gracias*' will tell the server to pass you by.

An invitation to partake in *mate* is a cultural treat and not to be missed, although the drink is an acquired taste and novices will find it very hot and bitter at first (adding sugar can be an option).

Mate is rarely served in restaurants or cafes, but you can buy a thermos, *mate* gourd, *bombilla* and a bag of herb at any large supermarket. Cure your gourd by filling it with hot water and *yerba* and letting it soak for 24 hours. Nearly all restaurants, cafes and hotels are used to filling thermoses, sometimes charging a small amount. Simply whip out your thermos and ask: '*¿Podía calentar agua para mate?*' ('Would you mind heating water for *mate*?'). And start making friends.

day and into the night and often have a long list of both food and drinks. Cafes, bars and pubs usually have a more limited range of snacks and meals available, though some can offer full meals. A *tenedor libre* (literally, 'free fork') is an all-you-can-eat restaurant; quality is usually decent, but a minimum-drink purchase is often mandatory and costs extra.

Argentines eat little for breakfast – usually just a coffee with *medialunas* (croissants – either *de manteca*, sweet, or *de grasa*, plain). Tostadas (toast) with *manteca* (butter) or *mermelada* (jam) is an alternative, as are *facturas* (pastries). Higher-end hotels and B&Bs tend to offer heartier breakfasts.

Vegetarians & Vegans

Health foods, organic products and vegetarian restaurants are available in Argentina's biggest cities, but outside of them you'll have to search harder.

Most restaurant menus include a few vegetarian choices, and pastas are a nearly ubiquitous option. Pizzerias and *empanaderías* (empanada shops) are good bets – look for empanadas made with *acelga* (chard) and *choclo* (corn). If you're stuck at a *parrilla*, your choices will be salads, omelets, pasta, baked potatoes, *provoleta* (a thick slice of grilled provolone cheese) and roasted vegetables. *Pescado* (fish) and *mariscos* (seafood) are sometimes available for pescatarians.

Sin carne means 'without meat,' and the words *soy vegetariano/a* ('I'm a vegetarian') will come in handy when explaining to an Argentine why you don't eat their nation's renowned steaks.

Vegans will have a much harder time in Argentina; there isn't a word for 'vegan.' Make sure homemade pasta doesn't include egg, and that fried vegetables aren't cooked in lard (*grasa*; *manteca* means butter in Argentina). You'll need to be creative to survive here. One tip: look for accommodations with a kitchen, so you can shop for and cook your own food. Good luck.

Plan Your Trip

Travel with Children

While Argentina is best known for its steak, gauchos and tango – not your top kid-friendly themes – there is plenty this country has to offer your little ones. There are dinosaur museums to wow at, beach resorts to splash around in and plenty of outdoor activities to use up all that extra energy. You'll find Argentina makes a good, interesting and, yes, at times challenging but fun family destination.

Argentina for Kids

Argentina is remarkably child-friendly in terms of general travel safety and people's attitudes towards families. This is a country where family comes first.

Argentine parents will often send unaccompanied pre-adolescents on errands or neighborly visits. While you're not likely to do this, you can usually count on your children's safety in public.

Argentina's numerous plazas and public parks, many with playgrounds, are popular gathering spots for families. This is a country where people frequently touch each other, so your children may be patted on the head by friendly strangers. Kids are a great ice-breaker and certainly make it easier for you to meet the locals.

And remember that families stay out very late in this country – it's common to see young kids and babies out past midnight with their parents. There's no early curfew and everyone's out having fun, so consider doing the same!

Best Regions for Kids

Buenos Aires

Argentina's capital holds plenty of museums, parks and shopping malls – many with fun areas for kids.

Atlantic Coast

Beaches and more beaches – bring swimsuits and sunscreen and start building castles.

Mendoza

Wine tasting is off limits for the kids, but you can go skiing, dog sledding and white-water rafting.

Iguazú

Waterfalls and wildlife galore, plus thrilling boat rides that guarantee a fun soaking.

Península Valdés

Rich with wildlife, such as splashy whales, smelly elephant seals and super-cute penguins.

Bariloche

Outdoor activities are the draw here – go hiking, rock climbing, horseback riding and rafting.

Children's Highlights

Watching Wildlife

- Visit **Güirá Oga zoo** (p202) and **Parque das Aves** (☎3529-8282; www.parquedasaves.com.br; admission AR$25; ⏲8:30am-5:30pm) in the Iguazú Falls area
- **Esteros del Iberá** (p175) is full of marsh deer, black caimans and adorable capybaras
- Check out the southern right whales, elephant seals and suit-wearing penguins on **Península Valdés** (p406)
- **Parque Temaikén** (p77), just outside BA, is an excellent zoo with photogenic animals

Energy Burners

- **Parque de la Costa** (p77), just outside BA in Tigre, offers roller coasters and other theme-park fun
- **Complejo Termal Cacheuta** (p333), outside Mendoza, is a thermal-baths complex with wave pool and waterslides
- The Andes mountains offer great skiing around Bariloche and Mendoza

Rainy Days

- Kids can overnight in their pajamas at **Museo Paleontológico Egidio Feruglio** (p411), Trelew's dinosaur museum
- **Museo de La Plata** (p119) is Argentina's best natural history museum – the taxidermy and skeletons are especially awesome
- Shopping centers have kid-centric amusements, such as playgrounds, video arcades, toy stores and ice-cream shops
- **The Glaciarium** (p455), El Calafate's slickest museum, highlights the wonders of glaciers

Outdoor Fun

- El Calafate's super-active **Glaciar Perito Moreno** (p464) is a wonder to behold for all ages
- The beaches on Argentina's Atlantic coast are family-friendly and offer up plenty of sand, surf and sun
- Horseback rides and folkloric shows are highlights during your stay on an *estancia* (ranch)
- The petrified forests of Patagonia (p423) aren't all that petrifying – unless you're a tree

Planning

Outdoor activities are best experienced outside the winter months of June through August (with the exception of skiing, of course). Small kids often get discounts on such things as motel stays, museum admissions and restaurant meals. Supermarkets offer a decent selection of baby food (expensive), infant formulas, disposable diapers, wet wipes and other necessities. Big pharmacies such as Farmacity also stock some of these items.

Strollers on crowded and uneven sidewalks can be a liability, so consider bringing a baby carrier. Public bathrooms are often poorly maintained, and baby changing tables are not common.

Au pairs and babysitters are available (mostly in BA); do a search at www.baexats.org for recommendations.

In reviews, very child-friendly destinations have been marked with 👪.

Sweet Dreams

The great majority of hotels accept children without any problems; the most upscale may even offer babysitting services. The only places with minimum age restrictions might be small boutique hotels or guesthouses. Hostels are usually not the best environment for kids, but some welcome them.

During summer reserving a hotel with a pool might be a good idea. Also look for places with kitchenettes. Apartments are available, especially in BA; in less-urban holiday destinations look for *cabañas* (cabins) with full kitchens. Larger campgrounds often have *cabañas*, common cooking facilities and sometimes play structures.

Dining

Most restaurants offer a selection of food suitable for children, such as vegetables, pasta, pizza, meat and chicken. Empanadas make good healthy snacks that are fun to eat, and don't forget to take the kids out for ice cream – it's a real Argentine treat!

Transportation

When it comes to public transport, Argentines are usually very helpful. Taxis and *remises* (call taxis) are common and affordable in most towns.

Regions at a Glance

As the eighth-largest country in the world, Argentina boasts nearly every kind of environment, from glaciated mountain peaks to cacti-dotted deserts to animal-rich swamplands and shrubby arid steppes. Outdoor fun-seekers will find their blissful adventures, beachcombers their warm stretches of sand and wine lovers their luscious vineyards.

The bigger cities, such as Buenos Aires and Córdoba, boast endless nightlife, entertainment, shopping and restaurants, along with a dose of culture, such as excellent museums, tango dance halls and colonial history. Argentina offers pretty much everything you might be looking for in a destination, so choose your desires, give yourself enough time to experience them all, and just take off!

Buenos Aires

Food
Nightlife
Tango

Steaks & More

There are plenty of fine steak houses in Buenos Aires. But you'll also find dozens of ethnic restaurants covering cuisines from Mexico, Brazil, India, China, Thailand, the Middle East…and practically anywhere else.

Burn the Midnight Oil

Buenos Aires is indeed the city that never sleeps. After dinner (often ending after midnight) *porteños* (Buenos Aires residents) head out for a drink, then hit the nightclubs after 2am. Other events happen at a more 'reasonable' hour, but you get the idea – this city loves staying up late.

Sultry Dancing

Ah, the tango. There's no denying the attraction of this sexy dance. And BA boasts countless dance venues and classes, along with world-class competitions. Put on your dancing shoes and get ready to fall in love – you're in the heart of tango land here.

p52

The Pampas & the Atlantic Coast

Beaches
Gaucho Culture
Hiking

Life's a Beach

In January coastal cities such as Mar del Plata, Pinamar and Necochea become heaving hubs full of sun-bronzed Argentines lying on hot sands during the day and partying all night long.

Gaucho Culture

This quintessential icon's heyday was centuries ago, but today the culture is kept alive in San Antonio de Areco, where an annual festival celebrates the gaucho's life. You can also visit an *estancia* (ranch), where horseback riding, gaucho demonstrations and *asados* (barbecues) are highlights.

Hiking

The ancient, worn-down mountain ranges of the Pampas aren't as spectacular as the youthful Andes. But around Sierra de la Ventana are some hikes that offer dramatic views of surrounding landscapes, – including one where you peek through a rock 'window.'

p116

Iguazú Falls & the Northeast

Water Features
Wildlife
Festivals

Wide Rivers, Mighty Iguazú

Towns and cities along the region's two major rivers are focused on great waterside strips for boating, strolling, eating and partying, while large fish attract anglers. Up north, Iguazú, the world's most impressive waterfalls, will leave you in awe.

Cute Capybaras

The Esteros del Iberá wetlands hold an astonishing wealth of creatures, including snapping caimans, colorful bird life and roly-poly capybaras. A long hop north brings you to Iguazú's national park and jungle ecosystem, equally rich in distinct wildlife species.

Carnaval

Brazil's proximity to this zone has left a legacy in the exuberant Carnaval celebrations. The most famous is in little Gualeguaychú, a short trip from Buenos Aires, but Corrientes and Posadas lose nothing by comparison.

p150

Salta & the Andean Northwest

Indigenous Culture
Colonial Cities
Activities

Before Columbus

The northwestern peoples witnessed the Inca; then the Spanish arrived. Centuries later, the ruins of cities remain, but the food, daily life and handicrafts speak of a persisting, living and changing culture.

Historic Towns

The northwestern cities are Argentina's oldest, and there's an unmistakable time-honored feel to them. Venerable churches, stately facades and handsome plazas planted with lofty trees – together with the relaxed pace of life – give these places an ambience unlike any other.

Out & About

The Andes dominate the geography here and boast excellent climbing, walking, and 4WD excursions. But there are also subtropical national parks replete with bird and animal life, and top-notch hang gliding and paragliding offer the opportunity to see how things look from above.

p217

Córdoba & the Central Sierras

Historic Buildings
Nightlife
Paragliding

Oldies but Goodies

The Jesuit legacy in Córdoba extends beyond wine making and higher education – they also constructed some fabulous buildings. Córdoba city boasts an entire block of well-preserved Jesuit architecture, and further examples are scattered around the province.

Bring on the Night

Catch an independent movie or a play, dance the night away or grab a few quiet drinks in a cozy bar – whatever you're looking for, Córdoba's young population and vibrant cultural scene make finding it a snap.

Take to the Skies

If you've ever even been vaguely tempted to try paragliding, this is the place to do it – the world-famous launch sites of La Cumbre and Merlo are home to scores of instructors offering tandem flights that will have you soaring with the condors.

p282

Mendoza & the Central Andes

Wine Tours
Mountains
Rafting

Hear it on the Grapevine

Get to the heart of Argentina's magnificent wine culture by visiting the vineyards, talking to the winemakers and seeing how it all comes together, from planting the vine to tasting the final, delicious product.

Lofty Ambitions

Snowcapped year-round and dominating the horizon, the Andes are one of Argentina's iconic images. Get up close and personal with them by climbing Aconcagua, the Americas' highest peak, or hitting the slopes in Mendoza's world-class ski resorts.

Wet & Wild

All that snowmelt from the Andes does more than just irrigate the grapevines. It also feeds a couple of rivers that gush down from the mountains, giving rafters the ride of their lives.

p315

Bariloche & the Lake District

Activities
Village Life
Paleontology

Get Out There

There's always something to do in the Lake District, a true year-round destination. Powder hounds hit the slopes in season at the province's top-notch ski resorts while the rest of the year the mountain trails, hikers' refuges and expansive vistas make it a trekker's paradise.

Kicking Back

One of the joys of traveling through this region is discovering small alpine villages nestled in the forest, surrounded by breathtaking mountain scenery – the perfect remedy for big-city blues.

Jurassic Parks

Some truly huge animals used to roam these parts, including the world's largest dinosaur and the world's largest carnivore. The sites where they were discovered are open to the public to teach a humbling lesson in size.

p353

Patagonia

Hiking
Wildlife-watching
Adventure

Wild Hiking

Iconic hikes around Fitz Roy and Torres del Paine bring deserved fame to the trails of Patagonia. But if you have time, check out the millennial forests of Parque Nacional Los Alerces and the electric turquoise lakes of ultra-remote Parque Nacional Perito Moreno.

Creature Feature

Abundant marine life makes the coast, and Península Valdés in particular, the hub for watching wildlife, but there's also the subtle allure of Patagonia's guanaco herds, soaring condors and ñandús that sprint across the steppe.

Real Adventure

Riding on an *estancia*, driving RN40, glacier chasing or just getting deep into the Andean wilderness: Patagonia is all about unfettered freedom and the allure of the unexpected.

p397

Tierra del Fuego

Hiking
Sea Travel
Winter Sports

Hoof it

Austral summer's long days make for backpacking bliss. Dientes de Navarino is the iconic Fuegian trek but the enchanted forests of Parque Nacional Tierra del Fuego also give a quick dose of big nature.

Set Sail

You don't have to round Cape Horn to find magic in these southern seas. Sail the Beagle Channel in search of marine life and indigenous ruins, boat through the Chilean fjords or paddle a sea kayak.

Winter Wonderland

Brave a winter journey to the frozen ends of the earth. From June to October, snow makes Ushuaia adventure central. Whoosh down the slopes of Cerro Castor, ski cross-country or zoom over the snowdrifts driven by sled dogs. Crackling bonfires, seafood banquets and comfy lodges cap the day.

p488

Uruguay

Beaches
Estancias
Food & Wine

A Beach for Every Taste

Beachside bliss wears many faces on Uruguay's Atlantic coast: chasing the perfect surf break at La Pedrera, getting friendly with sea lions at Cabo Polonio or scanning the sands for international celebrities at Punta del Este.

Wide Open Skies

Uruguay's gaucho soul lies in its vast interior landscapes. For a taste of traditional ranch life, spend a few nights on an *estancia*, riding horseback into an endless horizon by day and savoring the warmth of the fire and the brilliance of the stars by night.

Carnivore Paradise

Something's always grilling in Uruguay. The classic *parrillada* (mixed grill) of steak, pork chops, chorizo and *morcilla* (blood sausage) is enough to make any carnivore swoon, especially when accompanied by a glass of tannat from one of the country's up-and-coming wineries.

p513

On the Road

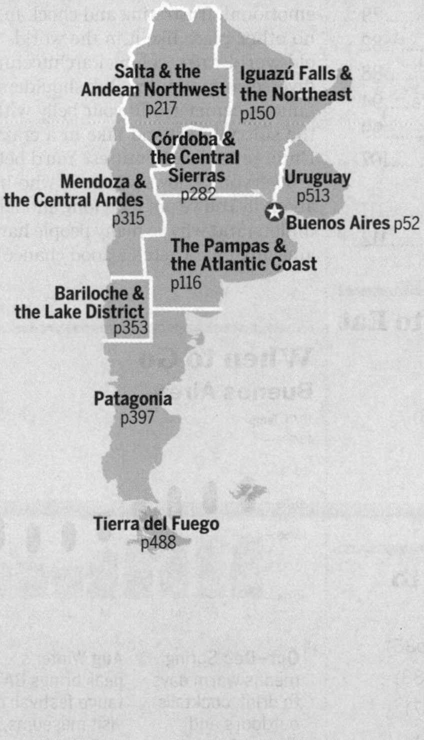

Salta & the Andean Northwest p217
Iguazú Falls & the Northeast p150
Córdoba & the Central Sierras p282
Mendoza & the Central Andes p315
Uruguay p513
Buenos Aires p52
The Pampas & the Atlantic Coast p116
Bariloche & the Lake District p353
Patagonia p397
Tierra del Fuego p488

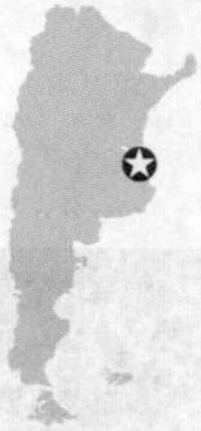

Buenos Aires

Best Places to Eat

- ➜ Hernán Gipponi Restaurant (p94)
- ➜ Las Pizarras (p93)
- ➜ Oviedo (p92)
- ➜ Sarkis (p93)
- ➜ Malvón (p93)

Best Places to Stay

- ➜ Poetry Building (p86)
- ➜ Miravida Soho (p88)
- ➜ The 5th Floor (p87)
- ➜ Casa Calma (p85)

Why Go?

Whip together a beautiful metropolis with gourmet cuisine, awesome shopping and frenzied nightlife – and you get Buenos Aires. It's a rough-hewn mix of Paris' architecture, Rome's traffic and Madrid's late-night hours, all spiked with Latin American flavor. BA is cosmopolitan, seductive, emotional, frustrating and chock-full of attitude, and there's no other place like it in the world. Seek out classic BA: the old-world cafes, colonial architecture, curious markets and diverse communities. Rub shoulders with Evita at Recoleta's famous cemetery, fill your belly with luscious steaks, dance the sultry tango and take in a crazy *fútbol* (soccer) match. Unforgettable adventures? You'd better believe it.

Everyone knows someone who has been here and raved about it. You've put it off long enough. Come to BA and you'll understand why so many people have fallen in love with this amazing city. There's a good chance you'll be one of them.

When to Go

Buenos Aires

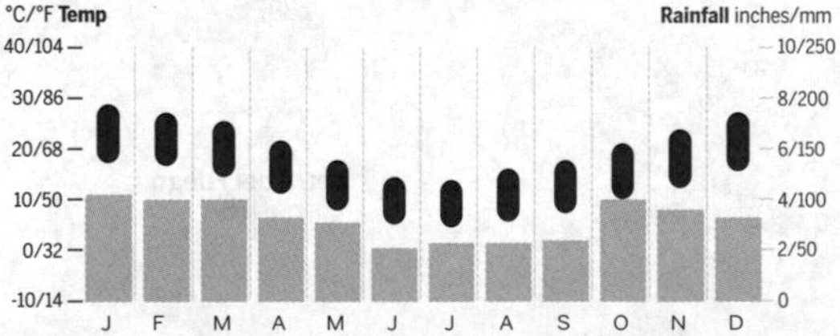

Oct–Dec Spring means warm days to drink cocktails outdoors and admire blooming jacarandas.

Aug Winter's peak brings BA's tango festival; or visit museums, art galleries and cultural centers.

Mar–May Explore BA in fall and catch the city's Independent Film Festival in April.

Supper Clubs

A hot BA trend continues to be *puertas cerradas* (closed-door restaurants). These prix fixe restaurants are sometimes only open on weekends and are great for meeting fellow diners, since the limited tables are often communal and the atmosphere is intimate. Most restaurants won't tell you the address until you make reservations (mandatory, of course). But if you want that feeling of being somewhere 'secret' – and eating special food – these places are highly appealing.

BUENOS AIRES 101

BA is a huge metropolis, but most places of interest are in just a few, easily accessible neighborhoods.

The heart of the city is **Microcentro**; it's small enough to walk around fairly easily. Just east is **Puerto Madero**, with scenic docklands and a large ecological park. Further south is **San Telmo**, known for its lovely colonial architecture and Sunday fair. South of here is **La Boca**, famed for colorful houses clad in corrugated metal.

West of the Microcentro sits **Congreso**, BA's seat of politics, boasting some stately buildings. To the north is upscale **Retiro**, home to the city's main train station and bus terminal. And just northwest lie **Recoleta** and **Barrio Norte**, boasting some of BA's most expensive real estate and dotted with art museums, fancy shops and luxurious mansions.

Further north is **Palermo**, an upper middle-class suburb with spacious parks, plenty of shopping and heaps of restaurants; it's subdivided into the trendy neighborhoods of Palermo Soho, Palermo Hollywood and Las Cañitas, among others. And edging Palermo's borders are **Belgrano** and **Once**, both home to concentrations of ethnic Chinese, Korean, Peruvian and Jewish people.

BA's Ezeiza airport is about 35km south of the city center.

Top Five Buenos Aires Splurges

- Hit the lovely spa at the five-star Four Seasons (p86) hotel
- Reserve a seat or two at the closed-door restaurant iLatina (p90)
- Find that perfect Victrola in a San Telmo antiques shop
- Set aside a day, head to the countryside and go horseback riding
- Head to the airport in a luxury car from Silver Star Transport (p112)

PESKY INFLATION

Be warned: while accurate at time of research, prices quoted here are likely to rise rapidly. Unofficial inflation rates hover around 25% (officially it's 10%). Check before booking.

Because of Argentina's high inflation, hotels and certain other businesses sometimes quote in US dollars. We've chosen to publish prices in the currency quoted to us during research, so keep an attentive eye for AR$ and US$ as you look through the listings!

Fast Facts

- Population: 2.9 million
- Area: 203 sq km
- Telephone area code: ☎011
- Annual per capita meat consumption: 58kg (129lb)

Must-try Foods

- *Bife de chorizo:* sirloin steak
- *Empanadas:* baked, savory turnovers
- *Helado*: arguably the best ice cream in the world

Resources

- Argentina Independent: www.argentinaindependent.com
- Pick up the Fork: www.pickupthefork.com

Buenos Aires Highlights

❶ Commune with BA's rich and famous dead at **Cementerio de la Recoleta** (p71)

❷ Absorb some history and see the presidential offices at **Plaza de Mayo** (p56)

❸ Check out the very popular Sunday **antiques fair** (p108) at Plaza Dorrego in San Telmo

❹ Feast on tasty steaks or more exotic cuisine in Palermo's **Las Cañitas** (p93)

❺ Marvel at amazingly high leg kicks and sexy moves at a **tango show** (p99)

❻ Shop in the fun and stylish designer boutiques of **Palermo Viejo** (p109)

❼ Party all night long in BA's chic and super-happening **nightclubs** (p94) in Palermo

❽ Attend a loud, exciting and always passionate ***fútbol* game** (p80)

❾ Strolling, shopping and people-watching on always-bustling **Calle Florida** (p56)

❿ Wander **El Caminito** (p67) and watch weekend buskers in La Boca

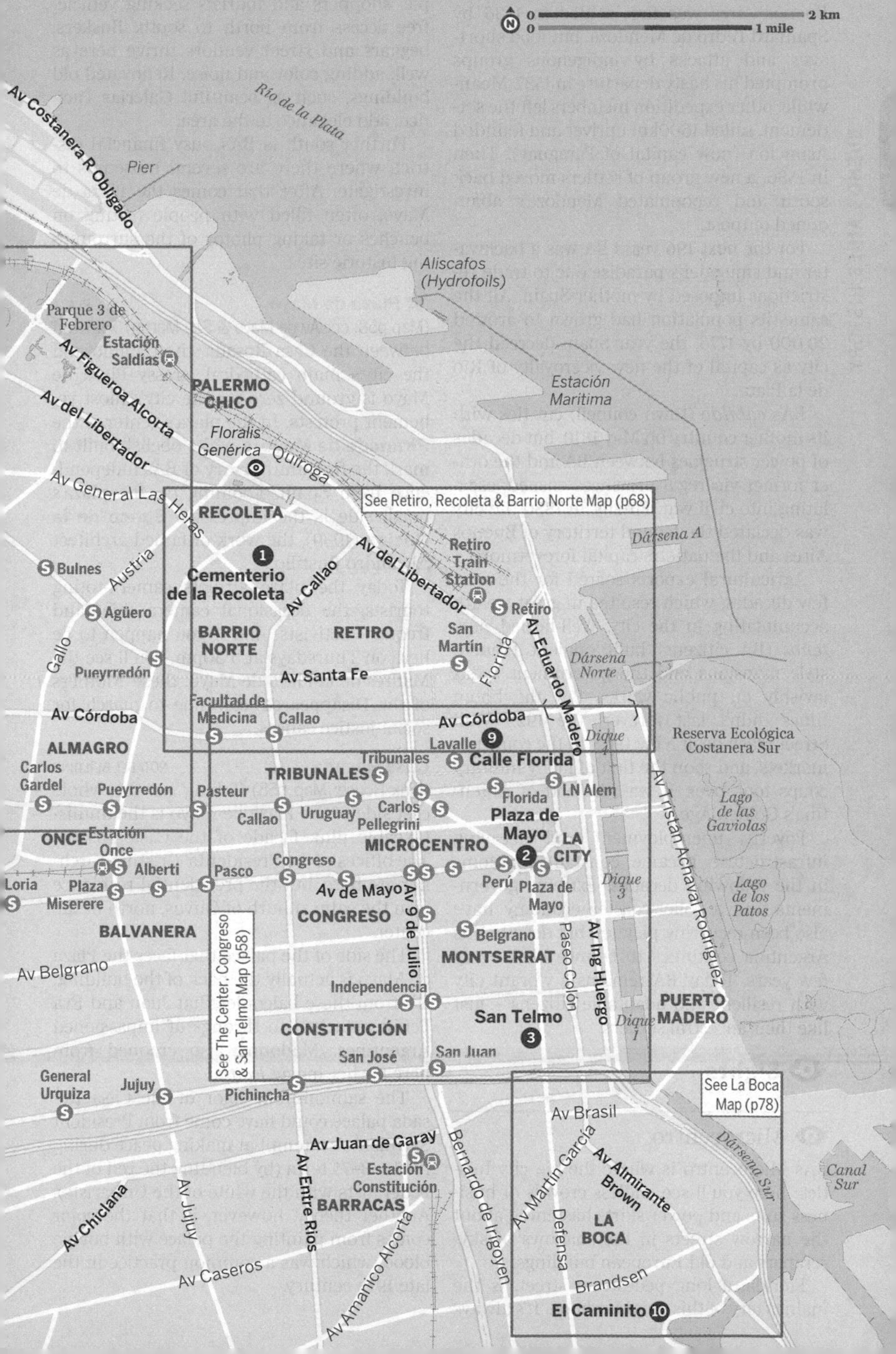

0 2 km
0 1 mile
Río de la Plata
Av Costanera R Obligado
Pier
Aliscafos (Hydrofoils)
Estación Maritima
Parque 3 de Febrero
Estación Saldías
Av Figueroa Alcorta
Av del Libertador
PALERMO CHICO
Floralis Genérica
Quiroga
Av General Las Heras
See Retiro, Recoleta & Barrio Norte Map (p68)
RECOLETA
1
Cementerio de la Recoleta
Av Callao
Av del Libertador
Retiro Train Station
Retiro
Dársena A
Bulnes
Austria
Agüero
Gallo
Pueyrredón
BARRIO NORTE
RETIRO
San Martín
Florida
Av Eduardo Madero
Dársena Norte
Av Santa Fe
Facultad de Medicina
Callao
Av Córdoba
Av Córdoba
Lavalle
9
Dique 4
Reserva Ecológica Costanera Sur
ALMAGRO
Carlos Gardel
Pueyrredón
Pasteur
Tribunales
TRIBUNALES
Calle Florida
LN Alem
Av Tristán Achaval Rodríguez
Lago de las Gaviolas
Callao
Uruguay
Carlos Pellegrini
Florida
Plaza de Mayo
ONCE
Estación Once
MICROCENTRO
LA CITY
2
Alberti
Loria
Plaza Miserere
Pasco
Congreso
Perú
Plaza de Mayo
Dique 3
Lago de los Patos
Av de Mayo
Av 9 de Julio
CONGRESO
BALVANERA
See The Center, Congreso & San Telmo Map (p58)
Belgrano
Paseo Colón
Av Ing Huergo
MONTSERRAT
Av Belgrano
Independencia
PUERTO MADERO
San Telmo
3
Dique 1
CONSTITUCIÓN
San José
San Juan
General Urquiza
Jujuy
Pichincha
See La Boca Map (p78)
Av Brasil
Dársena Sur
Av Juan de Garay
Estación Constitución
Bernardo de Irigoyen
Av Martín García
Av Almirante Brown
Canal Sur
BARRACAS
Av Chiclana
Av Jujuy
Av Entre Ríos
Defensa
LA BOCA
Av Amancio Alcorta
Av Caseros
Brandsen
El Caminito
10

History

Buenos Aires was first settled in 1536 by Spaniard Pedro de Mendoza, but food shortages and attacks by indigenous groups prompted his hasty departure in 1537. Meanwhile, other expedition members left the settlement, sailed 1600km upriver and founded Asunción (now capital of Paraguay). Then in 1580, a new group of settlers moved back south and repopulated Mendoza's abandoned outpost.

For the next 196 years BA was a backwater and smuggler's paradise due to trade restrictions imposed by mother Spain. All the same, its population had grown to around 20,000 by 1776, the year Spain decreed the city as capital of the new viceroyalty of Río de la Plata.

BA's *cabildo* (town council) cut ties with its mother country on May 1810, but decades of power struggles between BA and the other former viceregal provinces ensued, escalating into civil war. Finally, in 1880 the city was declared the federal territory of Buenos Aires and the nation's capital forevermore.

Agricultural exports soared for the next few decades, which resulted in great wealth accumulating in the city. Well-heeled *porteños* (BA citizens) built opulent French-style mansions and the government spent lavishly on public works. But the boom times didn't last forever: the 1929 Wall Street crash dealt a big blow to the country's markets, and soon the first of many military coups took over. It was the end of Argentina's Golden Age.

Poverty, unemployment and decaying infrastructure became constant problems in the following decades. Extreme governments and a roller-coaster economy have also been recurring plagues, but despite this Argentina continues to bounce back every few years. Today BA remains a vibrant city with resilient and adaptable citizens – just like their ancestral settlers.

Sights

Microcentro

BA's Microcentro is where the big city hustles: here you'll see endless crowds of business suits and power skirts hastening about the narrow streets in the shadows of skyscrapers and old European buildings.

Florida, a long pedestrian street, is the main artery of this neighborhood. It's always jammed during the day with businesspeople, shoppers and tourists seeking vehicle-free access from north to south. Buskers, beggars and street vendors thrive here as well, adding color and noise. Renovated old buildings, such as beautiful Galerías Pacífico, add elegance to the area.

Further south is BA's busy financial district, where there are several museums to investigate. After that comes the Plaza de Mayo, often filled with people resting on benches or taking photos of the surrounding historic sites.

★Plaza de Mayo PLAZA

(Map p58; cnr Av de Mayo & San Martín) Planted between the Casa Rosada, the Cabildo and the city's main cathedral, grassy Plaza de Mayo is ground zero for the city's most vehement protests. In the plaza's center is the **Pirámide de Mayo**, a white obelisk built to mark the first anniversary of BA's independence from Spain. Looming on the plaza's north side is the impressive **Banco de la Nación** (1939), the work of famed architect Alejandro Bustillo.

Today the plaza attracts camera-toting tourists, the occasional camera thief and frequent activists. And if you happen to be here on Thursdays at 3:30pm, you'll see the Madres de la Plaza de Mayo; these 'Mothers of the Disappeared' continue to march for social-justice causes.

Casa Rosada NOTABLE BUILDING

(Pink House; Map p58) Taking up the whole east side of the Plaza de Mayo is the unmistakeable pink facade of the Casa Rosada. The offices of 'La Presidenta' Cristina Kirchner are here, but the presidential residence is in the calm suburb of Olivos, north of the center.

The side of the palace that faces the Plaza de Mayo is actually the back of the building. It's from these balconies that Juan and Eva Perón preached to throngs of impassioned Argentines. Madonna also crooned from here for her movie *Evita*.

The salmon-pink color of the Casa Rosada palace could have come from President Sarmiento's attempt at making peace during his 1868–74 term (by blending the red of the Federalists with the white of the Unitarists). Another theory, however, is that the color comes from painting the palace with bovine blood, which was a common practice in the late 19th century.

Off-limits during the military dictatorship of 1976–83, the Casa Rosada is now reasonably accessible to the public. Free half-hour **tours** (☎4344-3600; ⏲10am-6pm Sat & Sun) **FREE** are offered.

Museo del Bicentenario MUSEUM
(Map p58; ☎4344-3802; www.museobicentenario.gob.ar; cnr Av Paseo Colón & Hipólito Yrigoyen; ⏲10am-6pm Wed-Sun Apr-Nov, 11am-7pm Wed-Sun Dec-Mar) **FREE** Behind the Casa Rosada you'll notice a glassy wedge marking this airy and sparkling underground museum, housed within the brick vaults of the old *aduana* (customs house). Head down into the open space, which has over a dozen side rooms – each dedicated to a different era of Argentina's tumultuous political history. There are mostly videos (in Spanish) and a few artifacts to see, along with temporary art exhibitions and an impressive restored mural by Mexican artist David Alfaro Siqueiros. A pleasant cafe-restaurant provides nourishment and rest.

Catedral Metropolitana CATHEDRAL
(Map p58; ⏲7:30am-6:30pm Mon-Fri, 9am-7pm Sat & Sun) This solemn cathedral was built on the site of the original colonial church and not finished until 1827. It's a significant religious and architectural landmark, and carved above its triangular facade and neoclassical columns are bas-reliefs of Jacob and Joseph. The spacious interior is equally impressive, with baroque details and an elegant rococo altar.

The cathedral is also a national historical site that contains the tomb of General José de San Martín, Argentina's most revered hero.

The cathedral is also a national historical site that contains the tomb of General José de San Martín, Argentina's most revered hero. Outside the cathedral you'll see a flame keeping his spirit alive.

Cabildo MUSEUM
(Map p58; ☎4342-6729; www.cabildonacional.com.ar; Bolívar 65; AR$10; ⏲10:30am-5pm Wed-Fri, to 6pm Sat & Sun) This mid-18th-century town hall building is now a museum. It used to have colonnades that spanned the Plaza de Mayo, but the building of surrounding avenues unfortunately destroyed them. Inside you'll find a few mementos of the early 19th-century British invasions, some paintings in colonial and early independence-style, and the occasional temporary exhibit. On Thursday and Friday, a lively crafts market sets up in the patio – and the cafe here is a great place to relax. Tours in Spanish offered.

Galerías Pacífico LANDMARK
(Map p58; ☎5555-5110; cnr Florida & Av Córdoba; ⏲10am-9pm) Covering an entire city block, this beautiful French-style building has fulfilled the commercial purpose that its designers envisioned when they constructed it in 1889. Galerías Pacíficos is now a shopping center – dotted with lovely fairy lights at night – and boasts upscale stores along with a large food court (which has longer hours than the stores). The excellent Centro Cultural Borges takes up the top floor. Tours are

BUENOS AIRES IN...

Two Days

Start with a stroll in **San Telmo** and duck into some antiques stores. Walk north to the **Plaza de Mayo** (p56) for a historical perspective, then wander the **Microcentro**, perhaps veering east to **Puerto Madero** – a great spot for a break.

Keep heading northward into **Retiro** and **Recoleta**, stopping off at the **Museo Nacional de Bellas Artes** (p71) to admire some impressionism. Be sure to visit the **Cementerio de la Recoleta** (p71) to commune with BA's bygone elite. For dinner and nightlife, **Palermo Viejo** is hard to beat.

On day two, take in the **Congreso** neighborhood or head to **La Boca**. Shop in **Palermo Viejo** and at night catch a **tango show** or a performance at the **Teatro Colón** (p106).

Four Days

On your third day consider taking a day trip to **Tigre**, or **Colonia** in Uruguay. On the fourth day you can take a **tour** or a **tango lesson**, check out **Palermo's parks** or head to the **Mataderos fair** (if it's a weekend). Be sure to find yourself a good steak restaurant for your last meal.

The Center, Congreso & San Telmo

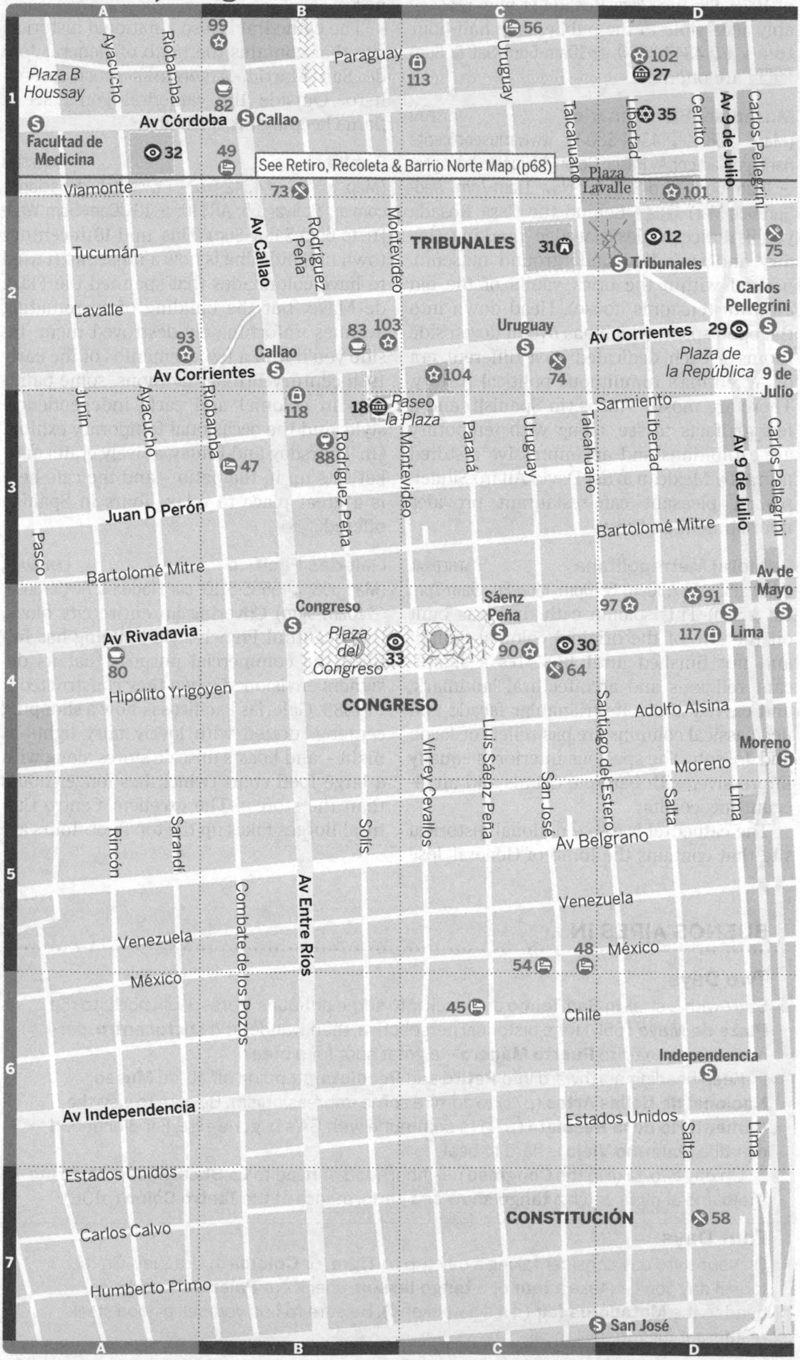

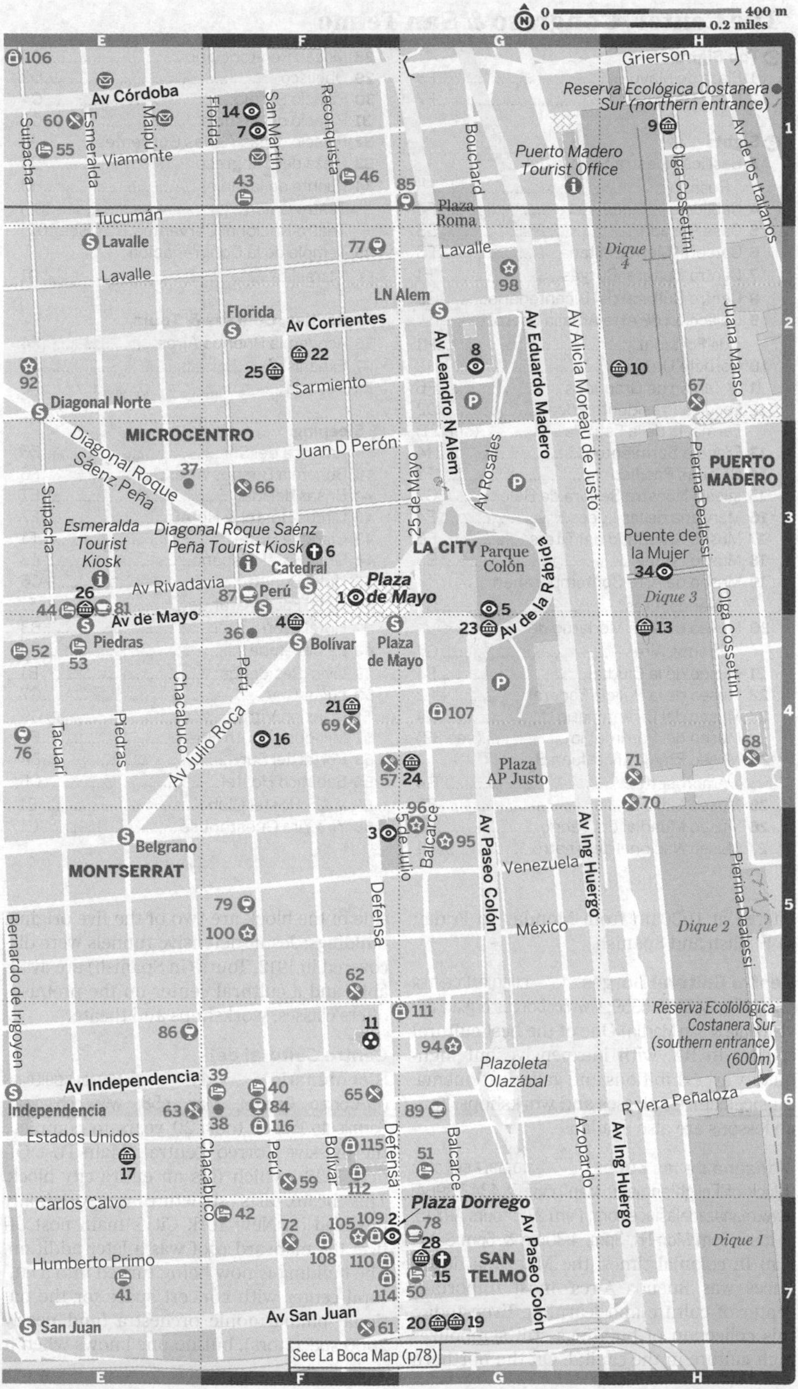
0 400 m
0 0.2 miles
E
F
G
H
1
2
3
4
5
6
7
106
Av Córdoba
Suipacha
Esmeralda
Maipú
Florida
San Martín
Reconquista
Bouchard
Grierson
Reserva Ecológica Costanera Sur (northern entrance)
Av de los Italianos
Olga Cossettini
Puerto Madero Tourist Office
60
55
Viamonte
14
7
43
46
85
9
Plaza Roma
Tucumán
Lavalle
77
Lavalle
Dique 4
98
LN Alem
Florida
Av Corrientes
Av Eduardo Madero
Av Alicia Moreau de Justo
Juana Manso
22
25
8
10
Sarmiento
Av Leandro N Alem
67
92
Diagonal Norte
MICROCENTRO
Juan D Perón
Pierina Dealessi
PUERTO MADERO
Diagonal Roque Sáenz Peña
37
66
25 de Mayo
Av Rosales
Suipacha
Esmeralda Tourist Kiosk
Diagonal Roque Saénz Peña Tourist Kiosk
6
Catedral
LA CITY
Parque Colón
Av de la Rábida
Puente de la Mujer
34
26
Av Rivadavia
87
Perú
Plaza de Mayo
1
Dique 3
Olga Cossettini
44
81
Av de Mayo
4
5
23
13
52
Piedras
53
36
Bolívar
Plaza de Mayo
Perú
Chacabuco
21
107
69
Tacuarí
Piedras
Av Julio Roca
16
76
68
Plaza AP Justo
57
24
71
70
96
3
Balcarce
95
Belgrano
MONTSERRAT
Defensa
Av Paseo Colón
Av Ing Huergo
Venezuela
Pierina Dealessi
79
100
México
Dique 2
Bernardo de Irigoyen
62
111
Reserva Ecológica Costanera Sur (southern entrance) (600m)
86
11
94
Plazoleta Olazábal
Av Independencia
39
40
65
R Vera Peñaloza
Independencia
63
38
84
116
89
Estados Unidos
Chacabuco
Perú
Bolívar
115
Defensa
Balcarce
Azopardo
Av Ing Huergo
17
51
59
112
Carlos Calvo
42
Plaza Dorrego
72
105
109
2
78
Dique 1
108
110
28
Humberto Primo
15
SAN TELMO
Av Paseo Colón
41
114
50
Av San Juan
San Juan
61
20
19
See La Boca Map (p78)

The Center, Congreso & San Telmo

offered at 11:30am from Monday to Friday, in English and Spanish.

Centro Cultural Borges CULTURAL CENTER
(Map p58; ☎5555-5359; www.ccborges.org.ar; cnr Viamonte & San Martín) One of the best cultural centers in BA, with inexpensive but high-quality art exhibitions and galleries, cinema, music, lectures, classes and workshops. Tango lessons are also available.

Manzana de las Luces NOTABLE BUILDING
(Block of Enlightenment; Map p58; ☎4342-3964; www.manazadelasluces.org; Perú 272; tours AR$15; ⏱tours 3pm Mon-Fri, 3pm, 4:30pm & 6pm Sat & Sun) In colonial times, the Manzana de las Luces was Buenos Aires' most important center of culture and learning. Even today, this collection of buildings still symbolizes high culture in the capital. On the northern side of the block are two of the five original buildings; Jesuit defensive tunnels were discovered in 1912. Tours (in Spanish) are available, and a cultural center on the premises offers classes, workshops and theater.

Centro Cultural del Bicentenario NOTABLE BUILDING
(Ex-Correo Central; Map p58; www.ccb.gov.ar; Sarmiento 151) It took 20 years to complete the massive Correo Central (Main Post Office; 1928), which fills an entire city block. This beaux arts structure was originally modeled on New York City's main post office; the mansard roof was a later addition. The building is now being turned into a cultural center with concert space for the national philharmonic orchestra (and nearly 2000 spectators), but no one knows when it

Eating

57 Aldo's Vinoteca F4
58 Aramburu D7
59 Bar El Federal F6
60 Broccolino E1
61 Café San Juan F7
62 Café San Juan La Cantina F5
63 Casal de Catalunya E6
64 Chan Chan C4
65 El Desnivel F6
66 Granix F3
67 i Central Market H2
68 i Fresh Market H4
69 La Panadería de Pablo F4
70 La Parolaccia del Mare H4
71 La Parolaccia Trattoria H4
72 Origen Café F7
73 Parrilla Peña B1
74 Pizzería Güerrín C2
75 Tomo 1 .... D2
Vita .... (see 36)

Drinking & Nightlife

76 Alsina E4
77 Bahrein F2
78 Bar Plaza Dorrego G7
79 Boutique F5
80 Café de los Angelitos A4
81 Café Tortoni E3
82 Clásica y Moderna B1
83 El Gato Negro B2
84 Gibraltar F6
85 La Cigale G1
86 La Puerta Roja E6
87 London City F3
88 Maluco Beleza B3
89 Pride Cafe G6

Entertainment

Academia Nacional del Tango .... (see 26)
90 Ávila Bar C4
Café de los Angelitos .... (see 80)
Café Tortoni .... (see 81)
91 Cantares D4
92 Confitería Ideal E2
93 El Beso A2
94 El Viejo Almacén G6
95 La Trastienda G5
96 La Ventana G5
97 Los 36 Billares D4
98 Luna Park G2
99 Notorious B1
100 Tango Queer F5
101 Teatro Colón D1
102 Teatro Nacional Cervantes D1
103 Teatro Presidente Alvear B2
104 Teatro San Martín C2
105 Todo Mundo F7

Shopping

106 Arte y Esperanza E1
107 Arte y Esperanza G4
108 Cualquier Verdura F7
109 Feria de San Telmo F7
110 Gil Antiguedades F7
111 Materia Urbana G6
112 Mercado de San Telmo F6
113 Portobello Vintage Boutique C1
114 Punto Sur F7
115 Vinotango F6
116 Walrus Books F6
117 Wildlife D4
118 Zival's B3

will open; check it out during your tenure and cross your fingers.

Museo de la Ciudad MUSEUM
(Map p58; ☎4343-2123; Defensa 219; admission AR$1; ⏲11am-7pm Mon-Fri, 10am-8pm Sat & Sun) This upstairs museum was closed at research time due to major restoration, but in the future you should expect both permanent and temporary exhibitions on *porteño* life and history here. Downstairs is a large hall showcasing salvaged doors and ancient hardware. Nearby, at the corner of Adolfo Alsina and Defensa, is the **Farmacia de la Estrella** (Map p58) (1835), a functioning homeopathic pharmacy with gorgeous woodwork and elaborate late-19th-century ceiling murals depicting health-oriented themes. Occasionally the museum opens via its Adolfo Alsina 412 door.

Museo Etnográfico Juan B Ambrosetti MUSEUM
(Map p58; ☎4331-7788; www.museoetnografico.filo.uba.ar; Moreno 350; admission AR$4; ⏲1-7pm Tue-Fri, 3-7pm Sat & Sun) This small but attractive anthropological museum was created by Juan B Ambrosetti not only as an institute for research and university training, but also as an educational center for the public. On display are archaeological and anthropological collections from the Andean Northwest and Patagonia. Beautiful indigenous artifacts are also featured, while an African and Asian room showcases some priceless pieces.

Basílica Nuestra Señora del Rosario NOTABLE BUILDING
(Map p58; ☎tours in Spanish 4331-1668; cnr Defensa & Av Belgrano; ⏲Tours admission by appointment only Mon-Fri, at 3:30pm & 4:30pm Sun) This

18th-century Dominican basilica has a colorful history. On its left tower are the replicated scars of shrapnel from fire against British troops who holed up here during the 1806 invasion. Tours in Spanish are available; you can see the flags that were captured from the British.

Museo de la Policía Federal MUSEUM
(Map p58; ☎4394-6857; San Martín 353, 7th fl; ⏰2-7pm Tue-Fri) FREE This quirky police museum displays a whole slew of uniforms and medals, along with 'illegal activities' exhibits (cockfighting and gambling), drug paraphernalia (including a fake arm stuck with a needle!) and even a stuffed police dog. The forensic room way in the back was being remodeled at research time – it may or may not keep its grisly photos and dummies of hacked-up murder victims; something to keep in mind if you bring the kids.

Museo Mitre MUSEUM
(Map p58; ☎4394-8240; San Martín 336; admission AR$15; ⏰1-5pm Mon-Fri) This museum is located in the colonial house where Bartolomé Mitre – Argentina's first legitimate president elected under the constitution of 1853 – resided with his family. Mitre's term ran from 1862 to 1868, and he spent much of it leading the country's armies against Paraguay. Two courtyards, salons, an office, a billiards room and Mitre's old bedroom are part of this complex. Since part of the museum is open air, you may find it closed during heavy rain.

Museo Mundial del Tango MUSEUM
(Map p58; ☎4345-6967; Av de Mayo 833, 1st fl; admission AR$20; ⏰2:30-7:30pm Mon-Fri) Located below the Academia Nacional del Tango (p99) is this tango museum – for fans of the dance only. Just a couple of large rooms are filled with tango memorabilia, from old records and photos to historic literature and posters. Tango shoes are also featured, but the highlight has to be one of Carlos Gardel's famous fedora hats.

Puerto Madero

The newest and least conventional of the capital's 48 official barrios is Puerto Madero, located east of the Microcentro. Once an old waterfront, it's now a wonderful place to stroll, boasting cobbled paths and a long line of attractive brick warehouses that have been converted into ritzy lofts, business offices and upscale restaurants. Today this neighborhood holds some of BA's most expensive real estate.

In the mid-19th century the city's mudflats were transformed into a modernized port for Argentina's burgeoning international commerce. Puerto Madero was completed in 1898, but it had exceeded its budget – and by 1910 the amount of cargo was already too great for the new port. Only the 1926 completion of Retiro's Puerto Nuevo solved these problems.

Reserva Ecológica Costanera Sur NATURE RESERVE
(☎4893-1588; Av Tristán Achavat Rodríguez 1550; ⏰8am-7pm Tue-Sun Nov-Mar, to 6pm Apr-Oct) FREE The beautifully marshy land of this 350-hectare nature reserve has become a popular site for weekend picnics and walks. Bring binoculars if you're a birder – over 200 bird species can be spotted, along with river turtles, iguanas and nutria. Further in at the eastern shoreline of the reserve you can get a close-up view of the Río de la Plata's muddy waters.

Tours are given on weekends; monthly Friday night full moon tours are also available (call for schedules). On warm weekends and holidays you can rent bikes just outside either the northern or southern entrances.

Colección de Arte Amalia Lacroze de Fortabat MUSEUM
(Museo Fortabat; Map p58; ☎4310-6600; www.coleccionfortabat.org.ar; Olga Cossettini 141; admission AR$35; ⏰noon-8pm Tue-Sun) Rivaling Palermo's Malba for cutting-edge looks is this stunning art museum, prominently located at the northern end of Puerto Madero. It shows off the collection of billionairess, philanthropist and socialite Amalia Lacroze de Fortabat, Argentina's wealthiest woman. There are galleries devoted to Antonio Berni and Raúl Soldi (both famous Argentine painters), and works by international stars like Dali, Klimt, Rodin and Chagall; look for Warhol's colorful take on Fortabat herself in the family portrait gallery.

Faena Arts Center ARTS CENTER
(☎4010-9233; www.faenaartscenter.org; Aime Paine 1169; admission AR$40, free Mon; ⏰varies depending on exhibition) This very large, airy art space – in a beautifully renovated flour mill – highlights the contemporary dreams of local and international artists and designers. You should expect the most cutting-edge exhibits that utilize these spaces to the maximum – think rope nets hanging from the

ceiling or light pyramids reaching for the sky. Check the website for upcoming shows.

Fragata Sarmiento MUSEUM

(Map p58; ☎ 4334-9386; Dique 3; admission AR$2; ⏲ 10am-7pm) Over 23,000 Argentine naval cadets and officers have trained aboard this 85m sailing vessel, which traveled around the world 37 times between 1899 and 1938. On board are detailed records of its lengthy voyages, a gallery of its commanding officers, plenty of nautical items including old uniforms, and even the stuffed remains of Lampazo (the ship's pet dog), serenely posed. Peek into the ship's holds, galley and engine room and note the hooks where sleeping hammocks were strung up.

Corbeta Uruguay MUSEUM

(Map p58; ☎ 4314-1090; Dique 4; admission AR$2; ⏲ 10am-7pm) This 46m-long military ship did surveys along Argentina's coast and supplied bases in Antarctica until it was decommissioned in 1926, after 52 years of service. Displayed below the main deck are interesting relics from Antarctica expeditions, such as crampons and snowshoes, along with historical photos and nautical items. Check out the tiny kitchen, complete with *mate* supplies (of course).

Puente de la Mujer BRIDGE

(Map p58; Dique 3) The striking Puente de la Mujer (Women's Bridge) is Puerto Madero's signature monument. Unveiled in 2001, this gleaming-white structure spans Dique 3 and resembles a sharp fishhook or even a harp – but is supposed to represent a couple dancing the tango. Designed by acclaimed Spanish architect Santiago Calatrava and mostly built in Spain, this 160m-long pedestrian bridge cost AR$6 million and rotates 90 degrees to allow water traffic to pass – when it's functioning, that is.

Congreso

Congreso is an interesting mix of old-time cinemas and theaters, bustling commerce and hard-core politics. The buildings still hold that European aura, but there's more grittiness here than in the Microcentro: it has a more local city feel, with an atmosphere of faded elegance and fewer fancy crowds.

Separating Congreso from the Microcentro is Av 9 de Julio, 'the widest street in the world!,' as proud *porteños* love to boast. While this may be true – it's 16 lanes at its widest – the neighbouring streets Cerrito and Carlos Pellegrini make it look even broader.

Teatro Colón NOTABLE BUILDING

(Map p58; ☎ 4378-7127; www.teatrocolon.org.ar; Tucumán 1171; tours AR$110; ⏲ tours 9am-5pm) This gorgeous and impressive seven-story building is one of BA's most prominent landmarks. It's the city's main performing-arts venue and the only facility of its kind in the country, a world-class forum for opera, ballet and classical music with astounding acoustics. Occupying an entire city block, the Colón can seat 2500 spectators and provide standing room for another 500. The theater's opening night was a presentation of Verdi's *Aïda,* and visitors have been wowed ever since. Worthwhile backstage tours run frequently.

Plaza del Congreso PLAZA

(Map p58; ☎ 4010-3000, ext 2410; ⏲ tours 12:30pm & 5pm Mon, Tue, Thu & Fri) At the western end of Av de Mayo lies Plaza del Congreso, often dotted with cooing pigeons and families feeding them. The **Monumento a los Dos Congresos** honors the congresses of 1810 in Buenos Aires and 1816 in Tucumán, both of which led to Argentine independence. The enormous granite steps symbolize the high Andes, and the fountain at its base represents the Atlantic Ocean.

West of the plaza is the colossal green-domed **Palacio del Congreso** (Congress building). Modeled on the Capitol in Washington, DC, and topped by an 85m dome, the palace was completed in 1906. Free guided tours are offered in English and Spanish. Go to the entrance at Hipólito Yrigoyen, 1849; bring photo ID.

Palacio Barolo NOTABLE BUILDING

(Map p58; ☎ 4381-1885; www.palaciobarolo.com; Av de Mayo 1370; standard tours AR$80, longer tours incl glass of wine AR$150; ⏲ standard tours 4-7pm Mon-Thu, longer tours 8pm Wed & Fri & 8:30pm Thu) One of the Congreso area's most striking buildings is this 22-story concrete edifice. The building's unique design was inspired by Dante's *Divine Comedy*; its height (100m) is a reference to each canto (or song), the number of its floors (22) to verses per song, and its divided structure to hell, purgatory and heaven.

Finished in 1923, Palacio Barolo was BA's highest skyscraper until the construction of Edificio Kavanagh, in Retiro. At the top is a lighthouse with an amazing 360-degree view of the city.

1

ANDREW BAIN/GETTY IMAGES ©

2

4

JOAO CANZIANI/GETTY IMAGES ©

MICHAEL TAYLOR/GETTY IMAGES ©

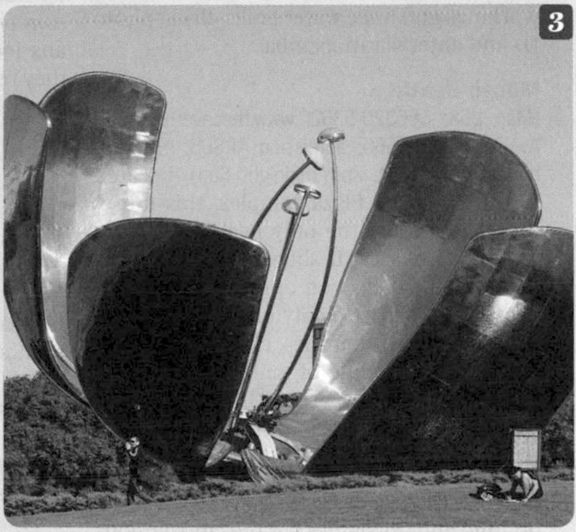

LONELY PLANET/GETTY IMAGES ©

1. El Caminito (p69)
La Boca's most famous street contains buildings with colorful facades.

2. Teatro Colón (p63)
Buenos Aires' much loved theater regularly hosts performances by prominent figures.

3. Floralis Genérica (p71)
This giant sculptural flower, built in 2002 by Eduardo Catalano, has petals that close up at night.

4. Obelisco (p66)
This 67m-high monument keeps a watchful eye over Av 9 de Julio.

Teatro Nacional Cervantes NOTABLE BUILDING
(Map p58; ☎4815-8883; www.teatrocervantes.gov.ar; Libertad 815) Six blocks southwest of Plaza San Martín, you can't help but notice the lavishly ornamented Cervantes theater. It's showing its age, with worn carpeting and rough edges, but improvement projects are planned. Until then, enjoy the elegance – however faded – with a tour (call for current schedules).

On the corner and attached to the theater is the low-key **Museo Nacional del Teatro** (Map p58; ☎4815-8883, ext 156; cnr Av Córdoba & Libertad; ⏲10am-6pm Mon-Fri) FREE. Check out the gaucho suit worn by Carlos Gardel.

Palacio de las Aguas Corrientes NOTABLE BUILDING, MUSEUM
(Map p58; cnr Av Córdoba & Riobamba) FREE Swedish engineer Karl Nyströmer and Norwegian architect Olaf Boye helped create this gorgeous and eclectic waterworks building. On the 2nd floor is the small and quirky **Museo del Patrimonio** (Map p58; ☎6319-1104; ⏲9am-1pm Mon-Fri, tours in Spanish 11am Mon, Wed & Fri) FREE. The collection of pretty tiles, faucets, handles, ceramic pipe joints and plenty of old toilets and bidets is well lit and displayed. Guided visits offer a backstage glimpse of the building's inner workings and huge water tanks. Bring photo ID and enter via Riobamba.

Museo Beatle MUSEUM
(Map p58; ☎6320-5362; www.thecavern.com.ar; Av Corrientes 1660; admission AR$50; ⏲10am-midnight Mon-Sat, 2pm-midnight Sun) Located in the Paseo La Plaza complex, this museum claims to be the only Beatles museum in South America. It showcases the Beatles memorabilia collection of owner Rodolfo R Veasquez – expect plenty of records, collector plates, toys, figurines, eight-track tapes, games and a couple of guitars from musicians related to the group. To find the museum, follow the 'The Cavern' signs.

Obelisco LANDMARK
(Map p58; cnr Avs 9 de Julio & Corrientes) At Avs 9 de Julio and Corrientes lies the city's famous Obelisco, 67m high and built in 1936; it's the destination of *porteño* sports fans when they have a big win to celebrate.

Plaza Lavalle PLAZA
The plaza is surrounded by the austere neoclassical **Escuela Presidente Roca** (Map p58) (1902), the French-style **Palacio de Justicia** (Map p58; Talcahuano 550; Ⓢ Línea B Uruguay) (1904) and the landmark Teatro Colón. Nearby is the **Templo de la Congregación Israelita** (Map p58), Argentina's largest synagogue.

San Telmo

Full of charm and personality, San Telmo is one of BA's most attractive and historically rich barrios. Narrow cobbled streets and low-story colonial housing retain an old-time feel, though the tourist dollar continues to bring about changes.

Historically, San Telmo is famous for the violent street fighting that took place when British troops, at war with Spain, invaded the city in 1806. British forces advanced up narrow Defensa, but an impromptu militia drove the British back to their ships. The victory gave *porteños* confidence in their ability to stand apart from Spain, even though the city's independence had to wait another three years.

After this, San Telmo became a fashionable, classy neighborhood. In the late 19th century, however, a yellow-fever epidemic hit, driving the rich north into present-day Recoleta. Many older mansions were subdivided and became *conventillos* (tenements) to house poor families. Years ago these *conventillos* attracted artists and bohemians looking for cheap rent, but these days they're more likely to be filled with fancy shops, cheap hostels or rich expats.

★ **Plaza Dorrego** PLAZA
(Map p58) After Plaza de Mayo, Plaza Dorrego is the city's oldest plaza. It dates to the 18th century and was originally a pit stop for caravans bringing supplies into BA from around Argentina. At the turn of the 19th century it became a public square, surrounded by colonial buildings that survive to this day. There's still a wonderful old-time atmosphere here and cafe-restaurants like Bar Plaza Dorrego will definitely take you back in time – if you can ignore the nearby Starbucks.

Plaza Dorrego is the heart of San Telmo's famous Sunday *feria* (street markets; see boxed text, p108).

El Zanjón de Granados ARCHAEOLOGICAL SITE
(Map p58; ☎4361-3002; www.elzanjon.com.ar; Defensa 755; 1hr tour Mon-Fri AR$90, 30min tour Sun AR$60; ⏲tours 11am, noon, 2pm & 3pm Mon-Fri, every 30min 1-6pm Sun) One of the more unique places in BA is this amazing ur-

ban architectural site. A series of old tunnels, sewers and cisterns (built from 1730 onwards) were constructed above a river tributary and provided the base for one of BA's oldest settlements, which later became a family mansion, then tenement housing and some shops. It's best to reserve ahead for tours.

Museo de Arte Moderno de Buenos Aires MUSEUM

(Mamba; Map p58; ☎4342-3001; www.museodeartemoderno.buenosaires.gob.ar; Av San Juan 350; admission AR$5, free Tue; ⏲11am-7pm Tue-Fri, to 8pm Sat & Sun) Housed in a recycled tobacco warehouse, this spacious and newly remodeled museum shows off the works of both national and international contemporary artists. Expect temporary exhibitions showcasing everything from photography to industrial design, and from figurative to conceptual art. There's also an auditorium, and there are plans to integrate the old cinema museum next door, too – and add a cafe and gift shop.

Museo de Arte Contemporáneo Buenos Aires MUSEUM

(MACBA; Map p58; ☎5299-2010; www.macba.com.ar; Av San Juan 328; admission AR$25; ⏲noon-7pm Mon & Wed-Fri, 11am-7:30pm Sat & Sun) Art lovers shouldn't miss this fine museum, which specializes in geometric abstraction drawn from the technology-driven world that surrounds us today (think architecture, maps and computers). So rather than traditional paintings, you'll see large, colorful and minimalist pieces meant to inspire reflection.

Museo Penitenciario MUSEUM

(Map p58; ☎4361-0917; museopenitenciarioargentino.blogspot.com.ar; Humberto Primo 378; ⏲2-6pm Thu, Fri & Sun) FREE Dating from 1760, this building was a convent and later a women's prison before it became a penal museum in 1980; reconstructed jail cells give an idea of the prisoners' conditions. Don't miss the homemade playing cards and shivs, plus the tennis balls used to hide drugs. A prison infirmary is also exhibited. Next door, the neocolonial and baroque **Iglesia Nuestra Señora de Belén** (Map p58; Humberto Primo 340) was a Jesuit school until 1767, when the Bethlemite order took it over.

Museo Histórico Nacional MUSEUM

(Map p78; ☎4307-1182; Defensa 1600; ⏲11am-6pm Wed-Sun) FREE Located in Parque Lezama is the city's national historical museum. It's dedicated to exhibiting items related to Argentina's revolution on May 25, 1810.

Inside, exhibits are a bit sparse, but at least they're neatly displayed. There are several portraits of presidents and other major figures of the time, and you can peek into a recreated version of José de San Martín's bedroom – he was a military hero and liberator of Argentina (along with other South American countries).

Mercado de San Telmo MARKET

(Map p58; Defensa, Bolívar, Carlos Calvo & Estados Unidos block; ⏲9am-8pm) This market was built in 1897 by Juan Antonio Buschiazzo, the same Italian-born Argentine architect who designed Cementerio de la Recoleta. It occupies the inside of an entire city block, though you wouldn't be able to tell just by looking at the modest sidewalk entrances. The wrought-iron interior (note the amazing original ceiling) makes it one of BA's most atmospheric markets; locals shop here for fresh produce and meat. Peripheral antique stalls offer luggage, wine decanters and other treasures. More stalls are open on weekends.

La Boca

Blue collar and raffish to the core, La Boca is still very much a locals' neighborhood. In the mid-19th century La Boca became home to Spanish and Italian immigrants who settled along the Riachuelo, the sinuous river that divides the city from the surrounding province of Buenos Aires. Many came during the booming 1880s and ended up working in the many meat-packing plants and warehouses here, processing and shipping out much of Argentina's vital beef exports.

LA BOCA WARNING

La Boca is not the kind of neighborhood for casual strolls – it can be downright rough in spots. Don't stray far from the riverside walk, El Caminito or La Bombonera Stadium, especially while toting expensive cameras. And certainly don't cross the bridge over the Riachuelo. There's nothing you'd really want to see outside the touristy areas, anyway. Buses 29, 64 and 152 go from Palermo or the city center to La Boca. Taxis are best after dark.

Retiro, Recoleta & Barrio Norte

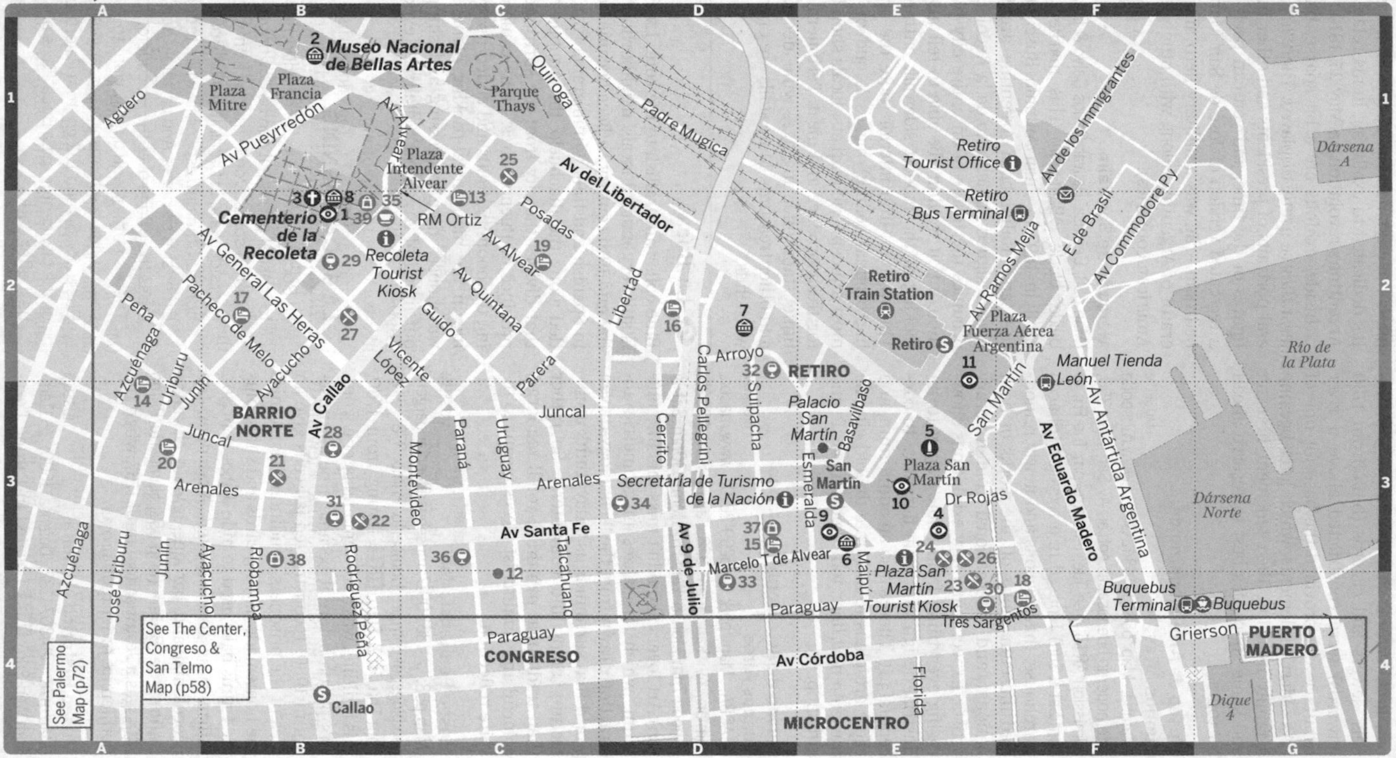

Retiro, Recoleta & Barrio Norte

After sprucing up the shipping barges, the port dwellers splashed leftover paint on the corrugated-metal sidings of their own houses – unwittingly giving La Boca what would become one of its claims to fame. Unfortunately, some of the neighborhood's color also comes from the rainbow slick of industrial wastes on the river.

El Caminito, near the southern edge of La Boca, is the barrio's most famous street, and on weekends busloads of camera-laden tourists come here for photographs and to browse the small crafts fair, while watching tango dancers perform for spare change. A riverside pedestrian walkway offers a close-up sniff of the Riachuelo, while a few museums provide mental stimulation.

★ Fundación Proa — MUSEUM

(Map p78; ☎ 4104-1001; www.proa.org; Av Don Pedro de Mendoza 1929; admission AR$15; ⌚ 11am-7pm Tue-Sun) Only the most cutting-edge national and international artists are invited to show at this elegant art museum, which features high ceilings, white walls and large display halls. Stunning contemporary installations utilize a wide variety of media and themes, while the rooftop terrace is *the* stylish place in La Boca for relaxing with a drink or snack – it boasts a view of the Riachuelo. Plenty of cultural offerings include talks, lectures, workshops, music concerts and cinema screenings.

★ Museo de Bellas Artes de La Boca Benito Quinquela Martín — MUSEUM

(Map p78; ☎ 4301-1080; Av Don Pedro de Mendoza 1835; suggested donation AR$10; ⌚ 10am-6pm Tue-Fri, 11am-6pm Sat & Sun) Once the home and studio of Benito Quinquela Martín (1890–1977), this fine-arts museum exhibits his works and those of more contemporary Argentine artists. The top floor displays Martín's surrealist paintings, whose broad, rough brush strokes and dark colors use the port, silhouettes of laboring men, smokestacks and water reflections as recurring themes. There are outdoor sculptures on the rooftop terraces, and the top tier has awesome views of the port.

Museo de la Pasión Boquense — MUSEUM

(Map p78; ☎ 4362-1100; www.museoboquense.com; Brandsen 805; admission from AR$60; ⌚ 10am-6pm) High tech and spiffy, this *fútbol* museum chronicles the rough-and-tumble neighborhood of La Boca, La Bombonera

Stadium, *fútbol* idols' histories, video highlights, the championships, the trophies and, of course, the gooooals. There's a 360-degree theater in a giant *fútbol*-ball auditorium, an old jersey collection and a gift shop. The museum is right under the stadium, a couple of blocks from the tourist part of El Caminito; get a tour of the pitch for a few extra pesos.

Retiro

Well-located Retiro is one of the ritziest neighborhoods in BA – but it hasn't always been this way. The area was the site of a monastery during the 17th century and later became the *retiro* (country retreat) of Agustín de Robles, a Spanish governor. Since then, Retiro's current Plaza San Martín – which sits on a bluff – has played host to a slave market, a military fort and even a bullring. Things are more quiet and exclusive these days.

Plaza San Martín PLAZA
(Map p68) French landscape architect Carlos Thays designed the leafy Plaza San Martín, which is surrounded by some of BA's most impressive public buildings. The park's most prominent monument is the obligatory equestrian **statue of José de San Martín**; important visiting dignitaries often come to honor the country's liberator by leaving wreaths at its base. On the downhill side of the park you'll see the **Monumento a los Caídos de Malvinas** (Map p68), a memorial to the young men who died in the Falklands War (Guerra de las Malvinas).

Palacio Paz NOTABLE BUILDING
(Círculo Militar; Map p68; ☎4311-1071, ext 147; www.palaciopaz.com.ar; Av Santa Fe 750; tours in English/Spanish AR$55/45; ⏲English tours 3:30pm Wed & Thu, Spanish tours 11am & 3pm Wed-Fri, 11am Sat) Once the private residence of José C Paz – founder of the still-running newspaper *La Prensa* – this opulent, French-style palace (1909) is the grandest in BA. Inside are ornate rooms, salons and halls with wood-tiled floors, marble walls and gilded details. Nearly all materials came from Europe and were then assembled here; there's also a modest garden out back.

Museo de Arte Hispanoamericano Isaac Fernández Blanco MUSEUM
(Palacio Noel; Map p68; ☎4327-0228; www.museofernandezblanco.buenosaires.gob.ar; Suipacha 1422; admission AR$5; ⏲2-7pm Tue-Fri, 11am-7pm Sat & Sun) Dating from 1921, this museum is in an old mansion of the neocolonial Peruvian style that developed as a reaction against French influences in turn-of-the-19th-century Argentine architecture. Its exceptional collection of colonial art includes silverwork from Alto Perú (present-day Bolivia), religious paintings and baroque instruments. There's little effort to place items in any historical context, but everything is in great condition and well lit, and the curved ceiling in the main salon is beautifully painted. There's also a peaceful garden.

Museo de Armas MUSEUM
(Weapons Museum; Map p68; ☎4311-1071, ext 179; www.museodearmas.com.ar; Av Santa Fe 702; admission AR$10; ⏲1-7pm Tue-Fri, 2-7pm Sat) Even if you've spent time in the armed forces, you probably have never seen so many weapons of destruction. This maze-like museum exhibits a frighteningly large but excellent collection of over 3000 bazookas, grenade launchers, cannons, machine guns, muskets, pistols, armor, lances and swords; even the gas mask for a combat horse is on display. The evolution of rifles and handguns is especially thoroughly documented, and there's a small but impressive Japanese weapons room.

Torre de los Ingleses LANDMARK
(Torre Monumental; Map p68; ☎4311-0186; Plaza Fuerza Aérea Argentina; ⏲10am-6pm Mon-Fri, 10am-6:30pm Sat & Sun) FREE Standing prominently across from Plaza San Martín, this 76m-high miniature version of London's Big Ben was a donation from the city's British community in 1916. You can enter inside the base of the tower, where there are a few historical photos, but folks aren't allowed up the elevator.

Edificio Kavanagh NOTABLE BUILDING
(Map p68; Florida 1035) This handsome 120m art deco apartment building was the tallest skyscraper in Latin America at the time of its construction in 1935.

Recoleta & Barrio Norte

BA's wealthiest citizens live and breathe in Recoleta, the city's most exclusive and fashionable neighborhood. In the 1870s many upper-class *porteños* relocated here from San Telmo during a yellow-fever epidemic. Today you can best see the wealth of this sumptuous quarter on **Av Alvear**, where many of the old mansions (and newer international boutiques) are located.

Full of lush parks, classy museums and French architecture, Recoleta is best known for its Cementerio de la Recoleta. The **Plaza Intendente Alvear** hosts the city's most popular crafts fair. A little further north is the 20m-high sculptural flower **Floralis Genérica**, whose giant metal petals closed up at night until the gears broke.

Barrio Norte is a subneighborhood southwest of Recoleta, but the lines are blurred.

★ **Cementerio de la Recoleta** CEMETERY
(Map p68; ☎0800-444-2363; cnr Junín & Guido; ⏲7am-5:30pm) FREE This cemetery is arguably BA's number-one attraction, and a must on every tourist's list. You can wander for hours in this amazing city of the dead, where countless 'streets' are lined with impressive statues and marble sarcophagi. Peek into the crypts and check out the dusty coffins – most of which hold the remains of the city's most elite sector of society – and try to decipher the history of its inhabitants.

Past presidents, military heroes, influential politicians and the just plain rich and famous have made it past the gates here. Hunt down Evita's grave (see box, p71) and don't forget your camera – there are some great photo ops here.

Free tours are offered in English at 11am Tuesday and Thursday and in Spanish at 9:30am, 11am, 2pm and 4pm from Tuesday to Sunday (weather permitting). For a great map and information, order Robert Wright's PDF guide (www.recoletacemetery.com); touts also sell maps at the entrance.

Basílica de Nuestra Señora del Pilar CHURCH
(Map p68; ☎4806-2209; Junín 1904; museum AR$6) The centerpiece of this gleaming white colonial church, built by Jesuits in 1716, is a Peruvian altar adorned with silver from Argentina's northwest. Inside, head to the left to visit the small but historic cloisters **museum** (open 10:30am to 6:15pm Monday to Saturday and 2:30pm to 6:15pm Sunday); it's home to religious vestments, paintings, writings and interesting artifacts.

★ **Museo Nacional de Bellas Artes** MUSEUM
(Map p68; ☎5288-9945; www.mnba.org.ar; Av del Libertador 1473; ⏲12:30-8:30pm Tue-Fri, 9:30am-8:30pm Sat & Sun) FREE This is Argentina's most important national arts museum and contains many key works by Benito Quinquela Martín, Xul Solar, Eduardo Sívori and other Argentine artists of the 19th and 20th centuries. There are also impressive international works by European masters such as Cézanne, Degas, Picasso, Rembrandt, Toulouse-Lautrec and Van Gogh. Everything is well displayed, and there's also a cinema, concerts and classes.

EVITA'S GRAVE

She's Recoleta's biggest star, and everyone who visits Cementerio de la Recoleta wants to see her final resting place. Here's how to find it: Go up to the first major 'intersection' from the entrance, where there's a statue. Turn left, continue until a mausoleum blocks your way, go around it to the right and turn right at the wide 'street.' After three blocks look to the left and you'll likely see people at her site, along with bunches of flowers.

Palermo

Palermo is heaven on Earth for BA's middle class. Its large, grassy parks – regally punctuated with grand monuments – are popular destinations on weekends, when families fill the shady lanes, cycle the bike paths and paddle on the peaceful lakes. Many important museums and elegant embassies are also located here, and certain subneighborhoods of Palermo have become some of the city's hottest destinations for shopping and nightlife.

Palermo's green spaces haven't always been for the masses. The area around **Parque 3 de Febrero** was originally the 19th-century dictator Juan Manuel de Rosas' private retreat and became public parkland after his fall from power. Within these green spaces you'll now find a zoo, planetarium and several gardens. Just south of the zoo is **Plaza Italia**, Palermo's main transport hub.

One of the capital's most trendsetting areas is **Palermo Viejo**, a scenic neighborhood with colonial buildings and plenty of fine shopping, dining and nightlife; it's further subdivided into Palermo Soho and Palermo Hollywood. The heart of this neighborhood is **Plaza Serrano** (Map p72), a small but very popular plaza surrounded by bars and restaurants, and host to a small weekend arts fair. Another popular but much smaller neighborhood to the north is **Las Cañitas**; many restaurants and other nightspots here

Palermo

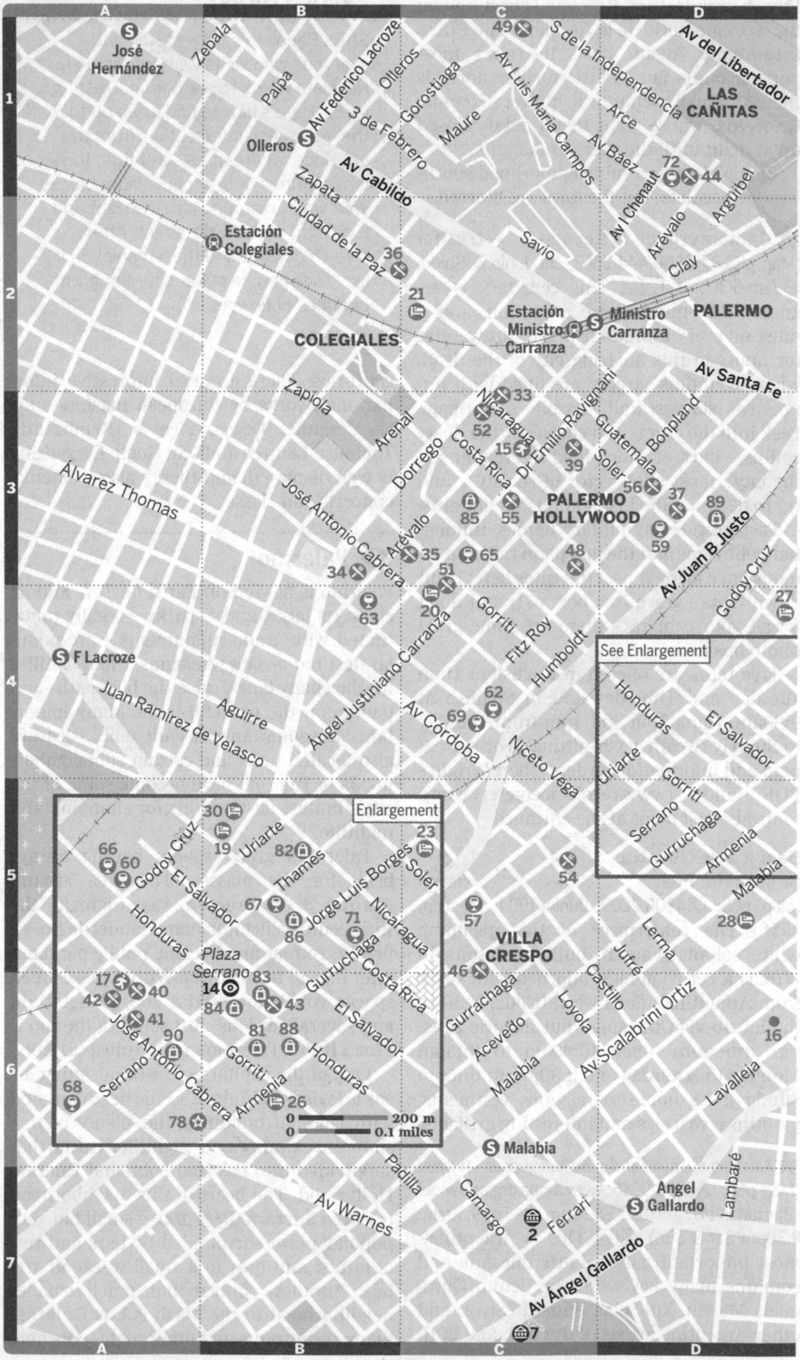
A
B
C
D
1
2
3
4
5
6
7
José Hernández
Zebala
Palpa
Av Federico Lacroze
Olleros
Gorostiaga
3 de Febrero
Maure
Olleros
Av Cabildo
Zapata
Ciudad de la Paz
S de la Independencia
Av Luis María Campos
Arce
Av Báez
Av del Libertador
LAS CAÑITAS
Av I Chenaut
Arévalo
Arguibel
Savio
Clay
Estación Colegiales
Estación Ministro Carranza
Ministro Carranza
PALERMO
COLEGIALES
Av Santa Fe
Zapiola
Arenal
Nicaragua
Dr Emilio Ravignani
Guatemala
Bonpland
Soler
Dorrego
Costa Rica
Álvarez Thomas
José Antonio Cabrera
Arévalo
PALERMO HOLLYWOOD
Av Juan B Justo
Godoy Cruz
Gorriti
Fitz Roy
Humboldt
Ángel Justiniano Carranza
F Lacroze
Juan Ramírez de Velasco
Aguirre
Av Córdoba
Niceto Vega
See Enlargement
Honduras
El Salvador
Uriarte
Gorriti
Serrano
Gurruchaga
Armenia
Malabia
Enlargement
Godoy Cruz
Uriarte
Thames
Jorge Luis Borges
Soler
El Salvador
Nicaragua
Honduras
Plaza Serrano
Gurruchaga
Costa Rica
El Salvador
José Antonio Cabrera
Gorriti
Honduras
Serrano
Armenia
0 200 m
0 0.1 miles
VILLA CRESPO
Lerma
Jufré
Castillo
Loyola
Gurrachaga
Acevedo
Malabia
Av Scalabrini Ortiz
Lavalleja
Malabia
Padilla
Camargo
Av Warnes
Ferrari
Angel Gallardo
Lambaré
Av Ángel Gallardo
49
72
44
36
21
33
52
15
39
56
37
89
85
55
59
48
35
65
34
51
20
63
27
62
69
30
19
82
23
66
60
67
86
71
17
40
42
14
83
43
84
41
90
81
88
68
26
78
54
57
28
46
16
2
7

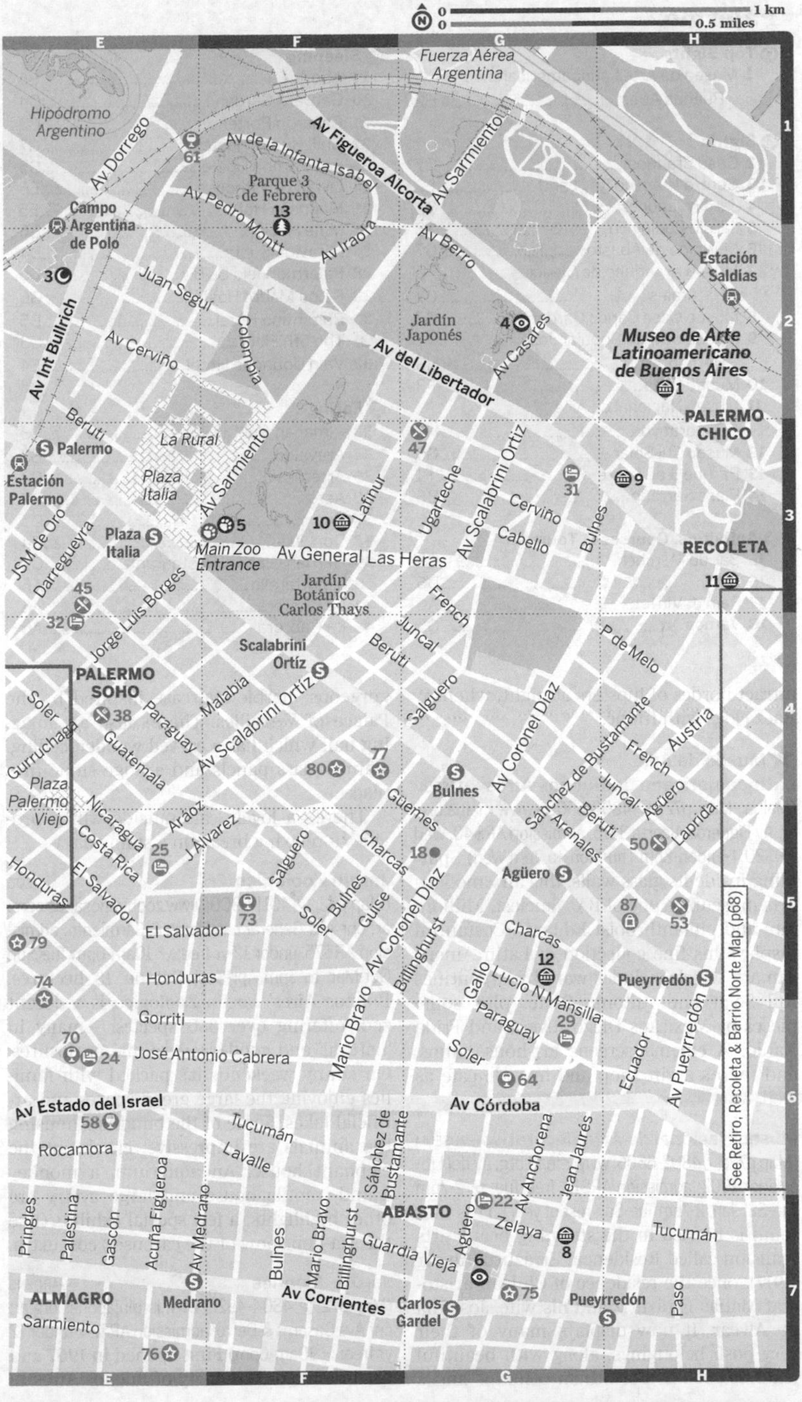
0 1 km
0 0.5 miles
E
F
G
H
1
2
3
4
5
6
7
Fuerza Aérea Argentina
Hipódromo Argentino
Av Dorrego
61
Av de la Infanta Isabel
Parque 3 de Febrero
13
Av Figueroa Alcorta
Av Sarmiento
Av Pedro Montt
Campo Argentina de Polo
Av Iraola
Av Berro
3
Juan Seguí
Estación Saldías
Av Int Bullrich
Colombia
Jardín Japonés
4
Av Casares
Museo de Arte Latinoamericano de Buenos Aires
1
Av Cerviño
Av del Libertador
Beruti
La Rural
PALERMO CHICO
Palermo
47
Estación Palermo
Plaza Italia
Av Sarmiento
Lafinur
Ugarteche
Av Scalabrini Ortiz
31
9
Cerviño
Cabello
Bulnes
JSM de Oro
Darregueyra
Plaza Italia
5
Main Zoo Entrance
10
Av General Las Heras
RECOLETA
11
45
Jorge Luis Borges
Jardín Botánico Carlos Thays
French
32
Juncal
P de Melo
Beruti
Scalabrini Ortíz
PALERMO SOHO
Malabia
Av Scalabrini Ortíz
Salguero
Av Coronel Díaz
Sánchez de Bustamante
Soler
38
Paraguay
French
Austria
Gurruchaga
Guatemala
77
80
Bulnes
Juncal
Agüero
Plaza Palermo Viejo
Nicaragua
Aráoz
Güemes
Arenales
Beruti
Laprida
Costa Rica
J Álvarez
25
Salguero
Charcas
18
50
Honduras
El Salvador
Bulnes
Agüero
73
Soler
Guise
Av Coronel Díaz
87
53
79
El Salvador
Billinghurst
Charcas
12
74
Honduras
Gallo
Lucio N Mansilla
Pueyrredón
Gorriti
Mario Bravo
Paraguay
29
70
24
José Antonio Cabrera
Soler
Ecuador
Av Pueyrredón
64
Av Estado del Israel
Av Córdoba
58
Tucumán
Sánchez de Bustamante
Av Anchorena
Jean Jaurés
Rocamora
Lavalle
Acuña Figueroa
22
Pringles
Palestina
Gascón
Av Medrano
ABASTO
Bulnes
Mario Bravo
Billinghurst
Guardia Vieja
Agüero
Zelaya
8
Tucumán
6
ALMAGRO
Medrano
Av Corrientes
Carlos Gardel
75
Pueyrredón
Paso
Sarmiento
76
See Retiro, Recoleta & Barrio Norte Map (p68)

Palermo

attract hordes of hipsters at night, when Av Báez clogs with traffic.

★ Museo de Arte Latinoamericano de Buenos Aires MUSEUM

(Malba; Map p72; ☎4808-6500; www.malba.org.ar; Av Figueroa Alcorta 3415; admission AR$40, Wed AR$20; ⊙noon-8pm Thu-Mon, to 9pm Wed) Sparkling inside its glass walls, this airy modern arts museum is one of BA's fanciest. Millionaire and philanthropist Eduardo Costantini displays his fine collection of Latin American art, which includes work by Argentines Xul Solar and Antonio Berni, plus some pieces by Mexicans Diego Rivera and Frida Kahlo. A cinema screens art-house films, and there's a gift shop and upscale cafe as well.

Museo Nacional de Arte Decorativo MUSEUM

(Map p72; ☎4802-6606; www.mnad.org; Av del Libertador 1902; admission AR$15, free Tue; ⊙2-7pm Tue-Sat Jan, 2-7pm Tue-Sun rest of year) This museum is housed in the stunning beaux arts mansion called Residencia Errázuriz Alvear (1917), once the residence of Chilean aristocrat Matías Errázuriz and his wife, Josefina de Alvear. It now displays many of their very posh belongings, along with beautiful features such as Corinthian columns and a gorgeous marble staircase inspired by the Palace of Versailles. There's also an amazing hall which has a carved wooden ceiling, stained-glass panels and a huge stone fireplace.

There's a lovely cafe outside which provides a relaxing break on a sunny day.

Jardín Zoológico ZOO

(Map p72; ☎4011-9900; www.zoobuenosaires.com.ar; cnr Avs General Las Heras & Sarmiento; admission AR$75, under 12 yr free; ⊙10am-6pm Tue-Sun Oct-Mar, to 5pm Apr-Sep) Set on 18 hectares, Buenos Aires' Jardín Zoológico is a decent zoo, offering over 350 species – many in 'natural' and good-sized animal enclosures. On sunny weekends it's packed with families enjoying the large green spaces and artificial lakes. Some of the buildings housing the animals are impressive; check out the elephant house. An aquarium, a monkey island, reptile house and large aviary are other highlights; a few special exhibits (like the sea-lion show or the carousel) cost extra.

Jardín Japonés GARDENS

(Map p72; ☎4804-4922; www.jardinjapones.org.ar; cnr Avs Casares & Berro; admission AR$24, under 12 yr free; ⊙10am-6pm) First opened in 1967 and then donated to the city of Buenos Aires in

43 La Esquina de las Flores	B6
44 Las Cholas	D1
45 Las Pizarras	E3
46 Malvón	C5
47 Malvón	G3
48 Miranda	C3
49 Natural Deli	C1
50 Natural Deli	H5
51 Olsen	C3
52 Oui Oui	C3
53 Oviedo	H5
54 Sarkis	C5
55 Siamo nel Forno	C3
56 Sudestada	D3

Drinking & Nightlife

57 878	C5
58 Amerika	E6
59 Casa Coupage	D3
60 Congo	A5
61 Crobar	E1
62 El Carnal	C4
63 Frank's Bar	B4
64 Glam	G6
65 Home Hotel	C3
66 Kika	A5
67 Magdalena's Party	B5
68 Mundo Bizarro	A6
69 Niceto Club	C4
70 Sitges	E6
71 Sugar	B5
72 Van Koning	D1
73 Verne	F5

Entertainment

74 Bach Bar	E5
75 Esquina Carlos Gardel	G7
76 La Catedral	E7
77 La Peña del Colorado	F4
78 La Viruta	A6
79 Salon Canning	E5
80 Thelonious Bar	F4

Shopping

81 Bolivia	B6
82 Bolivia	B5
83 Calma Chicha	B6
84 Feria Plaza Serrano	B6
85 Hermanos Estebecorena	C3
86 Lo de Joaquin Alberdi	B5
87 Patio del Liceo	H5
88 Rapsodia	B6
89 Sugar & Spice	D3
90 Zival's	A6

1979 (on the centenary of the arrival of Argentina's first Japanese immigrants), Jardín Japonés is one of the capital's best-kept gardens – and makes a wonderfully peaceful rest stop. Inside there's a Japanese **restaurant** along with lovely ponds filled with koi and spanned by pretty bridges. Japanese culture can be experienced through occasional exhibitions and workshops on ikebana, haiku, origami, *taiko* (Japanese drumming) and other events.

Museo Evita MUSEUM
(Map p72; ☎4807-0306; www.museoevita.org; Lafinur 2988; admission AR$20; ⏰11am-7pm Tue-Sun) Everybody who's anybody in Argentina has their own museum, and Eva Perón (1919–52) is no exception. Museo Evita immortalizes the Argentine heroine with plenty of videos, historical photos, books, old posters and newspaper headlines. However, the prize memorabilia has to be her wardrobe: dresses, shoes, handbags, hats and blouses lie proudly behind glass, forever pressed and pristine. Even Evita's old wallets and perfumes are on display. Our favorite is a picture of her kicking a *fútbol* – in heels.

Attached to the museum is a pleasant restaurant with a wonderfully leafy patio.

Museo de Arte Popular José Hernández MUSEUM
(Map p72; ☎4803-2384; www.museohernandez.buenosaires.gob.ar; Av del Libertador 2373; admission AR$5, free Sun; ⏰1-6:30pm Wed-Fri, 10am-7pm Sat & Sun) This museum was being remodelled at research time, but the emphasis here is on both traditional and contemporary arts and crafts, mostly from Argentina. Expect to see intricate gaucho-related silverwork like knives and *mate* sets, Mapuche textiles like ponchos, and folk crafts from the country's northern regions. The back halls hold changing exhibits.

Museo Xul Solar MUSEUM
(Map p72; ☎4824-3302; www.xulsolar.org.ar; Laprida 1212; admission AR$20; ⏰noon-8pm Tue-Fri, to 7pm Sat, closed Feb) Xul Solar was a painter, inventor, poet and friend of Jorge Luis Borges. This museum (located in his old mansion) showcases over 80 of his unique and colorful yet subdued paintings. Solar's Klee-esque style includes fantastically themed, almost cartoonish figures placed in surreal cubist landscapes. It's great stuff, and bizarre enough to put him in a class of his own. Tours in Spanish are available Tuesday and Thursday at 4pm and Saturday at 3:30pm.

Tierra Santa THEME PARK
(☎0800-444-3467; www.tierrasanta-bsas.com.ar; Av Costanera R Obligado 5790; adult/child 3-11yr AR$60/30; ⏲9am-9pm Fri, noon-10pm Sat, Sun & holidays Apr-Nov, 4pm-midnight Fri-Sun & holidays Dec-Mar) Even respectful, devout Catholics will find this – the 'world's first religious theme park' – a very tacky place. It boasts animatronic dioramas of Adam and Eve and the Last Supper, but its *pièce de résistance* is a giant Jesus rising from a fake mountain – aka the resurrection – every half-hour. It's just north of Palermo, near the water.

Centro Islámico Rey Fahd MOSQUE
(Map p72; ☎4899-0201; www.ccislamicoreyfahd.org.ar; Av Int Bullrich 55) This landmark mosque, built by Saudis on land donated by former president Carlos Menem, is southeast of Las Cañitas. Free tours in Spanish are offered on Tuesday, Thursday and Saturday at noon (bring your passport, dress conservatively and enter via Av Int Bullrich).

Belgrano

Bustling Av Cabildo, the racing heartbeat of Belgrano, is an overwhelming jumble of noise and neon; it's a two-way street of clothing, shoe and houseware shops that does its part to support the mass consumerism of *porteños*.

Only a block east of Av Cabildo, **Plaza Belgrano** is the site of a modest but fun weekend crafts fair.

Near the plaza stands the Italianate **Iglesia de la Inmaculada Concepción**, a church popularly known as 'La Redonda' because of its impressive dome. Four blocks northeast of Plaza Belgrano is **Barrancas de Belgrano**, an attractive park on one of the few natural hillocks in the city. And nearby, just across the train tracks, Belgrano's small **Chinatown** offers decent Chinese restaurants and cheap goods.

Museo de Arte Español Enrique Larreta MUSEUM
(☎4784-4040; www.museolarreta.buenosaires.gov.ar; Juramento 2291; admission AR$5; ⏲1-7pm Mon-Fri, 10am-8pm Sat & Sun) Hispanophile novelist Enrique Larreta (1875–1961) resided in this elegant colonial-style house across from Plaza Belgrano, which now displays his private art collection to the public. It's a grand and spacious old building, and contains classic Spanish art, period furniture, wood-carved religious items, shields and armor. The wood and tiled floors are beautiful, and everything is richly lit. Tours in Spanish are given at 5pm Monday to Friday, and 4pm and 6pm on Saturday and Sunday. Be sure to stroll the lovely gardens out back.

Once & Around

BA's most ethnically colorful neighborhood is Once, with sizable groups of Jews, Peruvians and Koreans. The cheap market around Once train station always bustles, with vendors selling their goods on sidewalks and crowds everywhere.

Museo Argentino de Ciencias Naturales MUSEUM
(Natural Science Museum; Map p72; ☎4982-6595; www.macn.secyt.gov.ar; Av Ángel Gallardo 490; admission AR$10; ⏲2-7pm) Way over to the west, the oval Parque del Centenario is a large open space containing this excellent natural-science museum. On display are large collections of meteorites, rocks and minerals, seashells, insects and dinosaur skeleton replicas. Life-size models of a basking shark and ocean sunfish are impressive, and the taxidermy and skeleton rooms are especially good. Bring the kids; they can mingle with the hundreds of children who visit on school excursions.

Museo Casa Carlos Gardel MUSEUM
(Map p72; ☎4964-2071; Jean Jaurés 735; admission AR$5, free Wed; ⏲11am-6pm Mon & Wed-Fri, 10am-7pm Sat & Sun) Small but noteworthy is this tribute to tango's most famous voice. Located in Gardel's old house, this museum traces his partnership with José Razzano and displays old memorabilia like photos, records and news clippings. There isn't a whole lot to see, so it's best for real fans or just the curious; look for the cluster of colorfully painted buildings. Free tango classes offered Wednesday and Friday at 6pm, and Saturday at 3pm.

Mercado de Abasto NOTABLE BUILDING
(Map p72; ☎4959-3400; www.abasto-shopping.com.ar; Av Corrientes 3247; ⏲10am-10pm) The historic Mercado de Abasto (1895) has been recycled by US-Hungarian financier George Soros into one of the most beautiful shopping centers in the city. The building, once a large vegetable market, received an architectural prize in 1937 for its Av Corrientes facade. It holds more than 200 stores, a large

cinema, a large food court and a kosher McDonald's (the one upstairs).

Activities

The extensive greenery in Palermo provides good areas for recreation, especially on weekends when the ring road around the rose garden is closed to motor vehicles. Recoleta has grassy parks also, if you can avoid the dog piles. Best of all is the Reserva Ecológica Costanera Sur, an ecological paradise just east of Puerto Madero; it's excellent for walks, runs, bike rides and even a bit of wildlife viewing.

Cycling

BA is not the best city to cycle around, but things are getting better; a bike lane system was introduced in 2010 and is expanding. A free bike-share program also exists, though it's more geared toward BA residents (one-hour rental limits).

The city's best places for two-wheeled exploration are Palermo's parks and the Reserva Ecológica Costanera Sur – on sunny weekends you can rent bikes at these places. You can also join city bike tours, which include bicycle and guide (see p79); these tour companies sometimes offer bike rentals. And if you're around on the first Sunday of each month, check out BA's version of Critical Mass (www.masacriticabsas.com.ar).

Horseback Riding

Caballos a la Par HORSEBACK RIDING
(☎15-5248-3592, 4384-7013; www.caballos-alapar.com) If you want to get out of town for a few hours and hop on a horse, forget those touristy *estancias* (ranches) and check out Caballos a la Par. Guided rides are given in a provincial park about an hour's drive from BA.

Fútbol

Inspired by watching professional *fútbol* teams play the game? Well, you can partake

BUENOS AIRES FOR CHILDREN

Palermo's **Parque 3 de Febrero** (Map p72; cnr Avs del Libertador & de la Infanta Isabel; 🚌10, 34, 130) is a huge park, and on weekends traffic isn't allowed on the ring road (rent bikes, boats and in-line skates nearby). Other good stops here include a planetarium, a zoo and a Japanese garden. If you're downtown and need a nature break, there's the Reserva Ecológica Costanera Sur (p62), a large nature preserve with good bird-watching.

Shopping malls make safe destinations for families – one of the best is the Mercado de Abasto (p76), which boasts a full-blown children's 'museum' (ie fancy playground) and mini-amusement park.

In San Telmo, check out the puppet museum, **Museo Argentino del Títere** (Map p58; ☎4307-6917; www.museoargdeltitere.com.ar; Estados Unidos 802; ⊙9:30am-12:30pm & 3-6pm Tue, Wed & Fri, 3-6pm Thu, Sat & Sun) FREE, which has inexpensive weekend shows.

Recoleta's **Museo Participativo de Ciencias** (Map p68; ☎4806-3456; www.mpc.org.ar; Junín 1930; admission AR$40; ⊙vary widely, see website) is a hands-on science museum with interactive learning displays. In Caballito is the good Museo Argentino de Ciencias Naturales (p76).

Christian parents might want to take the kids to Tierra Santa (p76), a unique and tacky (but fun) religious theme park. Not far away is Parque Norte (p78), a large water park that's perfect on a hot day.

Tigre, north of the city, makes a great day excursion. Get there via the Tren de la Costa; it ends right at **Parque de la Costa** (☎4002-6000; www.parquedelacosta.com.ar; General B Mitre 2; admission Tue & Wed from AR$52, Thu-Sun from AR$97), a typical amusement park with fun rides.

Outside the city is the exceptional zoo, **Parque Temaikén** (☎034-8843-6900; www.temaiken.com.ar; RP25, Km1, Escobar; adult/child 3-10yr AR$82/64; ⊙10am-7pm Tue-Sun Dec-Feb, to 6pm Mar-Nov). Only the most charming animal species are on display (think meerkats, pygmy hippos and white tigers), roaming freely around natural enclosures. An excellent aquarium comes with touch pools, and plenty of interactive areas provide mental stimulation.

To help calm down temper tantrums, visit one of BA's dozens of excellent ice-cream shops.

La Boca

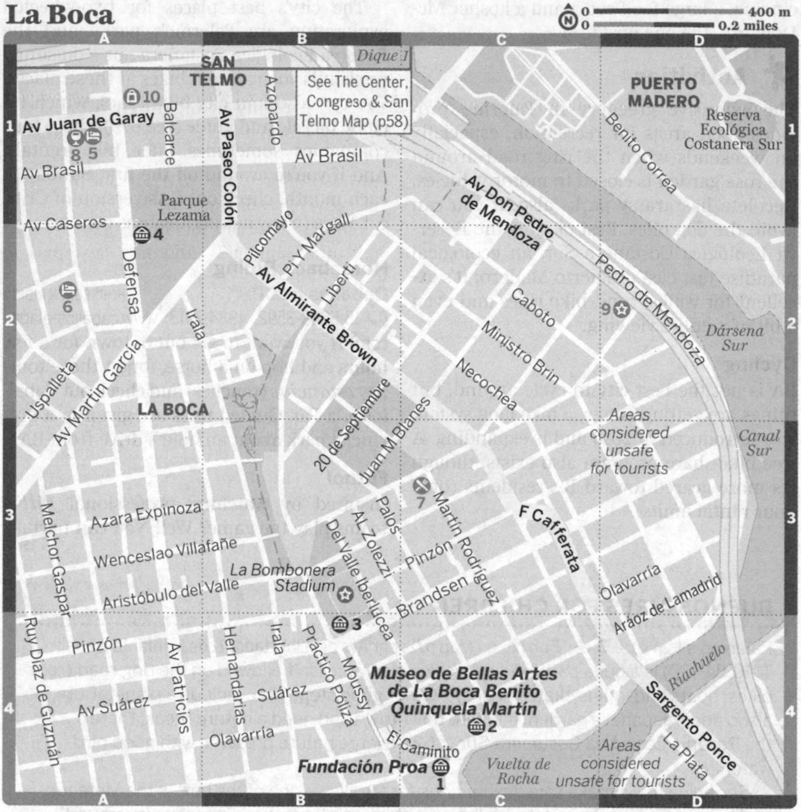

yourself – just contact **FC Buenos Aires Fútbol Amigos** (www.fcbafa.com) to join fellow travelers, expats and locals for some pick-up fun. The best part might be the *asados* (barbecues) that often happen after the games, plus, of course, the friends you make on the pitch.

Swimming

Finding a good swimming hole isn't easy in BA – unless you're lucky enough to be staying at a hotel with a decent pool (or are OK with splashing around indoors at the nearest gym).

Parque Norte SWIMMING
(☎4787-1382; www.parquenorte.com; Avs Cantilo & Guiraldes; admission Mon-Fri AR$70, Sat AR$90, Sun AR$100; ⊙9am-8pm Mon-Fri, 8am-10pm Sat & Sun) When the temperatures and humidity skyrocket, head north to this large water park. It's great for families, with huge shallow pools (perhaps 1.2m at their deepest), plus a large water slide and lots of umbrellas and lounge chairs. There are plenty of grassy areas in which to enjoy a picnic or *mate*. Bring towels.

Courses

Visitors have many opportunities to study almost anything in BA. Most cultural centers offer a wide variety of classes at affordable rates.

Language

BA is a major destination for students of Spanish, and good institutes are opening up all the time. Nearly all organize social activities and homestay programs, and all have private classes.

For something different, try **Spanglish** (www.spanglishexchange.com). It's set up like speed dating: you'll speak five minutes in English and five in Spanish, then switch partners.

La Boca

Top Sights
1 Fundación Proa C4
2 Museo de Bellas Artes de La Boca Benito Quinquela Martín C4

Sights
3 Museo de la Pasión Boquense B4
4 Museo Histórico Nacional A2

Sleeping
5 Bonito San Telmo A1
6 Casa y Mundo Bolivar A2

Eating
7 Il Matterello C3
Proa Cafe .... (see 1)

Drinking & Nightlife
8 Doppelgänger A1

Entertainment
9 Usina del Arte D2

Shopping
10 Moebius A1

When you're looking for an institute, it's always best to ask around for current recommendations.

Academia Buenos Aires LANGUAGE COURSE
(Map p58; ☎4345-5954; www.academiabuenosaires.com; Hipólito Yrigoyen 571, 4th fl)

DWS LANGUAGE COURSE
(Map p72; ☎4777-6515; www.dwsba.com.ar; Av Córdoba 4382)

Expanish LANGUAGE COURSE
(Map p58; ☎5252-3040; www.expanish.com; Juan D Perón 698)

Rayuela LANGUAGE COURSE
(Map p58; ☎4300-2010; www.spanish-argentina.com.ar; Chacabuco 852, 1st fl, No 11)

Vamos LANGUAGE COURSE
(Map p72; ☎5352-0001; www.vamospanish.com; Av Coronel Díaz 1736)

VOS LANGUAGE COURSE
(Map p68; ☎4812-1140; www.vosbuenosaires.com; Marcelo T de Alvear 1459)

Photography

Foto Ruta PHOTOGRAPHY
(☎6030-8881; www.foto-ruta.com) This workshop was started by two expat women who send folks out into neighborhoods with a few 'themes' to photograph – then everyone watches the slide show.

Tours

There are plenty of organized tours, from the large tourist-bus variety to guided bike rides to straight-up walks. Some travel agencies also offer tours (p111), including some very adventurous ones.

Companies offer tours in English and possibly other languages, and most have private tour options, too.

BA Walking Tours WALKING TOUR
(☎15-5773-1001; www.ba-walking-tours.com) Day, night, historic and tango tours.

Biking Buenos Aires BICYCLE TOUR
(☎4040-8989; www.bikingbuenosaires.com) Friendly American and Argentine guides take you on a variety of tours of BA, including graffiti and architecture tours.

Buenos Aires Bus BUS TOUR
(☎5239-5160; www.buenosairesbus.com; tour AR$120) Hop-on, hop-off roofless bus that runs frequently over two dozen stops (see website for details).

Buenos Tours WALKING TOUR
(☎5984-2444; www.buenostours.com) Well-run private tours guided by friendly, knowledgeable and responsible local expats. Great website, too.

Cultour WALKING TOUR
(☎15-6365-6892; www.cultour.com.ar) Good tours run by teachers and students from the University of Buenos Aires (UBA). Prepare to learn the historical and cultural facets of Buenos Aires.

Graffitimundo STREET-ART TOUR
(☎15-3683-3219; www.graffitimundo.com) Excellent tours of some of BA's best graffiti, by those in the know. Learn artists' history and the local graffiti culture. Several tours available, including a La Boca 'Hidden Walls' tour. Stencil workshops, too.

Urban Biking BICYCLE TOUR
(☎4314-2325; www.urbanbiking.com) One-day cycling tours – including an alternative 'nightlife' bike trip – bike and kayak excursions to Tigre.

Festivals & Events

Check with tourist offices for other happenings and for exact dates, as some vary from year to year.

Going to a Fútbol Game

In a land where Maradona is God, going to see a *fútbol* (soccer) game can be a religious experience. The *superclásico* between the Boca Juniors and River Plate has been called the number one sporting event to see before you die, but even the less-celebrated games will give you insight into Argentina's national passion.

Attending a regular match isn't too difficult. Keep an eye on the clubs' websites, which inform when and where tickets will be sold; often they're sold at the stadium before the game. You'll get a choice between *populares* (bleachers) and *plateas* (seats). Try to avoid the *populares*; these can get really rowdy and can sometimes be dangerous.

If you want to see a *clásico* – a match between two major teams – getting a ticket is much harder. Boca doesn't even put tickets for its key matches on sale; all tickets go to *socios* (members). Instead, you're better off going with an agency such as Tangol or via organizations like www.fcbafa.com or www.landingpad.com. It won't be cheap, but it's much easier (and safer, with less chance of fake tickets) getting a ticket this way.

However, if you do want to chance getting your own *clásico* or *superclásico* ticket, you can always look online at www.buenosaires.craigslist.org or www.mercadolibre.com.ar. If you're confident in your bargaining skills, scalpers exist, too.

Dress down, and try to look inconspicuous when you go. Take minimal cash and keep your camera close. You probably won't get in with water bottles, and food and drink in the stadium is meager and expensive. Arrive early to enjoy the insane build-up to the game. Most importantly – don't wear the opposing team's colors.

Clockwise from top left

1. Spectators, La Bombonera Stadium
2. Maradona mural, El Caminito (p69) **3.** *Superclásico* (p585), La Bombonera Stadium

TEAMS

Buenos Aires has two-dozen professional football teams – the most of any city in the world. Here are some of them:

» **Boca Juniors** (☎4309-4700; www.bocajuniors.com.ar)

» **River Plate** (☎4789-1200; www.cariverplate.com.ar)

» **Racing** (☎4371-9995; www.racingclub.com)

» **Independiente** (☎4229-7600; www.clubaindependiente.com/en)

» **San Lorenzo de Almagro** (☎4918-4237; www.sanlorenzo.com.ar)

LONELY PLANET/GETTY IMAGES ©

2

KEREN SU/GETTY IMAGES ©

3

LONELY PLANET/GETTY IMAGES ©

Festival Internacional de Cine Independiente FILM
(www.bafici.gov.ar; ⌚Apr) Highlights national and international independent films at venues all around BA.

Arte BA ART
(www.arteba.com; ⌚May) Popular event highlighting contemporary art, introducing exciting new young artists, and showing off top gallery works.

Anniversary of Carlos Gardel's death ANNIVERSARY
(⌚Jun) Anniversary of Carlos Gardel's death on June 24, 1935. Fans make a pilgrimage to Chacarita cemetery and tango events happen around BA.

Festival y Mundial de Tango TANGO FESTIVAL
(www.tangobuenosaires.gob.ar; various venues; ⌚Aug) Masterful tango performances, tango movies, classes, workshops, conferences and competitions in venues all over BA.

Vinos y Bodegas WINE
(www.expovinosybodegas.com.ar; ⌚Sep) A can't-miss vent for wine aficionados, offering vintages from over 100 Argentine *bodegas* (wineries).

Creamfields MUSIC
(www.creamfieldsba.com; ⌚Nov) BA's answer to the UK's outdoor, all-night, cutting-edge electronic-music and dance party, with dozens of international DJs and bands.

Buenos Aires Jazz FESTIVAL
(www.buenosairesjazz.gob.ar; ⌚Nov/Dec) In late November or early December, this jazz festival attracts jazz musicians of all stripes. Concerts and films also take place.

Campeonato Abierto de Polo SPORTS
(www.aapolo.com; ⌚Dec) Watch the world's best polo players and their gorgeous horses thunder up and down Palermo's polo fields.

Sleeping

Over the last decade Buenos Aires has seen its accommodation options increase exponentially. Boutique hotels and guesthouses, especially, have mushroomed in neighborhoods such as San Telmo and Palermo, and hostels are a dime a dozen. You shouldn't have trouble finding the type of place you're looking for, but it's still a good idea to make a reservation beforehand – especially during any holidays or the busy summer months of November through January.

Some places will help with transportation to and from the airport if you reserve ahead of time. The most expensive hotels will take credit cards but cheaper places might not (or may include a surcharge for credit card payment). Some kind of breakfast, whether it be continental or buffet, is included nearly everywhere; the same goes for wi-fi and air-con.

Prices at top-end hotels often vary depending on occupancy levels, and are usually quoted in US dollars. As a general rule, calling ahead or reserving via websites usually results in better pricing. At Hostelling International (HI) hostels, buying a membership card gives a discount off listed prices. Another hostel club is www.minihostels.com.

Any prices listed here are for high season (roughly November to February). Rates can skyrocket during peak seasons (Christmas and Easter) or drop during slow seasons.

Microcentro

As well as being very central, the Microcentro has the widest range and the largest number of accommodations in the city. Toward the north you'll be close to the popular pedestrian streets of Florida and Lavalle, as well as the neighborhoods of upmarket Retiro and Recoleta. The Plaza de Mayo area contains the bustling banking district and many historical buildings, and is within walking distance of San Telmo. During the day the whole area is very busy, but nights are much calmer as businesspeople flee the center after work. Don't expect creative cuisine in this area – for that you'll have to head to Palermo.

Milhouse Youth Hostel HOSTEL $
(Map p58; ☎4345-9604; www.milhousehostel.com; Hipólito Yrigoyen 959; dm AR$90-95, d AR$330-350; ❄@📶; Ⓢ Línea A Av de Mayo) BA's premiere party hostel, this popular HI spot offers a plethora of activities and services. Dorms are good and private rooms can be very pleasant; most surround an appealing open patio. Common spaces include a bar-cafe (with pool table) on the ground floor, a TV lounge on the mezzanine and a rooftop terrace above. A gorgeous annex building nearby offers similar services.

Portal del Sur HOSTEL $
(Map p58; ☎4342-8788; www.portaldelsurba.com.ar; Hipólito Yrigoyen 855; dm US$14-17, s/d

US$50/70; ❄@📶; Ⓢ Línea A Piedras) Located in a charming old building, this is one of the city's best hostels. Beautiful dorms and sumptuous, hotel-quality private rooms surround a central common area, which is rather dark but open. The highlight is the lovely rooftop deck with views and attached bar and lounge. Offers free tango and Spanish lessons and a walking tour; plenty of other activities available.

V & S Hostel Club HOSTEL $

(Map p58; ☎4322-0994; www.hostelclub.com; Viamonte 887; dm US$15, r from US$60; ❄@📶; Ⓢ Línea C Lavalle) 🍃 One of the best in town, this attractive, central and ecofriendly hostel is located in a pleasant older building. The common space, which is also the dining and lobby area, is good for socializing. The spacious dorms are carpeted and the private rooms are excellent; all have their own bathroom. A nice touch is the tiny outdoor patio in back.

Gran Hotel Hispano HOTEL $

(Map p58; ☎4345-2020; www.hhispano.com.ar; Av de Mayo 861; s/d AR$360/490; ❄@📶; Ⓢ Línea A Piedras) The tiny stairway lobby here isn't an impressive start, but upstairs there's a sweet atrium area with covered patio. Most rooms are modern and carpeted; those in front are biggest, and those on the top floor are brightest. There's also a pleasant outside sun terrace. It's a popular, central and well-tended place, so reserve ahead. Pay in cash for a 10% discount.

Claridge Hotel HOTEL $$

(Map p58; ☎4314-2020; www.claridge.com.ar; Tucumán 535; d US$160; ❄@📶🏊; Ⓢ Línea B Florida) One of downtown BA's finest hotels, the Claridge features a relatively grand entrance for the area, where space is scarce. Standard rooms, with their tiny bathrooms, aren't as fancy as you'd think, so go for a suite (some with balcony and Jacuzzi) if you want something special. The spa and pool are highlights. Prices vary widely, so check beforehand.

Hotel Facón Grande HOTEL $$$

(Map p58; ☎4312-6360; www.hotelfacongrande.com; Reconquista 645; r AR$1270; ❄@📶; Ⓢ Línea B Florida) For those seeking a touch of the country in Buenos Aires, there's this (slightly) gaucho-themed hotel. The lobby is

SHORT- & LONG-TERM RENTALS

Many travelers visiting Buenos Aires love the city so much that they want to stay longer and find an apartment. But snagging a pad isn't as easy as it could be: renters often need to commit to two years and nearly always need a *porteño*'s bond to guarantee monthly payments – an almost impossible combination for most foreigners.

To cater to this demand, dozens of apartment websites have popped up in recent years. These sites charge significantly more than locals would pay, but they don't have those pesky requirements either. You can view pictures of rental properties, along with prices and amenities. Usually the photos match what you will get, but not always; if you'd like someone to check out an apartment before you rent it, Madi Lang at BA Cultural Concierge (p109) can make sure the place isn't on a busy street, in an outlying neighborhood or near a construction site.

- www.bytargentina.com
- www.apartmentsba.com
- www.buenosaireshabitat.com
- www.oasisba.com
- www.santelmoloft.com
- www.stayinbuenosaires.com
- www.jaimejensen.com

If you're just looking for a room, check www.spareroomsba.com. Or look for longer-term guesthouses (where rooms usually share bathrooms) at www.casalosangelitos.com and www.lacasademarina.com.ar. And there's always the Buenos Aires branch of Craigslist.

Another good option for short- or long-term stays is dealing directly with owners via sites like www.airbnb.com, www.homeaway.com or www.flipkey.com. For free stays don't forget www.couchsurfing.com.

decorated in rustic furniture and cowhide-covered pillows, and rooms are modern and comfortable. The location on pedestrian Reconquista is good and there's an intimate vibe that's rare in hotels of this size. Get a top-floor room for views.

Congreso

Congreso contains many of the city's older theaters, cinemas and cultural centers. Lively Av Corrientes has many modest shops, services and bookstores. The Plaza del Congreso area is always moving, sometimes with mostly peaceful public demonstrations. Generally, this area is not quite as packed as the Microcentro and has a less business and touristy flavor, but it still bustles day and night.

Sabatico Hostel HOTEL $

(Map p58; ☎4381-1138; www.sabaticohostel.com.ar; México 1410; dm AR$100, r AR$400-500; ❄@📶; Ⓢ Línea E Independencia) This well-maintained hostel is located off the beaten path in an atmospheric neighborhood. Rooms are small but pleasant and the good common areas include a nice kitchen, dining and living room, airy patio hallways and a pleasant rooftop terrace with *asado* grill and hammocks in summer. There's occasional live music on weekends, plus a ping-pong table, foosball and bike rentals.

Hotel Lyon APARTMENT $$

(Map p58; ☎4372-0100; www.hotel-lyon.com.ar; Riobamba 251; d/tr/q AR$530/650/770; ❄@📶; Ⓢ Línea B Callao) If you're a traveling family or group and on a budget, this place is for you. The two- and three- bedroom apartments available here are basic and no-frills but very spacious, and all include entry halls, large bathrooms and separate dining areas with fridges (but no kitchens). Up to five people can be accommodated in each apartment. Reserve ahead.

Hotel Bonito BOUTIQUE HOTEL $$

(Map p58; ☎4381-2162; www.bonitobuenosaires.com; Chile 1507, 3rd fl; r US$90-105; ❄@📶; Ⓢ Línea E Independencia) Lovely boutique hotel with just five artsy, gorgeous rooms mixing the traditional and contemporary. Some have a loft, cupola sitting area or Jacuzzi; floors can be wooden or acid-finished concrete. There's a warm atmosphere, with a small bar area and a good, sizable breakfast. It's in a nontouristy, very local neighborhood within walking distance of Congreso and San Telmo.

La Cayetana HOTEL $$

(Map p58; ☎4383-2230; www.lacayetanahotel.com.ar; México 1330; r US$130-180; ❄@📶; Ⓢ Línea E Independencia) Located south of Congreso in Montserrat, this is a beautiful 1850s guesthouse offering 11 simple, colorful rooms, all decorated differently with rustic yet upscale furniture. The rooms surround three lovely outdoor patios, which are accented with original tiles and leafy plants – the last one has a grassy garden. Breakfast includes fresh fruit, yogurt and eggs to order. It's a quiet little paradise in a nontouristy neighborhood. Reserve ahead.

Livin' Residence APARTMENT $$

(Map p58; ☎5258-0300; www.livinresidence.com; Viamonte 1815; studios US$100, 1-bedroom apt US$110, 2-bedroom apt US$160; ❄📶; Ⓢ Línea D Callao) One of the better deals in town, especially if you're traveling in a group, are these studio and one- or two-bedroom apartments. All have a simple, contemporary feel, with tasteful furniture, flat-screen TVs, small kitchens and balconies. There's a tiny rooftop terrace with Jacuzzi, *asado* and nearby gym room. Security is good; reserve ahead.

San Telmo & Constitución

South of the Microcentro, San Telmo has some of the most traditional atmosphere in Buenos Aires. Buildings are more charming and historical than those in the center, and tend to be only a few stories high. Many restaurants and fancy boutiques have opened here in recent years, and there are some good bars, tango venues and other nightspots for entertainment. Most accommodation options here are hostels, humble hotels or upscale guesthouses rather than five-star hotels.

Constitución is just west of San Telmo, and much less touristy.

America del Sur HOSTEL $

(Map p58; ☎4300-5525; www.americahostel.com.ar; Chacabuco 718; dm AR$120-130, d AR$450-480; ❄@📶; Ⓢ Línea C Independencia) This gorgeous boutique-like hostel is the fanciest of its kind in Buenos Aires, and built especially to be a hostel. Beyond reception is a fine bar-bistro area with large, elegant wooden patio. Clean dorms with four beds all have amazingly well-designed bathrooms, while private rooms are tastefully decorated and better than those at many midrange hotels. A multitude of services are also on offer.

Circus Hostel & Hotel HOSTEL $

(Map p58; ☎4300-4983; www.hostelcircus.com; Chacabuco 1020; dm US$24, r from US$80; ; Línea C Independencia) From the trendy lounge in front to the wooden deck-surrounded wading pool in back, this hotel-hostel exudes hipness. Both dorms and private rooms, all small and simple, have basic furniture and their own bathrooms. There's a pool table and a slick TV area, too, but no kitchen.

Brisas del Mar HOTEL $

(Map p58; ☎4300-0040; www.hotelbrisasdelmar.com.ar; Humberto Primo 826; r AR$120, without bathroom AR$100; ; Línea C San Juan) Long-running old cheapie hotel with no luxuries – except for cable TV. Has basic but decent budget rooms, the cheapest ones with shared bathrooms – try for an upstairs one, as they're brighter. All face tiled hallways lined with plants, and there's a very rustic, unstocked kitchen. No breakfast.

Bohemia Buenos Aires HOTEL $

(Map p58; ☎4115-2561; www.bohemiabuenosaires.com.ar; Perú 845; r from AR$420; ; Línea C Independencia) With its slight upscale-motel feel, this good-value San Telmo hotel offers 22 simple and neat rooms, most good-sized, if a bit antiseptic with their white-tiled floors. None of the rooms has a bathtub, so instead of taking a soak enjoy the peaceful grassy backyard and small interior patios. The breakfast buffet is a plus, and there's a restaurant.

Casa y Mundo Bolivar BOUTIQUE HOTEL $$

(Map p78; ☎4300-3619; www.casabolivar.com; Bolívar 1701; studios & apt US$70-90; ; 29) Fourteen spacious studios and loft apartments with kitchenettes have been renovated into attractive modern spaces – some with original details such as carved doorways or painted ceilings – at this amazing mansion. Separate entrances join with hallways connecting through the complex, and there are lovely garden patios in which to relax. No breakfast, but there's a cafe-restaurant.

Three-day minimum stay; long-term guests preferred.

Bonito San Telmo GUESTHOUSE $$

(Map p78; ☎4362-8451; www.bonitobuenosaires.com; Av Juan de Garay 458; r US$90-105; ; 29) The busy avenue outside seems unlikely to offer such a paradise, but after you climb the stairs you'll be surrounded by contemporary touches, from the grand piano in the living room to the elegant dining nook in back. Six lovely rooms are available (including one with kitchenette), but the best features are the lush rooftop terraces, complete with San Telmo views. Reserve ahead.

★ **Mansión Vitraux** BOUTIQUE HOTEL $$

(Map p58; ☎4878-4292; www.mansionvitraux.com; Carlos Calvo 369; r US$135-160; ; Línea C Independencia) Almost too slick for San Telmo, this glass-fronted boutique hotel offers 12 beautiful rooms, all in different colors. All have either flat-screen or projection TV, and bathrooms boast very contemporary design. The breakfast buffet is in the basement wine bar, and a tasting is included in your stay. There is also a large Jacuzzi, a dry sauna and a fancy rooftop terrace with small lap pool.

Retiro

Retiro is a great, central place to be, *if* you can afford it – many of BA's most expensive hotels, along with some of its richest inhabitants, are settled here. Close by are leafy Plaza San Martín, the Retiro bus terminal and train station and many upscale stores and business services. Recoleta and the Microcentro are just a short stroll away.

Hotel Tres Sargentos HOTEL $

(Map p68; ☎4312-6082; www.hotel3sargentos.com.ar; Tres Sargentos 345; s/d AR$300/380; ; Línea C San Martín) A great deal for the location, this simple budget hotel has a decent lobby and is located on a pedestrian street. The carpets in the halls need changing, but the ones in the simple, comfortable rooms are clean enough. Some rooms even offer a bit of a view – ask for a floor up high.

★ **Casa Calma** BOUTIQUE HOTEL $$$

(Map p68; ☎4312-5000; www.casacalma.com.ar; Suipacha 1015; r US$220-240; ; Línea C San Martín) Those with stuffed wallets and of an ecoconscious mind now have their perfect hideaway in BA: this central, environmentally friendly and luxurious hotel. Rooms are beautifully pristine and relaxing (some even have sauna or Jacuzzi), with Zen-like baths and serene atmosphere. It's a world away from outside the front door, where BA noisily buzzes by.

Four Seasons HOTEL $$$
(Map p68; ☎4321-1200; www.fourseasons.com/buenosaires; Posadas 1086; d from US$665; ; Línea C San Martín) No surprise here – the Four Seasons offers all the perks that define a five-star hotel, such as great service and white terry-cloth robes. Rooms are large and beautiful, with contemporary furnishings and decorations, and the finest suites are located in an old, luxurious mansion next door (go for the presidential – it's US$10,000 per night).

There's also a gorgeous spa, an outdoor heated swimming pool and a top-notch restaurant.

Recoleta & Barrio Norte

Most of the accommodations in Recoleta are expensive, and what cheap hotels there are tend to be full much of the time. Buildings here are grand and beautiful, befitting the city's richest barrio, and you'll be close to Recoleta's famous cemetery, along with its lovely parks, museums and boutiques.

Reina Madre Hostel HOSTEL $
(Map p72; ☎4962-5553; www.rmhostelbuenosaires.com; Av Anchorena 1118; dm AR$95-105, s/d AR$215/235; ; Línea D Pueyrredón) This wonderful hostel is clean, safe and well run. It's in an old building that has plenty of personality, with high ceilings and original tiles, and all rooms are comfortable and modern (and share bathrooms). There's a cozy living room with balcony and small kitchen plus lots of dining tables, but the highlight is the wooden-deck rooftop with *asado*. Pet cat on premises.

Yira Yira Guesthouse GUESTHOUSE $
(Map p58; ☎4812-4077; www.yirayiraba.com; Uruguay 911, No 1B; s/d US$45/65; ; Línea D Callao) This casual, intimate apartment-home is run by the helpful Paz, who lives onsite. The floors are wooden and the ceilings high, and there are just four large rooms (all with shared bathrooms) facing the central living area with tiny patio. It's a good place to meet other travelers and is centrally located near downtown. Reserve ahead.

Hotel Lion D'or HOTEL $
(Map p68; ☎4803-8992; www.hotel-liondor.com.ar; Pacheco de Melo 2019; s AR$300-320, d AR$360-420, tr AR$400-560; ; Línea D Pueyrredón) These digs have their charm (it's an old embassy), but rooms vary widely – some are small, basic and dark, while others are grand. Despite some rough edges, all are good value and most have been modernized for comfort. The old marble staircase and elevator are fabulous, and there's a nice rooftop area. Cheap breakfast option; some rooms share bathrooms.

Art Suites APARTMENT $$
(Map p68; ☎4821-6800; www.artsuites.com.ar; Azcuénaga 1465; d AR$850-1450; ; Línea D Pueyrredón) The 15 luxurious, modern and spacious apartments here are all bright and boast minimalist decor, full kitchens or kitchenettes, sunny balconies and slick, hip furniture. Windows are double-paned for quiet, staff speak English and security is excellent. Continental breakfast included. Long-term discounts are available; reserve ahead. An annex offers more apartments.

★ **Poetry Building** APARTMENT $$$
(Map p68; ☎4827-2772; www.poetrybuilding.com; Junín 1280; apt US$175-235; ; Línea D Pueyrredón) These gorgeous studios and one- or two-bedroom apartments are perfect for families or small groups. Each one is different, eclectically decorated with reproduction antique furniture, and all come with fully stocked kitchens. Some boast an outdoor balcony or patio, but there's also a beautiful common terrace with soaking pool. Amenities include flat-screen TVs, plus an in-room iPod and cell-phone rentals.

Alvear Palace Hotel HOTEL $$$
(Map p68; ☎4808-2100; www.alvearpalace.com; Av Alvear 1891; r from US$640; ; 130) The classiest, most traditional hotel in BA. Old-world sophistication and superior service will help erase the trials of your long flight into town, while the bathtub Jacuzzi, Hermès toiletries and Egyptian-cotton bed sheets aid your trip into dreamland. There's also an excellent restaurant, elegant tea room, cigar bar, fine spa, indoor swimming pool and butler service.

Palacio Duhau – Park Hyatt HOTEL $$$
(Map p68; ☎5171-1234; www.buenosaires.park.hyatt.com; Av Alvear 1661; d from US$655; ; 130) If it's good enough for presidents, diplomats and Tom Cruise, it's good enough for you. The luxurious Park Hyatt takes up a city block and consists of two wings, including the Palacio Duhau, a renovated mansion. There's a gorgeously terraced garden with fountains and patios, plus a fine spa, indoor pool, wine and cheese bar, and art gallery. Excellent service.

Palermo

About a 10-minute taxi ride from the city center (and also well connected by bus and Subte lines), Palermo is the top choice for many travelers. Not only is it full of extensive parklands – which are great for weekend jaunts and sporting activities – but you'll have heaps of cutting-edge restaurants, happening bars, designer boutiques and hip dance clubs at your fingertips. Most of these places are located in the extensive subneighborhood of Palermo Viejo, which is further divided into Palermo Soho and Palermo Hollywood.

Chill House Hostel HOSTEL $

(Map p72; 4861-6175; www.chillhouse.com.ar; Agüero 781; dm AR$85, d AR$250-360; @; Línea B Carlos Gardel) One of the coolest-vibe hostels in BA is at this remodeled old house, boasting high ceilings and a rustic artsy style. There are two dorms, eight private rooms with bathroom (No 6 is especially nice) and an awesome rooftop terrace where weekly *asados* take place. Run by a French and Argentine team; free bike rentals, too.

Eco Pampa Hostel HOSTEL $

(Map p72; 4831-2435; www.hostelpampa.com.ar; Guatemala 4778; dm US$20, s/d US$70/85; @; Línea D Plaza Italia) Buenos Aires' first 'green' hostel is this casual spot sporting vintage furniture, low-energy light bulbs and a recycling system. The rooftop is home to a small veggie garden, compost pile and solar panels. Dorms are a good size and each of the eight private rooms comes with bathroom and flat-screen TV (most have air-con).

There's another branch further north in **Belgrano** (Iberá 2858).

Caserón Porteño GUESTHOUSE $$

(Map p72; 4554-6336; www.caseronporteno.com; Ciudad de la Paz 344; s AR$550-680, d AR$680-850; @; Línea D Olleros) Catering especially to tango dancers is this fine guesthouse with 10 simple but tastefully furnished rooms. All have private bathrooms, but four have them located outside the actual rooms. Behind the lush garden there's a small dance studio where classes take place, while other common spaces include a relaxing rooftop terrace and a kitchen for guest use.

Palermo Viejo B&B GUESTHOUSE $$

(Map p72; 4773-6012; www.palermoviejobb.com; Niceto Vega 4629; s/d US$75/85; @; 140) This small and intimate B&B is located in a remodeled *casa chorizo* – a long, narrow house. The six rooms all front a leafy outdoor patio hallway and are simple but quite comfortable; two have lofts. All come with fridge and a good breakfast. RSVP or call them ahead of time – they often leave on errands in the afternoon.

Abode GUESTHOUSE $$

(Map p72; 4774-3331; www.abodebuenosaires.com; Costa Rica 5193; r US$90-150; @; Línea D Palermo) Run by an expat couple who live on the premises, Abode is a very intimate and homey guesthouse. Each of the four simple yet comfortable rooms comes with its own bathroom, and the largest has a balcony. The highlight: a wonderful rooftop terrace, where you can enjoy your full English breakfast. By reservation only; no walk-ins. Friendly dog on premises.

Livian Guesthouse GUESTHOUSE $$

(Map p72; 4862-8841; www.livianguesthouse.com; Palestina 1184; r US$90-150; @; 106, 160) Located in a lovely old building in an untouristy section of Palermo is this chill guesthouse. There are 10 colorful yet tasteful rooms on offer, one with its own terrace and most with private bathroom (a few share bathrooms or have a private bathroom down the hall). There are pleasant living-room spaces and a pretty back garden, too.

★ **The 5th Floor** B&B $$

(Map p72; 4827-0366; www.the5thfloorba.com; r US$90-170; @; Línea D Scalabrini Ortíz) This upscale B&B offers seven elegant rooms, three with private balcony. All are tastefully decorated with art-deco furniture and modern amenities. The common living room is great for chatting with the English owner, a polo enthusiast, and there's also a pleasant back patio with lovely tile details. Occasional closed-door dining events happen here. Excellent breakfast. Address given upon reservation.

Rugantino Hotel HOTEL $$

(Map p72; 4773-2891; www.rugantinohotel.com; Uriarte 1844; r US$115; @; Línea D Palermo) This small and intimate hotel is located in a 1920s building and run by an Italian family. Various tiny terraces and catwalks connect the seven simple but beautiful rooms, all decked out in hardwood floors and modern styling – combined with a few antiques. The climbing vine–greenery in the small central courtyard well is soothing, and you can expect espresso for breakfast.

Cabrera Garden B&B $$
(Map p72; ☎4777-7668; www.cabreragarden.com; José Antonio Cabrera 5855; r US$145-250; ❄@📶🏊; 🚌140) One of BA's loveliest stays is this three-room B&B run by a Polish-German gay couple. The remodelled 1920s building boasts a beautiful grassy garden with small patio and pool, and there's a wonderful living room in which to hang out. Rooms are very comfortable and all different, with modern conveniences like flat-screen TV and iPod docks.

English, German and Polish spoken; reserve ahead.

Vain Boutique Hotel BOUTIQUE HOTEL $$$
(Map p72; ☎4776-8246; www.vainuniverse.com; Thames 2226; r US$190-300; ❄@📶; Ⓢ Línea D Plaza Italia) Fifteen elegant rooms, all with high ceilings and wooden floors, are in this nicely renovated building. All are modern in that white, minimalist way, and boast sofas and small desks. The highlight, however, is the wonderfully airy, multilevel living room with attached wooden-decked terrace – a great place to enjoy breakfast. Small bar-restaurant in the lobby; reserve ahead for discounts.

Mine Hotel HOTEL $$$
(Map p72; ☎4832-1100; www.minehotel.com; Gorriti 4770; d US$205-270; ❄@📶🏊; 🚌55) This hip boutique hotel offers 20 good-size rooms; some come with Jacuzzi and balcony and all have a desk and natural decor touches. Get one overlooking the highlight of the hotel: the peaceful backyard, which comes complete with small wading pool. There's a small bistro for the buffet breakfast, and Mine even attempts to be somewhat eco-friendly (reusing towels, low-energy bulbs, recycling).

★ **Miravida Soho** GUESTHOUSE $$$
(Map p72; ☎4774-6433; www.miravidasoho.com; Darregueyra 2050; r US$205-280; ❄@📶; Ⓢ Línea D Plaza Italia) Run by a friendly and helpful German couple, this gorgeous guesthouse comes with six beautiful and elegant rooms. All are very comfortable and one has a private terrace. There's a wine cellar, bar-lounge area for evening wine tastings, a small and relaxing patio, and even an elevator. It serves good, full breakfasts; reserve ahead (10% discount if you pay cash).

★ **Magnolia Hotel** BOUTIQUE HOTEL $$$
(Map p72; ☎4867-4900; www.magnoliahotel.com.ar; J Álvarez 1746; r US$255-350; ❄@📶; Ⓢ Línea D Scalabrini Ortíz) This classy boutique hotel is in a gorgeously restored old house. Its eight impeccably groomed rooms are bathed in muted colors and fitted with elegant furniture; some have a patio or balcony. Common spaces are beautiful, and the gorgeous rooftop terrace is strewn with cushy lounges. Other pluses include a welcome drink and a little patio for breakfast.

Eating

Eating out in Buenos Aires is a gastronomical highlight. Not only are the typical *parrillas* (steak houses) a dime a dozen, but the city's Palermo Viejo neighborhood boasts the most varied ethnic cuisine in the country. You can find Armenian, Brazilian, Mexican, Indian, Japanese, Southeast Asian and Middle Eastern cuisines – and even fusions of several. Most are acceptable and some are exceptional.

Microcentro eateries tend to cater to the business crowd, while nearby Puerto Madero is full of elegant and pricey restaurants. Congreso is pretty traditional cuisine-wise, except for its 'Little Spain' neighborhood. Recoleta is another expensive area with touristy but fun dining options near the cemetery. San Telmo keeps attracting more and more worthwhile restaurants.

Reservations are usually unnecessary except at the most popular restaurants – or perhaps on weekends. Except at five-star restaurants, wait staff provide simply adequate service – nothing fancy. Upscale restaurants charge a *cubierto,* a small cover charge for utensil use and bread. This doesn't include the tip, which should be at least 10%.

A good website for BA restaurants is www.guiaoleo.com (in Spanish); for good blogs in English there are www.saltshaker.net and www.pickupthefork.com.

Microcentro

Granix VEGETARIAN $
(Map p58; ☎4343-4020; Florida 165, 1st fl; all-you-can-eat AR$85; ⏲11am-3:30pm Mon-Fri; 🥬) Stepping into this large, modern lacto-ovo-vegetarian eatery will make you wonder if *porteños* have had enough steak already. Pick from the many hot appetizers and mains; there's also a great salad bar and plenty of desserts. It's only open for week-

day lunches, and located in a shopping mall (look for the stairs on the right). Takeout is available.

Aldo's Vinoteca ARGENTINE $$

(Map p58; ☎4334-2380; Moreno 372; mains AR$70-100; ⏰11am-midnight Sun-Thu, to 1am Fri & Sat) Located under the Moreno Hotel, this restaurant-wine shop is an upscale eatery serving a small but tasty menu of meat, seafood and pasta dishes, all amid walls lined with wine. What makes this place unique, however, is that the wine is sold at *retail* prices – thus making it easier to sample (and buy) the nearly 500 labels available.

★**Tomo 1** MODERN ARGENTINE $$$

(Map p58; ☎4326-6695; Carlos Pellegrini 521; mains AR$190-320; ⏰noon-3pm & 5:30pm-midnight Mon-Fri, 5:30pm-midnight Sat) At renowned Tomo 1, European-influenced Chef Federico Fialayre promotes a blend of Italian and Spanish cooking methods in dishes featuring seasonal produce, homemade pasta and fresh fish. For a splash-out, sample his famed cuisine with a three-course prix fixe menu (lunch/dinner AR$370/430); it comes with amuse-bouches, two glasses of wine, mineral water, coffee and petits fours.

Puerto Madero

Central Market MODERN ARGENTINE $$

(Map p58; ☎5775-0330; Av Macacha Güemes 302; mains AR$80-135; ⏰8am-midnight) In the morning, this pleasant airy restaurant has a coffee counter for espresso and scones; in the afternoon there are *panini* (Italian-style sandwiches) and a gourmet deli and a kitchenwares shop to poke around; and by night, the fancy dining room serves contemporary Argentinian dishes. Great waterfront seating on warm days for people-watching. Another branch, **i Fresh Market** (Map p58; ☎5775-0330; www.icentralmarket.com.ar; Villaflor 300; ⏰8am-midnight), is in Dique 3.

La Parolaccia Trattoria ITALIAN $$

(Map p58; ☎4343-1679; www.laparolaccia.com; Av Alicia Moreau de Justo 1052; mains AR$80-140; ⏰noon-midnight Sun-Thu, to 2am Fri & Sat) This popular Italian eatery specializes in delicious homemade pastas. Reserve one of the few tables with a water view, then enjoy sweet-potato gnocchi, gorgonzola ravioli or *cappelletti* (a small stuffed pasta) in four cheeses. If you're here at midday, the lunch menu is a great deal (available Monday to Saturday). A nearby branch, **La Parolaccia del Mare** (Map p58; Av Alicia Moreau de Justo 1170), specializes in seafood.

Congreso

Pizzería Güerrín PIZZERIA $

(Map p58; ☎4371-8141; Av Corrientes 1368; slices AR$8; ⏰11am-1am Sun-Thu, to 2am Fri & Sat) A quick pit-stop on Av Corrientes is this cheap but classic pizza joint. Just point at a pre-baked slice behind the glass counter and eat standing up with the rest of the crowd. Or sit down and order one freshly baked – this way you can also choose from a greater variety of toppings for your pizza.

★**Chan Chan** PERUVIAN $

(Map p58; ☎4382-8492; Hipólito Yrigoyen 1390; mains AR$35-65; ⏰noon-4pm & 8pm-midnight Tue-Sun) Thanks to fair prices and relatively quick service, this colorful Peruvian eatery is jam-packed at lunchtime with office workers devouring plates of *ceviche* (seafood cured in citrus) and *ajiaco de conejo* (rabbit and potato stew). There are also plenty of *arroz chaufa* (Peruvian-style fried rice) dishes, easily downed with a tangy pisco sour or a pitcher of *chicha morada* (a sweet fruity drink).

STEAK – OUTSIDE THE BOX

Going to a *parrilla* is great, but there are other options for amazing steak experiences.

Adentro (www.adentrodinnerclub.com) This *puerta cerrada* is like being at a good friend's *asado*. You'll get stuffed on delicious appetizers, then move on to amazing meat.

Argentine Experience (www.theargentineexperience.com) Learn the story of Argentina's beef and how to make empanadas and *alfajores* (cookie sandwiches). Plus you'll eat a supremely tender steak.

Steaks by Luis (www.steakbuenosaires.net) An upscale *asado* experience where you'll nibble on cheese and sip boutique wine while watching large hunks of meat being grilled.

Parrilla Tour (www.parrillatour.com) Start with a *choripán* (traditional sausage sandwich), then an empanada. You'll finish at a local *parrilla*.

Parrilla Peña PARRILLA $
(Map p58; ☎4371-5643; Rodríguez Peña 682; mains AR$50-90; ⊙noon-4pm & 8pm-midnight Mon-Sat, noon-4pm Sun) This simple, traditional and long-running *parrilla* is well known for its excellent-quality meats and generous portions. The service is fast and efficient and it's great value. Don't expect many tourists – this is a locals' sort of place. Also on offer are homemade pastas, salads and *milanesas* (breaded steaks), along with several tasty desserts and a good wine list.

★ **Aramburu** GOURMET $$$
(Map p58; ☎4305-0439; www.aramburuesto.com.ar; Salta 1050; prix fixe AR$390; ⊙8:30-11pm Tue-Sat) 'Molecular' dining has taken Buenos Aires by storm, and Chef Gonzalo Aramburu is leading the pack. The set 12-course meal might take you up to three hours to enjoy, each artistically created plate just a few bites of gastronomic delight. Expect enlightening tastes, textures, smells, plus unique presentations and a highly memorable meal. Located in the edgy but upcoming neighborhood of Montserrat.

San Telmo & Constitución

El Desnivel PARRILLA $
(Map p58; ☎4300-9081; Defensa 855; mains AR$45-80; ⊙noon-4:30pm & 7pm-1am Mon-Fri, noon-1am Sat & Sun) This famous and long-running *parrilla* joint packs in both locals and tourists, serving them treats like chorizo sandwiches and *bife de lomo* (tenderloin steak). The sizzling grill out front is torturous while you wait for a table (which could be in the large back room) – get here early, especially on weekends.

Origen Café INTERNATIONAL $
(Map p58; ☎4362-7979; Humberto Primo 599; mains AR$50-70; ⊙8am-10pm Tue-Fri & Sun, to 9:30pm Mon & Sat) Modern but unpretentious, this stylish corner bistro spills out onto the wide sidewalks; snag an outdoor table on a sunny afternoon. The creative menu features health-conscious dishes from stir-fries and whole-wheat pizzas to homemade soups and green salads. There's an emphasis on vegetarian food, and the cappuccinos are served in delightfully oversized mugs.

Bar El Federal ARGENTINE $
(Map p58; ☎4300-4313; cnr Perú & Carlos Calvo; mains AR$35-110; ⊙8am-2am Sun-Thu, to 4am Fri & Sat) Dating from 1864, this historic bar has a classic, somewhat rustic atmosphere accented with original wood and tile, and an eye-catching antique bar. The specialties here are sandwiches (especially turkey) and *picadas* (shared appetizer plates), but there are also lots of pastas, salads, desserts and tall mugs of icy beer.

Casal de Catalunya CATALAN $$
(Map p58; ☎4361-0191; Chacabuco 863; mains AR$60-100; ⊙8pm-midnight Mon, noon-4pm & 8pm-midnight Tue-Sat, noon-4pm Sun) Located in BA's Catalan cultural center is this excellent Catalan restaurant. Big on seafood, its specialties run from garlic shrimp to fresh mussels and clams in tomato sauce to fish of the day with *aioli* (a garlic and olive oil sauce). Other typical dishes include *jamón serrano* (prosciutto-like ham), seafood paella and suckling pig. Don't miss the luscious *crema catalana* for dessert.

La Panadería de Pablo MODERN ARGENTINE $$
(Map p58; ☎4331-4683; Defensa 269; mains AR$70-110; ⊙9:30am-6pm Mon-Wed, 9:30am-midnight Thu & Fri, 8pm-midnight Sat, 10am-7pm Sun) Enter this modern restaurant and be comforted by the awesome design, airy spaces and cozy booths. Try the smoked salmon salad with avocado, rib-eye marinated in rosemary and thyme, or Yamani rice stir-fries. There are a few elegant pizzas and pastas, too, along with over a dozen cocktails to

TOP CLOSED-DOOR RESTAURANTS

Puertas cerradas (closed-door restaurants) offer an exclusive atmosphere as they're usually located in the chef's own homes. Expect communal tables, but don't worry – your fellow diners are usually interesting. You'll get the address after booking.

Some of BA's best *puertas cerradas* include **iLatina** (www.ilatinabuenosaires.com/en), serving exquisite Colombian food; **Casa Saltshaker** (www.casasaltshaker.com), where you'll sample ex–New Yorker Dan Perlman's culinary creations; **NOLA** (www.nolabuenosaires.com), home to New Orleans–fusion dishes; **Casa Felix** (www.colectivofelix.com/casa-felix), a pescatarian's delight; and **Cocina Sunae** (www.cocinasunae.com), for near-authentic Asian-fusion meals.

MEATLESS IN BUENOS AIRES

Argentine cuisine is internationally famous for its succulent grilled meats, but this doesn't mean vegetarians – or even vegans – are completely out of luck.

Most restaurants, including *parrillas*, serve a few items acceptable to most vegetarians, such as green salads, omelets, pizza and pasta. Key words to beware of include *carne* (beef), *pollo* (chicken), *cerdo* (pork) and *cordero* (lamb). *Sin carne* means 'without meat' and the phrase *soy vegetariano/a* (I'm a vegetarian) can come in handy.

Close to the Microcentro there's Granix (p88) and **Vita** (Map p58; ☎4342-0788; www.vitamarket.com.ar; Hipólito Yrigoyen 583; mains AR$34-36; ⏰8am-8pm Mon-Fri, 10am-8pm Sat, noon-7pm Sun; 🖉). **Broccolino** (Map p58; ☎4322-7754; www.broccolino.com; Esmeralda 776; mains AR$50-120; ⏰noon-11:30pm) specializes in pasta – it's not meat-free, but there are many vegetarian choices.

The Palermo Viejo area has more upscale options, including Bio (p93), **Arevalito** (Map p72; ☎4776-4252; Arévalo 1478; mains AR$40; ⏰9am-midnight Mon-Sat; 🖉) and **Artemesia** (Map p72; ☎4776-5484; Gorriti 5996; ⏰lunch & dinner). **La Esquina de las Flores** (Map p72; ☎4832-8528; Gurruchaga 1630; ⏰8:30am-8pm Mon-Fri, till 8:30pm Sat, 10am-6pm Sun) is a long-running veggie cafeteria/health shop.

Even raw foodists have an option: gourmet, vegan, raw-live food, organic when possible, delivered to your door. Check out www.cocinaverde.com.

choose from. You'll also find a great patio in back for warm days, plus breakfast offerings.

★Café San Juan INTERNATIONAL **$$$**
(Map p58; ☎4300-1112; Av San Juan 452; mains AR$125-150; ⏰12:30-4pm & 8pm-1am) Having studied in Milan, Paris and Barcelona, celebrity TV-chef Leandro Cristóbal now runs the kitchen at this renowned San Telmo bistro. Start with fabulous tapas, then delve into the grilled Spanish octopus, *molleja* (sweetbreads) canneloni and the amazing pork *bondiola* (deliciously tender after nine hours' roasting). Most of the seafood is flown in daily from Patagonia. Reserve for lunch and dinner.

If you can't get a table here, try the **Café San Juan La Cantina** (Map p58; ☎4300-9344; Chile 474; mains AR$125-150; ⏰noon-3.30pm & 8.30pm-midnight Tue-Sun), located a few blocks away and with a different menu.

La Boca

★Proa Cafe CAFE **$**
(Map p78; ☎4104-1003; www.proa.org/eng/cafe.php; Av Don Pedro de Mendoza 1929; mains AR$45-80; ⏰11am-7pm Tue-Sun) Chef Lucas Angelillo presides over this airy eatery, located on the top floor of Fundación Proa. Stop in briefly for a fresh juice and gourmet sandwich, or stay longer and order a meat, seafood or pasta dish. Don't miss the rooftop terrace on a warm, sunny day – you'll get good views of the Riachuelo, hopefully without its corresponding scents.

Il Matterello ITALIAN **$$**
(Map p78; ☎4307-0529; Martín Rodríguez 517; mains AR$80-120; ⏰noon-midnight Tue-Sat) This Genovese trattoria serves up awesome lasagne bolognese and *tagliatelle alla rucola* (tagliatelle with arugula). For a special treat, however, try the *tortelli bianchi con burro foso al aglio* (pasta pillows stuffed with chard and Parmesan in a burned garlic sauce). For dessert there's a great tiramisu and seasonal *crostate* (cream-filled pastry). Also in **Palermo** (Map p72; ☎4831-8493; cnr Thames & Gorriti).

Retiro

Filo ITALIAN **$$**
(Map p68; ☎4311-0312; www.filo-ristorante.com; San Martín 975; mains AR$75-110; ⏰noon-1am) Popular with the business lunch crowd, this large, pop art–style Italian pizzeria tosses great thin-crust pies with fresh toppings – try a pie piled high with prosciutto and arugula. Other tasty choices include *panini,* gourmet salads, various pastas and a whirlwind of desserts. The menu is extensive – there's something to please just about everyone here.

Dadá INTERNATIONAL **$$**
(Map p68; ☎4814-4787; San Martín 941; mains AR$75-130; ⏰noon-2am Mon-Thu, to 5am Fri & Sat) The tiny bohemian Dadá, with walls painted red and a bar cluttered with wine bottles, feels like an unassuming neighborhood bar in Paris. Order something savory off the bis-

tro menu – the fresh guacamole and home-made potato chips are perfect for sharing. At night you can dine on grilled salmon and down an expertly mixed cocktail.

Dill & Drinks INTERNATIONAL $$
(Map p68; ☎4515-0675; www.dillanddrinks.com; San Martín 986; mains AR$70-140; ⏰noon-6pm Mon, to 2am Tue-Fri, 2pm-2am Sat) Here's an intimate bar-restaurant with contemporary and trendy design. Order the daily lunch special, which includes a principal plate and two cocktails (!), the latter made with fresh juices and fruits. Bring your own Negroni recipe; it'll be filed away in the venue's collection. Dishes are made with quality ingredients, like shrimp risotto or pork medallions in honey mustard.

★**Elena** MODERN ARGENTINE $$$
(Map p68; ☎4321-1728; www.elenaponyline.com; Four Seasons, Posadas 1086; mains AR$200-250; ⏰6:30-11am, 12:30-3:30pm & 7:30pm-1am) If you're looking for a splurge night out, Elena should be your destination. Located in the Four Seasons hotel, this highly rated restaurant uses the best ingredients and cooking methods to create superb dishes. Order the dry-aged rib-eye steak or seared prawns with charred baby fennel for something really special. Expect the cocktails, desserts and service to be five-star as well.

Recoleta & Barrio Norte

Cumaná ARGENTINE $
(Map p68; ☎4813-9207; Rodriguez Peña 1149; mains AR$40-50; ⏰noon-4pm & 8pm-1am) To sample Argentina's regional cuisine, check out this colorful, budget-friendly eatery with huge picture windows and an old-fashioned adobe oven. Cumaná specializes in delicious *cazuela,* stick-to-your-ribs stews filled with squash, corn, eggplant, potatoes and meat. Also popular are the empanadas, *locro* (corn-and-meat stew) and *humita* (corn, cheese and onion tamales). Come early to avoid a wait.

El Sanjuanino ARGENTINE $
(Map p68; ☎4805-2683; Posadas 1515; empanadas AR$13, mains AR$40-70; ⏰noon-4pm & 7pm-1am) This long-running, cozy little joint probably has the cheapest food in Recoleta, attracting both penny-pinching locals and thrifty tourists. Sit either upstairs or downstairs (in the basement) and order spicy empanadas, tamales or *locro* (corn-and-meat stew). The curved brick ceiling adds to the atmosphere, but many take their food to go – Recoleta's lovely parks are just a couple of blocks away.

Como en Casa ARGENTINE $
(Map p68; ☎4816-5507; www.tortascomoencasa.com; Riobamba 1239; lunch mains AR$45-70; ⏰8am-midnight Tue-Sat, 8am-8:30pm Sun & Mon) This gorgeous, upscale cafe-restaurant has a very elegant atmosphere and attracts Recoleta's wealthiest. It's best feature is the shady patio, complete with large fountain and surrounded by grand buildings, a must on a warm day. For lunch there are fancy sandwiches, salads, wraps and stir-fries, while dinner options include goulash, shrimp ragout and spinach gnocchi. Plenty of luscious desserts, plus breakfast, too.

Natural Deli CAFE, DELI $
(Map p72; ☎4822-1228; www.natural-deli.com; Laprida 1672; mains AR$50-72; ⏰8am-midnight Mon-Sat, 9am-midnight Sun; 🖉) Modern, organic cafe offering fresh dishes with a natural bent. Choose from creative gourmet sandwiches and wraps, fresh salads or stir-fries. There are also fresh juices and *licuados* (blended fruit smoothie), plus many organic gourmet products are sold. Great for breakfast; muffins, scones, brownies and even key lime pie available. Also in **Las Cañitas, Palermo** (Map p72; ☎4514-1776; Gorostiaga 1776; ⏰8am-midnight Mon-Sat, 9am-midnight Sun).

Rodi Bar ARGENTINE $
(Map p68; ☎4801-5230; Vicente López 1900; mains AR$50-90; ⏰7am-1am) A great option for well-priced, unpretentious food in upscale Recoleta. This traditional corner restaurant with fine old-world atmosphere and extensive menu offers something for everyone, from inexpensive combo plates to relatively unusual dishes like marinated beef tongue.

★**Oviedo** MEDITERRANEAN $$
(Map p72; ☎4822-5415; Beruti 2602; mains AR$90-140; ⏰noon-midnight Mon-Sat) Famed chef Martin Rebaudino brings a contemporary Spanish flair to seafood (the fish is shipped daily from Mar del Plata) and serves up melt-in-your-mouth *cochinillo* (suckling pig) dishes that are well worth writing home about. The desserts are homemade, as are the breads. A fantastic wine list and cordial service make Oviedo a fine dining experience that you'll be pleased to shell out for.

Palermo

Oui Oui INTERNATIONAL $

(Map p72; ☎4778-9614; www.ouioui.com.ar; Nicaragua 6068; mains AR$40-70; ⏰8am-8pm Tue-Sun) *Pain au chocolat* and shabby chic? *Oui.* This charming and popular French-style cafe produces the goods – dark coffee, buttery croissants and jars of tangy lemonade – and boasts a small and cozy interior. Choose also from creative salads, gourmet sandwiches and luscious pastries. Its annex, **Almacén Oui Oui** (Map p72; cnr Dorrego & Nicaragua; ⏰8am-9pm Tue-Sun), is on the same block and stays open an hour later.

Las Cholas ARGENTINE $

(Map p72; ☎4899-0094; Arce 306; mains AR$40-75; ⏰noon-4pm & 8pm-midnight) Good food and bargain prices keep this popular corner eatery packed. Choose from typical *parrilla* cuts or traditional Argentine foods like *locro* and *cazuela* (meat and veggie stews). Negatives include uncomfortable chairs, spotty service and the owner's large dog roaming the dining room.

★**Sarkis** MIDDLE EASTERN $

(Map p72; ☎4772-4911; Thames 1101; mains AR$55-90; ⏰noon-3pm & 8pm-1am) The food is well-priced at this long-standing Middle Eastern restaurant – come with a group to sample many exotic dishes. Start with the hummus platter, *baquerones* (marinated sardines), *keppe crudo* (raw meat) or *parras rellenas* (stuffed grape leaves), then follow up with kebabs, couscous with lentils or lamb in yogurt sauce. Less busy at lunchtime; expect a long wait for dinner.

★**Malvón** BAKERY $$

(Map p72; ☎4774-2563; www.malvonba.com.ar; Serrano 789; mains AR$50-130; ⏰8am-8:30pm) Famous for its US-style weekend brunch – which features pancakes, French toast and eggs Benedict – Malvón is an eatery with a wonderfully rustic yet upscale atmosphere. The gourmet sandwiches are tasty, but there are also great bagels, burgers, tapas and baked treats like scones, muffins and pecan pie. Expect a wait on the weekend. Also in **Palermo** (Map p72; Lafinur 3275).

★**Siamo nel Forno** PIZZERIA $$

(Map p72; ☎4775-0337; Costa Rica 5886; pizza AR$65-95; ⏰8pm-midnight Tue-Thu & Sun, to 1am Fri & Sat) Possibly the city's best Naples-style pizzas, made with quality ingredients and finished in a wood-fired oven so the thin crusts char beautifully. Try the Margherita, with tomatoes, fresh mozzarella, basil and olive oil; the Champignon & Prosciutto comes with mushrooms, ham and goat cheese. Also bakes up excellent calzoni.

Bio VEGETARIAN $$

(Map p72; ☎4774-3880; www.biorestaurant.com.ar; Humboldt 2192; mains AR$68-100; ⏰11am-midnight Sun-Thu, to 1am Fri & Sat; 🖉) The supremely health-conscious should make a beeline for this casual corner joint, which specializes in healthy, organic and vegetarian fare. Try the quinoa risotto, seitan stir-fry, Mediterranean couscous or mushrooms a la Bahiana (Brazilian-style). Don't miss the refreshing ginger lemonade. Also caters to celiacs, vegans and raw foodists.

★**Las Pizarras** INTERNATIONAL $$

(Map p72; ☎4775-0625; Thames 2296; mains AR$80-90; ⏰8pm-midnight Tue-Sun) At this unpretentious yet excellent restaurant, Chef Rodrigo Castilla cooks up a changing rainbow of eclectic dishes such as grilled venison or rabbit stuffed with cherries and pistachios. Those with meeker stomachs can choose the asparagus and mushroom risotto or any of the homemade pastas. The chalkboard menu on the wall adds to the casual atmosphere.

Astor MODERN ARGENTINE $$

(Map p72; ☎4554-0802; www.astorbistro.com; Ciudad de la Paz 353; mains AR$80-90; ⏰12:30-3:30pm Mon-Wed, 12:30-3:30pm & 8:30pm-midnight Thu & Fri, 8:30pm-midnight Sat) French-trained Chef Antonio Soriano presides over the kitchen at this contemporary restaurant in a residential neighborhood. The few main dishes change weekly but are always delicious and beautifully presented, accented with edible flowers. If you order the tasting menu (AR$149), bring your appetite – it's nine courses. To watch your meals being created, sit at the bar, which offers a view of the open kitchen.

Miranda PARRILLA $$

(Map p72; ☎4771-4255; www.parrillamiranda.com; Costa Rica 5602; mains AR$70-125; ⏰8am-1am Sun-Thu, to 2am Fri & Sat) Fashionable Miranda is the *parrilla* of choice for those looking for both style and substance. It's a pleasant modern steakhouse with concrete walls, high ceilings and rustic wooden furniture, but high-quality grilled beef is the main attraction here – try the popular *ojo de bife*. If you score a sidewalk table on a warm day, life doesn't get much better.

★Don Julio PARRILLA $$
(Map p72; ☎4832-6058; Guatemala 4699; mains AR$80-120; ⊙noon-4pm & 7:30pm-1am) Classy service and a great wine list add an upscale bent to this traditional corner steakhouse. The *bife de chorizo* is the main attraction here, but the exposed-brick interior, original floor tiles and cowhide tablecloths enhance the sensory experience, and the gourmet salads – served with a flourish by the uberprofessional wait staff – are a treat.

Olsen SCANDINAVIAN $$
(Map p72; ☎4776-7677; Gorriti 5870; mains AR$105-125; ⊙noon-midnight Tue-Sat, 10:30am-midnight Sun) With its hip, relaxed vibe, too-cool crowd and dramatic central fireplace, Olsen could easily be located in the frosty climes of Scandinavia. Chef German Martitegui's dishes are limited but inspired, and the vodka selection – over 60 – is superlative. Luxuriate with an exotic cocktail in the lovely front garden, or try the popular Sunday brunch. Limited menu between lunch and dinner.

Sudestada ASIAN $$
(Map p72; ☎4776-3777; Guatemala 5602; mains AR$105-135; ⊙noon-3:15pm & 8pm-midnight Mon-Thu, to 1am Fri & Sat) Sudestada's well-earned reputation comes from its well-prepared curries, stir-fries and noodle dishes, all inspired by the cuisines of Thailand, Vietnam, Malaysia and Singapore. Don't forgo an exotic cocktail or delicious lychee *licuado* (milkshake). Note that if you order something spicy, it's actually spicy. The popular set-lunch special offers fantastic value.

La Cabrera PARRILLA $$$
(Map p72; ☎4831-7002; José Antonio Cabrera 5099; mains AR$115-150; ⊙12:30-4:30pm & 8:30pm-1am Mon-Thu, to 2am Fri & Sat, 12:30pm-1am Sun) Hugely popular for grilling up BA's most sublime meats. Steaks come in 200g or 400g sizes and arrive with heaps of little complimentary side dishes. Come at 7pm for 'happy hour,' when everything is 40% off – just make sure you get here early enough to score a table. Additionally, here's an annex at **José Antonio Cabrera 5127** (Map p72), but do expect a long wait at both locations.

★Hernán Gipponi Restaurant MODERN ARGENTINE $$$
(Map p72; ☎3220-6820; www.hgrestaurant.com.ar; Soler 5862; mains AR$120-135, set menu AR$260, wine pairings AR$160 extra; ⊙7:30am-midnight Mon-Fri, 8am-midnight Sat & Sun) Located in the Fierro Hotel, this exceptional restaurant offers highly sophisticated, Spanish-influenced dishes created by chef Hernán Gipponi. Order the seven-course tasting menu for the full experience – it's pricey but worth it. Set menu on weekday lunches runs AR$150; the six-course weekend brunch costs AR$175 and is a must. On Monday night, everyone sits at one communal table. Reserve ahead.

Drinking & Nightlife

Cafes are an integral part of *porteño* life, and you shouldn't miss popping into one of these beloved hangouts to sip dainty cups of coffee and nibble biscuits with the locals. There are plenty of cafes in the city, and while you're walking around seeing the sights you're bound to run across one and find an excuse for a break. Some cafes are old classics and will take you back in time.

Most cafes serve all meals and everything in between: breakfast, brunch, lunch, afternoon tea, dinner and late-night snacks. Generally they open early in the morning and late into the evening.

In a city that never sleeps, finding a good drink is as easy as walking down the street. Whether you're into trendy lounges, Irish pubs, traditional cafes or sports bars, you'll find them all within the borders of BA.

Argentines aren't huge drinkers and you'll be lucky to see one rip-roaring drunk. One thing they *do* do, however, is stay up late. Most bars and cafes are open until two or three in the morning, and often until 5am on weekends – or until the last customer stumbles out the door.

If you like to party with young, heavy-drinking crowds, check out **Buenos Aires Pub Crawl** (☎15-5464-1886; www.pubcrawlba.com).

BA's *boliches* (nightclubs) are the throbbing heart of its world-famous nightlife. To be cool, don't arrive before 2am (or even 3am) and dress up. Payment for admission and drinks is nearly always in cash only.

Check out the website www.vuenosairez.com for current happenings. For one of BA's biggest and most unique parties, check out **La Bomba de Tiempo** (www.labombade

tiempo.com; Sarmiento 3131; AR$50; ⌚ Mon 7pm); it's at 7pm every Monday at Ciudad Cultural Konex.

Microcentro

La Cigale BAR

(Map p58; ☎ 4893-2332; 25 de Mayo 597; ⌚ noon-4pm & 6pm-close) This upstairs bar-restaurant is very popular with both office workers (during the day) and music-industry folks (later in the evening). There's either live music or DJs most nights, but it's best known for its 'French Tuesday,' when electronica and exotic cocktails draw heavy crowds. Fusion foods are served for both lunch and dinner.

Café Tortoni CAFE

(Map p58; ☎ 4342-4328; www.cafetortoni.com.ar; Av de Mayo 829) BA's oldest and most famous cafe, the classic Tortoni has become so popular with foreigners that it's turned into a tourist trap. Still, it's practically an obligatory stop for any visitor to town: order a couple of *churros* (fried pastry dough) with your hot chocolate and forget about the inflated prices. There are also tango shows nightly (AR$150 to AR$200) – reserve ahead.

London City CAFE

(Map p58; ☎ 4343-0328; Av de Mayo 599) This classy and historic cafe (being remodelled at research time) has been serving java enthusiasts for over 50 years, and claims to have been the spot where Julio Cortázar wrote his first novel. Your hardest work here, however, will most likely be choosing which pastry to try with your fresh cup of coffee.

Bahrein CLUB

(Map p58; ☎ 6225-2731; www.bahreinba.com; Lavalle 345; ⌚ Wed, Fri & Sat) Attracting a good share of BA's tattooed youth, Bahrein is a hugely popular downtown club housed in an old bank (check out the 'vault' in the basement). On the ground floor is the lounge-like Funky Room where resident DJs spin house music and electronica. Downstairs is the happening Xss discotheque, an impressive sound system and a dance floor for hundreds.

Congreso

Café de los Angelitos CAFE

(Map p58; ☎ 4314-1121; Av Rivadavia 2100; ⌚ 8am-midnight) Originally called Bar Rivadavia, this cafe was once the haunt of poets, musicians, even criminals, which is why a police commissioner jokingly called it '*los angelitos*' (the angels) in the early 1900s. Recently restored to its former glory, this historic cafe is now an elegant hangout for coffee or tea; it also puts on tango shows in the evening.

Clásica y Moderna CAFE

(Map p58; ☎ 4812-8707; www.clasicaymoderna.com; Av Callao 892; ⌚ 8am-2am Mon-Sat, 5pm-2am Sun) Catering to the literary masses since 1938, this cozy and intimate bookstore-restaurant-cafe continues to ooze history from its atmospheric brick walls. It's nicely

WINE TASTING AND MORE

Big on wine? There are a few ways in Buenos Aires to find out what Argentina's best grapes have to offer.

For private wine tastings, your best bet is with **Anuva Wines** (☎ 15-5768-8589; www.anuvawines.com). Try five boutique vintages with food pairings; it will also ship wine purchases to the USA. For informal tastings, inquire at **Pain et Vin** (Map p72; ☎ 4832-5654; Gorriti 5132), a casual wine and bread shop. **Bar du Marché** (Map p72; ☎ 4778-1050; www.bardumarchepalermo.com; Nicaragua 5946; ⌚ 9:30am-midnight Mon-Sat) is a low-key bistro offering 50 wines by the glass, while **Gran Bar Danzón** (Map p68; Libertad 1161) is an upscale lounge-restaurant that also has a good selection of wines by the glass.

Many *puertas cerradas* (closed-door restaurants) offer fine wines with their meals; **Casa Coupage** (Map p72; ☎ 4833-6354; www.casacoupage.com.ar; Soler 5518), run by an Argentine sommelier couple, is especially wine oriented.

For wine shops, try Lo de Joaquin Alberdi (p109) in Palermo – it offers tastings as well. In San Telmo, **Vinotango** (Map p58; ☎ 4361-1101; Estados Unidos 488; ⌚ 10:30am-9pm) is a good destination. Aldo's Vinoteca (p89) is a restaurant that sells wines at retail prices – even when you eat there.

In the event that you need a wine consultant, check out www.0800-vino.com.

lit, serves fine, simple meals and offers nightly live performances of folk music, jazz, bossa nova and tango. Mercedes Sosa (may she rest in peace), Susana Rinaldi and Liza Minnelli have all chirped here.

El Gato Negro TEAHOUSE, CAFE
(Map p58; ☎4374-1730; Av Corrientes 1669; ⏰9am-10pm Mon, to 11pm Tue, to midnight Wed & Thu, to 2am Fri & Sat, 3-11pm Sun) Tea-lined wooden cabinets and a spicy aroma welcome you to this pleasant little sipping paradise. Enjoy imported cups of coffee or tea, along with breakfast and dainty *sandwiches de miga* (thin, crustless sandwiches, traditionally eaten at tea time). Imported teas and coffees are sold in bulk, and a range of exotic herbs and spices are also on offer.

Maluco Beleza CLUB
(Map p58; ☎4372-1737; www.malucobeleza.com.ar; Sarmiento 1728; ⏰Wed & Fri-Sun) Located in an old mansion is this popular Brazilian *boliche*. It gets packed with upbeat revellers moving to samba fusion and others watching half-naked dancers writhing on the stage. For a more sedate atmosphere, climb the stairs, where it's more laid-back. If you're craving Brazilian cuisine, get here at 8:30pm on Wednesday, when dinner and a show are on tap.

San Telmo

★**Bar Plaza Dorrego** CAFE
(Map p58; ☎4361-0141; Defensa 1098; ⏰8am-2am Sun-Thu, to 3am Fri & Sat) You can't beat the atmosphere at this traditional joint; sip your *submarino* (hot milk with chocolate) by a picturesque window and watch the world pass by, or grab a table on the busy plaza. Meanwhile, traditionally suited waiters, piped-in tango music, antique bottles, and scribbled graffiti on walls and counters might take you back in time.

La Puerta Roja BAR
(Map p58; ☎4362-5649; Chacabuco 733; ⏰5pm-late) There's no sign at this upstairs bar – just look for the red door. It has a cool, relaxed atmosphere with low lounge furniture in the main room and a pool table tucked behind. This is a traditional place, so you won't find fruity cocktails on the menu – but there's good international food like curries, tacos and chicken wings.

Gibraltar PUB
(Map p58; ☎4362-5310; Perú 895; ⏰noon-4am) One of BA's classic pubs, the Gibraltar has a cozy atmosphere and a good bar counter for those traveling alone. It's also a great place for fairly authentic foreign cuisine – try the Thai, Indian or English dishes (full English breakfast offered from noon to 5pm). For a little friendly competition, head to the pool table in the back.

Doppelgänger COCKTAIL BAR
(Map p78; ☎4300-0201; Av Juan de Garay 500; ⏰7pm-close Tue-Fri, 8pm-close Sat) This cool, emerald-hued corner bar is one of the only places in BA where you can count on a perfectly mixed martini. That's because Doppelgänger specializes in vermouth cocktails. The atmosphere is calm and the lengthy menu is fascinating: start with the journalist, a martini with a bitter orange twist, or channel Don Draper and go for the bar's bestseller – an old-fashioned.

Boutique CLUB
(Map p58; ☎4543-3894; www.museumclub.com.ar; Perú 535; ⏰Wed, Fri & Sat) This cavernous disco is best known for its Wednesday-night 'after-office' party (read: meat market), which starts at the normally ungodly early hour of 7pm and runs to the ungodly early finishing hour of 2am. It's a huge space with multiple balconies and a great sound system highlighting '80s and '90s pop music. Note the amazing building, an old factory designed by Eiffel – who also did that somewhat famous Parisian landmark.

Retiro

★**Florería Atlántico** COCKTAIL BAR
(Map p68; ☎4313-6093; Arroyo 872; ⏰7pm-close Mon-Sat) One of BA's hottest bars, this basement speakeasy is located within a flower shop, adding an air of mystery and likely a main reason for its success. Hipsters, artists, chefs, businessmen and expats all flock here for the excellent cocktails, whether they're classic or unique – and the lack of gas lines means all of the delicious tapas and main dishes are cooked on the *parrilla* grill.

Milión COCKTAIL BAR
(Map p68; ☎4815-9925; www.milion.com.ar; Paraná 1048; ⏰6pm-2am Sun-Wed, to 3am Thu, to 4am Fri & Sat) This elegant and sexy bar takes up three floors of a renovated old mansion. The garden out back is a leafy paradise, overlooked by a solid balcony

that holds the best seats in the house. Nearby marble steps are also an appealing place to lounge with a frozen mojito or basil daiquiri, the tastiest cocktails on the menu. Downstairs, the restaurant serves passable international dishes.

Recoleta & Barrio Norte

La Biela CAFE

(Map p68; ☎4804-0449; www.labiela.com; Av Quintana 600; ⏰7am-2am Sun-Thu, to 3am Fri & Sat) A Recoleta institution, this classic landmark has been serving the *porteño* elite since the 1950s. The outdoor front terrace is unbeatable on a sunny afternoon, especially when the nearby weekend *feria* (street market) is in full swing.

Buller Brewing Company BAR

(Map p68; ☎4808-9061; www.bullerpub.com; RM Ortiz 1827; ⏰noon-1am Mon-Wed, to 2am Thu & Sun, to 4am Fri & Sat) Yes, it's a microbrewery in Buenos Aires, and in Recoleta, no less. Six kinds of beer are brewed on the premises, including a stout, hefeweisen, pilsen and a honey beer. Alcohol content ranges from 4.5% to 8.5%. There's a great outdoor patio in front and an extensive menu of snacks and sandwiches. Also in **Retiro** (Map p68; Paraguay 428).

Casa Bar SPORTS BAR

(Map p68; ☎4816-2712; www.casabarbuenosaires.com; Rodríguez Peña 1150; ⏰7pm-3am Wed-Fri, to 5am Sat) This recycled antique house turned sports bar offers a large selection of spirits and microbrews, along with a wine list stocked with higher-end bottles. You'll also find nachos, pizza and spicy hot wings on the menu, plus happy-hour specials from 7pm to 10pm. It's also a great spot to watch sports on TV, especially American football and baseball.

Basement Club CLUB

(Map p68; ☎4812-3584; Rodríguez Peña 1220; ⏰Thu-Sat) This cool but unpretentious subterranean club is known for first-rate DJ lineups, pounding house music and a diverse young crowd. Thanks to the Shamrock, which is the ever-popular Irish pub upstairs, this place sees plenty of traffic throughout the night. Come at 3am to see the club in full swing, or choose to descend the stairs after enjoying a few pints at ground level.

Palermo

Many hotels and restaurants in Palermo have great bars, such as **Home Hotel** (Map p72; ☎4778-1008; www.homebuenosaires.com; Honduras 5860; ⏰8am-midnight). For the hippest scene in town, head to Plaza Serrano (in Palermo Viejo) and settle in at one of the many trendy bars surrounding the plaza.

★Verne COCKTAIL BAR

(Map p72; ☎4822-0980; Av Medrano 1475; ⏰9pm-2am Sun-Wed, to 4am Thu-Sat) Upscale yet casual bar with slight Jules Verne theme. Cocktails are the specialties here, whipped up by one of BA's best bartenders, Fede Cuco. A few tables, some cushy sofas and an airy outdoor patio offer a variety of seating good options, but plant yourself at the bar to see drinks being made.

Magdalena's Party BAR

(Map p72; ☎4833-9127; www.magdalenasparty.com; Thames 1795; ⏰11am-2am Tue & Wed, 11am-4am Thu & Fri, noon-4am Sat & Sun) Popular bar-restaurant with laid-back atmosphere and *buena onda* (good vibes). DJs spin from Thursday to Saturday nights, and with cheap drinks this is a good preclub spot; try the vodka lemonade by the pitcher. Happy hour runs from noon to midnight daily, and tasty expat-friendly food is served, such as freshly ground hamburgers, California-style burritos and organic coffee. Weekend brunch, too.

Frank's Bar COCKTAIL BAR

(Map p72; ☎4777-6541; www.franks-bar.com; Arévalo 1445; ⏰9pm-4am Wed-Sat) Very popular plush, elegant speakeasy bar that 'requires' a password (via telephone booth) to get in – or you could just sweet talk the bouncer. Inside it's a beautiful space with crystal chandeliers, billowy ceiling drapes and an exclusive feel. Classic cocktails from before the 1930s are stirred – never blended – and served to a crowd of locals and foreigners. Check out the balcony bar, too.

878 BAR

(Map p72; ☎4773-1098; www.878bar.com.ar; Thames 878; ⏰8pm-2am Sun-Thu, to 4am Fri & Sat) Hidden behind an unsigned door is this 'secret' bar – you have to ring the bell to get in, but it's hardly exclusive. Enter a wonderland of elegant low lounge furniture and red brick walls; for whiskey lovers there are over 80 kinds to try, but the cocktails are tasty, too. If you're hungry, tapas are available (reserve for dinners).

Sugar BAR

(Map p72; ☎4831-3276; www.sugarbuenosaires.com; Costa Rica 4619; ⏲7pm-5:30am Mon-Fri, 11am-5:30am Sat, 11am-3am Sun) This lively expat watering hole brings in a youthful nightly crowd with well-priced drink specials and comfort food like chicken fingers and buffalo wings. Watch sports on the two huge TV screens or come on Thursdays – also known as ladies' night – when things can get a little rowdy. On weekends, you can roll out of bed and arrive in time for eggs and mimosas.

Congo BAR

(Map p72; ☎4833-5857; www.barcongo.com.ar; Honduras 5329; ⏲8pm-4am Mon-Thu, 9pm-5am Fri & Sat) The highlight at this trendy bar is the beautiful back patio – *the* place to be seen on hot summer nights, with its slick bar, leafy atmosphere and comfy wood booths. The music is great, too, with DJs spinning from Wednesday to Saturday, and inside there are elegant low lounges in romantic spaces. A full food menu is available, along with strong cocktails.

El Carnal BAR

(Map p72; ☎4772-7582; www.carnalbar.com.ar; Niceto Vega 5511; ⏲7pm-5am Tue-Fri, 9pm-5am Sat) See and be seen – preferably in the open air with an icy vodka tonic in hand – on the rooftop terrace at this ever-popular watering hole. With its bamboo lounges and billowy curtains, the place can't be beat for a cool chill out on a warm summer night. Early in the week reggae rocks, while Thursday to Saturday means pop and '80s tunes.

Mundo Bizarro BAR

(Map p72; ☎4773-1967; www.mundobizarrobar.com; Serrano 1222; ⏲8pm-late) This red-lit, futuristically retro and stylish lounge bar is open pretty much all through the night on weekends, when everything from old-time American music to hip DJs to jazz stirs up the air waves. If you're feeling peckish, check out the American-inspired bar food, which ranges from Tex-Mex to burgers to hot apple pie with ice cream. Dance on the stripper pole after you've had a few drinks.

Van Koning PUB

(Map p72; ☎4772-9909; Av Báez 325; ⏲7pm-3:30am Sun-Thu, to 5am Fri & Sat) Wonderfully rustic spaces make this Dutch-themed pub feel like the inside of a boat; after all, it's a 17th century–style seafaring theme complete with dark wood beams, flickering candles and blocky furniture. Bars on two floors serve over 30 kinds of both local and imported brews, with at least three on draft. A magnet for expats; the first Wednesday of the month is Dutch night.

Pachá CLUB

(☎4788-4288; www.pachabuenosaires.com; Av Rafael Obligado 6151; ⏲Sat) Popular, long-running electronica club well-known for attracting famous international DJs who spin tunes for the sometimes drug-addled crowds. Laser light shows and a great sound system makes the chic crowds happy through the early morning light – be sure to bring your shades and watch the sun come up from the terrace.

Kika CLUB

(Map p72; www.kikaclub.com.ar; Honduras 5339; ⏲Tue-Sun) Being supremely well located near the heart of Palermo Viejo's bar scene makes Kika's Tuesday-night popular 'Hype' party (www.hype-ba.com) easily accessible for the trendy crowds. It's a mix of electro, rock, hip-hop, drum'n'bass and dubstep, all spun by both local and international DJs. Other nights see electronica, reggaeton, Latin beats and live bands ruling the roost.

Niceto Club CLUB

(Map p72; ☎4779-9396; www.nicetoclub.com; Niceto Vega 5510; ⏲Thu-Sat) One of the city's biggest crowd-pullers, the can't-miss event at Niceto Club is Thursday night's Club 69, a subversive DJ extravaganza featuring gorgeously attired showgirls, dancing drag queens, futuristic video installations and off-the-wall performance art. On weekend nights, national and international spin masters take the booth to entertain lively crowds with blends of hip-hop, electronic beats, cumbia and reggae.

Crobar CLUB

(Map p72; ☎4778-1500; www.crobar.com.ar; cnr Av de la Infanta Isabell & Freyre; ⏲Fri & Sat) Year after year, stylish Crobar remains one of BA's most popular nightlife spots. Friday usually features international DJs mashing up the latest electronic selections, while Saturday tends to feature more commercial or Latin beats. There's also a back room for those who prefer classic rock, '80s remixes and occasional live bands, while the main levels are strewn with mezzanines and catwalks that allow views from above.

☆ Entertainment

Nonstop Buenos Aires has endless possibilities for entertainment. Dozens of venues offer first-rate theatrical productions, independent or contemporary movies, sultry tango shows, raging dance parties and exciting sports matches.

Many newspapers publish entertainment supplements on Friday; the *Buenos Aires Herald* has a particularly handy one. Also check www.vuenosairez.com (in Spanish) and www.argentinaindependent.com (in English).

Major entertainment venues often require booking through **Ticketek** (☎5237-7200; www.ticketek.com.ar), which incurs a service charge. At *carteleras* (discount-ticket offices), you can buy tickets at 20% to 50% discount for many events like tango shows, theater performances, movies and concerts. Here are three offices:

Cartelera Baires TICKET OFFICE
(www.cartelerabaires.com; Av Corrientes 1382, inside Galería Apolo)

Cartelera Espectáculos TICKET OFFICE
(☎4322-1559; www.123info.com.ar; Lavalle 742)

Cartelera Vea Más TICKET OFFICE
(☎6320-5319; www.veamasdigital.com.ar; Av Corrientes 1660, Local 2)

Tango Shows

Sensationalized tango shows aimed at tourists are common and impressive (though 'purists' don't consider them authentic). These usually include various tango couples, an orchestra and a couple of singers. They last about 1½ hours and come with a dinner option. Nearly all of the shows require reservations, while some offer modest online discounts and pick-up from your hotel.

Modest shows are more intimate and cost far less, but you won't get the theatrics, the costume changes or the overall visual punch. For discount tickets to some shows, check the *carteleras*. The website www.tangotix.com can help you choose the right show depending on your needs; it also sells discounted tickets.

Some *milongas* (tango academies) occasionally put on affordable tango shows; check out Confitería Ideal (p104), La Viruta (p105) or **Academia Nacional del Tango** (Map p58; ☎4345-6967; www.anacdeltango.org.ar).

For free (or rather, donation) tango, head to San Telmo on a Sunday afternoon – or sometimes other days. Dancers do their thing in the middle of Plaza Dorrego, though it gets crowded. Another sure bet is weekends on El Caminito in La Boca.

Café de los Angelitos TANGO SHOW
(Map p58; ☎4952-2320; www.cafedelosangelitos.com; Av Rivadavia 2100; show from US$90, show & dinner from US$130) Angelitos puts on one of the best shows in BA. It's tango – but also a bit more. The performers dress in top-notch costumes and use interesting props, like drapes and moving walls. They also dance to modern tunes like Bajofondo, and despite a nightclub feel – especially due to the lighting – it's tastefully and creatively done.

Rojo Tango TANGO SHOW
(☎4952-4111; www.rojotango.com; Faena Hotel & Universe, Martha Salotti 445; show US$210, dinner & show US$290) This sexy performance is the tango show to top all others – especially with its hefty price tag. Offering only 100 seats, the Faena's cabaret room is swathed in blood-red curtains and gilded furniture. The show itself loosely follows the history of tango, starting from its cabaret roots to the modern fusions of Ástor Piazzolla. The orchestra is first-rate, there are plenty of sexy period costumes and even a brief (shock!) nudity scene. This is tango foreplay at its best.

El Viejo Almacén TANGO SHOW
(Map p58; ☎4307-7388; www.viejoalmacen.com; cnr Balcarce & Av Independencia; show from US$90, show & dinner from US$140) One of Buenos Aires' longest-running shows (since 1969), this venue is a charming old building from the 1800s. A good dinner is served at a multistory restaurant in the main building, then everyone heads across the street to the small theater with intimate stage. The show starts with a quick movie about the tango show's history, then moves on to the highly athletic dancers with plenty of glitz. One highlight is the exceptionally good *folklore* segment.

La Ventana TANGO SHOW
(Map p58; ☎4334-1314; www.laventanaweb.com; Balcarce 431; show from US$90, dinner & show from US$140) This long-running basement venue is located in an old converted building with rustic brick walls. The tango show is excellent and includes a folkloric segment with Andean musicians and a display of *boleadores*

(Continued on p104)

The Tango

A lone woman, dressed in slit skirt and high heels, sits at a small table. She glances around, in search of the subtle signal. Her gaze suddenly locks onto a stranger's eyes, and there it is: the *cabeceo*. She nods and rises to meet him; the new pair head toward the dance floor.

History of Tango

The tango hasn't always been quite so mysterious, but it does have a long and somewhat complex history. Though the exact origins can't be pinpointed, some believe the dance started in Buenos Aires in the 1880s. Legions of European immigrants, mostly lower-class men, arrived in the great village of Buenos Aires to seek their fortunes. Missing their motherlands and the women they left behind, they sought out bars, cafes and bordellos to ease the loneliness. Here the men cavorted with waitresses and prostitutes, helping to evolve a dance blending machismo, passion and longing, with an almost fighting edge to it.

Small musical ensembles were soon brought in to accompany early tangos, playing tunes influenced by pampas, *milonga* verse, Spanish and Italian melodies, and African *candombe* drums. (The *bandoneón,* a small accordion, was brought into these sessions and has since become an inextricable part of the tango orchestra.) Here the tango song was also born. It summarized the new urban experience for the immigrants and was filled with nostalgia for a disappearing way of life. Themes ranged from profound feelings about changing neighborhoods, to the figure of the mother, or from male friendship to betrayal by women. Sometimes raunchy lyrics were added.

The perceived vulgarity of the dance was deeply frowned upon by the reigning elites, but it did manage to influence some brash young members of the upper classes, who took the novelty to Paris and created a craze – a dance that became an acceptable outlet for human desires, expressed on the dance floors of elegant cabarets. The trend spread around Europe and to the USA, and 1913 was considered by some to be 'the year of the tango.' When the evolved dance returned to Buenos Aires, now refined and famous, the tango finally earned the respectability it deserved. The golden years of tango were just beginning.

Tango at a Milonga Today

Buenos Aires is full of *milongas* (dance schools or halls), from classic venues with old-time atmosphere to hip warehouse spaces where dancers wear jeans. In other words, there's something for everyone.

At an established *milonga*, finding a good, comparable partner involves many levels of hidden codes, rules and signals that dancers must follow. In fact, some men will only proposition an unknown woman after the second song, so as not to be stuck with a bad dancer. After all, it's considered polite to dance at least to the end of a set (four songs) with any partner; if you are given a curt

---

1. Tango dancers (p99), Buenos Aires
2. Musician playing the *bandoneón*

1

2

'*gracias*' after just one song, consider yourself excused.

Your position in the area surrounding the dance floor can be critical. Ideally, you should sit where you have easy access to the floor and to other dancers' line of sight. You may notice singles sitting up front, while couples sit further back. Generally couples are considered 'untouchable' – for them to dance with others, they either enter the room separately, or the man may signal his intent by asking another woman to the floor. Now 'his' woman becomes available to others.

The *cabeceo* – the quick tilt of the head, eye contact and uplifted eyebrows – can happen from way across the room. The woman to whom the *cabeceo* is directed either nods yes and smiles, or pretends not to have noticed. If she says yes, the man gets up and escorts her to the floor. If she pretends not to have seen him, it's considered a rejection. When you're at a *milonga* and don't want to dance with anyone, don't look around too much – you could be breaking some hearts.

Don't be surprised to see different *milongas* put on at a single venue, depending on the time or day. Each *milonga* can be run by a different promoter, so each will have its own vibe, style, music and table arrangement, as well as age levels and experiences.

For good information on Buenos Aires' tango scene and how to navigate it, get a copy of Sally Blake's practical guide *Happy Tango: Sallycat's Guide to Dancing in Buenos Aires, 2nd edition* (www.sallycatway.com/happytango). You can pick up free tango magazines at *milongas* and tango shoe shops (of which there are many in Buenos Aires).

Tango classes are often available in the same venue as *milongas*, in the hours before they start, but you can find them everywhere from youth hostels to cultural centers – some are even included free when you book a fancy tango show. Tourist-oriented classes are often taught in English.

ROBERT FRERCK/GETTY IMAGES ©

En tu muerte y por tu nombre
lloraron hasta los hombres

2

DANITA DELIMONT/GETTY IMAGES ©

1. *Milonga* (public tango event), Buenos Aires **2.** Painting of famous tango singer Carlos Gardel (p586)

So what is the appeal of the tango? Experienced dancers will say that the rush from a blissful tango connection with a stranger can lift you to exhilarating heights. The dance can also become addictive – once you have fallen for the passion and beauty of the tango's movements, you can spend your life trying to attain a physical perfection that can never be fully realized. The true *tanguero* simply attempts to make the journey as graceful as possible.

TOP MILONGAS

- Salon Canning (p104)
- Club Gricel (p104)
- Confitería Ideal (p104)
- El Beso (p105)
- La Catedral (p104)

(Continued from p99)

(balls on cords that gauchos used to tangle up prey). There's also a patriotic tribute to Evita as a singer belts out 'Don't Cry for Me, Argentina.' The dinner offers a wide variety of tasty main dishes – unusual for tango shows. Gala Tango is a more upscale experience and happens upstairs.

Esquina Carlos Gardel TANGO SHOW
(Map p72; ☎4867-6363; www.esquinacarlosgardel.com.ar; Carlos Gardel 3200; show from US$96, dinner & show from US$140) One of the fanciest tango shows in town plays at this impressive 430-seat theater, an old cantina right next to the lovely shopping mall Mercado de Abasto (p76). The Abasto neighborhood was once Carlos Gardel's old stomping ground, and he even hung out at this locale. The memorable show starts with a good film about the area, then goes on to highlight top-notch musicians and performers.

Café Tortoni TANGO SHOW
(Map p58; ☎4342-4328; www.cafetortoni.com.ar; Av de Mayo 829; show AR$150-200) Nightly tango shows (reserve ahead) take place at this historic yet very touristy place; the shows are fine if you don't expect too much. Get your ticket the day of or one day beforehand at the cafe between 11am and 5pm (cash only).

Los 36 Billares TANGO SHOW
(Map p58; Av de Mayo 1265) Dating from 1894, this is one of the city's most historic cafe-bars. As its name implies, it's big on pool and billiard tables (check out the basement); the back room is full of men shuffling cards for a poker game. Tango shows, highlighting different singers and dancers every night, happen at 9pm from Monday to Wednesday; tango classes also available.

Todo Mundo TANGO, FLAMENCO
(Map p58; ☎4362-2354; Pasaje Anselmo Aieta 1095) This restaurant puts on free tango, flamenco and other types of shows, but you do have to order at least AR$100 worth of food – basic Argentine fare like empanadas, pasta and *parrilla* (mixed grill). Tango shows happen on Monday and Thursday nights, while flamenco flutters on Friday and Saturday nights. Expect rock, salsa, folk and jazz on other nights; all shows start around 10:30pm.

Milongas

Milongas are dance events where people strut their tango skills. The atmosphere at these events can be modern or historical, casual or traditional. Most have tango DJs that determine musical selections, but a few utilize live orchestras.

Milongas either start in the afternoon and run until 11pm, or start at around midnight and run until the early-morning light (arrive late for the best action). Classes are often offered beforehand.

For a unique outdoor experience, head to the bandstand at the Barrancas de Belgrano, where the casual *milonga* **La Glorieta** (www.glorietadebelgrano.com.ar) takes place on Saturday and Sunday evenings around 7pm.

Salon Canning MILONGA
(Map p72; ☎4832-6753; www.parakultural.com.ar; Av Scalabrini Ortiz 1331) Some of BA's finest dancers (no wallflowers here) grace this traditional venue with its great dance floor. Well-known tango company Parakultural often stages good events here involving live music, tango DJs, singers and dancers. Expect big crowds and plenty of tourists.

Club Gricel MILONGA
(☎4957-7157; www.clubgriceltango.com.ar; La Rioja 1180) This old classic (far from the center; take a taxi) often has big crowds, especially on Monday. It attracts an older, well-dressed clientele – along with plenty of tourists. There's a wonderful springy dance floor and occasionally live orchestras.

Confitería Ideal MILONGA
(Map p58; ☎4328-7750; www.confiteriaideal.com; Suipacha 384, 1st fl) This institution (since 1912) is the mother of all historic tango halls, with classes and *milongas* offered daily. Live orchestras occasionally accompany dancers, and there are dinner-tango shows on Friday and Saturday. The actual cafe section could use a facelift, as it's a bit dim, stodgy and impersonal, but it remains a classic. Featured in the film *The Tango Lesson*.

La Catedral MILONGA
(Map p72; ☎15-5325-1630; www.lacatedralclub.com; Sarmiento 4006) If tango can be youthful, trendy and hip, this is where you'll find it. The grungy warehouse space is very casual, with funky art on the walls, thrift-store furniture and dim atmospheric lighting. It's more like a young bohemian nightclub than anything else, and there's no implied dress code – you'll see plenty of jeans on the dancers. Great for cheap alcohol; the best-known *milongas* occur regularly on a Tuesday night.

GAY & LESBIAN BUENOS AIRES

In July 2010 Argentina became the first Latin American country to legalize same-sex marriage. Since then BA has become a huge gay destination, lending momentum to local events such as the **Marcha del Orgullo Gay** (Gay Pride Parade; www.marchadelorgullo.org.ar; Nov) and the **Queer Tango Festival** (www.festivaltangoqueer.com.ar).

To mix with local gays, check out popular bars like loud **Sitges** (Map p72; www.facebook.com/fiestaplop; cnr Federico Lacroze & Álvarez Thomas) and casual **Flux** (Map p68; 5252-0258; Marcelo T de Alvear 980; 7pm-3am Sun-Thu, to 4am Fri & Sat). The coffee shop **Pride Café** (Map p58; 4300-6435; Balcarce 869; 9am-8pm Mon-Fri, 11am-8pm Sat & Sun;) attracts mixed crowds. For a fun night of guided drinking and partying, there's **Out & About Pub Crawl** (www.outandaboutpubcrawl.com).

The best nightclubs are rough-and-tumble **Amerika** (Map p72; 4865-4416; www.ameri-k.com.ar; Gascón 1040; Fri-Sun) sexy-beautiful **Glam** (Map p72; 4963-2521; José Antonio Cabrera 3046; Thu-Sat) and **Alsina** (Map p58; 4331-3231; www.palacioalsina.net; Adolfo Alsina 940; Sun, plus 1 Fri per month). Current hot gay parties include **Fiesta Plop** (www.plop-web.com.ar), the monthly **Fiesta Dorothy** (www.fiestadorothy.com) and **Rheo** (www.rheo.com.ar).

An especially gay-friendly accommodation is **Lugar Gay** (Map p58; 4300-4747; www.lugargay.com.ar; Defensa 1120; dm US$25, s US$50-70, d US$80-95), a casual guesthouse that also acts as an information center. **Casa Brandon** (Map p72; 4858-0610; www.brandongayday.com.ar; Luis Maria Drago 236; 8pm-late Wed-Sun) is an art gallery-cultural center.

Good general websites are www.thegayguide.com.ar and www.nighttours.com/buenosaires. For free gay literature, look for *La Otra Guía*, *Gay Maps* (www.gmaps360.com) and *The Ronda* (www.theronda.com.ar).

There aren't many places catering exclusively to lesbians. Try long-running and intimate **Bach Bar** (Map p72; 15-5184-0137; www.bach-bar.com.ar; José Antonio Cabrera 4390), but otherwise there are the gay spots listed above. **La Fulana** (www.lafulana.org.ar) is a lesbian cultural center.

Finally, gay classes and *milongas* (tango academies) are given at La Marshall Milonga (p105) and **Tango Queer** (Map p58; www.tangoqueer.com).

La Viruta MILONGA
(Map p72; 4774-6357; www.lavirutatango.com; Armenia 1366, basement) Popular basement venue. Good beginner tango classes are available before *milongas* – translating into many inexperienced dancers on the floor earlier on – so if you're an expert get here late (after 3:30am). Music can run the gamut from tango to rock to cumbia to salsa earlier in the evening, with more traditional tunes later. Tango shows also on offer.

El Beso MILONGA
(Map p58; 4953-2794; Riobamba 416, 1st fl) A traditional and popular place, El Beso attracts some very good dancers – you should be very confident of your dancing skills if you come here. Located upstairs, it has good music and a cozy feel.

On Friday night, El Beso hosts the far less traditional **La Marshall Milonga** (http://lamarshallmilonga.com.ar) (gay *milonga*) for all who want to try a change of roles in their tango.

Live Music

Smaller venues showcase mostly local groups; international stars tend to play at large venues such as *fútbol* stadiums or **Luna Park** (Map p58; 5279-5279; www.lunapark.com.ar; cnr Bouchard & Av Corrientes). Clásica y Moderna (p95) occasionally hosts jazz groups.

With so many *porteños* boasting Spanish ancestry, it's not surprising that there are a few flamenco venues in town. Most are located in Congreso's Spanish neighborhood, near the intersection of Salta and Av de Mayo.

Música folklórica (folk music) also has its place in BA. There are several *peñas* (folk-music clubs) in the city, but other venues occasionally host *música folklórica* – keep your eyes peeled.

Usina del Arte CONCERT VENUE
(Map p78; http://agendacultural.buenosaires.gob.ar; Agustín Caffarena 1) This restored old

electricity factory is a valiant attempt to breathe new life to an edgy section of La Boca. It's a gorgeous red brick building complete with scenic clock tower, and its symphony concert hall is now the home to Buenos Aires' philharmonic and national symphony orchestras.

La Trastienda ROCK, REGGAE
(Map p58; ☎5533-5533; www.latrastienda.com; Balcarce 460) This large, atmospheric theater welcomes over 700, features a well-stocked bar, and showcases national and international live-music acts almost nightly. Look for headers such as Charlie García, Divididos, José González, Damien Rice and Conor Oberst. Get tickets at the office here or check www.tuentrada.com.ar.

Notorious JAZZ
(Map p58; ☎4813-6888; www.notorious.com.ar; Av Callao 966) This stylish, intimate joint is one of Buenos Aires' premier jazz venues. Up front you can buy CDs of various music genres, while in the back the restaurant-cafe (overlooking a verdant garden) hosts live shows nearly every night at 9:30pm. Log on to the website for schedules; most performances are jazz, but there's also Brazilian music.

Thelonious Bar JAZZ
(Map p72; ☎4829-1562; www.theloniousclub.com.ar; Salguero 1884, 1st fl; ⏲9pm-1am Wed-Thu, to 3am Fri & Sat) Up the stairs in an old mansion lies this dimly lit jazz bar, with high brick ceilings and a good sound system. Come early to snag a seat (or reserve one ahead of time) and partake in the Argentine menu and good range of cocktails. Thelonious is known for its classic and contemporary Argentine jazz lineups, though international musicians sometimes entertain.

Ávila Bar FLAMENCO
(Map p58; ☎4383-6974; Av de Mayo 1384; ⏲Thu-Sat) Offering flamenco for many years now is this cozy little Spanish restaurant with good traditional food. Main dishes can include rabbit, paella and seafood stews. Shows have older, experienced dancers and cost AR$220 (drinks not included). They start around 10:30pm and reservations are a must on weekends.

Cantares FLAMENCO
(Map p58; ☎4381-6965; www.cantarestablao.com.ar; Av Rivadavia 1180; show $AR90; ⏲shows 9pm Fri & Sat) This flamenco venue, in the old Taberna Español, once hosted the Spanish poet Federico García Lorca. It's a small basement space with only 85 seats, providing a wonderfully intimate place for the highly authentic dances. An a la carte dinner is on offer; reserve in advance. Flamenco classes also available.

La Peña del Colorado FOLK
(Map p72; ☎4822-1038; www.lapeniadelcolorado.com; Güemes 3657; ⏲8pm-4am) Nightly music shows (mostly folkloric) start at 10pm and are memorable at this rustic restaurant, and after midnight audience members pick up nearby guitars to make their own entertainment. There's also tasty northern Argentine food on offer, including *locro* (a corn-and-meat stew), *chipá* (chewy cheese balls) and *humitas de Chala* (like tamales) – the spicy empanadas are excellent.

Teatro Colón CLASSICAL MUSIC
(Map p58; ☎4378-7100; www.teatrocolon.org.ar; Cerrito 628) BA's premier venue for the arts, with ballet and opera as well as classical music.

Theater

Av Corrientes, between Avs 9 de Julio and Callao, has traditionally been the capital's center for theater, but there are now dozens of venues throughout the city.

Teatro Nacional Cervantes THEATER
(Map p58; ☎4816-4224; www.teatrocervantes.gov.ar; Libertad 815) Architecturally gorgeous theater featuring three halls, a grand lobby and red-velvet chairs. Has good productions at affordable prices.

Teatro San Martín THEATER
(Map p58; ☎0800-333-5254; www.complejoteatral.gob.ar; Av Corrientes 1530) This major venue has several auditoriums (the largest seats over 1000 people) and showcases international cinema, theater, dance and classical music.

Teatro Presidente Alvear THEATER
(Map p58; ☎4373-4245; www.complejoteatral.gob.ar; Av Corrientes 1659) Inaugurated in 1942 and named after an Argentine president whose wife sang opera, this theater holds over 700 and shows many musical productions, including ballet. Occasional free shows are on offer.

Cinemas

BA is full of cinemas, both historical neon classics and slick modern multiplexes. The traditional cinema districts are along pedestrian Lavalle (west of Florida) and on Av Corrientes, but newer cineplexes are spread throughout the city; most large shopping malls have one.

Check out the *Buenos Aires Herald* for original titles of English-language films. Except for kids' films, most movies are in their original language (with Spanish subtitles).

Shopping

Shopping is practically a sport for many Buenos Aires' citizens, who despite steeply rising inflation continue to shop as if there's no tomorrow. As the saying goes, 'An Argentine will make one peso and spend two.'

In the Microcentro, Florida is a multipurpose pedestrian strip that buzzes with shoppers, while Av Santa Fe is a bit less pedestrian-friendly but equally prominent as the city's main shopping artery. San Telmo is ground zero for antiques, and Av Pueyrredón near Once train station is *the* place for cheap (and lower-quality) clothing. Jewelry shops are found on Libertad south of Av Corrientes. Leather jackets and bags are cheapest on Calle Murillo (500–600 block), in Villa Crespo.

For both brand-name and avant-garde fashions, Palermo Viejo is the place to be. This neighborhood, split by railroad tracks into Palermo Soho and Palermo Hollywood, has the most concentrated number of clothing boutiques between Plaza Serrano and Plaza Palermo Viejo. You'll find housewares and plenty of knickknack shops here, too.

As in other Western countries, bargaining is not acceptable in most stores. High-price items such as jewelry and leather jackets can be exceptions, especially if you buy several. At street markets you can try negotiating for better prices – just keep in mind you may be talking to the artists themselves, who generally don't make much money. San Telmo's antiques fair, the Feria de San Telmo, is an exception: prices here are often inflated for tourists.

Microcentro & Congreso

Arte y Esperanza CRAFT

City (Map p58; ☎4343-1455; www.arteyesperanza.com.ar; Balcarce 234; ⌚9am-6pm Mon-Fri) Retiro (Map p58; ☎4393-3270; Suipacha 892) This store sells fair-trade, handmade products that include many from Argentina's indigenous craftspeople. Shop for jewelry, pottery, textiles, *mate* gourds, baskets, woven bags and animal masks.

Portobello Vintage Boutique VINTAGE

(Map p58; ☎4811-2619; Paraguay 1554; ⌚noon-8pm Mon-Fri) Excellent vintage clothing boutique. Find that special jacket, dress, shirt and bottom from the 1940s on up. All clothes are in great condition and sold at affordable prices. A few jewelry and other accessories are also for sale.

Zival's MUSIC

(Map p58; www.zivals.com; Av Callao 395; ⌚9:30am-9:30pm Mon-Sat) This is one of the better music stores in town, especially when it comes to tango, jazz and classical music. Listening stations are a big plus, and many books are also for sale. There's also a branch in **Palermo Viejo** (Map p72; Serrano 1445).

Wildlife OUTDOOR EQUIPMENT

(Map p58; ☎4381-1040; Hipólito Yrigoyen 1133; ⌚10am-8pm Mon-Fri, to 1pm Sat) If you're looking to buy (or sell) all manner of outdoor and camping equipment before traveling on from Buenos Aires, this is the place. Crampons, knives, tents, backpacks, climbing ropes, foul-weather clothing, military gear and even the occasional mule saddle can be found at this somewhat offbeat and musty shop.

San Telmo

Walrus Books BOOKS

(Map p58; ☎4300-7135; Estados Unidos 617; ⌚noon-8pm Tue-Sun) Run by an American photographer, this tiny shop is probably the best English-language bookstore in BA. Thousands of new and used literature and nonfiction books line the shelves, and there's a selection of Latin American classics translated into English. Bring your quality books (including Lonely Planet guides!) to trade; literary workshops offered, too.

Cualquier Verdura CLOTHING, HOMEWARES

(Map p58; ☎4300-2474; Humberto Primo 517; ⌚noon-8pm Thu-Sun) Located in a lovely, refurbished old house, this fun store sells eclectic items from vintage clothing to funny soaps (look for these in the 'bathroom') to recycled floppy-disc lamps to contemporary knickknacks and novelty toys. Wander through the outdoor patio and note the stained-glass windows on the wall, plus the *mate*-drinking Buddha just above the fountain.

Materia Urbana ART, HOMEWARES
(Map p58; ☎4361-5265; www.materiaurbana.com; Defensa 702; ⏰11am-7pm Wed-Fri, 2-7pm Sat, 10:30am-7pm Sun) This innovative design shop shows the work of over 100 local artists; one-of-a-kind finds include offbeat line drawings, abstract photography, carved wood statuettes, leather animal organizers, clothes, and jewelry made from silver, wood, and coral. There's nearly constant foot traffic at Materia Urbana, especially during the street fair on Sunday.

Punto Sur CLOTHING
(Map p58; ☎4300-9320; www.feriapuntosur.com.ar; Defensa 1135; ⏰11am-7:30pm) This is a great clothing store highlighting the works of over 60 Argentine designers. Creativity is rampant and it's a fun walk-through for unique funky threads, including interesting knitwear, colorful skirts, printed T-shirts, jewelry and accessories, cool handbags and even a few shoes. These are definitely clothes that make a statement.

Moebius CLOTHING
(Map p78; ☎4361-2893; Defensa 1356; ⏰3-8pm Mon, noon-8pm Tue-Sat) This funky little shop's racks are crowded with owner-designer Lilliana Zauberman's kaleidoscopic products: 1970s-style jersey dresses, whimsical ruffled bikinis, skirts printed with koi fish and frog patterns, cherry-red trench coats and handbags made from recycled materials. Around 60 designers sell their work here, so there's always something different, fun and new to keep an eye out for.

Gil Antiguedades ANTIQUES
(Map p58; Humberto Primo 412; ⏰11am-1pm & 3-7pm Tue-Sun) A window display of Great Gatsby–style flapper dresses and vintage nightgowns pulls the passerby into San Telmo's finest antiques emporium. Decorative objects like china teapots and leather hatboxes are overshadowed by the stunning array of silk slips and lacy Victorian gowns – John Galliano, Catherine Deneuve and Salvatore Ferragamo are among the famous people who've stopped by for inspiration on visits to Buenos Aires.

Recoleta & Retiro

El Ateneo BOOKS
(Map p68; Av Santa Fe 1860; ⏰9am-10pm Mon-Thu, to midnight Fri & Sat, noon-10pm Sun) Buenos Aires' landmark bookseller stocks a limited number of books in English, including Lonely Planet guides. There are several branches within the city, but this one – the Gran Splendid – is in a gorgeous old renovated cinema.

BUENOS AIRES STREET MARKETS

Some of BA's best crafts and souvenirs are sold at its many street markets, often by the artists themselves. You may have to sort through some tacky kitsch, but you'll also find creative and original art. Often there is also 'free' (ie donation) entertainment from casual performers.

Tourists and locals alike flock to the famous Sunday **Feria de San Telmo** (Map p58; Defensa; ⏰10am-6pm Sun; 🚌10, 22, 29, 45, 86), which brings together hundreds of street vendors, buskers and shoppers. You'll find jewelry, souvenirs, knickknacks, artwork, clothing, old collectibles, hand-made crafts and much more. It's a tight and crowded scene, so be prepared to bump into people – and watch your bag carefully.

Recoleta's hugely popular **Feria Artesanal** (Map p68; Plaza Intendente Alvear; ⏰10am-7pm) has dozens of booths and a range of creative goods. Hippies, mimes and tourists mingle; nearby restaurants provide refreshment. It runs on weekends and is located just outside the cemetery.

Costume jewelry, hand-knit tops, *mate* gourds, leather accessories and a whole lot of junk fill the crafts booths at small but lively **Feria Plaza Serrano** (Map p72; ⏰10am-8pm Fri-Sun) on fashionable Plaza Serrano in Palermo.

The unique **Feria de Mataderos** (☎Mon-Fri 4342-9629, Sat 4687-5602; www.feriademataderos.com.ar; cnr Avs Lisandro de la Torre & de los Corrales; ⏰11am-8pm Sun Apr–mid-Dec, 6pm-midnight Sat late Jan–mid-Mar) is far off in the barrio of Mataderos, but it's worth hiking out here for the shows of horsemanship, folk dancing and cheap authentic treats. From downtown, take bus 126, 155 or 180 (one hour). Confirm hours beforehand; it closes for a couple weeks 'between' seasons.

Autoría ART, ACCESSORIES
(Map p68; ☎5252-2474; www.autoriabsas.com.ar; Suipacha 1025; ⏲9:30am-8pm Mon-Fri, 10am-6pm Sat) This cool designer's showcase – stocked with edgy art books, sculptural fashions, whimsical leather desk sculptures and unique jewelry of all materials (silk cocoons!) – strives to promote Argentine designers. Especially interesting are the recycled materials – check out the bags made of tyvek, inner tubes, firehoses or even old sails. Products are of high quality and prices are accessible.

Palermo

Rapsodia FASHION
(Map p72; ☎4831-6333; www.rapsodia.com; Honduras 4872; ⏲10am-9pm) With fabrics from linen to leather and details like fringe and sequins, this large and popular boutique is a must for fashion mavens. Old and new are blended into creative, colorful styles with exotic and bohemian accents. Locals covet their dresses and jeans; over a dozen branches in the city.

Bolivia CLOTHING
(Map p72; ☎4832-6284; Gurruchaga 1581; ⏲11am-8pm Mon-Sat, 3-8pm Sun) There's almost nothing here that your young, hip and possibly gay brother wouldn't love, from the stylish plaid shirts to the skin-tight jeans to the military-styled jackets. Metrosexual to the hilt, and paradise for the man who isn't afraid of patterns, plaid or pastels. Also on **Nicaragua** (Map p72; ☎4832-6409; Nicaragua 4908; ⏲11am-8pm Mon-Sat, 3-8pm Sun).

Calma Chicha HOMEWARES
(Map p72; ☎4831-1818; www.calmachicha.com; Honduras 4909; ⏲10am-8pm Mon-Fri, 11am-8pm Sat, 1-7pm Sun) Calma Chicha specializes in creative homewares and accessories that are locally produced from leather, faux leather, sheepskin, cowhide and brightly hued fabric. Look for butterfly chairs, throw rugs, leather placemats, bright pillows and cowskin bags.

Patio del Liceo MALL
(Map p72; ☎4822-9433; Av Santa Fe 2729; ⏲2-8pm Mon-Sat) Wonderful little shopping mall with funky, casual and very artsy vibe. In the past few years, young struggling artists have taken over and created an artistic hub here, filling it with various small stores, exhibition spaces and workshops. You'll find a couple of bookshops, a record store and some design stores. For refreshment there's a small cafe called Baby Snakes.

Hermanos Estebecorena CLOTHING
(Map p72; ☎4772-2145; www.hermanosestebecorena.com; El Salvador 5960; ⏲11am-8pm Mon-Sat) The Estebecorena brothers apply their highly creative skills toward smartly designed tops, jackets that fold into bags, polo-collar work shirts and even supremely comfortable, nearly seamless underwear. The focus is on original, highly stylish, very functional men's clothing that makes the artsy types swoon. Selection is limited, but what's there really counts.

Lo de Joaquin Alberdi FOOD, WINE
(Map p72; ☎4832-5329; www.lodejoaquinalberdi.com; Jorge Luis Borges 1772; ⏲11am-9:30pm Mon-Sat, noon-9:30pm Sun) Nationally produced wines for every taste and budget line the racks and cellar of this attractive wine shop. Tastings happen Thursday and Friday at 7:30pm (double-check ahead of time) and include four wines and some cheeses; the cost is AR$100.

Sugar & Spice FOOD, WINE
(Map p72; ☎4777-5423; www.sugarandspice.com.ar; Guatemala 5419; ⏲10am-7pm Mon-Fri, 9am-1pm Sat) Nibble the exotic (for Argentina, at least) creations of Frank Almeida, a long-time American expat. Herb cookies, almond biscotti, hazelnut panettone and peanut-butter brownies soothe homesick taste buds, and daily baked bagels, muffins and scones are also available.

Information

CONCIERGE SERVICES

BA Cultural Concierge (☎15-3876-5937; www.baculturalconcierge.com) This service helps you plan itineraries, arrange airport transportation, run errands, get a cell phone, reserve theater tickets, scout out a potential apartment, plus more to help your trip run smoothly.

EMERGENCY

Ambulance (☎107)
Police (☎911, 101)
Tourist Police (Comisaría del Turista; ☎0800-999-5000, 4346-5748; Av Corrientes 436; ⏲24hr) Provides interpreters for travel insurance reports.

INTERNET ACCESS & TELEPHONE

Internet cafes and *locutorios* (telephone offices) with internet access are very common in the center; you can often find one by just walking a couple of blocks in any direction. Rates are cheap and connections are fast. Most cafes and restaurants have free wi-fi.

You can rent a desk, cubicle, office or meeting room via **Areatres** (☎5353-0333; www.areatresworkplace.com; Malabia 1720; ⊙8:30am-8pm Mon-Fri). There are fax and copy services, complete internet connections, networking social events – even a Zen-like patio. Also at **Humboldt 2036** (☎5258-7600; www.areatresworkplace.com; Humboldt 2036).

MEDIA

BA's most popular newspapers are the entertaining, tabloid-like *Clarín* and the more moderate and upper-class *La Nación*. *Página 12* provides a leftist perspective, while *Ámbito Financiero* is the voice of the business sector. For news in English there's the *Buenos Aires Herald*.

MEDICAL SERVICES

Dental Argentina (☎4828-0821; www.dentalargentina.com.ar; Laprida 1621, 2B) Dental services with English-speaking professionals.

Hospital Británico (☎4309-6400; www.hospitalbritanico.org.ar; Perdriel 74)

Hospital Italiano (☎4959-0200; www.hospitalitaliano.org.ar; Juan D Perón 4190)

MONEY

Banks and *cambios* (money-exchange offices) are common in the city center; banks have longer lines and more limited opening hours but may offer better rates. You're on your own if you use the ubiquitous shady figures (ie unofficial moneychangers) on Florida, offering '*cambio, cambio, cambio*' to passing pedestrians. Just remember there are quite a few fake bills floating about. For important information on Argentina's 'Blue Market' - or rather, black market for US dollars, see p604.

American Express (☎4310-3000)

MasterCard (☎0800-444-5220)

Visa (☎4379-3400)

POST

The post office has branches located all over the city.

Correo Internacional (Map p68; ☎4316-1777; Av Antártida Argentina; ⊙10am-5pm Mon-Fri) Only for shipping international parcels over 2kg.

DHL Internacional (Map p58; ☎0810-122-3345; www.dhl.com.ar; Av Córdoba 783) Many branches around town.

Federal Express (Map p58; ☎0810-333-3339; www.fedex.com; Maipú 753)

OCA (Map p58; ☎4311-5305; www.oca.com.ar; Viamonte 526) For domestic packages.

TOURIST INFORMATION

There are several small government tourist offices or kiosks in BA; hours vary throughout the year. The official tourism site of Buenos Aires is www.bue.gov.ar and the government site is www.buenosaires.gov.ar.

Diagonal Roque Saénz Peña Tourist Kiosk (Map p58; cnr Florida & Diagonal Roque Saénz Peña)

Esmeralda Tourist Kiosk (Map p58; cnr Av Rivadavia & Esmeralda)

Plaza San Martín Tourist Kiosk (Map p68; cnr Florida & Marcelo T de Alvear)

TRAVELING SAFELY IN BUENOS AIRES

While crime does exist in BA (as it does in any big city) and you'll notice that *porteños* are very security conscious, in general BA is fairly safe. In many places you can comfortably walk around at all hours of the night, even as a lone woman, as people generally stay out very late. However, be careful at night in some neighborhoods, including Constitución (around the train station), the eastern border of San Telmo, and La Boca (where, outside tourist streets, you should be careful even during the day).

Crime against tourists is almost always of the petty sort, such as pickpocketing in crowded markets or buses, or bag snatches when you're not looking – things smart travelers can guard themselves against. Be wary of the old 'mustard trick' – someone pointing out 'bird droppings' or whatever on your clothing, placed there by an accomplice, and offering to clean it up (while your valuables go off with the accomplice).

Other things to watch out for are fake bills. Most people get them in dark environments like taxis or nightclubs, but even Ezeiza's *cambios* (exchange houses) have been known to pass them. Get to know your bills; check www.santelmoloft.com/2011/07/22/fake-money-in-argentina for good tips.

Minor nuisances include the lack of respect shown by vehicles toward pedestrians, lax pollution controls and high noise levels.

If you've been robbed in some way, contact the tourist police (p109) to file a claim; they provide interpreters. For more safety tips, see p605.

Puerto Madero Tourist Office (Map p58; Dique 4)

Recoleta Tourist Kiosk (Map p68; Av Quintana 596)

Retiro Tourist Office (Map p68; ⌚7:30am-2:30pm Mon-Fri) In Retiro bus terminal, across from bus bay 36.

Secretaría de Turismo de la Nación (Map p68; ☎4312-2232; www.turismo.gov.ar; Av Santa Fe 883; ⌚9am-7pm Mon-Fri) Mostly info on Argentina but helps with BA.

TRAVEL AGENCIES

Along with the travel agencies listed following, Madi Lang at BA Cultural Concierge (p109) can help organize trips around Argentina for a reasonable price.

Anda Responsible Travel (☎3221-0833; www.andatravel.com.ar; Agüero 1050, 4A) Most notable for its La Boca tour, which introduces travelers to local organizations working toward improving the lives of its citizens. Also does many tours around Argentina that benefit local citizens, which are sometimes indigenous groups.

Say Hueque (☎5258-8740; www.sayhueque.com; Thames 2062) This independent travel agency specializes in customized adventure trips all around Argentina, and will also make air, bus and hotel reservations. It offers various BA tours as well. Also downtown (☎5258-8740; www.sayhueque.com; Viamonte 749, 6th fl), and in San Telmo (☎5352-9321; Chile 557).

Tangol (☎4363-6000; www.tangol.com; Florida 971, Suite 31) Do-all travel and tour agency that offers everything from guided *fútbol* games to country-wide packages. Also offers unusual activities including helicopter tours and skydiving. Another branch in San Telmo (Defensa 831).

Getting There & Away

AIR

Buenos Aires is Argentina's international gateway and easily accessible from North America, Europe and Australasia, as well as other capital cities in South America.

Almost all international flights arrive at BA's Ezeiza airport, about 35km south of the center. This modern airport has good services such as ATMs, restaurants and duty-free shops, an internet cafe and limited wi-fi.

Most domestic flights use Aeroparque Jorge Newbery airport, a short distance north of downtown BA. Flight information for both airports, in English and Spanish, is available at ☎5480-6111 or www.aa2000.com.ar.

BOAT

BA has a regular ferry service to and from Colonia and Montevideo, both in Uruguay. Ferries leave from **Buquebus terminal** (Map p68; ☎4316-6500; www.buquebus.com; cnr Avs Antártida Argentina & Córdoba). There are many more launches from September to April.

BUS

BA's modern **Retiro bus terminal** (Retiro; Map p68; www.tebasa.com.ar; Av Antártida Argentina) is 400m long, three floors high and has bays for 75 buses. The bottom floor is for cargo shipments and luggage storage, the top for purchasing tickets and the middle for everything else. The **information booth** (☎4310-0700; ⌚6am-midnight) will help you find the right long-distance bus (or check the terminal's website); it's located near the escalators at the southern end of the terminal. Other services include a tourist office (p111) on the main floor across from bus bay 36, ATMs, telephone offices (some with internet), cafes and many small stores.

You can buy a ticket to practically anywhere in Argentina and departures are fairly frequent to the most popular destinations. Prices vary widely according to bus company, class, season and inflation. Reservations are not necessary except during peak seasons (January, February and July).

Retiro bus terminal is connected to the local bus system, but it's a giant snarl and hard to figure out. There's a nearby Subte station and Retiro train station. Street taxis are numerous, though *remises* (call taxis) are generally more secure – there are several *remise* booths near the bus bay; all are open 24 hours.

Buses from Buenos Aires

DESTINATION	COST (AR$)	DURATION (HR)
Bariloche	1000	20
Córdoba	450	11
Foz do Iguaçu (Brazil)	870	19
Mar del Plata	300	5½
Mendoza	650	17
Montevideo (Uruguay)	410	8
Puerto Madryn	800	20
Punta del Este (Uruguay)	450	11
Rosario	190	4
Salta	980	21
Santiago (Chile)	1000	20
Ushuaia	1050	20

TRAIN

Privately run trains connect Buenos Aires' city center to its suburbs and nearby provinces. The three main central stations are served by Subte.

Trains from Buenos Aires

DESTINATION(S)	STATION	CONTACT
Tigre, Rosario, Córdoba & Tucumán	Retiro	**Línea Mitre** (☎0800-222-8736; www.mitresarmiento.com.ar)
Southern suburbs & La Plata	Constitución	**Línea Roca** (☎0800-362-7622; www.ugofe.com.ar/general_roca)
Bahía Blanca, Tandil & Mar del Plata	Constitución	**Ferrobaires** (☎0810-666-8736; www.ferrobaires.gba.gov.ar)
Southwestern suburbs & Luján	Once	**Línea Sarmiento** (☎0800-222-8736; www.mitresarmiento.com.ar)

ℹ Getting Around

TO & FROM AIRPORTS

Chauffeur-Driven Car

For a special treat, reserve a luxury car from **Silver Star Transport** (☎in Argentina 15-6826-8876, in the USA 214-502-1605; www.silverstarcar.com); you'll be driven by native English speakers from Ezeiza to the destination of your choice (US$150). There are car-rental booths at Ezeiza, but we do not recommend renting a car for your stay in Buenos Aires.

Bus

If you're really on a penny-pinching budget, take public bus 8 from Ezeiza, which costs AR$6 and can take up to two hours to reach the Plaza de Mayo area. Catch it outside the Aerolíneas Argentinas terminal (Terminal B), a 200m walk from the international terminal. You'll need coins; there's a Banco de la Nación located just outside customs.

Shuttle

If you're alone, the best way to and from Ezeiza aiport is taking a shuttle with transfer companies such as **Manuel Tienda León** (MTL; Map p68; ☎4315-5115; www.tiendaleon.com; Av Eduardo Madero 1299, Ezeiza airport). You'll see its stand immediately as you exit customs, in the transport 'lobby' area. Frequent shuttles cost AR$80 to AR$95 per person to the city center, run all day and night and take 40 to 60 minutes, depending on traffic. They'll deposit you either at the MTL office (from where you can take a taxi) or at some limited central addresses.

Another shuttle service, directed at independent travelers, is **Hostel Shuttle** (☎4511-8723; www.hostelshuttle.com.ar). Check the website for prices, schedules and drop-off destinations (only at certain hostels), and try to book ahead. You can also try www.minibusezeiza.com.ar.

Shuttles between Ezeiza and Aeroparque Jorge Newbery airport (the domestic airport) cost AR$95; from Aeroparque to the center AR$30.

Taxi

If taking a taxi, avoid MTL's overpriced taxi service. Instead, go past the transport 'lobby' area outside customs, walk past the taxi touts and you'll see the freestanding city taxi stand (with a blue sign saying **Taxi Ezeiza** (☎5480-0066; www.taxiezeiza.com.ar; ⏲24hr)). At the time of writing it charged AR$270 to the center. Note that if you pre-arrange your taxi back to Ezeiza after your stay in BA, the rate can be 20% cheaper.

Taxis between Aeroparque and the city center cost around AR$80.

BICYCLE

Vehicular traffic in BA is dangerous and hardly respectful toward bicycles but things are improving, with an expanding bike-lane system and a bike-share program (mainly for residents). Some areas call out for two-wheeled exploration, such as Palermo's parks and the Reserva Ecológica Costanera Sur. On weekends and some weekdays you can rent bikes at these places.

You can also join a city bike tour (see p79).

BUS

To understand BA's huge, complex bus system buy a *Guia T* (bus guide); they're sold at any newsstand, but try to find the handy pocket version or check www.omnilineas.com and click on 'city buses.' Most routes run 24 hours.

Local buses *(colectivos)* take either coins or a magnetic bus card called SUBE (see boxed text, 113), but won't take bills. Bus ticket machines on board give small change from coins. Offer your seat to the elderly, pregnant and women with young children.

CAR

Most local drivers are reckless, aggressive and even willfully dangerous. They ignore speed limits, signs, lines and signals, and will tailgate. Buses are a nightmare to reckon with, potholes are everywhere, and congestion and parking are a pain.

Public transportation is great and taxis are cheap and plentiful but if you still insist on renting a car, you'll need to be at least 21 years of age and have a valid driver's license, credit card and passport; an international driver's license isn't necessary.

Avis (☎4326-5542; www.avis.com.ar; Cerrito 1535)

Hertz (☎4816-8001; www.hertz.com.ar; Paraguay 1138) Also home to Thrifty Car Rental.

New Way (☎4515-0331; www.new-wayrentacar.com; Marcelo T de Alvear 773) Local, friendly and cheap.

SUBTE (SUBWAY)

BA's **Subte** (www.subte.com.ar) is the quickest way to get around the city, though it can get mighty hot and crowded during rush hour – and is a haven for pickpockets. It consists of Líneas (Lines) A, B, C, D, E and H. Four parallel lines run from downtown to the capital's western and northern outskirts, while Línea C runs north–south and connects the two major train stations of Retiro and Constitución. Línea H runs from Once south to Av Caseros, with plans to expand it.

One-ride magnetic cards for the Subte cost AR$3.50. To avoid queues buy several rides at once or get a SUBE card (see boxed text, p113).

Trains operate from 5am to around 10:30pm Monday to Saturday and 8am to around 10pm Sunday and holidays. Service is frequent on weekdays; on weekends you'll wait longer. At some stations platforms are on opposite sides, so be sure of your direction before passing through the turnstiles.

TAXI & REMISE

Buenos Aires' numerous and relatively inexpensive taxis are conspicuous by their black-and-yellow paint jobs. They click every 200m (or every minute of waiting time) and cost 20% more after 6pm. Make sure that the meter's set to the current price when you start your ride. Drivers do not expect a big tip, however, it's customary to let them keep small change. Taxis that are on the lookout for passengers will have a red light lit on the upper right corner of their windshield.

Most cab drivers are honest workers making a living, but there are a few bad apples. Try not to give them a 100 peso note for a small fare; sometimes they're short on change, but there have been cases where the driver quickly and deftly replaces a larger bill with a smaller (or fake) one. One solution is to state how much you are giving them and ask if they have change for it ('¿Tiene usted cambio de un cien?' – 'Do you have any change for a hundred?').

Be wary of receiving counterfeit bills. If you're suspicious this might happen, note aloud the last three numbers/letters on a bill as you're giving it to him.

At night the driver will turn on the light *(luz)* so you can carefully check your change (look for a watermark on bills). They'll do the same with your bills. And make sure you get the right change.

Pretend to have an idea of where you're going; a few taxis offer the 'scenic' route (though also be aware there are many one-way streets in BA). A good way to do this is to give the taxi driver an intersection rather than a specific address. Also, if you are obviously a tourist going to or from a touristy spot, don't ask how much the fare is beforehand; this makes it tempting to quote a higher price rather than simply using the taxi's meter.

Try to snag an 'official' taxi, usually marked by a roof light and license number printed on the doors. Official drivers must display their license on the back of their seat or dashboard; write down the details in case of problems or forgotten items.

You can also call a *remise* (call taxi) instead of hailing street cabs. *Remises* look like regular cars and don't have meters. They do cost a bit more than street taxis but are more secure, since an established company sends them out. Any hotel or restaurant will be happy to call a *remise* for you.

SUBE CARD

If you're planning on staying in BA for a while, the **SUBE card** (www.sube.gob.ar) is a very handy and inexpensive rechargeable card that you can use for the Subte, local buses and some trains. It saves you money and you don't have to keep a stash of coins on hand. Get it at some *kioskos* and Correo Argentino or OCA post offices around the city (check the website for locations or look for the SUBE logo at businesses). Ezeiza airport and Retiro bus terminal also have Sube booths where you can get and recharge this card. You'll need your passport or a copy. Charging the card itself is easy, and can be done at many kiosks or Subte stations.

AROUND BUENOS AIRES

Tigre & the Delta

The city of Tigre (35km north of BA) and the surrounding delta region is a popular weekend getaway for weary *porteños*. Latte-colored waters – rich with iron from the jungle streams flowing from inland South America – offer hidden gems in this marshy region. Glimpse into how locals live along peaceful canals, with boats as their only transportation. All along the shorelines are signs of water-related activity, from kayaking to canoeing to sculling.

Sights & Activities

Museo de Arte Tigre MUSEUM
(☎4512-4093; Paseo Victorica 972; admission AR$15; ⊙9am-7pm Wed-Fri, noon-7pm Sat & Sun) Tigre's fanciest museum is located in an old (1912) social club. This beautiful art museum showcases famous Argentine artists from the 19th and 20th centuries. The building itself is worth a visit.

Puerto de Frutos MARKET
(Sarmiento 160; ⊙10am-6pm) At this popular market, vendors sell housewares, furniture, wicker baskets, souvenirs and knickknacks; there are restaurants too. Weekends are busiest.

Museo Naval MUSEUM
(Naval Museum; ☎4749-0608; Paseo Victorica 602; admission AR$10; ⊙8:30am-5:30pm Mon-Fri, 10:30am-6:30pm Sat & Sun) This worthwhile museum traces the history of the Argentine navy with an eclectic mix of historical photos, model boats and airplanes, artillery displays and pickled sea critters.

Museo del Mate MUSEUM
(☎4506-9594; www.elmuseodelmate.com; Lavalle 289; admission AR$15; ⊙11am-6pm Wed-Sun) For something special, visit this museum with over 2000 items dedicated to the national drink. There's a small outdoor *mate* 'bar' as well.

Tours

Frequent commuter launches depart from Estación Fluvial (behind the tourist office) for various destinations in the delta (AR$45 to AR$68 round-trip). A popular destination is the Tres Bocas neighborhood, a half-hour boat ride from Tigre, where you can take residential walks on thin paths connected by bridges over narrow channels. There are several restaurants and accommodations here. The Rama Negra area has a quieter and more natural setting with fewer services, but is an hour's boat ride away.

Several companies offer inexpensive boat tours (AR$60 to AR$120, one to two hours), but commuter launches give you flexibility if you want to go for a stroll or stop for lunch at one of the delta's restaurants.

Bonanza Deltaventura ADVENTURE TOUR
(☎4409-6967; www.deltaventura.com) Adventures include canoe trips, bike rides and horseback rides.

El Dorado Kayak KAYAKING
(☎15-4039-5858; www.eldoradokayak.com) Kayaking tours deep inside the delta; all equipment and lunch included.

Sleeping & Eating

Tigre's huge delta region is dotted with dozens of accommodations, including camping, B&Bs, *cabañas* (cabins) and beach resorts. Since many are reached only by boat, most provide meals. Tigre's tourist office has photos and information on all accommodations and many are listed on its website. Book on weekends and holidays, when prices can rise significantly.

Tigre's cuisine is not cutting-edge, but dining can be atmospheric. For an upscale meal on Paseo Victorica, the city's pleasant riverside avenue, try **María Luján** (☎4731-9613; Paseo Victorica 611; mains AR$80-150; ⊙8:30am-midnight), which has a great patio. Another good eatery is bohemian **Boulevard Saenz Peña** (☎5197-4776; Blvd Sáenz Peña 1400; breakfast mains AR$35-75, dinner mains AR$60-70; ⊙10:30am-6pm Wed-Sat, 8:30pm to close Thu-Sat), offering healthy breakfasts and gourmet sandwiches. Ask the tourist office about the various restaurants in the delta.

The following accommodations are in the city of Tigre itself.

Posada de 1860 HOSTEL $
(Tigre Hostel; ☎4749-4034; www.tigrehostel.com.ar; Av Libertador 190; dm US$12, r from US$70; ❄@ᯤ) This odd hostel is in two buildings; one is the original mansion with eight private rooms with bathroom and large garden boasting great hangout decks, while the second is a nearby homey building with dorms and private rooms that all share bathrooms.

Hotel Villa Victoria GUESTHOUSE $$

(☎4731-2281; www.hotelvillavictoria.com; Liniers 566; r Sun-Fri from AR$557, Sat from AR$702; ❄@📶🏊) Run by an Argentine-Swedish family, this boutique hotel is more like a fancy guesthouse. Only six simple yet elegant rooms are available, and there's a pool in the large grassy garden. Swedish, French and English are spoken.

Casona La Ruchi GUESTHOUSE $$

(☎4749-2499; www.casonalaruchi.com.ar; Lavalle 557; r without bathroom AR$550; @📶🏊) This family-run guesthouse is in a beautiful old 1893 mansion. Most of the four romantic bedrooms have balconies; all have shared bathrooms with original tiled floors. There's a pool and large garden out back.

ℹ Information

Tourist Office (☎4512-4497; www.vivitigre.gov.ar; Mitre 305; ⏲8am-6pm) Located behind McDonald's.

ℹ Getting There & Away

BUS

Take bus 60 (marked 'Panam') straight to Tigre (1½ hours).

BOAT

Sturla Viajes has a commuter boat to Tigre that leaves from Grierson 400 in Puerto Madero, but it's only at 6.10pm Monday to Friday (AR$35). However, you can take its Tigre tour directly from Puerto Madero, which includes boat transport and a trip around the Delta (round-trip AR$260).

TRAIN

From Retiro train station you can take a 'Tigre' train straight to Tigre (one hour). The best way to reach Tigre, however, is via the **Tren de la Costa** (tickets AR$40) – a pleasant light-rail train with attractive stations and views. This train line starts in the suburb of Olivos: to get there, take a train from Retiro train station and get off at Mitre station, then cross the bridge to the Tren de la Costa. Buses 59, 60 and 152 also go to the Tren.

The Pampas & the Atlantic Coast

Includes ➡

Best Places to Eat

➡ Época de Quesos (p130)
➡ El Viejo Hobbit (p139)
➡ Los Troncos (p136)
➡ Taberna Baska (p144)
➡ Cervecería Modelo (p120)

Best Places to Stay

➡ Villa Nuccia (p144)
➡ Hotel Água Pampas (p132)
➡ Paradores Draghi (p123)
➡ Hotel Sirenuse (p144)
➡ Estancia Ave María (p127)

Why Go?

The seemingly endless fertile grasslands that make up the pampas financed Argentina's golden years over a century ago, and the area is still the nation's economic powerhouse, producing most of Argentina's famous beef.

These humble pampas are often overlooked by travelers, but there are hidden gems here and there. A visit to lovely San Antonio de Areco offers a taste of living gaucho culture, while the picturesque hills around Tandil and Sierra de la Ventana offer plenty of opportunities for outdoor recreation. And the Atlantic coast's bustling beaches make a great escape from Buenos Aires' summer heat.

You can also spend a few days in one of the region's many historic *estancias* (ranches), where the huge sky and faded elegance of Argentina's past can all be experienced firsthand.

When to Go

Mar del Plata

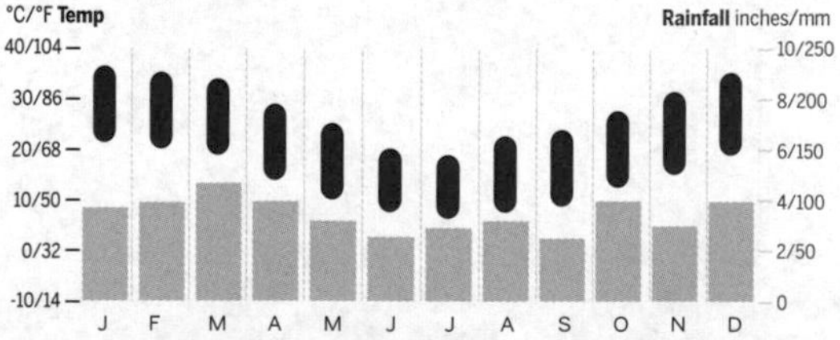

Jan–Feb Summer means great weather for the beach resorts, though prices and crowds skyrocket.

Oct–Nov & Mar–Apr Spring and fall are fine times to explore Tandil and Sierra de la Ventana.

Early Nov The gaucho celebration Día de la Tradición takes place in San Antonio de Areco.

NORTHERN PAMPAS

The pampas is both a general term for a large geographic region of fertile plains and the name of the province that lies to the west of Buenos Aires. The pampas grasslands roll southwards from the Río de la Plata to the banks of the Río Negro, stretching west towards the Andes and all the way up to the southern parts of Córdoba and Santa Fe provinces, taking in the entire Buenos Aires and La Pampa provinces.

The rich soil and lush natural grasses of the northern pampas make it Argentina's best cattle-raising country. The region yields plentiful hides, beef, wool and wheat for global markets, stamping Argentina on the world's economic map.

From the mid-19th century the province of Buenos Aires was the undisputed political and economic center of the country. When the city of Buenos Aires became Argentina's capital, the province submitted to national

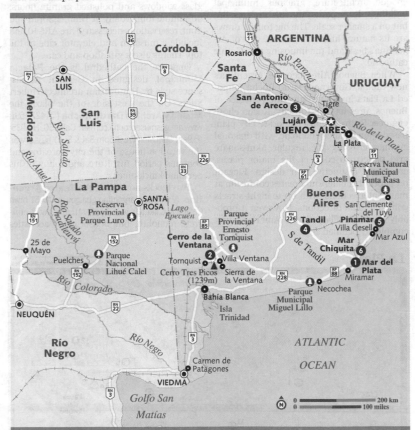

The Pampas & the Atlantic Coast Highlights

1. Soak up the sun and crowds in the Atlantic Coast's largest city, **Mar del Plata** (p139)
2. Peek through a natural rock 'window' atop the mountain **Cerro de la Ventana** (p132)
3. Go gaucho in **San Antonio de Areco** (p122), the Pampas' prettiest town
4. Sample some country life – and deli meats and cheese – in **Tandil** (p125)
5. Go windsurfing, kiteboarding or cycling in the beach resort of **Pinamar** (p135)
6. Explore the lagoon, spot flamingos or just chill out in **Mar Chiquita** (p138)
7. Join the masses on their holy pilgrimage to **Luján** (p120)

authority but didn't lose its influence. By the 1880s, after a brief but contentious civil war, the province responded by creating its own provincial capital in the model city of La Plata.

La Plata

☎0221 / POP 654,000

Just over an hour from Buenos Aires, this bustling university town has the same belle époque architecture, gracious municipal buildings, leafy parks and nightlife as BA, but on a smaller scale. The big tourist draws are its natural history museum, one of Argentina's best, and the imposing neo-Gothic cathedral.

When Buenos Aires became Argentina's new capital, Governor Dardo Rocha founded La Plata in 1882 to give the province of Buenos Aires its own top city. Rocha chose engineer Pedro Benoit's elaborate city plan, based upon balance and logic, with diagonal avenues crossing the regular 5km-square grid pattern to connect the major plazas, creating a distinctive star design. Elegant on paper, this blueprint creates confusion at many intersections, with up to eight streets going off in all directions. However, it probably made La Plata South America's first completely planned city.

Sights

La Plata's main sights are all within walking distance of each other. Near Plaza Moreno is the neo-Gothic **cathedral** (☎423-3931; www.catedraldelaplata.com; Plaza Moreno; ⏲10am-7pm; tower 11am-6pm Tue-Fri, 12:30-6pm Sat & Sun), which was begun in 1885 but not inaugurated until 1932, with tower construction only completed in 1999. The cathedral was inspired by medieval predecessors in Cologne and Amiens, and has fine stained glass windows and polished granite floors; 90-minute tours (daily at 11am, 2:30pm and 4pm, reservations necessary) are AR$40 and include a museum and elevator ride to the top. There's also a gift shop and cafe.

Opposite the cathedral is the **Palacio Municipal**, designed in German Renaissance style by Hanoverian architect Hubert Stiers. On the west side of the plaza, the **Museo y Archivo Dardo Rocha** (☎427-5591; www.amigosmuseorocha.com.ar; Calle 50, No 935; ⏲9am-5pm Mon-Fri, 3-6pm Sat & Sun) FREE was the vacation house of the city's creator and contains period furniture and many of his personal knickknacks.

Two blocks northeast, the **Teatro Argentino** (www.teatroargentino.gba.gov.ar; Av 51 btwn Calle 9 & Calle 10) is a fantastically ugly concrete monolith, but boasts great acoustics

La Plata

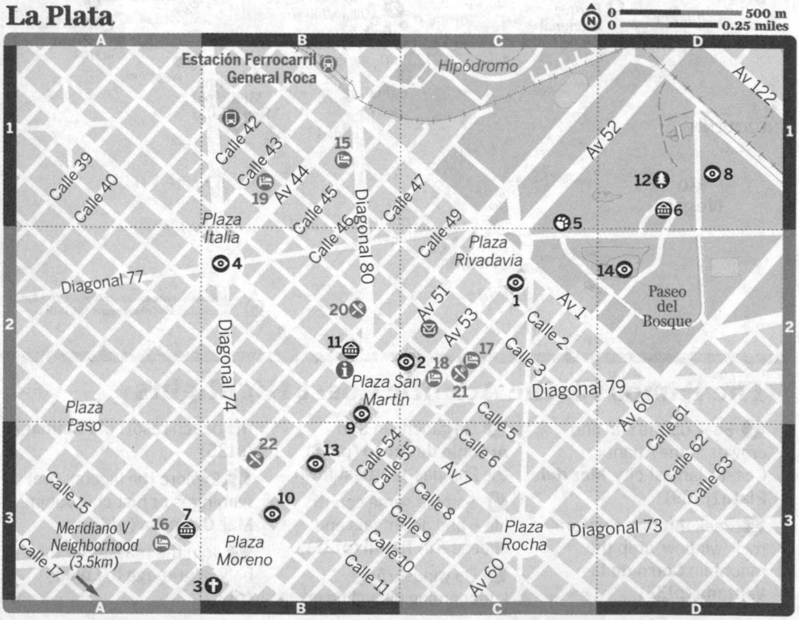

and quality performances: ballet, symphony orchestras and opera. Two blocks further northeast, in front of Plaza San Martín, is the ornate **Palacio de la Legislatura**, also in German Renaissance style. Nearby, catch the French Classic **Pasaje Dardo Rocha**, once La Plata's main train station and now the city's major cultural center, containing two museums. Also close by is the Flemish Renaissance **Casa de Gobierno**, housing the provincial governor and his retinue. On Sundays, check out the lively **feria artesanal** (crafts fair; Plaza Italia) on Plaza Italia.

Plantations of eucalyptus, gingko, palm and subtropical hardwoods cover **Paseo del Bosque**, parkland expropriated from an *estancia* at the time of the city's founding. It attracts a collection of strolling families, smooching lovers and sweaty joggers. Various interesting sights are strewn within, such as a small lake with paddleboats for rent; the open-air **Teatro Martín Fierro**, which hosts music and drama performances; the **Observatorio Astronómico** (☎423-6593; www.facebook.com/observatorio.laplata; AR$3; ⏲8pm Fri & Sat); the modest **Jardín Zoológico** (☎427-3925; admission AR$15; ⏲10am-6pm Tue-Sun); and the star attraction, **Museo de La Plata** (☎425-7744; www.museo.fcnym.unlp.edu.ar; admission AR$6, Tue free ; ⏲10am-6pm Tue-Sun). This excellent museum features the paleontological, zoological, archaeological and anthropological finds of famous Patagonian explorer Francisco P Moreno, The eclectic collection includes Egyptian tomb relics, Jesuit art, amusing taxidermy, amazing skeletons, mummies, fossils, rocks and minerals, scary insects and reconstructed dinosaurs. Arrange English tours in advance; it's worth visiting on weekends when school groups aren't around.

One of Argentina's most famous homes is **Casa Curutchet** (☎421-8032; casacurutchet@capba.org.ar; Av 53, No 320; admission AR$40; ⏲10:30am-2pm Tue-Fri, closed Jan), designed by French-Swiss architect Le Corbusier for Pedro Curutchet, an Argentine surgeon. It's a beautiful piece of modern architecture and was featured in the award-winning movie *El hombre de al lado* (The Man Next Door; 2009). Reserve in advance for tours.

To catch La Plata's main sights, hop on the **Bus Turístico** (☎429-5711; www.buenosaires.tur.ar/busturistico) FREE, a free open-roofed tourist bus that runs on Saturday and Sunday afternoons, four times daily. Loops start and end in Plaza Moreno and take one hour.

La Plata

Sights

1 Casa Curutchet ... C2
2 Casa de Gobierno ... C2
3 Cathedral ... B3
4 Feria Artesanal ... B2
5 Jardín Zoológico ... C1
6 Museo de La Plata ... D1
7 Museo y Archivo Dardo Rocha ... A3
8 Observatorio Astronómico ... D1
9 Palacio de la Legislatura ... B2
10 Palacio Municipal ... B3
11 Pasaje Dardo Rocha ... B2
12 Paseo del Bosque ... D1
13 Teatro Argentino ... B3
14 Teatro Martín Fierro ... D2

Sleeping

15 Benevento Hotel ... B1
16 Catedral Hotel ... A3
17 Hostel del Bosque ... C2
18 San Marco Hotel ... C2
19 Único Ecohostel ... B1

Eating

20 Carnes Don Pedro ... B2
21 Cervecería Modelo ... C2
22 Wilkenny ... B3

Sleeping

Hostel del Bosque HOSTEL $
(☎489-0236; www.hosteldelbosque.com.ar; Calle 54, No 460; dm AR$85-105, r AR$260; @📶) Superbly located within easy walking distance of all downtown attractions, this hostel in a modern building block has tight four- to eight-bed dorms, friendly staff, a rooftop terrace and a great back patio garden with *parrilla*. Book ahead for the one en suite private room.

Único Ecohostel HOSTEL $
(☎423-2626; www.hostelunico.com; Calle 4, No 565; dm AR$100-160, d AR$400-480; ❄📶) This gleaming modern hostel is conveniently located only a block from the bus station, with air-con, bedside reading lamps and en suite bathrooms in all dorms, and ecofriendly amenities including solar hot water. The downside? It's a bit sterile and institutional feeling, the neighborhood isn't the greatest and the doubles are overpriced.

Catedral Hotel HOTEL $
(☎483-0091; www.hcatedral.com.ar; Calle 49, No 965; s/d AR$250/380; 📶) A simple but well-run budget hotel, just two blocks west of the cathedral plaza.

Benevento Hotel HOTEL $$
(☎423-7721; www.hotelbenevento.com.ar; Calle 2, No 645; s AR$384-500, d AR$500-630; ❄@🛜) This charmingly renovated hotel just a few blocks from the bus station offers beautiful rooms with high ceilings and cable TV. Most have wood floors, plus balconies overlooking the busy street; top-floor rooms are the most modern and sport views.

San Marco Hotel HOTEL $$
(☎422-9322; www.sanmarcohotel.com.ar; Calle 54, No 523; s/d AR$439/650; ❄🛜) This comfortable three-star enjoys a prime location in the heart of town, between Plaza San Martín and Paseo del Bosque.

Eating & Drinking

A 10-minute taxi ride from the center, in the historic bohemian neighborhood Meridiano V, you'll find **Bar Imperio** (www.facebook.com/barimperiolp; Calle 17 btwn Calles 70 & 71; ⏲7pm-late Wed-Sun), **Mirapampa** (☎451-3798; www.facebook.com/MirapampaBar; cnr Calles 17 & 71; ⏲6pm-late Wed-Sun) and **Ciudad Vieja** (☎452-1674; www.ciudadviejaweb.com.ar; cnr Calles 17 & 71; ⏲9pm-late Wed-Fri, noon-late Sat & Sun), all restaurant-bars offering live music from Wednesday to Sunday nights. There's also a weekend crafts fair, **Feria en la Esquina** (www.feriaenlaesquina.com.ar; cnr Calles 17 & 71; ⏲3:30-7:30pm Sat & Sun), plus theater, cinema and cultural centers – no wonder it's popular with students.

Carnes Don Pedro ARGENTINE $
(Diagonal Norte 1005; per kg AR$70; ⏲10:30am-9:30pm Mon-Sat) For a great cheap takeout option, pile up your choices at the buffet here, then head to nearby Plaza San Martín for a picnic. There's plenty of food, from fresh salads to *parrilla* (mixed grill) to many cooked meat and vegetable dishes.

★**Cervecería Modelo** ARGENTINE $$
(www.cerveceriamodelo.com.ar; cnr Calles 5 & 54; mains AR$52-89; ⏲8am-1:30am; 🛜) Dating from 1894, its ceiling hung with hams and peanut shells strewn on the floor, this classic place serves snacks, meals and ice-cold ales to a happy crowd. There are great sidewalk tables, and it's not too old to boast a big-screen TV and wi-fi.

Wilkenny ARGENTINE $$
(cnr Calle 11 & 50; mains AR$59-85; ⏲8am-1am) This popular place with a traditional Irish-pub feel serves a decent range of food such as salads, sandwiches and pastas. The nightly happy hour features a rotating cast of whiskies and beers. There's also occasional live music.

Information

Municipal tourist office (☎427-1535; www.laciudad.laplata.gov.ar/turismo; cnr Calles 7 & 50, Pasaje Dardo Rocha; ⏲10am-8pm) Just off Plaza San Martín.

Post office (cnr Calle 4 & Av 51)

Getting There & Away

Plaza (www.grupoplaza.com.ar) runs bus 129 from Buenos Aires to La Plata every 15 to 20 minutes (AR$18, 1¼ hours). It leaves from the side street Martínez Zuvería, adjacent to Plaza Canadá in front of Buenos Aires' Retiro train station, making stops along Ave 9 Julio and at Constitución train station.

La Plata's **bus terminal** has plenty of connections to other parts of Argentina.

La Plata is also served by Buenos Aires' Línea Roca (p112) suburban train line, with half-hourly services from the Constitución station (AR$5.75, 1¼ hours).

Buses from La Plata

DESTINATION	COST (AR$)	DURATION (HR)
Bahía Blanca	347-432	8-10
Bariloche	868-989	24
Córdoba	390-450	10
Mar del Plata	207	5
Mendoza	605-690	15

Luján

☎02323 / POP 106,000

Luján is a compact riverside town that several times per year overflows with pilgrims making their way to Argentina's most important shrine. It boasts a huge Spanish-style plaza with imposing neo-Gothic cathedral, as well as a couple of interesting museums. The riverside area is lined with restaurants and barbecue stands selling *choripan* (a spicy pork sausage in a crunchy roll). You can rent boats for a paddle, while a chairlift carries sightseers over the grubby river – an oddly charming touch.

Sights

Basílica Nuestra Señora de Luján CHURCH
(crypt admission AR$10; ⏲basilica 8am-7pm, crypt 10:15am-5pm Mon-Fri, 10am-6pm Sat & Sun) Luján's undisputed focal point is this

HOME, HOME ON THE...FEEDLOT?

Juicy, grass-fed steaks have always been one of Argentina's biggest tourist attractions. But these days, this type of beef has nearly disappeared. Stuffing cattle into pens and feeding them grain is becoming a standard way of raising cattle for market. Today, over 80% of Argentina's cows slaughtered each year experience their last few months in a feedlot.

Factory-farmed meat is a fairly recent phenomenon in Argentina. The country's agriculturally rich and vast pampas plains were ideal grounds for raising free-range beef, and up until 2001 around 90% of cattle ate only their natural food: grass. But in the last decade several developments have changed this. The price of agricultural crops such as soybeans, of which Argentina is one of the world's top producers, has skyrocketed, making it more lucrative to grow the legume than dedicate space to cattle. A severe drought in recent years dealt another blow to the beef industry – there just wasn't enough grass to feed the herds.

But perhaps the biggest factor detrimental to the grass-fed cattle has been government subsidies for feedlot development, with the intention of producing beef more quickly than before. It's less profitable to raise a fully grass-fed cow – which takes much longer to reach maturity – than a grain-fed one. And the Argentine government also passed legislation keeping beef prices artificially low within its borders, while at the same time using taxes to discourage cattle ranchers from making profits by exporting beef. So even more ranchers have turned pastureland into soy or corn rows to stay alive.

At this rate, practically all Argentine cattle will soon live out their last few months in dirt-floor corrals, with their movements restricted, eating an un-cowlike diet of grains. They'll be shot full of immunizations and antibiotics, which are crucial to treating ailments brought on by these unnatural conditions. Their beef will be slightly less flavorful and nutritious, yet more tender – due to the lower percentage of muscle, plus higher fat. And the modern world of commercial beef production will finally have caught up to Argentina, wiping away a part of its history, reputation...and perhaps some of that famous Argentine pride.

imposing neo-Gothic basilica, built from 1887 to 1935 and made from a lovely rose-colored stone that glows in the setting sun. The venerated statue of the Virgin sits in the high chamber behind the main altar. Under the basilica you can tour a crypt that's inhabited by Virgin statues from all over the world. Masses take place in the basilica several times a day.

Complejo Museográfico Enrique Udaondo MUSEUM
(☎420245; www.amigosmuseolujan.com.ar; admission AR$5; ⏲12:30-4:30pm Wed, 11:30am-4:30pm Thu & Fri, 10:30am-5:30pm Sat, Sun & holidays) On the west side of Luján's gargantuan basilica plaza, this gorgeous colonial-era museum complex rambles with several display rooms, pretty patios and gardens. The Sala General José de San Martín showcases Argentina's battles for independence, while the Sala de Gaucho contains some beautiful *mate* (a bitter ritual tea) ware, horse gear and other gaucho paraphernalia.

Museo de Transporte MUSEUM
(admission AR$5; ⏲12:30-4:30pm Wed, 11:30am-4:30pm Thu & Fri, 10:30am-5:30pm Sat, Sun & holidays) Luján's transportation museum displays a remarkable collection of horse-drawn carriages from the late 1800s, the first steam locomotive to serve the city from Buenos Aires and a monster of a hydroplane that crossed the Atlantic in 1926. The most offbeat exhibits, however, are the stuffed and scruffy remains of Gato and Mancha, the hardy Argentine criollo horses ridden by adventurer AF Tschiffely from Buenos Aires to New York. This trip took 2½ years, from 1925 to 1928.

Festivals & Events

On the first Saturday in October, Día de la Virgen de Luján, throngs of the faithful walk the 65km from the Buenos Aires neighborhood of Liniers to Luján – a journey of up to 18 hours. Other large gatherings occur on May 8 (Virgin's Day), the first weekend in August (the colorful Peregrinación Boliviana), the last weekend in September (the 'gaucho' pilgrimage – watch

LA VIRGENCITA

Argentina's patron saint is a ubiquitous presence – you can spot her poster on butcher-shop walls, her statue in churches throughout the country and her image on the dashboards of taxis. She wears a triangular blue dress, stands on a half-moon and radiates streams of glory from her crowned head.

In 1630 a Portuguese settler in Tucumán asked a friend in Brazil to send him an image of the Virgin for his new chapel. Unsure what style of Virgin was required, the friend sent two – including one of the Immaculate Conception. After setting out from the port of Buenos Aires, the cart bearing the statues got bogged down near the river of Luján and only moved when the Immaculate Conception was taken off. Its owner took this as a sign, and left the statue in Luján so that a shrine could be built there. The other statue continued its journey to the northwest.

Since then the Virgin of Luján has been credited with a number of miracles – from curing tumors and sending a fog to hide early settlers from warring Indians, to protecting the province from a cholera epidemic. She was rewarded for her trouble in 1886 when Pope Leo XIII crowned her with a golden coronet set with almost 500 pearls and gems.

Every year millions of pilgrims from throughout Argentina visit Luján's basilica, where the original 17th-century statue is still displayed, to honor the Virgin for her intercession in affairs of peace, health, forgiveness and consolation. If you arrive here during the massive pilgrimage on the first Sunday in October, you'll spot families of exhausted pilgrims snoozing in the square, enjoying barbecues by the river and filling plastic bottles with holy water from the fountain.

for horses) and December 8 (Immaculate Conception Day).

Sleeping & Eating

Luján can easily be seen on a day trip from Buenos Aires. If you decide to overnight on a weekend, however, be sure to reserve ahead.

Pilgrims won't go hungry here – the central parts of San Martín, 9 de Julio and the riverfront are all lined with restaurants.

Hostel Estación Luján HOSTEL $

(☎429101; www.estacionlujanhostel.com.ar; 9 de Julio 978; dm/d/tr/q AR$160/300/350/400; ❄@🛜) Nicer than it looks from the outside, this small, modern hostel offers four clean rooms sleeping three to six, some with balcony overlooking the basilica half a block away. There's free kitchen use and a large common area. Avoid Saturdays, when rates jump.

Hotel Hoxón HOTEL $$

(☎429970; www.hotelhoxon.com.ar; 9 de Julio 760; s AR$315-380, d AR$505-590; ❄@🛜🏊) The best and biggest in town (and getting bigger with a new annex opening in 2014), this place two blocks north of the basilica has modern, clean and comfortable rooms. Superiors are carpeted and come with fridge and air-con. There's also a swimming pool with raised sundeck.

★L'Eau Vive FRENCH $$$

(☎421774; leauvivedeargentina.com.ar; Constitución 2112; mains around AR$120; ⏲noon-2:30pm & 8:30-10pm Tue-Sat, noon-2:30pm Sun) Just 2km from the town center you'll find this friendly French restaurant run by Carmelite nuns from around the world. Taxis here cost about AR$30, or take bus 501 from the center.

Information

Post office (Mitre 575)

Tourist office (☎427082; turismo@lujan.gov.ar; ⏲9am-6pm) In a domed, yellow building near the river in Parque Ameghino, at the west end of Lavalle.

Getting There & Away

Lujan's **bus terminal** (Av de Nuestra Señora de Luján & Almirante Brown) is three blocks north of the basilica. From Buenos Aires, take bus 57 (AR$17, two hours), operated by **Transportes Atlántida** (☎434957). It leaves every half-hour from outside the Plaza Italia or Once train stations.

San Antonio de Areco

☎02326 / POP 20,000

Nestled among lush farmlands, San Antonio de Areco (commonly known as Areco) is one of the prettiest towns in the pampas. About 115km northwest of Buenos Aires, it welcomes many day-tripping *porteños* (residents of Buenos Aires) who come for the peaceful atmosphere and picturesque colonial streets. The town dates from the early 18th century and preserves a great deal of criollo (people of pure Spanish descent born in the New World) and gaucho traditions, especially among its artisans, who produce very fine silverwork and saddlery. Gauchos from all over the pampas show up for November's Día de la Tradición, where you can catch them and their horses strutting the cobbled streets in all their finery.

San Antonio de Areco's compact town center and quiet streets are very walkable. Around the Plaza Ruiz de Arellano, named in honor of the town's founding *estanciero* (ranch owner), are several historic buildings, including the **iglesia parroquial** (parish church).

The **puente viejo** (old bridge; 1857), across the Río Areco, follows the original cart road to northern Argentina. Once a toll crossing, it's now a pedestrian bridge that leads to San Antonio de Areco's main attraction, the Museo Gauchesco Ricardo Güiraldes.

Areco shuts down during siesta time in the afternoon.

Sights

Museo Gauchesco Ricardo Güiraldes MUSEUM
(cnr R Güiraldes & Sosa; 11am-6pm Wed-Mon) FREE Recently reopened after sustaining flood damage in 2009, this sprawling museum in Parque Criollo dates to 1938 and includes an old flour mill, a re-created *pulpería* (tavern), a colonial-style chapel and a 20th-century reproduction of an 18th-century *casco* (ranch house). Displays include horse gear, gauchesco artwork and rooms dedicated to Ricardo Güiraldes, author of the novel *Don Segundo Sombra*.

Museo y Taller Draghi MUSEUM
(www.draghiplaterosorfebres.com; Lavalle 387; admission AR$25; 9am-1pm & 4-7pm Mon-Sat, 10am-1pm Sun) This small museum, attached to the silversmith workshop of the locally renowned Draghi family, highlights an exceptional collection of silver *facónes* (gaucho knives), beautiful horse gear and intricate *mate* paraphernalia. There's also some jewelry and leather bags; everything is for sale.

Museo Las Lilas MUSEUM
(www.museolaslilas.org; Moreno 279; admission AR$50; 10am-8pm Thu-Sun mid-Sep–mid-Mar, to 6pm rest of year) Florencio Molina Campos is to Argentines what Norman Rockwell is to Americans: a folk artist whose themes are based on comical caricatures. This pretty courtyard museum displays his famous works.

Festivals & Events

San Antonio de Areco is the symbolic center of Argentina's vestigial cowboy culture, and puts on the country's biggest gaucho celebration for **Día de la Tradición** (a 10-day event in early to mid-November; call the tourist office for exact dates). If you're in the area, don't miss it; attractions include a horseback procession through the town, displays of horsemanship, folk dancing and craft exhibitions. Main events take place at Parque Criollo. Note that events can sometimes be postponed by rain, as they were in 2013.

Sleeping

While San Antonio is a popular destination for day trips out of Buenos Aires, it's worth hanging around as there are some lovely places to stay. Book on weekends, when prices go up.

Areco Hostel HOSTEL $
(453120; www.arecohostel.com.ar; Arellano 121; dm/d/tr AR$120/280/420) In an atmospheric old building facing the central square, San Antonio's newest and nicest hostel offers one spacious four-bed dorm with working fireplace, a pair of larger dorms and a lone private room up front. The clean, tiled guest kitchen, narrow but grassy backyard and friendly management add to the appeal.

Hostal de Areco HOTEL $
(456118; www.hostaldeareco.com.ar; Zapiola 25; s/d Sun-Thu AR$250/270, r Fri & Sat AR$330;) Clustered with two other hotels, which aren't as personable but do have pools, this humble place has a pleasant salon and a nice large grassy garden in back. Rooms are simple but comfortable.

★ **Paradores Draghi** GUESTHOUSE $$
(455583; www.paradoresdraghi.com.ar; Matheu 380; s Sun-Thu only AR$450, d AR$580; @) Large, comfortable rooms (two with kitchenette) are available at this tranquil place. There's a grassy garden with beautiful pool,

San Antonio de Areco

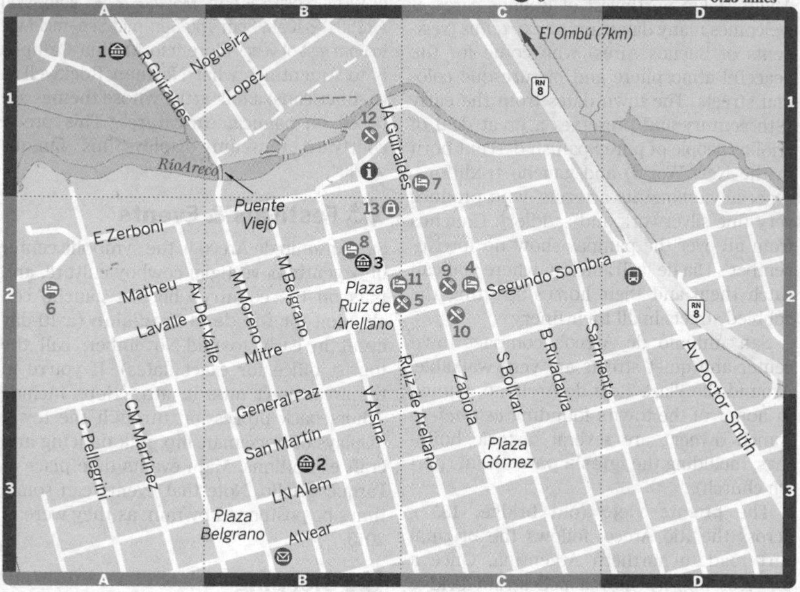

greenhouse breakfast room and two patios in which to relax.

Antigua Casona GUESTHOUSE $$
(☎456600; www.antiguacasona.com; Segundo Sombra 495; r Sun-Thu AR$600, Fri & Sat AR$660; ❄📶) This restored traditional home offers five high-ceilinged, lovely rooms with wooden floors, all set around covered tile hallways and brick patios. One room with outside bathroom costs less. Breakfast is good, and there are bikes available for rent.

Estancias

Private transfers directly from Buenos Aires to these *estancias* is available for an extra charge (see websites).

Estancia La Cinacina ESTANCIA $$$
(☎452045; www.lacinacina.com.ar; Zerboni s/n; d midweek/weekend AR$1000/1500; ❄🏊) On the edge of town, this touristy *estancia* offers comfortable lodgings in a pretty park setting. Weekend rates include daily horseback rides.

La Porteña ESTANCIA $$$
(☎in Buenos Aires 15-5626-7347; www.laporteniadeareco.com; RN8, Km110; día de campo AR$600, d incl full board AR$1800-2400; 🏊) Lovely grounds and historic location – this is where Ricardo Güiraldes wrote his gaucho epic *Don Segunda Sombra*. Good but not luxurious facilities and plentiful food; polo lessons available.

El Ombú ESTANCIA $$$
(☎492080; www.estanciaelombu.com; RP31, Cuartel VI, Villa Lía; día de campo AR$600, s/d incl full board AR$1500/2500; ❄🏊) This 300-hectare working *estancia* is located about 20km from Areco. You can watch and even take part in managing cattle herds – or play golf and tennis at a nearby country club.

Eating

Boliche de Bessonart ARGENTINE $
(cnr Zapiola & Segundo Sombra; picadas AR$10-65; ⏲11am-late Tue-Sun) Its shelves and walls filled with dusty bottles and and old gaucho photos, this weatherbeaten corner bar has been run by the Bessonart family for 60 years. Crowds of locals pour in nightly for *picadas* (shared appetizer plates), accompanied by beers or Fernet (a bitter aromatic spirit) mixed with Coca Cola.

La Esquina de Merti ARGENTINE $
(Arellano 147; mains AR$40-82; ⏲9am-midnight) Right on the plaza is this cafe-restaurant with great old feel. Typical *parrilla* is on offer, but there are also *milanesas* (breaded cutlets), pasta and some finer dishes too.

San Antonio de Areco

Sights

1 Museo Gauchesco Ricardo Güiraldes A1
2 Museo Las Lilas B3
3 Museo y Taller Draghi B2

Sleeping

4 Antigua Casona C2
5 Areco Hostel B2
6 Estancia La Cinacina A2
7 Hostal de Areco C1
8 Paradores Draghi B2

Eating

9 Almacén Ramos Generales C2
10 Boliche de Bessonart C2
11 La Esquina de Merti C2
12 Puesto La Lechuza B1

Shopping

13 La Olla de Cobre B2

Puesto La Lechuza PARRILLA $
(☎470136; Victorino Althaparro 423; mains AR$45-75; ⏰noon-3pm & 8pm-midnight Sat, noon-3pm Sun) Best on a warm day, when you can enjoy a lunch of empanadas (baked savory turnovers) or barbecued beef under the trees near the river. Live guitar music on Saturday nights; open weekends only.

Almacén Ramos Generales ARGENTINE $$
(www.ramosgeneralesareco.com.ar; Zapiola 143; mains AR$65-140; ⏰noon-3pm & 8pm-midnight) Come to this traditional local mainstay if you want an old-time atmosphere in which to eat fish, meat or pasta dishes.

Shopping

San Antonio de Areco's artisans are known throughout the country. *Mate* paraphernalia, *rastras* (silver-studded belts) and *facónes,* produced by skilled silversmiths, are the most typical items. The tourist office has an extensive list of artists and their trades.

La Olla de Cobre FOOD
(☎453105; laolladecobre.com.ar; Matheu 433; ⏰10am-1pm & 3-7:30pm Wed-Mon) For a gift of artisanal chocolates or *alfajores* (cookie-type sandwiches), try this shop just north of the square. It also serves coffee and hot chocolate.

Information

There are a few banks with ATMs along Alsina.
Post office (cnr Alvear & Av Del Valle)
Tourist office (☎453165; www.sanantoniodeareco.tur.ar; cnr E Zerboni & Ruiz de Arellano; ⏰10am-7pm Mon-Fri, 8am-8pm Sat & Sun)

Getting There & Away

Areco's **bus terminal** (Av Smith s/n) is five blocks east of the central square. **General Belgrano** (☎454059; www.gralbelgrano.com.ar) and **Chevallier** (☎453904; www.nuevachevallier.com) run frequent buses to/from Buenos Aires (AR$61 to AR$69, two hours). There are also buses to Luján (AR$40, 45 minutes).

SOUTHERN PAMPAS

Spreading out from the capital, the pampas region extends south beyond the borders of Buenos Aires province and west into the province of La Pampa.

In the southern part of Buenos Aires province, the endlessly flat plain is punctuated by sierras (hills). The Sierras de Tandil are ancient mountain ranges, worn to soft, low summits with heights that barely reach 500m. A little to the west, Sierra de la Ventana's jagged peaks rise to 1300m, attracting hikers and climbers.

Further west again, in the province of La Pampa, are the modest granite boulders of Parque Nacional Lihué Calel.

The hillside towns of Tandil and Sierra de la Ventana offer outdoor activities and a relaxing country atmosphere, while La Pampa's provincial capital of Santa Rosa is a decent resting point for overland travelers on their way west or south.

Tandil

☎0249 / POP 124,000

Pretty Tandil sits at the northern edge of the Sierras de Tandil, a 2.5-million-year-old mountain range worn down to gentle, grassy peaks and rocky outcroppings – perfect for rock climbing and mountain biking. It exudes a rare combination of laid-back country charm with the energy of a thriving regional city. The town center is leafy and relaxed, with many places observing the afternoon siesta. Later in the evening, however, locals crowd the squares and streets, shopping and partaking in the city's cultural offerings. On a side note, Tandil is known for nurturing a disproportionate number of Argentina's tennis stars – the latest of whom is Juan Martín del Potro.

THE GLORIOUS GAUCHO

If the melancholy *tanguero* (tango dancer) is the essence of the *porteño* (resident of Buenos Aires), then the gaucho represents the pampa: a lone cowboylike figure, pitted against the elements, with only his horse for a friend.

In the early years of the colony the fringe-dwelling gauchos lived entirely beyond the laws and customs of Buenos Aires, eking out an independent and often violent existence in the countryside. They slaughtered cattle roaming free and unsupervised on the fertile pampas and drank *mate*, the caffeine-rich herbal tea.

As the colony grew, cattle became too valuable to leave unprotected. Foreign demand for hides increased and investors moved into the pampas to take control of the market, establishing the *estancia* (ranch) system, in which large landholdings were handed out to a privileged few. Many freewheeling gauchos became exploited farmhands, while those who resisted domestication were threatened with prison or the draft.

By the late 19th century those in charge felt the gaucho had no place in modern Argentina. President Sarmiento (who governed 1868–74) declared that 'fertilizing the soil with their blood is the only thing gauchos are good for' – and already much gaucho blood had been spilled, their horsemanship making them excellent infantrymen for Argentina's civil war and the brutal campaigns against the Indians.

Like so many heroes, the gaucho only won love and admiration after his demise. His physical bravery, honor and lust for freedom are celebrated in José Hernández's 1872 epic poem *Martin Fierro* and Ricardo Güiraldes' novel *Don Segundo Sombra*. His rustic traditions form part of Argentina's sophisticated folk art, with skilled craftspeople producing intricate silver gaucho knives and woven ponchos, while his image is endlessly reproduced – most amusingly in Florencio Molina Campos' caricatures.

These days, the gaucho-for-export is much easier to spot than the real deal, especially in folkloric shows at many *estancias*. But the gaucho's descendants can be found on cattle farms throughout the pampas, riding over the plains in their dusty *boinas* (a kind of beret) and *bombachas* (riding pants). And on special occasions, such as the Día de la Tradición, they sport their best horse gear and show off their riding skills.

The town arose from Fuerte Independencia, a military outpost established in 1823. In the early 1870s it was the scene of one of the province's most remarkable battles, when renegade gauchos gathered in the hills before going on a murderous rampage against landowners and recent immigrants. Eventually the immigrants prevailed, and the culinary skills they brought from Europe have made the area an important producer of specialty foods. Today Tandil is famous for its cheeses and cured meats, which can be sampled throughout town.

Sights

The walk to **Parque Independencia** from the southwestern edge of downtown offers good views of the city, particularly at night, while the central **Plaza de Independencia**, surrounded by the typical municipal buildings and a church, is where the townspeople stroll in the evenings.

Calvario, a hill ostensibly resembling the site of Christ's crucifixion, attracts visitors at Easter, when a passion play is held.

At the north edge of town the Piedra Movediza (a 300-ton 'rocking stone') teetered precariously atop **Cerro La Movediza** for many years before finally falling in 1912. A 'replica' nonmoving stone was built in 2007. Take bus 503 (blue).

For more good views, head 4.5km west of town to **Cerro El Centinela** (www.cerrocentinela.com.ar), a hilltop park named for its sentinel-like rock formation. Up top you'll find two restaurants and a **chairlift** (AR$45; ⏲11:30am-5pm Fri, 10:30am-5:30pm Sat & Sun) that can whisk you further up the ridgeline. It's only open weekends outside warm months; a taxi here will cost you around AR$30.

Museo Tradicionalista Fuerte Independencia MUSEUM
(☎443-5573; www.museodelfuerte.org.ar; 4 de Abril 845; admission AR$20; ⏲2:30-6:30pm Tue-Sun Mar-Nov, 4-8pm Tue-Sun Dec-Feb) This historical museum exhibits a large and varied collection on Tandil's history. Photographs (captioned in Spanish) commemorate major

events, and the place is filled with relics – from carriages to ladies' gloves – donated by local families.

Museo de Bellas Artes MUSEUM
(☎443-2067; Chacabuco 357; admission AR$5; ⊙8:30am-12:30pm & 4:30-8:30pm Mon-Fri, 4-8pm Sat & Sun) This downtown museum has temporary exhibits of Argentine and international artists.

Reserva Natural Sierra del Tigre PARK
(admission AR$30; ⊙9am-7pm in summer, till 5:30pm in winter, closed if raining) This park is 6km south of Tandil, at the end of Calle Suiz, off Av Don Bosco. The rocky hills are fun to climb, and in spring the reserve is filled with fragrant wildflowers. The peaks offer views of the town to one side and the patchwork pampean farms stretching out from the other. A somewhat incongruous collection of animals – llamas and donkeys among them – have free run of the park, while their natural predator, the puma, is sadly caged. Taxis here cost around AR$40 one way; arrange pickup for a return ride.

Activities

The **Dique del Fuerte**, only 12 blocks south of Plaza Independencia, is a huge reservoir that you can easily walk around in a couple of hours. In summer, the Balneario Municipal runs several **swimming pools** and you can rent **canoes** and **kayaks**. There are also a few restaurants nestled along its shoreline.

Gabriel Barletta (☎450-9609; cabalgatasbarletta@yahoo.com.ar; 4hr tour AR$300) offers excellent four-hour horseback rides in the Reserva Natural Sierra del Tigre or other surrounding areas. For details on other outdoor activities around town, including bike rentals, trekking, canoeing, rappelling, mountain biking and rock climbing, ask the tourist office for its comprehensive list of tour operators and rental agencies.

Sleeping

Reservations are a must during summer, Easter week and holiday weekends. If you have your own transport, the many *cabañas* (cabins) along Av Don Bosco are a good option – the tourist office provides lists of fully equipped cabins, many of which have pools.

Casa Chango HOSTEL $
(☎442-2260; www.casa-chango.com.ar; 25 de Mayo 451; dm/s without bathroom AR$100/150, d with/without bathroom AR$380/320; @🛜) The marginal dorms at this centrally located hostel are somewhat redeemed by bright and attractive common areas with colorful tiles, high ceilings and other historical features. Two dorms have six beds, one has eight; avoid the lone 18-bed dorm and the private doubles, which offer poor value for money.

Gran Hotel Roma HOTEL $
(☎442-5217; www.hotelromatandil.com.ar; Alem 452; s/d AR$220/320; 🛜) It's bare-bones basic and definitely showing its age, but this budget hotel enjoys a convenient location only a block from Tandil's main plaza, and there's free wi-fi and parking.

Lo de Titi GUESTHOUSE $$
(☎442-0926; www.lodetiti.com.ar; Lobería 1050; r AR$710; ❄🛜🏊) Just four fine, big rooms are available at this awesome place. It has a huge grassy garden, colorful eclectic decor and great common room with kitchen use.

Belgrano 39 B&B B&B $$
(☎0249-15-4607076, 442-6989; hutton@speedy.com.ar; Belgrano 39; r AR$500; 🛜🏊) There's only room for two people, but this peaceful B&B, run by a one-of-a-kind British woman with encylopedic knowledge of Tandil, is well worth seeking out. It features a cozy room flanked by a large lovely garden and pool, with off-street parking available. Advance reservation required.

Las Acacias GUESTHOUSE $$
(☎442-3373; www.posadalasacacias.com.ar; Brasil 642; r AR$670; @🛜🏊) Located in an atmospheric former dairy at the eastern edge of town, this wonderful place with rustic atmosphere and tasteful decor has nine rooms surrounded by greenery.

★ **Estancia Ave María** ESTANCIA $$$
(☎442-2843; www.avemariatandil.com.ar; s/d midweek AR$1100/1450, weekend AR$1350/1800; @🛜🏊) This historic and beautiful 300-hectare *estancia* offers big rooms with views of the hills, and comfortable common areas. Prices include breakfast and dinner, plus activities such as horseback rides. It's 9km west of town.

Eating

Grill Argentino ARGENTINE $
(Gral Rodríguez 552; mains AR$38-76; ⊙noon-3pm & 7:30pm-midnight) This centrally located, cavernous dining hall half a block off the plaza is popular for its efficient service and its reasonably priced, abundant servings of

JENNY ACHESON/GETTY IMAGES ©

1. Traditional Argentinian barbecue **2.** *Bandoneón* player
3. Gaucho with horses **4.** Man with traditional *mate* drink

2

VIVIANE PONTI/GETTY IMAGES ©

Staying on an Estancia

One of the best ways to enjoy the open spaces of the pampas is to visit an *estancia* (ranch). Argentina's late-19th-century belle epoque saw wealthy families adorn their ranches with lavish homes and gardens.

Those glorious days being long gone, many of these establishments are open to tourists. The *día de campo* (day in the country) usually includes a huge *asado* (barbecue) with drinks, a tour of the historic home, and use of the property's horses, bicycles and swimming pool. Some places offer a *show gauchesco,* featuring folk dances and feats of horsemanship, while others host polo matches. *Estancias* are a sustainable tourism option, helping to preserve part of the country's past while providing an impressive guest-to-tree ratio. Most offer overnight stays, which include meals and activities.

4

ESTANCIA OPTIONS

The following options are all within a few hours' drive of Buenos Aires:

Los Dos Hermanos (☎011-4723-2880; www.estancialosdoshermanos.com) Best for horseback riding.

La Oriental (☎02364-15-640866; www.estancia-laoriental.com) Lovely house and setting.

La Candelaria (☎02227-494132; www.estanciacandelaria.com) Extravagant French-style castle.

Siempre Verde (☎02292-498555; www.estanciasiempreverde.com) Historic 1000-hectare ranch near Tandil.

La Margarita (☎011-4951-0638; www.estancialamargarita.com) Unique, 'self-catering' option.

Guapa Polo (☎15-6733-5612; www.guapapolo.com.ar) Learn to play polo.

Argentine classics such as *milanesas* with fries, pasta and steaks.

★ Época de Quesos ARGENTINE $$
(www.epocadequesos.com/tandil; cnr San Martín & 14 de Julio; mains AR$46-88; ⏲9am-10pm Mon-Thu, to 11pm Fri-Sun) Stuffed with tourists on a busy weekend, this place sells over 40 local cheeses and dozens of cured meats, which you can sample. Snag a table in the pleasant garden out back and order a sampler plate with specialty beer to match; regular main dishes are also available.

Tierra de Azafranes INTERNATIONAL $$
(☎443-6800; www.tierradeazafranes.com.ar; cnr San Martín & Av Santamarina; mains AR$58-79; ⏲noon-3pm & 8:30pm-midnight Wed-Mon) This hip and smartly decorated restaurant is known for its fish, pastas, risottos and paella. Don't miss the seafood stew (AR$73) on Wednesday night or the *brochettes colgantes* (AR$66), showy skewers of meat or seafood and vegetables suspended vertically from a hook at your table.

Aquí No Es INTERNATIONAL $$
(Chile 735; mains AR$50-100; ⏲10am-4pm Tue-Sat) A relaxing place for lunch, this bohemian eatery invites you to linger with its artsy vibe, casual garden with pool, and an ever-changing five-item menu built around fresh organic ingredients.

Drinking & Nightlife

For a small city, Tandil has several good bars.

Antares BAR
(9 de Julio 758; ⏲7:30pm-late Wed-Mon) The attractive, modern Tandil branch of this well-known brewery sports copper tap cylinders behind the bar and live music Thursday and Sunday nights.

Antique Bistro BAR
(Gral Rodríguez 687; ⏲8am-late) A sophisticated mood prevails at this tiny old-fashioned piano bar, where live folk and tango bands perform from 11:30pm onwards Wednesday through Sunday.

Shopping

Syquet FOOD
(www.syquet.com.ar; cnr Gral Rodríguez & Mitre; ⏲9am-1pm & 5-9pm Mon-Thu, 9am-9:30pm Fri & Sat, 10am-9pm Sun) Sells a tantalizing array of local cheeses, salamis and hams, along with other regional products.

Talabartería Berruti SOUVENIRS
(9 de Julio 757; ⏲9:15am-1pm & 4:30-8:30pm Mon-Sat) Especially good for leather, this store also stocks an assortment of *mates*, knives, silverwork and ponchos.

Information

There are plenty of banks with ATMs in the center.

Post office (Gral Pinto 623)

Tourist office (☎444-8698; www.tandil.gov.ar; Rodríguez 445; ⏲9am-8pm Mon-Sat, 9am-1pm Sun) Opposite Tandil's central plaza. There's another branch at the bus terminal (closed Sunday).

Getting There & Away

Tandil's **bus terminal** (☎432092; Av Buzón 400) is 12 blocks east of the main plaza. Walk, take bus 505 (AR$4.25) or you can catch a taxi (which will cost you about AR$20) from in front of the terminal.

Trains from Buenos Aires' Constitución station (*primera*/Pullman class AR$100/120, seven hours) arrive in Tandil on Tuesday and Friday nights and head back on Wednesday and Sunday nights, but double check as service can be suspended.

Buses from Tandil

DESTINATION	COST (AR$)	DURATION (HR)
Buenos Aires	187-205	5½
Córdoba	524-597	16
La Plata	149	5½
Mar del Plata	81	3
Mendoza	556-641	16
Necochea	69	3

Getting Around

Tandil's excellent public transportation system (per ride AR$4.25) reaches every important sight. Bus 500 (yellow) goes to Dique del Fuerte, buses 501 (red) and 505 (brown) go to the bus terminal, and bus 503 (blue) goes to Cerro La Movediza, plus the university and the bus terminal.

Sierra de la Ventana

☎0291 / POP 5000

Sierra de la Ventana's main attraction is the wealth of outdoor activity it offers: hiking up nearby peaks, trout fishing and bathing in the streams and pools, riding on horseback or bicycle through the hills, and climbing or rappelling among the rocks. Weekends fill with families from around the province coming to enjoy the picturesque hills.

🏃 Activities

Lots of outdoor pursuits are on offer in this region, and you can tackle most on your own. For hiking guides try **Luan & Ventur** (☑ 15-416-3786; luanventur.com.ar), which goes to Garganta del Diablo, the only way to explore that gorge. It also organizes rappelling, horseback riding and other tours.

For bike rentals head to **El Tornillo** (☑ 0291-15-431-1812; Roca 142; bike rental per hr/day AR$30/120; ⊙ 10am-7pm, closed in afternoons during hot weather), half a block south of the train station. The river area behind Hotel Alihuen is popular for splashing about.

👉 Tours

Sergio Rodriguez Turismo   GUIDED TOUR (☑ 491-5355; www.sergiorodrigueztur.com.ar; cnr Av San Martín & Iguazú) Sergio Rodriguez Turismo offers a variety of tours in the area, including visits to a nearby winery and an *estancia*.

🛏 Sleeping

Book ahead in summer and during long weekends. The tourist office has an extensive list of *cabañas*.

Alihuen Hotel   HOTEL $ (☑ 491-5074; www.lasierradelaventana.com.ar/ alihuen; cnr Tornquist & Frontini; s/d AR$150/300; 🛜 ⛵) About four blocks from the main drag, near the river, is this charmingly old-style hotel on grassy grounds. It's hardly luxurious, with creaky wood floors and simple furnishings, but there's plenty of atmosphere. An adjacent building has more modern rooms.

Hostería Maiten   HOTEL $ (☑ 491-5073; www.hosteriamaiten.blogspot.com. ar; Iguazú 93; s/d AR$150/220; 🛜) Sixteen very basic but clean rooms with open-shower bathrooms cluster around a flagstoned garden patio at this central, friendly and family-run place.

Hotel Atero   HOTEL $ (☑ 491-5002; cnr San Martín & Güemes; s/d AR$200/300; ❉🛜) The town's most centrally located hotel has comfortable rooms (some with balconies overlooking the main street) and an attached restaurant.

Camping Yamila   CAMPGROUND $ (☑ 0291-15-418-9266; www.campingyamila.8m. com; campsites per person AR$50) Four blocks north of the main street, this dusty but tree-shaded spot offers campsites with picnic tables and great river access.

🍴 Eating

Some restaurants close one or more days per week outside the December-to-March summer months.

Parrilla Rali-Hué   PARRILLA $ (☑ 491-5220; San Martín 307; mains AR$43-65; ⊙ noon-2:30 & 8-11pm) It's beef only at this casual joint, where locals flock to dine on the *parrillada* for two – good value at AR$130.

Sol y Luna   ARGENTINE $$ (☑ 491-5316; San Martín 628; mains AR$67-98; ⊙ noon-3pm & 8pm-midnight Thu-Tue; 🍴) This attractive place on the main drag serves up good homemade pastas and lighter dishes such as fresh trout accompanied by freshly sauteed vegetables. There are some purely vegetarian options as well.

La Comarca   ARGENTINE $$ (☑ 491-5629; Tornquist 125; mains AR$80-130; ⊙ 8-11pm) In a grand yellow house on a tree-lined side street, this romantic spot features refined dishes such as orange-braised pork with apple sauce, lamb with mint, chocolate mousse and crepes flambéed in rum.

ℹ Orientation

The town is divided into two sections by Río Sauce Grande. The main street, Av San Martín, lies south of the river, as do the bus and train stops and most other services.

ℹ Information

Banco Provincia (San Martín 260) The town's only bank; it has ATMs.
Post office (cnr Av Roca & Alberdi)
Tourist office (☑ 491-5303; www.sierradelaventana.org.ar; Av del Golf s/n; ⊙ 8am-8pm) Across the tracks from the train station.

ℹ Getting There & Around

Condor Estrella (☑ 491-5091; www.condor-estrella.com.ar) buses to Buenos Aires (AR$319, nine hours, six times weekly) and Bahía Blanca (AR$44, 2½ hours, twice daily) leave from a small office on Av San Martín, a block from the YPF gas station. There are additional services to Bahía Blanca with local *combi* (long-distance van) companies such as **Expreso Cabildo**

WORTH A TRIP

VILLA VENTANA

Just 17km northwest of Sierra de la Ventana is the peaceful village of Villa Ventana. There's nothing much to do here except wander the dusty streets, which meander through pretty residential neighborhoods full of pine trees, and investigate the ruins of South America's first casino (by guided tour only; see the tourist office). Villa Ventana is also a closer base than Sierra de la Ventana from which to visit Parque Provincial Ernesto Tornquist.

There are several places to stay, though none are budget. **Cabañas La Ponderosa** (☎0291-491-5491; www.laponderosacabanias.com.ar; cnr Cruz del Sur & Hornero; cabañas from AR$320; 📶), diagonally across from the minibus stop, has good-sized, homey and comfortable wood *cabañas* (cabins), some with loft and all with kitchenette. For a splurge, try **Hotel Água Pampas** (☎0291-491-0210; www.aguapampas.com.ar; Las Piedras btwn Hornero & Canario; r from AR$652; ❄@📶🏊), whose spa, tea room and restaurant complement gorgeous rooms built from local stone and recycled wood, right down to the hollow-log bathtubs. Prices drop on weekdays and from April to mid-December.

Transporte Silver minibuses connect Villa Ventana with Sierra de la Ventana (AR$11.50, 25 minutes) three to five times daily depending on the season; *remises* (taxis) cost AR$80. The **tourist office** (☎0291-491-0095; ⏰8am-6pm Mon-Thu, to 7pm Fri-Sun, to 8pm daily Jan & Feb) is located at the town's entrance.

(☎491-5247; cnr San Martín & Iguazú, in remise office; AR$55) and **Norte Bus** (☎0291-15-468-5101; San Martín 155; AR$80); the latter provides door-to-door service.

Ferrobaires (www.ferrobaires.gba.gov.ar) operates twice-weekly train service (Wednesdays and Fridays) from Sierra de la Ventana to Buenos Aires (AR$86 to AR$158) and Bahía Blanca (AR$37 to AR$73); additional trains run from Buenos Aires to Tornquist, 48km away.

Transporte Silver (☎0291-491-5383; Av San Martín 156) runs a thrice-daily door-to-door service (five times daily December to March) from Sierra de la Ventana to Villa Ventana (AR$11.50, 25 minutes) and Parque Provincial Ernesto Tornquist (AR$16, 40 minutes).

Parque Provincial Ernesto Tornquist

This 67-sq-km **park** (☎491-0039; adult/child AR$10/4; ⏰8am-5pm Dec-Mar, 9am-5pm Apr-Nov), 22km from Sierra de la Ventana, draws visitors from throughout the province. There are two entrances. The first is 5km west of Villa Ventana and home to the **Centro de Visitantes**, which has a small display on local ecology. The main hike here is **Cerro Bahía Blanca** (two hours rountrip), offering great views. There are also **Cuevas con Pinturas Repustres** (cave paintings), but you can only visit these with a guided tour, available from various agencies around Sierra de la Ventana.

The park's highlight, however, is at its other entrance, 3km further west. The five-hour (round-trip) hike to 1150m **Cerro de la Ventana** leads to a window-shaped rock formation near its peak. The climb offers dramatic views of surrounding hills and the distant pampas. Register with rangers before 11am at the trailhead, and take plenty of water and sun protection.

Less demanding destinations accessible from the Cerro de la Ventana trailhead include **Piletones** (2½ hours round-trip) and **Garganta Olvidada** (one hour round-trip). To visit the gorge and waterfall pool at **Garganta del Diablo** (six hours round-trip), you must go with a tour company.

Transportes Silver minibuses head to the park three to five times daily from Sierra de la Ventana (AR$16, 40 minutes) and Villa Ventana (AR$11, 15 minutes). For better timing to catch the park opening, arrange for a *remise* (taxi) to take you to the park from Sierra de la Ventana (around AR$140).

Santa Rosa

☎02954 / POP 103,000

About 600km from Buenos Aires – and a long way from pretty much anywhere else – Santa Rosa is unlikely to be of interest unless you find yourself traveling overland, in which case it's a convenient stopping point and transport hub. It's a pleasant enough place, however, with a small-town feel, friendly people and busy plaza area.

Sights & Activities

Laguna Don Tomás, 1km west of the city center, is the place for locals to sail, swim, play sports or just stroll.

Museo Provincial de Historia Natural MUSEUM
(422693; Quintana 116; 8am-noon & 2-5:30pm Mon-Fri, 6-9pm Sun) FREE This museum has Spanish-language displays about pampas ecosystems, a large taxidermy collection of local birds and mammals, and a few live snakes and dinosaur fossils.

Sleeping & Eating

Residencial Atuel HOTEL $
(422597; www.atuel.aehglp.org.ar; Luro 356; s/d AR$195/330;) Just steps from the bus terminal, this friendly place has worn but tidy rooms with cable TV. It's certainly good enough for one night.

Hotel Calfucurá HOTEL $$
(433303; www.hotelcalfucura.com; Av San Martín 695; s/d from AR$385/486;) Santa Rosa's best hotel, with a modern atmosphere, handy location near the bus terminal and very comfortable carpeted rooms. In summer, worth it for the pool.

Las Viñas Bar & Restó ARGENTINE $$
(385385; Av San Martín 142; mains AR$48-120; 8:30am-2am) This stylish eatery half a block from the main square draws a cosmopolitan local crowd with its nicely presented pasta, pizzas and meat dishes. The daily special (main course, drink and dessert) is good value at AR$75.

Information

You'll find several ATMs in the city center.

Post office (cnr Lagos & Rivadavia)

Provincial tourist office (424404; www.turismolapampa.gov.ar; cnr Luro & San Martín; 7am-9pm Mon-Fri, 9am-1pm & 4-9pm Sat & Sun) Across from the bus terminal; longer hours in January and February.

Getting There & Away

Aerolíneas (427588; Pico 267) flies to Buenos Aires. The airport is 3km from downtown. A taxi between the airport and the center costs approximately AR$30.

The **bus terminal** (Luro 365) is seven blocks east of the plaza. A convenient alternative for travelers to Bahía Blanca is the door-to-door afternoon minibus service (AR$190) offered by **Vivian Tours** (421200; www.viviantours.com.ar; cnr Luro & Rosas), three blocks south of the terminal.

For car rentals try **Sixt** (414600; www.sixt.com.ar; Lisandro de la Torre 96), with downtown and airport locations and good online rates.

BUSES FROM SANTA ROSA

DESTINATION	COST (AR$)	DURATION (HR)
Bahía Blanca	190	5
Bariloche	513-575	12
Buenos Aires	327-432	8
Mendoza	435-515	12
Neuquén	291-342	8
Puerto Madryn	360-419	10

Reserva Provincial Parque Luro

02954

Home to a mix of introduced and native species, as well as over 150 species of bird, this 76-sq-km **reserve** (499000; www.parqueluro.gov.ar; admission AR$4; 9am-7pm) is a peaceful place to spend time away from the city. Avoid Sundays if you don't like crowds, however, and bring water and sun protection in the baking summer.

At the turn of the 20th century a wealthy local, Doctor Pedro Luro, created Argentina's first hunting preserve here, importing exotic game species such as red deer and European boar. He also built an enormous French-style mansion to accommodate his European guests. As sport hunting fell out of vogue and the European aristocracy suffered the upheavals of WWI and the Great Depression, Luro went broke. The reserve was sold, then neglected, its animals escaping through the fence or falling victim to poachers.

Since its acquisition by the province in 1965 Parque Luro has served as a refuge for native species such as puma and wild fox, along with exotic migratory birds including flamingos. One of the park's biggest draws, however, is during the fall mating season of the red deer. In March and April the males bellow loudly (called 'la Brama') to attract female harems, while scuffling among themselves. There are **guided visits**

(AR$100; ⏰7-9pm Mar & Apr) to witness this spectacle.

Hourly tours of the **Castillo** (per person AR$8), Luro's mansion, offer insight into the luxurious eccentricities that Argentine landowners could indulge. As the story goes, Luro was only able to obtain the gorgeous walnut fireplace by purchasing an entire Parisian restaurant. Besides the museum, there's a **Sala de Carruajes** – a collection of turn-of-the-century carriages.

The park's sights are all located around a 6km ring road; reach the **Centro de Interpretación** by following the road 2.2km from the entrance. The basic **restaurant** and **campsites** (☎499000; per adult/child AR$50/30) are 500m beyond that (take food, though there's a small store). And 300m further up the road are nice **cabañas** (☎499000; 2-/3-/4-/5-person cabaña AR$280/330/380/420) that sleep up to five. A few short nature walks veer off the ring road.

Parque Luro is 35km south of Santa Rosa. From the bus terminal, catch the **Dumascat** (☎437090; www.dumascat.com.ar) bus bound for General Acha and ask to be dropped off at the park entrance (AR$10, 30 minutes, four daily), then find out when a bus returns to Santa Rosa. Alternatively, rent a car in Santa Rosa.

Parque Nacional Lihué Calel

☎02952

In the local indigenous language of Pehuenche, Lihué Calel means Sierra de la Vida (Range of Life), and describes a series of small, isolated mountain ranges and valleys that create unique microclimates in a nearly featureless pampean landscape.

This desertlike **park** (☎436595; www.lihuecalel.com.ar; admission free; ⏰8am-7pm) is a haven for native cats such as puma and yagouaroundi. You can spot armadillo, guanaco, mara (Patagonian hare) and vizcacha, while birdlife includes the rhealike ñandú and many birds of prey such as the carancho (crested caracara).

Lihué Calel receives only about 400mm of rainfall per year, but sudden storms can create brief waterfalls over granite boulders near the visitor center. Even when the sky is cloudless, the subterranean streams in the valleys nourish the *monte* (a scrub forest with a surprising variety of plant species). Within the park's 10 sq km exist 345 plant species, nearly half the total found in the entire province.

The most rewarding hike in the area is the hour-long climb to the 589m peak **Cerro de la Sociedad Científica Argentina**; watch for flowering cacti such as *Trichocereus candicans* between boulders. From the summit there are outstanding views of the entire sierra and surrounding marshes and salt lakes.

About 10km by car from the visitor center is the **Casona**, the ruins of the old house of former Estancia Santa María. Another 2km further along, the road peters out at the parking lot for the **Valle de las Pinturas**, where a 600m trail leads down a rock-strewn valley to some petroglyphs. These same two attractions are accessible to walkers via a 9km footpath from the visitor center.

More information is available at the **visitor center**, where there's a small museum. Spring is the best time to visit; flowers bloom and temperatures aren't too hot.

Sleeping

Near the visitor center is a comfortable and free campground with shade trees, firepits (bring wood), picnic tables, flush toilets and showers. Stock up on food before arriving; the nearest decent supplies are at the town of Puelches, 32km south.

Parador de la Sierra MOTEL $
(☎436101; r from AR$120) The closest lodging is this rustic motel on the highway 1km south of the park entrance (or 1.5km from park headquarters via a trail), with a handful of OK rooms and a restaurant.

Getting There & Away

Parque Nacional Lihué Calel is 228km southwest of Santa Rosa, and there are no direct buses to the park. Most southbound buses (ie to Neuquén or Bariloche) can drop you off on the highway near the entrance, or snag the daily minibus that heads to Puelches (AR$100, three hours). Check with the provincial tourist office for details.

Driving (rent a car in Santa Rosa) is the best way to visit the park.

ATLANTIC COAST

Argentines can justly claim to have Latin America's highest peak (Cerro Aconcagua), its widest avenue (Buenos Aires' 9 de Julio) and perhaps its prettiest capital, but its beaches aren't tropical paradises strewn with palm trees. There's no white sand here, the winds can be fierce and the water is cloudy rather than turquoise. Despite all this, Argentina's beaches are hardly unpleasant places in summer, and each January and February they reliably attract tens of thousands of well-heeled *porteños* escaping the capital's unrelenting heat. In fact, so many people flock to the shore that at times you might have a hard time finding a free spot to spread your towel.

So, if you don't mind the lively summer crowds, the Atlantic Coast offers a wonderful escape. And if you want to avoid the summer crowds, simply visit in the shoulder months of December and March, when the weather is still warm enough to enjoy the beaches and their activities. In the dead of winter, however, coastal towns here take on an abandoned feel and the foul weather can become downright depressing. Mar del Plata is an exception – the coast's largest city offers things for visitors to do all year round.

Accommodation prices vary widely along the coast, depending on the season. They rise sharply from mid-December through February, when reservations are crucial (and a few places require minimum stays). Prices then start declining in March but rise again during Easter, after which most places close down until November. At the places that do stay open, bargains can be found during these cooler months.

Unless otherwise specified, prices and opening hours listed here are for the January-to-February high season. In other months opening hours (especially at tourist offices and restaurants) are much shorter.

San Clemente del Tuyú

☎ 02252 / POP 12,000

With absolutely none of the glamour or glitz of the resorts down the coast, family-oriented San Clemente is a favorite for low-key beachgoers. There are reasonably priced accommodations near the waterfront, including **Brisas Marinas** (☎ 522219; www.brisas-marinas.com.ar; Calle 13, No 50; r AR$350-390;) and **Hotel 5 Avenue** (☎ 521035; Calle 5, No 1561; s/d AR$230/300;), and plenty of restaurants on the main drag, Calle 1. The **tourist information office** (☎ 42-3249; turismocentrosc@lacosta.gob.ar; Av Costanera btwn Calles 2 & 63; ⏲ 8am-midnight Jan & Feb, 9am-8pm Mar-Dec) is across from the beach.

A few kilometers north of San Clemente del Tuyú are several protected areas, including **Reserva Natural Municipal Punta Rasa** (whose beach is popular with kiteboarders) and **Parque Nacional Campos del Tuyú** (home of the rare pampas deer).

For tamer wildlife there's **Mundo Marino** (www.mundomarino.com.ar; adult/child under 11 AR$189/126; ⏲ 10am-8pm Jan & Feb, 10am-6pm Mar-Dec, weekends only Apr-Nov), South America's largest marine park. Another attraction is the popular recreation center **Termas Marinas** (www.termasmarinas.com.ar; adult/child under 11 AR$115/83; ⏲ 10am-8pm Jan & Feb, 10am-6pm Mar-Dec), featuring mineral-rich thermal baths.

From San Clemente's **bus terminal** (cnr Avs Naval & Talas del Tuyú), about 25 blocks from the town center, frequent buses run to Buenos Aires (AR$185 to AR$205, 4½ hours) and Pinamar (AR$46, 2½ hours).

Pinamar

☎ 02254 / POP 25,000

Located about 120km northeast of Mar del Plata, Pinamar's warm waters make a very popular destination for middle-class *porteños*. It's a busy place in summer. For a bit more tranquillity, head to the southern and more residential neighborhoods of Ostende and Valeria. Even further south is woodsy Cariló, Argentina's most exclusive resort and home to expensive houses, fashionable restaurants and sandy side roads.

Pinamar was founded and designed in 1944 by architect Jorge Bunge, who figured out how to stabilize the shifting dunes by planting pines, acacias and pampas grass. It was once the refuge for the country's upper echelons, but is now somewhat less exclusive and more laid-back.

Activities

The main activity in Pinamar is simply relaxing and socializing on the beach, which stretches all the way from north of the town down to Cariló. But the area also offers a wealth of outdoor activities, from windsurfing and waterskiing to horseback riding and fishing. You can also ride bicycles in the wooded areas near the golf course, or through the leafy streets of nearby Cariló.

For bike rentals, try **Leo** (☎ 48-8855; Av Bunge 1111; per hr/day AR$30/80; ⏲ 9am-9pm), on the main street near the tourist office. If you want to learn how to kiteboard, go to Sport Beach, the last *balneario* (bathing area) located about 5km north of Av Bunge. There are many more options for activities – ask at the tourist office.

Festivals & Events

Pinamar's film festival, **Pantalla Pinamar** (www.pantallapinamar.com), takes place in March and there are concerts and parties on the beach around New Year.

Sleeping

Reservations are a must in January, when some places have a one-week minimum stay. Best options for the budget-minded are near the southern beaches of Ostende and Valeria, though you'll also find some cheaper hotels and *hospedajes* (family homes) along Calle del Cangrejo, north of the tourist office.

Hostel Pinamar HOSTEL $
(☎482908; www.hostelpinamar.com; cnr Mitre & Nuestras Malvinas, Ostende; dm AR$149-209; ⊙late Nov-Easter; Wi-Fi) In Ostende, about 10 blocks south of Pinamar's center, this hostel with six- to sixteen-bed dorms and a well-equipped kitchen is perfectly situated just steps from the beach. The newly remodeled building – which is actually a tiny remnant of Pinamar's historic Atlantic Palace Hotel – dates to 1928. Look for it behind Hotel Soleado.

Camping Saint Tropez CAMPGROUND $
(☎482498; www.sainttropezpinamar.com.ar; Quintana 178, Ostende; 2-person camp site with tent AR$120-200; ⊙Dec-Mar) Due to its location near the beach at Ostende, this small camping site fills up in summer. Apartments are also available (from AR$400). Take the 'Montemar' bus from the bus station (AR$4).

Cabañas Pinaforet CABAÑAS $$
(☎409277; www.pinaforet.com.ar; cnr Apolo & Jason; 4-person cabaña per night Mar-Nov AR$400, Dec AR$500-700, per week Jan & Feb AR$7000; air-con, Wi-Fi) This sweet cluster of five spacious log cabins set among piney grounds is only a few paces from the bus terminal and within a few minutes' walk of the town center and beach. Each sleeps up to four people, making this a great budget option in low season. In high season, only weekly rentals are available.

Hotel Mojomar HOTEL $$
(☎407300; www.hotelmojomar.com.ar; Burriquetas 247; d AR$658-1075, ste AR$810-1190; air-con, Wi-Fi) This upscale but not luxurious hotel is nicely located three blocks off Av Bunge, and only a block from the beach. It has a beautiful lobby and small, comfortable rooms; those with partial sea view cost about 10% extra. A pair of more expensive suites come with air-con, plasma TV and whirlpool tubs.

La Vieja Hostería BOUTIQUE HOTEL $$$
(☎482804; www.laviejahosteria.com.ar; Del Tuyú 169; r AR$700-1450) In a beautifully remodeled 1940s house, Pinamar's nicest boutique hotel has elegantly appointed rooms, inviting common areas (including a poolside deck and a patio with massage tents) and a perfect location, just south of the main street and two blocks in from the beach.

Eating

The beach is lined with restaurants that serve beach grub such as fried calamari and burgers.

★**Los Troncos** ARGENTINE $$
(☎490717; cnr Eneas & Lenguado; mains AR$45-130; ⊙noon-3pm & 8pm-midnight Thu-Tue) In business for four decades, this beloved backstreet eatery is often packed with locals even in low season. Vintage black-clad waiters and lime green decor lend it a convivial old-school ambiance, while the menu includes everything from roast meats to seafood stews to homemade pastas, all done to perfection.

Jalisco MEXICAN $$
(www.jalisco.com.ar; Bunge 456; mains around AR$100; ⊙1-3:30pm & 7:30pm-1:30am) At this popular Tex-Mex eatery on Pinamar's main street, the fun begins at the entryway, adorned with cactus-shaped lamps and *papel picado* (colorful Mexican-style paper cutouts). Menu choices range from fajitas and quesadillas to pasta and seafood dishes. There's a second location in Cariló.

Acqua & Farina PIZZERIA $$
(☎570278; cnr Cerezo & Boyero, Cariló; mains AR$49-88; ⊙8pm-2am daily Dec-Mar, 8pm-11:30pm Fri-Sat & noon-3:30pm Sat-Sun Apr-Nov) Head to Cariló for the best thin-crust pizza around, as well as fresh salads and homemade pastas. Located in Cariló plaza, the last stop for the local Montemar bus.

Cantina Tulumei SEAFOOD $$
(Bunge 64; mains AR$50-140; ⏲ noon-4pm & 8pm-1am) Hit the outdoor deck at this main-street eatery, one block in from the waterfront, for reasonably priced, quality seafood. Fish is prepared in at least a dozen different sauces, or go for appetizers such as the shrimp omelet and octopus salad. Homemade pastas also available.

Tante INTERNATIONAL $$
(www.tante.com.ar; De las Artes 35; mains AR$47-134, afternoon teas AR$31-77; ⏲ noon-11:30pm) Three blocks inland from the beach, just off Av Bunge, this classy restaurant, bar and tearoom was once the home of a well-known 1950s soprano. Nowadays it serves up German, French and alpine specialties such as fondue, crepes, goulash, wurst and sauerkraut. Afternoon teas featuring stollen, strudel and other homemade pastries are also tempting. There's a second location in Cariló.

Information

Municipal tourist office (☎491680; turismo@pinamar.gov.ar; cnr Av Bunge & Shaw; ⏲ 8am-8pm Mon-Fri, 10am-8pm Sat, 10am-5pm Sun)

Post office (cnr Jasón & Eneas)

Getting There & Away

Pinamar's **bus terminal** (☎403500; Jason 2250) is about eight blocks north of the town center, just off Av Bunge. Destinations include Buenos Aires (AR$225, five to six hours), Mar del Plata (AR$69, 2½ hours) and San Clemente del Tuyú (AR$46, 2½ hours). There are frequent buses to nearby Villa Gesell (AR$20, 30 to 45 minutes).

For the southern beaches of Ostende (AR$4), Valeria (AR$5) and Cariló (AR$6), catch a Montemar local bus just outside the long-distance terminal or at stops along Av Bunge.

By the time you read this, trains may or may not be running from Buenos Aires Constitución train station to Pinamar's Estación Divisadero, about 2km north of town.

Villa Gesell

☎02255 / POP 30,000

Smaller and less flashy than its neighbors Pinamar and Mar del Plata, laid-back Villa Gesell is still a hit with the younger crowd. Uniquely for the coastal towns, it offers a wood-planked beach boardwalk, making walks along the sands much easier. It's also known for summer choral performances and rock and folk concerts, and there are plenty of outdoor activities to enjoy. The town is compact, with most services located on its main drag, Av 3, three blocks from the beach.

In the 1930s merchant, inventor and nature lover Carlos Gesell designed this resort of zigzag streets, planting acacias, poplars, oaks and pines to stabilize the shifting dunes. He envisioned a town that merged with the forest he had created, but it wasn't long before high-rise vacation shares began their malignant growth and the trees started to disappear.

Sights & Activities

For a totally different atmosphere visit **Mar de las Pampas**, an exclusive woodsy neighborhood that's a 15-minute bus ride south from Villa Gesell's bus terminal. It has sandy streets, expensive lodging (rented only by the week in summer) and upscale services – all dropped into a pine forest. The beach here is less crowded, too. Beyond Mar de las Pampas is **Mar Azul**, another (less exclusive) beach town.

Feria Artesanal MARKET
(crafts fair; Av 3 btwn Paseos 112 & 113) There's a nightly handicrafts fair from mid-December to mid-March. Expect lots of handmade jewelry, carved wood, paintings and souvenirs. The rest of the year it's a weekend-only event.

Muelle de Pesca FISHING
(Playa & Paseo 129) Gesell's 15m fishing pier offers year-round fishing for mackerel, rays, shark and other marine species.

Windy SURFING
(☎462616; www.windyplayabar.com.ar; cnr Paseo 104 & beach) You can rent surf gear from Windy, down on the beachfront.

Casa Macca BICYCLE RENTAL
(☎468013; Av Buenos Aires; per hr/day AR$25/70) For bicycle rentals try Casa Macca. It's located between Paseo 101 & Av 5.

Aventura Faro Querandí ADVENTURE SPORTS
(☎468989; cnr Av 3 & Paseo 132; tours AR$150) Aventura Faro Querandí runs four-hour tours in 4WD jeeps to a local lighthouse – a combination of hair-raising dune-bashing and excellent photo opportunities.

Sleeping

Campgrounds charge from AR$80 upwards per person per night. Most close at the end of March, but two at the southern end of town on Av 3 (at the beach) are open all year: **Autocamping Casablanca** (☎470771; www.autocampingcasablanca.com; Av 3; camp site per person AR$76-96; 📶) and **Camping Monte Bubi** (☎470732; www.montebubi.com.ar; cnr Av 3 & Paseo 168; camp site per person AR$86-144; 📶). Both have lots of services and *cabaña*-style accommodations. The Mar Azul bus from the terminal goes right by.

★ **La Deseada Hostel** HOSTEL $
(☎473276; www.ladeseadahostel.com.ar; cnr Av 6 & Paseo 119; dm AR$260; @📶) Teeming with young Argentines in January but tranquil off-season, this ultrahomey hostel sits atop a sloping evergreen-fringed lawn in a residential area between the bus terminal and the center, six blocks from the beach. Eight-bed dorms, plus private rooms in low season, are complemented by spacious, comfy common areas and a nice guest kitchen. Breakfast is served till 1pm.

Residencial Viya HOMESTAY $$
(☎462757; www.gesell.com.ar/viya; Av 5, No 582, btwn Paseos 105 & 106; d AR$440; 📶) A labor of love for world-traveler owners Oscar and Nilda Rodriguez, this old-school, family-run *residencial* (budget hotel) features simple rooms surounding a well-tended garden on a quiet residential street. Family dogs Pedro and Carmela offer the perfect cure for anyone missing pets back home. Rates are slashed in half during the off-season.

Hotel Tamanacos HOTEL $$
(☎468753; www.tamanacos.com.ar; cnr Paseo 103bis & Av 1; r AR$500-700; ❄📶🏊) One block from the beach, this cute hotel has some nice common areas, particularly the front deck. The 21 small, homey rooms have tiny baths, but with beach umbrellas provided you won't be in them most of the time. Guests enjoy access to the sauna, gym and tiny heated pool downstairs. Rooms facing away from the beach have air-con.

Belle Maison B&B $$
(☎462335; www.bellemaison.com.ar; Calle 4, btwn Paseos 106 & 107; r AR$400-700; @📶) At this large house in a residential neighborhood near the center, five rooms are available – the best one sits apart from the other four, which are clustered together along a shared hallway. Common spaces include a small garden and a pleasant bar area.

Eating & Drinking

Windy Playa Bar ARGENTINE $
(☎460430; www.windyplayabar.com; cnr Paseo 104 & beach; sandwiches AR$32-72; ⏲8am-3am) The beers are overpriced, but the sandwiches are good and the views superb from this

OFF THE BEATEN TRACK

MAR CHIQUITA

A humble and windy little gem, the beachside village of Mar Chiquita is home to **Albúfera Mar Chiquita**, a 35km-long lagoon with huge biodiversity – over 220 bird and 55 fish species live within its waters. There's good fishing in the area, and the beach is popular with windsurfers and kiteboarders – or just for hanging out for a bit.

Half a block in from the lagoon, **Hostería Bariloche** (☎0223-469-1254; www.hosteriabariloche.com.ar; cnr Beltran & Echeverría; r per person AR$170; @) is a friendly, family-run place with 10 rooms and apartments. It also rents wind-sports equipment and gives lessons when conditions in the lagoon permit. Campers can head to **Camping Santa Rosa** (☎0223-469-1300; cnr Rivera del Sol & playa; 4-person campsites AR$150).

The **visitor center** (☎0223-469-1288; saladeinterpretacion@hotmail.com; cnr Belgrano & Rivera del Sol; ⏲9am-8pm Dec-Easter, 9am-4pm Mon-Fri & 10am-6pm Sat & Sun rest of year) is beside the lagoon, a few blocks inland from the beach. Between December and March it organizes four-hour tours around the lagoon (per person AR$80, reserve ahead, minimum group size 10). Bring money – the closest ATM is 4km away in Mar de Cabo.

Mar Chiquita is 34km north of Mar del Plata. **Rápido del Sud** (☎0223-494-2507; www.el-rapido.com.ar) runs frequent buses that can drop you at the highway roundabout 2.5km outside Mar Chiquita (AR$21, 45 minutes). For transport into town your best bet is local bus 221 from Mar del Plata (AR$7.50, 1½ hours, every two hours in summer, every four hours rest of year); it goes all the way to the beach and the lagoon's edge.

casual beachside bar at the foot of Paseo 104. It's a great place for a mid-afternoon break from the sun and sand.

Rancho Hambre EMPANADAS **$**
(www.ranchohambre.com; Av 3, No 871; empanadas AR$9; ⏲noon-3pm & 7:30pm-late, closed Sun lunch & all day Wed) This main-street hotspot features 30 varieties of empanadas, from the humble (minced beef) to the more elaborate (arugula, parmesan and walnuts, or bacon with mozzarella and muscat-infused prunes).

★ **El Viejo Hobbit** PUB **$$**
(☎465851; www.gesell.com.ar/hobbit; Av 8 btwn Paseos 11 & 12; snacks AR$45-80, fondue AR$125-255; ⏲6pm-late Fri & Sat Apr-Nov, daily Dec-Mar) An obligatory stop for beer lovers and Tolkien fans, this whimsical backstreet bar plunges you straight into Hobbit land from the minute you pass through its beautiful round front door. Several beers brewed on-site complement a menu focused on fondue. There's a cozy 2nd floor, plus a backyard with an artificial waterfall and a miniature Hobbit house for kids to play in.

Las Margaritas ITALIAN **$$**
(☎456377; Av 2, No 484; mains AR$78-110; ⏲8pm-midnight Thu-Sat Mar-Nov, daily Dec-Feb) Charmingly cozy and quiet, this place serves excellent homemade pasta, including the house specialty, *ravioles negros Margarita* (shrimp and squid-ink ravioli). The tiramisu is also good. Reserve in summer.

La Delfina PARRILLA **$$**
(cnr Paseo 104 & Av 2; mains AR$54-99; ⏲noon-3pm & 8pm-midnight) A huge menu means there's something for everyone at this popular *parrilla*, from the 'El Supremo' *bife de chorizo* (steak with two eggs and bacon) to a low-calorie section and everything in between.

Sutton 212 INTERNATIONAL **$$**
(☎460674; cnr Paseo 105 & Av 2; mains AR$60-90; ⏲5pm-dawn) This lively restaurant with ample outdoor deck seating serves dishes ranging from Mediterranean to Asian fusion, along with gourmet crepes, sushi and sandwiches. DJs and live music keep things buzzing later in the evening, when the place becomes a happening bar.

ℹ Information

Post office (cnr Av 3 & Paseo 108)
Tourist office (☎478042; turismocentro@villagesell.gov.ar; Paseo 107 btwn Avs 2 & 3; ⏲8am-8pm, to midnight Jan & Feb) Conveniently located in the center. There's another branch at the **bus terminal** (cnr Av 3 & Paseo 140; ⏲5am-midnight mid-Dec–Easter, 8am-8pm rest of year).

ℹ Getting There & Away

The **bus terminal** (cnr Av 3 & Paseo 140) is 30 blocks south of the town center. Destinations include Buenos Aires (AR$226 to AR$252, 5¼ hours) and Mar del Plata (AR$55, two hours). You can buy bus tickets in the town center at **Central de Pasajes** (☎472480; cnr Av 3 & Paseo 107), which saves you a trip to the bus terminal.

For Pinamar, take El Rápido's direct bus (AR$20, 30 minutes) or Montemar's hourly local service (AR$14.50, 45 minutes) via Cariló, Valeria and Ostende.

Local buses into town (AR$4, 15 minutes) leave every 20 minutes from a shelter just across Av 3 from the long-distance terminal.

Mar del Plata

☎0223 / POP 593,000

Four hundred kilometers from Buenos Aires lies Mar del Plata ('Mardel'), the premier Argentine beach destination for *porteños*. If you end up here on a summer weekend, you'll be guaranteed to say 'Wow, this beach is crowded.' There might be a couple of places where you could get in a few swimming strokes without taking somebody's eye out, but mostly it's shoulder-to-shoulder sun-frazzled bodies. After spending a few days on its comically packed sands, watching street performers on the beachside Plaza Colón or exploring the wonders of the port, however, you might get the sense of adoration that the country feels for this place.

During the week, and especially outside of summer, the crowds disperse, hotel prices drop and the place takes on a more relaxed feel. Out-of-season visitors will find that Mardel is a large city with plenty of attractions other than its beach.

Rivadavia becomes a pedestrian street only during the summer months; San Martín is always pedestrian.

History

Europeans were slow to occupy this stretch of the coast, so Mardel was a late bloomer. Not until 1747 did Jesuit missionaries try to evangelize the southern pampas' indigenous people; the only reminder of their

Mar del Plata

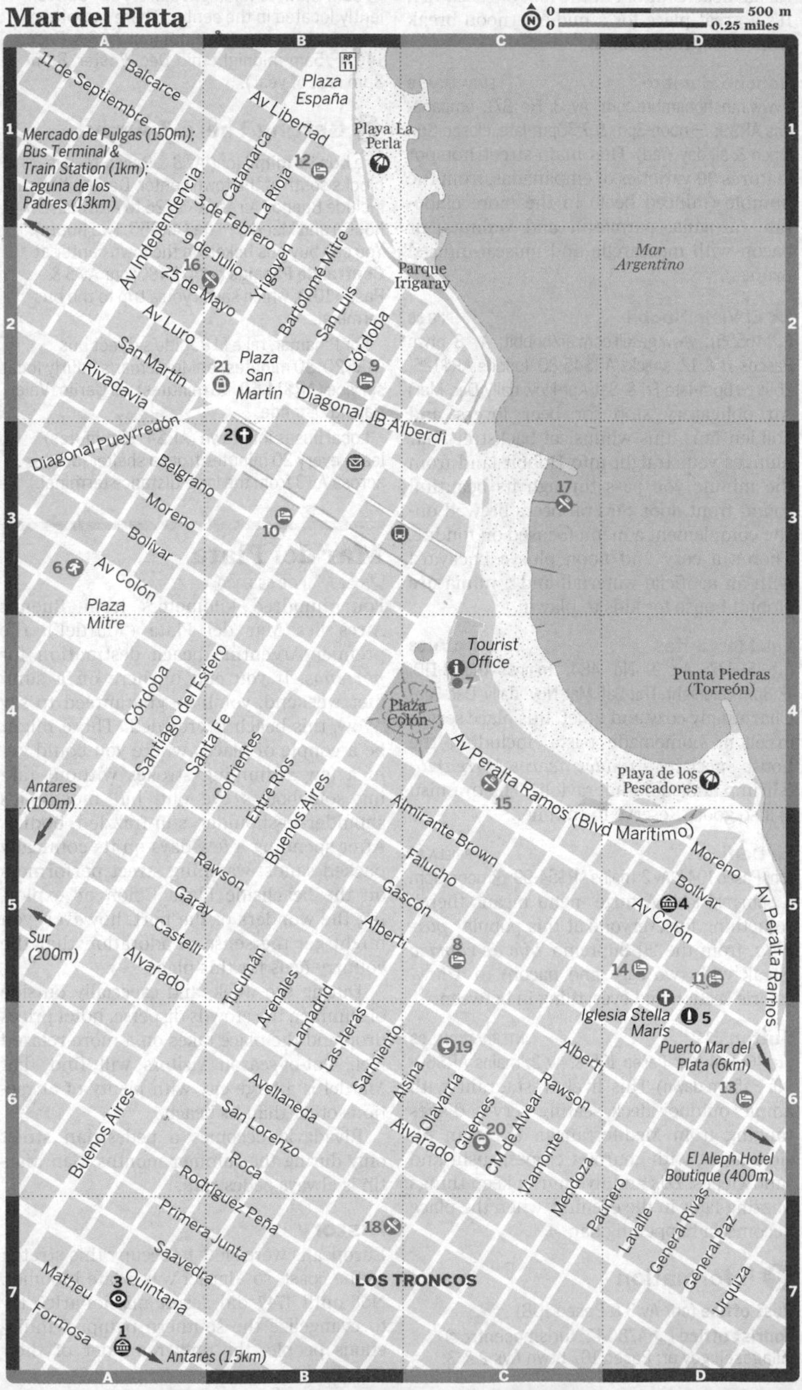

Mar del Plata

Sights

1 Archivo Museo Histórico Municipal Roberto T Barili A7
2 Catedral de los Santos Pedro y Cecilia B3
3 Centro Cultural Villa Victoria A7
4 Museo Municipal de Arte Juan Carlos Castagnino D5
5 Torre Tanque D6

Activities, Courses & Tours

6 Bicicletería Madrid A3
7 Paseos Para Gente Inquieta C4

Sleeping

8 Che Lagarto Hostel C5
9 City Hotel B2
10 Etoile B3
11 Hotel Sirenuse D5
12 La Pergola Hostel B1
13 Playa Varese Inn D6
14 Villa Nuccia D5

Eating

15 Alito C4
16 Montecatini B2
17 Pescadores C3
18 Tisiano B7

Drinking & Nightlife

19 Almacén Estación Central C6
20 La Bodeguita del Medio C6

Shopping

21 Diagonal de los Artesanos B2

efforts is a chapel replica near Laguna de los Padres.

More than a century later Portuguese investors established El Puerto de Laguna de los Padres. Beset by economic problems in the 1860s, the investors sold out to Patricio Peralta Ramos, who founded Mar del Plata proper in 1874. Peralta Ramos helped develop the area as a commercial and industrial center, and later as a beach resort. By the turn of the last century many wealthy *porteño* families owned summer houses, some of which still grace Barrio Los Troncos.

Since the 1960s the so-called Pearl of the Atlantic has lost some of its exclusivity, with the Argentine elite seeking refuge in resorts such as nearby Pinamar or Punta del Este (Uruguay). Still, Mar del Plata remains the most thriving of all of Argentina's beach towns.

Sights

Puerto Mar del Plata — PORT

Mar del Plata is one of Argentina's most important fishing locations and seafood-processing centers, and its port area, 8km south of the city center, is worth a visit. At the entrance to the port, just off Av de los Trabajadores (formerly Av Martínez de Hoz), you'll see a large cluster of seafood restaurants surrounding a parking lot. This is the **Centro Comercial del Puerto**, a good place to grab a bite to eat; just pick a place that looks busy.

You can also take your bus directly to the port's scenic and slightly touristy wharf, called the **Banquina de Pescadores**, which lies beyond the restaurant cluster – this saves you a 10-minute walk through an ugly industrial area. This picturesque wharf is home to dozens of orange fishing boats and the fisherfolk who follow their routine here. You might see a sea lion's head poking out of the water; these animals have established a large colony – all male – nearby on the *escollera sur* (southern jetty).

To get to this jetty, tromp south of the wharf about a block or so (there is no real path) and go past the port's security entrance, then turn left onto the road. This is another ugly industrial area, but eventually becomes the more pleasant jetty that leads 2km out to sea. On the way you'll pass a graveyard of **ruined ships**, half-sunken and rusting in the sun, and are likely see the colony of male sea lions lazing on a beach or behind a section of chain-link fence. And at the tip of the windy *escollera sur* you'll find a restaurant, which offers nourishment, along with panoramic views of the city.

Local bus 511 goes all the way to the wharf from downtown; you'll need a magnetic card to board. Bus 221 only reaches the seafood restaurants at the port's entrance. A taxi from downtown costs around AR$50.

Museo Municipal de Arte Juan Carlos Castagnino — MUSEUM

(Av Colón 1189; admission AR$10, Wed free; 1-7pm Mon & Wed-Fri, 3-8pm Sat & Sun) Built in 1909 as the summer residence of a prominent Argentine family, the turreted Villa Ortiz Basualdo now houses this fine-arts museum; its interior exhibits paintings, photographs and sculptures by Argentine artists.

Archivo Museo Histórico Municipal Roberto T Barili MUSEUM
(Lamadrid 3870; admission AR$10; ⌚8am-5pm Mon-Fri, 2-6pm Sat & Sun) In the Villa Emilio Mitre (1930), a former summer residence of the Argentine oligarchy, this museum houses a superb collection of late-19th-century photographs, along with other exhibits recalling Mar del Plata's colorful past.

Centro Cultural Villa Victoria CULTURAL CENTER
(☎492-0569; Matheu 1851; admission AR$10; ⌚10am-1pm & 5-9pm Jan & Feb, 1-7pm Wed-Mon Mar-Dec) Victoria Ocampo, founder of the literary journal *Sur*, hosted literary salons with prominent intellectuals from around the world at this, her summer chalet. It's now a cultural center that features changing art and cultural exhibitions.

Catedral de los Santos Pedro y Cecilia CHURCH
(www.catedralmardelplata.org.ar; ⌚8am-8pm) Facing the leafy Plaza San Martín, this neo-Gothic building features gorgeous stained glass, an impressive central chandelier from France, English tiled floors and occasional choral concerts.

Torre Tanque TOWER
(☎451-4681; Falucho 995; ⌚8am-4:45pm Mon-Fri) FREE This interesting medieval-style water storage tower, atop Stella Maris hill, was finished in 1943 and is still functioning. It offers awesome views over Mar del Plata and further out to sea.

Aquarium Mar del Plata AQUARIUM
(☎467-0700; www.mdpaquarium.com.ar; Av Martínez de Hoz 5600; adult/3-10yr AR$139/99; ⌚10am-6pm Fri-Sun Apr-Nov, daily Dec-Mar) Located 14km south of the center, near the lighthouse, is Mar del Plata's aquarium. Animals on display include penguins, flamingos, crocodiles and lots of fish. There are sea-lion, dolphin and waterskiing shows, along with a cinema. You can also swim with sharks (among other watery creatures) and sit on the beach. Get here on bus 221 or 511D.

Laguna de los Padres LAKE
A popular weekend destination for *marplatenses* (residents of Mar del Plata), this lake (13km from Mardel along RN226) offers a bucolic setting and countless activities, including bird-watching, fishing, water sports, biking, hiking and rock climbing. You can camp near the lake, and there are good places to eat in the pleasant town of Sierra de los Padres, 4km further west. Bus 717 (from Av Luro in Mardel) goes to Sierra de los Padres, passing by the lake's northern shore en route.

The area was first settled in 1746 as a Jesuit Mission aimed at rounding up the nomadic tribes of the area – there's a replica of the original chapel by the lake's shore.

Beaches

Mar del Plata's beaches are mostly safe and swimmable. Downtown fronts onto the most central beach, **Playa Bristol**, with its wharf and restaurant; the boardwalk here, next to the casino area, is always packed with activity. The next beach to the north is **Playa La Perla**, favored by a younger crowd and filled with *balnearios* (bathing resorts, or sections of beach with services such as beach chairs and parasols). To the south of Punta Piedras (Torreón) are **Playa Varese** and **Cabo Corrientes**, a pair of small beaches that are protected by small rocky headlands.

South of these beaches, at the more fashionable end of town, lies Playa Grande, also crowded with *balnearios*. About 11km south of the center, just past the port, you'll find the huge **Punta Mogotes** complex – slightly more relaxed and favored by families, who fill the *balnearios* to overflowing in January. This is also the location of **Playa Waikiki**, a popular spot for surfing.

Beyond the lighthouse is a less urbanized area. Though the beaches here are still filled with yet more *balnearios* in the summer, they're a quieter option. And for the adventurous, there's **Playa Escondida** (www.playaescondida.com.ar), some 25km south of Mardel and possibly Argentina's only legal nude beach. Bus 221 gets you there.

Activities

Mar del Plata and its surrounds offer plenty of opportunity to enjoy outdoor activities and adventure sports.

Biking is a good, green way to get around town. The streets of Los Troncos are relatively calm and pleasant for cycling. Bicycles can be rented from **Bicicletería Madrid** (☎494-1932; Yrigoyen 2249; per hr/day AR$30/120; ⌚9am-1pm & 3-7pm).

Surf is best in March or April. **Kikiwai Surf School** (☎485-0669; www.kikiwaisurfclub.com.ar; Av Martínez de Hoz 4100), run by surf pioneer Daniel Gil, offers surfing classes and rents boards; find it at Waikiki beach (about 11km south of center).

LITERARY LADY OF LA PLATA

She was 'the most beautiful cow in the pampas' according to French novelist Pierre Drieu, and Jorge Luis Borges called her 'the most Argentine of women.' In the 1920s and 1930s Victoria Ocampo gathered writers and intellectuals from around the globe to her home, Villa Victoria, creating a formidable literary and artistic salon.

Ocampo never went to university, but her voracious appetite for knowledge and love of literature led her to become Argentina's leading lady of letters. She founded the literary magazine *Sur*, which introduced writers such as Virginia Woolf and TS Eliot to Argentine readers. She was also an inexhaustible traveler and a pioneering feminist, and was loathed for her lack of convention. A ferocious opponent of Peronism, chiefly because of Perón's interference with intellectual freedom, Ocampo was arrested at Villa Victoria at the age of 63. In jail she entertained her fellow inmates by reading aloud and acting out scenes from novels and films.

If Victoria is remembered as a lively essayist and great patroness of writers, her younger sister, Silvina, was the literary talent, writing both short stories and poetry. Silvina won several literary prizes for her works, and in 1940 married Adolfo Bioy Casares, a famous Argentine writer and friend of Jorge Luis Borges.

As the sea lions attest, Mar del Plata is one of the best spots for fishing in Argentina. The rocky outcrop at **Cabo Corrientes**, just north of Playa Grande, is a good spot to try, as are the two breakwaters – **Escollera Norte** and **Escollera Sur** – at the port. Freshwater fishing is popular at Laguna de los Padres, while **Mako Team** (493-5338; www.makoteam.com.ar) offers ocean fishing excursions.

The rocky cliffs by the sea and the hills of Sierra de los Padres make for excellent climbing and rappelling. **Acción Directa** (474-4520; www.acciondirecta.com.ar; Av Libertad 3902) runs a school – it also offers mountain biking, canoeing and overnight active camping trips.

Horseback riding and skydiving are also possibilities – contact the tourist office for details.

Tours

Crucero Anamora BOAT TOUR
(489-0310; www.cruceroanamora.com.ar) This 30m boat offers harbor tours several times daily in summer (AR$125) and twice daily on weekends in winter from Dársena B at the port.

Paseos Para Gente Inquieta WALKING TOUR
(Blvd Marítimo) In high season the municipal tourist office conducts free organized tours to Mardel's port and museums as well as more unusual sights such as an *alfajor* or textile factory. Reserve ahead at the main tourist office.

Festivals & Events

The city's **International Film Festival** (www.mardelplatafilmfest.com) takes place in November. Launched in 1950, it's South America's most important film festival.

In January Mar del Plata also celebrates the **Fiesta Nacional de los Pescadores** (Fisherman's Festival; www.patronespescadores.com.ar), which features locals cooking up seafood feasts, along with a traditional procession.

Another large celebration is February's **Fiesta Nacional del Mar** (National Sea Festival), which includes the election and coronation of a 'Sea Queen.'

Sleeping

Prices start climbing in November and December, peak in January and February, then drop off in March. Reserve ahead in summer. In the off-season some accommodations close their doors.

Mar del Plata's crowded campgrounds are mostly south of town; the tourist office provides information about their facilities.

La Pergola Hostel HOSTEL $
(493-3695; www.lapergolahostel.com.ar; Yrigoyen 1093; dm AR$110-130, d AR$360; @ wifi) Lovingly managed by Reike practitioners Florencia and Eduardo, this hostel occupies a cool old Tudorlike building dating to 1929. Most of the four- to eight-bed wood-floor dorms and one private room have nifty architectural details, balconies and/or partial sea views. Other perks include a rooftop terrace with

pergola, a guest kitchen, a basement games/dining area and a 300-title video library.

Che Lagarto Hostel HOSTEL $
(451-3704; www.chelagarto.com; Alberti 1565; dm/d/tr AR$150/400/600; @ wi-fi) Opened in 2011, this hostel has it all: friendly staff, central location close to Mardel's best nightlife and shopping, and squeaky-clean private rooms and dorms sleeping a maximum of five people. There's also a guest kitchen and a pleasant downstairs common area with three shared computers.

★**Hotel Sirenuse** HOTEL $$
(451-9580; www.hotelsirenuse.com.ar; Mendoza 2240; d AR$550-650; air-con @ wi-fi) Friendly, family-run and supremely cozy, this place on Stela Maris hill just a few blocks from Playa Varese is one of Mardel's best values. All rooms have a warm and homey feel, with a European touch – not a surprise given that the owners are of Italian descent. Various languages spoken.

City Hotel HOTEL $$
(495-3018; www.cityhotelmardelplata.com; Diagonal JB Alberdi 2561; d AR$660-770, apt AR$1080-1230; wi-fi) This large, worker-owned cooperative hotel has an old-school feel and pleasant back garden. It's worth paying a bit extra for the larger 'superior' rooms with bathtubs; the front ones have balconies. There are also six two-room 'apartments' (no kitchen), perfect for families.

Etoile HOTEL $$
(493-4968; www.hoteletoilemdq.com.ar; Santiago del Estero 1869; d AR$600; wi-fi) Its central location and spacious carpeted rooms (some with long 'entry' space and sofa) make this place good value. Get a quieter room in the back – they're still bright. Buffet breakfast.

Playa Varese Inn HOTEL $$
(451-1813; www.playavareseinn.com.ar; Gascón 715; s AR$320-440, d AR$440-620; @ wi-fi) Fifteen simple, comfortable and good-sized rooms with concrete floors are on offer at this nice little *hostería* (lodging house). It's just 1½ blocks from the beach and has cable TV. Reserve ahead; it's popular.

★**Villa Nuccia** GUESTHOUSE $$$
(451-6593; www.villanuccia.com.ar; Almirante Brown 1134; d AR$850-1075; air-con @ wi-fi pool) Run by affable world travelers José Luis and Paula, this beautiful guesthouse offers nine elegant and spacious rooms, five in a renovated home, plus four with air-con and brand-new bathrooms in a modern annex; all but one come with whirlpool tubs. There's a grassy lawn out back with a swimming pool and Jacuzzi; afternoon tea service is offered.

El Aleph Hotel Boutique BOUTIQUE GUESTHOUSE $$$
(451-4380; www.elalephmdq.com.ar; LN Alem 2542; r AR$900-1400; air-con @ wi-fi pool) Located on a residential street a couple of blocks south of Playa Varese, this upscale place in a converted family home offers eight lovely rooms set around a grassy yard with small pool. Amenities include spacious bathrooms, plasma TVs and frigobars. The feel is exclusive but relaxed, with afternoon tea and homemade cakes. Reservations necessary; no children under 10.

Eating

Mar del Plata's numerous restaurants, pizzerias and snack bars often struggle to keep up with impatient crowds between December and March, and there are always long lines. For fresh seafood head south of town to the port, which has several restaurants cooking up the catch of the day.

Taberna Baska SPANISH $$
(480-0209; 12 de Octubre 3301; mains AR$50-110; noon-3pm Tue-Sun, 8:30pm-midnight Tue-Sat) Just inland from the port is this renowned Basque restaurant, running for over 50 years. Checkered tablecloths and dignified waiters give it an old-school atmosphere that nicely complements terrific traditional dishes such as garlic shrimp, mixed seafood stews, paella, *pulpo* (octopus), *bacalao* (cod) and fish in seven different sauces. For dessert try the delicious *natillas* (egg custard topped with cinnamon sugar).

Sur SEAFOOD $$
(493-6260; Alvarado 2763; mains AR$45-110; 8pm-midnight) Brick walls hung with nautical-themed prints form a cozy backdrop for this seafood place, long popular for its cordial service and fair prices. Specials all revolve around fish and shellfish, including *sorrentinos Sur* (pasta pouches filled with shrimp and salmon) and whole fish cooked in a variety of ways.

Tisiano ITALIAN $$
(486-3473; San Lorenzo 1332; mains AR$80-100; 8:30pm-midnight) Tucked into a back patio off the main street, this locally recommended restaurant serves fine Italian food,

from salmon carpaccio and squash *sorrentinos* (large, round filled pastas) to shrimp linguine and seven kinds of gourmet salad.

La Marina SEAFOOD $$
(12 de Octubre 3147; mains AR$40-110; ⏲noon-3:30pm Thu-Tue & 8pm-midnight Thu-Mon) You won't find seafood any fresher or more affordable than at this down-to-earth place opposite the port. In business since 1957, its specialties range from crispy *rabas* (fried squid rings) to the delicious *cazuela especial La Marina*, a seafood stew jam-packed with fish, shrimp, squid and mussels simmered in white wine, cream and saffron.

Alito ARGENTINE $$
(☎492-1741; www.alitomdp.com.ar; cnr Las Heras & La Costa; mains AR$46-119; ⏲11:45am-4pm & 8pm-midnight) With indoor and outdoor seating across from the waterfront near Plaza Colón, Alito is popular for its central location, wide-ranging menu and well-priced daily specials. For best value, come at lunchtime Monday through Thursday, when AR$85 gets you a complete meal including appetizer, main course, dangerously sweet homemade tiramisu and a glass of champagne or limoncello.

Montecatini ARGENTINE $$
(☎492-4299; www.montecatini.com.ar; cnr La Rioja & 25 de Mayo; mains AR$41-90; ⏲noon-3pm & 8pm-midnight; 👪) For solid, good-value dishes, make like the locals and head to this large, modern and popular restaurant. There's something for everyone – meat, fish, pasta, *milanesas,* stir-fries, sandwiches – and portions are generous. Good for families and large groups; several branches around town.

Pescadores SEAFOOD $$
(☎493-1713; Blvd Marítimo & Av Luro; AR$43-113; ⏲noon-3pm & 8pm-midnight) Located out on the fishing pier, this seafood restaurant offers great water views – especially from its 2nd floor (open in summer only). The menu runs through typical Mardel offerings of meat, pasta and seafood, but you're here for the views.

Viento en Popa SEAFOOD $$$
(☎489-0220; Av de los Trabajadores 257; mains AR$100-150; ⏲12:30-2:30pm & 8:30pm-12:30am) One of the port's most renowned restaurants, Viento en Popa specializes in seafood, though you'll also find beef, chicken and pasta dishes on the menu. Only the freshest ingredients are used for the fried calamari, seafood stew and various sautéed fish plates.

Drinking & Nightlife

At the Playa Grande end of town, the areas along Irigoyen and LN Alem, between Almafuerte and Rodríguez Peña, are popular nightlife magnets.

Antares BREWPUB
(☎492-4455; www.cervezaantares.com; Córdoba 3025; ⏲7pm-late) The eight homebrews on tap at Mar del Plata's only microbrewery include imperial stout, pale ale and barley wine – excellent cures for the Quilmes blues. Food is available and there is live music most weekends.

Almacén Estación Central BAR
(cnr Alsina & Garay; ⏲8pm-late) Reopened under new management in 2013, this trendy corner bar in a spiffed-up century-old building gets packed with revelers every night.

La Bodeguita del Medio BAR
(Castelli 1252; ⏲7pm-late) Named after one of Hemingway's favorite haunts, this atmospheric joint serves two-for-one mojitos between 7pm and 9pm. The Cuban dishes and bar snacks go down well, and there's occasional live music.

Shopping

Calle Güemes is lined with upscale stores.

Diagonal de los Artesanos CRAFT, MARKET
(Plaza San Martín; ⏲6pm-late) Vendors set up their stalls every summer evening on Plaza San Martín to sell everything from *mate* gourds and knives to sweaters and silverwork. Open Friday and Saturday afternoons outside summer.

Mercado de Pulgas MARKET
(Plaza Rocha; ⏲10am-6pm Fri-Sun) This relaxed flea market, selling everything including the kitchen sink, is at 20 de Septiembre between San Martín and Av Luro, seven blocks northwest of Plaza San Martín.

Information

There are several money exchanges along San Martín and Rivadavia, including **Jonestur** (www.jonestur.com; San Martín 2574) and **La Moneta** (www.lamoneta.com; Rivadavia 2623).

Post office (cnr Av Luro & Santiago del Estero)

Tourist office (☎495-1777; www.turismomardelplata.gov.ar; Blvd Marítimo 2240; ⏲10am-

8pm Mar-Dec, to 10pm Jan & Feb) Centrally located and exceptionally helpful.

Getting There & Away

AIR

From Mardel's Ástor Piazzolla International Airport, 10km north of town, **Aerolíneas Argentinas** (☎496-0101; www.aerolineas.com.ar; Moreno 2442) and **Sol** (www.sol.com.ar) have several daily flights to Buenos Aires.

BUS

Mar del Plata's sparkling bus terminal is next to the train station, about 2km northwest of the beach. To reach the center, cross Av Luro in front of the terminal and take local bus 511, 512 or 513 heading southeast; taxis cost about AR$25.

In the city center, the ticket agency **Central de Pasajes** (☎493-7843; cnr San Martín & Corrientes; ⏲10am-8pm) sells long-distance bus tickets for most companies, saving you a trip to the terminal.

Buses from Mar del Plata

DESTINATION	COST (AR$)	DURATION (HR)
Bahía Blanca	242	7
Bariloche	880	18-20
Buenos Aires	252-281	5½
Córdoba	612-699	16-18
Mendoza	725	18-20
Necochea	64	2¼
Pinamar	69	2½
Puerto Madryn	588	17
Tandil	81	3
Villa Gesell	55	2

TRAIN

The **train station** (☎475-6076; www.sofse.gob.ar; Av Luro 4700 at Italia; ⏲6am-midnight) is adjacent to the bus terminal, 2km from the beach. Trains with *primera* (AR$170) and Pullman (AR$200) class service run between Mar del Plata and Buenos Aires' Constitución station (six hours) three times weekly in each direction. The fancier *Marplatense* service (AR$210, 5¾ hours) runs only once weekly, leaving Buenos Aires early Friday evening and returning from Mar del Plata late Sunday afternoon. A lower-priced daily service (AR$102) had been suspended indefinitely at the time of research. Reserve tickets well ahead in summer.

Getting Around

The **airport** (☎478-0744) is 10km north of the city. Take bus 542, marked 'aeropuerto' (AR$3.25, 30 minutes) from the corner of Blvd Marítimo and Belgrano. Taxis cost around AR$60.

Despite Mar del Plata's sprawl, frequent buses reach just about every place in town. However, most buses (including the airport bus) require *tarjetas de aproximación* (magnetic cards) that must be bought ahead of time at *kioskos* (newsstands) and charged up. Popular bus 221 is an exception: it takes coins.

Colectivos MDP (www.colectivosmdp.com.ar) provides useful maps of all local bus routes on its website. The tourist office can also help with transport details.

Car rentals are available downtown at **Alamo** (☎495-2935; Córdoba 2270).

Necochea

☎02262 / POP 85,000

Totally pumping in summer and near dead in winter, Necochea's beach-town feel is undisturbed by the highrises that keep springing up. With nearly 70km of beachfront, it's fairly certain that you'll find a spot to lay your towel. Windy Necochea lures surfers year-round with its excellent waves. Other bonuses include walking and horseback riding opportunities in foresty Parque Municipal Miguel Lillo, and some of the best-value lodging on the coast.

Sights & Activities

The dense pine woods of **Parque Provincial Miguel Lillo**, a large greenbelt along the beach, are widely used for cycling, horseback riding, walking and picnicking. Horses and bikes can both be rented inside the park.

The Río Quequén Grande, rich in rainbow trout and mackerel, also allows for easy rafting and kayaking, particularly around the falls at **Saltos del Quequén**. Local outfitter **Mundo Bonito** (☎15-658998; www.facebook.com/mundobonito) organizes both river and ocean kayak trips.

At the village of **Quequén** at the river's mouth, several stranded shipwrecks offer good opportunities for exploration and photography below sculpted cliffs. The **faro** (lighthouse) is another local attraction.

With some of the best waves along the Atlantic coast, Necochea is a hit with surfers. **Monte Pasubio Surf Camp** (☎451482; www.montepasubio.com.ar; cnr Av 502 & Calle 529), across the river in Quequén, is a beachside surf school where you can camp, arrange classes and rent boards during the summer.

Sleeping

Note that some accommodations are only open December to March.

Jamming Hostel HOSTEL $
(☎517210; www.jamminghostel.com.ar; Calle 502, No 1685; dm AR$120-150, d AR$350) Big on skateboarding and surfing culture, this mediterranean-style hostel with a lively on-site bar-restaurant is near the beach in nearby Quequén, 6km from Necochea's bus terminal (a taxi costs around AR$35).

Hostería del Bosque HOTEL $$
(☎420002; www.hosteria-delbosque.com.ar; Calle 89, No 350; r AR$730-830;) Four blocks in from the beach, this homey yet elegant family-run *hostería* is by far the most atmospheric place to stay in town. Rooms are large and comfortable, and some have views of Parque Lillo across the street. Nice grassy garden in back.

Cabañas Río Quequén CABINS, CAMPGROUND $$
(☎421562; www.cabaniasrioquequen.com; cnr Calle 22 & Río Quequén; 2-person camp site AR$150, d AR$585;) Pleasantly situated on the banks of the Río Quequén, off a dead-end residential street 2.5km from the bus terminal and 3.5km from Necochea's downtown waterfront, these *cabañas* are surrounded by grassy, tree-shaded grounds, with a camping zone, a sandy river beach, a children's play area and kayaks available for river excursions.

Hotel Mirasol HOTEL $$
(☎525158; www.mirasolhotel.com.ar; Calle 4bis, No 4133; s/d AR$300/430;) Enjoying a prime location on Plaza San Martín, half a block from the pedestrian zone and two blocks from the beach, this friendly place offers comfortable budget rooms year-round; best value are the three upstairs units with air-con and windows overlooking the square. Included breakfast is served at the cafe across the plaza.

Eating & Drinking

There are several dining options around Plaza San Martín. Many of the *balnearios* have eateries where you can grab a bite beachside. In low season many restaurants are only open on weekends.

For a drink, check out the bars on Calle 87 between Calles 4 and 6.

El Loco PARRILLA $
(☎422761; Av 10, No 3204; mains AR$40-75; ⊙noon-3pm & 8pm-midnight Tue-Sun) Brimming with locals, this classic neighborhood *parrilla* with blazing fire, brick walls and simple wooden tables serves steaks cooked to order, accompanied by delicious side dishes such as roasted red peppers or fried potatoes with garlic and parsley. El Loco is

WORTH A TRIP

MIRAMAR

If you've got kids consider a side trip to Miramar, a family-friendly destination with a long, wide beach and gentle waves (surfable in spots). Compared to Mar del Plata, 45km to the north, Miramar is fairly low-key – but like any other Argentine resort it does get crowded in summer.

The **tourist office** (☎02291-420190; www.miramar.tur.ar; cnr Calle 21 & Costanera; ⊙8am-9pm), located at the beach, has details about various activities around town, including horseback riding, golfing and fishing. Miramar is known for its surf, more easily accessible at the north end of town where there are a few surf schools.

For accommodations, consider **Aventureiro Hostel** (☎02291-430981; www.aventureiro.com.ar; Calle 16, No 1067; dm AR$120-175, r AR$300-390;), an average hostel but just a couple of blocks from the beach; or the pleasant-enough **Hotel Danieli** (☎02291-432366; www.hoteldanielimiramar.com.ar; Calle 24, No 1114; d AR$480-600 Mar-Dec, d incl obligatory half board AR$800-1100 Jan & Feb;). From Mar del Plata, buses (AR$16, one hour) run regularly to Miramar's bus terminal at Av 40 and Calle 15, within six blocks of the center.

Those looking for downright isolation can head to **Mar de Sud**, a small town 16km south of Miramar. It's known for its rustic atmosphere, black-rock beach and fishing waters – and claims some hotel ruins as a main tourist attraction. There are no tall buildings here and much fewer services than its neighbor, so if you're looking to get away from the crowds this should be your stop.

halfway between Plaza San Martín and the Río Quequén. Reservations are a must on weekend nights.

Ernnan's CAFE $
(☎521427; Calle 83; mains AR$42-80; ⏰8am-late) Directly opposite Necochea's main square, this high-ceilinged cafe with sidewalk seating and free wi-fi makes a great place for a snack any time of day, serving everything from *medialunas* (croissants) and gourmet sandwiches to pizza, paella and homemade *sorrentinos* (large, round filled pastas).

Antares BREWPUB $$
(☎421976; www.cervezaantares.com; Calle 4, No 4266; mains AR$70-100; ⏰8pm-late Wed-Sun Apr-Nov, daily Dec-Mar) One block in from the beach, this is yet another branch of the beautiful bar-restaurant chain. There's a decent selection of pub-style food, along with several craft-style beers (actually brewed in Mar del Plata).

Taberna Española SPANISH $$
(☎520539; cnr Calle 83 & 8; mains AR$75-189; ⏰noon-3pm & 8pm-midnight) Head here for fine seafood, Spanish-style. Deals include the *plato del día* (daily special), served with coffee or dessert for AR$65, and a three-course menu (starter, main dish and dessert) for AR$100.

Information

Post office (Calle 6, No 4065)

Tourist office (☎438333; www.necochea.tur.ar; cnr Avs 2 & 79; ⏰8am-9pm Dec-Mar, 10am-4pm Apr-Nov) On the beach; also at the **bus terminal** (Av 58, btw Calle 47 & Av 45; ⏰mid-Dec–Mar).

Getting There & Away

The **bus terminal** (Av 58, btwn Calle 47 & Av 45) is 3.5km from the beach; taxis to the center cost AR$25 to AR$30, or take local bus 513 (AR$3), marked 'playa'. Destinations include Buenos Aires (AR$312, seven hours), Mar del Plata (AR$64, 2¼ hours), Tandil (AR$69, three hours) and Bahía Blanca (AR$175, five hours).

Bahía Blanca

☎0291 / POP 291,000

Grandiose buildings, an attractive plaza and boulevards lined with shade trees lend oft-overlooked Bahía Blanca the feel of a cosmopolitan city in miniature. Its chief advantage is as a resting point during overland trips from Buenos Aires to Patagonia, but it's not entirely without interest.

The hordes of sailors who dock here, at what is now South America's largest naval base, attest to Bahía Blanca's militaristic beginnings. In an early effort to establish military control on the periphery of the pampas, Colonel Ramón Estomba situated the pompously named Fortaleza Protectora Argentina at the natural harbor of Bahía Blanca in 1828.

Sights

Downtown attractions worth a look are the city's neoclassical performing arts center, **Teatro Municipal** (Alsina 425), and the **Museo de Arte Contemporáneo** (☎459-4006; Sarmiento 450; ⏰9am-8pm Tue-Fri, 4-8pm Sat & Sun) FREE, showcasing local and national artists.

On weekends an afternoon **artisans market** takes over Plaza Rivadavia, opposite the Municipalidad.

Museo del Puerto MUSEUM
(☎457-3006; www.museodelpuerto.blogspot.com; cnr Guillermo Torres & Cárrega; voluntary donation requested; ⏰9am-noon Mon-Fri, 4-8pm Sat & Sun) In the Ingeniero White neighborhood on the outskirts of town and housed in a colorfully painted former customs building that's dwarfed by the massive grain elevators and fortresslike power plant next door, this engaging museum is a tribute to the region's immigrants, and includes an archive with documents, photographs and recorded oral histories. The best time to visit is for a weekend afternoon tea, when local groups prepare regional delicacies, each week representing a different immigrant group; the scene is especially animated in winter, when there's often live music. Take bus 500 from the Plaza (30 to 40 minutes).

Sleeping

The most pleasant place to stay is near central Plaza Rivadavia, where you'll also find a wide selection of restaurants and cafes.

Bahía Blanca Hostel HOSTEL $
(☎452-6802; www.hostelbahiablanca.com; Soler 701; dm AR$70, s/d AR$130/170, s/d without bathroom AR$90/150; @📶) Located in an ancient hotel 1km east of the plaza, this hostel has friendly staff, a spacious kitchen and a games area with pool, ping-pong and foosball. Basic rooms surround an old patio; the cheapest share bathrooms. Transient male

workers rent upstairs rooms by the month, so it lacks that usual cozy 'international' hostel flavor.

Firenze Hotel HOTEL **$**
(☎455-7746; www.firenzehotel.com.ar; Rondeau 39; s/d AR$220/300; ❄📶) A good deal for its location, this small hotel just around the corner from the plaza has 17 simple rooms in a remodeled old building.

Hotel Muñiz HOTEL **$$**
(☎456-0060; www.hotelmuniz.com.ar; O'Higgins 23; s/d from AR$280/419; ❄@📶) Centrally located in a beautiful old building, the Muñiz offers four levels of decent but unmemorable rooms linked by long tiled hallways. The lobby has great old atmosphere.

Eating

Bambú BUFFET **$$**
(Chiclana 298; buffet AR$78-88; ⏲noon-3pm & 8:30pm-midnight) The best deal in town for the hungry is this *tenedor libre* (all-you-can-eat restaurant) efficiently run by a Chinese family. Choose from heaps of cooked dishes (many with Asian flavor), along with Argentine *asado* (barbecue grill); drinks are extra. There's takeout too.

El Mundo de la Parrilla PARRILLA **$$**
(www.elmundodelaparrilla.com; Av Colón 379; mains AR$40-120; ⏲8pm-late Mon, noon-3pm & 8pm-late Tue-Sun) It can get busy at this buzzing *parrilla,* which locals agree is the best in town. The *tenedor libre* (AR$100) sees an endless procession of succulent grilled meats brought to your table. Salad bar and drinks are extra.

★ **Gambrinus** ARGENTINE **$$**
(www.gambrinus1890.com; Arribeños 174; mains AR$43-120; ⏲noon-3pm & 8pm-late) Downtown's most atmospheric dining option is this traditional, old-time restaurant that dates from the 19th century. The menu features a mix of Argentine classics and German specialties such as wurst and sauerkraut. A vivacious local crowd and walls plastered with vintage ads and knickknacks enhance the welcoming vibe.

Information

Post Office (Moreno 34)

Tourist Kiosk (☎481-8944; turismo@bb.mun.gba.gov.ar; cnr Drago & Av Colón; ⏲9am-6pm Mon-Fri, 9:30am-1pm & 2:30-6pm Sat) The bus terminal (Brown 1700) also has a tourist office.

Getting There & Away

AIR

Aerolíneas Argentinas (☎456-0561; www.aerolineas.com.ar; San Martín 298), **LAN** (☎0810-999-9526; www.lan.com; Chiclana 344) and **Sol** (☎0810-444-4765; www.sol.com.ar) all offer flights from Bahía Blanca's airport, 15km east of town (AR$110 by taxi; there are no buses).

BUS

Bahía Blanca's **bus terminal** (Brown 1700) is about 2km southeast of Plaza Rivadavia. Taxis to the city center cost AR$30 to AR$40; local buses 514 and 517 run to the bus station from the stop in front of Banco de la Nación on Plaza Rivadavia; you'll have to buy a magnetic card at a newsstand to use them (there's no *kiosco* at the terminal).

There are several businesses – including *locutorios* (private telephone offices) and travel agent **Dakar** (☎456-2030; cnr Alsina & Chiclana; ⏲9am-8pm Mon-Fri, 9am-1pm & 5-8pm Sat) – right at the south end of Plaza Rivadavia that sell bus tickets, saving you a trip to the bus terminal for information. These different businesses sell different bus companies' tickets, so ask around if you want a particular schedule, company or price.

Travelers to Sierra de la Ventana have three options: **Condor Estrella** (☎491-5091; www.condorestrella.com.ar) runs two daily buses (AR$44, 2½ hours); **Expreso Cabildo** (☎491-5247) has a twice-daily bus-plus-van service (AR$55, two hours, buy ticket from driver at platform 1); and **Norte Bus** (☎0291-15-468-5101) operates a shuttle (AR$80, 1½ hours).

Buses from Bahía Blanca

DESTINATION	COST (AR$)	DURATION (HR)
Bariloche	584	12-14
Buenos Aires	417	9
Córdoba	396	13-15
Mar del Plata	242	7
Mendoza	600	16
Neuquén	288	7½
Sierra de la Ventana	44	2½
Trelew	355	10-12

TRAIN

Ferrobaires (www.ferrobaires.gba.gov.ar) runs trains from **Estación Ferrocarril Roca** (☎452-9196; Cerri 750) to Buenos Aires' Constitución station every day except Monday and Saturday, at around 7:30pm (AR$95 to $AR170, 14 to 15 hours). On Wednesday and Friday these trains serve Sierra de la Ventana (AR$37 to AR$73, three hours). At the time of research, Ferrobaires and Tren Patagónico were working to re-establish the train service south to Carmen de Patagones.

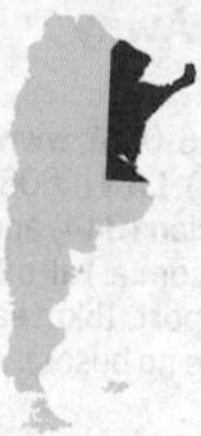

Iguazú Falls & the Northeast

Includes ➡

Best Parks & Reserves

- Parque Nacional Iguazú (p197)
- Parque Nacional do Iguaçu (p200)
- Reserva Provincial Esteros del Iberá (p175)
- Parque Nacional El Palmar (p183)

Best Places to Stay

- La Alondra (p171)
- Rancho de los Esteros (p177)
- Boutique Hotel de la Fonte (p204)
- Los Silos (p163)

Why Go?

Northeast Argentina is defined by water. Muscular rivers roll through flatlands that they flood at will, while fragile wetlands support myriad birdlife, snapping caimans and cuddly capybaras. The peaceful Río Iguazú, meandering through the jungle between Brazil and Argentina, dissolves in fury and power in the planet's most awe-inspiring waterfalls.

The river then flows into the Paraná, one of the world's mightiest watercourses, which surges southward, eventually forming the Río de la Plata near Buenos Aires. Along it are some of the country's most interesting cities: elegant Corrientes, colonial Santa Fe and booming Rosario, as well as Posadas, gateway to the ruined splendor of the area's Jesuit missions.

Dotted throughout are excellent parks that represent the region's biological diversity. The Esteros del Iberá harbor a particularly astonishing richness of wildlife.

When to Go

Puerto Iguazú

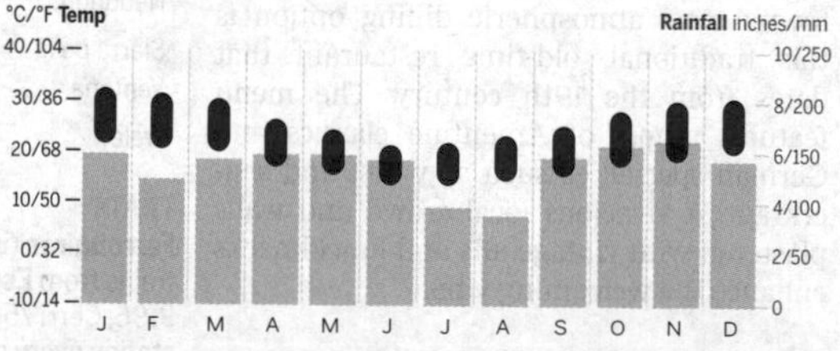

Feb Hot weather and flashy Carnaval celebrations in Gualeguaychú, Corrientes and Posadas.

Aug Cool and dry; spot animals in the Esteros del Iberá gathered around scarce water sources.

Sep–Oct Not too cold, hot or crowded. Iguazú flowing well but flooding and rain less likely.

ALONG THE RÍO PARANÁ

The mighty Paraná, the continent's second-longest river at 4000km (after the Amazon at 6405km), dominates the geography of Northeast Argentina. The cities along it have their town centers a sensible distance above the shorelines of this flood-prone monster, but have a *costanera* (riverbank) that's the focus of much social life. The river is still important for trade, and large oceangoing vessels ply it to and beyond Rosario, the region's top urban destination.

The Paraná is the demesne of enormous river fish – surubí, dorado and pacú, among others – that attract sports fishers from around the world. Their distinctive flavors enliven the menus of the region's restaurants; make sure you try them.

Rosario

☎0341 / POP 1.19 MILLION

Boom times are back for Rosario, birthplace of both the Argentine flag and 'Che' Guevara, and an important river port. The derelict buildings of the long *costanera* have been converted into galleries, restaurants and skate parks, and the river beaches and islands buzz with life in the summer. The center – a curious mishmash of stunning early-20th-century buildings overshadowed by ugly apartments – has a comfortable, lived-in feel, and the down-to-earth *rosarinos* (people from Rosario) are a delight. All are very proud of Rosario-born-and-bred Lionel Messi, golden boy of world *fútbol* (soccer).

History

Rosario's first European inhabitants settled here informally around 1720. After independence Rosario quickly superseded Santa Fe as the province's economic powerhouse, though, to the irritation of *rosarinos*, the provincial capital retained political primacy.

The Central Argentine Land Company, an adjunct of the railroad, was responsible for bringing in agricultural colonists from Europe, for whom Rosario was a port of entry. From 1869 to 1914 the city's population grew nearly tenfold, though a decline of economic and shipping activity during the 1960s led to a drop in Rosario's population and power.

Nationalistic Argentines cherish Rosario, home to a monument to the nation's flag, as Cuna de la Bandera (Cradle of the Flag).

Sights

Though it's a private home and you can't enter, you may want to check out the apartment building at **Entre Ríos 480** (Entre Ríos 480), where the newborn Ernesto 'Che' Guevara had his first home.

Costanera RIVERBANK

Rosario's most attractive feature is its waterfront, where an area of once derelict warehouses and train tracks has largely been reclaimed for the fun of the people. It stretches some 15km from its southern end at Parque Urquiza to the city's northern edge, just short of the suspension bridge that crosses into Entre Ríos province. It's an appealing place to wander and watch what's going on, from the plentiful birdlife and impromptu *fútbol* games to massive cargo ships surging past on the river.

Costanera Sur RIVERBANK

The grassy zone below downtown includes plenty of space for jogging and courting, as well as the Estación Fluvial (p154) building, which offers boat trips and eating and drinking options. Heading further north, you pass various cultural venues before reaching the **Parque de España** and its mausoleumlike edifice. Beyond here is a zone of bars and restaurants that gets lively at weekends, and then the city's contemporary art museum.

Costanera Norte RIVERBANK, BEACH

In summer this strip beginning 5km north of downtown attracts the crowds to its beaches. The mediocre public beach of **Rambla Catalunya** is backed by a promenade and bar-restaurants; beyond, the best beach is **Balneario La Florida** (admission AR$12; ⏲9am-8pm Oct-Apr), with services and a safe bathing area. Picturesque stalls behind it sell river fish. The 'Linea de la Costa' bus heads here: downtown it runs west along Rioja before turning north up Roca.

★Monumento Nacional a La Bandera MONUMENT

(www.monumentoalabandera.gob.ar; Santa Fe 581; ⏲9am-6pm Tue-Fri, 9am-noon & 2-6pm Sat & Sun, 2-6pm Mon) Manuel Belgrano, who designed the Argentine flag, rests in a crypt beneath this colossal stone obelisk built where the blue-and-white stripes were first raised. If rampant nationalism isn't your thing, it's nevertheless worth taking the elevator to the top (AR$5) for the great views over the waterfront, Río Paraná and its islands.

Iguazú Falls & the Northeast Highlights

❶ Drop your jaw in stunned amazement at the beauty and power of the **Iguazú Falls** (p195)

❷ Get personal with the mighty Paraná in livable, lovable **Rosario** (p151)

❸ Coo at the cute capybaras of the **Reserva Provincial Esteros del Iberá** (p175)

❹ Munch delicious freshwater fish by the Río Uruguay in pretty **Colón** (p181)

❺ Ponder a unique experiment in humanity at the ruined **Jesuit missions** (p186)

❻ Admire the sculptures in **Resistencia** (p210) then hit the

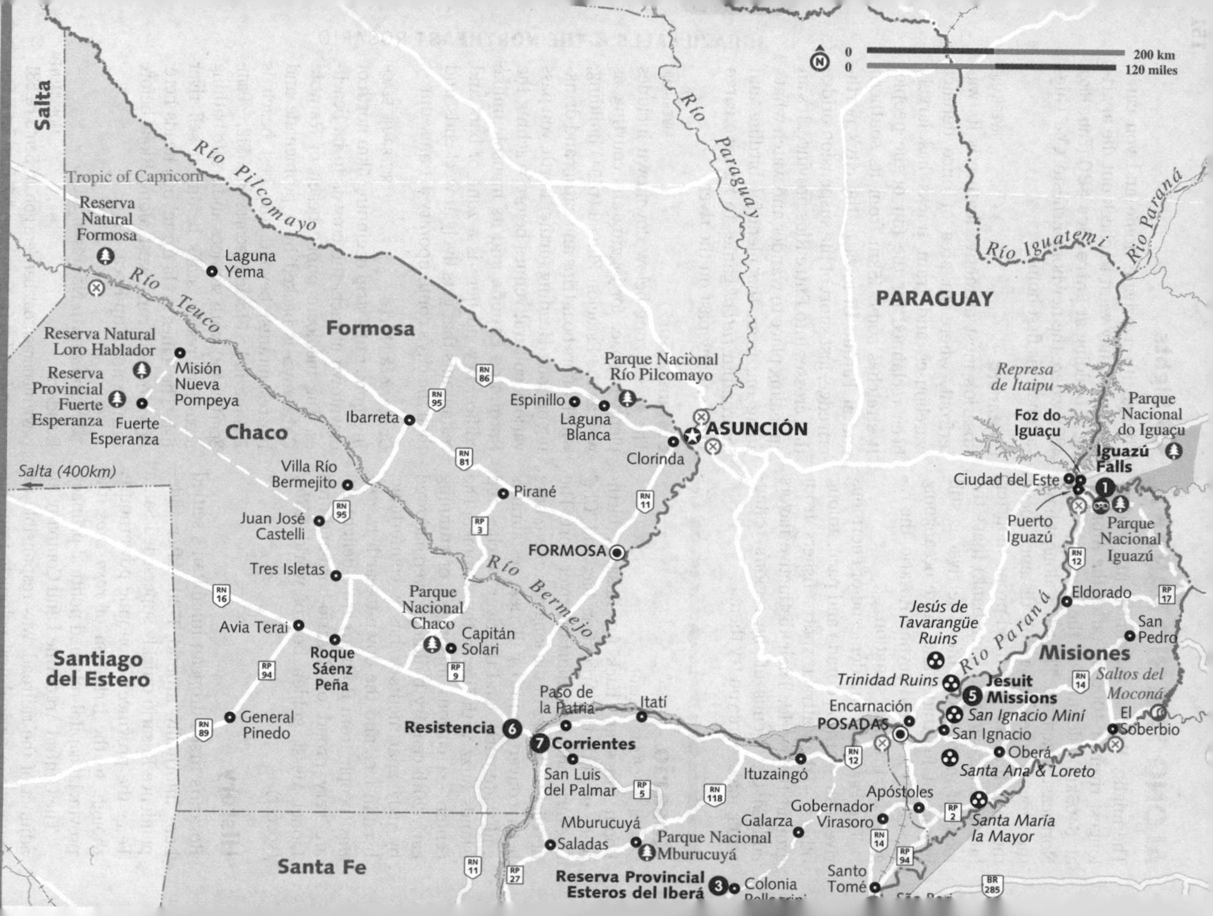

'impenetrable' Chaco, a bastion of traditional indigenous culture

7 Live it up at one of the region's classic Carnaval celebrations in **Gualeguaychú** (p180) or **Corrientes** (p171)

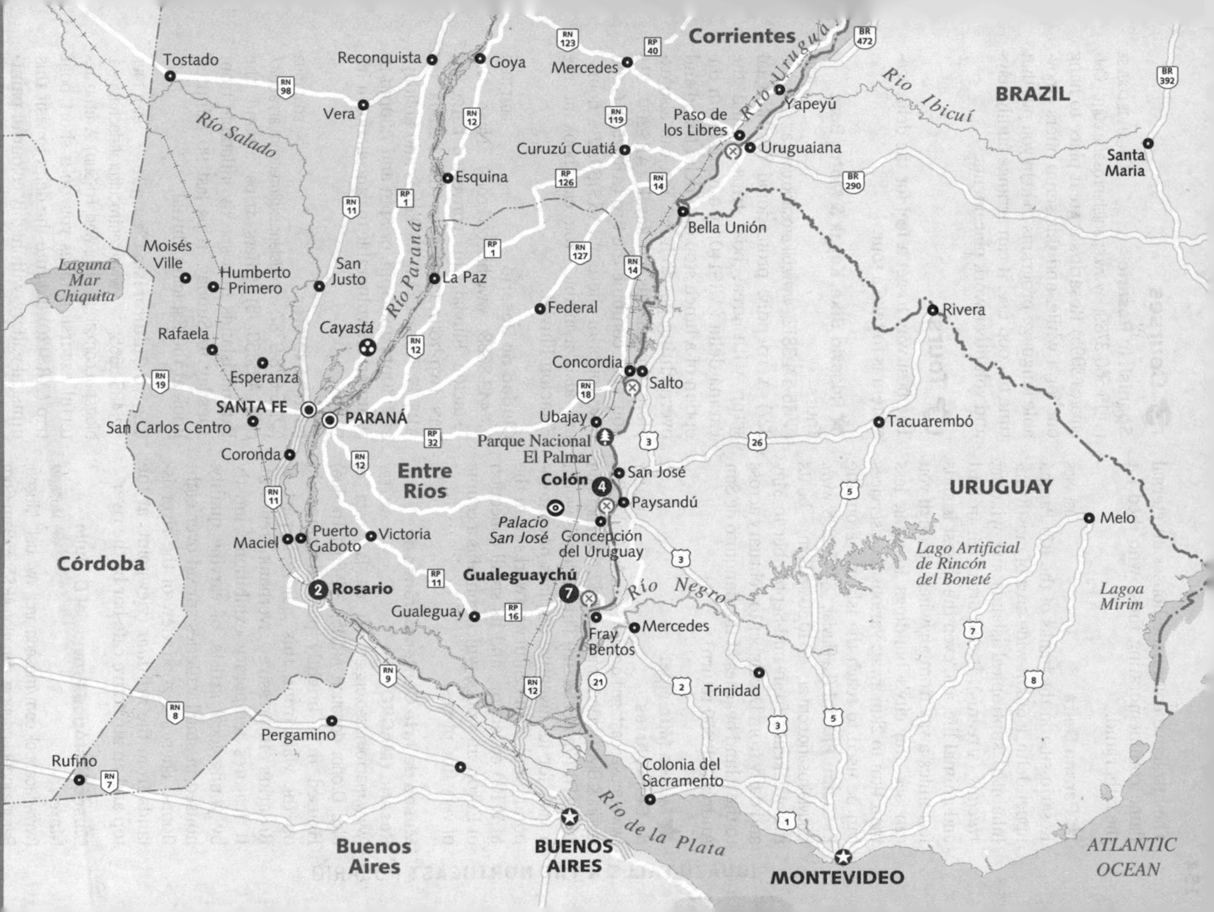

The attractive colonnade houses an eternal flame commemorating those who died for the fatherland.

★ **Paraná Delta** ISLANDS
Rosario sits on the banks of the Río Paraná upper delta, a 60km-wide area of mostly uninhabited subtropical islands and winding *riachos* (streams). It's an area rich in bird and animal life, and even the closest islands feel miles away from anywhere, though you can see the city's buildings looming less than 1km to 2km away. Various boat services can be used to reach the islands. From the **Estación Fluvial** (La Fluvial; ☎447-3838; www.lafluvialrosario.com.ar; ⏲10.30am-6pm) boats run weekends from mid-September to May and daily from December to February across to the island beaches at the Banquito de San Andrés (AR$60 return).

★ **Museo Municipal de Bellas Artes** GALLERY
(www.museocastagnino.org.ar; cnr Av Carlos Pellegrini & Blvd Oroño; admission AR$7; ⏲2-8pm Mon & Wed-Fri, 1-7pm Sat & Sun) This gallery is worth a visit for its inventive displays of contemporary and 20th-century artworks from the MACRO collection, and its small collection of European works, which contains a couple of very fine pieces.

Museo de Arte Contemporáneo de Rosario (MACRO) GALLERY
(www.macromuseo.org.ar; Av de la Costa at Blvd Oroño; donation AR$15; ⏲2-8pm Thu-Tue) Housed in a brightly painted grain silo on the waterfront, this gallery is part of Rosario's impressive riverbank renewal. It features temporary exhibitions, mostly by young local artists, of varying quality, housed in small galleries spread over eight floors. There's a good view of the river islands from the *mirador* (viewpoint) at the top and an attractive cafe-bar by the river.

Museo Histórico Provincial Dr Julio Marc MUSEUM
(www.facebook.com/museomarc; Av del Museo, Parque Independencia; donation AR$5; ⏲9am-6pm Tue-Fri, 2-7pm Sat & Sun, 3-8pm Sat & Sun Dec-Mar) The well-presented collection features plenty of post-independence exhibits plus excellent displays on indigenous cultures from all over Latin America. Particularly interesting is the collection of baroque religious art from the southern Andes. Information in Spanish only. It's closed when *fútbol* is on in the adjacent stadium.

Courses

Spanish in Rosario LANGUAGE COURSE
(☎15-560-3789; www.spanishinrosario.com; Catamarca 3095) Rosario's a great place to hang out for a while, and this setup offers enjoyable language programs to help you put that time to good use. It can arrange family stays and volunteer work placements.

Tours

The best way to get a feel for the delta ecosystem is to take a tour.

★ **Rosario Bike, Kayak & Motor Boat Tours** TOUR
(☎15-571-3812; www.bikerosario.com.ar; Zeballos 327) A friendly, professional multilingual setup with great boat trips around the Paraná delta (AR$140, two hours) with the option of a lunch stop on a delta island and overnighting possibilities. You can also explore the islands by kayak (AR$200, 2½ hours) or combine the two (AR$250). Good bike tours of the city (AR$160, 2½ hours) are also available. You can book at the Estación Fluvial.

Ciudad de Rosario BOAT TOUR
(☎449-8688; www.barcocr1.com) Near the Estación Fluvial, this converted barge offers two-hour cruises on the Paraná for AR$65; it leaves on weekends and holidays at 2:30pm and 5pm, or 5pm and 7:30pm in summer. It's vulnerable to cancellation if it's windy.

Island Explorer BOAT TOUR
(☎15-628-9287; www.islandexplorer.com.ar; adult/child AR$150/75) Offers trips around the Paraná islands in a speedy inflatable from Tuesday to Sunday. Trips last 90 minutes. Book at the Estación Fluvial.

Centro Cultural Isla Charigüé BOAT TOUR
(☎485-5665; www.centroculturalislacharigue.blogspot.com.ar; ⏲Mon, Wed, Fri-Sun) A characterful excursion takes you on a short boat trip (AR$120) out into the delta to visit this unusual gallery, with highly colourful paintings depicting riverine wildlife, as well as other delta-related art and poetry. Book at the Estación Fluvial.

Festivals & Events

Rosario packs out for the October 12 long weekend. Many hotels and hostels double their prices and fill up well ahead of time.

Semana de la Bandera FIESTA
Climaxing in ceremonies on June 20, the anniversary of the death of Manuel Belgrano, Flag Week is Rosario's major fiesta.

Sleeping

There are over 40 hostels, mostly devoted to the weekend Buenos Aires party crowd, and a herd of midrange hotels, several operated by **Solans** (www.solans.com). Prices generally drop midweek.

Hotel La Paz HOTEL $
(☎421-0905; www.hotellapazrosario.com.ar; Barón de Maua 36; s/d AR$250/280; ❄@📶) Well positioned on Plaza Montenegro, and still looking good after nearly 70 years in operation, this welcoming budget hotel offers value for money. Family rooms at the front have balconies overlooking Plaza Montenegro.

La Casa de Pandora HOSTEL $
(☎679-9314; www.lacasadepandora.com.ar; Entre Ríos 583; dm AR$70; @📶) Small, arty and welcoming, this is one of many Rosario hostels but does some of the important basics – cleaning, for example – much better than many competitors. It's a cute spot with attractive dorms, a kitchen and a petite courtyard. Various workshops – yoga, dance, folk music – are held during the week.

Hostel La Comunidad HOSTEL $
(☎424-5302; www.lacomunidadhostel.com; Roca 453; dm/d AR$70/210; @📶) Occupying a gorgeous old Rosario building, this spot has lofty ceilings and a light, airy feel. The dorms have handsome wooden bunks and floorboards; a cute private room is also available. There's a bar, lounge area and – except at weekends – a peaceful vibe.

La Casona de Don Jaime II HOSTEL $
(☎530-2020; www.lacasonadedonjaime.com; San Lorenzo 1530; dm/d AR$90/320; ❄@📶) There's plenty of punch for your peso at this friendly hostel. It's quiet and clean, with a climbing wall on the patio. Dorm beds have plenty of headroom and air-con is available for a little extra. Upstairs are rather smart themed private rooms. Discounts midweek and for Hostelling International (HI) members.

Rosario Inn HOSTEL $
(☎421-0358; www.rosarioinnhostel.com.ar; Sargento Cabral 54; dm/d AR$80/180; @📶) Right opposite the massive customs building near the river, this colorful hostel makes up in location and laid-back atmosphere what it lacks in facilities. Set around patios, it offers a helpful welcome, good social scene and activities. The six-bed dorms are comfortable enough; bathrooms are just adequate.

★**Barisit House Hotel** HOTEL $$
(☎447-6464; www.barisit.com.ar; Laprida 1311; s/d AR$450/550; ❄@📶) Go for one of the upstairs front rooms in this converted historic house to enjoy the romance of original floorboards, high ceilings, windows and balconies. The modern rooms are similarly attractively decorated and significantly more quiet. The personal small-hotel atmosphere is a real drawcard. Rates are 20% cheaper midweek.

Esplendor Savoy Rosario HOTEL $$
(☎429-6000; www.esplendorsavoyrosario.com; San Lorenzo 1022; r standard/superior AR$692/830, ste AR$1037; ❄@📶🏊) Even among the many elegant early-20th-century buildings of Rosario, this art nouveau gem is a standout. It's a flawless contemporary conversion; rooms feature modern conveniences that blend well with the centenarian features. An indoor pool, elegant cafe-bar and roof garden are among the attractions. It's popular for events, so don't expect a peaceful stay.

Hotel Plaza del Sol HOTEL $$
(☎426-4448; www.hotelesplaza.com; San Juan 1055; s/d AR$590/790; ❄@📶🏊) Despite a tired facade, the renovated rooms here feel new and look good; most are very spacious, all have balconies, and beds are comfortable. It's the best of the clutch of hotels on Plaza Montenegro; there's a gym, sauna, sundeck and heated indoor pool on the 11th floor, as well as helpful service. It's decent value, especially if you grab a discount by shopping around online.

1412 HOTEL $$
(☎448-7755; www.1412.com.ar; Zeballos 1412; r AR$532; ❄📶) Comfortably stylish, this decent-value new hotel is perfectly located for sorties to the Pellegrini restaurant strip. The handsome lobby offers free tea, coffee and cakes all day, while the rooms are pleasingly and flawlessly modern.

Plaza Real HOTEL $$
(☎440-8800; www.plazarealhotel.com; Santa Fe 1632; r standard/superior/luxury AR$677/800/883; ❄@📶🏊) Luxurious rooms, apartments and suites are to be had in this business hotel with rooftop pool. Fine facilities, a

Rosario

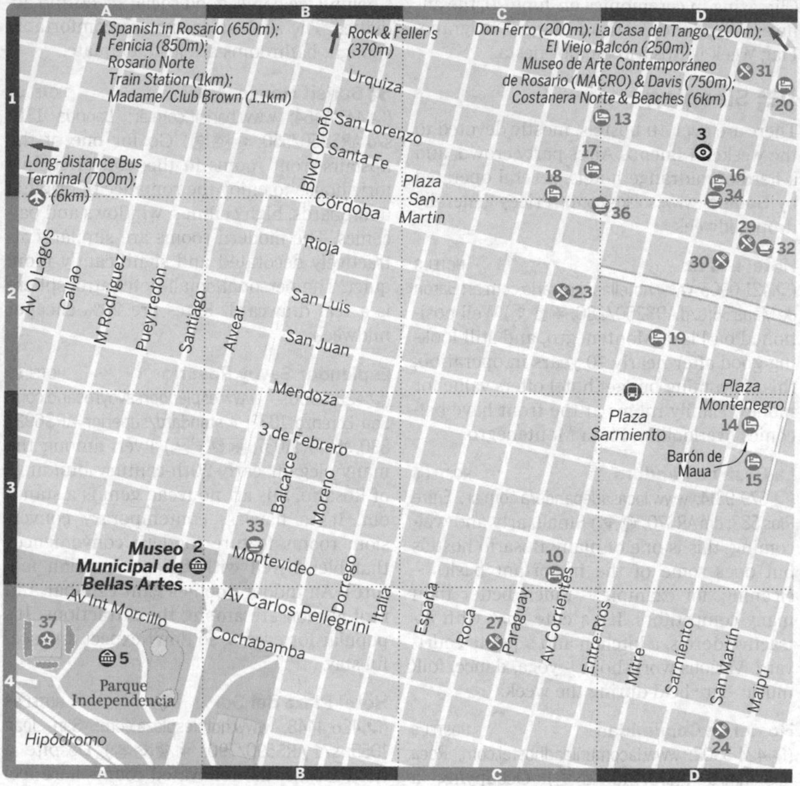

cracking breakfast and polite friendly service make it a reliable choice.

Roberta Rosa de Fontana Suites APARTMENT $$
(☎449-6767; www.rrdfsuites.com.ar; Entre Ríos 914; s/d AR$450/500; ❄📶) Situated very centrally above a colorful cafe, these rooms are modern and commodious, with brushed concrete ceiling, black floors and a small kitchenette. They come in various sizes, making it a good family option.

Ros Tower HOTEL $$$
(☎529-9000; www.rostower.com.ar; Mitre 295; r from AR$1020; ❄@📶≋) Great service and facilities in this sleek business-spa hotel with top river views from many rooms.

Eating

Central Rosario seems empty come supper time. That's because half the city is out on Av Carlos Pellegrini. Between Buenos Aires and Moreno there is a vast number of family-friendly eateries, including barn-like *parrillas* (steak restaurants), dozens of pizza places, several all-you-can-eat buffet joints, plus bars and a number of excellent ice-creameries. Just stroll along and take your pick. Most places have terraces facing onto the street.

★ **La Marina** SPANISH $
(1 de Mayo 890; mains AR$30-60; ⏰noon-4pm & 8pm-midnight Mon-Sat) Just above the flag monument, this basement place, which is decorated with faded Spanish tourism posters, is a top spot for inexpensive and really delicious seafood, like *rabas* (calamari) or succulent river fish on the grill. It doesn't take bookings, so be prepared to wait for a table, as it's deservedly popular. Be sure not to confuse it with the restaurant located above it.

Lo Mejor del Centro PARRILLA $
(Santa Fe 1166; mains AR$55-100; ⏲11.30am-3.30pm & 8pm-midnight or later) When this *parrilla* went bust, the staff were left high and dry, but the local government let them reopen it as a cooperative, and what a great job they've done. The meat's as good as you'll taste in Rosario, but you can also enjoy homemade pasta, paella, creative salads and a warm, convivial buzz at the tightly packed tables. The lunchtime set menu is terrific value.

El Ancla ARGENTINE $
(Maipú 1101; mains AR$35-70; ⏲lunch & dinner) One of Rosario's many beloved corner restaurants, this well-frequented local has an appealingly venerable interior and an authentic feel. The food – with lots of inexpensive single-plate meals – is reliably good and you always seem to get a friendly welcome. A good budget choice.

De Buen Humor ICE CREAM $
(www.debuenhumorhelados.com.ar; Rioja 1560; cones AR$17-30; ⏲10am-10pm;) Ice cream here comes from happy cows, they say. We can't vouch for that, but anyone with a sweet tooth will be mooing contentedly at the optimism-filled decor, patio seating, and tasty cones, concoctions and fruit salads.

Rincón Vegetariano VEGETARIAN $
(turinconvegetariano.blogspot.com; Mitre 720; mains AR$25-35; ⏲9am-4pm Mon-Sat;) This mostly vegetarian place is focused on healthy eating and weight loss and offers a huge range of meat-free hot and cold dishes to eat in or take out. There are always all sorts of deals going, with an all-you-can-eat buffet at lunchtime.

Zazpirak Bat BASQUE $$
(www.zazpirakbat.com; Entre Ríos 261; mains AR$50-95; ⏲8pm-12.30am Tue-Sat, 12.30-4pm Sun) From outside, this Basque cultural center gives few clues that there's a restaurant inside, and the menu seems a little humdrum at first glance. But what a place this is. Fish and seafood are prepared to give maximum expression to the natural flavors; it's all delicious, quantities are enormous, and the salads are particularly praiseworthy.

Escauriza SEAFOOD $$
(☎454-1777; www.escaurizaparrilla.com.ar; cnr Bajada Escauriza & Paseo Ribereño; mains AR$70-120; ⏲lunch & dinner) Just behind the Florida beach in the northern part of the city, this legendary place is one of Rosario's best spots to eat seafood. The enormous open dining area is redolent with the aromas of chargrilling river fish and plump fried calamari. Service, quality and quantity are all highly impressive. Book, get there at noon, or wait and wait if you want to lunch here on a summer weekend.

La Estancia PARRILLA $$
(www.parrillalaestancia.com.ar; Av Carlos Pellegrini 1501; mains AR$65-110; ⏲noon-3.30pm & 8pm-1am;) A sound choice on the Pellegrini strip, this typical upmarket grillhouse has really excellent cuts of meat – the *vacío* is special – allied with enough waiters that you'll never have to, er, wait. The only downsides are the closely spaced tables and mediocre wine list.

Amarra2 ARGENTINE $$
(☎447-7550; www.amarrarestaurante.com.ar; cnr Buenos Aires & Av Belgrano; mains AR$75-115;

Rosario

11am-3.30pm daily, 7.30pm-midnight or later Mon-Sat;) Smart but relaxed, this restaurant opposite the tourist office has a stylish split-level interior and serves up some very imaginative dishes, beautifully presented and prepared. Its specialty is fish, but the meat is also delicious. There are always interesting offers and specials available, usually including paella.

El Viejo Balcón PARRILLA **$$**
(cnr Italia & Wheelwright; mains AR$60-100; lunch & dinner) Be prepared to wait for a table at this long-time Rosario favorite in a *parrilla*-rich zone by the river. The meat is generously proportioned and of excellent quality: staff will even listen to how you want it cooked. There's enough on the menu here (crepes, pastas) to cater for all tastes.

La Chernia, El Chucho y La Cholga SEAFOOD **$$**
(www.rubenmolinengo.com; cnr JM de Rosas & Mendoza; mains AR$60-110; noon-3pm & 8pm-midnight) Step back a century in time as you walk into this beautifully decorated romantic corner restaurant. The long menu is all fish, from local river varieties to stews and soups bursting with tasty seafood. Shared platters for two are an enjoyable and good-value way to go here.

Don Ferro PARRILLA **$$**
(www.puertoespana.com.ar; Paraná riverbank; mains AR$60-115; 11am-3.30pm & 8pm-1am;) The handsomest restaurant in town, this is exquisitely set in an old brick railroad shed, with a delightful terrace on the platform, excellent service and seriously delicious meat. The menu is wide-ranging, though, and has mixed-grilled vegetables and more meaty options than most. Wines are very overpriced. It's on the riverbank near España.

Don Leo PARRILLA **$$**
(www.donleoparrilla.com; Av Carlos Pellegrini 971; mains AR$55-90; lunch & dinner) The angled timber ceiling and floorboards succeed in giving this *parilla* the feel of a rural grill restaurant, but its popular terrace on the Pellegrini strip brings home the urban reality. Excellent *parrilla* options and a reasonably priced wine list make it a smart choice. Packs out at weekends.

Davis ARGENTINE **$$$**
(435-7142; www.complejodavis.com; Av de la Costa 2550; mains AR$85-130, bar snacks AR$40-65; lunch & dinner;) Occupying Rosario's

most charming position, right on the river below the contemporary art museum with 180-degree views, is a smart restaurant inside a glass cube, and outdoor riverside seating with an overpriced bar menu of sandwiches and similar. The eats are much better inside – try the riverfish platter for two – but have a beer on the deck first to make the most of the location.

Drinking & Nightlife

Rosario has a great number of *restobares*, which function as hybrid cafes and bars and generally serve a fairly standard selection of snacks and plates. Many are good for a morning coffee, an evening glass of wine – or anything in between.

Espiria CAFE
(www.facebook.com/culturaespiria; Montevideo 2124; 8am-8pm Mon-Tue, 8am-1am Wed-Fri, 9am-1am Sat, 10am-1am Sun;) Perfect for combining with a visit to the nearby Museo Municipal de Bellas Artes, this enchanting cafe-bookshop-gallery occupies a beautiful house that has stained glass and an enticing patio. Innovative food, good breakfasts, coffees and juices make this one of Rosario's most relaxing spots.

Pasaporte CAFE, BAR
(cnr Maipú & Urquiza; 8am-late Mon-Sat;) Sublimely cozy with a pretty terrace and timeworn wooden furniture, this is a favorite for morning coffee with workers from the customs department opposite. But it also has a great evening atmosphere, particularly when the rain's pouring outside.

El Cairo CAFE, BAR
(www.barelcairo.com; cnr Sarmiento & Santa Fe; 7am-1am Mon-Thu, 7am-3am Fri & Sat, 4pm-1am Sun;) High-ceilinged and elegant, with huge panes of glass for people-watching (and vice versa), this classic Rosario cafe is good at any time of day, but especially in the evening, when it mixes a decent cocktail and puts on good Argentine pub grub. This is also one of the rare places that serve *mate* (a bitter ritual tea).

La Sede CAFE
(www.barlasede.com.ar; Entre Ríos 599; 8am-midnight or later;) In a striking modernist building, this is a very Argentine cafe with a literary feel and art exhibited on the walls. Come here to read a book, enjoy the draft beer, cakes and quiches or, at weekends, catch an offbeat live performance in the cozy downstairs space.

Fenicia BREWPUB
(www.feniciabrewing.com.ar; Francia 168; noon-late Tue-Fri, 6pm-late Sat & Sun;) You can smell the malt at this brewpub, where the delicious ales are produced right beneath your feet. It's a fine place to start exploring this bar-rich nightlife zone, and it also does a handy line in quesadillas, burgers and salads. The roof terrace is good on a warm evening. It's northwest of the city center, near the train station.

Popurrí CAFE
(Santa Fe 1510; 9am-8pm Mon-Fri, plus 10am-8pm Sat Apr-Sep;) Halfway between hipster and hippie, this lives up to its name with colorfully eclectic decor. Great juices and smoothies are accompanied by tasty, wholesome homestyle fare: omelets, sandwiches, or whatever takes their fancy that day (light meals AR$20 to A$40).

Rock & Feller's BAR
(www.rockandfellers.com.ar; cnr Blvd Oroño & Jujuy; 10am-late;) This enormous bar is a striking sight with its wall-to-wall guitar-hero decoration, good-looking bar and terrace area, and comfy padded stools cmblazoned with rock icons. Based on the much-imitated Hard Rock Café template, this is very popular locally for its atmosphere and menu of pizzas, sandwiches and the like. The only thing missing, at least when we visited, was rock music.

Moore CLUB
(www.facebook.com/moorerosario; Estación Fluvial; Thu-Sat Mar-Nov) One of the few central nightclubs, this is atmospherically located in the Estación Fluvial building with an outdoor deck and a consistently packed upstairs dance floor.

Madame/Club Brown CLUB
(www.mdmdisco.com; cnr Brown & Francia; 11pm-5:30am Fri-Sat) Claiming to be Latin America's biggest club, this massive, stylish former factory complex draws people from Buenos Aires at weekends.

Entertainment

There are lots of tango places in Rosario; grab the monthly listings booklet from the tourist office.

La Casa del Tango TANGO CENTER (www.facebook.com/casadeltangorosario; Av Illia 1750; ⌚9am-2pm) This tango center has info on performances and classes around town, often offers fun, very cheap evening lessons, and stages various events. The 9pm Saturday sessions are regular, and a great deal at AR$30. There's also a good cafe and restaurant. It's on the riverbank road near the junction with España.

Sports

Rosario has two rival *fútbol* teams with several league titles between them. **Newell's Old Boys** (☎421-1180; www.nob.com.ar; Parque Independencia) plays in red and black at Estadio Marcelo Bielsa, where the club is based, and has a long, proud history of producing great Argentine *fútbol* players. **Rosario Central** (☎421-0000; www.rosariocentral.com; cnr Blvd Avellaneda & Génova) plays in blue and yellow stripes at Estadio 'El Gigante de Arroyito'. Buy tickets from the stadiums from two hours before the match.

Shopping

Mercado de Pulgas del Bajo MARKET (Av Belgrano; ⌚2-8pm Sat, noon-8pm Sun) A small handicrafts market by the tourist office, where dealers sell everything from silverwork to leather goods. There are several other weekend markets held along the riverbank, including an excellent Sunday retro market near where Oroño meets the 'coast.'

Information

There are numerous places to get online, and plenty of spots offer free wi-fi, including Plaza 25 de Mayo and the pedestrian zone (network: mr_gratuita).

Several 24-hour pharmacies are in the city center, including on the corner of San Lorenzo and Entre Ríos.

Banks and ATMs are all over, with a cluster along Santa Fe near Plaza 25 de Mayo.

There are many *locutorios* (private telephone offices) around the city center.

Hospital Clemente Álvarez (☎480-8111; Av Carlos Pellegrini 3205) Southwest of the city center.

Sicómoro Ciber (Laprida 966; per hr AR$7; ⌚8am-2am Mon-Sat, 10am-2am Sun; wi-fi) Internet access.

Tourist Office (☎480-2230; www.rosarioturismo.com; Av del Huerto; ⌚9am-7pm) On the riverbank in the city center.

Getting There & Away

AIR

Aerolíneas Argentinas (☎0810-222-86527; www.aerolineas.com.ar; España 840; ⌚10am-6pm Mon-Fri, 9am-noon Sat) Flies daily to Buenos Aires.

Gol (www.voegol.com.br) Serves São Paulo in Brazil.

Sol (☎0810-444-4765; www.sol.com.ar) Flies daily to Buenos Aires and also services Mendoza, Córdoba, Montevideo and Punta del Este, among others.

BUS

The **long-distance bus terminal** (☎437-3030; www.terminalrosario.com.ar; Cafferata & Santa Fe) is 25 blocks west of the city center. From downtown, any bus along Santa Fe will do the trick. To get to the city center, take a bus marked 'Centro' or 'Plaza Sarmiento.' It's about AR$25 to AR$30 in a taxi.

Rosario is a major transportation hub and there are direct daily services to nearly all major destinations, including international services.

Manuel Tienda León (☎409-8000; www.mtl-rosario.com.ar; San Lorenzo 935) offers a direct service to or from Buenos Aires' international airport for AR$400. It does hotel pickups.

Buses from Rosario

DESTINATION	COST (AR$)	DURATION (HR)
Buenos Aires	170	4
Córdoba	230	5-7
Corrientes	430	9-11
Mendoza	385	12-15
Paraná	70	3
Posadas	596	14-15
Salta	696	15-17
Santa Fe	64	2½-3½
Tucumán	520	12-13

TRAIN

From **Rosario Norte train station** (www.ferrocentralsa.com.ar; Av del Valle 2750), unreliable services run several times weekly to Buenos Aires (AR$21 to AR$54, six to eight hours). Other trains run by **Ferrocentral** (www.ferrocentralsa.com.ar; tickets AR$21-54) that stop here en route between Buenos Aires and Córdoba, and Buenos Aires and Tucumán, do offer a more interesting trip but are often booked out well in advance.

Take bus 138 from San Juan and Mitre to the train station.

Getting Around

TO/FROM THE AIRPORT

To get to the **airport** (Fisherton; ☎451-6300; www.aeropuertorosario.com; Av Jorge Newbery s/n), 8km west of town, a taxi will charge around AR$80.

BICYCLE

For bike rental, head to Rosario Bike, Kayak & Motor Boat Tours (p154), which has well-equipped town bikes for AR$60/80 per half/full day or AR$300 per week. You'll need your passport and an AR$200 deposit. It usually has bikes available at the Estación Fluvial too.

BUS

From the local bus terminal on Plaza Sarmiento, bus services run virtually everywhere (see www.rosariobus.com.ar). Have the AR$3.75 fare in coins. You can buy a rechargeable card for AR$10 at any kiosk (AR$3.20 per trip).

Santa Fe

☎0342 / POP 526,100

There's quite a contrast between Santa Fe's relaxed center, where colonial buildings age gracefully in the humid heat and nobody seems to get beyond an amble, and a Friday night in the Recoleta district where university students in dozens of bars show the night no mercy. Capital of its province, but with a small-town feel, Santa Fe is an excellent place to visit for a day or two.

Santa Fe de la Veracruz (its full title) was moved here in 1651 from its original location at Cayastá, 75km to the north. In 1853 Argentina's first constitution was ratified by an assembly that met here; these days ambitious riverfront rehabilitation has added extra appeal to this historic city.

Santa Fe's remaining colonial buildings are within a short walk of Plaza 25 de Mayo, the town's functional center. Av San Martín, north of the plaza, is the major commercial street and part of it forms an attractive *peatonal* (pedestrian district) with palm trees and terraces.

To the east, a bridge crosses the river, then a tunnel beneath the Paraná connects Santa Fe with its twin city of Paraná in Entre Ríos.

Sights

★Convento y Museo de San Francisco MONASTERY
(Amenábar 2257; admission AR$5; ⏲8am-noon & 4-7pm Mon-Sat) The principal historical landmark is this Franciscan monastery and museum, built in 1680. While the museum is mediocre, the church is beautiful, with an exquisite wooden ceiling. The lovely cloister has a real colonial feel and is full of birdsong and the perfume of flowers. The monastery is still home to a handful of monks.

On your left as you enter the church is a fine polychrome Christ by grumpy Spanish master Alonso Cano, sent as a sympathy gift by the Queen of Spain when the town moved in 1649. By the altar, a stone marks the tomb of a priest who was killed by a jaguar taking refuge in the church during the 1825 flooding.

★Museo Histórico Provincial MUSEUM
(www.museobrigadierlopez.gob.ar; Av San Martín 1490; admission AR$5; ⏲8:30am-12:30pm & 3:30-8:30pm Tue-Fri, 5:30-8:30pm Sat & Sun) In a lovable 17th-century building, this museum has a variety of possessions and mementos of various provincial governors and *caudillos* (provincial strongmen), as well as some religious art and fine period furnishings, including a sedan chair once used to carry around the Viceroy of Río de la Plata. The opening hours indicated are for summer: it doesn't close mid-afternoon the rest of the year.

Museo Etnográfico y Colonial Provincial MUSEUM
(25 de Mayo 1470; donation AR$4; ⏲8:30am-12:30pm & 3-7pm Tue-Fri, 8:30am-12:30pm & 4-7pm Sat & Sun) Run with heartwarming enthusiasm by local teachers, this museum features a chronological display of stone tools, Guaraní ceramics, jewelry, carved bricks and colonial objects. Highlights of the museum include a set of *tablas* – a colonial game similar to backgammon – and a scale model of both original Santa Fe settlements. Afternoon opening hours tend to vary.

Plaza 25 de Mayo SQUARE
The center of colonial Santa Fe is a peaceful square framed by fine buildings. The vast **Casa de Gobierno** (Government House) was built in 1909 and replaced the demolished *cabildo* (town council building), seat of the 1852 constitutional assembly. On the square's east side, the exterior simplicity of the Jesuit **Iglesia de la Compañía** masks an ornate interior. The **cathedral** is a little underwhelming by comparison, and dates from the mid-18th century.

Santa Fe

Top Sights

1 Convento y Museo de San Francisco A7
2 Museo Histórico Provincial A7

Sights

3 Casa de Gobierno A7
4 Cathedral A6
5 Iglesia de la Compañía A6
6 Museo Etnográfico y Colonial Provincial A7
7 Plaza 25 de Mayo A6

Activities, Courses & Tours

8 Costa Litoral B4

Sleeping

9 Hostal Santa Fe de la Veracruz A3
10 Hotel Constituyentes B3
11 Hotel Emperatriz B3
12 Hotel Galeón B3

Eating

13 Club Social Sirio Libanés B3
14 La Boutique del Cocinero B3
15 Merengo A6
16 Restaurante España A3

Drinking & Nightlife

17 Chopería Santa Fe A1

Tours

Costa Litoral BOAT TOUR

(☎456-4381; www.costalitoral.net; Dique 1) From the redeveloped harbor area, a large catamaran runs weekend trips around the river islands (adult/child AR$70/50, two hours, 11am Saturday and Sunday) or to Paraná (adult/child AR$95/70, 5½ hours, 2pm Saturday and Sunday) with a couple of hours to explore the city. Book tickets in the bar opposite the dock.

Sleeping

The area around the bus terminal is the budget-hotel zone. Nearly all hotels offer a discount for cash payment, or a surcharge for card payment. To keep things simple, cash prices are listed here. Most offer free parking.

Hotel Constituyentes HOTEL $

(☎452-1586; www.hotelconstituyentes.com.ar; San Luis 2862; s/d AR$220/300, without bathroom AR$120/180; ❄@📶) Spacious rooms, low prices and proximity to the bus terminal are the main drawcards of this relaxed place. It's not luxury, but the owners are always looking to improve things and it makes a pleasant budget base. Rooms at the front suffer from street noise. Breakfast is AR$20 extra.

Hostal Santa Fe de la Veracruz HOTEL $
(455-1740; www.hostalsf.com; Av San Martín 2954; s/d standard AR$315/387, superior AR$447/518;) Decorated with indigenous motifs, this hotel on the pedestrian street offers polite service, spacious superior rooms and decent, slightly downbeat standards. It'll soon be time for redecorating though – those dozen shades of beige are looking a little dated. Siesta fans will love the 6pm checkout.

Hotel Emperatriz HOTEL $
(453-0061; emperatrizhotel.wordpress.com; Irigoyen Freyre 2440; s/d AR$250/350;) With a decayed but noble facade and other-era fittings, this hotel seems to have slipped under the radar of the 21st century. The rooms are small and not luxurious – there are various sizes and prices – but they're clean. It's a rather charming slice of old-time Argentina that won't be around in a few years' time. No cards.

★**Los Silos** HOTEL $$
(450-2800; www.hotellossilos.com.ar; Dique 1; s/d AR$760/850;) Santa Fe's decaying waterfront has been smartened up, and this excellent hotel is the star. Brilliantly converted from grain silos, it features original, rounded rooms with marvelous views and plenty of modern comfort. The vistas from the rooftop pool, spa and sundeck are even better, and service is excellent throughout. A handsome cafe and great play area for kids are other highlights; there's also an attached casino.

Hotel Galeón HOTEL $$
(454-1788; www.hotelgaleon.com.ar; Belgrano 2759; s/d AR$345/420;) Bright, unusual, and all curved surfaces and weird angles, this cheery place is a breath of fresh air. There's a variety of room types available, none of which is a conventional shape; the beds are seriously comfortable and the bathrooms pleasant. It's handy for the bus, too.

Eating

The best zones for cheap eats are across from the bus terminal, and the nightlife zone of La Recoleta.

Club Social Sirio Libanés MIDDLE EASTERN $
(25 de Mayo 2740; mains AR$30-65; 11.30am-2.30pm & 7-11.30pm Tue-Sun) Hidden down a passageway leading to a gym, this offers tasty, well-prepared Middle Eastern–style dishes as well as river fish, pasta and *parrilla* options; it's a pleasingly unusual place to eat. There's outdoor seating in the interior patio. Kitchen closes at 2pm lunchtimes.

Merengo BAKERY $
(www.alfajoresmerengo.com; Av General López 2634; alfajores from AR$3; 9am-12:30pm & 3-8pm) In 1851 Merengo stuck two biscuits together with *dulce de leche* (milk caramel) and invented the *alfajor*, now Argentina's favorite snack. They're still going strong: this, on the plaza, is one of several branches.

La Boutique del Cocinero INTERNATIONAL $$
(456-3864; www.laboutiquedelcocinero.com; Irigoyen 2443; dinner AR$190; dinner Fri & Sat) This innovative chef's shop has an open kitchen out the back, where staff will teach you to cook various styles of food in their Tuesday and Thursday evening classes. Best are the weekend dinners, which might be Indian, sushi, Lebanese or anything else: those who have booked turn up, make the dinner, supervised by a chef, then sit down to eat it together with a decent wine. Great fun. Book ahead.

El Quincho de Chiquito SEAFOOD $$
(cnr Brown & Obispo Vieytes; set menu AR$95; lunch & dinner) This legendary local institution is *the* place for river fish, on the *costanera* 6km north of downtown. There are few frills and no choice: four or five courses of delicious surubí, sábalo or pacú are brought out; you can repeat as often as you want. Drinks are extra but cheap.

It's around AR$35 each way in a taxi (staff will call you one to take you back) or catch bus 16 from any point on the waterfront road (AR$3.25).

Restaurante España ARGENTINE $$
(www.lineaverdehoteles.com; Av San Martín 2644; mains AR$80-110; lunch & dinner;) This hotel restaurant on the pedestrian street is a lovely space, with high ceilings, attentive staff and an old-fashioned feel. There's a huge menu that covers the range of fish (both locally caught and from the sea), steaks, pasta, chicken and crepes, with a few Spanish dishes thrown in to justify the name. The wine list is a winner, too.

Nesta ARGENTINE $$
(☎15-531-6718; www.facebook.com/nesta.restobar; Maipú 1964; mains AR$40-80; ⊙lunch & dinner) The nostalgic decor of this handsome house in a quiet leafy barrio makes a welcome evening retreat. A small menu of pizzas, vegetarian options and a couple of well-prepared meat dishes is accompanied by reggae or chillout beats. Worth booking at weekends.

Drinking & Nightlife

Santa Fe's nightlife centers on the intersection of 25 de Mayo and Santiago del Estero, the heart of the area known as La Recoleta, which goes wild on weekend nights – a crazy contrast to the sedate pace of life downtown. Places change name and popularity rapidly, so just take a look around the dozens of bars and clubs.

Chopería Santa Fe CAFE, BAR
(www.choperiasantafe.com.ar; San Jerónimo 3498; ⊙9am-late;) Santa Fe is a brewing town, and there's nowhere better to try the local lager than this historic corner pub. It's a huge affair, with streetside tables, a cypress-shaded terrace and an immense interior. A wide range of Argentine bar food – *picadas* (shared appetizer plates), sandwiches, pizzas and the like – is available to soak it up.

Entertainment

The city's best *fútbol* team, **Colón** (☎459-8025; www.clubcolon.com.ar; cnr Dr Zavalla & Pietranera), is in the top division. It plays at the Brigadier Estanislao López stadium, where you can also pick up tickets.

Information

Telephone and internet shops are all over, including in the bus terminal. Several banks with ATMs can be found along the *peatonal*.

Hospital Provincial José María Cullen (☎457-3340; Av Freyre 2150)

Municipal Tourist Office (☎457-4123; www.santafeturismo.gov.ar; Belgrano 2910; ⊙8am-8pm) In the bus terminal.

Provincial Tourist Office (☎458-9476; www.turismosantafe.com.ar; cnr Amenábar & Av San Martín; ⊙7am-1pm Mon-Fri) Helpful office for provincial exploration.

Tourist Information Booth (www.santafeturismo.gov.ar; Av San Martín s/n; ⊙7am-1pm & 4-8pm Mon-Fri, 9am-1pm & 4-8pm Sat) At the southern end of the pedestrian strip.

Getting There & Away

Aerolíneas Argentinas (www.aerolineas.com.ar) has six weekly flights to Buenos Aires (AR$430). **Sol** (☎0810-444-4765; www.sol.com.ar) flies the same route. The airport is 7km south of town on RN 11. A *remise* (booked taxi) will cost about AR$50.

From the **bus terminal** (☎457-4124; www.terminalsantafe.com; Belgrano 2910) there are bus services throughout the country.

BUSES FROM SANTA FE

DESTINATION	COST (AR$)	DURATION (HR)
Buenos Aires	252	6
Córdoba	200	5
Corrientes	329	8
Paraná	6	40min
Posadas	509	12
Resistencia	315	7
Rosario	64	2
Salta	784	16
Tucumán	472	11

Cayastá

An interesting day trip from Santa Fe takes you to that city's original location, the **Cayastá ruins** (Santa Fe la Vieja; ☎03405-493056; www.santafe-conicet.gov.ar/santafelavieja; RP1, Km78, Cayastá; admission AR$2; ⊙9am-1pm & 3-7pm Tue-Fri, 10am-1pm & 4-7pm Sat & Sun Oct-Mar, 9am-1pm & 2-6pm Tue-Fri, noon-6pm Sat & Sun Apr-Sep), picturesquely set beside the Río San Javier, which has eroded away a good portion of them.

There's ongoing archaeological excavation and conservation, but the most fascinating find by far has been the **Iglesia de San Francisco**. The Spanish and mestizo inhabitants of old Santa Fe were buried directly beneath the earth-floored church, and nearly 100 graves have been excavated, including those of Hernando Arias de Saavedra ('Hernandarias'), the first locally born governor of Río de la Plata province, and his wife, Jerónima, daughter of Juan de Garay, who founded Santa Fe and Buenos Aires. The skeletons have now been replaced by replicas, but it's still a spooky, atmospheric place.

You can also see the remains of two other churches (there were originally six) and the *cabildo* (town council building), as well as a handsome reconstructed period house. Near the site entrance is an attractive **museum** housing finds, including fine indigenous pottery with parrot and human motifs.

Last entry is strictly one hour before closing. If you want to visit in the morning, you will have to get the 9am bus here from Santa Fe.

There's a mediocre restaurant at the site and a couple of decent *parrillas* in town. Several spots both in Cayastá and along the RP1 offer cabin-type lodgings and boat trips on the river.

Cayastá is 76km northeast of Santa Fe on RP1 and served regularly from Santa Fe's bus terminal (AR$30, 1½ hours). Ask the driver to drop you at *'las ruinas,'* 1km short of Cayastá itself.

Paraná

☎0343 / POP 247,700

Unpretentious Paraná seems surprised at its own status as capital of Entre Ríos province. Perched on the hilly banks of its eponymous river, it's a sleepy, slow-paced city. Paraná was the capital of the Argentine Confederation (which didn't include Buenos Aires) from 1853 to 1861.

A tunnel beneath the main channel of the Paraná connects the city to Santa Fe.

Sights

★Museo Histórico de Entre Ríos Martiniano Leguizamón MUSEUM
(cnr Buenos Aires & Laprida; donation AR$4; 8am-12:30pm & 3-8pm Tue-Fri, 9am-noon & 5-8pm Sat, 9am-noon Sun) Flaunting local pride, this modern museum on Plaza Alvear contains information on the short-lived Republic of Entre Ríos and the battle of Monte Camperos, as well as *mate* paraphernalia and numerous solid wooden desks and portraits of Urquiza. Much of it was the collection of a local poet.

★Museo y Mercado Provincial de Artesanías HANDICRAFTS
(Av Urquiza 1239; 8am-1pm & 4-7pm Mon-Fri, 8am-1pm Sat, 9am-noon Sun) FREE Promoting handicrafts from throughout the province, this is a likable little place. Ask the curator to explain things to you; you'll be amazed at the intricacy of some of the work, such as the hats made from tightly woven palm fibers.

Costanera RIVERBANK
From the northern edge of downtown, Parque Urquiza slopes steeply downward to the banks of the Río Paraná. During summer the waterfront fills with people strolling, fishing and swimming. There's a public beach, Playa El Parque, west of the Paraná Rowing Club's private strand, but a better strip of sand, Playas de Thompson, is 1km further east, beyond the port.

Tours

Baqueanos del Río BOAT TOUR
(☎15-611-9170; baqucanosdelrio@ecourbano.org.ar; tours per person AR$50) Offers river excursions in wooden boats. Guides know a lot about the river and its ecosystem. Ring or email to book. Boats leave from the eastern end of the *costanera,* by the tourist office. At weekends in summer you can often just show up and wait for the next departure.

Costa Litoral BOAT TOUR
(☎423-4385; www.costalitoral.net; Buenos Aires 212) At weekends, this outfit runs afternoon one-way trips to Santa Fe and one-hour cruises on the river (adult/child AR$50/30) in a large catamaran.

Paraná en Kayak KAYAKING
(☎422-7143; www.paranaenkayak.com.ar) Easy kayak trips on the river as well as longer routes.

Sleeping

★Paraná Hostel HOSTEL $
(☎422-8233; www.paranahostel.com.ar; Pazos 159; dm/d AR$90/195) Right in the mix in central Paraná, this hostel has good security, a tree-shaded back patio and garden, as well as smart furnishings, decent facilities and comfy dorms. Upstairs are attractive, airy private rooms that share a bathroom. Rooms with air-con cost AR$10 more.

Las Mañanitas HOTEL $
(☎407-4753; www.lasmanianitas.com.ar; Carbó 62; s/d AR$300/350) There's a summer-house feel about this delightfully relaxed little budget place, which has nine rooms alongside a courtyard and garden with pool. The rooms are unremarkable, though well-priced – some are darkish duplexes, others simpler and lighter – but it's the grace of the whole ensemble that makes this a winner. Some of the plumbing could do with a refit.

Paraná

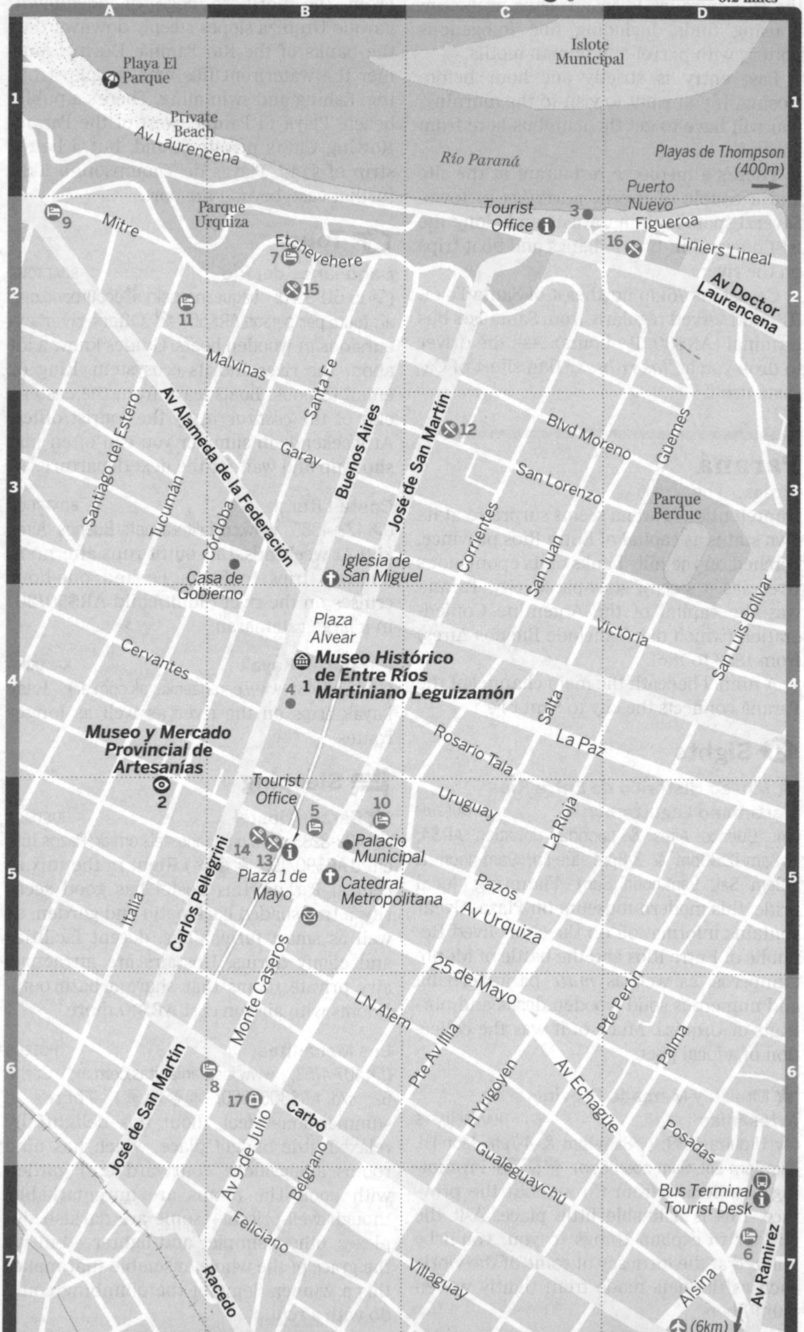
0 400 m
0 0.2 miles
Playa El Parque
Private Beach
Av Laurencena
Islote Municipal
Río Paraná
Playas de Thompson (400m)
Puerto Nuevo
Tourist Office
3
Figueroa
16
Liniers Lineal
Av Doctor Laurencena
9
Mitre
Parque Urquiza
7
Etchevehere
15
11
Malvinas
Santa Fe
Av Alameda de la Federación
Buenos Aires
José de San Martín
12
Blvd Moreno
Güemes
Garay
Santiago del Estero
Tucumán
Córdoba
San Lorenzo
Parque Berduc
Corrientes
San Juan
Iglesia de San Miguel
Casa de Gobierno
Plaza Alvear
Victoria
San Luis Bolívar
Cervantes
Museo Histórico de Entre Ríos Martiniano Leguizamón
1
4
Salta
La Paz
Museo y Mercado Provincial de Artesanías
2
Rosario Tala
Uruguay
Tourist Office
5
10
La Rioja
14
13
Palacio Municipal
Plaza 1 de Mayo
Catedral Metropolitana
Pazos
Italia
Carlos Pellegrini
Av Urquiza
Monte Caseros
25 de Mayo
Pte Perón
LN Alem
Pte Av Illia
Palma
José de San Martín
8
17
Carbó
H Yrigoyen
Av Echagüe
Av 9 de Julio
Belgrano
Gualeguaychú
Posadas
Bus Terminal
Tourist Desk
Feliciano
6
Villaguay
Racedo
Alsina
Av Ramírez
(6km)
A B C D
1 2 3 4 5 6 7

Paraná

Top Sights

Activities, Courses & Tours

Sleeping

Eating

Shopping

Hotel Bristol HOTEL **$**
(☎431-3961; Alsina 221; s/d AR$150/250; ❄📶) Right by the bus terminal, this budget hotel is well kept and quiet. Simple rooms with small bathrooms offer decent value.

Posada del Rosedal GUESTHOUSE **$$**
(☎422-3148; www.posadadelrosedal.com.ar; Santiago del Estero 656; s/d AR$300/510; ❄📶) Five rooms and a lovely little garden patio set on a quiet street just back from the riverside park: all you need for a dose of Paraná relaxation. Simple, compact, spotless rooms, helpful staff, and, in spring, a riot of flowering plants are plus points, as is the family room up at the back. More than the sum of its parts.

Maran Suites HOTEL **$$**
(☎423-5444; www.maran.com.ar; cnr Alameda de la Federación & Mitre; s AR$568, d AR$760-807; ❄@📶🏊) Towering over the western end of Parque Urquiza, this sleek modern hotel has a rare combination of style and warm-hearted personal service. Try to get a room as high up as possible, for city or river views. All the rooms are very spacious and decorated with flair; the 'presidential' suites (AR$1080) are big enough to get lost in and boast a Jacuzzi with memorable vistas over the water.

Gran Hotel Paraná HOTEL **$$**
(☎422-3900; www.hotelesparana.com.ar; Av Urquiza 976; s AR$515-644, d AR$623-779; ❄@📶) Fine service is a major plus at this large hotel on the main square, Plaza 1 de Mayo. There are two grades of room, all recently refurbished and spacious. If you don't mind a bit of traffic noise, try for a balcony on the square. Massages and Pilates are available, and there's a high-quality restaurant.

Howard Johnson Mayorazgo HOTEL **$$$**
(☎420-6800; www.hjmayorazgo.com.ar; Etchevehere; r AR$1054; ❄📶🏊) The long curved facade of this remodeled five-star dominates the waterfront from above. All the rooms face the river, are very spacious, and offer great views from large windows. A little bit extra gets you a balcony, but those rooms are lower down. There's an indoor and outdoor pool, spa, gym and a large casino. You'll find better rates online.

Eating

Flamingo Grand Bar CAFE **$**
(www.flamingograndbar.com.ar; cnr Av Urquiza & José de San Martín; light meals AR$30-60, set lunches AR$60-72; ⏰8am-10pm; 📶) Smart seats and a plaza-side location make this a favorite throughout the day, from morning croissants and juices through to *lomitos* (steak sandwiches) and lunch specials to decent à la carte dishes and *picadas*.

Don Charras PARRILLA **$$**
(☎422-5972; cnr José de San Martín & San Lorenzo; mains AR$70-120; ⏰11.30pm-3.30pm & 7.30pm-12.30am or later Tue-Sun; 📶) Thatched and atmospheric, this *parrilla* is a popular Paraná choice. Fridays and Saturdays see special fire-roasted options, but you can enjoy the usual chargrilled selection and solicitous service otherwise. Deep-pan stews are designed to share between three or more. Starters, drinks and the salad bar are scandalously overpriced, but the meat comes out in most generous portions.

Lola Valentina de los Pipos ARGENTINE **$$**
(☎423-5234; www.facebook.com/lolavalentina.parana; cnr Córdoba & Mitre; mains AR$70-120; ⏰11am-2.30pm & 8pm-midnight Mon-Fri, 11am-3pm & 8pm-1am Sat & Sun) With a cheerful but formal atmosphere and politely correct service, this evocative corner restaurant serves up delicious homemade pastas and some

1

KRZYSZTOF DYDYNSKI/GETTY IMAGES ©

2

4

MARIANA ELIANO/GETTY IMAGES ©

IAN TROWER/GETTY IMAGES ©

1. Iguazú Falls (p195)
Viewing this jaw-dropping sight is one of the highlights of a visit to Argentina.

2. San Ignacio Miní (p191)
The best preserved mission ruins in all of Argentina.

3. Toucan
This colorful species can be easily seen al Parque Nacional Iguazú.

4. Reserva Provincial Esteros del Iberá (p175)
Stunning wetlands that contain an abundant array of wildlife and aquatic plants.

JOHN W BANAGAN/GETTY IMAGES ©

great dishes using fish from the nearby Paraná.

Giovani ARGENTINE $$
(☎423-0527; Av Urquiza 1045; mains AR$60-110; ⏰11.30am-3.30pm & 8pm-midnight; 📶) With as-it-should-be service and thoughtful touches such as free coffee, this stylish restaurant in the center of town serves excellent meats from the *parrilla* and delectable pasta. There's a good range of fish dishes and a rather refined, romantic atmosphere.

Quincho del Puerto FISH $$
(Av Doctor Laurencena 350; fish AR$70-95; ⏰11am-2.30pm & 7-11.30pm, later on Sat & Sun) Popular spot for river fish just back from the *costanera*. There are various options, including the tasty (but bony) pacú and surubí. There are also pasta and *parrilla* options for those who don't fancy the finny tribes.

Drinking & Nightlife

Paraná is quiet midweek, but gets busier on Friday and Saturday nights. Most of the action is at the eastern end of the riverfront around Liniers Lineal.

Shopping

A recommended place to buy quality handicrafts is the Museo y Mercado Provincial de Artesanías (p165).

Centro de Artesanos HANDICRAFTS
(☎422-4493; cnr Av 9 de Julio & Carbó; ⏰9am-1pm & 4-8pm Apr-Oct, 9am-1pm & 5-9pm Nov-Mar) Traditional *artesanías* (handicrafts) are on display and for sale here. There's some very high-quality ware, and prices are fair.

Information

There are several banks with ATMs within a couple of blocks of Plaza 1 de Mayo. Dozens of places offer internet access and phone calls. There are various free wi-fi networks around the town center and along the *costanera*.

Hospital San Martín (☎423-4545; www.hospitalsanmartin.org.ar; Presidente Perón 450)

Tourist office (☎423-0183; www.turismoparana.gov.ar; Plaza 1 de Mayo s/n; ⏰8am-8pm) Helpful, with good brochures. There's another branch by Río Paraná (Laurencena & San Martín; ⏰8am-8pm), and a desk in the bus terminal (⏰8am-8pm).

Getting There & Around

The airport is 6km south of town, accessible only by *remise* (AR$35). Aerolineas Argentinas and **LAER** (☎0810-777-5237; www.laersa.com.ar) serve Buenos Aires.

The **bus terminal** (☎422-1282) is opposite Plaza Martín Fierro. Buses 1, 4, 5 and 9 run between the terminal and the town center. Paraná is a hub for provincial bus services, but Santa Fe is more convenient for long-distance trips. Buses leave every 30 minutes for Santa Fe (AR$6, 40 minutes).

BUSES FROM PARANÁ

DESTINATION	COST (AR$)	DURATION (HR)
Buenos Aires	270	6½-8
Colón	121	4-5
Concordia	137	4-5
Córdoba	218	6
Paso de los Libres	289	6-9
Rosario	70	3

Corrientes

☎0379 / POP 352,600

Stately Corrientes sits below the confluence of the Paraná and Paraguay rivers just across the water from its twin city, Resistencia. One of the nation's most venerable cities, it has elegant balconied buildings dating from the turn of the 20th century that lend a time-worn appeal to its colorful streets. The *costanera* is everybody's destination of choice for strolling, licking ice creams or sipping *mate* with friends.

Corrientes is a magnet for regional indigenous crafts; Guaraní culture has a strong presence. The city is famous for both its Carnaval and for being the setting of Graham Greene's novel *The Honorary Consul*.

Sights & Activities

Various operators run boat trips on the Paraná; the tourist office has a list.

★**Museo de Artesanías Tradicionales Folclóricas** MUSEUM
(Quintana 905; ⏰8am-8pm Mon-Fri, 9am-noon & 4-7pm Sat) FREE This intriguing museum in a converted colonial house has small displays of fine traditional *artesanía* (handicrafts) as well as a good shop, but the highlight is watching the students being taught to work leather, silver, bone and wood by master craftspeople. Other rooms around the courtyard are occupied by working artisans who will sell to you directly. The museum

guides are enthusiastic, knowledgeable and friendly.

Museo Histórico de Corrientes MUSEUM
(9 de Julio 1044; 8am-noon & 4-8pm Tue-Fri, 9am-noon & 4-7pm Sat) FREE This museum is set around an attractive patio and exhibits weapons, antique furniture, coins, and items dealing with religious and civil history. It's a little bit higgledy-piggledy, but staff are proud of the exhibition and keen to chat. The room on the War of the Triple Alliance is the most interesting.

Teatro Juan de Vera THEATRE
(San Juan 637; ticket office 9am-12.30pm & 6-9pm Tue-Fri, 10am-1pm & 6-9pm Sat) FREE A striking belle-epoque building; ask at the ticket office if you can have a peek inside to see the beautiful treble-galleried theater and its painted ceiling. The cupola retracts when management fancies a starlit performance.

Festivals & Events

Corrientes' traditionally riotous **Carnaval Correntino** competes with Gualeguaychú's for the title of the country's best. Celebrated over four consecutive weekends starting nine weeks before Easter, Carnaval's parades along the *costanera* attract participants from neighboring provinces and countries, with huge crowds.

Sleeping

Many Corrientes hotels offer a 10% discount for paying cash.

Bienvenida Golondrina HOSTEL $
(443-5316; www.bienvenidagolondrina.com; La Rioja 455; dm AR$85, s/d AR$200/280;) Occupying a marvelous centenarian building, all high ceilings, stained glass and artistic flourishes, this hostel makes a great base a few steps from the *costanera*. Comfortable wide-berthed dorm beds have headroom, facilities (including free bikes) are great, and the warmly welcoming management couldn't be more helpful.

Hotel Victoria HOTEL $
(443-5547; www.hotelvictoriaweb.com.ar; Av España 1050; s/d AR$200/280;) This decent budget choice is near Plaza JB Cabral. The doubles are far better than the twins or cramped singles.

★ **La Alondra** BOUTIQUE HOTEL $$
(443-5537; www.laalondra.com.ar; Av 3 de Abril 827; r standard/executive/ste AR$800/925/1100;) Sumptuously furnished with dark-wood antiques, this wonderfully renovated house is an oasis of relaxation from the unappealing main road. Most of the rooms that surround a small finger-shaped pool are suites boasting plush king-sized beds and characterful bathrooms fitted with claw-foot tubs. The newer area has been characterfully created from a former industrial space. Wonderfully handsome public areas and classy service add up to a most impressive package.

La Rozada BOUTIQUE HOTEL $$
(443-3001; www.larozada.com; Plácido Martínez 1223; s/d AR$550/625, with balcony AR$575/650;) This excellent option near the riverfront has commodious apartments and suites unusually set in the tower in the courtyard of an appealing 19th-century, battleship-gray historic building. Fine views are on offer from most rooms – a balcony room is slightly more expensive – and there's an attractive bar-restaurant. Guests can use the pool at the nearby rowing club.

CHAMAMÉ

Tango? What's that? Up here it's all about *chamamé*, one of the country's most intoxicating musical forms. Rooted in the polka, which was introduced by European immigrants, it is also heavily influenced by Guaraní culture. Its definitive sound is the accordion, which is traditionally accompanied by the guitar, the *guitarrón* (an oversized guitar used for playing bass lines), the larger *bandoneón* (accordion) and the *contrabajo* (double bass). Of course, a *conjunto* (band) is hardly complete without a singer or two.

Chamamé is as much a dance as it is a musical genre, and it's a lively one. It is a dance for a couple, except when the man takes his solo *zapateo* (tap dance). Corrientes province is the heart of *chamamé* and is therefore the easiest place to find a live performance. Check out the Spanish-only website www.corrienteschamame.com.ar for details of performances, and online tunes to introduce you to the genre. There's a two-week *chamamé* festival in early January.

Corrientes

Astro Apart Hotel

HOTEL $$

(☎ 446-6112; www.astroapart.com; Bolívar 1285; s/d AR$350/420; ❄@📶) Top value is to be had at this modern place, which features sizable, handsome white rooms with great beds and large windows. They come with a simple kitchen and offer plenty of handy facilities as reasonably priced extras.

Orly Hotel

HOTEL $$

(☎ 442-0280; www.hotelorlycorrientes.com.ar; San Juan 867; s/d budget AR$220/288, standard AR$361/462, superior r AR$576; ❄@📶🏊) Spruce and spotless, this professional and attractive three-star job overlooks a small plaza. It's divided in two; the older standard rooms are fine but smallish, and wi-fi doesn't reach all of them. The midpriced rooms are identical, but with a better TV: not worth the upgrade. The superiors, however, are great, with huge beds, modish couches and good bathrooms. The sauna, pool, Jacuzzi and gym add to the value.

Corrientes Plaza Hotel

HOTEL $$

(☎ 446-6500; www.hotel-corrientes.com.ar; Junín 1549; s/d AR$330/430; ❄@📶🏊) A good deal on the plaza in the heart of modern Corrientes, the Plaza has spacious, faultless modern rooms with LCD television, modern bathrooms and most with minibar. There's a gym and an outdoor pool, staff are friendly and there's a good breakfast spread. All in all, a very good deal.

Turismo Hotel Casino

HOTEL $$$

(☎ 446-2244; www.turismohotelcasino.com.ar; Entre Ríos 650; r AR$1380-1518, ste AR$1670-1837; ❄@📶🏊) By the casino on the riverfront, this stately old place has had a complete refit. It's now an excellent hotel, with modern rooms that are huge, elegantly and artistically furnished, but cozy and quiet. River views cost a little extra; it doesn't cost much to upgrade to a sizable suite; other drawcards include the big pool with plenty of chaise longues, and spa facilities.

Corrientes

Eating

El Quincho PARRILLA $
(cnr Pujol & Roca; parrillada for 2 AR$140-180; lunch & dinner) Rustic and welcoming, this Corrientes classic sits on a roundabout a short walk east of the town center. El Quincho is more about Argentine grill staples such as chorizo and *morcilla* (blood sausage) than fancy cuts of steak; there's always a deal on *parrilla* that comes out cheaper than the price we've listed here – expect about AR$50 a person plus drinks. Quality is good; quantity is enormous

Martha de Bianchetti CAFE, BAKERY $
(cnr 9 de Julio & Mendoza; pastries from AR$5; 8am-1pm & 4-11pm Mon-Sat;) This old-fashioned Italian-style bakery and cafe serves mind-altering pastries and excellent coffee; each cup comes with *chipacitos* (small cheese pastries). All the yummy treats are warm when the doors open.

Enófilos ARGENTINE $$
(443-9271; Junín 1260; mains AR$74-93; 11.30am-3.30pm & 8pm-12.30am Mon-Sat;) An *enófilo* is a wine lover, so the cellar gets plenty of attention at this attentive upstairs restaurant on the *peatonal*. The wine 'list' is displayed in a small temple at the room's center; traditional *correntino* ingredients such as succulent surubí river fish are given creative flair, and fine cuts of meat are showcased to advantage with sauces and fresh vegetables. The international menu is more hit-and-miss.

Sábato ARGENTINE $$
(Pago Largo 829; mains AR$70-90; 7pm-1am daily, noon-3pm Sat & Sun;) Just off the *costanera*, this upbeat spot has bright lights and white walls enlivened by prints of gaucho paintings. The menu is good for cuts from the grill, but also does a nice line in river fish prepared in a varicty of ways. The empanadas (baked savory turnovers) are a tasty way to start.

La Costa ARGENTINE $$
(cnr Av Costanera General San Martín & 9 de Julio; mains AR$50-90; Tue-Sun;) On the *costanera* this two-level modern place has a buzzy atmosphere, and serves a wide variety of Argentine dishes, including great *parrillada*. It's popular in the evenings, but you'll appreciate the river views from the floor-to-ceiling windows more over lunch.

Drinking & Nightlife

The area near the intersection of Junín and Buenos Aires contains several bars and clubs pumping along at weekends. The *costanera* also receives some action, with several bars and *boliches* (nightclubs) in the Costanera Sur zone south of the bridge to Resistencia.

Entertainment

Yacarú Porá LIVE MUSIC
(445-8800; www.yacarupora.com.ar; Av Centenario 4350; live music Wed-Sun evenings) This *parrilla* some 25 blocks east of the town center is one of the province's best places to listen to *chamamé*. There's a live show nightly Wednesdays to Sundays – sit down and hoe into the wine and good-quality meat, then take to the floor. Think AR$30 in a cab from downtown. Thursday has all-you-can-eat pasta and pizza.

Shopping

Museo de Artesanías Tradicionales Folclóricas HANDICRAFTS
(Quintana 905; 8am-8pm Mon-Fri, 9am-noon & 4-7pm Sat) This shop, which is attached to the museum, sells a wide variety of traditional artisan-made handicrafts at fair prices.

La Casa de Chamamé MUSIC
(Pellegrini 1790; ⏲9am-noon & 4-9pm Mon-Fri) This CD shop specializes in Corrientes' roots music, plus you can listen before you buy.

Information

Call shops and internet places are easy to find. There are many banks with ATMs on 9 de Julio between La Rioja and Córdoba. There are various irregularly open information offices around town.

Information Booth (Long-distance bus terminal; ⏲6:30am-12:30pm & 4:30-7:30pm)

Provincial Tourist Office (☎442-7200; www.turismocorrientes.gov.ar; 25 de Mayo 1330; ⏲7:30am-2pm & 3:30-8:30pm Mon-Fri, plus public holiday weekends) The most helpful tourist office.

Getting There & Away

Aerolíneas Argentinas (☎442-3918; www.aerolineas.com.ar; Junín 1301; ⏲8am-12:30pm & 4:30-8pm Mon-Fri, 9am-noon Sat) flies to Buenos Aires daily. It also flies there from nearby Resistencia.

The **long-distance bus terminal** (☎441-4839; Av Maipú 2400) is 3km southeast of the town center. Nearby Resistencia has better long-distance bus connections to the west and northwest. Buses to Resistencia (AR$5, 40 minutes) leave frequently from the **local bus terminal** (cnr Av Costanera General San Martín & La Rioja). Faster are the shared taxis that zip you into Resistencia for AR$10. They leave from the same intersection, and also from the corner of Av 3 de Abril and San Juan.

BUSES FROM CORRIENTES

DESTINATION	COST (AR$)	DURATION (HR)
Buenos Aires	548	12-14
Córdoba	525	11-14
Mercedes	99	3
Paraná	250	8
Paso de los Libres	175	5
Posadas	175	4
Puerto Iguazú	362	9
Rosario	430	10-12
Salta	474	13
Santa Fe	329	7-9

Getting Around

Local bus 109 (AR$2.70) goes to the **airport** (☎445-8358; RN 12), about 10km east of town. Bus 103 runs between the local bus terminal, downtown and the long-distance bus terminal on Av Maipú. A taxi to/from the long-distance bus terminal will cost AR$25 to AR$30.

Mercedes

☎03773 / POP 40,700

The main access point for the spectacular Esteros del Iberá wetlands, Mercedes is a rather handsome gaucho town with a mightily easy pace to life. Its claim to fame is the nearby – and completely surreal – roadside shrine to the gaucho Antonio Gil, an enormously popular religious phenomenon.

Sleeping & Eating

Hotel Sol HOTEL $
(☎420283; San Martín 519; r AR$300; ❄📶) Situated two blocks down from the plaza, this welcoming spot is built around a stunning patio: a riot of plants, birdsong and gleaming chessboard tiles. The high-ceilinged old rooms that open off it are good value for the price; there are also some very attractive modern rooms (double AR$390) up at the back.

Hotel Horizontes HOTEL $
(☎420489; Gómez 734; s/d AR$182/340; ❄📶) A block from the bus terminal, this bare but very clean hotel offers good value for spare, spotless rooms with compact bathrooms. Streetside ones suffer from some traffic noise.

Hotel Itá Pucú HOTEL $
(☎421015; Batalla de Salta 645; r per person AR$120; ❄📶) This friendly low-roofed budget hotel has a sort of spaghetti-western feel, and rickety but OK rooms that open onto a peaceful grassy garden. Breakfast is extra.

Hotel Manantiales Mercedes HOTEL $$
(www.manantialeshoteles.com; cnr Pujol & Sarmiento) Not quite open when we passed through, this brand-new hotel and casino on the square looked like becoming Mercedes' top option.

Sal y Pimienta ARGENTINE $
(Gómez 665; mains AR$35-50; ⏲lunch & dinner; 📶) A local favorite, this uncomplicated place near the bus terminal has a wide-ranging menu and unbeatable prices for its tasty meats, river fish, pastas and pizzas. The *lengua* (tongue) makes a great starter, and service is smart.

Shopping

Manos Correntinas HANDICRAFTS
(San Martín 499; 9am-noon & 5-8pm Mon-Fri, 9am-noon Sat) Manos Correntinas is a friendly handicrafts gallery and shop that displays the work of a cooperative of local craftspeople.

Information

Most services are along San Martín, which links the bus terminal with the plaza.

Centro de Interpretación (15-412216; www.mercedescorrientes.gov.ar; cnr Gómez & Caá Guazú; 7am-1pm & 3-9pm) Three blocks north and a block east of the bus terminal, this information office is helpful.

Bus terminal tourist information (6am-noon & 2-8pm) At the bus terminal. Doesn't always fulfill its timetable. The best for info on transport to Colonia Pellegrini.

Getting There & Away

The **bus terminal** (420165; cnr San Martín & Perreyra) is six blocks west of the plaza. Buses run regularly both ways. Destinations include Buenos Aires (AR$339, eight to 10 hours), Paso de los Libres (AR$42, two hours) and Corrientes (AR$99, three to four hours).

Reserva Provincial Esteros del Iberá

This stunning wetland reserve is home to an abundance of bird and animal life, and is one of the finest places to see wildlife in South America. Although tourism has been increasing substantially in recent years, Los Esteros del Iberá remains comparatively unspoiled. The main base for visiting the park is the sleepy village of **Colonia Pellegrini**, 120km northeast of Mercedes; it offers a variety of excellent accommodations. Rural *estancias* (ranches) in the larger area also make excellent bases.

The lakes and *esteros* (lagoons covered with abundant aquatic vegetation) are shallow, fed only by rainwater, and thick with vegetation. Vegetation accumulates to form *embalsados* (floating islands), and this fertile habitat is home to a stunning array of life. Sinister black caimans bask in the sun while capybaras feed around them. Other mammals include the beautiful orange-colored marsh deer, howler monkeys (officially the world's noisiest animal), the rare maned wolf, coypu, otters and several species of bat.

The birdlife is simply extraordinary; there are some 350 species present in the reserve, including colorful kingfishers, delicate hummingbirds, parrots, spoonbills, kites, vultures, several species of egret and heron, cormorants, ducks, cardinals and the enormous southern screamer, which would really light up Big Uncle Bob's eyes at a Christmas roast. *Ibera: Vida y Color* (AR$50 to AR$70), on sale at various places around town, is a useful wildlife guide with beautiful photos of most of the birds, plants and animals you may see.

Tours

The Laguna Iberá is only a small part of the 13,000-sq-km area of the Esteros. Some 80km north, at Galarza, is the Laguna Galarza and the larger Laguna de Luna, which also can be explored by boat.

Upmarket lodges can organize these activities; if you are staying at one they are usually included in the price. If not, the best place to organize boat trips and other excursions is the campsite (from where most trips leave). Note that few guides speak English; if you want an English-speaking guide, it's best to go through one of the lodges.

Night Walks & Horseback Rides WALKING TOUR
You can take guided night walks here (AR$75 for two hours). Longer guided walks are also available, as are horseback rides (AR$100), although these are more for the ride's sake than for wildlife-spotting.

Boat Trips BOAT TOUR
The best way to appreciate the area is by boat. The classic trip is a two- to three-hour excursion in a *lancha* (small motorboat; AR$120 to AR$150), which takes you around the Laguna Iberá and its *embalsados*. You'll see myriad bird and animal life, elegant lilies, water hyacinths and other aquatic plants. The guide will punt you remarkably close to the creatures. You can also take a night trip; go prepared with plenty of insect repellent!

Sleeping

Colonia Pellegrini

Colonia Pellegrini's accommodations are mushrooming, with more than 30 at last count. They are divided between *hospedajes*, usually simple rooms behind a family home,

GAUCHITO GIL

Spend time on the road anywhere in Argentina and you're bound to see at least one roadside shrine surrounded by red flags and votive offerings. These shrines pay homage to Antonio Gil, a Robin Hood–like figure whose burial place 9km west of Mercedes attracts hundreds of thousands of pilgrims every year.

Little is known for sure about 'El Gauchito,' as he is affectionately known, but many romantic tales have sprung up to fill the gaps. What is known is that he was born in 1847 and joined the army – some versions say to escape the wrath of a local policeman whose fiancée had fallen in love with him – to fight in the War of the Triple Alliance.

Once the war ended, Gil was called up to join the Federalist Army, but went on the run with a couple of other deserters. The trio roamed the countryside, stealing cattle from rich landowners and sharing it with poor villagers, who in turn gave them shelter and protection. The law finally caught up with the gang, and Gil was hung by the feet from the espinillo tree that still stands near his grave, and beheaded.

So how did this freeloading, cattle-rustling deserter attain saintlike status? Moments before his death, Gil informed his executioner that the executioner's son was gravely ill. He told the soldier that if he were buried – not the custom with deserters – the man's son would recover.

After lopping off Gil's head, the executioner carried it back to the town of Goya where – of course – a judicial pardon awaited Gil. On finding that his son was indeed seriously ill, the soldier returned to the site and buried the body. His son recovered quickly, word spread and a legend was born.

'Gauchito' Gil's last resting place is now the site of numerous chapels and storehouses holding thousands of votive offerings – including T-shirts, bicycles, pistols, knives, license plates, photographs, cigarettes, hair clippings and entire racks of wedding gowns – brought by those who believe in the gaucho's miracles. January 8, the date of Gil's death, attracts the most pilgrims.

and posadas (inns) or *hosterías,* comfortable lodges that offer full-board rates and excursions. Multiday packages are usually the best value here. Most accommodations can book a transfer from Mercedes or Posadas for you.

Posada Rancho Jabirú GUESTHOUSE $
(☎03773-15-413750; www.posadaranchojabiru.com.ar; Yaguareté s/n; s/d AR$120/240; ❄📶) The best of the options in this price category. Set in a carefully tended garden, it has spotless rooms sleeping up to five in a pretty bungalow. It's run by the friendly folk of Yacarú Porá restaurant next door.

Hospedaje San Cayetano GUESTHOUSE $
(☎03773-15-400929; www.argentinaparamirar.com.ar; cnr Guazú Virá & Aguapé; s/d AR$150/250; ❄📶🏊) This friendly choice, with its plunge pool, kitchen and *parrilla,* is constantly improving, and offers excellent budget twins, doubles and family rooms with good beds and showers. Rooms can be shared if others want to, and prices are a little negotiable. The boss runs good boat trips and transfers. Beethoven the parrot covers front-of-house.

Hospedaje Los Amigos GUESTHOUSE $
(☎03773-15-493753; hospedajelosamigos@gmail.com; cnr Guazú Virá & Aguapé; r per person AR$80; ❄) This excellent budget choice, with a kindly owner, offers spotless rooms with big beds and decent bathrooms for a pittance. You can also eat simply but well here: attractively inexpensive full-board rates are available.

Hospedaje Iberá GUESTHOUSE $
(☎03773-15-627261; www.hospedajeibera.com.ar; cnr Guazú Virá & Ysypó; r per person AR$100) Set behind a shop, this has a range of clean and spacious rooms with fan and hot-water bathroom.

Camping Iberá CAMPGROUND $
(☎03773-15-629656; www.ibera.gov.ar; Mbiguá s/n; per person 1st/subsequent days AR$55/40, vehicle AR$30) This municipal campground by the lake is a great place with grassy pitches, nearly all with their own *quincho* (thatched-roof building). This is where to go for boat trips; it's also worth checking out the view as the sun sets. Book ahead as it's not huge.

Rancho Iberá LODGE $$
(☎ 03773-15-412661; www.posadaranchoibera.com.ar; d AR$420; 📶) Attractively decorated rooms with narrow beds surround a tranquil veranda and garden at this friendly, central place.

La Antigua Posada GUESTHOUSE $$
(☎ 03773-15-401111; iberalaantiguaposada@hotmail.com; s/d AR$300/400; ❄) Cool, large, high-ceilinged rooms along a veranda. It has an appealing cafe and very welcoming owners.

★ **Rancho de los Esteros** LODGE $$$
(☎ 03773-15-493041; www.ranchodelosesteros.com.ar; cnr Ñangapiry & Capivára; s US$200, d standard/superior US$380/400, incl all meals & excursions; ❄📶🏊) This exquisitely peaceful lakeside retreat is run with traditional Argentine country hospitality by its owners. Four gorgeous, super-spacious rooms – they can fit a family – surround a beautifully maintained wetland garden full of birdsong. The traditional architecture, attentive hosts, tasty meals and lakeside shelter to watch the spectacular sunsets make this a very special place.

Posada de La Laguna LODGE $$$
(☎ 03773-499413; www.posadadelalaguna.com; Guazú Virá s/n; d incl full board & activities US$400; ❄📶🏊) Simple and elegant, in wide grounds by a lake, this lodge has bright white rooms with great beds and paintings by the owner. The emphasis is on relaxation (ie no TV), and staff pull it off, with friendly service, guided trips and good meals. The rooms in the building closer to the lake are slightly more charming, those in the other building are more private.

Ñandé Retá LODGE $$$
(☎ 03773-499411; www.nandereta.com; r AR$1167; ❄@📶🏊) This place has been around longer than any, and is still one of the most pleasing. Surrounded by pines and eucalypts, it's got a peaceful, hidden-away feel that is highly seductive. It's very family friendly, the rooms are colorful, service excellent and the pool is a decent size. Good value.

Aguapé Lodge LODGE $$$
(☎ 03773-499412; www.iberaesteros.com.ar; Yacaré s/n; s/d all-inclusive US$290/469; 📶🏊) This luxurious colonial-style posada is in a beautiful setting above the lake. It has attractive, high-ceilinged rooms, all-white walls and dark wood, along a veranda looking over the lawn to the water, and a wide variety of excursions. Cheaper 'rustic' rooms in another building are smaller, but also have plenty of character. Service is excellent.

Ecoposada del Estero LODGE $$$
(☎ 03773-15-443602; www.ecoposadadelestero.com.ar; Yaguareté s/n; s/d AR$1050/1620; 📶🏊) 🌿 Best in town for bird-watching, this is warmly run by a couple who know the area intimately. Ecological design has resulted in comfortable adobe buildings with wide verandas and attractive homemade wooden furnishings from various recycled materials. Their excursions are great but you'll see plenty from here – the lodge sits right on the edge of an *estero* and has abundant birdlife and a high observation platform.

Irupé Lodge LODGE $$$
(☎ 0376-443-8312; www.ibera-argentina.com; Yacaré s/n; s/d US$150/200, superior US$200/250; ❄📶🏊) On the lake near the causeway, this rustic lodge makes you feel very welcome. While the rooms are satisfactory, the artistic wooden furniture, the pool and the views across the water are the highlights. The superior rooms are a lot better, more attractive and sizable with greater privacy, air-con and private verandas. This price doesn't include excursions. Argentines pay around 15% less.

🛏 Around Reserve Provincial Esteros del Iberá

Estancia Rincón del Socorro LODGE $$$
(☎ 03782-497073; www.rincondelsocorro.com; s/d incl full board & excursions US$480/640; 📶🏊) Off the Mercedes road, 31km south of Pellegrini, this ranch, owned by ecocampaigner Doug Tompkins, is a place in which to come to terms with the big sky and abundant wildlife. It's substantial country comfort rather than luxury; the pretty rooms interconnect, making them great for family stays, while freestanding cabins sleep two. Around the complex, vast lawns blend into pastureland and contemplation. If this isn't remote enough, head over to San Alonso, its sister *estancia*, only reachable by plane.

Hotel Puerto Valle LODGE $$$
(☎ 03786-425700; www.hotelpuertovalle.com; RN12, Km1282; s/d US$244/376; ❄📶🏊) This luxurious, private option is on the bank of the Paraná – huge here, above the Yacyreta dam – near the northeastern tip of the Esteros. The

LOCAL KNOWLEDGE

ECOLOGICAL ISSUES IN THE IBERÁ

The Iberá ecosystem is delicate. US entrepreneurs-turned-conservationists Douglas and Kristine Tompkins have bought large tracts of private land adjoining the Reserva Provincial Esteros del Iberá and propose to donate them to the Corrientes government, if it puts them and the existing Iberá reserve under the control of the Argentine government as a national park.

But many locals are far from thrilled. What seemed a straightforward act of ecological philanthropy became a hot potato, pitting landowners, agribusiness and politicians against each other.

Beneath this part of northern Argentina – and extending into Brazil, Uruguay and Paraguay – is the Guaraní Aquifer, an immense body of underground water of increasing political importance. This has led some to see the Tompkins' involvement as a cover for a neocolonialist grab for resources.

Check out www.theconservationlandtrust.org and www.proyectoibera.org for the Tompkins' position. We asked Douglas Tompkins to comment:

Why the opposition?

Conservation encounters opposition wherever it is. Not one national park was created in the US without drawn-out battles with locals. Conservation is a political act and when it has to do with what one does with land then you are treading in hot political territory. A local cultural shift takes time and you also have to do your part well. We certainly make our share of mistakes, but fortunately they've been small ones. Overall we win people across to our side as the years go by.

Aquifer

The Guaraní aquifer is a nonissue. It's massive, somewhere around 1.2 million sq km. Iberá is a mere 1.3 million *hectares* of that. One percent. A shallow surface wetland with little to do with the deep aquifer. The Iberá's importance as a water source is also overestimated by people trying to make some kind of political or social noise. The Paraná passes more water than the whole Iberá under the Corrientes–Resistencia bridge every 18 hours.

Dangers

The industrial rice plantations and the big industrial tree plantations of even-aged exotic monocultures. Then on top of that you have arrogant fools who flout laws and build dikelike roads for dozens of kilometers disrupting the hydrology. Those are the big three threats to the wetlands. Some bad grazing practices exist, but they are mild in comparison.

What message would you like to convey to the Iberá's people?

The formation of a national park would bring benefits to the entire area and province, help biodiversity conservation and be a point of pride for locals. And, of course ,a big economic development component with the advent of lots of tourism. It would be the largest national park in Argentina, the province would benefit by the tourism and the nation would pay the costs for operating the park, a kind of double win for the province and its citizens.

Life goes on as usual for everyone, it is only the 560,000 hectares of provincial land, coupled with 175,000 hectares of foundation land that would constitute a national park. Beyond that all landowners just continue on. Zero change for them. The only thing that will change is the value of their land will go up, just like all land does when a park is declared next to them virtually anywhere in the world.

You're trialing the reintroduction of giant anteaters?

This project is already an unqualified success. We have lots of animals in the wild again, reproducing nicely and healthily. One of the most successful things we have ever done in conservation. We are very happy about it. Now we are partially through the reintroduction of the pampa deer and starting on the jaguar, which is a big undertaking.

rooms – some in the historic original building, others in annexes – are impeccable, with great river views. Meals and service are excellent. Excursions to the Iberá, their cayman farm, the monkey path and along the river are included if you are staying here.

There should be a spa complex by the time you read this. Half- and full-board (double from US$752) rates are offered.

Eating

All of the midrange and top-end accommodations options provide meals for their guests. If you ask in advance, and they have space, most of them allow nonguests too. There are other simple options in town. Eating hours are early: sit down before 2pm for lunch and before 9pm for dinner.

Yacarú Porá ARGENTINE $
(cnr Caraguatá & Yaguareté; mains AR$45-70; ⏲ lunch & dinner; 📶) Run with charm and enthusiasm, this bungalow guarantees a warm welcome. The food is prepared to order and features generous portions of meat, chicken dishes, pasta, salads, omelets and *milanesas* (breaded cutlets).

Los Carros ARGENTINE $
(cnr Mburucuyá & Yaguareté; mains AR$40-50; ⏲ lunch & dinner) Likeable and family-run, this simple place, with the picturesque horse carts it's named for in the yard, does tasty home-cooked food adorned with fresh vegetables and herbs from the garden. There's no menu and a limited selection: if you fancy local specialities, order in advance. Get here before 9pm for dinner.

Information

Note that as yet there is no bank or ATM in Colonia Pellegrini, so take plenty of cash. Wi-fi is widespread but at the time of research there were no public computers outside the lodges.

Municipal tourist office (info.turismo@ibera.gov.ar; ⏲ 8am-7pm) At the entrance to the village, after crossing the causeway en route from Mercedes, this is the best source of general information.

Visitor center (⏲ 8am-6pm) The reserve's visitor center, on the Mercedes side of the causeway, has a good exhibition on local wildlife (Spanish only) and an audiovisual presentation. The short path opposite the visitor center gives you a sporting chance of seeing howler monkeys up close, and other paths here introduce you to the different plants and habitats of the area.

Getting There & Away

The road from Mercedes to Colonia Pellegrini (120km) is drivable in a normal car except after rain. Bus services (AR$35, three to four hours) are basic and unreliable; check at the bus terminal information office. The most reliable departure is Crucero del Norte (Itatí II) at 12:30pm Monday through Friday, and 9:30am Saturday, returning from Pellegrini at 4am Monday to Friday, with an extra 5pm departure on Friday.

Iberá Bus (☎ 03773-15-482836) runs unreliably from the old bus terminal in Mercedes (corner of Alvear and Pujol, two blocks east and one south of the new bus terminal) at 1pm Monday to Friday and 9am Saturday (AR$50), returning from Pellegrini at 4.30am Monday to Saturday.

A faster and more comfortable way to get there is by 4WD. This costs around AR$150 to AR$180 per person if there are enough people, more if not. Get a list of operators through the information booth at the Mercedes bus terminal: there are several. At time of research the most useful were **Rayo** (☎ 03773-15-443536, 03773-420184) and **Monzón** (☎ 03773-15-443536), who theoretically departed daily. In Pellegrini, register for return journeys at the shop at the corner of Guazú Virá and Curupí. If it hasn't been raining, you could also get a *remise* from Mercedes if there's a group of you.

The road from Posadas is much worse (take the turning between Gobernador Virasoro and Santo Tomé in a normal car). Drivers charge AR$1500 to AR$1800 for a charter to Posadas, or AR$1300 to Gobernador Virasoro, from where frequent buses travel the 80km on to Posadas.

There's no gas station in Pellegrini; the closest are in Mercedes and at the main road junction near Santo Tomé. Fill up before you head in. A couple of places in Pellegrini can sell you petrol and diesel.

Be aware that car-rental companies in Posadas may refuse you service if you mention that the Iberá is one of your destinations.

ALONG THE RÍO URUGUAY

The second of the two great rivers that converge above Buenos Aires to form the Río de la Plata, the Uruguay divides the country of the same name from Argentina, and also forms part of the border with Brazil. Bridges provide access to these neighbors, whose influences have blended with those of indigenous and immigrant groups in the area. The riverside towns on the Argentine side offer plenty and are popular summer and weekend destinations.

GUALEGUAYCHÚ CARNAVAL

A mellow riverside town, **Gualeguaychú** (www.gualeguaychu.info) is quiet out of season but kicks off in summer, with the country's longest and flashiest Carnaval celebration. Make a stop here any weekend from mid-January to late February and you'll find things in full swing. The main venue is the Corsódromo, where admission is AR$120 to AR$150 most nights.

There's a string of decent budget hotels along Bolívar between Bartolomé Mitre and Monseñor Chalup, and three hostels in town.

Gualeguaychú is easily reached by bus from Buenos Aires (3½ hours), Paraná and other towns along the Río Uruguay. Gualeguaychú is also a crossing point to Uruguay: the town of Fray Bentos lies just across the bridge.

Concepción del Uruguay

03442 / POP 89,300

Set around a stately plaza, Concepción is a typical riverside town, wondering what to do with itself now that trade on the Río Uruguay has died off. It makes a decent stopover on the way north, has a couple of excellent places to stay and boasts the Palacio San José outside town.

Sights

The principal sights in the town itself are around the noble main plaza, where the earthy-pink-colored basilica, Palacio San José, holds the remains of Justo José de Urquiza.

Palacio San José PALACE
(www.palaciosanjose.com.ar; RP39, Km30; adult/child AR$15/3; 8am-7pm Mon-Fri, 9am-6pm Sat & Sun) Topped by twin towers and surrounded by elegant gardens, Justo José de Urquiza's ostentatious pink palace is 33km west of Concepción. Set around an arched patio, with a walled garden out the back, it was built partly to show up Urquiza's arch rival in Buenos Aires, Juan Manuel de Rosas, and partly to show the power and wealth of Entre Ríos province. From Concepción, **Sarbimas** (427777) will take up to four people there and back in a *remise*, including a two-hour wait, for AR$180.

Local *caudillo* (provincial strongman) Urquiza was largely responsible for Rosas' downfall in 1852 and the eventual adoption of Argentina's modern constitution. Sometime allies such as Domingo Sarmiento and Bartolomé Mitre supped at Urquiza's 8.5m dining-room table and slept in the palatial bedrooms. The bedroom in which Urquiza was murdered by a mob sent by Ricardo López Jordán is a permanent shrine, created by Urquiza's wife.

Another option for getting there is a tour: Turismo Pioneros will take two people for AR$100, including guided visit. You could also jump off a Caseros-bound bus and walk 3km to the palace. There's a mediocre restaurant at the palace and picturesque grounds for picnicking.

Sleeping

Residencial Centro GUESTHOUSE $
(427429; www.nuevorescentro.com.ar; Moreno 130; r AR$220;) The best budget deal in town has a variety of rooms around a courtyard near the plaza. They vary slightly in price depending on size and if they have air-con; there's more light in the ones upstairs.

Antigua Fonda HOTEL $
(433734; www.antiguafonda.com.ar; España 172; s/d AR$240/340;) Though you wouldn't know, this has been created from part of what was once a historic Concepción hotel. Pleasing rooms in shades of cream surround the small grassy garden, with artistic touches and a relaxing vibe. No breakfast, but there's a kitchen you can use. It's a block west and three south of the plaza.

La Posada GUESTHOUSE $
(425461; Moreno 166; r per person AR$120) A simple budget place that's nothing special but the best deal in town for solo travelers.

★ **Antigua Posta del Torreón** BOUTIQUE HOTEL $$
(432618; www.postadeltorreon.com.ar; Almafuerte 799; s/d/superior d US$72/108/124;) This intimate and classy hotel a block west and four south of the plaza offers a real haven for a relaxing stay. It's an elegantly refurbished 19th-century mansion, with plenty of original features and rooms surrounding a

postcard-pretty courtyard complete with fountain and small swimming pool. The superiors are worth the upgrade: much more spacious, with lovely furniture.

Eating

Café de la Plaza CAFE $

(www.cafedelaplazabar.com.ar; cnr Urquiza & Galarza; light meals AR$35-60; ⊙8am-2pm & 5pm-late; ☜) On the northwest corner of the plaza, this offbeat place has a bit of everything, with a terrace, chessboard tiles, tasty coffee, wooden bench booths, food and regular live music.

El Conventillo de Baco ARGENTINE $$

(☎433809; España 193; dishes AR$55-90; ⊙11am-3pm & 8pm-midnight) This handsome and totally recommendable spot has both indoor and outdoor dining in an attractive patio space and specializes in well-prepared river fish and seafood, with dishes like calamari stew and glazed pork as specialties. Good value.

Information

Telecentro Uruguay (3 de Febrero 63; internet per hr AR$10; ⊙7am-2pm & 5pm-midnight) Internet and phone calls just off the plaza.

Tourist office (☎442850; www.concepcionturismo.gov.ar; cnr Galarza & Supremo Entrerriano; ⊙8am-8pm) The handiest tourist office is a block east of the plaza. In high summer it opens until 10pm.

Getting There & Around

The **bus terminal** (☎422352; cnr Galarza & Chiloteguy) is 10 blocks west of the plaza. Bus 1 runs between them; a *remise* costs AR$10. A train arrives here from Paraná on Fridays and returns on Sundays (AR$26, eight hours).

BUSES FROM CONCEPCIÓN

DESTINATION	COST (AR$)	DURATION (HR)
Buenos Aires	160	4
Colón	14	¾
Concordia	46	2½
Gualeguaychú	22	1
Paraná	86	5

Colón

☎03447 / POP 24,800

The most appealing destination for riverside relaxation in Entre Ríos, Colón is a very popular summer getaway for Argentine holidaymakers. Its population almost doubles in January, but the pretty town takes it all in its stride. With numerous places to stay, a thriving handicrafts scene and worthwhile, out-of-the-ordinary restaurants, it's a great place to be. It's also a base for visiting the Parque Nacional El Palmar.

One of three main Entre Ríos border crossings, Colón is connected to the Uruguayan city of Paysandú by the Puente Internacional General Artigas. The center of the action is Plaza San Martín, a block back from the river, and the street 12 de Abril running up to it.

Sights & Activities

Strolling around the riverbank and quiet leafy streets is the highlight here. There are numerous *artesanía* shops selling everything from *mate* gourds to pickled coypu Colón has a thermal spa (see the boxed text, p183).

Tours

Ita i Cora Aventura BOAT TOUR

(☎423360; www.itaicora.com; San Martín 97; 2hr tour AR$190) The best option for getting out on the river. Its standard tour is a charismatic two-hour affair taking in sand flats and a forest trail in the middle of the Río Uruguay. Excellent English spoken.

Festivals & Events

Fiesta Nacional de la Artesanía HANDICRAFTS

This crafts fair in February in Parque Quirós features live folkloric entertainment.

Sleeping

There are numerous summer campgrounds, cabins, bungalows and apartments available for rent. Look for signs saying *'Alquilo a turistas.'* The tourist office can supply you with a list of official accommodations.

La Casona de Susana HOSTEL, GUESTHOUSE $

(☎428043; www.lacasonadesusana.com.ar; cnr 3 de Febrero & Paysandú; dm AR$80-200, d from AR$300; ❄☜☒) Run with a kind heart rather than ruthless efficiency, this is an unusual and welcoming hostel between the bus terminal and the river. Shared or private accommodations are available in three different room grades – from simple but serviceable en suite dorms to plush, colorful modern rooms. There's a pretty pool out back (extra for the cheapest rate) and kitchen use.

ENTERING URUGUAY

There are three main crossings linking Argentina with its eastern neighbor Uruguay. From south to north these are Gualeguaychú–Fray Bentos, Colón–Paysandú (cars pay an AR$60 toll on this bridge) and Concordia–Salto. All three are open 24 hours.

★Hostería 'Restaurant del Puerto' HOTEL $$
(☎422698; www.hosteriadecolon.com.ar; Alejo Peyret 158; r from AR$450; ❄@🛜🏊) In what has a strong claim to be Colón's loveliest house (on its prettiest street), this has characterful rooms decorated faithfully in the style of the 1880 building, with enormous windows, plenty of wood and noble rustic furniture. Family duplexes (AR$650) are a good deal, as are midweek discounts. There's a restaurant serving good dinners, and a heated pool and Jacuzzi out back. No cards.

Hotel Plaza HOTEL $$
(☎421043; www.hotel-plaza.com.ar; cnr 12 de Abril & Belgrano; d standard/superior AR$780/980; ❄@🛜🏊) This Colón staple has been around for a century, but it certainly never looked like this before. A sleek refit has left it looking modern and glistening. The rooms aren't quite as posh; the superiors are the new ones, with quality bathrooms. But the combination of plaza-side location (some rooms in each category have balconies) and decent-sized heated pool out the back make it a winner.

Centro Apart Hotel APARTMENT $$
(☎423858; www.centroaparthotel.com.ar; 12 de Abril 442; d AR$500; ❄@🛜) On the main street – head straight down Sourigues from the bus terminal to reach it – this complex offers large, comfortable apartments with decent kitchen that are a good deal for anybody and great for families. Prices are signficantly reduced in the low season. There are numerous similar apartment complexes around town.

Hotel Costarenas HOTEL $$$
(☎425050; www.hotelcostarenas.com.ar; cnr Av Quirós & 12 de Abril; d AR$990, with view AR$1187-1535; ❄@🛜🏊) This favorite of weekending *porteños* (residents of Buenos Aires) offers smart riverside accommodation and a decent spa complex (included), indoor and outdoor pools, and a good restaurant. Rooms are well equipped, but the interior rooms are pricey for their size and lack of view. Those with a view are much lighter and larger but significantly more expensive.

Eating & Drinking

El Sótano de los Quesos DELI $
(www.elsotanodelosquesos.com.ar; cnr Chacabuco & Av Costanera; mixed plates for 1/2 people AR$50/90; ⏲5-10pm Thu-Fri, 12:30am-10pm Sat & Sun; 🖉) Near the tourist office, this intriguing spot serves a wide variety of artisanal cheeses and other delicacies at pretty thatched tables on a lawn looking over the port. There's also locally made wine and beer on hand, and a cellar shop whose aromas will almost compel you to buy. It's open more frequently in high summer.

La Cantina ARGENTINE $
(Peyret 79; mains AR$30-60; ⏲11am-2:30pm & 8:30pm-midnight) Just off the plaza, this likable family-run restaurant does a nice line in uncomplicated and filling fare, with sizable chicken and beef dishes taking their place alongside tasty homemade pasta and river-fish options, including surubí empanadas.

★La Cosquilla del Ángel ARGENTINE $$
(☎423711; cnr San Martín & Balcarce; mains AR$75-100; ⏲11.30am-3.30pm & 8pm-midnight Wed-Mon; 🛜) Colón's best restaurant combines elegant, romantic decor, a big welcome and service with a whimsical and unpretentious approach, particularly in the curiously named dishes and the intriguing restaurant name, which translates as 'The Angel's Tickle.' Many dishes combine sweet and savory flavors; try the *mollejitas* (or *mollejas;* sweetbreads). The pasta is recommended and the wine list is above average.

Restaurant del Puerto ARGENTINE $$
(www.hosteriadecolon.com.ar; Peyret 158; mains AR$55-80; ⏲8pm-midnight Thu-Tue; 🛜) In a lovely old building near the river, this restaurant does tasty dinners with good service and plenty of imaginative river-fish dishes. It's good for a light dinner, with plenty of salad vegetables and fruit used. No cards.

El Viejo Almacén ARGENTINE $$
(☎422216; cnr Urquiza & Paso; mains AR$55-100; ⏲11am-3pm & 7.30pm-midnight) 🍃 A block from the plaza and with a quiet, brick-walled interior decorated with old-time photos, this place has a wide-ranging menu including great homemade pasta, delicious

empanadas, river fish and *parrilla* options. Portions aren't as big as in some places, but the vegetables come from its organic garden.

Shopping

La Casona HANDICRAFTS

(www.artesanoslacasona.com.ar; 12 de Abril 106; 9:30am-12:30pm & 5:30-8:30pm) On the corner of the Plaza San Martín, this is a co-operative selling a wide range of handmade goods.

Information

Tourist office (421233; www.colon.gov.ar; cnr Gouchón & Av Costanera; 7am-8pm Mon-Thu, 7am-9pm Fri, 8am-9pm Sat, 8am-8pm Sun) Occupies the former customs building, built by Urquiza. There is also an office in the bus terminal (open 9am to 7pm).

Getting There & Around

Colón's **bus terminal** (421716; cnr Rocamora & 9 de Julio) is seven blocks inland (roughly west) of the river and eight blocks north of the main shopping and entertainment street, 12 de Abril. A *remise* into the town center costs around AR$15.

Destinations include Buenos Aires (AR$144, 4½ hours), Gualeguaychú (AR$34, two hours) via Concepción (AR$14, 40 minutes), Concordia (AR$35, two hours) via Ubajay (AR$18, one hour) and Paysandú, Uruguay (AR$50, 45 minutes, one to five daily).

Parque Nacional El Palmar

03447

On the west bank of the Río Uruguay, midway between Colón and Concordia, the 8500-sq-km **Parque Nacional El Palmar** (493049; www.elpalmarapn.com.ar; RN 14, Km199; admission AR$50) preserves the last extensive stands of yatay palm on the Argentine littoral. In the 19th century the native yatay covered large parts of Entre Ríos, Uruguay and southern Brazil, but the intensification of agriculture, ranching and forestry throughout the region destroyed much of the palm savanna.

Reaching a maximum height of about 18m, with a trunk diameter of 40cm, larger specimens clustered throughout the park create a striking and soothing subtropical landscape that lends itself to photography. The grasslands and the gallery forests along the watercourses shelter much wildlife.

Park admission (valid for 48 hours) is collected at the entrance on RN 14 from 7am to 7pm, but the gate is open 24 hours.

Sights & Activities

Main facilities are 12km from the entrance down a good dirt road. Here, the **visitor center** (8am-7pm) has displays on natural history. You can organize canoeing, cycling and horseback-riding trips here. Decent dirt roads lead off the main access road to three viewpoints. **Arroyo Los Loros**, a short distance north of the campground by gravel road, is a good place to observe wildlife. South of the visitor center is Arroyo El Palmar, a pleasant stream accessed at two viewpoints, **La Glorieta** and **El Palmar**. These have short marked trails, and the latter has a hide for bird-watching. There are three other short trails near the visitor center, and another bird-watching hide near the Río Uruguay. Guided walks are available by prior arrangement.

There is river access for swimming and boating from the campground.

Sleeping & Eating

In Ubajay there are basic rooms in the bus terminal complex as well as other cheap lodgings.

Camping El Palmar CAMPGROUND $

(423378; campsites per adult/child/tent AR$45/20/30) This sociable campground by the visitor center is the only place to stay in the park. It has shady, level campsites, hot showers and electricity. The shop here sells snacks and food, including slabs of beef for the barbecues; opposite, there's a restaurant.

THERMAL SPAS ALONG THE URUGUAY

Most of the towns along the Río Uruguay – Gualeguaychú, Colón and Concordia for starters – have tapped the region's abundant geothermal aquifers to create appealing thermal spa complexes: a major focus of domestic tourism in these parts. They are well-equipped places with several indoor and outdoor pools of various temperatures. Entry to most of them is around AR$60 to AR$70. Check www.termasdeentrerios.gov.ar for a complete list.

THE GAUCHO JUDÍO

The gaucho is one of Argentina's archetypal images, but it's a little-known fact that many a gaucho was of Jewish origin. The first recorded instance of mass Jewish immigration to Argentina was in the late 19th century, when 800 Russian Jews arrived in Buenos Aires, fleeing persecution from Czar Alexander III.

The Jewish Colonization Association, funded by a German philanthropist, began distributing 100-hectare parcels of land to immigrant families; the first major colony was **Moisés Ville** in Santa Fe province, which became known at the time as Jerusalem Argentina. Today there are only about 300 Jewish residents left in town (15% of the population), but many traditions prevail: the tiny town boasts four synagogues, the bakery sells Sabbath bread, and kids in the street use Yiddish slang words such as 'schlep' and 'schlock.'

These rural Jews readily assimilated into Argentine society, mixing their own traditions with those of their adopted country, so it was not unusual to see a figure on horseback in baggy pants, canvas shoes and skullcap on his way to throw a hunk of cow on the *asado* (barbecue). Many descendants have since left the land in search of education and opportunities in the cities. Argentina's Jews number about 200,000, making them Latin America's largest Jewish community.

To learn more about the *gauchos judíos*, visit the Museo Judío de Entre Ríos in Concordia.

La Aurora del Palmar LODGE, CAMPGROUND **$$**
(☎421549; www.auroradelpalmar.com.ar; RN14, Km202; campsites AR$30 plus per adult AR$30, s/d without shower AR$200/300, d/q from AR$400/550;) Between Ubajay and El Palmar's entrance, this property is cattle ranch and citrus farm, plus has a protected palm forest as spectacular as those in the national park itself. It's an original, well-run place with shady campsites, family duplex rooms in a pretty bungalow, and rustic wooden rooms in renovated railway carriages. There's a good swimming pool and a restaurant. Canoeing, horseback riding and palm safaris are available.

Getting There & Away

El Palmar is on RN 14, a major national highway, so there are frequent north–south bus services. Any bus running north towards Concordia will drop you at the park entrance, 12km from the visitor center. You could walk or hitchhike from here; otherwise, stay on the bus for a further 6km to Ubajay, from where a *remise* will cost you around AR$100 to the visitor center. Ask the call shop alongside the bus terminal to call you one.

The easiest way to get here is by *remise* from Colón, where you can arrange a return trip plus two hours at the park, covering all the trails, for AR$380 (up to four people). A recommended driver for his good park knowledge is **Ariel** (☎03447-15-452451).

Concordia

☎0345 / POP 149,500

This pleasant agricultural service town on the Río Uruguay won't keep you spellbound for weeks at a time, but makes a convenient stop for a night. It's a citrus town – you can smell the tang in the air at times – and has a fine central plaza, riverside beaches and fishing. It also offers a border crossing, via the Represa Salto Grande hydroelectric project, to the Uruguayan city of Salto.

Sights & Activities

Museo Regional de Concordia MUSEUM
(cnr Entre Ríos & Ramírez; 7am-1pm & 2-8pm Mon-Fri, 9am-6pm Sat & Sun) FREE This down-at-heel museum covers Italian immigration and also has some fine old furniture. The main point of interest is the fabulous building, which blends French neorenaissance architecture with art nouveau touches. At the time of research it was closed for much-needed restoration.

Museo Judío de Entre Ríos MUSEUM
(☎421-4088; www.museojudioer.org.ar; Entre Ríos 476; donation AR$15; 8:30am-12:30pm Sun-Tue & Thu-Fri) Three rooms detailing the arrival and struggles of the Jewish gauchos, their way of life and the Holocaust seen through the eyes of those who experienced it. Also temporary exhibitions.

Castillo San Carlos
RUIN

(admission AR$15; ⊙9am-noon & 3-6pm) In the riverside Parque Rivadavia, at the northeastern edge of town, this ruined castle was built in 1888 by a French industrialist who mysteriously abandoned the property years later. French writer Antoine de Saint-Exupéry briefly lived here; there's a monument to his *The Little Prince* nearby.

🛏 Sleeping

Hotel Pellegrini
HOTEL $

(☑422-7137; hotelpellegrini@gmail.com; Pellegrini 443; s/d AR$200/300; 🖥) By far the best budget choice, three blocks south of the plaza, this friendly family-run place offers spotless rooms with TV and bathroom. You'll definitely need to book ahead, as it's popular.

Hotel Concordia
HOTEL $

(☑421-6869; La Rioja 518; s/d AR$230/330; ❋🖥) This cheap and cheerful choice occupies a cavernous building. Rooms vary in light, size and mattress quality. Bathrooms, some accessed via in-room stairs, are decent.

Hotel Salto Grande
HOTEL $$

(☑421-0034; www.hotelsaltogrande.net; Urquiza 581; s/d AR$458/578; ❋@🖥🏊) Just south of the main plaza, this polished, modern hotel offers excellent service at fair prices. There are several grades of room; the more expensive ones have better views and a minibar, but aren't a great deal better than the regular ones.

🍴 Eating

El Reloj
PIZZA $

(Pellegrini 580; pizza AR$40-60; ⊙11am-3.30pm & 7pm-1am Mon-Sat; 🖥) This spacious brick-walled pizzeria has good ambience and a staggering selection of options. A haven for the indecisive as staff don't grumble about doing half-and-halfs. It also does *parrilla*. Look out for specials deals operating almost nightly.

Malaika
ARGENTINE $$

(☑422-4867; 1 de Mayo 59; mains AR$60-100; ⊙8am-2am; 🖥☑) A relaxed and handsome option on the plaza. This cafe-bar serves a variety of tasty meals, with salads, pizza, pasta, snacks and more elaborate fare, including plenty of vegetarian options as well as daily specials. Its decent wine list, caring service and the romantic mood seal the deal.

ℹ Information

Tourist Office (☑421-3905; www.concordia.tur.ar; cnr Pellegrini & Mitre; ⊙8am-9pm) On the plaza. The information desk at the bus terminal (cnr Justo & Hipólito Yrigoyen) also has tourist info.

ℹ Getting There & Away

There are flights to Buenos Aires with **LAER** (☑0810-777-5237; www.laersa.com.ar). The **bus terminal** (☑421-7235; cnr Justo & Hipólito Yrigoyen) is 13 blocks north of Plaza 25 de Mayo. Four daily buses (none on Sunday) go to Salto, Uruguay (AR$40, 1¼ hours).

From the port beyond the east end of Carriego, launches cross the river to Salto (AR$30, 15 minutes) four times between 8:30am and 6:30pm Monday to Saturday.

BUSES FROM CONCORDIA

DESTINATION	COST (ARS)	DURATION (HR)
Buenos Aires	218	6
Colón	35	2
Concepción	46	3
Corrientes	179	7-8
Paraná	134	4½
Paso de los Libres	113	4
Posadas	294	7½

ℹ Getting Around

Bus 2 (AR$3) takes Yrigoyen south from the bus terminal to the town center. On its northward run catch it on Pellegrini in front of Banco de la Nación. A taxi to the bus terminal from the town center should cost about AR$20.

Paso de los Libres

☑03772 / POP 40,500

The name (meaning 'Crossing of the Free') is the most romantic thing about this border town on the banks of the Río Uruguay. It faces the larger Brazilian city of Uruguaiana on the opposite bank, and is connected to it by a well-used bridge. There's little to detain the traveler but the town has plenty of cross-border life, a picturesque central plaza and decent sleeping and eating options.

🛏 Sleeping & Eating

Hotel Las Vegas
HOTEL $

(☑423490; Sarmiento 554; s/d AR$180/300; ❋🖥) Despite the burgundy carpets and

'70s feel, this isn't so old and is a well-kept budget place in the town center. The rooms are dark but comfortable and have adequate bathrooms. Rooms up the back have more light and space. Ask for air-con if you want it: you do.

Hotel Alejandro Primero HOTEL $$
(☎424100; www.alejandroprimero.com.ar; Coronel López 502; s/d AR$350/500; ❄@📶🏊) A surprisingly good hotel, this has an elegant and old-fashioned lobby and restaurant area and slightly less impressive but very spacious rooms. Ask for one with views over the river and Uruguaiana in Brazil on the other side. There's also a pleasant outdoor pool and garden area.

El Nuevo Mesón ARGENTINE $
(Colón 587; mains AR$40-80; ⏰11am-3pm & 7.30pm-midnight) Smartly turned out in black and white – the waiters seem to be camouflaged – this offers really well-prepared dishes. There's pizza, *parrilla* and more elaborate creations, but it's all fairly priced and very tasty indeed. Grab a table outside if the weather's fine.

Information

There's no tourist office, but there are maps of town all over the town center. ATMs are on the plaza and along Av Colón.

Libres Cambio (Av Colón 901; ⏰8-11.50am & 3.30-5.50pm Mon-Fri) Changes money. There's another branch at the international bridge that also opens on Saturday.

Getting There & Away

The **bus terminal** (☎425600) is 1km from the town center. There are services to Buenos Aires (AR$300, eight to nine hours), Posadas (AR$176, five hours) and Corrientes (AR$152, five hours) via Mercedes (AR$42, three hours).

Buses to Uruguaiana (AR$3), Brazil, leave frequently from 7am onwards, stopping on Av San Martín at Av Colón and across from the bus terminal (by the castlelike building).

The frontier is open 24 hours. Travelers report that you can transit to Uruguay without requiring a Brazilian visa here, but don't bank on it.

Getting Around

Minibuses (AR$2) run from the corner below the bus terminal into town. A taxi to the town center is AR$20.

MISIONES

The narrow northeastern province of Misiones juts out like an Argentine finger between Brazilian and Paraguayan territory and is named for the Jesuit missions that were established in the region, the ruins of which are a major attraction. Today San Ignacio Miní is the best restored; it and other ruins (including those across the border in

OFF THE BEATEN TRACK

YAPEYÚ

It would be untruthful to call this delightfully peaceful place a one-horse town: there are many horses, and the sound of their hooves thumping the reddish earth in the evening is one of the nicest things about it. Yapeyú is a great spot to relax; the sort of place where locals will greet you on the street.

An hour north of Paso de los Libres by bus, Yapeyú was founded in 1626 as the southernmost of the Jesuit missions. It's also famous for being the birthplace of the great Argentine 'Liberator,' José de San Martín.

You can examine the Jesuit ruins – the **museum** (⏰8am-noon & 3-6pm Tue-Sun) FREE here has a comprehensive overview of all the missions – and admire the ornate building that now shelters the ruins of the house where San Martín was born in 1778.

Right on the plaza between these two major sights, **Hotel San Martín** (☎03772-493120; Sargento Cabral 712; s/d AR$190/300; ❄) is a simple, welcoming place set around an echoey inner courtyard. For something more upmarket, head to the modern riverside bungalows at **El Paraíso Yapeyú** (☎03772-493056; www.paraisoyapeyu.com.ar; cnr Paso de los Patos & San Martín; bungalow for 2/4 people AR$420/600; ❄🏊), where you can also camp.

There are four to five daily buses (AR$29, one hour) to/from Paso de los Libres and daily services to Posadas in the other direction. More buses stop on the highway at the edge of the town.

Paraguay) are easily accessed from the provincial capital, Posadas. Buses churn through Misiones en route to the Iguazú Falls in the north of the province, but a detour will take you to another stunning cascade – the Saltos del Moconá on the Río Uruguay.

The landscape here is an attraction. Approaching Misiones from the south you will see a change to gently rolling low hills, stands of bamboo, and fields of papaya and manioc. The highway passes tea and *mate* plantations growing from the region's trademark red soil – the province is the main producer of *mate,* Argentina's staple drink.

Posadas

0376 / POP 319,500

Capital of Misiones, and a base for visiting the Jesuit ruins after which the province is named, Posadas is a modern city that gazes across the wide Río Paraná to Encarnación in Paraguay. It's a stopover on the way north, but has plenty of charm of its own, if little in the way of sights.

Sights

The Jesuit missions (p190) are the area's big attraction.

Costanera RIVERBANK

In the afternoon, the *costanera* comes alive. It's a favorite spot for joggers, cyclists, dog walkers, *mate* sippers, hot-dog vendors and young couples staring at the lights of Paraguay across the water. Pride of place goes to 'Andresito,' a huge stainless-steel sculpture of Guaraní provincial strongman Andrés Guacarurí (Guazurary), looking like the Tin Man in search of a heart.

Palacio del Mate GALLERY

(Rivadavia 1846; 8am-12:30pm & 4-8pm Mon-Fri, 5-8pm Sat) Better than Posada's couple of desultory museums, this art gallery has temporary exhibitions and some displays on the *mate*-growing process.

Fundación Artesanías Misioneras GALLERY

(www.famercosur.com.ar; cnr Alvarez & Arrechea; 8am-8pm) FREE Guaraní culture is strong in this part of Argentina, and you'll see Guaraní artists selling their wares throughout the town center. Particularly fine pieces are displayed and sold here. There's another branch on the *costanera.* Don't bank on them keeping to opening hours.

Tours

Many operators around town offer tours to the Iguazú Falls, the Jesuit missions and the Esteros del Iberá.

Guayrá TOUR

(443-3415; www.guayra.com.ar; San Lorenzo 2208) Very helpful tour agency offering half-day tours to the Jesuit missions, the Paraguayan missions, Saltos del Moconá and more. Based in the Hotel Libertador.

Misión Paraná CRUISE

(15-433-4001; www.misionparana.com; Vieja Estación, Av Costanera; cruise per person AR$300-370; tickets sold 11am-1pm & 4:30-8:30pm) Runs dinner cruises on the Paraná Wednesday through Saturday. Drinks and dancing included. Look for discount flyers in your hotel.

Festivals & Events

Posadas celebrates **Carnaval** (in February or March, depending on the year) with great gusto.

Sleeping

Posadeña Linda HOSTEL $

(443-9238; www.hostelposadenalinda.com; Bolívar 1439; dm/d AR$100/270;) Run with a caring attitude, this excellent narrow hostel a short walk from the plaza offers a genuine welcome, comfortable bunks and a patio with a tiny plunge pool. It's colorful and relaxing with good facilities, although the kitchen could be better. Despite the street number, you'll find it between 1411 and 1419.

Residencial Misiones GUESTHOUSE $

(443-0133; Av Azara 1960; s/d AR$90/130) Offering seriously cheap rooms in a characterful central building, this is a budget option for those who want a clean, inexpensive sleep. The mattresses are in reverse gear, but it gains points for the low prices and the staff's caring attitude. Rooms vary in quality, so have a look at a few. All have bathroom.

Le Petit Hotel HOTEL $

(443-6031; www.hotellepetit.com.ar; Santiago del Estero 1630; s/d AR$300/400;) Peaceful and simple, this budget place is run by a kindly, helpful couple and features dark, clean, adequate rooms with big bathrooms around a leafy patio. It's a quiet, safe residential zone but only seven blocks from the heart of things.

Posadas

Posadas

Sights

1 Andresito Statue C1
2 Costanera C1
3 Fundación Artesanías Misioneras B1
4 Palacio del Mate C3

Activities, Courses & Tours

5 Guayrá B4
6 Misión Paraná D4

Sleeping

7 City Hotel B3
8 Hotel Julio César B4
9 Hotel Posadas Urbano B3
10 Le Petit Hotel C5
11 Posadeña Linda C3
12 Residencial Misiones B3

Eating

13 Cavas B3
14 El Rayo B3
15 Itakua C1
16 La Querencia B3
17 La Tradicional Rueda C1

Drinking & Nightlife

18 La Nouvelle Vitrage B3

City Hotel HOTEL $
(☎ 443-9401; www.misionescityhotel.com.ar; Colón 1754; s/d AR$250/420; ❄@☏) Bang on the plaza, the City has just about the biggest sign in a big-sign town. The rooms are old-fashioned and vary; some are rather uninspiring with lino floors, but others, right up on the 10th and 11th floors, are nicer, with plenty of air and picturesque views from what's just about the city's highest point. Cheaper during low season.

★ **Hotel Posadas Urbano** HOTEL $$
(☎ 444-3800; www.hahoteles.com; Bolívar 2176; s/d/ste AR$696/808/1095; ❄@☏≋) The new kid on the Posadas block has rapidly become top dog with its wide array of facilities and great central location. The bright, large carpeted chambers all have great bathrooms, balconies and big windows with views over town. Suites add space but little else. The atrium pool space, art exhibitions, gym and spa facilities, and appealing lounge area add points.

Hotel Julio César HOTEL $$
(☎ 442-7930; www.juliocesarhotel.com; Entre Ríos 1951; s/d AR$480/550, superior AR$540/620; ❄@☏≋) This four-star job in the city center has light, spacious, summery rooms with fridge and pleasing bathrooms. The slightly pricier superior rooms are basically identical but have flatscreen TV and sit on higher floors with wide views.

Eating

A Posadas speciality is *galeto* (chargrilled chicken pieces stuffed with bacon, red peppers and butter). It's delicious.

El Rayo CAFETERIA $
(Bolívar 2089; light meals AR$30-50; ⏲ 6am-4pm Mon-Fri, 5pm-1am Sat) No frills and effective, this joint is thronged at lunchtime for its delicious empanadas, *lomitos* and good-value pizza. Service comes with a smile, too. Thumbs up.

★ **La Tradicional Rueda** PARRILLA $$
(☎ 442-5620; Arrechea & Av Costanera; mains AR$60-90; ⏲ 11am-3.30pm & 7.30-midnight or later; ☏) Stylish and traditional in feel, with uniformed waiters and sturdy wooden seats, this two-level grill restaurant is in a prime riverside position: look for the wooden wheel outside. There is excellent service; quality meats and a nice line in salads and river fish put this a class above most *parrilla* places.

La Querencia PARRILLA $$
(☎ 443-7117; Bolívar 322; mains AR$60-90; ⏲ 10.30am-3.30pm & 7pm-1am Mon-Sat, 11am-4pm Sun; ☏) On the plaza, this upmarket *parrilla* specializes in delicious *galeto*. Also memorable are the brochettes (giant spikes with various delicious meats impaled upon them). The salads are also unusually well prepared. The service is great and the atmosphere here is always a highlight.

Cavas ARGENTINE $$
(www.cavas-resto.com.ar; Bolívar 1729; mains AR$60-100; ⏲ 11.30am-3pm & 8pm-1am; ☏) Unashamedly visitor-oriented, this place just off the plaza still produces excellent food. It's a romantic locale, with several worthwhile river-fish dishes and formally correct service.

Itakua FUSION $$
(Costanera s/n; mains AR$55-100; ⏲ noon-3pm & 7pm-late; ☏) This spacious and stylish bar-restaurant is in the heart of the riverside strip. Traditional Argentine ingredients are given zip with eclectic European influences: brie, pesto and sauerkraut accompany local meats here. Quality is reliable, as is the buzzy atmosphere.

Drinking & Nightlife

Most of the weekend action happens down at the *costanera*, where a knot of eateries, bars and clubs go loud and late. To get to the action, dead north up Buenos Aires and its continuation for some nine blocks from the city center.

La Nouvelle Vitrage CAFE
(Bolívar 1899; ⏲ 8am-late; ☏) With a vaguely French feel, this amiable cafe, located on the plaza, has a comfy interior and a terrace perfect for watching everyday life in Posadas go by.

Information

There are several ATMs around the plaza, and call centers and internet places nearby.

Hospital General R Madariaga (☎ 444-7775; www.hospitalposadas.gov.ar; Av López Torres 1177) About 1.5km south of downtown.

Misiones Tourist Office (☎ 444-7539; www.turismo.misiones.gov.ar; Colón 1985; ⏲ 8am-8pm) Has well-informed staff.

Getting There & Away

At the time of research, train service from Buenos Aires to Posadas had been suspended.

AIR

Aerolíneas Argentinas (442-2036; Ayacucho 1724) flies daily to Buenos Aires.

BUS

Buses to Encarnación (AR$10), Paraguay, leave every 20 minutes, stopping at the corner of San Lorenzo and Entre Ríos. With border formalities, the trip can take more than an hour, but is usually quicker.

Everyone gets out to clear Argentine emigration. The bus may leave without you; hang onto your ticket to catch the next one. The same happens on the Paraguayan side. There's a tourist office by Paraguayan immigration, and official moneychangers hanging around. Get small denominations: a 100,000 guarani note is hell to change.

Posadas' bus terminal can be reached from downtown by bus 8, 15, 21 or 24 (AR$3.50). It's around AR$50 in a taxi.

Bus services to San Ignacio (AR$24 to AR$31, one hour) depart roughly half-hourly.

OFF THE BEATEN TRACK

VISITING THE PARAGUAYAN MISSIONS

From Posadas (or San Ignacio) there's a very rewarding day trip to two of the Jesuit missions in Paraguay. The ruined but majestic churches at Trinidad and Jesús de Tavarangüe have been carefully restored and preserve some fabulous stonework.

From Posadas, cross by bus to Encarnación and get off at the bus terminal. From here, buses (most marked Ciudad del Este) run roughly half-hourly to Trinidad (G7000, 50 to 60 minutes). Get the driver to let you off at the turnoff to the ruins; it's then a 700m walk.

The **Trinidad ruins** (7am-7pm Apr-Sep, 7am-5:30pm Oct-Mar) are spectacular, with the red-brown stone of the church contrasting strongly with the flower-studded green grass and surrounding hillscapes. There is much decoration preserved: scalloped niches still hold timeworn sculptures, and the font and elaborate baroque pulpit are impressive. Doorways are capped with fine, carved decoration. You can climb to the top of one of the walls; an earlier church and bell tower have also been restored. There's a hotel and restaurant by the ruins.

Walk back to the main road and turn right. At the gas station 200m further on is the turnoff to **Jesús de Tavarangüe**, 12km away. Shared taxis (G7500) wait here to fill, and buses pass every two hours. You can get a taxi to take you to Jesús de Tavarangüe, wait for you and bring you back to the turnoff for about G30,000.

The restored **church** (7am-7pm Apr-Sep, 7am-5:30pm Oct-Mar) was never finished. The spectacular trefoil arches (a nod to Spain's Moorish past) and carved motifs of crossed swords and keys make it perhaps the most picturesque of all the Jesuit ruins. The treble-naved church, with green grass underfoot, is on a similarly monumental scale as Trinidad. You can climb the tower for views of the surrounding countryside.

Back on the main road, buses back to Encarnación stop by the gas station. Buses back to Posadas leave from the bus stop outside the bus terminal, opposite the school.

A joint ticket for the ruins at Trinidad, Jesús and San Cosme (southwest of Encarnación) is G25,000; it's valid for three days.

You may need a visa to enter Paraguay. Currently, Americans, Canadians, Australians and New Zealanders do; Israelis, Brits and other EU citizens don't. A single-entry visa from the Paraguayan consulate in Posadas can be ready in about an hour. You'll need passport photos, a copy of your passport, proof of an onward ticket and possibly proof of sufficient funds (a credit card may do). You can try going through without stamping in, but you risk a fine if caught.

You can also visit the ruins from San Ignacio: get the bus to Corpus, then cross to Paraguay on the ferry (8am to 5pm Monday to Friday). They'll usually let you pay for a day entry (US$15) so you don't need a visa. Various tour operators in both Posadas and San Ignacio offer day trips to the Paraguayan ruins.

Buses from Posadas

DESTINATION	COST (AR$)	DURATION (HR)
Buenos Aires	584	12-14
Corrientes	135	4
Paso de los Libres	205	5
Puerto Iguazú	142	4½-5½
Resistencia	197	5
Rosario	596	13-15
Tucumán	600	17

Getting Around

Bus 28 (AR$3.50) goes to the airport from San Lorenzo (between La Rioja and Entre Ríos). A *remise* costs about AR$60. There are various car-rental agencies at the airport and in town.

San Ignacio

0376 / POP 6300

The best preserved of the Argentine missions, San Ignacio Miní is the central attraction of this small town north of Posadas. You could visit from Posadas or on your way to Iguazú, but a better idea is to stay the night. The hotels are comfortable, and you'll have a chance to check out the excellent sound-and-light show at the ruins. San Ignacio is a good base for visiting other mission ruins, both in Argentina and Paraguay.

San Ignacio is 56km northeast of Posadas via RN12. From the highway junction Av Sarmiento leads 1km to the town center, where Rivadavia leads six blocks north to the ruins.

Sights

San Ignacio Miní RUIN

(www.misiones-jesuiticas.com.ar; entrance Calle Alberdi s/n; joint missions ticket AR$70; 7am-6pm Apr-Sep, 7am-7pm Oct-Mar) These mission ruins are the most complete of those in Argentina: atmospheric and impressive for the quantity of carved ornamentation still visible and for the amount of restoration. The interpretation center provides good background information, and the ruins themselves feature interactive panels providing multilingual audio.

Admission includes entry to the nearby ruins at Santa Ana and Loreto and also to Santa María la Mayor, a little further afield.

There is a worthwhile sound-and-light show (foreigners AR$70) at the ruins every non-rainy night.

First founded in 1610 in Brazil, but abandoned after repeated attacks by slavers, San Ignacio was established here in 1696 and functioned until the Jesuit expulsion. The ruins, rediscovered in 1897 and restored between 1940 and 1948, are a great example of 'Guaraní baroque.' At its peak, the settlement had a Guaraní population of nearly 4000.

The interpretation center is an impressive display with plenty of unbiased information (in Spanish and English) about the missions from both Jesuit and Guaraní perspectives. You can listen to Guaraní music, including some religious pieces composed at the missions, and inspect a virtual model of San Ignacio as it would have been.

There are free guided tours (multilingual) of the ruins. You first pass between rows of Guaraní houses before arriving at the plaza, on one side of which is the enormous red sandstone church. Impressive in its dimensions, it is the focal point of the settlement. While the red-brown stone is very picturesque in its contrast with the green grass, the buildings were originally white. Before lime was available, it was obtained by burning snail shells.

Times for the nightly show vary according to number of groups. It's a touching, at times haunting, experience played out in various locations using projections onto a mist of water spray, giving a ghostlike quality. Headsets offer a variety of languages.

Casa de Horacio Quiroga HOUSE

(Av Quiroga s/n; admission AR$20; 8am-6pm) Uruguayan writer Horacio Quiroga was a get-back-to-nature type who found his muse in the rough-and-ready Misiones backwoods lifestyle. His simple house at the southern end of town (a 30-minute walk) was built by himself out of stone.

To reach it, you walk along a trail through sugarcane, where panels (in English, too) detail the events of a deeply tragic life so full of shotgun accidents and doses of cyanide it's almost funny. Grand views of the Paraná inspired Quiroga to write his regionally based stories.

Activities

Head down to the Parque Provincial Teyú Cuaré, a protected peninsula on the Río

Paraná, for forest walking and cycling, views, river beaches and Guaraní heritage.

Tours

Tierra Colorada TOUR
(☎15-437-6220; maicolback@gmail.com; RN12) This all-round helpful operator just below the bus terminal – look for the Misionerita restaurant – runs tours to the Paraguayan missions (per person for four people AR$250), or to the Moconá falls (AR$300). It also hires bikes, runs kayaking trips on the river and visits to Guaraní settlements, stores baggage, books buses and gives impartial tourist information.

Sleeping & Eating

Various simple eating options – serving burgers, pizzas and *milanesas* – crowd the streets around the ruins; most are open during the day only.

Hotel La Toscana HOTEL $
(☎447-0777; www.hotellatoscana.com.ar; cnr H Irigoyen & Uruguay; s/d AR$180/260;) In a peaceful part of town half a block from the highway, this simple, welcoming Italian-run place is a relaxing retreat indeed. Cool and spacious basic rooms surround a great pool, deck and garden area. It's a top spot to unwind for a few days and offers great value.

Hotel San Ignacio HOTEL $
(☎447-0047; www.hotelsanignacio.com.ar; cnr Sarmiento & San Martín; s/d AR$180/290, 4-person cabana AR$420; @) Located bang in the town center, this is an excellent choice for its clean, quiet, comfortable rooms, great bathrooms, benevolent owners, and an attached bar and internet cafe. The A-frame cabins out the back are great value for groups. The bar does simple food. You may never find it easier to be the best pool player in town, but the foosball is a different story. No breakfast.

Adventure Hostel HOSTEL $
(☎447-0955; www.sihostel.com; Independencia 469; dm AR$72-84, d AR$270; @) Next to the plaza two blocks south of the church, this well-run, motivated place has comfortable dorms with only three (beds) or four (bunks) berths, decent private rooms and excellent facilities. There's everything from climbing wall to pool (both kinds), ping-pong and seesaws in the spacious grassy grounds. It does traditional Misiones breakfasts and decent dinners, rents bikes, has powered sites for motorhomes and offers HI discount.

La Carpa Azul ARGENTINE $
(www.lacarpaazul.com; Rivadavia 1295; set meals AR$75-100; 6am-4pm;) Near the ruins entrance, this big blue tent serves basic three-course meals of roast meat (average) or river fish (good). It often takes evening group bookings, so you may find it open.

Information

Tourist office (6:30am-10:30pm) At the highway junction.

Getting There & Away

The bus terminal is on the main road near the arch that marks the entrance to town. Services between Posadas (AR$16, one hour) and Puerto Iguazú (AR$90 to AR$120, four to five hours) are frequent, and there are plenty of connections to other major cities.

The Other Missions

Santa Ana & Loreto

Atmospherically decaying in the humid forest, these two Jesuit missions are both off RN12 between Posadas and San Ignacio.

At **Santa Ana** (www.misiones-jesuiticas.com.ar; 7am-7pm Oct-Mar, 7am-6pm Apr-Sep), which was founded in 1633 but moved here in 1660, dense forest has been partially removed to reveal a settlement that had over 7000 Guaraní inhabitants at its peak. The enormous 140-sq-meter plaza attests to the importance of the settlement.

The muscular church's thick walls and photogenic strangler figs lend a dramatic effect to what must have been a magnificent building, though none of its decorative embellishments remain. To the right side of the church is the cemetery, which was used by villagers into the later half of the 20th century but is now neglected. Behind the church, a channel and reservoir remain from what was a sophisticated irrigation system.

Loreto (www.misiones-jesuiticas.com.ar; 7am-7pm Oct-Mar, 7am-6pm Apr-Sep), founded in 1632, has fewer visible remains than Santa Ana, and you may feel it's not worth the effort to visit via public transportation. The old adobe latrine and a chapel are partially restored, but the jungle is king here again and it's difficult to interpret the tumbled mossy stones among the trees. It's undeniably atmospheric, though. It was one of the more important missions; a printing press was built here – the first in the southern part of the continent.

Admission for both Loreto and Santa Ana is via a **joint ticket** (admission AR$70; ⌚ valid for 15 days)that includes San Ignacio Miní and Santa María la Mayor. Guided tours are

A TRIUMPH OF HUMANITY

For a century and a half from 1609, a great social experiment was carried out in the jungles of South America by the Society of Jesus (the Jesuits). Locating themselves in incredibly remote areas, priests set up *reducciones* (missions), where they established communities of Guaraní whom they evangelized and educated, while at the same time protecting them from slavery and the evil influences of colonial society. It was a utopian ideal that flourished and led Voltaire to describe it as 'a triumph of humanity which seems to expiate the cruelties of the first conquerors.'

For the Guaraní who were invited to begin a new life in the missions, there were many tangible benefits, including security, nourishment and prosperity. Mortality declined immediately and mission populations grew rapidly. At their peak the 30 Jesuit *reducciones* that were spread across what's now Argentina, Brazil and Paraguay were populated by more than 100,000 Guaraní. Each mission had a minimum of Europeans: two priests was the norm, and the Guaraní governed themselves under the Jesuits' spiritual authority. The Jesuits made no attempt to force the Guaraní to speak Spanish and only sought to change those aspects of Guaraní culture – polygamy and occasional cannibalism – that clashed with Catholic teaching. Each Guaraní family was given a house and children were schooled.

The typical *reducción* consisted of a large central plaza, dominated by the church and *colegio*, which housed the priests and also contained art workshops and storerooms. The houses of the Guaraní occupied the rest of the settlement in neat rows; other buildings might include a hospital, a *cotiguazú* that housed widows and abandoned wives, and a *cabildo* (town council building) where the Guaraní's chosen leader lived.

The settlements were self-sufficient; the Guaraní were taught agriculture and food was distributed equally. As time went on and the missions grew, wooden buildings were replaced by stone ones and the churches, designed by master architects with grandiose utopian dreams, were stunning edifices with intricate baroque stonework and sculpture comparable with the finest churches being built in Europe at the time.

Indeed, the missions' most enduring achievement was perhaps artistic. The Guaraní embraced the art and music they were introduced to and, interweaving European styles with their own, produced beautiful music, sculpture, dance and painting in 'Guaraní baroque' style. The Jesuits' religious music strongly attracted the Guaraní to Catholicism.

However, mission life necessarily had a martial side. Raiding parties of *bandeirantes* (armed bands) from Brazil regularly sought slaves for sugar plantations, and the Jesuits were resented by both Spanish and Portuguese colonial authorities. There were regular skirmishes and battles until a notable victory over an army of 3000 slavers at Mbororó in 1641 ushered in a period of comparative security.

The mission period came to an abrupt end. Various factors, including envy from the colonial authority and settlers, and a feeling that the Jesuits were more loyal to their own ideas than those of the Crown, prompted Carlos III of Spain to ban them from his dominions in 1767, following the lead of Portugal and France. With the priests gone, the communities were vulnerable and the Guaraní gradually dispersed. The decaying missions were then ruined in the wars of the early 19th century.

The 1986 film *The Mission* is about the last days of the Jesuit missions. Most intriguing is the casting of a Colombian tribe, the Waunana (who had had almost no contact with white people) as the Guaraní.

Almost nothing remains of several of Argentina's 15 missions, but those well worth visiting include San Ignacio Miní in San Ignacio, Loreto and Santa Ana; Yapeyú; and Santa María la Mayor. The fabulous Paraguayan missions at Jesús de Tavarangüe and Trinidad can be easily visited on a day trip too. There are others to visit not too far away in southern Brazil.

THE OTHER FALLS

Apart from Iguazú, the remote and unusual Saltos del Moconá also live long in the memory. A geological fault in the bed of the Río Uruguay divides the river lengthwise and water spills over the shelf between the two sections, creating a waterfall some 3km long and up to 15m high, depending on the water level.

Most important: the falls aren't always visible; if the river is high, you're out of luck. Ring ahead to find out. December to March is normally the best time to visit.

The falls are at the eastern edge of Misiones province, roughly equidistant from Posadas and Puerto Iguazú. From Posadas, several daily buses leave for El Soberbio (four hours); from here it's 63km to the falls: there are three daily bus services. There's also a daily bus from Puerto Iguazú directly to the falls (AR$165, four hours), allowing you to see them on a long day trip from there.

At the end of the road, you cross the Río Yabotí (if it's high you won't be able to go further) and arrive in the **Parque Provincial Moconá** (www.parquesaltosmocona.com.ar; RP 2; admission AR$50; ⏲9am-5pm). Here there's a visitor center, walking trails with views of the falls, boat excursions to get you up close to them (AR$120), and a restaurant.

Various operators, including most accommodations in the area, run boat trips to the falls from points further away: these are recommended, as you get to see Brazilian and Argentine jungle reserves on each side, an attraction in itself.

El Soberbio is an interesting place, a service center for a lush agricultural area growing tobacco, citronella and manioc. There's a ferry crossing to Brazil, and blond heads are everywhere, a legacy of German and Eastern European immigrants joining the indigenous Guaraní population. Ox carts are still widely used for transport.

The several places to stay include spotless motel-style **Hostal Del Centro** (☎03755-495133; cnr Rivadavia & San Martín; s/d AR$125/250; ❄📶), right in the center of town but built around a grassy courtyard; rooms are good for this price and there's a kitchen you can use.

Several upmarket jungly lodges, simple cabins and campsites are closer to the falls. These include the following:

Refugio Moconá (www.refugiomocona.com.ar; RP2; tent/dm/d AR$100/120/350) Six kilometers short of the falls, these are the closest accommodations and offer pleasant grassy camping, simple rooms in a rustic wooden building and good meals. Some impressive cabins with decks overlooking the river below are being built. There are boat trips to the falls, ziplines, rappelling, kayaking and guided walks available. Day use of the trails is AR$25.

Don Enrique Lodge (☎011-4732-3502; www.donenriquelodge.com.ar; s/d AR$1100/1720; 📶) Beautiful wooden bungalows in a very remote location with the river below make for a romantic getaway. Delicious food and welcoming hosts seal the deal. Rate is full board, with guided walks and other activities included. The turnoff is 16km from El Soberbio, then it's another 16km up a rough road. Staff will take you the last few kilometers in a pickup.

Posada La Misión (☎011-15-3415-0500; www.lodgelamision.com.ar; RP2; s/d AR$480/580, master AR$690/790; ❄📶🏊) This superbly situated spot sits on the riverbank 35km from El Soberbio. There are two types of room: rustic ones with fan and beautiful 'master suites' with air-con, veranda with view and modern bathroom with Jacuzzi. Rates are half-board and include some excursions if you stay two nights or more.

included in the admission price. The missions have small museums and kiosks at their entrances.

ℹ Getting There & Away

Buses heading north from Posadas stop at the turnoffs on RN12 for both sites. Santa Ana's is at Km1382.5, from where it's a 700m walk to the ruins. Loreto's is at Km1389, with a 2.5km walk. It can be intensely hot, so take plenty of water. From San Ignacio, an hourly bus (AR$10) leaves from the center to the turnoffs for both missions – some actually drop off at the Loreto ruins themselves. This makes it easy to see both in a day trip from San Ignacio. You can get a *remise* from San Ignacio to take you to both, including waiting time, for about AR$200.

Santa María la Mayor

Further afield, this is the fourth **mission** (RP2, Km43; ⌚7am-7pm Oct-Mar, 7am-6pm Apr-Sep) on the joint admission ticket. A sizable plaza is the main feature, with the church very ruinous. The settlement was a large one, with printing press and prison; the chapel is a 20th-century addition. It's a relaxing place surrounded by jungle that's great for bird-watching, with toucans and trogons easily spotted.

The ruins are on the RP2 between Concepción de la Sierra and San Javier, 110km southeast of Posadas. To get there, take a bus from Posadas to Concepción de la Sierra. There, change to a San Javier–bound service and ask the driver to let you off at the ruins, which are some 25km down the road. You can get a San Javier–bound bus direct from Posadas, but make sure it runs via the ruins; some go a different way.

IGUAZÚ FALLS

One of the planet's most awe-inspiring sights, the Iguazú Falls are simply astounding. A visit is a jaw-dropping, visceral experience, and the power and noise of the cascades – a chain of hundreds of waterfalls nearly 3km in extension – live forever in the memory. An added benefit is the setting: the falls lie split between Brazil and Argentina in a large expanse of national park, much of it rainforest teeming with unique flora and fauna.

The falls are easily reached from either side of the Argentine–Brazilian border, as well as from nearby Paraguay. Both Argentina's Puerto Iguazú and Foz do Iguaçu, on the Brazilian side, have a wide choice of accommodations.

History & Environment

Álvar Núñez Cabeza de Vaca and his 1542 expedition were the first Europeans to view the falls. According to Guaraní tradition the falls originated when an Indian warrior named Caroba incurred the wrath of a forest god by escaping downriver in a canoe with a young girl, Naipur, with whom the god was infatuated. Enraged, the god caused the riverbed to collapse in front of the lovers, producing a line of precipitous falls over which Naipur fell and, at their base, turned into a rock. Caroba survived as a tree overlooking it.

Geologists have a more prosaic explanation. The Río Iguazú's course takes it over a basaltic plateau that ends abruptly just short of the confluence with the Paraná. Where the lava flow stopped, thousands of cubic meters of water per second now plunge down as much as 80m into sedimentary terrain below. Before reaching the falls, the river divides into many channels with hidden reefs, rocks and islands separating the many visually distinct cascades that together form the famous *cataratas* (waterfalls). In total, the falls stretch around 2.7km.

Seeing the Falls

The Brazilian and Argentine sides offer different views and experiences. Go to both (perhaps to the Brazilian first) and hope for sun. The difference between a clear and an overcast day at the falls is vast, only in part because of the rainbows and butterflies that emerge when the sun is shining. Ideally you should allow for a multiple-day stay to have a better shot at optimal conditions.

While the Argentine side – with its variety of trails and boat rides – offers many more opportunities to see individual falls close up, the Brazilian side yields the more panoramic views. You can easily make day trips to both sides of the falls, no matter which side of the border you base yourself. Many people choose to see both sides in one day, but it's a rush.

National Parks

The Brazilian and Argentine sides of the falls are both national parks: Parque Nacional do Iguaçu and Parque Nacional Iguazú, respectively. High temperatures, humidity and rainfall encourage a diverse habitat: the parks' rainforest contains more than 2000 identified plant species, countless insects, 400 species of bird, and many mammals and reptiles.

Resembling Amazonian rainforest, the Iguazú-area forests consist of multiple levels, the highest a closed 30m canopy. Beneath it are several additional levels of trees, plus a dense ground-level growth of shrubs and herbaceous plants. One of the most interesting is the guapoy (strangler fig), an epiphyte that uses a large tree for support until it finally asphyxiates its host.

Iguazú Falls

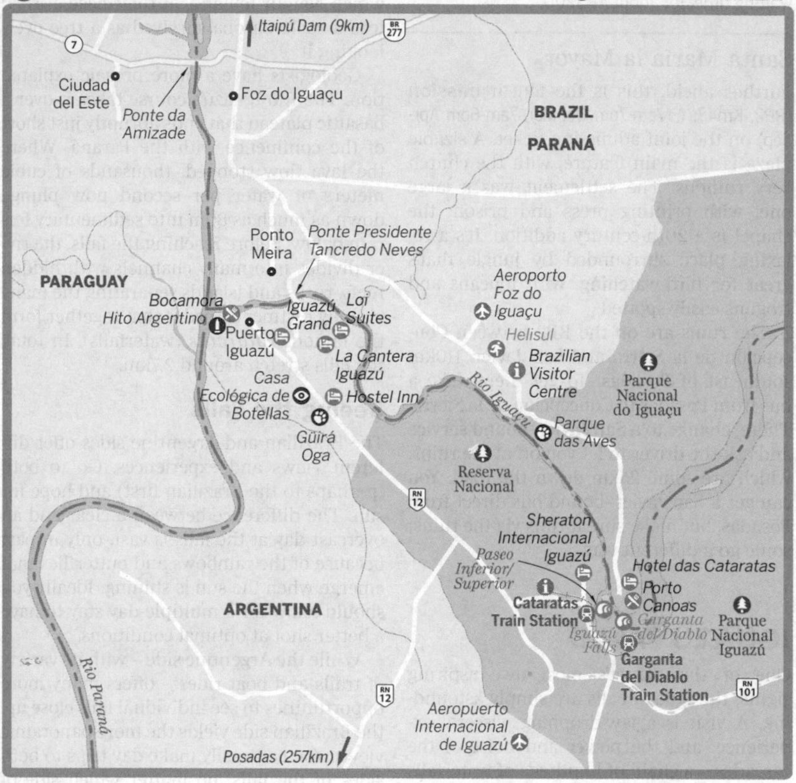

Mammals and other wildlife are present but not easily seen, because many are either nocturnal or avoid humans – which is not difficult in the dense undergrowth. This is the case, for instance, with large cats such as the puma and jaguar. The largest mammal is the tapir, but most common is the coati, a relative of the raccoon. It is not unusual to see iguanas; and watch out for snakes.

Tropical bird species add a dash of color, with toucans and various species of parrot easily seen. The best time to see birds is in the early morning along the forest trails.

Despite regular official denials, the heavy impact of so many visitors to the area has clearly driven much of the wildlife further into the parks, so the more you explore the region away from the falls themselves the more you'll see.

Dangers & Annoyances

The river currents are strong and swift; tourists have been swept downriver and drowned. Of course, don't get too close to the falls proper.

The heat and humidity are often intense and there's plenty of hungry insect life, so pack sunscreen and repellent.

On both sides, you're almost certain to encounter coatis. Don't feed them; though these clownish omnivores seem tame, they become aggressive around food and will bite and scratch. Both parks have a medical point in case of coati attack.

You are likely to get soaked, or at least very damp, from the spray at the falls, so keep your documents and camera protected in plastic bags. You can buy plastic ponchos at the visitor centers on both sides.

Readers have noted that the stamps on sale at the Argentine side of the park can only be posted in the park itself or large cities.

Parque Nacional Iguazú

03757

On the Argentine side, this **park** (491469; www.iguazuargentina.com; adult/6-12yr AR$170/115, car entry AR$40; 8am-6pm) has plenty to offer, and involves a fair amount of walking. The spread-out complex at the entrance has various amenities, including lockers, an ATM (you have to pay for everything in cash in pesos) and a restaurant. There's also an exhibition, **Yvyrá-retã**, with a display on the park and Guaraní life essentially aimed at school groups. The complex ends at a **train station**, from which a train runs every half-hour to the Cataratas train station, where the waterfall walks begin, and to the Garganta del Diablo. You may prefer to walk: it's only 650m along the **Sendero Verde** path to the Cataratas station, and a further 2.3km to the Garganta, and you may well see capuchin monkeys along the way.

There's enough here to detain you for a couple of days; admission is reduced by 50% if you visit the park again the following day. You need to get your ticket stamped when leaving on the first day to get the discount.

Sights

Walking around is the best way to see the falls, with sets of paths offering different perspectives over the cascades. It really is worth getting here by 9am: the gangways are narrow and getting stuck in a conga line of tour groups in searing heat and humidity takes the edge off the experience.

Two circuits, the **Paseo Superior** (650m) and **Paseo Inferior** (1400m), provide most of the viewing opportunities via a series of trails, bridges and *pasarelas* (boardwalks). The Paseo Superior is entirely level and gives good views of the tops of several cascades and across to more. The Paseo Inferior descends to the river (mostly wheelchair accessible), passing delightfully close to more falls on the way. At the end of the path a free launch makes the short crossing to **Isla San Martín**, an island with a trail of its own that gives the closest look at several falls, including **Salto San Martín**, a huge, furious cauldron of water. It's possible to picnic and swim on the lee side of the island, but don't venture too far off the beach. When the water is high – and this is the case more often than not – island access is shut off. At the same junction you can buy tickets for the popular boat rides under the falls.

From Cataratas train station, train it or walk the 2300m to the Garganta del Diablo stop, where an 1100m walkway across the placid Río Iguazú leads to one of the planet's most spectacular sights, the **Garganta del Diablo** (Devil's Throat). The lookout platform is perched right over this amazingly powerful and concentrated torrent of water, a deafening cascade plunging to an invisible destination; the vapors soaking the viewer blur the base of the falls and rise in a smoke-like plume that can often be seen several kilometers away. It's a place of majesty and awe, and should be left until the end of your visit. The last train to the Garganta leaves at 4pm, and we recommend taking it, as it'll be a somewhat less crowded experience. If you walk, you'll see quite a lot of wildlife around this time of day, too.

Activities

Relatively few visitors venture beyond the immediate area of the falls to appreciate the park's forest scenery and wildlife, but it's well worth doing. On the falls trails you'll see large lizards, coatis and several species of bird, but you'll see much more on one of the few trails through the dense forest.

Sendero Macuco WALKING

This jungle trail leads through dense forest to a nearly hidden waterfall, **Salto Arrechea**. The first 3km of the trail to the top of the waterfall is almost completely level, but there is a steep, muddy drop down to the base of the falls and beyond to the Río Iguaçu, about 650m in all. Figure about 1¼ hours each way from the trailhead.

You can swim at the waterfall. Early morning is best, with better opportunities to see wildlife. Last entry is at 3pm. There's a map-guide available at the information desks.

Tours

Explorador Expediciones JUNGLE TOUR

(491469; www.rainforestevt.com.ar) Using knowledgeable guides, this is the best option for appreciating Parque Nacional Iguazú's flora and fauna. It offers combined driving-walking excursions: the Safari a la Cascada takes you to the Arrechea waterfall (AR$220, 90 minutes); better is the Safari en la Selva (AR$280, two hours), a trip in an untouristed part of the park that includes explanations of Guaraní culture.

1

3

MARGIE POLITZER/GETTY IMAGES ©

VISIONSOFAMERICA/JOE SOHM/GETTY IMAGES ©

MARK NEWMAN/GETTY IMAGES ©

The Iguazú Falls

There are few more impressive sights on the planet than this majestic array of cascades on the border of Argentina and Brazil. Set in luxurious tropical jungle, the falls are accessible, and provide a primal thrill that will never be forgotten.

Brazilian Side

1 Hit the Brazilian side first to appreciate the wide panorama from its short viewing path within a birdlife-rich national park. Cascade after cascade is revealed, picturesquely framed by tropical vegetation before you end up below the impressive Salto Floriano (p201).

Garganta del Diablo

2 The highlight of the falls is the 'Devil's Throat.' Stroll out over the placid Iguazú river before gazing in awe as it drops away beneath you in a display of primitive sound and fury that leaves you breathless (p197).

Argentine Side

3 Two spectacular walkways, one high, one low, get you in close to torrents of water of extraordinary power. Expect awesome photos, expect to get wet, and expect to be exhilarated (p197).

Boat Trips

4 Not wet enough yet? Then prepare to be absolutely drenched. Zippy motorboats take thrillseekers right in under one of the biggest waterfalls on the Argentine side. More sedate canoeing and rafting excursions are also available on the Brazilian side (p197 and p200).

Jungle Trails

5 The waterfalls aren't the only thing on offer. National parks on both sides of the river offer various easy-to-medium trails through the jungle that give great wildlife-watching opportunities (p197 and p200).

Clockwise from top left

1. Foz do Iguaçu (p207) **2.** Garganta del Diablo (p197) **3.** Iguazú Falls (p195)

You don't need the falls admission ticket; morning departures can include hotel pickup and afternoon departure includes a transfer back to Puerto Iguazú. Best to book a day or more in advance by phone or at its information booths at the falls.

Iguazú Jungle Explorer BOAT TOUR
(☎421696; www.iguazujungle.com) Offers several river adventures on the Argentine side of the Iguazú falls. Most popular is the short boat trip leaving from the Paseo Inferior that takes you right under one of the waterfalls for a high-adrenaline soaking (AR$180).

Full Moon Walks WALKING TOUR
(☎491469; www.iguazuargentina.com) For five consecutive nights per month, these guided walks visit the Garganta del Diablo. There are three departures nightly. The first, at 8pm, offers the spectacle of the inflated rising moon; the last, at 9:30pm, sees the falls better illuminated. Don't expect to see wildlife. The price (AR$300) includes admission and a drink; dinner is extra (AR$90). Book in advance as numbers are limited. Extra buses from Puerto Iguazú cater for moonwalkers.

Sleeping & Eating

There's one hotel within Parque Nacional Iguazú. Numerous snack bars offer predictably overpriced fare. Their food is awful; bring a (coati-proof) picnic, eat at one of the two buffet restaurants or lunch at the Sheraton.

Sheraton Iguazú HOTEL $$$
(☎491800; www.sheraton.com/iguazu; r standard with forest/falls view US$430/503;) With a privileged position within Parque Nacional Iguazú itself and looking right upriver to the Garganta del Diablo, this backs it up with professional service and spacious rooms with balconies: superiors are similar to standards but newer. The jungle-side view is pretty too. There's a good outdoor pool area, as well as a heated pool and spa indoors. Rooms are substantially cheaper online.

The restaurant has a limited selection (mains AR$105 to AR$180). In-room wi-fi costs extra.

La Selva BUFFET $$$
(www.iguazuargentina.com; all you can eat AR$150; 11am-3:30pm) During your visit, this restaurant, close to the Parque Nacional Iguazú's main entrance, will get talked up so much you'll fear the worst, but it's actually OK, with a buffet of hot and cold dishes, and all-you-can-eat *parrillada*. It's well overpriced but information kiosks give out vouchers offering a substantial discount so head there first.

Fortín BUFFET $$$
(www.fortincataratas.com; all-you-can-eat AR$135; 10am-4pm) Well located near the Paseos Inferior and Superior falls walkways, this offers a mediocre and overpriced buffet spread with *parrilla* choices. Bargain hard for a better deal. A beer on the deck is a decent alternative.

Getting There & Away

Parque Nacional Iguazú is 20km southeast of Puerto Iguazú. From Puerto Iguazú's bus terminal, buses leave every 20 minutes for the park (AR$35, 40 minutes) between 7:20am and 7.20pm, with return trips between 7:50am and 7:50pm. The buses make flag stops at points along the highway. A taxi from town to the park entrance is AR$100.

Parque Nacional do Iguaçu (Brazil)

This Brazilian **park** (☎3521-4400; www.cataratasdoiguacu.com.br; adult/2-12yr R$48.80/7.50; tickets 9am-5pm) is entered via an enormous visitor center, with snack bar, ATMs and lockers (R$10), among other amenities. Parking here costs R$15, but it's free at the Parque das Aves opposite.

Tickets can be purchased by credit card or with a variety of currencies. All catering outlets take cards, so day-trippers won't need to obtain Brazilian currency. Double-decker buses await to take you into the park proper. Keep your eyes peeled for animals. The last bus back from the falls is at 6:30pm.

The park is open for guided evening walks once a month on the night of the full moon.

Sights & Activities

The double-decker bus that takes you into Parque Nacional do Iguaçu makes two stops before the main falls stop. These are trailheads for excursions that cost extra. If you plan to do any of these, chat with one of the agents touting them around the park visitor center; they can get you a discount.

ENTERING BRAZIL

Many nationalities require visas to enter Brazil. At the time of writing these included citzens of the USA, Australia, Canada and Japan. EU citizens did not. Download the application form at https://scedv.serpro.gov.br and take it to a Brazilian consulate. You can use the one in **Puerto Iguazú** (☎03757-420192; Córdoba 264; visa fee Australia/Canada/Japan/USA/other AR$238/442/170/1088/136; ⏲8am-noon Mon-Thu, 8-11am Fri), which may be cheaper than in your home country. You'll need a return ticket, a photo and a bank or credit card statement. If you get there early, it can usually be ready by the next working day and same day may be possible.

That said, it is usually – *but not always* – possible to take a day trip by bus to the Brazilian falls without a visa. You'll have to catch the Foz do Iguaçu–bound bus, not the one that goes direct to the Brazilian falls. Argentine officials will stamp you out; stay on the bus when it passes Brazilian immigration and don't blame us if you're out of luck that day and get sent back. *Remise* and taxi drivers can usually get you through without immigration formalities too.

★Cataratas do Iguaçu WATERFALL

The main Iguazú waterfall observation trail provides you with unforgettable vistas, and this is where it starts. Located by the Hotel das Cataratas, it is the third, and principal, bus stop on the route that takes you into the Parque Nacional do Iguaçu. From here you walk 1.5km down a paved trail with brilliant views of the falls on the Argentine side, the jungle and the river below. Every twist of the path reveals a more splendid vista until the trail ends right under the majestic Salto Floriano, which will give you a healthy sprinkling of water via the wind that it generates.

A boardwalk leads out to a platform with majestic vistas, with the Garganta del Diablo close at hand, and a perspective down the river in the other direction. If the water's high, it's unforgettable; a rainbow is visible in the spray on clear afternoons.

From here an elevator heads up to a viewing platform at the top of the falls at Porto Canoas, the last stop of the double-decker buses. Porto Canoas has boat excursions, an internet terminal, a gift shop, a couple of snack bars and a buffet restaurant.

Trilha do Poço Preto HIKING

(☎3529-9627; www.macucoecoaventura.com.br; per person R$135) This 9km trail takes you on a guided journey through the jungle on foot, by bike or on a trailer. It ends at Taquara Island above the falls, where you can kayak or take a boat cruise to Porto Canoas. You can also return via the Bananeiras Trail. The trailhead is the first stop on the bus route into Parque Nacional do Iguaçu.

Bananeiras Trail WALKING

(☎3529-9627; www.macucoecoaventura.com.br; per person R$105) This is a 1.6km walk passing lagoons and observing aquatic wildlife, which ends at a jetty where you can take boat rides or silent 'floating' excursions in kayaks down to Porto Canoas. It is accessed from the second stop on the bus route into Parque Nacional do Iguaçu.

Macuco Safari BOAT TRIP

(☎3574-4244; www.macucosafari.com.br; per person R$140, without boat segment R$70) This two-hour safari includes a 3km trailer ride through the jungle, a 600m walk to a small waterfall and then a boat ride up toward the Iguazú falls. Don't confuse it with the Macuco trail on the Argentine side. This safari is accessed from the second stop on the bus route into Parque Nacional do Iguaçu.

Cânion Iguaçu ADVENTURE SPORTS

(☎3529-6040; www.campodedesafios.com.br) At the beginning of the main Parque Nacional do Iguaçu waterfall trail is this activity center offering rafting (R$80), abseiling (R$70), rock climbing (R$50) and a canopy tour (R$70). It's at the third stop on the bus route into Parque Nacional do Iguaçu.

Helisul SCENIC FLIGHTS

(☎3529-7474; www.helisul.com; flights R$255) By the Parque Nacional do Iguaçu visitor center, this setup runs 10-minute chopper jaunts at 450m over the Brazilian side of the falls. The environmental impact is questionable, but it's undeniably exhilarating. There are open panels in the windows for unimpeded photography.

Sleeping & Eating

★Hotel das Cataratas HOTEL $$$
(☎2102-7000; www.hoteldascataratas.com; BR469, Km32; r from R$1309;) In the Parque Nacional do Iguaçu near the falls, this excellent hotel appeals enormously for location, though only a few rooms have falls views, and those only partial. It's decorated throughout in understated, elegant Portuguese colonial style, with tiling in the bathrooms and dark wood in the bedrooms. Public areas have cozy appeal, and the fine pool area is surrounded by birdsong. Service is excellent.

Be sure to climb the belvedere for the view. Online rates are much better.

Porto Canoas BUFFET $
(buffet R$45; ⏲noon-4pm) Situated at the end of the main trail at the Parque Nacional do Iguaçu, this restaurant has a long pleasant terrace overlooking the river just before it descends into the maelstrom – a great spot for a beer – and an OK buffet lunch with plenty of salads and hot dishes.

Getting There & Around

'Parque Nacional' buses run from Foz do Iguaçu's urban bus terminal (pay entering the terminal) to the park (R$2.85, 45 minutes) every 22 minutes between 6am and 7pm, then hourly until midnight, stopping along Avs Juscelino Kubitschek and das Cataratas.

Taxis from Foz to the park entrance cost R$40.

From Puerto Iguazú, there's a direct bus to the Brazilian falls four times a day (AR$60 return, 40 minutes), with departures from 8:10am to 2pm and returns from 11am to 5pm (Brazilian time). This stops at Brazilian immigration and collects passports. You can also take the regular bus to Foz do Iguaçu and get off a couple of stops after crossing the international bridge. Cross the road, and wait for the Parque Nacional bus. Repeat at the same stop on the way back. See 'Entering Brazil' (p201).

Puerto Iguazú

☎03757 / POP 82,200

Booming Puerto Iguazú sits at the confluence of the Ríos Paraná and Iguazú and looks across to Brazil and Paraguay. It doesn't really feel like Argentina any more. There's no town center and little feeling of community – everyone is here to see the falls or to make a buck out of them. Still, it's quiet, safe and has good transportation connections; there are also many excellent places to stay and eat.

Sights & Activities

There's little to see in the town itself, but 1km west of the town center along Av Tres Fronteras is the **Hito Argentino**, a small obelisk at the impressive confluence of the Ríos Paraná and Iguazú. From here you can see Brazil and Paraguay, with similar markers on their sides. A fairly desultory *artesanía* market is also here.

Güirá Oga ZOO
(www.guiraoga.com.ar; RN12, Km5; admission AR$75; ⏲9am-6pm, last entry 5pm) Out of town on the way to Parque Nacional Iguazú, this is an animal hospital and center for rehabilitation of injured wildlife. It also carries out valuable research into the Iguazú forest environment and has a breeding program for endangered species. You get walked around the jungly park by one of the staff, who explains (English available) heaps about the birds and animals and the sad stories of how they got there. The visit takes about 80 minutes.

Casa Ecológica de Botellas NOTABLE BUILDING
(http://lacasadebotellas.googlepages.com; RN12, Km5; admission AR$30; ⏲8am-7pm Sep-May, 8:30am-6:30pm Jun-Aug) About 200m down a side road off the Iguazú Falls road, this fascinating place is well worth a visit. The owners have used packaging materials – plastic bottles, juice cartons and the like – to build not only an impressive house but also furnishings and a bunch of original handicrafts that make unusual gifts. The guided visit will talk you through their techniques.

Tours

Numerous local operators offer day tours to the Brazilian side of the Iguazú falls (AR$150 to AR$250 depending on what's included), some taking in the Itaipu dam and Paraguay shopping as well. Many have offices at the bus terminal.

Cruceros Iguazú BOAT TOUR
(☎421111; www.crucerosiguazu.com; Zona Puerto, Local 3; AR$180) Daily late-afternoon cruises on the Paraná and Iguazú rivers in a large catamaran.

Iguazú Bike Tours CYCLING TOUR
(☎422623; www.iguazubiketours.com.ar; Raúl Alfonsín 119) These guys run anything from gentle jaunts through the nearby forest to long

vehicle-supported rides through the lesser-visited corners of Parque Nacional Iguazú.

Sleeping

There are numerous sleeping options for all budgets, including a string of resort-type hotels between town and Parque Nacional Iguazú. In the streets around the bus terminal are many hostels. Another option is the Sheraton Iguazú (p200) at the falls themselves. Many places don't accept credit cards or slap a hefty surcharge on.

Garden Stone HOSTEL $
(☎420425; www.gardenstonehostel.com; Av Córdoba 441; dm/d AR$100/300; ❄📶🏊) The best feature of this amiably run hostel is its perfectly relaxing garden area, where there's a pool. Other good things include handiness for the bus terminal, good kitchen, tasty included breakfast, decent dorms and general peaceful vibe.

Timbó Hostel HOSTEL $
(☎422698; www.timboiguazu.com.ar; Av Misiones 147; dm AR$70, s/d AR$170/300; ❄@📶🏊) This sweet spot at the center of town is a welcome respite from the hustle and bustle. With a peaceful little garden and pool area, spacious (if dark and musty) dorms, pretty private rooms and a surprisingly decent breakfast under a thatched roof, it's a good deal.

Residencial Lola GUESTHOUSE $
(☎423954; residenciallola@hotmail.com; Av Córdoba 255; s/d AR$120/200; @📶) Plenty of price gouging goes on in Puerto Iguazú, but it stops at Lola's front door. This cheap, cheerily run spot is very close to the bus terminal and features compact, clean rooms with bathroom for a pittance. No sign.

Hotel Lilian HOTEL $
(☎420968; hotellilian@yahoo.com.ar; Beltrán 183; s/d AR$300/345; ❄@📶) Run by a hospitable family that isn't out to rip tourists off, this friendly place offers plenty of value, with its bright and cheerful rooms around a patio. The superior rooms – worth the small extra outlay – have a balcony and heaps of natural light. All the bathrooms are spacious and spotless. Things get done the way they should here.

Hostel Inn HOSTEL $
(☎421823; www.hostel-inn.com; RN12, Km5; dm/r AR$89/403; ❄@📶🏊) This is more resort than hostel, and you get a lot for your pesos, as the spotless place is set in expansive grounds and has a big pool and all the backpacker-friendly facilities you can imagine. The dorms are commodious and air-conditioned; the ones in separate buildings in the garden tend to be a little quieter.

Most readers love it to bits, though some complain about Cool Hostel Syndrome (CHS): you'll know whether it's for you or not. It's a way into town, but buses stop right outside. Offers 10% HI discount.

Marco Polo Inn HOSTEL $
(☎425575; www.marcopoloinniguazu.com; Av Córdoba 158; dm/d AR$95/432; ❄@📶🏊) Built motel-style, this hostel is opposite the bus terminal. The dorms are darkish but come with lockers and private bathroom, and there's a host of other facilities. It's popular, so book. Offers 10% HI discount.

Noelia HOSTEL, GUESTHOUSE $
(☎420729; www.hostelnoelia.com; Beltrán 119; dm AR$60, d AR$270, without bathroom AR$220; ❄📶🏊) On a quiet street, this has crowded but decent dorms with private bathroom at a sharp price, and musty but OK-value private rooms. It's an easygoing, tranquil place with a pool and simple open kitchen.

Irupé Mini GUESTHOUSE $
(☎420711; irupeiguazu@yahoo.com.ar; Av Misiones 88; s/d AR$80/150, d with air-con AR$200; ❄📶) This is very basic but offers friendliness, location and decent value for cheap private rooms, which are tight, with tiny bathrooms. Go for rooms at the back, which have more light. It will offer dorm rates if it's not too full.

Jasy Hotel HOTEL $$
(☎424337; www.jasyhotel.com; San Lorenzo 154; r US$110; ❄📶🏊) Original and peaceful, these 10 two-level rooms, with a great design for family sleeping, climb a hill like a forest staircase and are all equipped with a balcony gazing over plentiful greenery. Artful use of wood is the signature; you'll fall in love with the bar and deck area. Prepare to stay longer than planned.

> **ℹ CHANGING THE CLOCKS**
>
> From mid-October to mid-February, southern Brazil changes the clocks for summer, putting it an hour ahead of Argentina, which doesn't observe daylight saving time.

Puerto Iguazú

Guest House Puerto Iguazú GUESTHOUSE $$
(☎423346; www.guesthousepuertoiguazu.com; Lindtron 14; r US$140, without bathroom US$105, ste US$175; ❄📶🏊) In a hidden-away plot overlooking the Río Iguazú, the friendly owners have set up a real haven here. There are just four rooms, elegant and comfortable; two share a good bathroom. You can use the spacious kitchen, watch birds in the garden, or kick back on the poolside terrace with river views. Overpriced but pleasing.

Jardín de Iguazú HOTEL $$
(☎424171; www.hoteljardindeiguazu.com.ar; Bompland 274; r AR$922; ❄📶🏊) In many ways a standard midrange hotel, this appeals for its handy central location, competent staff, pleasant pool and Jacuzzi, and comfortably bland modern rooms. The standard rooms aren't super-spacious, so if that's important to you, upgrade to a superior, which costs very little extra.

Hotel La Sorgente HOTEL $$
(☎424252; www.lasorgentehotel.com; Av Córdoba 454; s/d AR$690/975; ❄@📶🏊) Set around a verdant garden, life couldn't be easier here – if you can't face the long walk around the pool, take the bridge across it. Plain, somewhat musty twin rooms have queen-sized beds; cozier upstairs doubles overlook the pool and banana plants. Breakfast, served in the authentic Italian restaurant, gets the seal of approval, too. Cheaper if you pay cash.

★ **Boutique Hotel de la Fonte** HOTEL $$$
(☎420625; www.bhfboutiquehotel.com; cnr Corrientes & 1 de Mayo; r US$190-270; ❄@📶🏊) The mark of a good hotel is constant improvement, and this place adds great features so fast we can barely keep up. It's a secluded, enchanting spot, featuring characterful individual rooms and suites around a tree-filled courtyard garden that's romantically

Puerto Iguazú

Activities, Courses & Tours
1 Cruceros Iguazú A1

Sleeping
2 Garden Stone C2
3 Guest House Puerto Iguazú D1
4 Hotel La Sorgente C2
5 Hotel Lilian D3
6 Irupé Mini C2
7 Jardín de Iguazú C2
8 Jasy Hotel D2
9 Marco Polo Inn C3
10 Noelia D4
11 Residencial Lola C3
12 Timbó Hostel B3

Eating
13 Aqva C3
14 Color C3
15 Feria B1
16 La Misionera B3
17 La Rueda C4
18 La Vitrina C4
19 Lemongrass B2
20 María Preta B3
21 Terra C3

Drinking & Nightlife
22 Buena Vida B3
23 Cuba Libre B2

lit at night. One of the welcoming owners is an architect, and it shows, in the numerous small decorative touches as well as the artistic design.

An outdoor hot tub, small spa complex, saltwater pool, and all-over style and elegance are other great features. The other owner is a chef who runs one of the town's best restaurants, De La Fonte (p206), so you're in luck there too. A standout.

La Cantera Iguazú LODGE $$$
(☎493016; www.iguazulodgelacantera.com; Selva Iryapú s/n; r from US$200; ❄@🛜≋) Nestled in deep forest 1.5km off the falls road, this enchanting, intimate lodge has appealing 'tierra' rooms with balcony in wooden buildings that in some cases still have trees growing through them. The upper-level 'jungle' rooms offer better views and have a hammock. Cheaper 'forest' rooms are attractive but less rustic. Biking, guided walks and visits to the Guaraní hamlets are included.

Loi Suites RESORT $$$
(☎498300; www.loisuites.com.ar; Selva Iryapú s/n; r US$492-783; ❄@🛜≋) Spectacularly set in the jungle yet just a few kilometers from town, this giant complex has several buildings connected by walkways. It's decorated in relaxed country style and features a huge tree-surrounded pool area as its highlight. Rooms are spacious and comfortable; upgrade to a balcony for bird-watching opportunities. But charging extra for spa use and in-room wi-fi seems outrageous at these rates. Online prices are usually lower.

Iguazú Jungle Lodge HOTEL $$$
(☎420600; www.iguazujunglelodge.com; cnr Yrigoyen & San Lorenzo; r US$224-304; ❄🛜≋👪) A little corporate in feel, but with a very secluded location considering it's on the edge of town, this offers spacious, well-equipped accommodations with quality beds and jungle balcony in a resort-style complex surrounding a large pool. Staff are multilingual and very helpful. It's a great option for families, with games room and suites. Good onsite restaurant.

Iguazú Grand HOTEL $$$
(☎498050; www.iguazugrand.com; RN12, Km1640; r from US$502; ❄@🛜≋👪) Don't let the tacky ads for the attached casino put you off this place, just short of the bridge across to Brazil. It's a huge upmarket complex, classically decorated, with a variety of excellent rooms, pretty grounds, a great pool area, spa (included) and top restaurant. Facilities are first class, and children are made very welcome. It's cheaper online.

Eating

Restaurants in Puerto Iguazú are pricey but generally of good quality, and open early for dinner to cater for tourists. Credit cards aren't widely accepted: ask beforehand or carry cash.

Feria MARKET $
(La Feirinha; cnr Av Brasil & Félix de Azara; picadas for 2 AR$60-90; ⏲8am-midnight) A really nice place to eat is this market in the north of town. It's full of stalls selling Argentine wines, sausages, olives and cheese to visiting Brazilians, and several of them put out *picadas*, other simple regional dishes and cold beer. There's folk music some nights and a good evening atmosphere.

La Misionera BAKERY $

(☎424580; P Moreno 210; empanadas AR$6-8; ⏲11am-11:30pm) Excellent empanadas with a big variety of fillings, as well as delivery option.

Lemongrass CAFE $

(www.facebook.com/lemongrassiguazu; Bompland 231; snacks AR$15-30; ⏲8:30am-2pm & 5-10pm Mon-Sat; 📶) There's something very likable about this artistic little side-street cafe. Good fresh juices, decent coffee, delicious sweet temptations and tasty savory tarts are the way to go. Beers and *caipirinhas* (Brazilian cocktails) are also available.

★ **María Preta** ARGENTINE $$

(☎420441; www.facebook.com/MariaPretaRestaurant; Av Brasil 39; mains AR$52-88; ⏲11am-3pm & 7pm-midnight or later; 📶✎) The indoor-outdoor eating area and evening guitarist make this a popular dinner choice, whether it's for steaks that are actually cooked the way you want them, for a wide range of typical Argentine-Spanish dishes, or for something a little snappier: caiman fillet.

Bocamora ARGENTINE $$

(☎420550; www.bocamora.com; Av Costanera s/n; mains AR$60-110; ⏲noon-midnight Tue-Sun; 📶) A superbly romantic location overlooking three nations is reason enough to come to this place just down the hill from the Argentine border marker. It specializes in grilled meats and well-prepared plates of river fish; the food is competent and tasty, service is great and the view is just breathtaking.

Color PARRILLA, PIZZA $$

(☎420206; www.parrillapizzacolor.com; Av Córdoba 135; mains AR$55-95; ⏲lunch & dinner; 📶) This popular indoor-outdoor pizzeria and *parrilla* packs them into its tightly spaced tables, so don't discuss state secrets. But the prices are fair for this strip, and the meat comes out redolent of wood smoke; the wood-oven pizzas and empanadas are also very toothsome.

Terra ASIAN $$

(☎421931; Av Misiones 125; mains AR$60-90; ⏲dinner; 📶✎) Chalked signatures of myriad satisfied customers mark the walls of this chilled bar-restaurant that specializes in well-prepared wok dishes, with teriyaki salmon, pasta and salads as other options. The streetside terrace fills fast.

La Vitrina PARRILLA $$

(Av Victoria Aguirre 773; mains AR$50-92; ⏲lunch & dinner) This homey barn of a place is the place to come for great *asado de tira* (ribs) among other *parrilla* delicacies. It's less touristy than some and has enticing outdoor seating. There's live music at weekends.

De La Fonte ITALIAN $$$

(www.bhfboutiquehotel.com; cnr Corrientes & 1 de Mayo; mains AR$110-180; ⏲8pm-midnight Tue-Sun; 📶) The domain of a talented Italian chef, this exquisite hotel restaurant is superstrong on presentation, whether it be the homemade pasta or inventive artist-themed creations with fish or meat. An open kitchen furnishes elegant indoor and outdoor dining in this beautiful courtyard oasis. Degustation menus showcase the array of culinary ability on display.

La Rueda ARGENTINE $$$

(☎422531; www.larueda1975.com; Av Córdoba 28; mains AR$80-125; ⏲5:30pm-midnight Mon-Tue, noon-midnight Wed-Sun; 📶) A mainstay of upmarket eating in Puerto Iguazú, this culinary heavyweight still packs a punch. The salads are imaginative and delicious, as are the river-fish (dorado, pacú and surubí) creations. The homemade pasta is cheaper but doesn't disappoint. Service is good but slow.

Aqva ARGENTINE $$$

(☎422064; www.aqvarestaurant.com; cnr Av Córdoba & Thays; mains AR$80-135; ⏲noon-midnight; 📶) Solicitous service and plenty of flavor keep this split-level corner spot filled with buzz of contented diners. The quality of the meat is excellent, and this is also a recommended spot to get to know some of the region's river fish.

🍷 Drinking & Nightlife

Tourism and Brazilians from Foz do Iguaçu looking for a cheap night out on the weakened peso make Puerto Iguazú's nightlife lively. Action centers on Av Brasil, where a string of bars attract evening drinkers. Unsubtle **Cuba Libre** (www.facebook.com/cuba.megadisco; cnr Av Brasil & Paraguay; ⏲from 11pm Wed-Sun) around the corner gets the cross-border crowd living it up on the dance floor.

Buena Vida BAR

(P Moreno 254; ⏲10am-2am; 📶) Half a block from the main bar zone, this split-level outdoor spot feels secluded. It's an attractive setup done out in dark wood with corrugated metal, and offers sandwiches, picadas, empanadas and the like (light meals AR$25 to AR$50) as well as good mixed drinks and beer specials.

Information

Currency exchange places are along Av Victoria Aguirre downtown. There are various free wi-fi zones around town.

Hospital (☎420288; cnr Av Victoria Aguirre & Ushuaia)

Macro (cnr Av Misiones & Bompland) ATM.

Tourist kiosk (Bus terminal; ⏲7am-7pm) Downstairs in the bus terminal.

Tourist office (☎420800; www.iguazuargentina.com; Av Victoria Aguirre 311; ⏲7am-1pm & 2-9pm Mon-Fri, 8am-noon & 4-8pm Sat & Sun) Main tourist office.

Getting There & Away

Aerolíneas Argentinas (☎420168; Av Victoria Aguirre 295; ⏲8am-noon & 3-7pm Mon-Fri, 8am-1pm Sat) flies from Iguazú three to seven times daily to Buenos Aires, once to Salta and twice weekly to Rio de Janeiro. **LAN** (www.lan.com) flies the Buenos Aires route three times daily.

The **bus terminal** (☎42-3006; cnr Avs Córdoba & Misiones) has departures for all over the country. There's a morning bus Monday to Saturday to the Saltos del Moconá waterfall (AR$165, four hours), with a day trip possible.

There are Brazilian domestic services across the border in Foz do Iguaçu. Some buses to Brazilian destinations leave from Puerto Iguazú or offer a free connection in a taxi.

BUSES FROM PUERTO IGUAZÚ

DESTINATION	COST (AR$)	DURATION (HR)
Buenos Aires	765	17-18
Córdoba	887	22
Corrientes	413	9
Posadas	142	4½-6
Resistencia	377	9-10
San Ignacio	90-120	4-5

Getting Around

Four Tourist Travel (☎420681, 422743; M Moreno 58) runs an airport shuttle for AR$40 per person that meets incoming flights; from town, it needs to be booked in advance. A *remise* costs AR$100. The airport is 25km from town.

Frequent buses cross to Foz do Iguaçu, Brazil (AR$8/R$4, 35 minutes), and to Ciudad del Este, Paraguay (AR$20, one hour), from 7am to 7pm from the local side of the bus terminal. There are four daily buses direct to the Brazilian side of the Iguazú falls (AR$60 return).

A taxi to Foz costs around AR$140; to the Brazilian side of the Iguazú falls it's AR$230 return. Avoid the *remise* office at the bus terminal: it's more expensive than other offices around. Always negotiate.

Foz do Iguaçu (Brazil)

☎045 / POP 263,500

Hilly Foz is base camp for the Brazilian side of the Iguazú falls, and gives you a chance to get a feel for a Brazilian town. It's much bigger and more cosmopolitan than Puerto Iguazú, and has a keep-it-real feel that its Argentine counterpart lacks. It's not particularly pretty, but there's something appealing about it nonetheless.

Sights

Itaipu DAM

(☎0800-645-4645; www.turismoitaipu.com.br; Tancredo Neves 6702; panoramic/special tour R$24/60; ⏲regular tour hourly 8am-4pm) This binational dam is the world's second-largest hydroelectric power station and, at some 8km long and 200m high, is a memorable sight, especially when the river is high and a vast torrent of overflow water cascades down the spillway.

The visitor center, 12km north of Foz, has regular tours and the more detailed *circuito especial* (eight daily, minimum age 14), which takes you into the power plant itself.

Public buses (R$2.85, 30 minutes) head here every 15 minutes from the urban bus terminal.

The project was controversial: it plunged Brazil into debt and necessitated large-scale destruction of rainforest and the displacement of 10,000 people. But it cleanly supplies nearly all of Paraguay's energy needs, and 20% of Brazil's.

A variety of other attractions within the complex include a museum, wildlife park and river beaches.

Parque das Aves ZOO

(www.parquedasaves.com.br; admission R$28; ⏲9am-5pm) Near the Parque Nacional do Iguaçu entrance is this large bird park. It has a huge assortment of our feathered friends, mostly Brazilian, with good information in English and Spanish. Walk-through aviaries get you up close and personal with toucans, macaws and hummingbirds.

Foz do Iguaçu (Brazil)

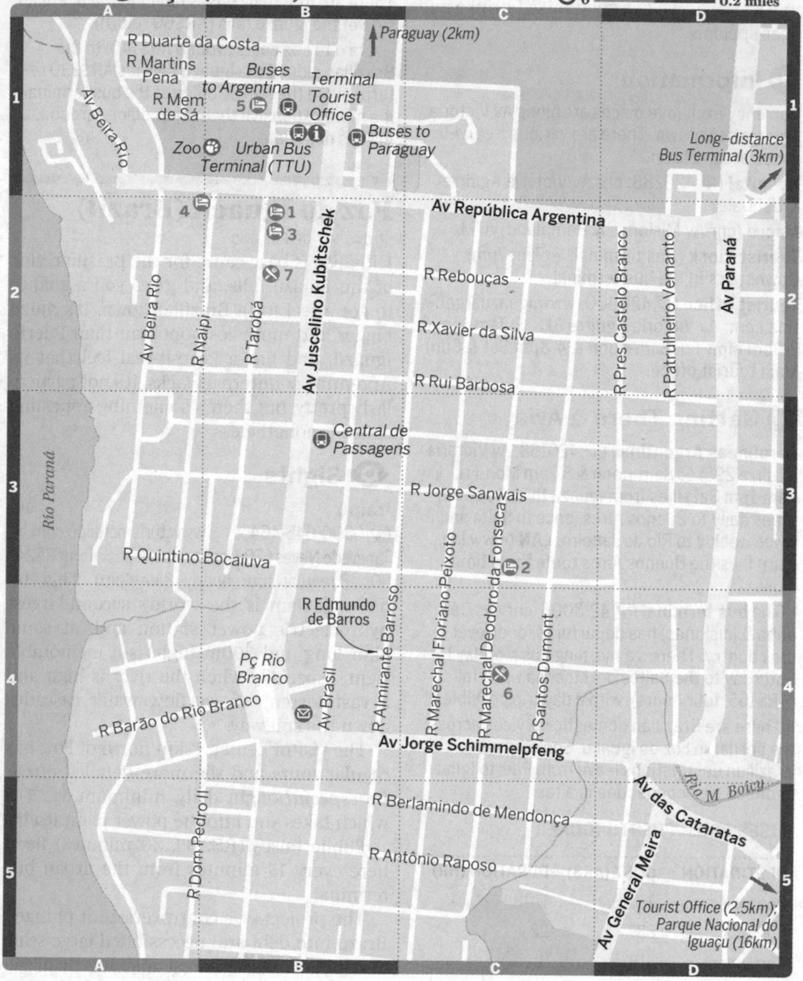

Sleeping

Normally you'll get a rate up to 40% lower than rack rates. Don't be afraid to ask for a discount.

★**Pousada Sonho Meu** GUESTHOUSE $
(☎3573-5764; www.pousadasonhomeufoz.com.br; R Mem de Sá 262; s/d R$160/210; ❄@📶🏊) What from the outside looks like an administrative building becomes a delightful oasis barely 50m from the urban bus terminal. Rooms are simply decorated with bamboo; there's a standout pool (complete with a mini *catarata*!), breakfast area and outdoor guest kitchen, and a warm welcome throughout. Cash only. Prices can be half those indicated here.

Iguassu Guest House HOSTEL $
(☎3029-0242; www.iguassuguesthouse.com.br; R Naipi 1019; dm/d R$40/120; ❄@📶🏊) Great facilities and welcoming management mark this out from the Foz hostel herd. There's a small pool out the back, it's spotless, and there's a really good open kitchen and lounge area. Dorms vary in size; private rooms are very compact but comfortable. The urban bus terminal is just around the corner.

Foz do Iguaçu (Brazil)

Sleeping

1 Hotel Del Rey B2
2 Hotel Rafain Centro C3
3 Hotel Tarobá B2
4 Iguassu Guest House A2
5 Pousada Sonho Meu B1

Eating

6 Armazém C4
7 Búfalo Branco B2

Hotel Rafain Centro HOTEL **$$**
(☎3521-3500; www.rafaincentro.com.br; R Marechal Deodoro da Fonseca 984; s/d R$272/347; ❄@📶🏊) Much more appealing than some of the hulking megahotels around town, the Rafain is a recently renovated, four-star place with plenty of style, artistic detail and friendly staff. Rooms are simple with large balconies and there's a cracking pool and terrace. Prices can come down substantially. Great facilities.

Hotel Tarobá HOTEL **$$**
(☎2102-7700; www.hoteltarobafoz.com.br; R Tarobá 1048; s/d R$210/256; ❄@📶🏊) You'll likely need to book for this place that's handy for the urban bus terminal. Value is high here considering the facilities and professional staff; the tiled rooms are bright and spacious and all have minifridge and cable TV. There's also a sauna and small gym. Breakfast is excellent.

Hotel Del Rey HOTEL **$$**
(☎2105-7500; www.hoteldelreyfoz.com.br; R Tarobá 1020; s/d R$255/290; ❄@📶🏊) Friendly, spotless and convenient. The rooms are spacious and comfortable, facilities are excellent and the breakfast buffet is huge.

Eating

It's easy to eat cheaply. Many places will serve you a soft drink and *salgado* (baked or fried snack) for as little as R$4, and cheap locals offer buffet lunches for R$10 to R$15. Thanks to the Lebanese community, there are dozens of shawarma (kebab) places.

Armazém BRAZILIAN **$$**
(☎3572-0007; www.armazemtrapiche.com.br; R Edmundo de Barros 446; mains R$30-60; ⏲6pm-midnight daily & 11.30am-3.30pm Sat & Sun; 📶) A block off Av Jorge Schimmelpfeng, this well-frequented high-ceilinged restaurant serves top-shelf Brazilian food. From starters like cheese-laden carpaccio to delicious chicken, cod and beef mains, all just about enough for two, it delivers on taste. There are various special nights, and even a sushi-bar annex. The wine list covers the whole Southern Cone. It does free hotel pickups and drop-offs.

Búfalo Branco CHURRASCARIA **$$**
(☎3523-9744; www.bufalobranco.com.br; Rebouças 530; all-you-can-eat R$60; ⏲noon-11pm; 📶✎) This spacious Foz classic continues to draw locals and tourists alike for its classy but overpriced *rodízio* (all-you-can-eat mixed grill cut at your table), which features delicious roast meats, including excellent beef, as well as more unusual choices such as chicken hearts and turkey balls. The salad bar is great, and includes tasty Lebanese morsels and sushi rolls. Look diffident outside the door and you might get a cheaper deal.

Drinking & Nightlife

Make sure you have the classic Brazil experience: an ice-cold bottle of beer in a plastic insulator served in a no-frills local bar with red plastic seats. Unbeatable. For a healthier tipple, juice bars give you the chance to try exotic fruits such as *acerola, açaí* or *cupuaçu.*

Nightlife in the city centers on Av Jorge Schimmelpfeng. A row of big indoor-outdoor bars here all specialize in *chopp* (draft beer) and do decent food designed to share.

Orientation

Foz is at the confluence of the Ríos Iguaçu (Iguazú) and Paraná; international bridges connect it to Puerto Iguazú, Argentina and Ciudad del Este, Paraguay. Av das Cataratas leads 20km to the Brazilian side of the Iguazú falls, passing the Argentina bridge on the way.

Information

Hotels and restaurants (and just about everything else including buses) in town accept US dollars, Paraguayan guaranis and Argentine pesos, but it's always cheaper to pay in Brazilian reals. There's currency exchange at the border. Handy ATMs are in the Muffato supermarket, a block past the urban bus terminal.

HSBC (Av Brasil 1131) One of several banks with an ATM around this area.

Paraguayan Consulate (☎3523-2898; R Marechal Deodoro da Fonseca 901; ⏲8:30am-12:30pm & 1:30-4pm Mon-Fri) Four-hour turnaround for visas (US$80 to US$160 depending

OFF THE BEATEN TRACK

MISIONES JUNGLE WITHOUT THE CROWDS

The Iguazú jungle is a fabulous habitat for birds, plants, insects and mammals, but mass tourism at the falls means you're unlikely to see as much wildlife as you might wish. One option for seeing more is to head east to the other end of the park. Around the *mate*-growing town of Andresito are several lodges, including excellent **Surucuá** (0376-15-4371046; www.surucua.com; Andresito; s/d incl all meals US$140/220). Run by a welcoming young Misiones couple, this is right in the jungle. Comfortable rustic accommodations and delicious home-cooked meals featuring local ingredients are supplemented by activities including jungle walks and memorable kayak trips among river islands. It's a bird-watcher's paradise, with over 200 species recorded including trogons, toucans, hummingbirds and manakins. Relaxation is guaranteed with no mobile or internet coverage. Multinight stays are cheaper and you will be picked up from Andresito, served by four daily buses from Puerto Iguazú (AR$50, 2½ hours).

on nationality). At the Paraguayan border, you may be able to get in for the day without one, or buy a three-day entry there.

Tourist office (0800-451516; www.iguassu.tur.br; Av Cataratas 2330; 7am-11pm) Unhelpfully located out of town on the way to the Iguazú falls. The phone number is toll-free and English speaking. There's a handier tourist office located in the urban bus terminal (7:30am-6pm).

Getting There & Away

There are daily flights to Rio de Janeiro, Curitiba and São Paulo among other cities in Brazil.

Long-distance buses services include Curitiba (10 hours), São Paulo (16 hours) and Rio de Janeiro (22 hours). You can buy tickets at many central travel agencies, including **Central de Passagens** (3528-8284; www.centraldepassagens.com; Av Juscelino Kubitschek 526).

Getting Around

For the airport or falls, catch the 'Aeropuerto/Parque Nacional' bus from the urban bus terminal or one of the stops along Av Juscelino Kubitschek; the trip takes 30 to 40 minutes and costs R$2.85, paid as you enter the terminal. A taxi costs about R$40.

The **long-distance bus terminal** (3522-3336; Av Costa e Silva 1601) is 5km northeast of downtown. To get downtown, taxi it for R$20 or walk downhill to the nearby bus stop and catch any 'Centro' bus (R$2.85).

Buses to Puerto Iguazú (R$4/AR$10) run along Rua Mem de Sá alongside the urban bus terminal half-hourly from 8am until 8pm; they stop along Av Juscelino Kubitschek. Buses for Ciudad del Este, Paraguay (R$4), run every 15 minutes (half-hourly on Sundays); catch them on Av Juscelino Kubitschek opposite the urban bus terminal.

THE GRAN CHACO

The Gran Chaco is a vast alluvial lowland, stretching north from Santa Fe and Córdoba provinces, across the entirety of Chaco and Formosa, and into Paraguay, Bolivia and Brazil. It reaches far to the west, drying up as it goes: the western side, known as the Chaco Seco (Dry Chaco), has been dubbed the Impenetrable, due to its severe lack of water across an endless plain of thorn scrub.

Deforestation continues apace here, with vast areas being cleared to plant soya, of which Argentina is now one of the world's major producers. However, the planting has seriously affected Toba tribes, whose traditional environment is being destroyed.

Crossing the Gran Chaco from Formosa to Salta along the northern RN81 is brutal and can take nearly two days, but taking the RN16 from Resistencia proves much faster.

Resistencia

0362 / POP 385,700

This provincial capital is perched on the edge of the barely populated Chaco wilderness. It isn't the most likely candidate for the garland of artistic center of northern Argentina, yet baking-hot Resistencia has strong claims to that title – its streets are studded with sculpture (600 or more) and there's a strong boho-cultural streak that represents a complete contrast to the tough cattle-and-scrub solitudes that characterize the province.

Sights

★Sculptures SCULPTURE

At last count, more than 600 sculptures graced the city, a number that increases with every Bienal. The streets are packed with them, especially around the plaza and north up Av Sarmiento. Every Bienal, a brochure is printed with a sculpture walking tour around the city. Get hold of the latest one at **MusEUM** (www.bienaldelchaco.com; Av Wilde 1100; ⌚9:30-11:30am & 4-8pm Mon-Fri, 9:30-11:30am & 6-8pm Sat) FREE, an open-air workshop on the north side of Parque 2 de Febrero.

Several of the most impressive pieces are on display here, and this is where the Bienal is held. Locals can buy pieces at a symbolic cost, but they have to display them streetside.

★Museo del Hombre Chaqueño MUSEUM

(JB Justo 280; ⌚8am-noon & 3-7pm Mon-Fri) FREE This small but excellent museum is run by enthusiastic staff (some English spoken) who talk you through displays covering the three main pillars of Chaco population: indigenous inhabitants (there are some excellent ceramics and Toba musical instruments on display); criollos; and 'gringos,' the wave of mostly European immigration

INDIGENOUS GROUPS OF THE GRAN CHACO

With some 50,000 members, the **Toba** of the Gran Chaco is one of Argentina's largest indigenous groups, but their existence is nonetheless frequently ignored. Toba protests highlight the stark reality that many communities suffer from abandoned government facilities and, in some, people actually die of starvation. Few Argentines have much idea about the struggles of this *pueblo olvidado* (forgotten people).

As a traveler, it's easy to zip through the sun-scorched Chaco without ever noticing the presence of indigenous people, except, perhaps, for the crafts sold at government-sponsored stores or along the roadside. In Resistencia the Toba live in barrios (neighborhoods) that are separated from the rest of the city. And those who don't live in the city either live in towns that travelers rarely visit (such as Juan José Castelli or Quitilipi) or deep within the Argentine Impenetrable. If you know the way, you'll find Toba *asentamientos* (settlements) that are unlike anything else in Argentina. People live in extreme poverty (although there's always a church) and, except for the occasional government-built health center, nearly all buildings are made of adobe, with dirt floors and thatched roofs.

The Toba refer to themselves as Komlek (Qom-lik) and speak a dialect of the Guaycurú linguistic group, known locally as Qom. They have a rich musical tradition (the Coro Toba Chelaalapi, a Toba choir founded in 1962, has Unesco World Heritage designation). Along with basket weaving and ceramics, the Toba are known for their version of the fiddle, which they make out of a gas can.

The region's most numerous indigenous group is the **Wichí**, with a population of over 60,000. Because the Wichí remain extremely isolated (they live nearly 700km from Resistencia, in the far northwest of Chaco province and in Formosa and Salta provinces) they are the most traditional of its groups. They still obtain much of their food through hunting, gathering and fishing. The Wichí are known for their wild honey and their beautiful *yica* bags, which they weave with fibers from the chaguar plant, a bromeliad native to the arid regions of the Chaco. Like the Toba, most Wichí live in simple adobe huts.

The **Mocoví** are the Gran Chaco's third-largest indigenous group, with a population of 17,000, concentrated primarily in southern Chaco province and northern Santa Fe. Until the arrival of Europeans the Mocoví sustained themselves primarily through hunting and gathering, but today they rely mostly on farming and seasonal work. They are famous for their burnished pottery, which is the most developed of the Chaco's indigenous pottery.

For more information on the Toba, Wichí or Mocoví, stop by Resistencia's **Centro Cultural Leopoldo Marechal** (☎0362-445-2738; Pellegrini 272; ⌚8:30am-12:30pm & 4:30-7:30pm Mon-Fri), which has crafts exhibits and a shop sponsored by the Fundación Chaco Artesanal, and the same city's Museo del Hombre Chaqueño. You can also journey into the Impenetrable to visit the Toba or Wichí.

Resistencia

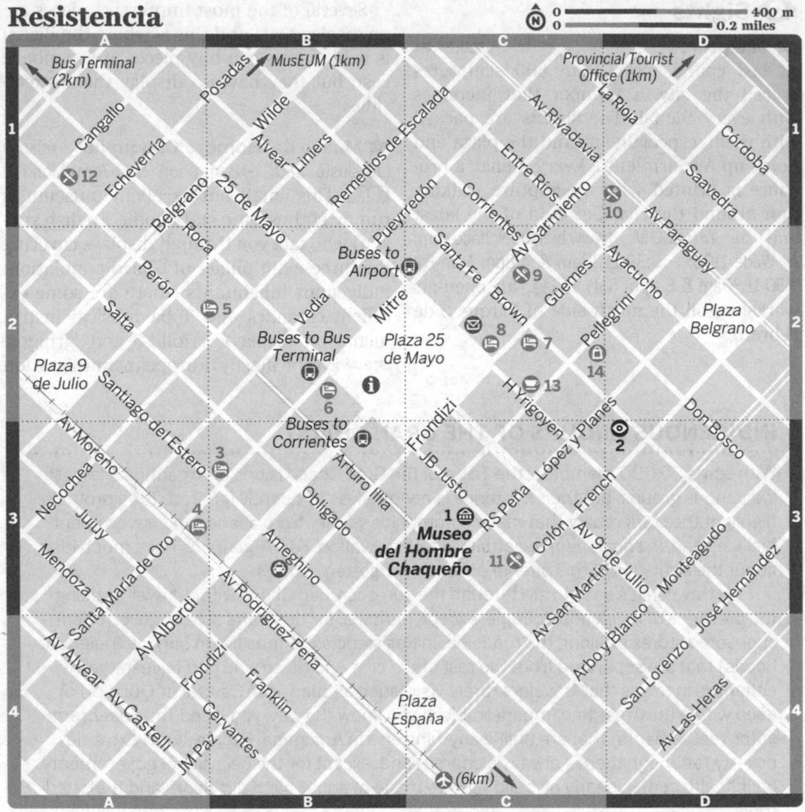

from the late 19th century onwards. Best is the mythology room upstairs, where you'll get to meet various quirky characters from Chaco popular religion.

El Fogón de los Arrieros CULTURAL CENTER
(Brown 350; admission AR$10; ⌚8am-8pm Mon-Fri, 9am-1pm Sat) Founded in 1943, this is a cultural center, art gallery and bar that for decades has been the driving force behind Resistencia's artistic commitment and progressive displays of public art. It is famous for its eclectic collection of art objects from around the Chaco and Argentina. The museum also features the wood carvings of the local artist and cultural activist Juan de Dios Mena. Check out the irreverent epitaphs to dead patrons in the memorial garden; it's called 'Colonia Sálsipuedes' (leave if you can).

Festivals & Events

Bienal de Escultura SCULPTURE
(www.bienaldelchaco.com) In the third week of July in even years, this event brings 10 renowned Argentine and international sculptors to town. Arranging themselves around the fountain at MusEUM, they have seven days to complete a sculpture under the public gaze. The medium changes every time.

Sleeping

Hotel Colón HOTEL $
(☎442-2277; www.colonhotelyapart.com; Santa María de Oro 143; s/d/apt AR$278/388/468; ❄@🛜) Art deco fans mustn't miss this 1920s classic, a few steps south of Plaza 25 de Mayo. It's an amazingly large and characterful building with some enticingly curious period features. The refurbished rooms are great – make sure you get one – and there are good-value apartments available too.

Resistencia

Hotel Alfil HOTEL $
(☎442-0882; Santa María de Oro 495; s/d AR$150/220; ❄📶) A few blocks south of Plaza 25 de Mayo, the old-fashioned Alfil is a reasonable budget choice. Interior rooms are dark but worthwhile if the significant street noise in the exterior rooms (with their strangely inaccessible balconies) will bother you. Air-con is AR$20 extra, but it's a decent deal despite the lack of breakfast.

★ **Hotel Amerian** HOTEL $$
(☎445-2400; www.hotelcasinogala.com.ar; Perón 330; s/d AR$593/660; ❄@📶🏊) This swish casino-hotel is the city's smartest choice, with various grades of room and slick service. Rooms are excellent for these rates: very spacious, attractively stepped and with a dark, elegant, vaguely Asian feel to the decor. As well as the slot machines, there's a sauna, gym and self-contained spa complex. The big outdoor pool with bar is a highlight.

Niyat Urban Hotel HOTEL $$
(☎444-8451; www.niyaturban.com.ar; Yrigoyen 83; s/d AR$465/520; ❄@📶) Shiny and confident, this hotel alongside Plaza 25 de Mayo offers excellent service and plenty of value for its gleaming but very compact modern rooms, which boast great bathrooms, comfy beds and big flat-screen TVs. Some look over the plaza. There's also a gym with vistas and a small spa complex with saunas and outdoor Jacuzzi.

Hotel Covadonga HOTEL $$
(☎444-4444; www.hotelcovadonga.com.ar; Güemes 200; s/d AR$495/535; ❄@📶🏊) With an excellent location close to Plaza 25 de Mayo, this upmarket hotel has fine facilities, including a pool, sauna and Jacuzzi, and personable staff. The public areas are slickly furnished, and the renovated rooms feature streetside balconies and attractive wooden floors. While they still exist, unrenovated rooms are significantly cheaper (AR$295/395).

Casa Mía HOTEL $$
(☎442-5026; www.casamiahotel.com.ar; Santa María de Oro 368; s/d AR$320/445; ❄@📶) Neat, fairly unadorned but modern rooms with good bathrooms. Nice touches such as some art and plants about the place, and helpful service.

Eating

La Bianca ARGENTINE $
(Colón 102; dishes AR$50-80; ⏰11am-3.30pm & 8pm-midnight Wed-Mon) Busy and bustling, this long-time local split-level favorite keeps 'em coming for its well-priced pasta, pizza and soufflés. There's also meat and salad dishes in generous quantities. A cheap and cheerful option.

Parrillada Don Abel PARRILLA $
(Perón 698; mains AR$50-90; ⏰11am-3.30pm & 7.30pm-midnight or later, closed dinner Sun) This homey *parrilla* is decorated with photos of satisfied customers and serves substantial portions of pasta and grilled surubí, in addition to the usual beef. It has a convivial family buzz to it at the weekend.

Juan Segundo ARGENTINE $$
(Av Paraguay 24; mains AR$70-110; ⏰8pm-1am daily, lunch 11.30am-3pm Sat & Sun; 📶) With a casually elegant chessboard-tiled interior and appealing outdoor tables in this upmarket zone of the city, this place offers decent *parrilla* choices and salads, and even better fish and meat dishes with well-prepared sauces.

OFF THE BEATEN TRACK

PENETRATING 'EL IMPENETRABLE'

If you have a yen to get off the beaten track, the more remote areas of the Chaco are for you. Key access point for the Impenetrable is **Juan José Castelli**, 115km north of Roque Sáenz Peña, and served by four daily buses from Resistencia (AR$110, five hours) and several from Roque. From Castelli, you can head west along *ripio* (gravel) roads to remote Fuerte Esperanza (buses and shared *remises* run this route), which has two nature reserves in its vicinity: **Reserva Provincial Fuerte Esperanza** and **Reserva Natural Loro Hablador**. Both conserve typical dry Chaco environments, with algarrobo and quebracho trees, armadillos, peccaries and many bird species. **Loro Hablador**, 40km from Fuerte Esperanza, has a good campground and short walking trails with ranger guides. Fuerte Esperanza has two simple *hospedajes* (guesthouses). Further north, **Misión Nueva Pompeya** was founded in 1899 by Franciscans who established a mission station for Matacos in tough conditions. The main building, with its square-towered church, is a surprising sight in such a remote location. There are cheap hotels in town.

In the north of the region, in Formosa province, the **Bañado de Estrella** is a vast wetland environment that's one of Argentina's standout bird-watching spots. The river Bermejo divides Chaco and Formosa provinces and, at the time of research, the westernmost crossing was the bridge northeast of Castelli, near Villa Río Bermejito.

Various operators offer excursions and packages, which include visits to the reserves, Misión Nueva Pompeya and indigenous communities in the area. **EcoTurChaco** (Carlos Aníbal Schumann; ☎0364-15-446-8128; www.ecoturchaco.com.ar; Av San Martín 500, Juan José Castelli) comes recommended, and also runs a campground and lodge in Villa Río Bermejito, a riverside settlement 67km northeast of Juan José Castelli.

Be warned: in summer the temperatures are extreme out here.

Coco's Resto ARGENTINE $$
(☎442-3321; Av Sarmiento 266; mains AR$60-100; ⏲11.30am-3pm & 8pm-midnight Mon-Sat, lunch Sun; Wi-Fi) Stylishly occupying two front rooms of a house, this intimate, well-decorated restaurant is popular with suited diners from the nearby state parliament. A wide-ranging menu of pastas, meats soused in various sauces and a long wine list make this a pleasant Chaco choice.

Drinking & Nightlife

El Fogón de los Arrieros BAR, TANGO
(Brown 350; ⏲opens for events) This cultural center's bar presents regular live music and small-scale theatrical events, including Thursday night tango (AR$20).

El Viejo Café CAFE
(Pellegrini 109; ⏲7am-late Sun-Thu, 1pm-late Fri & Sat; Wi-Fi) In an elegant old edifice, with an eclectically decorated interior, this is a fine choice any time of day. Its terrace is sweet for a sundowner, and it gets lively later on weekends, when there's usually live music. Solid if unspectacular meals (mains AR$40 to A$70) are also available

Shopping

There's a selection of *artesanía* stalls on the southern side of Plaza 25 de Mayo.

Fundación Chaco Artesanal HANDICRAFTS
(fundacionchacoartesanal@gmail.com; Pellegrini 272; ⏲8:30am-12:30pm & 4:30-7:30pm Mon-Fri) Selection of indigenous crafts as well as CDs from the Toba choir.

Information

There are several ATMs around Plaza 25 de Mayo and lots of internet places around the central streets.

Hospital Perrando (☎445-2583; Av 9 de Julio 1099)

Provincial tourist office (☎443-8880; www.chaco.travel; Av Sarmiento 1675; ⏲6:30am-8pm) A half-hour walk from the center, this regional tourist office has reasonably up-to-date information on the further-flung parts of the Chaco.

Terminal tourist office (www.chaco.travel; ⏲7am-8pm Mon-Fri, 7-9:30am & 6-8:30pm Sat & Sun) In the bus terminal.

Tourist office (☎445-8289; Roca 20; ⏲7:30am-noon & 4-8pm Mon-Sat, 5-8pm Sun)

In a kiosk on the southern side of Plaza 25 de Mayo. Good bilingual city information.

Getting There & Away

Aerolíneas Argentinas (☎444-5551; Justo 184; ⌚8am-12:30pm, 4:30-8pm Mon-Fri, 8am-noon Sat) flies to Buenos Aires daily.

Resistencia's **bus terminal** (☎446-1098; cnr MacLean & Islas Malvinas) serves destinations in all directions. Buses zip between Corrientes and Resistencia (AR$7, 40 minutes) frequently. You can also catch a bus (AR$3.50) to Corrientes from the city center, on Av Alberdi just south of Plaza 25 de Mayo. Faster are **shared taxis** (Frondizi 416; ⌚24hr) (AR$10, 20 minutes).

BUSES FROM RESISTENCIA

DESTINATION	COST (AR$)	DURATION (HR)
Asunción (Paraguay)	125	5
Buenos Aires	548	13-14
Córdoba	513	10-13
Posadas	197	4½-5½
Puerto Iguazú	377	9-10
Salta	460	12
Santiago del Estero	355	8½-10½
Tucumán	435	11-12

Getting Around

Aeropuerto San Martín is 6km south of town on RN11; take bus 2 from the northwest corner of Plaza 25 de Mayo. The bus terminal is a AR$40 taxi ride from the city center, or you can take bus 3 or 9 from opposite the Hotel Colón. Don't walk it: travelers have reported muggings.

Parque Nacional Chaco

Preserving several diverse ecosystems that reflect subtle differences in relief, soils and rainfall, this very accessible **park** (☎03725-499161; www.parquesnacionales.gov.ar; admission free; ⌚Solari 9am-4pm, park 24hr) protects 150 sq km of the humid eastern Chaco. It is 115km northwest of Resistencia via RN16 and RP9. The access town is Capitán Solari.

Activities

Hiking and **bird-watching** are the principal activities here. From the main campground there are two short trails, one leading to viewpoints over lakes. A longer 12km road, suitable for cars, bikes and horses, heads south to the Panza de Cabra lake.

Sleeping & Eating

The park's main campground is equipped with power, toilets, drinking water and rentable bikes. Though vendors sometimes appear at weekends, you should bring all your own food. There are various sleeping options in Capitán Solari and closer to the park. The closest is **José Luis Ávalos** (☎03725-15-400608; s/d AR$120/180; ❄), less than 1km away.

Getting There & Away

Capitán Solari is 2½ hours from Resistencia by bus. La Estrella runs five buses daily (AR$38).

From Capitán Solari, the park office may be able to organize transportation for you – it's worth ringing – otherwise you can walk, hitchhike or take a *remise* (AR$40 to AR$50) the 5km to the park. The road may be impassable for motor vehicles in wet weather.

Roque Sáenz Peña

☎0364 / POP 96,900

Something of a frontier town, Presidencia Roque Sáenz Peña is well out in the Chaco, and is a gateway to the 'Impenetrable' beyond. It is known for its thermal baths, fortuitously discovered by drillers seeking potable water in 1937, and makes an appealing stop, with a rugged, friendly feel.

Sights & Activities

Parque Zoológico ZOO
(adult/child AR$10/2; ⌚9am-6pm Mon-Fri, 8am-6:30pm Sat & Sun) At the junction of RN16 and RN95, 4km east of downtown, the town's spacious zoo and botanical garden emphasizes birds and mammals found in the Chaco region, alongside a few lions, tigers and bears. Featured species are tapir and jaguar, but there are also crocodiles, llamas, monkeys, a bafflingly large chicken pen, snakes, condors and vultures.

Complejo Termal Municipal SPA
(www.elchacotermal.com.ar; Brown 545; ⌚7am-10pm) Roque's famous thermal baths draw their saline water from 150m below ground. The complex, around since the 1930s, is now a top-class facility, offering thermal baths (AR$60) in individual rooms, saunas and Turkish baths (AR$40), and a big pool with water jets and retractable roof (AR$60).

OFF THE BEATEN TRACK

NORTH TOWARD PARAGUAY

Daily buses run from Resistencia to Asunción, Paraguay's capital, making the crossing in Argentina's far north at **Clorinda**, a chaotic border town with little of interest beyond its bustling markets.

To stop somewhere more interesting en route, try baking-hot **Formosa**, a medium-sized city and provincial capital two hours north of Resistencia on the bus. Hotels, restaurants and services can be found along Av 25 de Mayo, which links the sleepy plaza with the waterfront on the Río Paraguay – the best place to stroll once the temperatures drop.

About 6km out of town, **Laguna Oca** offers good bird-watching. For more, hit **Parque Nacional Río Pilcomayo** (☎03718-470-045; www.parquesnacionales.gov.ar; RN86; ⏲8am-6pm), 126km northwest of Formosa and 55km west of Clorinda. Daily buses connect these towns with **Laguna Blanca**, an easy-paced citrus town, where you'll find inexpensive lodgings – **Residencial Guaraní** (☎03718-470024; cnr San Martín & Sargento Cabral; r per person AR$120) is the standout – and *remises* that will take you into the national park. In the park itself, the main feature is also called **Laguna Blanca**, where rangers can take you out in boats to spot caiman.

Treatments on offer include kinesiology, massage and aromatherapy.

Sleeping

Hotel Presidente HOTEL $
(☎442-4498; San Martín 771; s/d AR$170/260; ❄@📶) Well-run and inexpensive, this is a pleasing place right in the heart of town, with friendly staff and rooms with comfortable beds, fridge and hairdryer.

★**Atrium Gualok** HOTEL $$
(☎442-0500; www.atriumgualok.com.ar; San Martín 1198; s/d AR$490/520; ❄📶🏊) Right next to the spa complex, this fine modern hotel gives a feeling of space throughout. Rooms are indeed set around a lofty central atrium and are sleek, minimalist and great value for its standard. There's an enticing pool area and the hotel has its own spa complex and casino. Substantial discount for paying cash. Single rate includes half-board.

Eating

Bien, José! PARRILLA $
(25 de Mayo 531; mains AR$30-50; ⏲7.30pm-midnight; 📶) Warm personal service melds with delicious meat empanadas and decent *parrilla* choices at this good-value restaurant. Every generation is called José here, so ask one of them what the daily special is and enjoy.

Giuseppe PIZZA $
(Moreno 680; pizzas from AR$40; ⏲lunch & dinner) This place has slightly staid decor but is extremely popular in the evening for its tasty pizza and interesting pasta combinations. Try not to sit down the side – the kitchen belts out so much heat you expect brimstone and horned waiters.

Ama'nalec ICE CREAM $
(Moreno 601; ice creams from AR$15; ⏲8am-11:45pm) This busy corner place does tempting little pastries and very tasty ice cream, a godsend in Roque's paralyzing heat. It has some unusual flavors – figs in cognac is worth a lick.

Atrium Gualok RESTAURANT $$
(☎442-0500; www.atriumgualok.com.ar; San Martín 1198; mains AR$60-90; ⏲11am-3.30pm & 7pm-midnight; 📶) In a town of few gourmet choices, this hotel restaurant does its best with modern design and well-presented pastas, meats and more at fair prices.

Information

Av San Martín has several banks with ATMs and numerous internet/telephone places. There's tourist information available in the Complejo Termal Municipal.

Getting There & Away

The **bus terminal** (☎420280; Petris btwn Avellaneda & López) is seven blocks east of downtown; take bus 1 from Mitre. There are regular buses to Resistencia (AR$68, two hours), and services running west to Tucumán, Santiago del Estero, Mendoza and Salta also stop here.

Salta & the Andean Northwest

Includes ➡

Best National Parks

- ➡ Parque Nacional Calilegua (p245)
- ➡ Parque Nacional Talampaya (p280)
- ➡ Parque Nacional El Rey (p233)

Best Places to Stay

- ➡ Estancia las Carreras (p264)
- ➡ Killa (p239)
- ➡ Kkala (p228)
- ➡ Posada El Arribo (p244)

Why Go?

Argentina's northwest sits lofty, dry and tough beneath the mighty Andes. Nature works magic here with stone: weird, wonderful, tortured rockscapes are visible throughout.

There's a definite Andean feel with traditional handicrafts, llamas, indigenous communities and Inca ruins, and the high, arid puna (Andean highlands) stretching into Chile and Bolivia. The region's cities were Argentina's first colonial settlements and have special appeal.

Several popular routes await. From travelers' favorite Salta, head through a national park studded with cactus sentinels to gorgeous Cachi, then down through traditional weaving communities in the Valles Calchaquíes to Cafayate, home of some of Argentina's best wines. Another route from Salta soars upwards to the puna mining settlement of San Antonio de los Cobres, heads north to the spectacular salt plains of the Salinas Grandes, and then down to the visually wondrous and history-rich Quebrada de Humahuaca.

When to Go

Salta

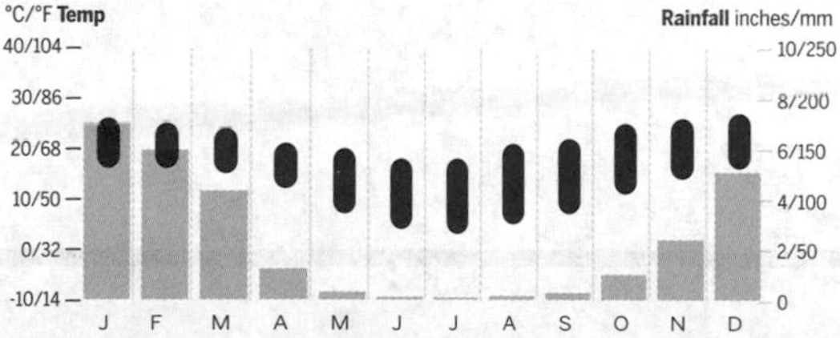

Feb Temperatures high but Carnaval celebrations worth seeing.

Jul & Aug Chilly up on the puna (Andean highlands), but pleasant around the Salta region.

Sep & Oct Top compromise: fewer tourists in Salta and acceptable spring temperatures.

Salta & the Andean Northwest Highlights

1. Wonder at nature's palette in the **Quebrada de Humahuaca** (p246)
2. Observe weavers at work in the memorable **Valles Calchaquíes** (p232)
3. Cleanse your lungs in the crisp mountain air of **Tafí del Valle** (p263)
4. Hit Wild West **Chilecito** (p278), the base for uplifting mountain excursions
5. Soak up the colonial ambiance and relax in the enticing boutique hotels of sophisticated **Salta** (p221)
6. Taste the torrontés at northern Argentina's wine capital of **Cafayate** (p236)

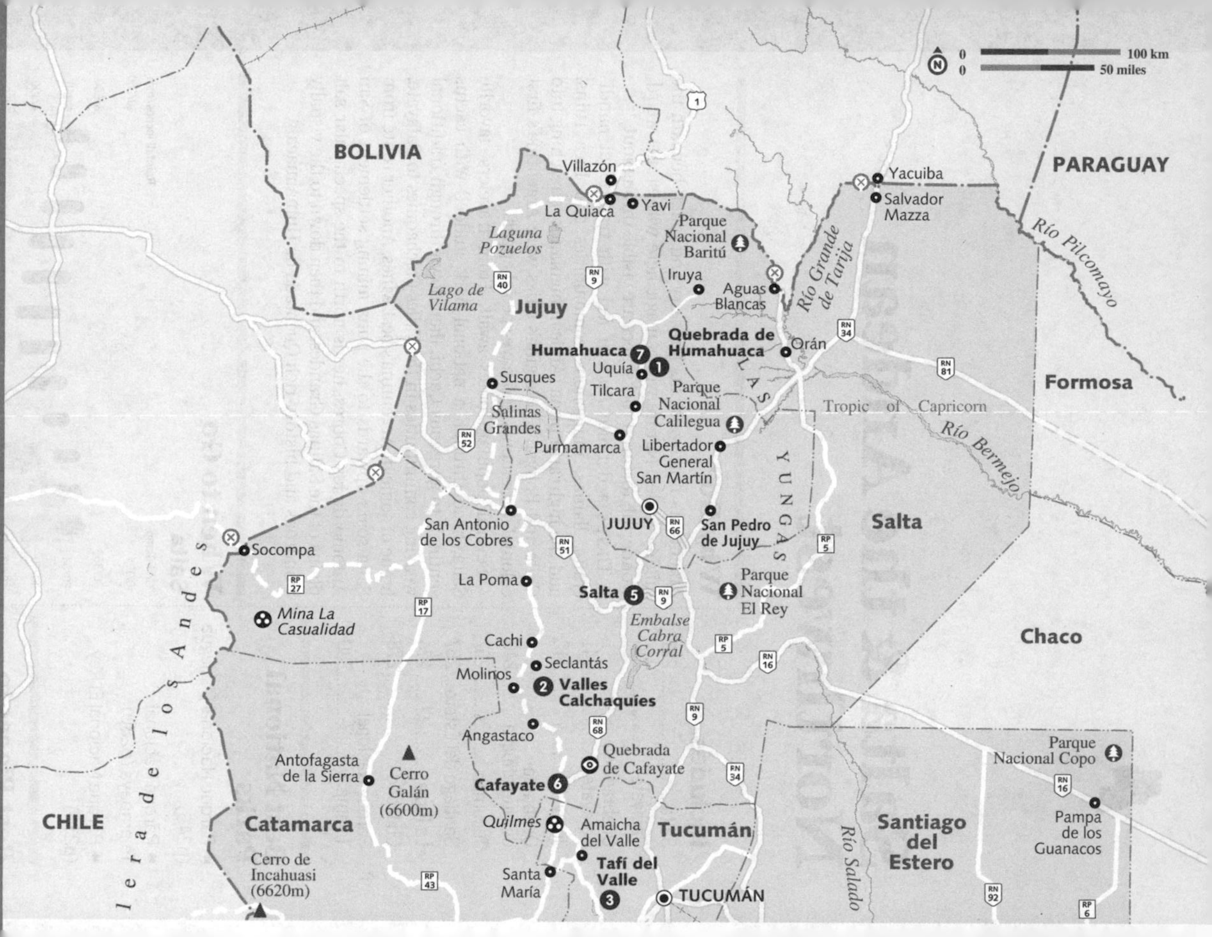

7 Try the regional **cuisine** (p254) of the far northwest, where llama meat and quinoa replace beef and pasta on the menu.

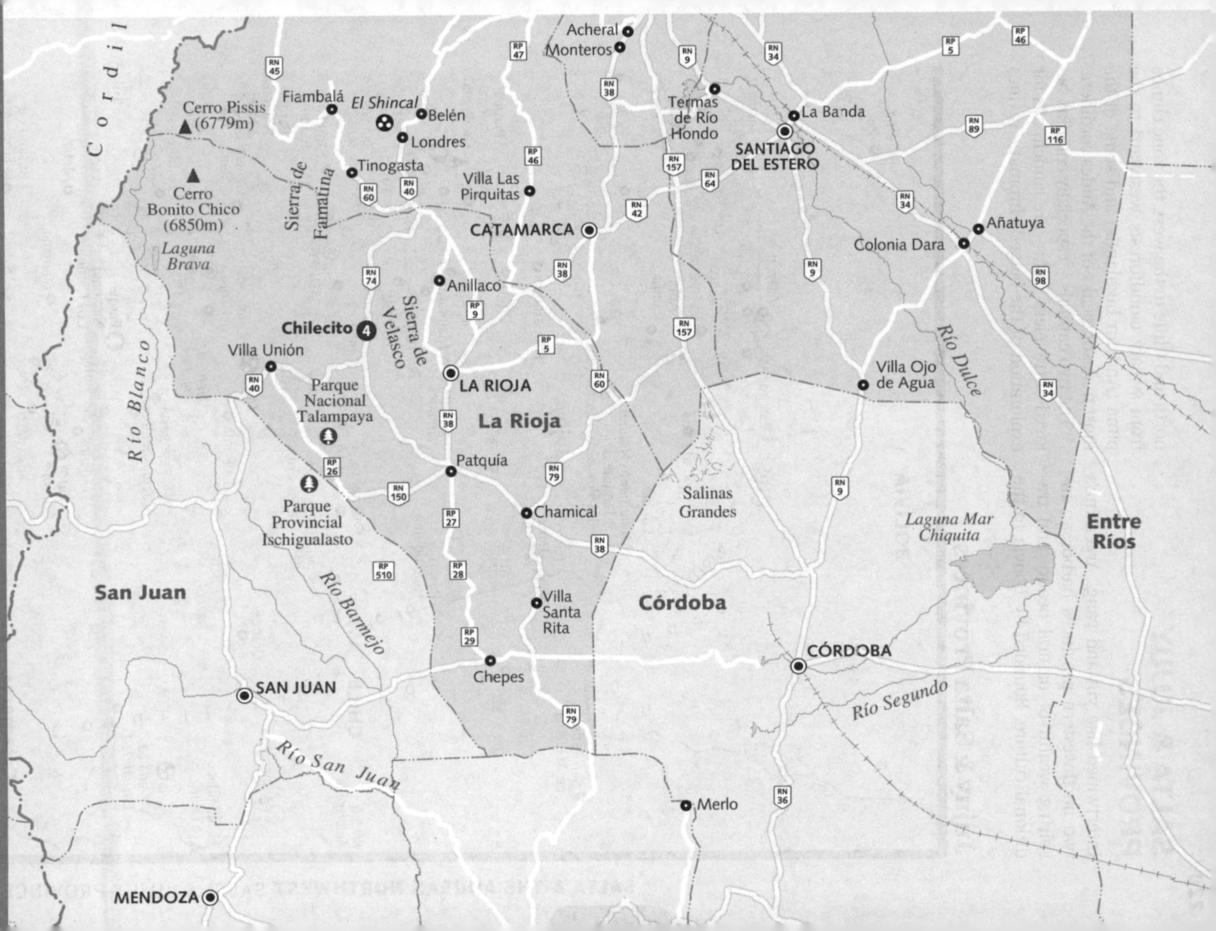

SALTA & JUJUY PROVINCES

Intertwined like yin and yang, Argentina's two northwestern provinces harbor an inspiring wealth of natural beauty and traditional culture. Bounded by Bolivia to the north and Chile to the west, the zone climbs from sweaty cloudforests westward to the puna (Andean highlands) and some of the most majestic peaks of the Andes cordillera.

The two capitals – especially colonial, beloved-of-travelers Salta – are launchpads for exploration of the jagged chromatic ravines

Jujuy & Salta Provinces

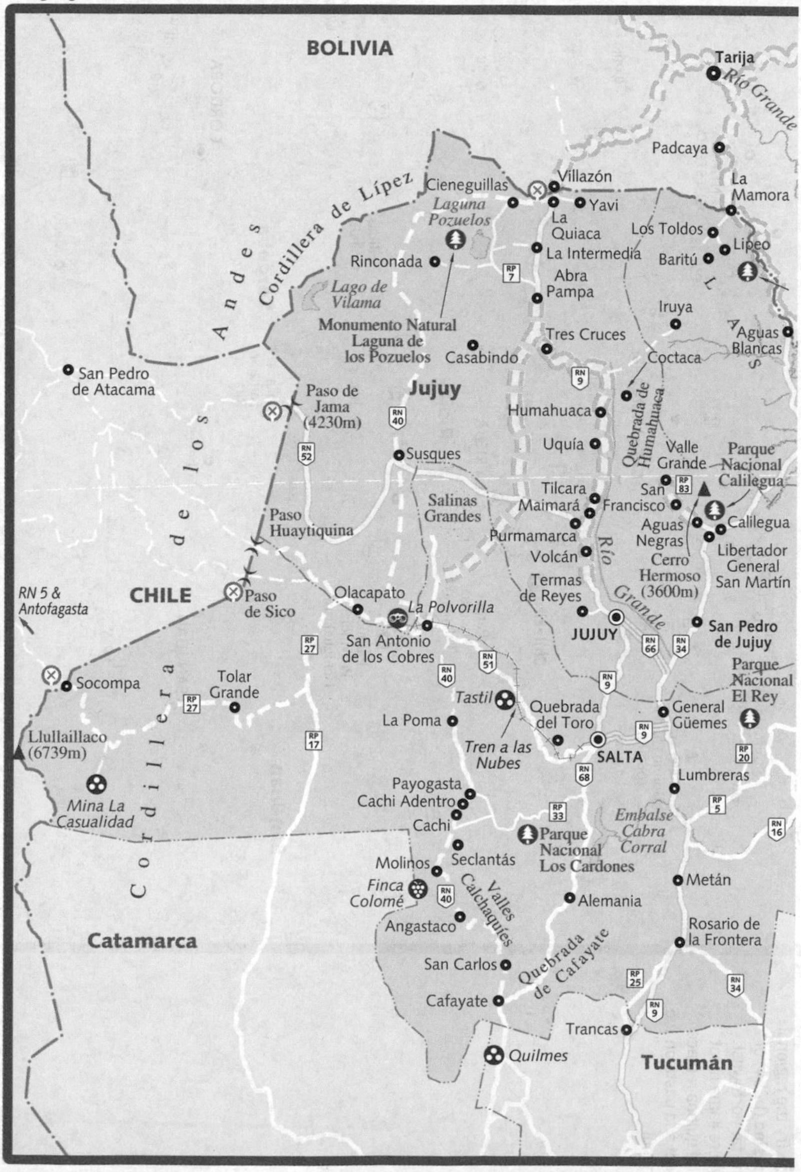

of the Quebrada de Cafayate and Quebrada de Humahuaca; for the villages of the Valles Calchaquíes, rich in artisanal handicrafts; for the stark puna scenery; for nosing the aromatic Cafayate torrontés whites; or for exploration in the national parks of Calilegua or El Rey.

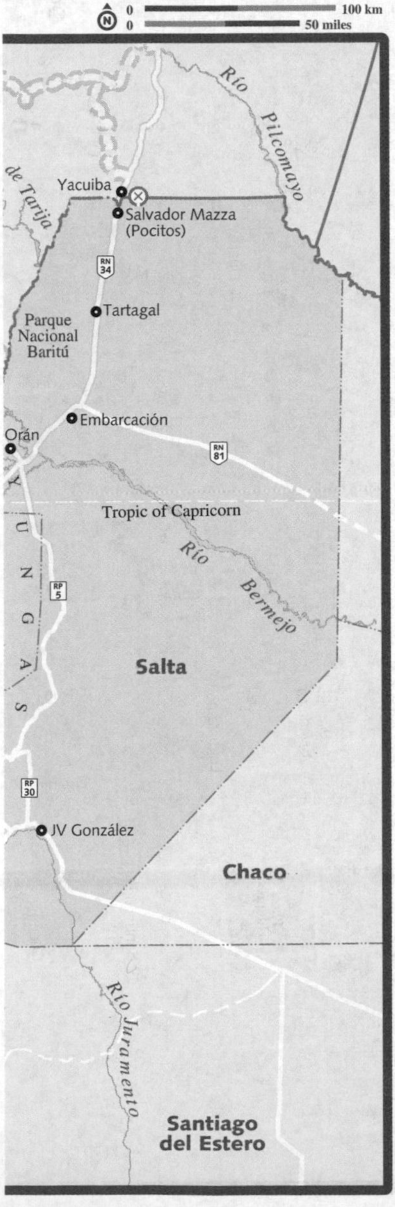

Salta

0387 / POP 655,600 / ELEV 1187M

Sophisticated Salta is a favorite of many, engaging active minds with its outstanding museums, and lighting romantic candles with its plaza-side cafes and the live *música folklórica* (folk music) of its popular *peñas* (folk-music clubs). It offers the facilities – and the traffic and noise – of a large town, retains the comfortable vibe of a smaller place and preserves more colonial architecture than most places in Argentina.

Founded in 1582, it's now the most touristed spot in northwest Argentina, with numerous accommodation options. The center bristles with tour agents: this is the place to get things organized for onward travel. A very popular option is to hire a car here to explore the surrounding area.

Sights

★Museo de Arqueología de Alta Montaña MUSEUM

(MAAM; www.maam.gob.ar; Mitre 77; Argentines/foreigners AR$30/40; 11am-7:30pm Tue-Sun) One of northern Argentina's premier museums, this has a serious and informative exhibition focusing on Inca culture and, in particular, the child sacrifices left on some of the Andes' most imposing peaks.

The centerpiece of the display is the mummified body of one of three children (rotated every six months) discovered at the peak of Llullaillaco in 1999. It was a controversial decision to display the bodies and it is a powerful experience to come face-to-face with them.

Intricately plaited hair and clothes are perfectly preserved, and their faces reflect – who knows? – a distant past or a typical 21st-century Salta face; a peaceful passing or a tortured death. You decide.

The grave goods impress by their immediacy, with colors as fresh as the day they were produced. The *illas* (small votive figurines of animals and humans) are of silver, gold, shell and onyx, and many are clothed in textiles. It's difficult to imagine that a more privileged look at pre-Columbian South American culture will ever be offered us. Also exhibited is the 'Reina del Cerro,' a tomb-robbed mummy that ended up here after a turbulent history. Good videos give background. There's a library as well as a cafe-bar with terrace and wi-fi.

Salta

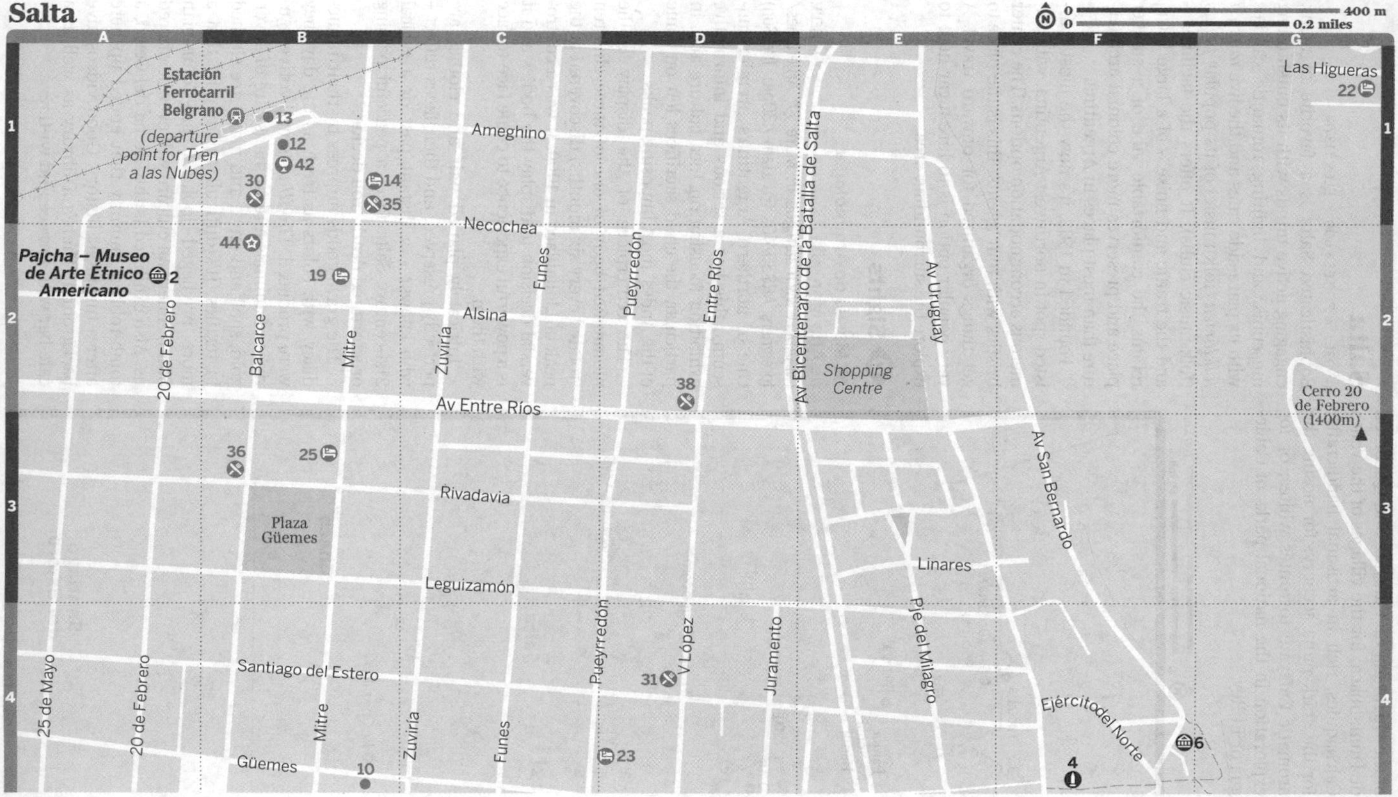
0 400 m
0 0.2 miles
A
B
C
D
E
F
G
1
2
3
4
Estación Ferrocarril Belgrano
(departure point for Tren a las Nubes)
13
12
42
30
14
35
44
19
Pajcha – Museo de Arte Étnico Americano 2
Las Higueras 22
Cerro 20 de Febrero (1400m)
Ameghino
Necochea
Alsina
Av Entre Ríos
Rivadavia
Leguizamón
Santiago del Estero
Güemes
Plaza Güemes
Shopping Centre
25 de Mayo
20 de Febrero
Balcarce
Mitre
Zuviría
Funes
Pueyrredón
Entre Ríos
Av Bicentenario de la Batalla de Salta
Av Uruguay
Av San Bernardo
Linares
Pje del Milagro
Juramento
V López
Ejército del Norte
38
36
25
31
23
10
4
6

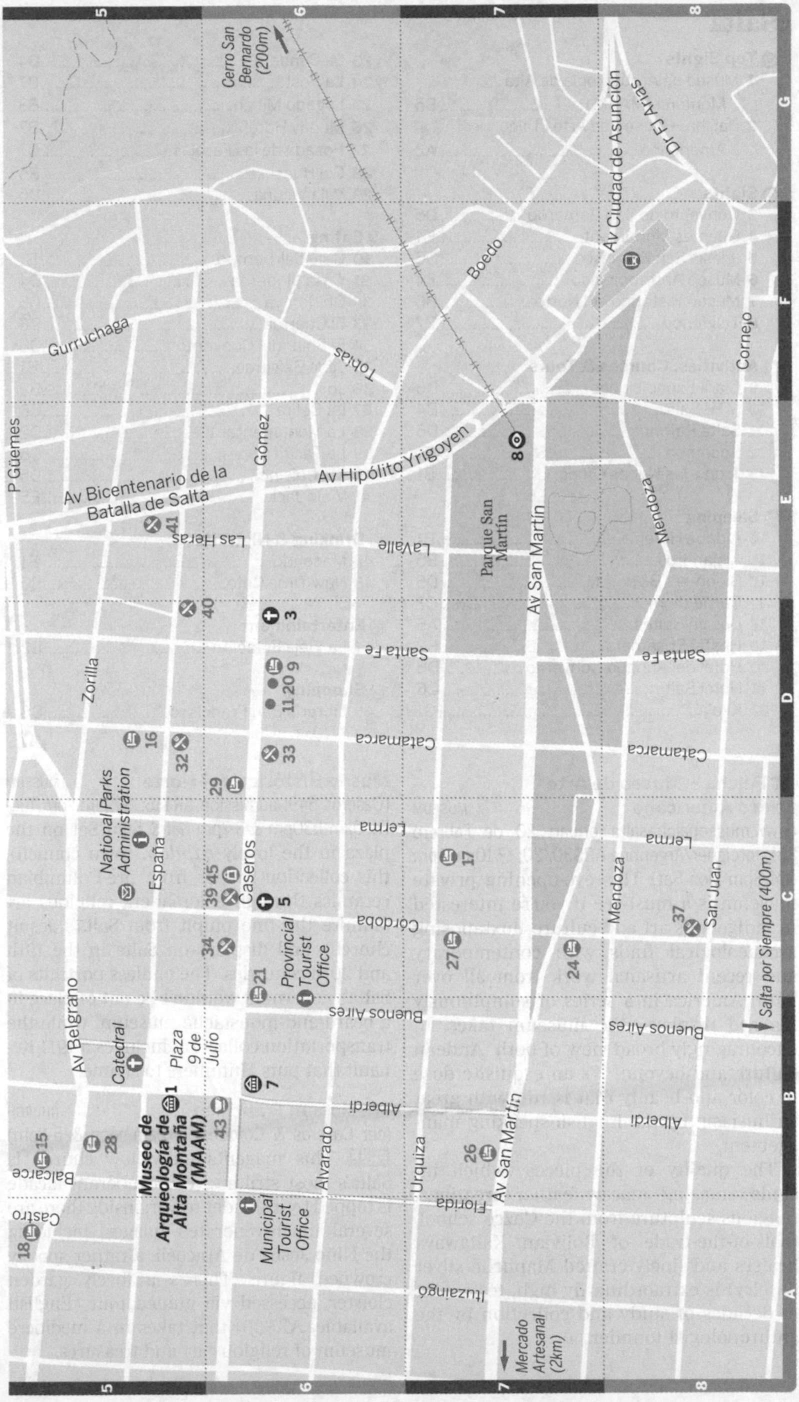
Cerro San Bernardo (200m)
P Güemes
Gurruchaga
Tobías
Boedo
Av Ciudad de Asunción
Dr FJ Arias
Cornejo
Av Bicentenario de la Batalla de Salta
Av Hipólito Yrigoyen
Gómez
Las Heras
LaValle
Parque San Martín
Av San Martín
Mendoza
Zorilla
Santa Fe
Catamarca
National Parks Administration
España
Caseros
Lerma
Provincial Tourist Office
Córdoba
Buenos Aires
Salta por Siempre (400m)
San Juan
Av Belgrano
Catedral
Plaza 9 de Julio
Museo de Arqueología de Alta Montaña (MAAM)
Alberdi
Urquiza
Balcarce
Alvarado
Municipal Tourist Office
Florida
Castro
Ituzaingó
Mercado Artesanal (2km)
A
B
C
D
E
F
G
5
6
7
8

Salta

Top Sights

1	Museo de Arqueología de Alta Montaña (MAAM)	B5
2	Pajcha – Museo de Arte Étnico Americano	A2

Sights

3	Convento de San Bernardo	D6
4	Güemes Monument	F4
5	Iglesia San Francisco	C6
6	Museo Antropológico	F4
7	Museo Histórico del Norte	B6
8	Teleférico	E7

Activities, Courses & Tours

9	Clark Expediciones	D6
10	MTB Salta	B4
11	Salta Rafting	D6
12	Socompa	B1
13	Tren a las Nubes Office	B1

Sleeping

14	Aldaba Hotel	B1
15	Alejandro I	B5
16	Bloomers B&B	D5
17	Carpe Diem	C7
18	Design Suites	A5
19	Hostal Prisamata	B2
20	Hotel del Antiguo Convento	D6
21	Hotel Salta	C6
22	Kkala	G1
23	La Candela	D4
24	La Posta	C7
25	Legado Mítico	B3
26	Munay Hotel	B7
27	Posada de las Farolas	C7
28	Sol Huasi	B5
29	Villa Vicuña	D6

Eating

30	Café del Tiempo	B1
31	Casa Moderna	D4
32	Chirimoya	D5
33	El Charrúa	D6
34	El Solar del Convento	C6
35	José Balcarce	B1
36	Jovi II	B3
37	La Céfira	C8
38	La Monumental	D2
39	La Tacita	C6
40	Ma Cuisine	D5
41	Viejo Jack	E5

Drinking & Nightlife

42	Macondo	B1
43	New Time Café	B6

Entertainment

44	La Vieja Estación	B2

Shopping

45	Librería San Francisco	C6

★ Pajcha – Museo de Arte Étnico Americano — MUSEUM

(www.museopajchasalta.com.ar; 20 de Febrero 831; foreigner/Argentine AR$30/20; ⏲10am-1pm & 4-8pm Mon-Sat) This eye-opening private museum is a must-see if you're interested in indigenous art and culture. Juxtaposing archaeological finds with contemporary and recent artisanal work from all over Latin America in a series of sumptuously realized displays, the museum takes an encouragingly broad view of both Andean culture and beyond. It's an exquisite dose of color and beauty that is run with great enthusiasm by the English-speaking management.

The quality of the pieces (which include amazing macaw-feather creations, religious sculpture from the Cuzco school, tools-of-the-trade of Bolivian Kallawaya healers and finely crafted Mapuche silver jewelry) is extraordinarily high, testament to decades of study and collection by the anthropologist founder.

Museo Histórico del Norte — MUSEUM

(Caseros 549; admission AR$15; ⏲9am-7pm Tue-Fri, 9am-1:30pm & 3-7pm Sat & Sun) Set on the plaza in the lovely *cabildo* (town council), this collection ranges from pre-Columbian ceramics through colonial-era religious art (admire the fine pulpit from Salta's Jesuit church), and displays on Salta in the 19th and 20th centuries. The endless portraits of Salta's governors wouldn't be out of place in a beard-and-moustache museum, while the transportation collection includes a 1911 Renault that puts Hummers to shame.

Iglesia San Francisco — CHURCH

(cnr Caseros & Córdoba; ⏲9am-noon & 5-8pm) FREE This magenta-and-yellow church is Salta's most striking. The exuberant facade is topped by a slender tower; inside there are several much-venerated images, including the Niño Jesús de Aracoeli, a rather spooky crowned figure. There's a lovely garden cloister, accessed via guided tour (English available, AR$30) that takes in a mediocre museum of religious art and treasures.

Convento de San Bernardo CONVENT
(cnr Caseros & Santa Fe; pastries 9am-noon, 4-6pm) Only Carmelite nuns may enter this 16th-century convent but visitors can approach the blindingly whitewashed adobe building (consider sunglasses) to admire its carved, 18th-century algarrobo-wood door and buy nun-made pastries. The church is visitable before Mass (7am to 8:30am weekday & Sunday mornings, 7pm to 8pm Saturday evenings).

Cerro San Bernardo HILL
For outstanding views of Salta, take the **teleférico** (431-0641; one way/round-trip AR$30/50; 10am-7pm) from Parque San Martín up to the top of this hill, a 1km ride will take you eight minutes. Alternatively, take the trail starting at the **Güemes monument**. Atop is a cafe (whose terrace has the best views), a watercourse and *artesanía* (handicraft) shops.

Museo Antropológico MUSEUM
(www.antropologico.gov.ar; cnr Ejército del Norte & Polo Sur; admission AR$5; 8am-7pm Mon-Sat) Has good representations of local ceramics, especially from the Tastil ruins (Argentina's largest pre-Inca town), and some well-designed displays in its attractive, purpose-built spaces.

Courses

Salta appeals as a spot for a Spanish course, and there are several operators. Search online for recent recommendations.

Tours

Salta is the base for a range of tours, offered by numerous agencies, with a high concentration on Buenos Aires, between Caseros and Alvarado. Popular trips head to Cafayate (AR$300), Cachi (AR$325), San Antonio de los Cobres (the *Tren a las Nubes* route; AR$335), the same adding Salinas Grandes and Purmamarca (AR$590) and more.

For trips beyond the standard excursions we recommend:

Alternativa Salta 4WD TOUR
(15-502-5588; www.alternativasalta.com) Runs brilliant multiday 4WD trips into the spectacular, remote highlands of northwestern Argentina.

Clark Expediciones BIRD-WATCHING
(497-1024; www.clarkexpediciones.com) Professional agency offering trips with English-speaking guides to national parks and remote uplands. The staff are serious about bird-watching: trips include a half-/full day in the Reserva del Huaico, which is a 60-hectare cloud forest reserve 8km west of Salta; two days to Parque Nacional El Rey; and multiday tailored itineraries.

MTB Salta MOUNTAIN BIKING
(15-527-1499; www.mtbsalta.com; Güemes 569) Arranges a variety of excellent mountain biking and hiking tours around the province, ranging from half-days in the nearby forests to multiday excursions in the Valles Calchaquíes.

Norte Trekking HIKING
(15-509-3299; www.nortetrekking.com) Trips to Parque Nacional El Rey, multiday hikes and mountain-climbing, with some guaranteed departure dates listed on its website. They also do excellent 4WD excursions into the mountainous western part of the province.

Salta Rafting RAFTING
(421-3216; www.saltarafting.com; Caseros 177) Runs two-hour white-water rafting trips on the Class III Río Juramento, 100km from Salta (AR$330 including a barbecue lunch; transportation to/from Salta AR$150 extra). At the same location are spectacular 400m ziplines across a canyon (four-line trip AR$250).

Sayta HORSEBACK RIDING
(15-683-6565; www.sayta.com.ar; Chicona) This *estancia* (ranch) 40km from Salta runs excellent horseback-riding days, with gaucho culture and optional *asado* (barbecue). You can stay overnight. A half-day with/without lunch costs AR$420/300, and full-board accommodation for a night is AR$480 (with a day's riding AR$800). Prices include transfers from Salta.

Socompa TOUR
(431-5974; www.socompa.com; Balcarce 998) This professionally run setup runs highly recommended tours into the Andean highlands. Its flagship 5-day Puna Experience takes in the best of the Altiplano (high plain) scenery of Catamarca and Salta provinces using comfortable accommodations and multilingual guides.

Sleeping

Salta has dozens of hostels, and, like elsewhere, some are cleaner than others. Boutique hotels and apartments tend to pop

TREN A LAS NUBES

The *Tren a las Nubes* (Train to the Clouds), Argentina's most famous rail trip, heads from Salta down the Lerma Valley before ascending multicolored Quebrada del Toro, continuing past Tastil ruins and San Antonio de los Cobres, before reaching the trip's highlight – a stunning viaduct spanning a desert canyon at **La Polvorilla**, 4220m above sea level.

The trip is a touristy one, with piped music and Spanish and English commentary. It's a long day – leaving Salta at 7am, and not getting back until nearly midnight. You only stop twice, at the viaduct and at San Antonio, and you only get ten to fifteen minutes in each. If you opt to return by bus (recommended), it's a couple of hours quicker. Other options combine the train with tours to places such as Purmamarca and Salinas Grandes.

The price includes mediocre snacks; you can book a place in the dining car for fuller meals (set menus AR$110). You're not meant to take food on board. Vendors sell empanadas (baked savory turnovers) and coca leaves for the altitude. There are medical staff on board in case of altitude sickness.

The train runs Saturdays from April to mid-December with extra departures at busy times, and the return trip costs AR$950, or AR$1175 if you return by bus. Book tickets online, at the **office** (☎422-3033; www.trenalasnubes.com.ar; Ameghino & Balcarce; ⏰8am-9:30pm Mon-Fri, 5:30-11:30am Sat) at Salta station or at travel agents in town. Look out for discount vouchers around town.

Many Salta tour operators run trips along the road paralleling the train's route (AR$390), which is also a spectacular ascent. Most don't include the viaduct. You could also just get the bus to San Antonio de los Cobres and get a cab to La Polvorilla from there.

up like mushrooms – there's always some interesting brand-new offering besides the listings we include here.

Salta por Siempre HOSTEL $
(☎423-3230; www.saltaporsiempre.com.ar; Tucumán 464; dm AR$80-120, s/d AR$180/300; @📶) It's eight blocks south of the plaza, but well worth the trudge to this super-friendly hostel. The quiet and handsome building has glisteningly clean, colorful rooms with bathrooms – some dorms have beds while others have bunks – plus a proper kitchen and attractive shared spaces. Breakfast is included. The owners tend to do interesting things with their dorm prices, which they quote much cheaper on some online sites than others, so check around.

Munay Hotel HOTEL $
(☎422-4936; www.munayhotel.com.ar; Av San Martín 656; s/d AR$240/360; ❄📶) With everything you could want in a budget hotel – a handy location, staff who are pleased to see you, well-furnished and clean bedrooms, shower curtains and breakfast – this is a fine choice. It's located on a busy, chaotic street but is very central. Some rooms are small, but they're happy to move you to a better one if they can.

La Posta GUESTHOUSE, HOSTEL $
(☎422-1985; hostallaposta@gmail.com; Córdoba 368; dm/s/d AR$85/200/300; 📶) This simple but enchanting guesthouse makes a great budget choice for those looking for a quiet, peaceful central stay. Caring owners keep it spotless, and the en suite rooms are excellent. Dorms have breathing room and lockers, and breakfast is a tasty one with decent coffee. An appealingly relaxing place. It may be moving so check ahead.

Hostal Prisamata HOSTEL $
(☎431-3900; www.hostalprisamata.com; Mitre 833; dm/s/d AR$70/130/190; @📶) Hammocks in the patio and a great location a street away from the Calle Balcarce action make this friendly, well-kept hostel a top spot. The kitchen is decent and there's a barbecue out the back; it's worth the small extra spend for the dorms with fewer beds.

Sol Huasi HOSTEL $
(☎422-7521; www.hostalsolhuasi.com; Belgrano 671; dm/d AR$60/160; @📶) Super-centrally located, this is a basic hostel located in a cool old house, with plenty of lounging space. There are decent bathroom facilities and a relaxed vibe. Very friendly staff make this a great place to meet people and party. Early sleepers are probably better off elsewhere.

Camping Municipal Carlos Xamena CAMPGROUND $
(423-1341; Av Libano; per person/tent/car AR$8/16/16;) This place has 500 tent sites and a huge lake-like pool (it takes ten days to fill). It's typically loud in summer and at weekends. Take bus 3B from Ituzaingó between San Martín and Mendoza. There's a supermarket near the campground.

★ **Carpe Diem** B&B $$
(421-8736; www.carpediemsalta.com.ar; Urquiza 329; s/d AR$650/750;) There's a real home-away-from-home feel about this B&B that's full of thoughtful touches, like home-baked bread at breakfast, enticing places to sit about with a book and a computer with internet connection in the attractive rooms, stocked with noble antique furniture. Singles with shared bathroom in the appealing grassy garden are small but a good deal at AR$350.

La Candela HOTEL $$
(422-4473; www.hotellacandela.com.ar; Pueyrredón 346; d AR$520-920;) Decked out like a country villa with an L-shaped pool and grassy garden, this is nevertheless central and features excellent staff, good facilities and comfortable rooms, including a duplex apartment out the back. Different grades of room differ chiefly by size. The decor is one of easy elegance, with an eclectic range of art on the walls.

Aldaba Hotel HOTEL $$
(421-9455; www.aldabahotel.com; Mitre 910; s AR$516-783, d AR$702-929;) A block away from the *peña* (folk-music club) action of Calle Balcarce, this intimate, comfortable place is nevertheless superbly quiet and tranquil. Run with a solicitous personal touch, it's decorated with restrained elegance, and boasts super-comfortable beds and friendly service. Superior rooms are slightly larger than the compact standards and deluxes have great hydromassage showers. Numerous hospitable details make this a standout.

Bloomers B&B B&B $$
(422-7449; www.bloomers-salta.com.ar; Vicente López 129; s AR$530, d AR$600-700;) Book ahead to grab one of the five rooms at this exquisitely stylish yet comfortable guesthouse. The second B here stands for brunch, served until noon. The color-themed rooms are all different and all delightful. It's like staying at a friend's – you can use the kitchen – but few of our friends have a place this pretty.

Villa Vicuña BOUTIQUE HOTEL $$
(432-1579; www.villavicuna.com.ar; Caseros 266; r from AR$835;) Beautifully realized in modern antique style, this is a welcome newcomer in a central location that boasts luminous, easy-on-the-eye rooms in a typical, elegant Salta house. There's a feeling of light and space throughout; the back garden with pool is a highlight, as are numerous decorative details and pleasant service.

Finca Valentina ESTANCIA $$
(15-415-3490; www.finca-valentina.com.ar; RN51 Km6; s/d standard US$125/155, s/d superior US$138/165;) Only the chirping of birds and cicadas breaks the silence at this fabulously peaceful ranch a few kilometers beyond the airport and a twenty-minute drive from the center. The comfortable, homey elegance focuses on cool white spaces and plenty of lounging potential on verandas. An excellent breakfast is included and other meals are available.

Hotel del Antiguo Convento HOTEL $$
(422-7267; www.hoteldelconvento.com.ar; Caseros 113; s/d standard AR$392/490, d superior AR$565;) Rooms are modern and sunny at this central hotel and there's a great little pool area out the back. A duplex apartment next to it sleeps four and goes for AR$690. Superiors on the top floor are excellent, with extra facilities.

Posada de las Farolas HOTEL $$
(421-3463; www.posadalasfarolas.com.ar; Córdoba 246; s/d AR$280/450;) Good value for neat, clean air-con rooms in the center, some of which look onto tiny garden patios. It's run by decent people, is spotless and is a pleasingly reliable choice. They make the effort at breakfast time, too.

Hotel Salta HOTEL $$
(426-7500; www.hotelsalta.com; Buenos Aires 1; s/d standard AR$600/875, s/d superior AR$845/1180;) You pay extra for location here (but what a location) on a corner of the postcard-pretty central plaza, in a stately, traditional hotel. Facilities are good and service excellent, but the rooms are a tad disappointing. Try to grab one with a view of the church and Cerro San Bernardo. Superiors are bigger than the compact standards, and have bathtubs. Heavily discounted in quiet times.

★ **Kkala** BOUTIQUE HOTEL $$$
(☎ 439-6590; www.hotelkkala.com.ar; cnr Las Higueras & Papaya; r US$240-360; ❄@📶🏊) Tucked away in the upmarket residential barrio (suburb) of Tres Cerritos, this peaceful place makes relaxation easy. Exquisite rooms, suites and public areas surround a small garden with heated pool; the higher grades come with views and their own Jacuzzi. Decks with city vistas make perfect spots for a sundowner from the honesty bar. It normally doesn't take kids under 12.

Legado Mítico BOUTIQUE HOTEL $$$
(☎ 422-8786; www.legadomitico.com; Mitre 647; r standard/superior/deluxe US$255/275/295; ❄@📶) The elegant rooms, some faithful to the style of this noble old Salta house, some with a lightly-worn indigenous theme, are reason enough to book in at this tranquil central retreat, particularly if you grab one of the downstairs ones with their own secluded bamboo-strewn patio. Courteous service and an atmosphere of refined relaxation are other high points. No under 12s.

Design Suites HOTEL $$$
(☎ 011-5199-7465; www.designsuites.com; Av Belgrano 770; r/ste US$248/284; ❄@📶🏊) We're not 100% sure whether the look of this place – all exposed concrete and urban-trendy design – works in a colonial city such as Salta, but it's an undeniably attractive space. The excellent, quiet rooms have hydromassage tubs and almost floor-to-ceiling windows offering super town views. The rooftop pool-and-spa space is another great spot to linger over the vistas. Service is willing and the restaurant is very good.

Alejandro I HOTEL $$$
(☎ 400-0000; www.alejandro1hotel.com.ar; Balcarce 252; r standard/superior/executive AR$1320/1460/1650; ❄@📶🏊) Salta's most upmarket big hotel is visible, for better or worse, from the whole city. The rooms are slick and modern, and get pricier and larger as you move higher up the building. There are all the five-star facilities, including a tour desk, and English-speaking service is efficient.

✖ Eating

It's a toss-up between Salta and Tucumán for Argentina's best empanadas, but they're wickedly toothsome in both places. Locals debate the merits of fried (in an iron skillet – juicier) or baked (in a clay oven – tastier).

★ **Chirimoya** VEGETARIAN $
(www.facebook.com/chirimoya.vegetariano; España 211; mains AR$30-60; ⏲ 9am-3pm & 9pm-midnight Mon-Fri, 9pm-midnight Sat; 📶✓) Colorful and upbeat, this vegan (some honey used) cafe-restaurant makes an enticing stop. Delicious blended juices and organic wines wash down daily-changing specials served in generous portions. It's all delicious: it does deliveries, too.

Casa Moderna DELI $
(Vicente López 423; light meals AR$40-70; ⏲ 10am-2pm & 6-11pm Mon-Sat; 📶) Excellent cheeses, cured meats and preserves are on sale in this charismatic deli. Out the back – including a pretty little garden patio – are tables where you can enjoy gourmet sandwiches, a glass of wine, or delicious *picadas* (shared appetizer plates).

Jovi II ARGENTINE $
(www.jovidos.com.ar; Balcarce 601; mains AR$40-75; ⏲ 12.30-3.30pm & 8pm-midnight) A long terrace overlooking the palms of Plaza Güemes is just one reason to like this popular local restaurant that does a huge range of dishes well, without frills and in generous portions. Several rabbit dishes, tasty fish and a succulent plate of the day are backed up by excellent service.

La Monumental PARRILLA $
(Entre Ríos 202; mains AR$40-75; ⏲ 12.30-3pm & 8pm-12.30am) The fluorescent lighting and phalanx of fans mark this out as a classic neighborhood grill. Generous quantities, including an impressive array of free nibbles, cheap house wine and decent meat seal the deal. Half-portions are more than enough for one. Don't confuse it with the more upmarket restaurant with the same name diagonally opposite.

Viejo Jack PARRILLA $
(Av Bicentenario de la Batalla de Salta 145; mains AR$50-80; ⏲ 12.30-3.30pm & 8pm-1am or later) Far enough out of the tourist zone to be authentic, but not so far it's a pain in the backside to get to, this is a down-to-earth spot very popular with locals for its *parrillada* (mixed grill including steak) and pasta. The serves are huge – designed for two to four – but you'll get a single portion (still enough for two) for 70% of the price.

La Tacita EMPANADAS $
(Caseros 396; empanadas AR$4.50; ⏲ 8am-11pm) This very basic little eatery offers some

of the city's best empanadas in a no-frills setting.

El Charrúa ARGENTINE, PARRILLA $$
(www.parrillaelcharrua.com.ar; Caseros 221; mains AR$75-110; ⌚noon-3.30pm & 7pm-12.30am, later Sat & San; 📶) Bright and homey, this popular restaurant goes way beyond the normal *parrilla* (steak restaurant) focus and includes regional dishes, including lots of trout preparations. Service and quality are generally reliable, and the price is fair for this standard.

Ma Cuisine FUSION $$
(☎421-4378; www.macuisineresto.com.ar; España 83; mains AR$55-90; ⌚8pm-midnight Tue-Sat; 📶) The refreshingly crisp interior of this likeable little place sees a variety of changing dishes – pasta, fish and meat well-prepared and served with things such as noodles or stir-fried vegetables – chalked up on the board. The friendly young couple that run it lived in France, so there's a certain Gallic influence at work.

El Solar del Convento ARGENTINE $$
(☎421-5124; Caseros 444; mains AR$70-90; ⌚lunch & dinner; 📶) Warmly decorated and popular, this reliable touristy choice offers solicitous service – the free aperitif wins points – and a varied menu. It specializes in *lomo* (sirloin) with tasty sauces, and also has fish dishes and *parrillada* options. The wine list offers lots of (priced-up) provincial choices.

La Céfira PASTA $$
(Córdoba 481; mains AR$50-80; ⌚dinner Mon-Sat, lunch Sun; 📶) This handsome dining room a few blocks south of the center is a cut far above the usual gnocchi-with-four-cheese-sauce joints. Delicious homemade pasta includes such temptations as squid-ink ravioli with crab, or spinach fettuccini with salmon and caper sauce.

THE CHILDREN GIVEN TO THE MOUNTAIN

The phrase 'human sacrifice' is sensationalist, but it is a fact that the Inca culture from time to time offered the lives of high-born children to please or appease their gods. The Inca saw this as an offering to ensure the continuing fertility of their people and the land. The high peaks of the Cordillera de los Andes were always considered sacred, and were chosen as sites for the sacrifices. The Inca felt that the children didn't die as such, but were reunited with their forefathers, who watched over the communities from the highest peaks.

The children, carefully selected for the role, were taken to the ceremonial capital of Cuzco, where they were the centerpieces of a large celebration – the *capacocha*. Ceremonial marriages between them helped to cement diplomatic links between tribes across the Inca empire. At the end of the fiesta, they were paraded twice around the plaza, and then had to return home in a straight line – an arduous journey that could take months. Once home, they were feted and welcomed, and then taken into the mountains. They were fed, and given quantities of *chicha* (an alcoholic drink made from fermented maize) to drink. When they passed out, they were taken up to the peak of the mountain and entombed, sometimes alive, presumably never to awaken, and sometimes having been strangled or killed with a blow to the head.

Three such children were found in 1999 near the peak of **Llullaillaco**, a 6739m volcano some 480km west of Salta, on the Chilean border. It's the highest known archaeological site in the world. The cold, low pressure and lack of oxygen and bacteria helped to preserve the bodies almost perfectly. The Doncella (Maiden) was about 15 at the time of death, and was perhaps an *aclla* (a 'virgin of the sun'), a prestigious role in Inca society. The other two, a boy and girl both aged six to seven (the girl damaged by a later lightning strike), had cranial deformations that indicated they came from high-ranking families. They were accompanied each by an *ajuar* (a selection of grave goods), which included textiles and small figurines of humanoids and camelids.

The mummies' transfer to Salta was controversial. Many felt they should have been left where they were discovered, but this, once the location was known, would have been impossible. Whatever your feelings on them, and the role of archaeology, they offer an undeniably fascinating glimpse of Inca religion and culture.

Café del Tiempo CAFE, ARGENTINE **$$**
(www.cafe-del-tiempo.com.ar; Balcarce 901; dishes AR$55-105; ⏱6pm-3am Mon-Thu, 11am-4am Fri-Sun; 📶) Decked out to resemble a Buenos Aires cafe, this has prices to match but offers a stylish terrace in the heart of the Balcarce zone; a top spot for a drink. There's some sort of performance or live music every night. The menu includes llama dishes and international offerings such as chop suey, and the *picadas* (shared appetizer plates) are great for a group.

José Balcarce ARGENTINE **$$$**
(☎421-1628; www.cocinadealtura.com.ar; cnr Mitre & Necochea; mains AR$80-130; ⏱8pm-12:15am) Exposed stone walls and solicitous service set the scene for a satisfying upmarket dining experience here. Starters such as llama carpaccio could be followed by sea bass or other highland-type dishes involving lamb or trout. Ingredient quality is excellent, and presentation is good without showing off. The wine list sees each grape variety described in human terms.

Drinking & Nightlife

Peñas are the classic Salta night-time experience. The two blocks of Balcarce north of Alsina, and the surrounding streets, are the main nightlife zone. Bars and clubs around here tend to follow the typical boom-bust-reopen-with-new-name pattern, so just follow your nose.

Macondo BAR
(www.facebook.com/macondo.barensalta; Balcarce 980; ⏱7pm-3am Mon-Fri, until 5am Sat & Sun; 📶) After all the *folklórica* (folk music) on this street, the indie '90s-'00s mix in this trendy bar might come as a relief. Popular with locals and tourists, it keeps it lively until late. There's live music most nights.

New Time Café CAFE
(Caseros 602; ⏱6:30am-2am; 📶) In the race for the accolade of Salta's best plaza cafe, this two-level corner spot wins by several lengths. It offers shady (in the afternoon) tables, great views of the *cabildo*, Cerro San Bernardo and cathedral, and wi-fi. Live music some nights.

Shopping

An artisan's market sets up every Sunday along Balcarce, stretching a couple of blocks south from the station.

Mercado Artesanal HANDICRAFTS
(Av San Martín 2555; ⏱9am-9pm) 🍃 For souvenirs, this provincially sponsored market is noteworthy. Articles include indigenous handicrafts, such as hammocks, string bags, ceramics, basketry, leatherwork and ponchos. Take bus 5A from downtown.

Librería San Francisco BOOKS
(Caseros 362; ⏱9am-1pm & 5-9pm Mon-Fri, 9am-1pm Sat) Decent selection of English books, mostly classics.

PEÑAS

Salta is famous Argentina-wide for its *folklórica* (folk music), far more national in scope than tango. A *peña* is a bar or social club where people eat, drink and gather to play and listen, traditionally in the form of an impromptu jam session.

These days, the Salta *peña* is quite a touristy experience, a dinner-show with CD sales and tour groups; nevertheless, it's a great deal of fun. Traditional fare is empanadas and red wine but most places offer a wider menu of meat and regional dishes.

Peña heartland is Calle Balcarce, between Alsina and the train station. There are several here, along with other restaurants, bars and *boliches* (nightclubs) – it's Salta's main nightlife zone.

Some are a lot better and more traditional than others. A couple of the best:

La Casona del Molino (☎434-2835; Luis Burela 1; mains AR$40-70; ⏱9pm-5am Tue-Sun) This former mansion, about 20 blocks west of Plaza 9 de Julio, is a Salta classic with several spacious rooms with performers who work around the tables rather than on a stage. The food is of very good quality. Get there early-ish to guarantee a table. There's a AR$50 cover Thursday to Saturday.

La Vieja Estación (☎421-7727; Balcarce 885; cover charge AR$50; ⏱7pm-3am) The best established of the Balcarce *peñas*, with a stage, wooden tables and a good atmosphere. Music starts at 10pm. Top empanadas and other regional food (mains AR$40 to AR$85).

ℹ Information

There are lots of ATMs around the central streets, and call centers and internet places are plentiful.

Citibank (cnr España & Balcarce) Changes euros and dollars, has a high ATM withdrawal limit.

Hospital San Bernardo (☎432-0445; www.hospitalsanbernardo.com.ar; Tobías 69)

Municipal Tourist Office (☎437-3340; www.saltalalinda.gov.ar; Caseros 711; ⊙8am-9pm Mon-Fri, 9am-9pm Sat & Sun) Gives out maps.

National Parks Administration (APN; ☎431-2683; www.parquesnacionales.gov.ar; España 366; ⊙8:30am-2:30pm Mon-Fri) On the 3rd floor of the Aduana building, offers information and advice on the region's national parks. Contact before going to El Rey. There are plans afoot for a new park interpretation and information center in Salta.

Provincial Tourist Office (☎431-0950; www.turismosalta.gov.ar; Buenos Aires 93; ⊙8am-9pm Mon-Fri, 9am-8pm Sat & Sun) Top marks – friendly, efficient and multilingual. Ask staff about provincial road conditions.

ℹ Getting There & Away

AIR

Salta's **airport** is 9.5km southwest of town on RP51. **Andes** (☎0810-777-26337; www.andesonline.com; Caseros 459; ⊙9am-1pm & 4:30-8pm Mon-Fri, 9am-1pm Sat) flies thrice weekly to Buenos Aires with connection to Puerto Madryn. **Aerolíneas** (☎0810-222-86527; www.aerolineas.com.ar; Caseros 475; ⊙9am-12:45pm & 4:30-8:15pm Mon-Fri, 9am-12:45pm Sat) flies six times daily to Buenos Aires and also to Puerto Iguazú and Mendoza. **LAN** (☎0810-9999-526; www.lan.com; Caseros 476; ⊙9am-1pm & 5-8pm Mon-Fri) flies to Buenos Aires three times daily.

BUS

Salta's **bus terminal** (Av Hipólito Yrigoyen) has frequent services around the country. There's an ATM and left-luggage services.

Three companies run to San Pedro de Atacama, Chile (9 to 10 hours, AR$430), with daily departures at 7am via Jujuy and Purmamarca. They continue to Calama, Antofagasta, Iquique and Arica (AR$700).

Ale Hermanos goes once or twice daily to San Antonio de los Cobres (AR$55, 5½ hours) and two to three times daily to Cachi (AR$67, 4½ hours).

For Puerto Iguazú, change in Posadas. For Bariloche, change in Mendoza. Companies can sell through-tickets.

Buses from Salta

DESTINATION	COST (AR$)	DURATION (HR)
Buenos Aires	860-980	18-22
Cafayate	86	4
Córdoba	521	11-14
Jujuy	63	2
La Quiaca	190	8
La Rioja	382	10-12
Mendoza	750	18-20
Puerto Iguazú	710	24
Resistencia	350	10-12
Salvador Mazza	210	6½
Santiago del Estero	271	7
Tucumán	177	4½

CAR

Renting a car in Salta is a very popular option to see the northwestern highlands and valleys. There are dozens of agencies: get several quotes, as there are frequent special offers. Typically, it's AR$350 to AR$450 per day for a week's hire, triple that for a 4WD. You can find some good online offers booking well in advance.

Companies, even big names, are mostly slipshod operations. Mechanical problems are common, and don't expect state-of-the-art roadside assistance: you're often better sorting minor problems out yourself. Most offer big discounts for paying cash. Complaints are frequent: we don't recommend specific operators. A list of providers is available on the turismo.salta.gov.ar webpage.

The stretch between San Antonio de los Cobres and La Poma (en route to Cachi) is often 4WD only, but the *ripio* (gravel) road between San Antonio and Salinas Grandes is normally passable. Always check with the provincial tourist office for current conditions.

You can't take rental cars into Bolivia, but it is possible to take them into Chile by paying a bit extra and giving a few days' notice.

ℹ Getting Around

Bus 8A from San Martín near Buenos Aires runs to the airport (AR$2.50), otherwise it's a AR$60 taxi ride.

Several local buses (AR$2.50) connect downtown with the bus terminal. For AR$6, you can buy a chargeable *tarjeta magnética* (magnetic bus card) for local buses to avoid having to carry the correct change.

Valles Calchaquíes

One of Argentina's most seductive off-the-beaten-track zones is a winning combination of rugged landscapes, traditional workshops, strikingly attractive adobe villages and some top wines. Small but sophisticated Cafayate, with its wineries and paved highway, presents quite a contrast to more remote settlements such as Angastaco or Molinos, while Cachi, accessible from Salta via a spectacular road that crosses the Parque Nacional Los Cardones, is another peaceful and popular base. Vernacular architecture in these valleys merits special attention – even modest adobe houses sport neoclassical columns or Moorish arches.

The indigenous Diaguita (Calchaquí) here put up some of the stiffest resistance to Spanish rule.

Parque Nacional Los Cardones

Flanking the winding RP33 from Salta to Cachi across the Cuesta del Obispo, this takes its name from the cardón (candelabra cactus), the park's most striking plant species. In the treeless Andean foothills and puna, the cardón has long been an important source of timber for rafters, doors, window frames and similar uses. You see it often in the region's traditional buildings.

Los Cardones is free to enter and has no services – though a visitor center on the main road is gradually being renovated – but there is a modern **park office** (☎03868-496005; loscardones@apn.gov.ar; Payogasta; ⏲8am-3pm Mon-Fri) in Payogasta, 11km north of Cachi. Take plenty of water and protection from the sun. Buses between Salta and Cachi will stop for you, but verify times. Most people disembark at Valle Encantada, the most accessible, picturesque part of the park.

Cachi

☎03868 / POP 2600 / ELEV 2280M

The biggest place by some distance hereabouts – you'll hear locals refer to it as 'the city' – enchanting Cachi is nevertheless little more than a village surrounded by stunning scenery. Overlooked by noble mountains, it boasts fresh highland air, sunny days and crisp nights. The cobblestones, adobe houses, tranquil plaza and opportunities to explore the surrounds mean that it's the sort of place that eats extra days out of your carefully planned itinerary.

Sights

Museo Arqueológico MUSEUM
(AR$10 donation; ⏲10am-7pm Mon-Fri, 10am-6pm Sat, 11am-3pm Sun) On the plaza, this is a well-presented and professionally arranged account of the surrounding area's cultural evolution, with good background information (in Spanish) on archaeological methods. Don't miss the wall in the secondary patio, composed of stones with petroglyphs.

Next door **Iglesia San José** (1796) has graceful arches and a barrel-vaulted ceiling of cardón wood. The confessional and other features are also cardón, while holy water lives in a large *tinaja* (oil jar).

Activities

A short walk from Cachi's plaza brings you to a **viewpoint** and then the picturesque hilltop **cemetery**; nearby is a rather unlikely airstrip.

There's a handful of rather unremarkable **archaeological sites** dotted around the valley; these make destinations for picturesque hikes or drives. There's a winery in town, and others within easy driving distance.

Many locals hire out **horses**; look for signs or ask in the tourist office.

Valley Walking WALKING
Just over an hour's walk from Cachi, Cachi Adentro is a tiny village where not a lot happens: you can swing on the seats in the demi-plaza or sip a soda from the store. It's a particularly lovely walk in summer, when streams and cascades are alive with water.

From here, you could return a longer way (20km total): bear left past the church and then take a left down the road signposted to Las Trancas. This winds around the valley and eventually crosses the river; shortly afterwards, turn left at the church (heading right leads 2km to the lovely Algarrobal campground); and this will lead you back to Cachi via the hamlet of La Aguada. This section is spectacular in the late afternoon.

Tours

★**Santiago Casimiro** HIKING, MOUNTAINEERING
(☎15-638545; santiagocasimiro@hotmail.com; Bar rio Cooperativa Casa 17) A highly recommended local guide for hiking and mountaineering trained in mountain rescue and first aid. He's the man to speak to if you want to tackle the rather imposing Nevado de Cachi peak.

OFF THE BEATEN TRACK

PARQUE NACIONAL EL REY

East of Salta, this **national park** (elrey@apn.gov.ar) FREE is at the southern end of the Yungas subtropical corridor and protects a gloriously biologically diverse habitat.

It's a beautiful, varied landscape ranging from meadowlands and low scrub forest to subtropical cloudforest. There are various well-marked trails, some accessible by vehicle. You'll see lots of birdlife, and mammals such as peccaries and brown brocket deer are often spotted. **Laguna Los Patitos**, 2km from park headquarters, offers opportunities to observe waterbirds. Longer trails lead to moss-covered **Pozo Verde**, a three- to four-hour climb to an area teeming with birdlife. Other trails are of similar day-trip length and involve multiple river crossings. Shorter 2km **Sendero La Chuña** heads out from the campsite and is a good introduction to this ecosystem.

There is free **camping** at the park's headquarters, with a huge grassy area for tents, toilets, drinkable water, cold showers and evening power but no shop. Contact the APN office in Salta for up-to-date info. The closest non-camping accommodation is at a curious ecological community 4km down the park road from the turnoff.

From the access road on the RP5, it's 37km on gravel to the park entrance and a further ten to the trailheads and campsite. The park access road fords several streams that are impassable in a normal car if it's been raining (likely from December to March). You can also arrange guided visits from Salta. Last fuel is at the General Güemes–Salta junction, 160km from the park, so make sure you fill up there.

Urkupiña OUTDOORS
(☎491317; uk_cachi@hotmail.com; Zorrilla s/n) Runs cycling trips, hiking and quad-bike excursions, trips to Cachi Adentro or nearby archaeological sites for around AR$100 to AR$150, and longer jaunts along RN40 in both directions; this can be a good way to reach Cafayate (AR$300).

Sleeping

Nevado de Cachi GUESTHOUSE $
(☎491912; Ruiz de los Llanos s/n; s/d AR$100/160, s without bathroom AR$60; 📶) Just off the plaza, this is decent budget choice has rooms around a grapevine-draped patio. Beds are comfortable, and bathrooms – both shared and private – work well enough. Prices are slightly negotiable and vary by room; the dearer upstairs ones are the best. Overall, a bargain. Breakfast not included.

La Mamama HOSTEL $
(☎491305; Suárez 590; dm/r without bathroom AR$50/100) A welcoming spot at the quiet end of a central street, with kitchen use, simple rooms with saggy mattresses and a Cachi-casual feel.

Hospedaje Don Arturo GUESTHOUSE $
(☎491087; www.hospedajedonarturo.blogspot.com; Bustamante s/n; s/d AR$120/200, without bathroom AR$90/160; 📶) Very solid budget choice: rooms are cramped but spotless; the best feature is the lounge area and back deck looking over the riverbed.

Viracocha HOSTEL $
(☎15-685-2445; www.hostelcachi.com.ar; Ruiz de los Llanos s/n; dm/d AR$85/350; 📶) Central and relaxed, this likeable hostel has good dorms featuring sturdy bunk beds with plenty of headroom. The attached restaurant is romantically lit but more hit-and-miss.

Camping Municipal CAMPGROUND, HOSTEL $
(☎491902; oficinadeturismo.cachi@gmail.com; campsites per person AR$30-40, dm/cabin AR$30/250; 🏊) On a hill southwest of the plaza, this offers shaded sites with barbecues surrounded by hedges; the municipal pool is here. There's also a hostel with dorms (AR$12) and cabins (AR$125); reserve at the tourist office.

★**Miraluna** APARTMENTS $$
(☎458002; www.miraluna.com.ar; La Aguada; apt for 2/4 AR$650/950, large apt for 4 AR$1050; 📶🏊) 🍃 Seven kilometers from town in the hamlet of La Aguada, these beautifully romantic, rustic cabins come in three sizes and have a spectacular, fabulously peaceful setting in a working vineyard surrounded by breathtaking mountain and valley views. Breakfast features tasty home-baked bread, and other light meals are available. You can also help yourself to vegetables from the organic garden.

El Cortijo BOUTIQUE HOTEL $$

(☎491034; www.elcortijohotel.com; Av ACA s/n; s/d AR$440/555; ❄📶) Opposite the ACA Hostería Cachi entrance, this stylish small hotel offers rooms that aren't large but are decorated with finesse, and some – particularly 'Los Padres,' with its own private terrace with loungers (doubles AR$660) – have fabulous views of the sierra. There's also an excellent on-site restaurant and helpful staff. Good value.

ACA Hostería Cachi HOTEL $$

(☎491105; www.soldelvalle.com.ar; Av ACA s/n; s/d AR$475/710; ❄@📶🏊) With its hilltop position, this family friendly hotel has the best views in town, and there are worse ways to spend your day than relaxing poolside checking them out. Rooms are unexciting but picturesquely surround a patio; the grassy grounds are great and there's even a little farm zoo.

Hostería Villa Cardón GUESTHOUSE $$

(☎491701; casadetetacuara@gmail.com; Aranda s/n; d AR$480-540; 📶) The friendly young owners bend over backwards here to make your stay a pleasant one, and the white, minimalist, comfortable rooms opening off a courtyard on a quiet backstreet are perfect for relaxation. Breakfast is a highlight, and the overall package is faultless. The teahouse out front is great, too. Single rates available off-season.

La Merced del Alto HOTEL $$$

(☎490020; www.lamerceddelalto.com; s/d US$188/218; @📶🏊) Built of traditional whitewashed adobe with ceramic floors and cane ceilings, this hotel across the river from town is designed to look like an historic monastery. It offers excellent facilities and great peace and quiet, with cool, restrained rooms looking over either the hills beyond (slightly more expensive) or the interior patio. Public areas include a most inviting lounge, a good restaurant, and a rustic spa area (extra charge). Service is multilingual and top-notch. Substantially cheaper for Argentines.

Eating

For local dishes such as *locro* (a spicy stew of maize, beans, beef, pork and sausage) and *humitas* (stuffed corn dough, resembling Mexican tamales), look for non-touristy *confiterías* (cafes offering light meals) and *comedores* (basic cafeterias).

Oliver PIZZA $

(Ruíz de los Llanos 160; mains AR$28-80; ⏲7am-midnight; 📶✎) On the plaza, this homey, multilevel, wooden-tabled restaurant is a reliable choice for tasty pizza, bruschetta and a couple of creative meaty mains. The terrace on the plaza is also a fine place for a sundowner.

Ashpamanta ARGENTINE $$

(Bustamante s/n; dishes AR$45-90; ⏲12.30-3pm & 7.30-11pm; ✎) Compact and snug, this likable little place has a short but tasty menu of pasta, salads and a couple of more elaborate mains – quinoa risotto or panfried fillets with vegetables – that are prepared in an open kitchen behind the bar.

Information

Tourist Office (☎491902; oficinadeturismo.cachi@gmail.com; Güemes s/n; ⏲9am-9pm) On the plaza.

Getting There & Away

Two to three daily buses run between Salta (AR$67, 4 hours) and Cachi: a spectacular ride up to the Cuesta del Obispo pass, then through cactus-studded Parque Nacional Los Cardones. Seclantás is serviced daily (AR$19) and Molinos four times weekly (AR$28), while three buses Monday through Saturday run to Cachi Adentro (AR$6.50, 30 minutes).

Buses run north to La Poma, an old hacienda town that, as far as public transport goes, is the end of the line. The road beyond, to San Antonio de los Cobres, is an arduous, spectacular ascent criss-crossing a river via lonely goat farms to a 4895m pass. It's only passable in a non-4WD at certain times (normally September to December); phone the **police** (☎0387-490-9051) for advice. Otherwise, approach San Antonio the long way round.

For Cafayate, you can get as far as Molinos, from where you can hitch or get a remise to Angastaco, which has bus service to Cafayate. A tour from Cachi is another option.

Seclantás

☎03868 / POP 300 / ELEV 2100M

Charmingly peaceful Seclantás is the spiritual home of the Salta poncho. There are many weavers' workshops in town, and north of here, along the eastern branch of the road to Cachi, artisans' homes invite you to drop in and peruse their wares: the stretch of road has been dubbed the **Ruta de los Artesanos**. One of them, Señor Tero, wove a poncho worn by Pope John Paul II.

Places to stay in Seclantás cluster around the plaza. **Hostería La Rueda** (☎498041; cnr Cornejo & Ferreyra; s/d with bathroom AR$130/180, without bathroom AR$100/150) is hospitable and spotless, featuring comfortable, pretty, common areas and decent rooms. The campground is just behind the church, and has a public pool as well as cabins.

There's a daily bus from Cachi to Seclantás; it continues to Molinos on some days.

Molinos

☎03868 / POP 900 / ELEV 2020M

If you thought Cachi was laid-back, wait until you see Molinos, a lovely backwater with a collection of striking colonial buildings and beautiful adobe houses; a stroll through the streets will reveal some real gems. Molinos takes its name from the still-operational flour mill on the Río Calchaquí; its picturesque appeal is augmented by shady streets and good accommodations. There's an ATM on the plaza.

Sights

Centro de Interpretación Molinos MUSEUM, WORKSHOP
(www.naturalezaparaelfuturo.org; Cornejo s/n; donation AR$10; 8am-7:30pm) This restored historic house has a good English/Spanish display on the region's culture and history, and tourist information. It's also a space for artisans – especially weavers – to work and sell their crafts, one of a number of inspiring sustainable projects around here funded from various sources.

Criadero Coquera & Casa Entre Rios CAMELIDS, HANDICRAFTS
(8am-12:30pm & 3:30-7pm Mon-Sat) FREE About 1.5km west of Molinos, this is where the government's agricultural research arm raises vicuñas: you can feed these beautiful creatures (any time; just walk on up the side) with straw. Here also is the Casa de Entre Ríos, where there's a fine artisans' market with spectacular ponchos and wall-hangings woven from sheep, llama, and vicuña wool for sale.

Iglesia San Pedro Nolasco CHURCH
(8am-8pm) FREE The town's lovely 17th-century church in the Cuzco style features twin bell towers and a cactus-wood ceiling.

Sleeping & Eating

A couple of down-home places do decent cheap meals.

★ **Hacienda de Molinos** HOTEL $$
(☎494094; www.haciendademolinos.com.ar; Cornejo s/n; r standard/ superior AR$750/950; @) Across from the church, this colonial, adobe hacienda is also known as the Casa de Isasmendi, after Salta's last colonial governor, who lived and died here. It's been picturesquely restored, with sober, handsome rooms with inviting beds, antique furniture, cane ceilings and great bathrooms, set around lovely patio

WORTH A TRIP

COLOMÉ BODEGA

Fine wines are produced at this ecological **bodega** (☎03868-494200; www.bodegacolome.com; tasting AR$73; 10:30am-6pm), which is set (as they say hereabouts) 'where the devil lost his poncho,' some 18km down a spectacular gravel road west from Molinos. The vineyards enjoy a stunning natural setting, surrounded by hills and mountains that seem to change color hourly. Forward thinking on several fronts is also in evidence: the complex is electrically self-sufficient, has funded substantial infrastructural improvements in the local community and boasts a stunning **museum** (2-6pm) FREE designed by artist James Turrell, with a permanent exhibition of nine of his works. These are utterly memorable installations involving light and the strange frontiers of our own perception; it's a remarkable place. Both bodega and museum visits should be booked ahead by phone or email (museo@colomeargentina.com), though you can often just turn up, too. As well as tastings, the bodega serves delicious salads and sandwiches (AR$52 to AR$65) and a meat option. The *estancia* hotel (doubles US$550) only opens for group bookings, but it's worth enquiring, for if you coincide with a group, rooms may be available.

Some 9 kilometers beyond Colomé, Bodega El Humanao is also worth a visit for its beautifully balanced cabernet-malbec blend, among its other wines.

spaces. It's on the edge of the village and utterly peaceful. There's an overpriced but reasonable restaurant (open noon to 3:30pm and 7:30pm to 10:30pm).

Los Cardones de Molinos GUESTHOUSE $
(☎494061; cardonesmolinos@hotmail.com; cnr Sarmiento & San Martín; s/d AR$200/350, without bathroom AR$150/250;) This is an excellent sleeping choice, with comfortable rooms with cactus furniture. You're treated as one of the family and can use the kitchen; breakfast is included, there's a washing machine, and the exceptionally welcoming and accommodating owner is a great source of local advice.

Getting There & Away

There's a bus to Molinos from Salta (AR$95, six hours) via Cachi (AR$28, two hours) on Monday, Wednesday, Friday and Sunday. It returns at 7am Monday, Tuesday, Thursday and Saturday. Shared *remises* (taxis) run thrice daily to Salta (AR$120) via Cachi.

Local *remise* operators such as recommended **Sergio Rueda** (☎0387-15-447-8446) run to Angastaco (around AR$300) on demand and can also take you to Colomé (AR$180 with waiting) and other wineries.

Angastaco

☎03868 / POP 900 / ELEV 1955M

Tiny Angastaco sits among some of the most dramatically tortuous rockscapes of the valley route. Forty kilometers south of Molinos and 54km north of San Carlos, it's an oasis with vineyards, fields of anise and cumin, and the ruins of an ancient *pucará* (walled city).

Angastaco has an ATM and gas station. There is an **archaeological museum** (Pl Principal s/n; 7:30am-1:30pm Mon-Fri) FREE and irregularly attended tourist information in the municipal building.

Hospedaje El Cardón (☎15-459-0021; Martínez s/n; r per person with/without bathroom AR$70/60) is a decent budget choice. It's 50m to your right if you're standing facing the church. Grand **Hostería Angastaco** (☎491123; s/d AR$85/150;) is very abandoned but friendly and offers good value for its simple high-ceilinged rooms with cardón cactus-wood furniture. There's a simple restaurant and summer-only pool. Five kilometers north of the turnoff to town, **Finca El Carmen** (☎15-412-5900; www.vallesdelcarmen.com.ar; RN40 Km4427; s/d AR$350/450) is an intriguing place to stay on an historic ranch whose adobe buildings include an 18th-century Jesuit church. Hospitality is excellent and decent meals are available.

At research time, the only public transportation was buses heading south to San Carlos and Cafayate at 6am Monday to Saturday and 5pm Monday, Friday, and Sunday. For Molinos, 40km north, transports (ask around) run the route for AR$300 to AR$350 total. They'll often meet the Cafayate bus, where you can share the fare with other passengers. See Molinos for contact numbers. Otherwise, it's a hitchhike: best done from the main road, where there's shade and a cafe.

San Carlos

☎03868 / POP 1900 / ELEV 1624M

A sizable traditional village, San Carlos, 22km north of Cafayate, is connected to it by paved road, a pleasant shock if you're arriving from the north. Most visitors push on through, but there's a special place to stay here in **La Casa de los Vientos** (☎15-456525; www.casadelosvientos.com.ar; Barrio Cemitigre; d/q AR$300/500; @), signposted off the main road at the Cachi end of town. Built in the traditional manner of adobe, with terracotta tiles and cane ceilings, it incorporates some ingenious environmental innovations. The owners are potters, and the rooms (all different) are decorated with rustic flair and beauty. There's a heated indoor pool and a very genuine welcome.

Cafayate

☎03868 / POP 13,300 / ELEV 1683M

Argentina's second center for quality wine production, Cafayate is a popular tourist destination but still has a tranquil small-town feel. It's spectacularly scenic, with the green of the vines backed by soaring mountains beyond, and is one of northwest Argentina's most seductive destinations. It's easily reached from Salta via the tortured rockscapes of the Quebrada de Cafayate; it's also a major stop on RN40 and the Valles Calchaquíes route. With a selection of excellent accommodations for every budget, and several wineries to visit in and around town, it invites laying up for a while to explore the surrounding area. Also, check out the excellent *artesanía*.

Cafayate is famous for its torrontés, a grape that produces aromatic dry white wine, but the bodegas hereabouts also produce some fine reds from cabernet sauvignon, malbec and tannat.

Sights & Activities

Museo de la Vid y El Vino MUSEUM
(www.museodelavidyelvino.gov.ar; Av General Güemes; foreigners/Argentines AR$30/10; ⊙10am-7.30pm Tue-Sun) This impressive museum gives a good introduction to the area's wine industry. The atmospheric first section, which deals with the viticultural side – the life of the vines – through a series of poems and images, is particularly appealing. The second part covers the winemaking side, and there's a cafe where you can try and buy. English translations are good throughout.

Bodega El Esteco WINERY
(☎421283; www.elesteco.com.ar; tours AR$25; ⊙tours 10am, 11am, noon, 2:30pm, 3:30pm, 4.30pm, 5:30pm & 6:30pm Mon-Fri, 10am, 11am & noon Sat & Sun) This corporate affair on the northern edge of town is a smart and attractive winery producing some of the region's best wines. The tasting is a little spartan though.

Salvador Figueroa WINERY
(☎421125; Pasaje 20 de Junio, 25; AR$10; ⊙9:30am-12:30pm & 3:30-7pm) This tiny friendly family winery in town produces only 8000 bottles of torrontés and malbec per year with small hand-operated equipment.

Bodega de las Nubes WINERY
(☎422129; www.bodegamounier.com; AR$15; ⊙9:30am-5pm Mon-Fri, 9:30am-1:30pm Sat) Five kilometers west of Cafayate along the road to Río Colorado (it's signposted 'Mounier'), this small, organic and friendly winery has a fabulous position at the foot of the jagged hills. It also does tasty deli plates here. Ring ahead if you want to eat. Grape-picking day in March is lots of fun, with volunteers welcomed.

Bodega Nanni WINERY
(☎421527; www.bodegananni.com; Chavarría 151; tours free, tasting AR$15; ⊙10:30am-1pm & 2:30-6:30pm Mon-Sat, 11am-1pm & 2:30-6pm Sun) FREE The half-hourly tour and tastings of four young wines are short and bright here: a small, central winery with a lovely grass patio. Its wines are organic, uncomplicated and drinkable. There's an on-site restaurant, too.

El Porvenir WINERY
(☎422007; www.elporvenirdecafayate.com; Córdoba 32; ⊙9am-1pm daily, plus 3-6pm Tue-Sat) This well-run bodega focuses on quality wine production. The tour is free, but generous tastings cost from AR$45, depending on which wines you want to try.

Bodega Etchart WINERY
(☎421310; www.bodegasetchart.com; RN40) Two kilometers south of town, this produces some six million bottles of quality torrontés, cabernet and malbec per year. Visits were off at the time of research but are due to resume. Check for updates.

Museo Arqueológico MUSEUM
(cnr Colón & Calchaquí; admission by donation; ⊙11:30am-9pm Mon-Fri, 11:30am-3pm Sat) This private museum's collection was left by enthusiastic archaeologist Rodolfo Bravo and merits a visit. Sourced mostly from grave sites within a 30km radius from Cafayate, the excellent array of ceramics, from the black and gray wares of the Candelaria and Aguada cultures to late Diaguita and Inca pottery, are well displayed across two rooms. While there's not much explanation, the material speaks for itself.

Río Colorado WALKING, SWIMMING
A beautiful 6km walk southwest of town leads you to Río Colorado. Follow the river upstream (best with a guide) for about 1½ hours to get to a 10m **waterfall**, where you can swim. There's a second waterfall and further cascades further up. Look out for **rock paintings** on the way . If you ride to the trailhead, you can leave your bike at the nearby house for a few pesos. Combinable with a visit to Bodega de las Nubes.

Warning: if the river is high after rains in January and February, the route to the waterfall becomes strenuous and dangerous. Sudden torrents can come down quickly from the mountains at any time of year, so always keep an eye upstream while bathing.

Tours

The standard minibus tour of the Quebrada leaves in the afternoon, when the colors are more vivid, and costs around AR$150. Three- to four-hour treks in the Quebrada and Río Colorado are also popular. Day-long trips to Cachi (AR$500) are tiring, while Quilmes (AR$160) can be visited more cheaply in a taxi if there are two or more of you. Horseback rides range from a couple of hours

Cafayate

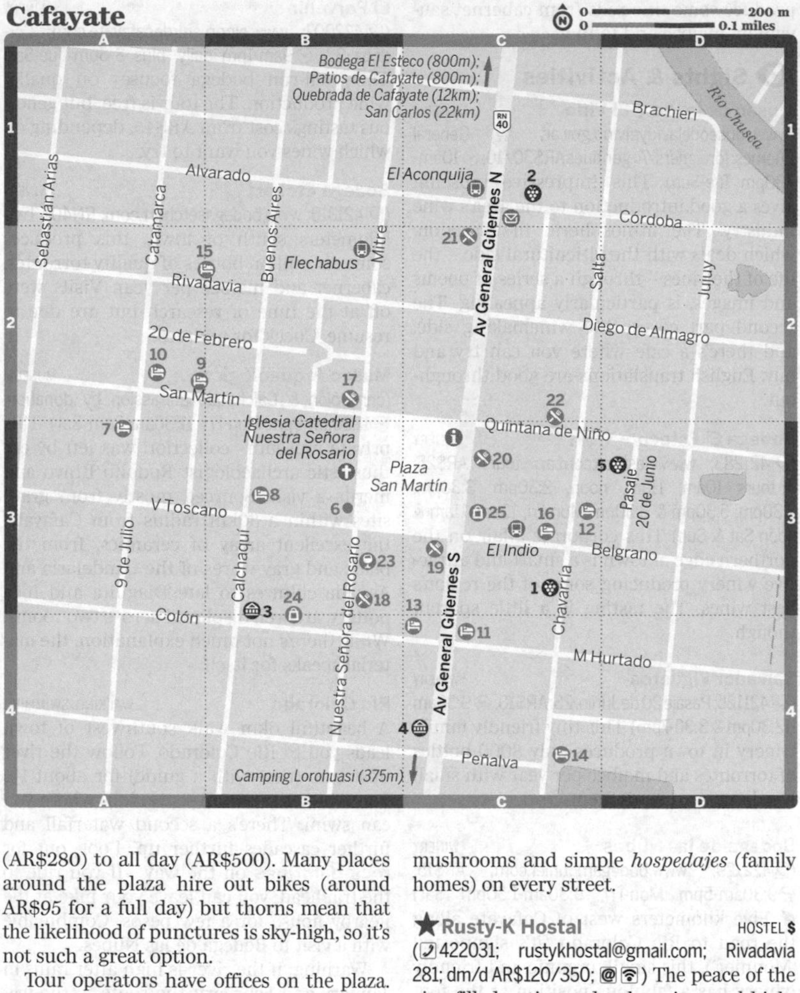

(AR$280) to all day (AR$500). Many places around the plaza hire out bikes (around AR$95 for a full day) but thorns mean that the likelihood of punctures is sky-high, so it's not such a great option.

Tour operators have offices on the plaza. Most are mediocre but the Quebrada scenery speaks for itself. **Majo Viajes** (☎422038; majoviajes@gmail.com; Nuestra Señora del Rosario 77) is better than many.

Festivals & Events

The **Serenata a Cafayate** (www.serenata-cafayate.com.ar) in February, is a very worthwhile three-day *folklore* festival; **Fiesta de la Virgen del Rosario**, on October 4, is the town fiesta and gets lively.

Sleeping

Cafayate has numerous places to stay, with new boutique hotels popping up like mushrooms and simple *hospedajes* (family homes) on every street.

★ Rusty-K Hostal HOSTEL $
(☎422031; rustykhostal@gmail.com; Rivadavia 281; dm/d AR$120/350; @ wi-fi) The peace of the vine-filled patio garden here is a real highlight, as is the friendliness and spotlessness of the rooms and dorms. Cute doubles and an excellent attitude make this Cafayate's budget gem. These prices are for high summer and drop substantially out-of-season. Book ahead.

Casa Árbol GUESTHOUSE, HOSTEL $
(☎422238; www.facebook.com/casaarbolcafayate; Calchaquí 84; dm/d AR$75/240; wi-fi) There's something really pleasant about this casual spot. Run by a young family, it has airy, beautiful decor and a really genuine welcome. Pretty, spotless rooms and a four-bed dorm share two bathrooms. There are plans for an attached wine bar, too.

Cafayate

Sights

Activities, Courses & Tours

Sleeping

Eating

Drinking & Nightlife

Shopping

Hostal del Valle GUESTHOUSE $
(☎421039; www.welcomeargentina.com/hostaldelvalle; San Martín 243; s/d AR$300/378; ❄📶) This enticing place offers myriad pot plants, and pretty rooms with large, inviting beds and excellent bathrooms. Smaller, darker rooms downstairs are a little cheaper and still worthwhile. Breakfast is mediocre but served in a rooftop conservatory with privileged views.

Hostal Ñusta GUESTHOUSE $
(☎421852; www.aparthotelcafayate.com; Catamarca 15; d AR$350-445; ❄@📶) 🍃 This generously run central guesthouse has a variety of rooms, some a bit cramped; superiors have air-con. It's all spotless, and the good vibe makes it more than the sum of its parts.

Hostel Ruta 40 HOSTEL $
(☎421689; www.hostel-ruta40.com; Av General Güemes 178; dm/d AR$110/380; @📶) Dorms are darkish and can be a little stuffy, but facilities and atmosphere are good at this central hostel. Prices drop substantially outside of high summer. Breakfast is included, there are decent private rooms and there's a kitchen. HI discount applies.

Camping Lorohuasi CAMPGROUND $
(RN40 Sur; campsites per person/tent AR$10/10, dm AR$25; 🏊) This campground 10 minutes' walk from the center along Av General Güemes is one of several in this area. It can get dusty when the wind blows. Facilities – including a high-season pool – are OK, and there are constricted but cheap dorm beds in weird little hexagonal cabins.

★ **Killa** BOUTIQUE HOTEL $$
(☎422254; www.killacafayate.com.ar; Colón 47; s/d/sup d AR$700/860/1300; ❄📶🏊) Classy, comfortable and well run, this handsome and recommendable hotel has colonial style and is given warmth by its creative use of natural wood, stone and local *artesanía*. The gorgeous rooms – not a TV in sight – have great bathrooms, and the upstairs suites – worth the extra investment – have cracking views and private balcony spaces. There's a pretty pool area and impeccable hospitality.

Villa Vicuña BOUTIQUE HOTEL $$
(☎422145; www.villavicuna.com.ar; Belgrano 76; d/ste US$150/190; ❄@📶) Peacefully set around twin patios, this offers an intimate retreat with beautiful, spotless rooms with French doors, big beds and reproduction antique furniture. Rooms are in two styles: one more colonial in feel, with dark wood and religious icons. There are numerous helpful little details, service and breakfast are good, and you can lose hours deciphering the offbeat mural sculpture in the courtyard.

Portal del Santo HOTEL $$
(☎422400; www.portaldelsanto.com.ar; Chavarría 250; s/d AR$700/800; ❄@📶🏊) Cool white elegance is the stock-in-trade of this hospitable hotel resembling a colonial palace with arched arcades. Lower rooms open onto both the front porch and the inviting garden-pool area; top-floor chambers (double/suite AR$900/1200) have mountain views and even more space. Suites sleep four. The owners are helpful and put on a great breakfast.

Hotel Munay HOTEL $$
(☎15-585-4718; www.munayhotel.com.ar; Chavarría 64; s/d AR$290/400; ❄📶🏊) The elegant

simplicity and clean uncluttered lines of this hotel seem to reflect the surrounding sierra. Rooms are unadorned, attractive and spotless, with good bathrooms. Excellent value, helpful service and a hospitable atmosphere make this a sound choice.

Cabañas Luna y Sol APARTMENTS **$$**
(☎421852; www.cabaniascafayate.com; 9 de Julio 31; d/q AR$612/1055;) An enticing option for families and couples, these cute apartments come with kitchenette and living area; the larger ones are duplex, with two sleeping areas. There's also a little pool and sustainable initiatives. Discount for cash payment.

Patios de Cafayate HOTEL **$$$**
(☎422229; www.patiosdecafayate.com; RN40; r US$280-407;) Though just a short walk north of town, this secluded place is a seductive getaway. Set in a beautiful centenarian *estancia*, it's a classy, elegant spot with helpful professional service. Rooms are classically colonial, with noble dark wood furniture, local *artesanía,* and perspectives over either the surrounding vineyards or the garden area, which includes a great swimming pool. Enter through the El Esteco winery.

Eating

There are many similar options around the plaza, offering adequate local dishes backed by live *folklórica* music at weekends.

★**Casa de las Empanadas** ARGENTINE **$**
(Mitre 24; dozen empanadas AR$60; 11am-3pm & 7-11pm) Decorated with the scrawls of contented customers, this no-frills place has a wide selection of empanadas that are all absolutely delicious. Local wine in ceramic jugs and *humitas* and *tamales* can round out the meal. If it's closed, head to its other **branch** (Nuestra Señora del Rosario 156; dozen empanadas AR$60).

★**Quilla Huasi** NORTHWEST ARGENTINE **$**
(www.facebook.com/quillahuasi; Quintana de Niño 70; mains AR$30-60; 11.30am-3.30pm & 7.30-11.30pm Wed-Mon) A cute little place with tasty versions of regional favorites like *humitas, tamales* and *locro*. Other unexpected things crop up, like osso buco that's been stewed in local wine. Service is caring and excellent and there's appealing outdoor seating, too. Top value.

Heladería Miranda ICE CREAM **$**
(Av General Güemes; cones AR$15-35; 1:30pm-midnight) A frequent dilemma in Argentina is whether to go for a rich red cabernet or a dry white torrontés, but it doesn't usually occur in ice-cream parlors. It does here: the Miranda's wine sorbets are Cafayate's pride and joy, but other fresh fruit flavors, including a *tuna* (cactus-fruit) one, are also delicious.

El Terruño ARGENTINE **$$**
(☎422460; www.terruno.todowebsalta.com.ar; Av General Güemes 30; mains AR$60-95; noon-3.30pm & 7.30pm-midnight;) Plaza-side seating and polite service are backed up by the food at this restaurant, which curiously has two menus, one of which is less traditional, with dishes such as inventive seafood-based salads, and well-prepared mains, including plenty of fish dishes. This is Cafayate's most reliable midrange option.

El Rancho NORTHWEST ARGENTINE **$$**
(www.elranchocafayate.com.ar; Toscano 4; mains AR$35-79; noon-3pm & 7.30pm-midnight or 1am) A cut above the string of hit-and-miss places around the plaza, this has a short, simple menu of local dishes, including *locro* and some good chicken plates. It's owned by a bodega, so competition wines are overpriced. It appeals on winter nights, with a crackling fire, and the nights when a blind guitarist plays unobtrusive *folklórica*.

Drinking

★**Chato's Wine Bar** WINE BAR
(Nuestra Señora del Rosario 132; 7-11pm) Run by a cordial English-speaking boss, this unusual place is decorated with warmth and style. It's the only proper wine bar in Cafayate, with a list of some 200 varieties available by the glass, and a great place for a tasting session, a drink in friendly surroundings, or a chat about wine or anything else. You can munch on a *picada* so it doesn't go to your head.

Shopping

There are numerous *artesanía* shops around the central plaza. The **Mercado Artesanal** (Av General Güemes; 9am-10pm) cooperative features many locals' high-quality work at more-than-fair prices. For fine silver, check out the workshop of **Jorge Barraco** (Colón 157).

Information

There are banks with ATM on the plaza, as well as phone/internet places.

Tourist Office (☎422442; Plaza San Martín; ⏰8am-9pm) On the northeast corner of the plaza.

Getting There & Away

Flechabus (Mitre s/n) runs five to six daily services to Salta (AR$86, four hours) and one or two to Angastaco (AR$32, two hours) via San Carlos (two to five daily, 30 mins, AR$9). **Aconquija** (cnr Av General Güemes & Alvarado) leaves two to four times daily for Tucumán (AR$145 to AR$164, five to 6½ hours) via Amaicha and Tafi del Valle (AR$83 to AR$103, 2½ to four hours); some go via Santa María (AR$45, two hours). Counterintuitively, quicker buses are cheaper. **El Indio** (Belgrano s/n) runs once daily to Salta and Santa María.

Getting Around

Taxis congregate opposite the cathedral and can be useful for reaching bodegas and other destinations. If there's none around, call ☎422128. To Quilmes with waiting time costs around AR$300, to San Carlos one-way it's AR$60, to Angastaco AR$200.

Quebrada de Cafayate

North of Cafayate, the Salta road heads through the barren and spectacular Quebrada de Cafayate, a wild landscape of richly colored sandstone and unearthly rock formations. Carved out by the Río de las Conchas, the canyon's twisted sedimentary strata exhibit a stunning array of tones, from rich red ochre to ethereal green. While you get a visual feast from the road itself – it's one of the country's more memorable drives or rides – it's worth taking time to explore parts of the canyon. The best time to appreciate the Quebrada is in the late afternoon, when the low sun brings out the most vivid colors.

A short way north of Cafayate, Los Médanos is an extensive dune field that gives way to the canyon proper, where a series of distinctive landforms are named and signposted from the road. Some, such as El Sapo (the Toad) are underwhelming, but around the Km46-47 mark, the adjacent Garganta del Diablo (Devil's Throat) and Anfiteatro (Amphitheatre) are much more impressive. Gashes in the rock wall let you enter and appreciate the tortured stone, whose clearly visible layers have been twisted by tectonic upheavals into extraordinary configurations.

These landmarks are heavily visited, and you may be followed by locals hoping for some pesos for a bit of 'guiding.' *Artesanía* (handicrafts) sellers and musicians hover too, but there's no reliable place to buy food or water.

> **COCA CHEWING**
>
> In the northwest, you'll see signs outside shops advertising *coca* and *bica*. The former refers to the leaves, mainly grown in Peru and Bolivia, which are also used to produce cocaine. *Bica* refers to bicarbonate of soda, an alkaline that, when chewed along with the leaves (as is customary among Andean peoples), releases their mild stimulant effect and combats fatigue, altitude sickness and hunger. Chewing coca and possessing small amounts for personal use is legal, but only in Argentina's northwestern provinces. Taking them back down south or into Chile is illegal, and there are plenty of searches.

Getting There & Away

There are several ways to see and explore the canyon. Tours from Salta are brief and regimented; it's much better to take a tour or taxi from closer Cafayate. Biking it from Cafayate is possible, but regular punctures makes this an unreliable option.

You could also combine the bus with walking and maybe hitching. Be aware of bus schedules between Salta and Cafayate, and carry food and plenty of water in this hot, dry environment. A good place to start exploration is the Garganta del Diablo; several other attractions are within easy walking distance of here.

San Antonio de los Cobres

☎03873 / POP 4300 / ELEV 3775M

This dusty mining town is on the puna 168km west of Salta, and over 2600m above it. It's suffered since the deterioration of the region's mining and associated railway, but is a typical highland settlement, with adobe houses, near-deserted streets and a serious temperature drop after sundown. It's worth stopping in to get the feel of this facet of Andean life. You can head north from here to the Quebrada de Humahuaca via the Salinas Grandes and Purmamarca, and, some of the year, south to Cachi.

Sights

There's little to see in town – though the sunsets are spectacular – but 16km to the west is the viaduct at La Polvorilla, the last stop of the *Tren a las Nubes*. You can climb up a zigzag path to the top of the viaduct and walk across it. *Remises* in San Antonio charge about AR$120 for the return journey.

Sleeping & Eating

Simple restaurants dot Belgrano; good bets for empanadas, *milanesas* (breaded cutlets) and other local staples.

El Palenque GUESTHOUSE $
(☎490-9019; hostalelpalenque@hotmail.com; Belgrano s/n; d without bathroom AR$140, tr AR$210) Welcoming and tidy, this fine choice is a few blocks from the center, past the church. It looks closed from outside, but it's not. Superclean rooms are insulated and (comparatively) warm; there's hot water and sound family ownership.

Hotel de las Nubes HOTEL $$
(☎490-9059; www.hoteldelasnubes.com; Caseros 441; s/d AR$510/630; wifi) The best place to stay and eat in town, this has simple decoration in its comfortable-enough rooms, which boast doubleglazing and heating. Book ahead. The restaurant (mains AR$79 to AR$95; open noon to 2pm and 7pm to 9.30pm) serves a short menu of local dishes; overpriced but tasty enough.

Getting There & Away

One to two daily buses run from Salta (AR$55, 5½ hours) with Ale Hermanos. See also the *Tren a las Nubes* (p226). Precious little transportation runs over the Paso de Sico to Chile these days; ask around town for trucks due to leave. From San Antonio, a good *ripio* (gravel) road runs 97km north, skirting the Salinas Grandes to intersect with the paved RP52.

Salinas Grandes

Bring sunglasses for this spectacular **salt plain** in a remote part of the puna, at some 3350m above sea level. A lake that dried up in the Holocene Era, this is now a 525-sq-km crust of salt up to half a meter thick. On a clear day, the blinding contrast between the bright blue sky and the cracked and crusty expanse of white is spellbinding.

The *salinas* (salt plains) are in Salta province, but most easily reached by heading west along paved RP52 from Purmamarca in Jujuy province. About 5km west of the intersection of RP52 and the good *ripio* road that heads 97km to San Antonio de los Cobres, there's a saltmining building; opposite, you can head onto the salt pan to check out the rectangular basins from which the salt is periodically dug out. Artisans sell stone carvings and llamas made from salt. A couple of places to buy drinks and food are on the road nearby.

The only way of reaching the *salinas* by public transportation is to jump off a Chile- or Susques-bound bus from Jujuy or Purmamarca. Check timetables carefully before doing this; on some days it's possible to catch a bus back to Purmamarca a couple of hours later, but on other days it's not. This road has enough traffic to hitchhike.

Otherwise, grab a *remise* from Purmamarca, or take a tour from Purmamarca, Tilcara, Jujuy or Salta. From the latter, it's a hellishly long day, unless you opt to overnight.

The *salinas* are spectacular, but the otherworldly *salares* (salt flats) of southwestern Bolivia are even more so; if you're heading that way (or have already been), you might want to prioritize other attractions.

Jujuy

☎0388 / POP 265,300 / ELEV 1201M

Of the trinity of northwestern cities, San Salvador de Jujuy (or simply Jujuy) lacks Salta's colonial sophistication or Tucuman's urban vibe and is often bypassed by travelers. Nevertheless, it has a livable feel, enticing restaurants and is the most culturally indigenous of any of Argentina's cities.

The city was founded in 1593, after two previous incarnations were razed by indigenous groups who hadn't given planning permission. The province bore the brunt of conflict throughout the independence wars, with Spain launching repeated invasions down the Quebrada de Humahuaca from Bolivia; Jujuy was famously evacuated during what is known as the *éxodo jujeño*.

The city's name is roughly pronounced *hoo-hooey;* if it sounds like an arch exclamation of surprise, you're doing well.

Jujuy

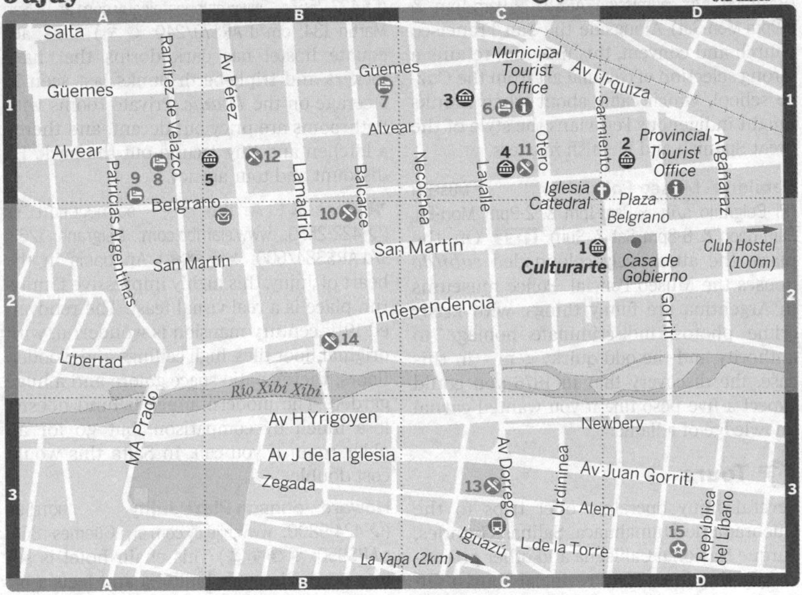

Sights

★Culturarte GALLERY

(www.facebook.com/museoculturartejujuy; cnr San Martín & Sarmiento; 8am-9pm Mon-Fri, 10am-noon & 5-8pm Sat, 5-8pm Sun) FREE An attractive modern space, this showcases exhibitions by well-established Argentine contemporary artists. There's also a cafe-bar with a great little balcony elevated over the street.

Museo Arqueológico MUSEUM

(Lavalle 434; admission AR$5; 8am-8pm Mon-Fri) The standout exhibit is a vivid 3000-year-old fertility goddess figure, depicted with snakes for hair and in the act of giving birth. She's a product of the advanced San Francisco culture, which existed in Las Yungas from about 1400 BC to 800 BC. There's also a selection of skulls with cranial deformities (practiced for cosmetic reasons) and mummified bodies.

Museo Temático de Maquetas Tupac Amaru MUSEUM

(Alvear 1152; 8am-11pm) FREE Set up by and housed in the headquarters of an indigenous political organization, this rather charming museum tells the history, traditions and mythology of indigenous Argentina in a series of rather entertaining dioramas. If you can read Spanish, you'll find copious information here on these subjects.

Jujuy

Top Sights

1 Culturarte ... C2

Sights

2 Cabildo & Museo Policial ... D1
3 Museo Arqueológico ... C1
4 Museo Histórico Franciscano ... C1
5 Museo Temático de Maquetas Tupac Amaru ... B1

Sleeping

6 Hostería Carlos Alvear ... C1
7 Howard Johnson Plaza Jujuy ... B1
8 Munay Hotel ... A1
9 Posada El Arribo ... A1

Eating

10 Krysys ... B2
11 Madre Tierra ... C1
12 Manos Jujeñas ... B1
13 Mercado del Sur ... C3
14 Viracocha ... B2

Entertainment

15 El Coya Bolívar ... D3

Museo Histórico Franciscano MUSEUM
(Belgrano s/n; admission AR$5; ⏲9am-1pm & 5-9pm Mon-Sat) Alongside the San Francisco church and convent, this museum retains a strong selection of colonial art from the Cuzco school, which came about when monks taught indigenous Peruvians the style of the great Spanish and Flemish masters.

Cabildo & Museo Policial MUSEUM
(Pl Belgrano s/n; ⏲8am-1pm & 2-9pm Mon-Fri, 9am-noon & 6-8pm Sat & Sun) FREE On the plaza, the attractively colonnaded *cabildo* houses the Museo Policial. Police museums in Argentina are funny things, with grisly crime photos, indiscriminate homage to authority and the odd quirky gem – in this case, the discovery that in 1876 you could expect a five peso fine if you wanted carnal knowledge of a llama.

Tours

Several Jujuy operators offer trips to the Quebrada de Humahuaca, Salinas Grandes, Parque Nacional Calilegua and other provincial destinations. The Provincial Tourist Office (p245) can give you a full listing.

Festivals & Events

In August, Jujuy's biggest event, the week-long **Semana de Jujuy**, commemorates Belgrano's evacuation of the city during the wars of independence.

Sleeping

Lots of cheap *residenciales* (budget hotels) stock the chaotic streets around the bus terminal.

Munay Hotel HOTEL $
(☎422-8435; www.munayhotel.com.ar; Alvear 1230; s/d AR$240/360; 📶) This good-value budget hotel offers small but comfortable and spotless rooms in a nice little package a couple of blocks away from the action. Service is friendly and parking is available for AR$50 extra.

Hostería Carlos Alvear GUESTHOUSE $
(☎422-2982; restojujuy@gmail.com; Alvear 627; s/d AR$170/275, without bathroom AR$80/160; 📶) A variety of rooms is tucked away here behind a popular central restaurant. They're clean and OK for the price, but make sure you select carefully (upstairs) as some of those with shared bathroom tend to be somewhat poky. The further back, the quieter it gets.

Club Hostel HOSTEL $
(☎423-7565; www.clubhosteljujuy.com.ar; San Martín 134; dm/d AR$70/240; @📶) This adequate hostel has dark dorms that have lockers and triple-berth bunks last seen in steerage on the *Titanic*. Private rooms with bathrooms are pricy but decent, and there's a kitchen and tiny Jacuzzi out the back. HI discount and tour agency.

★ **Posada El Arribo** BOUTIQUE HOTEL $$
(☎422-2539; www.elarribo.com; Belgrano 1263; s/d AR$384/600; ❄@📶🏊) An oasis in the heart of Jujuy, this highly impressive family-run place is a real visual feast. The renovated 19th-century mansion is wonderful, with original floor tiles, high ceilings and wooden floors; there's patio space galore and a huge garden. The modern annex behind doesn't lose much by comparison, but go for an older room if you can. In Salta this would cost double.

Howard Johnson Plaza Jujuy HOTEL $$
(☎424-9800; www.hjjujuy.com.ar; Güemes 864; r AR$950; ❄@📶🏊) This chain hotel is set in a borderline-ugly building and feels a bit impersonal but makes up for it with really excellent facilities, including a sizable pool, spa and gym. Rooms are spacious and comfortable.

Eating

Jujuy's lively **Mercado del Sur**, opposite the bus terminal, is a genuine trading post where indigenous Argentines swig *mazamorra* (a cold maize soup) and peddle coca leaves. Simple eateries around here serve hearty regional specialties; try *chicharrón con mote* (stir-fried pork with boiled maize) or spicy *sopa de maní* (peanut soup).

Madre Tierra BAKERY, CAFE $
(www.facebook.com/MadreTierraRestauranteNaturista; Belgrano 619; snacks AR$15-40; ⏲6:30am-3pm & 4-10:30pm Mon-Sat; 🌿) This place is a standout. The vegetarian food – there's a daily set menu – is excellent and the sandwiches and pizzas can be washed down with fresh juice or organic beer. There's lovely garden patio seating and the bakery out the front does wholesome breads.

Manos Jujeñas NORTHWEST ARGENTINE $
(Av Pérez 381; mains AR$35-60; ⏲11am-3pm & 7-11pm Tue-Sun) 🍃 One of Jujuy's best addresses for no-frills traditional slow-food cooking, this fills up with a contented buzz on weekend evenings. There are several

classic northeastern dishes to choose from, but it's the *picante* – marinated chicken or tongue or both with onion, tomato, rice and Andean potatoes – that's the pride of the house.

Viracocha NORTHWEST ARGENTINE $
(cnr Independencia & Lamadrid; mains AR$40-70; noon-3.30pm & 7.30pm-12.30am) Atmospheric vaulted restaurant serving excellent traditional dishes such as *picantes* of any meat you can think of, pickled llama, and warming peanut soup.

★ **Krysys** ARGENTINE $$
(Balcarce 272; mains AR$60-75; noon-3pm & 9pm-1am Mon-Sat, noon-3pm Sun;) The best *parrilla* option is this central, upscale place offering all your barbecued favorites in a relaxed atmosphere. But there's plenty more on the menu, with a range of tasty sauces to go with the chicken, pork or beef, and various appetizing starters. Prices are fair, and you'll get the meat the way you want it cooked.

Drinking & Nightlife

Jujuy's folkloric *peñas* have live music at weekends. Fun **El Coya Bolívar** (15-472-5311; Lisandro de la Torre 634; music Fri & Sat), near the bus terminal, has three bands on Friday and Saturday nights, while little and legendary **La Yapa** (402-0637; Mejías 426, Barrio Malvinas; 8pm-late Fri & Sat) is further away. The big *boliches* (nightclubs) are out on RN9 south of town.

Orientation

The center of town sits between the Xibi Xibi and Grande rivers. The bus terminal is across the former: travelers have reported incidents around here so invest in a cab if arriving by night.

Information

There are many central banks with ATMs. Call centers and internet places abound.

Hospital Pablo Soria (422-1228; cnr Patricias Argentinas & Av Córdoba)

Municipal Tourist Office (402-0246; turismo@municipiodejujuy.gov.ar; cnr Alvear & Otero; 7am-1pm & 2-8pm Mon-Fri, 7am-10pm Sat & Sun) Friendly and central. There's another at the bus terminal.

Provincial Tourist Office (422-1343; www.turismo.jujuy.gov.ar; Gorriti 295; 7am-10pm Mon-Fri, 8am-9pm Sat & Sun) Excellent office on the plaza with good brochures and staff.

Getting There & Away

AIR

Aerolíneas (422-2575; www.aerolineas.com; Av Pérez 355; 8:30am-12:15pm & 4:30-8:15pm Mon-Fri, 8:30am-12:15pm Sat) services Buenos Aires once or twice daily.

BUS

The old-school **bus terminal** (422-1375; cnr Av Dorrego & Iguazú) has provincial and long-distance services, but Salta has more choice.

Daily buses going from Salta to Chile stop here.

Buses from Jujuy

DESTINATION	COST (AR$)	DURATION (HR)
Buenos Aires	918	20-23
Córdoba	540	12-16
Humahuaca	40	2
La Quiaca	70	4-5
Mendoza	738	20
Purmamarca	30	1¼
Salta	63	2
Salvador Mazza	229	7
Tilcara	27	1¾
Tucumán	198	5

Getting Around

El Cadillal airport is 33km east of the center. A **shuttle service** (15-432-2482; AR$45) leaves from the cathedral to coincide with flights, otherwise it's AR$200 in a *remise*.

If you're after a rental car, **Avis** (424-9800; www.avis.com; Güemes 864) or **Hertz** (422-9582; www.hertz.com; San Martín 944) are central; there are also branches at the airport.

Las Yungas

Jujuy province's eastern portion is a humid, fertile subtropical zone where arid, treeless altiplano gives way to montane forest and, in places, dense cloudforest. Two national parks, with abundant, colorful birdlife and harder-to-spot mammals such as pumas, tapirs and jaguars, allow you to explore this ecosystem.

Parque Nacional Calilegua

This accessible, beautiful, biodiverse park stretches up the Serranía de Calilegua range to peaks offering boundless views above the forest and across El Chaco to the east.

The spectacular 22km road through the park ascends from 550m to 1700m, taking you through the three types of forest that characterize the park's different altitude layers and offering spectacular views.

Along this road are trailheads for nine marked hikes, from 10-minute strolls to tough descents down to river level. The best places for bird and mammal watching are near the stream courses in the early morning or late afternoon. Most trailheads are within easy walking distance of the park entrance. Rangers offer guiding services on the longer trails.

From Valle Grande, beyond the park boundaries to the west, it's possible to hike in a week to Humahuaca along the Sierra de Zenta, or to Tilcara.

The ranger station at Aguas Negras, the **park entrance** (calilegua@apn.gov.ar; ⏲9am-6pm) FREE, is the best source of information about trails and conditions. There's another ranger station at Mesada de las Colmenas, halfway along the road through the park.

The free **campground** is at the entrance. It has bathrooms and shower, but no power, drinking water or shop.

Libertador General San Martín is a sizable sugarcane town with little charm but several places to stay. Little Calilegua is more appealing, with a tumbledown tropical feel and a deafening chorus of cicadas around the historic Sala de Calilegua estate.

Jardín Colonial (☎03886-430334; eljardin colonial@hotmail.com; San Lorenzo s/n; r per person from AR$100;) is a characterful, haphazardly-run centenarian bungalow with attractive rooms and a verdant, sculpture-filled garden. It's cheap and very casual: there are no locks on the rooms and you're left to your own devices. Toucans roost in the trees opposite.

Numerous buses between Jujuy/Salta and Salvador Mazza stop at Libertador General San Martín and Calilegua, and some will let you off at the junction for the park, 3km north of Libertador's center and 2km south of Calilegua. It's 8km from here to the Aguas Negras ranger station; there's enough traffic to hitchhike. It's also easy to taxi it from either town.

BOLIVIA VIA SALVADOR MAZZA OR AGUAS BLANCAS

RN34 continues past Calilegua to Argentina's northernmost settlement, Salvador Mazza (also known as Pocitos), a major border with Bolivia. Cross the **frontier** (⏲24hr), and take a shared taxi 5km to the larger Bolivian settlement of Yacuiba, which has buses to Tarija and Santa Cruz. There's no Bolivian consulate, so get your visa in Jujuy or Salta if you need one. Salvador Mazza is served by numerous buses from Jujuy, Salta and other northern cities.

Another crossing in this area is the international bridge between Aguas Blancas and Bermejo, with good onward bus connections to Tarija. Aguas Blancas is served by bus from Salta, but there are more frequent connections to Orán, from where shared taxis leave for Aguas Blancas from opposite the bus station. Direct services are available between Salta and Tarija (Juarez, AR$350, 8 hours).

Quebrada de Humahuaca

North of Jujuy, the memorable Quebrada de Humahuaca snakes its way upward toward Bolivia. It's a harsh but vivid landscape, a dry yet river-scoured canyon overlooked by mountainsides whose sedimentary strata have been eroded into spectacular scalloped formations that reveal waves of colors. The palette of this Unesco World Heritage–listed valley changes constantly, between shades of creamy white and rich, deep reds; the rock formations in places recall a necklace of sharks' teeth, while in others they look like the backbone of some unspeakable beast.

Dotting the valley are dusty, picturesque, indigenous towns offering a fine variety of places to stay, plus historic adobe churches, and homey restaurants serving warming *locro* (a stew of maize, beans, pumpkin, and meat) and llama fillets. The region has experienced a tourism boom in recent years and gets very full in summer, when accommodation prices soar.

There are many interesting stops along this colonial post route between Potosí (Bolivia) and Buenos Aires; buses run every 40 minutes or so, so it's quite easy to jump off and on as required. The closest place to hire a car is Jujuy. The Quebrada shows its best side early in the morning, when colors are more vivid and the wind hasn't got up.

Purmamarca

0388 / POP 510 / ELEV 2192M

Little Purmamarca, 3km west of the highway, sits under the celebrated Cerro de los Siete Colores (Hill of Seven Colors), a spectacular, jagged formation resembling the marzipan fantasy of a megalomaniac pastry chef. The village is postcard-pretty, with ochre adobe houses and ancient algarrobo trees by the bijou 17th-century church. This, and its proximity to Jujuy, has made it very touristy; if you're looking for an authentic Andean village, move on. Nevertheless, Purmamarca is an excellent place to shop for woven goods; a flourishing market sets up on the plaza every day.

Apart from shopping for handicrafts, make sure you take the easy but spectacular 3km walk around the *cerro* (hill), whose striking colors are best appreciated in the morning or evening sunlight.

CARNAVAL IN THE QUEBRADA

Argentina's most intriguing Carnaval celebrations take place right the length of the Quebrada in February/March. Indigenous traditions melded with the customs of the Spanish conquerors to create a vibrant hybrid that kicks off on the Saturday 50 days before Easter Sunday. In each town, a devil figure is dug up from where he was buried the previous year and paraded into town amid much noise, triggering an eight-day bender of dancing and copious drinking.

Sleeping

El Pequeño Inti GUESTHOUSE $

(490-8089; Florida s/n; s/d AR$230/260) Small and enticing, this fine little choice is just off the plaza. Offering value (for two), it has unadorned rooms with comfortable beds and marine-schemed bathrooms.

Mama Coca HOSTEL $

(490-8434; mamacocapurma@hotmail.com; Rivadavia s/n; dm/d AR$80/190;) Right by where the buses stop, this casual hostel is a simple place to hole up behind a restaurant. It's friendly, with a small vine-shaded patio. Dorms have a decent amount of space. No kitchen or breakfast.

★ **Los Colorados** APARTMENTS $$

(490-8182; www.loscoloradosjujuy.com.ar; Chapacal s/n; s/d/q AR$700/900/1550;) Looking straight out of a science-fiction movie, these strange but inviting apartments are tucked right into the *cerro,* and blend in with it. They are stylish, spacious and cozy; fine places to hole up for a while and a great option for families.

★ **Huaira Huasi** HOTEL $$

(490-8070; www.huairahuasi.com.ar; RN52, Km5; d/apt for four AR$666/1655; @) One of a handful of characterful hotels on the main road above town, this stands out for its majestic valley views and handsome terracotta-colored adobe buildings. There are two apartments that sleep five, and they are just beautifully decorated with local fabrics and cardón wood; rooms are obviously smaller but still lovely. Good value.

Terrazas de la Posta HOTEL $$

(490-8053; www.terrazasdelaposta.com.ar; d standard/superior AR$720/850;) Handsome rooms with spacious bathrooms share a veranda with great sierra views. Superiors are newer and larger, with air-con and eye-catching modern styling.

Eating

Tierra de Colores NORTHWEST ARGENTINE $

(Libertad s/n; mains AR$40-70; 11am-3.30pm & 7-11pm) A likeably rustic dining area with cane ceiling is a venue for delicious traditional food, served in generous portions. Juicy *tamales,* toothsome *locro* and sizable llama brochettes are the way to go. Service is pleasant, and there's somewhat touristy but enjoyable live music at lunch and dinnertime.

El Churqui de Altura NORTHWEST ARGENTINE $$

(Salta s/n; mains AR$55-90; noon-3:30pm & 7:30-10:30pm) Substantially overpriced, but dishes of local trout, goat or llama stews and oven-cooked empanadas are pretty tasty. It only opens lunchtimes if it's busy.

Information

There's an ATM on the plaza.

Tourist Office (490-8443; Florida s/n; 7am-7pm, extended hours Jan-Feb) Just off the plaza.

Getting There & Away

Buses to Jujuy (AR$30, 1¼ hours) run regularly; others go to Tilcara (AR$6 to AR$10, 30

The Quebrada de Humahuaca

The tortured rockscapes and palette of mineral colors that changes through the day make this arid valley a highlight of the northwest. Exploring the indigenous villages and towns strung along it is a delight.

Iruya

1 A long, rickety drive over a spectacular mountain pass, this remote village preserves a traditional and indigenous feel. Surrounded by imposing cliffs and mountains, it's a place whose slow pace obliges you to step off the frenzied wheel for a day or three (p254).

Purmamarca

2 This small town is dominated by its surrounding crags, which feature some of the valley's most vibrant mineral colorings. The focus of things here is the great artisan market on the square (p247).

Tilcara

3 A range of excellent small hotels, stunning landscapes, excursions and the cactus-studded ruins of an indigenous fortress make this many travelers' favorite base in the Quebrada (p250).

Humahuaca

4 The valley's largest town has an authentic feel and makes a good base for the region. Picturesque cobbled streets, fair-trade handcrafts and typical northwestern dishes, such as *locro* or llama stew are highlights (p253).

Uquía

5 This village has the region's standout church, a beautiful 17th-century structure whose interior famously features paintings of the main angels packing muzzle-loading weaponry (p253).

1

DEMETRIO CARRASCO/GETTY IMAGES ©

4

RALF HETTLER/GETTY IMAGES©

Clockwise from top left
1. Iruya (p254) **2.** Market, Purmamarca (p247)
3. Pucará, Tilcara (p250) **4.** Local fabrics

YADID LEVY/GETTY IMAGES ©

DANITA DELIMONT/GETTY IMAGES ©

CHILE VIA SUSQUES

The paved road climbs doggedly from Purmamarca through spectacular bleak highland scenery to a 4150m pass, then crosses a plateau partly occupied by the Salinas Grandes. You hit civilization at **Susques**, 130km from Purmamarca, which has gas and an ATM.

Susques is well worth a stop for its terrific village **church** (admission by donation; ⏲8am-6pm). Dating from 1598, it has a thatched roof, cactus-wood ceiling and beaten-earth floor, as well as charismatic, naïve paintings of saints on the whitewashed adobe walls. There's a tourist office on the main road, and basic places to stay. From Susques RN40 heads south to San Antonio de los Cobres via the Polvorilla viaduct. It's a lonely road: check conditions before heading down it.

Daily buses run from Jujuy to Susques (AR$70, four to five hours) via Purmamarca (AR$58).

Beyond Susques, the road continues 154km to the Paso de Jama (4230m), a spectacular journey. This is the Chilean border, although Argentine **emigration** (⏲8am-midnight) is some way before it. There's gas here. No fruit, vegetables or coca leaves are allowed into Chile – they check. The paved road continues toward San Pedro de Atacama. Buses from Salta and Jujuy travel this route.

minutes) and Humahuaca (AR$30, 1¼ hours). You can get a cab (AR$10) to the main road junction where more buses pass.

Purmamarca has no gas station; the closest can be found 25km north, at Tilcara, or south, at Volcán. Westward, the nearest is in Susques, a 130km climb away.

Tilcara

☎0388 / POP 4360 / ELEV 2461M

Picturesque Tilcara is many people's choice for their Quebrada de Humahuaca base. The mixture of local farmers getting on with a centuries-old way of life and arty urban refugees looking for a quieter existence has created an interesting balance on the town's dusty streets.

Sights

Pucará RUIN

(admission incl Museo Arqueológico Argentines/Latin Americans/others AR$15/20/30, Mon free; ⏲9am-6pm) This reconstructed pre-Columbian fortification is 1km south of the center across an iron bridge. Its situation is undeniably strategic, commanding the river valley both ways and, though the site was undoubtedly used before, the ruins date from the 11th to 15th centuries. There are great views and, seemingly, a cardón cactus for every soul that lived and died here. For further succulent stimulation, there's a cactus garden by the entrance.

The 1950s reconstruction has taken liberties; worse yet is the earlier, ridiculous monument to pioneering archaeologists bang where the plaza would have been. Nevertheless, you can get a feel of what would have been a sizable fortified community. Most interesting is the 'church,' a building with a short paved walkway to an altar; take note of the niche in the wall alongside.

Museo Arqueológico MUSEUM

(Belgrano 445; admission incl pucará Argentines/Latin Americans/others AR$15/20/30, Mon free; ⏲9am-6pm) This well-presented collection of regional artifacts in a striking colonial house has some pieces from the *pucará* (walled city), and exhibits give an insight into the life of people living around that time. The room that is dedicated to ceremonial masks is particularly impressive.

Activities

You'll see phone numbers for *cabalgatas* (horseback rides) everywhere, and most accommodations can arrange it for you. Guides for walks around the area congregate at the tourist office.

Garganta del Diablo HIKING

(AR$5 admission) Of several interesting walks around Tilcara, most popular is the 4km hike to Garganta del Diablo, a pretty canyon and waterfall. Head toward the *pucará,* but turn left along the river before crossing the bridge. Swimming is best in the morning, when the sun is on the pool.

Tilcara Mountain Bike BICYCLE RENTAL
(☎15-500-8570; tilcarabikes@hotmail.com; Belgrano s/n; per hr/day AR$20/100 ; ⏲9am-7pm) A friendly setup just past the bus terminal that hires out well-maintained mountain bikes and provides a helpful map of routes in the area.

Tours

Several operators around town run trips up and down the Quebrada and to the Salinas Grandes. A recommended guide for the spectacular multiday trek to the Calilegua national park is **Juan Pablo Maldonado** (☎15-504-5322).

Caravana de Llamas TREKKING
(☎15-408-8000; www.caravanadellamas.com; cnr Corte & Viltipico) A highly recommended llama-trekking operator running half-day (AR$300 to AR$420) and full-day (AR$600 to AR$900) excursions of varying difficulty around Tilcara, and in the Salinas Grandes, and multiday excursions, including a six-day marathon from Tilcara to the Las Yungas forested lowlands. The guide is personable and well informed about the area. Llamas are pack animals: you walk, they carry the bags. Drop by to meet the llamas (AR$45) even if you're not planning a trip.

Festivals & Events

Tilcara celebrates several festivals during the year, the most notable of which is January's **Enero Tilcareño**, with sports, music and cultural activities. August's indigenous **Pachamama** (Mother Earth) festival is also worthwhile.

Sleeping

There's a huge variety, with numerous upmarket boutique hotels and dozens of simple hostels, guesthouses, and good-value rooms in private homes (the tourist office keeps a list of these).

Malka GUESTHOUSE, HOSTEL $
(☎495-5197; www.malkahostel.com.ar; San Martín s/n, Barrio Malka; dm/d AR$115/400, cabin for 4 AR$650;) This rustic complex is a special place, both hotel and hostel. The welcoming owners, secluded, shady situation, thoughtfully different dorms, and smart stone-clad rooms with hammocks and deckchairs out front make it the sort of retreat you end up staying longer in than you expected. A relaxing yoga room with courses is another reason to linger. Good breakfast included and HI discount.

Facing the church, head left for a block, then turn right and follow this road.

Antigua Tilcara GUESTHOUSE, HOSTEL $
(☎15-502-0144; www.antiguatilcara.com.ar; Sorpresa 484; dm/s/d standard AR$80/250/420, s/d superior AR$300/500; @) Run with real enthusiasm and offering a genuine welcome, this excellent place offers a spacious dorm with single beds and two grades of room, both handsome. Superiors are worth the small extra investment for extra space and views. There's a great cafe-bar area with vistas, cracking breakfasts, a small kitchen, and various sustainable practices. A top place.

Albahaca Hostel HOSTEL $
(☎15-585-5994; www.albahacahostel.com.ar; Padilla s/n; dm/d AR$45/160;) Simple but well-priced and very friendly, with decent dorms, comfortable private rooms and a sociable roof terrace. A place to make friends.

★**Posada de Luz** LODGE $$
(☎495-5017; www.posadadeluz.com.ar; Ambrosetti 661; r AR$550-750; @) With a nouveau-rustic charm, this little place is a fantastic spot to unwind for a few days. More expensive rooms have sitting areas, but all feature adobe walls, cane ceilings, pot-bellied stoves and individual terraces with deckchairs and views out over the valley. Pretty grounds include a BBQ area and children's playground; excellent personal service is a real highlight.

Con los Ángeles LODGE $$
(☎495-5153; www.posadaconlosangeles.com.ar; Gorriti 156; s/d standard AR$460/510, d superior AR$630; @) The lovely, extensive grassy garden complete with sun loungers comes as a surprise coming from the street. Warmly run by a friendly young family, this features stylish common areas and thoughtfully decorated king-bedded rooms arrayed along the lawn. Dinners are available for guests.

Rincón de Fuego BOUTIQUE HOTEL $$
(☎427-1432; www.rincondefuego.com; Ambrosetti 445; s/d standard AR$550/680, s/d superior AR$680/830; @) Romantic and welcoming, this posada is tucked away in the higher part of town; it's a fine spot to retreat to with someone you love. Effective, artistic use of bare stone and adobe lends much atmosphere; the rooms are darkish but seductive, with woodstoves. Superiors are especially great, with space to spare and beautiful

artisanal llama-wool carpets. Breakfast features bread baked in the patio's clay oven.

Cerro Chico CABIN $$

(☎15-404-2612; www.cerrochico.com; d/q AR$450/650; 📶🏊) Two kilometers from town down a dirt road, this attractive complex of cabins climbs a hill with gorgeous Quebrada views and a remote, relaxing feel. The standard cabins are compact but handsome, and the pool area is a great little spot. Turn left straight after crossing the bridge into Tilcara and follow the signs.

Patio Alto HOTEL, HOSTEL $$

(☎495-5792; www.patioalto.com.ar; Torrico 675; dm/s/d AR$228/828/900; @📶) Great vistas from the coziness of your large bed are the highlight of the handsome modern rooms at this top-of-the-town hotel. A good breakfast, afternoon tea and thoughtful details are included. There are also downstairs (but upmarket) dorms that are every bit as nice, with four single beds, cane lockers and kitchen use; the only thing missing is the view.

Aguacanto LODGE $$

(☎495-5817; www.aguacanto.com.ar; Corte 333; d/apt AR$520/750; 📶) Spruce rooms and apartments surrounding a lawn featuring hammocks and one of Tilcara's most amazing views. Service is very friendly. Prices drop off-season.

Eating

Ma'koka CAFE $

(Belgrano s/n; sandwiches AR$25-35; ⏰8:30am-1pm & 3-9pm; 📶) With a gloriously eclectic music mix and interesting texts on the area and the Andes in general, this likeable bookshop-cafe has the best coffee in town as well as tasty cakes and top sandwiches on bread made from coca or local corn varieties.

Peña de Carlitos NORTHWEST ARGENTINE $

(www.lapeniadecarlitos.com.ar; Lavalle 397; dishes AR$25-45; ⏰10am-midnight) This cheery long-standing local restaurant with scrawls of happy customers adorning the walls offers live folkloric music with no cover charge from 9:30pm every night. There's more of a mix of locals and visitors than in most places, and low-priced ok-quality regional dishes. Try the llama empanadas.

★ **El Nuevo Progreso** ARGENTINE $$

(☎495-5237; www.facebook.com/elnuevoprogreso; Lavalle 351; mains AR$65-80; ⏰6-11:30pm; 🍷) An engaging atmosphere and delicious tourist-oriented cuisine features imaginatively prepared llama dishes, excellent meat plates, interesting veggie options and great salads. Service can be a bit stand-offish but it's well worthwhile.

El Patio ARGENTINE $$

(☎495-5044; Lavalle 352; mains AR$55-75; ⏰noon-3pm & 6.30-10.30pm Wed-Mon; 🍷) Tucked away between plaza and church, this has a lovely shaded patio and garden seating. It offers a wide range of tasty salads, inventive llama dishes and a far-from-the-madding-crowd atmosphere.

Arumi NORTHWEST ARGENTINE $$

(Lavalle 660; mains AR$40-80; ⏰6pm-midnight) Art on the walls, regular live events and a comfortably attractive evening ambience are allied with highland ingredients of good quality here. Delicious *tamales* and pleasingly honest stews take their place alongside tasty llama and beef with sauces and homemade pastas and pizzas. Service is caring.

Information

There are several central internet places and call centers as well as a bank with ATM just off the plaza on Lavalle.

Tourist Office (☎495-5135; mun_tilcara@cootepal.com.ar; Belgrano 366; ⏰8am-9pm daily Jan-Feb, 8am-7pm Mon-Sat, 9am-noon Sun) Good information on walks and has a list of accommodation prices. It is often open Sunday afternoons despite the official hours.

Getting There & Away

The bus terminal is on the main street, Belgrano, but more services stop at the main road junction. There are services roughly every 45 minutes to Jujuy (AR$27, 1½ hours), and north to Humahuaca (AR$13, 45 minutes) and La Quiaca (AR$62, 3½ hours). Several services daily hit Purmamarca (AR$6, 30 minutes) and Salta (AR$99, 3½ hours).

Around Tilcara

Maimará, 8km south, is a typical adobe valley settlement set beneath the spectacular and aptly named Paleta del Pintor (Painter's Palette) hill. Its hillside cemetery is a surprising sight with a picturesque backdrop, but the friendly village has more to offer, with decent accommodations and a winery.

Part of a chain that ran from Lima to Buenos Aires during viceregal times, **Posta de Hornillos** (admission AR$5; ⏰8:30am-6pm) is a beautifully restored staging post 11km south of Tilcara. The interesting exhibits include leather suitcases, some impressively fierce swords and a fine 19th-century carriage.

Uquía

03887 / POP 530 / ELEV 2818M

It's not often that you imagine the heavenly hosts armed with muzzle-loading weapons, but in this roadside village's fabulous 17th-century **church** (admission by donation; 10am-noon & 2-4pm) that's just what you see. A restored collection of Cuzco-school paintings – the *ángeles arcabuceros* (arquebus-wielding angels) – features Gabriel, Uriel et al putting their trust in God but keeping their powder dry. There's also a gilt altarpiece with fine painted panels. Follow the road uphill past the church, keep going past the cemetery, and you'll reach the Quebrada de las Señoritas, with beautiful orange rock formations.

By the church, **Hostal de Uquía** (490523; Av Belgrano; d AR$260;) is a neat place with decent if saggy-bedded rooms decorated with local fabrics. At busy times, it does meals but the best lunch option is a couple of blocks uphill. **Cerro La Señorita** (Viltipoco s/n; mains AR$40-65; lunch) is a bastion of delicious home cooking and baking, with standout desserts made using fresh produce from the garden.

Humahuaca

03887 / POP 7990 / ELEV 2989M

The Quebrada's largest settlement is also its most handsome, with atmospheric cobblestoned streets, adobe houses and quaint plazas. You can feel the nearby puna here, with chilly nights, thinner air and a quiet indigenous population. Humahuaca is less altered by tourism than the towns further south, though there are good handicrafts shops, and folk musicians strum and sing in the restaurants.

Sights & Activities

Built in 1641, Humahuaca's **Iglesia de la Candelaria** (Buenos Aires) faces Plaza Gómez. Nearby, the lovably knobbly **cabildo** is famous for its clock tower, where a life-size figure of San Francisco Solano emerges at noon to deliver a benediction. From the plaza, a staircase climbs to rather vulgar **Monumento a la Independencia**.

Hasta las Manos HIKING, SANDBOARDING
(15-497-6148; juan_rumel@yahoo.com.ar) Recommended for exciting multiday treks to the Calilegua national park, with a stunning change in terrain as you descend into the subtropical forest systems. It also hires bikes and offers sandboarding at Abra Pampa, day-hikes and high-mountain excursions.

Festivals & Events

Humahuaca observes February 2 as the day of its patron, the **Virgen de Candelaria**.

Sleeping

The boutique hotel boom hasn't yet hit Humahuaca, which keeps it real with cheap family-run accommodations and a couple of midrange hotels. Prices given are for summer; they rise for Carnaval and drop for the rest of the year.

Hostal La Soñada GUESTHOUSE $
(421228; www.hostallasoniada.com; San Martín s/n; r AR$320;) Just across the tracks from the center, this is run by a kindly local couple and features spotless rooms with colorful bedspreads and good bathrooms. Breakfast is served in the attractive common area, and guests are made to feel welcome.

La Humahuacasa HOSTEL $
(15-412-0868; www.humahuacasa.com.ar; Buenos Aires 740; dm/d AR$80/250;) Artistic and welcoming, this is central and offers appealingly cozy dorms around a small patio. It's an involved, social place with a decent kitchen and a good vibe about it.

Posada La Churita GUESTHOUSE $
(421055; http://posadalachurita.webege.com; Buenos Aires 456; r per person AR$100) Run by warm-hearted and motherly Olga, this is one of a few unheated cheapies on this street. In theory the rooms – spick and span, with individual beds – are dorms, but you may well get one to yourself. Shared bathrooms are clean and hot water reliable. Guests have use of the kitchen and a common area.

Hostería Naty GUESTHOUSE $
(421022; www.hosterianaty.com.ar; Buenos Aires 488; s/d AR$240/270;) In the heart of town, this has friendly management and rooms of varying shapes and sizes at a fair price. The ones around the outside patio are quieter. Breakfast is included and there's parking round the back.

Solar de la Quebrada HOTEL $$
(☎421986; www.solardelaquebrada.com.ar; Santa Fé 450; r AR$430;) This is an attractive hostelry with characterful rooms decorated with local art: superiors are substantially more spacious for not many extra pesos. Like so many places around here, it suffers from absent owners, but nonetheless it's a decent deal with showers offering just about the best water pressure in the Quebrada.

Eating & Drinking

Most places offer a very competitive lunchtime set meal for AR$40 to AR$60.

Aisito NORTHWEST ARGENTINE $
(Buenos Aires 435; mains AR$25-55; 11am-3pm & 7-11pm) Warmly decorated and blessed with caring service, this is a pleasing option for well-priced local cuisine. Tasty baked empanadas take their place alongside well-blended stirfries and succulent llama. There's excellent live music at weekends, and nightly in summer.

Mikunayoc NORTHWEST ARGENTINE $
(cnr Corrientes & Tucumán; mains AR$40-80; 11am-3.30pm) The wide-ranging menu here includes several interesting llama dishes, cordial service and a range of empanadas which feature intriguing fillings. The salads are also a good bet. It's a pleasant, colorful place so you can forgive the odd lapses.

K'Allapurca NORTHWEST ARGENTINE $
(Belgrano 210; mains AR$28-60; 11.30am-3pm & 8-11pm;) Tasty llama stews plus pizza, pasta and more at this oversized but welcoming main street restaurant.

Casa Vieja NORTHWEST ARGENTINE $$
(cnr Buenos Aires & Salta; mains AR$60-90; 8am-11:30pm;) Perhaps better for a relaxing drink than a meal, this warm and attractive corner spot is hung with basketry and large dreamcatchers. It serves various local dishes, overpriced, but including several appealing veggie options.

Shopping

The handicrafts market, near the defunct train station, has woolen goods, souvenirs and atmosphere. Near the plaza, **Manos Andinas** (Buenos Aires 401; 8am-noon & 3:30-9pm) sells fair-trade *artesanía*.

Information

There are several central internet places. The **tourist office** (Plaza Gómez s/n; 7am-7pm Mon-Fri, 7am-noon Sat, extended hours Jan-Feb) is in the *cabildo;* there's also an ATM on this plaza. The tourist office on the highway is shut, but young rascals outside sell pamphlets that the other office gives out free.

Getting There & Away

The **bus terminal** (cnr Belgrano & Entre Ríos) is three blocks south of the plaza. There are regular buses to Salta (AR$117, 4½ hours), Jujuy (AR$40, 2¼ hours), and La Quiaca (AR$40, three hours). There are three to four daily buses to Iruya (AR$40, three hours).

Iruya

☎03887 / POP 1070 / ELEV 2780M

There's something magical about Iruya, a remote village just 50km from the main road but a world away in other respects. It makes a great destination for a few days for proper appreciation of the Quebrada de Humahuaca region away from the highway. There's some epic hiking around the town.

The journey is worthwhile in itself. Turning off RN9, 26km north of Humahuaca, the *ripio* road ascends to a spectacular 4000m pass at the Jujuy–Salta provincial boundary. Here, there's a massive *apacheta* (travelers' cairn). Plastic bottles are from liquid offerings to the Pachamama.

You then wind down into another spectacular valley and eventually reach Iruya, with its pretty yellow-and-blue church, steep streets, adobe houses and spectacular mountainscapes (with soaring condors). It's an indigenous community with fairly traditional values, so respect is called for. Chatting with the friendly locals is a highlight here, as is the excellent hiking in the surrounding mountains and valleys. Local guides are available. It's also worth visiting other communities in the valley, such as pretty San Isidro.

There's a bank with ATM and an internet place, both on San Martín.

Sleeping

There are many cheap accommodations in people's homes, costing AR$35 to AR$50 per person in a private room.

Milmahuasi HOSTEL $
(☎15-445-7994; www.milmahuasi.com; Salta s/n; dm/s/d AR$100/280/400;) This hostel

and guesthouse is brilliantly run by people with a real passion for Iruya. Well-travelled Víctor can explain anything from the best hikes to the local geology: ask about the wifi project. Both dorms and private rooms are spotless and rustically attractive, with great comfortable mattresses. Good breakfast is included, and evening vegetarian specials are offered, plus chats on the cultural background. HI discount.

Federico III HOTEL $
(☎15-629152; www.complejofedericoiii.com.ar; cnr San Martín & Salta; r per person AR$150) Just above the plaza at the bottom of town; this has pretty, heated whitewashed rooms around a little courtyard. You can grab a room with a view; those without compensate with a TV. There's also a bar and restaurant, and it runs a pretty campsite (AR$15 per person) across the river.

Hostería Iruya HOTEL $$
(☎482002; www.hoteliruya.com; San Martín 641; s/d AR$600/770, with view AR$750/870; wi-fi) At the top of the town, this place has simple light white rooms with wide beds, a spacious common area and a picturesque stone terrace with memorable views. It's worth the extra cash for the big-windowed rooms with valley vistas. There's a decent restaurant.

Eating

Several simple eateries serve local cuisine. By far the best is **Comedor Iruya** (Comedor Tina; ☎15-404-3606; cnr Lavalle & San Martín; dishes AR$25-40; ⏱lunch & dinner), on the road about 500m before town. Here, genial Juan and Tina serve delicious home-style meat and salad dishes in a cozy atmosphere.

Getting There & Away

Buses from Humahuaca (AR$40, three hours) leave three to four times daily; there is also a daily bus from Tilcara (AR$53, four hours) and other connecting services.

The *ripio* road often becomes impassable in summer due to rain. You'll often see villagers hitchhiking – a good way to meet locals.

La Quiaca

☎03885 / POP 13,800 / ELEV 3442M

Truly the end of the line, La Quiaca is 5171km north of Ushuaia, and a major crossing point to Bolivia. It's a cold, windy place that has decent places to stay, but little to detain you.

BOLIVIA VIA LA QUIACA

Crossing from La Quiaca to Villazón, Bolivia, walk, taxi or bus it to the bridge, then walk across, clearing **immigration** (⏱24 hours). Bolivia is much nicer than Villazón promises, so head past the cut-price stalls and straight to the bus terminal or train station. Cheap but reliable accommodation options are by the bus terminal and the plaza if you need. Buses and minibuses head to Tupiza (1½ hours),La Paz (20 hours) and elsewhere. The train station (www.fca.com.bo for timetables) is 1.5km north of the border crossing, with four weekly services to Tupiza (three hours), Uyuni (six hours) and Oruro (13 hours). Bolivia is one hour behind northern Argentina. For a quick Villazón visit, clear Argentine immigration but don't get stamped into Bolivia. La Quiaca has a Bolivian consulate.

After leaving the Quebrada de Humahuaca, paved RN 9 passes through **Abra Pampa**, a forlorn windy town 90km north of Humahuaca, and climbs through picturesque and typical altiplano landscapes. Look for the endangered vicuña off main routes.

La Quiaca is divided by its defunct train tracks; most services are west of them. North of town, a bridge crosses the river to Villazón, Bolivia.

Sleeping & Eating

Hostel El Apolillo HOSTEL $
(☎422388; www.elapolillohostel.blogspot.com; Árabe Siria 146; dm/d AR$70/250; @wi-fi) This traveler's rest is conscientiously run by a cordial couple, and has a colorful patio, comfortable dorms, good kitchen area, and a very cozy en-suite private room. It makes an ecological effort, with solar heating and other sustainable practices, and there's a pool table.

Copacabana Hostel GUESTHOUSE $
(☎423875; www.hostelcopacabana.com.ar; Pellegrini 141; r per person without bathroom AR$75; @wi-fi) Across the tracks and a block up the street with the Banco de la Nación on the corner, this place offers small, rather sweet heated pink rooms with shared bathroom and amiable staff. Ongoing renovations will

add more rooms and facilities. Handily, the staff can reserve Bolivian trains for you. HI discount.

Hostería Munay HOTEL $
(☎423924; www.munayhotel.com.ar; Belgrano 51; s/d AR$240/360; 📶) Set back from the pedestrian street (you can still drive in), this is a decent option with heated rooms decorated with *artesanía*. You can often negotiate a discount. It's not wonderful but it's the best hotel in town.

Hotel de Turismo HOTEL $
(☎423390; laquiacahotel@gmail.com; cnr Árabe Siria & San Martín; s/d AR$230/330; @📶) In decline but acceptable, this hotel offers adequate heated rooms with parquet floors and decent bathrooms. The restaurant (mains AR$40 to AR$80) is the town's most reliable eating option.

Information

Change money on the Bolivian side of the border or at the bus terminal. Call centers and internet places abound.

Banco Macro (Árabe Siria 441) Has an ATM.

Information Kiosk (Av España s/n; ⏲10am-1pm & 4-8pm) Run by a hostel, this offers decent information opposite the bus terminal.

Tourist Office (☎422644; turismo@laquiaca.com.ar; ⏲7am-7pm) Branches at the border, and at the southern entrance to town. Often shut.

Getting There & Away

The chaotic **bus terminal** (cnr Belgrano & España) has frequent connections to Jujuy (AR$70, four to five hours), Salta (AR$150, 7 hours), and good-value services to Buenos Aires (AR$520, 28 hours). There is no transportation to Bolivia, but a few Argentine long-distance buses leave directly from Villazón's bus station.

Yavi

☎03885 / POP 210 / ELEV 3440M

Picturesque, indigenous Yavi, 16km east of La Quiaca via paved RP 5, is a great detour and lazy little hideaway, with the tumbledown romanticism of its adobe streets and two fascinating colonial-era buildings.

Sights & Activities

Local walks can take you to even smaller, rural Yavi Chico or along the river to see cave paintings. A longer excursion takes you to pretty Laguna Colorada.

★ **Iglesia de Yavi** CHURCH
(Marqués Campero s/n; admission by donation; ⏲9am-1pm & 2-6pm) Built by the local marquis in the late 17th century, Yavi's intriguing church – one of northern Argentina's most fascinating – preserves stunning altarpieces in sober baroque style, covered in gold leaf and adorned with excellent paintings and sculptures, mostly from the Cuzco school. The translucent onyx windows also stand out.

Casa del Marqués Campero MUSEUM
(Marqués Campero s/n; admission AR$5; ⏲8am-1pm & 2-6:30pm) The house of the marquis who built the church in the late 17th century is now a museum. It displays beautifully restored furniture, exhibits on puna life and a charming library.

Sleeping & Eating

As well as a decent campground by the museum (AR$20 per person), Yavi has several simple places to stay.

La Casona HOSTEL $
(☎422316; mccalizaya@hotmail.com; cnr Pérez & San Martín; dm/d AR$50/220) Simple but likeable, this has gnarled wooden floors and rustic rooms with stoves for winter nights.

Hostería Pachamá GUESTHOUSE $
(☎423235; www.pachamahosteria.net; cnr Pérez & RN5; s/d AR$100/200) At the entrance to town, with rather charming rooms set around an adobe courtyard, and a pretty eating area.

Getting There & Away

Remises (AR$12, 20 minutes) run to Yavi from La Quiaca's Mercado Municipal on Hipólito Yrigoyen; departures are much more frequent in the early morning. Otherwise, it's AR$70 in a taxi.

TUCUMÁN & AROUND

Though the country's second-smallest province, Tucumán has played a significant role in Argentina's story. It was here that independence was first declared, and its massive sugar industry is of great economic importance.

Tucumán city is full of heat and energy, in complete contrast to the lung-cleansing air of Tafí del Valle, up in the hills to the west. Beyond, Argentina's most important pre-Columbian site is Quilmes, on the Cafayate road. South of Tucumán, Santiago del Estero is a backwater with an enjoyably sleepy feel.

Tucumán

0381 / POP 967,000 / ELEV 420M

Baking hot, energetic and brash, (San Miguel de) Tucumán, the cradle of Argentine independence, is the nation's sixth-largest city and feels like it, with a metropolitan bustle that can come as quite a shock after the other, more genteel, northwestern provincial capitals. You may prefer it at night, when the fumes and heat of the day have lulled, and cafes and bars come to life.

Tucumán's blue-collar feel and down-to-earthness is complemented by a lively cultural scene, steps ahead of its serene neighbors. There's world-class paragliding and hang-gliding in the hills west of town.

History

Founded in 1565, Tucumán distinguished itself when it hosted the congress that declared Argentine independence in 1816. Unlike other northwestern colonial cities, Tucumán successfully reoriented its economy after independence. At the southern end of the sugarcane zone, it was close enough to Buenos Aires to take advantage of the capital's growing market. By 1874 the railway reached the city, permitting easy transportation and rapid growth. Economic crises have hit hard in the past but sugarcane's growing use as a fuel source means there's plenty of optimism about the future.

Sights

Casa de la Independencia MUSEUM
(Casa Histórica; Congreso 151; adult/child AR$10/free; 10am-6pm, to 7pm late Jul) Unitarist lawyers and clerics declared Argentina's independence from Spain on July 9, 1816, in this late-colonial mansion (although the Federalists boycotted the proceedings). Portraits of the signatories line the walls of the original room. There's plenty of information in Spanish on the lead-up to these seismic events, and English guided tours (free) are available.

There's a sound-and-light show nightly except Thursday; entry is AR$10/5 per adult/child. Get tickets at the tourist office.

Alongside the building are areas with handicrafts stalls and stands selling traditional foods.

Museo Folclórico Manuel Belgrano MUSEUM
(Av 24 de Septiembre 565; 9am-1pm & 5-9pm Tue-Fri, 5-9pm Sat & Sun) FREE Occupying a colonial house, this pleasant museum features a good collection of traditional gaucho gear, indigenous musical instruments (check out the armadillo *charangos*) and weavings, as well as some pottery.

Casa Padilla MUSEUM
(25 de Mayo 36; 9am-12:30pm & 4:30-8:30pm, 4:30-8:30pm Sat & Sun) FREE Alongside the Casa de Gobierno, this partly-restored mid-19th-century house belonged to provincial governor José Frías (1792–1874), then to his mayor son-in-law Ángel Padilla. European art, Chinese porcelain and period furniture make up the collection.

Tours

Tour operators offer excursions from sedate city strolls to canoeing, challenging hikes and paragliding; the city has hosted the Paragliding World Cup. Most paragliding operators are based in San Javier in the hills to the west. The tourist office can supply a fuller list. One worthwhile hike is the beautiful 72km trek from Tucumán to Tafí del Valle. Many do it in three days, but it's mostly uphill, so four is more relaxed. Find waypoints on www.wikiloc.com (search for Yerba Buena-Tafí).

Montañas Tucumanas OUTDOOR ACTIVITIES
(15-467-1860; www.montanastucumanas.com) A cordial, professional setup offering hiking, climbing, canyoning, rappelling and more.

Tucumán Parapente PARAGLIDING
(15-444-7508; www.tucumanparapente.com.ar) Excellent tandem paragliding flights over the Yungas forests, as well as instruction. One of many operators.

Turismo del Tucumán TOUR
(422-7636; www.turismodeltucuman.com; Crisóstomo Álvarez 360) Guided trips to spots of interest around the province, including the Yungas circuit (AR$175), Tafí del Valle (AR$250) and Quilmes (AR$375).

Walter 'Paco' Castro PARAGLIDING
(pacoflight@hotmail.com) A reader-recommended hang-gliding instructor offering tandem flights.

Festivals & Events

Celebrations of the **Día de la Independencia** (Argentina's Independence Day) on July 9 are vigorous. *Tucumanos* (people who live in Tucumán) also celebrate the **Batalla de**

Tucumán

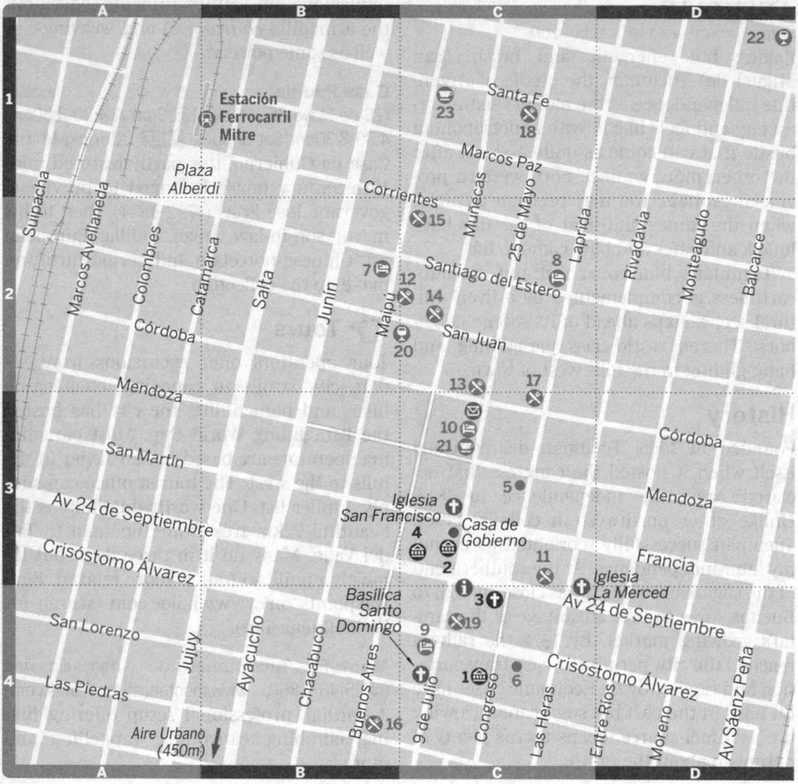

Tucumán (Battle of Tucumán) on September 24.

Sleeping

A La Gurda HOSTEL $

(☎497-6275; www.lagurdahostel.com.ar; Maipú 490; dm/s/d AR$80/190/280; ❄@📶) Upstairs in a lovely old house, this very pleasant hostel offers ten-bed dorms with lockers and ok-value private bunk rooms with air-con. There's a pool table and excellent bathroom facilities, bar service and a kitchen; everything's spotless. Management is helpful and friendly.

Casa Calchaquí GUESTHOUSE $

(☎425-6974; www.casacalchaqui.com; Lola Mora 92, Yerba Buena; s/d/q AR$250/350/550; ❄@📶🏊) Six kilometers west of the center in the upmarket barrio of Yerba Buena, this is a welcome retreat. Comfortably rustic rooms surround a relaxing garden space complete with hammocks, bar service and mini-pool. Yerba Buena has good restaurants and nightlife. Grab a taxi (AR$35) or bus 102 or 118 from opposite the bus terminal.

The street is off Av Aconquija (at 1100): the Banco Galicia is on the corner. They also have bikes for hire. Ask about their rustic cabins in a spectacular off-piste setting near Amaicha del Valle.

★ **Tucumán Center** HOTEL $$

(☎452-5555; www.tucumancenterhotel.com.ar; 25 de Mayo 230; s/d AR$690/780; ❄@📶🏊) It's hard to fault this upmarket, business-class hotel bang in the center. Service and facilities – including an outdoor pool and access to a proper gym just down the road – are first-rate, and the huge beds are mighty comfortable. Suites come with space to spare and a bathtub with bubbles. This place offers excellent value.

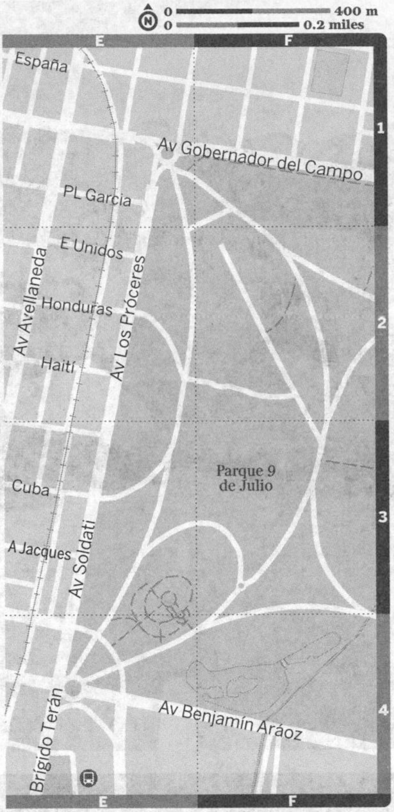

Tucumán

Sights

1 Casa de la Independencia C4
2 Casa Padilla C3
3 Catedral C4
4 Museo Folclórico Manuel Belgrano C3

Activities, Courses & Tours

5 Montañas Tucumanas C3
6 Turismo del Tucumán C4

Sleeping

7 Λ La Gurda B2
8 Amerian Tucumán C2
9 Hotel Premier C4
10 Tucumán Center C3

Eating

11 El Portal C3
12 Fon C2
13 Il Postino C2
14 La Leñita C2
15 La Sirio-Libanesa C2
16 Lotos B4
17 Mi Nueva Estancia C3
18 Setimio C1
19 Shitake C4

Drinking & Nightlife

20 Costumbres Argentinas C2
21 Filipo C3
22 La Casa de Yamil D1
23 Plaza de Almas C1

Aire Urbano BOUTIQUE HOTEL $$

(☎424-2397; www.aireurbano.com; Ayacucho 681; s/d standard AR$538/650, d superior AR$725;) A few blocks south of the center opposite a plaza, this small oasis is a welcome find. There's a pool, sauna and Jacuzzi out on the grassy patio and a tastefully decorated lounge area. Rooms are great; all feature king beds. Superior rooms are larger and come complete with their own hydromassage tub.

Amerian Tucumán HOTEL $$

(☎430-0100; www.amerian.com; Santiago del Estero 425; s/d AR$763/835;) Modern and efficient, this offers good-sized comfortable modern rooms with king beds and large flatscreens. Windows are double-glazed to help with the noise, and facilities include pillow menu, netbooks to lend and a small gym. Staff are generally excellent.

Hotel Premier HOTEL $$

(☎431-0381; www.hotelpremier.com.ar; Crisóstomo Álvarez 510; s/d AR$350/430;) A block off the square, this modernized hotel is a decent deal, particularly if you can bag a better online rate. The renovated rooms are spacious, with flatscreen TV, comfortable queen beds and town views. The aircon sometimes struggles with the Tucumán heat. The on-site restaurant is worthwhile.

Eating

Tucumán is famous for its excellent eggy empanadas, which you'll find everywhere.

★ **Mi Nueva Estancia** PARRILLA $

(☎430-7049; Córdoba 401; mains AR$50-75; lunch & dinner;) Delicious! That's the verdict on the cuts of meat at this popular grill restaurant, but the salad bar and other menu choices also win points. Value is great here for both quality and quantity, and service is friendly and efficient.

MICHAEL TAYLOR/GETTY IMAGES ©

1. Indigenous culture
The Andean Northwest is Argentina's richest zone in which to explore pre-Columbian culture

2. Quebrada de Cafayate (p241)
A wild and spectacular landscape is carved out by the Río de las Conchas.

3. Iglesia San Francisco (p224)
Salta's most striking landmark is topped by a slender tower.

4. Purmamarca (p247)
A picturesque village watched over by a striking *cerro* (hill).

DAMIEN SIMONIS/GETTY IMAGES ©

OLIVIER CIRENDINI/GETTY IMAGES ©

El Portal NORTHWESTERN ARGENTINE $
(☎422-6024; www.empanadaselportal.com.ar; Av 24 de Septiembre 351; empanadas AR$6, mains AR$60; ⏲10am-11pm) Half a block east of Plaza Independencia, this rustic indoor/outdoor eatery has a tiny but perfectly formed menu, based around empanadas, *locro* and the like. Delicious and authentic.

La Sirio-Libanesa MIDDLE EASTERN $
(Maipú 575; set menu for 1/2 AR$52/80-95; ⏲11am-3pm & 8pm-midnight; ✎) The restaurant at the Syrian-Lebanese society offers tasty Levantine cuisine that makes a welcome change of scene. Mashed eggplant, tasty *kipe naye* (marinated raw mincemeat) and tabouleh salad all feature; there are several set menus, as well as à la carte.

Il Postino PIZZA, PASTA $
(cnr 25 de Mayo & Córdoba; pizza & pasta AR$42-70; ⏲7am-2am; ✎) Pizza and pasta are served with panache in this atmospheric brick warehouse eatery. It's popular with everyone, and you often have to wait for a table. It's worth it: the standard (of the pizza especially) is sky-high. It also serves tapas-sized snacks. There's another branch nearby at Junín 86.

Fon VEGETARIAN $
(Maipú 435; buffet AR$45; ⏲noon-3:30pm Mon-Sat; ✎) The lunchtime buffet at this vegetarian restaurant has mostly Chinese dishes, with a few local favorites such as *ensalada rusa* (Russian salad) and empanadas thrown in. It's not gourmet, but it does the job. Similar veggie restaurants can be found at Buenos Aires 294 (**Lotos** (Buenos Aires 294; ⏲11am-3pm Mon-Sat; ✎)) and 9 de Julio 86 (**Shitake** (9 de Julio 86; ⏲lunch Mon-Sat; ✎)).

La Leñita PARRILLA $$
(☎422-9196; San Juan 633; mains AR$60-100; ⏲11am-3.30pm & 8pm-1am) One of the better *parrilla* restaurants around in this part of the world, this stands out for service and the good quality of the meat. Try *picana* (rump steak) or the delicious *mollejitas* (sweetbreads). Staff sing *folklore* music halfway through the night.

Setimio ARGENTINE $$$
(☎431-2792; www.setimio.com; Santa Fe 512; dishes AR$70-120; ⏲food 7:30pm-1:30am Mon-Wed, to 2am Thu-Sat) Wall-to-wall bottles decorate this smart wine shop and restaurant, whose menu features Spanish-style tapas, lots of salads, and well-prepared fish dishes among other gourmet toothsome delights. Several wines are available by the glass, and you can pick any of the several hundred bottles from the shelves for a small corkage fee. It opens as a wine shop in the mornings.

Drinking & Nightlife

From Thursday to Saturday nights, the action is in the Abasto region, on Calle Lillo. Follow San Lorenzo west from the town center, and you'll hit the middle of the zone. There are dozens of bars and nightclubs – take your pick. Other *boliches* can be found in Yerba Buena, 6km west of the town center.

Filipo CAFE
(Mendoza 501; licuados AR$27; ⏲7am-1am Mon-Thu, 7am-3am Fri-Sat, 8am-1am Sun) Glasses gleaming on the gantry, outdoor tables and bow-tied waiters make this a great cafe. Top espresso, prize-worthy apple *licuados* (blended fruit drinks), and beer served as if it were Bollinger are the highlights.

Plaza de Almas CAFE
(www.plazadealmas.com; Maipú 791; mains AR$40-70; ⏲8pm-late) This intimate and engaging multilevel place is popular with under-40 *tucumanos* and is one of the best of the city's many combination cafe-bar-restaurant-cultural centers. The short but interesting menu offers a range of kebabs and salads, among other international-style choices.

Costumbres Argentinas BAR
(www.facebook.com/costumbresargentinas.bar; San Juan 666; ⏲9:30pm-4am Wed-Sun) Though the address seems like a contradiction in terms, this unusual, popular and welcoming bar has an arty bohemian vibe and sometimes puts on live music. The big two-level beer garden is the place to be on summer nights. Simple food is also available.

La Casa de Yamil LIVE MUSIC
(☎422-8487; http://lacasadeyamil.com.ar; España 153; ⏲live music dinner Fri & Sat, lunch Sun) This untouristy *parrilla* is very popular for its Friday and Saturday night live *folklore* music; there's also a Sunday lunchtime session. The food's good, and there are plenty of traditional northwestern dishes such as *tamales* to try.

Information

Tucumán is bristling with internet cafes and call centers, and downtown ATMs.

Hospital Padilla (☎429-0969; Alberdi 550)

Tourist Office (☎430-3644; www.tucumanturismo.gob.ar; Av 24 de Septiembre 484; ⏲8am-10pm Mon-Fri, 9am-9pm Sat & Sun) On the plaza, helpful and knowledgeable. There's another office in the shopping center at the bus terminal, open the same hours.

Getting There & Away

AIR

Aerolíneas (☎431-1030; www.aerolineas.com.ar; 9 de Julio 110; ⏲9am-1pm & 5-8pm Mon-Fri, 9am-12:30pm Sat) and **LAN** (☎422-0606; www.lan.com; San Juan 426; ⏲9am-1pm & 5-8pm Mon-Fri) fly several times daily to Buenos Aires.

BUS

Tucumán's **bus terminal** (☎400-2000; Brígido Terán 350; 📶) is a major affair with 60 platforms and plenty of shops and services. The bus information booth is outside, by the supermarket.

Buses from Tucumán

DESTINATION	COST (AR$)	DURATION (HR)
Buenos Aires	623	15-17
Cafayate	138	6½
Catamarca	116	3½
Córdoba	300	7-9
Jujuy	174	5
La Quiaca	318	9-11
La Rioja	195	6
Mendoza	515	13-15
Puerto Iguazú	630	21
Resistencia	398	11-12
Salta	156	4¼
Salvador Mazza	319	12
Santiago del Estero	68	2
Tafí del Valle	48	2½-3

TRAIN

Argentina's trains aren't what they used to be, but Tucumán is still connected to Buenos Aires (via Santiago del Estero and Rosario) twice a week from the beautiful **Estación Mitre** (☎430-9220; www.ferrocentralsa.com.ar; Pl Alberdi s/n) in the northwest of town. Services frequently take hours longer than advertised, visibility isn't great, food is ordinary, hygiene is low, but it's an old-fashioned experience that might appeal to those who are in no hurry or are on a strict budget. Because it's so cheap, it books up well in advance.

At time of research, trains were leaving Buenos Aires' Retiro station at 7:30am on Monday and Friday for the 27-hour journey. From Tucumán, trains left at 5pm on Wednesday and 7.40pm on Saturday.

The trip costs AR$45/70/130 in *turista* (2nd class)/1st class/Pullman (reclinable seats) or AR$800 for two in a sleeper. There's a bar/restaurant on the train.

Getting Around

Aeropuerto Benjamín Matienzo is 8km east of downtown. Bus 121 and 124 head there from the terminal; a *remise* costs around AR$60 from the town center.

For getting around the city, local buses (AR$3.50) clearly mark their major destinations on the front.

There are several car-rental places, including multinationals. A reliable choice is **Móvil Renta** (☎431-0550; www.movilrenta.com.ar; San Lorenzo 370).

Tafí del Valle

☎03867 / POP 3300 / ELEV 2100M

This lovely hill town is where Tucumán folk traditionally head to take refuge from the summer heat. The journey is a spectacular one: a narrow river gorge with dense subtropical forest on all sides opens onto a misty valley beneath the snowy peaks of the Sierra del Aconquija. The precipitous mountain road merits a window seat.

Tafí makes a fine spot to hang out for a few days, with crisp mountain air, many budget accommodations and a laid-back scene. There are also memorable historic ranches to stay at.

Sights & Activities

Several people around town hire out horses (look for *'alquilo caballos'* or *'cabalgatas'*) for rides in the valley. The tourist office can give you details of the **Ruta del Artesano**, with a number of visitable handicraft workshops in and around town. Download the pdf from www.tucumanturismo.gov.ar.

Capilla La Banda CHURCH, MUSEUM

(Av José Frías Silva; admission AR$10; ⏲8am-6pm) This 18th-century Jesuit chapel, acquired by the Frías Silva family of Tucumán after the Jesuits' expulsion and then expanded in the 1830s, was restored to its original configuration in the 1970s. Note the escape tunnel under the altar. A small collection of funerary urns, Cuzco-school religious art,

DAY-TRIPPING FROM TUCUMÁN

The fertile, hilly area northwest of Tucumán is known as **Las Yungas**, and offers plenty of appealing day trips to get you out of the hot, busy city. The tourist offices offer good information on destinations like the reservoir of **El Cadillal**, offering camping, swimming, a 'ski-lift' and windsurfing, or the **Parque Sierra de San Javier**, a university-operated reserve offering guided walks. El Simoqueño (ticket booth 3) runs regular buses from Tucumán's bus terminal to El Cadillal (AR$9, one hour), while BerBus (no ticket booth, leaves from platforms 57 to 59; AR$11 to AR$20) runs to San Javier (where there are a few places to stay) and the reserve. Tour operators also run trips out here and this is the paragliding area.

ecclesiastical vestments and period furniture is displayed.

The chapel is a short walk from downtown. Cross the river bridge and you'll see it on your left after 750m.

Walks around Tafí HIKING

Hiking in the mountains around Tafí is an attractive prospect. An easy, well-marked hike climbs **Cerro El Pelao** for views over the town. The path starts on the left as soon as you've crossed the bridge. It takes about 1¼ hours to climb. From the same road you can walk a pleasant 10km to **El Mollar**, following the river and the reservoir, visit the menhir park and get the bus back.

Other hills include 3000m **Matadero**, a four- to five-hour climb; 3600m **Pabellón** (six hours); and 4500m **El Negrito**, reached from the statue of Cristo Redentor on RN 307 to Acheral. Trails are badly marked, and no maps available; you can hire guides: ask at the tourist office.

You can walk from here to Tucumán (p257).

Sleeping

There are many choices. Prices rise in January when Tafí gets packed. Unheated rooms can get distinctly chilly any time of year.

Nomade Hostel HOSTEL $
(☎15-307-5922; www.nomadehostel.com.ar; Los Castaños s/n; dm/d incl dinner AR$100/250; @ wi-fi) Relaxed and welcoming, a 10-minute walk from the bus terminal. Turn right, follow the road round the bend, and veer right. Rates include breakfast and tasty home-cooked dinners. Atmosphere here is excellent. HI discount.

Hotel Virgen del Valle HOTEL $
(☎421016; virgendelvalle@tafidelvalle.com; Los Menhires s/n; d AR$360; ❄ @ wi-fi) Just off the main drag in the heart of town, this features spacious, comfortable rooms around a small courtyard. It's not luxury but it's a good deal at this price.

Hospedaje Celia GUESTHOUSE $
(☎421170; Belgrano 443; r per person AR$90) Set back from the road 100m uphill from the church, offers bright, white and comfortable rooms in a tranquil setting with heating and private bathroom. There are inconveniences – no sockets, for example – but staff will charge things for you and the price is right.

Camping Los Sauzales CAMPGROUND $
(☎421880; lossauzales@tafidelvalle.com; Los Palenques s/n; per person/tent AR$20/25, per car AR$15-25) Run-down but pleasant grassy campsite about 750m west of the plaza. Also has simple cabins and bungalows (AR$100 to AR$175).

★ **Estancia Las Carreras** ESTANCIA $$
(☎421473; www.estancialascarreras.com; RP325 Km13, Las Carreras; d AR$750; wi-fi) In a visually striking location, surrounded by hills great for hiking and horse-riding, this spot offers only the lowing of cattle to disturb the tranquility. An historic Jesuit ranch and working farm and cheese factory, it offers superb accommodations in this characterful 18th century complex. Public areas are wonderful too, and there are few better bases for relaxation in this part of Argentina. It's 13km from Tafí in the village of Las Carreras.

★ **Estancia Los Cuartos** ESTANCIA $$
(☎15-587-4230; www.estancialoscuartos.com; Av Critto s/n; d AR$470-540; @ wi-fi) Oozing character from every pore, this lovely spot with grazing llamas lies between the bus terminal and town center. Two centuries old, it feels like a museum, with venerable books lining antique shelves, and authentic rooms redolent with the smell of aged wood and woolen blankets but with great modern bathrooms. Newer rooms offer less history but remain true to the feel of the place. Traditional cheeses are also made here.

Las Tacanas ESTANCIA $$
(☎421821; www.estancialastacanas.com; Perón 372; d AR$780; @ 📶) Impeccably preserved and decorated, this fabulous historic complex in the center of town – but feeling like a rural retreat – was once a Jesuit *estancia* and is a memorable place to stay. Adobe buildings, more than three centuries old, house a variety of tasteful, rustic rooms with noble furniture and beamed ceilings. Don't expect modern luxury: it's the character and history that you're paying for.

Hostería Lunahuana HOTEL $$
(☎421330; www.lunahuana.com.ar; Av Critto 540; s/d AR$575/805; @ 📶) This stylish and popular hotel has rooms decorated with flair – some have mezzanines accessed by spiral staircases. The whole place is decked out with interesting and tasteful decorations, and service is professional and friendly.

Descanso de las Piedras CABIN $$
(☎15-570-1266; www.descansodelaspiedras.com; Madre Teresa de Calcuta s/n; s/d/q AR$350/550/950; 📶) Welcoming and social, these cute cabins and rooms surround a grassy area with solar-heated pool, vegetable garden, ducks and llamas, and a burbling stream. It's a relaxing retreat a twenty-minute walk from the center and a great option for families, with cabins sleeping up to seven available. Cross the bridge and follow the signs. Cheaper off-season.

Hotel Tafí HOTEL $$
(☎421007; www.hoteltafiweb.com.ar; Belgrano 177; s/d AR$430/540; 📶) Reliable option with a ski-lodge feel and helpful staff. The medium-sized rooms have gleaming bathrooms, wood-tile floors and mountain views. There's a pleasant rocky garden, and the huge fireplace makes the comfortable lounge area the place to be on a chilly night.

Eating & Drinking

The eating scene is along Perón. Try the tasty local Kkechuwa artisanal beers.

El Rancho de Félix NORTHWESTERN $
(www.ranchodefelix.com.ar; cnr Belgrano & Perón; mains AR$40-65; ⏲11am-3.30pm & 7-11pm; 📶) This big, warm thatched barn of a place is incredibly popular for lunch. Regional specialties such as *locro* and *humitas* feature heavily on the menu, but *parrilla* and pasta are also on offer. It sometimes doesn't open evenings if things are quiet in town.

Don Pepito PARRILLA $$
(www.donpepitodetafi.com.ar; Perón 193; mains AR$45-95; ⏲11am-3.30pm & 7.30pm-midnight) It looks touristy, the level of service varies, and it charges too much for extras, but the meat is truly excellent. Bypass the set *parrilladas* and order off the menu. Kidneys, *bife de chorizo* or *chivito* (goat) are all fine choices and are served in generous portions. There's often live entertainment (small surcharge).

Orientation

Tafí's center is a triangle of three streets. Av Critto is the main drag. If you turn left out of the bus terminal, you're following it into the center. Off it, Perón is the center of activity, and Belgrano climbs from Perón past the church.

Information

Several places offer phone calls and internet access.

Banco Tucumán (cnr Av Critto & Perón) ATM.

Casa del Turista (☎15-643-8337; Los Faroles s/n; ⏲8am-10pm) On the pedestrian street.

Getting There & Away

Tafí's **bus terminal** (☎421025; Av Critto) is 400m east of the center. Aconquija has six to nine buses a day to Tucumán (AR$50, three hours). Buses head the other way to Santa María (AR$55, two hours, four to five daily) and Cafayate (AR$80, 3½ hours, two to five daily) via Amaicha del Valle and the Quilmes ruins turnoff.

The road from Tucumán is beautiful, and the road to Santa María, Quilmes and Cafayate is scenic, crossing the 3050m pass known as Abra del Infiernillo (Little Hell Pass).

Around Tafí del Valle

A beautiful circular drive or cycle is a circuit of the valley (some 47km). Highlights include standout views and the Jesuit *estancia*, hotel and cheese factory of Las Carreras (p264) (guided visits AR$15 including coffee; visit at 5pm to see the milking). At pretty El Mollar, at the other end of the valley from Tafí, you can visit the **Parque de los Menhires** (Plaza s/n, El Mollar; ⏲9am-7pm Tue-Fri, 2-7pm Sat & Sun) FREE on the plaza, a collection of more than 100 carved standing stones found in the surrounding area. They were produced by the Tafí culture some 2000 years ago.

Tour companies in Tafí run mediocre excursions round this circuit (AR$200). If there's more than one of you, a remise will do it for less. Aconquija buses head to El Mollar, and also to Las Carreras. The final stop on the Las Carreras route is El Rincón, from where a 4km downhill walk will take you to El Mollar, allowing you to do the full valley circuit.

Santa María

☎03838 / POP 10,800 / ELEV 1900M

Actually within Catamarca province, this fine stopover between Tafí del Valle and Cafayate, and is a handy base for the Quilmes ruins.

The attractive plaza, nine blocks north of the bus terminal, is the center of town. A helpful **tourist office** (☎421083; www.santamariadeyokavil.com.ar; Pl General Belgrano s/n; ⏲7am-11pm Mon-Fri, 8am-11pm Sat & Sun), with heroic opening hours, is located under the trees in the square itself. On one corner of the plaza, the recommended **Museo Arqueológico Eric Boman** (cnr Belgrano & Sarmiento; ⏲9am-1pm & 6-8pm Mon-Fri, 10am-1pm & 6-8pm Sat) FREE has a worthwhile collection of ceramics and gold and silver grave jewelry from this important archaeological zone. Ask to see the back room, where a whole lot more elaborately decorated funerary urns are stored. Next door is an **artesanía cooperative**, selling woven goods and other handicrafts at more-than-fair prices.

There are many places to stay in town, including welcoming **Residencial Pérez** (☎420257; hotelperez@hotmail.com; San Martín 94; s/d AR$120/200), with spotless rooms set around a viney courtyard behind a cafe near the plaza (no sign).

There are several buses daily to Tucumán (AR$113, five hours) via Tafí del Valle (AR$55, two hours) and two daily to Cafayate (AR$43, two hours) via Quilmes. Several buses and minibuses a week go to Belén (AR$70, four hours). *Remises* from the terminal to the center cost AR$7.

Amaicha del Valle

☎03892 / POP 3210

On the main road between Tafí del Valle and Cafayate, this dusty settlement has an indigenous feel and, indeed, is famous for its **Pachamama festival** in February, which includes music, dancing and a llama sacrifice to bless the harvest. Ornate and unusual **Museo de Pachamama** (admission AR$30; ⏲8:30am-6:30pm Mon-Sat) combines a picturesque collection of indigenous art and artifacts with the sculpture and tapestries of the artist who designed the striking indoor-outdoor building.

Amaicha is useful for getting to the ruins at Quilmes, and has several places to stay, including hostels and campgrounds. Buses between Tafí (AR$51, 1½ hours) and Cafayate (AR$40, 1½ to 2½ hours) stop here.

Quilmes

☎03892

Dating from about AD1000, **Quilmes** (admission AR$20; ⏲8am-7pm) was a complex indigenous urban settlement that occupied about 30 hectares and housed as many as 5000 people. The Diaguita inhabitants survived contact with the Inca, which occurred from about AD 1480 onward, but could not outlast the siege of the Spaniards, who in 1667 deported the remaining 2000 people to Buenos Aires.

Quilmes' thick walls underscore its defensive purpose, but clearly this was more than just a *pucará* (walled city). Dense construction radiates from the central nucleus. For revealing views of the extent of the ruins, climb as high as you can; there are trails on either side up to the remains of watchtowers that also offer great perspectives. Be prepared for intense sun with no shade, and a large fly population keen on exploring your facial orifices.

Legal battles between the Diaguita community and the government mean the hotel and restaurant are long closed, but the museum at the site is due to reopen: just as well, for it's difficult to interpret the ruins without it. Friendly folk selling local ceramics sell cold drinks and will look after your bags; there's also a place at the main road junction that will do it.

Getting There & Away

Buses between Cafayate and Santa María or Tafí drop off at the junction; from there it's a 5km walk or hitchhike to the ruins. Otherwise, get off at Amaicha del Valle, where a *remise* will charge around AR$100 one-way to the ruins: bargain to get a decent price including waiting time. Often a few people want to go, so you can share costs. A *remise* from Cafayate or Santa María is also inexpensive and tours to Quilmes run from Cafayate and Tafí.

Santiago del Estero

☎0385 / POP 360,900

Placid Santiago enjoys the distinction of the title 'Madre de Ciudades' (Mother of Cities) for this, founded in 1553, was the first Spanish urban settlement in what is now Argentina. Sadly, it boasts no architectural heritage from that period, but still makes a pleasant stop.

Santiagueños (residents of Santiago del Estero) enjoy a nationwide reputation for, to put it politely, valuing rest and relaxation over work. Nevertheless, there's plenty of bustle around the town center, particularly in the evenings when life orbits around the pretty plaza and adjoining pedestrian streets.

Sights

★Centro Cultural del Bicentenario MUSEUM, GALLERY

(CCB; www.ccbsantiago.gov.ar; Pellegrini 149 & Libertad s/n; admission AR$5; 9am-2pm & 4-9pm Tue-Sun) This excellent cultural center is an airy, modern space housing three museums, all imaginatively displayed; the highlight is the **anthropological collection**, with a stunning array of indigenous ceramics as well as jewelry and flutes. Fossils of mastodons and glyptodonts, an extinct family of creatures that somewhat resembled large armadillos, also impress.

The sparsely labeled **historical museum** is attractively set around the patio of Santiago's most noble building and touches on slavery, the strife of the 19th century, and the role of women. The top floor **art gallery** features good temporary exhibitions. All info is in Spanish. The downstairs cafe is a popular meeting place.

Parque Aguirre PARK, RIVERSIDE

This enormous eucalypt- and casuarina-filled area has a disgracefully neglected **zoo** – those poor tigers will have someone's hand off one day – campgrounds, swimming pool and a **costanera** (riverside road). It's a fine place for a wander, with plenty to keep the kids entertained, and has a few *confiterías* and bars.

Festivals & Events

Marcha de los Bombos PROCESSION

(www.marchadelosbombos.com.ar) During the last week of July, *santiagueños* celebrate the founding of the city. The centerpiece is this boisterous procession into the center by thousands of locals banging all manner of drums.

Sleeping

Hotel Avenida HOTEL $

(☎421-5887; www.havenida.com.ar; Pedro León Gallo 403; s/d AR$200/380;) You have to feel for these people: they set up a welcoming little hotel, beautifully decorated with indigenous art and right opposite the bus terminal. Then the city moved the bus terminal to the other side of town. Nevertheless, it's well worth the short walk from the center. Spotless, renovated, friendly and always improving: a great little place.

Campamento Las Casuarinas CAMPGROUND $

(☎421-1390; Parque Aguirre; per person/tent AR$3/5) This cheap municipal campground is normally a pleasant, shady area, less than 1km from Plaza Libertad, but on Friday night a big party scene takes over for the weekend.

Hotel Savoy HOTEL $$

(☎421-1234; www.savoysantiago.com.ar; Tucumán 39; s/d AR$330/440; @) With a sumptuous entrance and gorgeous curving staircase, this place looks like a palace at first glance. Sadly, there are no four-poster beds or servants fanning you with ostrich feathers, but the remodeled rooms are comfortable, with decent showers, and the service is attentive. It's excellently located and has a rather nice little heated outdoor pool, once you find it.

Hotel Carlos V HOTEL $$

(☎424-0303; www.carlosvhotel.com; Independencia 110; s/d standard AR$480/720, d superior

TERMAS DE RÍO HONDO

Halfway between Santiago del Estero and Tucumán, and served by regular buses between them, this place is renowned nationwide as a winter destination for its thermal water, and its nearly 200 hotels all have hot mineral baths. If you fancy a spa treatment, it's a good stop, though there's little else of interest beyond its famous chocolates and *alfajores* (filled sandwich cookies). You can get some great hotel deals here online, especially from November to April when much of town shuts down.

Santiago del Estero

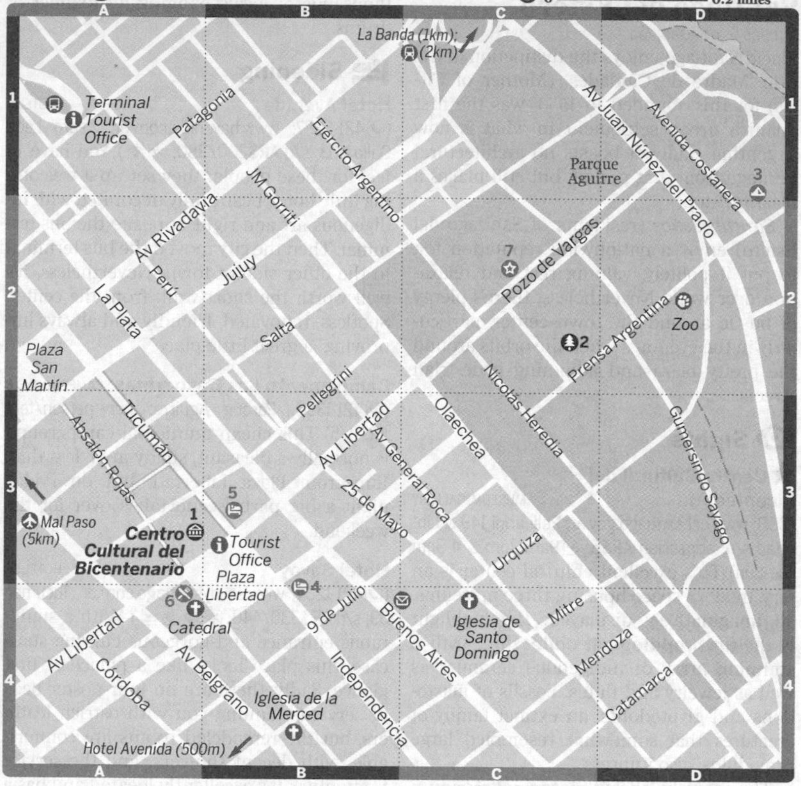

AR$960; ❄@📶🏊) By far the most luxurious option in town, this has a great central location and spacious rooms with business-level facilities, large comfortable beds and carpet. Some rooms have a balcony while superiors are larger with table and chairs. There's a gym and sauna as well as the indoor pool.

Eating & Drinking

Head to Roca between Salta and Libertad for a selection of popular cafes, bars and modish salon restaurants. This is the main eating and drinking area.

Mía Mamma ARGENTINE **$$**
(24 de Septiembre 15; mains AR$45-80; ⏲noon-3pm & 9pm-12:15am) Set back from the plaza, this is a discreet and reliable restaurant with well-dressed waiters who see to your every need. There's a salad bar with plenty of vegetables (AR$49, or AR$35 with a main) and a wide choice of food that includes enormous *parrilla* options as well as tasty *arroz a la valenciana* (paella).

Entertainment

El Patio del Indio Froilán TRADITIONAL MUSIC
(www.elindiofroilan.com.ar; Av Libertador Norte s/n, Barrio Boca del Tigre; ⏲Sun) For over 40 years now, indigenous local hero Froilán González has been making drums from the trunks of the ceibo tree. They are used by some of the biggest names in Latin music. On Sundays, locals and visitors gather at this open space and workshop to eat empanadas, investigate drum-making and listen and dance to live music. Great scenes.

La Casa del Folclorista TRADITIONAL MUSIC
(www.facebook.com/lacasadelfolcloristaSDE; Pozo de Vargas s/n; ⏲noon-3pm, 9pm-1am Tue-Sun) On the way to the riverfront, this big barn of a *peña* has live folk bands Thursday through

Santiago del Estero

Top Sights
1 Centro Cultural del Bicentenario A3

Sights
2 Parque Aguirre C2

Sleeping
3 Campamento Las Casuarinas D1
4 Hotel Carlos V B4
5 Hotel Savoy B3

Eating
6 Mía Mamma A4

Entertainment
7 La Casa del Folclorista C2

Sunday and cheap *parrilla* and empanadas any time. The music kicks off around 11pm.

Information

There's free wi-fi in the plaza.

Terminal Tourist Office (8am-1pm, 3-9pm) In the bus terminal.

Tourist Office (421-3253; www.turismosantiago.gob.ar; Libertad 417; 7am-9pm Mon-Fri, 10am-1pm, 3-5:20pm Sat, 10am-1pm Sun) On the plaza.

Getting There & Away

AIR

Aerolíneas (422-4335; www.aerolineas.com.ar; 24 de Septiembre 547; 8:30am-12:30pm & 5:30-9pm Mon-Fri, 9am-12:30pm Sat) fly five times weekly to Buenos Aires.

BUS

Santiago's swish **bus terminal** (www.tosde.com.ar; Chacabuco 550) is six blocks northwest of Plaza Libertad. For Salta and Catamarca, there are better connections via Tucumán. Bus 20 (AR$2.50) heads into town, but it's only AR$8 in a taxi.

Buses from Santiago del Estero

DESTINATION	COST (AR$)	DURATION (HR)
Buenos Aires	615	13-16
Catamarca	145	4½
Córdoba	249	5-6
La Rioja	303	7-8
Resistencia	355	8-10
Salta	271	6-7
Tucumán	93	2

TRAIN

Santiago del Estero's twin town La Banda is on the line between Tucumán (4½ hours) and Buenos Aires' Retiro station (22 hours). Bus 117 does a circuit of Santiago's center before heading across the river to the station.

Getting Around

Bus 119 (AR$2.50) goes to **Aeropuerto Mal Paso** (SDE; 434-3651; Av Madre de Ciudades), 6km northwest of downtown. A taxi costs AR$25.

CATAMARCA & LA RIOJA

Comparatively little visited by travelers, these provinces are wonderful fun to explore, and are rich in scenery and tradition. Both were home to important pre-Columbian cultures and consequently the region contains many important archaeological sites. The landscape rises westwards into the Andes, with some of the country's most spectacular highland scenery accessible by tour or 4WD: it's an utterly memorable landscape.

Catamarca

0383 / POP 195,100 / ELEV 530M

Vibrant Catamarca has a completely different feel to the other towns of this size within the region. San Fernando del Valle de Catamarca, to give the city its full name, has a lovely central plaza filled with robust jacaranda, araucaria, citrus and palm trees, and streets dotted with noble buildings. A few blocks west, Parque Navarro's huge eucalypts scent the air and are backed by the spectacular sierra beyond.

Sights

Sights outside of town easily accessible by bus include the grotto where the town's Virgin was found, a reservoir, indigenous ruins, and the picturesque foothills around Villa Las Pirquitas. The tourist office will explain them all and show you where to get the bus.

★**Museo Arqueológico Adán Quiroga** MUSEUM
(Sarmiento 450; 8am-1pm & 3-9pm Mon-Fri, 8am-8pm Sat, 10am-6pm Sun) FREE This fine archaeological museum displays a superb collection of pre-Columbian ceramics from several different cultures and eras. Some

Catamarca

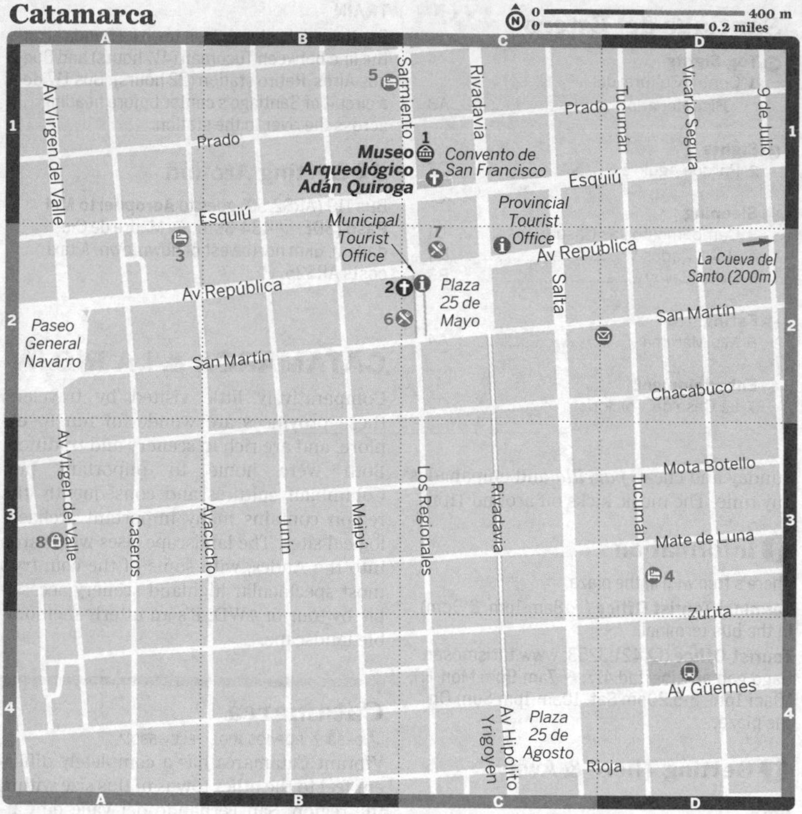

exhibits – particularly the black Aguada ceramics with their incised, stylized animal decoration – are of truly remarkable quality. Also present are a couple of mummies found at 5000m, a spooky shrunken head from the Amazon, and trays used to snort lines of ground tobacco. There's also a colonial and religious section. Closed weekends in January.

Catedral Basílica de Nuestra Señora del Valle CATHEDRAL
(Pl 25 de Mayo; ⏲9am-9pm) This 19th century cathedral shelters the Virgen del Valle, patron of Catamarca and one of northern Argentina's most venerated images. Her back faces towards the church; you can get a look at her face by ascending to the Camarín, which is a chapel accessed down the side of the building and decorated with stained glass panels telling her story.

Festivals & Events

The **Fiesta de Nuestra Señora del Valle** takes place for two weeks after Easter as hordes of pilgrims come to honor the Virgen del Valle. On her saint's day, December 8, she is similarly feted.

Sleeping

Most hotels offer discounts for cash payments.

Residencial Tucumán GUESTHOUSE $
(☎442-2209; Tucumán 1040; s/d AR$190/240; ❄📶) This well-run, immaculately presented *residencial* has comfortable, spotless rooms, is excellent value and is about a one-minute walk from the bus terminal. There are other nearby options if it's full.

San Pedro Hostel HOSTEL $
(☎445-4708; www.hostelsanpedro.com.ar; Sarmiento 341; dm AR$70; @📶🏊) This hostel feels

Catamarca

Top Sights

Sights

Sleeping

Eating

Shopping

as though it is in gentle decline, but has a big back garden that includes cactuses, a *parrilla* and a tiny pool. Dorms are OK: they pack plenty of bunks in, but it's not usually very busy. It's very relaxed – as is the cleaning.

★ **Hotel Casino Catamarca** HOTEL $$
(☎443-2928; www.hotelcasinocatamarca.com; Esquiú 151; r standard/superior AR$541/840; ❄@🛜≋) They've got space to spare at this peaceful but central hotel, which features handsome modern design and bags of facilities. The rooms are more than ample in size, with white sheets contrasting with wooden floors. Some have balconies; superiors add minibar, king-size beds and hydromassage tubs. There's a restaurant, gym, small spa complex, and a long pool and lawn area. And a casino, of course.

Eating

The main nighttime action is in a zone north of the center on and around Av Gobernador Galíndez.

Caravati CAFE $
(Sarmiento 683; dishes AR$40-70; ⏲8am-3pm & 6pm-2am; 🛜) The most inviting of the plaza's terraces, this is named after the Italian architect who designed much of central Catamarca, including the cathedral alongside. The handsome interior is popular for a good line in pizzas, sandwiches and more substantial dishes, including a worthwhile AR$60 weekday lunch.

La Cueva del Santo SPANISH $$
(☎446-3544; www.facebook.com/lacueva.delsanto; Av República 1162; pintxos AR$10-22, dishes AR$54-65; ⏲from 9pm Tue-Sat) The somewhat patchy Catamarca dining scene has been given a real boost by this sweet spot opposite the striking 19th-century hospital. It deals in authentic Spanish fare: the highlight are delicious Basque-style cold and hot *pintxos* (canape-type tapas). It's a sociable, fun experience. Operates reduced hours in summer – check Facebook.

Salsa Criolla PARRILLA $$
(www.salsa-criolla.com.ar; Av República 546; all-you-can-eat AR$99; ⏲11.30am-3pm & 7.30-11.30pm Tue-Sun) On the plaza, this is a high-class all-you-can-eat *parrillada*. It doesn't try to stuff you with chorizo first like in some places – rather, it insists on tempting you with high-quality cuts long after you've insisted you don't want any more. There are à la carte options.

Shopping

Catamarca enthusiastically promotes its fine natural products; the region is well known for wines, olive oil, walnuts, jams and conserves. There are several shops stocking these along Sarmiento and Rivadavia near the plaza.

Mercado Artesanal y Fábrica de Alfombras HANDICRAFTS
(Av Virgen del Valle 945; ⏲7am-1pm & 3-9pm Mon-Fri, 8am-8pm Sat & Sun) For Catamarca's characteristic hand-tied rugs, visit this artisans' market. The market also sells ponchos, blankets, jewelry, red onyx sculptures, musical instruments and basketry. Adjacent is a carpet-weaving workshop, where they'll happily show you around (free). It's only open mornings from Monday to Friday.

Information

Banks with ATMs are around the plaza.

Municipal Tourist Office (Sarmiento 620; ⏲8am-9:30pm) Just outside the cathedral.

Provincial Tourist Office (☎443-7791; www.turismocatamarca.gov.ar; cnr Rivadavia & República; ⏲9am-9pm) Helpful desk in a shopping arcade on a corner of the plaza.

Getting There & Around

AIR

Aerolíneas (☎442-4460; www.aerolineas.com.ar; Sarmiento 589; ⏲8am-1pm & 6-9pm Mon-

OFF THE BEATEN TRACK

THE WILD NORTHWEST

If you like getting off the beaten track, you're sure to appreciate out-of-the-way Antofagasta de la Sierra in the far northwest of Catamarca province, 300 kilometers beyond Belén. This puna village sits at 3320 meters amid spectacular landscape.

Driving yourself or by tour from Belén or Catamarca you can take in other sights in the area: the spectacular pumice fields of Campo de Piedra Pomez, remote volcanoes, the salt flats and hamlet of Antofalla, and flamingo-stocked lakes.

It's particularly worth visiting in early March for the livestock- and traditional culture-based Fiesta de la Puna. There's accommodation available in family homes or the **Hostería de Antofagasta** (03835-471001; Principal s/n, Antofagasta de la Sierra; s/d AR$100/200). It's freezing in winter. Buses run here from Catamarca via Belén at 6.15 am Wednesdays & Fridays (12 to 15 hours, AR$150), returning at 10am on Mondays and Fridays.

Fri, 9am-1pm Sat) has five weekly flights from Buenos Aires. Minivans run from the terminal to **Aeropuerto Felipe Varela** (443-0080), some 22km east of town on RP33, to coincide with flights, or it's AR$80 in a *remise*.

BUS

Catamarca's spruce **bus terminal** (442-3415; Av Güemes 850) includes a shopping complex and cinema. There are services around the province and the country, including to Tucumán (AR$116, four hours), La Rioja (AR$79, two hours) and Buenos Aires (AR$585, 14 to 16 hours).

Belén

03835 / POP 12,300 / ELEV 1250M

Slow-paced Belén, a stop on RN40, feels like, and is, a long way from anywhere, and will appeal to travelers who like things small-scale and friendly. It's one of the best places to buy woven goods, particularly ponchos. There are many *teleras* (textile workshops) around town, turning out their wares made from llama, sheep and alpaca wool. The nearby ruins of El Shincal are another reason to visit.

Sights

Museo Cóndor Huasi MUSEUM
(cnr Belgrano & San Martín; admission AR$3; 8am-1pm & 4-8pm Mon-Fri) Upstairs at the end of a shopping arcade at a corner of the plaza, this museum has a good archaeological collection with a range of ceramics from different eras of settlement in the region.

Arañitas Hilanderas TEXTILE WORKSHOP
(www.arañitashilanderas.com.ar; Av Virgen de Belén s/n; 9:30am-noon, 2-6:30pm) A good place to see weavers at work. Follow Belgrano past the Hotel Belén to find it.

Rua Chaky TEXTILE WORKSHOP
(461068; ruachaky@argentina.com; Barrio 17 de Agosto, Casa 28; 9:30am-noon, 2-6:30pm) FREE Watch shawls and ponchos being made at this friendly workshop is on the other side of the main road from town, a short stroll from the center.

Tours

★ **Chaku Aventuras** TOUR
(463976; www.chakuaventuras.com.ar; Rivadavia 37; 2/3-day tours AR$1600/2500) This well-run setup run excellent excursions into the west and northwestern highlands of the province. A two-day trip takes in the Adobe Route, the Fiambalá hot springs and the mighty mountains near the Chilean border; a three-day trip heads northwest to Antofagasta and the spectacular puna scenery in that region. May have moved to Calle Belgrano below the Hotel Belén by the time you read this.

Sleeping & Eating

Fredy Hostal GUESTHOUSE $
(461230; www.amarillasinternet.com/fredyhostal; Av Calchaquí 461; s/d/tr AR$120/170/210;) One of a handful of cheap places on the main road through town, this is hospitable and features appealing rustic rooms around a patio with cactus garden. Air-con is a little extra.

★ **Hotel Belén** HOTEL $$
(461501; www.belencat.com.ar; cnr Belgrano & Cubas; s/d AR$310/410, sup s/d AR$360/470; @) A surprising presence in town, this stylish hotel has dark, comfortable rooms featuring exposed rock bathrooms, indigenous art, an archaeological collection and very comfortable beds. If you can ignore a few creaks and quirks – sound travels way too easily between bathrooms, service

is patchy and not everything works all the time – it's a very characterful stay at a decent price.

1900 ARGENTINE $

(☎461100; Belgrano 391; mains AR$45-60; ⏲12:30-3pm & 9pm-1:30am) Beyond-the-call service is the key to this highly enjoyable restaurant a block down from the plaza. It's very popular, but it hates to turn people away, so a Tetris-like reshuffling of tables is a constant feature. Prices are more than fair, and there are a number of large platters designed to be shared. Well-mixed salads and juicy brochettes are highlights.

Shopping

There's a marquee off the plaza with a number of *artesanía* stalls selling ponchos, camelid-wool clothing and foot-trodden local wine. For more upmarket woven goods, **Familia Avar Saracho** (☎461091; avarsaracho@hotmail.com; Roca 144; ⏲10am-11pm) has reasonable prices and arranges shipping.

Information

There's a bank at the corner of General Paz and Lavalle, near the tourist office.

Tourist Office (☎461304; www.turismodebelen.com.ar; General Paz 180; ⏲7am-1pm & 2-10pm) Also has a small mineral exhibition. There's an irregularly attended office next to the bus station.

Getting There & Away

Belén's **bus terminal** (cnr Sarmiento & Rivadavia) is one block south and one west of the plaza. Catamarca (AR$89, four to five hours) is served several times daily. Night services run to La Rioja and Córdoba, and several weekly buses and minibuses go to Santa María (AR$70, four hours) – a scenic journey.

Around Belén

Londres & El Shincal

Only 15km southwest of Belén, sleepy Londres dates from 1558, though it moved several times before returning here in 1612, and the inhabitants fled again during the Diaguita uprising of 1632. Its name (London) celebrated the marriage of the prince of Spain (later Philip II) to Mary Tudor, queen of England, in 1555.

Seven kilometers west are the Inca ruins of **El Shincal** (admission AR$5; ⏲8am-sunset). Founded in 1470, the town occupied a commanding position in the foothills of the mountains, surveying the vast valley to the south. The setting is spectacular, with fantastic views and great atmosphere. The *ushno* (ceremonial platform) and *kallanka* (possibly a barracks) have been restored. Two hillocks aligned to the rising and setting sun probably served as both lookouts and altars. Entrance includes an explanation of the somewhat neglected museum.

Five to six buses Monday to Saturday run from Belén to Londres (AR$5) and the ruins. A *remise* from Belén with waiting time is around AR$170. There's a campground between Londres and the ruins, and a cabin complex. Londres also has a couple of basic *residenciales*.

Beyond Londres, Chilecito is 200km south in La Rioja province along RN 40, if you have transportation. The drive is a spectacular one, with the imposing Sierra Famatina to the west and Sierra de Velasco to the east. The road is excellent.

Western Catamarca

☎03837

Western Catamarca province is well worth exploring, with historic adobe churches, vineyards, and stunning views from the hot springs above Fiambalá, an oasis town set in an arid valley among dunes and spectacular mountainscapes that have been favorite terrain for the Dakar rally since it moved here from Africa. In the far west, a cluster of awe-inspiring 6000m peaks form the planet's second-loftiest ensemble after the Everest region. The main settlements are Tinogasta and Fiambalá, 50km apart. If you don't have transport, tours from Belén or Catamarca are the best ways to see the area.

Sights & Activities

Ruta del Adobe HISTORIC BUILDINGS

FREE The road between Tinogasta and Fiambalá is designated the 'adobe route' for its ensemble of fantastic historic buildings with thick walls of mud, straw and dung and cane roofs supported by algarrobo beams. Buildings are signposted off the road and include former inns and little museums. This was an important trade route to Bolivia and Peru. On public transport you can check out the Iglesia de San Pedro, at the southern entrance to Fiambalá, and the adjacent Comandancia de Armas.

Termas de Fiambalá HOT SPRINGS
(Fiambalá; AR$30; ⏲7am-10pm) From Fiambalá 15km east into the mountains, these thermal springs emerge from rock and cascade down the mountainside in a series of pools: the highest at around 40°C, cooler ones below. The views over the desert valley are epic. It's best after 5pm when there's more shade. Weekends are rowdy. There's a campsite and various simple accommodation options here. It's AR$100 in a *remise* from Fiambalá.

Museo del Hombre MUSEUM
(Azarelli s/n, Fiambalá; AR$10; ⏲7:30am-1:30pm & 3:30-8pm Mon-Fri, 8am-1pm & 3-8pm Sat & Sun) This interesting local museum has sections on geology and archaeology, with high-quality ceramics and two haunting Inca mummies with their well-preserved funerary goods. Another room is dedicated to mountaineering, giving details of famous expeditions to the province's fourteen 6000m-plus peaks.

Los Seismiles MOUNTAINS
FREE West of Fiambalá, the paved road winds its way up into some serious mountains, topping out at the Chilean border. It's a stunning drive, with no services apart from a white-elephant hotel halfway between Fiambalá and the frontier. Los Seismiles are the peaks over 6000m, and you'll see several of them, including Ojos del Salado (6879m), the world's highest volcano.

Even more awe-inspiring scenery is accessed via a lonely mining road that leads 90km to Monte Pissis, the Americas' third-highest peak. It's about 5 hours return to a viewpoint (50km) over this imposing mountain, with hauntingly beautiful blue, black and turquoise lakes in the foreground. Due to its isolation, this is best by tour – operators in Belén and Catamarca can arrange it.

Sleeping & Eating

Fiambalá has lots of simple lodgings and a hostel. Camping is possible, but beware of frequent high winds and sandstorms.

★**Casa Grande** BOUTIQUE HOTEL
(☎421140; www.casagrandetour.com; Moreno 801, Tinogasta; d AR$650; ❄📶🏊) This standout option in Tinogasta occupies an historic adobe building that has been added to and given sublime original decorative touches by the welcoming owners. Cozy rustic rooms are traditionally built with cane ceilings; there's a beautiful Jacuzzi room and outdoor pool, and inventive meals, including excellent salads, are available. It rents sandboards and bikes.

Hostería Municipal HOTEL
(☎496291; www.fiambala.gov.ar; Almagro s/n, Fiambalá; s/d AR$180/290; ❄📶) The heart of Fiambalá is this place built around an unattractive shaded courtyard. Rooms are decent, and there's a restaurant serving simple meals.

Information

Fiambalá Tourist Office (☎496250; www.fiambala.gov.ar; Pl Principal s/n, Fiambalá; ⏲7am-9pm Mon-Fri, 8am-9pm Sat & Sun) On the plaza.

Getting There & Away

There are three or more daily buses from Catamarca to Tinogasta and Fiambalá (5¾ hours, AR$125). A few weekly reach La Rioja and Córdoba. Five weekly buses link Belén and Tinogasta (AR$35).

La Rioja

☎0380 / POP 178,900 / ELEV 500M

Encircled by the Sierra de Velasco's graceful peaks, La Rioja is quite a sight on a sunny day. And there are plenty of those: summer temperatures rise sky-high in this quiet, out-of-the-way provincial capital. Even if you're on a short highlights tour, you might consider stopping off (it's halfway between Mendoza and Salta) to take a tour to the Talampaya and Ischigualasto national parks.

Sights

La Rioja is a major devotional center, so many landmarks are ecclesiastical in nature.

★**Museo Folklórico** MUSEUM
(Pelagio Luna 811; admission by donation; ⏲9am-12:30pm & 4:30-8:30pm Tue-Sun) This hugely worthwhile museum is set in a wonderful early-17th-century adobe building, and has fine displays on various aspects of the region's culture. Themes include *chaya* (local La Rioja music), the Tinkunaco festival, weaving and winemaking. The informative guided tour is excellent if your Spanish is up to it.

Convento de Santo Domingo CHURCH
(cnr Pelagio Luna & Lamadrid; ⏲9:30am-12:30pm & 6-8pm Mon-Fri) FREE Built in 1623 by the

EL TINKUNACO – CONFLICT RESOLUTION IN THE 16TH CENTURY

The fascinating and moving El Tinkunaco ceremony is a symbolic representation of the resolution of the clash of cultures that occurred at the birth of La Rioja. When Juan Ramírez de Velasco founded the city in 1591, he blithely ignored the fact that the land was owned and farmed by the Diaguita, who naturally took exception to their territory being carved up among Spanish settlers. They rebelled in 1593, and a bloody conflict was averted by the mediation of the friar Francisco Solano, later canonized for his efforts. The Diaguita trusted the cleric and listened to his message. They agreed to down their arms on two conditions: that the Spanish *alcalde* (mayor) resign; and that his replacement be the Christ child. The Spaniards agreed and peace was made. The new mayor became known as Niño Jesús Alcalde.

The Tinkunaco (the word means 'meeting' in Quechua) commemoration commenced not long afterwards. Every year at noon on December 31, two processions – one representing the Spaniards, one the Diaguita – cross town to the Casa de Gobierno. The processions meet, and solemnly all fall to their knees before the image of the Niño Jesús Alcalde, then embrace. It's a powerful moment with its message about cultural differences and compromises.

Diaguita under the direction of Dominican friars, this is Argentina's oldest monastery. The date appears in the carved algarrobo doorframe, also the work of Diaguita artists. You'll also find a museum of religious art on-site.

Museo de la Ciudad/Museo de Bellas Artes MUSEUM
(Pelagio Luna 248; donation AR$5; 9am-noon & 4-8pm) The city makes a big effort rehabilitating old buildings for cultural ends. This complex is the most recent effort: the art gallery shows temporary exhibits while the city museum's display of historical items and photos is beautifully curated though not of massive interest. The beautiful restoration and enthusiastic staff make it worth dropping by.

Activities

Several operators run excursions around the province, and may include visits to the Parque Nacional Talampaya, which invariably includes the nearby Parque Provincial Ischigualasto (also known as 'Valle de la Luna') in San Juan province. These companies also offer excursions to high, remote parts of the Andes in the western part of the province.

Águila Blanca HANG-GLIDING, PARAGLIDING
(Hugo Ávila; 445-1635; www.turismoaguilablanca.com; Av Ramírez de Velasco Oeste 4900 (Km7) Offers instruction and tandem flights, as well as accommodation.

Tours

Corona del Inca TOUR
(442-2142; www.coronadelinca.com.ar; Pelagio Luna 914) Offers various excursions to provincial highlights.

Terra Riojana TOUR
(442-0423; www.terrariojana.com.ar) Terra Riojana operates a variety of tours around the province.

Runacay TOUR
(03825-470368; www.runacay.com) Offer tours around Talampaya and Ischigualasto National Parks, as well as good trips to Laguna Brava and other lofty destinations.

Festivals & Events

Taking place at noon on December 31, El Tinkunaco is one of Argentina's most interesting ceremonies (see boxed text, p275).

La Chaya CARNAVAL
The local variant of Carnaval. Its name, derived from a Quechua word meaning 'to get someone wet,' should give you an idea of what to expect. The musical style associated with the festival is also called *chaya*.

Sleeping

La Rioja's hotels often discount if you pay cash and aren't afraid to bargain.

Pucará Hotel HOTEL $
(443-7789; hotelpucara-larioja@hotmail.com; República de Siria 79; s/d AR$200/320;) Cool and tranquil, this newish hotel has

La Rioja

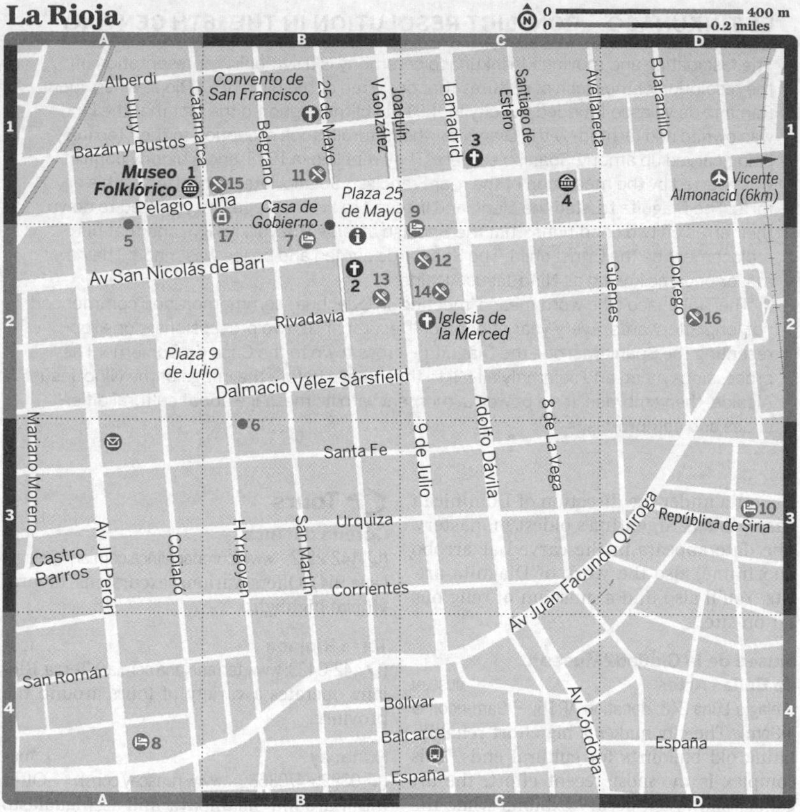

simple but comfortable lodgings in a quiet barrio. The friendly young owners have made it a welcoming place with stonework and traditional art decorating public areas and the clean, dark rooms with decent mattresses. It's La Rioja's best budget hotel.

Hostel Apacheta HOSTEL $

(☎ 15-444-5445; www.apachetahostel.com.ar; Av San Nicolás de Bari 669; dm/d AR$80/200; ❄ 📶) Wood has been put to imaginative uses in this central hostel. Furniture made from pallets and packing crates combines with antiques to make a pleasantly original design. It's a simple place; dorms feature a variety of beds and bunks, with air-con and plenty of room to move. You can rent bikes here.

Hotel Talampaya HOTEL $$

(☎ 442-2005; Av JD Perón 1290; s/d AR$300/500; ❄ @ 📶 🏊) A conversion from what was formerly a government hotel, this rather oversized, lugubrious building has rooms that are good at this price (especially the singles), and have decent bathrooms, safes and noisy balconies.

Naindo Park Hotel HOTEL $$$

(☎ 447-0700; www.naindoparkhotel.com; Av San Nicolás de Bari 475; s/d AR$884/1017; ❄ @ 📶 🏊) Just off the plaza, and dominating it assertively, La Rioja's finest hotel has an excellent level of service, a fistful of facilities and prices to match. The rooms are commodious and good-sized, if in need of a dash of vim. Still, they have original art on the walls and decent views.

Eating

Regional dishes to look for include *locro*, juicy empanadas, *chivito asado* (barbecued goat), *humitas*, *quesillo* (a cheese specialty) and olives. Cheap local wines are a good bargain in restaurants.

La Rioja

El Marqués ARGENTINE $

(Av San Nicolás de Bari 484; meals AR$30-55; 8am-1am) This simple but effective local eatery just off the plaza puts many pricier restaurants to shame. Sandwiches, traditional local dishes, pasta, pizza, omelets and grilled meats are well prepared and fairly priced. It's something of a bargain and the fruit *licuados* are delicious, too.

Café del Paseo CAFE $

(cnr Pelagio Luna & 25 de Mayo; light meals AR$30-60; 7:30am-3pm & 5:30pm-1am;) This is your spot on the corner of the plaza to observe La Rioja life. Executives with I-gadgets mingle with families and tables of older men chewing the fat over another slow-paced La Rioja day.

Orígenes ARGENTINE $$

(442-8036; www.origeneslarioja.com.ar; cnr Catamarca & Pelagio Luna; mains AR$50-85; 11am-4pm & 7pm-12.30am;) Smart and enthusiastic, this occupies a corner of an enormous, handsome 19th-century school, now turned cultural center. It draws on local traditions but brings a modern chef's expertise to bear on them. The result is excellent in many ways, including the inspiring salads, a meal in themselves. Prices are more than fair.

La Vieja Casona ARGENTINE $$

(442-5996; www.lacasonalunch.com.ar; Rivadavia 457; mains AR$55-90; lunch & dinner) Cheerfully lit and decorated, this is a cracking place with a great range of regional specialties, creative house choices and a menu of standard Argentine dishes – the *parrillada* here is of excellent standard. There's a fair selection of La Rioja wines, too, and wonderful smells from the busy kitchen.

Stanza ITALIAN $$

(443-0809; www.lastanzaresto.com.ar; Dorrego 164; mains AR$50-85; noon-3pm & 8-11pm Tue-Sun) One of the best places in town, this stylish restaurant serves imaginative pasta dishes that are a cut above most places, as well as other Italian favorites such as saltimbocca. The attractive interior is supplemented by an enticing courtyard terrace.

Joaquín FUSION $$$

(www.facebook.com/joaquin.resto.7; Rivadavia 537; mains AR$65-110; 8pm-1:30am Sun-Thu, 8pm-3am Fri & Sat;) A relaxed spot for indoor our outdoor dining, this offers a short, tasty menu of well-presented, well-thought-out dishes, as well as satisfying fresh pasta tossed with basil. Service is slow and prices on the high side, but it's a deservedly popular local meeting place.

Shopping

La Rioja is famous for weaving and silverwork that combine indigenous techniques with Spanish designs and color combinations.

Fittingly for a place named after Spain's most famous wine region, La Rioja wine has a national reputation.

Mercado Artesanal de La Rioja HANDICRAFTS

(Pelagio Luna 792; 9am-12:50pm & 5-8:50pm Tue-Sat, 9am-12:50pm Sun) La Rioja crafts are exhibited and sold here, as are other popular artworks at prices lower than most souvenir shops. Afternoon closing is earlier in winter.

Information

Municipal Tourist Office (Plaza 25 de Mayo; 8am-1pm & 3-9pm Mon-Fri, 8am-9pm Sat & Sun) In a kiosk on the plaza itself.

Provincial Tourist Office (442-6345; www.turismolarioja.gov.ar; 8am-1pm, 4-9pm) On the roundabout next to the bus terminal in the south of town.

Getting There & Away

AIR

Aerolíneas Argentinas (☎442-6307; www.aerolineas.com.ar; Belgrano 63; ⌚8am-1pm & 5:30-8:30pm Mon-Fri, 8:30am-12:30pm Sat) Flies six times weekly to and from Buenos Aires.

BUS

La Rioja's **bus terminal** (Av Circunvalación s/n) is picturesquely backed by the sierra. It's a long walk south from downtown.

For Chilecito, **La Riojana** (☎443-5279; Buenos Aires 154; ⌚9:15am-1:15pm & 6:15-9:15pm Mon-Fri, 9:30am-1pm & 7-9pm Sat, 9:30am-12:30pm & 6-9pm Sun) minibuses run three times daily (AR$86, 2½ hours), a little quicker than the bus. Minibuses leave from the **minibus terminal** (☎446-8562; Artigas 750) seven blocks south of the plaza, though you can board at the office beforehand.

Buses from La Rioja

DESTINATION	COST (AR$)	DURATION (HR)
Belén	101	5
Buenos Aires	630	14-17
Catamarca	82	2
Chilecito	80	3
Córdoba	250	6-7
Mendoza	335	8
Salta	382	10
San Juan	240	6
Santiago del Estero	303	7-8
Tucumán	205	6½

Getting Around

Aeropuerto Vicente Almonacid (☎442-7239) is 7km east of town on RP5. A taxi costs around AR$50. From the bus terminal to downtown is about AR$20. Local buses (AR$3.50) run between terminal and center, including numbers 2, 6, 7, 8 and 4B.

Chilecito

☎03825 / POP 33,700 / ELEV 1080M

With a gorgeous situation among low rocky hills and sizable snowcapped peaks, Chilecito, a stop on spectacular RN40, has several interesting things to see, including an amazing abandoned cableway leading to a mine high in the sierra. With the intense heat, mining heritage and slopes around town dotted with cardón cactus, Chilecito has a Wild West feel and is definitely the most appealing place to spend a few quiet days in this part of the country. It's also a base for worthwhile excursions into the sierra.

History

To enable the mining of gold, silver and copper from the Sierra de Famatina, a cablecar was constructed running from Chilecito, at the end of the railway line, to La Mejicana, at an altitude of 4603m, more than 3.5km above Chilecito and nearly 40km away. With nine stations, a tunnel and 262 towers, the amazing project was completed in 1904. Men and supplies were carried to the mine, operated by a British firm, in four hours. WWI put an end to it and the line started to decay, although local miners continued using it until the 1930s.

Sights

★Museo del Cablecarril — MUSEUM, CABLECAR

(Av Presidente Perón s/n; donation AR$5; ⌚8am-1pm & 2-6pm) This old cablecar station documents the extraordinary engineering and mining project that created modern Chilecito at the beginning of the 20th century. The simple, picturesque museum preserves photos, tools and documents, as well as communications equipment, including an early cellphone. You'll be shown the museum (in Spanish) then taken to the cablecar terminus itself – a rickety spiral staircase climbs to the platform, where ore carts now wait silently in line. It's best in late afternoon with sun bathing the rusted metal and snowy sierras.

With a car, you can investigate the second and third cablecar stations, too. Guided tours visit the final stop of La Mejicana, high in the sierra.

The museum is on the main road at the southern entrance to town, a block south of the bus terminal.

Cristo del Portezuelo — MONUMENT

(Maestro s/n) FREE Head down Maestro from the plaza to reach this recent addition: a huge statue of Christ on a platform accessed by a 200-step ascent flanked by terraced cactus gardens. Views from the top give super perspectives over town, local couples canoodle secure at the feet of the saviour. There's a

WESTERN RIOJA TRIPS

The western portion of La Rioja province is fascinating, with plenty of intriguing destinations in the sierras. The towns of Chilecito and Villa Unión are launchpads for a range of excellent excursions. Parque Nacional Talampaya is one appealing trip, which also takes in the Ischigualasto provincial park and (from Chilecito) crosses the picturesque Miranda pass. For some serious 4WD mountain action, head up to the abandoned mine at La Mejicana (4603m), an ascent that takes in some amazing scenery and a broad palette of colors, including a striking yellow river. Deeper into the sierras by the Chilean border is sizable Laguna Brava, a flamingo-filled lake surrounded by awesomely bleak and beautiful Andean scenery. Higher still, at 5600m, is the sapphire-blue crater lake of Corona del Inca, only accessible in summer.

Operators in Chilecito such as **Salir del Cráter** (☎03825-423854; www.salirdelcrater.com.ar), **Inka Ñan** (☎03825-422418; www.inkanan.com.ar; 25 de Mayo 37) and **Cuesta Vieja** (☎03825-424874; www.cuestavieja.com; Joaquín V González 467) run these trips, which cost around AR$400 to AR$1100 per person depending on numbers. In Villa Unión, a good operator is Runacay (p275). There's usually a minimum of two people, but they'll try and put a group together.

cafe, and a painfully slow funicular (AR$10) for weary legs.

Molino de San Francisco MUSEUM
(Ocampo 63; admission AR$5; ⏱7am-noon & 2-7pm) Chilecito founder Don Domingo de Castro y Bazán owned this colonial flour mill, which houses an eclectic assemblage of archaeological tools, antique arms, early colonial documents, minerals, traditional wood and leather crafts, banknotes, woodcuts, cellphones and paintings. It's four blocks west of the plaza.

La Riojana WINERY
(☎423150; www.lariojana.com.ar; La Plata 646; ⏱tours on the hour from 10am-3pm Mon-Fri, 10am-noon Sat) FREE La Riojana cooperative is the area's main wine producer, and a sizable concern. A good free tour shows you through the bodega – think large cement fermentation tanks rather than rows of musty barrels – and culminates in a generous tasting. It's a block north and five west of the plaza.

Sleeping

Posada del Sendero GUESTHOUSE $
(☎425489; www.posadadelsendero.com.ar; Pje Spilimbergo, San Miguel; s/d AR$190/290; ❄ 📶 🏊) Tucked away on the edge of town, 2km from the plaza, this sweet spot looks over a vineyard and the hilly surrounds of Chilecito. Eight unpretentious but appealing rooms give on to a common space and a garden with small pool. It's utterly peaceful. Welcoming hosts put on a good breakfast: for other meals, there's a barbecue or you can dial restaurant delivery.

Hotel Ruta 40 HOTEL $
(☎422804; www.hotelruta40.com.ar; Libertad 68; s/d AR$150/220, without bathroom AR$120/200; ❄ 📶) A laid-back budget hotel a couple of blocks from the plaza, this comfortable spot offers a variety of rooms with decent enough beds and clean, spacious bathrooms. Check out a few – some look over a vine-covered patio to the hills beyond.

Hostal Mary Pérez GUESTHOUSE $
(☎423156; hostal_mp@hotmail.com; Florencio Dávila 280; s/d AR$150/250; 📶) A neat little *residencial* in the northeast of town that is more like a family-run hotel. The place is spotless – you may get high on the smell of cleaning products – and rooms come with TV and phone. They also offer apartments for two or four.

Hotel ACA Chilecito HOTEL $
(☎422201; www.hotelchilecitoaca.com.ar; T Gordillo 101; s/d standard AR$230/300, s/d superior AR$285/400; ❄ @ 📶 🏊) With a quiet location near where the town ends among rocky hills, this ACA establishment is tired but offers value for money. There's space to burn, with a garden and cavernous recreation room with pool table. Rooms are light, bright and pleasant, with tiled floors and gleaming bathrooms. There's also a restaurant.

MAC Royal Suites HOTEL $$$
(☎422002; www.macroyalsuites.com; 19 de Febrero 361; s/d/ste US$376/564/815; ❄ @ 📶 🏊)

Mimicking the surrounding hills' color but still out-of-place in low-rise Chilecito, this modern hotel bears the initials of the casino magnate owner. Facilities, which include indoor and outdoor pools, saunas, a cactus garden and modern gym, are great. Rooms are stylish and spacious, with hydromassage bathtub and elegant furniture. Still, it seems overpriced: cynical locals nod knowingly. Service, though, is warm and enthusiastic.

Eating & Drinking

El Rancho de Ferrito ARGENTINE $

(Av Pelagio Luna 647; mains AR$35-55; 11am-3pm & 7-11pm Tue-Sun) A block west and seven north of the plaza, this inviting local restaurant is worth every step. You've seen the menu before – except for house specialties such as *cazuela de gallina* (chicken stew: yum), and local wines – but the quality, price and authentic atmosphere make it truly excellent.

La Posta ARGENTINE $$

(425988; cnr 19 de Febrero & Roque Lanús; mains AR$50-100; noon-3.30pm & 8pm-midnight) Warmly decorated and stylish, with shelves of deli products on sale, the cuisine and service here doesn't live up to the ambience or the prices but can provide a satisfying dinner nonetheless. Kid (*cabrito*) is a specialty – try it stewed in torrontés wine. Follow 19 de Febrero four blocks north from the plaza.

Yops CAFE

(AE Dávila 70; 9:15am-2pm & 8:30pm-2am Mon-Sat) Simple but atmospheric, this bohemian spot is comfortably Chilecito's best cafe, serving fine coffee, cold beer and decent mixed drinks. Watch the locals' epic chess battles.

Information

The plaza has banks with ATMs and internet/telephone places.

Tourist Office (422688; www.emutur.com.ar; Castro y Bazán 52; 8am-10pm;) Enthusiastic staff and good material. Half a block off the plaza. There's also a booth at the bus terminal.

Getting There & Away

The **bus terminal** (Av Presidente Perón s/n;) is 1.5km south of the center. It's a spectacular trip from La Rioja (AR$80, three hours), passing the red rock formations of Los Colorados en-route, with the snowcapped Sierra de Famatina in the background. There are direct services from Chilecito to farther-flung destinations like Buenos Aires. **La Riojana** (424710; Maestro 61) minibuses also do the La Rioja run a little quicker for a few pesos more. There are no buses north to Belén; to avoid the lengthy backtrack you could take a tour to El Shinkal.

Parque Nacional Talampaya

03825 / ELEV 1300M

The spectacular rock formations and canyons of this dusty desert national park are evidence of erosive action of water that these days is hard to believe existed here. The sandstone cliffs are amazing, as are the distant surrounding mountainscapes. Talampaya is relatively close to fossil-rich Parque Provincial Ischigualasto in San Juan province and it's easy to combine the two if you have transport or visit with a tour.

Sights & Activities

You must enter by guided visit, arranged at the visitor center. The standard 2½-hour (AR$165) or longer 4½-hour excursions (AR$240), taking in more remote sights, are in comfortable minibuses and there's little walking involved; nevertheless, take water and protection from the fierce sun. Guided walks (AR$120 to AR$200) and trips on bicycles are also available; a more appealing way of exploring if the heat's not too intense, though you'll still likely have to pay for transport into the park if you're on foot. There are night excursions when there's a full moon.

Cañon de Talampaya ROCK FORMATIONS

(8:30am-5:30pm) Focus of visits is this spectacular dry (usually) watercourse bounded by sheer sandstone cliffs. Condors soar on thermals, and guanacos, rheas and maras can be seen in the shade of algarrobo trees along the sandy canyon floor. A series of enigmatic petroglyphs carved into oxidized sandstone slabs are the first stop on the standard visit, followed by, in the canyon itself, such highlights as the Chimenea del Eco, whose impressive echo is a guaranteed hit, the Catedral formation and the clerical figure of El Monje.

Ciudad Perdida & Cañon Arco Iris ROCK FORMATIONS

(8:30am-5:30pm) In another part of the park, accessed from the road 14km before reaching the main park entrance, these impressive formations are accessed via guided 4WD tours which only leave once full (3 to 4 hours; AR$160).

Sendero Triásico DINOSAUR FOSSILS

This 'Triassic' path takes you past life-size replicas of dinosaurs whose fossilized remains have been found in the Talampaya area.

Sleeping & Eating

There's shadeless camping at the visitor center (AR$25 per person), which has decent toilets and showers. There's also a cafe here serving meals and cold drinks.

There are simple accommodations in Pagancillo, 29km north. A further 29km up the road, larger Villa Unión has several cabin and hotel options, some quite stylish. The park website www.talampaya.gov.ar has a useful pdf detailing accommodation options.

Information

The **visitor center** (☎470356; www.talampaya.gov.ar; ⏲excursions 8am-5pm inclusive mid-Sep-Apr, 8:30am-4:30pm inclusive May-mid-Sep) is just off the RP26. Here you pay the AR$50 admission (AR$25 for Argentine citizens, free for under-17s), and arrange guided visits. Entry is valid for two days and includes a free jaunt introducing biological and cultural aspects of the park. Don't sweat if you miss the jaunt: you get most of this info on park tours, too.

Getting There & Away

Buses from La Rioja to Pagancillo and Villa Unión will leave you at the park entrance (AR$80, 3½ hours), from where it's only a 500m walk to the visitor center. The earliest bus (Facundo) leaves La Rioja at 7am, giving you plenty of time to make a day-trip. There's a daily bus between Villa Unión, 58km up the road, and Chilecito (AR$70, three hours) over the spectacular Miranda pass. It leaves Villa Unión at 3pm; you can make it if you cadge a lift off someone in your tour group.

If you want to see Talampaya and Ischigualasto in one day, tour operators in La Rioja will do it for around AR$500 per person. You could also take a *remise* - from La Rioja think AR$1500 for up to four passengers; from Villa Unión they are somewhat less.

Córdoba & the Central Sierras

Includes ➡

Best Places to Eat

- ➡ El Bistro del Alquimista (p303)
- ➡ Rincón Suizo (p308)
- ➡ La Nieta (p292)
- ➡ Kasbah (p299)
- ➡ El Paseo (p307)

Best Places to Stay

- ➡ 279 Boutique B&B (p303)
- ➡ Hotel Azur (p292)
- ➡ Andamundos Hostel (p308)
- ➡ Hospedaje Casa Rosita (p306)
- ➡ Estancia La Estanzuela (p314)

Why Go?

Argentina's second city bursts with life. Home to not one but seven major universities, Córdoba has a young population that ensures an excellent nightlife and a healthy cultural scene. Córdoba also boasts a fascinating history, owing its architectural and cultural heritage to the Jesuits, who set up shop here when they first arrived in Argentina.

The rolling hill country out of town is dotted with places that could grab your attention for a day or a month, including five Jesuit missions that make for an easy day trip from the capital.

Adventure buffs also head to the hills, where the paragliding is excellent, or a couple of national parks offer excellent trekking opportunities.

Further to the southwest, the Valle de Conlara and Sierras Puntanas offer a real chance to get away from the crowds and into the heart of the countryside.

When to Go

Córdoba

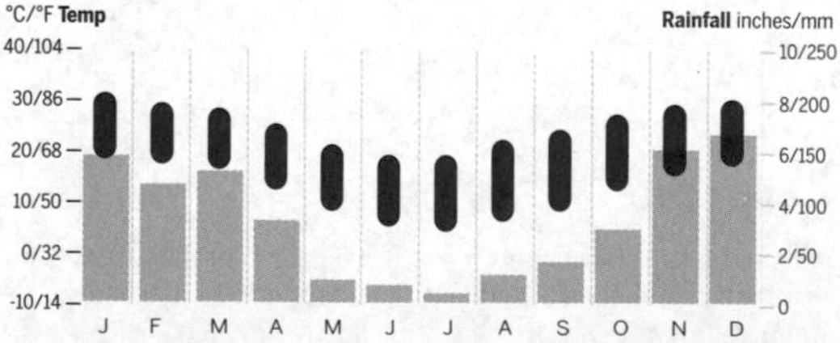

Nov–Feb During the day, cool off riverside in the Sierras. At night, hit Córdoba's bars.

Jul–Sep Chances of snow at higher altitudes. Low rainfall makes for good trekking weather.

Mar–Jun Clear, cool days with occasional rain – ideal for outdoor activities.

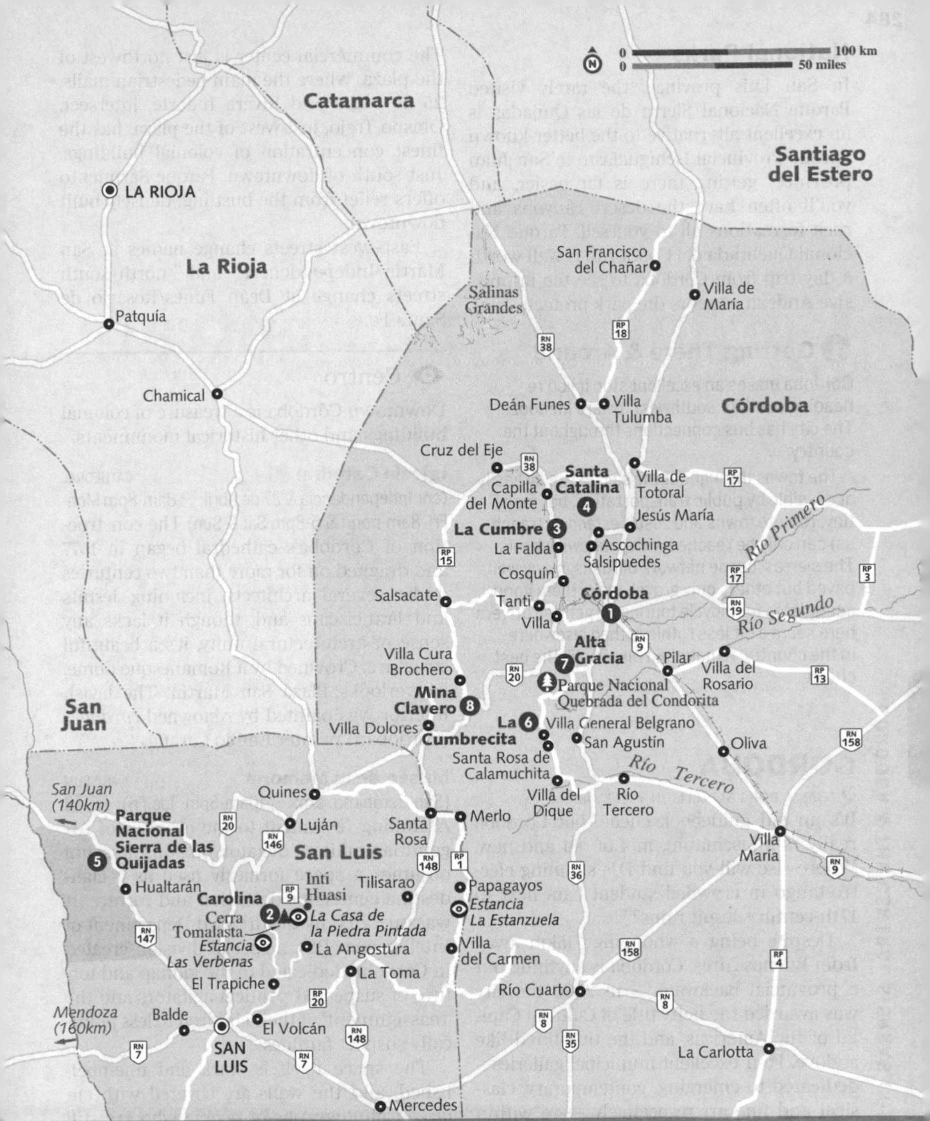

Córdoba & the Central Sierras Highlights

1. Lap up the culture and wander the gorgeous streets of the stately city of **Córdoba** (p284)
2. Check out ancient caves, rock art and highland scenery around **Carolina** (p313)
3. Get high with the paragliding fanatics at **La Cumbre** (p298)
4. Take a breather at the atmospheric 17th-century Jesuit *estancia* (ranch) of **Santa Catalina** (p302)
5. Break in your hiking boots among the surreal rock formations of **Parque Nacional Sierra de las Quijadas** (p312)
6. Mellow out in the pedestrian-only mountain village of **La Cumbrecita** (p306)
7. Visit Che's house in **Alta Gracia** (p300)
8. Cool off riverside in the quaint resort town of **Mina Clavero** (p307)

National Parks

In San Luis province, the rarely visited Parque Nacional Sierra de las Quijadas is an excellent alternative to the better-known Parque Provincial Ischigualasto in San Juan province: getting there is far easier, and you'll often have the desert canyons and rock formations all to yourself. Parque Nacional Quebrada del Condorito is well worth a day trip from Córdoba to see the impressive Andean condors the park protects.

Getting There & Around

Córdoba makes an excellent stop if you're heading south or southwest toward Mendoza. The city has bus connections throughout the country.

The towns throughout the sierras are all easily accessible by public transportation, but many tiny, remote towns and Jesuit *estancias* (ranches) can only be reached with your own wheels. The sierras' dense network of roads, many well paved but others only gravel, make them good candidates for bicycle touring; Argentine drivers here seem a bit less ruthless than elsewhere in the country. A mountain bike is still the best choice.

CÓRDOBA

0351 / POP 1.317 MILLION / ELEV 400M

It's an old guidebook cliché, but Córdoba really *is* a fascinating mix of old and new. Where else will you find DJs spinning electro-tango in crowded student bars next to 17th-century Jesuit ruins?

Despite being a whopping 715km away from Buenos Aires, Córdoba is anything but a provincial backwater – in 2006 the city was awarded the hefty title of Cultural Capital of the Americas, and the title fitted like a glove. Four excellent municipal galleries – dedicated to emerging, contemporary, classical and fine art respectively – are within easy walking distance of each other and the city center.

Sights

There's plenty to see, so allow yourself at least a couple of days for wandering around. Most churches are open roughly from 9am to noon and from 5pm to 8pm. Museum opening hours change regularly depending on the season and the administration.

Most colonial sites lie within a few blocks of Plaza San Martín, the city's urban nucleus. The commercial center is just northwest of the plaza, where the main pedestrian malls, 25 de Mayo and Rivera Indarte, intersect. Obispo Trejo, just west of the plaza, has the finest concentration of colonial buildings. Just south of downtown, Parque Sarmiento offers relief from the bustling, densely built downtown.

East–west streets change names at San Martín/Independencia and north–south streets change at Deán Funes/Rosario de Santa Fe.

Centro

Downtown Córdoba is a treasure of colonial buildings and other historical monuments.

Iglesia Catedral CATHEDRAL

(cnr Independencia & 27 de Abril; 8am-8pm Mon-Fri, 8am-noon & 5-8pm Sat & Sun) The construction of Córdoba's cathedral began in 1577 and dragged on for more than two centuries under several architects, including Jesuits and Franciscans and, though it lacks any sense of architectural unity, it's a beautiful structure. Crowned by a Romanesque dome, it overlooks Plaza San Martín. The lavish interior was painted by renowned *cordobés* (Córdoban) painter Emilio Caraffa.

Museo de la Memoria MUSEUM

(San Jerónimo s/n; 10am-6pm Tue-Fri) FREE A chilling testament to the excesses of Argentina's military dictatorship, this museum occupies a space formerly used as a clandestine center for detention and torture. It was operated by the dreaded Department of Intelligence (D2), a special division created in Córdoba dedicated to the kidnap and torture of suspected political agitators and the 'reassignment' of their children to less politically suspect families.

The space itself is stark and unembellished, and the walls are covered with enlarged photographs of people who are still 'missing' after 30 years. There's not much joy here, but the museum stands as a vital reminder of an era that human-rights groups hope will never be forgotten.

Museo Histórico Provincial Marqués de Sobremonte MUSEUM

(0351-433-1661; Rosario de Santa Fe 218; admission AR$10; 10:30am-3pm Mon-Fri) It's worth dropping into this museum, one of the most important historical museums in the country, if only to see the colonial house it occupies: an 18th-century home that once belonged to Rafael Núñez, the colonial governor of Córdoba and later viceroy of the Río de la Plata. It has 26 rooms, seven interior patios, meter-thick walls and an impressive wrought-iron balcony supported by carved wooden brackets.

Cripta Jesuítica MUSEUM
(cnr Rivera Indarte & Av Colón; admission AR$5; ⏲10am-3pm Mon-Fri) Built at the beginning of the 18th century by the Jesuits, the Cripta Jesuítica was originally designed as a novitiate and later converted to a crypt and crematorium. Abandoned after the Jesuit expulsion, it was demolished and buried around 1829 when the city, while expanding Av Colón, knocked the roof into the subterranean naves and built over the entire structure. It remained all but forgotten until 1989 when Telecom, while laying underground telephone cable, accidentally ran into it.

The city, with a new outlook on such treasures, exquisitely restored the crypt and uses it regularly for musical and theatrical performances and art exhibits. Entrances lie on either side of Av Colón in the middle of the Rivera Indarte pedestrian mall.

Museo Municipal de Bellas Artes Dr Genaro Pérez GALLERY
(Av General Paz 33; ⏲10am-8pm Tue-Sun) FREE This art gallery is prized for its collection of paintings from the 19th and 20th centuries. Works, including those by Emilio Caraffa, Lucio Fontana, Lino Spilimbergo, Antonio Berni and Antonio Seguí, chronologically display the history of the *cordobés* school of painting, at the front of which stands Genaro Pérez himself. The museum is housed in Palacio Garzón, an unusual late-19th-century building named for its original owner; it also has outstanding changing contemporary art exhibits.

Plaza San Martín & Around PLAZA
Córdoba's lovely and lively central plaza dates from 1577. Its western side is dominated by the white arcade of the restored **Cabildo** (colonial town-council building), completed in 1785 and containing three interior patios, as well as basement cells. All are open to the public as part of the **Museo de la Ciudad** (Independencia 30; admission AR$2; ⏲9:30am-12:30pm & 3:30-6pm), a block to the south.

Occupying nearly half a city block, **Iglesia de Santa Teresa y Convento de Carmelitas Descalzas de San José** (cnr Caseros & Independencia; ⏲6-8pm) was completed in 1628 and has functioned ever since as a closed-order convent for Carmelite nuns. Only the church itself is open to visitors.

★ Manzana Jesuítica NOTABLE BUILDING
Córdoba's beautiful Manzana Jesuítica (Jesuit Block), like that of Buenos Aires, is also known as the Manzana de las Luces (Block of Enlightenment), and was initially associated with the influential Jesuit order.

Next door, the Colegio Nacional de Monserrat (p287) dates from 1782, though the college itself was founded in 1687 and transferred after the Jesuit expulsion. Though the interior cloisters are original, the exterior was considerably modified in 1927 by restoring architect Jaime Roca, who gave the building its present baroque flare.

In 2000 Unesco declared the Manzana Jesuítica a World Heritage site, along with five Jesuit *estancias* (ranches) throughout the province.

➡ Museo Histórico de la Universidad Nacional de Córdoba MUSEUM
(Obispo Trejo 242; guided visits per person AR$10; ⏲tours Mon-Sat, in English 10am & 5pm, in Spanish 11am & 3pm) In 1613 Fray Fernando de Trejo y Sanabria founded the Seminario Convictorio de San Javier, which, after being elevated to university status in 1622, became the Universidad Nacional de Córdoba. The university is the country's oldest and contains, among other national treasures, part of the Jesuits' Grand Library and the Museo Histórico de la Universidad Nacional de Córdoba.

Guided visits are the only way to see the inside and are well worth taking. The guides let you wander through the Colegio and peek into the classrooms while students run around.

➡ Iglesia de la Compañía de Jesús CHURCH
(cnr Obispo Trejo & Caseros; ⏲7am-1pm, 5-8pm) FREE Designed by the Flemish Padre Philippe Lemaire, this church dates from 1645 but was not completed until 1671, with the successful execution of Lemaire's plan for a cedar roof in the form of an inverted ship's hull. Lemaire, unsurprisingly, was once a boat builder. Inside, the church's baroque altarpiece is made from carved Paraguayan cedar from Misiones province.

The Capilla Doméstica, completed in 1644, sits on Caseros, directly behind the church. Its ornate ceiling was made with

Córdoba

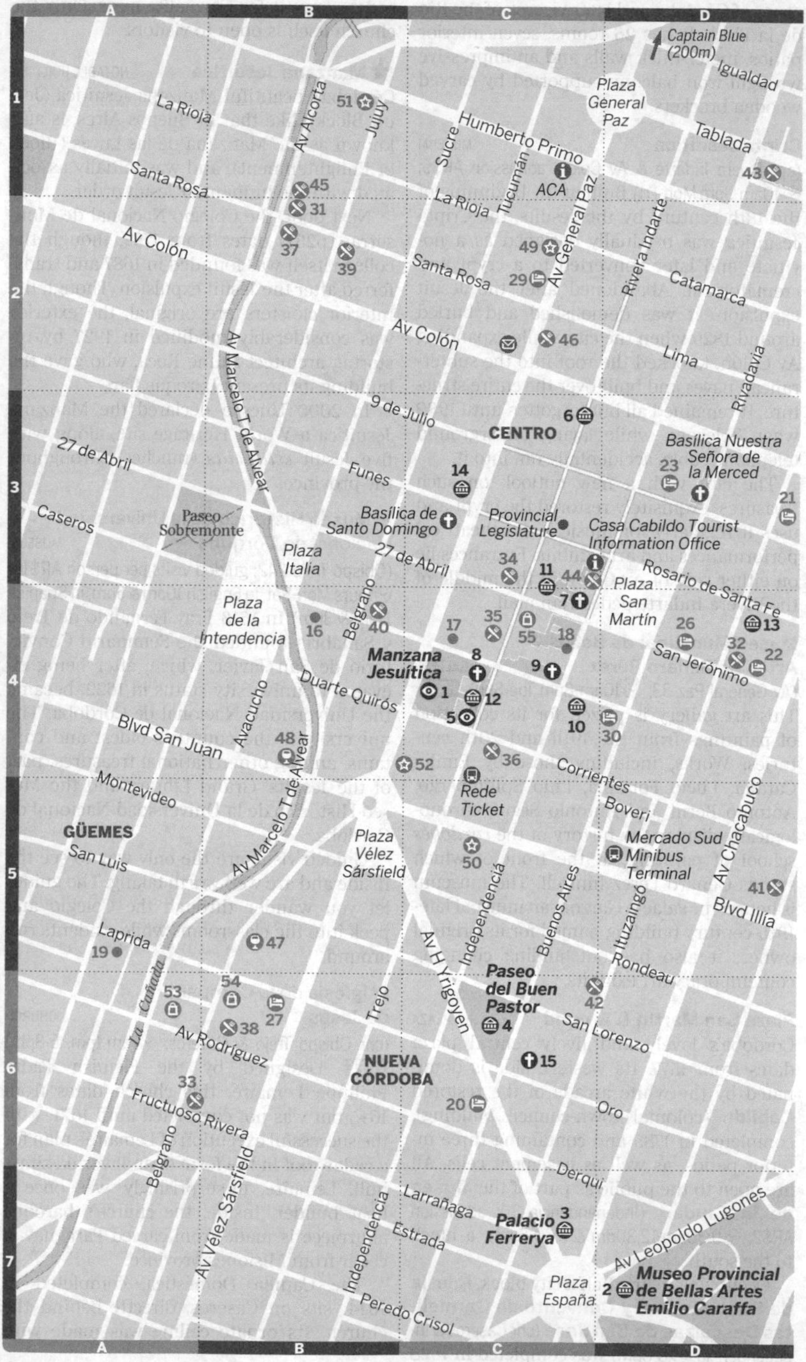
A
B
C
D
1
2
3
4
5
6
7
Captain Blue (200m)
Igualdad
Plaza General Paz
Tablada
La Rioja
Jujuy
Av Alcorta
51
Humberto Primo
Sucre
Tucumán
ACA
Av General Paz
Rivera Indarte
43
Santa Rosa
45
31
La Rioja
37
39
Av Colón
49
29
Santa Rosa
Catamarca
Av Colón
46
Lima
Rivadavia
Av Marcelo T de Alvear
9 de Julio
6
CENTRO
Basílica Nuestra Señora de la Merced
23
27 de Abril
Funes
14
21
Caseros
Paseo Sobremonte
Basílica de Santo Domingo
Provincial Legislature
Casa Cabildo Tourist Information Office
Plaza Italia
27 de Abril
34
11
44
Rosario de Santa Fe
Plaza San Martín
7
Plaza de la Intendencia
Belgrano
16
40
17
35
55
18
26
13
32
22
San Jerónimo
Manzana Jesuítica
8
9
Duarte Quirós
Avacucho
1
12
5
10
30
Blvd San Juan
48
Av Marcelo T de Alvear
36
52
Corrientes
Montevideo
Rede Ticket
Boveri
GÜEMES
Plaza Vélez Sársfield
San Luis
50
Mercado Sud Minibus Terminal
Av Chacabuco
41
Independencia
Buenos Aires
Ituzaingó
Blvd Illía
Laprida
19
47
Av H Yrigoyen
Rondeau
La Cañada
53
54
27
Paseo del Buen Pastor
42
Trejo
4
San Lorenzo
38
Av Rodríguez
NUEVA CÓRDOBA
15
33
Fructuoso Rivera
20
Oro
Belgrano
Av Vélez Sársfield
Derqui
Larrañaga
Independencia
Palacio Ferrerya
3
Av Leopoldo Lugones
Estrada
Plaza España
2
Museo Provincial de Bellas Artes Emilio Caraffa
Peredo Crisol

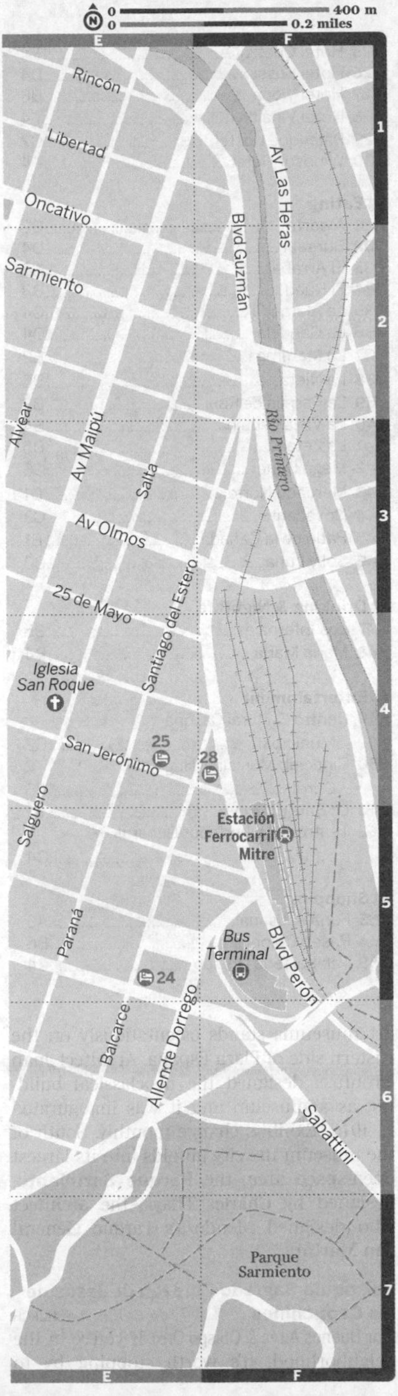

cowhide stretched over a skeleton of thick taguaro cane and painted with pigments composed partially of boiled bones.

➡ Colegio Nacional de Monserrat NOTABLE BUILDING

(Obispo Trejo 294) The Colegio Nacional de Monserrat dates from 1782, though the college itself was founded in 1687 and transferred after the Jesuit expulsion. Though the interior cloisters are original, the exterior was considerably modified in 1927 by restoring architect Jaime Roca, who gave the building its present baroque flare.

Nueva Córdoba & Güemes

Before the northwestern neighborhoods of Chateau Carreras and Cerro de las Rosas lured the city's elite to their peaceful hillsides, Nueva Córdoba was the neighborhood of the *cordobés* aristocracy. It's now popular with students, which explains the proliferation of brick high-rise apartment buildings. Still, a stroll past the stately old residences that line the wide Av H Yrigoyen reveals the area's aristocratic past.

Once a strictly working-class neighborhood, Güemes is now known for the eclectic antique stores and artisan shops that line the main drag of Belgrano, between Rodríguez and Laprida. Its weekend *feria artisanal,* one of the country's best, teems with antique vendors, arts and crafts and a healthy dose of Córdoba's hippies. It's within the same block as the **Museo Iberoamericano de Artesanías** (cnr Belgrano & Laprida; 10am-5pm Mon-Fri, 10am-8pm Sat, 2-8pm Sun) FREE, which houses beautiful crafts from throughout South America. A good way back to the city center is along La Cañada, an acacia-lined stone canal with arched bridges.

★ Paseo del Buen Pastor GALLERY

(Av H Yrigoyen 325; 10am-8pm) FREE This cultural center/performance space was built in 1901 as a combined chapel, monastery and women's prison. In mid-2007 it was reinaugurated to showcase work by Córdoba's young and emerging artists. There are a couple of hip cafe-bars in the central patio area where you can kick back with an Appletini or two. The attached chapel (which has been deconsecrated) hosts regular live-music performances – stop by for a program, or check Thursday's edition of the local newspaper *La Voz del Interior* for details.

Córdoba

Top Sights
1 Manzana Jesuítica ... C4
2 Museo Provincial de Bellas Artes Emilio Caraffa ... D7
3 Palacio Ferrerya ... C7
4 Paseo del Buen Pastor ... C6

Sights
Cabildo ... (see 44)
5 Colegio Nacional de Monserrat ... C4
6 Cripta Jesuítica ... C3
7 Iglesia Catedral ... C4
8 Iglesia de la Compañía de Jesús ... C4
9 Iglesia de Santa Teresa y Convento de Carmelitas Descalzas de San José ... C4
10 Museo de la Ciudad ... C4
11 Museo de la Memoria ... C3
12 Museo Histórico de la Universidad Nacional de Córdoba ... C4
13 Museo Histórico Provincial Marqués de Sobremonte ... D4
Museo Iberoamericano de Artesanías ... (see 53)
14 Museo Municipal de Bellas Artes Dr Genaro Pérez ... C3
15 Parroquia Sagrado Corazón de Jesús de los Capuchinos ... C6

Activities, Courses & Tours
16 Able Spanish School ... B4
17 Facultad de Lenguas ... C4
18 Nativo Viajes ... C4
19 Tsunami Tango ... A5

Sleeping
20 Gaiadhon Hostel ... C6
21 Hostel Alvear ... D3
22 Hotel Azur ... D4
23 Hotel Garden ... D3
24 Hotel Heydi ... E5
25 Hotel Quetzal ... E4
26 Hotel Sussex ... D4
27 Hotel Viena ... B6
28 Hotel Viña de Italia ... F4
29 Palenque Hostel ... C2
30 Windsor Hotel ... D4

Eating
31 Alcorta ... B2
32 Bursatil ... D4
33 El Arrabal ... A6
34 El Ruedo ... C3
35 La Alameda ... C4
36 La Candela ... C4
37 La Mamma ... B2
38 La Nieta ... B6
39 La Parrilla de Raul ... B2
40 La Vieja Esquina ... B4
41 La Zeta ... D5
42 Mega Doner ... C6
43 Mercado Norte ... D1
44 Novecento ... C3
45 Patio de la Cañada ... B1
46 Sol y Luna ... C2

Drinking & Nightlife
47 Los Infernales ... B5
48 Maria Maria ... B4

Entertainment
49 Centro Cultural Casona Municipal ... C2
50 Cineclub Municipal Hugo del Carril ... C5
51 La Sala del Rey ... B1
52 Teatro del Libertador General San Martín ... C4

Shopping
53 Feria Artisanal ... A6
54 Paseo Colonial ... B6
55 Talabartería Crespo ... C4

★ **Palacio Ferrerya** GALLERY
(Av H Yrigoyen 551; admission AR$12; ⏲10am-8pm Tue-Sun) This Nueva Córdoba landmark was built in 1914 and designed by Ernest Sanson in the Louis XVI style. The building itself is amazing, and has recently been converted into a fine-arts museum, featuring more than 400 works in 12 rooms spread over three floors. If you're into art or architecture, this place is a don't miss.

★ **Museo Provincial de Bellas Artes Emilio Caraffa** GALLERY
(Av H Yrigoyen 651; admission AR$10; ⏲10am-8pm Tue-Sun) One of the city's best contemporary art museums stands ostentatiously on the eastern side of Plaza España. Architect Juan Kronfuss designed the neoclassical building as a museum and it was inaugurated in 1916. Exhibits change monthly. South of the museum the city unfolds into its largest open-space area, the **Parque Sarmiento**, designed by Charles Thays, the architect who designed Mendoza's Parque General San Martín.

Parroquia Sagrado Corazón de Jesús de los Capuchinos CHURCH
(cnr Buenos Aires & Obispo Oro) If you're in the neighborhood, it's worth stopping by to

check out this marvelous neo-Gothic church built between 1928 and 1934, whose glaring oddity is its missing steeple (omitted on purpose to symbolize human imperfection). Among the numerous sculptures that cover the church's facade are those of Atlases symbolically struggling to bare the spiritual weight of the religious figures above them (and the sins and guilt of the rest of us).

Courses

Córdoba is an excellent place to study Spanish; in many ways, being a student is what Córdoba is all about. Lessons cost about AR$70 per hour for one-on-one tuition or AR$800 per week in small classes.

Facultad de Lenguas LANGUAGE
(0351-433-1075, ext 30 0351-433-1073; www.lenguas.unc.edu.ar; Av Vélez Sársfield 187; 8am-1pm & 3-7pm Mon-Fri) Part of the Universidad Nacional de Córdoba.

Able Spanish School LANGUAGE
(0351-422-4692; www.ablespanish.com.ar; Tucumán 76; 9am-8pm Mon-Sat) Offers accommodation and afternoon activities at extra cost and discounts for extended study.

Tsunami Tango DANCE
(0351-15-313-8746; www.tsunamitango.blogspot.com.ar; Laprida 453) Tango classes and *milongas* (tango halls) Tuesday to Sunday. The website lists times.

Tours

All of the city's hostels and most hotels can arrange tours within the city and around the province.

City Tours WALKING TOUR
(in Spanish/English AR$30/50) Absorb Córdoba's rich history by taking one of the guided walking tours that depart at 9:30am and 11:30am Monday to Friday from Casa Cabildo. Reserve a day in advance if you want a tour in English. There are also free thematic tours on an irregular basis – ask at the tourist office to see the schedule.

Festivals & Events

During the first three weeks of April the city puts on a large **crafts market** (locally called 'FICO') at the city fairgrounds, in the north near Chateau Carreras stadium. Bus 31 from Plaza San Martín goes there. Mid-September's **Feria del Libro** is a regional book fair.

Sleeping

Hotels on and around Plaza San Martín make exploring the center a cinch, but you'll have to walk several blocks for dinner and nightlife. Hotels along La Cañada and in Nueva Córdoba, on the other hand, mean that going out to dinner and hitting the bars is a simple matter of walking down the street.

Centro

Hostel Alvear HOSTEL $
(0351-421-6502; www.alvearhostel.com.ar; Alvear 158; dm/d from AR$60/200; @) An excellent location and spacious dorms set in an atmospheric old building make Alvear one of the better hostels in the downtown area.

Palenque Hostel HOSTEL $
(0351-423-7588; www.palenquehostel.com.ar; Av General Paz 371; dm from AR$80, d without bathroom AR$220; @) By far the prettiest hostel in Córdoba, the Palenque occupies a classic old house and retains much of its original charm. Facilities are extensive, including laundry area, air-con and nightly cooking classes. Dorms are large, with plenty of room to move.

Hotel Quetzal HOTEL $
(0351-426-5117; www.hotelquetzal.com.ar; San Jerónimo 579; s/d AR$200/300; @) Offers spacious, minimalistic, modern rooms. It's a surprisingly tranquil option in a busy neighborhood.

Hotel Garden HOTEL $$
(0351-421-4729; www.garden-hotel.com.ar; 25 de Mayo 35; s/d AR$350/480, apt AR$450;) About as central as it gets. The large, modern rooms here are probably the best deal in this price range and certainly the best deal in the downtown area. Breakfast is served in a cafe around the corner. Staff can also hook you up with some very good-value apartments in various locations around the downtown area.

Hotel Viña de Italia HOTEL $$
(0351-425-1678; www.hotelvinadeitalia.com.ar; San Jerónimo 611; s/d AR$220/300;) There's a bit of elegance left in this 150-room hotel, and the midsize rooms include TV, phone, air-con and heating. The rooms aren't nearly as graceful as the lobby, but they're still a good deal.

1

YADID LEVY/GETTY IMAGES ©

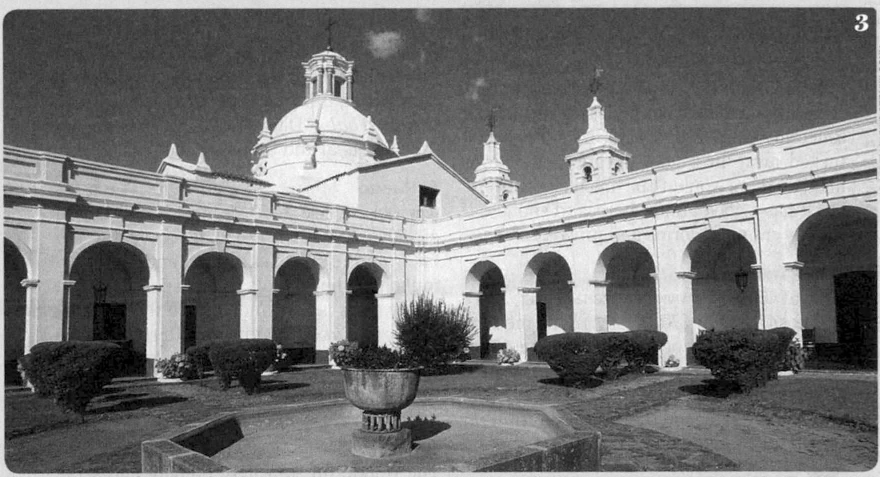

ARCO IMAGES GMBH/ALAMY ©

1. Parque Nacional Sierra de las Quijadas (p312)
Otherworldly rock formations make for great hiking opportunities.

2. Iglesia Catedral (p284)
Córdoba's beautiful church is crowned by a Romanesque dome.

3. Estancia Santa Catalina (p302)
This Jesuit *estancia* is one of the Sierra's most beautiful and is a Unesco World Heritage site.

Windsor Hotel HOTEL $$
(☎0351-422-4012; www.windsortower.com; Buenos Aires 214; r/ste AR$678/858;) In a great downtown location, the Windsor is one of the few classic hotels in town with any real style. The lobby's all dark wood and brass, and the rooms have been tastefully renovated with modern fittings.

Hotel Heydi HOTEL $$
(☎0351-422-2219; www.hotelheydi.com.ar; Blvd Illía 615; s/d AR$320/400;) This is the best of the bunch near the bus terminal: a modern, immaculate place with friendly, professional staff.

Hotel Sussex HOTEL $$
(☎0351-422-9070; www.hotelsussexcba.com.ar; San Jerónimo 125; s/d AR$320/495;) Another wonderful lobby (this one sporting vaulted ceilings, grand piano and fine art) leads on to more workaday rooms. At this price, you'd want to be getting plaza views.

★**Hotel Azur** BOUTIQUE HOTEL $$$
(☎0351-424-7133; www.azurrealhotel.com; San Jerónimo 243; r AR$800-1200; @) Surprisingly one of a kind here in Córdoba, the Azur mixes minimal chic with eclectic local and international furnishings to pull off a very stylish little boutique hotel. Rooms are all they should be and the common areas (including rooftop deck and pool area) are extremely inviting.

Nueva Córdoba & La Cañada

Gaiadhon Hostel HOSTEL $
(☎0351-15-800-5923; www.gaiadhonhostel.com.ar; Buenos Aires 768; dm AR$70-80, s/d without bathroom AR$150/230;) A cozy little hostel tucked away in a good location. If it ever filled up there wouldn't be much elbow room, but it has a good atmosphere, and spotless if slightly cramped dorms and private rooms.

Hotel Viena HOTEL $$
(☎0351-460-0909; www.hotelviena.com.ar; Laprida 235; s/d AR$290/370; @) This modern hotel in the heart of Nueva Córdoba offers bright, clean rooms and an excellent breakfast buffet. There are lots of nooks for sitting in the lobby area, and there's a restaurant on the premises. Good choice.

Eating

Mercado Norte MARKET $
(cnr Rivadavia & Oncativo; set meals from AR$35; 8am-3pm Mon-Sat) Córdoba's indoor market has delicious and inexpensive food, such as pizza, empanadas (baked savory turnovers) and seafood. Browsing the clean stalls selling every imaginable cut of meat, including whole *chivitos* (goat) and pigs, is a must.

Sol y Luna VEGETARIAN $
(General Paz 278; mains from AR$45; 12-3:30pm;) A fantastic selection of vegetarian offerings. Pay by the kilo or choose from the limited selection of set meals.

Bursatil CAFE $
(San Jerónimo & Ituzaingó; mains AR$35-60; 8am-6pm Mon-Sat;) Stylish, modern cafes are starting to pop up in the old part of town, and Bursatil is one of the finest. There's a cool modern interior, good coffee and a small, Asian-inspired menu.

Patio de la Cañada PARRILLA $
(☎0351-427-0628; Alcorta 360; mains AR$40-100; 12:30-11:30pm;) This is one of the better-value *parrillas* (steakhouses) around, offering top-quality meats at reasonable prices. The all-you-can-eat *parrilla* (mixed grill; AR$95) is especially good value.

La Parrilla de Raul PARRILLA $
(cnr Jujuy & Santa Rosa; mains AR$35-70; 12-11:30pm;) Of Córdoba's *parrillas,* this is probably one of the most famous. *Parrillada* (mixed grill including steak) for two costs only AR$40, not including extras such as drinks or salad.

Mega Doner MIDDLE EASTERN $
(Ituzaingó 528; set meals AR$30-50; 11-1am) Conveniently located in Nueva Córdoba's bar district, this place specializes in real giro *doner kebabs*. Daily lunch specials are an excellent deal and there's outdoor seating.

El Ruedo CAFE $
(cnr Obispo Trejo & 27 de Abril; mains around AR$50; 8am-10pm;) It doesn't stray too far from the steak, sandwich and pizza formula here, but the plaza-side spot under big shady trees is a winner, as are the *limonadas con soda* (lemon juice with soda water) on a hot day.

★**La Nieta** FUSION $$
(☎0351-468-1920; Belgrano 783; mains AR$70-120; 9pm-1am Tue-Fri, 4:30pm-1am Sat & Sun;) The wonderful staff here prepare and serve a changing menu of delectable regional specialties, creative pastas and house recipes. Be sure to save room for dessert. Check out the lovely upstairs terrace, which catches breezes

LOCAL FLAVOR

Looking to chow down with Córdoba's student crowd? Pull up a stool at any of the following, where the empanadas, beer and *locro* (spicy corn and meat stew) flow freely.

La Alameda (Obispo Trejo 170; empanadas AR$5, locro AR$30; ⌚ noon-11:30pm) Pull up a bench and wash down your homemade empanadas with some ice-cold beer. Then write some graffiti on the wall.

La Candela (Duarte Quirós 67; empanadas AR$5.50, locro AR$35; ⌚ 11am-1am) Rustic and wonderfully atmospheric, run by three cranky but adorable señoras.

La Vieja Esquina (cnr Belgrano & Caseros; empanadas AR$4.50, locro AR$32; ⌚ 11am-6pm Mon-Sat) A cozy little lunch spot with stools and window seating. Order at the bar.

and gives ample people-watching ops on the street below.

El Arrabal ARGENTINE $$
(☎ 0351-460-2990; Belgrano 899; mains AR$80-120; ⌚ 11:30am-1am Tue-Sun; wi-fi) One of the few old-style restaurants in Nueva Córdoba (OK, so it may be a reconstruction), servng slightly pricey but imaginative regional and house specialties. It's packed out for the dinner tango show (AR$25 to AR$50) at 11pm Thursday to Saturday. Make a reservation.

La Mamma ITALIAN $$
(cnr Santa Rosa & Alcorta; mains AR$80-130; ⌚ noon-1am Tue-Sat; wi-fi) Probably Córdobás most famous pasta restaurant, with an excellent selection that goes far beyond the standard Argentine offerings. The Grande Mamma sauce (featuring caramelized onions, cream cheese, mushrooms and greens) comes highly recommended.

Novecento INTERNATIONAL $$
(☎ 0351-423-0660; cnr Rosario de Santa Fe & Independencia; mains AR$55-90; ⌚ 9am-4pm Mon-Fri; wi-fi) There are few more atmospheric options for dining downtown than this cute little cafe-restaurant, set in the courtyard of the historic *cabildo* (town council) building. The menu ticks all the 'classic' boxes and throws in a few welcome surprises.

La Zeta MIDDLE EASTERN $$
(cnr Corrientes & Salguero; mains AR$50-80; ⌚ 11am-11pm) Excellent Middle Eastern food (with a couple of Mediterranean faves thrown in) provides a welcome dash of variety. There's not much to be said for the decor, but the flavors more than make up for that.

Alcorta STEAKHOUSE $$
(☎ 0351-424-7452; Av Alcorta 330; mains AR$80-120; ⌚ 12-11:30pm; wi-fi) This upmarket *parrilla,* esteemed for its grilled meats (many say they're the best in town), also serves delicious pasta and fish. Try the *mollejitas al sauvignon blanc* (sweetbreads in a white-wine sauce).

Drinking & Nightlife

Córdoba's drink of choice is Fernet (a strong, medicinal-tasting herbed liquor from Italy), almost always mixed with Coke. If you don't mind a rough morning, start in on the stuff.

Nightlife in Córdoba basically divides itself into three areas. All the bright young things bar-hop in Nueva Córdoba – a walk along Rondeau between Avs H Yrigoyen and Chacabuco after midnight gives you a choice of dozens of bars, mostly playing laid-back (or ribcage-rattling) electronic music. For a slightly older crowd and a more laid-back scene, check out the bars on Belgrano, in the blocks around the artisańs market.

Across the river to the north on Av Las Heras between Roque Sáenz Peña and Juan B Justo (the area known locally as Abasto) are the discos and nightclubs. Go for a walk along here and you'll probably pick up free passes to some, if not all, of them.

Los Infernales BAR
(Belgrano 631; ⌚ 6pm-1am Tue-Sun) A laid-back bar playing an eclectic range of music. Live music Thursday to Sunday and a big *patio cervecero* (beer garden) make this a standout.

Maria Maria CLUB
(cnr San Juan & Alvear; ⌚ 9pm-late Thu-Sun) An ever-popular spot for drinks and dancing, attracting a good range of locals, travelers and expats.

Captain Blue CLUB
(Las Heras 124; ⌚ 8pm-late Wed-Sat) One of the best spots in town to catch Latin dance grooves such as salsa and bachata. Weekends it often has live bands.

WORTH A TRIP

LOS GIGANTES

This spectacular group of rock formations, 80km west of Córdoba, is fast becoming Argentina's rock-climbing capital. The two highest peaks are the granite giants of Cerro de La Cruz (2185m) and El Mogote (2374m). There are numerous Andean condors – the park is only 30km from Parque Nacional Quebrada del Condorito, and the birds have slowly taken to this area as well. The area is home to the tabaquillo tree, with its papery peeling bark, which is endangered in Argentina and only found here and in Bolivia and Peru.

Getting here is complicated. **Sarmiento** (0351-433-2161) buses leave Córdoba's main bus terminal at 8am Wednesday to Monday and 6am on Tuesday (AR$55, two hours). The bus pretty much turns around and comes back again, meaning you have to spend the night. Schedules change frequently, so be sure to check.

Get off at El Crucero (tell the driver you're going to Los Gigantes). From there it's a 3km walk to La Rotonda, where there is a super-basic **hospedaje** (03541-498370; camp site per person AR$25, dm AR$75, per person kitchen use AR$25) and a small store (beer, soft drinks and snacks only), which is open on weekends.

At La Rotonda you can hire guides (AR$85) to show you around the cave complexes and take you to the top of Cerro de La Cruz. It's not a long hike, but there is some tricky rock scrambling involved. Guides are recommended because the maze of trails through the rocks can be hard to follow and if the fog comes down you can easily get lost.

Some of the Córdoba hostels and tour operators such as **Nativo Viajes** (0351-424-5341; Independencia 174; 9am-6pm Mon-Fri, 10am-3pm Sun) offer trekking excursions and day trips to Los Gigantes. Córdoba's tourist office maintains a list of rock-climbing guides.

Entertainment

La Voz del Interior, the main Córdoba newspaper, has a reasonably comprehensive entertainment section every Thursday with show times and the like.

Cuarteto music (a Córdoba invention) is big here and played live in many venues. Unfortunately, it's also the gangsta rap of Argentine folk music and tends to attract undesirable crowds. **La Sala del Rey** (Humberto Primero 439; from 9pm Thu-Sat) is a respectable venue and the best place to catch a *cuarteto* show.

Centro Cultural Casona Municipal CULTURAL CENTER
(cnr Av General Paz & La Rioja; 8am-8pm Sun-Fri, 10am-10pm Sat) Shows contemporary and avante garde art, hosts concerts and offers month-long art and music courses.

Teatro del Libertador General San Martín THEATER
(0351-433-2319; Av Vélez Sársfield 365; admission AR$40-200; box office 9am-9pm) It's well worth going to a performance here, if only to see the opulence of the country's most historic theater. The building was completed in 1891, and the floor was designed to be mechanically raised level with the stage, so seats could be removed, allowing for grand parties for the aristocracy of the early 1900s.

Cineclub Municipal Hugo del Carril CINEMA
(0351-433-2463; www.cineclubmunicipal.org.ar; Blvd San Juan 49; admission AR$10; box office 9am-late) For a great night (or day) at the movies, pop into this municipal film house, which screens everything from art flicks to Latin American award winners and local films. Stop by for a program. There's also live music and theatrical performances here.

Shopping

Antique stores line Calle Belgrano in barrio Güemes, where there is also a **feria artisanal** (Artisans' Market; cnr Rodriguez & Belgrano; 5-10pm Sat & Sun), one of the country's best. You'll find Argentine handicrafts at several stores downtown.

Paseo Colonial ACCESSORIES
(Belgrano 795; 10am-9pm Mon-Sat, 5-10pm Sun) To find out what the city's hip young designers have been working on, slip into this little arcade, featuring a variety of small shops selling clothes, homewares and jewelry.

Talabartería Crespo SOUVENIRS
(☎0351-421-5447; Obispo Trejo 141; ⏲8am-6pm Mon-Sat) Leather goods made from *carpincho* (a large rodent that makes a beautifully spotted leather) are the specialty here. Sweaters, knives and *mate* (a bitter ritual tea) paraphernalia grace the shelves as well.

ℹ Information

MEDICAL SERVICES

Emergency hospital (☎0351-421-0243; cnr Catamarca & Blvd Guzmán)

MONEY

Cambios (money-exchange offices) and ATMs are on Rivadavia north of the plaza; both are also at the main bus terminal and airport.

Cambio Barujel (cnr Rivadavia & 25 de Mayo; ⏲9am-6pm Mon-Fri, 9am-2pm Sat)

Maguitur (25 de Mayo 122; ⏲9am-6pm Mon-Fri, 9am-2pm Sat) Charges 3% on traveler's checks.

POST

Main Post Office (Av General Paz 201; ⏲8am-6pm Mon-Fri & 9am-1pm Sat)

TOURIST INFORMATION

ACA (Automóvil Club Argentino; ☎0351-421-4636; cnr Av General Paz & Humberto Primo; ⏲24hr) Argentina's auto club; good source for provincial road maps.

Casa Cabildo Tourist Information Office (☎0351-434-1200; Independencia 30; ⏲8am-8pm) The provincial and municipal tourist boards occupy the same office in the historic Casa Cabildo. There are also branches located at the airport and the bus terminal.

TRAVEL AGENCIES

Asatej (☎0351-422-9453; www.asatej.com; Av Vélez Sársfield 361, Patio Olmos, Local 412; ⏲8am-6pm Mon-Fri & 9am-1pm Sat) On the 3rd floor of Patio Olmos shopping center. Non-profit student travel agency with great staff. Open to all ages and nonstudents.

ℹ Getting There & Away

AIR

Córdoba's international airport, **Ingeniero Ambrosio Taravella** (☎434-8390) is about 15km northwest of the city center.

Aerolíneas Argentinas/Austral (☎0351-482-1025; Av Colón 520) has offices downtown and flies several times daily to Buenos Aires, Salta and Puerto Iguazú. **Sol** (☎0810-122-7765; www.sol.com.ar) flies to Rosario and Mendoza and **Aero Chaco** (☎0810-345-2422; www.aerochaco.net) flies to Resistencia.

BUS

Córdoba's **bus terminal** (NETOC; ☎0351-434-1692; Blvd Perón 300) is about a 15-minute walk from downtown. **Rede Ticket** (Obispo Trejo 327; ⏲8am-9pm Mon-Sat) sells tickets for all the major bus companies without charging commission. Its downtown location is handy for booking in advance.

In the new terminal (across the road, accessed by tunnel), several bus companies offer services to the same destinations as those offered by the minibus terminal. Be aware that those buses that leave from the terminal stop everywhere, which often adds another hour to the journey time.

Several companies offer service to Chilean destinations, including Santiago (AR$562, 16 hours), although some involve changing buses in Mendoza.

Buses from Córdoba

DESTINATION	COST (AR$)	DURATION (HR)
Bahía Blanca	550	12
Bariloche	1048	22
Buenos Aires	530	10
Catamarca	275	5-6
Corrientes	598	12
Esquel	1218	25
Formosa	618	12
Jujuy	713	12
La Rioja	280	7
Mendoza	535	10
Merlo	140	5½
Montevideo (Uruguay)	734	15
Neuquén	765	17
Paraná	248	6
Puerto Iguazú	1170	22
Puerto Madryn	958	18-20
Resistencia	581	13
Río Gallegos	1830	40
Rosario	260	6
Salta	687	12
San Juan	365	14
San Luis	295	6
San Martín de los Andes	1048	21
Santiago del Estero	284	6
Tucumán	390	8

MINIBUS

Frequent minibuses leave from **Mercado Sud minibus terminal** (Blvd Illia near Buenos Aires). Most go direct, while some stop at every little town along the way. It's worth asking, as this can shave an hour off your travel time.

In summer there may be direct buses to La Cumbrecita, but it will probably be quicker to go first to Villa General Belgrano.

Minibuses from Córdoba

DESTINATION	COST (AR$)	DURATION (HR)
Alta Gracia	14	1
Capilla del Monte	52	3
Cosquín	29	1¼
Jesús María	19	1
La Cumbre	45	3
Mina Clavero	50	3
Villa Carlos Paz	16	1
Villa General Belgrano	45	2

TRAIN

Trains leave Córdoba's **Estación Ferrocarril Mitre** (☎0351-426-3565; Blvd Perón s/n) for Rosario (AR$22/34/69 in *turista/primera/*Pullman class, nine hours) and Buenos Aires' Retiro station (AR$30/50/90/300 in *turista/primera/*Pullman/*camarote*, 17 hours) at 2:40pm on Sundays and Wednesdays. There is a dining car and bar on board. Tickets often sell out weeks in advance, especially in the *camarote* (two-person sleeping cabin), so book as soon as possible.

Trains to Cosquín (AR$6.50, two hours) leave from **Estación Rodriguez del Busto** (☎0351-477-6195; Cardeñosa 3500) on the northwest outskirts of town at 8:44am and 10:55am daily, with an extra noon service on weekends. The R4 bus stops at 27 de Abril 160 en route to the station or it's an AR$35 taxi ride.

ℹ Getting Around

The airport is 15km north of town via Av Monseñor Pablo Cabrera. Intercórdoba goes to/from the airport from the main bus station (AR$5). A taxi into town should cost around AR$100.

Buses require rechargeable magnetic cards or *cospeles* (tokens), both of which are available from nearly every kiosk in town. Rides cost AR$2.50.

A car is very useful for visiting some of the nearby Jesuit *estancias* that cannot be reached by bus. Depending on seasonal demand, economy cars cost around AR$250 with 200km. Try **Alamo** (☎0351-499-8436; Duarte Quirós 1300, Sheraton Hotel; ⏰9am-6pm) or **Europcar** (☎0351-481-7683, 0351-422-4867; Entre Ríos 70; ⏰9am-6pm Mon-Fri, 9am-1pm Sat).

THE CENTRAL SIERRAS

Nowhere near as visually spectacular as the nearby Andes, the Central Sierras more than make up for it by being way more hospitable. The area is dotted with little towns that are worth a quick visit or a longer stay, and is connected by an excellent road network with frequent bus services.

From the hippie chic of paragliding capital La Cumbre to the over-the-top kitsch of Villa Carlos Paz, you'd have to be one jaded traveler not to find something to your liking here. Kicking back is easily done – the riverside village of Mina Clavero is a favorite, as are the ex-Jesuit centers of Alta Gracia and Jesús María. Things get decidedly Germanic down south, and the pedestrian-only La Cumbrecita is not to be missed for *spaetzle* (German egg noodles), bush walks and swimming holes.

Cosquín

☎03541 / POP 19,500 / ELEV 720M

Cosquín is known throughout the country for its **Festival Nacional del Folklore** (www.aquicosquin.org), a nine-day national folkmusic festival that has been held in the last week of January since 1961. The town gets packed for the festival, stays busy all summer and goes pleasantly dead the rest of the year. The slightly more hardcore **Cosquín Rock Festival** used to be held here, until the neighbors decided that teenagers with wallet chains, studded wristbands and piercings weren't really the tourist trade they were looking for. The festival relocated a few years ago to the banks of the nearby (and aptly named) Lago San Roque.

East of town, 1260m **Cerro Pan de Azúcar** offers good views of the sierras and, on a clear day, the city of Córdoba. An **aerosilla** (chairlift; return AR$50; ⏰9am-6pm) runs to the summit regularly in the summer – check with the tourist office in the off season. A taxi to the base should cost about AR$90/120 one way/return with a half-hour wait.

Across the river from the center of town (turn left after the bridge), Av Belgrano forms 4km of waterfront promenade – a great place

Central Sierras

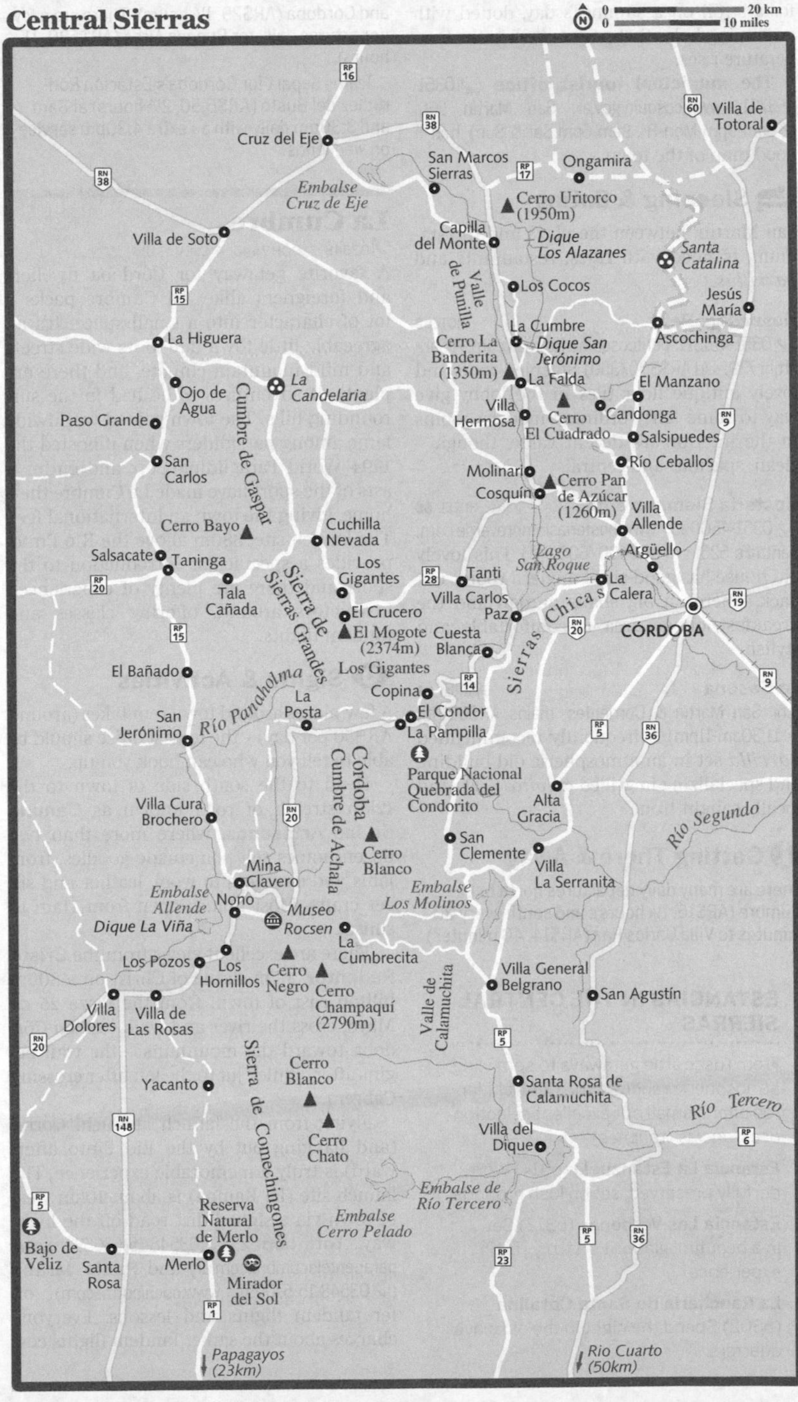

for a stroll on a summer's day, dotted with swimming holes that pack out when the temperature rises.

The **municipal tourist office** (☎0351-453701; www.cosquin.gov.ar; San Martín 560; ⏰8am-9pm Mon-Fri, 9am-6pm Sat & Sun) has a good map of the town.

Sleeping & Eating

San Martín, between the plaza and the stadium, is lined with cafes, restaurants and *parrillas*.

Hospedaje Petit HOTEL $
(☎0351-451311; petitcosquin@hotmail.com; A Sabattini 739; s/d AR$300/350) Steepled roofs and lovely antique floor tiles in the lobby give way to some fairly ordinary modern rooms in the interior. It's decent value, though – clean, spacious and central.

Hostería Siempreverde HOTEL $$
(☎0351-450093; www.hosteriasiempreverde.com; Santa Fe 525; s/d AR$400/600; 📶) This lovely old house has good-sized modern rooms out back. There's a big shady garden and the breakfast/lounge area is comfortable and stylish.

La Casona PARRILLA $
(cnr San Martín & Corrientes; mains AR$60-90; ⏰11:30am-11pm) A frequently recommended *parrilla* set in an atmospheric old building and specializing in grilled *chivito* (goat) and locally caught trout.

Getting There & Away

There are many daily departures north to La Cumbre (AR$16, 1¼ hours); and south every 20 minutes to Villa Carlos Paz (AR$14, 40 minutes) and Córdoba (AR$29, 1¼ hours). There are a few departures daily for Buenos Aires (AR$530, 11 hours).

Trains depart for Córdoba's Estación Rodriguez del Busto (AR$6.50, 2½ hours) at 8am and 3:30pm daily with an extra 4:30pm service on weekends.

ESTANCIAS IN THE CENTRAL SIERRAS

From rustic little getaways to sprawling, atmospheric ranches, the Central Sierras offer a small but excellent selection of *estancias* (ranches).

Estancia La Estanzuela (p314) Wonderfully preserved, set on lush grounds.

Estancia Las Verbenas (p312) Set in a beautiful glade, it's a truly rustic experience.

La Ranchería de Santa Catalina (p302) Spend the night in the old slave quarters.

La Cumbre

☎03548 / POP 7540 / ELEV 1141M

A favorite getaway for Córdoba dwellers and foreigners alike, La Cumbre packs a lot of character into a small space. It's an agreeable little town due to its wide streets and mild mountain climate, and there are plenty of adventures to be had in the surrounding hills. The town gained worldwide fame among paragliders when it hosted the 1994 World Paragliding Cup, and enthusiasts of the sport have made La Cumbre their home, giving the town an international feel. The launch site, 380m above the Río Pinto, provides a spectacular introduction to the sport and there are plenty of experienced instructors around, offering classes and tandem flights.

Sights & Activities

A few places around town rent bikes (around AR$50 per day) – the tourist office should be able to tell you who can hook you up.

Head to the south side of town to the 12km stretch of road known as **Camino de los Artesanos**, where more than two dozen homes sell homemade goodies, from jams and chutneys to wool, leather and silver crafts. Most homes open from 11am to sunset.

There are excellent views from the **Cristo Redentor**, a 7m statue of Christ on a 300m hilltop east of town; from the Plaza 25 de Mayo, cross the river and walk east on Córdoba toward the mountains – the trail begins after a quick jut to the left after crossing Cabrera.

Flying from the launch at Cuchi Corral (and hanging out by the Río Pinto afterward) is truly a memorable experience. The launch site (La Rampa) is about 10km west of town via a signed dirt road off the highway. **Toti López** (☎03548-15-636592; www.parapentelacumbre.com.ar) and **Pablo Jaraba** (☎03548-15-570951; www.cuchicorral.com) offer tandem flights and lessons. Everyone charges about the same. Tandem flights cost

AR$600 for a half-hour; full courses cost AR$6000.

At the **Aeroclub La Cumbre** (☎03548-452544; Camino a los Troncos s/n; ⏰9am-7pm) you can arrange everything from tandem flights to ultralights and parachute jumps. Ask for Andy Hediger (former paragliding world champion).

Hacer Cumbre (☎03548-15-638424; www.hacercumbre.com; Caraffa 270; ⏰9am-1pm & 4-8pm) offers pretty much everything else in the area, including treks, 4WD off-roading and horseback tours in the breathtaking countryside around Cerro Ongamira.

Sleeping

The proprietors of most places can arrange any activities available in La Cumbre.

Hostel La Cumbre HOSTEL $
(☎03548-451368; www.hostellacumbre.com; San Martín 186; dm AR$90, r AR$300, without bathroom AR$250; @📶🏊) A couple of blocks behind the bus terminal, this converted English mansion is one of the most impressive hostels in the Sierras. Views from the front balcony are superb.

Camping El Cristo CAMPGROUND $
(☎03548-451893; Monseñor P Cabrera s/n; campsites AR$20) Below the Cristo Redentor east of town, La Cumbre's exceptional campgrounds are only a short tramp from the center.

Hostería Pastoral HOTEL $$
(☎03548-452787; www.hosteriapastoral.com.ar; Moreno 480; s/d AR$450/500, with spa access AR$500/550; @📶🏊) A cozy ski-lodge atmosphere, homey lounge areas and a huge yard with swimming pool make up for the somewhat outdated rooms. If not, the spa with Jacuzzi, sauna and massages may tip the scales.

Eating & Drinking

★**Kasbah** ASIAN $
(Alberdi & Sarmiento; mains AR$50-100; ⏰12:30pm-12:30am; 📶) You may not be expecting a good Thai curry out here, but this cute little triangular restaurant comes up with the goods. Also on offer is a range of Chinese and Indian dishes.

Khushka ARGENTINE $
(25 de Mayo 185; mains AR$50-100; ⏰noon-1am; 📶) If you're looking for a spicy stew and a good selection of northern Argentine-influenced dishes, this one's worth checking out. There's also a good wine list and live music on weekends.

El Pungo PUB
(www.elpungopub.com.ar; Camino de los Artesanos s/n; cover from AR$30; ⏰noon-late Sat & Sun) This somewhat legendary watering hole attracts musicians from all over the country (Argentine folk musicians Charly Garcia and Fito Paez have played here).

Information

Banco de la Provincia de Córdoba (cnr López y Planes & 25 de Mayo; ⏰9am-1pm Mon-Fri) Has an ATM.

Tourist office (☎03548-452966; www.lacumbre.gov.ar; Av Caraffa 300; ⏰8am-9pm Apr-Jun & Aug-Nov, to midnight Dec-Mar & Jul) Across from the bus terminal in the old train station. Friendly staff will supply a handy map of the town and surroundings.

Getting There & Away

Buses depart regularly from La Cumbre's convenient **bus terminal** (General Paz, near Caraffa), heading northward to Capilla del Monte (AR$11, 30 minutes) or south to Cosquín (AR$15, 1¼ hours), Villa Carlos Paz (AR$28, 1½ hours), San Marcos (AR$21, one hour) and Córdoba (AR$45, 2½ hours). Minibuses (which take about half an hour less) are the fastest way to Córdoba. There is also a direct service to Buenos Aires (AR$650, 12½ hours).

San Marcos de las Sierras

☎03549 / POP 930 / ELEV 625M

Once a moribund hill town, San Marcos got an injection of life in the late '60s when the hippies discovered its mild climate, way-off-the-grid isolation and good farmland, and began flocking here. Over the decades, curious tourists began appearing, having heard about the hippie town in the Sierras, and eventually the town's emphasis shifted from agriculture and handicraft manufacture to tourism.

Taken aback by the swing towards capitalism, many of the old crew moved out but traces of San Marcos' hippie heritage remains – the community has successfully campaigned against the use of genetically modified crops in the valley as well as sealed roads and even a gas station in town. These days the town makes for a pleasant getaway and the creekside location in a pretty valley is as enticing as ever.

There's no bus terminal, but buses arrive and depart from a stop near the main plaza. The **tourist office** (☑03549-496452; www.sanmarcossierras.gov.ar; cnr Libertad & Sarmiento; ☉9am-6pm) has a good map of the town and surrounds and decent info on walks and upcoming events. There's an ATM in the Municipal building on Sarmiento, but bring cash in case it isn't working.

◉ Sights & Activities

San Marcos enjoys a fabulous natural setting, and there are some excellent walks just out of town, including the riverside walk to the **Viejo Molino** (admission AR$5; ☉9am-3pm), a 17th-century flour mill that was used to grind the town's cereals until the 1950s. The tourist office has a good area map.

Museo Hippie MUSEUM
(AR$20; ☉11am-6pm Thu-Mon) 🕊 Far more interesting for the stream-of-consciousness commentary on the evolution of the hippie movement in Argentina (dating back to the Greek Philosophers) than the actual artifacts it holds, this small museum on the northern outskirts of town is worth a visit – if nothing else, it's a pleasant walk out there.

🛏 Sleeping & Eating

Restaurants and cafes surround the main plaza. Most accommodations are within a kilometer of here.

Hostel Agrimon HOSTEL $
(☑03549-496397; posadaargimon@infovia.com.ar; Sarmiento 341; dm/d AR$110/300; @ 🕸) A sweet little hostel right in front of the main plaza. Dorms are spacious, sleeping four, and come with private bathrooms; doubles are good value, too. A shady garden out back and an OK kitchen and living area round out the deal.

Camping La Quebrada CAMPGROUND $
(☑03549-496137; Av Siete Colores s/n; campsites per person AR$35) Shady campsites on the riverfront. Facilities include *parrillas* (barbecues) and reasonable bathrooms.

Madre Tierra HOTEL $$
(☑03549-496394; secretosdemadretierra@hotmail.com; San Martín 650; s/d AR$400/500; ✴🕸🕸) Probably the most formal setup in town, with stylish, modern rooms (a bit on the small side) arranged around a good-sized swimming pool. It's about 500m over the bridge north of the plaza.

Kaparece INTERNATIONAL $
(Libertad 112; mains AR$35-60; ☉8am-midnight) This cute little place has the most varied menu in town, with a good range of salads and sandwiches and some good-value set lunches (AR$65).

❶ Getting There & Away

There are five buses daily from La Cumbre (AR$21, one hour). Buses also pass through here en route from Cruz del Eje to Córdoba (AR$55, four hours).

Jesús María
☑03525 / POP 31,600

Sleepy little Jesús María earns its place on the map by being home to one of the most atmospheric Jesuit *estancias* in the region – the Unesco-listed **Museo Jesuítico Nacional de Jesús María** (☑03525-420126; admission AR$10, Tue free; ☉8am-9pm Tue-Fri). The church and convent were built in 1618 and are set on superbly landscaped grounds. The Jesuits, after losing their operating capital to pirates off the Brazilian coast, sold wine they made here to support their university in colonial Córdoba. The museum has good archaeological pieces from indigenous groups throughout Argentina, informative maps of the missionary trajectory and well-restored (though dubiously authentic) rooms.

Jesús María is also home to the annual **Fiesta Nacional de Doma y Folklore** (www.festival.org.ar), a 10-day celebration of gaucho horsemanship and customs beginning the first weekend of January. The festival draws crowds from all over the country – and accusations of animal cruelty from animal-rights groups, who argue that whipping horses and making them perform acrobatics in front of noisy crowds under bright lights is tantamount to torture.

Most people do Jesús María as a day trip from Córdoba. Frequent minibuses (AR$19, one hour) leave Córdoba's Mercado Sud terminal and bus terminal daily.

Alta Gracia
☑03547 / POP 48,100 / ELEV 550M

Set around a 17th-century Jesuit reservoir, Alta Gracia is a tranquil little mountain town of winding streets and shady parks. The star attraction here is the 17th-century Jesuit *estancia,* whose exquisite church, nighttime lighting, and lovely location between a tiny

CLOSE ENCOUNTERS

It's not just the freaks and hippies. Even normal-looking people in Capilla del Monte have stories about strange lights appearing in formation in the night skies over nearby Cerro Uritorco. The stories go way back, too. In 1935 Manuel Reina reported seeing a strange being, dressed in a tight-fitting suit, while he was out walking on a country road. In 1986 Gabriel and Esperanza Gómez saw a spaceship so big that its lights illuminated the surrounding countryside. The next day a burn mark measuring 122m by 64m was found at the point where it reportedly landed.

A couple of years later, 300 people witnessed another ship, which left a burn mark 42m in diameter. And in 1991 another burn mark was found. This one measured 12m in diameter, with a temperature of 340°C. Geologists were called in and they claimed that nearby rocks had recently been heated to a temperature of 3000°C.

Why all this activity around Capilla del Monte? This is where it gets really weird. One theory is that *Ovnis* (UFOs) visit the area because Cerro Uritorco is where the knight Parsifal brought the Holy Grail and the Templar Cross at the end of the 12th century. He did this to lay them beside the Cane of Order, which had been made 8000 years before by Lord Voltán of the Comechingones, the indigenous tribe that inhabited this region.

Another theory is that they are drawn here because underneath Uritorco lies Erks, a subterranean city, which, according to 'hermetic scientists,' is where the future regeneration of the human species will take place. Inside you'll find the Esfera Temple and the three mirrors used to exchange data with other galaxies, and where you can see the details of the life of every human being.

The official explanation? Good ol' meteorological phenomena, caused by supercharged ion particles in the atmosphere, mixed in with a healthy touch of mass hysteria.

Whatever you believe, one thing's for sure: all this hype isn't hurting little Capilla del Monte's tourist industry one bit. Until recently, the only people climbing Uritorco were goatherds and a few interested townsfolk. These days, numbers can approach 1000 per day, all hoping to catch a glimpse of the mysterious lights.

If you want to climb Uritorco (1950m) you must start the climb before midday, and begin your descent by 3pm. The 5km hike to the top affords spectacular views. From Capilla del Monte, catch a taxi or walk the 3km to the base of the mountain.

Capilla del Monte is a comfortable enough place to base yourself – the town has plenty of restaurants and lodging; the **tourist office** (☎03548-481903; www.capilladelmonte.gov.ar; cnr Av Pueyrredón & Buenos Aires; ⌚8am-8pm) in the old train station has mounds of information. For more info on UFOs in the area, drop in to the **Centro de Informes Ovni** (☎03548-482485; www.ciouritorco.org; Juan Cabus 397; ⌚10am-4pm). There is a frequent bus service south to Córdoba (AR$52, three hours), stopping at all towns on the RN38, and long-distance service to Buenos Aires.

reservoir and the central plaza make it one of the most impressive of Córdoba province's Unesco World Heritage sites. Revolutionary Che Guevara spent his adolescence in Alta Gracia and his former home is now a museum. Many people come on day trips from Córdoba, but the city is emerging as a destination in its own right and as a base for exploring the southern sierras.

The **tourist office** (☎03547-428128; www.altagracia.gov.ar; Reloj Público, cnr Av del Tajamar & Calle del Molino; ⌚7am-10:30pm summer, to 7pm winter) occupies an office in the clock tower. The best source of English-language information is at www.ilovealtagracia.com.

Sights & Activities

Jesuit Estancia NOTABLE BUILDING

From to 1762, Jesuit fathers built the **Iglesia Parroquial Nuestra Señora de la Merced** (west side of Plaza Manuel Solares) FREE, the *estancia's* most impressive building. Directly south of the church, the colonial Jesuit workshops of **El Obraje** (1643) are now a public school. Beside the church is the **Museo Histórico Nacional del Virrey Liniers** (☎03547-421303; www.museoliniers.org.ar; admission AR$15, Wed free; ⌚9am-1pm & 3-7pm Tue-Fri, 9:30am-12:30pm & 3:30-6:30pm Sat, Sun & holidays), named after former resident Virrey Liniers, one of the last officials to

WORTH A TRIP

ESTANCIA SANTA CATALINA

One of the most beautiful of the Sierra's Unesco World Heritage sites, the Jesuit *estancia* (ranch) of **Santa Catalina** (03525-421600; www.santacatalina.info; admission AR$15; 10am-1pm & 2-6pm Tue-Sun, closed Jan, Feb, Jul & Semana Santa), some 20km northwest of Jesús María, is a quiet, tiny place, where the village store occupies part of the *estancia,* and old-timers sit on the benches outside and watch the occasional gaucho ride past on a horse. Much of the *estancia* is off-limits to visitors, but guided **tours** (each site AR$10) are available, taking in the chapel, cloisters and novitiate, where unmarried slave girls were housed.

The grounds themselves, while a fraction of their former selves, are lovely and well maintained and you can easily while away an hour or two wandering around. Outside the *estancia,* around the back, is the original reservoir built by the Jesuits, now slowly being overtaken by tall-stemmed lilies.

Santa Catalina is the only Unesco World Heritage *estancia* still under private ownership. Part of the family owns and operates **La Ranchería de Santa Catalina** (03525-424467; s without bathroom AR$260, d AR$750;), a lovely inn, restaurant (meals from AR$80) and crafts store in the *ranchería*. It has only two rooms, which occupy the former slave quarters and, while small, are carefully decorated and retain their original stone walls. Three more rooms with bathrooms are being constructed, using traditional techniques. The place is run by a friendly couple who are more than willing to fill you in on the illustrious story of the *estancia,* from Jesuit times to the present.

A taxi out here from Jesús María costs about AR$160.

occupy the post of Viceroy of the River Plate. If you want to know every last historical detail, guided tours in English (AR$30 per person; held at 10am, 11:30am, 3:30pm and 5pm) are available and recommended – you need to call to reserve one day in advance. If you just have a passing interest, each room has an information sheet in English, which gives you a fair understanding of what's going on.

Directly north of the museum, across Av Belgrano, the **Tajamar** (1659) is one of the city's several 17th-century dams, which together made up the complex system of field irrigation created by the Jesuits.

Museo Casa de Ernesto Che Guevara MUSEUM
(Avellaneda 501; admission AR$75; 2-7pm Mon, from 9am Tue-Sun) In the 1930s, the family of youthful Ernesto Guevara moved here because a doctor recommended the dry climate for his asthma. Though Che lived in several houses – including the house in Rosario, where he was born – the family's primary residence was Villa Beatriz, which was purchased by the city and restored as this museum.

Its cozy interior is now adorned with a photographic display of Che's life, and a couple of huge photographs commemorating a recent visit from Fidel Castro and Hugo Chávez. If you think you've been on the road for a while, check out the map detailing Che's travels through Latin America – whatever you think of the man's politics, you have to admit he was well traveled. A small selection of Che paraphernalia (including cigars, of course) is on sale.

Tours

El Trebol OUTDOORS
(turismoaventuraeltrebol@hotmail.com) Offers an interesting range of tours in the pretty countryside surrounding Alta Gracia, on horseback or in van to places such as outlying Jesuit sites or the very worthwhile observatory. Also on offer is a fascinating historical walking tour of the city.

Sleeping & Eating

A number of cafe-bar-restaurants with sidewalk seating are scattered along Av Belgrano, in the three blocks downhill from the Jesuit museum.

La Yola Hostel HOSTEL $
(03547-15-467063; Belgrano 152; dm/d AR$80/160;) Alta Gracia's coziest little hostel has OK dorms, spacious doubles and an unbeatable main-street location.

★279 Boutique B&B BOUTIQUE HOTEL $$
(☎03547-424177; www.279altagracia.com; Giorello 279; r AR$450; 📶) 🍃 Alta Gracia's best accommodations by far only offer two rooms, but that just adds to the charm. Run by an ex–New York photographer, it's a stylish, intimate place with just the right blend of old features rescued from the original house and slick modern styling.

Breakfast is fantastic, the location's great and attention to detail is superb. More like this, please.

★El Bistro del Alquimista FUSION $$
(Castellanos 351; meals AR$100-120; ⏲Mon-Sat 9pm-midnight; 📶) This is the way the gourmet scene in Argentina *should* be heading: an open kitchen with chefs doubling as waitstaff and well-presented, innovative dishes served up in a casual atmosphere with super-attentive service. The four-pass menu changes daily and the wines all come from boutique winemakers.

Getting There & Away

Minibuses depart regularly for Córdoba (AR$14, one hour) a block uphill from the *estancia*. The **bus terminal** (Tacuarí at Perón) near the river also has departures for Córdoba and Buenos Aires (AR$550, 13 hours). Buses to Villa General Belgrano stop every hour on RP5, about 20 blocks along Av San Martín from the town center.

Villa General Belgrano

☎03546 / POP 7800 / ELEV 720M

More a cultural oddity than a full-blown tourist attraction, the village of Villa General Belgrano flaunts its origins as a settlement of unrepatriated survivors from the German battleship *Graf Spee,* which sank near Montevideo during WWII.

The annual Oktoberfest, held during the first two weeks of October, draws beer lovers from all over the world. In summertime the village slowly fills with holidaymakers enjoying the tranquil streets and the evergreen-dotted countryside. Unless you're really excited about microbrew beer, *torta selva negra* (Black Forest cake) and goulash, Villa General Belgrano can be seen in a day trip from Córdoba or nearby La Cumbrecita. Despite its decidedly Germanic flavor, you'd be lucky to hear any of the modern-day inhabitants speaking the language of the old country.

Sights & Activities

If you're up for a stroll, a lovely path runs between Corrientes and El Quebracho, alongside the Arroyo La Toma, a creek one block back from the main street.

Lookout tower LOOKOUT
(Roca 168; admission AR$10; ⏲9am-8pm) For an overview of the town and surrounds, make your way up to the lookout tower attached to the tourist office.

Friedrich BICYCLE RENTAL
(☎03546-461451; Roca 224; ⏲9am-6pm Mon-Sat) Friedrich rents mountain bikes for AR$20/100 per hour/day.

Sleeping & Eating

In the December-to-March high season, hotel prices rise and rooms fill quickly. Unless you book weeks before Oktoberfest, plan on hitting the festival as a day trip from Córdoba.

There are numerous restaurants along the main strip of Roca and San Martín.

Albergue El Rincón HOSTEL $
(☎03546-461323; Fleming 347; campsite per person/dm/d AR$70/100/170) 🍃 This beautiful Dutch-owned hostel, surrounded by forest, has excellent, spacious dorm rooms, outdoor and indoor kitchens, a *parrilla* and its own biodynamic farm. Outstanding breakfasts cost AR$25. It's a good 900m walk from behind the bus terminal to the entrance gate; follow the signs.

WORTH A TRIP

OKTOBERFEST IN VILLA GENERAL BELGRANO

If you're in the Sierras around the start of October, consider hitting Villa General Belgrano, which celebrates its German heritage with a 10-day, nationally recognized Oktoberfest. While the beer runs as freely as it does at Oktoberfests all over the world, there are also parades, endless concerts and other cultural presentations. The festival also features so much delicious street food that you'll be loosening a couple of buttons on your Lederhosen, even if you're not a drinker.

For more info on the festival, have a look at www.vgb.gov.ar/oktoberfest.

The Legend of Che

One of Cuba's greatest revolutionary heroes, in some ways even eclipsing Fidel Castro himself, was an Argentine. Ernesto Guevara, known by the common Argentine interjection 'che,' was born in Rosario in 1928 and spent his first years in Buenos Aires. In 1932, after Guevara's doctor recommended a drier climate for his severe asthma, Guevara's parents moved to the mountain resort of Alta Gracia.

He later studied medicine in the capital and, in 1952, spent six months riding a motorcycle around South America, a journey that opened Guevara's eyes to the plight of South America's poor.

After his journey, Guevara traveled to Central America, finally landing in Mexico, where he met Fidel Castro and other exiles. The small group sailed to Cuba on a rickety old yacht and began the revolution that overthrew Cuban dictator Fulgencio Batista in 1959. Unfulfilled by the bureaucratic task of building Cuban socialism, Guevara tried, unsuccessfully, to spread revolution in the Congo, Argentina and finally Bolivia, where he was killed in 1967.

Today Che is known less for his eloquent writings and speeches than for the striking black-and-white portrait as the beret-wearing rebel – an image gracing everything from T-shirts to CD covers – taken by photojournalist Alberto Korda in 1960.

In 1997, on the 30th anniversary of Che's death, the Argentine government issued a postage stamp honoring Che's Argentine roots. You can take a look at the stamps and other Che memorabilia by visiting Alta Gracia's modest Museo Casa de Ernesto Che Guevara (p302).

OLIVIER CIRENDINI/GETTY IMAGES ©

Clockwise from top left

1. Postcards **2.** Museo Casa de Ernesto Che Guevara (p302), Alta Gracia **3.** Mural, Plaza Dorrego (p66), Buenos Aires

2

AARON MCCOY/GETTY IMAGES ©

TRAVEL INK/GETTY IMAGES ©

Posada Aitué HOTEL $$
(☎03546-463439; www.aitueposada.com; Sársfield 75; s/d from AR$400/600) This lovely Alpine-style chalet is a short walk from the center. Pay another AR$200 and you get a sitting room, kitchenette and hydro-massage bath.

Blumen INTERNATIONAL $$
(Roca 373; mains AR$80-120; ⏲noon-11pm Tue-Sun) With one of the widest menus in town, Blumen serves up good, tasty, if slightly expensive, dishes. It's a great spot for a few drinks – the huge shady beer garden is all wooden tables and pagodas, with plenty of space in between and the microbrew beer flowing readily.

Information

The **tourist office** (☎03546-461215; www.elsitiodelavilla.com; Roca 168; ⏲8:30am-8:30pm) is on the main street, as are banks with ATMs.

Getting There & Away

The bus terminal is a few blocks uphill from the main street. Buses leave every hour for Córdoba (AR$45, two hours), and daily for Buenos Aires (AR$485, 11 hours). There are seven departures daily for La Cumbrecita (AR$34, one hour).

La Cumbrecita

☎03546 / POP 550 / ELEV 1300M

The pace of life slows waaaay down in this alpine-styled village, nestled in the forest in the Valle de Calamuchita. The tranquility is largely thanks to the town's pedestrian-only policy. It's a great place to kick back for a few days and wander the forest trails leading to swimming holes, waterfalls and scenic lookouts.

Visitors must park their cars in the dirt parking lot (AR$50) before crossing the bridge over Río del Medio by foot.

The helpful **tourist office** (☎03546-481088; www.lacumbrecita.gov.ar; ⏲8:30am-9pm summer, 10am-6pm winter) is on the left, just after you cross the bridge into town.

Sights & Activities

Hiking is the best reason to visit La Cumbrecita. Short trails are well marked and the tourist office can provide a crude but useful map of the area. A 25-minute stroll will take you to **La Cascada**, a waterfall tucked into the mountainside. **La Olla** is the closest swimming hole, surrounded by granite rocks (people jump where it's deep enough). **Cerro La Cumbrecita** (1400m) is the highest point in town, about a 20-minute walk from the bridge. Outside town, the highest mountain is the poetically named **Cerro Wank** (1715m); a hike to the top takes about 40 minutes.

For guided hikes further into the mountains, as well as horseback riding (AR$200 for four hours), trout fishing and mountain biking, contact **Viviendo Montañas** (☎03546-481172; www.viviendomontanas.blogspot.com; Las Truchas s/n; ⏲9am-1pm & 3-8pm), which has an office on the main road in town. The company can also take you trekking to the top of **Cerro Champaquí** (2790m), the highest peak in the Sierras (a two-day trek).

Sleeping & Eating

La Cumbrecita has more than 20 hotels and *cabañas* (cabins) in the surrounding hills; the tourist office is a good resource. Make reservations in summer (January and February), during Easter and during Villa General Belgrano's Oktoberfest.

Hospedaje Casa Rosita HOMESTAY $
(☎03546-481003; Calle Principal s/n; s/d without bathroom AR$200/300) A humble little *hospedaje* (family home) set in a charming house by the river at the entrance to the village. If you can, go for room 1, which has a bay window overlooking the river.

Hostel Planeta HOSTEL $
(☎03546-15-409847; dm AR$90, r per person AR$140; 📶) The best hostel in town is reached via a steep path next to the Hotel Las Verbenas tennis court. It's set in a lovely traditional house and has a good dining area and kitchen, reasonable dorms and killer views.

Hotel La Cumbrecita HOTEL $$
(☎03546-481052; www.hotelcumbrecita.com.ar; s/d AR$350/700; ❄📶🏊) Built on the site of the first house in La Cumbrecita, this rambling hotel has some excellent views out over the valley. Rooms aren't huge, but most have fantastic balconies. The extensive grounds include a gym and tennis courts.

Restaurante Bar Suizo EUROPEAN $
(Calle Pública s/n; mains AR$50-90; ⏲8am-10pm; 📶) Pull up a wooden bench under the pine tree and try some of the excellent Swiss-German options such as *spaetzle* with wild-mushroom sauce.

WORTH A TRIP

THERE'S SOMETHING WEIRD IN THEM THAR HILLS

For some reason, Córdoba's Sierras region is one of the quirkiest in Argentina, and the great thing about traveling in the region is that every once in a while you stumble upon something truly wonderful and unexpected. Here are a few of our favorites:

Capilla del Monte This otherwise sleepy little hill town is world-famous among UFO watchers who come here in the hope of communing with the extraterrestrials from on top of the mystical Cerro Uritorco.

Villa General Belgrano (www.elsitiodelavilla.com/oktoberfest) The town's strong German heritage gives it a very European flavor, which really takes off as the beer starts flowing in Oktoberfest (see boxed text, p303).

Carlos Paz (www.villacarlospaz.gov.ar/turismo) Like a mix between Vegas and Disneyland, this lakeside getaway is dotted with theme hotels (the Great Pyramids, the Kremlin) and centered around a massive cuckoo clock.

Museo Rocsen (www.museorocsen.org; admission AR$40; ⌚9am-sunset) Near the tiny town of Nono, outside of Mina Clavero, the 27,000-plus pieces on display here form probably the most eclectic collection of trash/treasure you're ever likely to see.

Hotel Eden (admission by tour AR$30; ⌚10am-6pm) Take a guided tour of this once-extravagant, now-decaying hotel, built in 1897, where the guest list included Albert Einstein, the Duke of Savoy and several Argentine presidents. Inside the hotel is the **Miniature Train Museum**, a strangely captivating museum devoted to, you guessed it, very small trains.

★**El Paseo** PARRILLA **$$**
(mains AR$60-90; ⌚noon-midnight Thu-Sun) Out by the La Olla swimming hole, this place serves up a good *parrilla*, plus all the Germanic standards. It's great for afternoon beer.

ℹ Getting There & Away

From Villa General Belgrano, **Transportes Pajaro Blanco** (☎03546-461709; ⌚8am-8pm) has seven departures to La Cumbrecita (AR$34, one hour) from 7am to 7:30pm. The last bus back from La Cumbrecita leaves at 8:40pm. In summer there may be occasional minibuses from Córdoba's Mercado Sud terminal.

Parque Nacional Quebrada del Condorito

ELEV 1900-2300M

This national park protects 370 sq km of stunning rocky grasslands across the Pampa de Achala in the Sierras Grandes. The area, particularly the *quebrada* (gorge) itself, is an important condor nesting site and flight training ground for fledgling condors. A 9km, two- to three-hour hike from the park entrance at **La Pampilla** leads to the Balcón Norte (North Balcony), a clifftop over the gorge where you can view the massive birds circling on the thermals rising up the gorge. You can visit easily as a day trip from Córdoba or on your way to Mina Clavero.

Any bus from Córdoba to Mina Clavero will drop you at La Pampilla (AR$34, 1½ hours), where a trailhead leads to the gorge. To return to Córdoba (or on to Mina Clavero), flag a bus from the turnoff. Hostels in Córdoba arrange day tours to the park.

For more information on the park, contact **Intendencia del PN Quebrada del Condorito** (☎03541-433371; Resistencia 30; ⌚9am-6pm Mon-Fri) in Villa Carlos Paz.

Mina Clavero

☎03544 / POP 8500 / ELEV 915M

Really jumping in summertime, Mina Clavero pretty much empties out for the rest of the year, leaving visitors to explore the limpid streams, rocky waterfalls, numerous swimming holes and idyllic mountain landscapes at their own pace.

Mina Clavero is 170km southwest of Córdoba via RN20, the splendid Nuevo Camino de las Altas Cumbres (Highway of the High Peaks). It sits at the confluence of Río de Los Sauces and Río Panaholma, in the Valle de Traslasierra.

The **tourist office** (☎470171; www.minaclavero.gov.ar; Av San Martín 1464; ⏰7am-midnight Dec-Mar, 9am-9pm Apr-Nov) has standard brochures and a useful map of town.

Sights & Activities

Mina Clavero's *balnearios* (swimming areas) get mobbed in summer, but are often empty the rest of the year. The boulder-strewn gorges of the Río Mina Clavero are easily explored. A lovely *costanera* (riverside road) has been constructed, running from the pedestrian bridge all the way to the **Nido de Aguila**, the best swimming hole around – this makes for a great afternoon stroll. From there head west along the Río de Los Sauces and you'll hit **Los Elefantes**, a *balneario* named for its elephant-like rock formations. A 3km walk south along the river will take you to **Villa Cura Brochero**, where you'll find black pottery that is characteristic of this region.

Sleeping

Many accommodations close around the end of March, when the town almost rolls up the sidewalks.

★Andamundos Hostel HOSTEL $
(☎03544-470249; www.andamundoshostel.com.ar; San Martín 554; dm/d AR$80/220; @ 📶) A rustic little setup a couple of blocks from the center of town. The big yard backing onto the river is a bonus.

Hostería Arenas HOTEL $$
(☎03544-478829; www.hosteriaarenas.com.ar; Lugones 1501; s/d AR$500/600; 📶 🏊) The functional, modern rooms here may lack flavor but that's more than made up for by the fantastic riverside location and good-sized swimming pool. Rooms without river views cost 10% less.

Eating

Most of Mina Clavero's restaurants are along San Martín. Head south over the river for more upscale *parrillas* and restaurants.

★Rincón Suizo CAFE $
(Champaqui 1200; mains AR$40-80; ⏰11am-10pm) This comfy teahouse on the river prides itself on its homemade ice creams, delicious Swiss food (including fondue, raclette and ratatouille) and *torta selva negra*.

MINA CLAVERO SHORTCUT

The Río Mina Clavero splits the town in two. If you arrive at the bus terminal, take the pedestrian bridge across the river – it takes you straight into the downtown area. Otherwise you have to go the long way around.

Palenque INTERNATIONAL $
(San Martín 1191; mains AR$40-80; ⏰11-1am; 📶) Funky works of art on the walls and live music on the weekends make this a popular spot. It's a great place for drinks and the snacks and meals are a good deal, too.

La Mamita PARRILLA $
(cnr San Martín & Recalde; mains AR$50-90; ⏰noon-4pm & 8pm-midnight) The most frequently recommended *parrilla* in town, this place serves up tasty empanadas and good-value set meals; located in front of the plaza.

Getting There & Away

The **bus terminal** (Mitre 1191) is across the Río Mina Clavero from the town center. There are several daily buses to Córdoba (AR$55, three hours) and at least three a day to Merlo (AR$39, 2½ to three hours). Minibuses to Córdoba are faster (AR$45, 2½ hours).A couple of buses per day depart for Buenos Aires (AR$524, 13 hours). For destinations in San Juan and Mendoza provinces, go to nearby Villa Dolores (AR$21, one hour).

SAN LUIS & AROUND

The little-visited province of San Luis holds a surprising number of attractions, made all the better by the fact that you'll probably have them all to yourself.

The province is popularly known as La Puerta de Cuyo (the door to Cuyo), referring to the combined provinces of Mendoza, San Luis, La Rioja and San Juan.

The regional superstar is without doubt the Parque Nacional Sierra de las Quijadas, but the mountain towns along the Valle de Conlara and Sierras Puntanas are well worth a visit if you're looking to get off the tourist trail.

Merlo

02652 / POP 17,000 / ELEV 890M

At the top of the Valle de Conlara, the mountain town of Merlo is a growing resort known for its gentle microclimate (the local tourist-industry buzzword) in a relatively dry area. The town is located 200km northeast of San Luis, tucked into the northeast corner of San Luis province.

The **municipal tourist office** (02652-476078; www.villademerlo.gov.ar; Coronel Mercau 605; 8am-8pm) has maps and information on hotels and campgrounds.

Sights & Activities

For a sweeping view of the town and valley, head up to the *miradores* (lookouts) overlooking town. Taxis charge around AR$400 to take you to the Mirador del Sol, halfway up the mountain, and then another 12km to the Mirador de los Condores, which is on top of the mountain ridge and gives views in both directions. There's a **confíteria** (mains AR$60-90; 8am-7pm) up here and, if the wind is right, you can watch the parasailing maniacs taking off from the nearby launchpad.

Two kilometers from the center, in Rincón del Este, on the road to the Miradors, the **Reserva Natural de Merlo** (admission free; daylight hr) is a lovely spot for creekside walks up to a couple of swimming holes. Tour operators in the park offer a range of activities including guided walks, ziplines and rock climbing. **El Rincon del Paraiso** (set meals around AR$70; 8am-6pm), about 400m from the park entrance, is a beautiful, shady restaurant in the middle of the park – a great place for lunch or a couple of drinks.

Serranias Tour (02652-474737; serraniastour@merlo-sl.com.ar; Avenida del Sol 186; 9am-1pm & 3-8pm Mon-Fri, 9am-1pm Sat) is one of the many established tour operators in town. It offers tours to the nearby archaeological/paleontological park at Bajo de Veliz (half day AR$200), and a trip combining the nature reserve and Miradors de Sol and de los Condores (half-day AR$150). This company can hook you up with parasailing operators – flights cost around AR$600 and last 20 to 30 minutes, depending on wind conditions.

Sleeping

Merlo Hostel HOSTEL $
(02652-476928; www.merlohostel.com.ar; Av del Sol 1025; dm AR$95; @) A sweet little family-home-turned-hostel. Dorms could be bigger, but there are good hangout areas, it's an excellent central location and this is one of the few true budget options in town.

Hostería Cerro Azul HOTEL $$
(02652-478648; www.hosteriacerroazul.com.ar; cnr Saturno & Jupiter; r AR$400;) This bright, modern hotel just off the main drag offers big rooms with spacious bathrooms. The lounge-dining area is gorgeous, with high cathedral ceilings.

Eating & Drinking

Cirano ITALIAN $
(Av del Sol 280; mains AR$60-100; noon-1am;) Ignore the flashing fairy lights – there are some good-value eats on offer here, and an excellent set lunch or dinner for AR$46.

WORTH A TRIP

EL VOLCÁN

A small village nestled in the hills east of San Luis, El Volcán (there is no volcano here, by the way) is a laid-back summer getaway spot. The star attraction is the river that runs through the middle of town, where Balneario La Hoya, a series of natural rock pools, offers shady swimming spots and picnic areas.

El Volcán is close enough to San Luis to make it an easy day trip, but there are plenty of cabins for rent, especially during summer.

Hotel El Volcán (0266-449-4044; Banda Norte s/n; s/d AR$300/450;) is the only real hotel in the village. It's a sprawling complex set on shady grounds that run down to the river. The hotel closes off-season – call to make sure it's open. **El Mantial** (Balneario La Hoya; mains AR$35-60; 8am-9pm) has decent food and great views out over the river. Portions are big and service is quick, if somewhat impersonal.

Regular buses run to and from San Luis' main bus terminal (AR$8, 30 minutes).

★Tono ARGENTINE $$
(Av del Sol 690; mains AR$80-120; ⏲noon-1am; 📶) Specializing in regional foods and using lots of local ingredients, this place is a good bet anytime, but Thursday to Saturday nights feature live *trova* (folk) bands, making it even better.

La Cerveceria BAR
(Av del Sol 515; ⏲2pm-late; 📶) If you're looking for a beer, this is your spot – there are eight different types of microbrew on offer, plus the national and imported standbys, sidewalk seating and snacks.

Getting There & Away

Long-distance buses leave from the **new bus terminal** (RN 1 at Calle de las Ovejas), about eight blocks south of the town center.

Buses from Merlo

DESTINATION	COST (AR$)	DURATION (HR)
Buenos Aires	502	12
Córdoba	160	6
Mendoza	305	8
Mina Clavero	60	3
San Luis	72	4

Getting Around

Local buses leave from the **old bus terminal** (☎02652-492858; cnr Pringles & Los Almendres) in the center of town. There are departures for Piedra Blanca (AR$7, 20 minutes), Bajo de Veliz (AR$25, one hour), Papagayos (AR$25, one hour) and the nearby artisan village of Cerro de Oro (AR$10, 30 minutes).

San Luis

☎0266 / POP 170,000 / ELEV 700M

Even people from San Luis will tell you that the best the province has to offer lies outside of the capital. That said, it's not a bad little town – it has a few historic sights and the central Plaza Pringles is one of the prettiest in the entire country. The town's main nightlife strip, Av Illia, has a decent concentration of bars, cafes and restaurants, and makes for a fun night out.

Located on the north bank of the Río Chorrillos, San Luis is 260km from Mendoza via RN7, and 456km from Córdoba via RN148.

Sights

The center of town is the beautiful tree-filled Plaza Pringles, anchored on its eastern side by San Luis' handsome 19th-century **cathedral** (Rivadavia). Provincial hardwoods such as algarrobo (carob tree) were used for the cathedral's windows and frames, and local white marble for its steps and columns.

On the north side of Plaza Independencia is the provincial **Casa de Gobierno** (Government House). On the south side of the plaza, the **Iglesia de Santo Domingo** (cnr 25 de Mayo & San Martín) and its convent date from the 1930s, but reproduce the Moorish style of the 17th-century building they replaced. Take a peek at the striking algarrobo doors of the attached **Archivo Histórico Provincial**, which is around the corner on San Martín.

Dominican friars at the **mercado artesanal** (cnr 25 de Mayo & Rivadavia; ⏲8am-1pm Mon-Fri), next to Iglesia de Santo Domingo, sell gorgeous handmade wool rugs as well as ceramics, onyx crafts and weavings from elsewhere in the province.

Also stroll over to the lovely former **train station** (Avs Illia & Lafinur) for a look at its green corrugated-metal roofs and decorative ironwork dating from 1884.

Tours

Las Quijadas Turismo TOUR
(☎0266-443-1683; San Martín 874; ⏲9am-1pm & 4-8pm Mon-Sat) Tours to Parque Nacional Sierra de las Quijadas, La Angostura and Inti Huasi.

Sleeping

San Luis' better hotels cater to a business crowd, filling up quickly on weekdays and offering discounts on weekends.

San Luis Hostel HOSTEL $
(☎0266-442-4188; www.sanluishostel.com.ar; Falucho 646; dm/tw AR$80/190; @📶🏊) San Luis' best and most central hostel has it all, from pool table to DVD library, excellent kitchen and shady backyard with barbecue. The 16-person dorms (segregated for male and female) could be a bit more atmospheric, but apart from that it's pure gold.

Hotel Castelmonte HOTEL $$
(☎0266-442-4963; www.castelmontehotel.com.ar; Chacabuco 769; s/d AR$210/305; ❄📶) An excellent-value midrange hotel. Spacious rooms have wooden parquetry floors and

good firm beds. While central, it's set back from the road, keeping things nice and quiet.

Vista Suites & Spa BUSINESS HOTEL $$$
(☎0266-442-5794; www.vistasuites.com.ar; Av Illia 526; s/d from AR$770/890; ❄@📶🏊) The latest addition to San Luis' seemingly saturated business hotel scene features way-slick design, a gourmet restaurant, day spa, indoor pool and all the other comforts you'd expect for the price.

Eating & Drinking

Traditional San Luis dishes include *empanadas de horno* (baked empanadas) and *cazuela de gallina* (chicken soup).

There are numerous laid-back bars along Av Illia. As is the deal all over the country, they start late and end late. Go for a stroll and see which one you like.

Maria Bonita MEXICAN $
(Illia 392; mains from AR$50; ⏲noon-2am; 📶) Decent Mexican food can be hard to come by in Argentina, and this place is about as good as it gets. Big sizzling fajita platters are a winner, as is the selection of Mexican beers and tequilas.

Aranjuez CAFE $
(cnr Pringles & Rivadavia; mains AR$40-70; ⏲8am-11:30pm; 📶) A fairly standard cafe-bar-restaurant on the plaza, this one gets a mention for the sidewalk tables out on the pedestrian thoroughfare which make it a great spot for drinks, snacks and people-watching.

Orientation

On the north bank of the Río Chorrillos, San Luis is 260km from Mendoza via RN7 and 456km from Córdoba via RN148.

The commercial center is along the parallel streets of San Martín and Rivadavia between Plaza Pringles in the north and Plaza Independencia in the south. Most services for travelers are within a few blocks of the plaza, with the exception of the bus terminal.

Information

Several banks, mostly around Plaza Pringles, have ATMs.

ACA (Automóvil Club Argentino; ☎0266-442-3188; Av Illia 401; ⏲24 hr) Auto club; good source for provincial road maps.

Post office (cnr Av Illia & San Martín; ⏲8am-6pm Mon-Fri & 9am-1pm Sat)

Regional hospital (☎0266-442-2627; Av República Oriental del Uruguay 150) On the eastward extension of Bolívar.

Tourist office (☎0266-442-3957; www.turismo.sanluis.gov.ar; cnr Av Illia & Junín; ⏲9am-9pm) The helpful staff can supply a good map of the town and its attractions plus offer good advice on regional sights.

Getting There & Around

AIR

San Luis airport (☎0266-442-2427) is 3km northwest of the center; taxis cost around AR$25.

Aerolíneas Argentinas (☎0266-442-5671; Av Illia 472; ⏲9am-6pm Mon-Fri, 9am-1pm Sat) flies daily to Buenos Aires.

BUS & CAR

San Luis' new **bus terminal** is on the eastern edge of town. For Provincial destinations, including El Volcán (AR$8, 30 minutes), Carolina (AR$18, two hours), Inti Huasi (AR$20, 2½ hours) and Balde (AR$13, 45 minutes), you can get a bus from here or the **downtown stop** (cnr Bolivar & San Martín), which saves you a trek out to the terminal.

Buses to the center (AR$2.50) leave from in front of the Toyota dealership, across the road from the terminal.

There are long-distance departures daily to most tourist destinations. For destinations such as Neuquén and Bariloche, you might have to head first to Mendoza or San Rafael.

Hertz (☎cell phone 0266-15-4549002; Av Illia 305; ⏲9am-7pm) is the local car-rental agency.

Buses from San Luis

DESTINATION	COST (AR$)	DURATION (HR)
Buenos Aires	800	11
Córdoba	295	7
Mendoza	200	5
Rosario	485	9
San Juan	248	5
San Rafael	174	5
Santa Fe	543	12

Around San Luis

Balde

☎0266

This small village, 35km west of San Luis, is remarkable only for its thermal baths. The municipal complex is a decidedly down-at-heel affair, while a new spa resort offers oodles of comfort in gorgeous surrounds.

Centro Termal Municipal (☎0266-449-9319; Av Esteban Agüero s/n; 1hr baths per person AR$18, campsites AR$20, 2-person cabin AR$300; ⏰baths 8am-6pm) offers small rooms with a bath and a bed to relax, rented by the hour. They're clean enough and decent value for a quick dip. Cabins (located across the road) are spacious for two.

Los Tamarindos (☎0266-444-2220; www.jardinesdetamarindos.com; Av Esteban Agüero s/n; s/d AR$400/500, cabins s/d AR$450/550; ⏰baths 8am-6pm) is a wonderful thermal baths complex featuring a couple of public pools for day use – an outdoor one at 26°C (AR$30 per person) and a lovely, clean indoor one (AR$45 for both). The rooms here are standard, with small baths fed by hot spring water, but the cabins are a real treat: they're much more spacious and have a separate tub where you can get neck deep in the water.

Regular buses run to and from San Luis' bus terminal to the bus terminal at Balde (AR$10, 45 minutes), which is a short walk to either of the complexes.

Parque Nacional Sierra de las Quijadas

Fans of the *Road Runner* cartoon will feel oddly at home among the red sandstone rock formations in this rarely visited **national park** (☎02652-490182; sierradelasquijadas@apn.gov.ar; admission AR$50) The park comprises 1500 sq km of canyons and dry lake beds among the Sierra de las Quijadas, the peaks of which reach 1200m at Cerro Portillo. Recent paleontological excavations by the Universidad Nacional de San Luis and New York's Museum of Natural History unearthed dinosaur tracks and fossils from the Lower Cretaceous, 120 million years ago.

Despite the shortage of visitors here, access to the park is excellent: buses from San Luis to San Juan will drop visitors at the park entrance and ranger station just beyond the village of Hualtarán, about 110km northwest of San Luis via RN147 (San Juan is 210km to the northwest). At this point, a 6km dirt road leads west to a viewpoint overlooking the **Potrero de la Aguada**, a scenic depression beneath the peaks of the sierra that collects the runoff from much of the park and is a prime wildlife area. At the ranger station you can hire guides; two-hour, 3km treks to see the famous dinosaur footprints leave hourly between 9am and 4pm and cost AR$80 per person. Four-hour treks to a 150m-deep canyon in the park leave at 1:30pm and cost AR$150. A minimum group size of two people applies to both treks.

Other **hiking** possibilities in the park are excellent, but the complex canyons require a tremendous sense of direction or, preferably, the assistance of a local guide. Even experienced hikers should beware of summer rains and flash floods, which make the canyons extremely dangerous.

There's a shady free **campground** near the overlook, and a small store with groceries and drinks, including very welcome ice-cold beer.

Buses from San Juan to San Luis pass every hour or so, but they don't always stop. It's sometimes possible to catch a lift from the park entrance to the overlook.

Valle de las Sierras Puntanas

From San Luis the RP9 snakes its way northwards, following the course of the Río Grande. Along the way, small villages are slowly developing as tourist destinations while still retaining much of their original character. The picturesque mining town of Carolina and nearby Inti Huasi cave are highlights of the region, and the landscapes higher up in the valley, with their rolling meadows and stone fences, probably resemble the Scottish highlands more than anything you've seen in Argentina so far.

Estancia Las Verbenas

Set in a gorgeous glade in the Valle de Pancanta, this **estancia** (☎0266-429-6151; www.lasverbenas.com.ar; RP9, Km68; per person incl full board AR$320; 📶) does rustic to the hilt, with plenty of hearty food served up among animal-skin decoration and rough-hewn furniture. Rooms are basic but comfortable. Three-hour horseback-riding tours (AR$120 per person) to a nearby waterfall are bound to be a highlight of your stay here. The sign-posted entrance to the property is located just after the bridge on the highway, from where it's another kilometer or so to the farmhouse. If you're coming by bus, call and staff will pick you up from the highway.

Carolina

02651 / POP 250 / ELEV 1610M

Nestled between the banks of the Río Grande and the foothills of Cerro Tomalasta (2020m), Carolina is a photogenic little village of stone houses and dirt roads. Take away the power lines and you could be stepping back in time 100 years. The region boomed in 1785 when the Spanish moved in to exploit local gold mines that had first been used by the Inca. Nobody uses street addresses in Carolina – the town is small enough to navigate without them.

Sights & Activities

One of the quirkier museums in the country, **Museo de Poesia** (10am-6pm Tue-Sat) FREE honors San Luis' favorite son, poet Juan Crisóstomo Lafinur. The museum has a few artifacts from the poet's life, plus handwritten homages to the man by some of Argentina's leading poets.

Across the creek and up the hill from the poetry museum is a small **stone labyrinth**, set on the hilltop. It should provide an hour or so of entertainment (or, if your sense of direction is really bad, days of frustration).

Huellas Turismo (02652-490224; www.huellasturismo.com.ar; 9am-1pm & 3-7pm) is the local tour operator, and can set you up with tours of the local gold mine, rock-climbing and rappelling trips on Cerro Tomalasta, and tours of Inti Huasi, La Casa de la Piedra Pintada and La Angostura.

Sleeping & Eating

Accommodations are improving in Carolina, but if you can't find a place, ask in the restaurants for a *casa de familia* (room in a private house with shared bathroom), which rents for around AR$80 per person.

La Posta del Caminante HOTEL $
(0266-445-2000; www.lapostadelcaminante.com.ar; RP9 s/n; s/d AR$250/390, without bathroom AR$210/350;) Carolina's one hotel is set in a gorgeous stone building on the edge of town. A lovely seminatural rock swimming pool out the back completes the picture. The hotel is open mainly in summer, so if you're set on staying here, call ahead.

Rincón del Oro Hostel HOSTEL $
(02651-490212; Pringles s/n; dm/d without bathroom AR$80/170;) Set on a hilltop overlooking town, this great little hostel has a rustic, intimate feel despite its 57-bed capacity.

La Tomalasta CAFETERIA $
(mains AR$35-60; 8am-11pm) Good-value home-cooked meals. If it looks like it's closed, go around the back to the general store and ask them to open up.

Getting There & Away

Regular buses run from Carolina to San Luis (AR$18, two hours), passing through El Volcán. Some continue on to Inti Huasi (AR$5, 30 minutes).

Around Carolina

INTI HUASI

This wide, shallow **cave** (admission free; daylight hr), the name of which means 'house of the sun' in Quechua, makes an interesting stop, as much for the gorgeous surrounding countryside as for the cave itself. Radiocarbon dating suggests that the cave was first inhabited by the Ayampitín some 8000 years ago. There are regular buses here from San Luis (AR$20, 2½ hours), passing through Carolina (AR$5, 30 minutes).

LA CASA DE LA PIEDRA PINTADA

Coming from Carolina, 3km before the Inti Huasi cave, a dirt track turns off to Paso de los Reyes. From the turnoff, it's an easy walk to **La Casa de la Piedra Pintada** (admission free), where more than 50 rock carvings are easily visible in the rock face. Follow the road until you reach an open meadow at the base of Cerro Sololasta and you'll see the new cable-and-wood walkway up the cliff face that gives you access to the site. Once you're finished with the rock art, continue up the hill for spectacular views out over the Sierras Puntanas.

The road used to be signposted, but isn't any more, making finding this place a little tricky – you can ask for directions at Inti Huasi, or pay someone to guide you for a nominal fee.

Valle de Conlara

Heading northeast to Merlo from San Luis, the landscape changes dramatically as the road climbs into the hills. As you leave San Luis the land is arid and desertlike; Papagayos has its own unique vistas, punctuated by palm trees, while Merlo is a lush mountain town.

Estancia La Estanzuela

Set on a Jesuit mission dating from 1750, this gorgeous **estancia** (☎02656-420559; www.estanzuela.com.ar; 1 or 2 people incl full board AR$1200;) has been left in near-original condition from the days when it was a working farm. Floors are wood or stone, walls are meter-thick adobe and many ceilings are constructed in the traditional gaucho style. The house is decorated like a museum, with antique furniture, paintings and family heirlooms galore. A small pond that the Jesuits built for irrigation serves for romantic rowboat outings and there is plenty of horseback riding and nature walking to be done. This is a very special – near-magical – place and the minimum three-night stay should not be hard to adhere to. Prices include meals, drinks and activities.

The property is located 2km off RP1, between Villa del Carmen and Papagayos. The closest public transportation is to Papagayos from Merlo. Reservations for rooms are essential and must be made at least two days in advance. If you don't have your own transportation, ask about getting picked up in Papagayos or San Luis.

Papagayos

☎02656 / POP 430

Possibly the last thing you're expecting to see in this part of the world is a valley full of palm trees, but that's exactly where this small town is situated. On the banks of the Arroyo Papagayos, the town is surrounded by huge Caranday palms, giving the area a certain notoriety for handicrafts made from their trunks and branches.

Small stores (mostly attached to workshops) selling these *artesanias en palma* are scattered around town. **Rosa López** (in front of plaza) has the best range. The tourist office can provide a map showing all the store locations, along with other local attractions.

The *arroyo* (creek) is a good place to cool off – its length is dotted with swimming holes. For a more formal swimming environment, the Balneario Municipal offers swimming pools, picnic and barbecue areas.

For horseback riding and treks to local waterfalls and swimming spots out of town, ask at the tourist office or Hostería Los Leños.

The **Oficina de Turismo** (☎02656-481868; www.papagayos.gov.ar; RP 1 s/n; ⏲8am-8pm) is useful for contacting guides and arranging tours, and has decent maps of the town.

Hostería Los Leños (☎02656-481812; www.hosterialoslenios.blogspot.com; Av Comechingones 555; r AR$350;), the best-looking hotel in town, has fresh new rooms with spacious bathrooms and a good-sized swimming pool. Also on offer are excellent home-cooked meals (mains AR$40 to AR$70) and staff can set you up with a picnic lunch if you're off on a day trip.

From Papagayos' main plaza there are regular buses to Merlo (AR$9, one hour).

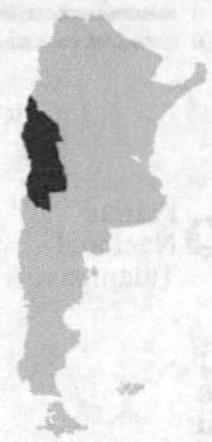

Mendoza & the Central Andes

Includes ➡

Best Wineries

- ➡ Di Tomasso (p332)
- ➡ Salentein (p337)
- ➡ Viñas de Segisa (p347)
- ➡ Pulenta Estate (p337)

Best National & Provincial Parks

- ➡ Parque Provincial Aconcagua (p336)
- ➡ Parque Provincial Volcán Tupungato (p338)
- ➡ Parque Provincial Payunia (p342)
- ➡ Parque Provincial Ischigualasto (p352)

Why Go?

A long, narrow sliver of desert landscape, the Mendoza region is home to two of Argentina's claims to fame – the Andes and wine. The city itself is lively and cosmopolitan and the surrounding area boasts hundreds of wineries offering tours – an educational (and occasionally intoxicating) way to spend an afternoon or a month.

If you can put your glass down for a minute, there's plenty more to keep you busy. Just down the road is Aconcagua, the Americas' highest peak and a favorite for mountain climbers the world over. A couple of ski resorts give you the chance to drop into fresh powder while Mendoza's tour operators offer up a bewildering array of rafting, mountain biking and paragliding options.

To the north, often-overlooked San Juan province is well worth a visit, as much for its small but important selection of wineries as for the surreal desert landscape of the Parque Provincial Ischigualasto.

When to Go

Mendoza

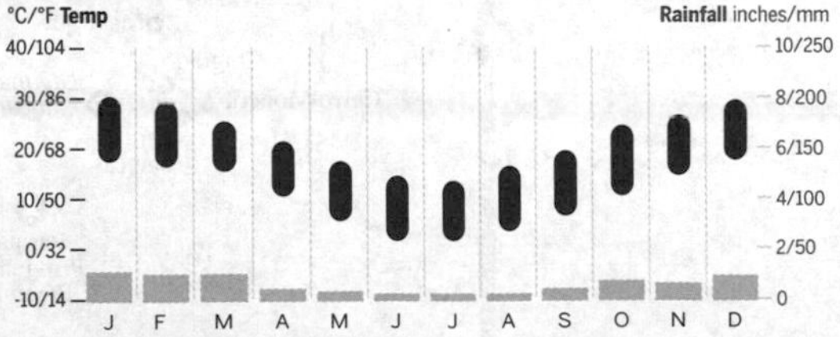

Dec–Mar Hot, dry weather makes this the perfect time to climb the region's highest peaks.

Apr–Jun Autumn is spectacular, thanks to the colors of Mendoza's trees and grapevines.

Jul–Sep Ski season paints the Andes white – breathtaking sight, even for nonskiers.

Mendoza & the Central Andes Highlights

1. Carve tracks in fresh powder on the world-class slopes of **Las Leñas** (p343)
2. Grab some wheels and treat yourself to a tour of the wineries in **Maipú** (p332)
3. Get away from the crowds and into the stunning Valle de Calingasta in **Barreal** (p348)
4. Discover dinosaur fossils embedded in bizarre rock formations in **Parque Provincial Ischigualasto** (p352)
5. Make the scene in any number of hip bars on Av Arístides in **Mendoza** (p328)
6. Soak those aching traveling bones in the thermal complex at **Cacheuta** (p333)
7. Touch the roof of the Americas on **Cerro Aconcagua** (p336), the highest peak in the Western Hemisphere

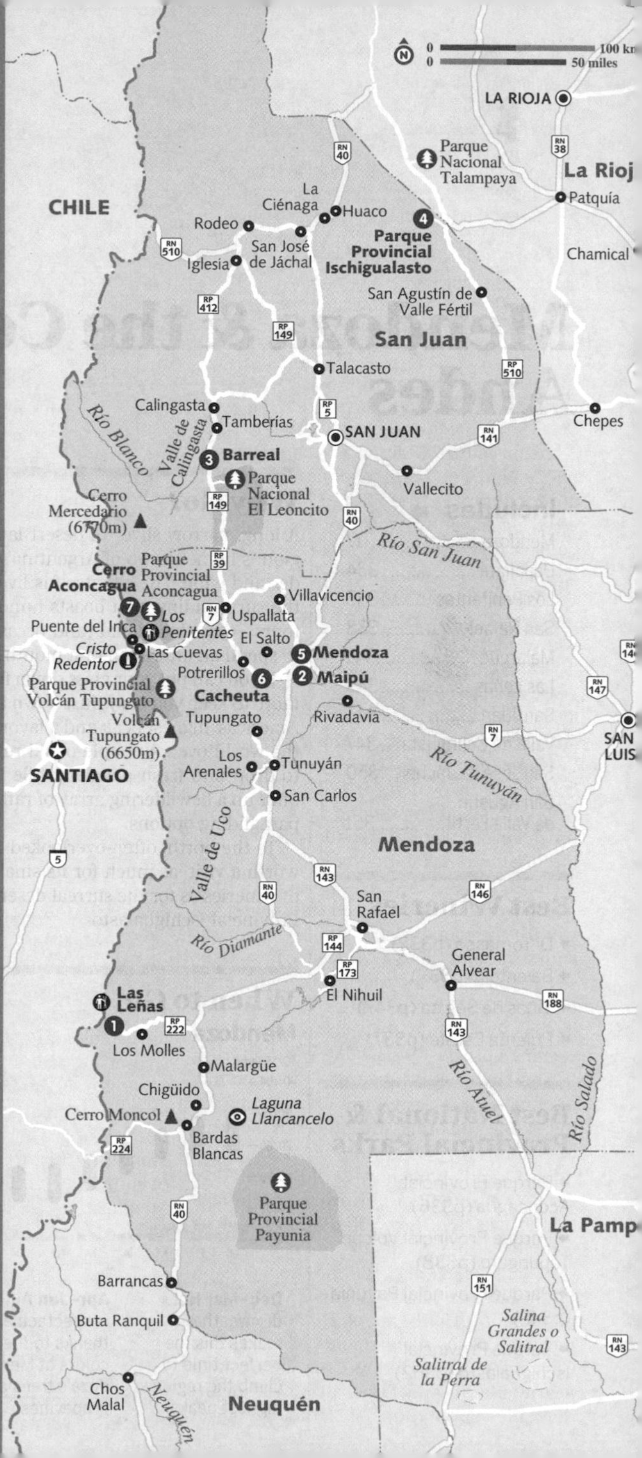

Getting There & Away

With flights to/from nearby Santiago (Chile), Mendoza has the region's only international airport. There are regular flights to Mendoza, San Juan and San Luis from Buenos Aires. During ski season there are usually flights to Malargüe, near Las Leñas ski resort. Bus transportation is excellent throughout the province. If you're heading south to the Lake District, the fastest way can be to head to Neuquén city, but if you don't mind taking it slow, a seldom-explored section of RN40 between Mendoza and Neuquén provinces can be a worthwhile detour.

Mendoza

0261 / POP 1.1 MILLION / ELEV 703M

A bustling city of wide, leafy avenues, atmospheric plazas and cosmopolitan cafes, Mendoza is a trap. Even if you've (foolishly) only given it a day or two on your itinerary, you're bound to end up hanging around, captivated by the laid-back pace while surrounded by every possible comfort.

Ostensibly it's a desert town, though you wouldn't know unless you were told – *acequias* (irrigation ditches) that run beside every main road and glorious fountains that adorn every main plaza mean you'll never be far from the burble of running water.

Lively during the day, the city really comes into its own at night, when the bars, restaurants and cafes along Av Arístides fill up and overflow onto the sidewalks with all the bright young things, out to see and be seen.

All over the country (and in much of the world), the name Mendoza is synonymous with wine, and this is the place to base yourself if you're up for touring the vineyards, taking a few dozen bottles home or just looking for a good vintage to accompany the evening's pizza.

The city's wide range of tour operators also makes it a great place to organize rafting, skiing and other adventures in the nearby Andes.

Mendoza is 1050km west of Buenos Aires via RN7 and 340km northwest of Santiago (Chile) via the Los Libertadores border complex.

Strictly speaking, the provincial capital proper is a relatively small area with a population of only about 115,000, but the inclusion of the departments of Las Heras, Guaymallén and Godoy Cruz, along with nearby Maipú and Luján de Cuyo, means that the population of Gran Mendoza (Greater Mendoza) swells to a little over one million.

CUYO

The provinces of Mendoza, San Juan, San Luis and La Rioja are traditionally known as the Cuyo, a term which is derived from the indigenous Huarpe word *cuyum*, meaning 'sandy earth.' The Huarpes were the original practitioners of irrigated agriculture in the region, a legacy still highly visible throughout the region today. The term is one you'll encounter often, whether in the names of local bus companies, businesses and newspapers, or in everyday conversation.

The city's five central plazas are arranged like the five-roll on a die, with Plaza Independencia in the middle and four smaller plazas lying two blocks from each of its corners. Be sure to see the beautifully tiled Plaza España.

Av San Martín is the main thoroughfare, crossing the city from north to south, and Av Las Heras is the principal commercial street.

A good place to orient yourself is the **Terraza Mirador** (9 de Julio 500, City Hall; free; 9am-1pm) **FREE**, which is the rooftop terrace at **City Hall** (9 de Julio 500), offering panoramic views of the city and the surrounding area.

Sights

★**Museo Fundacional** MUSEUM

(cnr Alberdi & Videla Castillo; admission AR$15; 9am-8pm Mon-Sat, 3-8pm Sun) Mendoza's Museo Fundacional protects excavations of the colonial *cabildo* (town council), destroyed by an earthquake in 1861. At that time, the city's geographical focus shifted to the west and south to its present location. A series of small dioramas depicts Mendoza's history, and works through all of human evolution as though the city of Mendoza were the climax (and maybe it was).

★**Museo Municipal de Arte Moderno** GALLERY

(Plaza Independencia; 9am-8pm Tue-Sun) This municipal museum is a relatively small but well-organized facility with modern and contemporary art exhibits. Free concerts

Mendoza

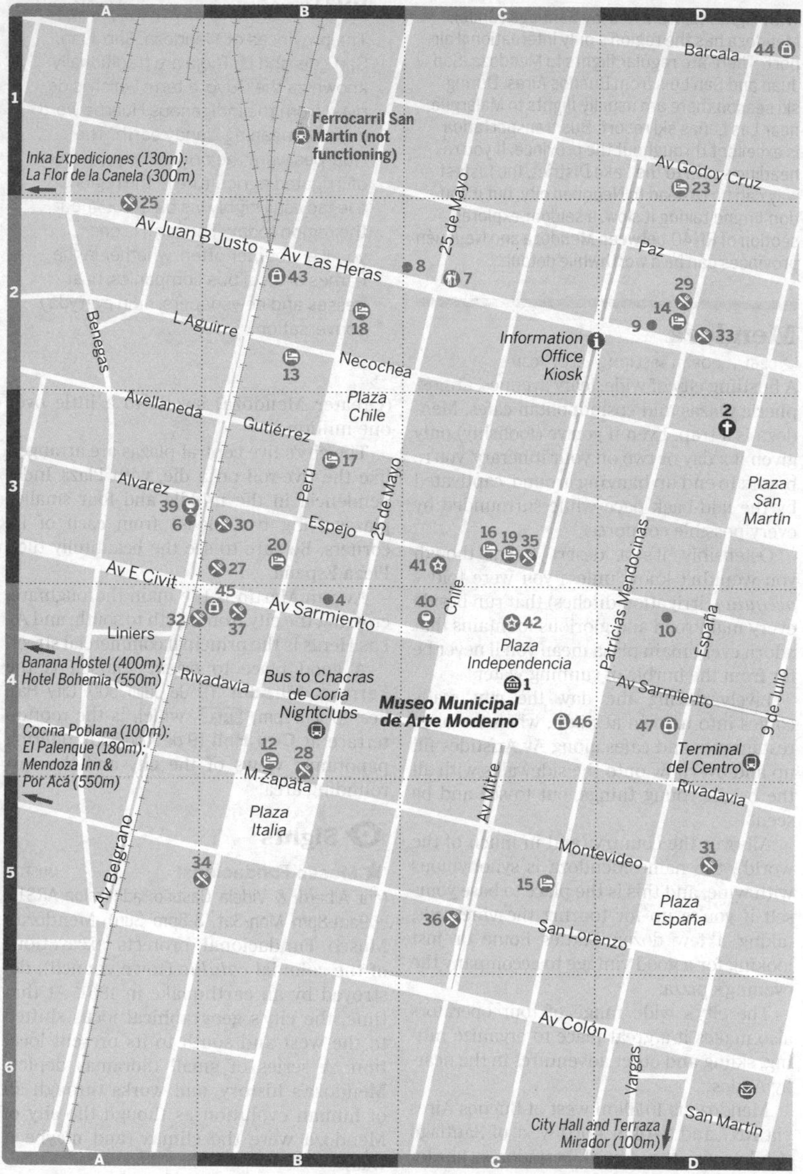

and theatrical performances are usually held here on Sunday nights at 8pm; make sure you stop by for the weekly program. The museum is located underground at the Plaza Independencia.

Museo Histórico General San Martín MUSEUM
(Remedios Escalada de San Martín 1843; admission AR$5; ⏲9am-1pm & 3-8pm Mon-Fri) Honors José de San Martín, the general who liberated Argentina from the Spanish and whose

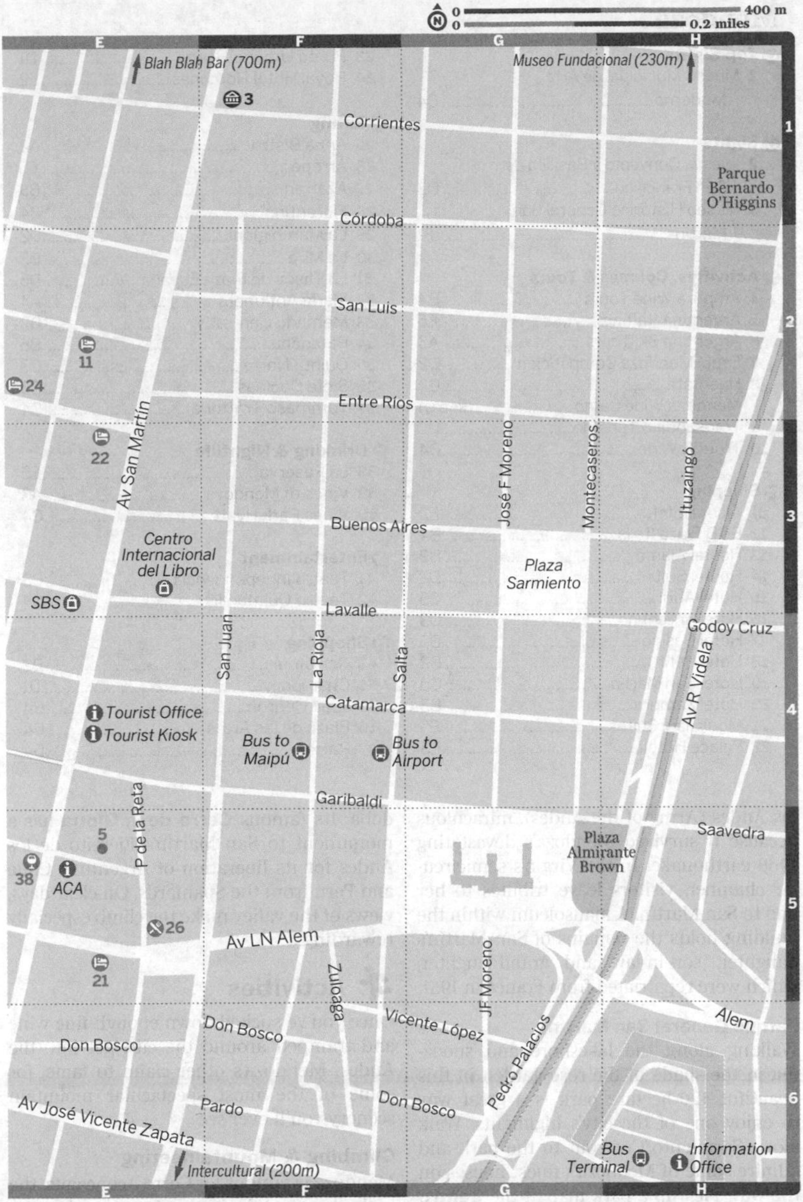

name graces parks, squares and streets everywhere; the Libertador is dear to Mendoza, where he resided with his family and recruited and trained his army to cross into Chile. The museum is in a small arcade off Av San Martín.

Iglesia, Convento y Basílica de San Francisco CHURCH
(Necochea 201; ⌚9am-1pm Mon-Sat) Many *mendocinos* (people from Mendoza) consider the image at this church of the Virgin of Cuyo, patron of San Martín's Ejército de

Mendoza

Top Sights
1 Museo Municipal de Arte Moderno ... C4

Sights
2 Iglesia, Convento y Basílica de San Francisco ... D3
3 Museo Histórico General San Martín ... F1

Activities, Courses & Tours
4 Ampora Wine Tours ... B4
5 Argentina Rafting ... E5
6 Argentina Ski Tours ... A3
7 Esquí Mendoza Competición ... C2
8 Huentata ... C2
Mendoza Wine Camp ... (see 6)
9 Transandino Turismo ... D2
10 Trout & Wine ... D4

Sleeping
11 Alcor Hotel ... E2
12 B&B Plaza Italia ... B4
13 Hostel Alamo ... B2
14 Hostel Suites ... D2
15 Hotel Abril ... C5
16 Hotel Argentino ... C3
17 Hotel Casino ... B3
18 Hotel Petit ... B2
19 Hotel San Martín ... C3
20 Hotel Zamora ... B3
21 Modigliani Suites ... E5
22 Palace Hotel ... E3
23 Punto Urbano Hostel ... D1
24 Royal Hotel Horcones ... E2

Eating
25 Anna Bistro ... A2
26 Arrope ... E5
27 Azafrán ... B3
28 Florentino ... B4
29 La Marchigiana ... D2
30 La Mira ... B3
31 La Tasca de Plaza España ... D5
32 Maria Antioneta ... A4
33 Mercado Central ... D2
34 Patancha ... B5
35 Quinta Norte ... C3
36 Siete Cocinas ... C5
37 Tommaso Trattoria ... B4

Drinking & Nightlife
38 La Reserva ... E5
39 Vines of Mendoza ... A3
40 Vines Park Hyatt ... C4

Entertainment
41 Teatro Independencia ... C3
42 Teatro Quintanilla ... C4

Shopping
43 Carrefour ... B2
44 Chamonix ... D1
45 Juan Cedrón ... B4
46 Plaza de las Artes ... C4
47 Raices ... D4

los Andes (Army of the Andes), miraculous because it survived Mendoza's devastating 1968 earthquake. In the Virgin's semicircular chamber, visitors leave tributes to her and to San Martín. A mausoleum within the building holds the remains of San Martín's daughter, son-in-law and granddaughter, which were repatriated from France in 1951.

Parque General San Martín PARK
Walking along the lakeshore and snoozing in the shade of the rose garden in this beautiful 420-hectare park is a great way to enjoy one of the city's highlights. Walk along Sarmiento/Civit out to the park and admire some of Mendoza's finest houses on the way. Pick up a park map at the **Centro de Información** (☎0261-420-5052, ext 22; cnr Avs Los Platanos & Libertador; ⏰9am-5pm), just inside the impressive entry gates, shipped over from England and originally forged for the Turkish Sultan Hamid II. The park was designed by Carlos (Charles) Thays in 1897, who also designed Parque Sarmiento in Córdoba. Its famous **Cerro de la Gloria** has a monument to San Martín's Ejército de los Andes for its liberation of Argentina, Chile and Peru from the Spaniards. On clear days, views of the valley make the climb especially rewarding.

Activities

Once you've sucked down enough fine wine and tramped around the city, get into the Andes, Mendoza's other claim to fame, for some of the most spectacular mountain scenery you'll ever see

Climbing & Mountaineering

Mendoza is famous for Cerro Aconcagua, the highest mountain in the Americas, but the majestic peak is only the tip of the iceberg when it comes to climbing and mountaineering here. The nearby Cordón del Plata boasts several peaks topping out between 5000m and 6000m, and there are three important rock-climbing areas in the province:

Los Arenales (near Tunuyán), El Salto (near Mendoza) and Chigüido (near Malargüe).

Pick up a copy of Maricio Fernandez' full-color route guide (Spanish only), *Escaladas en Mendoza*, at **Inka Expediciones** (☎0261-425-0871; www.inka.com.ar; Av Juan B Justo 345; ⏲9am-6pm Mon-Fri, 9am-1pm Sat). For up-to-date information and a list of recommended guides, contact the **Asociación Argentina de Guías de Montaña** (www.aagm.com.ar).

For climbing and hiking equipment, both rental and purchase, visit **Chamonix** (☎0261-425-7572; www.chamonix-outdoor.com.ar; Barcala 267; ⏲9am-1pm & 3-6pm Mon-Sat).

Skiing & Snowboarding

Los Penitentes has the best skiing near Mendoza, although further south, Las Leñas has arguably the best skiing in South America. For standard ski and snowboard equipment rental, try **Esquí Mendoza Competición** (☎0261-429-7944; Av Las Heras 583; ⏲9am-8pm) or any of the shops along Av Las Heras. In high season, all charge AR$120 to AR$200 per day for a skis-boots-poles package and about AR$200 per day for a snowboard with boots. Most rent gloves, jackets and tire chains, as well. If you're an intermediate or advanced skier, Argentina Ski Tours (p321) can set you up with much better equipment.

White-Water Rafting

The major rivers are the Mendoza and the Diamante, near San Rafael. Most agencies offer full-day descents (from AR$650) and multiday expeditions. Transport costs AR$80 extra. Well-regarded Argentina Rafting operates a base in Potrerillos but you can book trips at its Mendoza (p321) office.

Courses

Intercultural LANGUAGE COURSE
(www.spanishcourses.com.ar; República de Siria 241; ⏲9am-8pm Mon-Sat) Offers group and private Spanish classes and internationally recognized exams. Can also help find longer-term accommodation in Mendoza.

Tours

Numerous agencies organize climbing and trekking expeditions, rafting trips, mule trips and cycling trips.

Argentina Rafting ADVENTURE TOUR
(☎0261-429-6325; www.argentinarafting.com; Amigorena 86; ⏲9am-6pm Mon-Sat) Rafting, mountain biking, kayaking, paragliding and rock climbing, among other activities.

Argentina Ski Tours SKI TOUR
(☎0261-423-6958; www.argentinaskitours.com; Belgrano 1194 B; ⏲11am-8:30pm Mon-Fri, 5:30pm-8:30pm Sat) Full-service ski tours and lessons in Spanish or English. Best quality ski-equipment rental in town. Also brokers a range of on-mountain accommodations.

Transandino Turismo ADVENTURE TOUR
(☎0261-423-7993; www.transandinoturismo.com.ar; Las Heras 341, lcl 3; ⏲9am-1pm & 4-9pm Mon-Fri, 9am-3pm Sat) Offers a range of adrenaline-packed activities, including skydiving, zip-lining and paragliding.

Huentata GUIDED TOUR
(☎0261-425-7444; www.huentata.com.ar; Av Las Heras 699; ⏲9am-8pm) Conventional travel agency that organize trips in and around town. Possibilities include half-day tours of the city (AR$110), and day tours of the Cañon del Atuel (AR$300), Villavicencio (AR$150) or the high cordillera around Potrerillos, Vallecito and Uspallata (AR$250).

Wine Tours

For the casual sipper, a self-guided tour of Maipú or any of the bodega tours offered by various travel agencies around town will likely satisfy. There are also a few companies operating out of Mendoza offering deluxe wine tours. They're not cheap, but small group sizes, English-speaking guides and access to exclusive vineyards are among the benefits. Most also offer tours of the Valle de Uco, an important new wine-growing region 150km south of Mendoza that's near-impossible to explore by public transport and is only just starting to appear on tour-agency itineraries.

All of the operators listed below can set you up with horseback tours of the vineyards, too, usually a full-day affair with gourmet lunch included (US$190).

Trout & Wine TOUR
(☎0261-425-5613; www.troutandwine.com; Espejo 266; ⏲9am-1pm & 3-8pm Mon-Sat) Organizes custom-designed full-day tours of Luján de Cuyo (US$150) and the Uco Valley (US$160) with a maximum group size of eight. From November to March it runs fly-fishing tours in the Valle de Uco for US$310, which include all gear and a barbecue lunch out in the highlands accompanied by – you guessed it – some very fine wines.

(Continued on p326)

Mendoza's Wine

Since the Jesuits first planted vines in northern Argentina more than 500 years ago, Argentine wine has gone from strength to strength, and the country is now recognized as one of the leading international wine producers. If you're at all interested in wine, make sure the Mendoza area is firmly on your itinerary.

From Humble Beginnings...

The first major improvement in Argentine wine came with the arrival of European immigrants in the 19th century. These folks brought varieties from their home countries, replacing the Jesuits' criollo vines with 'noble' varieties such as merlot and cabernet sauvignon. The new grapes brought a minimal increase in quality but, even so, Argentine wine remained a very domestic product, often to be enjoyed with a big blast of soda to take the edge off.

Then, as if from nowhere, Argentine wines hit the world stage with a vengeance, and these days a Mendoza merlot has just as much (if not more) cachet than a comparably priced Chilean red.

While the wineries have definitely improved their marketing, in the end it all comes down to quality – Argentine wines are good and they just keep getting better. One of the keys to successful wine making is controlled irrigation. A big rain before a harvest can spoil an entire crop, but this is something winemakers in the desert-like Mendoza region don't have to worry about. Nearly every drop of water is piped in, and comes as beautiful fresh snowmelt from the Andes.

Desert vineyards have another advantage – the huge variation between daytime and nighttime temperatures. Warm days encourage sugar production and help the grapes grow a nice thick skin. Cool nights ensure good acidity levels, and low humidity means bugs and fungus aren't a problem.

The techniques are improving, too – better hygiene standards, the further replacement of old 'criollo' vines with

MENDOZA SHOPPING LIST

Spoiled for choice? Here are our top picks:

Reds

- Chacra 55 Pinot Noir 2011 (AR$330)
- Matias Riccitelli Malbec Vineyard Selection 2011 (AR$165)
- Domaine St Diego 9 Lunas 2010 (AR$150)
- O Fournier Alfa Crux 2006 (AR$300)

Whites

- Catena Zapata White Stone Chardonnay 2009 (AR$500)
- Cobos Bramare Chardonnay 2011 (AR$95)
- Doña Paula Estate Sauvignon Blanc 2013 (AR$75)
- Gimenez Riili Perpertumm Torrontes 2012 (AR$59)

1. Grape harvesters at a winery, Luján de Cuyo (p332)
2. Mendoza wine

1

'noble' varieties such as malbec, cabernet sauvignon, merlot and syrah, and the practice of aging wines in smaller oak barrels (with a lifespan of a few years) rather than large barrels (which would be used for up to 70 years) have all had positive effects.

You can't talk about Argentine wines without talking price-to-quality ratio. The country's economic crash in 2001 was a boon for exporters as prices plummeted and, overnight, Argentine wine became a highly competitive product. Land here is (relatively) cheap and labor so inexpensive that nearly every grape in the country is handpicked, a claim that only top-end wines in other countries can make.

Touring the Vineyards

As Mendoza's wine industry grows so does its sister industry of wine tourism. These days it's not whether you can do a wine tour, but which one and how.

There are options for every budget. If you're watching your pesos, biking around the Maipú region is an excellent-value option. Wineries here are close together and their tour prices are low, so you can visit several in a day and taste some decent wines without breaking the bank. Be aware that this is a very popular way to spend the day, and some wineries will herd you through like cattle to make space for the next group.

If you're not a cyclist but not ready to commit to a full-on wine tour either, a good middle option is the satellite town of Luján de Cuyo, 19km south of Mendoza. You can bus and taxi around the area with minimal planning, hit three or four wineries, and be back in Mendoza before nightfall.

Those who can afford a little more and are interested in learning about techniques in a relaxed setting should consider a tour. You'll avoid the crowds, and sometimes get to meet the winemakers. The gourmet lunch at one of the wineries and top-shelf tastings that come with these tours may tip the scales, too. Tour companies can organize custom tours for the

DEDÉ VARGAS/GETTY IMAGES ©

YADID LEVY/GETTY IMAGES ©

1. Mendoza vineyards in autumn **2.** Vines of Mendoza wine bar (p329)

serious connoisseur, designed to take in the specific wineries, regions or even wines that you are particularly interested in.

If you have the time and money, the best way to tour the region is strictly DIY. Rent a car in Mendoza, buy one of the winery maps on sale at every newsstand and create your own itinerary. Make the most of your freedom by visiting the Valle de Uco – home to some of the Mendoza region's most cutting-edge wineries. It's about 150km south of the city, but there are plenty of wineries offering accommodation and even specialty wine lodges – you can stay out there and tootle around to your heart's content. Be warned, though – Argentina has a zero-tolerance law for driving under the influence. If you were to get pulled over after a heavy day in the tasting room, you could be in big trouble.

SHIPPING WINE

While it's illegal to post wine from Argentina, countries such as the USA and Canada have no restriction on how much you can bring home in your luggage, provided you pay duty. And duty can be as low as US$5 for 40 bottles for the US.

If you are planning on transporting wine, it's best to stop in at a specialty wine store where they can pack bottles to avoid breakage (remember that many airlines have restrictions on bottles in hand luggage).

(Continued from p321)

Mendoza Wine Camp TOUR
(☎0261-423-6958; www.mendozawinecamp.com; Belgrano 1194 B; ⏰11am-8:30pm Mon-Fri, 5:30-8:30pm Sat) A young company whose tours tend more towards interaction and education. Also offers a great *asado* (barbecue grill) cooking class day trip. Prices run to about AR$770 per day.

Ampora Wine Tours TOUR
(☎0261-429-2931; www.mendozawinetours.com; Av Sarmiento 647; ⏰9am-9pm Mon-Sat, 5-9pm Sat & Sun) A well-established operation that concentrates on midrange and top-end wines. It has tours leaving every day to Luján de Cuyo (US$170) and the Uco Valley (US$180). Tours focus more on tasting than winemaking techniques.

Festivals & Events

Mendoza's biggest annual event, the **Fiesta Nacional de la Vendimia** (National Wine Harvest Festival), lasts about a week, from late February to early March. It features a parade on Av San Martín with floats from each department of the province, numerous concerts and *folklórico* (folk music) events, and it all culminates in the coronation of the festival's queen in the Parque General San Martín amphitheater.

Sleeping

Note that hotel prices rise from January to March, most notably during the wine festival in early March. Some hostels in Mendoza will only rent you a bed if you buy one of their tours.

★**Hostel Alamo** HOSTEL $
(☎0261-429-5565; www.hostelalamo.com.ar; Necochea 740; dm AR$85-95, d with/without bathroom AR$240-350/200; @) An impeccable hostel in a great location, the Alamo offers roomy four-bed dorms, great hangout areas and a wonderful backyard with a small swimming pool.

Mendoza Inn HOSTEL $
(☎0261-438-0818; www.mendozahostel.com; Av Arístides Villanueva 470; dm AR$75-85, d AR$240; @) This place is in a great location and features friendly, bilingual staff, making it one of the city's better hostels. Common areas are on the spacious side and the large shady backyard and pool are definite pluses.

Hotel Casino HOTEL $
(☎0261-425-6666; www.nuevohotelcasino.com.ar; Gutiérrez 668; s/d AR$260/300;) Facing on to Plaza Chile, the Hotel Casino offers some good, spacious rooms and some smallish, ordinary ones. They're all clean and comfortable, but have a look at a few before deciding.

Punto Urbano Hostel HOSTEL $
(☎0261-429-5281; www.puntourbanohostel.com; Av Godoy Cruz 332; dm AR$70, d with/without bathroom AR$260/220; @) Just north of the city center, this hostel maintains an air of intimacy despite its grand proportions. The dorms are regular, but the doubles are extremely good value – spacious, with wide-screen TVs and tastefully decorated bathrooms. The large backyard – good for smoking, drinking, barbecuing and generally hanging out – is an added bonus.

Royal Hotel Horcones HOTEL $
(☎0261-425-0045; www.hotelhorcones.com; Av Las Heras 145; s/d AR$200/280; @) A good deal on very central, spacious rooms. The wallpaper could do with a change, but the parquetry floors and sunny patio area are winners.

Banana Hostel HOSTEL $
(☎0261-423-3354; www.bananahostel.com.ar; Julio A Roca 344; dm AR$85-100, d with/without bathroom AR$280/200; @) Spacious hostel set in the quiet residential neighborhood known as La Quinta. The common areas are great, as is the big backyard and huge swimming pool.

Hostel Suites HOSTEL $
(☎0261-423-7018; www.hostelsuitesmendoza.com; Mendocinas 1532; dm from AR$75, d AR$300; @) A definite step above most other hostels in town, this one is well designed and well organized, offering a decent deal on dorms and hotel-style doubles. Free activities, tours, a good kitchen, rooftop terrace and a central location round out the picture.

Hotel Petit HOTEL $
(☎0261-423-2099; www.petit-hoteles.com.ar; Perú 1459; s/d AR$240/300;) An excellent, central location, friendly welcome and big buffet breakfast make up for the slightly cramped rooms at this clean but aging hotel.

Hotel Abril HOTEL $
(☎0261-429-0027; www.hotel-abril.com; Mendocinas 866; s/d from AR$360/389; @) A modern hotel with touches of class, the Abril

never really lives up to its 'boutique' claims, but is a pretty good deal for the price, amenities and location.

Hotel Zamora HOTEL $

(☎0261-425-7537; Perú 1156; s/d AR$240/300; ❄📶) With a lot more style than most in this price range, this sweet little family-run hotel offers comfortable rooms, a buffet breakfast and a charming courtyard with tinkling fountain and Spanish tile-work.

★**Modigliani Suites** APARTMENT $$

(☎0261-429-9222; www.modiglianisuites.com; Alem 41; apt AR$515-1030; ❄📶) Good value furnished apartments are extremely hard to come by in Mendoza, but these ones are fantastic. The owner-architect has a keen eye for detail and the charming suites have just that right mix of minimalist cool and pleasing decoration. The on-site art gallery is an added bonus, as are the contemporary works that grace each apartment.

Alcor Hotel HOTEL $$

(☎0261-438-1000; www.alcorhotel.com.ar; General Paz 86; s/d AR$360/415; ❄📶) One block from busy Av Las Heras, this is a recently renovated hotel that has maintained a few of its original charms. Rooms are big, light and well proportioned, with some comfy touches. Discounts apply for stays longer than three days.

Hotel San Martín HOTEL $$

(☎0261-438-0677; www.hsm-mza.com.ar; Espejo 435; s/d AR$490/520; ❄@📶) Fronting the plaza, this three-story brick hotel offers solid value. There's plenty of tasteful tile-work and rooms are spacious and comfortable with modern bathrooms and big windows.

Hotel Argentino HOTEL $$

(☎0261-405-6300; www.argentino-hotel.com; Espejo 455; s/d from AR$580/640; ❄@📶🏊) Right on the central plaza, this business-class hotel has some fine features, including large rooms and a decent-sized swimming pool. Pay extra for a balcony overlooking the plaza.

Palace Hotel HOTEL $$

(☎0261-423-4200; www.hotelpalace.com.ar; Av Las Heras 70; s/d AR$230/400; ❄📶) The fading '70s charm of this large hotel is compensated for by its great, central location and a few classy decorations left over from the good ol' days. Rooms are generously sized and those at the front boast views out over the busy avenue.

B&B Plaza Italia B&B $$$

(☎0261-423-4219; www.plazaitalia.net; Montevideo 685; r AR$684; ❄📶) This five-room B&B is hard to beat when it comes to friendliness and delicious breakfasts. The house is lovely, the owners (who speak English) are divine, and the living room is just right for reading. It's like being at home.

Hotel Bohemia BOUTIQUE HOTEL $$$

(☎0261-420-0575; www.bohemiahotelboutique.com; Granaderos 954; s/d AR$570/672; ❄@📶🏊) Somewhat out of place in Mendoza's otherwise workaday hotel scene, this repurposed family home features slick design, comfortable common areas and small but well-appointed rooms featuring minimalist decoration. It's about eight blocks west of the Plaza Independencia.

Eating

Some of Mendoza's best restaurants, often with outdoor seating and lively young crowds, are along Av Arístides Villanueva, the western extension of Av Colón. West of Plaza Independencia, Av Sarmiento is lined with the city's most traditional, albeit touristy, *parrillas* (steak restaurants), while east of the plaza along the Sarmiento *peatonal* (pedestrian street), you'll find numerous sidewalk cafes with outdoor seating. The Sarmiento cafes are required visiting for coffee. The renovated **Mercado Central** (cnr Av Las Heras & Patricias Mendocinas; mains from AR$55; ⏲8:30am-11pm) is a good hunting ground for reasonably priced set meals.

El Palenque ARGENTINE $

(Av Arístides Villanueva 287; mains AR$60-90; ⏲11am-1am Mon-Sat) Don't miss this superb, extremely popular restaurant styled after an old-time *pulpería* (tavern), where the house wine is served in traditional *pinguinos* (white ceramic penguin-shaped pitchers). The food and appetizers are outstanding, and the outside tables are always full and fun.

La Flor de la Canela PERUVIAN $

(Av Juan B Justo 426; mains AR$40-60; ⏲noon-1am Wed-Mon) Need something spicy? Check out this authentic, bare-bones Peruvian eatery a few blocks from the center. What it lacks in atmosphere it makes up for in flavor.

Cocina Poblana MIDDLE EASTERN $

(Av Arístides Villanueva 217; dishes from AR$50; ⏲12-3pm & 7pm-1am Mon-Sat) The very tasty, inexpensive Middle Eastern food here (hummus, falafel, dolmas) comes as a welcome break from all that steak. The shish kebab served with tabouleh salad is a definite winner.

Quinta Norte ARGENTINE $
(Av Mitre & Espejo; set meals AR$50, mains AR$50-75; ⌚8am-midnight) Sidewalk dining right across from the plaza. The menu's not huge, but there are some good dishes and the set lunches are some of the best in town. A great place to grab a coffee and recharge the batteries.

Arrope VEGETARIAN $
(Primitiva de la Reta 927; AR$10 per 100 grams; ⌚8am-3pm) Feeling a little meat-heavy? Slip into this cozy vegetarian cafe/restaurant and choose from a wide range of animal-free goodies on the buffet table.

★ **Anna Bistro** FUSION $$
(Av Juan B Justo 161; mains AR$80-120; ⌚12:30pm-1am) One of Mendoza's best-looking restaurants offers a wonderful garden area, cool music and carefully prepared dishes.

Patancha INTERNATIONAL $$
(Perú 778; mains from AR$70; ⌚noon-midnight) A cute little place serving up some great tapas alongside traditional favorites such as *humitas* (stuffed corn dough resembling Mexican tamales) and the occasional surprise such as seafood stir-fry. The AR$55 set lunch is a bargain.

La Tasca de Plaza España SPANISH $$
(☎0261-423-3466; Montevideo 117; mains AR$90-120; ⌚1-3pm Thu & Fri, 7:30pm-midnight daily) With excellent Mediterranean and Spanish tapas (mostly seafood), great wines, intimate atmosphere, good art and friendly service, La Tasca is one of Mendoza's best.

Florentino FUSION $$
(Montevideo 675; mains from AR$90; ⌚8:30pm-12am) One of the more innovative restaurants downtown, it specializes in lighter dishes combining flavors you're unlikely to find elsewhere. Vegetarian and celiac options available.

Siete Cocinas ARGENTINE $$
(San Lorenzo & Mitre; mains AR$100-160; ⌚8pm-1am) Promising a gastronomical tour of Argentina's seven regional cuisines, this place delivers handsomely with delicacies such as goat cheese ravioli, slow-cooked pork and Patagonian lamb-and-mushroom pie.

Tommaso Trattoria ITALIAN $$
(Av Sarmiento 762; mains AR$80; ⌚11:30am-midnight) An excellent, trilingual (Italian, Spanish and English) menu featuring a good range of creative regional Italian dishes. The wine list is impressive and the tables out the front are the place to be on a balmy evening.

Maria Antioneta INTERNATIONAL $$
(Belgrano 1069; mains AR$80-130; ⌚8am-11pm; 📶) The wonderful, fresh blend of flavors on the menu here are echoed in the design of the dining room – a pleasing mix of retro and modern styling. Everything's well presented and flavorful and accompanied by an excellent selection of wines and desserts.

La Marchigiana ITALIAN $$
(Patricias Mendocinas 1550; mains AR$80-120; ⌚12-3pm & 7pm-1am) Mendoza's most frequently recommended Italian restaurant. The decor may seem stark, but the service is warm and a few Argentine twists to the classic Italian menu keep things interesting.

La Mira FUSION $$
(Av Belgrano 1191; mains AR$75-120; ⌚9am-midnight) Delicious, innovative dishes in a relaxed environment. Each dish comes as a full meal (some with side orders of vegetables) and there's a small but respectable wine list.

Azafrán FUSION $$$
(☎0261-429-4200; Av Sarmiento 765; mains AR$110-160; ⌚12-3pm & 7pm-1am Mon-Sat) It's hard to figure out what's the bigger draw here – the rustic-chic decor, the small but creative menu or the extensive wine list. Who cares? Enjoy them all.

Drinking & Nightlife

For a great night on the town, walk down Av Arístides Villanueva, where it's bar after bar; in summer, entire blocks fill with tables and people enjoying the night. On the other side of town is the Tajamar, which is similar, but more laid-back and bohemian. This area is your best bet to hear live music.

Wine is available pretty much everywhere in Mendoza (right down to gas stations), but there are a few places that are considered specialists.

Finding a dance floor generally means abandoning downtown for one of two areas: the northwest suburb of El Challao, or Chacras de Coria, along the RP82 in the southern outskirts. The former is reached by bus 115 from Av Sarmiento. Chacras de

Coria is reached from the stop on La Rioja between Catamarca and Garibaldi by taking bus 10, interno (internal route number) 19, or from the corner of 25 de Mayo and Rivadavia by taking bus 10, interno 15. In both cases simply asking the driver for los boliches (the nightclubs) is enough to find the right stop. The nightclubs in both El Challao and Chacras de Coria are all right next to each other, and you can walk along to take your pick from the ever-changing array. **La Guanaca** (Ruta Panamericana s/n , Chacras de Coria; ⏲10pm-5:30am Fri & Sat) was the hot club out here at the time of research – with a bit of luck it may still be going by the time you arrive.

Many visitors to Mendoza (and *mendocinos* for that matter) find the effort involved getting to these places far outweighs the fun they have while there, often opting for the smaller bars along Av Arístides Villanueva. One exception is **La Mala** (Escalada 2273; admission AR$20-33; ⏲11pm-late), in the Tajamar nightlife precinct. It gets a good crowd and was the hottest club around at the time of writing.

Por Acá BAR
(Av Arístides Villanueva 557; ⏲8pm-late Wed-Sat) Purple and yellow outside and polka-dotted upstairs, this bar-lounge gets packed after 2am, and by the end of the night, dancing on the tables is not uncommon. Good retro dance music.

La Reserva GAY
(Rivadavia 34; admission free-AR$50; ⏲from 9pm Tue-Sat) This small, nominally gay bar packs in a mixed crowd and has outrageous drag shows at midnight every night, with hardcore techno later.

Vines of Mendoza WINE BAR
(Belgrano 1194; ⏲3-10pm) This friendly, central wine bar (where everybody, down to the security guards, seems to speak English) offers flights (tastings of five selected wines) and top-shelf private tastings. It also offers wine-appreciation classes which give you an idea of how to taste wine – a great idea before hitting the bodegas.

Blah Blah Bar BAR
(Escalada 2307; ⏲from 6pm) A Tajamar favorite, Mendoza's version of a dive bar is hip but restrained, with a casual atmosphere and plenty of outdoor seating.

Vines Park Hyatt WINE BAR
(Chile 1124; ⏲11am-midnight) In the super-formal surrounds of Mendoza's best-looking hotel, this is a relaxed and intimate wine bar offering wine by the glass, cheese platters and tapas.

☆ Entertainment

Check the tourist offices or museums for a copy of *La Guía,* a monthly publication with comprehensive entertainment listings. *Los Andes,* the daily rag, also has a good entertainment section.

Theater & Live Music

For everything from live music to avante-garde theater, check the program at the **Centro Cultural Tajamar** (Escalada 1921; admission free-AR$35; ⏲from 8pm) in the Tajamar district.

The main theaters in town are **Teatro Quintanilla** (☎0261-423-2310; Plaza Independencia) and the nearby **Teatro Independencia** (☎0261-438-0644; cnr Espejo & Chile).

Shopping

Av Las Heras is lined with souvenir shops, leather shops, chocolate stores and all sorts of places to pick up cheap Argentine trinkets. Items made of *carpincho* (spotted tanned hide of the capybara, a large rodent) are uniquely Argentine and sold in many of the stores.

Unless you are looking for a very obscure top-of-the-range bottle (or a sales assistant who knows what they're talking about), the best place to buy wine in town, in terms of price and variety, is the supermarket **Carrefour** (Avs Las Heras & Belgrano; ⏲8am-10pm). Specialty wine stores stock finer wines, have staff who speak at least a little English and can pack your bottles for shipping.

Plaza de las Artes MARKET
(Plaza Independencia; ⏲5-11pm Fri-Sun) Outdoor crafts market in the Plaza Independencia.

Raices HANDICRAFTS
(Av España 1092; ⏲8am-7pm Mon-Fri, 8am-1pm Sat) High-quality weavings, *mate* (a bitter ritual tea), jewelry and more. There is another location nearby on Av Sarmiento 162.

Juan Cedrón WINE
(Av Sarmiento 278; ⏲9am-1pm & 4-9pm Mon-Sat) A small but well-chosen selection lines the walls. Doubles as a wine bar. Occasional tastings and sidewalk tables.

Centro Internacional del Libro BOOKS (☎0261-420-1266; Lavalle 14; ⏰9am-6pm Mon-Fri, 9am-2pm Sat) Small selection of classics and best-sellers in English.

SBS BOOKS (Gutiérrez 54; ⏰9am-6pm Mon-Sat) A large range of novels in English, Lonely Planet guidebooks, maps and wine-related literature. Also TOEFL resources and textbooks for Spanish students.

Information

DANGERS & ANNOYANCES

Mendoza has long been one of Argentina's safer destinations, but economic woes have caught up here, too, resulting in an increased number of street crimes. Tourists are rarely the target here and the city is still a safe place, but there are a few things to watch out for. Bag snatching and pickpocketing (particularly when the victim is wandering around with their hands full) are on the rise, as is the practice of snatching MP3 players from joggers in the park.

The areas around the bus terminal and on Cerro de la Gloria (in Parque General San Martín) now have an increased police presence, but are still considered dangerous at night. Increased caution is recommended during the early afternoon, too, as police tend to take the siesta along with everybody else. There have been several reports of people picking locks on hostel lockers – if you have something really valuable, leave it at your hostel's reception or, better yet, in its safe.

EMERGENCY

Servicio Coordinado de Emergencia (☎0261-428-0000) Call for an ambulance.

IMMIGRATION

Immigration Office (☎0261-424-3512; Av San Martín 1859; ⏰9am-4pm Mon-Fri) In Godoy Cruz, south of the city center.

MEDIA

La Guía This free monthly events magazine is a must-have if you plan on keeping up with Mendoza's hectic cultural scene. Pick up a copy at any tourist office.

Wine Republic (www.wine-republic.com) An excellent English-language magazine focusing on wine but also featuring good reviews of up-and-coming restaurants, Mendoza gossip and a couple of entertaining articles. Pick up a copy at Vines of Mendoza (p329) or Trout & Wine (p321).

MEDICAL SERVICES

Hospital (☎0261-420-0063/0600; cnr José F Moreno & Alem)

MONEY

There are many ATMs downtown. The following two banks are architectural landmarks; Banco Mendoza is massive.

Banco de la Nación (cnr Necochea & 9 de Julio; ⏰9am-1pm Mon-Fri)

Banco Mendoza (cnr Gutiérrez & San Martín; ⏰9am-1pm Mon-Fri)

Cambio Santiago (Av San Martín 1199; ⏰8am-6pm Mon-Fri, 9am-1pm Sat & Sun) Charges 2% commission on traveler's checks.

POST

Post Office (Av San Martín at Colón; ⏰8am-6pm Mon-Fri, 9am-1pm Sat)

TOURIST INFORMATION

ACA (Automóvil Club Argentina; ☎0261-420-2900; cnr Av San Martín & Amigorena; ⏰24 hr) Argentina's auto club; good source for provincial road maps.

Municipal Tourist Offices (www.turismo.mendoza.gov.ar) Bus Terminal; (☎0261-431-5000; ⏰8am-8pm) City Hall (⏰8am-8pm) The municipality has information offices at the bus terminal and city hall.

Tourist Kiosk (☎420-1333; Garibaldi; ⏰8am-6pm) This helpful kiosk near Av San Martín is the most convenient information source.

Tourist Office (☎0261-420-2800; www.turismo.mendoza.gov.ar; Av San Martín 1143; ⏰8am-10pm Mon-Fri) Good maps; plenty of brochures.

TRAVEL AGENCIES

Asatej (☎0261-429-0029; mendoza@asatej.com.ar; Av Sarmiento 223; ⏰9am-1pm & 4pm-9pm Mon-Fri, 9am-2pm Sat) Recommended student and discount travel agency.

Getting There & Away

AIR

Aerolíneas Argentinas/Austral (☎0261-420-4185; Av Sarmiento 82; ⏰10am-6pm Mon-Fri, 10am-1pm Sat) The airlines share offices; Aerolíneas flies several times daily to Buenos Aires.

LANChile (☎0261-425-7900; Rivadavia 135; ⏰10am-7pm Mon-Fri) LANChile flies twice daily to Santiago de Chile.

Sol (☎0810-444-4765; www.sol.com.ar) Flies to direct Córdoba and Neuquén, with connections further afield.

BUS

Mendoza is a major transport hub so you can travel to just about anywhere in the country. Mendoza's **bus terminal** (☎0261-431-3001; Av de Acceso Este & Costanera) has domestic and international departures. You can book tickets at no extra cost downtown at the **Terminal del Centro** (9 de Julio 1042; 9am-1pm & 5-9pm).

Domestic

Several companies send buses daily to Uspallata (AR$30, two hours) and Los Penitentes (AR$36, four hours), the latter for Aconcagua.

During the ski season several companies go directly to Las Leñas (about AR$160, seven hours).

A number of companies offer a morning bus service to the Difunta Correa Shrine (AR$120 return, departs 7:30am) in San Juan province; the journey is three hours each way and the bus waits three hours before returning. Buses to Maipú leave from the stop on La Rioja between Garibaldi and Catamarca.

Buses from Mendoza

There are daily departures from Mendoza's bus terminal to most destinations in the following table, and sometimes upwards of 10 to 20 per day to major cities. Prices reflect midseason fares.

DESTINATION	COST (AR$)	DURATION (HR)
Bahía Blanca	790	16
Bariloche	900	20
Buenos Aires	375	13-17
Catamarca	458	10
Córdoba	535	10
Jujuy	896	22
Malargüe	95	5
Mar del Plata	835	19
Neuquén	574	10-12
Resistencia	1050	24
Río Gallegos	1982	41
Rosario	335	12
Salta	995	18
San Juan	134	2½
San Luis	200	3½
San Rafael	48	3
Tucumán	592	14

International

Numerous companies cross the Andes every day via RN7 (Paso de Los Libertadores) to Santiago, Chile (AR$400, seven hours), Viña del Mar (AR$400, seven hours) and Valparaíso (AR$420, eight hours). The pass sometimes closes due to bad winter weather; be prepared to wait (sometimes days) if weather gets extreme.

Several carriers have connections to Lima, Perú (AR$2500, 60 to 70 hours), via Santiago, Chile.

International buses depart from the main bus terminal. Companies are at the eastern end of the terminal.

Getting Around

TO/FROM THE AIRPORT

Plumerillo International Airport (0261-520-6000; Acceso Norte s/n) is 6km north of downtown on RN40. Bus 68 ('Aeropuerto') from Calle Salta goes straight to the terminal.

BUS

Mendoza's bus terminal is really just across the street from downtown. After arriving, walk under the Videla underpass and you'll be heading toward the center, about 15 minutes away. Otherwise, the 'Villa Nueva' trolley (actually a bus) connects the terminal with downtown.

Local buses cost AR$4.10 – more for longer distances – and require a magnetic Redbus card, which can be bought at most kiosks in denominations of AR$5 and AR$10. Most *lineas* (bus lines) also have *internos* (internal route numbers) posted in the window; for example, *linea* 200 might post *interno* 204 or 206; watch for both numbers. *Internos* indicate more precisely where the bus will take you.

CAR

Car-rental agencies are at the airport and along Primitivo de la Reta.

Avis (0261-447-0150; Primitivo de la Reta 914; 8:30am-8:30pm Mon-Fri, 8:30am-1pm & 5:30-8pm Sat & Sun)

Localiza (0261-429-6800; Primitivo de la Reta 936, Local 4; 8am-8pm Mon-Fri, 9am-1pm & 5-8pm Sat & Sun)

National/Alamo (0261-429-3111; Primitivo de la Reta 928; 8am-8pm Mon-Fri, 8:30am-1pm & 4-8pm Sat & Sun)

Around Mendoza

Wineries

Thanks to a complex and very old system of river-fed aqueducts, land that was once a desert now supports 70% of the country's wine production. Mendoza province is wine country, and many wineries near the capital offer tours and tasting. Countless tourist agencies offer day tours, hitting two or more wineries in a precisely planned day, but it's also easy enough to visit on your own. Hiring a *remise* (taxi) is also feasible. Some winery tours and tastings are free, though some push hard for sales at the end, and you never taste the *good* stuff without paying. Malbec, of course, is the definitive Argentine wine.

With a full day it's easy to hop on buses and hit several of the area's most appealing wineries in the outskirts of neighboring

WORTH A TRIP

MAIPÚ: A GOURMET EXPERIENCE

The small town of Maipú, just out of Mendoza, is so packed with wineries, olive oil farms and other gourmet businesses that it's easy to hit five or six in a day. All offer tours and most finish proceedings with at least a small sampling of their produce.

Accordingly, a few companies in Maipú rent bikes, making a day tour of the area an excellent outing, and a lot more fun than the often rushed half-day wine tours on offer from Mendoza tour agencies.

To get to Maipú, catch the 173 bus from the bus stop on La Rioja in Mendoza and get off at the triangular roundabout. Bike-hire competition here is serious business (there have been fistfights in the street between operators) and the main companies are all within walking distance of each other. Go for a stroll and see who has the best wheels. Among operators are **Mr Hugo Bikes** (☎0261-497-4067; www.mrhugobikes.com; Urquiza 2228; bikes per day AR$40; ⏰9am-7pm Mon-Sat) and **Coco Bikes** (☎0261-481-0862; Urquiza 1781; bikes per day AR$30; ⏰9am-6pm Mon-Sat). All will supply you with a (basic) map of the area and may throw in goodies like water and discount vouchers for tastings.

Reservations are not necessary at any of the following.

Carinae (☎0261-499-0470; www.carinaevinos.com; Aranda 2899; tours AR$35; ⏰10am-6pm daily) is the furthest south you really want to go – it's a small, French-owned winery producing a lovely rosé and some good reds. Tour fees are deducted from any wine purchases you make.

Across the road is **LAUR** (www.laursa.com.ar; Aranda 2850; tours AR$10; ⏰10am-6pm Mon-Sat), a 100-year-old olive farm. The 15-minute tour tells you everything you need to know about olive oil production and is followed by a yummy tasting session.

Heading back to Urquiza, go past the big roundabout and venture north. The first winery you come to is **Di Tomasso** (☎0261-587-8900; www.familiaditommaso.com; Urquiza 8136; tours AR$25; ⏰10am-6pm Mon-Sat), a beautiful, historical vineyard dating back to the 1830s. The tour includes a quick pass through the original cellar section.

Heading north again, take a right on Moreno to get to **Viña del Cerno** (☎0261-481-1567; www.elcerno.com.ar; Moreno 631; tours AR$25; full tasting AR$60; ⏰10am-6pm Mon-Sat), a small, old-fashioned winery supervised by its two winemaker owners. The underground cellar complex is atmospheric, but tastings can be a little rushed.

Making your way back to Urquiza, drop in at Tempus Alba, a large, modern winery that offers a quick self-guided tour of the installations and a very tasty lunch menu (mains AR$37 to AR$67) in their restaurant overlooking the vines.

Back on Urquiza, continue north until you get to the big roundabout. Turn right and follow the signs to **Historia y Sabores** (Carril Gómez 3064; tastings AR$25; ⏰10am-6pm Mon-Fri, 9am-1pm Sat). Seven families run this little chocolate- and liqueur-making operation. Tours are brief, but the lovely rustic surrounds and comfy bar (where you're offered a free shot of liqueur) make it a worthwhile stop.

Along Urquiza, keep heading north until you get to where you got off the bus, take a right on Montecaseros and continue for 500m to reach **Bodega La Rural** (☎0261-497-2013; www.bodegalarural.com.ar; Montecaseros 2625; tours AR$50; ⏰9am-1pm & 2-5pm Mon-Fri) Winery tours here are fairly standard (and you probably have the idea by now) but the museum is fascinating – displaying a huge range of winemaking equipment from over the years, including a grape press made from an entire cowskin. Tours in Spanish leave on the hour. If you want one in English, call ahead, or you can simply walk around on your own.

Maipú, only 16km away. For a look at what the cutting-edge wineries are doing, consider renting a car or going on a tour of the Valle de Uco. Another option is the area of Luján de Cuyo, 19km south of Mendoza, which also has many important wineries. Buses to Maipú leave from La Rioja, between Garibaldi and Catamarca in central Mendoza; buses to wineries in Luján de Cuyo leave from Mendoza's bus terminal.

Mendoza's tourist office on Garibaldi near Av San Martín provides a basic but helpful map of the area and its wineries. Also look for the useful three-map set *Wine Map: Wine and Tasting Tours.*

Luigi Bosca WINERY
(0261-498-1974; www.luigibosca.com.ar; San Martín 2044, Luján de Cuyo; guided visits AR$45; Mon-Sat by reservation only) Luigi Bosca, which also produces Finca La Linda, is one of Mendoza's premier wineries. If you're into wine, don't miss it. Tours are available in Spanish and English. Take bus 380 (AR$4.10, one hour) from platform 53 in Mendoza's bus terminal.

Bodegas Chandon WINERY
(0261-490-9968; www.bodegaschandon.com.ar; RN40, Km29, Agrelo, Luján de Cuyo; guided visits AR$30; Mon-Sat by reservation only) The modern Bodegas Chandon is popular with tour groups and known for its sparkling wines (champagne). Tours are available in Spanish and English. Take bus 380 (AR$3, one hour) from platform 53 in Mendoza's bus terminal.

Catena Zapata WINERY
(0261-413-1100; www.catenawines.com; Calle Cobos 5519, Agrelo, Luján de Cuyo; visits/tours by appointment 10am-6pm Mon-Sat) Catena Zapata is one of Argentina's most esteemed wineries. Tours are fairly mundane but are conducted in English, German or Spanish. Tasting – if you put down the cash – can be educational indeed. Get there by taxi (cheaper if you catch a bus to Luján de Cuyo and grab one from there).

Cacheuta

02624 / POP 640 / ELEV 1237M

About 40km southwest of Mendoza, in the department of Luján de Cuyo, Cacheuta is renowned for its medicinal thermal waters and agreeable microclimate.

The open-air thermal-baths complex **Complejo Termal Cacheuta** (02624-490139; www.termascacheuta.com; RP82, Km41; admission AR$75; 10am-6pm) is one of the best in the country due to its variety of pools and dramatic setting on the side of a valley. Midweek is the best time to come as weekends get crowded with kids splashing around on the waterslide and in the wave pool, and the air runs thick with the smoke from a thousand *parrillas*.

There is lodging at the lovely **Hotel & Spa Cacheuta** (02624-490153; www.termascacheuta.com; RP82, Km38; s/d with full board from AR$1020/1740;), where prices include a swimming pool, hot tubs and massage, in addition to optional recreation programs. Nonguests may use the baths for around AR$240 per person.

Campers can pitch a tent at **Camping Termas de Cacheuta** (02624-482082; RN7, Km39; campsite per person AR$35).

Expreso Uspallata (in Mendoza 0261-438-1092) runs daily buses to Cacheuta (AR$45, 1½ hours).

Potrerillos

02624 / ELEV 1351M

Set above the newly built Potrerillos reservoir in beautiful Andean precordillera, Potrerillos is one of Mendoza's white-water hot spots, usually visited during a day's rafting trip from the capital.

Located about 1km uphill from the ACA campground, **Argentina Rafting** (02624-482037; Ruta Perilago s/n) offers rafting and kayaking on the Río Mendoza. Trips range from a 5km, one-hour Class II float to a 50km, five-hour Class III–IV descent over two days. Organize trips at the Mendoza office (p321) or at the base here in Potrerillos.

El Puesto Hostel HOSTEL $
(02624-467-4356; www.elpuestohostel.com.ar; Av Los Condores s/n; dm AR$80) This newish hostel has four- to six-bed dorms in a tranquil setting. Table tennis and darts are on hand to keep you entertained and hearty traditional meals are available (AR$55 to AR$80).

Camping del ACA CAMPGROUND
(02624-482013; RN7, Km50; campsites members /nonmembers AR$50/60) Camping del ACA offers shady sites near the reservoir just below the new town.

Villavicencio

0261 / ELEV 1800M

If you've ordered mineral water from any restaurant or cafe in Argentina, odds are you've ended up with a bottle of Villavicencio on your table. These springs are the source, and their spectacular mountain setting once hosted the prestigious thermal baths resort of the **Gran Hotel de Villavicencio** (8am-8pm) FREE. Popular with the Argentine elite during the middle of the 20th century, the resort has been closed for more than a decade; promises have floated around for years that it would 'soon' reopen.

Panoramic views from the hair-raising winding turns leading to Villavicencio make the journey an attraction in itself. There is free camping alongside the attractive **Hostería Villavicencio** (☎0261-439-6487; meals AR$80-130; ⌚10:30am-6pm), which has no accommodations but serves gourmet meals in charming surrounds.

There is no public transportation to the valley. Nearly every tour operator in Mendoza offers half-day tours (AR$150) that take in the hotel grounds, the bottling plant and short walks in the surrounding countryside.

Uspallata

☎02624 / POP 3800 / ELEV 1751M

A humble little crossroads town on the way to the Chilean border, Uspallata is an oasis of poplar trees set in a desolate desert valley. The polychrome mountains surrounding the town so resemble highland Central Asia that director Jean-Jacques Annaud used it as the location for the epic film *Seven Years in Tibet*.

The town first gained fame as a low-budget base for the nearby ski fields at Los Penitentes, but has recently been coming into its own with a few companies offering treks, horseback riding and fishing expeditions in the surrounding countryside.

There's a post office and a Banco de la Nación, which has an ATM. The **tourist office** (☎02624-420009; RN7 s/n; ⌚8am-9pm) is across from the YPF gas station. It has good information on local sights and activities and some very basic (but still useful) area maps.

Sights

A kilometer north of the highway junction in Uspallata, a signed lateral leads to ruins and a museum at the **Museo Las Bóvedas** (admission free; ⌚11am-5pm) FREE, a smelting site since pre-Columbian times. An easy 8km walk north of town brings you to **Cerro Tunduqueral** (⌚11am-6:30pm), where you'll find sweeping views and Inca rock carvings.

Tours

Uspallata Aventura ADVENTURE TOUR
(☎0261-15-598-813535; ⌚9am-6pm Mon-Sat, 9am-1pm & 4-8pm Sun) Uspallata Aventura offers a range of outdoor activities, including horseback riding, mountain-bike tours, rock climbing, trekking and 4WD off-roading. It also rents mountain bikes for AR$15/60 per hour/day.

Fototravesías 4x4 GUIDED TOUR
(☎0261-15-508-9049; www.fototravesias4x4.com) Fototravesías 4x4, near the main intersection, offers exciting 4WD tours in the surrounding mountains. The owner is a photographer and is especially amenable to ensuring travelers get good shots.

Sleeping & Eating

In the summer high season (when climbers from around the world descend on the area), reservations are wise.

Hostel International Uspallata HOSTEL $
(☎15-466-7240; www.hosteluspallata.com.ar; RN7 s/n; dm/d AR$80/250) Friendly hostel 7km east of town with plain but comfortable rooms. Dinner (AR$70 to AR$100) is available. There's good hiking from the hostel and you can rent bikes and horses here. Ask the bus driver to drop you at the front before you hit Uspallata.

Hotel Portico del Valle HOTEL $$
(☎02624-420103; Las Heras s/n; s/d AR$550/650) A recently constructed, vaguely modern hotel right on the crossroads. It's nothing fancy, but fine for a few days.

Hostería Los Cóndores HOTEL $$
(☎02624-420002; www.loscondoreshotel.com.ar; Las Heras s/n; s/d AR$600/700; ❄️) Close to the junction, this is the finest hotel in the center of town. There's plenty of space, modern furnishings, and a gut-busting breakfast buffet is included in the price.

★ **Café Tibet** CAFE $
(cnr RN7 & Las Heras; mains AR$45-80; ⌚8am-11pm) No visit to Uspallata would be complete without at least a coffee in this little oddity. The food is nothing spectacular, but the decor, comprising leftover props from *Seven Years in Tibet*, is a must for fans of the surreal.

El Rancho PARRILLA $$
(cnr RN7 & Cerro Chacay; mains AR$80-130; ⌚12-3pm & 7pm-1am Tue-Sun) This is the coziest and most reliable *parrilla* in town, serving all the usual, plus a good roasted *chivo* (goat).

Getting There & Away

Expreso Uspallata (☎0261-432-5055) runs several buses daily to and from Mendoza (AR$30, 2½ hours). Buses continue from Uspallata to Las Cuevas (AR$35, two hours), near the Chilean border, and stop en route at Los Penitentes, Puente del Inca and the turnoff to Laguna Los Horcones for Parque Provincial Aconcagua. They can be flagged from all of these locations on their return to Uspallata from Las Cuevas.

Andesmar has daily morning departures to Santiago (AR$400, six hours) and Valparaíso (AR$400, seven hours) in Chile.

There's been talk for some time of a new bus service which will connect Uspallata with Barreal in San Juan province – it may well be operating by the time you read this.

All buses leave from the Expreso Uspallata office in the little strip mall near the junction.

Los Penitentes

☎02624 / ELEV 2581M

So named because the pinnacles resemble a line of monks, **Los Penitentes** (☎0261-429-9953; www.lospenitentes.com) has both excellent scenery and snow cover (in winter). It's 165km west of Mendoza via RN7, and offers downhill and cross-country skiing at an altitude of 2580m. Lifts (AR$215 to AR$295 per day) and accommodations are modern, and the vertical drop on some of its 21 runs is more than 700m. Services include a ski school (private lessons start around AR$205), equipment rentals (skis AR$100 per day, snowboards AR$120) and several restaurants and cafeterias.

In high ski season (July and August) and during peak climbing season (December through to March), it's recommended to make reservations up to a month in advance.

Sleeping

Hostel Los Penitentes HOSTEL $

(☎in Mendoza 0261-425-5511; www.penitentes.com.ar; dm AR$165-216) A cozy converted cabin, owned by Mendoza's HI Campo Base, it accommodates 38 people in extremely close quarters, and has a kitchen, wood-burning stove and three shared bathrooms. It's all good fun with the right crowd. Lunch and dinners are available for AR$30 to AR$50 each.

Hotel & Hostería Ayelén HOTEL $$

(☎in Mendoza 0261-425-3443; s/d from AR$450/800) A four-star resort hotel with comfortable accommodations in the main hotel and cheaper rooms in the *hostería* (lodging house) alongside. The hotel is slowly getting fixed up by its new owners, so the decor in some rooms leaves a bit to be desired. The restaurant is fantastic, though, and consistently gets rave reviews.

Hostería Los Penitentes HOTEL $$

(☎in Mendoza 0261-524-4708; www.hosteriapenitentes.com; d from AR$790) This modest *hostería* with plain, comfortable rooms has a restaurant and bar and offers full board with ski passes.

Refugio Aconcagua HOTEL $$

(☎in Mendoza 0261-424-1565; www.refugioaconcagua.com.ar; r with half-board per person AR$490) There's nothing fancy about the rooms at this place, but they're an OK size and considering you're in the middle of the resort, with a private bathroom and two meals a day, they're a good deal. The restaurant here serves up big, hearty set meals (AR$60 to AR$150) and is open year-round.

Puente del Inca

☎0261 / ELEV 2270M

One of Argentina's most striking natural wonders, this stone bridge over the Río de las Cuevas glows a dazzling orange from the sediment deposited by the warm sulfuric waters. The brick ruins of an old spa, built as part of a resort and later destroyed by flood, sit beneath the bridge, slowly yielding their form to the sulfuric buildup from the thermal water that trickles over, around and through it. Due to the unstable nature of the structure, the area has been closed off and you can't cross the bridge or enter the hot baths any more, but you can still get some fairly wild photos.

Puente del Inca enjoys a spectacular setting, and whether or not you climb, it's a good base for exploring the area. Trekkers and climbers can head north to the base of Aconcagua, south to the pinnacles of Los Penitentes, or even further south to 6650m Tupungato.

About 1km before Puente del Inca (directly across from Los Puquios), the small **Cementerio Andinista** is a cemetery for climbers who died on Aconcagua.

Sleeping & Eating

In summer, free camping is possible at the nearby mini ski resort of **Los Puquios** (☎0261-429-5007; www.lospuquios.com.ar) FREE. There are two accommodations options at Puente del Inca. A string of restaurants by the roadside offer filling but unexciting meals from around AR$80.

Hostel El Nico HOSTEL $
(☎0261-592-0736; elnicohostel@gmail.com; dm/d AR$150/400) A cozy little hostel sleeping 14 people. Can organize treks in summer and snowshoe/skiing expeditions in winter.

Hostería Puente del Inca HOTEL $$
(☎0261-596-6022; www.hosteriapdelinca.com.ar; s/d AR$450/600) Although closed at the time of research, this place offers reasonable rooms and a huge restaurant serving decent value set meals. It's the most comfortable in the area and fills up fast in climbing season.

Getting There & Away

A few buses a day leave from Mendoza's bus terminal for Puente del Inca (AR$45, four hours), passing through Uspallata. If you're on a day trip, check return times with the driver – you don't want to get stuck up here. Buses from Chile pass through but are often full and won't stop to pick you up.

Nearly every Mendoza tour operator offers day tours to Puente del Inca, often combined with Las Cuevas.

Parque Provincial Aconcagua

North of RN7, nearly hugging the Chilean border, Parque Provincial Aconcagua protects 710 sq km of the wild high country surrounding the western hemisphere's highest summit, 6962m Cerro Aconcagua. Passing motorists (and those who can time their buses correctly) can stop to enjoy the view of the peak from **Laguna Los Horcones**, a 2km walk from the parking lot just north of the highway.

During trekking season there are rangers stationed at: Laguna Los Horcones; the junction to Plaza Francia, about 5km north of Los Horcones; at Plaza de Mulas on the main route to the peak; at Refugio Las Leñas, on the Polish Glacier Route up the Río de las Vacas to the east; and at Plaza Argentina, the last major camping area along the Polish Glacier Route.

Only highly experienced climbers should consider climbing Aconcagua without the relative safety of an organized tour.

Cerro Aconcagua

Often called the 'roof of the Americas,' the volcanic summit of Aconcagua covers a base of uplifted marine sediments. The origin of the name is unclear; one possibility is the Quechua term Ackon-Cahuac, meaning 'stone sentinel,' while another is the Mapuche phrase Acon-Hue, signifying 'that which comes from the other side.'

Italian-Swiss climber Mathias Zurbriggen made the first recorded ascent in 1897. Since then, the peak has become a favorite destination for climbers from around the world, even though it is technically less challenging than other nearby peaks. In 1985 the Club Andinista Mendoza's discovery of an Incan mummy at 5300m on the mountain's southwest face proved that the high peaks were a pre-Columbian funerary site.

Reaching the summit requires a commitment of at least 13 to 15 days, including acclimatization time; some climbers prefer the longer but more scenic, less crowded and more technical Polish Glacier Route.

Potential climbers should acquire RJ Secor's climbing guide *Aconcagua* (Seattle, The Mountaineers, 1999). The website www.aconcagua.com.ar and Mendoza government's website, www.aconcagua.mendoza.gov.ar, are also helpful.

Nonclimbers can trek to **base camps** and **refugios** beneath the permanent snow line. On the Northwest Route there is also the relatively luxurious Hotel Refugio Plaza de Mulas which has been plagued by ownership troubles over the years – if you'd like to stay there, check with trekking operators if it's operating.

Permits

From December to March permits are obligatory for both trekking and climbing in Parque Provincial Aconcagua; park rangers at Laguna Los Horcones will not permit visitors to proceed up the Quebrada de los Horcones without one. Fees vary according to the complex park-use seasons. Permits cost AR$800/1600 for trekkers (three/seven days) and AR$55000 for climbers (20 days) during high season (December 15 through to January 31); AR$700/1400 for trekkers and AR$4400 for climbers during midseason (December 1 to December 14 and February 1 through to February 20); and AR$700/1400 (trekking) and AR$3500 (climbing) in low season (November 15 through to November 30 and February 21 through to March 15). Argentine nationals pay about 30% of overseas visitors' fees at all times. These fees climb (steeply) each year – check www.aconcagua.mendoza.gov.ar for the latest information.

TOURING THE VALLE DE UCO

Seriously remote and woefully signposted, the Valle de Uco – home to some of Mendoza's top wineries – is best visited on a guided tour. If you've got the time and patience, though, you can easily rent a car in Mendoza to make the trip.

The valley is an easy day trip from Mendoza, but there are some wonderfully atmospheric places to stay out here, including **Tupungato Divino,** (02622-448948; www.tupungatodivino.com.ar; cnr RP89 & Calle los Europeos; s/d US$120/150;) **Posada Salentein** (02622-429000; www.bodegasalentein.com; RP89 s/n; r with full board from US$187;) and **Casa Antucura** (0261-15-3390491; www.casaantucura.com; Barandica s/n, Tunuyán; r from AR$1720;)

If you're looking for a lunch stop, most of the above wineries offer gourmet meals. Otherwise, **Ilo** (02622-488323; cnr Cabral & Belgrano, Tupungato; mains AR$80-140; 12-3pm & 8pm-12am Mon-Sat) is generally considered the best in Tupungato – the good range of seafood dishes makes it a winemakers' favorite.

Reservations are essential for touring any of the following 'must sees' in the region:

Pulenta Estate (0261-440-0066; www.pulentaestate.com; RP86; 9am-5pm Mon-Fri, 9am-1pm Sat) A boutique winery started by the ex-owners of the Trapiche label. Tours of the beautiful modern facility focus on tasting, not production.

Andeluna Estate (02622-423226, ext 13; www.andeluna.com.ar; RP89, Km11; 10am-5pm) Tastings of the wonderful wines produced here take place in a charming old-world style tasting room. There are also great mountain views from the patio.

La Azul (02622-423593; www.bodegalaazul.com.ar; RP89 s/n; 10am-5pm Mon-Sat) A small winery producing excellent malbecs. Tours are in Spanish only, but focus mainly on tasting – you're in and out in 20 minutes.

Salentein (02622-429000; www.bodegasalentein.com; RP89 s/n; 9am-5pm Mon-Sat) A state-of-the-art, Dutch-owned winery that's distinctive for its on-site contemporary-art gallery and its method of moving grapes and juice by hand and gravity, rather than by machine.

Francois Lurton (0261-441-1100; www.francoislurton.com; RP94, Km21) An ultramodern facility run by two French brothers from a famous winemaking family, producing one of the best Mendoza torrontés on the market. Excellent tours with impressive tasting areas and barrel room.

Organized tours rarely, if ever, include the park entrance fee. Fees should be paid in Argentine pesos but can be paid in US dollars, and you must bring your original passport with you when you pay the fee. The permit start-date takes effect when you enter the park.

All permits are available only in Mendoza at the provincial tourist office.

Routes

There are three main routes up Cerro Aconcagua. The most popular one, approached by a 40km trail from Los Horcones, is the **Ruta Noroeste** (Northwest Route) from Plaza de Mulas, 4230m above sea level. The **Pared Sur** (South Face), approached from the base camp at Plaza Francia via a 36km trail from Los Horcones, is a demanding technical climb.

From Punta de Vacas, 15km southeast of Puente del Inca, the longer but more scenic **Ruta Glaciar de los Polacos** (Polish Glacier Route) first ascends the Río de las Vacas to the base camp at Plaza Argentina, a distance of 76km. Climbers on this route must carry ropes, screws and ice axes, in addition to the usual tent, warm sleeping bag and clothing, and plastic boots. This route is more expensive because it requires the use of mules for a longer period.

Mules

The cost of renting cargo mules, which can carry about 60kg each, has gone through the roof: the standard fee among outfitters is AR$920 for the first mule from Puente del Inca to Plaza de Mulas, though two mules cost only AR$1453.

For mules, contact Rudy Parra at Aconcagua Trek or Fernando Grajales. If you're going up on an organized tour, the mule situation is, of course, covered.

Tours

Many of the adventure-travel agencies in and around Mendoza arrange excursions into the high mountains. It is also possible to arrange trips with some overseas-based operators.

Several guides from the **Asociación Argentina de Guías de Montaña** (www.aagm.com.ar) lead two-week trips to Aconcagua, including **Pablo Reguera** (www.pabloreguera.com.ar) and **Mauricio Fernández** (www.summit-mza.com.ar).

All guides and organized trips are best set up online or by telephone *at least* a month in advance. Everything – guides, mules, hotels etc – must be booked far in advance during peak climbing months.

See following for a list of some of the area's most established and experienced operators.

Daniel Alessio Expediciones HIKING
(www.alessio.com.ar) Located in Mendoza; contact online.

Fernando Grajale HIKING
(www.grajales.net) Contact online.

Inka Expediciones HIKING
(☎0261-425-0871; www.inka.com.ar; Juan B Justo 345, Mendoza) Fixed and tailor-made expeditions.

Rudy Parra's Aconcagua Trek HIKING
(☎0261-15-466-5825; www.rudyparra.com; Barcala 484) Contact online

Getting There & Away

The two park entrances – Punta de Vacas and Laguna Los Horcones – are directly off RN7 and are well signed. The Los Horcones turnoff is only 4km past Puente del Inca. If you're part of an organized tour, transport will be provided. To get here by bus, take an early morning Expreso Uspallata bus from Mendoza. Buses bound for Chile will stop at Puente del Inca, but often fill up with passengers who are going all the way through.

From Los Horcones, you can either walk back along the RN7 to Puente del Inca or, otherwise, time your buses and catch a Mendoza-bound bus back down.

Las Cuevas & Cristo Redentor

☎02624 / ELEV 3200M

Pounded by chilly but exhilarating winds, the rugged high Andes make a fitting backdrop for Cristo Redentor, the famous monument erected after a territorial dispute between Argentina and Chile was settled in 1902. The view is a must-see either with a tour or by private car (a tunnel has replaced the hairpin road to the top as the border crossing into Chile), but the first autumn snowfall closes the route. You can hike the 8km up to El Cristo via trails if you don't have a car.

Parque Provincial Volcán Tupungato

Tupungato (6650m) is an impressive volcano, partly covered by snowfields and glaciers, and serious climbers consider the mountain a far more challenging, interesting and technical climb than Aconcagua. The main approach is from the town of **Tunuyán**, 82km south of Mendoza via RN40, where the **tourist office** (☎02622-422193, 488097; República de Siria & Alem; ⏰8am-8pm) can provide info. Many of the outfitters who arrange Parque Provincial Aconcagua treks can also deal with Tupungato.

San Rafael

☎0260 / POP 118,000 / ELEV 690M

A busy, modern town whose streets are lined with majestic old sycamores and open irrigation channels, San Rafael reveals its charms slowly – if you have a few days, it's worth giving it a chance. It's not exactly Mendoza, but it's getting there.

There is nothing to do in town – part of its allure, really – except wander its shady streets and plazas or while the day away in a cafe. There are, however, several esteemed wineries within biking distance that are well worth a visit.

Sights & Activities

San Rafael is flat (hence the proliferation of bike riders here), and when in Rome…get a bike. Several places around town rent out clunkers, but if you're looking for a smooth ride, try **Ciclos Adelcor** (Av H Yrigoyen & Los

San Rafael

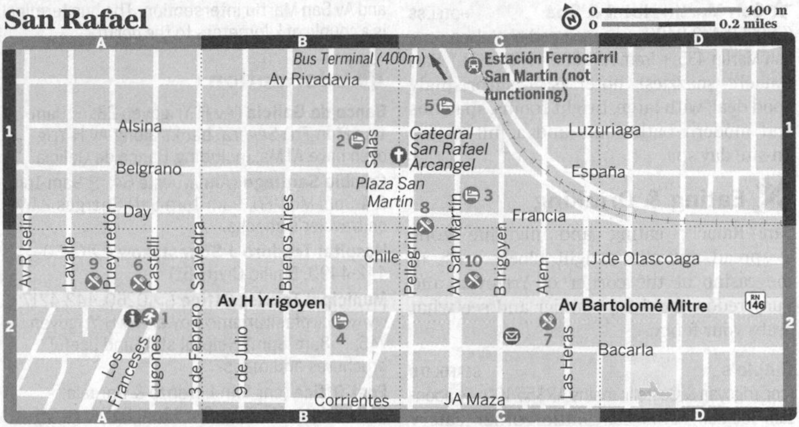

Franceses; per hour AR$10; 9am-1pm & 4-8pm Mon-Sat).

There are a few wineries within walking or cycling distance of town offering free tours and tasting. Head west on RN143, which has a welcome bike path along its side. The modern and highly regarded **Bianchi Champañera** (0260-443-5600; www.vbianchi.com; cnr RN143 & Valentín Bianchi; tours AR$15; 9am-noon & 2-5pm Mon-Sat) is the furthest west, but still only 6km away. Tours are friendly, offering visitors a glimpse into the making of sparkling wine (champagne), and English is spoken.

A couple of kilometers out of town, **Suter** (0260-442-1076; www.sutersa.com.ar; Av H Yrigoyen 2850; short tours free; 9:30am-12:30pm & 2-5pm Mon-Fri) is a rather unromantic, modern affair, but a worthwhile stop for some discounted wine. For AR$220 you can set up a half-day tour, visiting the vineyards with an agronomist, tasting specialty wines and eating a big lunch in the vineyard.

For info about these and other wineries in the area, contact the tourist office.

Sleeping

Hotel España HOTEL $
(0260-442-1192; www.hotelespanasrl.com.ar; Av San Martín 270; s/d from AR$260/320;) It may not scream 'Spain,' but the mod 1960s-ish interior is definitely unique. Rooms in the 'colonial' sector open onto a delightful pool area, making them more attractive (and a better deal) than the spacious rooms in the pricier 'celeste' sector.

San Rafael

Activities, Courses & Tours
1 Ciclos Adelcor A2

Sleeping
2 Hostel Tierrasoles B1
3 Hotel España C1
4 Hotel Jardín B2
5 San Martín Hotel & Spa C1

Eating
6 Diablo's A2
7 La Pagoda C2
8 Las Duelas C1
9 Malbec A2
10 Nina C2

Hostel Tierrasoles HOSTEL $
(0260-443-3449; www.tierrasoles.com.ar; Alsina 245; dm AR$75 d with/without bathroom AR$240/220;) Simply the best-looking hostel in town has OK-sized dorms and a couple of good sitting areas. The inviting backyard (with barbecue for guest use) rounds out the picture.

Hotel Jardín HOTEL $
(0260-443-4621; www.hoteljardinhotel.com.ar; Av H Yrigoyen 283; s/d AR$200/300;) There is indeed a garden here – or better said, a courtyard – filled with baroque touches such as fountains and sculptures of nude Greek figures. Rooms face onto it and are big and comfortable, if slightly soulless.

Camping El Parador CAMPGROUND $
(0260-442-7983; Isla Río Diamante; campsites AR$45) Located about 6km south of downtown.

★ San Martín Hotel & Spa HOTEL $$
(☎0260-442-0400; www.sanmartinhotelspa.com; San Martín 435; r from AR$600;) San Rafael's snazziest hotel is a surprisingly good deal, with large, bright rooms, spacious and modern bathrooms and a full-service on-site day spa.

Eating & Drinking

San Rafael's eating and nightlife zone is spread out along eight blocks west of the casino at the corner of Yrigoyen and Pueyrredón. Go for a wander and see what grabs your fancy.

Diablo's SEAFOOD $
(cnr Yrigoyan & Castelli; mains AR$55-100; noon-1am Tue-Sun) This cozy little corner eatery features a great range of tapas, surprisingly fresh seafood dishes, some good local wines and an impressive range of imported and microbrew beers.

Nina PIZZERIA $
(Av San Martín & Olascoaga; mains AR$50-100; 8am-1am;) The menu doesn't stretch much beyond pizzas and sandwiches, but this is a good coffee spot and becomes a happening bar with live music later.

La Pagoda BUFFET $
(Av Bartolomé Mitre 188; tenedor libre AR$65; 12-3pm & 8-11:30pm) Anybody familiar with the *tenedor libre* (all-you-can-eat) scene in Argentina won't find too many surprises here, but the food (Argentine and Chinese) is fresh enough – get there early – and there's certainly plenty of it.

Las Duelas INTERNATIONAL $$
(Paseo Pelligrini 190; mains AR$50-100; 9am-late) A fine little sidewalk cafe on a semi-pedestrian strip, specializing in good sandwiches and salads and a couple of inventive main courses.

Malbec PARRILLA $$
(cnr Av H Yrigoyen & Pueyrredón; mains AR$80-120; noon-1am) San Rafael's most frequently recommended *parrilla* holds no surprises, but has a good range of pastas and salads and, yes, some big juicy steaks.

Orientation

San Rafael is 230km southeast of the city of Mendoza via RN40 and RN43, and 189km northeast of Malargüe via RN40. Most areas of interest in town are northwest of the Av H Yrigoyen and Av San Martín intersection. The bus terminal is a couple of kilometers to the north.

Information

Banco de Galicia (Av H Yrigoyen 28; 9am-1pm Mon-Fri) Several banks along Av H Yrigoyen have ATMs, including Banco de Galicia.

Cambio Santiago (Almafuerte 64; 9am-1pm & 4-9pm Mon-Fri, 9am-1pm Sat) Charges 2.5% on traveler's checks.

Hospital Teodoro J Schestakow (☎0260-442-4490; Emilio Civit 151)

Municipal Tourist Office (☎0260-442-4217; www.sanrafaelturismo.gov.ar; Av H Yrigoyen 745; 8am-8pm) Helpful staff and useful brochures and maps.

Post Office (cnr San Lorenzo & Barcala; 8am-6pm Mon-Fri, 9am-1pm Sat)

Getting There & Around

Aerolíneas Argentinas/Austral (☎0260-443-8808; Av H Yrigoyen 395; 10am-6pm Mon-Fri, 10am-1pm Sat) flies daily except on Sunday to and from Buenos Aires.

If you're headed to Patagonia, there's one minibus per day that leaves from the bus terminal for Buta Ranquil (AR$231, eight hours) in Neuquén province via Malargüe. It leaves at 6pm daily except on Saturday and seats sell out very quickly. It's recommended that you book (and pay) a couple of days in advance to ensure a seat.

San Rafael's new **bus terminal** (☎0260-442-7720; General Paz 800) is an AR$20 taxi ride from downtown.

Renta Autos (☎0260-442-4623; www.renta-deautos.com.ar; Av H Yrigoyen 797; 9am-6pm Mon-Fri, 9am-1pm & 5-8pm Sat & Sun) Renta Autos offers the best deals on car rentals in town.

BUSES FROM SAN RAFAEL

San Rafael's bus terminal has regular daily departures to the following destinations.

DESTINATION	COST (AR$)	DURATION (HR)
Bariloche	670	16
Buenos Aires	675	14
Córdoba	406	11
Las Leñas	53	3
Malargüe	53	3
Mar del Plata	750	16
Mendoza	60	3
Neuquén	439	9
San Luis	174	4

Cañon del Atuel & Valle Grande

South of San Rafael along the Río Atuel, RP173 passes through a multicolored ravine that locals compare to Arizona's Grand Canyon, though much of the 67km Cañon del Atuel has been submerged by four hydroelectric dams. Nevertheless, there is whitewater rafting on its lower reaches, and several operators at the tourist complex of Valle Grande, midway down the canyon, do short but scenic floats down the river, and other trips.

RP173 turns to dirt road past the dam at Valle Grande, and continues through the scenic Cañon del Atuel to the podunk village of El Nihuil, 79km from San Rafael – you'll need a private vehicle or tour group if you want to see this stretch.

Activities

Sport Star OUTDOORS
(0260-15-4581068; www.sportstar.com.ar; RP173, Km35; 10am-5pm) Offers the widest range of activities, including trekking, horseback riding, kayaking, mountain-bike tours, canoes and rappelling.

Sleeping & Eating

Cabañas Río Azul CABIN $$
(0260-442-3663; www.complejorioazul.com.ar; RP173 Km33; cabin for 2/4 persons AR$400/600;) Most places to stay in the canyon cater to large groups and are rather unpleasant, but this place offers comfortable cabañas with a lovely grassy area over the river – a great spot to while away a day or two in the sun, especially in off-season.

Hotel Valle Grande HOTEL $$
(0260-15-4580660; RP173 Km35; r AR$600-900;) In the 'town' of Valle Grande, this three-star hotel offers the best accommodation around, in a lovely setting by the river, and a good restaurant, too.

Getting There & Away

Numerous San Rafael tour companies run day trips to Valle Grande, starting at AR$150. Regular buses run from San Rafael's bus terminal to Valle Grande (AR$15, one hour). Buses to El Nihuil take the alternative RP144, which doesn't go through the canyon.

Malargüe

0260 / POP 21,600 / ELEV 1400M

Despite serving as a base for Las Leñas, one of Argentina's snazzier ski resorts, Malargüe is a mellow little town and popular as a cheaper alternative to the luxury hotels on the mountain. The dry precordillera that surrounds the town is geologically distinct from the Andes proper, and two fauna reserves, Payén and Laguna Llancancelo, are close by. Caving is possible at Caverna de Las Brujas and Pozo de las Animas. The nearby Parque Provincial Payunia is a 4500-sq-km reserve with the highest concentration of volcanic cones in the world.

Due to Malargüe's remote location, it's a great spot for stargazing, and the **Planetarium** (0260-447-2116; Villegas & Aldeo; tours AR$30; 5-9pm) is an excellent, state-of-the-art complex featuring some freaky architecture and some reasonably entertaining audiovisual presentations.

Activities

Several companies offer excellent 4WD and horseback-riding excursions, and if you don't have a car, these are generally the best way to get into the surrounding mountains. Possible day trips include Caverna de Las Brujas (AR$430 per person, which includes AR$60 park entrance fee and obligatory guide), Los Molles and Las Leñas (AR$400) and the marvelous Laguna Llancancelo and Malacara volcano (AR$430 plus AR$65 entry fee). One of the most exciting drives you might ever undertake is the 12-hour 4WD tour through Parque Provincial Payunia (AR$550); be sure your tour stops at all the sites – those that combine the visit with Laguna Llancancelo only visit half the sites in Payunia.

Karen Travel (0260-447-2226; www.karentravel.com.ar; Av San Martín 54) and **Payunia Travel** (0260-447-2701; www.payuniatravel.com; Av San Martín 581) are among the well-established agencies in town offering tours.

Sleeping

Malargüe has abundant, reasonably priced accommodations. Prices quoted here are for ski season (June 15 through to September 15) and drop by up to 40% the rest of the year. Singles are nonexistent during ski season, when you'll likely be charged for however many beds are in the room.

Hostel Nord Patagonia HOSTEL $

(0260-453-7071; www.nordpatagoniahostel.com.ar; Inalican 52 Este; dm/d AR$120/320;) Malargüe's best hostel is a cozy affair, right on the plaza. Dorms are spacious and spotless with private bathrooms, the living areas are warm and homey and there's a well-stocked kitchen.

Camping Municipal Malargüe CAMPGROUND $

(0260-447-0691; Alfonso Capdevila s/n; campsites AR$50) At the northern end of town, 300m west of Av San Martín, this is the closest place to camp.

El Nevado APARTMENT $$

(0260-15-440-0712; www.aparthotelnevado.com.ar; Puebla 343; apt from AR$550;) Excellent value apartments available by the day or for longer stays. They come with fully equipped kitchens, separate sleeping areas and a cute little garden out back.

Hotel de Turismo HOTEL $$

(0260-447-1042; Av San Martín 224; s/d AR$300/500) The Turismo's a good standby – there are plenty of rooms (which are nothing special) so it rarely fills up. Downstairs, the restaurant-cafe lifts the tone with a few charming touches.

Hotel Bambi HOTEL $$

(0260-447-1237; Av San Martín 410; s/d AR$300/450) Friendly hotel with clean but faded rooms featuring renovated bathrooms. Probably the most comfortable place downtown for the price.

★ **Microtel Inn** BOUTIQUE HOTEL $$$

(0260-447-2300; www.microtelmalargue.com.ar; RN40 s/n; s/d AR$1000/1200;) At the northern edge of town, the most luxurious hotel for miles around lays it all on – buffet breakfast, art gallery, indoor pool... Rooms are spacious and modern and come complete with hydromassage tubs which are a welcome sight after a hard day's workout on the slopes.

Eating

★ **El Quincho de María** ARGENTINE $

(Av San Martín 440; mains AR$50-100; 12-11pm) The finest dining in the center is at this cozy little *parrilla* where everything from the gnocchi to the empanadas (baked savory turnovers) is handmade. Be sure not to miss the mouth-watering shish kebabs for AR$60.

Los Olivos ARGENTINE $$

(San Martín 409; mains AR$80-110; 12-11:30pm) A good range of well-prepared food here – the menu is split into 'gourmet' (offering regional faves like goat and trout) and 'classic', with inventive twists on Argentine standards.

Information

Banco de la Nación (cnr Av San Martín & Inalicán; 9am-1pm Mon-Fri) One of several banks downtown with ATMs.

Post Office (cnr Adolfo Puebla & Saturnino Torres; 8am-6pm Mon-Fri, 9am-1pm Sat)

Tourist Office (0260-447-1659; www.malargue.gov.ar; RN40, Parque del Ayer; 8am-8pm) Helpful tourist office with facilities at the northern end of town, on the highway. A small kiosk (9am-9pm) operates out of the bus terminal.

Getting There & Around

From Malargüe's **bus terminal** (cnr Av General Roca & Aldao) there are several direct buses to Mendoza daily (AR$95, five hours), plus others requiring a change in San Rafael (AR$53, three hours). Outside of winter, there's no public transport for Los Molles or Las Leñas.

Transportes Leader (447-0519; San Martín 775) operating out of the Club Los Amigos pool hall has one minibus leaving for Buta Ranquil (AR$179, five hours) in Neuquén at 9pm Sunday to Friday. Seats sell out fast – it's recommended that you book (and pay) at least two days in advance.

For winter transportation to Los Molles and Las Leñas ski resorts, contact any of the recommended travel agencies. They offer a round-trip shuttle service, including ski rentals, from AR$120 to AR$150 per person.

Around Malargüe

0260

Geologically distinct from the Andean mountains to the west, the volcanically formed landscapes surrounding Malargüe are some of the most mind-altering in Argentina and have only recently begun to receive tourist attention. Visiting the following places is impossible without your own transportation, though Malargüe's excellent travel agencies can arrange excursions to all of them.

Just over 200km south of Malargüe on the RN40, the spectacular **Parque Provincial Payunia** is a 4500-sq-km reserve with a higher concentration of volcanic cones (over 800 of them) than anywhere else in the world. The scenery is breathtaking and shouldn't be missed. The 12-hour 4WD tours or three-day horseback trips offered by most of the agencies in Malargüe are well worth taking.

Lying within its namesake fauna reserve about 60km southeast of Malargüe, **Laguna Llancancelo** is a high mountain lake visited by more than 100 species of birds, including flamingos.

Caverna de Las Brujas is a magical limestone cave on Cerro Moncol, 72km south of Malargüe and 8km north of Bardas Blancas along RN40. Its name means 'Cave of the Witches.' The cave complex stretches for 5km. Guided tours (admission and flashlights included in the price) take two to three hours. Tours depart with a minimum group size of two, although getting more people together will bring down the per-person cost. Check with tour operators in Malargüe for details.

Los Molles

Before Las Leñas took over as the prime ski resort in the area, Los Molles was the only place around where you could grab a poma (ski lift). These days it's a dusty windswept village that would be slowly sinking into obscurity if not for its reasonably priced accommodation alternatives for those wishing to be near, but not in, Las Leñas, and its favored status for rock climbers, hikers and other rugged outdoor types. The village straddles RP222, which is 55km northwest of Malargüe. Karen Travel in Malargüe offers a range of activities in the dramatic countryside that surrounds the village.

Hostel Pehuenche (☎011-15-4035-2339; www.caphostel.com; dm AR$130-205) is one of the best setup hostels in the country, offering a bar, 'digital playroom', transfers to Las Leñas and extra-snuggly duck-down duvets.

The most modern and best equipped of the hotels here, **Hotel Los Molles** (☎0261-15-691-5029; www.losmolleshotel.com.ar; RP222, Km30; s/d AR$835/1114) features big rooms with balconies facing out over the valley. A decent restaurant serves good-value set meals (AR$75).

Buses heading between Malargüe (AR$35, one hour) and Las Leñas (AR$15, 30 minutes) pass through the village.

Las Leñas

☎0260

Designed primarily to attract wealthy foreigners, **Las Leñas** (☎0260-447-1281; www.laslenas.com; ⊙mid-Jun-late-Sep) is Argentina's most self-consciously prestigious ski resort. Since its opening in 1983 it has attracted an international clientele who spend their days on the slopes and nights partying until the sun comes up. Because of the dry climate, Las Leñas has incredibly dry powder.

Its 33 runs cover 33 sq km; the area has a base altitude of 2200m, but slopes reach 3430m for a maximum drop of 1230m. Outside the ski season Las Leñas is also attempting to attract summer visitors who enjoy weeklong packages, offering activities such as mountain biking, horseback riding and hiking.

Las Leñas is 445km south of Mendoza and 70km from Malargüe, all via RN40 and RP222.

Lift Tickets & Rentals

Prices for lift tickets vary considerably throughout the ski season. Children's tickets are discounted about 30%. One-day tickets range from AR$321 in low season to AR$472 in high season (week passes are AR$1710 to AR$2517). Also available are three-day, four-day, two-week and season passes.4

Rental equipment is readily available and will set you back about AR$250 per day for skis or snowboards.

Sleeping & Eating

Las Leñas has a small village with five luxury hotels and a group of 'apart hotels', all under the same management. They are generally booked as part of a weeklong package, which includes lodging, unlimited skiing and two meals per day. Despite the country's economic troubles, rates for foreigners staying in Las Leñas have changed little. All bookings are done either online at www.laslenas.com or centrally through **Ski Leñas** (☎011-4819-6060, in Buenos Aires 011-4819-6000; ventas@laslenas.com; Cerrito 1186, 8th fl).

Apart Hotel Gemenis (weekly per person from US$1484) and **Apart Hotel Delphos** (weekly per person from US$1520) offer similar packages without meals but do have well-equipped kitchenettes.

There are also small apartments with two to six beds and shared bathrooms, equipped for travelers to cook for themselves. Budget travelers can stay more economically at Los Molles, 20km down the road, or at Malargüe, 70km away.

Restaurants in the village run the gamut, from cafes, sandwich shops and pizzerias to upscale hotel dining rooms. The finest restaurant of all is Las Cuatro Estaciones, in Hotel Piscis.

Hotel Acuario HOTEL $$$

(s/d weekly from US$4126/5160;) The most humble of the hotels here is still very comfortable, and, with 'only' 40 rooms, cozier than other options.

Hotel Escorpio HOTEL $$$

(s/d weekly from US$3265/4080;) This 47-room hotel is nominally three stars, but still top-notch, with an excellent restaurant. Guests can use facilities at the Hotel Piscis.

Hotel Aries HOTEL $$$

(r weekly from US$5160;) Aries is a four-star hotel with a sauna, gym facilities, a restaurant and luxuriously comfortable rooms.

Virgo Hotel & Spa HOTEL $$$

(s/d weekly from US$4126/5160;) The newest hotel in the village, this one goes all out, with a heated outdoor swimming pool, sushi bar, whirlpool bath and cinema.

Hotel Piscis HOTEL $$$

(s/d weekly from US$6037/6740;) The most extravagant of Las Leñas' lodgings is the five-star, 99-room Hotel Piscis. This prestigious hotel has wood-burning stoves, a gymnasium, sauna, an indoor swimming pool, the elegant Las Cuatro Estaciones restaurant, a bar, a casino and shops. Rates depend on time of the season, and are based on double occupancy.

Getting There & Away

There is a bus service operating in season from Mendoza (AR$130, 6½ hours), San Rafael (AR$60, three hours) and Malargüe (AR$35, 1½ hours).

South along the Ruta Nacional 40

From Malargüe the RN40 winds its way through rugged desert landscapes and into Neuquén province. Despite what many will tell you, there *is* public transportation along this route. Transportes Leader runs minibuses between San Rafael and Buta Ranquil Sunday to Friday, stopping in Malargüe. From Buta Ranquil there are connections to Neuquén and Chos Malal, but you may get stuck for the night. There's no real reason to be here, but there are a couple of cheap hotels, one nice accommodations option, and enough restaurants and cafes to keep you from starving.

San Juan

0264 / POP 109,100 / ELEV 650M

Living in the shadow of a world-class destination like Mendoza can't be easy and, to its credit, San Juan doesn't even try to compete. Life in this provincial capital moves at its own pace, and the locals are both proud of and humble about their little town.

No slouch on the wine production front, San Juan's wineries are refreshingly low-key after the Mendoza bustle, and the province's other attractions are all within easy reach of the capital. Most come here en route to Parque Provincial Ischigualasto.

In 1944 a massive earthquake destroyed the city center, and Juan Perón's subsequent relief efforts are what first made him a national figure. The city goes dead in summer, especially on Sunday, when all of San Juan heads to the nearby shores of Dique Ullum for relief from the sun.

Sights

If you need a little perspective on things, make your way up the **Lookout Tower** (cnr Mendoza & Rivadavia; admission AR$10; 9am-1pm & 5-9pm) for a sweeping view out over the town and surrounding countryside.

Museum hours change often, so check with the tourist office for updated information.

Casa Natal de Sarmiento MUSEUM

(Sarmiento 21 Sur; admission AR$15; 9am-7pm Mon-Fri, 9am-2pm Sat, 11am-6pm Sun) Casa Natal de Sarmiento is named for Domingo Faustino Sarmiento, whose prolific writing as a politician, diplomat, educator and journalist made him a public figure within and beyond Argentina. Sarmiento's *Recuerdos de Provincia* recounted his childhood in this house and his memories of his mother. It's now a museum.

Museo de Vino Santiago Graffigna MUSEUM

(0264-421-4227; www.graffignawines.com; Colón 1342 Norte; 10am-7pm Mon-Sat, 10-4pm Sun) FREE Museo de Vino Santiago Graffigna is a wine museum well worth a visit. It also has a wine bar where you can taste many of San Juan's best wines. Take bus 12A from in front of the tourist office on Sarmiento (AR$3, 15 minutes) and ask the driver to tell you when to get off.

Tours

Tour operators in San Juan provide lots of options for taking in the sights.

Mario Agüero Turismo TOUR
(0264-422-0840; General Acha 17 Norte; 9am-1pm & 4-8pm Mon-Fri, 9am-1pm Sat) Offers organized tours including Parque Provincial Ischigualasto.

Triasico Turismo TOUR
(0264-422-8566; www.triasico.com.ar; Sarmiento 42 Sur; 9am-1pm & 4-8pm Mon-Sat) Specializes in Ischigualasto tours (AR$640, minimum two people) – come here if you're struggling to get a group together.

Sleeping

Zonda Hostel HOSTEL $
(0264-420-1009; www.zondahostel.com.ar; Caseros 486 Este; dm AR$80, s/d AR$150/200, s/d without bathroom AR$180/230;) A charming little hostel with some cozy hangout areas and stylish touches such as big bathrooms and parquetry floors. The location's handy, too – midway between the bus terminal and downtown.

Hotel Alhambra HOTEL $
(0264-421-4780; www.alhambrahotel.com.ar; Gral Acha 180 Sur; s/d AR$260/350;) Smallish, carpeted rooms with splashes of dark wood paneling, giving them a classy edge. Little touches such as leather chairs and gold ashtray stands in the hallways give it a kitschy appeal and the central location seals the deal.

Hotel del Bono Suite HOTEL $$
(0264-421-7600; www.hoteldelbono.com.ar; Mitre 75 Oeste; d/ste AR$622/966;) With some slick design features taking the edge off the corporate blandness, this is a good deal for the price, and the well-stocked kitchenettes and rooftop pool are added bonuses.

Albertina Hotel HOTEL $$
(0264-421-4222; www.hotelalbertina.com; Mitre 31 Este; r from AR$455; @) A slick, business-class hotel on the plaza. The rooms are a bit of a letdown, but bathrooms are big.

JUST A LOAD OF HOT AIR

While traveling through San Juan, especially in autumn and winter, you may become acquainted – through hearsay if not through experience – with one of the region's meteorological marvels: *el zonda*. Much like the chinook of the Rockies or the foehn of the European Alps, the *zonda* is a dry, warm wind that can raise a cold day's temperature from freezing to nearly 20°C (68°F). The *zonda* originates with storms in the Pacific that blow eastward, hit the Andes, dump their moisture and come whipping down the eastern slopes, picking up heat as they go. The wind, which varies from mild to howling, can last several days; *sanjuaninos* (people from San Juan) can step outside and tell you when it will end – and that it will be cold when it does. It's a regular occurrence, giving the region – and the *sanjuaninos* – severe seasonal varience, especially during winter.

Plaza Hotel HOTEL $$
(0264-422-5179; plazahotelsanjuan@hotmail.com; Sarmiento 344 Sur; s/d AR$270/420;) There's no plaza in sight, but the large, unrenovated rooms here represent fair value. Check out a few for better ventilation and light.

Eating

Most restaurants are right downtown, and many of the city's hippest eateries are around the intersection of Rivadavia and Entre Ríos.

Baró INTERNATIONAL $
(Rivadavia 55 Oeste; mains AR$50-90; 8am-11:30pm) This popular main-street cafe-restaurant has the best variety of pasta dishes in town and a relaxed atmosphere that make it a good stop for coffee or drinks at any time.

Soychú VEGETARIAN $
(Av José Ignacio de la Roza 223 Oeste; buffet AR$45; noon-9pm Mon-Sat, 11am-3pm Sun;) Excellent vegetarian buffet attached to a health-food store selling all sorts of groceries and a range of teas. Arrive early for the best selection.

★de Sánchez FUSION $$
(Rivadavia 61 Oeste; mains AR$90-120; ⏲noon-3pm & 8pm-midnight Tue-Sun) San Juan's snootiest downtown restaurant is actually pretty good. It has a creative menu with a smattering of seafood dishes, an adequate wine list (featuring all the San Juan heavy hitters) and a hushed, tranquil atmosphere.

Remolacha PARRILLA $$
(cnr Av José Ignacio de la Roza & Sarmiento; mains AR$70-120; ⏲12-3pm & 8pm-1am) One of the biggest *parrillas* in town, the dining room is a bit ordinary, but eating in the garden is a lush experience. Get a table by the picture windows looking into the kitchen and you'll be able to see your meal being hacked off the carcass before getting thrown on the flames. Excellent salads, too.

Shopping

Mercado Artesanal Tradicional MARKET
(Traditional Artisans Market; Centro de Difusión Cultural Eva Perón; ⏲10am-7pm Mon-Sat) The Mercado Artesanal Tradicional is an excellent local handicrafts market with an assortment of items for sale including ponchos and the brightly colored *mantas* (shawls) of Jáchal.

Orientation

San Juan is 170km north of Mendoza via RN40 and 1140km from Buenos Aires. Like most Argentine cities, San Juan's grid pattern makes orientation very easy; the addition of cardinal points – norte (north), sur (south), este (east) and oeste (west) – to street addresses helps even more. East–west Av San Martín and north–south Calle Mendoza divide the city into these quadrants. The functional center of town is south of Av San Martín, often referred to as Av Libertador.

Information

ACA (Automóvil Club Argentina; ☎0264-422-3781; 9 de Julio 802) Argentina's auto club; good source for provincial road maps.

Banco de San Juan (cnr Rivadavia & Entre Ríos; ⏲9am-1pm Mon-Fri) Has an ATM.

Cambio Santiago (General Acha 52 Sur; ⏲8am-6pm Mon-Fri, 9am-1pm Sat & Sun) Money exchange.

Hospital Rawson (☎0264-422-2272; cnr General Paz & Estados Unidos)

Post Office (Av José Ignacio de la Roza 259 Este; ⏲8am-6pm Mon-Fri, 9am-1pm Sat)

Tourist Office (☎0264-422-2431; www.turismo.sanjuan.gov.ar; Sarmiento 24 Sur; ⏲8am-7pm) Has a good map of the city and its surroundings plus useful information on the rest of the province, particularly Parque Provincial Ischigualasto.

Getting There & Away

AIR

Aerolíneas Argentinas/Austral (☎0264-421-4158; Av San Martín 215 Oeste; ⏲10am-6pm Mon-Fri, 10am-1pm Sat) Aerolíneas Argentinas/Austral flies twice daily to Buenos Aires except Sunday (once only).

BUS

From San Juan's **bus terminal** (☎0264-422-1604; Estados Unidos 492 Sur) you can book tickets to Santiago, Viña del Mar and Valparaíso in Chile but you'll have to change buses in Mendoza.

Except in summer, when there may be direct buses, service to Patagonian destinations south of Neuquén requires a change of bus in Mendoza, though through-tickets can be purchased in San Juan.

Buses from San Juan

Various companies serve the following destinations daily.

DESTINATION	COST (AR$)	DURATION (HR)
Barreal	80	4
Buenos Aires	850	14
Calingasta	70	3½
Catamarca	460	8
Córdoba	365	11
Huaco	65	3
Jujuy	776	20
La Rioja	345	7
Mendoza	105	3
Neuquén	685	15½
Rodeo	55	3½
Rosario	620	14
Salta	752	17
San Agustín de Valle Fértil	95	4½
San José de Jáchal	55	3
San Luis	248	5
Tucumán	635	13

Getting Around

Las Chacritas Airport (☎0264-425-4133) is located 13km southeast of town on RN20. A *remise* (taxi) costs AR$60.

OFF THE BEATEN TRACK

RUTA DEL VINO DE SAN JUAN

San Juan's winery tourism industry isn't quite as developed as that of Mendoza, but in a lot of ways that's a good thing. There are no crowds for a start, and tours are occasionally conducted by the winemakers themselves. A few wineries have got together to promote the Ruta del Vino de San Juan (the San Juan Wine Route). The best way to do it, if you want to hit them all in one day, is to hire a car. Starting from downtown San Juan, it's about a 40km return stopping at all the places listed here. It is feasible to do it by public transport and taxi, too. None of the wineries listed below require reservations.

The first stop on the route should be **Las Marianas** (☎0264-423-1191; www.bodegalasmarianas.com.ar; Calle Nuevo s/n; ⏲9am-8pm Mon-Sat) FREE. One of the prettiest wineries in the region, this one was built in 1922, abandoned in 1950 and reinstated in 1999. The main building is gorgeous, with thick adobe walls and a few examples of the original winemaking equipment lying around. The mountain views out over the vineyard are superb. If you're coming by bus, catch the 16 (AR$4.10, 40 minutes) near the corner of Santa Fe and Mendoza in San Juan. Get off at the corner of Calle Aberastain and Calle Nuevo, where you'll see a signpost to the winery (an 800m walk).

Making your way back to Calle Aberastain, turn right and follow the road south for 500m to **Viñas de Segisa** (☎0264-492-2000; www.saxsegisa.com.ar; Aberastain & Calle 15; ⏲9am-7pm Mon-Sat) FREE. This stately old winery has more of a museum feel than others. The tour of the underground cellar complex is excellent and tastings are generous.

If you're not up for a walk, now's the time to call a *remise* (taxi). If you are, make your way back north to Calle 14, turn right and continue for 5km until you hit RN40. Turning left, after about 1km you'll come to **Fabril Alto Verde** (☎0264-421-2683; www.fabrilaltoverde.com.ar; RN40, btwn Calle 13 & 14; ⏲9am-1pm & 2:30-6:30pm Mon-Fri) FREE, a big, state-of-the-art winery that sells 90% of its wine for export; tours here are in English or Spanish and come accompanied by a rather dreary promotional video. The award-winning organic brands Buenas Hondas and Touchstone are produced here.

Next, catch a 24 bus heading north on RN40 up to Calle 11. Turning right down Calle 11 for 300m brings you to **Miguel Mas** (☎0264-422-5807; miguelmas@infovia.com.ar; Calle 11 s/n; ⏲9am-5pm Mon-Fri) FREE This small winery makes some of the country's only organic sparkling wine (champagne) and other wine. The whole process – apart from inserting the cork in bottles – is done by hand. Tours (in Spanish only) take you through every step of the process.

Making your way back out to RN40, flag down a 24 bus, which will take you back to the bus terminal in San Juan.

If there's two or more of you, hiring a car to get to Ischigualasto can work out a better deal than taking a tour. One caveat being that many rental outfits try to steer you away from one-day rentals. The tourist office keeps a list of rental operators, including **Classic** (☎0264-422-4622; Av San Martín 163 Oeste; ⏲9am-7pm), across from the tourist office and **Trebol** (☎0264-422-5935; Laprida 82 Este; ⏲9am-8pm), inside the Alkazar Hotel.

Around San Juan

Only 18km west of San Juan, the 32 km sq **Dique Ullum** is a center for nautical sports: swimming, fishing, kayaking, waterskiing and windsurfing (though no rental equipment is available). Balnearios (beach clubs) line its shores, and hanging out for a day in the sun is part of being in San Juan. At night, many of the balnearios function as dance clubs. Bus 23 from Av Salta or Bus 29 from the San Juan bus terminal via Av Córdoba both go hourly to the dam outlet.

Valle de Calingasta

The Calingasta Valley is a vast smear of scenic butter cradled between the Andes and the rumpled, multicolored precordillera, and is one of the most beautiful regions in both San Juan and Mendoza provinces.

With the completion of two new reservoirs, the spectacular cliffside RP12 is

DIFUNTA CORREA

Legend has it that during the civil wars of the 1840s Deolinda Correa followed the movements of her sickly conscript husband's battalion on foot through the deserts of San Juan, carrying food, water and their baby son in her arms. When her meager supplies ran out, thirst, hunger and exhaustion killed her. But when passing muleteers found them, the infant was still nursing at the dead woman's breast. Commemorating this apparent miracle, her shrine at Vallecito is widely believed to be the site of her death.

Difunta literally means 'defunct,' and Correa is her surname. Technically she is not a saint but rather a 'soul,' a dead person who performs miracles and intercedes for people; the child's survival was the first of a series of miracles attributed to her. Since the 1940s her shrine, originally a simple hilltop cross, has grown into a small village with its own gas station, school, post office, police station and church. Devotees leave gifts at 17 chapels or exhibit rooms in exchange for supernatural favors. In addition, there are two hotels, several restaurants, a commercial gallery with souvenir shops, and offices for the nonprofit organization that administers the site.

Interestingly, truckers are especially devoted. From La Quiaca, on the Bolivian border, to Ushuaia in Tierra del Fuego, you will see roadside shrines with images of the Difunta Correa and the unmistakable bottles of water left to quench her thirst. At some sites there appear to be enough parts lying around to build a car from scratch!

Despite lack of government support and the Catholic Church's open antagonism, the shrine of Difunta Correa has grown as belief in her miraculous powers has become more widespread. People visit the shrine all year round, but at Easter, May 1 and Christmas, up to 200,000 pilgrims descend on Vallecito. Weekends are busier and more interesting than weekdays.

There are regular departures to Vallecito from San Juan and Mendoza.

now closed. Most maps will show the old road, but drivers have to take RP5 north to Talacasto, then the RP149, which snakes around west and then south to Calingasta.

Calingasta

02648 / POP 2200 / ELEV 1430M

Calingasta is a small agricultural town shaded by álamos (poplars) on the shores of Río de los Patos. There's little to do, though a visit to the 17th-century adobe chapel **Capilla de Nuestra Señora del Carmen** makes a nice stop on the way to Barreal. Looming on the horizon 7km out of town is **Cerro El Calvario**, the site of an indigenous cemetery where several mummies have been found. One example can be seen in Calingasta's small **archaeological museum** (admission AR$10; 10am-1pm & 4-8pm Tue-Sat), just off the main plaza.

The folks at Calingasta's **tourist information office** (02648-441066; www.calingastaturismo.gov.ar; RP12; 8am-8pm), at the entrance to town from San Juan, are helpful for sights and lodging in the area.

If you wish to spend the night, lay your head at the modest **Hospedaje Nora** (02648-421027; cnr Cantoni & Sarmiento; r per person AR$150), featuring simple but spacious rooms in a family house. Those in the building out the back are a better deal. There's a **municipal campground** (campsites AR$35) down by the river. The meals at **La Morocha** (mains from AR$40; 12-3pm & 6-11pm) will stave off your hunger – on offer are tasty empanadas and good-value set meals.

Two buses a day roll through town, heading for San Juan (AR$70, 3½ hours) and Barreal (AR$12, 30 minutes).

Barreal

02648 / POP 3460 / ELEV 1650M

Barreal's divine location makes it one of the most beautifully situated towns you'll likely ever come across. Sauces (weeping willows), álamos and eucalyptus trees drape lazily over the dirt roads that meander through town, and views of the Cordillera de Ansilta – a stretch of the Andes with seven majestic peaks ranging from 5130m to 5885m – are simply astonishing. Wandering along Barreal's back roads is an exercise in dreamy laziness.

Presidente Roca is the main drag through town, a continuation of RP149 that leads from Calingasta to Barreal and on to Parque

Nacional El Leoncito. Only a few streets have names; businesses listed without them simply require asking directions.

Sights & Activities

Wander down to the **Río de los Patos** and take in the sweeping views of the valley and the **Cordillera de Ansilta**, whose highest peak, **Ansilta**, tops out at 5885m. To the south, **Aconcagua** and **Tupungato** are both visible, as is the peak of **Cerro Mercedario** (6770m).

At the south end of Presidente Roca is a sort of triangular roundabout. Follow the road east (away from the Andes) until it leads into the hills; you'll see a small shrine and you can **hike** into the foothills for more stunning views. Follow this road for 3km and you'll come to a mining site (the gate should be open). Enter and continue for 1km to reach a **petrified forest**.

White-water rafting is excellent – more for the scenery than for the rapids themselves – and most trips start 50km upriver at **Las Hornillas**. Contact **Barreal Rafting** (0264-15-530-7764), the best-established rafting operator in town.

Las Hornillas (site of two *refugios* – rustic shelters – and a military outpost) also provides **climbing** access to the Cordón de la Rameda, which boasts five peaks over 6000m, including Cerro Mercedario. Climbing here is more technical than Aconcagua and many mountaineers prefer the area. Ramon Ossa, a Barreal native, is a highly recommended mountain guide and excursion operator who knows the cordillera intimately; contact him at **Cabañas Doña Pipa** (02648-441004; www.fortunaviajes.com.ar). He can arrange trips to Cerro Mercedario and expeditions across the Andes in the footsteps of San Martín, including mules and equipment.

Barreal is best known for **carrovelismo** (land sailing), an exhilarating sport practiced on a small cart with a sail attached. Fanatics come from miles away to whizz around out on the gusty, cracked lake bed at Pampa El Leoncito, about 20km from town and adjacent to the national park. **Rogelio Toro** (0264-15-671-7196; dontoro.barreal@gmail.com) hires the necessary equipment and also gives classes.

For access to the *refugio* at Las Hornillas, climbing information, guide services and **mountain bike** rental, visit Maxi at **Cabañas Kummel** (02648-441206; Presidente Roca s/n).

Sleeping & Eating

Posada Don Lisandro HOSTEL $
(0264-15-505-9122; www.donlisandro.com.ar; Av San Martín s/n; dm AR$70, d with/without bathroom AR$220/180) This newish *posada* (inn) is actually a 100-year-old house. The original cane-and-mud ceilings remain, as do a few sticks of room furniture. There's a kitchen for guest use and lovely, shady grounds to lounge around in.

★ **El Alemán** HOTEL $$
(0264-15-4119913; www.elalemanbarreal.com; r for 2/4 people AR$400/480) Down by the river, with sweeping views of the Andes, this German/Argentine-owned complex has some of the best-looking rooms in town. Rooms are cute and cozy and the lack of TVs adds to the overall tranquility of the place. There's an excellent restaurant on the premises, serving hearty dishes and superb breakfasts made from the freshest ingredients.

Call ahead to get picked up from the town center.

Restaurante Isidro ARGENTINE $$
(Presidente Roca s/n; mains AR$45-60; 8am-3pm & 8-11:30pm) This restaurant offers a fairly standard range of meats and pastas and some delicious meat empanadas. Also a good selection of wines from the San Juan region.

Information

Banco de la Nación (Presidente Roca s/n; 9am-1pm Mon-Fri) Has an ATM.

Tourist Office (02648-441066; turismo@calingasta.gov.ar; Presidente Roca s/n; 8am-8pm) Located beside the main plaza; offers a list of excursion operators and accommodations.

Getting There & Away

Barreal's right at the end of the line, but there are two departures per day for San Juan (AR$80, four hours), which pass through Calingasta (AR$12, 30 minutes).

There's been talk for some time of a bus service that will connect Barreal with Uspallata in Mendoza province – it may well be operating by the time you read this.

Parque Nacional El Leoncito

The 76-sq-km Parque Nacional El Leoncito occupies a former *estancia* (ranch) 22km south of Barreal. The landscape is typical of the Andean precordillera, though it's drier than the valley north of Barreal. Lately, its primary attraction is the Pampa de Leoncito, where a dry lake bed makes for superb land sailing. The high, dry and wide-open valley rarely sees a cloud, also making for superb stargazing. Hence, the park is home to the **Complejo Astronomico el Leoncito** (www.casleo.gov.ar), which contains two important observatories, the Observatorio El Leoncito and Observatorio Cesco. Night visits are also possible, but must be scheduled ahead of time by contacting the Complejo's **San Juan office** (☎0264-421-3653; Av. España 1512 sur, San Juan; ⏰9am-1pm & 3-6pm Mon-Fri).

Camping is not permitted here, but in the northwest corner of the park, Cascada El Rincon is a lovely, small waterfall set in a shallow canyon. If you're looking for somewhere to picnic and splash around on a hot day, this is your spot.

There is no public transport to the park, and with 17km of entrance road added to the 22km to get here from Barreal, it's certainly too far to walk and probably too far to ride. If you don't have your own transportation, contact Ramon Ossa at Cabañas Doña Pipa in Barreal – his informative tours of the park have been heartily recommended.

San José de Jáchal

☎02647 / POP 10,900 / ELEV 1170M

Founded in 1751 and surrounded by vineyards and olive groves, Jáchal is a charming village with a mix of older adobes and contemporary brick houses. *Jachalleros* (the local residents) are renowned for their fidelity to indigenous and gaucho craft traditions; in fact, Jáchal's reputation as the Cuna de la Tradición (Cradle of Tradition) is celebrated during November's **Fiesta de la Tradición**. Except during festival season, finding these crafts is easier in San Juan.

Across from the main plaza the **Iglesia San José**, a national monument, houses the **Cristo Negro** (Black Christ), or Señor de la Agonía (Lord of Agony), a grisly leather image with articulated head and limbs, brought from Potosí in colonial times.

Jáchal's accommodation scene isn't what you'd call thriving, but the **Hotel San Martín** (☎02647-420431; www.jachalhotelsanmartin.com; Echegaray 387; s/d AR$195/275; ❄@), a few blocks from the plaza, does the job. It's not quite as contemporary as it looks from the outside, but rooms are big and comfortable and the bathrooms are modern.

La Taberna de Juan (San Martín s/n; mains AR$70-100; ⏰noon-11pm) is a bright and cheery *parrilla* facing the plaza. Meat is the go here, but there's a range of pasta dishes and salads, too. Set lunches are particularly good value.

There are several daily buses to San Juan (AR$55, three hours) from Jáchal's **bus terminal** (cnr San Juan & Obispo Zapata).

Rodeo

☎02647 / POP 2600 / ELEV 2010M

Rodeo is a small, ramshackle town with picturesque adobe houses typical of the region, 42km west of San José de Jáchal.

Rodeo has recently become famous – world famous – for **windsurfing** and **kitesurfing**. The town is only 3km away from one of the best windsurfing sites on the planet: **Dique Cuesta del Viento**, a reservoir where, between mid-October and early May, wind speeds reach 120km/h nearly every afternoon, drawing surfers from around the globe. Even if you don't take to the wind, it's worth spending a day or two wandering around Rodeo and hanging out on the beach absorbing the spectacular views and watching the insanity of airborne windsurfers.

Inside the town hall, the **tourist office** (municipalidad_iglesia@yahoo.com.ar; ⏰8am-8pm) provides a list of places to stay and information on local attractions.

From San Juan's bus terminal, there are several departures daily for Rodeo (AR$30, 5½ hours).

Sleeping & Eating

Rancho Lamaral HOSTEL $
(☎0264-15-660-1197; www.rancholamaral.com; dm/d AR$100/280) On Playa Lamaral, on the shore of the reservoir, HI-affiliate Rancho Lamaral offers simple rooms in a refurbished adobe house. It also offers windsurfing classes and kitesurfing courses, and rents all equipment.

50 Nudos HOTEL $$
(☎011-15-5759-0525; www.50nudos.com; Puque s/n; s/d AR$238/420) 50 Nudos offers charming, rustic rooms. Follow the signs from the

OFF THE BEATEN TRACK

HUACO

Continuing north from San José de Jáchal on RN40, visitors pass through a beautiful landscape that is rich with folkloric traditions and rarely seen by foreigners. East of Jáchal RN40 climbs the precipitous Cuesta de Huaco, with a view of Los Cauquenes dam, before arriving at Huaco, a sleepy village 36km from Jáchal whose 200-year-old Viejo Molino (Old Mill) justifies the trip. Some visitors get captivated by Huaco's eerie landscape and middle-of-nowhere atmosphere. If you're one of them, you can stay at **Hostería Huaco** (☎0264-460-0779; www.hosteriahuaco.com.ar; Calle La Paz s/n; s/d AR$225/275; 📶🏊), a beautifully set up little hotel with great mountain views from the backyard pool.

One bus daily from Huaco heads to San Juan (AR$65, four hours), passing though Jáchal (AR$23, one hour) on the way.

Backtracking to RN510 and heading westward, you pass through the town of Rodeo and into the department of Iglesia, home of the precordillera thermal baths of Pismanta. RN510 continues west to Chile via the lung-busting 4765m Paso del Agua Negra (open summer only). South of Pismanta, RP436 returns to RN40 and San Juan.

main street to these. Optional are larger rooms with sitting area and breakfast served in your room.

La Surfera INTERNATIONAL $
(Santo Domingo s/n; mains AR$50-90; ⏰noon-1am; 🍃) La Surfera is on the main street in the center of town. This laid-back restaurant/cafe/reggae bar is HQ for Rodeo's surprisingly large hippy community. Vegetarian meals are predictably good; meat dishes could be better.

San Agustín de Valle Fértil

☎02646 / POP 4400

Reached via comically undulating highways that cut through the desert landscape, San Agustín de Valle Fértil makes an excellent base for trips to the nearby Parque Provincial Ischigualasto. It's a measure of just how dry the countryside is that this semiarid valley gets called 'fertile.'

Apart from visiting the park, there's not much to do around these parts, but the ponderous pace of life here, where people sit on the sidewalks on summer evenings greeting passersby, has mesmerized more than one visitor.

Sleeping & Eating

Eco Hostel HOSTEL $
(☎02646-420147; www.ecohostel.com.ar; Mendoza 42; dm/d AR$80/190; 📶🏊) One of the better hostels in town, with a great location half a block from the plaza and a tiny above-ground pool. Can arrange good-value tours to local sights, including Parque Provincial Ischigualasto.

Cabañas de Valle Pintada CABIN $$
(☎0264-434-5737; www.vallepintado.com.ar; cnr Tucumán & Mitre; r/cabin AR$300/500; 📶🏊) Some of the best value rooms and cabins in town, a block from the plaza. Rooms are spacious and spotless with a little kitchenette, and cabins sleep four comfortably. The lovely garden and good-sized pool are the cream on the pudding.

La Gran Picada INTERNATIONAL $
(Rivadavia s/n; mains AR$50-120; ⏰8am-1am) A cozy little bar-restaurant serving very tasty pizzas and *picadas* (shared appetizer plates) made from fresh regionally sourced ingredients. Wash it all down with a fantastic selection of imported beers.

Orientation

San Agustín lies among the Sierra Pampeanas, gentle sedimentary mountains cut by impressive canyons, 247km northeast of San Juan via RN141 and RP510, which continues to Ischigualasto and La Rioja. San Agustín is small enough that locals pay little attention to street names, so you may need to ask for directions.

Information

Municipal Tourist Office (Gral Acha; ⏰7am-1pm & 5-10pm Mon-Fri, 8am-1pm Sat) Across from the plaza. Can help arrange car or mule excursions into the mountain canyons and backcountry.

Post Office (cnr Laprida & Mendoza; ⏰8am-6pm Mon-Fri, 9am-1pm Sat)

Turismo Vesa (☎02646-420143; www.turismovesa.com; Mitre s/n) For tours to Parque Provincial Ischigualasto, Talampaya, El Chiflón and horseback riding.

Getting There & Away

From San Agustín's **bus terminal** (Mitre, btwn Entre Ríos & Mendoza) daily buses head to San Juan (AR$95, 4½ hours).

Parque Provincial Ischigualasto

Also known fittingly as **Valle de la Luna** (Valley of the Moon; admission AR$70; 8am-6pm), this park takes its name from the Diaguita word for 'land without life'. Visits here are a spectacular step – or drive, as the case may be – into a world of surreal rock formations, dinosaur remains and glowing red sunsets. The park is in some ways comparable to North American national parks such as Bryce Canyon or Zion, except that here, time and water have exposed a wealth of fossils (some 180 million years old, from the Triassic period).

The park's **museum** displays a variety of fossils, including the carnivorous dinosaur Herrerasaurus (not unlike Tyrannosaurus rex), the Eoraptor lunensis (the oldest-known predatory dinosaur) and good dioramas of the park's paleoenvironments.

The 630-sq-km park is a desert valley between two sedimentary mountain ranges, the Cerros Colorados in the east and Cerro Los Rastros in the west. Over millennia, at every meander in the canyon, the waters of the nearly dry Río Ischigualasto have carved distinctive shapes in the malleable red sandstone, monochrome clay and volcanic ash. Predictably, some of these forms have acquired popular names, including **Cancha de Bochas** (the ball court), **El Submarino** (the submarine) and **El Gusano** (the worm), among others. The desert flora of algarrobo trees, shrubs and cacti complement the eerie landforms.

From the visitor center, isolated 1748m **Cerro Morado** is a three- to four-hour walk, gaining nearly 800m in elevation and yielding outstanding views of the surrounding area. Take plenty of drinking water and high-energy snacks.

Tours

All visitors to the park must go accompanied by a ranger. The most popular tours run for three hours and leave on the hour (more or less), with cars forming a convoy and stopping at noteworthy points along the way, where the ranger explains (in Spanish only) exactly what it is you're looking at.

If you have no private vehicle, an organized tour is the only feasible way to visit the park. These are easily organized in San Agustín. Otherwise ask the tourist office there about hiring a car and driver. Tour rates (not including entry fees) are about AR$650 per person from San Juan (through any travel agency in town), or about AR$200 per person from San Agustín. Tours from San Juan generally depart at 5am and return well after dark.

A variety of other tours (around AR$50 per person) are available from the visitor center here. Options include spectacular full-moon tours (2½ hours) in the five days around the full moon, treks to the summit of Cerro Morado (three to four hours), and a 12km circuit of the park on mountain bikes.

Sleeping & Eating

There is camping at the **visitor center** (per person AR$30), which has a *confitería* (cafe) serving simple meals (breakfast and lunch) and cold drinks; dried fruits and bottled olives from the province are available. There are toilets and showers, but because water is trucked in, don't count on it. There's no shade.

Getting There & Away

Ischigualasto is about 80km north of San Agustín via RP510 and a paved lateral road to the northwest. Given its size and isolation, the only practical way to visit the park is by private vehicle or organized tour. Note that the park roads are unpaved and some can be impassable after rain, necessitating an abbreviated trip.

Bariloche & the Lake District

Includes ➡

Best Places to Eat

- Tres Catorce (p395)
- Corazón Contento (p377)
- Ñancú Lahuén (p374)
- Tinto Bistro (p374)
- La Trattoria de la Famiglia Bianchi (p360)

Best Places to Stay

- La Casona de Odile (p367)
- La Escondida (p385)
- Hostería Chimehuín (p383)
- Hostel Bajo Cero (p371)
- Hostería La Masía (p377)

Why Go?

Home to some of the country's most spectacular scenery, the Lake District is one of Argentina's prime tourist destinations. People come to ski, fish, climb, trek and generally bask in the cool, fresh landscapes created by the huge forests and glacier-fed lakes.

The paleontological sites and outstanding wineries just out of the city of Neuquén are well worth stopping off for en route; and way, way south is the resort town of Bariloche, with its picture-postcard location on the banks of the Lago Nahuel Huapi.

Getting away from the crowds is easily done. The lakeside villages of Villa Traful and San Martín de los Andes fill up for a short time in summer and are blissfully quiet the rest of the year. To the north, Chos Malal makes an excellent base for exploring nearby volcanoes, lagoons and hot springs.

When to Go

Bariloche

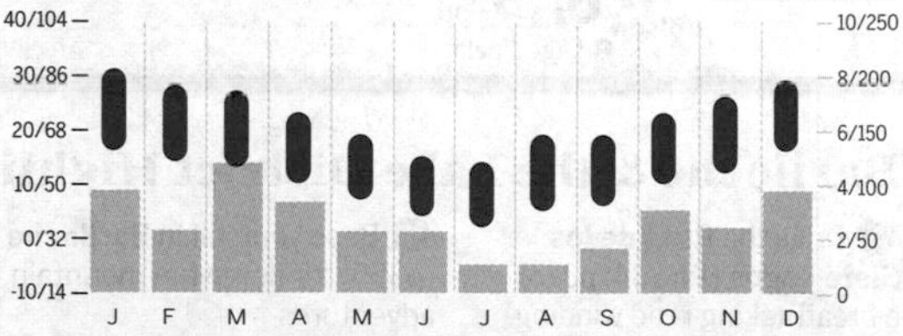

Mar–May Warm days and cool nights make this a great time to visit.

Jun–Sep Snow season means spectacular mountain vistas.

Oct–Dec Moderate temperatures and blooming wildflowers, so put your trekking boots on.

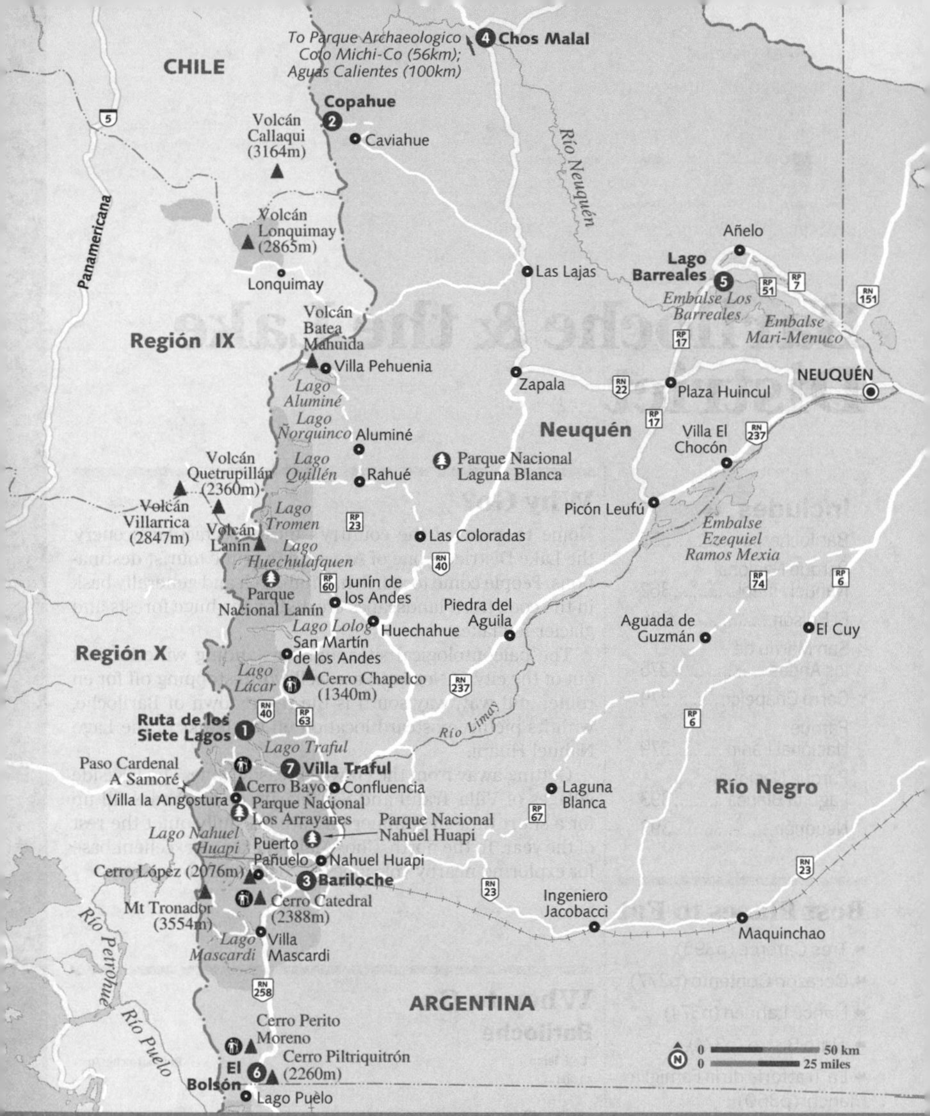

Bariloche & the Lake District Highlights

❶ Drive the **Ruta de los Siete Lagos** (RN234; p375, a breathtaking road winding between alpine lakes and pehuén forests

❷ Soak your worries away in a bubbling mud bath in the thermal resort town of **Copahue** (p386)

❸ Base yourself in **Bariloche** (p355) for some fun mountain adventures

❹ Get off the tourist trail in **Chos Malal** (p390) and out into its spectacular surrounds

❺ Follow in the footsteps of dinosaurs at **Lago Barreales** (p394)

❻ Hit the hippie market in **El Bolsón** (p366) for fresh fruits and other yummies

❼ Wind down for a few days surrounded by the gorgeous scenery of **Villa Traful** (p374)

National Parks

The spectacular but often crowded Parque Nacional Nahuel Huapi is the cornerstone of the Lake District's parks. Bordering it to the north, Parque Nacional Lanín gets fewer trail trampers and has equally spectacular sights, including Volcán Lanín and humbling pehuén forests. The tiny Parque Nacional Arrayanes is worth a day trip from Villa la Angostura to check out its beautiful cinnamon-colored arrayán trees.

Getting There & Away

The region's two primary ground transport hubs are Neuquén and Bariloche, where buses arrive from throughout the country. The main airports are in these cities, plus San Martín de los Andes, while smaller ones are in Zapala, Chos Malal and El Bolsón. All have flights to/from Buenos Aires.

Bariloche

0294 / POP 109,300 / ELEV 770M

Strung out along the shoreline of Lago Nahuel Huapi, in the middle of the national park of the same name, Bariloche (formally San Carlos de Bariloche) has one of the most gorgeous settings imaginable. This, combined with a wealth of summer and winter activities in the surrounding countryside, has helped it become, for better or worse, the Lake District's principal destination.

The soaring peaks of Cerros Catedral, López, Nireco and Shaihuenque (to name just a few) – all well over 2000m high – ring the town, giving picture-postcard views in nearly every direction.

These mountains aren't just for gazing, though – excellent snow coverage (sometimes exceeding 2m at the *end* of the season) makes this a winter wonderland, and a magnet for skiers and snowboarders.

In summertime the nature buffs take over, hitting the hills to climb, hike trails, fish for trout and ride mountain bikes and horses.

There's so much fun to be had that this town has become the destination for Argentine high school students' end of year celebrations. And if all this wasn't enough, Bariloche is also Argentina's chocolate capital and the only thing that approaches the amount of storefront window space dedicated to fresh chocolate is the infinite number of peculiar gnomes of all sizes and demeanors that is sold in nearly every shop downtown.

Officially founded in 1902, the city really began to attract visitors after the southern branch of the Ferrocarril Roca train line arrived in 1934 and architect Ezequiel Bustillo adapted Central European styles into a tasteful urban plan. Bariloche is now known for its alpine architecture, which is given a Patagonian twist through the use of local hardwoods and unique stone construction, as seen in the buildings of Bustillo's *centro cívico* (civic center).

The flip side of Bariloche's gain in popularity is uncontrolled growth: in the last two decades the town has suffered as its quaint neighborhoods have given way to high-rise apartments and time-shares. The silver lining is that many accommodations have remained reasonably priced.

Sights

Centro Cívico NEIGHBORHOOD

A stroll through Bariloche's center, with its beautiful log-and-stone buildings designed by architect Ezequiel Bustillo, is a must. Besides, posing for a photo with one of the barrel-toting Saint Bernards makes for a classic Argentine snapshot, and views over the lake are superb. The buildings house the municipal tourist office and the museum.

Museo de la Patagonia MUSEUM

(0294-442-2309; Centro Cívico; donation AR$20; 10am-12:30pm & 2-5pm Tue-Fri, 10am-6pm Sat) The museum is filled with archaeological and ethnographic materials, life-like stuffed animals and enlightening historical evaluations on such topics as Mapuche resistance to the Conquest of the Desert.

Activities

Bariloche and the Nahuel Huapi region are one of Argentina's major outdoor recreation areas, and numerous operators offer a variety of activities, particularly horseback riding, mountain biking and white-water rafting.

Mountaineering & Trekking

The national park office distributes a brochure with a map, adequate for initial planning, that rates hikes as easy, medium or difficult and suggests possible loops. Many of these hikes are detailed in Lonely Planet's *Trekking in the Patagonian Andes*.

Club Andino Bariloche (p361) provides loads of information (including on camping), and issues obligatory permits for trekking in Parque Nacional Nahuel Huapi. For

Bariloche

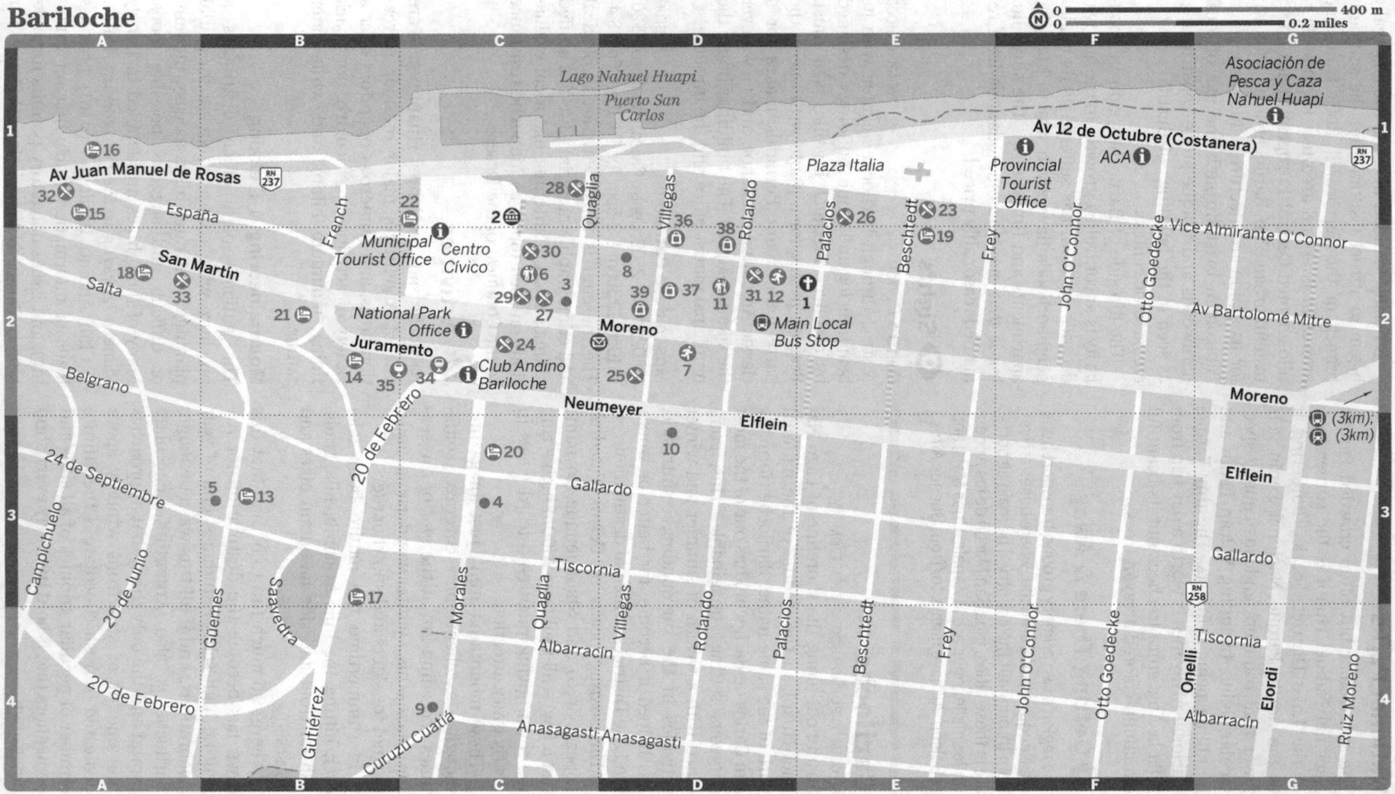
0 400 m
0 0.2 miles
A
B
C
D
E
F
G
1
2
3
4
Lago Nahuel Huapi
Puerto San Carlos
Asociación de Pesca y Caza Nahuel Huapi
Av 12 de Octubre (Costanera)
ACA
Provincial Tourist Office
Plaza Italia
Av Juan Manuel de Rosas
RN 237
España
French
Municipal Tourist Office
Centro Cívico
San Martín
Salta
National Park Office
Juramento
Club Andino Bariloche
Moreno
Main Local Bus Stop
Neumeyer
Elflein
Quaglia
Villegas
Rolando
Palacios
Beschtedt
Frey
John O'Connor
Otto Goedecke
Vice Almirante O'Connor
Av Bartolomé Mitre
(3km); (3km)
Belgrano
24 de Septiembre
20 de Febrero
Gallardo
Tiscornia
Albarracín
Campichuelo
20 de Junio
Güemes
Saavedra
Gutiérrez
Curuzú Cuatiá
Morales
Anasagasti
RN 258
Onelli
Elordi
Ruiz Moreno
1
2
3
4
5
6
7
8
9
10
11
12
13
14
15
16
17
18
19
20
21
22
23
24
25
26
27
28
29
30
31
33
32
34
35
36
37
38
39

Bariloche

Sights

1	Catedral Turismo	E2
2	Museo de la Patagonia	C1

Activities, Courses & Tours

3	Adventure Center	C2
4	Aguas Blancas	C3
5	Bariloche Moto Tours	B3
6	Baruzzi Deportes	C2
7	Bikeway	D2
8	Espacio	D2
9	EXtremo Sur	C4
10	La Montaña	D3
11	Martín Pescador	D2
12	Tom Wesley Viajes de Aventura	D2

Sleeping

13	Hospedaje Wikter	B3
14	Hostel 41 Below	B2
15	Hostel Los Troncos	A1
16	Hostel Patanuk	A1
17	Hostería La Paleta del Pintor	B3
18	Hostería La Sureña	A2
19	Hostería Piuke	E2
20	Hotel Carlos V	C3
21	Hotel Edelweiss	B2
22	Hotel Tirol	C1

Eating

23	Covita	E1
24	Días de Zapata	C2
25	El Boliche de Alberto	D2
26	Familia Weiss	E1
27	Helados Jauja	C2
28	Kostelo	C1
29	La Esquina	C2
30	La Marca	C2
31	La Marmite	D2
32	La Trattoria de la Famiglia Bianchi	A1
33	Rock Chicken	A2

Drinking & Nightlife

34	Los Vikingos	C2
35	South Bar	B2

Shopping

36	Abuela Goye	D2
37	Huitral-Hue	D2
38	Mamuschka	D2
39	Paseo de los Artesanos	D2

AR$30, its *Mapa General de la Guía de Sendas y Picadas* is cartographically mediocre, but has good trail descriptions and is indispensable for planning. It sells three additional trekking maps, all of which include mountain-bike trails.

Skiing

Nahuel Huapi's ski resort, Cerro Catedral (p364), was once South America's trendiest, and has been superseded only by Las Leñas (near Mendoza) and resorts in Chile. Las Leñas has far superior snow (dry powder), but it lacks Catedral's strong point: views. There's nothing like looking over the shimmering lakes of Nahuel Huapi from its snowy slopes.

Day passes run between AR$305 and AR$455, depending on the season. If you need lessons, stop into the ski schools at Cerro Catedral or Club Andino Bariloche. Two-hour private lessons run at about AR$720. For rental equipment, try **Baruzzi Deportes** (0294-442-4922; Urquiza 250; 9am-1pm & 3-6pm Mon-Fri, 9am-1pm Sat) or **Martín Pescador** (0294-442-2275; martinpescador@bariloche.com.ar; Rolando 257; 9am-1pm & 3:30-7pm Mon-Fri). Equipment is also available on-site. Sets of skis, boots and poles rent for between AR$125 and AR$165, and snowboarding gear between AR$175 and AR$225 per day, depending on the season.

Mountain Biking

Bicycles are ideal for the Circuito Chico (though this 60km loop demands endurance) and other trips near Bariloche; most roads are paved and even the gravel roads are good. Mountain-bike rental, including gloves and helmet, will cost you around AR$120 per day at a number of places. Try **Bikeway** (0294-445-6571; www.bikeway.com.ar; Moreno 237).

Fishing

Fly-fishing draws visitors from around the world to Argentina's accessible Andean-Patagonian parks, from Lago Puelo and Los Alerces in the south to Lanín in the north of the country.

On larger lakes, such as Nahuel Huapi, trolling is the preferred method, while fly-fishing is the rule on most rivers. The season runs mid-November to mid-April. For more information, contact the **Asociación de Pesca y Caza Nahuel Huapi** (Hunting & Fishing Club; 0294-442-1515; www.apcnh.com; cnr Costanera 12 de Octubre & Onelli; 9am-6pm Mon-Sat). For rental equipment and guide hire, try Baruzzi Deportes or Martín Pescador. Both offer guided fishing trips for about AR$3600 per day for one or two people (price is the same either way and includes all equipment, lunch, transport and guide). Fishing licenses (AR$180/540/720 per day/

week/season) are required and available at these shops.

Horseback Riding

Most travel agencies along Av Bartolomé Mitre offer horseback-riding trips.

Cabalgatas Carol Jones HORSEBACK RIDING
(0294-442-6508; www.caroljones.com.ar) For something special, contact the amiable Carol Jones, who offers half-day horseback riding from her family *estancia* (ranch) outside of town for AR$360 per person. The price includes transportation to/from town and an excellent *asado* (barbecue grill) outside. She also offers multiday pack trips by horse for AR$1000 per person per day.

Tom Wesley Viajes de Aventura OUTDOORS
(0294-443-5040; Av Bustillo, Km15.5) Offers horseback riding and mountain biking. This operator has been long in the business and has an excellent reputation.

Rafting & Kayaking

Rafting and kayaking on the Río Limay and the Río Manso have become increasingly popular in recent years. The best time to be on the rivers is November through February, though you can raft October through Easter.

EXtremo Sur RAFTING
(0294-442-7301; www.extremosur.com; Morales 765; 9am-6pm) In business since 1991, this outfit offers several trips on the Río Manso: the Manso Inferior (class II to III, AR$670 per person) is suitable for all ages; the Manso a la Frontera (class III to IV, AR$790 per person, ages 14 and up) is a fun and beautiful stretch of the river before the Chilean border.

There's also a three-day Expedición Río Manso (class III to IV), in which you camp riverside at excellent facilities.

Aguas Blancas RAFTING
(0294-443-2799; www.aguasblancas.com.ar; Morales 564; 9am-1pm & 3-7pm) This business has an excellent reputation and offers trips on the Río Manso.

Pura Vida Patagonia KAYAKING
(0294-15-4414053; www.puravidapatagonia.com.ar) Offers kayaking trips on the Lago Nahuel Huapi, ranging from half-day stints to overnight camp-'n'-kayak trips, custom-designed to match your skill level.

Paragliding

The mountains around Bariloche make for spectacular paragliding. If you wish to take to the sky, it will cost you around AR$600 for a 20-minute to half-hour tandem flight with, among others, **Parapente Bariloche** (0294-15-4552403; Cerro Otto base).

Courses

La Montaña LANGUAGE COURSE
(0294-452-4212; www.lamontana.com; Elflein 251; 10am-8pm Mon-Fri) This is a recommended Spanish school.

Tours

Countless tourist agencies along and near Av Bartolomé Mitre, such as Turisur, run minibus tours to the national park and as far south as El Bolsón. Prices range from AR$115 for a half-day trip along the Circuito Chico to AR$280 to San Martín de los Andes via the scenic Ruta de los Siete Lagos.

Adventure Center DRIVING TOUR
(0294-442-8368; www.adventurecenter.com.ar; Perito Moreno 30; 9am-6pm) Three-day trips down the fabled RN40 as far as El Calafate are offered from AR$1580 per person. Trips run from the end of October to April. Prices include accommodations, but national park entries and food are separate.

Bariloche Moto Tours MOTORBIKE TOUR
(0294-446-2687; www.barilochemototours.com) Organizes custom-tailored motorbike tours to everywhere between southern Patagonia and northern Chile and beyond.

Espacio BOAT TOUR
(0294-443-1372; www.islavictoriayarrayanes.com; Av Bartolomé Mitre 139) Espacio offers cruises on Nahuel Huapi lake in its 40ft catamaran *Cau Cau* during summer. Reserve your place two days in advance.

Festivals & Events

For 10 days in August, Bariloche holds its **Fiesta Nacional de la Nieve** (National Snow Festival).

In January and February the **Festival de Música de Verano** (Summer Music Festival) puts on several different events, including the **Festival de Música de Cámara** (Chamber Music Festival), the **Festival de Bronces** (Brass Festival) and the **Festival de Música Antigua** (Ancient Music Festival).

On May 3 is the **Fiesta Nacional de la Rosa Mosqueta**, celebrating the fruit of the wild shrub used in many regional delicacies.

Sleeping

From camping and private houses to five-star hotels, Bariloche's abundant accommodations make it possible to find good value even in high season, when reservations are a good idea. Prices peak during ski season (July and August), drop slightly during high season (January and February) and are lowest the rest of the year.

Hostel Los Troncos HOSTEL $
(☎0294-443-1188; www.hostellostroncos.com.ar; San Martín 571; dm/d from AR$85/250;) A step above most other hostels in town, the Troncos offers modern rooms with private bathrooms and cozy touches such as private reading lamps. There's also a range of super comfy hangout areas, an industrial-sized kitchen and a cute little courtyard garden.

Hostel 41 Below HOSTEL $
(☎0294-443-6433; www.hostel41below.com; Juramento 94; dm AR$80-90, d without bathroom AR$300; @) This is an intimate hostel with clean dorms, fine doubles (with good views) and mellow vibe. The kitchen and common room are excellent.

Hospedaje Wikter HOTEL $
(☎0294-442-3248; www.hospedajewikter.com.ar; Güemes 566; s AR$150;) Up the hill away from the center, this friendly little *hospedaje* offers spacious rooms in a bright, modern building. Bathrooms are bigger than most in this price range and some rooms have good views.

La Selva Negra CAMPGROUND $
(☎0294-444-1013; campingselvanegra@speedy.com.ar; Av Bustillo, Km2.900; campsites per person AR$55) Located 3km west of town on the road to Llao Llao, this is the nearest organized camping area. It has good facilities and, in the fall, you can step outside your tent to pick apples.

Hostel Patanuk HOSTEL $
(☎0294-443-4991; www.patanuk.com; Av JM de Rosas 585; dm/d AR$90/260;) Bariloche's only lakefront hostel is a definite winner. Big picture windows put you right in front of the water and mountains. Hardwood floors, a spacious kitchen and comfy lounge round out the picture.

Hotel Tirol HOTEL $$
(☎0294-442-6152; www.hosteriatirol.com.ar; Libertad 175; s/d AR$595/695; @) Right in the middle of town, this charming little lodge offers comfortable, spacious rooms. Those out the back have spectacular views out over the lake and to the mountain range beyond, as does the bright sitting/breakfast area.

Hostería La Paleta del Pintor HOTEL $$
(☎0294-442-2220; 20 de Febrero 630; s/d AR$230/420;) Everything about this place screams 'cute,' but the rooms are big and airy, with small but spotless bathrooms and big-screen TVs.

Hotel Carlos V HOTEL $$
(☎0294-442-5474; www.carlosvpatagonia.com.ar; Morales 420; s/d AR$1000/1200; @) At first glance a fairly standard business hotel, the Carlos V has plenty of hidden charm. That, the central location and the good-sized rooms make it hard to beat.

Hostería Katy HOTEL $$
(☎0294-444-8023; www.gringospatagonia.com; Av Bustillo, Km24.3; s/d AR$310/470; @) One of the closest *hosterías* (lodging houses) to the national park, this one's set in a charming family home. It's a family-run operation; the rooms are warm and comfortable, with big bathrooms and firm beds.

Hostería Piuke HOTEL $$
(☎0294-442-3044; res.piuke@gmail.com; F Beschtedt 136; s/d AR$350/450;) One of the better-value hotels down near the lakefront, this one has good-sized, comfortable rooms and some very hip retro '70s furnishings.

Hostería La Sureña HOTEL $$
(☎0294-442-2013; www.hosterialasurena.com.ar; San Martín 432; s/d AR$316/456;) A cozy, hectically decorated lobby leads on to a wide variety of rooms – some are spacious and well-appointed, others are workaday and cramped. Have a look at a few if you can.

Hotel Edelweiss HOTEL $$$
(☎0294-444-5500; www.edelweiss.com.ar; San Martín 202; r from AR$1320; @) One of the better business-class hotels in town, the Edelweiss manages to retain a warmth despite its size. All the facilities are here, including a fantastic 7th-floor day spa and swimming pool.

Eating

Bariloche has some of Argentina's best food, and it would take several wallet-breaking, belt-bursting and intestinally challenging weeks to sample all of the worthwhile restaurants. Regional specialties, including *cordero* (lamb, cooked over an open flame), *jabalí* (wild boar), *ciervo* (venison) and *trucha* (trout), are especially worth trying.

Covita VEGETARIAN $
(☎0294-442-1708; O'Connor 511; mains AR$30-60; ⏰12-3pm Mon-Sat, 7-11:30pm Thu-Sat; ✎) Wonderfully healthy cafe that caters to macrobiotic, vegan and even raw food diets. Choose from salads, stirfries, curries, and sushi. Fresh organic juices too.

La Marca INTERNATIONAL $
(Urquiza 240; mains AR$60-120; ⏰12pm-12am; 📶) Upscale *parrilla* (steak restaurant) with reasonable (for Bariloche) prices. Choose from the impressive range of brochettes (shasliks) – beef, chicken, venison, lamb and salmon. On a sunny day, grab a garden table at the side.

Helados Jauja ICE CREAM $
(Perito Moreno 14; ice cream from AR$20) Ask anyone in town who serves the best ice cream in Bariloche and they'll reply with one word: 'Jauja.' Many say it's the best in the country.

Rock Chicken FAST FOOD $
(San Martín 234; mains AR$49-75; ⏰10am-late) Late night munchies? Midday junk-food cravings? The beef, burgers and fried chicken here won't be winning any culinary awards, but they get the job done.

★La Trattoria de la Famiglia Bianchi ITALIAN $$
(☎0294-442-1596; España 590; mains AR$80-110; ⏰12-11:30pm; 📶) Finally, an Italian restaurant that offers something different. Excellent, creative pastas, a good range of meat dishes and some wonderful risottos, with ingredients such as seafood and wild mushrooms.

La Esquina CAFE $$
(Urquiza & Perito Moreno; mains AR$80-110; ⏰9-12am; 📶) The most atmospheric *confitería* (cafe offering light meals) in town has good coffee, reasonably priced sandwiches and burgers, and some good regional specialties.

Familia Weiss ARGENTINE $$
(Palacios 167; mains AR$80-125; ⏰12-4pm & 8pm-12am Mon-Thu, 12pm-12am Fri-Sun; 📶) A popular family restaurant offering good-value regional specialties such as venison, trout and goulash. The picture menu is handy for the Spanish-challenged, there's a good atmosphere and nightly live music.

El Boliche de Alberto PARRILLA $$
(☎0294-443-1433; Villegas 347; mains AR$92-107; ⏰12-3pm & 8pm-12am; 📶) It's worth dining at this esteemed *parrilla* simply to see the astonished look on tourists' faces when a slab of beef the size of a football lands on the table; it's the AR$100 *bife de chorizo* (the AR$80 portion is plenty).

Días de Zapata MEXICAN $$
(☎0294-442-3128; Morales 362; mains AR$80-150; ⏰12-3:30pm & 8pm-12:30am; 📶) A warm and inviting little Mexican restaurant. Dishes tend more toward the Tex Mex than you would think (the owners hail from Mexico City), but the flavors are good and the servings generous.

Kostelo INTERNATIONAL $$
(☎0294-443-9697; Quaglia 111; mains AR$80-120; ⏰12-3pm & 8pm-12am Tue-Sun; 📶) Modern and upscale bar-restaurant best for its location right near the lake. The food isn't bad, however – creative, well-presented and decent portions. Try to get a table with water view.

La Marmite ARGENTINE $$
(☎0294-442-3685; Av Bartolomé Mitre 329; mains AR$90-150; ⏰12pm-1am; 📶) A trusty choice for Patagonian standards such as trout and venison. Also the place to come for chocolate fondue (AR$220 for two), in case you haven't eaten enough of the stuff cold.

Drinking

Los Vikingos BAR
(cnr Juramento & 20 de Febrero; ⏰8pm-late) A laid-back little corner bar serving a good range of local microbrewery beers at excellent prices. The music's cool and the decor eclectic. DJs play on weekends.

South Bar BAR
(Juramento s/n; ⏰8pm-late) Mellow local pub where you can actually have a conversation while you drink your beer. Darts, too.

Shopping

Bariloche is renowned for its chocolates, and dozens of stores downtown, from national chains to mom-and-pop shops, sell chocolates of every style imaginable. Quality, of course, varies: make sure you don't get sick on the cheap stuff!

Mamuschka FOOD
(☎0294-442-3294; Av Bartolomé Mitre 298; ⊙9am-6pm) Quite simply, the best chocolate in town. Don't skip it. Seriously.

Abuela Goye FOOD
(☎0294-443-3861; Av Bartolomé Mitre 258; ⊙9:30am-7:30pm) One of Bariloche's long-time chocolate makers. Still small and still worth trying.

Huitral-Hue CLOTHING
(☎0294-442-6760; Villegas 250; ⊙9am-1pm & 3-8pm Mon-Sat) Good selection of traditional ponchos, textiles and wool sweaters.

Paseo de los Artesanos HANDICRAFTS
(cnr Villegas & Perito Moreno; ⊙daylight hrs) Local craftspeople display wares of wool, wood, leather, silver and other media here.

Orientation

The principal commercial area is along Av Bartolomé Mitre. Do not confuse VA O'Connor (also known as Vicealmirante O'Connor or Eduardo O'Connor) with similarly named John O'Connor, which cross each other near the lakefront. Similarly, Perito Moreno and Ruiz Moreno intersect near Diagonal Capraro, at the east end of the downtown area.

Information

Banks with ATMs are ubiquitous in the downtown area.

ACA (Automóvil Club Argentino; ☎0294-442-3001; Av 12 de Octubre 785) Argentina's auto club has provincial road maps.

Cambio Sudamérica (Av Bartolomé Mitre 63; ⊙9am-8pm Mon-Fri & 9am-1pm Sat) Change foreign cash and traveler's checks here.

Club Andino Bariloche (☎0294-442-2266; www.clubandino.com.ar; 20 de Febrero 30; ⊙9am-8pm in summer, 6-8pm Mon-Fri rest of year) Best source of hiking information on Nahuel Huapi. Gives information on hikers' refuges in the park.

Hospital (☎0294-442-6100; Perito Moreno 601) *Long* waits, no charge.

Municipal Tourist Office (☎0294-442-9850; www.barilochepatagonia.info; Centro Cívico; ⊙8am-9pm) It has many giveaways, including useful maps and the blatantly commercial but still useful *Guía Busch,* updated biannually and loaded with basic tourist information about Bariloche and the Lake District.

National Park Office (☎0294-442-3111; San Martín 24; ⊙8am-4pm Mon-Fri, 9am-3pm Sat & Sun)

Post Office (Moreno 175; ⊙8am-6pm Mon-Fri, 9am-1pm Sat)

Provincial Tourist Office (☎0294-442-3188/9, 0294-442-3188; secturrn@bariloche.com.ar; cnr Av 12 de Octubre & Emilio Frey; ⊙9am-7pm) Has information on the province, including an excellent provincial map and useful brochures in English and Spanish.

Getting There & Away

AIR

Aerolíneas Argentinas (☎0294-443-3304; Av Bartolomé Mitre 185; ⊙9am-7pm Mon-Fri, 9am-1pm Sat) has flights to Buenos Aires twice daily Monday through Wednesday and three times daily the rest of the week. In high season there are direct weekly flights to Córdoba and El Calafate and possibly Ushuaia.

LAN (☎0810-999-9526; www.lan.com; Av Bartolomé Mitre 534; ⊙9am-1pm & 4-8pm Mon-Sat) flies to Chile and Buenos Aires, and **LADE** (☎0294-442-3562; www.lade.com.ar; O'Connor 214; ⊙9am-3pm Mon-Sat) covers southern destinations.

BOAT

It's possible to travel by boat and bus to Chile aboard the Cruce de Lagos tour.

BUS

Bariloche's **bus terminal** (☎0294-443-2860) and train station are east of town across the Río Ñireco on RN237. Shop around for the best deals, since fares vary and there are frequent promotions. During high season it's wise to buy tickets at least a day in advance. The bus terminal tourist office is helpful.

The principal route to Chile is over the Cardenal A Samoré (Puyehue) pass to Osorno (AR$120, five hours) and Puerto Montt (AR$140, six hours), which has onward connections to northern and southern Chilean destinations. Several companies make the run.

BARILOCHE BUS CARDS

Bariloche's local buses work with magnetic cards that can be purchased at the **3 de Mayo ticket office** (☎0294-442-5648; Perito Moreno 480), downtown or at the bus terminal. You can also pick up handy *horarios* (schedules) for all destinations from these offices. Cards cost AR$15 (recharged with however much credit you want). You can also buy individual tickets, but for most routes a ticket will cost AR$7.50, while using the card costs AR$3.50. Some hostels loan cards to guests on payment of a deposit.

To San Martín de los Andes and Junín de los Andes, Albus, Transportes Ko-Ko and **Turismo Algarrobal** (☎0294-442-7698) take the scenic (though possibly chokingly dusty) Ruta de los Siete Lagos (RN234) during summer, and the longer, paved La Rinconada (RN40) route during the rest of the year.

Buses from Bariloche

The following services have at least three departures per day:

DESTINATION	COST (AR$)	DURATION (HR)
Bahía Blanca	643	12-14
Buenos Aires	1078	20-23
Córdoba	1048	22
El Bolsón	54	2
Esquel	174	4½
Junín de los Andes	101	3
Mendoza	725	19
Neuquén	353	7
Río Gallegos	800	28
San Martín de los Andes	125	4
San Rafael	595	15
Viedma	220	12
Villa la Angostura	52	1½

TRAIN

As troubled as any of the intercity train lines, when it's running the **Tren Patagonico** (☎02944-423172; www.trenpatagonico-sa.com.ar) leaves the **train station** (☎02944-423172), across the Río Ñireco next to the bus terminal. If it is operating, it generally leaves Bariloche for Viedma (16 hours) at 5pm on Sundays; fares will probably range from AR$169 in *economica* (economy) to AR$350 in *camarote* (1st-class sleeper). All this information is incredibly fluid – it's best to check with the tourist office beforehand.

Getting Around

TO/FROM THE AIRPORT

Bariloche's **airport** is 15km east of town via RN237 and RP80. A *remise* (taxi) costs about AR$100. Bus 72 (AR$7.50) leaves from the main bus stop on Perito Moreno.

BUS

At the main local bus stop, on Perito Moreno between Rolando and Palacios, **Codao del Sur** and **Ómnibus 3 de Mayo** run hourly buses to Cerro Catedral. Codao uses Av de los Pioneros, while 3 de Mayo takes Av Bustillo.

From 6am to midnight, municipal bus 20 leaves the main bus stop every 20 minutes for the attractive lakeside settlements of Llao Llao and Puerto Pañuelo. Bus 10 goes to Colonia Suiza 14 times daily. During summer three of these, at 8:05am, noon and 5:40pm, continue to Puerto Pañuelo, allowing you to do most of the Circuito Chico using public transport. Departure times from Puerto Pañuelo back to Bariloche via Colonia Suiza are 9:40am, 1:40pm and 6:40pm. You can also walk any section and flag down buses en route.

Ómnibus 3 de Mayo buses 50 and 51 go to Lago Gutiérrez every 30 minutes, while in summer the company's Línea Mascardi goes to Villa Mascardi/Los Rápidos three times daily. Ómnibus 3 de Mayo's Línea El Manso goes twice on Friday to Río Villegas and El Manso, on the southwestern border of Parque Nacional Nahuel Huapi.

Buses 70, 71 and 83 stop at the main bus stop, connecting downtown with the bus terminal.

CAR

Bariloche is loaded with the standard car-rental agencies and is one of the cheapest places to rent in the country. Prices vary greatly depending on season and demand, but usually come in around AR$400 per day with 200km.

Andes (☎0294-443-1648; www.andesrentacar.com.ar; San Martín 162; ⏰9am-6pm)

Budget (☎0294-444-2482; www.budgetbariloche.com; B Mitre 717; ⏰9am-7pm)

Hertz (☎0294-442-3457; www.milletrentacar.com.ar; Elflein 190; ⏰9am-9pm)

TAXI

A taxi from the bus terminal to the center of town costs around AR$25. Taxis within town generally don't go over the AR$15 mark.

Parque Nacional Nahuel Huapi

☎02944

One of Argentina's most-visited national parks, Nahuel Huapi occupies 7500 sq km in mountainous southwestern Neuquén and western Río Negro provinces. The park's centerpiece is Lago Nahuel Huapi, a glacial remnant over 100km long that covers more than 500 sq km. To the west, a ridge of high peaks separates Argentina from Chile; the tallest is 3554m Monte Tronador, an extinct volcano that still lives up to its name (meaning 'Thunderer') when blocks of ice tumble from its glaciers. During the

Parque Nacional Nahuel Haupi

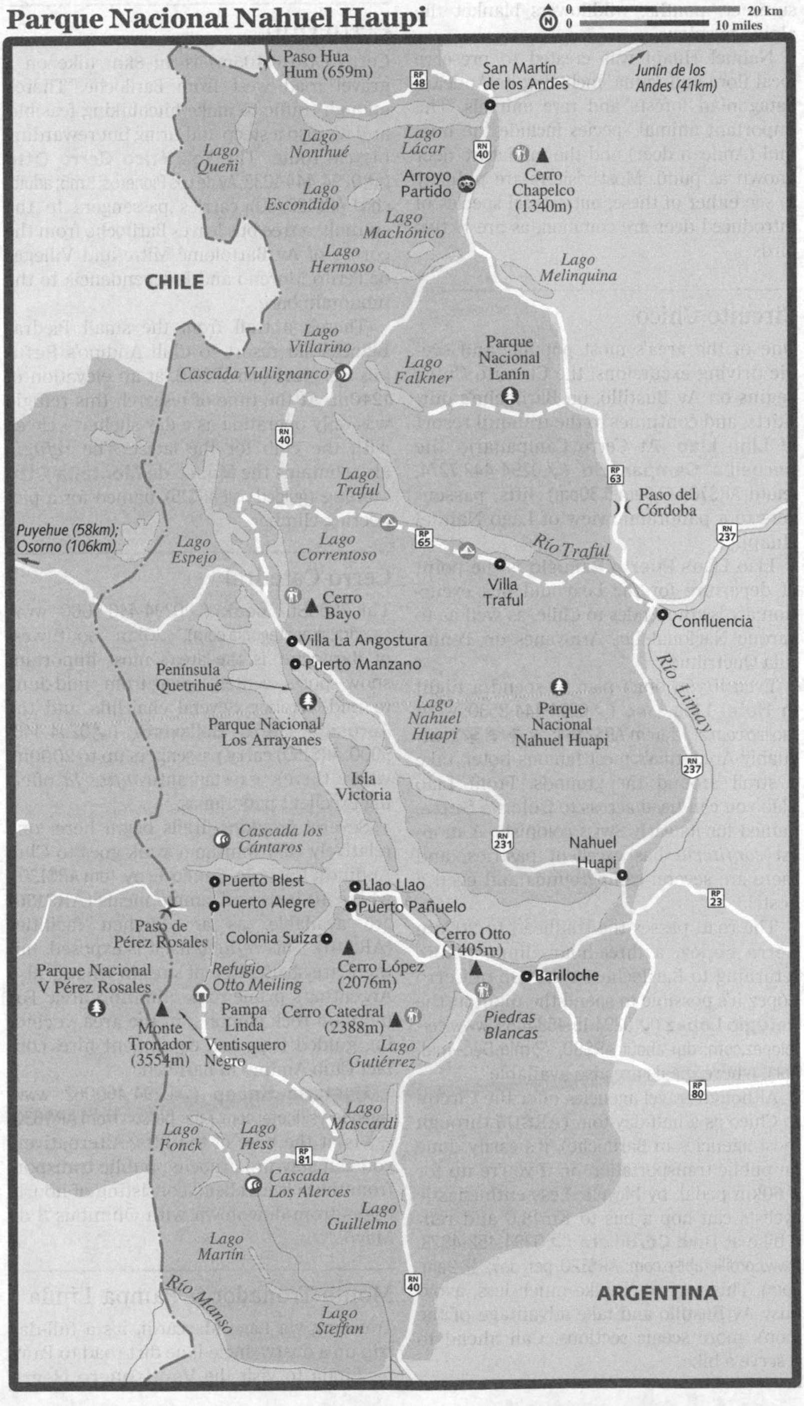

summer months, wildflowers blanket the alpine meadows.

Nahuel Huapi was created to preserve local flora and fauna, including its Andean-Patagonian forests and rare animals. The important animal species include the huemul (Andean deer) and the miniature deer known as pudú. Most visitors are unlikely to see either of these, but several species of introduced deer are common, as are native birds.

Circuito Chico

One of the area's most popular and scenic driving excursions, the Circuito Chico begins on Av Bustillo, on Bariloche's outskirts, and continues to the tranquil resort of **Llao Llao**. At Cerro Campanario the **Aerosilla Campanario** (☎0294-442-7274; return AR$70; ⏲9am-5:30pm) lifts passengers to a panoramic view of Lago Nahuel Huapi.

Llao Llao's **Puerto Pañuelo** is the point of departure for the boat and bus excursion across the Andes to Chile, as well as to Parque Nacional Los Arrayanes on Península Quetrihué.

Even if you don't plan to spend a night in **Hotel Llao Llao** (☎0294-444-8530; www.llaollao.com.ar; d from AR$2464;), arguably Argentina's most famous hotel, take a stroll around the grounds. From Llao Llao you can head across to **Colonia Suiza**, named for its early Swiss colonists. A modest *confitería* has excellent pastries, and there are several campgrounds and even a hostel.

The road passes the trailhead to 2076m **Cerro López**, a three-hour climb, before returning to Bariloche. At the top of Cerro López it's possible to spend the night at the **Refugio López** (☎0294-15-4584459; www.cerrolopez.com; dm about AR$90; ⏲mid-Dec–mid-Apr), where meals are also available.

Although travel agencies offer the Circuito Chico as a half-day tour (AR$115 through most agencies in Bariloche), it's easily done on public transportation or, if you're up for a 60km pedal, by bicycle. Less enthusiastic cyclists can hop a bus to Km18.6 and rent a bike at **Bike Cordillera** (☎0294-452-4828; www.cordillerabike.com; AR$120 per day; ⏲9am-6pm). This way you'll bike much less, avoid busy Av Bustillo and take advantage of the loop's more scenic sections. Call ahead to reserve a bike.

Cerro Otto

Cerro Otto (1405m) is an 8km hike on a gravel road west from Bariloche. There's enough traffic to make hitchhiking feasible, and it's also a steep and tiring but rewarding bicycle route. The **Teleférico Cerro Otto** (☎0294-444-1035; Av de Los Pioneros, Km5; adult/child AR$120/80) carries passengers to the summit; a free bus leaves Bariloche from the corner of Av Bartolomé Mitre and Villegas or Perito Moreno and Independencia to the mountain base.

There's a trail from the small Piedras Blancas ski resort to Club Andino's **Refugio Berghof** (dm AR$60), at an elevation of 1240m. At the time of research this refugio was only operating as a day shelter – check with the club for the latest. The *refugio* also contains the **Museo de Montaña Otto Meiling** (guided visit AR$15), named for a pioneering climber.

Cerro Catedral

This 2388m **peak** (☎0294-440-9000; www.catedralaltapatagonia.com), 20km southwest of Bariloche, is the area's most important snow-sports center, open from mid-June to mid-October. Several chairlifts and the **Aerosilla Cerro Bellavista** (☎0294-440-9000; AR$150) carry passengers up to 2000m, where there's a restaurant-*confitería* offering excellent panoramas.

Several **trekking** trails begin here: one relatively easy four-hour walk goes to Club Andino's **Refugio Emilio Frey** (dm AR$130), where 40 beds and simple meals (AR$130) are available, as are kitchen facilities (AR$40). This *refugio* itself is exposed, but there are sheltered tent sites in what is also Argentina's prime **rock-climbing** area. For more on rock climbing in the area, including guided trips and equipment hire, contact Club Andino in Bariloche.

Hostería Knapp (☎0294-460062; www.legendaryskihotel.com; r per person from AR$630;) is at the base of the lifts. Alternatively you can stay in Bariloche; public transport from there is excellent, consisting of hourly buses from downtown with Ómnibus 3 de Mayo.

Monte Tronador & Pampa Linda

Traveling via Lago Mascardi, it's a full-day trip up a dusty, single-lane dirt road to Pampa Linda to visit the **Ventisquero Negro**

(Black Glacier) and the base of Tronador (3554m). Visitors are rewarded with views of dozens of waterfalls that plunge over the flanks of extinct volcanoes.

From Pampa Linda – the starting point for several excellent **hikes** – hikers can approach the snow-line Club Andino **Refugio Otto Meiling** (dm AR$130) on foot (about four to six hours' hiking time) and continue to Laguna Frías via the **Paso de las Nubes**; it's a five- to seven-hour walk to an elevation of 2000m. It's also possible to complete the trip in the opposite direction by taking Cerro Catedral's ferry from Puerto Pañuelo to Puerto Blest, and then hiking up the Río Frías to Paso de las Nubes before descending to Pampa Linda via the Río Alerce. The *refugio* itself prepares delicious meals (around AR$130, kitchen use AR$45) and is well stocked with good wine and beer. You can hire a guide at the *refugio* to take you on a number of excursions, which range from a three-hour hike to a nearby glacier to the multiday ascent of Cumbre Argentina on Tronador.

Climbers intending to scale Tronador should anticipate a three- to four-day technical climb requiring experience on rock, snow and ice.

The road to **Pampa Linda** passes **Los Rápidos**, after which it becomes extremely narrow. Traffic is therefore allowed up to Pampa Linda until 2pm. At 4pm cars are allowed to leave Pampa Linda for the return trip. For AR$130 one way, Club Andino Bariloche has summer transport (end of November to April) to Pampa Linda at 8:30am daily, returning around 5pm. Buses depart from in front of Club Andino, and the 90km ride takes about 2½ hours. Park entry fees (AR$65) must be paid en route at the ranger station at Villa Mascardi (the bus stops so you can do this).

Sleeping

In addition to the campgrounds in the Bariloche area, there are sites at Lago Gutiérrez, Lago Mascardi, Lago Guillelmo, Lago Los Moscos, Lago Roca and Pampa Linda. *Refugios* are mostly open from December to the end of April. Reservations are not accepted – beds are allocated on a first come, first served basis but a space will always be found (maybe on the floor) for whoever arrives.

Within the park is a number of hotels tending to the luxurious, though there is also the moderately priced **Hostería Pampa Linda** (☎0294-449-0517; www.hosteriapampalinda.com.

THE CRUCE DE LAGOS

One of Argentina's classic journeys is the Cruce de Lagos, a scenic 12-hour bus-and-boat trip over the Andes to Puerto Montt, Chile. Operated exclusively by **Turisur** (☎0294-442-6109; www.cruceandino.com; Mitre 219; per person AR$1650), the trip begins around 8am in Bariloche (departure times vary) with a shuttle from Turisur's office to Puerto Pañuelo near Hotel Llao Llao. The passenger ferry from Puerto Pañuelo leaves immediately after the shuttle arrives so, if you want to have tea at Llao Llao, get there ahead of time on your own (but make sure you bought your ticket in advance). Service is daily in the summer, Monday to Friday the rest of the year. In winter (mid-April to September) the trip takes two days and passengers are required to stay the night in Peulla, Chile, where you have the choice of **Hotel Natura Patagonica** (☎in Chile 65-972289; www.hotelnatura.cl; s/d US$190/198; @ wifi) or the **Hotel Peulla** (☎in Chile 65-972288; www.hotelpeulla.cl; s/d US$124/131; @ wifi). There used to be a more economical option at Puerto Blest, but it was closed at time of research. Ask about this option at Turisur.

Bicycles are allowed on the boats, and sometimes on the buses (provided you dismantle them), so cyclists may end up having to ride the stretches between Bariloche and Pañuelo (25km), Puerto Blest and Puerto Alegre (15km), Puerto Frías and Peulla (27km), and Petrohué and Puerto Montt (76km); the tourist office may have info about alternative transportation between Petrohué and Puerto Montt for cyclists hoping to avoid the ride.

In winter it's not possible to purchase tickets only for segments of the trip (except between Puerto Pañuelo and Puerto Blest; AR$402). In summer (December to April) it's possible to buy just the boat sections (AR$523). Either way, if you're cycling Turisur will cut your rate slightly since you won't be riding the buses. Though the trip rarely sells out, it's best to book it at least a day or two in advance.

ar; s/d AR$580/720). For a real treat, stay at the secluded **Hotel Tronador** (☎0294-449-0556; www.hoteltronador.com; s/d from AR$890/1500; ⏲Nov–mid-Apr), at the northwest end of Lago Mascardi on the Pampa Linda road.

ℹ Information

A good source of information about the park is the Nahuel Huapi national park office in Bariloche.

For trekking maps and information about hiking in the region, see Lonely Planet's *Trekking in the Patagonian Andes* by Carolyn McCarthy or, if you read Spanish, the locally published *Las Montañas de Bariloche* by Toncek Arko and Raúl Izaguirre.

ℹ Getting There & Around

For road conditions in and around the national parks, call **Parque Nacional Estado de Rutas** (☎105) toll-free.

El Bolsón

☎0294 / POP 17,000 / ELEV 300M

It's not hard to see why the hippies started flocking to El Bolsón back in the '70s. It's a mellow little village for most of the year, nestled in between two mountain ranges. When summer comes, it packs out with Argentine tourists who drop big wads of cash and disappear quietly to whence they came.

In the last 30-odd years El Bolsón has been declared both a non-nuclear zone and an 'ecological municipality' (are you getting the picture yet?). What's indisputable is that just out of town are some excellent, easily accessible hikes that take in some of the country's (if possibly not the world's) most gorgeous landscapes.

The town welcomes backpackers, who often find it a relief from Bariloche's commercialism and find themselves stuffing their bellies with natural and vegetarian foods

El Bolsón

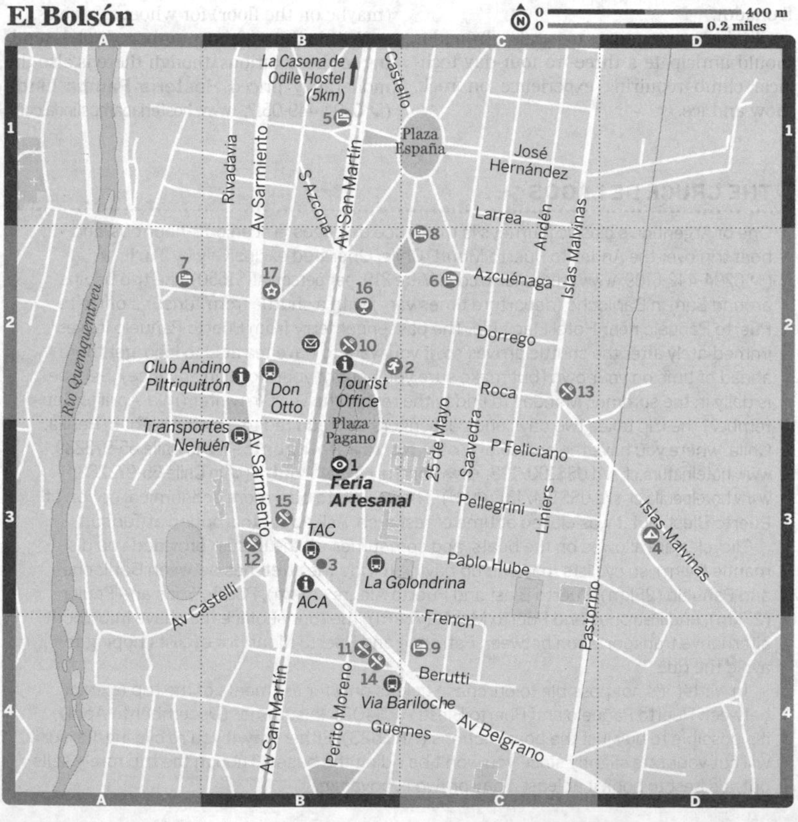

and the excellent beer, sweets, jams and honey made from the local harvest.

Rows of poplars lend a Mediterranean appearance to the local *chacras* (farms), most of which are devoted to hops (El Bolsón produces nearly three-quarters of the country's hops) and fruits.

Motorists should note that El Bolsón is the northernmost spot to purchase gasoline at Patagonian discount prices (although recent decreases in subsidies have seen the difference drop to around AR$1 per liter).

Sights & Activities

The principal landmark in town is the ovoid Plaza Pagano. Most services are nearby.

★Feria Artesanal MARKET

(⌚10am-4pm Tue, Thu & Sat) Local craftspeople sell their wares at this market, along the eastern edge of Plaza Pagano, which boasts over 300 artists, who make and sell everything from wooden cutting boards and *mate* (a bitter ritual tea) gourds to jewelry, flutes and marionettes. With numerous food vendors (adhering to the regulation that everything sold in the market must be handmade), it's also a chance to sample local delicacies. On sunny Sundays the *feria* (market) operates about half-tilt.

Grado 42 RAFTING

(☎0294-449-3124; www.grado42.com; Av Belgrano 406; ⌚8:30am-8:30pm Mon-Sat, 10:30am-1pm & 5-7pm Sun) For adventures in the surrounding countryside, this company offers extensive trekking, mountain biking and other tours around El Bolsón, and rafting on the Río Manso. Trips on the Manso Inferior (class II to III) cost AR$650 per person (including lunch); on the Manso a la Frontera (class II to IV) trips cost AR$740 (including lunch and dinner).

El Tabano BICYCLE RENTAL

(☎0294-449-3093; Perito Moreno 2871; ⌚9am-6pm Mon-Sat) Rents bikes for AR$30/100 per hour/day.

El Bolsón

Top Sights

Activities, Courses & Tours

Sleeping

Eating

Drinking & Nightlife

Entertainment

Shopping

Festivals & Events

Local beer gets headlines during the **Festival Nacional del Lúpulo** (National Hops Festival), over four days in mid-February. El Bolsón also hosts a weekend **jazz festival** (www.elbolsonjazz.com.ar) in December.

Sleeping

Budget travelers are more than welcome in El Bolsón, where reasonable prices are the rule rather than the exception.

★La Casona de Odile Hostel HOSTEL $

(☎0294-449-2753; www.odile.com.ar; dm/d AR$120/350; @📶) Five kilometers north of the center is one of the best hostels in the country. Set on two hectares of parklike riverside land, this is one of those places you come for a couple of days and find yourself there two weeks later.

Traveler-run, it's got all you could possibly want – good amenities, comfy dorms and rooms, an on-site microbrewery, yoga classes, massage cheap, hearty dinners and bike hire.

La Casa del Arbol HOSTEL $

(☎0294-472-0176; www.hostelelbolson.com; Perito Moreno 3038; dm from $70, d with/without bathroom from AR$190/270; @📶) A great little hostel, with a couple of good private rooms, spacious dorms and excellent kitchen, living and outdoor areas.

Hostería Luz de Luna HOTEL $
(☎0294-449-1908; www.luzdelunaelbolson.com.ar; Dorrego 150; s/d AR$200/300; 📶) Although spacious, the rooms here manage to retain a pleasant, homelike feel. Individual decoration and spotless bathrooms add to the appeal. Go for one upstairs for better light and views.

Residencial Valle Nuevo HOTEL $
(☎0294-449-2087; 25 de Mayo 2345; r AR$350) With spotless bathrooms, big-screen TVs and rocking views out the back onto mountain peaks, these are some of the best budget rooms in town. If you're coming in summer, book well ahead.

Camping Refugio Patagónico CAMPGROUND $
(☎0294-448-3888; www.refugiopatagonico.com.ar; Falkland Islands s/n; campsites per person AR$45; 📶) Not bad as far as campgrounds go – basically a bare field, but a pleasant stream burbles alongside it. Services are good, including *asados* and a modern toilet block.

La Posada de Hamelin GUESTHOUSE $$
(☎0294-449-2030; www.posadadehamelin.com.ar; Granollers 2179; s/d AR$390/450; 📶) A beautiful little rustic getaway. There are only four rooms, but they're all gorgeous, with exposed beams and rough hewn walls. The sunny upstairs dining area is a great place to munch on an empanada (baked savory turnover).

Hostería La Escampada HOTEL $$
(☎0294-448-3905; www.laescampada.com.ar; Azcuénaga 561; s/d AR$360/530; 📶) A refreshing break from El Bolsón's stale accommodation scene, the Escampada is all modern design with light, airy rooms and a relaxed atmosphere.

Comarca Hotel HOTEL $$
(☎0294-449-2235; www.comarcahotelbolson.com.ar; Av San Martín 3220; s/d from AR$530/720; ❄📶) El Bolsón's spiffiest hotel is a slick, business-class number. Standard rooms are fine, but an extra AR$70 buys you a king size bed, minifridge and sweeping mountain views.

✖ Eating

El Bolsón's restaurants lack Bariloche's variety, but food is consistently good value and often outstanding, thanks to fresh local ingredients and careful preparation. *Trucha arco iris* (rainbow trout) is the local specialty.

Feria Artesanal MARKET $
(⏲10am-4pm Tue, Thu & Sat) 🍃 The market is the best and most economical place to eat. Goodies here include fresh fruit, Belgian waffles with berries and cream, huge empanadas for AR$5, sandwiches, fritatas, *milanesa de soja* (soy patties), locally brewed beer and regional desserts.

La Salteñita FAST FOOD $
(Belgrano 515; empanadas AR$5; ⏲10am-9pm) For spicy northern empanadas, try this cheap rotisserie.

Jauja ICE CREAM $
(Av San Martín 2867; cones from AR$23; ⏲8am-11pm; 📶) The most dependable *confitería* in town serves up all your faves with some El Bolsón touches (such as homemade bread and strawberry juice) thrown in. The daily specials are always worth checking out – the risotto with lamb and wild mushrooms is divine. The attached ice-creamery is legendary – make sure you leave room for a kilo or two.

Otto Tipp ARGENTINE $$
(☎0294-449-3700; cnr Roca & Falkland Islands; mains AR$75-120; ⏲12pm-1am Dec-Feb, 8pm-1am Wed-Sat Mar-Jan; 📶) After a hard day of doing anything (or nothing) there are few better ways to unwind than by working your way through Mr Tipp's selection of microbrews. Guests are invited to a free sampling of the six varieties and there's a good selection of regional specialties, such as smoked trout and Patagonian lamb cooked in black beer.

Pasiones ARGENTINE $$
(cnr Belgrano & Beruti; mains AR$80-120; ⏲12-11:30pm; 📶) Specializing in excellent, homemade pastas, this sunny little spot has huge picture windows featuring some of the best views in town. Occasionally has live music.

Patio Venzano ARGENTINE $$
(cnr Sarmiento & Pablo Hube; mains AR$85-130; ⏲12am-12pm) On sunny days you'll want to arrive a little early to guarantee an outside table. No surprises on the menu (pasta, *parrilla*), but the atmosphere's a winner.

Las Brasas PARRILLA $$$
(☎0294-449-2923; cnr Av Sarmiento & Pablo Hube; mains AR$100-150; ⏲11:30am-12pm; 📶) The finest dining option in town. Las Brasas' signature dish is Patagonian lamb, but it offers other *parrilla* favorites, plus a variety of trout dishes.

Drinking & Nightlife

Barr 442 BAR
(☎0294-449-2313; Dorrego 442; ⊙Wed-Sat from 8pm) This venue doubles as a disco on Friday nights and often has live music on Saturday nights.

Entertainment

Centro Cultural Eduardo Galeano THEATER
(☎0294-449-1503; cnr Dorrego & Onelli) Small performance space featuring local (sometimes international) theater, music and dance. Stop by for a program or ask around town.

Shopping

El Bolsón is a craft-hunter's paradise. Besides the regular *feria artesanal* there are several other outlets for local arts and crafts.

Monte Viejo HANDICRAFTS
(cnr Pablo Hube & Av San Martín; ⊙9am-6pm) Quality ceramics, woodcrafts, silver and Mapuche textiles.

Information

ACA (Automóvil Club Argentino; ☎0294-449-2260; cnr Avs Belgrano & San Martín) Auto club; has provincial road maps.

Banco de la Nación (cnr Av San Martín & Pellegrini; ⊙9am-1pm) Has an ATM.

Club Andino Piltriquitrón (☎0294-449-2600; www.capiltriquitron.com.ar; Sarmiento, btwn Roca & Feliciano; ⊙6-8pm) Visitors interested in exploring the surrounding mountains can contact this office for information on hiking conditions, which *refugios* are open and general trail queries. Keeps a desk in the tourist office during hiking season.

Post Office (Av San Martín 2806; ⊙8am-6pm Mon-Fri, 9am-1pm Sat)

Tourist Office (☎0294-449-2604; www.elbolson.gov.ar) At the north end of Plaza Pagano. It has a good town map and brochures, plus thorough information on accommodations, food, tours and services. Maps of the surrounding area are crude but helpful. Superb staff.

Getting There & Away

El Bolsón has no central bus terminal, but most companies are on or near Av San Martín.

Via Bariloche (☎0294-445-5554; cnr Av Belgrano & Beruti) goes to Bariloche (AR$54, two hours) and Esquel (AR$98, two to three hours), and to points north of there, usually with a change in Neuquén (AR$380, eight hours).

TAC (☎0294-449-3124; cnr Av Belgrano & Av San Martín) also goes to Bariloche and Neuquén; the company sells tickets to Mendoza, Córdoba and other northern destinations, though you'll have to change buses in Neuquén.

Don Otto (☎0294-449-3910; Av Belgrano 406) goes to Bariloche and Comodoro Rivadavia (AR$455, 11 hours), with connections in Esquel for Trelew and Puerto Madryn.

Getting Around

BUS

Local bus service to nearby sights is extensive during the busy summer months, but sporadic in fall and winter, when you'll have to hire a taxi or take a tour. The tourist office provides up-to-date information. Local buses cost AR$1.50.

Transportes Nehuén (☎0294-449-1831; cnr Sarmiento & Padre Feliciano) has summer bus services to many local destinations.

La Golondrina (☎0294-449-2557; Pablo Hube & Perito Moreno) goes to Cascada Mallín Ahogado, leaving from the south end of Plaza Pagano; and to Lago Puelo, leaving from the corner of Av San Martín and Dorrego.

TAXI

Remises are a reasonable mode of transportation to nearby trailheads and campgrounds. Companies include **Radio Taxi** (☎0294-449-1224), **Patagonia** (☎0294-449-3907) and **Avenida** (☎0294-449 3599); call for rides.

Around El Bolsón

The outskirts of El Bolsón offer numerous ridges, waterfalls and forests for hikers to explore. With lots of time, and food and water, some of the following places can be reached by foot from town, though buses and *remises* to trailheads are reasonable. Mountain biking is an excellent way to get out on your own; for rentals try Maputur in El Bolsón.

Popular destinations include **Cabeza del Indio**, a lookout 7km from town and **Cascada Mallín Ahogado**, a small waterfall 10km north of town that provides access to the Club Andino Piltriquitrón's **Refugio Perito Moreno** (☎in El Bolsón 0294-448-3433; per night with/without sheets AR$65/30), a great base for several outstanding hikes. From here it's 2½ hours to the 2206m summit of **Cerro Perito Moreno** (☎0294-449-3912; lift pass AR$125-190, ski/snowboard rental AR$125/140) a small ski resort with a base elevation of 1000m.

Serious hikers head for the 2260m **Cerro Piltriquitrón** a granite ridge yielding panoramic views across the valley of the Río

Azul to the Andean crest along the Chilean border. Midway up is the **Bosque Tallado** (Sculpture Forest) and the Club Andino's **Refugio Piltriquitrón** (camping free, dm AR$50). Beds here are outstanding value, but bring your own sleeping bag. Moderately priced meals are available. From the *refugio* it's another two hours to the summit. Water is abundant along most of the summit route, but hikers should carry a canteen and bring lunch to enjoy at the top.

For more information on these and other hikes in the area and the various hikers' *refugios* operating, contact the Club Andino Piltriquitrón in El Bolsón.

In Chubut province, 15km south of El Bolsón, the **Parque Nacional Lago Puelo** protects a windy, azure lake suitable for swimming, fishing, boating, hiking and camping. By the waterfront the **Juana de Arco** (☎0294-449-8946; www.interpatagonia.com/juanadearco) takes passengers across the lake to Argentina's Pacific Ocean outlet at the Chilean border (AR$180, three hours). Hardcore hikers can walk into Chile from here – a tourist office at the dock has details.

Peuma Hue (☎0294-449-9372; www.peuma-hue.com.ar; s/d from AR$320/460) is a comfortable lakeside resort complex nestled between two rivers with great views of the mighty Piltriquitrón mountain range. There are both free and fee campgrounds at the park entrance, including **Camping Lago Puelo** (☎0294-449-9186; per person AR$45).

Regular buses go to Lago Puelo from El Bolsón in summer, but there's reduced service on Sunday and off-season.

Villa la Angostura

☎0294 / POP 11,100 / ELEV 850M

An upmarket resort town on the northwestern shore of Lago Nahuel Huapi, Villa la Angostura provides accommodations and services for nearby Cerro Bayo, a small but popular winter-sports center.

It's worthwhile stopping by in summer, too, for lake cruises and walks in the small but incredibly diverse Parque Nacional Los Arrayanes (a small peninsula dangling some 12km into the lake), and because this is the southern starting point for the breathtaking trip along the Ruta de los Siete Lagos.

The village consists of two distinct areas: El Cruce, which is the commercial center along the highway, and La Villa, nestled against the lakeshore, 3km to the south. Though La Villa is more residential, it still has hotels, shops, services and, unlike El Cruce, lake access.

Sights & Activities

Several outfitters in town offer trekking, horseback riding and guided mountain-bike rides, and the tourist office provides information on each. Mountain biking is a great way to explore the surrounding area.

Parque Nacional Los Arrayanes PARK
(admission AR$65) This inconspicuous, often overlooked park, encompassing the entire Quetrihué peninsula, protects remaining stands of the cinnamon-barked arrayán, a member of the myrtle family. In Mapudungun (language of the Mapuche) the peninsula's name means 'place of the arrayánes.'

The park headquarters is at the southern end of the peninsula, near the largest concentration of arrayánes, in an area known as **El Bosque**. It's a three-hour, 12km hike to the tip of the peninsula, on an excellent **interpretive nature trail**. You can also hike out and get the ferry back from the point, or vice versa. There are two small lakes along the trail. Regulations require hikers to enter the park before midday and leave it by 4pm in winter and around 6pm to 7pm in summer.

From the park's northern entrance at La Villa, a very steep 20-minute hike leads to two **panoramic overlooks** of Lago Nahuel Huapi.

Cabalgatas Correntoso HORSEBACK RIDING
(☎0294-15-451-0559; www.cabalgatacorrentoso.com.ar; Cacique Antriao 1850) For horseback riding (half-day to multiday trips). Contact Tero Bogani, who brings the gaucho side of things to his trips. Prices start at AR$300 for a three-hour outing.

Centro de Ski Cerro Bayo SKIING
(☎0294-449-4189; www.cerrobayoweb.com; full-day pass AR$250-420) From June to September, lifts carry skiers from the 1050m base up to 1700m at this 'boutique' (read small but expensive) winter resort, 9km northeast of El Cruce via RP66. All facilities, including rental equipment (AR$200 to AR$265), are available on-site.

Cerro Belvedere HIKING
A 4km hiking trail starts from Av Siete Lagos, northwest of the tourist office, and leads to an **overlook** with good views of Lago Correntoso, Nahuel Huapi and the surround-

ing mountains. It then continues another 3km to the 1992m summit. After visiting the overlook, retrace your steps to a nearby junction that leads to **Cascada Inayacal**, a 50m waterfall. If you're coming out here, get a map at the tourist office as the trails can be confusing.

Aquiles BICYCLE RENTAL
(Arrayanes 150; ⊙9am-1pm & 4-8pm) Rents quality mountain bikes for AR$120 per day.

Angostura Outdoors FISHING
(☑0294-15-4349319; www.angosturaoutdoors. com; Arrayanes 270 lcl 4; ⊙9am-1pm & 4-8pm) The waters around Villa la Angostura provide excellent fishing and these folks, the only specialized fly-fishing guides in the Villa, offer a range of tours including floats, boat tours, combined trekking and fishing trips and multiday excursions. With advance notice they can organize trips to Chile to fly fish for king salmon.

Vela Aventura BOAT TRIP
(☑cell phone 0294-15-451-2460; www.vela-aventura.com.ar) Offers sailboat rides around the lake. A three-hour trip costs about AR$760 for up to four people.

🛏 Sleeping

Except for camping and Angostura's growing hostel scene, accommodations are pricey; in summer, single rooms are almost impossible to find – expect to pay for two people.

Residencial Río Bonito GUESTHOUSE $
(☑0294-449-4110; www.riobonitopatagonia.com. ar; Topa Topa 260; d/tr AR$350/430; @🕾) Bright and cheery rooms in a converted family home a few blocks from the bus terminal. The big, comfortable dining-lounge area is a bonus, as are the friendly hosts and kitchen use for guests.

Camping Cullumche CAMPGROUND $
(☑0294-449-4160; moyano@uncu.edu.ar; Blvd Quetrihué s/n; campsites per person AR$35-50) Well signed from Blvd Nahuel Huapi, this secluded but large lakeside campground can get very busy in summer, but when it's quiet, it's lovely.

Verena's Haus HOTEL $$
(☑0294-449-4467; www.verenas-haus.com.ar; Los Taiques 268, El Cruce; s/d AR$180/280; 🕾) With all the heart-shaped motifs and floral wallpaper, this one probably doesn't qualify as a hunting lodge, but it is a good deal for

couples looking for a quiet, romantic spot. Rooms are big, spotless and packed with comfy features.

★**Hostel Bajo Cero** HOSTEL $$
(☑0294-449-5454; www.bajocerohostel.com; Río Caleufu 88; dm/d AR$150/500; @🕾) A little over a kilometer west of the bus terminal is this gorgeous hostel with large, well-designed dorms and lovely doubles. It has a nice garden and kitchen, plus airy common spaces.

Hotel Angostura HOTEL $$
(☑0294-449-4224; www.hotelangostura.com; Blvd Nahuel Huapi 1911, La Villa; s/d from AR$500/650, bungalow AR$800-1350; 🕾) Ignore the squishy rooms and the deer-antler light fittings – this is an awesome location. It's perched up on a clifftop overlooking the bay and the national park; your biggest problem here is going to be neck crick from checking out the view – no matter which way you're walking.

🍴 Eating

There are several restaurants and *confiterías* in El Cruce along Los Arrayanes and its cross streets.

Gran Nevada ARGENTINE $
(Av Arrayanes 106; mains AR$50-80; ⊙12am-11:30pm) With its big-screen TV (quite possibly showing a *fútbol* game) and big, cheap set meals, this is a local favorite. Come hungry, leave happy.

La Encantada ARGENTINE $$
(☑0294-449-5515; Cerro Belvedere 69, El Cruce; mains AR$90-150; ⊙12pm-12am; 🕾) A cute little cottage offering all of your Patagonian and Argentine favorites. The food is carefully prepared and beautifully presented, and the atmosphere is warm and inviting. The pizza is some of the best in town and there's a good selection of local beers and wines.

Los Troncos ARGENTINE $$
(Av Arrayanes 67, El Cruce; mains AR$80-120; ⊙8am-11pm; 🕾) Specializing in 'mountain food,' this lovely little place serves up a range of tempting dishes, such as deer stew, trout with almond sauce and wild mushroom stew.

Lancomilla PARRILLA $$
(Arrayanes 176; mains AR$80-130; ⊙12pm-12am; 🕾) The most popular *parrilla* on the main drag, this one does some good lamb dishes along with the standard offerings.

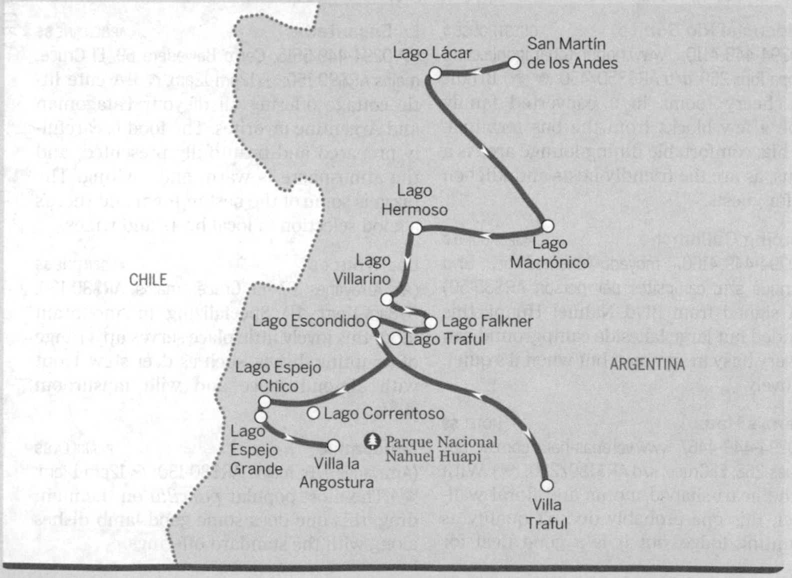
San Martín de los Andes
Lago Lácar
Lago Hermoso
Lago Machónico
Lago Villarino
CHILE
Lago Escondido
Lago Falkner
Lago Traful
ARGENTINA
Lago Espejo Chico
Lago Correntoso
Lago Espejo Grande
Parque Nacional Nahuel Huapi
Villa la Angostura
Villa Traful

JOHN ELK/GETTY IMAGES ©

JOHN ELK/GETTY IMAGES ©

Top: Lago Espejo Grande
Bottom: San Martín de los Andes (p375)

1 DAY DRIVE La Ruta de los Siete Lagos

A A spectacular road between towering, snow-capped mountains, crystal-clear lakes and dense pine forests, this is a 110km Lake District classic. Bike it in a few days, drive it in one, tour it or bus it – just don't miss it.

Starting at **San Martín de los Andes**, head out of town on the Ruta Nacional 40, skirting the banks of **Lago Lácar** and passing the Mapuche town of Curruhuinca. After 20km you'll come to the lookout at Arroyo Partido. From here it's a 5km downhill coast to a bridge over the Río Hermoso. Two short climbs and 5km later, you'll reach the dark-blue **Lago Machónico**. A further 5km brings you to a turnoff on the right, from where it's 2km of dirt road to **Lago Hermoso**, surrounded by mixed ñire and radale forests. Colored deer are common in this area, as are hunters, so be on the lookout (for both) when walking in the woods.

Entering the Parque Nacional Nahuel Huapi, it's 15km to the Cascada Vullignanco, a 20m waterfall made by the Río Filuco. Two kilometers on, the road runs between **Lago Villarino** and **Lago Falkner**, which has a wide sandy beach.

Two kilometers further on is **Lago Escondido**, from where it's 8km of downhill zigzag to a turnoff to the left. Follow this side (dirt) road for 2km to get to the north end of **Lago Traful**.

After 30km look for the **Villa Traful** turnoff – it's 27km from here to the villa, down a good dirt road, passing scenic lakeside bush campgrounds.

Sticking to the main road, though, you'll skirt the banks of **Lago Correntoso** and after 20km you'll come to a bridge and a disused *hostería* (lodging house). If you're looking for a side trip, just before the bridge, turn right and take the uphill road that ends at **Lago Espejo Chico** after 2km.

Continuing south, you'll catch glimpses of **Lago Espejo Grande** on the right through the trees. There are several lookouts along the road.

From here it's another 15km to a crossroads where you turn left, and 10km on asphalt to **Villa la Angostura**.

★Tinto Bistro
INTERNATIONAL $$$

(Av Arrayanes 256; mains AR$110-160; ⌚8:30pm-1am Mon-Sat) Besides the fact that the food (regional cuisine prepared with European flair) is excellent, the owner, Martín Zorreguieta, is the brother of Máxima, princess of the Netherlands. Feast on that.

Information

Banco de la Provincia (Calle Las Frambuesas btwn Cerro Belvedere & Nahuel Huapi, El Cruce; ⌚9am-1pm Mon-Fri) Has an ATM.

Post Office (Las Fuschias 121; ⌚8am-6pm Mon-Fri, 9am-1pm Sat) In a shopping gallery behind the bus terminal

Tourist Office (☎0294-449-4124; Arrayanes 9; ⌚8am-9pm daily)

Getting There & Away

Villa la Angostura's **bus terminal** (cnr Av Siete Lagos & Av Arrayanes, El Cruce) is across the street from the tourist office in El Cruce. Some buses stop in El Cruce on runs between Bariloche and San Martín de los Andes.

For Chile, **Andesmar** (☎0294-449-5217) goes over Paso Cardenal Samoré to Osorno (AR$240, 3½ hours).

There are numerous daily departures to Bariloche (AR$52, one hour) and two daily departures to Neuquén (AR$352, seven hours). Albus departs several times daily during summer to San Martín de los Andes (AR$70, four hours) by the scenic Ruta de los Siete Lagos. La Araucana runs daily services to Villa Traful (AR$38, two hours).

Getting Around

BOAT

Two companies run daily ferries from the dock (next to Hotel Angostura in La Villa) to the tip of Quetrihué peninsula, Parque Nacional Los Arrayanes (AR$110/220 one way/return, plus AR$65 national park entrance). Purchase tickets at the dock before hiking out, to secure a space on the return. The ride takes 45 minutes and you can put a bicycle on the boat.

BUS

Local buses cost AR$4 to go anywhere in town. Transportes 15 de Mayo runs hourly buses from the terminal to La Villa (15 minutes), up Av Siete Lagos to Lago Correntoso (15 minutes), and south down Av Arrayanes to Puerto Manzano on Lago Nahuel Huapi (15 minutes). From July through to September, and December through to March, 15 de Mayo runs six or seven daily buses to the ski resort at Cerro Bayo (AR$28, one hour).

TAXI

Taxis are the best means of getting to the trailheads, although some are served by local buses. Both leave from the local bus terminal on Av Siete Lagos, just north of Av Arrayanes.

Villa Traful

☎0294 / POP 360 / ELEV 720M

This little village enjoys an almost achingly beautiful location surrounded by mountains on the southern banks of Lago Traful. The place really packs out in January, February and Easter, when booking accommodations three months in advance is advised. The rest of the year, you may just have it to yourself. Depending on what you're into, November, December, March and April are great times to be here.

Getting here is half the fun – Villa Traful is 80km north of Bariloche via unpaved RP65.

Sights

Cascadas de Arroyo Blanco & Coa Có
WATERFALL, VIEWPOINT

These two waterfalls are a moderately easy, two-hour round-trip walk from town that can be done without a guide. Walk uphill on the street running beside the *guardaparque* (park ranger) office and follow the signs. From where the path forks at the open field it's 500m on the left to the 30m-high Coa Có. Return and take the other fork for 1km to the smaller Cascadas de los Arroyos Blancos. Far more spectacular than the actual waterfalls are the lookouts along the way, which give you a bird's-eye view of the forest, lake and mountains beyond.

Lagunas las Mellizas
LAKE, VIEWPOINT

Starting with a boat ride across the lake, this trek of moderate difficulty begins with a 2½-hour climb through cypress forests before reaching a lookout with views of the Lagunas Azul and Verde (Blue and Green Lagoons). If you've still got the legs for it, fording a stream gets you to an area with a variety of well-preserved Tehuelche rock paintings, dated at around 600 years old.

Tours

Eco Traful
TOUR

(☎0294-447-9139; ⌚10am-1pm & 4-7pm) A recommended agency that leads trips to Lagunas Las Mellizas (AR$230/320 per person walking/horseback) and Cerro Negro

(AR$120 per person), and organizes boat rides and fishing trips.

Sleeping & Eating

There are only a few places to stay unless you rent a *cabaña* (cabin; the tourist office has a complete listing).

There are also a couple of restaurants tucked into the trees and a general store.

Albergue & Camping Vulcanche HOSTEL $
(☎0294-447-9028; www.vulcanche.com; campsites per person AR$35, dm AR$80;) In a beautiful wooded area on the eastern edge of the village, this grassy campground and hostel has decent dorms and a good kitchen.

Hostería Villa Traful HOTEL $$
(☎0294-447-9005; cabanastraful@yahoo.com.ar; s/d from AR$350/420) A pleasant little mom-and-pop-run operation on the western edge of town. Rooms are aging but comfortable, there's a good restaurant on the premises, and the owners organize boating and fishing trips.

★ **Ñancú Lahuén** ARGENTINE $$
(mains AR$80-110; lunch & dinner;) A cute little log cabin set up in the center of the village. Trout dishes are the specialty (try 'em with the almond sauce), but the menu stretches to *parrilla* and a good range of salads as well.

Information

Banco de la Provincia de Neuquén, in the middle of the village, has an ATM that accepts Visa and MasterCard.

Tourist Office (☎0294-447-9099; www.villatraful.gov.ar; daily Dec-Feb, Sat-Wed Mar-Jan) Shares an office with the *guardaparque* (park ranger) in the middle of the village.

Getting There & Away

Villa Traful has better bus connections in summertime (December to February). La Araucana has daily services to Villa la Angostura (AR$38, two hours) and summer services to San Martín de los Andes (AR$55, 2½ hours). There are services from Bariloche (AR$40, two hours) daily in summer and three in summer.

San Martín de los Andes

☎02972 / POP 28,000 / ELEV 645M

Like a mellower version of Bariloche, San Martín has two peak periods: winter for skiing at Cerro Chapelco and summer for trekking, climbing etc in nearby Parque Nacional Lanín. Brave souls also swim in the chilly waters of Lago Lácar on the western edge of town. Between these times it's a quiet little town with a spectacular setting that retains much of the charm and architectural unity that once attracted people to Bariloche. A boat ride on the lake is pretty much a must if you're passing through, and if the snow's cleared (anytime from November onwards) and you're heading south, you should seriously think about leaving town via the scenically neck-straining Ruta de los Siete Lagos (RN234), which runs south to Villa la Angostura, Lago Nahuel Huapi and Bariloche.

Sights

Almost everything in San Martín de los Andes is within walking distance of the *centro cívico,* and the shady lakefront park and pier are a delightful place to spend an afternoon.

★ **Museo Primeros Pobladores** MUSEUM
(M Rosas; admission AR$5; 8:30am-12pm Wed-Fri, 5-8pm Mon, Wed & Fri, 11am-1pm Sat) Regional archaeological and ethnographic items such as arrowheads, spear points, pottery and musical instruments are the focus of this museum, located two doors north of the tourist office, near Av Roca.

Activities

Ruta de los Siete Lagos DRIVING
From San Martín, RN234 follows an eminently scenic but rough, narrow and sometimes dusty route past numerous alpine lakes to Villa la Angostura. It's known as the Ruta de los Siete Lagos (Seven Lakes Route) and its spectacular scenery has made the drive famous. Sections of the 110km route close every year due to heavy snowfalls – December to May is the best time to schedule this trip, but ask around for current conditions. Full-day tours from San Martín, Villa la Angostura and Bariloche regularly do this route, but there's also a scheduled bus service and, with a little forward planning, it's possible to drive/cycle it yourself.

HG Rodados BICYCLE RENTAL
(☎02972-427345; Av San Martín 1061; 9am-1pm & 4-8pm Mon-Fri, 9am-1pm Sat) Mountain biking is an excellent way to explore the surrounding area and a good way to travel the Ruta de los Siete Lagos. Rent bikes here for around AR$20/60 per hour/day.

San Martín de Los Andes

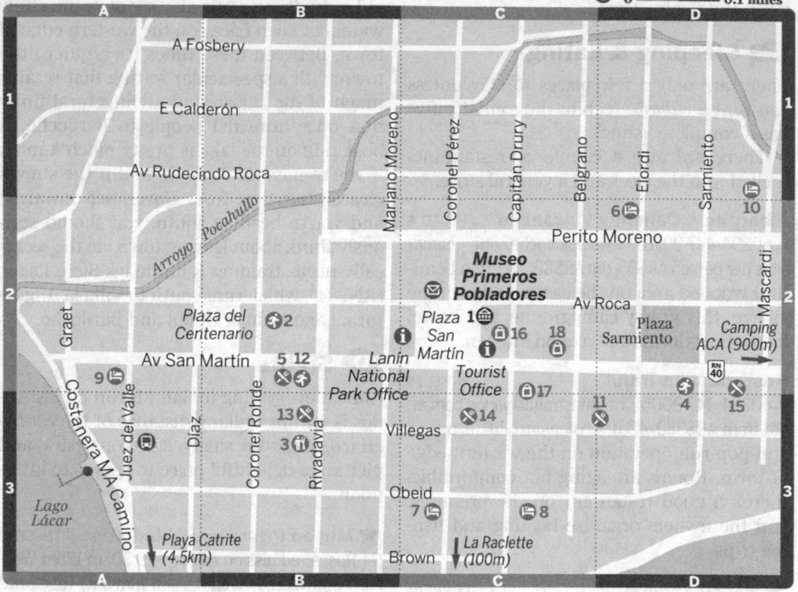

Mirador Bandurrias VIEWPOINT
(admission AR$5) A 2.5km steep, dusty hike ends with awesome views of Lago Lácar; be sure to take a snack or lunch. Tough cyclists can reach the *mirador* (viewing point) in about an hour via dirt roads.

Playa Catrite BEACH
Walk, bike or hitch to this protected rocky beach, 4km away down RN234 (there's a bus three times daily in summer). It has a laid-back restaurant with a nice deck.

Lanín Turismo RAFTING
(☎02972-425808; www.laninturismo.com; Av San Martín 431; ⏲9am-8pm Mon-Sat) With this outfit, rafting on the Río Meliquina, south of San Martín, or the Río Hua Hum to the west, costs about AR$350 for the day trip, including transfers. The river is spectacular and suitable for kids.

Andestrack OUTDOORS
(☎02972-420588; www.andestrack.com.ar; Coronel Rhode 782; ⏲9am-1pm & 3-8pm Mon-Sat) There are excellent opportunities for trekking and climbing in Parque Nacional Lanín. This is a young, enthusiastic company that has been highly recommended for mountain biking, canoeing, snowshoeing and dog sledding in the park.

Bumps SKIING
(☎02972-428491; www.skibumps.com.ar; Villegas 459; ⏲9am-6pm Mon-Sat) Skiing and snowboarding at nearby Cerro Chapelco attracts enthusiastic winter crowds. In San Martín, rental equipment is available from this store and at many other places along San Martín. Ski gear and snowboards cost between AR$130 to AR$170 per day to rent, plus you can also rent equipment on the mountain.

Festivals & Events

San Martín celebrates its founding on February 4 with speeches, parades and other festivities; the **parade** itself is an entertainingly incongruous mix of military folks, firefighters, gauchos, polo players and foxhunters.

Sleeping

As a tourist center, San Martín is loaded with accommodations, but they're relatively costly in all categories, especially in summer high season (January to March) and peak ski season (mid-July and August), when reservations are a must. Quality, however, is mostly high. In low season, prices can drop by 40%.

San Martín de Los Andes

El Oso Andaluz Hostel HOSTEL $
(02972-427232; www.elosoandaluz.com.ar; Elordi 569; dm/d from AR$80/250;) San Martín's coziest little downtown hostel has a good bed-to-bathroom ratio, atmospheric common areas and good value private rooms.

Camping ACA CAMPGROUND $
(02972-427332; Av Koessler 2175; campsites with 2-person minimum per person AR$60) This is a spacious campground on the eastern outskirts of town. However, you should try to avoid sites near the highway.

★ **Hostería La Masía** HOTEL $$
(02972-427688; www.hosterialamasia.com.ar; Obeid 811; s/d AR$450/700;) Taking the whole Edelweiss thing to the next level, La Masía offers plenty of dark-wood paneling, arched doorways and cast-iron light fittings. Rooms are big and comfortable and most have mountain views. Fireplaces warm the lobby, and the owners are usually around to make sure everyone feels at home. Superb.

La Posta del Cazador HOTEL $$
(02972-427501; www.postadelcazador.com.ar; San Martín 175; s/d AR$580/650;) A large, rather somber lodge that's heavy on the dark woods and hunting paraphernalia. The location's good and the serious-sized breakfast should set you up for the day.

Hostería Hueney Ruca HOTEL $$
(02972-421499; www.hosteriahueneyruca.com.ar; cnr Obeid & Coronel Pérez; s/d AR$320/480;) The big terracotta-tiled rooms here look onto a cute, well-kept little backyard. Beds are big and firm and bathrooms spacious, with glass-walled shower stalls.

La Raclette HOTEL $$
(02972-427664; www.laraclette.com.ar; Pérez; r AR$650;) Not suitable for claustrophobes, the narrow, low-ceilinged hallways here lead on to spacious, comfortable rooms. What really tips the scales are the downstairs common areas – a lounge-bar area and cozy little conversation pit centered around a big open fireplace.

Turismo Hotel HOTEL $$
(02972-427592; www.interpatagonia.com/hotelturismo; Mascardi 517; s/d AR$350/450;) A classic '70s ski lodge, right down to the stuffed deer's head and old-school pool table in the lobby. Rooms are comfortable enough, but best avoided if you have problems with glaring yellow paint jobs.

Eating

★ **Corazón Contento** CAFE $
(San Martín 467; mains around AR$60; 9am-11pm;) A cute little bakery-cafe serving up an excellent range of fresh and healthy snacks and meals. The salads are great and the freshly baked scones and muffins hit the spot.

Pizza Cala PIZZERIA $
(Av San Martín 1111; mains AR$45-90; 12pm-1am;) The local's choice for pizza is this ever-expanding place near the plaza. All the classics are here, plus some 'gourmet' options such as smoked trout, spinach and eggplant.

Doña Quela ARGENTINE $$
(San Martín 1017; mains AR$80-120; 12pm-1am;) Carefully prepared, well-presented dishes served up in an antique-packed dining room. Patagonian dishes such as deer with wild mushroom sauce are the stars, but it's all good, and comes accompanied by an impressive wine list.

Bamboo PARRILLA $$
(cnr Belgrano & Villegas; mains from AR$100; 12-4pm & 9pm-1am;) One reader claims

this upmarket *parrilla* serves 'the best meat in all of Argentina.' We haven't tried all the meat in Argentina (yet), so you be the judge.

La Casona ARGENTINE **$$**
(Villegas 744; mains AR$80-120; ⌚12-11pm; 📶) The cozy atmosphere belies the wide menu, with some good twists on regional favorites. Try the boar stew in black-beer sauce or the lamb and wild mushroom risotto.

El Mesón INTERNATIONAL **$$$**
(☎02972-424970; Rivadavia 885; mains AR$100-150; ⌚12-3pm & 9-11pm) This cute little place has one of the most creative menus in town, with plenty of trout dishes, paella and a couple of vegetarian options.

Shopping

Many local shops sell regional products and handicrafts.

Artesanías Neuquinas HANDICRAFTS
(☎02972-428396; M Rosas 790; ⌚9am-6pm Mon-Sat) A Mapuche cooperative that has high-quality weavings and wood crafts on offer.

El Carpincho ACCESSORIES
(Capitán Drury 814; ⌚9am-1pm & 3-6pm Mon-Sat) Gaucho regalia.

Patalibro BOOKS
(☎02972-421532; patalibro@yahoo.com.ar; Av San Martín 866; ⌚9am-8pm) Good selection of books on Patagonia in Spanish; some Lonely Planet titles and novels in English. Carries the excellent *Sendas y Bosques* park trail maps (AR$30).

Information

There are many other travel agencies along Av San Martín, Belgrano and Elordi that offer standard services as well as excursions.

ACA (Automóvil Club Argentino; ☎02972-429430; Av Koessler 2175; ⌚24 hr) Good source for provincial road maps.

Andina Internacional (☎02972-427871; Capitán Drury 876; ⌚9am-6pm) Money exchange, including traveler's checks.

Banco de la Nación (Av San Martín 687; ⌚9am-1pm Mon-Fri) Has an ATM.

Lanín National Park Office (Intendencia del Parque Nacional Lanín; ☎02972-427233; www.parquenacionallanin.gov.ar; Emilio Frey 749; ⌚8am-2pm Mon-Fri) The office provides limited maps as well as brochures and information on road conditions on the Ruta de los Siete Lagos.

Post Office (cnr Pérez & Roca; ⌚8am-6pm Mon-Fri, 9am-1pm Sat)

Ramón Carrillo Hospital (☎02972-427211; cnr Coronel Rohde & Av San Martín)

Tourist Office (☎02972-427347; www.sanmartindelosandes.gov.ar; cnr San Martín & Rosas; ⌚8am-9pm daily) Provides surprisingly candid information on hotels and restaurants, plus excellent brochures and maps.

Getting There & Away

AIR

There are regular flights from **Chapelco airport** (☎02972-428388; RN234) to Buenos Aires with **Aerolíneas Argentinas** (☎02972-410588; Mariano Moreno 859; ⌚8am-10pm Mon-Sat, 9am-9pm Sun).

BOAT

Naviera (☎02972-427380; naviera@smandes.com.ar; ⌚9:30am-7:30pm Mon-Sat, 10:30am-7:30pm Sun) sails from the **passenger pier** (Muelle de Pasajeros; Costanera MA Camino) as far as Paso Hua Hum on the Chilean border, at 10am. A dock has been under construction for several years at Hua Hum – when it is eventually completed, passengers will be able to disembark to cross the border into Chile. For now, you have to get off at Chachin, which is about an hour's walk from Hua Hum. Departure times do change; so call the ferry company or check with the tourist office. The fare is AR$260/400 one way/return.

BUS

The **bus terminal** (☎02972-427044; cnr Villegas & Juez del Valle) is a block south of the highway and 3½ blocks southwest of Plaza San Martín.

La Araucana (☎02972-420285) heads to Villa Traful daily during summer (AR$60, 2½ hours). If you're heading to Villa La Angostura or Bariloche during the summer, Albus regularly takes the scenic Ruta de los Siete Lagos (RN234) instead of the longer but smoother Rinconada route.

To get to Aluminé you must first change buses in Zapala or Junín de los Andes (where there are three departures per week).

Igi-Llaima (☎02972-428878) takes RP60 over Paso Tromen (also known as Mamuil Malal) to Temuco, Chile (AR$180, six hours), passing the majestic Volcán Lanín en route; sit on the left for views.

From San Martín there is direct service in summer via RN231 over Paso Cardenal A Samoré (Puyehue) to Osorno and Puerto Montt in Chile.

Buses from San Martín De Los Andes

There are frequent daily departures to the following destinations.

DESTINATION	COST (AR$)	DURATION (HR)
Bariloche	125	4½
Buenos Aires	1195	20-23
Junín de los Andes	30	1
Neuquén	342	6
Villa la Angostura	70	4
Zapala	154	3½

Getting Around

Chapelco airport (p378) is midway between San Martín and Junín. Any bus heading north out of San Martín can drop you at the entrance.

Transportation options slim down during low season. In summer Transportes Airen goes twice daily to Puerto Canoa on Lago Huechulafquen (AR$35) and will stop at campgrounds en route. **Albus** (02972-428100) goes to the beach at Playa Catrite on Lago Lácar (AR$18) several times daily, while **Transportes Ko-Ko** (02972-427422) runs four buses daily to Lago Lolog (AR$18) in summer only.

San Martín has no lack of car-rental agencies.

Alamo (02972-410811; Av San Martín 836, 2nd fl; 9am-6pm)

Sur (02972-429028; Villegas 830; 9am-6pm Mon-Fri, 9am-2pm Sat & Sun)

Cerro Chapelco

Located 20km southeast of San Martín, **Cerro Chapelco** (02972-427845; www.cerrochapelco.com) is one of Argentina's principal winter-sports centers, with a mix of runs for beginners and experts, and a maximum elevation of 1920m. The **Fiesta Nacional del Montañés**, the annual ski festival, is held during the first half of August.

Lift-ticket prices vary, depending on when you go; full-day passes run from AR$170 to AR$285 for adults, AR$140 to AR$240 for children. The slopes are open from mid-June to early October. The low season is mid-June to early July and from August 28 to mid-October; high season is around the last two weeks of July. Rental equipment is available on-site as well as in San Martín.

Transportes Ko-Ko runs two buses each day (three in summer; AR$35 return) to the park from San Martín's bus terminal. Travel agencies in San Martín also offer packages with shuttle service, or shuttle service alone (AR$55); they pick you up at your hotel.

Parque Nacional Lanín

Dominating the view in all directions along the Chilean border, the snowcapped cone of 3776m Volcán Lanín is the centerpiece of this **national park** (www.parquenacionallanin.gov.ar; admission free-AR$65), which extends 150km from Parque Nacional Nahuel Huapi in the south to Lago Ñorquinco in the north.

Protecting 3790 sq km of native Patagonian forest, Parque Nacional Lanín is home to many of the same species that characterize more southerly Patagonian forests, such as the southern beeches – lenga, ñire and coihue. The area does host some unique specimens, though, such as the extensive stands of the broadleaf, deciduous southern beech, raulí, and the curious pehuén (monkey puzzle tree; *Araucaria araucana*), a pinelike conifer whose nuts have long been a dietary staple for the Pehuenches and Mapuches. Note, though, that only indigenous people may gather *piñones* (pine nuts) from the pehuénes.

The towns of San Martín de los Andes, Junín de los Andes and Aluminé are the best bases for exploring Lanín, its glacial lakes and the backcountry.

At the time of writing admission was charged to enter the park only if you were heading towards Puerta Canoa.

Lago Tromen

This northern approach to **Volcán Lanín** (3776m), which straddles the Argentina-Chile border, is also the shortest and usually the earliest in the season to open for hikers and climbers. Before climbing Lanín, ask permission at the Lanín national park office in San Martín or, if necessary, of the *gendarmería* (border guards) in Junín. To prove that you are adequately equipped, it's obligatory to show equipment, such as plastic tools, crampons, ice axe and clothing – including sunglasses, sunblock, gloves, hats and padded jackets.

From the trailhead at the Argentine border station, it's five to seven hours to the **CAJA refugio** (capacity 20 people), at 2600m on the Camino de Mulas route; above that point, snow equipment is necessary. There's a shorter but steeper route along the ridge known as the Espina del Pescado. Trekkers can cross the Sierra Mamuil Malal to Lago Huechulafquen via Arroyo Rucu Leufu.

Parque Nacional Lanín

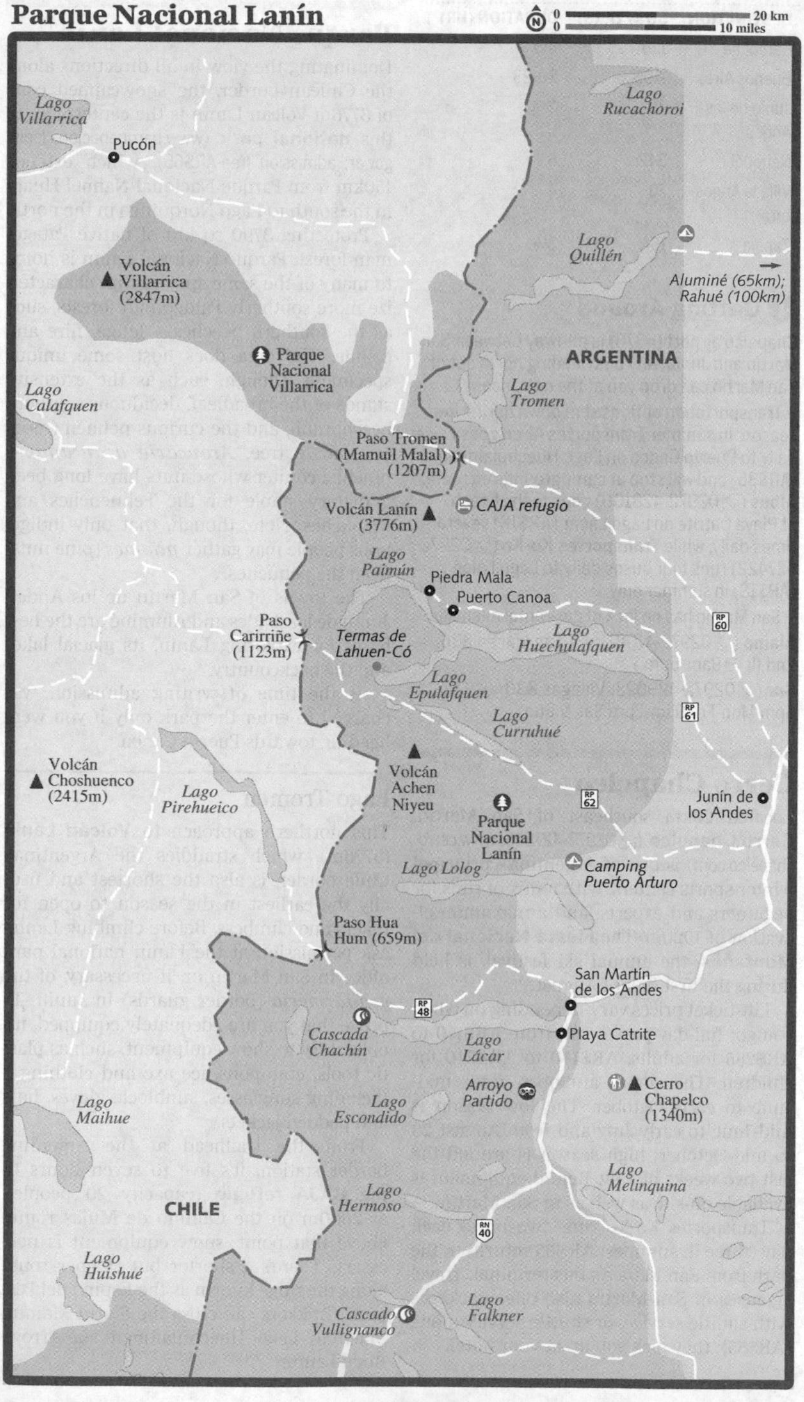

0 20 km
0 10 miles
Lago Villarrica
Pucón
Volcán Villarrica (2847m)
Parque Nacional Villarrica
Lago Calafquen
Lago Rucachoroi
Lago Quillén
Aluminé (65km); Rahué (100km)
ARGENTINA
Lago Tromen
Paso Tromen (Mamuil Malal) (1207m)
CAJA refugio
Volcán Lanín (3776m)
Lago Paimún
Piedra Mala
Puerto Canoa
Paso Carirriñe (1123m)
Termas de Lahuen-Có
RP 60
Lago Huechulafquen
Lago Epulafquen
Lago Currhué
RP 61
Volcán Choshuenco (2415m)
Lago Pirehueico
Volcán Achen Niyeu
RP 62
Junín de los Andes
Parque Nacional Lanín
Lago Lolog
Camping Puerto Arturo
Paso Hua Hum (659m)
San Martín de los Andes
RP 48
Cascada Chachín
Playa Catrite
Lago Lácar
Arroyo Partido
Cerro Chapelco (1340m)
Lago Maihue
Lago Escondido
Lago Melinquina
Lago Hermoso
CHILE
RN 40
Lago Huishué
Cascado Vullignanco
Lago Falkner

Contact Andestrack (p376) or the park office in San Martín to organize guides for climbing Lanín. The hike usually takes two days: you leave early the first and stay at the RIM *refugio* (shelter), rise before dawn the following day, hike to the summit and walk down. If you want to go up in winter, Andestrack can set you up with guides to hike up and board or ski down.

Lago Quillén

Situated in the park's densest pehuén forests, this isolated lake is accessible by dirt road from Rahué, 17km south of Aluminé, and has many good **campsites**. Other nearby lakes include **Lago Rucachoroi**, directly west of Aluminé, and **Lago Ñorquinco** on the park's northern border. There are Mapuche reservations at Rucachoroi and Quillén.

Lago Huechulafquen

The park's largest lake is also one of its most central and accessible areas. Despite limited public transportation, it can be reached from San Martín and – more easily – Junín de los Andes. RP61 climbs from a junction just north of Junín, west to Huechulafquen and the smaller Lago Paimún, offering outstanding views of Volcán Lanín and access to trailheads of several excellent hikes.

From the ranger station at **Puerto Canoa**, a good trail climbs to a viewpoint on Lanín's shoulder, where it's possible to hike across to Paso Tromen or continue climbing to either of two *refugios:* the **RIM refugio** belongs to the army's Regimiento de Infantería de Montaña, while the **CAJA refugio** belongs to the Club Andino Junín de los Andes. Both are fairly rustic but well kept and can be bases for attempts on the summit. The initial segment follows an abandoned road, but after about 40 minutes it becomes a pleasant woodsy trail along the **Arroyo Rucu Leufu**, an attractive mountain stream. Halfway to the *refugio* is an extensive **pehuén forest**, the southernmost in the park, which makes the walk worthwhile if you lack time for the entire route. The route to RIM's *refugio,* about 2450m above sea level, takes about seven hours one way, while the trail to CAJA's *refugio* takes a bit longer.

Another good backcountry hike circles **Lago Paimún**. This requires about two days from Puerto Canoa; you return to the north side of the lake by crossing a cable platform strung across the narrows between Huechulafquen and Paimún. A shorter alternative hike goes from the very attractive campground at **Piedra Mala** to **Cascada El Saltillo**, a nearby forest waterfall. If your car lacks 4WD, leave it at the logjam 'bridge' that crosses the creek and walk to Piedra Mala – the road, passable by any ordinary vehicle to this point, quickly worsens after a harsh winter. Horses are available for hire at Piedra Mala. Transportes Ko-Ko runs buses to Piedra Mala daily in summer from the San Martín bus terminal.

Campsites are abundant along the highway; travelers camping in the free sites in the narrow area between the lakes and the highway must dig a latrine and remove their own trash. If you camp at the organized sites (which, though not luxurious, are maintained), you'll support Mapuche concessionaires who at least derive some income from lands that were theirs before the state usurped them a century ago. Good campgrounds include **Camping Raquithue** (per person AR$35) and **Bahía Cañicul** (☎0297-249-0211; AR$35)

Noncampers should treat themselves to a stay at **Hostería Refugio Pescador** (☎0294-15-4255837; www.refugiodelpescador.com; r per person incl full board AR$650) or the three-star **Hostería Paimún** (☎02972-491758; www.hosteriapaimun.com.ar; r per person incl full board AR$720); both of these options cater to fishing parties.

Lago Lácar & Lago Lolog

From San Martín, at the east end of Lago Lácar, there is bus service on RP48, which runs along the lake to the Chilean border at Paso Hua Hum. You can get off the bus anywhere along the lake or get off at Hua Hum and hike to **Cascada Chachín**; bus drivers know the stop. From the highway, it's 3km down a dirt road and then another 20 minutes' walk along a trail to the waterfall. It's a great spot for a picnic.

About 15km north of San Martín de los Andes, Lago Lolog offers good fishing in a largely undeveloped area. You'll find free camping at **Camping Puerto Arturo**. Transportes Ko-Ko runs four buses daily in summer to Lago Lolog from San Martín (AR$15).

Information

The Lanín national park office in San Martín produces brochures on camping, hiking and

EXCURSIONS TO PARQUE NACIONAL LANÍN

In summer, buses leave the terminal in Junín several times a day for destinations within the national park, allowing you to hit the trails and camp in some beautiful areas. The buses run three 'circuits' and charge AR$34 one way.

Lago Huechulafquen & Puerto Canoa (via RP61)

From Puerto Canoa, on the north shore of the lake, there are three worthwhile hikes, including a 1½-hour round-trip walk to the Cascada del Saltillo and a seven-hour round-trip hike to **Cara Sur de Lanín** (south face of Volcán Lanín). For the latter, park rangers require you set out by 11am. Ranger stations are at the entrance to Huechulafquen and at Puerto Canoa. From Puerto Canoa, the boat **Jose Julian** (☎02972-428029; www.catamaranjosejulian.com.ar; AR$160) offers boat trips on the lake. Buses depart Junín's terminal twice in the morning (usually around 8am and 11am) and once in the afternoon (around 4pm). Be sure to catch the last bus back unless you plan to camp.

Circuito Tromen (via RN23 & RP60)

Buses depart twice daily to **Lago Tromen**, from where there is a 1½-hour round-trip walk along the river, passing a fine araucaria forest and a lookout with fabulous views of the lake. Another 45-minute walk takes you to the base of **Volcán Lanín's Cara Norte** (north face). This is one departure point for the two- to three-day ascent of Lanín. Park rangers inspect equipment and test any climbers who plan to go without a guide. To hire a guide, contact the tourist office in Junín. This is the access point for the CAJA *refugio* (shelter) and two military-owned *refugios*. Lago Tromen can also be reached by taking any bus that goes to Chile and getting off at Tromen.

Circuito Currhué (via RP62)

Buses depart once or twice daily for **Lago Currhué** and **Lago Epulafquen**; near the latter is a trailhead that leads to the **Termas de Lahuen-Có** (☎02972-424709; www.lahuenco.com; s/d from AR$1240/1580), about one hour's walking from the head. Package tours out here – including transportation, lunch and spa treatments – cost around US$100 and can be organized through the center or through tour operators in town. Luxurious rooms are available, should you want to spend the night. You can also hike from here to the crater of Volcán Achen Niyeu.

climbing in the park. Scattered throughout the park proper are several ranger stations, but they usually lack printed materials. The national park's **website** (www.parquenacionallanin.gov.ar) is full of useful information.

ℹ Getting There & Away

Although the park is close to San Martín and Junín, public transportation is not extensive. With some patience, hitchhiking is feasible in high season. Buses over the Hua Hum and Tromen passes, from San Martín and Junín to Chile, will carry passengers to intermediate destinations but are often full.

Junín de los Andes

☎02972 / POP 12,600 / ELEV 800M

A much more humble affair than other Lake District towns, Junín's a favorite for fly-fishers – the town deems itself the trout capital of Neuquén province and, to drive the point home, uses trout-shaped street signs. A couple of circuits leading out of town take in the scenic banks of the Lago Huechulafquen, where Mapuche settlements welcome visitors. Outside of peak season, these circuits are best done by private vehicle (or incredibly enthusiastic cyclists), but travel agents based here offer reasonably priced tours.

Sights & Activities

Junín's surroundings are more appealing than the town itself, but the museum is well worth seeing.

Museo Mapuche MUSEUM

(Padre Milanesio 751; ⏲9am-12:30pm & 2-7pm Mon-Fri, 9am-12:30pm Sat) The collection at this museum includes Mapuche weavings as well as a variety of archaeological pieces. Worth a visit.

Vía Cristi LANDMARK

Situated about 2km from the center of town, near the end of Av Antardida Argentina, Vía Cristi contains a collection of 22 sculptures, bas reliefs and mosaics winding its way up Cerro de la Cruz and vividly depicting the Conquest of the Desert, Mapuche Legends, Christian themes and indigenous history.

Trout Fishing FISHING

(AR$75/250/350 per day/week/season) The area around Junín is prime country for trout fishing, and the Río Aluminé, north of Junín, is an especially choice area. Catch-and-release is obligatory. Fishing permits are available through the tourist office.

Ciclismo Mavi BICYCLE RENTAL

(Felix San Martín 415; ⌚9am-1pm & 3-6pm) Rents mountain bikes for AR$20/100 per hour/day.

Tours

Picurú Turismo TOUR

(☎02792-492829; www.picuruturismo.tur.ar; Coronel Suárez 371; ⌚9am-6pm Mon-Fri, 9am-1pm & 4-7pm Sat) Recommended tour operator for trips into Parque Nacional Lanín and tours of Mapuche communities.

Festivals & Events

In January the **Feria y Exposición Ganadera** displays the best of local cattle, horses, sheep, poultry and rabbits. There are also exhibitions of horsemanship, as well as local crafts exhibits, but this is the *estanciero's* (*estancia* owner's) show.

In July, the Mapuche celebrate their crafts skills with the **Semana de Artesanía Aborigen**.

The **National Trout Festival** takes place in November.

Sleeping

High season coincides with fishing season (November through April); during low season, prices are lower than those that are quoted here.

Tromen Hostel HOSTEL $

(☎02972-491498; www.hosteltromen.com.ar; Lonquimay 195; dm/d AR$60/180; @ wi-fi) Junin's coziest hostel is set in a converted family home at the southern end of town. Double rooms are an excellent deal, dorms are OK and the living and kitchen areas are comfortable and well-equipped.

Camping Laura Vicuña CAMPGROUND $

(Ginés Ponte s/n; campsites per person AR$35; wi-fi) You won't find a much more sublime location for an urban campground: perched on an island in between two burbling creeks, with all the facilities, plus fully equipped cabins (three-night minimum).

★ **Hostería Chimehuín** HOTEL $$

(☎02972-491132; www.interpatagonia.com/hosteriachimehuin; cnr Coronel Suárez & 25 de Mayo; s/d AR$300/450; wi-fi) This is a beautiful spot a few minutes from the center of town. Book early and you'll have a good chance of snagging a room with a balcony overlooking the creek. Either way, rooms are big, warm and comfortable and the whole place has a tranquil air to it.

Rüpú Calel HOTEL $$

(☎02972-491569; Coronel Suárez 560; s/d AR$350/400; wi-fi) While they may look big and bare to some, the rooms here have a pleasing simplicity and are sparkling clean, as are the spacious bathrooms.

Eating

Junín's dining scene is slowly improving. Local specialties such as trout, wild boar and venison may be available.

Sigmund ARGENTINE $

(Juan M de Rosas 690; mains AR$60-90; ⌚noon-midnight; wi-fi) Fabulous trendy eatery with colorful artsy decor, healthy food and great *onda* (vibe). Choose from dozens of pizzas, pasta, sandwiches and salads, all delivered with friendly service.

Lespos PIZZERIA $

(Domingo Milanesio 520; mains AR$60-90; ⌚12pm-1am) An inviting little pizza and burger bar, with a better atmosphere than most. There's a wide range of pizzas on offer and a good music selection seals the deal.

Ruca Hueney PARRILLA $$

(☎02792-491113; cnr Colonel Suárez & D Milanesio; mains AR$80-120; ⌚12pm-12am; wi-fi) Ruca Hueney, Junín's oldest restaurant, is reliable and has the most extensive menu in town. Portions are large; service is abrupt. There's a cheaper takeout counter next door in case you were thinking about a picnic at the park across the street.

Orientation

The center is between the highway and the river. Don't confuse Av San Martín, runs on the west side of Plaza San Martín, with Félix San Martín, two blocks west.

Information

Banco de la Provincia de Neuquén (Av San Martín, btwn Coronel Suárez & General Lamadrid; 9am-1pm Mon-Fri) Opposite the plaza.

Club Andino Junín de los Andes (cnr Milanesio & Suárez local 3; 9am-6pm daily in summer, 3pm-6pm Mon-Fri rest of year) Behind the tourist office, this mountaineering club provides information on the Volcán Tromen climb as well as other excursions within the Parque Nacional Lanín.

Lanin National Park Office (02972-491160; cnr Milanesio & Suárez; 8am-9pm) Inside the tourist office. Has information on Parque Nacional Lanín.

Post Office (cnr Coronel Suárez & Don Bosco; 8am-6pm Mon-Fri, 9am-1pm Sat)

Tourist Office (02792-491160; junindelosandes.gov.ar; cnr Milanesio & Suárez; 8am-9pm) Enthusiastically helpful staff. Fishing permits and a list of licensed fishing guides available.

Getting There & Away

Junín and San Martín de los Andes share Chapelco airport, which lies midway between the two towns. There are regularly scheduled flights to Buenos Aires and Neuquén. A *remise* into town should run you about AR$60. Another option is walking the 1km out to the highway and flagging down a passing bus (AR$15, 25 minutes).

The **bus terminal** (02792-492038; cnr Olavarría & Félix San Martín) is three blocks from the main plaza. El Petróleo goes three times a week to Aluminé (AR$32, three hours).

BUSES FROM JUNÍN DE LOS ANDES

DESTINATION	COST (AR$)	DURATION (HR)
Buenos Aires	1164	22
Neuquén	319	6
San Martín de los Andes	30	1
Zapala	132	3

Aluminé

02942 / POP 4600 / ELEV 400M

Time seems to have stopped for Aluminé and, although it's an important tourist destination, it is less visited than destinations to the south. Situated 103km north of Junín de los Andes via RP23, it's a popular fly-fishing destination and offers access to the less-visited northern sector of Parque Nacional Lanín. The Río Aluminé also offers excellent white-water rafting and kayaking.

Sights & Activities

The tourist office keeps a list of available **fishing** guides and also sells fishing licenses (costing AR$180/540/720 per day/week/season).

Traditional Communities VILLAGES

The nearby Mapuche communities of **Aigo** and **Salazar**, on the 26km dirt road to **Lago Ruca Choroi** (in Parque Nacional Lanín), sell traditional weavings, araucaria pine nuts and, in summer, *comidas tipicas* (traditional dishes). Salazar is an easy, signposted 12km walk or bike ride out of town – just follow the river. Aigo is another 14km along.

Aluminé Rafting OUTDOORS

(02942-496322; www.interpatagonia.com/aluminerafting; Conrado Villegas 610; 9am-6pm Mon-Sat) For rafting on the Río Aluminé (best in November), as well as kayaking, fly-fishing, trekking and rock climbing.

Sleeping & Eating

If you're traveling in a group, ask the tourist office about its list of self-catering cabins – some just out of town – that offer good value for three or more people. High season coincides with the November-through-April fishing season.

Nid Car HOTEL $

(02942-496131; nidcaralumine@yahoo.com.ar; cnr Christian Joubert & Benigar; s/d AR$150/200) Very standard and slightly spacious rooms just uphill from the plaza. Cheapest in town and not a bad deal as long as you're not fussy.

Hotel de la Aldea HOTEL $$

(02942-496340; www.hoteldelaaldea.com.ar; cnr RP23 & Crouzielles; r with town/river view AR$660/750;) A sprawling brick wonderland out on the highway (a two-minute walk from the center of town), the Aldea is comfortable enough with modern, slightly cramped rooms. It's definitely worth paying the extra for the river views.

La Posta del Rey ARGENTINE $$

(C Joubert 336; mains AR$80-120; 8am-11pm;) Located inside the Hostería Aluminé, this is the best eating option in town, serving up all the Argentine standards plus some good Patagonian favorites such as lamb, venison and trout.

Information

Banco del Provincia del Neuquén (cnr Conrado Villegas & Torcuato Mordarelli; ⏰Mon-Fri 9am-1pm) Bank and ATM.

Tourist Office (☎02942-496001; info@alumine.gov.ar; Christian Joubert, Plaza San Martín; ⏰8am-8pm mid-Mar–Nov, 9am-9pm Dec–mid-Mar) For local info and maps, fishing permits, road conditions etc.

Getting There & Away

Aluminé's **bus terminal** (☎02941-496048) is just downhill from the plaza, an easy walk to any of the hotels listed here. Aluminé Viajes and Albus go daily to/from Neuquén (AR$195, six hours), Zapala (AR$110, three to 3½ hours) and San Martín de los Andes (AR$84, 4½ hours). There's one bus a day to Villa Pehuenia (AR$30, one hour) at 7:30pm.

Villa Pehuenia

☎02942 / POP 700 / ELEV 1200M

Villa Pehuenia is an idyllic little lakeside village situated on the shores of Lago Aluminé, 102km north of Junín de los Andes (via RP23 and Aluminé) and 120km west of Zapala, via RP13. There are several Mapuche communities nearby, including Puel, located between Lago Aluminé and Lago Moquehue.

The village lies at the heart of the Pehuen region, named of course after the pehuén (araucaria) trees that are so marvelously present. If you have a car, the Circuito Pehuenia is a great drive; it's a four- to six-hour loop from Villa Pehuenia past Lago Moquehue, Lago Ñorquinco, Lago Pulmarí and back around Lago Aluminé. Mali Viajes in Aluminé offers scenic back-road tours along this route in summer, starting from Aluminé.

Sights & Activities

Volcán Batea Mahuida VOLCANO

From the top of here (2010m) you can see eight volcanoes (from Lanín to the south to Copahue to the north) in both Argentina and Chile. Inside Batea Mahuida is a small crater lake. You drive nearly to the top (summer only) and then it's an easy two-hour walk to the summit.

Batea Mahuida SKIING

(☎02942-467711; www.cerrobateamahuida.com.ar; day pass AR$150-200) Volcán Batea Mahuida is the location of this small Mapuche-operated ski park, which is little more than a few snowy slopes with a T-bar and a Poma. If you're a Nordic skier, you're in better luck – a circuit goes around the park, taking in awesome views of the volcano and lakes.

Los Pehuenes ADVENTURE SPORTS

(☎02942-498029; www.pehuenes.com.ar; Centro Comercial; ⏰9am-1pm & 4-8pm) The local adventure-tourism operator offers rafting, trekking, horseback riding and 4WD off-roading trips.

Sleeping & Eating

Many businesses in Villa Pehuenia close down off season. Those listed here are open year-round. *Hosterías* and *cabañas* are spread around the Peninsula de los Coihues.

Hostería de las Cumbres HOTEL $$

(☎02942-498097; www.posadalascumbre.com.ar; d AR$500; 📶) Right down by the waterfront in the main part of town, this cozy little *hostería* has smallish rooms coming off way-narrow corridors. Lake views from the front rooms, however, make this one a winner.

★**La Escondida** HOTEL $$$

(☎02942-15-691166; www.posadalaescondida.com; r from AR$1700; 📶) A small *posada* (inn) tucked away down by the lakefront. There are just six rooms, all fitted out in fine detail and with decks overlooking the water. Sitting areas are sumptuous, the restaurant is one of the best in the village and there are good value cabins (without water views) on offer if you're traveling in a group.

Parador del Lago ARGENTINE $

(mains AR$60-120; ⏰11am-11pm; 📶) A fine selection of Patagonian goodies served up on pizzas, pastas and a few plated meals. Also boasts a great deck overlooking the lake and a small selection of microbrew beers.

Information

Banco de la Provincia del Neuquén (RP13 s/n; ⏰9am-1pm Mon-Fri) Next to the police station; has an ATM.

Oficina de Turismo (☎02942-498044; www.villapehuenia.gov.ar; RP13 s/n; ⏰9am-8pm) At the entrance to town; is extremely helpful and provides good maps of the region.

Getting There & Around

Exploring the area is tough without a car, though hitchhiking is definitely feasible in summer. **Destinos Patagonicos** (☎02942-498067; Centro Comercial) is the representative for Albus, the only bus company currently serving the village.

There are daily buses to Zapala (AR$159, 4½ hours), Neuquén (AR$254, seven hours) and Aluminé (AR$30, one hour).

Caviahue

☎02948 / POP 610 / ELEV 1600M

On the western shore of Lago Caviahue, the ski village of Caviahue lies at the southeast foot of Volcán Copahue. A better-looking village than Copahue, this one is growing rapidly, too – construction noise fills the air during summer.

Activities

Walks — WALKING

There are some good short walks from the village, including a popular day trek that goes up past the **Cascada Escondida** waterfall to **Laguna Escondida**. Another walk to the four waterfalls known as **Cascadas Agrio** starts from across the bridge at the entrance to town. The tourist office has an excellent map showing these and other walks around the area.

Hotel Caviahue — SPA

(treatments from AR$45) If you fancy a spot of pampering, this hotel has a day spa where you can enjoy a thermal bath and treatments.

Centro de Ski Cerro Caviahue — SKIING

(☎02948-495043; www.caviahue.com) A little under 2km west of Caviahue, this ski resort has seven chairlifts, and four Pomas, which take skiers all the way up to the peak of Volcán Copahue (2953m). Equipment hire (skis/snowboard around AR$140 per day) is also available on the mountain or in the village. Adult day passes range from AR$233 to AR$338, depending on the season.

Tours

Caviahue Tours — HIKING, OUTDOORS

(☎02948-495138; www.caviahuetours.com; Av Bialous Centro Comercial local 11; ⏲9am-1pm & 4-8pm) If you have a taste for adventure, this company organizes treks, including to Laguna Termal and Volcán Copahue, rents mountain bikes in summer and offers dog-sledding trips in winter.

Sleeping & Eating

Hebe's House — HOSTEL $

(☎02948-495238; www.hebeshouse.com.ar; Mapuche & Puesta del Sol; dm/d AR$150/420; ⏲Dec-Sep; 📶) Hebe crams them in to cozy but cramped dorms. It's set in a cute alpine building and offers kitchen access, laundry facilities and plenty of tourist information. If you're coming in winter, book well ahead.

Hotel Caviahue — HOTEL $$

(☎02948-495044; hotelcaviahue@issn.gov.ar; 8 de Abril s/n; s/d AR$500/700; 📶) A rambling, older-style hotel set up the hill, with views out over the village, lake and mountains. It's the only hotel open in the village year-round. Rates drop around 30% off-season. Also on the premises is the only restaurant (mains AR$60 to AR$100) in town to stay open year-round.

Information

Oficina de Turismo (☎02948-495036; www.caviahue-copahue.gov.ar; ⏲9am-8pm) At the entrance to town. Good maps and up-to-date info on local accommodations. There's another office in the *municipalidad* (city hall).

Getting There & Away

One bus daily runs to Neuquén (AR$157, 6½ hours) via Zapala (AR$110, 3½ hours). If you're headed for Chos Malal, you can shave a couple of hours off your travel time by getting off in Las Lajas (AR$78, 2½ hours) and waiting for a bus there. Check your connection times with the bus company **Cono Sur** (☎02942-432607) though – if you're going to get stranded, Zapala is the place to do it.

Copahue

☎02948 / ELEV 2030M

This small thermal springs resort stands on the northeastern side of its namesake volcano among steaming, sulfurous pools, including a bubbling hot-mud pool, the popular **Laguna del Chancho** (admission AR$15; ⏲8am-6pm). The setting, in a natural amphitheater formed by the mountain range, is spectacular, but the town isn't much to look at.

Copahue has been gaining in popularity, mainly with Argentine tourists, as the growth in tourist infrastructure shows. Due to snow cover, the village is only open from the start of December to the end of April.

The village centers on the large, modern **Complejo Termal Copahue** (☎0299-442-4140; www.termasdecopahue.com; Ortiz Velez; baths AR$45, spa treatments from AR$40), which offers a wide range of curative bathing programs.

The best hotel in the village, **Hotel Termas** (☎02948-495525; www.hoteltermascopahue.com.ar; Doucloux s/n; s/d from AR$450/628; 📶), features modern rooms, atmospheric common areas and an excellent restaurant serving both traditional Argentine and regional foods.

Residencial Codihue (☎02948-495543; codihue@futurtel.com.ar; Velez s/n; s/d AR$320/480) is the best budget option in town, with simple rooms just down the road from the thermal baths complex. Full board is available.

Parrillada Nito (Zambo Jara s/n; mains AR$80-150; ⏲12-11:30pm) is the most frequently recommended *parrilla* in town.

In summer, one bus runs on a daily basis to Neuquén (AR$187, seven hours) via Zapala (AR$117, four hours). There are no scheduled departures to Neuquén for the remainder of the year.

THE MAPUCHE

The Lake District's most prevalent indigenous group, the Mapuche, originally came from Chilean territory. They resisted several attempts at subjugation by the Inca and fought against Spanish domination for nearly 300 years. Their move into Argentina began slowly. Chilean Mapuche were making frequent voyages across the Andes in search of trade as far back as the 17th century. Some chose to stay. In the 1880s the exodus became more pronounced as the Chilean government moved into Mapuche land, forcing them out.

Another theory for the widespread move is that, for the Mapuche, the *puelmapu* (eastern land) holds a special meaning, as it is believed that all good things (such as the sun) come from the east.

Apart from trade, the Mapuche (whose name means 'people of the land' in Mapudungun, their language) have traditionally survived as small-scale farmers and hunter-gatherers. There is no central government – each extended family has a *lonko* (chief) and in times of war families would unite to elect a *toqui* (axe-bearer) to lead them.

The role of *machi* (shaman) was and still is an important one in Mapuche society. It is usually filled by a woman, whose responsibilities included performing ceremonies for curing diseases, warding off evil, dreamwork, and influencing weather, harvests, social interactions. The *machi* was also well schooled in the use of medicinal herbs but, as Mapuche access to land and general biodiversity in the region has decreased, this knowledge is being lost.

Estimates of how many Mapuche live in Argentina vary according to the source. The official census puts the number at around 300,000, while the Mapuche claim that the real figure is closer to 500,000.

Both in Chile and Argentina, the Mapuche live in humble circumstances in rural settings, or leave the land to find work in big cities. It is estimated that there are still 200,000 fluent Mapudungun speakers in Chile, where nominal efforts are made to revive the language in the education system. No such official program has been instituted in Argentina and, while exact numbers are not known, it is feared that the language here may soon become extinct.

Apart from loss of language, the greatest threat to Mapuche culture is the loss of land, a process that has been under way ever since their lands were 'redistributed' after the Conquest of the Desert and many Mapuche were relocated to reserves – often the lowest-quality land, without any spiritual significance to them. As with many indigenous peoples, the Mapuche have a special spiritual relationship with the land, believing that certain rocks, mountains, lakes and so on have a particular spiritual meaning.

Despite a relatively well-organized land-rights campaign, the relocation continues today, as Mapuche lands are routinely reassigned to large commercial interests in the oil, cattle and forestry industries. Defiant to the end, the Mapuche don't look like fading away any time soon. They see their cultural survival as intrinsically linked to economic independence and Mapuche-owned and -operated businesses are scattered throughout the Lake District.

1

GRANT DIXON/GETTY IMAGES ©

2
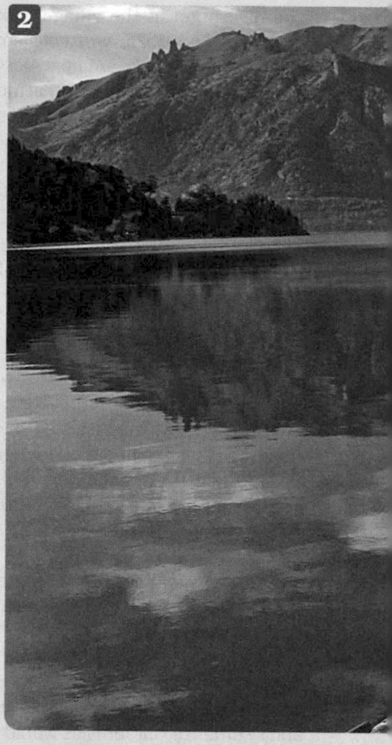

4
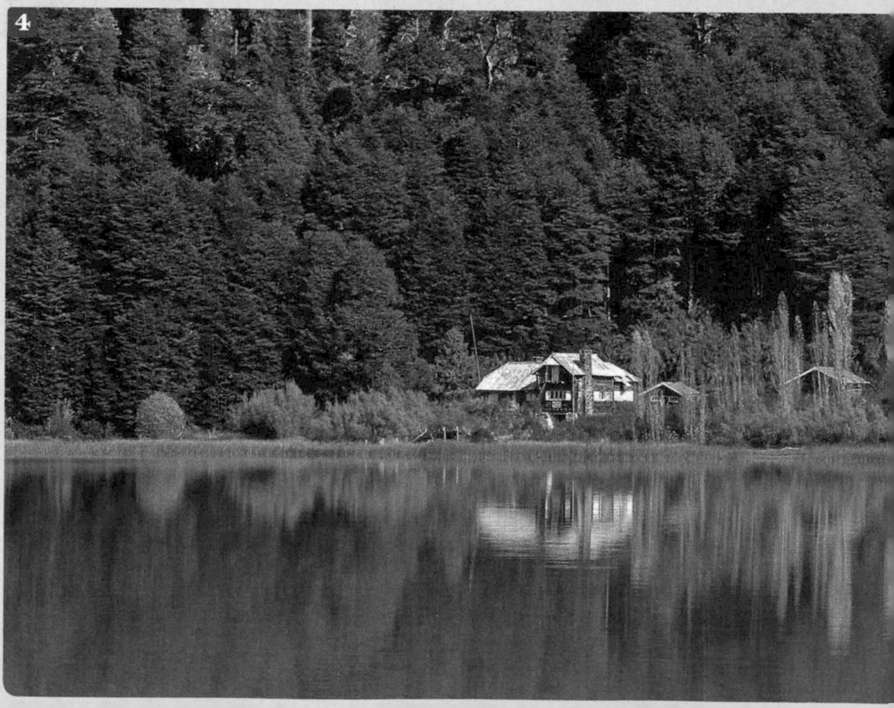

TUNART/GETTY IMAGES ©

THIRD CLIFF IMAGERY/ALAMY ©

THEO ALLOFS/CORBIS ©

1. Centro Cívico (p355)
Bariloche's civic center contains many log-and-stone buildings.

2. Lago Gutiérrez (p365)
Set up camp on the shore of this Lake District beauty, part of the Parque Nacional Nahuel Huapi.

3. Bariloche (p355)
The city's architecture has a Patagonian twist, using local hardwoods and unique stone construction techniques.

4. Parque Nacional Nahuel Huapi (p362)
This park was created to preserve local flora and fauna.

Chos Malal

☎02948 / POP 13,100 / ELEV 862M

Cruising through the stark, desertlike landscape north of Zapala doesn't really prepare you for arrival at this pretty little oasis town. Set at the convergence of Río Neuquén and Río Curi Leuvú, the town boasts two main plazas, bearing the names of the two superheroes of Argentina – San Martín and Sarmiento. Around the former is the majority of the historic buildings, including the Fuerte IV Division fort (go around the back for sweeping views out over the river valley). Five blocks south is Plaza Sarmiento, where you'll find banks and businesses.

Sleeping & Eating

Most accommodations are located between the two plazas. People in Chos Malal eat a lot of goat, and you may find yourself doing the same while you're there.

Alto Chos Malal HOTEL $
(☎02948-421263; www.altochosmalal.com.ar; Jujuy 60; s/d AR$200/300, apt AR$550;) The best budget deal in town has clean, spacious rooms half a block from Plaza Sarmiento.

Hostería Don Costa HOTEL $$
(☎02948-421652; www.doncostaweb.com.ar; Sarmiento 234; s/d AR$350/450;) Attractive, modern rooms set well back from the road in case Chos Malal ever has a noisy night. Rooms are on the small side (like, door-bumping-bed small), but excellent value for the price. Get one upstairs for a balcony, sunlight and ventilation.

Las Delicias de L'Traful BAKERY $
(Roca 80; pastries from AR$10; 7:30am-1:30pm & 4:30-9:30pm) A small bakery-cafe serving up yummy, super-fresh baked goods and excellent coffee.

El Viejo Caicallén PARRILLA $$
(General Paz 345; mains AR$80-110; noon-11pm Mon-Sat) The best *parrilla* in town is at this happy place, offering all sorts of meat dishes, pastas, salads and sandwiches. There are usually a couple of regional faves such as black butter trout and grilled goat to choose from, too.

Information

Banco de la Nación (cnr Sarmiento & Urquiza; 9am-1pm Mon-Fri) Has an ATM.

Hospital Zonal Gregorio Avárez (☎02948-421400; cnr Entre Ríos & Flores) English speaker usually on-site.

Tourist Information (☎02948-421425; turnorte@neuquen.gov.ar; 25 de Mayo 89; 8am-9pm) Has good maps of the town and surrounds.

Getting There & Away

Regular buses depart for Zapala (AR$105, three hours), Neuquén (AR$223, six hours). There's one bus per day to Varvarco (AR$80, three hours) at 2pm. Two minibuses a day leave for Buta Ranquil (AR$50, two hours) – if you want to connect to the bus for Mendoza catch the 4:30pm one.

North along the Ruta Nacional 40

Following the RN40 north from Chos Malal gives you more wild desert scenery, tiny windswept towns and expansive, empty vistas. Despite what many will tell you, there *is* public transportation along this route. **Transportes Leader** (☎in Buta Ranquil 02948-493268; cnr Malvinas & Jadull) runs minibuses between Buta Ranquil and San Rafael, Monday to Saturday (AR$231). There's a regular bus service from Neuquén and Chos Malal to Buta Ranquil, where you may get stuck for the night. There's no real reason to be here, but there are a couple of cheap hotels, one nice one, and enough restaurant-cafes to keep you from starving.

Zapala

☎02942 / POP 32,100 / ELEV 1200M

Taking its name as an adaptation of the Mapuche word *chapadla* (dead swamp), Zapala got off to a bad start, image-wise. Not much has changed. This is a humble little place where the locals amuse themselves with walks up and down the main street, punctuated by lengthy pauses on street corners.

Sights & Activities

The main excuse for rolling through town is to visit the nearby Parque Nacional Laguna Blanca, with its awesome array of birdlife, or to take advantage of the town's bus connections for the rarely visited northern reaches of the Lake District.

WORTH A TRIP

LAGUNA TERMAL TREK

This day trip, which should be possible in around eight hours, is easy enough to do on your own, leaving from Copahue. Due to snow conditions, it's only possible from December to April unless you bring special equipment. If you'd like to take the side route to the peak of Volcán Copahue, it's recommended that you go with an experienced guide. Caviahue Tours is among the many tour operators offering guides on this route.

From the Hotel Valle del Volcán at the upper (southwest) edge of the village, cross the little footbridge and climb briefly past a life-size statue of the Virgin. The well-worn foot track leads across a sparsely vegetated plain towards the exploded cone of Volcán Copahue, dipping down to lush, green lawns by the northern shore of the Lagunas Las Mellizas' western 'twin.' Follow a path along the lake's north side past little black-sand beaches and gushing springs on its opposite shore, to reach the start of a steam pipeline, one to 1¼ hours from the village. The roaring of steam from the subterranean Copahue Geothermal Field entering the *vapoducto* and irregular explosive blasts of discharging steam can be heard along much of the trek. Cross the lake outlet – further downstream is a wide, easy ford – then cut up southwest over snowdrifts past a tarn to meet a 4WD track at the edge of a small waterlogged meadow. Turn right and follow this rough road up around left (or take a vague trail marked with white paint splashes to its right until you come back to the road on a rocky ridge below a wooden cross). The 4WD track continues westward up through a barren volcanic moonscape to end under a tiny glacier on the east flank of Volcán Copahue, 1¼ to 1½ hours from the pipeline.

Ascend southwest over bouldery ridges, crossing several small mineral-and-melt-water streams. To the northwest, in Chile, the ice-smothered Sierra Velluda and the near-perfect snowy cone of Volcán Antuco rise up majestically. From the third streamlet (with yellowy, sulfur-encrusted sides), cut along the slope below a hot spring then climb to the top of a prominent gray-pumice spur that lies on the international border. Ascend the spur until it becomes impossibly steep, then traverse up rightward over loose slopes into a gap to reach Laguna Termal, 1¼ to 1½ hours from the end of the 4WD track (3½ to 4¼ hours from Copahue).

Filling Volcán Copahue's eastern crater, this steaming hot lake feeds itself by melting the snout of a glacier that forms a massive rim of ice above its back wall. Sulfurous fumes often force trekkers to retreat from the lake, but these high slopes also grant a wonderful vista across the vast basin (where both villages are visible) between the horseshoe-shaped Lago Caviahue (Lago Agrio) and the elongated Lago Trolope to the northeast. From here, more experienced trekkers can continue up to the summit of Volcán Copahue.

To get back to Copahue, retrace your ascent route. If you have a decent map of the area, you can follow the Arroyo Caviahue (Río Agrio) and RN26 back to town.

Warning

Particularly on windy days, acrid fumes rising from Laguna Termal can be overpowering due to sulfur dioxide gas (which attacks your airways). Approach the lake cautiously – don't even consider swimming in it. Less experienced trekkers are advised to go with an organized tour.

Centro Cultural ARTS CENTER
(San Martín & Chaneton; ⌚5-10pm) In front of the plaza, this hosts concerts and shows work by local artists and recently released Hollywood blockbusters.

Festivals

Zapala's **Feria de la Tradición**, held in the second week in November, showcases regional culture, with plenty of folk music, gaucho horse skill demonstrations, handicraft exhibits plus some delicious regional food on sale.

Sleeping & Eating

Be aware that Zapala has very limited accommodations options.

OFF THE BEATEN TRACK

NORTH OF CHOS MALAL

Heading north from Chos Malal brings you to a couple of wonderful, rarely visited attractions. Public transportation is rare and often nonexistent, but if you have the time and patience you'll be well rewarded.

Parque Archaeologico Colo Michi-Co

This small archaeological site features one of the most important collections of Pehuenche rock art in Patagonia. There are over 600 examples here, carved with symbolic figures and abstract designs. Getting to the site without a private vehicle is tricky. Buses leave Chos Malal at 2pm daily for the village of Varvarco (AR$80, three hours). From there, it's 9km south on the RP39 to the Escuela Colo Michi-Co (buses will drop you off), where you'll see a signpost leading to the park, an 8km walk away. Bring everything – there's nothing out here.

If all that walking doesn't excite you, contact **Señora La Gallega** (☎02948-421329) in Varvarco – there aren't any *remises* (taxis) there, but the señora should be able to hook you up with a car and driver, charging around AR$12 per kilometer, plus waiting time. Hitchhiking is common practice in the area, but be prepared for long waits.

Aguas Calientes

These excellent natural outdoor hot springs located at the foot of the Volcán Domuyo are spread over 20 sq km and feature three main sites. The main one at Villa Aguas Calientes is suitable for swimming; Las Olletas is a collection of bubbling mud pits and Los Tachos are geysers, spurting up to heights of 2m. The site is 40km north of Varvarco, where the last public transport terminates. If you don't have your own wheels and can get to Varvarco on your own, you can ask about hiring a driver with Señora La Gallega.

Hotel Pehuén HOTEL $
(☎02942-423135; cnr Etcheluz & Elena de la Vega; s/d AR$240/320; 📶) Despite its (rather mysterious) two-star status, this is the best budget deal in town, conveniently near the bus terminal, with clean rooms, an attractive (classy, even) lobby and a good restaurant below.

Hotel Hue Melén HOTEL $$
(☎02942-432109; www.hotelhuemelen.com; Almirante Brown 929; s/d AR$400/600; ❄📶) You may be faintly surprised by the quiet stylishness of this hotel-casino complex. King-size beds, full bathtubs, contemporary art on the walls...it's wonderful what gambling money can buy you.

El Chancho Rengo CAFE $
(cnr Av San Martín & Etcheluz; sandwiches AR$30-50; ⏰8am-11:30pm) It's reasonably likely that half the town saunters in here for an espresso every day. Its outdoor tables and good coffee and sandwiches make it great for a light bite.

Mayrouba ARGENTINE $$
(cnr Monti & Etcheluz; mains AR$80-120; ⏰8am-1am; 📶) The best-looking restaurant in town also serves up some of the tastiest fare. There are shades of Middle Eastern influence on the menu and Patagonian faves such as smoked trout. If you're up for a few drinks, it turns into a bar later on, with an impressive cocktail list.

Information

Banco de la Provincia del Neuquén (cnr Av San Martín & Etcheluz; ⏰9am-1pm Mon-Fri) Bank with ATM.

Laguna Blanca National Park Office (☎02942-431982; lagunablanca@apn.gov.ar; Av Ejercito Argentino 217; ⏰8am-3pm Mon-Fri) For information on Parque Nacional Laguna Blanca.

Tourist Office (☎02942-424296; RN22, Km1398; ⏰7am-9pm) Located on the highway, 2km west of town center.

Getting There & Away

Zapala's **bus terminal** (☎02942-421370; Etcheluz & Uriburu) is located about four blocks from Av San Martín. During summer there are frequent bus departures for Copahue (AR$117, four hours).

BUSES FROM ZAPALA

DESTINATION	COST (AR$)	DURATION (HR)
Aluminé	110	3½
Buenos Aires	1010	18
Chos Malal	105	3
Caviahue	105	3
Junín de los Andes	132	3
Laguna Blanca	28	½
Neuquén	98	3
San Martín de los Andes	154	3½
Temuco (Chile)	290	6
Villa Pehuenia	159	4½

Parque Nacional Laguna Blanca

At 1275m above sea level and surrounded by striking volcanic deserts, Laguna Blanca is only 10m deep, an interior drainage lake that formed when lava flows dammed two small streams. Only 30km southwest of Zapala, the lake is too alkaline for fish but hosts many bird species, including coots, ducks, grebes, upland geese, gulls and even a few flamingos. The 112.5-sq-km park primarily protects the habitat of the black-necked swan, a permanent resident.

Starting 10km south of Zapala, paved and well-marked RP46 leads through the park toward the town of Aluminé. If you're catching a bus, ask the driver to drop you off at the information center. If you don't have your own transport, ask at the National Parks office in Zapala if you can get a ride out with the rangers in the morning. A taxi to the park should charge around AR$320, including two hours' waiting time.

There is a small improved campground with windbreaks, but bring all your own food. There's a **visitor center** (9am-6pm Fri-Sun) with information displays and maps of walking trails, but there's no place to eat.

Neuquén

0299 / POP 231,200 / ELEV 265M

There are only two reasons to stop in Neuquén – the wealth of paleontological sites in the surrounding area, and the three excellent wineries just out of town. That said, the town has a strangely hypnotic effect, with its wide, tree-lined boulevards and liberal smattering of plazas.

At the confluence of the Río Neuquén and the Río Limay, Neuquén is the province's easternmost city. Most travelers hit Neuquén en route to more glamorous destinations in Patagonia and the Lake District – the town is the area's principal transport hub, with good connections to Bariloche and other Lake District destinations, to the far south and to Chile. Paved highways go east to the Río Negro valley, west toward Zapala and southwest toward Bariloche.

Sights

Wineries WINERY

Just outside of town are three of the most important Patagonian wineries – **NQN** (0299-489-7500; www.bodeganqn.com.ar; RP7, Picada 15; 9am-1pm & 2-4pm Mon-Fri, 10:30am-4:30pm Sat & Sun), **Fin del Mundo** (0299-555-5330; www.bodegadelfindelmundo.com; RP8, Km9, San Patricio Del Chañar; 10am-4pm Mon-Fri, 10am-5pm Sat) and **Schroeder** (0299-489-9600; www.familiaschroeder.com; Calle 7 Nte, San Patricio del Chañar; admission AR$30; 9am-5pm Mon-Fri, 10:30am-5:30pm Sat & Sun). Access to the vineyards is almost impossible without your own vehicle, but Turismo Arauquen can get you out there, often in combination with a paleontological tour.

Museo Nacional de Bellas Artes MUSEUM

(cnr Bartolomé Mitre & Santa Cruz; 10am-8pm Mon-Sat, 4-8pm Sun) Showcases fine arts from the region and often features traveling exhibitions.

Tours

Turismo Arauquen GUIDED TOUR

(0299-442-6476; www.arauquen.com; H Yrigoyen 720; 9am-7pm Mon-Fri, 9am-1pm Sat) Offers guided visits to paleontology sites of Lago Barreales, Plaza Huincul and Villa El Chocón for about AR$260 per person (minimum four), which can be combined with winery visits (AR$200 per person). If you have fewer than four people, winery tours happen every Saturday, guaranteed.

Sleeping

Neuquén's hotels mainly cater to the business set. Overall, the hotels are fairly unexciting in all ranges and less than great value for budget travelers.

BIG, BIG BONES

In 1989 a local Neuquenian named Guillermo Heredia discovered a dinosaur bone on his property 7km east of the town of Plaza Huincul. Paleontologists investigated the site and later unearthed a dozen bones belonging to what they named *Argentinosaurus huinculensis* – the largest known dinosaur in the world. The gargantuan herbivore, dating from the mid-Cretaceous period, measured an incredible 40m long and 18m high.

The sheer size of the *Argentinosaurus huinculensis* is difficult to fathom, which is why stopping to gawk at the replica skeleton at Plaza Huincul's **Museo Municipal Carmen Funes** (☎0299-496-5486; Córdoba 55; AR$10; ⏲9am-7pm Mon-Fri, 10:30am-8:30pm Sat & Sun) is a humbling lesson in size.

Along with Parque Provincial Ischigualasto in San Juan province, Neuquén is one of the earth's dinosaur hot spots. Here, three important paleontology sites – Plaza Huincul, Villa El Chocón and Centro Paleontológico Lago Barreales – lie within a couple of hours' drive from Neuquén city and will delight anyone even slightly interested in dinosaurs.

About 80km southwest of Neuquén city, Villa El Chocón boasts the remains of the 100-million-year-old, 14m, eight-ton, meat-eating *Giganotosaurus Carolinii*, the world's largest known carnivore. Discovered in 1993 by fossil hunter Rubén Carolini, the dinosaur is even bigger than North America's better known Tyrannosaurus rex. El Chocón is also home to giant dinosaur footprints along the shore of Ezequiel Ramos Mexía reservoir. (One local confessed how families used to fire up *asados* – barbecues – in the footprints before they knew what they were!)

For true dino-freaks, the best place to satiate the hunger for bones is the **Centro Paleontológico Lago Barreales** (☎0299-15-4182295; www.proyectodino.com.ar; Costa Dinosaurio; AR$40; ⏲9am-7pm), located 90km northwest of Neuquén. Here you can actually work – as in get your hands dirty digging – on-site with paleontologists in one of the world's only fully functioning dinosaur excavation sites open to the public. You can visit the museum and take a guided tour of the site in about 1½ hours, but the real pleasure comes from the unique opportunity offered by sticking around. Prices (which help fund research) are US$105 for one day, US$270 for two days/one night, or about US$780 for three days/two nights. Bear in mind that this is a working archaeological site, and visits (even day trips) should be organized well in advance. Under the supervision of renowned paleontologist and project director Jorge Calvo, you'll spend your days dusting off Cretaceous-period bones and picking at fossils, and your nights in the silence of the desert. As Calvo says, 'when you set to work picking at the soft rock, uncovering fossilized leaves and bones that are 90 million years old, you forget about the rest of the world – some people even forget to eat.'

From Neuquén's bus terminal, there are regular buses to Plaza Huincul (AR$35, 1¾ hours), and all buses between Neuquén and Zapala stop there. There are also regular buses to Villa El Chocón from Neuquén (AR$28, 1¼ hours). Centro Paleontológico Lago Barreales is a bit more difficult to reach; contact the site for driving directions or possible transportation options (there are no buses to the site). If you drive, take RP51, not RN7.

Punto Patagonico Hostel HOSTEL $
(☎0299-447-9940; www.puntopatagonico.com; Periodistas Neuquinas 94; dm AR$90, d AR$250; @📶) Neuquén's best hostel is a good deal – it's well set up with comfy dorms, spacious lounge and a good garden area.

Bardas Hotel HOTEL $$
(☎0299-442-2403; www.bardashotel.com.ar; Roca 109; s/d AR$420/630, superior AR$800; ❄📶) One of the smaller hotels in town is also one of the best looking. If rooms had just a little more panache you'd be tempted to call this a boutique hotel. Rooms are modern, but vary widely – generally those at the front are more spacious.

Parque Hotel HOTEL $$
(☎0299-442-5806; www.parquehotelnqn.com.ar; Av Olascoaga 271; s/d AR$210/310; 📶) There are a few charming touches in the spacious, tile-floored rooms here. Some are showing their age these days, but most have good views out over the busy street below.

Eating & Drinking

The many *confiterías* along Av Argentina are all pleasant spots for breakfast and morning coffee. There are numerous bars and *confiterías* in the area north of Parque Central and around the meeting of the diagonals.

Tres Catorce INTERNATIONAL $

(9 de Julio 63; mains AR$60-140; ⏲12pm-1am Tue-Sun; 📶) Neuquén's dining scene has improved considerably over the years, with this casually stylish eatery at the forefront. On offer are carefully prepared dishes, thoughtful garnishes and a small but well-selected range of boutique wines.

La Nonna Francesa INTERNATIONAL $

(☎0299-430-0930; 9 de Julio 56; mains AR$70-120; ⏲12-11pm Mon-Sat) Some of Neuquén's finest dining can be found at this French-Italian trattoria – the pastas are all extremely good, but the trout dishes are the absolute standouts.

Confitería Donato CAFE $

(cnr JB Alberdi & Santa Fe; mains AR$45-80; ⏲8am-11pm; 📶) Plenty of dark wood paneling and brass fittings give this place an old-time feel and the wraparound seats may have you lounging around for hours. The menu runs the usual *confitería* gamut, with plenty of sandwiches, cakes and coffee on offer. There's live music Friday to Sunday nights and the occasional tango show – drop in for the schedule.

Shopping

Paseo de los Artesanos HANDICRAFTS

(Av Independencia, Parque Central; ⏲10am-9pm Wed-Sun) Neuquén's largest selection of regional handicrafts is at this outlet, north of the old train station.

Artesanías Neuquinas HANDICRAFTS

(Brown 280; ⏲8am-1pm & 5-9pm Mon-Fri, 9am-1pm Sat) This provincially sponsored store offers a wide variety of high-quality Mapuche textiles and wood crafts.

Orientation

Known as Félix San Martín in town, the east–west RN22 is the main thoroughfare, and lies a few blocks south of downtown. Be sure not to confuse it with Av San Martín (ie sans the 'Félix'), the obligatory homage to Argentina's national icon. The principal north–south street is Av Argentina, which becomes Av Olascoaga south of the old train station. Street names change on each side of Av Argentina and the old train station. Several diagonal streets bisect the conventional grid.

Information

Neuquén's dozens of travel agencies are almost all located near downtown. Several banks cluster around the corner of Av Argentina and Juan B. Justo have ATMs.

ACA (Automóvil Club Argentino; ☎0299-442-2325; Diagonal 25 de Mayo at Rivadavia) Argentina's auto club; good source for provincial road maps.

Cambio Pullman (Ministro Alcorta 144; ⏲9am-7pm Mon-Sat) Money exchange.

Post Office (cnr Rivadavia & Santa Fe; ⏲8am-6pm Mon-Fri, 9am-1pm Sat)

Provincial Tourist Office (☎0299-442-4089; www.neuquentur.gov.ar; Félix San Martín 182; ⏲7am-9pm) Great maps and brochures. There's a more centrally located kiosk (Olascoaga s/n; ⏲8am-8pm) in the Central Park, at the corner of Olascoaga.

Regional Hospital (☎0299-443-1474; Buenos Aires 421)

Getting There & Away

AIR

Neuquén's **airport** (☎0299-444-0525) is west of town on RN22. **Aerolíneas Argentina/Austral** (☎0299-442-2411, 0299-442-2410, 0299-442-2409; Santa Fe 52) flies to Buenos Aires four times daily Monday to Friday and twice daily on weekends.

BUS

Neuquén is a major hub for domestic and international bus services. Accordingly, its **bus terminal** (☎0299-445-2300; cnr Solalique y Ruta 22), about 3.5km west of Parque Central, is well decked out, with restaurants, gift stores and even a luggage carousel! To get downtown take either a Pehueche bus (AR$4.10; buy a ticket at local 41) or a taxi (AR$35).

Several carriers offer services to Chile: Albus goes to Temuco (AR$306, 9 hours) via Zapala and Paso Pino Hachado.

Neuquén is a jumping-off point for deep-south Patagonian destinations. Northern destinations such as Catamarca, San Juan, Tucumán, Salta and Jujuy may require a bus change in Mendoza, though the entire ticket can be purchased in Neuquén.

Buses from Neuquén

The following table lists daily departures to nearly all long-distance destinations; provincial destinations are served numerous times daily.

DESTINATION	COST (AR$)	DURATION (HR)
Aluminé	195	6
Bahía Blanca	344	7½
Buenos Aires	947	17
Chos Malal	223	6
Córdoba	765	16
El Bolsón	380	7
Esquel	469	10
Junín de los Andes	319	6
Mendoza	525	13
Puerto Madryn	480	11
Río Gallegos	1399	29
San Martín de los Andes	342	6
San Rafael	385	10
Viedma	310	8
Villa la Angostura	352	7
Zapala	98	3

Getting Around

Neuquén is a good province to explore by automobile, but drivers should be aware that RN22, both east along the Río Negro valley and west toward Zapala, is a rough road with heavy truck traffic. If you're looking for a rental car, **Turismo Arauquen** (☎ 0299-442-6476; www.arauquen.com; H Yrigoyen 720) has the best rates in town.

Patagonia

Includes ➡

Best National Parks & Reserves

- ➡ Parque Nacional Los Glaciares (p452, p464)
- ➡ Reserva Faunística Península Valdés (p406)
- ➡ Parque Nacional Torres del Paine (p479)

Best Places to Stay

- ➡ Bahía Bustamante (p421)
- ➡ Del Nomade Hostería Ecologica (p409)
- ➡ La Casa de Paula (p412)
- ➡ Tierra Patagonia (p485)
- ➡ Nothofagus B&B (p449)

Why Go?

On South America's southern frontier, nature grows wild, barren and beautiful. Spaces are large, as are the silences that fill them. For the newly arrived, such emptiness can be as impressive as the sight of Patagonia's jagged peaks, pristine rivers and dusty backwater oases. In its enormous scale, Patagonia offers an innumerable wealth of potential experiences and landscapes.

Though no longer a dirt road, lonely RN40 remains the iconic highway that stirred affection in personalities as disparate as Butch Cassidy and Bruce Chatwin. On the eastern seaboard, paved RN3 shoots south, connecting oil boomtowns with ancient petrified forests, Welsh settlements and the incredible Península Valdés. Then there is the other, trendy Patagonia where faux-fur hoodies outnumber the guanacos. Don't miss the spectacular sights of El Calafate and El Chaltén, but remember that they're a world apart from the solitude of the steppe.

When to Go

El Calafate

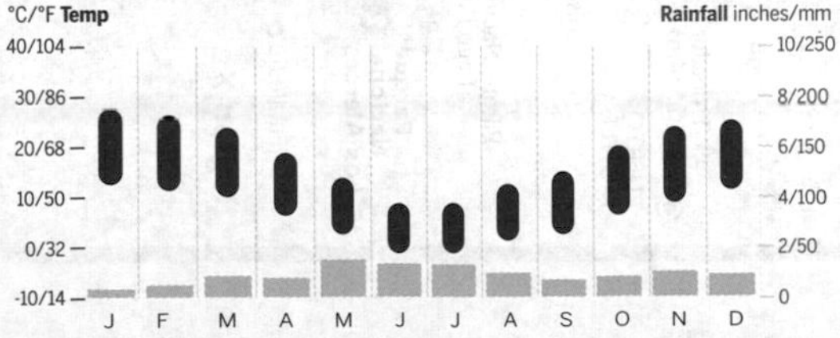

Nov–Mar The warmest months, ideal for *estancia* visits and driving Ruta 40.

Jun–mid-Dec Right whales migrate to Península Valdés.

Mid-Sep–early Mar Coastal fauna, including penguins, marine birds and sea lions, abounds.

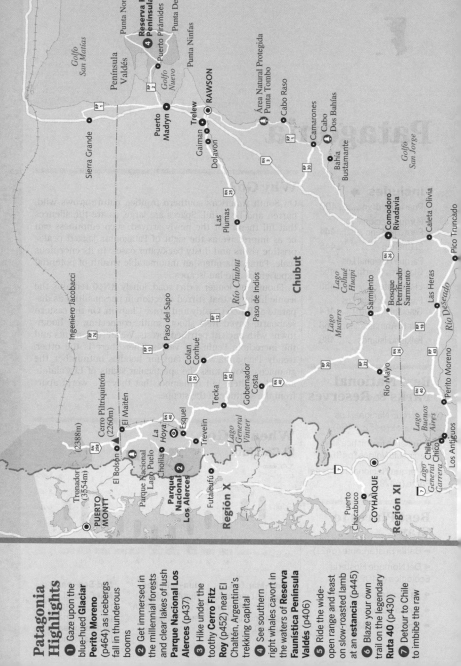

Patagonia Highlights

1. Gaze upon the blue-hued **Glaciar Perito Moreno** (p464) as icebergs fall in thunderous booms

2. Get immersed in the millennial forests and clear lakes of lush **Parque Nacional Los Alerces** (p437)

3. Hike under the toothy **Cerro Fitz Roy** (p452) near El Chaltén, Argentina's trekking capital

4. See southern right whales cavort in the waters of **Reserva Faunística Península Valdés** (p406)

5. Ride the wide-open range and feast on slow-roasted lamb at an **estancia** (p445)

6. Blaze your own trail on the legendary **Ruta 40** (p430)

7. Detour to Chile to imbibe the raw

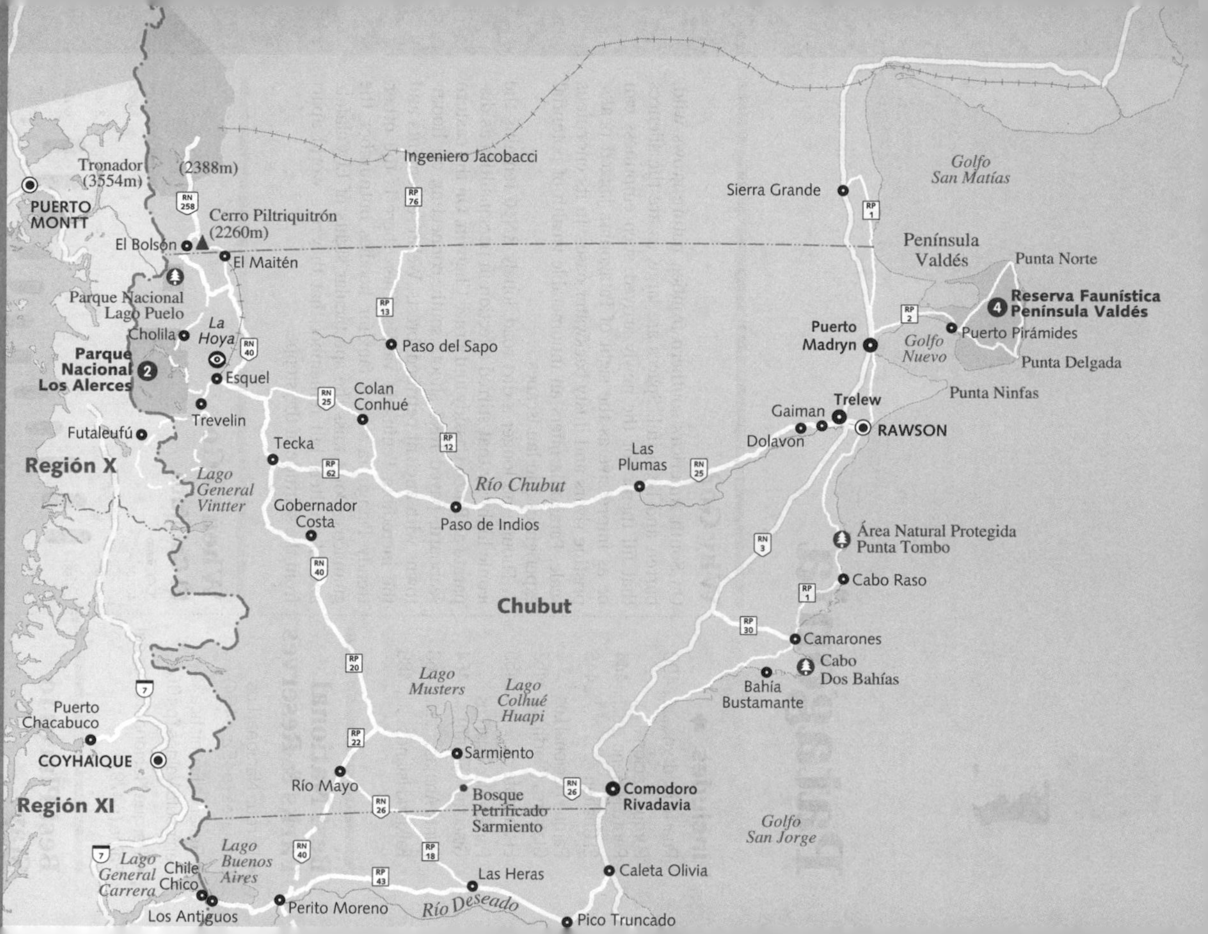

beauty of **Parque Nacional Torres del Paine** (p479)

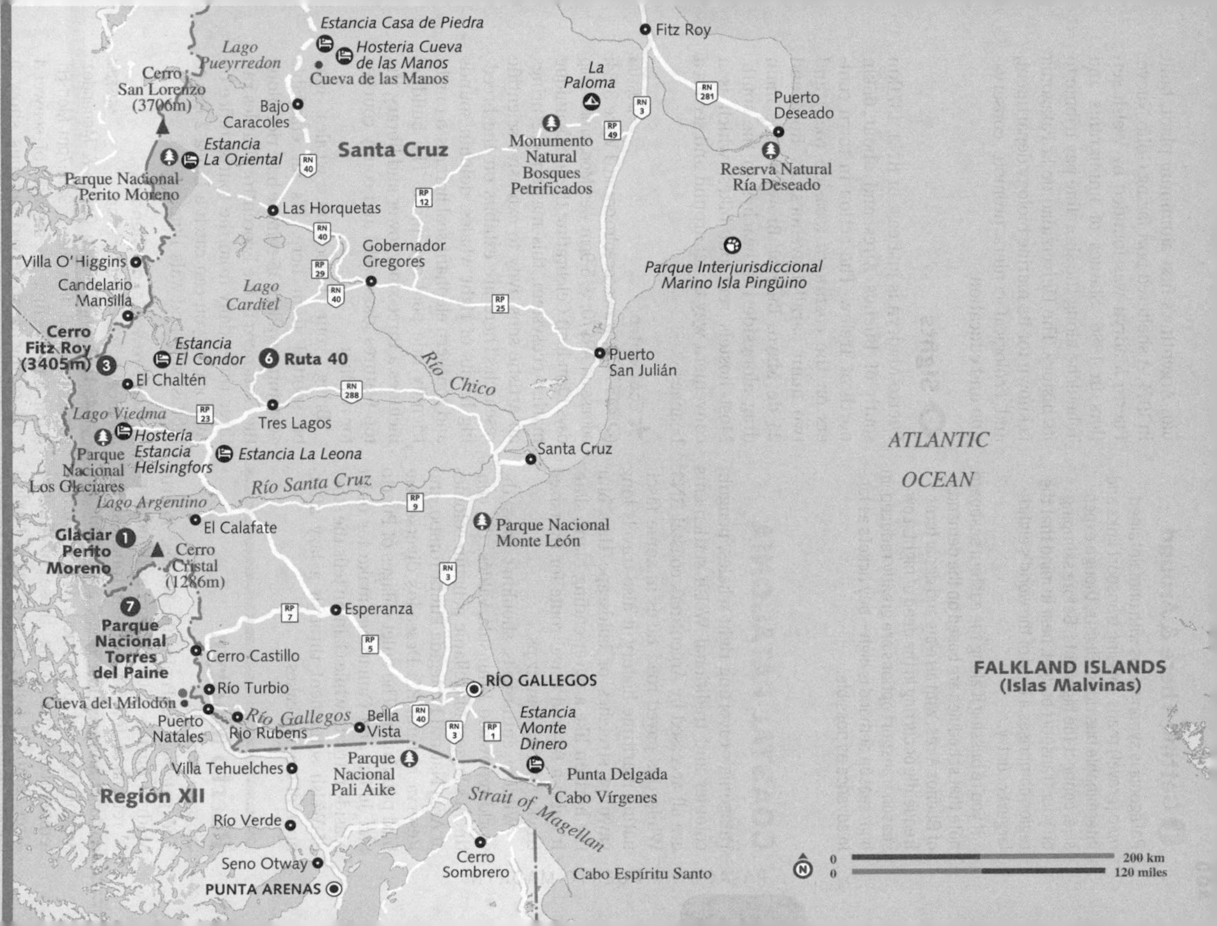

Getting There & Around

Patagonia is synonymous with unmaintained *ripio* (gravel) roads, missing transport links and interminable bus rides. Flights, though expensive, connect the highlights. Before skimping on your transport budget, bear in mind that the region comprises a third of the world's eighth-largest country.

If you're bussing it along the eastern seaboard, note that schedules are based on the demands of Buenos Aires, with arrivals and departures frequently occurring in the dead of night. Low-season transport options are greatly reduced. In high season demand is high – buy tickets as far in advance as possible.

COASTAL PATAGONIA

Patagonia's cavorting right whales, penguin colonies and traditional Welsh settlements are all accessed by Argentina's coastal RN3. While this paved road takes in some fascinating maritime history, it also travels long yawning stretches of landscape that blur the horizon like a never-ending blank slate. It's also a favored travel route for oversized trucks on long-haul trips.

Wildlife enthusiasts shouldn't miss the world-renowned Península Valdés, the continent's largest Magellanic penguin colonies at Área Natural Protegida Punta Tombo, and Reserva Natural Ría Deseado's diverse seabird population. The quiet villages of Puerto San Julián and Camarones make for quiet seaside retreats, while Gaiman tells the story of Welsh settlement through a lazy afternoon of tea and cakes.

Puerto Madryn

☎0280 / POP 81,300

The gateway to Península Valdés, Puerto Madryn bustles with tourism and industry. It retains a few small-town touches: the radio announces lost dogs, and locals are welcoming and unhurried. With summer temperatures matching those of Buenos Aires, Madryn holds its own as a modest beach destination, but from June to mid-December the visiting right whales take center stage. From July to September, these migrating whales come so close they can be viewed without taking a tour – either from the coast 20km north of town or from the town pier.

The sprawling city is the second-largest fishing port in the country and home to Aluar, Argentina's first aluminum plant, built in 1974. A sheltered port facing Golfo Nuevo, Puerto Madryn was founded by Welsh settlers in 1886. Statues of immigrants and Teheulche along the shoreline pay tribute to its history. The Universidad de la Patagonia is known for its marine biology department, and ecological centers promote conservation and education.

Sights

Puerto Madryn is just east of RN3, 1371km south of Buenos Aires and about 65km north of Trelew. The action in town centers on the *costanera* (seaside road) and two main parallel avenues, Av Roca and 25 de Mayo. Bulevar Brown is the main drag alongside the beaches to the south. Most hostels rent out bikes, which is a convenient way to get around and see area beaches.

★EcoCentro MUSEUM

(☎445-7470; www.ecocentro.org.ar; J Verne 3784; admission AR$70; ⏲5-9pm Wed-Mon, cruise ship days 10am-1pm) Celebrating the area's unique marine ecosystem, this masterpiece brings an artistic sensitivity to extensive scientific research. There are exhibits on the breeding habits of right whales, dolphin sounds and southern elephant-seal harems, a touch-friendly tide pool and more. The building includes a three-story tower and library, the top features glass walls and comfy couches for reading.

Bring your binoculars: whales may be spotted from here. It's an enjoyable 40-minute walk or 15-minute bike ride along the *costanera* to the Ecocentro. Shuttles run three times daily from the tourist office on Av Roca, or you can catch a Línea 2 bus to the last stop and walk 1km.

Museo Provincial de Ciencias Naturales y Oceanográfico MUSEUM

(☎445-1139; cnr Domecq García & Menéndez; admission AR$6, free Tue; ⏲9am-7pm Mon-Fri, 3-7pm Sat) Feeling up strands of seaweed and ogling a preserved octopus show a hands-on museum approach. The 1917 Chalet Pujol features marine and land mammal exhibits, preserved specimens, as well as collections of Welsh wares. Explanations in Spanish are geared to youth science classes, but the exhibits are visually informative and creatively presented. Make sure you head up to the cupola for views of the port.

Puerto Madryn

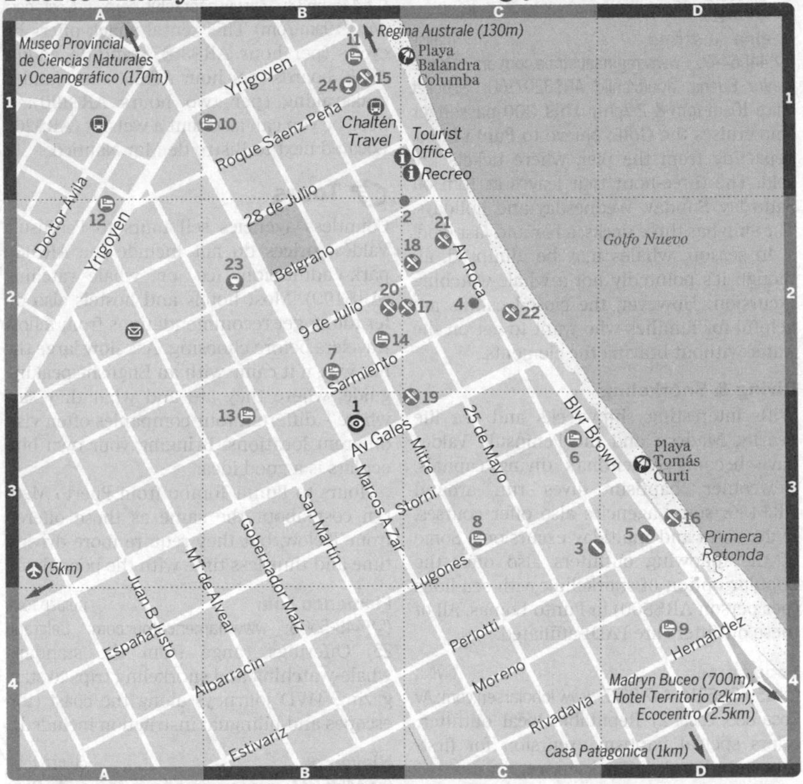

Puerto Madryn

Sights

1 Fundación Patagonia Natural B3

Activities, Courses & Tours

2 Flamenco Tour C2
3 Lobo Larsen C3
Napra Club .... (see 16)
4 Nievemar C2
5 Scuba Duba D3

Sleeping

6 Chepatagonia Hostel C3
7 El Gualicho B2
8 El Retorno C3
9 Hi! Patagonia Hostel D4
10 Hostería Las Maras B1
11 Hotel Bahía Nueva B1
12 La Casa de Tounens A2
13 La Tosca B3
14 Posada del Catalejo B2

Eating

15 Ambigú B1
16 Bistro de Mar Nautico D3
17 Bodegón C2
18 Guiseppe C2
19 Lupita C3
20 Mr Jones B2
21 Olinda C2
22 Plácido C2

Drinking & Nightlife

23 Cheers Patagonia B2
24 Margarita Bar B1

Fundación Patagonia Natural CONSERVATION ORGANIZATION
(☎445-1920; www.patagonianatural.org; Marcos A Zar 760; ⏲9am-4pm Mon-Fri) A well-run nongovernmental organization, Fundación Patagonia Natural promotes conservation and monitors environmental issues. Volunteers here diligently nurse injured birds and marine mammals to health.

Activities

Cruising

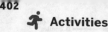

Regina Australe CRUISE

(☎4456447; www.reginaaustrale.com.ar; Muelle Piedra Buena; adult/child AR$320/160; ⊙ticket office 10am-1pm & 2-7pm) This 300-passenger ship cruises the Golfo Nuevo to Punta Lobo, departing from the pier, where tickets are sold. The three-hour tour leaves at 1pm on Saturday, Sunday, Wednesday and holidays. The ship has three decks, a bar and fast food.

In season, whales may be glimpsed, although it's pointedly not a whale-watching excursion. However, the closed cabins are helpful for families who want to get on the water without braving the elements.

Diving & Snorkeling

With interesting shipwrecks and sea life nearby, Madryn and the Península Valdés have become Argentina's diving capitals. Newcomer 'baptism' dives run around AR$450; some agencies also offer courses, night dives and multiday excursions. Some of the following outfitters also offer the popular option of snorkeling with sea lions (per person AR$800) in Punto Lomas. All of these outfitters are PADI-affiliated.

Lobo Larsen DIVING

(☎15-451-6314, 447-0277; www.lobolarsen.com; Av Roca 885, Local 2) Reputable local outfitter; offers special baptism excursion for first-timers and multilingual service.

Scuba Duba DIVING

(☎445-2699; www.scubaduba.com.ar; Blvr Brown 893) Quality operator.

Madryn Buceo DIVING

(☎0280-15-456-4422; www.madrynbuceo.com; Blvr Brown 1900) Offers dive baptisms, snorkeling with sea lions and regular outings, with hostel pickup service.

Windsurfing & Kayaking

In high season, a hut next to Bistro de Mar Nautico offers lessons and rents out regular and wide boards and kayaks by the hour. South of Muelle Piedrabuena, **Playa Tomás Curti** is a popular windsurfing spot.

★ **Huellas y Costas** KAYAKING

(☎15-466-4772, 447-0143; www.huellasycostas.com; 3-day kayak excursion US$1085) A praised outfitter offering multiday kayak excursions in small groups with bilingual guides. Whale-watching is a big element of these trips, though the price drops low season.

Napra Club WATER SPORTS

(☎445-5633; www.napraclub.com; Costanera s/n; ⊙9am-7pm) This rental shack offers bicycles (per hour AR$30), stand-up paddle (SUP) boards (per hour AR$80) and guided seakayaking (per two hours AR$190); if need be you can also rent a wetsuit (AR$20). Located next to Bistro de Mar Nautico.

Tours

Countless agencies sell tours to Península Valdés; prices do not include the AR$130 park admission fee or whale-watching (AR$490). Most hotels and hostels also offer tours; get recommendations from fellow travelers before choosing. Ask how large the bus was, if it came with an English-speaking guide, where they ate and what they saw where – different tour companies often visit different locations. Bringing your own binoculars is a good idea.

Tours to Punta Tombo from Puerto Madryn cost about the same as those offered from Trelew, but they require more driving time and thus less time with the penguins.

Flamenco Tour GUIDED TOUR

(☎445-5505; www.flamencotour.com; Belgrano 25) Offerings range from the standard whale-watching and snorkeling trips to stargazing 4WD journeys along the coast (telescopes and bilingual instruction included).

Nievemar GUIDED TOUR

(☎445-5544; www.nievemartours.com.ar; Av Roca 493) Amex representative. Excursions include whale-watching and visits to sea-lion colonies and the petrified forest.

Sleeping

Book ahead, especially if you want a double room. Tourist offices offer a comprehensive lodging list with prices that include nearby *estancias* (ranches) and rental apartments.

All hostels have kitchens and many offer pickup from the bus terminal, but most are a short, flat walk away.

Hi! Patagonia Hostel HOSTEL $

(☎445-0155; www.hipatagonia.com; Av Roca 1040; dm AR$100, tr/q AR$500/560, d/tr/q without bathroom AR$100/320/380/480; @) Reservations are essential at this sociable suburban-style house featuring both private rooms and dorm beds with down comforters, a cocktail bar in the grassy courtyard, bike rental, climbing wall and barbecues. New triples and quads feature private bathrooms. Owner Gaston is a consummate host as well as an amateur meteorologist (which helps when planning day trips).

La Tosca HOSTEL $
(☎445-6133; www.latoscahostel.com; Sarmiento 437; dm AR$125, d AR$300-375, ste AR$500; @📶) A tie for the best hostel in town is this cozy guesthouse where the owners and staff greet you by name. The creation of a well-traveled couple, La Tosca is modern and comfy, with a grassy courtyard, good mattresses, and varied breakfasts with homemade cakes. Double suites and a post-checkout bathroom with showers are wonderful additions. There's also bike rental.

La Casa de Tounens HOSTEL $
(☎447-2681; www.lacasadetounens.com; Passaje 1 de Marzo 432; s/d AR$200/300, dm/s/d without bathroom AR$80/180/240 ; @📶) A congenial nook near the bus station, run by a friendly Parisian-Argentine couple. With few rooms, personal attention is assured. There's a cozy stone patio strewn with hammocks, barbacue grill for guests and homemade bread for breakfast.

Chepatagonia Hostel HOSTEL $
(☎445-5783; www.chepatagoniahostel.com.ar; Storni 16; dm/tw/d AR$90/270/300; @📶) Just a stone's throw from the beach, this well-run hostel is owned by a friendly couple who book tours for guests and fire up the grill for barbecues twice a week. Adding to the appeal are comfortable beds and the possibility of glimpsing a breaching whale from the hostel balcony.

El Retorno HOSTEL $
(☎445-6044; www.elretornohostel.com.ar; Mitre 798; dm/tw AR$95/320; @📶) Run by the indefatigable Gladys, a den mother to travelers from all over. Besides dorms and snug doubles, there's a solarium, barbecue area and bike rental.

Posada del Catalejo HOSTEL $
(☎447-5224; www.posadadelcatalejo.com.ar; Mitre 46; dm AR$100, d/tr AR$360/400, d without bathroom AR$310; @) Located in an old-fashioned building that makes the place feel more like a budget B&B, with cool wall murals. Doubles are considerably nicer than the worn-out dorms. Staff are welcoming and breakfast includes homemade bread and *medialunas* (croissants).

Camping ACA CAMPGROUND $
(☎445-2952; info@acamadryn.com.ar; Camino al Indio; s/d campsites AR$65/95; ⊙closed May-Aug) These 800 gravel campsites are sheltered by trees to break the incessant wind. Although there are no cooking facilities, some snacks (and sometimes prepared meals) are available. To get there from downtown, city bus 2 goes within 500m of the campground; get off at the last stop (La Universidad).

El Gualicho HOSTEL $$
(☎445-4163; www.elgualicho.com.ar; Marcos A Zar 480; dm/d/tr/q AR$100/440/504/560; @📶) This sleek, contempo hostel provides very stylish digs, though mattresses are mysteriously cheap quality. We love the ample common spaces, with billiards and hammocks, but being truly massive (with 120 beds) makes it somewhat impersonal. Doubles have TV. Bikes are available for rent and a massive activity board keeps you posted.

La Posada Hotel INN $$
(☎447-4087; www.la-posada.com.ar; Mathews 2951; d/superior US$140/$168; @🏊) This modern inn amid rolling green lawns offers a quiet alternative to lodging in town. Its tidy, light-filled rooms with bright accents come with cable TV; in the garden there's a pool and barbecue grill. It's 2km south of the town center.

Casa Patagonica B&B $$
(☎445-1540; www.casa-patagonica.com.ar; Av Roca 2210; d/tr AR$380/410, without bathroom AR$270/350; @📶) Warm and relaxed, with homemade cakes for breakfast and a *quincho* (thatched-roof building) for cooking or barbecues. Lodgings are in a brick home with vaulted ceilings and impeccably kept rooms, five blocks from the beach and 1km south of the town center.

Hostería Las Maras INN $$
(☎445-3215; www.hosterialasmaras.com.ar; Marcos A Zar 64; s/d AR$530/590, superior AR$590/680; @) Brick walls, exposed beams and wicker furniture create an intimate setting for couples – in the lobby anyway. Guest rooms are just small, prim and servicable – if design matters to you, upgrade to a superior room.

Hotel Bahía Nueva HOTEL $$
(☎445-0145, 445-0045; www.bahianueva.com.ar; Av Roca 67; s/d/tr AR$552/655/790; @📶)

Stretching to resemble an English countryside retreat, the Bahía Nueva includes a foyer library and flouncy touches. Its 40 rooms are well groomed, but only a few have ocean views. Highlights include a bar with billiards and a TV (mostly to view movies and documentaries), as well as tour information.

Hotel Territorio BOUTIQUE HOTEL **$$$**
(447-1496; www.hotelterritorio.com.ar; Av Roca 33; d/tr/ste incl spa US$300/360/390; @) Set behind beautiful dunes with ocean views, this 36-room hotel is minimal chic – with polished concrete, plush modern furniture and an entire whale vertebrae gracing a yawning hall. Kids can use a spacious play room. The Punta Cuevas location is a trek from the town center, but there's a cool cocktail bar and a contemporary spa.

Eating

Mr Jones INTERNATIONAL **$**
(9 de Julio 116; mains AR$40-100; dinner) Serving a wealth of yummy stouts and reds, homemade pot pie, and fish and chips, this favorite local pub always delivers. Service is friendly but tends to be slow.

Bodegón CAFE **$**
(447-2547; 25 de Mayo 411; mains AR$60-80) With its tiny tables and brick walls, this intimate cafe wouldn't be out of place in Buenos Aires. As expected, it serves the classics: steak with fries, *cazuelas* (meat stews) and *milanesas,* with wine named for famous *fútbol* (soccer) teams. It's the ideal boy's night out.

Lupita MEXICAN **$**
(15-472-2454; Av Gales 195; mains AR$63-80; 8pm-1am) This tiny, colorful eatery serves up nachos and fajitas to travelers homesick for something spicy. While it's not straight out of Guadalajara, a valiant effort is made with homemade whole wheat tortillas and house salsas.

★**Olinda** ARGENTINE **$$**
(447-0304; Av Roca 385; mains AR$79; noon-4pm & 7:30pm-1am) With deck seating and a cool candlelit atmosphere, this contemporary cafe serves a range of tasty blackboard specials at good prices. Rotating offerings means the food is always fresh – think Patagonian lamb, local seafood and homemade bread. Set menus are a good deal.

Bistro de Mar Nautico SEAFOOD **$$**
(447-4289; Blvr Brown 860; mains AR$40-110; 8am-12am) With unbeatable beachfront atmosphere and bustling old-school waiters, this busy cafe does the job. Seafood lovers can get grilled fish or crisp calamari. There's also burgers, pizzas and even breakfast. After 8pm there's a limited menu.

Ambigú ARGENTINE **$$**
(www.ambiguresto.com.ar; cnr Av Roca & Roque Sáenz Peña; mains AR$60-105) Locals gravitate toward this corner cafe offering the full gamut of dishes. The setting is an elegant renovation of a historic bank building, backlit by warm colors.

Plácido ARGENTINE **$$**
(445-5991; www.placido.com.ar; Av Roca 506; mains AR$70-100; noon-3pm & 8pm-late) Chic and waterfront, this white-linen restaurant serves beautifully presented versions of traditional dishes such as shrimp in garlic and *cordero patagónico* (Patagonian lamb) in a minimalist setting. Try the shellfish sampler paired with a white from Bodega Fin del Mundo.

Guiseppe ITALIAN **$$**
(445-6891; 25 de Mayo 381; mains AR$80-100; noon-4pm & 8pm-1am) This Italian bistro hits just the right note with fresh pastas, gnocchi and pizza *a la piedra,* served up on classic red-checkered tablecloths. If you want something a little more exotic, go for the *risotto de langostinos* (with crawfish).

Drinking & Nightlife

Bars and dance clubs come and go, so ask locals what's *de moda* (in) now.

Margarita Bar PUB
(Roque Sáenz Peña; 11am-4am) With a trendy edge, this low-lit brick haunt has a laundry list of cocktails, a friendly bar staff and decent food (mains AR$25 to AR$600). On weekends there's dancing after 1:30am.

Cheers Patagonia PUB
(445-2249; Belgrano 323; noon-3pm & 8pm-late, closed Mon) The only spot with beers on tap (and good ones at that) as well as a well-priced wine list, Cheers has proved popular with locals and travelers alike. The sprawling interior patio is a boon in summertime. Food is contemporary and Argentine, with tapas leading to lamb dishes and seafood, with mixed reviews.

Information

Banco de la Nación (9 de Julio 127) Has an ATM and changes travelers checks.

Cambio Thaler (☎445-5858; Av Roca 497; ⏰9:30am-1pm & 6-8pm Mon-Fri, 10am-1pm & 7-9pm Sat & Sun) Poor rates for travelers checks.

Hospital Subzonal (☎445-1999; R Gómez 383)

Post Office (cnr Belgrano & Gobernador Maíz)

Recreo (cnr 28 de Julio & Av Roca; ⏰9am-1pm & 5-9pm Mon-Sat) Stocks a good selection of regional books, maps, and a few English-language novels and guidebooks. There is another branch (corner 25 de Mayo and Roque Sáenz Peña) in town.

Tourist Office (☎445-3504; www.madryn.gov.ar/turismo; Av Roca 223; ⏰7am-9pm Mon-Fri, 8am-9pm Sat & Sun Dec-Feb, limited hours Apr-Nov) Helpful and efficient staff, and there's usually an English or French speaker on duty. Check the *libro de reclamos* (complaint book) for traveler tips. There's another helpful desk at the bus terminal (open 7am to 9pm in high season).

Getting There & Away

Due to limited connections, it pays to book in advance, especially for travel to the Andes.

AIR

Though Puerto Madryn has its own modern airport 5km west of town, **Aeropuerto El Tehuelche**, most commercial flights still arrive in Trelew, 65km south.

Newcomer **Andes** (☎445-2355; www.andesonline.com; Av Roca 624) has flights to Buenos Aires' Aeroparque (AR$1380) several times a week. **Aerolíneas Argentinas** (☎445-1998; Av Roca 427) flies from Trelew but has a ticketing representative here.

BUS

Puerto Madryn's full-service **bus terminal** (www.terminalmadryn.com; cnr Ciudad de Nefyn & Dr Avila), behind the historic 1889 Estación del Ferrocarril Patagónico, has an ATM and a helpful tourist information desk. Bus timetables are clearly posted and large luggage lockers are available for rent.

Bus companies include **Andesmar** (☎447-3764), **Don Otto** (☎445-1675), **Mar y Valle** (☎447-2056), **Que Bus** (☎445-5805), **TAC** (☎445-7785) and **TUS** (☎445-1962). **Chaltén Travel** (☎445-4906; Av Roca 115) has buses to Esquel and offers connecting service north on RN40 (to Bariloche) or south (to Perito Moreno and El Chaltén).

The bus to Puerto Pirámides, operated by Mar y Valle (AR$40, 1½ hours), leaves at 9:45am and returns to Madryn at 6pm. Monday through Friday there are 6:30am and 4pm departures, returning at 8am and 1pm.

Buses from Puerto Madryn

DESTINATION	COST (AR$)	DURATION (HR)
Bariloche	463-602	14-15
Buenos Aires	768-640	18-20
Comodoro Rivadavia	233	6-8
Córdoba	816	18
Esquel	343-432	7-9
Mendoza	840-998	23-24
Neuquén	350	12
Río Gallegos	675-728	15-20
Trelew	25	1
Viedma	183	5-6

Getting Around

Rent a bicycle for travel in and around town. Taxis can be hired to Puerto Piramides (AR$550) and Punta Loma/Doradillo (AR$220).

TO/FROM THE AIRPORT

Southbound 28 de Julio buses to Trelew, which run hourly Monday through Saturday between 6am and 10pm, will stop at Trelew's airport on request.

Radio taxis, including **La Nueva Patagonia** (☎447-6000), take travelers to and from Madryn's airport for about AR$46, while **Eben-Ezer** (☎447-2474) runs a service (per person AR$90) to the Trelew airport.

CAR

A round-trip to Península Valdés is a little over 300km. A group sharing expenses can make car rental a relatively reasonable and more flexible alternative to taking a bus tour if you don't have to pay for extra kilometers – rent under clear terms.

Rates vary, depending on the mileage allowance and age and condition of the vehicle. The family-owned **Centauro** (☎0280-15-340400; www.centaurorentacar.com.ar; Av Roca 733) gets high marks as an attentive and competitively priced rental agency. Basic vehicles run AR$700 per day, with insurance and 400km included.

Around Puerto Madryn

Home to a permanent sea-lion colony and cormorant rookery, the **Reserva Faunística Punta Loma** (admission AR$50) is 17km southwest of Puerto Madryn via a good but winding gravel road. The overlook is about

15m from the animals, best seen during low tides. Many travel agencies organize two-hour tours (AR$180) according to the tide schedules; otherwise, check tide tables and hire a car or taxi, or make the trek via bicycle.

Continue on the same road for **Punta Ninfas**, a cliffside marked by a lighthouse, to see elephant seals on the beach. There's also a penguin colony forming here. Please exercise self-restraint and snap photos at a nonthreatening distance. It's 78km from Puerto Madryn on a dusty dirt road.

Twenty kilometers north of Puerto Madryn via RP1 is **Punta Flecha** observatory, a recommended whale-watching spot.

Coastal Río Negro

At the gateway to Patagonia, Viedma shares the lush Río Negro with sister city Carmen de Patagones. With stylish riverfront cafes, Viedma, the capital of Río Negro province, exhudes prosperity. Historic Carmen de Patagones is worth touring for its steep cobblestone streets and colonial stylings.

Heading south, La Ruta de los Acantilados is a beautiful stretch of Atlantic coastline. Repeated wave action has worn the ancient cliff faces (three million to 13 million years old) to reveal a wealth of fossils. While the area teems with activity in summer, it shuts down in the low season.

Balneario El Cóndor, 31km southeast of Viedma at the mouth of the Río Negro, has the largest parrot colony in the world, with 35,000 nests in its cliff faces. Its century-old lighthouse is Patagonia's oldest.

Some 30km further south, there's a permanent southern sea-lion colony at **La Lobería** (Reserva Faunística de Punta Bermeja), on the north coast of Golfo San Matías. The population peaks during spring, when males come ashore to fight other males and establish harems of up to 10 females. The females give birth from December onward. An observation balcony sits directly above the mating beaches, safe and unobtrusive. Buses from Viedma pass within 3km of the colony.

At the northwest edge of Golfo San Matías, 179km west of Viedma along RN3, the crowded resort of Las Grutas owes its name to its eroded sea caves. Thanks to an exceptional tidal range, the beaches can expand for hundreds of meters. The **Tourism Office** (☎02934-497470; www.lasgrutasturismo.com.ar; Galería Antares, Primera Bajada) has tide schedules. Buses leave hourly to San Antonio Oeste, 16km northeast, with more lodging.

Reserva Faunística Península Valdés

Home to sea lions, elephant seals, guanacos, rheas, Magellanic penguins and numerous seabirds, Unesco World Heritage site Península Valdés is one of South America's finest wildlife reserves. More than 80,000 visitors per year visit this sanctuary, which has a total area of 3600 sq km and more than 400km of coastline.

The wildlife viewing is truly exceptional, though the undisputed main attraction is the endangered *ballena franca austral* (southern right whale). The warmer, more enclosed waters along the Golfo Nuevo, Golfo San José and the coastline near Caleta Valdés from Punta Norte to Punta Hércules become prime breeding zones for right whales between June and mid-December.

One doesn't expect lambs alongside penguins, but sheep *estancias* occupy most of the peninsula's interior, which includes one of the world's lowest continental depressions, the salt flats of Salina Grande and Salina Chica, 42m below sea level. At the turn of the 20th century, Puerto Pirámides, the peninsula's only village, was the shipping port for the salt extracted from Salina Grande.

About 17km north of Puerto Madryn, paved RP2 branches off RN3 across the Istmo Carlos Ameghino to the entrance of the **reserve** (admission AR$130; ⏲8am-8pm daily). The **Centro de Interpretación** (⏲8am-8pm), 22km beyond the entrance, focuses on natural history, displays a full right whale skeleton and has material on the peninsula's colonization, from the area's first Spanish settlement at Fuerte San José to later mineral exploration. Don't miss the panoramic view from the observation tower.

If you are sleeping in Puerto Madryn but plan to visit the park on two consecutive days, ask a ranger to validate your pass so you can re-enter without charges.

Puerto Pirámides

☎0280 / POP HUMANS 570, WHALES 400–2700

Set amid sandy cliffs on a bright blue sea, this sleepy old salt port now bustles with tour buses and visitors clad in orange life

Reserva Faunística Península Valdés

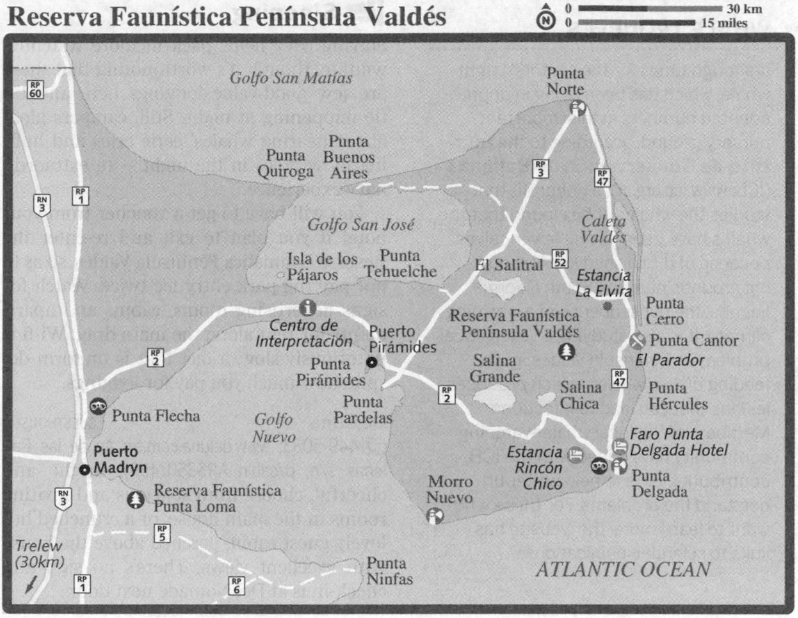

jackets. Whales mean whopping and ever-growing tourism here, but at the end of the day the tour buses split and life in this two-street town regains its cherished snail's pace.

Av de las Ballenas is the main drag, which runs perpendicular to Primera (1era) Bajada, the first road to the beach, stuffed with tour outfitters.

Activities

While most visitors focus on whale-watching, adventure offerings continue to grow.

Bicycles or kayaks can be rented and area *estancias* offer **horseback riding**. Or visitors can walk to the **sea-lion colony** less than 5km from town (though mostly uphill). It is a magnificent spot to catch the sunset, occasional whale sightings and views across the Golfo Nuevo toward Puerto Madryn. Time your visit with the tides; high tides finds all the sea lions swimming out to sea.

Tours

★ Patagonia Explorers KAYAKING
(☎0280-15-434-0618; www.patagoniaexplorers.com; Av de las Ballenas; 2hr kayak trip AR$380) This band of brothers (and sister) offer top-notch guided hikes and sea-kayaking trips. A new three-day trip on the Golfo San José includes paddling with sea lions and lots of wildlife-watching and wilderness camping. There's also full moon and sunset options. Check the website or drop by its office for more information.

Patagonia Scuba DIVING
(☎0280-15-457-8779; www.patagonia-scuba.com.ar; Av de las Ballenas s/n; diving baptism AR$400) A reputable PADI-certified outfitter offering diving trips and snorkeling with sea lions (AR$800). The best water visibility is in August. Check its Facebook page.

Whale-Watching Tours

This is the place to glimpse spy-hopping, breaching and tailing cetaceans on a **whale-watching excursion** (adult/child AR$470/235), arranged in Puerto Madryn or Puerto Pirámides. The standard trip lasts 1½ hours, but longer excursions are available.

When choosing a tour, check what kind of boat will be used: smaller, Zodiac-style inflatable rafts offer more intimacy but may be less comfortable. By law, outfitters are not allowed within 100m of whales without cutting the motor, nor allowed to pursue them.

Check your outfitter's policies. When the port is closed due to bad weather, tour bookings are usually honored the following day (although these days are more crowded).

WHALE TROUBLES

It's tough times for the southern right whale, which has been dying in unprecedented numbers in this important nursery ground, according to the **Instituto de Conservación de Ballenas** (ICB; www.icb.org.ar), a nonprofit that studies the whales. It has found that the whales have been having fewer calves because of diminished krill in feeding grounds near the South Georgia Islands, the consequence of a warming climate. It is also studying a vexing local problem on Península Valdés: gulls feeding off live whales, which produces lesions that can lead to infections. Members of the local whale-watching community have joined with the ICB, contributing data to help better understand the problems. For those who want to learn more, the website has links to scientific publications.

Outside of whale-watching season (June to December), boat trips aren't worthwhile unless you adore sea lions and shorebirds.

Bottazzi WHALE-WATCHING
(☎449-5050; www.titobottazzi.com; 1era Bajada) A recommended family business in its second generation and the only company with its own agency in Puerto Madryn. More personalized sunset cruises feature a smaller boat.

Southern Spirit WHALE-WATCHING
(☎449-5094; www.southernspirit.com.ar; 1era Bajada) A reputable outfitter, with plans in the works to bring something truly unique to whale-watching: underwater viewing. The semi-submergeable, custom-built *Yellow Submarine* with underwater windows is sure to provide a different perspective for 35 to 40 passengers.

Hydrosport WHALE-WATCHING
(☎449-5065; www.hydrosport.com.ar; 1era Bajada) In addition to whale-watching, runs dolphin-watching tours and has naturalists and submarine audio systems on board.

Whales Argentina WHALE-WATCHING
(☎449-5015; www.whalesargentina.com.ar; 1era Bajada) Offers quality trips with a bilingual guide; also runs personalized excursions on a four-seater semi-rigid boat.

Sleeping

Staying over helps pack in more watching wildlife, though it's worth noting that there are few good-value lodgings here and little happening at night. Still, campers gloat about hearing whales' eerie cries and huffing blow holes in the night – an extraordinary experience.

You will have to get a voucher from your hotel if you plan to exit and re-enter the Reserva Faunística Península Valdés, so as to not pay the park entry fee twice. Watch for signs advertising rooms, cabins and apartments for rent along the main drag. Wi-fi is notoriously slow, a fact that is uniform despite how much you pay for lodgings.

De Luna GUESTHOUSE $
(☎449-5083; www.deluna.com.ar; Av de las Ballenas s/n; d/cabin AR$350/450) Bright and cheerful, choose from spacious and inviting rooms in the main house, or a crunched but lovely guest cabin, perched above the house with excellent views. There's no sign and check-in is at Del Nomade next door.

Hostel Bahía Ballenas HOSTEL $
(☎15-456-7104; www.bahiaballenas.com.ar; Av de las Ballenas s/n; dm AR$100; ❄@📶) A bare-bones brick hostel with two enormous single-sex dorms; the 'Backpackers' sign will catch your eye. Rates include kitchen use, breakfast is extra (AR$20).

Camping Municipal CAMPGROUND $
(☎15-420-2760; per person AR$30) Convenient, sheltered gravel sites with clean toilets, a store and hot pay showers, down the road behind the gas station. Come early in summer to stake your spot. Avoid camping on the beach: high tide is very high.

La Casa de la Tía Alicia GUESTHOUSE $$
(☎449-5046; www.hosteriatiaalicia.com.ar; Av de las Ballenas s/n; d AR$400; 📶) A cozy spot for couples, this petal-pink house has just three cabin-style rooms in bright crayon-box colors around a cute garden area. There's in-room tea service, and the management has a conscientious approach of recycling water and composting.

Hidden House GUESTHOUSE $$
(☎449-5003, 15-464-4380; www.hiddenhousepatagonia.com; Segunda Bajada; s/d US$100/120; ❄📶) Lovely and partially tucked behind the dunes, this airy home is a fun destination, with flower boxes, friendly dogs and chair loungers in the dunes. Very personal

service is provided by chef host Mumo, who can cook up meals and put on a great barbecue. The street is unmarked, it's the second sea-access road.

Motel ACA MOTEL $$
(☎449-5004; www.motelacapiramides.com; Av Roca s/n; d AR$580; ❄📶) One of the better bets in town, though it can be noisy. The attached restaurant, open to the public, serves fresh seafood and offers bay views through huge glass windows.

Cabañas en el Mar CABINS $$
(☎15-466-1629; cabanasenelmar@gmail.com; Av de las Ballenas; 4-/5-person cabin AR$720/780; ❄📶) Smack in the center of all the action (it's right where the road splits to the waterfront), these comfortable new cabins are spotless, cool and well equipped. Bedrooms have a TV, and kitchens have full-sized refrigerators and stoves.

★**Del Nomade Hostería Ecologica** LODGE $$$
(☎449-5044; www.ecohosteria.com.ar; Av de las Ballenas s/n; d US$180; @📶) 🍃 Owned by a renowned Argentine nature photographer, these eight stylish ecolodge rooms have homey, minimalist style and homemade breakfasts. Maximum effort has been put into making it green – using wood from fallen trees, enzymatic water treatment, solar panels, composting and natural cleaning agents. You can get in the wildlife mood browsing the photo displays and stacks of *National Geographic* magazines.

Excursion lunch boxes are available (AR$60) as well as long-stay discounts.

Restingas Hotel LUXURY HOTEL $$$
(☎449-5101; www.lasrestingas.com; 1era Bajada; d garden/ocean view US$231/271; @📶🏊) A beachfront luxury hotel and spa with spacious rooms and an attractive glass-walled living room. While service appears lax, watching whales from your bedroom is a big plus. Guests praise the abundant buffet breakfast; its gourmet restaurant is open to the public.

Eating & Drinking

Restaurants flank the beachfront, down the first street to the right as you enter town. Note that water here is desalinated: sensitive stomachs should stick to the bottled stuff. If self-catering, it's best to haul your groceries from Puerto Madryn.

El Viento Viene CAFE $
(1era Bajada; mains AR$40-50; ⊙9am-7:30pm) This little nook is a charming spot for coffee, sandwiches and homemade pie, and also sells innovative arts and crafts.

La Estación SEAFOOD $$
(Av de las Ballenas s/n; mains AR$100; ⊙noon-midnight, closed Tue) This funky, fresh eatery is the ideal spot to crack open a bottle of wine and savor it. Though the vibe is casual, dishes like *langostinos a la plancha* (grilled prawns), fresh scallops and lamb sorrentinos are fit for kings. Reserve a table ahead, as there are precious few.

Guanaco PUB
(☎449-5046; Av de las Ballenas s/n; mains AR$35-85; ⊙6pm-12am Wed-Mon) Art installations on a covered porch announce this funky *cervecería* serving Hernan's artisan brews and other regional brews. The pub food, like pizzas, vegetarian stir-fry and steaks, is good too. A sure sign things are going well, it has been known to close for lack of inventory.

Information

A small **tourist office** (☎449-5048; www.puertopiramides.gov.ar; 1era Bajada; ⊙9am-2pm & 3-6pm) helps with travelers' needs. Visitors can access the internet at **India** (Av de las Ballenas; per hr AR$60; ⊙10:30am-8pm) and take out cash from the ATM at **Banco de Chubut** (Av de las Ballenas).

Getting There & Around

The Mar y Valle bus service travels from Puerto Madryn to Puerto Pirámides (AR$40, 1½ hours) at 9:45am and returns to Madryn at 6pm. Monday through Friday there are 6:30am and 4pm departures, returning at 8am and 1pm. Bus tours from Puerto Madryn may allow passengers to get off here.

Around Puerto Pirámides

If you're driving around the peninsula, take it easy. Roads are *ripio* and washboard, with sandy spots that grab the wheels. If you're in a rental car, make sure you get all the details on the insurance policy. Hitchhiking here is nearly impossible and bike travel is long and unnervingly windy.

ISLA DE LOS PÁJAROS

In Golfo San José, 800m north of the isthmus, this bird sanctuary is off-limits to humans, but visible through a powerful telescope. It contains a replica of a chapel built at Fuerte San José.

PUNTA DELGADA

In the peninsula's southeast corner, 76km southeast of Puerto Pirámides, sea lions and, in spring, a huge colony of elephant seals are visible from the cliffs. Enter the public dirt road right of the Faro Punta Delgada Hotel.

Sleeping

★Estancia Rincón Chico ESTANCIA $$$
(☎0280-447-1733; www.rinconchico.com.ar; d incl full board AR$2300; ⊙mid-Sep–Mar) With a prime location for wildlife-watching, this refined and recommended inn hosts university marine biologists, student researchers and tourists. Lodging is inside a modern, corrugated-tin ranch house with eight well-appointed doubles and a *quincho* for barbecues. In addition to guided excursions, there are paths for cycling and walking on your own.

Faro Punta Delgada Hotel LUXURY HOTEL $$$
(☎445-8444, 02965-15-406304; www.puntadelgada.com; d incl excursion US$308) A luxury hotel in a lighthouse complex that once belonged to the Argentine postal service. Horseback riding, 4WD tours and other activities are available. Nonguests can dine at the upscale restaurant serving *estancia* fare. Guided naturalist walks down to the beach leave frequently in high season.

PUNTA CANTOR & CALETA VALDÉS

In spring, elephant seals haul themselves onto the long gravel spit at this sheltered bay, 43km north of Punta Delgada. September has females giving birth to pups, while males fight it out defending their harem – a dramatic sight from the trails that wind down the hill. You may even see guanacos strolling the beach.

Tour groups fill up **El Parador** (☎474248; www.laelvira.com.ar; mains AR$50-100), a decent restaurant which offers a set lamb barbecue lunch (AR$195) cooked Patagonian-style as well as lighter fare. It is part of **Estancia La Elvira**, which is currently not open to the public as lodgings, though this status may change in the future. A few kilometers north of El Parador, there's a sizable colony of burrowing Magellanic penguins.

PUNTA NORTE

At the far end of the peninsula, solitary Punta Norte boasts an enormous mixed colony of sea lions and elephant seals. Its distance means it is rarely visited by tour groups. But the real thrill here is the orcas: from mid-February through mid-April these killer whales come to feast on the unsuspecting colonies of sea lions. The chances are you won't see a high-tide attack, but watching their dorsal fins carving through the water is enough to raise goose bumps.

There's a small but good **museum** that focuses on marine mammals, and has details

THE LITTLE PRINCE

From an apartment in Manhattan in 1941, a French pilot and writer, in exile from the battlefields of Europe, scripted what would become one of the most-read children's fables, *The Little Prince*. Antoine St-Exupéry, then 40 years old, had spent the previous 20 years flying in the Sahara, the Pyrenees, Egypt and Patagonia – where he was director of Aeropostal Argentina from 1929 to 1931. Intertwined in the lines of *The Little Prince* and Asteroid B612 are images of Patagonia ingrained from flights over the windy, barren landscape.

Legend has it that the shape of Isla de los Pájaros, off the coast of Península Valdés, inspired the elephant-eating boa constrictor (or hat, as you may see it), while the perfectly conical volcanoes on the asteroid are modeled on those seen en route to Punta Arenas, Chile. The author's illustrations show the little prince on mountain peaks resembling the Fitz Roy Range (one such peak now bears his name). And, possibly, meeting two young daughters of a French immigrant after an emergency landing in Concordia, near Buenos Aires, helped mold the character of the prince.

St-Exupéry never witnessed the influence his young character would enjoy. In 1944, just after the first publication of *The Little Prince*, he disappeared during a flight to join French forces-in-exile stationed in Algiers. His Patagonia years also figure in two critically acclaimed novels, *Night Flight* and *Wind, Sand and Stars*, both worthwhile reads on long Patagonia trips.

on the Tehuelche and the area's sealing history. There's also a **cafe** with basic snacks, open only if it's busy enough to warrant it.

Trelew

0290 / POP 98,000

Though steeped in Welsh heritage, Trelew isn't a postcard city. In fact, this uneventful midsized hub may be convenient to many attractions, but it's home to few. The region's commercial center, it's a convenient base for visiting the Welsh villages of Gaiman and Dolavon. Also worthwhile is the top-notch dinosaur museum.

Founded in 1886 as a railway junction, Trelew (tre-*ley*-ooh) owes its easily mispronounced name to the Welsh contraction of *tre* (town) and *lew* (after Lewis Jones, who promoted railway expansion). During the following 30 years, the railway reached Gaiman, the Welsh built their Salón San David (a replica of St David's Cathedral, Pembrokeshire), and Spanish and Italian immigrants settled in the area. In 1956 the federal government promoted Patagonian industrial development and Trelew's population skyrocketed.

Trelew is situated 65km south of Puerto Madryn via RN3.

The city center surrounds Plaza Independencia, with most services located on Calles 25 de Mayo and San Martín, and along recently renovated Av Fontana. East-west streets change names on either side of Av Fontana.

Sights

The tourist office sometimes has an informative walking-tour brochure, in Spanish and English, describing most of the city's historic buildings.

★Museo Paleontológico Egidio Feruglio MUSEUM

(442-0012; www.mef.org.ar; Av Fontana 140; adult/child AR$54/42; 9am-7pm) Showcasing the most important fossil finds in Patagonia, this natural-history museum offers outstanding life-sized dinosaur exhibits and more than 1700 fossil remains of plant and marine life. Nature sounds and a video accent the informative plaques, and tours are available in a number of languages. The collection includes local dinosaurs, such as the tehuelchesaurus, patagosaurus and titanosaurus.

With an international team, museum researchers helped discover a new and unusual species called Brachytrachelopan mesai, a short-necked sauropod. Egidio Feruglio was an Italian paleontologist who came to Argentina in 1925 as a petroleum geologist for YPF.

Kids aged eight to 12 can check out the 'Explorers in Pyjamas' program, which invites kids to sleep over and explore the museum by flashlight. The museum also sponsors interesting group tours to Geoparque Paleontológico Bryn Gwyn, in the badlands along the Río Chubut (25km from Trelew, or 8km south of Gaiman via RP5). The three-hour guided visits are a walk through time, visiting exposed fossils dating as far back as the Tertiary, some 40 million years ago.

Museo de Artes Visuales MUSEUM

(443-3774; Mitre 351; 8am-8pm Mon-Fri, 2-8pm Sat & Sun) FREE Adjoined to the tourist office, this small visual-arts museum features works on loan from the Museo Nacional de Bellas Artes in Buenos Aires, as well as some polished relics from Welsh colonization.

Museo Regional Pueblo de Luis MUSEUM

(442-4062; cnr Av Fontana & Lewis Jones; admission AR$2; 8am-8pm Mon-Fri, 2-8pm Sat & Sun) In a former train station, this small museum displays historical photographs, clothing and period furnishings of Welsh settlers, along with relics from the area's indigenous peoples.

Tours

Several travel agencies run excursions to Área Natural Protegida Punta Tombo (AR$330, plus AR$78 admission), some passing by Puerto Rawson on the way back to see Commerson's dolphins *(toninas overas)*, known as the world's smallest dolphin, when conditions are agreeable. The actual time at Punta Tombo is only about 1½ hours. Full-day trips to Península Valdés (AR$450) are also on offer, but going to Puerto Madryn first is a better bet: there are more options, prices are similar and there's less driving time.

Local tour agencies worth checking out include Amex representative **Nievemar** (443-4114; www.nievemartours.com.ar; Italia 20), which accepts travelers checks, as well as **Alcamar Travel** (442-1448; San Martín 146).

Trelew

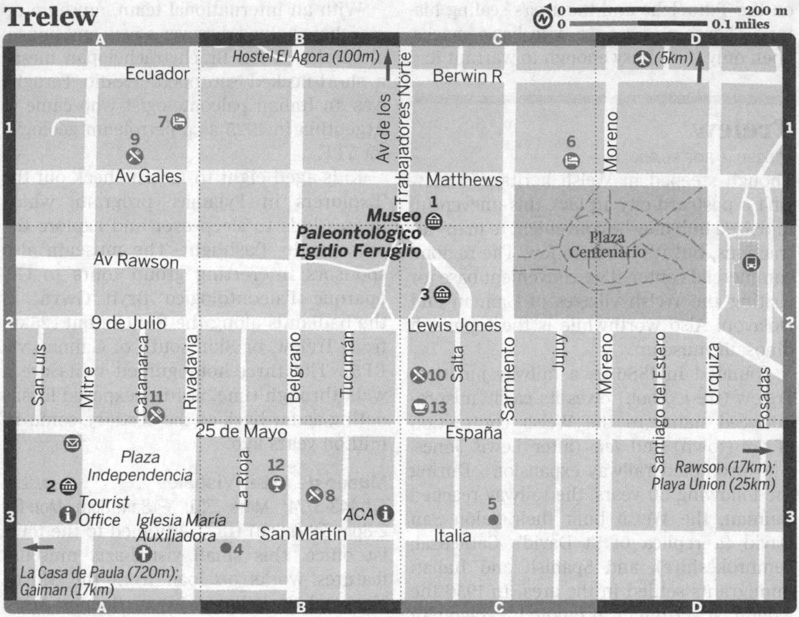

Festivals & Events

Gwyl y Glaniad FESTIVAL

On July 28 the landing of the first Welsh is celebrated by taking tea in one of the many chapels.

Eisteddfod de Chubut CULTURAL FESTIVAL

A Welsh literary and musical festival, held in late October. The tradition started in 1875.

Aniversario de la Ciudad FESTIVAL

October 20; commemorates the city's founding in 1886.

Sleeping

Trelew's accommodations are largely dated and geared toward the business traveler; in addition, spots fill up fast. Travelers can find more variety in nearby Puerto Madryn or Gaiman.

Hostel El Agora HOSTEL $

(442-6899; www.hostelagora.com.ar; Edwin Roberts 33; dm AR$100;) A backpacker haven, this cute brick house is sparkling and ship-shape. Features include a tiny patio, book exchange and laundry. It also does guided bicycle tours. It's two blocks from Parque Centenario and four blocks from the bus terminal.

Residencial Rivadavia GUESTHOUSE $

(443-4472; www.rivadaviahotel.com.ar; Rivadavia 55; s/d/tr AR$200/280/350;) Up on a hill, this small family-run hotel offers good value, though the rooms with gauzy curtains are somewhat faded. Breakfast costs extra.

★ **La Casa de Paula** B&B $$

(15-435-2240; www.casadepaula.com.ar; Marconi 573; s/d/tr US$100/120/130;) A haven after a day of sun and wind, artist Paula's house beckons with huge king beds covered in down duvets and woven throws. An eclectic and warm decor fills this modern home, with jazz on the radio and cozy living areas stacked with fashion mags. There's also a lush garden and an outstanding breakfast with homemade jam.

La Casona del Río B&B $$

(443-8343; www.lacasonadelrio.com.ar; Chacra 105; s/d/tr US$110/125/165;) Five km outside the city center, on the bank of the Río Chubut, this English-style B&B is a thoroughly charming refuge. Guest rooms are smart and bright, other features include a library, tennis court, gazebo and rental bikes.

Patagonia Suites Apart APARTMENT $$

(0280-453-7399, 442-1345; www.patagoniansuites.com; Matthews 186; d AR$671-775;) A

Trelew

Top Sights
1 Museo Paleontológico Egidio Feruglio C1

Sights
2 Museo de Artes Visuales A3
3 Museo Regional Pueblo de Luis C2

Activities, Courses & Tours
4 Alcamar Travel B3
5 Nievemar C3

Sleeping
6 Patagonia Suites Apart C1
7 Residencial Rivadavia A1

Eating
8 La Bodeguita B3
9 Majadero A1
10 Miguel Angel C2
11 Sugar A2

Drinking & Nightlife
12 Boru Irish Pub & Restobar B3
13 Touring Club C2

foxy addition to town, these 13 modern apartments (from studios to multiple bedrooms) feature wood details, hairdryers and corduroy bedspreads. They also come with fully equipped kitchens and cable TV. The complex faces Parque Centenario.

Eating

La Bodeguita ARGENTINE $
(Belgrano 374; mains AR$40-80; ⌚Tue-Sun) A popular stop for meats, pasta and seafood, this restaurant boasts attentive service and a family atmosphere.

Miguel Angel ITALIAN $$
(☎443-0403; Av Fontana 246; mains AR50-110; ⌚closed Mon) This chic eatery, outfitted with sleek white booths, departs from the everyday with savory dishes such as gnocchi and wild mushrooms, and pizza with bacon and basil on crisp, thin crust.

Sugar CONTEMPORARY $$
(25 de Mayo 247; mains AR$75-120;) Facing Plaza Independencia, this modern restaurant spices up a basic menu of classic Argentine fare with options like quinoa milanesas, stir-fried beef, grilled vegetables and herbed fish. There's salads and fresh juice on offer too. While it isn't gourmet, it's still a welcome change from Argentine same-old, same-old.

Majadero ARGENTINE $$$
(☎443-0548; Av Gales 250; mains AR$80-130; ⌚8pm-midnight Mon-Sat, noon-6pm Sun) Iron lamps and brickwork restore the romance to this 1914 flour mill – undoubtedly the nicest restaurant setting in town. On weekends it's busy, with the wood-fired *parrilla,* grilling steaks and even vegetables.

Drinking & Nightlife

★**Touring Club** CAFE
(Av Fontana 240; ⌚6:30am-2am) Old lore exudes from the pores of this historic *confitería* (café offering light meals; snacks AR$12), from the Butch Cassidy 'Wanted' poster to the embossed tile ceiling and antique bar back. Even the tuxedoed waitstaff appear to be plucked from another era. Service is weak and the sandwiches are only so-so, but the ambience is one of a kind.

Boru Irish Pub & Restobar PUB
(Belgrano 341; ⌚8pm-4am) Hip and attractive, featuring a beautiful wood bar and a row of cozy red booths, Boru serves up icy beer and plates piled high with french fries.

Information

ATMs and *locutorios* (private telephone offices) with internet are plentiful downtown and around Plaza Independencia.

ACA (Automóvil Club Argentino; ☎435197; cnr Av Fontana & San Martín) Argentina's auto club; good source for provincial road maps.

Post Office (cnr Av 25 de Mayo & Mitre)

Tourist Office (☎442-0139; cnr San Martín & Mitre; ⌚8:30am-8pm Mon-Fri, 9am-9pm Sat & Sun) Helpful and well stocked, with some English-speaking staff.

Getting There & Away

AIR

Trelew's airport is 5km north of town off RN3. Airport tax is AR$18.

The following are one-way base fares.

Aerolíneas Argentinas (☎442-0222; Rivadavia 548) flies direct daily to Buenos Aires (AR$782), and several times a week to Bariloche (AR$1220), Ushuaia (AR$1401) and El Calafate (AR$1914).

LADE (☎443-5740), at the bus terminal, flies to Comodoro Rivadavia weekly.

BUS

Trelew's full-service bus terminal is six blocks northeast of downtown.

For Gaiman (AR$8), **28 de Julio** (☎443-2429) has 18 services daily between 7am and 11pm (reduced weekend services), with most continuing to Dolavon (AR$10, 30 minutes). Buses to Rawson (AR$7, 15 minutes) leave every 15 minutes.

Mar y Valle (☎443-2429) and 28 de Julio run hourly buses to Puerto Madryn. Mar y Valle goes to Puerto Pirámides (AR$60, 2½ hours) daily at 8:15am, with additional service in summer. **El Ñandú** (☎442-7499) goes to Camarones (AR$100, four hours) at 8am on Monday, Wednesday and Friday.

Long-distance bus companies include **El Cóndor** (☎443-1675), **Que Bus** (☎442-2760), **Andesmar** (☎443-3535), **TAC** (☎443-9207), **TUS** (☎442-1343) and **Don Otto** (☎442-9496).

Of several departures daily for Buenos Aires, Don Otto has the most comfortable and most direct service. Only Don Otto goes to Mar del Plata, while TAC goes to La Plata. TAC and Andesmar service the most towns. For Comodoro Rivadavia there are a few daily departures with TAC, Don Otto or Andesmar, all of which also continue to Río Gallegos.

Buses from Trelew

DESTINATION	COST (AR$)	DURATION (HR)
Bahía Blanca	355	12
Bariloche	577	13-16
Buenos Aires	670	18-21
Comodoro Rivadavia	200	5-6
Córdoba	682	19
Esquel	307	8-9
La Plata	670	19
Mar del Plata	646	17-21
Mendoza	872-1045	24
Neuquén	385	10
Puerto Madryn	25	1
Río Gallegos	640	14-17
Viedma	242	8

Getting Around

From the airport, taxis charge AR$35 to downtown, AR$96 to Gaiman and AR$365 to Puerto Madryn. Car-rental agencies at the airport include **Hertz** (☎447-5247) and **Rent a Car Patagonia** (☎442-0898; www.rentacarpatagonia.com.ar; Rivadavia 86).

Around Trelew

Rawson, 17km east of Trelew, is Chubut's provincial capital, but nearby **Playa Unión**, the region's principal playground, has the capital attraction: Commerson's dolphins. Playa Unión is a long stretch of white-sand beach with blocks of summer homes and restaurants serving crisp, fresh *rabas* (calamari). Dolphin tours depart **Puerto Rawson** from April to December. For reservations, contact **Toninas Adventure** (☎0280-15-467-5741, 449-8372; www.facebook.com/ToninasAdventure).

To reach the beach, get off at Rawson's plaza or bus terminal and hop on a green 'Bahía' bus, which heads to Puerto Rawson before turning around.

Gaiman

☎0280 / POP 4730

Cream pie, dainty tea cakes, *torta negra* (a rich, dense fruit cake) and a hot pot of black tea – most visitors take an oral dose of culture when visiting this quintessential Welsh river-valley village. Locals proudly recount the day in 1995 when the late Diana, Princess of Wales, visited Gaiman to take tea (her teacup is still on display at Ty Te Caerdydd). Today about one-third of the residents claim Welsh ancestry and teahouses persist in their afternoon tradition, even though their overselling sometimes rubs the charm a little thin.

The town's name, meaning Stony Point or Arrow Point, originated from the Tehuelche who once wintered in this valley. After the Welsh constructed their first house in 1874, the two groups peacefully coexisted for a time. Later immigrant groups of criollos, Germans and Anglos joined. Gaiman's homey digs provide great value for lodgers, but the town offers little in the way of diversion beyond quiet strolls past stone houses with rose gardens after a filling teahouse visit.

Tiny Gaiman is 17km west of Trelew via RN25. Av Eugenio Tello is the main road, connecting the main town entrance to leafy Plaza Roca. Most of the teahouses and historic sites are within four blocks of the plaza. Across the river are fast-growing residential and industrial areas.

Sights

Gaiman is ideal for an informal walking tour, past homes with ivy trellises and drooping, oversized roses. Architecturally distinctive churches and chapels dot the town. **Primera Casa** (cnr Av Eugenio Tello & Evans; admission AR$15; ⏲11am-6pm) is the first house, built in 1874 by David Roberts. Dating from 1906,

WELSH LEGACY

The Welsh opened the door to settling Patagonia in 1865, though the newfound freedom cost them dearly. Few had farmed before and the arid steppe showed no resemblance to their verdant homeland. After nearly starving, they survived with the help of the Tehuelche, and eventually occupied the entire lower Chubut valley, founding the towns and teahouses of Rawson, Trelew, Puerto Madryn and Gaiman.

Today about 20% of Chubut's inhabitants have Welsh blood, but a revival of Welsh culture is dragging it back from the grave. According to Welsh historian Fernando Coronato, 'For the old principality of Wales, Patagonia meant its most daring venture.' This renewed bond means yearly British Council appointments of Welsh teachers and exchanges for Patagonian students. Curious Welsh tourists visit to time travel in their own culture, thanks to Patagonia's longtime isolation.

the **Colegio Camwy** (cnr MD Jones & Rivadavia) is considered the first secondary school in Patagonia.

Museo Histórico Regional Gales MUSEUM
(cnr Sarmiento & 28 de Julio; admission AR$5; ⏲3-8pm daily Dec-Mar, 3-7pm Tue-Sun Apr-Nov) The old train station houses this fine small museum holding the belongings and photographs of Gaiman pioneers.

Museo Antropológico MUSEUM
(cnr Bouchard & Jones; admission AR$15; ⏲11am-6pm) The Museo Antropológico offers humble homage to the indigenous cultures and history. Ask the tourist office for access. Nearby is the 300m **Túnel del Ferrocarril**, a brick tunnel through which the first trains to Dolavon passed in 1914.b

Sleeping

★Yr Hen Ffordd B&B $
(☎449-1394; www.yrhenffordd.com.ar; Jones 342; s/d/tr AR$250/300/350; Wi-Fi) This charming B&B is run by a young couple who give you a set of keys to the front door so you can come and go as you please. Rooms are simple but cozy, with cable TV and private bathrooms with great showers. In the morning, work up an appetite for the divine homemade scones.

Hostería Gwesty Tywi B&B $
(☎449-1292; www.hosteria-gwestytywi.com.ar; Chacra 202; s/d/tr AR$270/350/400; @Wi-Fi) Diego and Brenda run this wonderful Welsh B&B with large gardens and snug, frilly rooms. Breakfast includes a selection of jams, cold meats and bread. They are glad to help with travel planning and occasionally fire up the barbecue, to the delight of guests. It's a bit far from the town center.

Dyffryn Gwyrdd GUESTHOUSE $
(☎449-1777; patagongales@yahoo.com.ar; Av Eugenio Tello 103; s/d/tr AR$200/300/350; Wi-Fi) Open when the rest are not, this canary-yellow place features bright and simple carpeted rooms with fans and throw pillows. The bathrooms are dated but spotless, and there's a quiet bar and TV area.

Camping Bomberos Voluntarios CAMPGROUND $
(☎449-1117; cnr Av Yrigoyen & Moreno; adult/child AR$20/5) An agreeable campground with hot-water showers and fire pits

Eating & Drinking

Tarten afal, tarten gwstard, cacen ffrwythau, spwnj jam and *bara brith* and a bottomless pot of tea – hungry yet? Afternoon tea is taken as a sacrament in Gaiman – though busloads of tourists get dump-trucked in teahouses without warning. The best bet is to look for places without buses in front, or wait for their departure. Tea services usually run from 2pm to 7pm.

Siop Bara BAKERY $
(Tello 505; snacks AR$20; ⏲8am-1pm & 3-9pm) This Welsh bakery is the perfect quick, no-fuss stop for pastries, ice cream and excellent sandwiches.

Gwalia Lan ARGENTINE $$
(cnr Av Eugenio Tello & Jones; mains AR$50-106; ⏲12:30-3pm & 7:30pm-midnight Tue-Sat, 12:30-3pm Sun) Gwalia Lan is considered Gaiman's best restaurant; it serves homemade pasta and well-seasoned meat dishes that are consistently good. Service is attentive.

Ty Nain TEAHOUSE
(Yrigoyen 283; tea AR$95; ⏲closed May) It's been years since Ty Nain was written up in the *Washington Post* and *Los Angeles Times*, but the endorsements are still plastered on

OFF THE BEATEN TRACK

CABO RASO

Old Patagonia still lives, breathes and wind batters the occasional visitor on this rocky, arid coast replete with a reviving ghost town and near-secret surf spots.

Formerly a booming sheep ranching settlement founded in the late 1800s, the cape was abandoned by the 1950s. Now an Argentine family is attempting a quiet revival through sustainable tourism. At **El Cabo** (☎0280-15-467-3049, 0280-442-0354; www.caboraso.com.ar/servicios.html; RP1, Km294; campsite per person AR$20, dm AR$60, 4-6 person cabins AR$450-550) guests can rent simple stone houses from the original settlement under restoration or camp on the beach. Be aware: some installations are primative and night life is just a matter of throwing your head back and watching the milky way.

Access is via private vehicles. It's 80km north of Camarones via gravel roads and 55km south of Punta Tombo.

the front lawn. Inside an ivy-clad 1890 home, Ty Nain persists as one of the country's most traditional teahouses. The adjoining museum has some interesting Welsh artifacts.

★Ty Gwyn TEAHOUSE
(☎499-1009; 9 de Julio 111; tea AR$110) A favorite of locals, this white house serves cakes, jams and breads that are all homemade and fresh, *always*. With 30 years in business.

Ty Cymraeg TEAHOUSE
(☎449-1010; www.gaimantea.com; Matthews 74; tea AR$110) Teatime in this riverside house includes sumptuous pies and jams. The youngest member of the Welsh family that owns the place, an energetic 20-something named Miguel, is happy to explain Welsh traditions – from poetry competitions to the significance of carved wooden 'love spoons' – and his knowledge adds significantly to the experience.

Plas y Coed TEAHOUSE
(☎449-1133; www.plasycoed.com.ar; Jones 123; tea AR$110) Run by the original owner's great-granddaughter in a gorgeous brick mansion, Plas y Coed pleases the palette and senses, with friendly service, fresh cakes and serious crochet cozies for that steaming-hot pot. Rooms are also available for rent (doubles AR$280.)

Information

There's one ATM on Plaza Roca at Banco del Chubut, but it does not always work, so bring cash. *Locutorios* and internet can be found along the main drag.

Post Office (cnr Evans & Yrigoyen) Just north of the river bridge.

Tourist Office (☎449-1571; www.gaiman.gov.ar; cnr Rivadavia & Belgrano; ⊙9am-8pm Dec-Mar, 9am-6pm Apr-Nov) Ask for a map and guided tours of historic houses.

Getting There & Away

During the week, 28 de Julio buses depart for Trelew (AR$8) frequently from Plaza Roca, from 7am to 11pm (fewer services on weekends). Most buses to Dolavon (AR$8) use the highway, but some take the much longer gravel 'valley' route. *Remise* (taxi) services are cheaper in Gaiman than in Trelew; the trip to Trelew costs around AR$150 for up to four passengers.

Around Gaiman

To experience an authentic historic Welsh agricultural town, head to the distinctly nontouristy **Dolavon** (population 2500; www.dolavon.com.ar), 19km west of Gaiman via paved RN25. Welsh for 'river meadow,' the town offers pastoral appeal, with wooden waterwheels lining the irrigation canal, framed by rows of swaying poplars. The historic center is full of brick buildings, including the 1880 **Molino Harinero** (☎0280-449-2290; romanogi@infovia.com.ar; Maipú 61) with still-functioning flour mill machinery. It also has a cafe-restaurant, **La Molienda** (mains AR$80), serving handmade breads and pasta with local wines and cheeses. Call owner Romano Giallatini for opening hours.

Área Natural Protegida Punta Tombo

Continental South America's largest penguin nesting ground, **Área Natural Protegida Punta Tombo** (admission AR$78; ⊙8am-6pm Sep-Apr) has a colony of more than half a million Magellanic penguins and attracts many other birds, most notably king and rock cormorants, giant petrels, kelp gulls, flightless steamer ducks and black oystercatchers. A new management plan requires rangers to accompany visitors on rookery visits.

Trelew-based travel agencies run day-long tours but may cancel if bad weather makes the unpaved roads impassable. If possible, come in the early morning to beat the crowds. Most of the nesting areas in the 200-hectare reserve are fenced off: respect the limits and remember that penguins can inflict serious bites.

The **Centro Tombo** (8am-6pm) is an interpretive visitor center. Guests and tours park here and take a shuttle to the rookery. Shuttle frequency depends on demand, but it's greater in the morning. There's a bar and *confitería* on-site, but it's best to bring a picnic lunch.

Punta Tombo is 110km south of Trelew and 180km south of Puerto Madryn via well-maintained gravel RP1 and a short southeast lateral. Motorists can proceed south to Camarones via scenic but desolate Cabo Raso. If you can get a group together, it may be worth renting a car in Trelew or Puerto Madryn to come here.

Camarones

0297 / POP 1300

In the stiff competition for Patagonia's sleepiest coastal village, Camarones takes home the gold. Don't diss its languorous state: if you've ever needed to run away, this is one good option. Its empty beaches are conducive to strolling and townsfolk are masters of the art of shooting the breeze. It is also the closest hub to the lesser-known Cabo Dos Bahías nature reserve, where you can visit 25,000 penguin couples and their fuzzy chicks.

Spanish explorer Don Simón de Alcazaba y Sotomayor anchored here in 1545, proclaiming it part of his attempted Provincia de Nueva León. When the wool industry took off, Camarones became the area's main port. The high quality of local wool didn't go unnoticed by justice of the peace Don Mario Tomás Perón, who operated the area's largest *estancia,* Porvenir, on which his son (and future president) Juanito would romp about. The port flourished, but after Comodoro Rivadavia finished its massive port, Camarones was all but deserted.

In 2009 the paving of RN1 meant the start of direct bus services from Comodoro Rivadavia. To a moderate degree, tourism is increasing, so hurry to this coastal village now if you want to be able to say you knew Camarones way back when.

Tours

Patagonia Austral Expediciones TOUR
(0297-15-451-7660; patagoniaustralexpeditions@hotmail.com) Contact for fishing excursions and outings to see dolphins and the nearby islands.

Festivals

Fiesta Nacional del Salmón FISHING
A weekend of deep-sea fishing competitions featuring a free Sunday seafood lunch and the crowning of Miss Salmoncito, celebrated in February.

Sleeping & Eating

★**Camping Camarones** CAMPGROUND $
(0297-15-494-7080; www.campingcamarones.com; San Martín; campsites per person/vehicle AR$30/30; cabin s/d AR$180/300;) At the waterfront port, this peaceful campground with hot showers and electricity is run by a friendly older couple. Sonia can cook up fresh shrimp, seafood and salmon for guests with advance notice in summer. A basic store sells provisions.

Las Cabañas CABIN $
(15-400-0818, 15-422-2270; patagoniamara@hotmail.com; cnr Roca & Estrada; tr AR$350) Located opposite the plaza, these pastel shoebox cabins are good value. Like new (the grass hasn't even started growing yet), they feature small, clean bedrooms with a bathroom and kitchenette. If no one is here, ask at Alma Patagonica, which runs the cabins.

Hotel Indalo Inn HOTEL $$
(496-3004; www.indaloinn.com.ar; cnr Sarmiento & Roca; d/cabin AR$460/690) Currently the only game in town, Indalo could just as well be called indolent – guests seem almost a nuisance to staff. Remodeled rooms are a bit of a squeeze, but feature good bedding and strong showers. The cabins are more expensive but offer sea views.

Alma Patagonica CAFE $$
(cnr Sarmiento & Roca; pizza AR$75; 11am-midnight) A gem, this restored century-old frontier bar is run by enthusiastic hipsters with an eye on preserving local tradition. Homemade fish empanadas (baked, savory turnovers) are excellent, washed back with a massive cold beer. They also run Las Cabañas, located one block away.

Information

Tourist Office (☎496-3013; cnr Belgrano & Estrada; ⏲8am-7pm Mon-Fri, 9am-7pm Sat & Sun Dec-May) Very helpful, with maps, good tips on scenic outings and lodging information.

Getting There & Away

At a gas-station junction 180km south of Trelew, RP30 splits off from RN3 and heads 72km east to Camarones. Buses leave from the **bus terminal** (cnr 9 de Julio & Rivadavia). Transportes Ñandú buses go to Trelew (AR$100, four hours) at 4pm on Monday, Wednesday and Friday. Transportes ETAP goes to Comodoro Rivadavia (AR$100, 3½ hours) on Tuesday and Thursday at 1pm.

Local taxis make the 30-minute ride to Cabo Dos Bahías.

Cabo Dos Bahías

Thirty rough kilometers southeast of Camarones, the isolated **Cabo Dos Bahías** (admission AR$35; ⏲year-round) rookery attracts far fewer visitors than Punta Tombo, making it an excellent alternative. You'll be rewarded with orcas, a huge colony of nesting penguins in spring and summer, whales in winter, and a large concentration of guanacos and rheas. Sea birds, sea lions, foxes and fur seals are year-round residents.

You can pitch a tent for free at Cabo Dos Bahías Club Naútico or on any of the beaches en route from Camarones.

Comodoro Rivadavia

☎0297 / POP 175,200

Surrounded by dry hills of drilling rigs, oil tanks and wind-energy farms, tourism in the dusty port of Comodoro (as it's commonly known) usually means little more than a bus transfer. What this modern, hardworking city does provide is a gateway to nearby attractions with decent services. It sits at the eastern end of the Corredor Bioceánico highway that leads to Coyhaique, Chile.

Founded in 1901, Comodoro was once a transport hub linking ranches in nearby Sarmiento. In 1907 the town struck it rich when workers drilling for water found oil instead. With the country's first major gusher, Comodoro became a state pet, gaining a large port, airport and paved roads. Today it is a powerhouse in the now-privatized oil industry. Although the recession hit hard in 2001, this boomtown rebounded with a flashy casino, elegant shops and hot rods on the streets. Now it holds the dubious status of the largest consumer of plasma TVs in Argentina. Indeed, the recent arrival of Walmart has been a boon for the whole province.

Commerce centers on principal streets Avs San Martín and Rivadavia. Between Mitre and Belgrano, San Martín has upscale boutiques and shops unknown to most of Patagonia.

Sights

Museo Nacional del Petróleo MUSEUM

(☎455-9558; admission AR$25; ⏲9am-5pm Tue-Fri, 3-6pm Sat) Intransigent petroleum fans should head to Museo Nacional del Petróleo for an insider look at the social and historical aspects of petroleum development. Don't expect balanced treatment of oil issues – the museum was built by the former state oil agency YPF (it is now managed by the Universidad Nacional de Patagonia). While its historical photos are interesting, the detailed models of tankers, refineries and the entire zone of exploitation are best left to the die hard. Guided tours are available.

The museum is in the suburb of General Mosconi, 3km north of downtown. Take a *remise* from downtown (AR$40) or bus 7 'Laprida' or 8 'Palazzo' (AR$1.75, 10 minutes); get off at La Anónima supermarket.

Museo Regional Patagónico MUSEUM

(☎477-7101; cnr Av Rivadavia & Chacabuco; ⏲9am-6pm Mon-Fri, 11am-6pm Sat & Sun) FREE Decaying natural-history specimens overshadow some small yet entertaining archaeological and historical items, including well-crafted pottery, spear points and materials on early South African Boer immigrants.

Tours

Several agencies arrange trips to Bosque Petrificado Sarmiento and Cueva de las Manos.

Ruta 40 TOUR

(☎0294-452-3378; www.ruta-40.com) If you're really up for a road trip, contact Ruta 40. The small, multilingual outfitter is based in Bariloche but with some tours starting in Comodoro, like the eight-day journey Ruta 40 tour, with stops at Puerto Deseado, Cueva de las Manos and several lovely *estancias* before ending up in El Calafate. Consult for current rates and departure dates.

Circuito Ferroportuario TOUR

FREE The urban train tour Circuito Ferroportuario takes visitors on a circuit from the tourism office to visit containers, warehouses, historical installations and workshops on the port.

Sleeping

Catering mainly to business travelers and long-term laborers, lodging here fits two categories: the ritzy and the run-down. Brisk business means lodgings are overpriced and often full – book ahead.

Hotel Victoria HOTEL $$

(446-0725; www.hotelvictoriacrd.com.ar; Belgrano 585; s/d/tr AR$460/595/715) The friendliest hotel on the block, with soothing, good-sized rooms with firm twin beds, desks and cable TV, but oddly without internet. If the aroma of baking pastries is any indication, it's worth taking breakfast.

Lucania Palazzo Hotel HOTEL $$$

(449-9300; www.lucania-palazzo.com; Moreno 676; s/d AR$1060/1215;) Comodoro's answer to the Trump Towers, the sparkling Palazzo offers ocean views from every room and tasteful modern decor, although ventilation could be better. While its features only add up to those of a solid chain hotel, there's a decent restaurant and the eager staff offers helpful recommendations.

WAM BOUTIQUE HOTEL $$$

(406-8020; www.wamhotel.com.ar; Av Hipólito Yrigoyen 2196; d AR$1050;) Comodoro's only boutique effort is this shining new hotel just outside the town center, with an unfortunate office-building-like exterior. Rooms have a refreshing, contemporary look, with crisp white linens, neutral tones and glass-walled tubs. There's restaurant service and a gym. Guests have access to spa, Jacuzzi and pool included. Located just off the *costanera*, in a convenient but industrial area.

Eating

The oil boom in this part of the world has bankrolled a taste for fine dining. Look out for the free *Sabores del Sur* restaurant directory in your hotel.

Puerto Mitre PIZZERÍA $

(446-1201; Ameghino 620; mains AR$60) The place for pizza and classic Argentine empanadas, staple traveler fare.

Chocolates ICE CREAM $

(Av San Martín 231; cones AR$15;) Ice-cream junkies will appreciate this parlor's selection of velvety chocolate and rich *dulce de leche* flavors. If you're traveling with children, bring them here to ride the miniature carousel.

★ **La Tradición** PARILLA $$

(446-5800; Mitre 675; mains AR$50-120; closed Sun) A favorite of townsfolk, this elegant *parrilla* grills excellent beef, whole roast lamb and crisp shoestring fries in a setting of white linens and oil paintings (literally, since their subjects are oil rigs!)

Drinking

Molly Malone CAFE

(447-8333; cnr 9 de Julio & Av San Martín 292) Run by the Golden Oldies rugby club, this funky little resto-pub (mains AR$40 to AR$80) is a pleasant stop for breakfast, set lunch or an evening Quilmes. The food's just average but the atmosphere is fun and inviting.

Entertainment

Cine Teatro Español CINEMA

(447-7700; www.cinecr.com.ar; Av San Martín 668; tickets AR$15) A stately, old-fashioned cinema that offers a wide selection of Hollywood flicks.

Information

ACA (Automóvil Club Argentino; 446-0876; cnr Dorrego & Alvear) Maps and road info.

Banco de la Nación (cnr Av San Martín & Güemes) Most of Comodoro's banks and ATMs, including this one, are along Avs San Martín or Rivadavia.

Hospital Regional (444-2287; Av Hipólito Yrigoyen 950)

Post Office (cnr Av San Martín & Moreno)

Tourist Office (444-0664; www.comodoroturismo.gob.ar; Av Rivadavia 430; 8am-8pm Mon-Fri, 9am-3pm Sat & Sun) Friendly, well stocked and well organized. A desk at the bus terminal (open 8am to 9pm) is, at least in theory, open during the hours indicated.

Getting There & Away

The Corredor Bioceánico – RN26, RP20 and RP55 – is a straight highway link to Coyhaique, Chile, and its Pacific port, Puerto Chacabuco. Developers are promoting this commercial transport route as an alternative to the Panama Canal, since the pass is open year-round and it is the continent's shortest distance between ports on both oceans. Paved RN26, RP20 and RN40 lead to Esquel and Bariloche.

AIR

Aeropuerto General Mosconi (CRD; ☎454-8190) is 9km north of town.

Aerolíneas Argentinas (☎444-0050; Av Rivadavia 156) and **Lan Argentina** (☎454-8160; Airport) fly a couple of times daily to Buenos Aires (one way from AR$1268).

Comodoro is the hub for **LADE** (☎447-0585; Av Rivadavia 360), which wings it at least once a week to El Calafate (AR$776), Río Gallegos (AR$776), Trelew (AR$724), Ushuaia, Buenos Aires and points in between. Schedules and routes change as often as the winds.

BUS

The chaotic **bus terminal** (Pellegrini 730) receives all buses plying RN3. Stop at the helpful tourist desk to enquire about maps and travel assistance.

Most bus schedules are divided into northbound and southbound departures. **Andesmar** (☎446-8894) departs five times daily (between 1:15am and 3pm) for points north including Trelew, Rawson and Puerto Madryn.

TAC (☎444-3376) follows the same route and continues to Buenos Aires. **Etap** (☎447-4841) runs to Esquel and Río Mayo daily, to Sarmiento four times daily and to Coyhaique, Chile, at 8am on Wednesday and Saturday.

Sportman (☎444-2988) services Los Antiguos and connections to Chile Chico, via the town of Perito Moreno. **Taqsa/Marga** (☎447-0564) goes to Bariloche and El Calafate in the evening.

Schedules are in constant flux; upon arrival at the bus terminal, ask at each bus line's desk for information on departure times.

Buses from Comodoro Rivadavia

DESTINATION	COST (AR$)	DURATION (HR)
Bariloche	460	12
Buenos Aires	825-1040	24
Coyhaique, Chile	250	11
Esquel	305	10
El Calafate	670	14
Los Antiguos	250	5
Puerto Deseado	190	4
Puerto Madryn	276	6
Río Gallegos	440	10-12
Río Mayo	105	3½
Sarmiento	70	2
Trelew	240	5

Getting Around

Bus 8 'Directo Palazzo' (AR$1.75) goes directly to the airport from outside Comodoro's bus terminal. A taxi to the airport costs AR$60 from downtown.

Expreso Rada Tilly links the bus terminal to the nearby beach resort (AR$3) every 20 minutes on weekdays and every 30 minutes on weekends.

Rental cars are available from **Avis** (☎454-9471; Airport) and **Localiza** (☎446-1400; Airport). **Dubrovnik** (☎444-0073; www.rentacardubrovnik.com; Moreno 941) rents 4WD vehicles.

Puerto Deseado

☎0297 / POP 13,300

Some 125km southeast of the RN3 junction, RN281 weaves through valleys of rippling pink rock, past guanacos in tufted grassland, to end at the serene and attractive deep-sea-fishing town of Puerto Deseado. While the town is ripe for revitalization, it is also apparent that change takes a glacial pace here: witness the vintage trucks that rust on the streets like beached cetaceans. But the draw of the historic center, as well as the submerged estuary of Ría Deseado, that brims with seabirds and marine wildlife, make Puerto Deseado a very worthy detour.

In 1520 the estuary provided shelter to Hernando de Magallanes after a crippling storm waylaid his fleet; de Magallanes dubbed the area 'Río de los Trabajos' (River of Labors).

In 1586 English privateer Cavendish explored the estuary and named it after his ship *Desire,* its name today. The port attracted fleets from around the world for whaling and seal hunting, compelling the Spanish crown to send a squadron of colonists under the command of Antonio de Viedma. After a harsh winter, more than 30 of them died of scurvy. Those who survived moved inland to form the short-lived colony of Floridablanca. In 1834 Darwin surveyed the estuary, as did Perito Moreno in 1876.

Puerto Deseado is located two hours southeast of the RN3 junction at Fitz Roy via the dead-end RN281. The center of the town's activity is based around the axis formed by main streets San Martín and Almirante Brown.

DON'T MISS

BAHÍA BUSTAMANTE

A number of coastal reserves feature Patagonia's diverse marine life, but few illuminate the exuberance of this ecosystem like this historic 80-hectare **estancia** (☎0297-480-1000, in Buenos Aires 011-4778-0125; www.bahiabustamante.com; s/d/tr sea cottage incl full board & activities US$500/620/750, basic 3-person cottage US$145; 📶) located between Trelew and Comodoro Rivadavia. Romantics will love the sprawling steppe, rolling grass dunes and pebble beaches that beg you to bask in the slow rhythms of life on this deserted coast. Excursions are thoughtfully guided by bilingual naturalists, and include sea kayaking, trekking the on-site 65-million-year-old petrified forest and boat trips to see Magellanic penguins, sea lions and marine birds.

Another quirky footnote in Patagonian history, Bahía Bustamante was founded by an entrepreneurial Andalucian immigrant who used the abundant algae in the bay to manufacture agar agar, a natural food thickener. At one point hundreds of workers lived on the *estancia*, which became a kind of Wild West, complete with a police station and jail cell. In pre-settlement times, Tehuelches traveled the area, leaving behind their small tools and middens.

These days the much-reduced algae harvests also include comestible seaweed, which is mostly exported to Japan. An *estancia* tour explains the sheep farming operation, which is transitioning to better ecological practices. Grazing rotation promotes soil and native plant recovery and recently introduced Merino hybrids are better adapted to the ecosystem.

The *estancia* has the sleepy feel of a ghost village coming back to life. Its heart is the former general store, now converted to a rustic-chic living room and dining area where you might dine on local lamb or seaweed crepes with the grandsons of the founder, who now run the *estancia*. Lodgings are in comfortable seafront cabins with big red loungers recycled from shipping palettes. For a more economical approach, cabins facing the steppe offer an optional salad box with provisions from the on-site greenhouse, takeout from the restaurant and à la carte excursions.

Once you've come all this way, it's optimal to stay at least three days. The time to see fauna is between mid-September and early March, with January and February ideal to go swimming. Bird-watching is best during November hatching but it's also cool to watch sea lions nurse new pups in January. Most visitors fly into Comodoro, but if you have a car, it's worthwhile to take the scenic coastal route from nearby Camarones.

Sights & Activities

Estación del Ferrocarril Patagónico HISTORIC SITE
(admission by donation; 🕒4-7pm Mon-Sat) Train fans can check out the imposing English-designed train station off Av Oneto, built by Yugoslav stonecutters in 1908. Puerto Deseado was once the coastal terminus for a cargo and passenger route that hauled wool and lead from Chilean mines from Pico Truncado and Las Heras, located 280km northwest.

Vagón Histórico LANDMARK
(cnr San Martín & Almirante Brown; 🕒5-8pm) In the center of town, this restored 1898 wagon is famous as the car from which rebel leader Facón Grande prepared the 'Patagonia Rebellion.' In 1979 the car was almost sold for scrap, but disgruntled townspeople blocked the roads to stop the sale. A few blocks to the west lies the attractive **Sociedad Española** (San Martín 1176), c 1915.

Museo Regional Mario Brozoski MUSEUM
(☎487-1358; cnr Colón & Belgrano; 🕒10am-7pm Mon-Fri, 4-8pm Sat) FREE Displays relics of the English corvette *Swift*, sunk off the coast of Deseado in 1776. Divers continue to recover artifacts from this wreck, which was discovered in 1982.

Club Naútico WATER SPORTS
(☎0297-15-419-0468) Paddling and windsurfing can be enjoyed in summer. On the waterfront, it rents boards and kayaks (summer only). Depending on current conditions, sport fishing can be an option; inquire at the pier.

City Tour WALKING

A self-guided tour is a good start if you want to catch the vibes of Deseado. Pick up a *Guía Historica* map (in Spanish) from either tourist office.

Tours

Darwin Expediciones ADVENTURE TOUR

(0297-15-624-7554; www.darwin-expeditions.com; Av España 2601) Offers sea-kayaking trips, wildlife observation, and multiday nature and archaeology tours with knowledgeable guides. Its best seller is the ecosafari tour of Reserva Natural Ría Deseado (AR$300).

Los Vikingos ADVENTURE TOUR

(0297-15-624-4283, 0297-15-624-5141, 487-0020; www.losvikingos.com.ar; Estrada 1275) Trips on land and sea. Tours, some led by marine biologists, include Reserva Natural Ría Deseado and Monumento Natural Bosques Petrificados.

Sleeping

Ask at the tourist office about (relatively) nearby *estancias*.

Residencial Los Olmos HOTEL $

(487-0077; Gregores 849; s/d/tr AR$200/270/320;) A solid budget option kept spotless by a vigilant matron, this brick house has 19 small rooms with TV, ample heat and private bathrooms.

Camping Cañadón Giménez CAMPGROUND $

(0297-15-466-3815; RN281; per tent AR$30, 4-person cabins AR$150; year-round) Four kilometers northwest of town, but only 50m from the Ría Deseado, this campground is sheltered by forest and high rocky walls. Bare-bones cabins sleep four; bring your own linens. Showers (AR$20), hot water and simple provisions are available.

Tower Rock APARTMENT $$

(in Buenos Aires 011-3935-0188, 011-3935-0150; www.tower-rock.com; Pueyrredón 385 or Almirante Zar 305; apt US$80-165;) With studios and multiple bedroom apartments, this comfortable option offers peace and privacy. Apartments come fully equipped with outfitted kitchen, flatscreen TV, lock box and daily maid service. Hosts Patricia and Jorge are happy to answer questions.

Hotel Los Acantilados HOTEL $$

(487-2167; www.hotelosacantilados.com; cnr Pueyrredón & Av España; s/d standard AR$270/320, superior AR$410/485;) More inspiring from outside than in, these clifftop digs boast an extensive lounge with fireplace: the perfect chill spot. Superior rooms and the dining room look out on the waterfront, while standard rooms are plain with dated bathrooms.

Cabañas Las Nubes CABIN $$

(0297-15-403-2677; www.cabanaslasnubes.com.ar; Ameghino 1351; d/q cabins AR$520/620;) These deluxe two- and three-story hilltop cabins feature fully equipped kitchens and some ocean views. Unfortunately, the service lags.

Eating

Puerto Deseado has chicken rotisseries all over town, good for a quick bite.

Puerto Cristal SEAFOOD $$

(Av España 1698; mains AR$60-120; noon-3pm & 8pm-midnight, closed Wed) Bridezilla decor aside, this popular seafood haunt satisfies with sturdy portions of grilled fish, fried calamari and an extensive wine selection.

Puerto Darwin PUB $$

(www.darwin-expeditions.com; Av España 2581; mains AR$100; 9am-2am;) Featuring sandwiches, *picadas* and fish, this cafe run by Darwin Expediciones is easygoing and has views of the port. It's a hike from downtown and street numbers aren't labeled: keep walking along the water until you reach the other side of a fenced-in industrial area.

Information

Banks, ATMs, *locutorios* and internet options are all found along San Martín.

Banco de la Patagonia (San Martín & Almirante Brown)

CIS Tour (487-2864; www.cistours.com.ar; San Martin 916) Handles local tours and flight reservations.

Dirección Municipal de Turismo (487-0220; http://puertodeseado.tur.ar; San Martín 1525; 9am-8pm) Helpful with maps; there's another English-speaking desk at the bus terminal (Sargento Cabral 1302), but its hours are limited.

Hospital Distrital (487-0200; España 991)

Post Office (San Martín 1075)

Getting There & Around

The **bus terminal** (Sargento Cabral 1302) is on the northeast side of town, nine long blocks and slightly uphill from San Martín and Av Oneto. **Taxis** (☎487-2288, 487-0645) are metered.

There are five daily departures to Comodoro Rivadavia (AR$190, four hours) with **La Únion** (☎487-0188) and **Sportman** (☎487-0013). Sportman also goes to Río Gallegos (AR$510, 13 hours) twice daily. Schedules change frequently; inquire at the bus terminal about departures.

If you're thinking of getting off at godforsaken Fitz Roy (where locals claim the only thing to see is the wind!) to make progress toward Comodoro or Río Gallegos, think again: buses arrive at a demonic hour and the only place to crash is the campground behind Multirubro La Illusion.

Reserva Natural Ría Deseado & Parque Interjurisdiccional Marino Isla Pingüino

Flanked by sandy cliffs, these aquamarine waters create sculpted seascapes you won't forget. Considered one of South America's most important marine preserves, Ría Deseado is the unique result of a river abandoning its bed, allowing the Atlantic to invade 40km inland and create a perfect shelter for marine life. The recent designation of Parque Interjurisdiccional Marino Isla Pingüino (a mouthful, but essentially a national park) will likely expand offerings for visitors.

The marine life is abundant here. Several islands and other sites provide nesting habitats for seabirds, including Magellanic penguins, petrels, oystercatchers, herons, terns and five species of cormorant. Isla Chaffers is the main spot for the penguins, while Banco Cormorán offers protection to rock cormorants and the striking gray cormorant. Isla Pingüino has nesting rockhoppers (arriving mid-October) and elephant seals. Commerson's dolphins, sea lions, guanacos and ñandús (ostrich-like rheas) can also be seen while touring the estuary.

The best time to visit is December to April. Darwin Expediciones (p422) runs circuits that take in viewing of Commerson's dolphins, Isla Chaffers, Banco Cormorán as well as a walk to a penguin colony. The main attraction of the all-day Isla Pingüinos excursion (AR$700) is the punked-out rockhopper penguins with spiky yellow and black head feathers, but the tour also includes wildlife-watching, sailing and hiking. Tours have a four-person minimum. Los Vikingos (p422) makes similar excursions with bilingual guides and organizes overland trips.

Monumento Natural Bosques Petrificados

During Jurassic times, 150 million years ago, this area enjoyed a humid, temperate climate with flourishing forests, but intense volcanic activity buried them in ash. Erosion later exposed the mineralized *Proaraucaria* trees (ancestors of the modern *Araucaria,* unique to the southern hemisphere), up to 3m in diameter and 35m in length. Today the 150-sq-km **Monumento Natural Bosques Petrificados** (Petrified Forests Natural Monument; ⏲9am-9pm year-round) FREE has a small visitor center, English-language brochure and short interpretive trail, leading from park headquarters to the largest concentration of petrified

BIG FEET, TALL TALES

Say 'Patagonia' and most think of fuzzy outdoor clothes, but the name that has come to symbolize the world's end still invites hot debate as to its origin.

One theory links the term 'Patagón' to a fictional monster in a best-selling 16th-century Spanish romance of the period, co-opted by Magellan's crew to describe the Tehuelche as they wintered in 1520 at Puerto San Julián. Crew member and Italian nobleman, Antonio Pigafetta, described one Tehuelche as 'so tall we reached only to his waist…He was dressed in the skins of animals skillfully sewn together…His feet were shod with the same kind of skins, which covered his feet in the manner of shoes…The captain-general [Magellan] called these people Patagoni.'

Another theory suggests that the name comes from the Spanish *pata,* meaning paw or foot. No evidence corroborates the claim that the Tehuelche boasted unusually big feet (it's possible that the skins they wore made their feet seem exceptionally large). But it's good fodder for the genre of travelers' tales, where first impressions loom larger than life.

trees. Until its legal protection in 1954, the area was plundered for some of its finest specimens; these days you're not allowed to take home souvenirs.

The park is 157km southwest of Caleta Olivia, accessed from the good gravel RP49, leading 50km west from a turnoff at Km 2074 on RN3. There's no public transportation. Buses from Caleta Olivia leave visitors at the junction, but you may wait several hours for a lift into the park. Los Vikingos (p422) runs tours from Puerto Deseado.

There's basic camping and provisions at **La Paloma**, 20km before park headquarters. Camping in the park is prohibited.

Puerto San Julián

02962 / POP 7900

The perfect desolate-yet-charismatic locale for an art film, this small town bakes in bright light and dust, in stark contrast to the startling blue of the bay. Considered the cradle of Patagonian history, the port of San Julián was first landed in 1520 by Magellan, whose encounter with local Tehuelches provided the region's mythical moniker. Viedma, Drake and Darwin followed. While its human history is proudly put forth, the landscape speaks of geologic revolutions, with its exposed, striated layers, rolling hills and golden cliffs.

Puerto San Julián's first non-indigenous settlers came from the Falkland Islands (Islas Malvinas) with the late-19th-century wool boom. Scots followed with the San Julián Sheep Farming Company, which became the region's primary economic force for nearly a century. Recent growth has the city developing like never before with mining and seafood-processing industries; there's also a local university. For travelers, it is a relaxed and welcoming stop, as well as a great place to see Commerson's dolphins.

Sights & Activities

The most popular attractions are the museum and the penguin colony. Another option is trekking the coastline and checking out the abundant birdlife. For more information, consult the tourist information booth in the bus terminal, or the branch on the highway.

Museo Nao Victoria MUSEUM

(admission AR$15; 8am-9:30pm) Relive Magellan's landing at this museum and theme park with life-sized figures cloaked in armor and shown celebrating Mass and battling mutiny, at the port on a reproduction of the original ship.

Circuito Costero DRIVING

Take a *remise* or your own poor, abused rental car on the incredibly scenic 30km drive following Bahía San Julián on a dirt road. A series of golden bluffs divide beautiful beaches with drastic tides. The area includes a sea-lion colony and the penitent attraction of Monte Cristo (with its stations of the cross).

Tours

Banco Cormorán PENGUIN TOUR

(admision per person AR$150) The last census found 130,000 penguins inhabiting this stretch of Bahía San Julián, which you can visit by boat. The penguins stick around from September to April; when conditions permit, you'll be able to step off the boat and walk around an island where penguins swim, doze and guard their eggs. The tour also stops at Banco Justicia to see the cormorant rookeries and other seabirds. From December to March there's a good chance you'll see the Commerson's dolphin, known as the world's smallest dolphin.

Expediciones Pinocho TOUR

(454600; cnr Mitre & 9 de Julio; 2hr excursion per person AR$220 ; 9am-9pm Jan-Feb) Two-hour excursions on Bahía San Julián are run by a marine biologist-led team at Expediciones Pinocho.

Sleeping & Eating

Hotel Ocean HOTEL $

(452350; San Martín 959; s/d/tr AR$310/370/430;) This remodeled brick building has attractive, well-scrubbed rooms with firm beds and a backdrop of tropical tones. Friendly staff are happy to assist travelers – when you're tired and hungry and the bus has dropped you off in town around midnight (as it probably will), they'll help you find an open restaurant.

Camping Municipal CAMPGROUND $

(454506; Magallanes 650; tent AR$50, RV AR$70-100) On the waterfront at the north end of Vélez Sarsfield, this full-service campground has hot showers, laundry and windbreaks.

Hostería Miramar GUESTHOUSE $$

(454626; hosteriamiramar@uvc.com.ar; San Martín 210; s/d AR$350/420;) Natural light fills this cheerful waterfront option run by a local family. Eleven rooms, including a family-sized apartment, are super-clean with TV, carpeted floors and somewhat dated mint-green decor.

Hotel Bahía HOTEL **$$**
(☎453144; www.hotelbahiasanjulian.com.ar; San Martín 1075; s/d AR$385/450; @) This glass-front hotel feels decadent in a place like San Julián. Rooms are modern and beds firm, while TV and laundry service are perks. The cafe-bar is also open to the public.

Costanera Hotel HOTEL **$$**
(☎452300; www.costanerahotel.com; 25 de Mayo 917; s/d/tr AR$390/450/530;) After major renovations, this waterfront mainstay feels new again. Rooms are standard but tidy, and the restaurant is good.

La Rural PARRILLA **$**
(Ameghino 811; mains AR$40-80) Service is friendly at La Rural but the hearty food is somewhat mediocre. Still, pretty much all of San Julián seems to congregate at this unpretentious spot. Fareon offer ranges from meat and potatoes to grilled fish and pasta.

Restaurante Costanera Hotel ARGENTINE **$$**
(25 de Mayo 917; mains AR$45-85; noon-3pm & 8-11pm) Slightly formal but good value, this crisp hotel restaurant overcomes a bland setting with good wines and satisfying dishes like grandmother's potatoes, laced with cream and bacon.

Shopping

Centro Artesenal Municipal ARTS & CRAFTS
(Costanera s/n; 8am-8pm Mon-Fri) A cool co-operative selling handmade ceramics and woven goods.

Information

Banco Santa Cruz (cnr San Martín & Moreno) Has a Link ATM.

Dirección de Turismo (☎454396; www.sanjulian.gov.ar; Av San Martín 1552; 7am-12am Mon-Fri, 11am-11pm Sat & Sun) The main office is located in the bus terminal, with friendly service. A new office at the **rotunda** (RN3; 7am-12pm & 2-8pm Oct-Apr) is useful if you're traveling by car but not by bus, as the town is still a good distance away and transport is infrequent.

Post Office (cnr San Martín & Belgrano)

Getting There & Away

BUS

Most RN3 buses visit Puerto San Julián's **bus terminal** (San Martín 1552) at insane hours. Before settling for a bus that will drop you off in the port at 4am, try **Don Otto** (☎452072), which delivers southbound travelers to San Julián at civilized evening hours. **Via Tac** (☎454049) goes to Puerto Madryn (AR$440, 12 hours). **Andesmar** (☎454403) goes to Comodoro Rivadavia (AR$220, six hours). **Taqsa/Marga** (☎454667) goes to Bariloche and Río Gallegos (AR$220, 4½ hours) at 4am, where travelers can make connections south.

There are slightly more expensive door-to-door service options, all operating Monday to Saturday in the early morning hours. **Cerro San Lorenzo** (☎452403; Berutti 970) serves Gobernador Gregores at 8am (four hours).

Bus schedules may change, so always confirm departures ahead of time.

Parque Nacional Monte León

Inaugurated in 2004, this fine coastal national park protects over 600 sq km of striking headlands and archetypal Patagonian steppe, and 40km of dramatic coastline with bays, beaches and tidal flats. Once a hunting ground for nomads, and later frequented by the Tehuelche, this former *estancia* is home to abundant Magellanic penguins, sea lions, guanacos and pumas. Bring binoculars: the wildlife-watching is prime.

Hiking along the coastline, with its unusual geographic features, is best when low tide exposes stretches of sandy and rocky beach. In October 2006 the park's signature landscape attraction, **La Olla** (a huge cavelike structure eroded by the ocean), collapsed from repeated tidal action. Accessible at low tide, **Isla Monte León** is a high offshore sea stack heavily mined for guano between 1933 and 1960. Now it has been recolonized by cormorants, Dominican gulls, skuas and other seabirds. Use caution and know the tide tables before setting out: the tidal range is great, exposed rocks are slippery and the water returns quickly.

Nature trails split off from the main road, leading to the coast. The **penguin trail** crosses the steppe, leading to an overlook of the rookery. It's forbidden to leave the trail, but seeing these 75,000 couples shouldn't be difficult. The round-trip takes 1½ hours. Cars can reach the prominent cliff **Cabeza**

de León (Lion's Head), where a 20-minute trail leads to the park's sea lion colony.

Campers must stay in the designated camping area. The other lodging option is the charming **Hostería Monte León** (in Buenos Aires 011-4621-4780; www.monteleon-patagonia.com; s/d incl half-board US$390/234; Nov-Apr), a refurbished century-old *casco* (ranch house) of an 1895 *estancia*. The four-bedroom house retains the spartan style of the Patagonian farmhouse, and features iron-rod beds, basic tasteful furnishings and an open kitchen with iron wood stove.

For boat excursions or fly-fishing for steelhead, consult with the **park office** (www.pnmonteleon.com.ar). The park entrance is 30km south of Comandante Luis Piedrabuena or 205km north of Río Gallegos, directly off RN3. Watch for it carefully since signage is poor.

Río Gallegos

02966 / POP 95,800

Hardly a tourist destination, this coal shipping, oil-refining and wool-raising hub is a busy port with a few merits for travelers. Since the reign of the Kirchners, the capital city of their home province has been spruced up and spit polished. Outside of town, visitors can find some of the continent's best fly-fishing, traditional *estancias* and amazingly low tides (retreating 14m). Traveler services are good here but most zip through en route to El Calafate, Puerto Natales or Ushuaia.

Gallegos' economy revolves around nearby oilfields, with coal deposits shipped to ocean-going vessels at Punta Loyola. Home to a large military base, the city played an active role during the Falklands War (Guerra de las Malvinas). The main street, formerly Roca, was renamed Kirchner in honor of the former president.

Sights

Museo Provincial Padre Jesús Molina MUSEUM
(423290; cnr Av San Martín & Ramón y Cajal; 9am-8pm Mon-Fri, 3-8pm Sat & Sun) FREE Satiate your appetite for dinosaur dioramas and modern art at this museum offering exhibits on anthropology, paleontology, geology and fine arts. The Tehuelche ethnology exhibit includes fascinating photographs and local history.

Museo de Arte Eduardo Minnicelli MUSEUM
(436323; Maipú 13; 8:30am-7pm Tue-Fri, 2-6pm Sat & Sun) FREE Shows rotating exhibits from larger museums and paintings by Santa Cruz artists, with a mission to educate through art. Also a good spot to get news on local cultural gatherings.

Museo Malvinas Argentinas MUSEUM
(437618; cnr Pasteur & Av San Martín; 11am-6pm Mon-Fri, 10am-5pm Sat & Sun) FREE Perhaps a must-see for Brits, this museum gets inside the Argentine claim to the Islas Malvinas. Exhibits include signs made by ex-combatants and a video on the subject in English.

Plaza San Martín PLAZA
Pretty, with quiet benches in the shade of poplars and purple-blossom jacarandas.

Museo de los Pioneros MUSEUM
(437763; cnr Elcano & Alberdi; 10am-7pm) FREE In a prefabricated 1890s metal-clad house shipped from England, this museum has good displays on early immigrant life.

Funda Cruz CULTURAL CENTER
(G Lista 60) An attractive, imported, prefabricated wooden house. Once a customs office, it now hosts cultural activities as well as a *salón de té* (teahouse).

Tours

The large penguin rookery at Cabo Vírgenes, 140km southeast of Río Gallegos, can be visited from October to March. Excursions can be booked through **Al Sur Turismo** (436743; www.alsurturismo.com.ar; Errazuriz 194); an eight-hour trip costs AR$390 per person, with a minimum of three travelers (plus AR$15 park admission). Prices go up for smaller groups.

Sleeping

Since hotels cater mainly to business travelers, good-value budget accommodations are scarce.

El Viejo Miramar HOTEL $
(430401; hotelviejomiramar@yahoo.com.ar; Av Kirchner 1630; s/d AR$250/390) Snug carpeted rooms and spotless bathrooms make this affable choice a good one. Its personable owner makes guests feel at ease. Rates include breakfast (but not a second cup of coffee).

Hotel Covadonga HOTEL $
(420190; hotelcovadongargl@hotmail.com; Av Kirchner 1244; d AR$350, without bathroom

Río Gallegos

Río Gallegos

Sights

1 Funda Cruz C1
2 Museo de Arte Eduardo Minnicelli C3
3 Museo de los Pioneros A2
4 Museo Malvinas Argentinas C4
5 Museo Provincial Padre Jesús Molina C4
6 Plaza San Martín C3

Sleeping

7 El Viejo Miramar A3
8 Hotel Aire de Patagonia B3
9 Hotel Covadonga B3
10 Hotel Sehuen B2

Eating

11 Laguanacazul C1
12 Pizza Roma Express C3
13 RoCo C2

AR$300;) Good value and grandmotherly, the tidy Covadonga has large rooms with creaky floors, and a sunny living room with worn leather sofas. Rooms with private bathrooms are worth the upgrade. Cash discounts are offered.

Hostel Elcira HOSTEL $

(429856; Zuccarino 431; dm AR$80, d AR$180;) An impeccable yet kitschy family home with friendly hosts. It's far from the town center but just a 10-minute walk from the bus terminal.

★ **Hotel Aire de Patagonia** BOUTIQUE HOTEL $$

(444950; www.hotelairepatagonia.com.ar; Vélez Sarsfield 58; s/d AR$480/570;) Fresh and modern, this welcoming boutique hotel zings you up to your room in a hydraulic capsule elevator. Amenities include soft Egyptian cotton sheets, radiant floors and flatscreen TVs. The cute *confitería* is a good spot for a quiet espresso or board game.

Hotel Sehuen HOTEL **$$**
(☎425683; www.hotelsehuen.com; Rawson 160; d from AR$420) In a town short of budget rooms, this will do, but it seems overpriced. Rooms are tiny, thin walled and bathrooms positively tiny. Local newspapers and a basic buffet are available in the ample breakfast area.

Eating

Pizza Roma Express PIZZERIA **$**
(☎434400; Av San Martín 650; pizzas AR$30-60; ⏲11am-late) Cheap and casual, with service that's friendlier than you'll find elsewhere in town, this is where students and families dine on burgers, gnocchi and salads, and older gents share big bottles of cold Quilmes beer.

Laguanacazul GOURMET **$$**
(☎444114; cnr G Lista & Sarmiento; mains AR$80-150; ⏲noon-3pm & 8pm-midnight, closed Mon) Laguanacazul dares to take Patagonian cuisine to new places, with stir-fried trout and slow-cooked lamb with vegetables. The waterfront location is lovely and the interior quite stylish, but the service is practically snobbish; it's not advisable to come in here wearing grubby backpacker clothes.

RoCo ARGENTINE **$$**
(☎420203; Av Kirchner 1175; mains AR$50-90; ⏲8am-midnight, closed Sun) On the main thoroughfare, this upscale eatery pleases with swift service and a varied menu. Start with lamb empanadas, while main dishes include pasta, king crab and Patagonian lamb with fresh peas.

Information

Banks on Av Kirchner have ATMs. Internet is widely available in internet cafes and some restaurants.

ACA (Automóvil Club Argentino; ☎420477; Orkeke 10) Gas station, maps and traveler services.

Centro de Informes Turistico (Av San Martín s/n; ⏲Oct-Apr) Useful info kiosk on median strip.

Hospital Regional (☎420289; José Ingenieros 98)

Immigration Office (☎420205; Urquiza 144; ⏲9am-3pm Mon-Fri)

Municipal Tourist Office (☎436920; www.riogallegos.gov.ar; Av Beccar 126; ⏲8am-5pm Mon-Fri) A desk at the bus terminal keeps longer hours.

Post Office (cnr Avs Kirchner & San Martín)

Provincial Tourist Office (☎422702; Av Kirchner 863) Most helpful, with maps, bilingual staff and detailed info.

Getting There & Away

AIR

Río Gallegos' airport is 7km northwest of town.

The following are one-way base rates. **Aerolíneas Argentinas** (☎0810-2228-6527; Av San Martín 545) flies daily to Buenos Aires (AR$1267) and frequently to Ushuaia (AR$775). **LADE** (☎422316; Fagnano 53) flies several times a week to Buenos Aires, Río Grande (AR$492), El Calafate (AR$482), Comodoro Rivadavia (AR$776) and Ushuaia.

BUS

Río Gallegos' **bus terminal** (cnr RN3 & Av Eva Perón) is about 3km southwest of the city center. Companies include **El Pingüino** (☎442169), **Líder** (☎442160), **Bus Sur** (☎442687), **Andesmar** (☎442195), **Sportman** (☎442595) and also **TAC** (☎442042). Companies going to Chile include **Ghisoni** (☎457047), **Pacheco** (☎442765) and **Tecni-Austral** (☎442427). **Taqsa/Marga** (☎423130; www.taqsa.com.ar; Estrada 71) beelines straight from the airport to Puerto Natales and El Calafate.

Buses from Río Gallegos

DESTINATION	COST (AR$)	DURATION (HR)
Buenos Aires	1385	36-40
Comodoro Rivadavia	450	9-11
El Calafate	180	4
El Chaltén	300	9
Esquel	655	19
Puerto Madryn	726	15-20
Puerto Natales (Chile)	170	5-7
Puerto San Julián	205	4½
Punta Arenas (Chile)	120	5-6
Río Grande	355	8-10
Trelew	689	14-17
Ushuaia	500	12

Getting Around

It's easy to share metered taxis (AR$40) between the city center, the bus terminal and the airport. From Av Kirchner, buses marked 'B' or 'terminal' link the city center and the bus terminal (AR$5).

Car rental is expensive due to the poor conditions of the roads to most places of interest. Despite exchange rates, rental deals are often better in Punta Arenas, Chile. For local rentals, try **Riestra Rent A Car** (☎ 421321; www.riestrarentacar.com; Av San Martín 1508).

Around Río Gallegos

Visiting a working *estancia* affords an intimate glimpse into the unique Patagonian lifestyle. These are not luxury hotels, but homes that have been converted into comfortable lodgings. Meals are often shared with the owners, and token participation in the daily working life is encouraged. For *estancias* in Santa Cruz province, contact the provincial tourist office in Río Gallegos or see www.estanciasdesantacruz.com.

Named for gold once found on the coast, **Estancia Monte Dinero** (☎ 02966-15522663; www.montedinero.com.ar; s/d incl full board US$280/440; ⏲ Oct-Apr) is a comfortable, old-world lodging with intricate hand-painted doors, billiards and well-appointed rooms. All activities are included in the lodging rates. Dudes gor for the typical *estancia* activities – dog demos, shearing etc – and can also take trips to nearby **Cabo Vírgenes**, where Magellanic penguins nest September through March at Argentina's second-largest penguin rookery. History aficionados can appreciate that it's at Km0 of the historic RN40, as well as the *estancia* museum's intriguing display of an assortment of goods salvaged from shipwreck after the family Greenshyls sailed here from Ireland in 1886. Travel agencies in Río Gallegos offer day trips here starting in mid-November.

INLAND PATAGONIA

Save for the travel hubs of El Calafate and El Chaltén, RN40 and its offshoots are bit of a backwater. The ultimate road trip, RN40 parallels the backbone of the Andes, where ñandús doodle through sagebrush, trucks kick up whirling dust and gas stations rise on the horizon like oases.

Now that over two-thirds of the 1228km stretch between Esquel and El Calafate is paved, travel is considerably easier, although the rough parts remain pretty rough. For now, public transport stays limited to a few summer-only tourist shuttle services, and driving requires both preparation and patience.

RN40 parallels the Andes from north of Bariloche to the border with Chile near Puerto Natales, then cuts east to the Atlantic Coast. Highlights include the Perito Moreno and Los Glaciares national parks, the rock art of Cueva de los Manos and remote *estancias*.

This section picks up RN40 in Esquel, from where it continues paved until south of Gobernador Costa, where it turns to gravel. From there on down, gravel is interspersed with paved sections, mainly near population centers. At the time of writing, the last 130km before El Chaltén, the 120km further to El Calafate and 130km beyond it were paved.

Esquel

☎ 02945 / POP 32,400 / ELEVATION 570M

If you tire of the gnome-in-the-chocolate-shop ambience of Bariloche and other cutesy Lakes District destinations, regular old Esquel will feel like a breath of fresh air. Set in western Chubut's dramatic, hikeable foothills, Esquel is a hub for Parque Nacional Los Alerces and an easy-going, friendly base camp for abundant adventure activities – the perfect place to chill after hard travel on RN40.

Founded at the turn of the 20th century, Esquel is the region's main livestock and commercial center. It's also the historic southern end of the line for *La Trochita*, the narrow-gauge steam train. The town takes its name from Mapundungun, meaning either 'bog' or 'place of the thistles.'

RN259 zigzags through town to the junction with RN40, which heads north to El Bolsón and south to Comodoro Rivadavia. South of town, RN259 passes a junction for Parque Nacional Los Alerces en route to Trevelin.

Sights & Activities

Esquel's best attractions are of the outdoor variety, notably Parque Nacional Los Alerces and La Hoya. Esquel's nearby lakes and rivers offer excellent **fly fishing**, with the season running from November to April. You can purchase a license at the YPF gas station (p433) that houses the ACA. **Mountain biking** is a good way to get out of town and explore the surrounding hills and trails.

THE EPIC RUTA NACIONAL 40

Patagonia's RN40 is the quintessential road trip. But it's not for rushing – the weather can be wily and the gravel loose. It can seem to go on forever. But it is also magical, when after rattling along for hours, the interminable flat line of steppe bursts open with views of glacial peaks and gem-colored lakes. As it is paved, travel here is becoming easier. But long distances between gas stations and windy, unpaved sections still offer ample challenges.

Be Prepared

Travel with necessary repair equipment. If renting a car, carry two full-sized *neumáticos* (spare tires), check that the headlights work and that suspension, tires and brakes are in good shape. The gravel can puncture gas tanks, so have extra fuel on hand, as well as oil and generous supplies of food and water. Gas is subsidized in Patagonia, so fill up at each opportunity. Cell phones have no coverage outside of towns, so drivers must be self-sufficient.

Road Rules

The law requires seatbelts and headlights during daylight hours. Respect speed limits: 65km/h to 80km/h is a safe maximum speed. Sheep *always* have the right of way. Guanacos and ñandús are other potential hazards. Slow down, give them space and watch out for unsigned *guardaganados* (cattle guards).

Take the Backseat

Several travel agencies coordinate two- to five-day minivan transport along RN40 from El Calafate to Bariloche, via El Chaltén, Perito Moreno and Los Antiguos. Service follows fair weather, from mid-October/November to early April, depending on demand and road conditions. Pricier guided tours stretch the trip over four or five days.

If you're really up for a road trip, contact Ruta 40 (p418). The small, multilingual outfitter takes travelers on 10-day journeys on RN40 from Bariloche to El Calafate, with stops at Cueva de las Manos and several lovely *estancias*. Consult for current rates and departure dates.

Quicker, more straightforward travel along RN40 can be arranged through **Chaltén Travel** (☎011-4326-7282; www.chaltentravel.com; Sarmiento 559, piso 8, Buenos Aires), which runs northbound two-day shuttles, leaving at 8am from El Calafate, with accommodation in Perito Moreno. Southbound three-day shuttles leave Bariloche at 6:45am on odd-numbered days, with accommodations in Perito Moreno and El Chaltén. Buses stop in Los Antiguos as well. It is usually available from November to March. For the one-way trip, prices start at AR$1100 per person (not including accommodations or food). It's possible to hop on and off along the route, but space on the next shuttle cannot be reserved. Combinations to Puerto Madryn are also available for northbound travelers. Chaltén Travel has branches in El Calafate (p457), **El Chaltén** (☎493092, 493005; Av San Martín 635), Puerto Madryn (p405) and **Bariloche** (☎0294-442-3809; www.chaltentravel.com; Quaglia 262).

Some travelers have had good experiences with bus line Taqsa/Marga (p442), which offers high-season service north and south between El Calafate and Bariloche (AR$950, 28 hours, October to April), with stops in El Chaltén, Perito Moreno and Esquel.

Museo de Culturas Originarias Patagónicas MUSEUM
(☎451929; Nahuel Pan; donations accepted; ⏱2-5pm) **FREE** Displays a modest collection of Mapuche artifacts; *La Trochita* stops here.

Museo del Tren MUSEUM
(☎451403; cnr Roggero & Urquiza; ⏱8am-2pm Mon-Sat) **FREE** Just outside town, this train museum is in the Roca train station where *La Trochita*, Argentina's famous narrow-gauge steam train, stops. In summer several tour agencies sell tickets for round-trip rides on the antique train.

Cerro La Hoya SNOW SPORTS
(☎453018; www.cerrolahoya.com; admission AR$185, lift ticket adult/child AR$160/125; ⏱skiing

Jun-Oct) Despite wide open bowls and some of Argentina's best powder skiing, this 1350m resort is just starting to become well-known. While cheaper and less crowded than Bariloche, it is smaller and comparatively tame, ideal for families. Summer activities include hiking, chairlift rides and horseback riding. Equipment can be rented on-site or at sport shops in Esquel. Minibus transfers cost AR$60; taxis may be a better deal for groups. It's 13km north of Esquel.

Coyote Bikes BICYCLE RENTAL
(☎455505; www.coyotebikes.com.ar; Rivadavia 887; 2hr/day rental AR$60/130; ⊙9am-1pm & 3:30-8pm Mon-Fri, 9am-1pm Sat) For mountain-bike rentals and trail details in summer.

Tours

Independent and nationally certified guides **Estefanía Chereguini** (☎02945-549357; endlesspatagonia@gmail.com) and **Walter Oszust** (☎02945-682915; walteroszust@gmail.com), the creators of Huella Andina, lead guided hikes (from US$30 per day) in Parque Nacional Los Alerces and throughout Patagonia. English spoken.

Circuito Lacuestre BOAT TOUR
Numerous travel agencies sell tickets for the Circuito Lacustre boat excursion in Parque Nacional Los Alerces; buying a ticket in Esquel assures a place on the often-crowded trip. Full-day excursions, including the lake cruise, cost AR$195 when sailing from Puerto Chucao or AR$250 from Puerto Limonao, including transfers to and from the park.

Expediciones Patagonia Aventura ADVENTURE TOUR
(EPA; ☎457015; www.epaexpediciones.com; Av Fontana 482) Offers rafting, canyoning, horseback riding and trekking. Those white-water rafting (half-day AR$250 with transport) on Río Corcovado (90km away) can overnight at the recommended riverside hostel. Canopy tours, horseback riding and trekking use the mountain center, an attractive wooden lodge (full pension from AR$720) in Parque Nacional Los Alerces. Guests have access to kayaks, and camping is also available.

Festivals & Events

Semana de Esquel FESTIVAL
A week-long February event that celebrates the city's 1906 founding.

Fiesta Nacional de Esquí SKI FESTIVAL
(National Skiing Festival) Takes place in mid-September at La Hoya.

Sleeping

Esquel has many accommodations; check with the tourist office for more listings, which include cabins and apartments geared for ski vacations.

Sol Azul HOSTEL $
(☎455193; www.hostelsolazul.com.ar; Rivadavia 2869; dm AR$90; @📶) With the good looks of a mountain lodge, this welcoming hostel ups the ante with a sauna and a fully decked-out kitchen with industrial stoves lined with spices. There's also dinners serving local meat. Dorms are in a house at the back, with small but tidy bathrooms. It's a taxi ride to the center, on the northern edge of town. Breakfast is extra (AR$20).

Planeta Hostel HOSTEL $
(☎456846; www.planetahostel.com; Roca 458; dm AR$110, d AR$350; 📶) This old but boldly painted downtown house features friendly service but cramped rooms. Down comforters, a spotless communal kitchen and a flatscreen TV lounge are a cut above the usual.

Hostería La Chacra B&B $$
(☎452802; www.lachacrapatagonia.com; RN259, Km5; d/tr AR$400/500; @📶) If you want a shot of local culture, nothing is better than this country lodging in a 1970s home with ample bright rooms, generous gringo breakfasts and thick down bedding. The owner Rini is a consummate host and expert on local Welsh history. Get here via shuttle, taxi or Trevelin bus – they pass hourly.

Sur Sur HOTEL $$
(www.hotelsursur.com; Fontana 282; d/tr AR$450/550; 📶) A popular option, this family enterprise delivers warmth and comfort. Small tile rooms feature TV, fan and hair dryers, and the hallways are decked with regional photos taken by former guests. Breakfast is served buffet-style.

Hostería Angelina INN $$
(☎452763; www.hosteriaangelina.com.ar; Av Alvear 758; d/superior AR$350/390; @📶) Hospitable and polished, with a courtyard fountain, Angelina follows international standards with professional service and a good breakfast buffet.

DON'T MISS

THRU TREKKING PATAGONIA

The US has the Appalachian Trail, New Zealand has the Te Araroa Trail, and now Argentina has **Huella Andina** (huellaandina.desarrolloturistico.gov.ar), the country's first long-distance trail. Huella, literally 'footprint,' is the local term for footpaths.

The project was the brainchild of Estefanía Chereguini and Walter Oszust, two young mountaineers in Esquel. It took them three years to mark 430km of trails through the Andes with 31 stages. Huella Andina crosses from Neuquen to Chubut, passing through five national parks, including Parque Nacional Los Alerces, and private lands. Scenery shifts from araucaria to alerce forest, from mountain heights to river valleys and pristine lakes. It's marked by a couple of blue and white parallel bands.

Now managed by the Minsterio Nacional de Turismo, the project is expected to eventually feature over 600km of linked trails. Visit the website for details on trail stages and a map.

Plaza Esquel Hostería & Spa HOTEL **$$**
(☎457002; www.patagoniaandesgroup.com.ar; Av Ameghino 713; d/superior incl spa AR$530/630; @☎) On the plaza, this attractive *hostería* has small rooms with modern decor but a little wear and tear. The spa features a sauna and Jacuzzi, but not much ambience.

★**Las Bayas Hotel** BOUTIQUE HOTEL **$$$**
(☎455800; www.lasbayashotel.com; Av Alvear 985; d/tr AR$1540/1725) Simply lovely, this elegant boutique lodging sits head and shoulders above other hotels. Tasteful decor includes wood accents, warm woolen throws and modern accents. Spacious rooms feature LCD screens and DVD libraries, kitchenettes and tubs with massage jets. There's also spa services available and deep discounts in low season.

Hostería Canela B&B B&B **$$$**
(☎453890; www.canelaesquel.com; cnr Los Notros & Los Radales, Villa Ayelén; d/tr US$165/203, q apt US$290; ☎) Veronica and Jorge's refined B&B, tucked away in a pine forest 2km outside the town center, feels elegant and comfortable, an ideal match for mature guests. The English-speaking owners offer in-room tea service and the comfortable beds are topped with pristine white linens.

Eating

La Abuela ARGENTINE **$**
(Rivadavia 1109; mains AR$60-75; ⊙noon-3pm & 7:30-11pm Mon-Fri) Shoehorn yourself into this family nook decked out in lace tablecloths, and enjoy cheap gnocchi, homemade pasta and home-cooked classics like *puchero* (vegetable and meat stew) with a carafe of passable house wine.

Cheers PUB **$**
(☎457041; cnr Sarmiento & Av Alvear; mains AR$30-80; ⊙noon-late) Don't let the Irish-pub atmosphere fool you into thinking this is just another stock standard watering hole: Killarney's serves up good set lunches, too, and a range of hearty soups, salads and sandwiches with the Guinness, of course.

María Castaña CAFE **$**
(cnr 25 de Mayo & Rivadavia; snacks AR$30-60; ⊙9am-late) A favorite at this frilly cafe is waffles with *dulce de leche;* it's also good for breakfast, sandwiches and ice-cream sundaes. Grab an overstuffed chair at the back. It also serves more substantial fare.

La Luna ARGENTINE **$$**
(Av Fontana 656; mains AR$45-100; ⊙noon-4pm & 7pm-1am) This chic rock'n'roll restaurant-bar offers tasty spinach pizza, vegetable crepes, and heaped portions of steak and fries. The evening crowd spills out of wooden booths and brick nooks, drinking Patagonia's artisan beers.

Don Chiquino ITALIAN **$$**
(Amhegino 1641; mains AR$80; ⊙lunch & dinner) Of course, pasta is no novelty in Argentina, but the owner-magician performing tricks while you wait for your meal is. The ambience is happy-cluttered and dishes such as sorrentinos prove satisfying.

Drinking

Hotel Argentino BAR
(25 de Mayo 862; ⊙4pm-5am) This lanky and lowbrow Wild West saloon is much better suited to drinking than sleeping, but by all means stop by: the owner is friendly, the 1916 construction is stuffed with relics and sculptures, and the place gets more than a little lively on weekends.

☆ Entertainment

Dirección Municipal de Cultura CULTURAL CENTER
(☎451929; www.esquelsemueve.com.ar; Belgrano 330) Sponsors regular music, cinema, theater and dance.

Information

ACA (Automóvil Club Argentino; ☎452382; cnr 25 de Mayo & Av Ameghino; ⏰daylight hours;) Inside YPF gas station; sells fishing licenses.

Banco de la Nación (cnr Av Alvear & General Roca) Has an ATM and changes travelers checks.

Banco del Chubut (Av Alvear 1147) Has an ATM.

Hospital Regional (☎450009; 25 de Mayo 150)

Post Office (Av Alvear 1192) Next to the tourist office.

Tourist Office (☎451927; www.esquel.gov.ar; cnr Av Alvear & Sarmiento; ⏰7am-11pm) Well organized, helpful and multilingual, with an impressive variety of detailed maps and brochures.

Getting There & Around

AIR

Esquel's airport is 20km east of town off RN40. Taxis will set you back around AR$140.

Aerolíneas Argentinas (☎453614; Av Fontana 406) flies to Buenos Aires (one way from AR$965) several times a week.

BUS

Esquel's full-service **bus terminal** (cnr Av Alvear & Brun) is close to the town center.

Transportes Jacobsen (☎453528) goes to Futaleufú, Chile (AR$40, 1½ hours), at 8am and 6pm Monday and Friday. Buses go hourly to Trevelin (AR$10, 30 minutes), stopping near the corner of Av Alvear and 25 de Mayo on the way out of town.

In summer **Transportes Esquel** (☎453529; www.transportesesquel.com.ar) goes through Parque Nacional Los Alerces (AR$28, 1¼ hours) to Lago Futalaufquen at 8am daily (and also at 2pm and 6pm during January). The first bus goes all the way to Lago Puelo (AR$45, six hours), and stops in Lago Verde (AR$45) at 10:30am and Cholila at noon. An open ticket is available, which allows passengers to make stops along the way between Esquel and Lago Puelo or vice-versa. Do note that the service is reduced in low season.

Buses from Esquel

DESTINATION	COST (AR$)	DURATION (HR)
Bariloche	105-170	4¼
Buenos Aires	1160	25
Comodoro Rivadavia	300	8
El Bolsón	80	2½
Neuquén	355	10
Puerto Madryn	429	7-9
Río Gallegos	655	18
Trelew	307-407	8-9

TRAIN

The narrow-gauge steam train *La Trochita* departs from the diminutive **Roca train station** (www.latrochita.org.ar; cnr Roggero & Urquiza; ⏰8am-2pm Mon-Sat). There's a frequent tourist-oriented service to Nahuel Pan. For the timeless *Old Patagonian Express* feeling, your best bet is to catch a bus to El Maitén for the less touristy excursion to Desvio Thomae; however, this service is only available from time to time. You can confirm schedules online or via the tourist office.

CAR

Compact rentals start around AR$600 a day, including 100km and insurance. Try **Patagonia Travel Rent A Car** (☎455811, 02945-15-692174; www.patagoniatravelrentacar.com; Av Alvear 1041), which offers a good range of vehicles.

Trevelin

☎02945 / POP 6350 / ELEVATION 735M

Historic Trevelin (treh-*veh*-lehn), from the Welsh for town *(tre)* and mill *(velin),* is the only community in interior Chubut with a notable Welsh character. Easygoing and postcard pretty, this pastoral village makes a tranquil lodging alternative to the much busier Esquel (remember, everything is relative here), or an enjoyable day trip for tea. The surrounding countryside is ripe for exploration.

Just 22km south of Esquel via paved RN259, Trevelin centers around the octagonal plaza Coronel Fontana. Eight streets radiate from it, including the principal thoroughfare, Av San Martín (also the southward extension of RN259). RN259 forks west 50km to the Chilean border and to Futaleufú, 12km beyond.

Patagonian Wildlife

Thanks to deep ocean currents that bring nutrients and abundant food, the coast of southern Argentina plays host to bountiful marine life. To see them hunt, court, nest and raise their young renews one's sense of wonder along these lonely Atlantic shores.

Magellanic Penguin

1 Adorable and thoroughly modern, penguins co-parent after chicks hatch in mid-November. See the action at Punta Tombo (p416), Ría Deseado (p423) and Bahía Bustamante (p421).

Southern Sea Lion

2 Found year-round along the southern coast of Argentina, these burly swimmers feed on squid and the odd penguin.

Commerson's Dolphin

3 These small dolphins often join boaters in play. See them all year at Playa Unión (p414), in Ría Deseado (p423) and Puerto San Julián (p424).

Southern Right Whale

4 In spring, the shallow waters of Península Valdés (p406) attract thousands of these creatures to breed and bear young.

Orca

5 To witness raw nature at work, visitors flock to Punta Norte (p410) on Península Valdés, where these powerful creatures almost beach themselves in the hunt for sea lions, from mid-February to mid-April.

Southern Elephant Seal

6 Consummate divers, these monsters spend most of the year at sea. In austral spring, spy on their breeding colony at Punta Delgada (p410) on Península Valdés. Watch for beachmasters – dominant males controlling harems of up to 100 females.

1

4

Clockwise from top left

1. Magellanic penguins 2. Southern sea lions
3. Commerson's dolphin 4. Southern right whale

DAVID TIPLING/GETTY IMAGES ©

JUAN CARLOS MUNOZ/GETTY IMAGES ©

Sights

Museo Regional Molino Viejo MUSEUM
(☎480461; cnr 25 de Mayo & Molino Viejo; admission AR$30; ⊙11am-6pm Mon-Fri, 12:30-6:30pm Sat & Sun) Occupies the restored remains of a 1922 grain mill. At the time of research it was closed for renovation. It's a couple of blocks east of the plaza, at the end of 25 de Mayo.

Tumba de Malacara MONUMENT
(☎480108; admission AR$20; ⊙4:30-7pm) Horse lovers can pay their respects at this monument holding the remains of Malacara, a brave horse whose swift retreat saved its owner's hide. Town founder John Evans escaped with Malacara from murderbent Araucanians, who were retaliating for an attack by the Argentine army during the Conquista del Desierto. Located two blocks northeast of the plaza.

Festivals & Events

Aniversario de Trevelin FESTIVAL
Commemorates the founding of the city on March 19.

Eisteddfod FESTIVAL
The biggest Welsh celebration of the year, this multilingual festival where bards compete in song and poetry takes place at the end of October.

Sleeping

Circulo Policial CAMPGROUND $
(☎480947; Costanera Río Percy & Holdich; campsites per person AR$35; ⊙Jan-Feb, sometimes with extension depending on weather) Fine, grassy campsites with shade. From Av San Martín 600 block, walk two blocks west on Coronel Holdich and turn left down the gravel road.

Hostería Casa de Piedra LODGE $$
(☎480357; www.casadepiedratrevelin.com; Brown 244; d/tr AR$690/750; ❄📶) A haven for anglers and 4WD enthusiasts, this elegant stone lodge boasts a huge fireplace and rustic touches. Buffet breakfast includes yogurt, homemade bread, cakes and fruit.

Cabañas Wilson CABIN $$
(☎480803; www.wilsonpatagonia.com.ar; RP259 at RP71; 4-/6-person cabins AR$620/730; 📶) Savor the serenity surrounding these wood-and-brick cabins with log furniture on the edge of town. The cabins include daily cleaning service, extra covers and a barbecue deck. An abundant breakfast is optional.

Cabañas Oregon CABIN $$
(☎480408; www.oregontrevelin.com.ar; cnr Av San Martín & JM Thomas; 4-person cabin AR$600; 📶) Scattered around an apple orchard on the south side of town, these appealing log cabins come with handmade wooden furniture. Features include kitchen and TV, and there's also a swingset for kids. The on-site grill restaurant (buffet grill AR$100 to AR$150, closed Tuesday) is reputed as the best spot in town to eat meat, with good service.

Eating & Drinking

Just as visitors to Trelew flock to Gaiman, so visitors to Esquel head to Trevelin for Welsh tea. Teahouses are typically open from 3pm

LA TROCHITA: THE OLD PATAGONIAN EXPRESS

Clearly an anachronism in the jet age, Ferrocarril Roca's **La Trochita** (☎02945-451403), Argentina's famous narrow-gauge steam train, averages less than 30km/h on its meandering journey between Esquel and El Maitén – at top speed. The train Paul Theroux facetiously called *The Old Patagonian Express* provides both a tourist attraction and a service for local citizens..

Like many state projects, its completion seemed an interminable process, beginning in 1906 and reaching completion in 1945. It has suffered some of the oddest mishaps in railroad history. In the late 1950s and early 1960s, the train was derailed three times by high winds, and ice has caused other derailments. In 1979 it collided with a cow.

La Trochita's original 402km route between Esquel and Ingeniero Jacobacci was probably the world's longest remaining steam-train line. Belgian Baldwin and German Henschel engines refilled their 4000L water tanks at strategically placed *parajes* (pumps) every 40km to 45km. Most of the passenger cars, heated by wood stoves, date from 1922, as do the freight cars.

During summer the **Tren Turístico** (tickets AR$250; ⊙10am twice weekly, additional departures Jan-Feb) travels from Roca train station in Esquel to Nahuel Pan, 20km east. At Nahuel Pan, the train stops for photo ops and a small artisan market.

to 8pm. Often the portions are big enough to share – ask first if it's OK.

★ Nikanor ARGENTINE $$

(☎480400; Libertad 56; mains AR$75-130; ⏲12:30-2:30pm & 8:30-11pm) If you're not in the mood for tea, make this excellent home-style restaurant your first choice. A husband and wife team serve up raviolis stuffed with local lamb, a list of Argentine wines and flambé crepes for dessert. In a lovely, renovated early-20th-century home, with exposed brick, exposed beams and a window exposing the original adobe and bamboo construction.

Nain Maggie TEAHOUSE

(☎480232; www.casadetenainmaggie.com; Perito Moreno 179; tea service AR$110; ⏲10am-12:30pm & 3-8:30pm) Trevelin's oldest teahouse occupies a modern building but has high traditional standards. Along with a bottomless pot, there's cream pie, *torta negra* and scones.

La Mutisia TEAHOUSE

(☎480165; Av San Martín 170; tea service AR$110) Everything is reliably homemade at this teahouse.

Shopping

Mercado de Artisanos MARKET

This artisans market kills Plaza Coronel Fontana on Sundays in summer and on alternate Sundays the rest of the year.

Information

Banco del Chubut (cnr Av San Martín & Brown) Just south of the plaza, with an ATM.

Gales al Sur (☎480427; www.galesalsur.com.ar; Patagonia 186) Esquel buses stop at this travel agency, which also arranges tours.

Post Office (Av San Martín) Just south of the plaza.

Tourist Office (☎480120; www.trevelin.gov.ar) Helpful, with a free town map, information on local hikes and English-speaking staff.

Getting There & Away

The **bus terminal** (cnr Roca & RN40) faces the main plaza. Most services originate in Esquel. **Gales del Sur** (☎480427; RN259) has hourly buses to Esquel (AR$10, 30 minutes). Buses cross the border to Chile's Futaleufú (AR$40, one hour) on Monday and Friday at 8:30am and 6pm, plus Wednesday in summer.

Parque Nacional Los Alerces

☎02945

This collection of spry creeks, verdant mountains and mirror lakes resonates as unadulterated Andes. The real attraction, however, is the alerce tree *(Fitzroya cupressoides)*, one of the longest-living species on the planet, with specimens that have survived up to 4000 years. Lured by the acclaim of well-known parks to the north and south, most hikers miss this gem, which makes your visit here all the more enjoyable.

Resembling California's giant sequoia, the alerce flourishes in middle Patagonia's temperate forests, growing only about 1cm every 20 years. Individual specimens of this beautiful tree can reach over 4m in diameter and exceed 60m in height. Like the giant sequoia, it has suffered overexploitation because of its valuable timber. West of Esquel, this 2630-sq-km park protects some of the largest alerce forests that still remain.

Because the Andes are relatively low here, westerly storms deposit nearly 3m of rain annually. The park's eastern sector, though, is much drier. Winter temperatures average 2°C, but can be much colder. The summer average high reaches 24°C, but evenings are usually cool.

While its wild backcountry supports the seldom-seen huemul (Andean deer) and other wildlife, Los Alerces functions primarily as a trove of botanical riches which characterize the dense Valdivian forest.

Activities

As well as sailing and hiking, travel agencies in Esquel do fishing, canoeing, mountain biking, snorkeling and horseback riding.

Sailing

Traditionally, **Circuito Lacustre** is Los Alerces' most popular excursion and involves sailing from Puerto Limonao up Lago Futalaufquen and through the narrow channel of the Río Arrayanes to Lago Verde.

Low water makes it necessary to hike the short distance between Puerto Mermoud, at the north end of Lago Futalaufquen, and Puerto Chucao on Lago Menéndez. Launches from Puerto Chucao handle the second segment of the trip (1½ hours) to the northern nature trail **El Alerzal**, the most accessible stand of alerces. Another option (recommended) is to arrive at Puerto

Parque Nacional Los Alerces

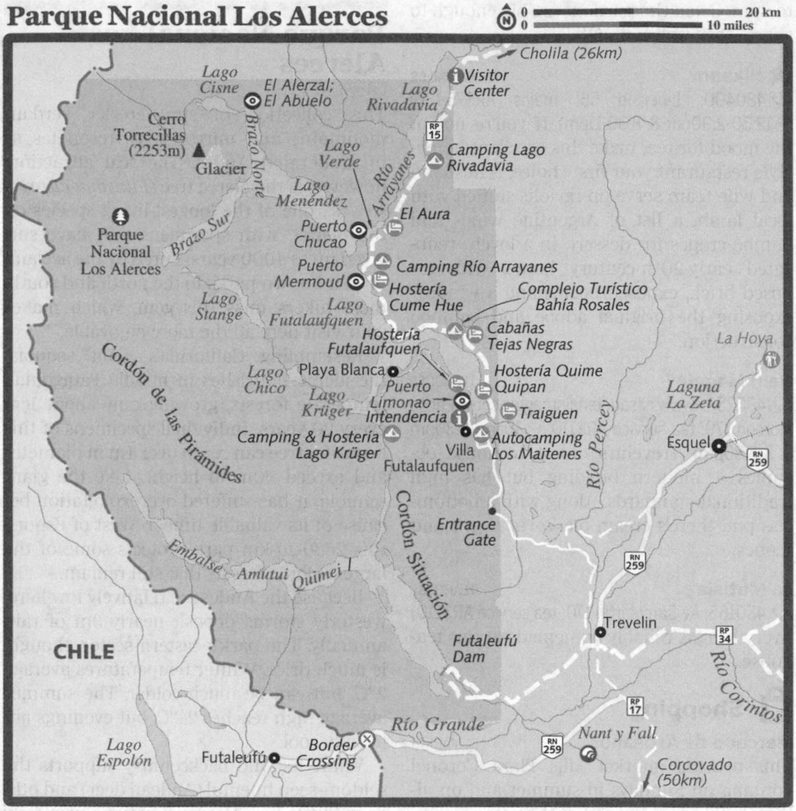

Chucao via a 1500m very scenic trail that crosses the bridge over Río Arrayanes.

The launch remains docked for over an hour at El Alerzal trailhead, sufficient for an unhurried hike around the loop trail that passes **Lago Cisne** and an attractive waterfall to end up at **El Abuelo** (Grandfather), a 57m-tall, 2600-year-old alerce.

From Puerto Limonao, the excursion costs AR$420; from Puerto Chucao it's AR$340. Departures are in the morning from Limonao and at noon from Chucao, returning to Chucao around 5pm and to Limonao at 7pm. In summer purchase tickets in Esquel to ensure a seat.

Hiking

Hikers must sign in at the one of the ranger stations before heading out.

Day hikes can be undertaken from several interpretive trails located near **Lago Futalaufquen**. There is also a 25km trail from **Puerto Limonao** along the south shore of Futalaufquen to **Hostería Lago Krüger**, which can be done in a long day, or broken up by camping at **Playa Blanca**. Boat excursions from Puerto Limonao to Lago Krüger cost AR$420 per person.

For longer hikes, see Lonely Planet's *Trekking in the Patagonian Andes*.

Sleeping & Eating

En route to the park, watch for roadside signs advertising ideal picnic goods: homemade bread, delicious Chubut cheese, fresh fruit and Welsh sweets. In Villa Futalaufquen there are a couple of basic grocery stores and a summer-only restaurant, but it's best to bring your own provisions.

Los Alerces has several full-service campgrounds, all of which have showers, grocery stores and restaurants on-site or nearby. Free (no services) and semi-organized campgrounds exist near most of these fee sites.

With a group, *cabañas* can be an affordable option.

Camping Río Arrayanes CAMPGROUND $
(☎454381; campsites per adult/child AR$60/40) A new campground, with showers, bathrooms and grills, located in one of the most scenic areas of the park.

Camping Lago Rivadavia CAMPGROUND $
(☎454381; campsites per adult/child AR$60/40) These idyllic spots at Lago Rivadavia's south end are sheltered in the trees with picnic tables and a boat launch. There's an electricity hookup, too. It's 42km north of Villa Futalaufquen.

Autocamping Los Maitenes CAMPGROUND $
(☎471006; campsites per adult/child AR$60/40) On a slip of grass between the main road and the lake, these spots have lovely water views. Sites include shade, electricity hookup and fire pits, 200m from the Intendencia.

Cabañas Tejas Negras CABIN $$
(☎471012, 471046; www.tejasnegras.com.ar; 4-/5-person cabins AR$900/1200) With a lawn like a golf course and a handful of prim A-frames, Nilda and Hector have hosted guests for 40 years. Think retreat: there are no *fútbol* matches on these greens where tranquility is savored. Note to parents – they only take kids who are well-behaved! Requires a three-night minimum.

Traiguen CABIN $$
(☎02945-15-68-3606; 4-person cabins AR$400; ⊙year-round) You might need good clearance to make it up the dirt road, but these few, ample cabins have lovely lake views and their going rate is a steal. Run by the *simpatico* Graciela and her giant tomcats.

Complejo Turístico Bahía Rosales CAMPGROUND $$
(☎02945-15-403413, 471044; 4-/6-person cabin AR$550/700) This sprawling complex with sporting facilities sits at the north end of Lago Futalaufquen, 1.5km from the main road via a dirt path. When we researched, the campgrounds were closed for the season; check for changes.

Hostería Quime Quipan INN $$
(☎471021; www.quimequipan.com.ar; d/tr from AR$575/645, 5-person apt/cabin AR$875/965; ⊙Nov-Apr;) In a breathtaking setting, this old-fashioned guesthouse offers pleasant but dated rooms – splurge for those with lake views. Nonguests can dine at the cozy, sunlit restaurant, an après-fishing pit stop. Wi-fi in the lobby only.

★**Hostería Futalaufquen** INN $$$
(☎471008; www.hosteriafutalaufquen.com; d incl half-board lake/forest view AR$1040/1250, 3-person cabin AR$1520) Exclusive and elegant, this country inn is on the quieter western shore of Lake Futalaufquen, 4.5km north of Villa Futalaufquen at the end of the road. It offers well-appointed doubles and log cabins (without kitchens). Activities ranging from kayaking to rappelling can be arranged from here. Afterwards, collapse by the fire with a plate of dessert.

Cabins come in varying size for up to eight guests. Make reservations at Sarmiento 635 in Esquel.

El Aura CABIN $$$
(Lago Verde Wilderness Resort; ☎in Buenos Aires 011-4816-5348; www.hosteriaselaura.com; 2-/4-person cabins incl full board US$340/510; ⊙Nov-April) Rustic yet ritzy, these raspy stone *cabañas* feature big cozy beds, panoramic

ON BUTCH CASSIDY'S TRAIL IN CHOLILA

Butch Cassidy, the Sundance Kid and Etta Place tried settling down and making an honest living near this quiet farming community outside the northeast entrance to Parque Nacional Los Alerces. The bandits' tale is recounted by Bruce Chatwin in the travel classic *In Patagonia*. Though the threesome's idyll only lasted a few years, their partially restored homestead still stands, just off RP71 at Km21, 8km north of Cholila. Cholila's enthusiastic **Casa de Informes** (☎02945-4980131, 02945-498040; www.turismocholila.gov.ar; RP71 at RP 15; ⊙Dec-Mar) has a helpful regional map and will gladly point you in the right direction.

To overnight in this funky Patagonian outpost, check out the hospitable **Piuke Mapu Hostel** (☎02945-15-685608; www.piukemapu.com; Av Soberanía Argentina 200; dm AR$65), located three blocks from the plaza. Young owners Laura and Dario also run a community garden and mountain refuge and guide local trekking and Alpine excursions.

forest views and earthy motifs. Anglers can rent motorized rafts to cast from Lago Futalaufquen's every nook and cranny. Guided trekking, horseback riding and fly-fishing are also offered. A gourmet restaurant and teahouse cater to travelers and guests. It's 35km north of Villa Futalaufquen.

Camping & Hostería Lago Krüger CAMPGROUND $$$
(☎02945-15-4424-7964; www.lagokrugger.com.ar; campsites per person AR$90, dm 2 nights AR$1100, d incl half-board 2 nights AR$2755) This attractive and relatively isolated lakefront mountain refuge is accessible by the 25km trail that leaves from Hostería Futalaufquen, or by launch from Puerto Limonao (AR$220).

Information

During the high season (Christmas to Semana Santa) foreigners pay AR$75 admission. In Villa Futalaufquen you'll find the **Intendencia** (Park Office; ☎471020, 471015; ⏲8am-9pm summer, 9am-4pm rest of year), the park administration center where rangers have details about hiking, camping and guided excursions. Get your fishing permits here. The headquarters also houses the **Museo y Centro del Interpretación**, which is a natural-history museum. The visitor center at the northern end of the park is only open between December and February.

Gobernador Costa

☎02945 / POP 2250

When you find a town where a child snaps the tourist's picture (and not the reverse), it's something of an anomaly. This rusted little cattle town abuts the yawning stretch of RN40 between Esquel and Río Mayo, at the intersection of RP20 for Sarmiento and Comodoro Rivadavia. Some 20km west of town, RP19 leads to **Lago General Vintter** and several smaller blue-ribbon lakes near the Chilean border; camping is possible along the shores.

Traveler services are few but reasonable. **Banco Chubut** (cnr Sarmiento & San Martín) has an ATM. The curious **JR Departamentos** (☎15-529537; d AR$220-280; Wi-Fi) has small but serviceable apartments that come with a deck of cards, kitchenette and cloud murals on a black backdrop: find Noemi at the main street pharmacy to check in. They also take Chilean pesos. Motel-style **Hotel Roca** (☎491126; Av Roca s/n; d AR$300; Wi-Fi) has tidy brick rooms and a restaurant. Meals can be taken from **Kaserita** (Aguado 128; mains AR$35-50; ⏲10am-2pm & 6-10:30pm), essentially a fresh pasta kitchen with folding-chair seating.

From the **bus terminal** (Av Roca s/n), buses go to Esquel and continue to Bariloche at 3:45am every day but Saturday. For Comodoro Rivadavia (AR$300, eight hours), buses leave twice daily. Both routes are paved.

WORTH A TRIP

BOSQUE PETRIFICADO SARMIENTO

Fallen giants scatter the pale sandstone landscape at this **petrified forest** (admission AR$20; ⏲dawn-dusk), 30km southeast of Sarmiento. The forest, brought here by strong river currents from the mountainous regions about 65 million years ago, has logs 100m in length and 1m wide. For travelers, this area is much more accessible than the Monumento Natural Bosques Petrificados further south.

Go with your own rental car, or ask at the tourist office in Sarmiento for *remise* rates for the 1½-hour round-trip. Try to stay through sunset, when the striped bluffs of Cerro Abigarrado and the multihued hills turn brilliantly vivid.

Located 10km west of Sarmiento, working cherry farm **Chacra Labrador** (☎0297-489-3329, 0297-15-404-3222; www.hosterialabrador.com; d AR$800; Wi-Fi) is a charming 1930s homestead offering bed and breakfast. Rooms are few but luxuriant, with big cozy beds, antique furniture, pots of tea and crackling fires.

The eager staff at Sarmiento's **tourist office** (☎0297-489-8220; cnr Infanteria 25 & Pietrobelli; ⏲8am-7pm Mon-Fri, 11am-5pm Sat & Sun) can provide *remise* rates, maps and lodging information. Sarmiento is 148km west of Comodoro along RN26 and RP20. Etap buses run daily to Comodoro Rivadavia (AR$70, two hours). **Buses Etap** (☎0297-4893058) goes to Río Mayo (AR$70, 1½ hours) go at 9:30pm daily.

Río Mayo

☎02903 / POP HUMANS 2800, SHEEP 800,000

The national capital of sheep shearing is a surprisingly humdrum place, save for the petroleum workers and waylaid gauchos practicing their wolf whistles on female *turistas*. This barren pit stop is 200km south of Gobernador Costa and 135km north of Perito Moreno.

The **Casa de Cultura** (☎420400; Ejército Argentino s/n; ⏰9am-noon & 3-6pm) kiosk houses a tourist office, with information on local mountain-biking options. **Banco del Chubut** (cnr Yrigoyen & Argentina) has an ATM.

January's **Festival Nacional de la Esquila** features merino wool-quality competitions and guanaco shearing in anticipation for the main event: the long-anticipated crowning of the national sheep-shearing queen.

The picture of eccentricity, **El Viejo Covadonga** (☎420020; San Martín 573; dm/s/d AR$120/180/360; wifi) features rooms with good down covers but varying in quality. Its coveted feature is the orange vinyl bar. **Hotel Akatá** (☎420054; San Martín 640; s/d AR$180/250; @ wifi)has meals and internet but little else; its wood-panel rooms are dark and airless. Otherwise the YPF is a good bet for a quick sandwich and coffee.

There are daily morning services from the **bus terminal** (☎420174; cnr Fontana & Irigoyen) to Comodoro Rivadavia (AR$105, 4½ hours) and Sarmiento (AR$75, two hours). Service goes twice weekly to Coyhaique, Chile (AR$120, six hours), currently Wednesday and Saturday. Schedules change regularly so check at the bus terminal. Heading south to Perito Moreno, there is currently 43 unpaved kilometers. The only regularly scheduled services on this rugged stretch of RN40 are summer-only backpacker shuttles.

Perito Moreno

☎02963 / POP 4620

Don't confuse this dull town with the jaw-dropping national park of the same name or the glacier near El Calafate – the only tourist attraction here is cruising the strip on Saturday night. A brief stopover en route to the more inviting Andean oasis of Los Antiguos, Perito Moreno does have a good range of services for a town on RN40, though area mining means hotels are often booked. Attractions Cueva de las Manos and Parque Nacional Perito Moreno are not far off. A dedicated archaeological museum, Museo Gradin, which exhibits a variety of archeological discoveries from the Rio de las Pinturas, was in the works at the time of research and promises to be a useful companion stop.

The town's glory came in 1898, when explorer Perito Moreno challenged Chile's border definition of *'divortum aquarum continental'* (which claimed the headwaters of Pacific-flowing rivers as Chilean territory) by rerouting Río Fénix, which flows through town, to Atlantic-bound Río Deseado. The river and the area remained Argentine, and the town took his name. The main drag, San Martín, leads north to RP43 and south to RN40; it's 128km south to Bajo Caracoles and 135km north of Río Mayo.

Tours

GuanaCondor Tours TOUR
(☎432303; jarinauta@yahoo.com.ar; Perito Moreno 1087; ⏰10am-noon & 4-8pm Mon-Wed & Sat, 5-8pm Sun) The experienced GuanaCondor Tours runs tours in summer to Cueva de las Manos (AR$350 per person), accessing the park via the former Estancia Los Toldos, with a challenging hike that adds considerably to the experience. Also ask about its trips to Monte Zeballos, a high mesa with excellent views, and the overnight trip to Paso Tehuelche.

Hugo Campañoli GUIDED TOUR
(☎432336) Hugo Campañoli is a local guide who takes groups of three or more to Cueva de las Manos on day trips.

Zoyen TOUR
(☎432207; www.zoyenturismo.com.ar; Peron 1008) Good local travel agency with trips to Cueva de las Manos in high season.

Sleeping & Eating

There are a couple of well-stocked *panaderías* (bakeries) and supermarkets along San Martín.

Hotel Americano HOTEL $
(☎432074; www.hotelamericanoweb.com.ar; San Martín 1327; s/d AR$195/300, d superior AR$350; wifi) Thriving Americano also has a decent grill and cafe that's busy in the evenings. Rooms vary widely – some lack windows, others can be quite cozy – so ask to see a few before deciding.

Hotel Belgrano HOTEL $
(☎432019; www.hotelbelgrano.guiapatagonia.net; San Martín 1001; dm/s/d AR$100/200/280) This big, boxy corner hotel has spacious concrete rooms with decent mattresses but not much ambience. Most folks shuffle in during the wee hours from Chaltén Travel shuttles.

Camping Municipal CAMPGROUND $
(Laguna de los Cisnes, off Mariano Moreno; per tent AR$30, plus per person AR$30, vehicles AR$25, 2-/6-person cabañas AR$200/300) The cheapest option for backpackers is this campground with rustic cabins on the south side of town. It's shaded by breezy poplars and has hot showers.

Chacra Kaiken Lodge B&B $$$
(☎0297-15-408-6996, 432079; www.chacrakaiken.com.ar; Yrigoyen 2012; d/tr from AR$550/740; wi-fi) A solid new option, this four-room B&B is run by Petty and Coco, lifelong area residents who used to run a well-known *estancia*. So in addition to a snug sleep, they offer a lovely setting and a fresh taste of real Patagonia.

Salón Iturrioz CAFE $
(cnr Rivadavia & San Martín; sandwiches AR$50; 7am-11pm; wi-fi) With cappucino and wi-fi, this charming brick corner cafe is a godsend to RN40. It's also a social hub, and the best place to get information on Museo Gradin across the street.

Information

Banco de Santa Cruz (cnr San Martín & Rivadavia) Has an ATM and changes travelers checks.

Hospital Distrital (☎432040; Colón 1237)

Post Office (cnr JD Perón & Belgrano)

Tourist Office (☎432732; peritomoreno@santacruzpatagonia.gob.ar; San Martín; 7am-11:30pm Mon-Fri, 8am-3pm Sat & Sun) Helpful, with a surprising number of pamphlets and brochures and information on homestay lodgings. There is also a desk at the bus terminal (access road to RN43).

Getting There & Away

LADE (☎432055; San Martín 1065) flies to El Calafate, Río Gallegos, Río Grande and Ushuaia.

The **bus terminal** (access road to RN43) sits behind the YPF rotunda at the northern entrance to town. Taxis (AR$15) provide the only transport between here and the town center, other than a flat 15-minute walk. Buses leave a few times daily for Los Antiguos (AR$52, 40 minutes), though departure times aren't reliable as they're usually scheduled to connect with incoming buses from RN40, which are often delayed. In the afternoon, starting at 3:50pm, multiple buses also head for Comodoro Rivadavia (AR$217, six hours) and Río Gallegos (AR$551, 16 hours) via RN3.

Several shuttle services also offering excursions serve travelers on RN40. From November to April, **Chaltén Travel** (☎02902-492212; www.chaltentravel.com) goes north to Bariloche (11 hours), departing from Hotel Belgrano in Perito Moreno at 8pm on even-numbered days. Shuttles leave Hotel Belgrano at 8am to head south to El Chaltén (11 hours) on odd-numbered days.

The bus company **Taqsa/Marga** (☎432675) now runs the entire stretch of RN40 between El Calafate and Bariloche several times a week starting at the end of October, stopping at El Chaltén, Bajo Caracoles, Perito Moreno and Esquel along the way.

Los Antiguos

☎02963 / POP 3360

Situated on the windy shores of Lago Buenos Aires, the agricultural oasis of Los Antiguos is home to *chacras* (small independent farms) of cherries, strawberries, apples, apricots and peaches. Before Europeans arrived, it was known as I-Keu-khon (Place of the Elders) to Tehuelches. It makes for an attractive crossing to Chile, and the stretch of road between Perito Moreno and Los Antiguos affords particularly spectacular lake views.

Volcán Hudson's 1991 eruption covered the town in ash, but farms have bounced back. In summer **Lago Buenos Aires**, South America's second-biggest lake, is warm enough for a brisk swim. The stunning **Río Jeinemeni** is a favored spot for trout and salmon fishing.

Most services in the town are located either on or near east–west Av 11 de Julio, which heads west to the Chilean frontier at Chile Chico, the region's most convenient border crossing. Perito Moreno and RN40 are 60km east.

Tours

Chelenco Tours TOUR
(☎15-6284-2177; www.chelencotours.tur.ar; Av 11 de Julio Este 584; 10am-1pm & 4:30-9:30pm) In a log cabin office, this tour operator offers trekking to Cueva de Las Manos as well as trips to the scenic road to Monte Zeballos, in addition to longer excursions.

Festivals

Fiesta de la Cereza CHERRY FESTIVAL
Rodeos, live music and the crowning of the national Cherry Queen during the second weekend of January. Artisan goods are sold and *peñas folklóricas* (Argentine folk music concerts) at private farms go on all night long – see the tourist information office for more information.

Sleeping & Eating

Hotel Los Antiguos Cerezos HOTEL $
(491132; hotel_losantiguoscerezos@hotmail.com; Av 11 de Julio 850; s/d/tr AR$270/360/440;) A large cement building with modern but somewhat sterile rooms with single beds, TV and a good dose of heat when you need it.

Albergue Padilla HOSTEL $
(491140; mia_padilla@hotmail.com; San Martín 44; dm/d AR$100/420;) Chaltén Travel shuttles deposit lodgers at this cash-only family-run institution after dark. Pineboard dorms share bathrooms with plenty of hot water; towels cost extra. Doubles are overpriced. The staff have RN40 shuttle tickets and the latest details on Chilean border crossing and ferries.

Camping Municipal CAMPGROUND $
(491265; Av 11 de Julio s/n; campsite/dm/cabin AR$50/200/300) Windbreaks help considerably at this lakeshore site 1.5km east of town. Dorms are in windowless cabins with hot showers available in the evening; whole cabins sleep up to four.

★ **Hostería Antigua Patagonia** HOTEL $$
(491038; www.antiguapatagonia.com.ar; RP43 Acceso Este; s/d/tr AR$504/590/730;) In a stunning setting, this plush lakefront complex has a dose of rustic, with wooden trunks in rooms, four-poster beds and a stone fireplace that begs you to curl up in front like a cat. Beds are comfortable, though the foam pillows disappoint. With good service, sauna, pool, and bikes and kayaks for guests. It's 2km east of town.

Hotel Mora HOTEL $$
(0297-15-420-7472; www.hotelmorapatagonia.com; Av Costanera 1064; s/d/tr 475/610/760;) With its corrugated tin facade and lovely outdoor deck, this lodging holds promise. The best rooms are doubles with lake views. Others run toward the basic end with fatigued mattresses and showerheads without stalls. Still, the deck overlooking a waterfront promenade is ideal for a sunset beer. There is a nice restaurant on-site.

Cabañas Rincon de los Poetas CABIN $$
(491051; Patagonia Argentina 226; d/tr/q AR$400/500/600) These snug and kitschy wooden cabins equipped with kitchenettes are nothing fancy, but they prove good value for groups and families. It's located two blocks from the town center.

Viva El Viento CAFE $$
(491109; www.vivaelviento.com; Av 11 de Julio 447; mains AR$85-130; 9am-9pm Oct-Apr;) This stylish cafe and restaurant serves up strong coffee and warm service. The menu offers fresh salads, pastas, excellent steak in pepper sauce and locally farmed Chubut trout. Service is attentive and the kitchen is willing to make adaptations for vegetarians.

Information

Banco de Santa Cruz (Av 11 de Julio 531) Has a 24-hour ATM.

Post Office (Gregores 19)

Tourist Information Office (491261; www.losantiguos.tur.ar; Av 11 de Julio 446; 8am-8pm) Helpful, with a map of town and farms selling fresh produce. The website has comprehensive lodging and transportation information in multiple languages.

Getting There & Around

The gradual paving of RN40 may alter transport options and times, so make sure you get current information.

Buses go several times daily to nearby Perito Moreno (AR$52, 40 minutes). Those in a rush to move on will find more transport links there to other parts of Patagonia. For Chile, **La Unión** (491078; cnr Perito Moreno & Patagonia Argentina) crosses the border to Chile Chico (AR$27) on weekdays at noon.

From mid-November to March, **Chaltén Travel** (www.chaltentravel.com) goes to El Chaltén on even-numbered days at 9am, stopping first in Perito Moreno.

A Chilean ferry run by **Naviera Sotramin** (56-0672-237958; Chile Chico; passenger/car CH$200/17,700) crosses Lago General Carrera daily from Chile Chico to Puerto Ibañez almost daily, a big shortcut to Coyhaique. If driving, make your reservation a week in advance and arrive 30 minutes before departure time. Alternatively, it's possible to continue overland around the lake's southern shore to Carretera Austral and Coyhaique.

Leiva Remise (☎491228) taxi service is useful when it's pouring rain and you need a ride to your hotel.

Cueva de las Manos

Unesco World Heritage site **Cueva de las Manos** (Cave of the Hands; admission AR$80; ⏲9am-7pm) features incredible rock art, a must-see if you pass through. Dating from about 7370 BC, these polychrome paintings cover recesses in the near-vertical walls with imprints of human hands, drawings of guanacos and, from a later period, abstract designs. Of around 800 images, more than 90% are of left hands; one has six fingers.

The approach is via rough but scenic provincial roads off RN40, abutting Río de las Pinturas. Drive with caution: bounding guanacos are abundant. There are three points of access: a 28km unpaved road from RN40, direct but with loose gravel; a route via Bajo Caracoles, with 46km of gravel roads; and another from the north side and Hostería Cueva de las Manos (closed in low season), with 22km of gravel and 4km on foot via a footbridge.

Guides in Perito Moreno organize day trips (around AR$350 per person plus park entrance fee). The trip from Perito Moreno is about 3½ hours (one way) over rocky roads. Once you arrive at the caves, free 45-minute guided walks are given every hour by knowledgeable staff. There's an information center and a basic *confitería* at the reception house near the southern entrance, but it's best to bring your own food.

On the doorstep of Argentina's best deposit of rock art, **Hostería Cueva de las Manos** (☎02963-432207, in Buenos Aires 011-5237-4043; www.cuevadelasmanos.net; dm/s/d/tr AR$140/520/620/720, 4-6 person cabin from AR$960; ⏲Nov-Apr), formerly Estancia Los Toldos, sits a short distance off RN40, 52km south of Perito Moreno. Guests can stay in cabins, the *hostería* or a 20-person dormitory. Rooms are plain but well appointed. Guests and tour groups can approach Cueva de los Manos via a scenic but challenging hiking trail (summer only) that starts from the *hostería*, descends the canyon and crosses Río de las Pinturas.

Rustic but welcoming **Estancia Casa de Piedra** (☎02963-432199; off RN40; campsites per person AR$35, dm AR$150; ⏲Jan-Feb), a basic ranch 76km south of Perito Moreno, has plain rooms and allows camping. It's a good spot for trekkers to hunker down: there are nearby volcanoes and you can take a beautiful day-long hike to the Cueva de las Manos via Cañon de las Pinturas (nonguests pay AR$30 for access). From the *estancia*, it's 12km to the canyon, then another 6km to the cave – estimate about 10 hours round-trip. Hikers should get an early start and bring their own food; guides can be contracted here but the trail is clear enough to go without one.

Bajo Caracoles

Blink and you'll miss this dusty gas stop. Little has changed since Bruce Chatwin dubbed it 'a crossroads of insignificant importance with roads leading all directions apparently to nowhere' in *In Patagonia* in 1975. If you're headed south, fill the tank, since it's the only reliable gas pump between Perito Moreno (128km north) and Tres Lagos (409km south). From here RP39 heads west to Lago Posadas and the Paso Roballos to Chile.

Lodgers put on a brave face for **Hotel Bajo Caracoles** (☎02963-490100; d AR$380), with old gas heating units that require a watchful eye. It also stocks basic provisions, serves decent coffee and has the only private telephone in town.

Heading south, RN40 is paved to Las Horquetas, a blip on the radar screen where RN40, RP27 and RP37 intersect. From here it's another 128km southeast via RP27 to Gobernador Gregores, which was almost completely paved at the time of research.

Parque Nacional Perito Moreno

Wild and windblown, **Parque Nacional Perito Moreno** (⏲visitor registration 9am-9pm, park open Oct-April) is an adventurer's dream. Approaching from the steppe, the massive snowcapped peaks of the Sierra Colorada rise like sentinels. Guanacos graze the tufted grasses, condors circle above, and wind blurs the surface of aquamarine and cobalt lakes. If you come here, you will be among 1200 yearly visitors – that is, mostly alone. Solitude reigns and, save for services offered by local *estancias*, you are entirely on your own.

Honoring the park system's founder, this remote but increasingly popular park encompasses 1150 sq km, 310km southwest of the town of Perito Moreno. Don't confuse this gem with Parque Nacional Los Glaciares (home to the Glaciar Perito Moreno) further south.

The sedimentary Sierra Colorada is a palette of rusty hues. Beyond the park boundary, glacier-topped summits such as 3706m **Cerro San Lorenzo** (the highest peak in the area) tower over the landscape. The highest peak within the park is Cerro Mié (2254m).

As precipitation increases toward the west, the Patagonian steppe grasslands along the park's eastern border become sub-Antarctic forests of southern beech, lenga and coihue. Because the base altitude exceeds 900m, weather can be severe. Summer is usually comfortable, but warm clothing and proper gear are imperative in any season. The water is pure but you must bring all food and supplies.

Sights & Activities

Behind the information center, a one-hour interpretive trail leads to **Pinturas Rupestres**, somewhat denigrated cave paintings with interpretive signs in English. Consult park rangers for backpacking options and guided walks to the pictographs at **Casa de Piedra** on Lago Burmeister, and to **Playa de los Amonites** on Lago Belgrano, where there are fossils.

Lago Burmeister is an eight-hour round-trip walk. The peninsula of **Lago Belgrano** has two hikes: an all-day walk around the perimeter or a four-hour round-trip to an interior lake. When conditions are very windy, the above options, and El Rincón, are the best: stay off the peaks!

From Estancia La Oriental, it's a 3½-hour hike to the summit of 1434m **Cerro León** for a dazzling panorama. Immediately east of the summit, the volcanic outcrop of **Cerro de los Cóndores** is a nesting site, with numbers of condors circling a 300m cliff. Pumas have also been spotted here and guanacos down below.

Sleeping & Eating

There are free campgrounds at the information center (barren and exposed; no fires allowed); on the steppe at Lago Burmeister, 16km north from the information center (more scenic and well sheltered among dense lenga forest); and at El Rincón, 15km south. Fires are not allowed. Campgrounds

ESTANCIAS IN PATAGONIA

Most assume *estancias* (ranches) are all about livestock, but these offbeat offerings prove otherwise.

A Wealth of Wildlife

Meet the neighbors – that would be the penguins, seabirds and elephant seals – around Península Valdés' Estancia Rincón Chico (p410).

Spot dozens of the namesake species of Estancia El Cóndor (p459) at this rugged mountain ranch north of El Chaltén.

View the diverse fauna of Magellanic penguins, sea lions, guanacos and pumas at Hostería Monte León (p426).

Breathtaking Beauty

Luxuriate among glaciers, lakes and the ragged Cerro Fitz Roy in the exclusive Hostería Estancia Helsingfors. (p467)

Explore the wonders of a petrified forest and sea islands inhabited solely by birds, penguins and sea lions at the magical Bahía Bustamante (p421).

Just Like Indiana Jones

Trek to Unesco World Heritage site Cueva de las Manos from Hostería Cueva de las Manos (p444), via the serpentine red-rock canyon of Río de las Pinturas.

The Bargain Bin

Grab your zzzs in a bunk bed and save some bucks: Estancia El Cóndor (p459), Hostería Cueva de las Manos and Estancia Casa de Piedra (p444) all offer affordable *refugio* (rustic shelter) lodgings. Some with higher price tags include all meals and excursions, delivering a lot for your money.

have pit toilets, picnic tables and potable water. Pack trash out.

Estancia La Oriental CAMPGROUND $$
(in Buenos Aires 011-4343-2366/9568; www.estanciasdesantacruz.com/LaOriental/laoriental.htm; 3-person tent US$25, s/d/tr/q US$140/175/230/260; Nov-Mar) At the foot of Cerro León and the end of the road on Lago Belgrano's north shore, La Oriental is the ideal base camp for exploring the park's varied backcountry. The ranch mostly caters to groups, and does a good job with food, 4WD and horseback-riding trips. Two-night stay required. Guests must register in the park before entering.

Gasoline at the *estancia* is for guests only. Transfers are available from RN40 (US$250).

Information

Visitors must register at the park's information center on the eastern boundary upon arrival. It's stocked with informative maps and brochures. Information can also be obtained at the National Parks Administration Office in Gobernador Gregores.

Getting There & Away

Access road RN37 is not transitable in winter, and the park is closed then anyway. In shoulder seasons the road may be impassable – check with the National Parks Administration Office in Gobernador Gregores before heading out.

Public transportation only goes to the junction of RN37 and RN40, and hitchhiking is a poor option (trailheads are far from the information center). If you're driving, carry spare gas and tires.

Gobernador Gregores

02962 / POP 4500

Sleepy Gobernador Gregores is one of the better stops on RN40, with hotels and shops offering a cheerful demeanor.

Gregores is 60km east of RN40 on RP25. It's the nearest town to Parque Nacional Perito Moreno (still 200km west) and an ideal spot to get supplies and arrange transportation. There's a very enthusiastic **tourist office** (491259; www.turismoengregores.com; Paseo 9 de Julio 610; 8am-2pm Mon-Fri) with comprehensive information on lodgings. The **National Parks Administration Office** (491477; San Martín 882; 9am-4pm Mon-Fri) can be helpful if you have plans to go to Parque Nacional Perito Moreno.

Seventy kilometers west of town via RP29, the waters of **Lago Cardiel** are well loved by anglers for blue-ribbon salmon and rainbow trout fishing. From the junction to the lake it's another 116km to **Tres Lagos**, where a jovial couple run a 24-hour YPF gas station, then another 123km west to El Chaltén. At present, the route to Tres Lagos is the last unpaved section of RN40 this far south.

Summer-only **Camping Nuestra Señora del Valle** (491398; gregoresturismo@yahoo.com.ar) FREE has showers, hot water and stone grills. Get a hot meal (AR$60), including excellent homemade pasta, friendly conversation and firm beds, at **Cañadón León** (491082; Roca 397; s/d/tr AR$260/360/390;), with 25 rooms that are ample and spotless. Reserve ahead. It also rents cars and provides regional transfers.

A new bus terminal is under construction. **Cerro San Lorenzo** (491340; cnr San Martín & Alberdi) buses leave for Puerto San Julián (AR$205, four hours) Monday to Saturday at 4pm or 6pm – ask at the office for exact departure times. **Taqsa/Marga** (02966-442003; Paralello 956) goes to Río Gallegos (AR$576, eight hours) daily.

Heading south on RN40, there are still 100 unpaved kilometers between Gobernador Gregores and useful gas stop Tres Lagos, though paving is ongoing.

El Chaltén

02962 / POP POP 1630

This colorful village overlooks the stunning northern sector of Parque Nacional Los Glaciares. Every summer thousands of trekkers come to explore the world-class trails that start right here. Founded in 1985, in a rush to beat Chile to the land claim, El Chaltén is still a frontier town, albeit an offbeat one, featuring constant construction, hippie values and packs of roaming dogs. Every year more mainstream tourists come to see what the fuss is all about, but in winter (May to September) most hotels and services board up and transportation links are few.

El Chaltén is named for Cerro Fitz Roy's Tehuelche name, meaning 'peak of fire' or 'smoking mountain' – an apt description of the cloud-enshrouded summit. Perito Moreno and Carlos Moyano later named it after the *Beagle's* Captain FitzRoy, who navigated Darwin's expedition up the Río Santa Cruz in 1834, coming within 50km of the cordillera.

El Chaltén

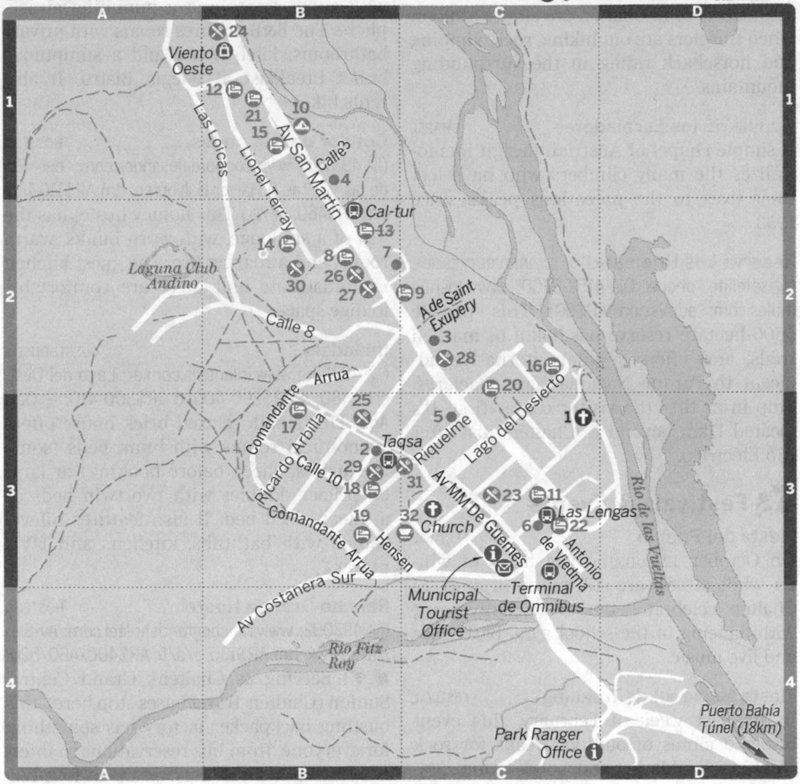

El Chaltén

Sights
1 Capilla de los Escaladores C3

Activities, Courses & Tours
Casa de Guias .... (see 27)
2 Chaltén Fishing B3
3 El Chaltén Mountain Guides C2
4 El Relincho B1
5 Fitzroy Expediciones C3
6 Las Lengas C3
7 Patagonia Mágica B2

Sleeping
8 Albergue Patagonia B2
9 Anita's House C2
10 Camping El Refugio B1
Camping El Relincho .... (see 4)
11 Condor de Los Andes C3
12 Destino Sur B1
13 Hostel Pioneros del Valle B2
14 Hostería El Puma B2
15 Hotel Poincenot B1
16 Inlandsis C2
17 Kaulem B3
18 Nothofagus B&B B3
19 Posada La Base B3
20 Posada Lunajuim C2
21 Rancho Grande Hostel B1
22 Senderos Hostería C3

Eating
23 Domo Blanco C3
24 El Muro B1
25 Estepa B3
26 Fuegia Bistro B2
27 La Cervecería B2
28 La Lucinda C2
29 La Tapera B3
Patagonicus .... (see 23)
30 Ruca Mahuida B2
31 Techado Negro C3

Drinking & Nightlife
32 La Chocolatería C3

Sights & Activities

The streets of El Chaltén are empty at noon when travelers are out hiking, rock climbing and horseback riding in the surrounding mountains.

Capilla de los Escaladores CHAPEL
A simple chapel of Austrian design memorializes the many climbers who have lost their lives to the precarious peaks since 1953.

Reserva Los Huemules NATURE PRESERVE
(☎satellite phone 011-4152-5300; www.loshuemules.com; admission AR$60) This private 5600-hectare reserve has 25km of marked trails, and offers a quiet alternative adjacent to Parque Nacional Los Glaciares. Stop in at the the visitor center first. It's located 17km beyond El Chaltén, just after Río Eléctrico.

Festivals & Events

Fiesta del Pueblo FESTIVAL
On October 12, on the wet heels of winter while streets are still mired in mud, El Chaltén celebrates the town anniversary, with dancing in the school gym, barbecues and live music.

Fiesta Nacional de Trekking FESTIVAL
In the last week of February, this event brings a circus of outdoor freaks for rock climbing, bouldering and woodcutting competitions, as well as running and mountain-bike races.

Sleeping

Reservations should be made at least one month in advance for the January to February high season – demand here is that great. Plus it would be particularly depressing to arrive in the dark with the wind howling and no bed waiting. One solution is to bring a bombproof tent – there's always space in the campgrounds.

Dorm beds fill up fast in summer. Unless otherwise noted, thin walls, cramped dorms and insufficient shared facilities are the norm.

Albergue Patagonia HOSTEL $
(☎493019; www.patagoniahostel.com.ar; Av San Martín 392; dm $AR120, s/d/tr AR$380/420/500, s/d without bathroom AR$280/300; ⊙Sep-May; @📶) A gorgeous and welcoming wooden farmhouse with helpful staff. Dorms in a separate building are spacious and modern, with good service and a humming atmosphere. The B&B features rooms with private bathrooms, kitchen use and a sumptuous buffet breakfast at Fuegia Bistro. It also rents bikes.

Condor de Los Andes HOSTEL $
(☎493101; www.condordelosandes.com; cnr Río de las Vueltas & Halvor Halvorsen; dm AR$110-130, s/d AR$460; @📶) This homey hostel has the feel of a ski lodge, with worn bunks, warm rooms and a roaring fire. The guest kitchen is immaculate and there are comfortable lounge spaces.

Inlandsis GUESTHOUSE $
(☎493276; www.inlandsis.com.ar; Lago del Desierto 480; s AR$290-400, d AR$300-410; ⊙Oct-Apr) This small, relaxed brick house offers economical rooms with bunk beds (some are airless, check before booking) or larger, pricier doubles with two twin beds or a queen-sized bed. It also features bilevel cabins with bathtubs, kitchens and DVD players.

Rancho Grande Hostel HOSTEL $
(☎493092; www.ranchograndehostel.com; Av San Martín 724; dm AR$130, s/d/tr AR$400/460/520; @📶) Serving as Chaltén's Grand Central Station (Chaltén Travel buses stop here), this bustling backpacker factory has something for everyone, from bus reservations to internet (extra) and cafe service. Clean four-bed rooms are stacked with blankets, and bathrooms sport rows of shower stalls. Private rooms have their own bathrooms and free breakfast.

Hostel Pioneros del Valle HOSTEL $
(☎491368; www.caltur.com.ar/pioneros/hostel.html; Av San Martín 451; dm AR$120; 📶) This behemoth has mixed six-bed dorms with in-room bathrooms, lockers and free wi-fi, in addition to a plasma TV. Run by a transport company, there's also travel and sleep packages.

Camping El Refugio CAMPGROUND $
(☎493221; Calle 3 s/n; campsites per person AR$60, dm A$90) This private campground is attached to a basic hostel – hot showers for campers are included in the fee. Sites are exposed and there is some sparse firewood (fires are OK).

Camping El Relincho CAMPGROUND $
(☎493007; www.elrelinchopatagonia.com.ar; Av San Martín 545; campsites per person/vehicle

AR$50/10, 4-person cabin AR$650) A private campground, with wind-whipped and exposed sites.

★**Nothofagus B&B** B&B $$
(☎493087; www.nothofagusbb.com.ar; cnr Hensen & Riquelme; s/d/tr AR$420/450/530, without bathroom AR$300/320/440; Oct-Apr; @ wifi) Attentive and adorable, this chalet-style inn offers a toasty retreat with hearty breakfast options. Practices which earn them the Sello Verde (green seal) include separating organic waste and replacing towels only when asked. Wooden-beam rooms have carpet and some views. Those with hallway bathrooms share with one other room.

Senderos Hostería B&B $$
(☎493336; www.senderoshosteria.com.ar; Perito Moreno s/n; s/d/ste from US$138/155/210) This contemporary, corrugated tin home offers wonderful amenities for trekkers seeking creature comforts. The on-site restaurant serves exquisite gourmet meals with excellent wines and attentive service, a real perk when you're spent from a day outdoors. Smart rooms have soft white sheets, firm beds, lock boxes and occasional Fitz Roy views.

Kaulem BOUTIQUE HOTEL $$
(☎493251; www.kaulem.com.ar; cnr Av Antonio Rojo & Comandante Arrua; s/d AR$870/980, d cabin AR$820; wifi) With a cozy lodge atmosphere, this boutique hotel is rustic and stylish, with just four rooms, all with Fitz Roy views, and an adjacent cabin. The buffet breakfast includes yogurt, homemade bread and fruit. Guests share a huge open dining and living area piped with good music and stocked with books and chess.

Anita's House CABIN $$
(☎493288; www.anitashouse.com.ar; Av San Martín 249; 2-/4-person cabin from AR$540/750; wifi) When the wind howls, these few modern cabins are a snug spot for groups, couples or families, smack in the center of town. Owner-run, the service is impeccable. Kitchens come fully equipped and there's room service and cable TV. Two-story cabins, with higher rates, are more spacious.

Posada Lunajuim INN $$
(☎493047; www.lunajuim.com; Trevisán 45; s/d/tr US$95/115/140; wifi) Combining modern comfort with a touch of the offbeat, this welcoming inn gets good reviews from guests. The halls are lined with the owner's monochrome sculptures and textured paintings, and a stone fireplace and library provide a rainy-day escape. Some nice touches include DIY box lunches and a buffet breakfast.

Posada La Base GUESTHOUSE $$
(☎493031; www.elchaltenpatagonia.com.ar; Calle 10, No 16; d/tr/q AR$520/640/760) A smart, sprawling house with spacious rooms that all face outside and have access to an immaculate kitchen. Large groups should book rooms 5 and 6, which share an inside kitchen with dining area. The reception area has a popular video loft with a multilingual collection. The rates we have indicated don't include the discount for two or more nights.

Hostería El Puma LODGE $$$
(☎493095; www.hosteriaelpuma.com.ar; Lionel Terray 212; s/d/tr AR$880/1100/1320; wifi) This luxury lodge with 12 comfortable rooms offers intimacy without pretension, as well as huge buffet breakfasts. The rock-climbing and summit photographs and maps lining the hall may inspire your next expedition, but lounging by the fireplace is the most savory way to end the day.

Destino Sur HOTEL $$$
(☎493360; www.hoteldestinosur.com; Lionel Terray 370; d/deluxe US$234/256) Storm this castle via the oversized medieval doors and a perfectly acceptable high-end hotel awaits. Indeed, with 24 rooms and floors yet to finish, it is an impressive block of stone, rod iron and finished wood. It also boasts the first elevator in town. Amenities include satellite TV, minibar and lockboxes in tasteful rooms with native accents, and there is a gym and spa with Jacuzzi and sauna.

Hotel Poincenot HOTEL $$$
(☎493252; www.hotelpoincenot.com; Av San Martín 668; s/d US$167/190; wifi) New and modern, this busy hotel has 20 rooms with flatscreen TV, and comfortable beds decked in down bedding and colorful throws. Spacious rooms include a cathedral-ceiling living room, dining area and bar. Service is professional and attentive.

Eating

Groceries, especially produce, are limited and expensive. Bring what you can from El Calafate.

★La Cervecería BREWPUB $
(Av San Martín 320; mains AR$50-90; ⊙noon-3pm & 8pm to late) That après-hike pint usually evolves into a night out in this humming pub with *simpatico* staff and a feisty female beer master. Savor a stein of unfiltered blond pilsner or turbid bock with pasta or *locro* (a spicy stew of maize, beans, beef, pork and sausage).

La Lucinda CAFE $
(Av San Martín 175; sandwiches AR$50; ⊙7am-midnight; 🅥) With homemade soups and stews, hot sandwiches (including good vegetarian options) and a selection of coffee, tea and wine. This artsy, sky-blue cafe is friendly and almost always open – a godsend when the weather is howling. Breakfast is served too.

Domo Blanco ICE CREAM $
(Av MM De Güemes s/n; snacks AR$15; ⊙2pm-midnight) Homemade ice cream made with fruit harvested from a local *estancia* and calafate bushes in town.

Fuegia Bistro INTERNATIONAL $$
(Av San Martín 342; mains AR$70-125; ⊙dinner Mon-Sat) Favored for its warm ambience and savory mains, this upscale eatery boasts good veggie options and a reasonable wine list. Try the homemade pasta with ricotta, spinach and fresh mushrooms, or trout with lemon.

Techado Negro CAFE $$
(Av Antonio Rojo; mains AR$45-110; ⊙7am-12am) With local paintings on the wall, bright colors and a raucous, unkempt atmosphere in keeping with El Chaltén, this homespun cafe serves up abundant, good-value and sometimes healthy Argentine fare. Think homemade empanadas, squash stuffed with *humita* (sweet tamale), brown rice vegetarian dishes, soups and pastas. It also offers box lunches.

El Muro ARGENTINE $$
(Av San Martín 912; mains AR$70-120; ⊙dinner) For ribsticking mountain food (think massive stir-fry, lentil stew or trout with crisp grilled veggies), head to this tiny outpost at the end of the road. Portions are abundant and desserts – such as warm apple pie or bread pudding – should practically be mandatory.

La Tapera TAPAS $$
(cnr Antonio Rojo & Riquelme; mains AR$75-120; ⊙lunch & dinner) This ambient eatery specializes in tapas but wintry staples such as pumpkin soup and grilled steak are also good options. On cold days, you can sit so close to the open fireplace that you'll have to peel off a layer.

Estepa PATAGONIAN $$
(cnr Cerro Solo & Av Antonio Rojo; mains AR$75-125; ⊙noon-1am Mon-Sat) Local favorite Estepa cooks up consistent, flavorful dishes such as lamb with calafate sauce, trout ravioli or spinach crepes.

Patagonicus PIZZERIA $$
(cnr Av MM De Güemes & Andreas Madsen; pizza AR$50-100; ⊙closed Wed & May-Sep) The best pizza in town, with 20 kinds of pizza, salads and wine served at sturdy wood tables surrounded by huge picture windows. Cakes and coffee are also worth trying.

Ruca Mahuida GOURMET $$$
(Lionel Terray 55; mains AR$90-135; ⊙7-11pm) Smoked trout, squash soufflé and salmon ravioli are a welcome departure from typical fare at this stone house with sheepskin benches. Though we wish it were more consistent, it has gotten some rave reviews.

Drinking

La Chocolatería CAFE
(Lago del Desierto 105; chocolate & coffee drinks AR$30-50; ⊙Nov-Mar) This irresistible chocolate factory tells the story of local climbing legends on the walls. It makes for an intimate evening out, with options ranging from spirit-spiked hot cocoa to wine and fondue.

Shopping

Viento Oeste BOOKS
(☎493200; Av San Martín 898) Sells books, maps and souvenirs and rents a wide range of camping equipment, as do several other sundries shops around town.

Information

Technologically speaking, El Chaltén is a study in contrasts: there's no cell phone reception and one ATM (located in the bus terminal), but you're likely to pick up a good wi-fi signal in your hotel room and you won't have any problem finding a long-distance call center or gas station. Euros and US dollars are widely accepted but credit cards are not, though some restaurants accept them. If you're coming from El Calafate, just take out the cash you'll need there and skip the possible complications in El Chaltén. Surf www.elchalten.com for a good overview of the town.

Chaltén Travel (☎493092; www.chaltentravel.com; cnr Av MM De Güemes & Lago del Desi-

OFF THE BEATEN TRACK

TREKKING INTO CHILE

Gonzo travelers can skirt the Southern Ice Field on foot to get from Argentina's Parque Nacional Los Glaciares and El Chaltén to Villa O'Higgins, the last stop on Chile's Carretera Austral. This one- to three-day trip can be completed between November and March. Bring all provisions, Chilean currency, plus your passport and rain gear. Boat delays are not unheard of, so be prepared to stay overnight and pack enough food. Here's the nuts and bolts:

➡ Grab the shuttle bus from El Chaltén to the south shore of Lago del Desierto, 37km away (AR$150, one hour).

➡ Usually a ferry travels to the north shore of Lago del Desierto (AR$150, 4½ hours) but at the time of writing this service was temporarily unavailable. Another option is to hike the coast (15km, five hours). Pass through Argentine customs and immigration here. Camping is allowed.

➡ From the north shore of Lago del Desierto, trek or ride to Laguna Larga (1½ hours). Camping is not allowed.

➡ Trek or ride to Laguna Redonda (1½ hours). Camping is not allowed.

➡ Trek or ride to Candelario Mansilla (two hours). Candelario Mansilla has lodging in a family farmhouse, guided treks and horse rental (riding or pack horse per day CH$20,000). Pass through Chilean customs and immigration here.

➡ Take the Hielo Sur catamaran (CH$42,000, four hours) from Candelario Mansilla, on the south edge of Lago O'Higgins, to Puerto Bahamondez. Trips go one to three times a week, usually on Saturday with some Monday or Wednesday departures. A bus goes from Puerto Bahamondez to Villa O'Higgins (CH$2100).

In Villa O'Higgins, **El Mosco** (☎0672-431819; patagoniaelmosco.com; Carretera Austral Km1240; campsites per person CH$5000, dm CH$9,000, d CH$40,000, s/d without bathroom CH$18,000/30,000) has good lodging options. For Chilean ferry information, consult **Hielo Sur** (☎0672-431821/822; www.villaohiggins.com) in O'Higgins.

erto) Books airline tickets and bus travel on RN40.

Municipal Tourist Office (☎493370; comfomelchalten@yahoo.com.ar; Terminal de Omnibus; ⏲10am-10pm) Friendly and extremely helpful, with lodging lists and good information on town and tours. English is spoken.

Park Ranger Office (☎493024, 493004; pnlgzonanorte@apn.gov.ar; donations welcome; ⏲9am-8pm Dec-Feb, 10am-5pm Mar-Nov) Many daytime buses stop for a short bilingual orientation at this visitor center, just before the bridge over the Río Fitz Roy. Park rangers distribute a map and town directory and do a good job of explaining Parque Nacional Los Glaciares' ecological issues. Climbing documentaries are shown at 2pm daily – great for rainy days. Open 10am-5pm low season.

Puesto Sanitario (☎493033; AM De Agostini 70) Provides basic health services.

ℹ Getting There & Away

El Chaltén is 220km from El Calafate via newly paved roads. A bicycle path heads from town to Hostería El Pilar, in Parque Nacional Los Glaciares. Bike rentals (per day AR$160) are available in various locations.

All buses go to the new **Terminal de Omnibus**, located near the entrance to town. For El Calafate (AR$200, 3½ hours), Chaltén Travel (p430) has daily departures at 7:30am, 1pm and 6pm in summer. **Cal-tur** (☎493079; Av San Martín 520) and **Taqsa/Marga** (☎493068; Av Antonio Rojo 88) also make the trip for the slightly cheaper price of AR$150. Service is less frequent in low season.

Las Lengas (☎493023; www.transportelaslengas.com.ar; Antonio de Viedma 95) shuttles directly to El Calafate's airport (AR$150) in high season and Rio Gallegos (AR$300, seven hours). It also has minivans that head to Lago Desierto (AR$150), Hostería El Pilar (AR$60) and Río Eléctrico (AR$60). There is also taxi service to El Calafate's airport available for AR$1200.

Chalten Travel goes to Bariloche on odd days of the month throughout the high season (AR$1100, two days), including an overnight stop in Perito Moreno (meals and accommodations are extra).

Parque Nacional Los Glaciares (North)

In the northern part of the park, the Fitz Roy Range – with its rugged wilderness and shark-tooth summits – is the de facto trekking capital of Argentina. It also draws world-class climbers for whom Cerro Torre and Cerro Fitz Roy are milestone ascents notorious for brutal weather conditions. But you don't have to be extreme to enjoy the numerous well-marked trails for hiking and jaw-dropping scenery – that is, when the clouds clear.

Parque Nacional Los Glaciares is divided into geographically separate northern and southern sectors. El Chaltén is the gateway town for the northern part of the park. El Calafate is the gateway town for the southern section of the park, which features the Glaciar Perito Moreno.

Activities

Before heading out for the following hikes, stop by the Park Ranger Office (p451) for updated trail conditions. The most stable weather for hiking comes not in summer but in March and April, when there is less wind (and fewer people). During June and July trails may be closed – check first with the Park Ranger Office.

Experienced backpackers can register to hike in the remote areas, which require some route finding. A first-person ranger update is necessary for these hikes. For more information on hiking, read Lonely Planet's *Trekking in the Patagonian Andes*.

Laguna Torre

If you have good weather – ie little wind – and clear skies, make this hike (three hours one way) a priority, since the toothy Cerro Torre is the most difficult local peak to see on normal blustery days.

There are two trail options which later merge. One starts at the northwestern edge of El Chaltén. From a signpost on Av San Martín, head west on Eduardo Brenner and then right to find the signposted start of the track. The Laguna Torre track winds up westwards around large boulders on slopes covered with typical Patagonian dryland plants, then leads southwest past a wet meadow to a junction with a trail coming in from the left after 35 to 45 minutes.

Starting from the southern end of El Chaltén, follow Lago del Desierto west past the edge of town, then drop to the riverbed, passing a tiny hydroelectric installation. At a signpost the route climbs away from the river and leads on through scattered lenga and ñire woodland (a small, deciduous southern beech species), with the odd wire fence to step over, before merging with a more prominent (signposted) path coming in from the right.

Continue up past a rounded bluff to the **Mirador Laguna Torre**, a crest with the first clear view up the valley to the extraordinary 3128m rock spire of Cerro Torre, set above a sprawling mass of intersecting glaciers.

The trail dips gently through stands of lenga, before cutting across open scrubby river flats and old revegetated moraines to reach a signposted junction with the Sendero Madre e Hija, a shortcut to Campamento Poincenot, 40 to 50 minutes on. Continuing upvalley, bear left at another signposted fork and climb over a forested embankment to cross a small alluvial plain, following the fast-flowing glacial waters of the Río Fitz Roy. You'll arrive at **Campamento De Agostini** (formerly Bridwell) after a further 30 to 40 minutes. This free campground (with pit toilet) gets busy; it serves as a base camp for Cerro Torre climbers. The only other nearby camping is in a pleasant grove of riverside lengas below Cerro Solo.

Follow the trail along the lake's north side for about an hour to **Mirador Maestri** (no camping).

Laguna de los Tres

This hike to a high alpine tarn is a bit more strenuous (four hours one way) than the hike to Laguna Torre. The trail starts from a yellow-roofed pack station. After about an hour there's a signed lateral to excellent free backcountry **campsites** at Laguna Capri. The main trail continues gently through windswept forests and past small lakes, meeting the Lagunas Madre and Hija trail. Carry on through wind-worn ñire forest and along boggy terrain to **Río Blanco** (three hours) and the woodsy, mice-plagued **Campamento Poincenot**. The trail splits before Río Blanco to Río Eléctrico. Stay left to reach a climbers' base camp. Here the trail zigzags steeply up the tarn to the eerily still, glacial **Laguna de los Tres** in close view of 3405m Cerro Fitz Roy. Be prepared for high, potentially hazardous winds and allow extra time.

Parque Nacional Los Glaciares (North)

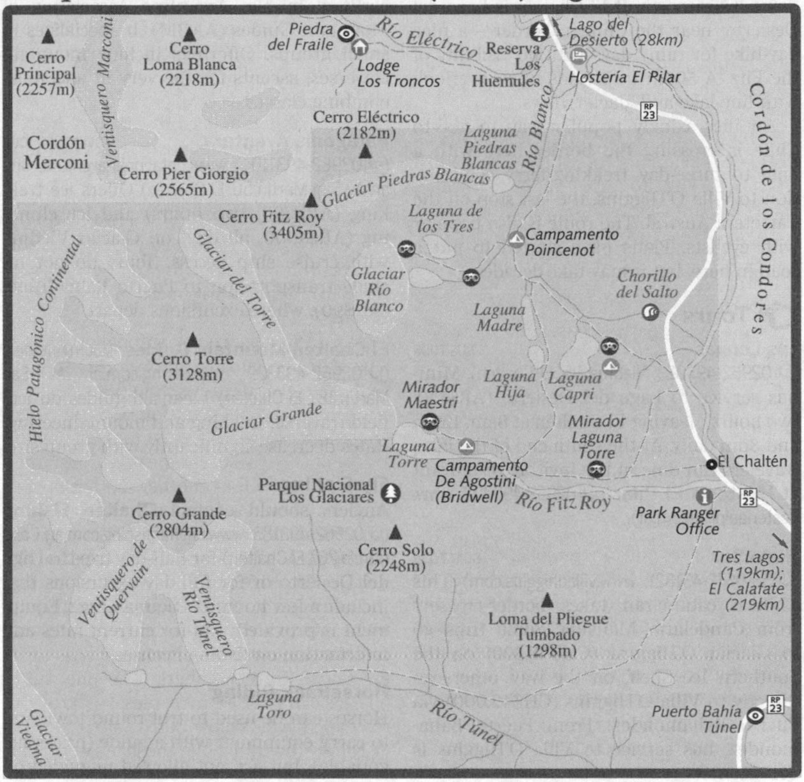

Piedra del Fraile

At Campamento Poincenot, the trail swings west to Laguna de los Tres or northeast along Río Blanco to Valle Eléctrico and Piedra del Fraile (eight hours from El Chaltén; five hours from the Río Blanco turnoff). From the turnoff, the latter trail leads to **Glaciar Piedras Blancas** (four hours), which ends with a scramble over massive granite boulders to a turquoise lake with dozens of floating icebergs. Pass through pastures and branches left up the valley along **Río Eléctrico**, enclosed by sheer cliffs, before reaching the private **Lodge Los Troncos** (campsites per person AR$75, dm AR$150-230) There's a restaurant but no guest kitchen. Dorm rates are cheapest with your own sleeping bag. Visitors must pay an entry fee (AR$150). Reservations are not possible since there are no phones – simply show up. The campground has a kiosk, restaurant and excellent services, and the owners can recommend trails.

Rather than backtrack, it's possible to head east, hopping over streams to RP23, the route back to El Chaltén. You'll pass the waterfall **Chorillo del Salto** on the way.

Buses to Lago del Desierto drop hikers at the Río Eléctrico bridge (AR$60).

Loma del Pliegue Tumbado & Laguna Toro

Heading southwest from the Park Ranger Office, this trail (four to five hours one way) skirts the eastern face of Loma del Pliegue Tumbado going toward Río Túnel, then cuts west and heads to Laguna Toro. It's the only hike that allows views of both Cerros Torre and Fitz Roy at once. It's also less crowded than the main routes. The hike is gentle, but prepare for strong winds and carry extra water.

Lago del Desierto & Chile

Some 37km north of El Chaltén is Lago del Desierto, near the Chilean border – a nice day-hike for rainy days with no visibility of the Fitz. A 500m trail leads to an overlook with fine lake and glacier views.

An increasingly popular way to get to Chile is crossing the border here with a one- to three-day trekking/ferry combination to Villa O'Higgins, the last stop on the Carretera Austral. The route is also popular with cyclists. Plans have started to put a road in here, but it may take decades.

Tours

Las Lengas BUS TOUR

(☎02962-493023; Viedma 95, El Chaltén) Minibus service to Lago del Desierto (AR$150, two hours), leaving El Chaltén at 8am, 12pm and 3pm daily. At the south end of the lake, travelers can dine in the inviting restaurant at **Hostería El Pilar** (☎02962-493002; www.hosteriaelpilar.com.ar).

Hielo Sur BOAT TOUR

(☎56-0672-431821; www.villaohiggins.com) This Chilean catamaran takes border-crossers from Candelario Mansilla. Some trips go to Glaciar O'Higgins (CH$68,500) on the Southern Ice Shelf, on the way, others go directly to Villa O'Higgins (CH$42,000) via Puerto Bahamondez. From Puerto Bahamondez, bus service to Villa O'Higgins is CH$2100.

Ice Climbing & Trekking

Many companies offer ice-climbing courses and ice treks, some including sleds pulled by Siberian huskies. Multiday guided hikes over the Hielo Patagónico Continental (Continental Ice Field) have the feel of polar expeditions. Catering to serious trekkers, this route involves technical climbing, including use of crampons and strenuous river crossings.

Fitzroy Expediciones MOUNTAINEERING

(☎02962-493178; www.fitzroyexpediciones.com.ar; Av San Martín 56, El Chaltén) Runs glacier-trekking excursions on Viedma Glacier, a five-day itinerary that includes trekking in the Fitz Roy and Cerro Torre area, as well as other excursions. Note that Fitzroy Expediciones does accept credit cards, unlike most businesses in town.

Casa de Guias MOUNTAINEERING

(☎02962-493118; www.casadeguias.com.ar; Lago del Desierto s/n, El Chaltén) Friendly and professional, with English-speaking guides certified by the Argentine Association of Mountain Guides (AAGM). It specializes in small groups. Offerings include mountain traverses, ascents for the very fit and rock-climbing classes.

Patagonia Aventura ADVENTURE TOUR

(☎02962-493110; www.patagonia-aventura.com.ar; Av San Martín 56, El Chaltén) Offers ice trekking (AR$780, two hours) and ice climbing (AR$1000, all day) on Glaciar Viedma with cruise ship access. Tours do not include transportaion to Puerto Bahía Túnel (AR$90), where excursions depart.

El Chaltén Mountain Guides MOUNTAINEERING

(☎02962-493329; www.ecmg.com.ar; Av San Martín 187, El Chaltén) Licensed guides do ice-field traverse, trekking and mountaineering. Rates decrease significantly with group size.

Fly-Fishing

Anglers should contact **Chaltén Fishing** (☎02962-493185; www.chaltenfishing.com.ar; Cabo García 267, El Chaltén) for half-day trips to Lago del Desierto or for full-day excursions that include a few hours at Laguna Larga. Equipment is provided; call for current rates and information on fishing licenses.

Horseback Riding

Horses can be used to trot round town and to carry equipment with a guide (prices negotiable), but are not allowed unguided on national-park trails. Outfitter **El Relincho** (☎02692-493007, in El Calafate 02902-491961; www.elrelinchopatagonia.com.ar; Av San Martín 505, El Chaltén; 4hr ride AR$450) takes riders to the pretty valley of Río de las Vueltas and also offers more challenging rides combined with a ranch barbecue. Cabin-style accommodations are also available.

Kayak & Canoe Trips

As El Chaltén grows, so do the aquatic offerings. Fitzroy Expediciones (p454) has half-day guided kayaking trips on the Río de las Vueltas that stop for lunch at the company's adventure camp. (Overnight stays are also available in the timber lodge and eight cabins, 17km north of town – ask at the office in El Chaltén for more info.) You can also book two-day canoe and camping trips to Río La Leona.

Lake Cruises

Patagonia Aventura (p454) offers cruises (per person AR$300, plus AR$90 transfer) on Lago Viedma with impressive views of the 40m Glaciar Viedma, grinding from Cerro Fitz Roy. Boat trips leave from Puerto Bahía Túnel and last 2½ hours.

Rock Climbing

Outfitters around town rent equipment; **Patagonia Mágica** (☎02692-486261; www.patagoniamagica.com; Fonrouge s/n, El Chaltén) runs one-day rock-climbing workshops for beginners. Experienced climbers can go on the Glaciar Laguna Torre with certified guides.

Sleeping

Free backcountry campgrounds have one pit toilet. Some sites have dead wood for windbreaks but fires are prohibited. Water is pure as glacial melt; only wash downstream from the campground and pack out all trash.

Getting There & Away

Parque Nacional Los Glaciares is just outside El Chaltén, which is convenient if you're driving your own car; otherwise, most excursions offer transfers in and out of the park for around AR$60.

El Calafate

☎02902 / POP 16,700

Named for the berry that, once eaten, guarantees your return to Patagonia, El Calafate hooks you with another irresistible attraction: Glaciar Perito Moreno, 80km away in Parque Nacional Los Glaciares. The glacier is a magnificent must-see, but its massive popularity has encouraged tumorous growth and rapid upscaling in once-quaint El Calafate. However, it's still a fun place to be with a range of traveler services. The strategic location between El Chaltén and Torres del Paine (Chile) makes it an inevitable stop for those in transit.

Located 320km northwest of Río Gallegos, and 32km west of RP11's junction with northbound RN40, El Calafate flanks the southern shore of Lago Argentino. The main strip, Av del Libertador General San Martín (typically abbreviated to Libertador), is dotted with cutesy knotted-pine souvenir shops, chocolate shops, restaurants and tour offices. Beyond the main street, pretensions melt away quickly: muddy roads lead to ad-hoc developments and open pastures.

January and February are the most popular (and costly) months to visit, but as shoulder-season visits grow steadily, both availability and prices stay a challenge.

Sights

★**Glaciarium** MUSEUM

(☎497912; www.glaciarium.com; adult/child AR$140/80; ⏰9am-8pm Sep-May, 11am-8pm May-Aug) Unique and exciting, this gorgeous museum illuminates the world of ice. Displays and bilingual films show how glaciers form, along with documentaries on continental ice expeditions and stark meditations on climate change. Adults suit up in furry capes for the *bar de hielo* (AR$100 including drink), a blue-lit below-zero club serving vodka or fernet and Coke in ice glasses.

The gift shop sells handmade and sustainable gifts crafted by Argentine artisans. It also hosts international cinema events. It's 6km from Calafate toward the national park. To get there, take the free hourly transfer from 1 de Mayo between Av Libertador and Roca.

Reserva Natural Laguna Nimez WILDLIFE RESERVE

(admission AR$40; ⏰daylight hours) Prime avian habitat alongside the lakeshore, north of town with a self-guided trail and staffed Casa Verde information hut with binocular rental (AR$35). It's a great place to spot flamingos – but watching birds from El Calafate's shoreline on Lago Argentino can be just as good.

Centro de Interpretacíon Historico MUSEUM

(☎497799; www.museocalafate.com.ar; Av Brown & Bonarelli; admission AR$48; ⏰10am-8pm Sep-May, 11am-5pm Jun-Aug) Small but informative, with a skeleton mold of Austroraptor Cabazaii (found nearby) and Patagonian history displays. The friendly host invites museum-goers for a post-tour *mate* (a bitter ritual tea).

Tours

Some 40 travel agencies arrange excursions to Glaciar Perito Moreno and other local attractions, including fossil beds and stays at regional **estancias**, where you can hike, ride horses or relax. Tour prices for Glaciar Perito Moreno (per person AR$120 to AR$1050) don't include the park entrance fee. Ask agents and other travelers about added benefits, such as extra stops, boat trips, binoculars or multilingual guides.

El Calafate

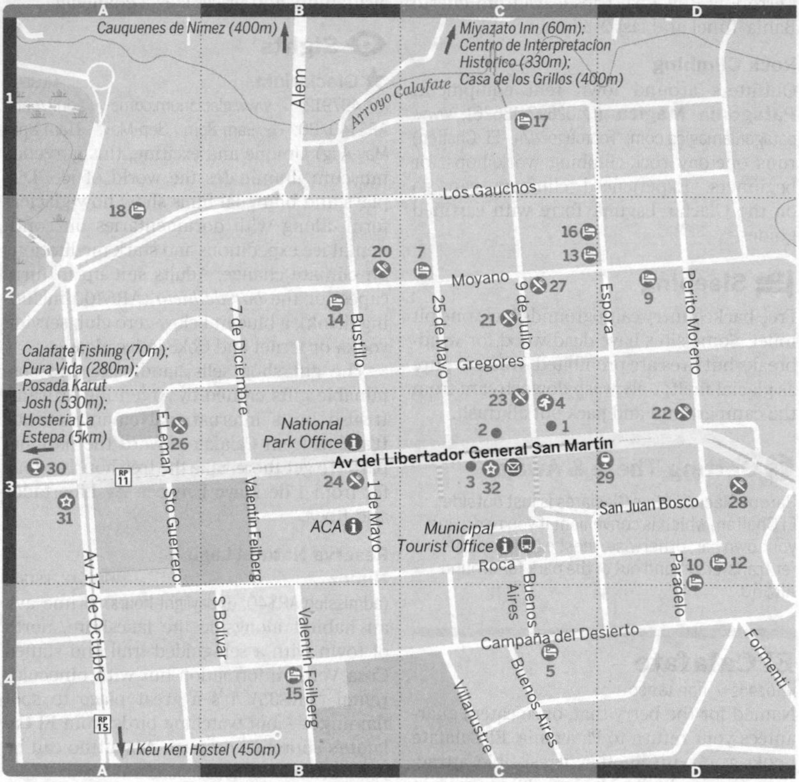

El Calafate

Activities, Courses & Tours

1 Cal-tur C3
2 Chaltén Travel C3
3 Glaciares Sur C3
4 Mar Patag C3
Overland Patagonia .... (see 11)

Sleeping

5 Albergue Lago Argentino C4
6 America del Sur E2
7 Calafate Hostel C2
8 Camping El Ovejero E2
9 Hospedaje Jorgito D2
10 Hostal Schilling D3
11 Hostel del Glaciar Libertador E3
12 Hotel La Loma D3
13 Hotel Michelangelo C2
14 Hotel Posada Los Álamos B2
15 Las Cabañitas B4
16 Lautaro C2
17 Los Dos Pinos C1
18 Los Sauces Casa Patagónica A2
19 Newenkelen E1

Eating

20 Cambalache B2
21 El Cucharón C2
22 La Anónima D3
23 La Fonda del Parillero C3
24 La Lechuza B3
25 La Tablita E3
26 Los Amigos A3
27 Mi Ranchito C2
28 Viva la Pepa D3

Drinking & Nightlife

el ba'r .... (see 4)
29 Librobar D3
30 Sholken A3

Entertainment

31 Don Diego de la Noche A3
32 La Toldería C3

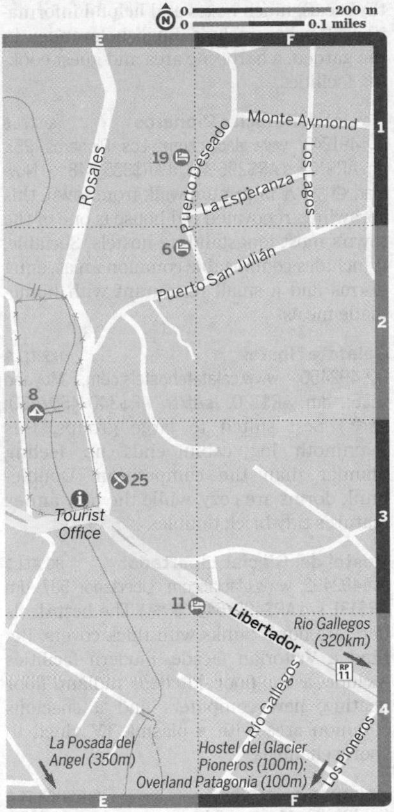

★ Glaciares Sur ADVENTURE TOUR
(☎491095; www.argospatagonia.com.ar; Libertador 1185; per person AR$880-990) Get glacier stunned *and* skip the crowds with these recommended day tours to the unexplored end of Parque Nacional Los Glaciares. Small groups drive to Lago Rocas with an expert multilingual guide to view Glaciar Frias. The adventure-tour option features a four-hour hike, the culture-tour option includes a traditional *asado* (barbecue grill) and off-hour visits to the Glaciar Perito Moreno.

Cal-tur TOUR
(☎491368; www.caltur.com.ar; Libertador 1080) Specializes in El Chaltén tours and lodging packages.

Chaltén Travel TOUR
(☎492480, 492212; www.chaltentravel.com; Libertador 1174) Recommended tours to Glaciar Perito Moreno, stopping for wildlife viewing (binoculars provided); also specializes in RN40 trips. Outsources some excursions to **Always Glaciers** (www.alwaysglaciers.com).

Overland Patagonia TOUR
(☎492243, 491243; www.glaciar.com) This outfit operates out of both Hostel del Glaciar Libertador and Hostel del Glaciar Pioneros. It organizes the alternative glacier trip, which includes hiking and navigating the lake.

Enjoy! ADVENTURE TOUR
(☎497722; www.enjoycalafate.com) A popular outfitter specializing in adventure tours, with bilingual guides leading activities like climbing Cerro Roca and Via Ferrata (assisted ascent), rappel and zipline. There's no office, guests are picked up at their hotels. Operations are based out of Estancia 25 de Mayo.

Calafate Fishing FLY-FISHING
(☎496545; www.calafatefishing.com; Libertador 1826; ⏲10am-7pm Mon-Sat) Calafate offers fun fly-fishing trips to Lago Roca (half-day AR$1050) and Lago Strobbel, where you can test rumors that the biggest rainbow trout in the world lives here.

Sleeping

Though lodgings are abundant, popular offerings may book well in advance. The core high season is January to February, although some places extend it from mid-October until April. Luxury hotels are being added at a quick clip, though not all offer the same standard. Look for deep discounts in low season.

The Municipal Tourist Office has a complete list of *cabañas* and apartment hotels, which are the best deals for groups and families. Most hostels offer pickup from the bus terminal.

Camping El Ovejero CAMPGROUND $
(☎493422; www.campingelovejero.com.ar; José Pantín 64; campsites per person AR$50; @ wifi) Woodsy, well-kept (and a little noisy) campsites with spotless showers with 24-hour hot water. Locals boast that the on-site restaurant is one of the best deals in town for grill food. Extras include private tables, electricity and grills. It's located by the creek just north of the bridge into town.

Lautaro GUESTHOUSE $
(☎492698; www.hospedajelautaro.com.ar; Espora 237; dm AR$95, s/d/t A$280/350/460, s/d without bathroom AR$250/280 ; ⊙closed Jul; @📶) Chill and homey, this refurbished guesthouse reflects the playful efforts of young owners Dario and Belen. It's central, with pretty rooms in a bold palette. Guests can order box lunches made with fresh bread or dine in on home-cooked meals that beat most local restaurants. There's also guest cooking facilities, free coffee and tea, and trip planning.

Hostal Schilling GUESTHOUSE $
(☎491453; http://hostalschilling.com; Paradelo 141; s/d/tr AR$280/350/430; 📶) Good value and centrally located, this friendly guesthouse is a good choice for travelers. Much is due to the family owners, Cecilia, Marcelo and Raimiro, who look after guests with a cup of tea or help with logistical planning. When we visited it was mid-renovation, so rooms vary widely, the best are well lit and roomy. It also has multiple living rooms and a restaurant.

They can also help with reservations for Estancia El Cóndor.

America del Sur HOSTEL $
(☎493525; www.americahostel.com.ar; Puerto Deseado 151; dm AR$130, d/q AR$540/600; @📶) This backpacker favorite has a stylish lodge setting with heated floors and views. Doubles are pleasant and uniform. It's a well-staffed social scene that boasts fun times, including nightly barbecues with salad buffet in high season.

I Keu Ken Hostel HOSTEL $
(☎495175; www.patagoniaikeuken.com.ar; FM Pontoriero 171; dm AR$120, cabin per person AR$400; @📶) With helpful staff, artisan beer and a pet sheep, this quirky hostel has proven popular with travelers. Features include inviting common areas, a deck for lounging and first-rate barbecues (with amnesty for the pet sheep). Its location, near the top of a steep hill, offers views and a workout.

Las Cabañitas CABIN $
(☎491118; www.lascabanitascalafate.com; Valentín Feilberg 218; dm AR$ 120, 2-/3-/4-person cabins AR$370/420/520, d/tr without bathroom AR$300/360; ⊙closed Jul; @📶) A restful spot with snug storybook A-frames with spiral staircases leading to loft beds and apartments. Guests have kitchen privileges. The energetic owner Gerardo also provides worthy meals, lunch boxes and helpful information. Touches include English lavender in the garden, a barbecue area and guest cooking facilities.

Hostel del Glaciar Pioneros HOSTEL $
(☎491243; www.glaciar.com; Los Pioneros 251; dm AR$105, s AR$296-413, d AR$385-448; ⊙Nov-Mar; @📶) A 15-minute walk from town, this sprawling, renovated red house is one of the town's most longstanding hostels. Sociable, it includes comfortable common areas, snug dorms and a small restaurant with homemade meals.

Calafate Hostel HOSTEL $
(☎492450; www.calafatehostels.com; Moyano 1226; dm AR$120, s/d/tr AR$340/450/560; @📶) Best suited to large groups, this mammoth log cabin ends up feeling blander than the competition. Double-bunk dorms are cozy, while the new annex features tidy brick doubles.

Hostel del Glaciar Libertador HOSTEL $
(☎492492; www.glaciar.com; Libertador 587; dm AR$131, s/d AR$495/544; @📶) The best deals here are dorm bunks with thick covers. Behind a Victorian facade, modern facilities include a top-floor kitchen, radiant floor heating, new computers and a spacious common area with a plasma TV glued to sports channels.

Hospedaje Jorgito GUESTHOUSE $
(☎491323; Moyano 943; r per person AR$130, without bathroom AR$100) The lovely Señora Virginia has received generations of travelers in her modest home, decorated with vintage Barbies, doilies and synthetic flowers. Rooms vary in size but are bright and well kept. Guests can use the large kitchen.

Albergue Lago Argentino HOSTEL $
(☎491423; Campaña del Desierto 1050; dm AR$100, s/d/tr AR$300/350/390) Run by Estela, who has been here for years, this pink property offers clean but squat basic dorms. The more appealing annex across the street has attractive and quiet garden rooms ideal for couples. Provides good local information and bike rentals. Close to the bus terminal.

Los Dos Pinos GUESTHOUSE $
(☎491632, 491271; www.losdospinos.com; 9 de Julio 358; campsites per person AR$50, dm/d/tr AR$100/390/520; 📶) This labyrinthine lodging has a supermarket selection of rooms, all adequate, though not charming. Dorms lack

OFF THE BEATEN TRACK

ESTANCIA EL CÓNDOR

A burly slice of heaven, this remote **estancia** (☎in Buenos Aires 011-4735-7704, satellite phone 011-4152-5400; www.cielospatagonicos.com; s/d bunkhouse US$100/150, s/d/tr casco incl full board & excursions US$255/400/540; ⊙Oct-Mar) sits tucked into the shores of Lago San Martín. A private nature reserve, tawny steppe, mossy beech forest and frozen mountaintops comprise its 40,000 hectares.

Even for Patagonia this landscape seems oversized – from the massive turquoise lake (known as O'Higgins on its Chilean side), to the 13 kinds of orchids and craggy cliffs where condors wheel on the wind. Riding enthusiasts could do a week on horseback without running out of fresh terrain; in addition, the adjoining mountain refuge of La Nana provides a basecamp even deeper in the wilderness. Trails are also apt for hiking, though river crossings should always be made with a guide. A day trip to the *condorera* (where condors nest) is a highlight.

The *estancia* occupies a curious footnote in Patagonian history. Its *puesto* (homestead) La Nana was home to an infamous Brit named Jimmy Radburn, who kidnapped a Tehuelche woman named Juana (with her consent – she had already been sold off by her father to pay a gambling debt) and came to this ultra-remote spot at the turn of the 20th century to raise a family. Currently La Nana is only accessible by a day-long hike or ride from the main *casco*.

Rates include all meals and excursions. Lodgings are comfortable but not luxuriant. The *casco* has six rooms, each with a private bathroom, a large stone fireplace and a small collection of literature on the region. Cheaper accommodations are at a more rustic bunkhouse. Meals include fresh vegetables from the greenhouse and meat from the ranch.

Visitors can drive on their own or take a five-hour transfer from El Calafate (US$65), with set departures on Monday and Friday. El Cóndor is located three hours from Tres Lagos, 118km off RN40, on the way to El Chaltén. Currently, there is no legal border crossing here.

insulation but have clean bathrooms and kitchen facilities.

Hosteria La Estepa BOUTIQUE HOTEL **$$**
(☎493551; www.hosterialaestepa.com; Libertador 5310; s/d US$80/100, deluxe US$100/120; @📶) Guests happily tuck into this snug, rustic lodging with panoramic lake views and farm antiquities. Of the 26 rooms, a handful have water views, the deluxe versions have small living areas. A sprawling 2nd-floor social area is strewn with regional maps and board games. The restaurant serves homemade meals. It's 5km west of the town center, toward the national park.

Cauquenes de Nimez B&B **$$**
(☎492306; www.cauquenesdenimez.com.ar; Calle 303, No 79; d US$85; ❄📶) Both modern and rustic, Gabriel's welcoming two-story lodge offers views of flamingos on the lake (from November through summer). Smart rooms decorated with corduroy duvets and nature photography also feature lockboxes and TVs. Personalized attention is a plus, as is the complimentary tea time with lavender muffins, and free bikes (donations support the nature reserve).

Posada Karut Josh B&B **$$**
(☎496444; www.posadakarutjosh.com.ar; Calle 12, No 1882, Barrio Bahía Redonda; d/tr AR$420/510) Run by an Italian-Argentine couple, this peaceful aluminum-sided B&B features big, bright rooms and a lovely garden with lake views. Breakfast is abundant and satisfying meals (AR$85) are also available.

Miyazato Inn B&B **$$**
(☎491953; www.interpatagonia.com/miyazatoinn; Egidio Feruglio 150, Las Chacras; s/d US$80/90; @) Resembling a simple Japanese inn, this elegant B&B wins points for personalized service. Breakfast include sweets and *medialunas*, and excursionists get a hot thermos of coffee or tea to go. It's a five-minute walk away from the center of town.

Newenkelen GUESTHOUSE **$$**
(☎493943; www.newenkelenposada.com.ar; Puerto Deseado 223; d/tr AR$360/430; @📶) Perched on a hill above town, this intimate option features six immaculate brick rooms with

tasteful bedding, tea in rooms and mountain views.

Casa de los Grillos B&B $$
(☎491160; www.casadegrillos.com.ar; Las Bandurrias s/n; s/d/apt AR$370/430/505) A quiet spot with fresh rooms, soft beds and attentive service. The backyard cabin offers shaggy bedspreads and all-new fixtures and appliances. There's self-service coffee, tea and spring water, and a *quincho* provides ample cooking and recreation space.

La Posada del Angel GUESTHOUSE $$
(☎495025; posadadelangelcalafate.com; Madre Teresa de Calcutta 909; d/q US$60/80;) Mature travelers or those who want a homey touch will appreciate this comfortable brick family home with just a few rooms for guests, as well as ample bathrooms, immaculate shared spaces and adorable pets. It's uphill from the town center.

Hotel La Loma INN $$
(☎491016; www.lalomahotel.com; Roca 849; r AR$334-558; @) Colonial furnishings and a lovely rock garden enhance this ranch-style retreat with opera on the hi-fi (old radio). Superior rooms are spacious and bright, antiques fill the creaky hallways, and reception boasts an open fire and plenty of books. Rates vary depending on the view and room quality.

Hotel Michelangelo HOTEL $$
(☎491045; www.michelangelohotel.com.ar; Moyano 1020; d/tr AR$/787/955; @) Tour groups favor this Swiss chalet–style lodging in the center of town. Recently renovated, with a chic lobby and living area with stone fixtures and low lighting. Guest rooms have tasteful, muted colors, high ceilings and full amenities.

Los Sauces Casa Patagónica LUXURY HOTEL $$$
(☎495854; www.casalossauces.com; Los Gauchos 1352; d/ste from US$290/360; @) With an award-winning restaurant, full spa and spacious, immaculately manicured grounds where exotic birds roam and staff members zip by in golf carts, Los Sauces feels less hotel than luxury compound. The varied monochromatic interiors are gorgeous, with first-class beds, huge flatscreen TVs and stone bathrooms with Jacuzzis.

Hotel Posada Los Álamos RESORT $$$
(☎491144; www.posadalosalamos.com; Moyano 1355; s/d/ste AR$1414/1539/2263; @) Considering the amenities, prices are pretty reasonable at Calafate's original resort. There's lush rooms, overstuffed sofas, spectacular gardens, tennis courts, putting greens and a spa. It's enough to make you almost forget about seeing Glaciar Perito Moreno.

Eating

For picnic provisions, small shops selling fresh bread, fine cheeses, sweets and wine are found on the side streets perpendicular to Libertador. Head to **La Anónima** (cnr Libertador & Perito Moreno) for cheap take-out and groceries.

La Fonda del Parillero PARILLA $
(9 de Julio 29; mains AR$37-57; 10am-12am) Skip the pretension and dine at this busy grill with a few sidewalk tables and takeout, particularly good if your hunger strikes late night. In addition to steaks, it also offers homemade pastas, pies and a variety of empanadas.

Viva la Pepa CAFE $
(Amado 833; mains AR$60-75; lunch & dinner) Decked out in children's drawings, this cheerful cafe specializes in crepes, but also offers great sandwiches with homemade bread (try the chicken with apple and blue cheese), fresh juice and gourds of *mate*.

★**Mi Ranchito** ARGENTINE $$
(☎490540; Moyano 1089; mains US$90-110; noon-3:30 & 8pm-midnight) Inspired and intimate, with the owners themselves cooking and serving oversized osso buco, delicious braided pastas stuffed with king crab, divine salads and sweetbreads with wilted spinach on toast. For dessert, chocolat fondant or passionfruit semifreddo are both worth the calorie hit, and more. In a tiny brick pioneer house with space for few. Reserve a few days ahead.

Pura Vida ARGENTINE $$
(☎493356; Libertador 1876; mains AR$65-100; dinner Thu-Tue;) Featuring the rare treat of Argentine home cooking, this offbeat, low-lit eatery is a must. Its longtime owners are found cooking up buttery spiced chicken pot pies and filling wine glasses. For vegetarians, brown rice and wok veggies or various salads are satisfying. Don't skip the decadent chocolate brownie with ice cream, steeped in warm berry sauce. Reserve ahead.

La Tablita PARRILLA $$
(Rosales 24; mains AR$80-120; lunch Thu-Tue, dinner daily) Steak and spit-roasted lamb are

the stars at this satisfying *parrilla,* popular beyond measure for good reason. For average appetites a half-steak will do, rounded out with a good malbec, fresh salad or garlic fries.

El Cucharón ARGENTINE $$
(9 de Julio 145; mains AR$80-120; ⊙lunch & dinner) This sophisticated eatery, tucked away in a small space a few blocks off the main street, is a relatively undiscovered gem and an excellent place to try the regional classic *cazuela de cordero* (lamb stew). The trout with lemon sauce and grilled vegetables is delicious, too.

Los Amigos SEAFOOD $$
(E Leman 40; mains AR$60-100; ⊙lunch & dinner) A real neighborhood restaurant run by a gregarious Uruguayan, Amigos specializes in seafood, but does standard Argentine fare too, with nice touches like marinated eggplant and peppers to spread on your bread.

Cambalache CAFE $$
(www.cambalacherestobar.com.ar; Moyano 1258; mains AR$65-110; ⊙noon-midnight) Housed in a restored tin house, this cheerful travelers' hub offers inexpensive wine and just average regional dishes like grilled steak, oversized pizzas and lamb stew.

La Lechuza PIZZERIA $$
(Libertador 1301; pizzas AR$52-100; ⊙noon-3pm & 6:30-11:30pm) Serves a classic selection of empanadas, salads and pizza on round wooden plates – try the sheep cheese and olive pizza with a local microbrew.

Drinking & Nightlife

Sholken BREWPUB
(Libertador 1630; ⊙8pm-2am) After a day in the wind and sun, this snug brewpub is a godsend. Beer is brewed on-site and the tiny kitchen (mains AR$80) churns out heaping trays of meats and cheeses and spicy beef empanadas. For vegetarians, the endive salad with walnuts, blue cheese and passion-fruit dressing is excellent.

Librobar PUB
(Libertador 1015) Upstairs in the gnome village, this hip bookshop-bar serves coffee, bottled beers and pricey cocktails. Peruse the oversized photography books on Patagonian wildlife or bring your laptop and take advantage of the free wi-fi.

el ba'r CAFE
(9 de Julio s/n; ⊙breakfast & lunch) This trendy patio cafe is the hot spot for you and your sweater-clad puppy to order espresso, *submarinos* (hot milk with melted chocolate bar), green tea or sandwiches (mains AR$60).

Entertainment

La Toldería CLUB
(☎491443; www.facebook.com/LaTolderia; Libertador 1177) This petite storefront opens its doors to dancing and live acts at night, probably the best spot to try if you're feeling boisterous.

Don Diego de la Noche LIVE MUSIC
(Libertador 1603; ⊙until 5am) This perennial favorite serves dinner and features live music like tango, guitar and *folklórico* (Argentine folk music).

Information

MEDICAL SERVICES

Hospital Municipal Dr José Formenti (☎491001; Roca 1487)

MONEY

Withdraw your cash before the weekend rush – it isn't uncommon for ATMs to run out on Sundays. If you are headed to El Chaltén, consider getting extra cash here.

Banco Santa Cruz (Libertador 1285) Changes travelers checks and has an ATM.

Thaler Cambio (Libertador 963; ⊙10am-1pm Mon-Fri, 5:30-7:30pm Sat & Sun) Usurious rates for travelers checks, but it is open on weekends.

POST

Post Office (Libertador 1133)

TOURIST INFORMATION

ACA (Automóvil Club Argentino; ☎491004; cnr 1 de Mayo & Roca) Argentina's auto club; good source for provincial road maps.

Municipal Tourist Office (☎491466, 491090; www.elcalafate.gov.ar; cnr Rosales & Libertador; ⊙8am-8pm) Has town maps and general information. There's also a **kiosk** (☎491090; www.elcalafate.gov.ar; cnr Libertador & Rosales; ⊙8am-8pm) at the bus terminal; both tourist offices have some English-speaking staff on hand.

National Park Office (☎491545; Libertador 1302) Offers brochures and a decent map of Parque Nacional Los Glaciares. It's better to get info here than at the park.

1

CHRISTOPHER GROENHOUT/GETTY IMAGES ©

4

DOUG ALLAN/GETTY IMAGES ©

ROLANDO GARIBOTTI/GETTY IMAGES ©

CHRISTOPHER GROENHOUT/GETTY IMAGES ©

Extreme Patagonia

More than 130 years ago, Lady Florence Dixie ditched high society to ride horses across the Patagonian steppe. Today, you can still fulfill a dream of scaling unnamed peaks, paddling alongside sea lions or tracing a glacier's edge.

Horseback Riding

1 *Estancias* (ranches; p445) remind us how good it is to ride without fences, to feel the heat of a campfire and sleep under the stars.

Ice Climbing

2 Adrenaline, check. Near El Chaltén, eco-camps help you tackle the surreal frozen terrain in Parque Nacional Los Glaciares (p452), where good guiding services make it accessible even to amateurs.

Glacier Trekking

3 More than a hike, it's a full-immersion aesthetic experience. Strap on crampons and explore these living sculptures in Torres del Paine (p479) or Parque Nacional Los Glaciares (p452 and p464).

Diving

4 Clear waters, nearby shipwrecks and cool marine life make Península Valdés (p406) the diving capital of Argentina, with the best visibility in August.

Sea Kayaking

5 Paddle with penguins and Commerson's dolphins in Ría Deseado (p423) and Bahía Bustamante (p421), or play alongside sea lions near Península Valdés (p406).

Driving Ruta Nacional 40

6 Watch herds of dusky guanaco, or the slow approach of shimmering peaks; the sky was never bluer or bigger than on this remote road (p430), an icon of slow travel that flanks the Andes.

Clockwise from top left

1. Horseback riding, El Calafate (p455) **2.** Rock climbing, Cerro Fitz Roy (p452) **3.** Glaciar Perito Moreno (p464) **4.** Diving, Reserva Faunística Península Valdés (p406)

TRAVEL AGENCIES

Most agents deal exclusively with nearby excursions and are unhelpful for other areas.

Tiempo Libre (☎491207; www.tiempolibreviajes.com.ar; Gregores 1294) Can book flights.

Getting There & Away

AIR

The modern **Aeropuerto El Calafate** is 23km east of town off RP11; the departure tax is US$38.

The following rates are one way. **Aerolíneas Argentinas** (☎492814, 492816; Libertador 1361) flies daily to Bariloche or Esquel (from AR$2061), Ushuaia (AR$630), Trelew (AR$1633), and Aeroparque and Ezeiza in Buenos Aires (from AR$1285).

LADE (☎491262; Jean Mermoz 168) flies a few times a week to Río Gallegos (AR$745), Comodoro Rivadavia (AR$753), Ushuaia and Buenos Aires. **Lan** (☎495548; 9 de Julio 57) flies to Ushuaia weekly.

BUS

El Calafate's hilltop **bus terminal** (Roca s/n) is easily reached by a pedestrian staircase from the corner of Libertador and 9 de Julio. Book ahead in high season, as outbound seats can be in short supply.

For Río Gallegos, buses depart four times daily; contact **Taqsa/Marga** (☎491843) or **Sportman** (☎492680). Connections to Bariloche and Ushuaia may require leaving in the middle of the night and a change of buses in Río Gallegos.

For El Chaltén, buses depart daily at 8am, 2pm and 6pm. Both **Caltur** (☎491368; www.caltur.com.ar; Libertador 1080) and Chaltén Travel (p457) head to El Chaltén and drive the RN40 to Bariloche (AR$1100, two days) during the summer.

For Puerto Natales, Chile, **Cootra** (☎491444) and **Turismo Zahhj** (☎491631) depart at 8am and 8:30am daily (three times weekly in low season), crossing the border at Cerro Castillo, where it may be possible to connect to Torres del Paine.

Buses from El Calafate

DESTINATION	COST (AR$)	DURATION (HR)
El Chaltén	150-200	3½
Bariloche	950	14*/28 summer/winter (*bus travels RN40 summer only)
Puerto Natales (Chile)	195	5
Río Gallegos	180	4

Getting Around

Airport shuttle **Ves Patagonia** (☎494355; www.vespatagonia.com) offers door-to-door service (one way/round-trip AR$60/100). There are several car-rental agencies at the airport. **Localiza** (☎491398; www.localiza.com.ar; Libertador 687) and **Servi Car** (☎492541; www.servi4x4.com.ar; Libertador 695) offer car rentals from convenient downtown offices.

Renting a **bike** is an excellent way to get a feel for the area and cruise the dirt roads by the lake. Albergue Lago Argentino offers rentals.

Around El Calafate

From El Calafate, paved RN40 cuts southeast across vast steppe for 95km, then jogs south at El Cerrito and turns to gravel. Staying on paved RP5 means a slow-going, five-hour, 224km bore of a trip southeast to Río Gallegos. From there, paved RP7 connects back to RN40 for the Chilean border crossing at Cerro Castillo–Cancha Carrera, Parque Nacional Torres del Paine and Puerto Natales.

Parque Nacional Los Glaciares (South)

Among Earth's most dynamic and accessible ice fields, Glaciar Perito Moreno is the stunning centerpiece of the southern sector of Parque Nacional Los Glaciares (admission AR$130, collected after 8am). It's 30km long, 5km wide and 60m high, but what makes it exceptional in the world of ice is its constant advance – it creeps forward up to 2m per day, causing building-sized icebergs to calve from its face. Watching the glacier is a sedentary park experience that manages to be thrilling.

The glacier formed as a low gap in the Andes allowed moisture-laden Pacific storms to drop their loads east of the divide, where they accumulate as snow. Over millennia, under tremendous weight, this snow has recrystallized into ice and flowed slowly eastward. The 1600-sq-km trough of Lago Argentino, the country's largest body of water, is evidence that glaciers were once far more extensive than today.

While most of the world's glaciers are receding, Glaciar Perito Moreno is considered 'stable.' Regardless, 17 times between 1917 and 2006, as the glacier has advanced, it has dammed the Brazo Rico (Rico Arm) of Lago Argentino, causing the water to rise. Several times the melting ice below has been unable to support the weight of the water behind it and the dam has collapsed in an explosion of water and ice. To be present when this spectacular cataclysm occurs is unforgettable.

Glaciar Perito Moreno is as much an auditory as a visual experience when huge icebergs calve and collapse into the **Canal de los Témpanos** (Iceberg Channel). This natural-born tourist attraction at Península de Magallanes is close enough to guarantee great views, but far enough away to be safe. A series of steel catwalks (almost 4000m total) and vantage points allow visitors to see, hear and photograph the glacier. Sun hits its face in the morning and the glacier's appearance changes as the day progresses and shadows shift.

There is a free shuttle from the parking area to the catwalks. A closed *refugio* with glass walls allows for glacier viewing in bad weather; there's also a snack bar and two-story restaurant Nativos, serving cappuccino and sandwiches to sightseers. If you bring a picnic, remember that it is difficult and costly to remove trash from the area – please pack yours out.

For student rates, visitors must have a student ID. The main gateway town to the park's southern sector, El Calafate, is 80km east of the glacier by road. It's where you'll find most operators for tours and activities.

Activities

Glaciar Perito Moreno

Beyond a short walk that parallels the shoreline at the boat dock and climbs to the lookout area, there are no trails in this sector of the park accessible without boat transportation. These nautical excursions allow you to sense the magnitude of Glaciar Perito Moreno, still from a safe distance. Tours do not include transfers to Parque Nacional Los Glaciares (AR$130 round-trip) and park entry fee.

Around El Calafate & PN Los Glaciares (South)

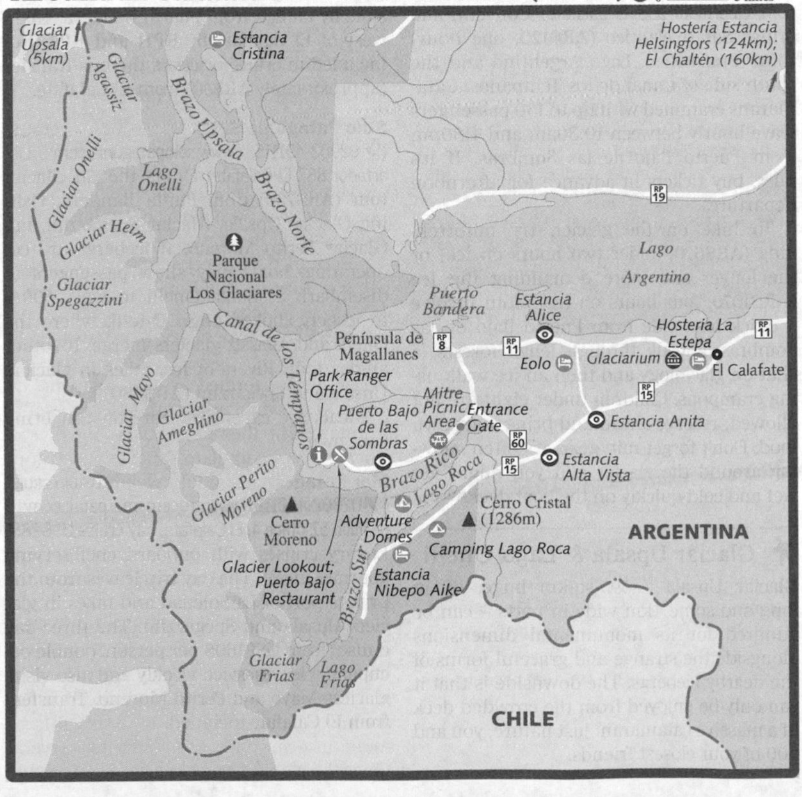

THE STORY OF GLACIERS

Ribbons of ice, stretched flat in sheets or sculpted by weather and fissured by pressure, glaciers have a raw magnificence that is mind-boggling to behold.

As snow falls on the accumulation area, it compacts to ice. The river of ice is slugged forward by gravity, which deforms its layers as it moves. When the glacier surges downhill, melted ice mixes with rock and soil on the bottom, grinding it into a lubricant that keeps pushing the glacier along. At the same time, debris from the crushed rock is forced to the sides of the glacier, creating features called moraines. Movement also causes cracks and deformities called crevasses.

The ablation area is where the glacier melts. When accumulation outpaces melting at the ablation area, the glacier advances; when there's more melting or evaporation, the glacier recedes. Since 1980 global warming has contributed greatly to widespread glacial retreat.

Another marvel of glaciers is their hue. What makes some blue? Wavelengths and air bubbles. The more compact the ice, the longer the path that light has to travel and the bluer the ice appears. Air bubbles in uncompacted areas absorb long wavelengths of white light so we see white. When glaciers calve into lakes, they dump a 'glacial flour' comprised of ground-up rock that gives the water a milky, grayish color. This same sediment remains unsettled in some lakes and diffracts the sun's light, creating a stunning palette of turquoise, pale mint and azure.

Hielo y Aventura ICE TREKKING, CRUISE
(☎02902-492205, 492094; www.hieloyaventura.com; Libertador 935, El Calafate) Conventional cruise Safari Nautico (AR$120, one hour) tours Brazo Rico, Lago Argentino and the south side of Canal de los Témpanos. Catamarans crammed with up to 130 passengers leave hourly between 10:30am and 4:30pm from Puerto Bajo de las Sombras. If it's busy, buy tickets in advance for afternoon departures.

To hike on the glacier, try minitrekking (AR$670, under two hours on ice) or the longer and more demanding Big Ice (AR$1070, four hours on ice). Both involve a quick boat ride from Puerto Bajo de las Sombras, a walk through lenga forests, a chat on glaciology and then an ice walk using crampons. Children under eight are not allowed; reserve ahead and bring your own food. Don't forget rain gear: it's often snowing around the glacier and you might get wet and cold quickly on the boat deck.

Glaciar Upsala & Lago Onelli

Glaciar Upsala – 595-sq-km huge, 60km long and some 4km wide in parts – can be admired for its monumental dimensions alongside the strange and graceful forms of the nearby icebergs. The downside is that it can only be enjoyed from the crowded deck of a massive catamaran: just nature, you and 300 of your closest friends.

On an extension of the Brazo Norte (North Arm) of Lago Argentino, it's accessible by launch from Puerto Bandera, 45km west of El Calafate by RP11 and RP8. Not included in cruise prices is the bus transfer (approximately AR$50) from El Calafate.

Solo Patagonia S.A. CRUISE
(☎02902-491115; www.solopatagonia.com; Libertador 867, El Calafate) Offers the All Glacier tour (AR$720) from Punta Bandera, visiting Glaciar Upsala, Glaciar Spegazzini and Glaciar Perito Moreno. If icebergs are cooperating, boats may allow passengers to disembark at Bahía Onelli to walk 500m to iceberg-choked **Lago Onelli**, where the Onelli and Agassiz glaciers merge. Its other all-day tour, Rivers of Ice, takes in glaciers Upsala and Spegazzini (AR$480).

Meals are expensive, but you can bring your own.

Mar Patag LUXURY CRUISE
(☎02902-492118; www.crucerosmarpatag.com; 9 de Julio 57, office 4, El Calafate; day cruise US$288) Luxury cruises with onboard chef serving gourmet meals. The day trip leaves from the private port of La Soledad and takes in glaciers Upsala and Spegazzini. The three-day cruise (from US$1608 per person, double occupancy) leaves twice weekly and also visits glaciers Mayo and Perito Moreno. Transfers from El Calafate included.

Lago Roca

The serene south arm of Lago Argentino, with lakeshore forests and mountains, features good hikes and pleasant camping. *Estancia* accommodations occupy this section of Parque Nacional Los Glaciares, where most visitors rarely travel. No entrance fee is charged. For transportation, contact Caltur.

Cerro Cristal HIKING

A rugged but rewarding 3½-hour hike, with views of Glaciar Perito Moreno and the Torres del Paine on clear days. The trail begins at the education camp at La Jerónima, just before the Camping Lago Roca entrance, 55km southwest of El Calafate along RP15.

Cabalgatas del Glaciar HORSEBACK RIDING

(☎495447; www.cabalgatasdelglaciar.com) Day and multiday riding or trekking trips with glacier panoramas to Lago Rocas and Paso Zamora on the Chilean border. Also available through Caltur.

Sleeping & Eating

★**Camping Lago Roca** CAMPGROUND $

(☎02902-499500; www.losglaciares.com/campinglagoroca; per person AR$70, cabin dm per 2/4 people AR$300/450) This full-service campground complete with restaurant-bar and located a few kilometers past the education camp makes for an excellent adventure base. The clean concrete-walled dorms provide a snug alternative to camping. Hiking trails abound, and the center rents fishing equipment and bikes and coordinates horseback riding at the nearby Estancia Nibepo Aike.

Hostería Estancia Helsingfors ESTANCIA $$$

(☎in Buenos Aires 011-5277-0195; www.helsingfors.com.ar; per person incl full board, transfer & activities s/d US$365/450; ⊙Oct-Apr) The simply stunning location ogling Cerro Fitz Roy from Lago Viedma makes for lots of love-at-first-sight impressions. Intimate and welcoming, this former Finnish pioneer ranch is a highly regarded luxury destination, though it cultivates a relaxed, unpretentious ambience. Guests pass the time on scenic but demanding mountain treks, rides and visits to Glaciar Viedma.

Transfers are made on Tuesday, Thursday and Saturday, otherwise you can order a chartered van. It's on Lago Viedma's southern shore, 170km from El Chaltén and 180km from El Calafate.

Estancia Cristina ESTANCIA $$$

(☎02902-491133, in Buenos Aires 011-4803-7352; www.estanciacristina.com; d 2 nights incl full board & activities US$1200; ⊙Oct-Apr) Locals in the know say the most outstanding trekking in the region is right here. Lodging is in bright, modern cabins with expansive views. A visit includes guided activities and boating to Glaciar Upsala. Accessible by boat, it's at Punta Bandera, off the northern arm of Lago Argentino.

Estancia Nibepo Aike ESTANCIA $$$

(☎02902-492797, in Buenos Aires 011-5272-0341; www.nibepoaike.com.ar; RP15, Km60; s/d incl full board & activities from US$290/440; ⊙Oct-Apr) This Croatian pioneer ranch, still a working cattle ranch, offers the usual assortment of *estancia* highlights, including demonstrations and horseback riding with bilingual guides. Rooms are simply lovely and high-quality photos give a sense of the regional history. Guests can also explore the surroundings on two wheels from the bicycle stash. Transfers to and from El Calafate are included.

Eolo LUXURY HOTEL $$$

(☎in Buenos Aires 011 4700-0075; www.eolo.com.ar; RP11; s/d incl full board from US$710/880) Ringed by miles of Patagonian steppe, this Relais & Chateaux property leaves the rustic life outside the double glass windows. Guests first see an interior courtyard filled with lavender. There's 17 tasteful guest rooms, a sauna, small pool and spa services. Beautiful antique *estancia* furniture and a collection of old regional maps and publications set the mood. Transfer included.

Adventure Domes CAMPGROUND $$$

(☎02962-493185; adventure-domes.com; per person US$250) Reviews have been mixed for this all-inclusive nature camp, which features hikes and ice trekking on the glacier and overnights in domes with comfortable beds, hot-water showers and all meals (lunch boxes for day trips). Provides transfers.

Getting There & Away

Glaciar Perito Moreno is 80km west of El Calafate via paved RP11, passing through the breathtaking scenery around Lago Argentino. Bus tours (AR$110 round-trip, AR$80 for transport only) are frequent in summer, or simply stroll down El Calafate's Libertador. Buses leave El Calafate in the early morning and afternoon, returning around noon and 7pm.

CHILEAN PATAGONIA

Rugged seascapes rimmed with glacial peaks, the stunning massifs of Torres del Paine and howling steppe characterize the other side of the Andes. Once you come this far, it is well worth crossing the border. Chilean Patagonia consists of the isolated Aisén and Magallanes regions, separated by the southern continental ice field. This area covers Punta Arenas, Puerto Natales and Parque Nacional Torres del Paine. For in-depth coverage of Chile, pick up Lonely Planet's *Chile & Easter Island*.

Most nationals of countries that have diplomatic relations with Chile don't need a visa. Upon entering, customs officials issue a tourist card, valid for 90 days and renewable for another 90; authorities take it seriously, so guard it closely to avoid the hassle of replacing it. If arriving by air, US citizens must pay a one-time reciprocal entry fee of US$160, valid for the life of the passport; Canadians pay US$132 and Australians US$95.

Temperature-sensitive travelers will quickly notice a difference after leaving energy-rich Argentina: in public areas and budget accommodations central heating is rare; warmer clothing is the norm indoors.

US cash is not widely accepted. Prices here are given in Chilean pesos (CH$).

Punta Arenas

☎0612 / POP 130,700

Today's Punta Arenas is a confluence of the ruddy and the grand, witnessed in the elaborate wool-boom mansions, the thriving petrochemical industry and its port status. Visitors will find it the most convenient base to travel around the remote Magallanes region, with good traveler services. Watch for more cruise-ship passengers and trekkers to replace the explorers, sealers and sailors of yesterday at the barstools – but save a spot for the old guard.

Founded in 1848 as a penal settlement and military garrison, Punta Arenas was conveniently situated for ships headed to Alta California during the gold rush. The economy took off only in the last quarter of the 19th century, after the territorial governor authorized the purchase of 300 purebred sheep from the Falkland Islands (Islas Malvinas). This experiment encouraged sheep farming and, by the turn of the century, nearly two million grazed the territory.

Sights & Activities

Museo Regional de Magallanes MUSEUM

(Museo Regional Braun-Menéndez; ☎244216; www.museodemagallanes.cl; Magallanes 949; admission CH$1000; ⏰10:30am-5pm Wed-Mon, closes at 2pm May-Dec) This opulent mansion testifies to the wealth and power of pioneer sheep farmers in the late 19th century. The well-maintained interior houses a regional historical museum (ask for booklets in English) and original exquisite French-nouveau family furnishings, from intricate wooden inlaid floors to Chinese vases.

In former servants' quarters, a downstairs cafe is perfect for a pisco sour while soaking up the grandeur.

Plaza Muñoz Gamero PLAZA

A central plaza of magnificent conifers surrounded by opulent mansions. Facing the plaza's north side, Casa Braun-Menéndez houses the private **Club de la Unión** (☎241489; admission CH$1000; ⏰10:30am-1pm & 5-8:30pm Tue-Fri, 10:30am-1pm & 8-10pm Sat, 11am-2pm Sun); the tavern, La Taberna, downstairs is open to the public. The nearby **monument** commemorating the 400th anniversary of Magellan's voyage was donated by wool baron José Menéndez in 1920.

Just east, the former **Sociedad Menéndez Behety** now houses Turismo Comapa. The **cathedral** sits west.

★**Cementerio Municipal** CEMETERY

(main entrance at Av Bulnes 949; ⏰7:30am-8pm) FREE Among South America's most fascinating cemeteries, with both humble immigrant graves and flashy tombs, like that of wool baron José Menéndez, which Bruce Chatwin described as a scale replica of Rome's Vittorio Emanuele monument. See the map inside the main entrance gate.

It's an easy 15-minute stroll northeast of Plaza Muñoz Gamero, or catch any taxi *colectivo* (shared taxi with specific route) in front of the Museo Regional Braun-Menéndez on Magallanes.

Museo Naval y Marítimo MUSEUM

(☎205479; www.museonaval.cl; Pedro Montt 981; adult/child CH$1200/600; ⏰9:30am-12:30pm & 2-5pm Tue-Sat) A naval and maritime museum with historical exhibits which include a fine account of the Chilean mission that rescued Sir Ernest Shackleton's crew from Antarctica. The most imaginative display is a replica ship complete with bridge, maps, charts and radio room.

Museo Regional Salesiano MUSEUM
(☎221001; Av Bulnes 336; admission CH$2500; ⏲10am-12:30pm & 3-6pm Tue-Sun) Especially influential in settling the region, the Salesian order collected outstanding ethnographic artifacts; those here tout the mission's role as peacemakers between the Yaghan and Ona and settlers.

Tours

Worthwhile day trips include tours to the **Seno Otway pingüinera** (penguin colony), 48km to the north. Tours (from CH$20,000) leave at 4pm daily October through March, weather permitting.

The town's first settlements at Fuerte Bulnes and Puerto Hambre comprise **Parque Historia Patagonia** (☎723195; www.phipa.cl; Km56 Sur; admission CH$12,000; ⏲9:30am-6:30pm). Visit with a tour group or a rental car.

Torres del Paine tours are abundant from Punta Arenas, but the distance makes for a very long day; it's best to organize transport from Puerto Natales.

If you have the time, a more atmospheric alternative to Seno Otway is the thriving Magellanic penguin colonies of **Monumento Natural Los Pingüinos** on Isla Magdalena. Five-hour ferry tours (adult/child CH$28,000/14,000) land for an hour at the island and depart the port on Tuesday through Sunday, December through February. Confirm times in advance. Book tickets through **Turismo Comapa** (☎200200; www.comapa.com; Magallanes 990) and bring a picnic.

Tours also go to destinations such as Parque Nacional Pali Aike.

Recommended agencies:

Turismo Aonikenk GUIDED TOUR
(☎228616; www.aonikenk.com; Magallanes 570) Recommended English-, German- and French-speaking guides. Offers Cabo Froward treks, visits to the king penguin colony in Tierra del Fuego, and cheaper open expeditions geared at experienced participants.

Inhóspita Patagonia HIKING
(☎224510; Navarro 1013) Offers hiking trips to Cabo Froward, the southernmost point on mainland South America.

Turismo Pali Aike GUIDED TOUR
(☎223301; www.turismopaliaike.com; Navarro 1129) Recommended tour company.

Sleeping

On the cruise-ship circuit, Punta Arenas has a plethora of hotels. Foreigners are not required to pay the additional 18% IVA charge if paying with US cash, travelers checks or credit card. Prices drop low season (mid-April to mid-October).

Hospedaje Magallanes B&B $
(☎228616; www.aonikenk.com; Magallanes 570; dm/s/d CH$12,000/29,000/32,000; @📶) A great, inexpensive option run by a German-Chilean couple, who are also Torres del Paine guides with an on-site travel agency. With just a few quiet rooms, there are often communal dinners or backyard barbecues by the climbing wall. Breakfast includes brown bread and strong coffee.

Hospedaje Independencia GUESTHOUSE $
(☎227572; www.chileaustral.com/independencia; Av Independencia 374; campsites per person $CH2000, dm CH$5000; @) One of the last die-hard backpacker haunts, with cheap prices and bonhomie to match. Despite the chaos, the rooms are reasonably clean and there are kitchen privileges, camping and bike rentals.

Hostal Fitz Roy GUESTHOUSE $
(☎240430; www.hostalfitzroy.com; Navarro 850; dm/d CH$8000/30,000, d without bathroom CH$25,000, 5-person cabin CH$35,000; @) This country house in the city offers rambling, good-value rooms and an inviting, old-fashioned living room to pore over books or sea charts. Rooms have phones and TVs.

Hostel Keoken GUESTHOUSE $
(☎244086; www.hostelkeoken.cl; Magallanes 209; s/d CH$25,000/30,000 with shared bathroom CH$15000/22,000; @) Increasingly popular with backpackers, Hostel Keoken features comfortable beds topped with fluffy white down comforters and serves homemade pastries for breakfast. The center of town is a few minutes' away on foot.

Al Fin del Mundo HOSTEL $
(☎710185; www.alfindelmundo.cl; O'Higgins 1026; dm CH$12,000, s/d without bathroom CH$20,000/32,000; 📶) On the 2nd and 3rd floors of a downtown building, these rooms are cheerful but due for updates. All share bathrooms with hot showers and there is a large kitchen, as well as a living area with a large TV, pool table and DVD library.

Punta Arenas

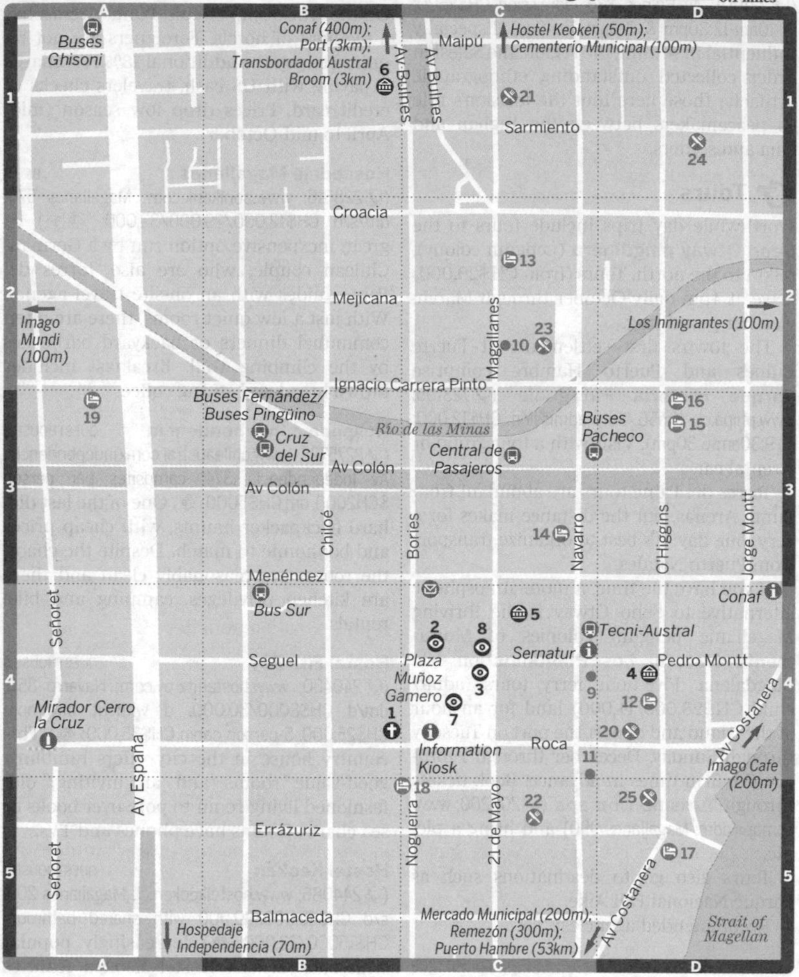

★**Ilaia Hotel** BOUTIQUE HOTEL $$
(☎723100; www.ilaia.cl; Carrera Pinto 351; d/tr from US$95/125; 📶) Playful and modern, this high-concept boutique hotel is run with all the warmth of a family home. Sly messages are written to be read in mirrors, rooms are simple and chic, and an incredible glass lookout room beams out on the Strait of Magellan. There's yoga and various therapies available. Healthy breakfasts include chapati bread, homemade jam, avocados, yogurt and more. Heads up: you won't find a TV here.

Hostal Terrasur INN $$
(☎225618; www.hostalterrasur.cl; O'Higgins 723; s/d CH$40,000/45,000; @📶) The slightly upscale Terrasur nurtures a secret-garden atmosphere, from its rooms with flowing curtains and flower patterns to the miniature green courtyard.

Hostal La Estancia GUESTHOUSE $$
(☎249130; www.estancia.cl; O'Higgins 765; d CH$45,000, dm CH$12,000, s/d without bathroom CH$20,000/35,000; @📶) An old downtown house with big rooms, vaulted ceilings and tidy shared bathrooms. Longtime owners

Punta Arenas

Sights

Activities, Courses & Tours

Sleeping

Eating

Drinking & Nightlife

Alex and Carmen are eager to help with travel plans. There's a book exchange, kitchen use, laundry and storage.

Hotel Plaza HOTEL $$
(☎241300; www.hotelplaza.cl; Nogueira 1116; s/d US$105/130; @) This converted mansion boasts vaulted ceilings, plaza views and historical photos lining the hall. Inconsistent with such grandeur, the country decor is unfortunate. But service is genteel and the location unbeatable.

Hotel Dreams del Estrecho LUXURY HOTEL $$$
(☎600-626-0000; www.mundodreams.com/detalle/dreams-punta-arenas; O'Higgins 1235; d/ste US$185/221; @ 📶 🏊) Parked at the water's edge, this glass oval high-rise brings a little Vegas to the end of the world. It's a glittery atmosphere, with new rooms that are spacious and luxuriant, but the showstopper is the swimming pool that appears to merge with the ocean. There's also a spa, casino and swank restaurant on-site.

Eating

Local seafood is an exquisite treat: go for *centolla* (king crab) between July and November or *erizos* (sea urchins) between November and July.

Café Almacen Tapiz CAFE $
(www.cafetapiz.cl; Roca 912; mains CH$5000; ⊙9am-9:30pm; 📶) Cloaked in alerce shingles, this lively cafe makes for an ambient coffee break. In addition to gorgeous layer cakes, it serves salads, and pita sandwiches with goat cheese, meats or roasted veggies.

Los Inmigrantes CAFE $
(www.inmigrante.cl; Quillota 559; mains AR$5000; ⊙noon-8pm) In the historic Croatian neighborhood, this cafe serves generous oversized sandwiches of salmon, cured meats or veggies on all kinds of bread, as well as decadent cakes. On display are interesting relics from Dalmatian immigrants.

Mercado Municipal MARKET $
(21 de Mayo 1465; ⊙8am-3pm) Fish and vegetable market with cheap 2nd-floor *cocinerías* (eateries).

Fuente Hamburg CHILEAN $
(Errázurriz 856; mains CH$2500-5000; ⊙10:30am-8:30pm Mon-Fri, 10:30am-3pm Sat) Shiny barstools flank a massive grill churning out quick bites. Grab a *churrasco* (thin-sliced beef) topped with tomatoes and green beans, served with fresh mayo on a soft bun.

Imago Cafe CAFE $
(Av Costanera s/n; mains CH$3000-6000; ⊙9:30am-9pm Mon-Fri, 11am-9pm Sat & Sun) A hip 2nd-story nook overlooking the city, with loose-leaf teas, fair-trade coffee and sandwiches.

Secreto de la Patagonia SELF-CATERING $
(Sarmiento 1029) Locally made artisan chocolates, goat cheese and preserved meats, worthy as gifts or park treats.

★**La Marmita** CHILEAN $$
(☎222056; www.marmitamaga.cl; Plaza Sampaio 678; mains CH$6000-10,000; ⊙lunch & dinner Mon-Sat) This classic bistro enjoys wild popularity for its lovely, casual ambience

and tasty fare. Besides fresh salads and hot bread, hearty dishes such as casseroles or seafood hark back to grandma's cooking, Chilean style. There's also a new take-out service.

Damiana Elena CHILEAN **$$**
(Magallanes 341; mains CH$7000-9000; ⏲dinner Mon-Sat) This elegant restaurant is in a romantic old house, off the beaten path in a residential neighborhood. The detour is worth it for the warm, sophisticated ambience and first-rate Chilean cuisine: highlights are salmon ceviche and grilled tilapia.

Remezón GOURMET **$$$**
(☎241029; www.patagoniasalvaje.cl; 21 de Mayo 1469; mains CH$5000-15,000; ⏲lunch & dinner) An innovative mainstay with homey atmosphere. Garlic soup made with fragrant beef broth is a good starter, even shared. Game dishes are the house specialty, but the delicate *merluza negra* (black hake) shouldn't be missed, served with *chupe de espinaca* (spinach casserole). Chef Luis also offers group cooking workshops that include a trip to the local market.

Sotito's SEAFOOD **$$$**
(☎243565; O'Higgins 1138; mains CH$5000-15,000; ⏲lunch & dinner) This seafood institution is popular with moneyed locals and cruise-ship travelers in search of a classy king crab feast. The decor may not be inspiring but the cuisine doesn't disappoint.

Drinking & Nightlife

La Taberna BAR
(Casa Braun-Menéndez, Plaza Muñoz Gamero; ⏲7pm-2am On-Fri, 7pm-3am Sat & Sun) This dark and elegant subterranean bar, with polished wood fixtures and cozy nooks reminiscent of an old-fashioned ship, is a classic old-boys' club. The rooms fill with cigar smoke later in the evening, but the opportunity to sip pisco sours in the classy Casa Braun-Menéndez shouldn't be missed.

Information

Travel agencies in the city center, along Roca and Navarro, change cash and travelers checks. All are open weekdays and Saturday, with a few open on Sunday morning. Banks with ATMs dot the city center.

Conaf (☎223841; Menéndez 1147) Has details on the nearby parks.

Hospital Regional (☎205000; cnr Arauco & Angamos)

Information Kiosk (☎200610; Plaza Muñoz Gamero; ⏲8am-7pm Mon-Sat, 9am-7pm Sun) South side of Plaza Muñoz Gamero.

Post Office (Bories 911) Located one block north of Plaza Muñoz Gamero.

Sernatur (☎241330; www.sernatur.cl; Navarro 999; ⏲8am-6pm Mon-Fri) Has friendly, well-informed, multilingual staff, and lists of accommodations and transportation. Also has a list of recommended doctors.

Sur Cambios (Navarro 1001) Exchanges money.

Getting There & Away

The tourist offices distribute a useful brochure that details all forms of transportation available.

AIR

Punta Arenas' airport is located 21km north of town.

LanChile (☎241100; www.lan.com; Bories 884) flies several times daily to Santiago (CH$229,000) with a stop in Puerto Montt (CH$127,000), and on Saturday to the Falkland Islands (round-trip CH$435,000). For national flights, book ahead online for the best deals. **Sky Airline** (☎710645; www.skyairline.cl; Roca 935) flies daily to Santiago, stopping in Puerto Montt or Concepcion.

Aerovías DAP (☎616100; www.aeroviasdap.cl; O'Higgins 891) From November to March flies to Porvenir (CH$29,000) several times daily Monday to Saturday, and to Puerto Williams (CH$75,000) at 10am Monday to Saturday. Luggage is limited to 10kg per person. It also offers airport transfers (CH$3000) for passengers.

BOAT

Transbordador Austral Broom (☎580089; www.tabsa.cl) Operates three ferries to Tierra del Fuego. The car/passenger ferry *Crux Australis* to/from Porvenir (per person/vehicle CH$5800/37,000, 2½ to four hours) usually leaves at 9am but has some afternoon departures; check the current online schedule. The faster Primera Angostura crossing (per person/vehicle CH$1600/13,900, 20 minutes), northeast of Punta Arenas, sails every 90 minutes between 8:30am and 11:45pm. Broom sets sail for Isla Navarino's Puerto Williams (reclining seat/bunk CH$93,000/130,000 including meals, 30 hours) three or four times per month on Wednesday only, and returning on Saturdays.

Cruceros Australis (☎in Santiago 02-442-3110; www.australis.com; ⏲Sep-May) Luxury four- and five-day cruises to Ushuaia and back. Turismo Comapa (p469) handles local bookings.

BUS

Buses depart from company offices, most situated within a block or two of Av Colón. Buy tickets several hours (if not days) in advance. The **Central de Pasajeros** (☎245811; cnr Magallanes & Av Colón) is the closest thing to a central booking office.

Bus Sur (☎614222; www.bus-sur.cl; Menéndez 552) Buses to El Calafate, Puerto Natales, Río Gallegos, Ushuaia and Puerto Montt.

Buses Fernández/Buses Pingüino (☎221429; www.busesfernandez.com; Sanhueza 745) Buses to Puerto Natales, Torres del Paine and Río Gallegos.

Buses Ghisoni (☎240646; www.busesbarria.cl; Av España 264) Comfortable buses to Río Gallegos, Río Grande and Ushuaia.

Buses Pacheco (☎242174; www.busespacheco.com; Av Colón 900) Buses to Puerto Natales, Río Gallegos and Ushuaia.

Tecni-Austral (☎222078; Navarro 975) Buses to Río Grande.

Cruz del Sur (☎227970; www.busescruzdelsur.cl; Sanhueza 745) Buses to Puerto Montt, Osorno and Chiloé.

Buses from Punta Arenas

DESTINATION	COST (CH$)	DURATION (HR)
Puerto Montt	45,000	32
Puerto Natales	5000	3
Río Gallegos	10,000	5-8
Río Grande	20,000	9
Ushuaia	30,000	10

Getting Around

TO/FROM THE AIRPORT

Buses depart directly from the airport to Puerto Natales. **Transfer Austral** (☎282854) runs door-to-door shuttle services (CH$3000) to/from town to coincide with flights. Buses Fernández does regular airport transfers (CH$3000).

BUS & TAXI COLECTIVO

Taxi *colectivos*, with numbered routes, are only slightly more expensive than buses (about CH$800, or a bit more late at night and on Sundays); far more comfortable and much quicker.

CAR

Cars are a good option for exploring Torres del Paine, but renting one in Chile to cross the border into Argentina can become prohibitively expensive due to international insurance requirements. If heading for El Calafate, it is best to rent your vehicle in Argentina. Purchasing a car to explore Patagonia has its drawbacks, as Chilean Patagonia has no through roads that link northern and southern Patagonia, so it is entirely dependent on the roads of Argentina or expensive ferry travel.

Punta Arenas has Chilean Patagonia's most economical rental rates, and locally owned agencies tend to provide better service. Recommended **Adel Rent a Car/Localiza** (☎235472; www.adelrentacar.cl; Pedro Montt 962) provides attentive service, competitive rates, airport pickup and good travel tips. Other choices include **Budget** (☎225983; O'Higgins 964), **Hertz** (☎248742; O'Higgins 987) and **Lubag** (☎710484; Magallanes 970).

Around Punta Arenas

Penguin Colonies

There are two substantial Magellanic penguin colonies near Punta Arenas. Easier to reach is **Seno Otway** (Otway Sound; admission CH$6000, road toll CH$1000; ⏲8am-6:30pm), with about 6000 breeding pairs, about an hour northwest of the city. The larger (50,000 breeding pairs) and more interesting **Monumento Natural Los Pingüinos** is accessible only by boat to Isla Magdalena in the Strait of Magellan.

Arrive via private vehicle or tour. If driving independently, pay attention as you head north on RN9 – it's easy to miss the small sign indicating the turnoff to the penguin colony.

Parque Nacional Pali Aike

Rugged volcanic steppe pocked with craters, caves and twisted formations, Pali Aike means 'devil's country' in Tehuelche. This desolate landscape is a 50-sq-km **park** (admission CH$1000) along the Argentine border. Mineral content made lava rocks red, yellow or green-gray. Fauna includes abundant guanaco, ñandú, gray fox and armadillo. In the 1930s Junius Bird's excavations at 17m-deep **Pali Aike Cave** yielded the first artifacts associated with extinct New World fauna such as the milodón and the native horse *Onohippidium*.

The park has several trails, including a 1.7km path through the rugged lava beds of the **Escorial del Diablo** to the impressive **Crater Morada del Diablo**; wear sturdy shoes or your feet could be shredded. There are hundreds of craters, some four stories high. A 9km trail from Cueva Pali Aike to **Laguna Ana** links a shorter trail to a site on the main road, 5km from the park entrance.

Parque Nacional Pali Aike is 200km northeast of Punta Arenas via RN9, Ch 255 and a graveled secondary road from Cooperativa Villa O'Higgins, 11km north of Estancia Kimiri Aike. There's also access from the Chilean border post at Monte Aymond. There is no public transport, but Punta Arenas travel agencies offer full-day tours.

Puerto Natales

☑ 0612 / POP 18,500

On the windswept shores of Seno Última Esperanza (Last Hope Sound), this formerly modest fishing village is now the well-trodden hub of the continent's number-one national park, Torres del Paine. Though tourism has transformed its rusted tin shop fronts into gleaming facades, Natales maintains its windswept charm, especially in the shoulder seasons.

The Navimag ferry through Chile's fjords ends and begins its trips here. Located 250km northwest of Punta Arenas via RN, Puerto Natales also offers frequent transport to El Calafate, Argentina.

⊙ Tours

Antares/Big Foot Patagonia ADVENTURE TOUR
(☑ 414611; www.bigfootpatagonia.com; Pedro Montt 161) Guide service specializing in Torres del Paine, Antares can facilitate climbing permits and made-to-order trips. It also has the concession for ice hikes in the park. Also runs kayak tours in the park.

Baqueano Zamora HORSEBACK RIDING
(☑ 613530; www.baqueanozamora.cl; Baquedano 534) Runs horseback-riding trips in Torres del Paine.

Knudsen Tour GUIDED TOUR
(☑ 414747; knudsentour@yahoo.com; Blanco Encalada 284) A well-regarded outfit, which has trips to El Calafate, Torres del Paine and alternative routes along Seno Último Esperanza.

Turismo 21 de Mayo GUIDED TOUR
(☑ 411978; www.turismo21demayo.cl; Eberhard 560) Organizes day-trip cruises and treks to the Balmaceda and Serrano glaciers.

🛏 Sleeping

Options abound, most with breakfast, laundry and lowered rates in the low season. Reserve ahead if arriving on the ferry. Hos-

tels often rent equipment and arrange park transport.

The Singing Lamb HOSTEL $
(☑ 410958; www.thesinginglamb.com; Arauco 779; dm CH$11,500-13,000, d CH$37,000; @🛜) ⏎ Sparkling clean and green (with compost, recycling, rainwater collection and linen shopping bags), this fresh hostel is run by a motherly Kiwi. The two long dorms feel a little institutional but thoughtful touches like central heating, a tasty breakfast (with eggs and homemade wheat toast) and sunroom compensate. To get here, follow Raimírez one block past Plaza O'Higgins.

Lili Patagonico's Hostal HOSTEL $
(☑ 414063; www.lilipatagonicos.com; Arturo Prat 479; dm CH$8000, s/d CH$22,000/30,000, without bathroom CH$16,000/22,000; @🛜) A sprawling house with a climbing wall, a variety of dorms, and colorful doubles with brand-new bathrooms and down comforters.

Hospedaje Nancy GUESTHOUSE $
(☑ 410022; www.nataleslodge.cl; Raimírez 540; d CH$26,000, without bathroom CH$18,000; @) Oft-praised for its adoptable hostess, Nancy, this two-story home offers lived-in rooms with kitchen privileges and internet access. It's a family environment with twin or double beds available.

Hostal Dos Lagunas GUESTHOUSE $
(☑ 414198; hostaldoslagunas@gmail.com; cnr Barros Arana & Bories; dm/d CH$10,000/$25,000) Alejandro and Andrea are attentive hosts, spoiling guests with filling breakfasts, steady water pressure and travel tips.

Hotel IF Patagonia BOUTIQUE HOTEL $$
(☑ 410312; www.hotelifpatagonia.com; Magellanes 73; s/d US$140/150; 🛜) ⏎ With brimming hospitality, IF (for Isabel and Fernando) is minimalist and lovely, with sustainability built into its design. Its bright, modern interior includes wool throws, down duvets and deck views of the fjord. Optional seafood dinners are prepared with the catch of the day.

Kau B&B $$
(☑ 415978; www.kaulodge.com; Costanera Pedro Montt 161; d CH$55,000; 🛜) ⏎ With a mantra of simplicity, this aesthetic remake of a box hotel is cozy and cool. Thick woolen throws, picnic-table breakfast seating and well-worn, recycled wood lend casual intimacy. Rooms boast fjord views, central heating, bulk toiletries, and safe boxes. The attached Coffee Maker espresso bar boasts

killer lattes and staff have tons of adventure information on tap.

Amerindia B&B $$
(☎411945; www.hostelamerindia.com; Barros Arana 135; d CH$43,000, without bathroom CH$33,000, 6-person apt CH$80,000; ⏲closed Jul; @📶) An earthy retreat with a woodstove, beautiful weavings and raw wood beams. Don't expect a hovering host; the atmosphere is chill. Guests wake up to cake, eggs and oatmeal in a cozy cafe open to the public, also selling organic chocolate and teas.

4Elementos GUESTHOUSE $$
(☎995246956; www.4elementos.cl; Esmeralda 811; d CH$30,000, dm/s/d/q without bathroom CH$12,000/20,000/25,000/40,000) A pioneer of Patagonian recycling, the passionate mission of this spare guesthouse is educating people about proper waste disposal. Includes Scandanavian breakfasts. Also rents camping equipment and sells basic provisions for hikers, including Trauko's famous organic whole wheat bread. By reservation only.

Patagonia Aventura HOSTEL $
(☎411028; www.apatagonia.com; Tomás Rogers 179; dm/s/d CH$9000/15,000/20,000; ⏲mid-Sep–mid-May; @📶) On Plaza de Armas, this comfortable hostel has ambient dorms with down duvets and an attached tour agency also renting bikes. No kitchen facilities.

Erratic Rock II B&B $$
(☎414317; www.erraticrock2.com; Benjamin Zamora 732; d CH$38,000, tr without bathroom CH$39,000; @📶) Billed as a 'hostel alternative for couples,' this cozy home offers spacious doubles with throw pillows and tidy bathrooms. Breakfasts in the bright dining room are abundant.

Casa Cecilia GUESTHOUSE $$
(☎613560; www.casaceciliahostal.com; Tomás Rogers 60; d CH$40,000, without bathroom CH$40,000) Well kept and central, Cecilia is a reliable mainstay with good showers, highly praised service and homemade wheat toast for breakfast. The only drawbacks are a small kitchen and cramped rooms.

★**The Singular Hotel** BOUTIQUE HOTEL $$$
(☎414040, bookings in Santiago 02-387-1500; www.thesingular.com; RN9, Km1.5; d/ste incl full board & excursions US$360/660; @📶🏊) Reclaiming the space of a regional landmark, the Singular occupies a former meatpacking and shipping facility on the sound. Heightened industrial design, like lobby chairs fashioned from old radiators, mixes with interesting vintage photos and antiques. The snug glass-walled rooms all have water views and the chic bar-restaurant (alongside the museum, open to the public) serves fresh local game.

Guests can use the spa with pool and explore the surroundings by bike or kayak. It's located in Puerto Bories, 6km from the city center.

Remota LODGE $$$
(☎414040, bookings in Santiago 02-387-1500; www.remota.cl; RN9, Km1.5; s/d US$300/350; @📶🏊) Socialites beware – isolation is the idea in this immense landscape. Though rooms are cozy, you'll probably want to spend all your time at 'the beach' – a glass-walled room with lounge futons that gape at the wild surroundings. Guests can choose an all-inclusive package that includes excursions, like treks in Torres del Paine, or a B&B option. Unlike most hotels, the exclusive Remota draws your awareness to what's outside: silence broadcasts gusty winds, windows imitate old stock fences and a crooked passageway pays tribute to *estancia* sheep corridors.

Hotel Indigo BOUTIQUE HOTEL $$$
(☎413609; www.indigopatagonia.cl; Ladrilleros 105; d/ste incl spa US$275/369; @📶) Hikers will head first to Indigo's rooftop Jacuzzis and glass-walled spa, but plush, restful rooms are stocked with apples and tea candles. Materials like eucalyptus, slate and iron overlap the modern with the natural to interesting effect. The star here is the fjord in front of you, which even captures your gaze in the shower.

✖ Eating

La Mesita Grande PIZZERIA $
(www.mesitagrande.cl; Arturo Prat 196; pizza CH$5500; ⏲lunch & dinner) Happy diners share one long, worn table for outstanding thin-crust pizza, quality pasta and organic salads.

La Casa Magna RESTAURANT $
(Manuel Bulnes 370; menu CH$3000; ⏲10:30am-midnight) Almost always open, this friendly no-frills eatery offers wonderful home cooking at bargain prices.

El Living CAFE $
(www.el-living.com; Arturo Prat 156; mains $2600-5000; ⏲11am-11pm Nov–mid April; 🖊) Indulge in the London lounge feel of this chill cafe.

Puerto Natales

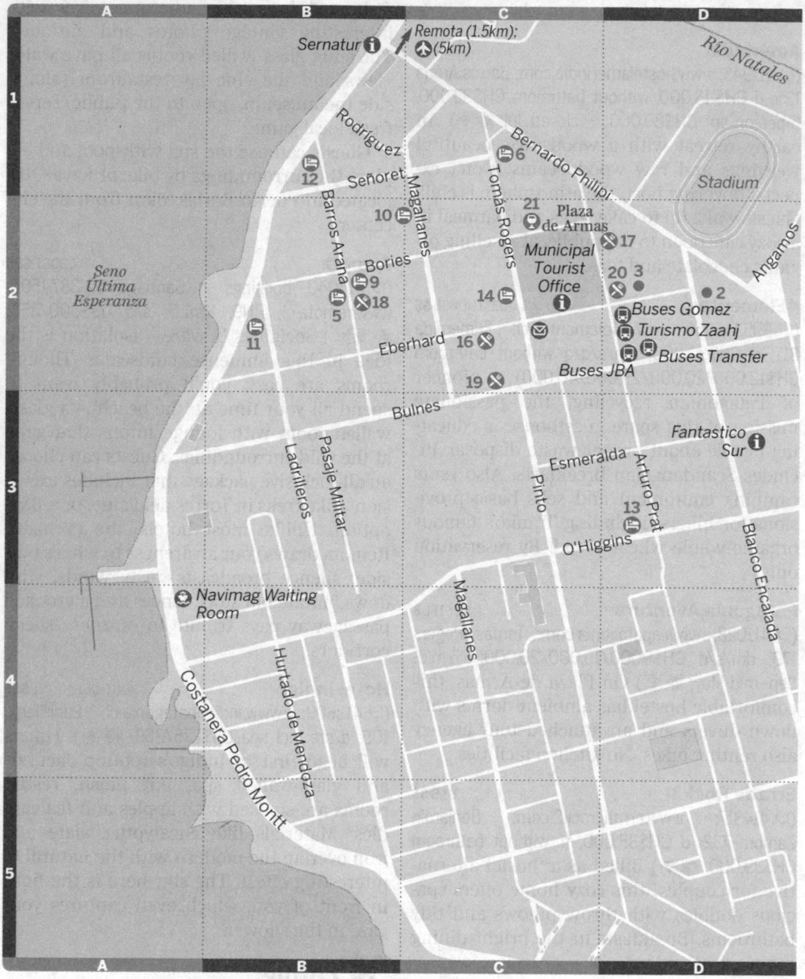

There's proper veg fare, stacks of European glossies and a stream of eclectic tunes.

★ Afrigonia FUSION $$

(Eberhard 343; mains CH$8000; ⏲lunch & dinner) Outstanding and wholly original, you won't find Afro-Chilean cuisine on any NYC menu. This romantic gem was dreamed up by a hardworking Zambian-Chilean couple. Fragrant rice, fresh ceviche and mint roasted lamb are prepared with succulent precision.

Cangrejo Rojo CAFE $$

(Santiago Bueras 782; mains CH$6000; ⏲9am-1:30pm & 3-10:30pm, closed Mon) Unfathomably friendly and cheap, this cute corrugated tin cafe serves pies, ice cream, sandwiches and hot clay pot dishes like seafood casserole or lamb chops. To get here, follow Baquedano four blocks south of Plaza O'Higgins to Santiago Bueras.

La Aldea MEDITERRANEAN $$

(www.aldearestaurant.cl; Barros Arana 132; mains CH$7000; ⏲8pm-12am) Chef Pato changes the offerings daily, but the focus is fresh and Mediterranean. Think grilled clams, lamb tagine and quinoa dishes. Get here early, there's only eight tables.

Puerto Natales

Activities, Courses & Tours

1 Baqueano Zamora........E4
2 Knudsen Tour........D2
3 Turismo 21 de Mayo........D2

Sleeping

4 4Elementos........E3
5 Amerindia........B2
6 Casa Cecilia........C1
7 Erratic Rock II........F4
8 Hospedaje Nancy........E3
9 Hostal Dos Lagunas........B2
10 Hotel IF Patagonia........B2
11 Hotel Indigo........B2
12 Kau........B1
13 Lili Patagonico's Hostal........D3
14 Patagonia Aventura........C2
15 The Singing Lamb........E5

Eating

16 Afrigonia........C2
17 El Living........D2
18 La Aldea........B2
19 La Casa Magna........C2
20 La Mesita Grande........D2

Drinking & Nightlife

21 Baguales........C2

Drinking

Baguales BREWERY
(www.cervezabaguales.cl; Bories 430; 7pm-2am daily, Sat & Sun only in winter;) Climber friends started this microbrewery as a noble quest for quality suds, and they have succeeded. Gringo-style burgers and generous veggie tacos will whet your appetite. Make sure you get here early to grab a booth, which comes complete with its own metered tap and a topo map to plan your route.

Information

INTERNET RESOURCES

The best bilingual portal for the region is www.torresdelpaine.cl.

MEDICAL SERVICES

Hospital (61 411582; Pinto 537)

MONEY

Most banks in town have ATMs.

Gasic (Manuel Bulnes 692) Decent rates on cash and travelers checks.

POST

Post Office (Eberhard 429)

TOURIST INFORMATION

Conaf (411438; Baquedano 847) National parks service administrative office.

Erratic Rock (410355; www.erraticrock.com; Baquedano 719) Aims to keep Torres del Paine sustainable with good visitor advice (staff give a free Torres del Paine introduction talk for trekkers daily at 3pm). Also promotes alternative options and rents gear. Guide service specializes in treks to Cabo Froward, Isla Navarino and lesser-known destinations.

Fantastico Sur (710050; www.fantasticosur.com; Esmeralda 661; 9am-1pm & 3-6pm Mon-Fri) Runs Refugios Torres, El Chileno, Los

Cuernos in Torres del Paine and offers park tours, guiding and trek planning services.

Municipal Tourist Office (☎614808; Plaza de Armas; ⏰8:30am-12:30pm & 2:30-6pm Tue-Sun) In the Museo Histórico, with attentive staff and region-wide lodgings listings.

Sernatur (☎412125; infonatales@sernatur.cl; Costanera Pedro Montt 19; ⏰9am-7pm Mon-Fri, 9:30am-6pm Sat & Sun) There's a second **office** (⏰9am-7pm Mon-Fri, 9:30am-6pm Sat & Sun) with the municipal tourist office on Plaza de Armas.

TRAVEL AGENCIES

Turismo Comapa (☎414300; www.comapa.com; Manuel Bulnes 541; ⏰9am-1pm & 3-7pm Mon-Fri, 10am-2pm Sat) Navimag ferry and airline bookings.

Vertice Patagonia (☎412742; www.vertice-patagonia.com; Ladrilleros 209) The place to book Refugios Grey and Paine Grande in Torres del Paine.

ℹ Getting There & Away

AIR

Puerto Natales' small airport currently does not offer commercial flights but this situation may change.

BOAT

For many travelers, a journey through Chile's spectacular fjords aboard the **Navimag Ferry** (☎411421; www.navimag.com; Pedro Montt 308)becomes a highlight of their trip. Departing every Tuesday from Puerto Natales, this four-day and three-night northbound voyage on the *Amadeo I* has become so popular it should be booked well in advance.

You can also try your luck. To confirm when the ferry is due, contact Turismo Comapa a couple of days before your estimated arrival date. The ferry transports cars and passengers. It leaves Puerto Natales and stops in Puerto Edén (or the advancing Glaciar Pía XI on southbound sailings) en route to Puerto Montt. Schedules vary according to weather conditions and tides. Disembarking passengers must stay on board while cargo is transported; those embarking have to spend the night on board.

Accommodations are in six-bunk cabins with private bathrooms. Fares include all meals (including veggie options if requested while booking, but bring water, snacks and drinks anyway) and interpretive talks. The per-person fare is US$500. Check online for current schedules, and an additional ferry that's planned for 2015.

BUS

Puerto Natales recently added a bus terminal, **Rodoviario** (Bus Terminal; Av España 1455), though companies continue to have offices in the center for ticket purchases.

A second road has been opened to Torres del Paine and, although it's gravel, it is much more direct than the alternative. Several tour operators use it. This alternative entrance goes alongside Lago del Toro to the Administración (park headquarters).

Buses leave for Torres del Paine two to three times daily at around 7am, 8am and 2:30pm. If you are headed to Mountain Lodge Paine Grande in the low season, take the morning bus to meet the catamaran (one way CH$12,000, two hours). Tickets may also be used for transfers within the park, so save your stub. Schedules are in constant flux, so double-check them before heading out.

Bus Sur (☎614220; www.bus-sur.cl; Baquedano 668) Buses to Punta Arenas, Torres del Paine, Puerto Montt, El Calafate, Río Gallegos and Ushuaia.

Buses Fernández/El Pingüino (☎411111; www.busesfernandez.com; cnr Esmeralda & Ramírez) Buses to Torres del Paine and Punta Arenas. Also goes direct to Puerto Natales from the airport.

Buses Gomez (☎415700; www.busesgomez.com; Arturo Prat 234) Buses to Torres del Paine.

Buses JBA (☎410242; Arturo Prat 258) Buses to Torres del Paine.

Buses Pacheco (☎414800; www.busespacheco.com; Ramírez 224) Buses head to Punta Arenas, Río Grande and Ushuaia.

Buses Transfer (☎412616; Manuel Bulnes 518) Buses to Torres del Paine, El Calafate and Ushuaia.

Cootra (☎412785; Baquedano 244) Bus to El Calafate daily at 8:30am.

Turismo Zaahj (☎412260; www.turismozaahj.co.cl; Arturo Prat 236/270) Buses to Torres del Paine and El Calafate.

Buses from Puerto Natales

DESTINATION	COST (CH$)	DURATION (HR)
El Calafate	14,000	5
Punta Arenas	5000	3
Torres del Paine	8000	2
Ushuaia	31,500	13

ℹ Getting Around

Note that car rental is fairly expensive and availability is limited; you'll likely get better rates in Punta Arenas or Argentina. Try **Emsa/Avis** (☎614388; Eberhard 577). Many hostels will rent out bikes.

Parque Nacional Bernardo O'Higgins

Virtually inaccessible, O'Higgins remains an elusive cache of glaciers. Only entered by boat, full-day excursions (CH$72,000 including lunch) to the base of Glaciar Serrano are run by Turismo 21 de Mayo (p474).

You can access Torres del Paine via boat to Glaciar Serrano. Passengers transfer to a Zodiac (a motorized raft), stop for lunch at Estancia Balmaceda and continue up Río Serrano, arriving at the southern border of the park by 5pm. The same tour can be done leaving the park, but may require camping near Río Serrano to catch the Zodiac at 9am. The trip, which includes park entry, costs CH$97,000 with Turismo 21 de Mayo.

Parque Nacional Torres del Paine

☎ 0612

Soaring almost vertically to nearly 3000m above the Patagonian steppe, the Torres del Paine (Towers of Paine) are spectacular granite pillars that dominate the landscape of what may be South America's finest **national park** (www.pntp.cl; high/low season in Chilean pesos only CH$18,000/5000).

Before its creation in 1959, the park was part of a large sheep *estancia*. Part of Unesco's Biosphere Reserve system since 1978, it shelters flocks of ostrich-like rheas (known locally as ñandús), Andean condors, flamingos and many other bird species. Conservation has been most successful with the guanaco *(Lama guanicoe)*, which grazes the open steppe where predatory pumas cannot approach undetected. Herds of guanacos don't even flinch when humans or vehicles approach.

Weather can be wildly changeable in this 1810-sq-km park. Expect to experience four seasons in a day. Sudden rainstorms and knock-down gusts are part of the adventure. Bring high-quality wet-weather gear, a synthetic sleeping bag and, if you're camping, a good tent.

Guided day trips from Puerto Natales are possible, but permit only a glimpse of what the park has to offer. Nature lovers should plan to spend anywhere from three to seven days.

In 2005 a hiker burned down 10% of the park using a portable stove in windy conditions. In 2011 another fire caused by an illegal camper burned down 16,200 hectares. Be conscientious and tread lightly – you are one of more than 120,000 yearly guests.

Activities

Torres del Paine's 2800m granite peaks inspire a mass pilgrimage of hikers from around the world. Most go for the circuit or the 'W' to soak in these classic panoramas, leaving other incredible routes deserted. The Paine Circuit (the 'W' plus the backside of the peaks) requires seven to nine days, while the 'W' (named for the rough approximation to the letter that it traces out on the map) takes four to five. Add another day or two for transportation connections.

Most trekkers start either route from **Laguna Amarga**. You can also hike from Administración, or take the catamaran from Pudeto to Lago Pehoé and start from there; hiking roughly southwest to northeast along the 'W' presents more views of black sedimentary peaks known as Los Cuernos (2200m to 2600m). Trekking alone,

WORTH A TRIP

CUEVA DEL MILODÓN

In the 1890s Hermann Eberhard discovered the remains of an enormous ground sloth just 24km northwest of Puerto Natales. Nearly 4m tall, the herbivorous milodón survived on the succulent leaves of small trees and branches, but became extinct in the late Pleistocene. The 30m-high **cave** (cuevadelmilodon.cl; admission CH$4000) pays homage to its former inhabitant with a life-size plastic replica of the animal. It's not exactly tasteful, but still worth a stop, whether to appreciate the grand setting and ruminate over its wild past or to take an easy walk up to a lookout point.

Camping (no fires) and picnicking are possible. Torres del Paine buses pass the entrance, 8km from the cave proper. There are infrequent tours from Puerto Natales; alternatively, you can hitchhike or share a taxi (CH$20,000). Outside of high season, bus services are infrequent.

Parque Nacional Torres del Paine

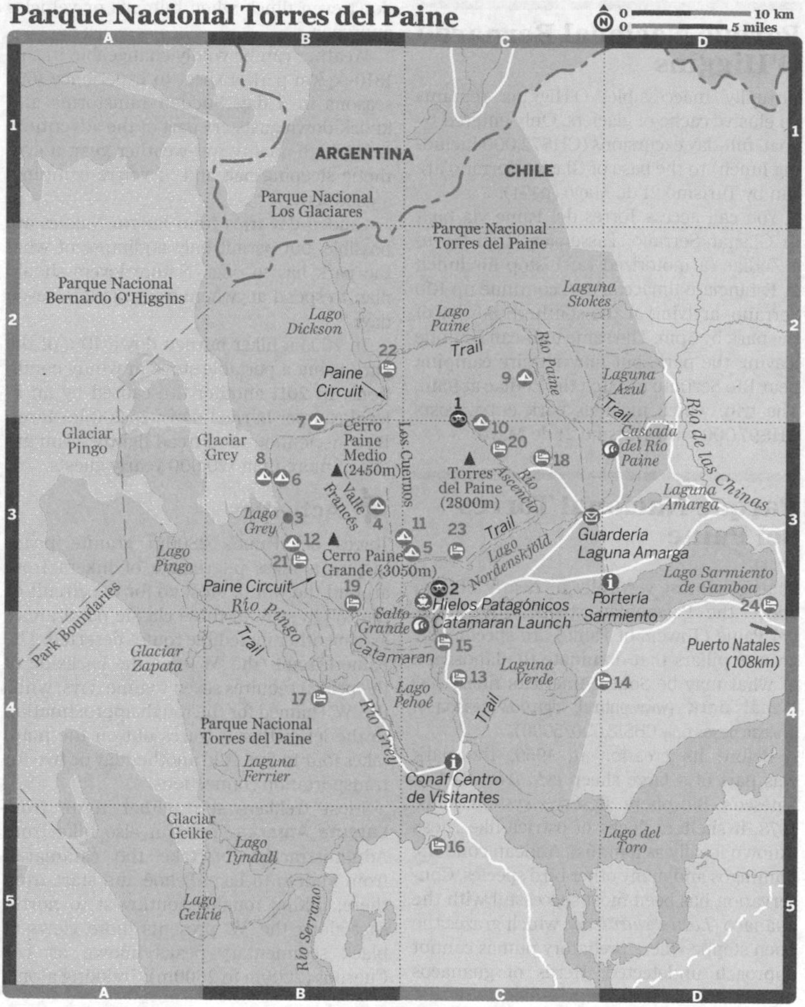

especially on the backside of the circuit, is unadvisable. Tour operators in Puerto Natales offer guided treks, which include all meals and accommodations at *refugios* or hotels. Per person rates decrease significantly in groups.

Hiking the 'W'

Most people trek the 'W' from right to left (east to west), starting at Laguna Amarga – accessible by a twice-daily 2½-hour bus ride from Puerto Natales. But hiking west to east – especially between Lago Pehoé and Valle Francés – provides superior views of Los Cuernos. To start the W from the west, catch the catamaran across Lago Pehoe, then head north along Lago Grey or Campamento Italiano, from which point excellent (and pack-free) day hikes are possible. The segments listed offer some of the W's most memorable walking opportunities.

The area between Lago Pehoé and Refugo Grey was primarily affected by the 2011 fire, with denuded landscapes where forests formerly stood. Volunteers have reforested the area but restoration is still long in coming.

Parque Nacional Torres del Paine

Sights

1	Mirador Las Torres	C2
2	Mirador Nordenskjöld	C3

Activities, Courses & Tours

3	Antares/Big Foot Patagonia	B3

Sleeping

4	Campamento Británico	B3
5	Campamento Italiano	C3
	Campamento Lago Dickson	(see 22)
6	Campamento Los Guardas	B3
7	Campamento Los Perros	B3
8	Campamento Paso	B3
9	Campamento Serón	C2
10	Campamento Torres	C3
	Camping Chileno	(see 20)
11	Camping Francés	C3
12	Camping Grey	B3
	Camping Las Torres	(see 18)
13	Explora	C4
14	Hostería Mirador del Payne	D4
15	Hostería Pehoé	C4
16	Hotel Cabañas del Paine	C5
17	Hotel Lago Grey	B4
18	Hotel Las Torres	C3
19	Mountain Lodge Paine Grande	B3
20	Refugio Chileno	C3
21	Refugio Grey	B3
22	Refugio Lago Dickson	B2
	Refugio Las Torres	(see 18)
23	Refugio Los Cuernos	C3
24	Tierra Patagonia	D3

Refugio Las Torres to Mirador Las Torres HIKING

(4hr one way) A moderate hike up Río Ascencio to a treeless tarn beneath the eastern face of the Torres del Paine for the closest view of the towers. The last hour is a knee-popping scramble up boulders (covered with knee- and waist-high snow in winter). There are camping and *refugios* at Las Torres and Chileno, with basic camping at Campamento Torres. In summer stay at Campamento Torres and head up at sunrise to beat the crowds.

Refugio Las Torres to Los Cuernos HIKING

(7hr one way) Hikers should keep to the lower trail as many get lost on the upper trail (unmarked on maps). There's camping and a *refugio*. Summer winds can be fierce.

Another option is to hike one hour further to Camping Francés, run by Fantastico Sur.

Los Cuernos/Lago Pehoé to Valle Francés HIKING

(5hr one way) In clear weather, the most beautiful stretch between 3050m Cerro Paine Grande to the west and the lower, still spectacular, Torres del Paine and Los Cuernos to the east, with glaciers hugging the trail. Camp at Campamento Italiano and Campamento Británico, in the heart of the valley, or at the valley entrance at Camping Francés.

Mountain Lodge Paine Grande to Refugio Grey HIKING

(4½hr) A relatively easy trail with a few challenging downhill scampers. Four hours one way from Lago Pehoé. The glacier lookout is another half-hour's hike away. With camping and *refugios* at both ends.

Mountain Lodge Paine Grande to Administración HIKING

(5hr) Up and around the side of Lago Pehoé, then through grassland along Río Grey. Not really part of the 'W,' but after the hike, cut out to the Administración to avoid backtracking to Laguna Amarga. Mountain Lodge Paine Grande can radio in and make sure that you can get a bus from Administración back to Puerto Natales. You can also enter the 'W' this way to hike it east to west.

Hiking the Paine Circuit

This loop takes in the 'W' hiking trail, plus the backside between Refugio Grey and Refugio Las Torres. The landscape is desolate yet beautiful. Paso John Garner (the extreme part of the trek) sometimes has knee-deep mud and snow. There's a basic *refugio* at Los Perros or there's rustic camping.

Many hikers start the Paine Circuit by entering the park (by bus) at Laguna Amarga, then hike for a few hours to Refugio and Camping Chileno. From there, the circuit continues counterclockwise, ending in Valle Francés and Los Cuernos.

Refugio Grey to Campamento Paso HIKING

(4hr heading north, 2hr going south) Hikers might want to go left to right (west to east), which means ascending Paso John Garner rather than slipping downhill.

Campamento Paso to Campamento Los Perros HIKING

(4hr) This route has plenty of mud and sometimes snow. Don't be confused by what

The 'W'

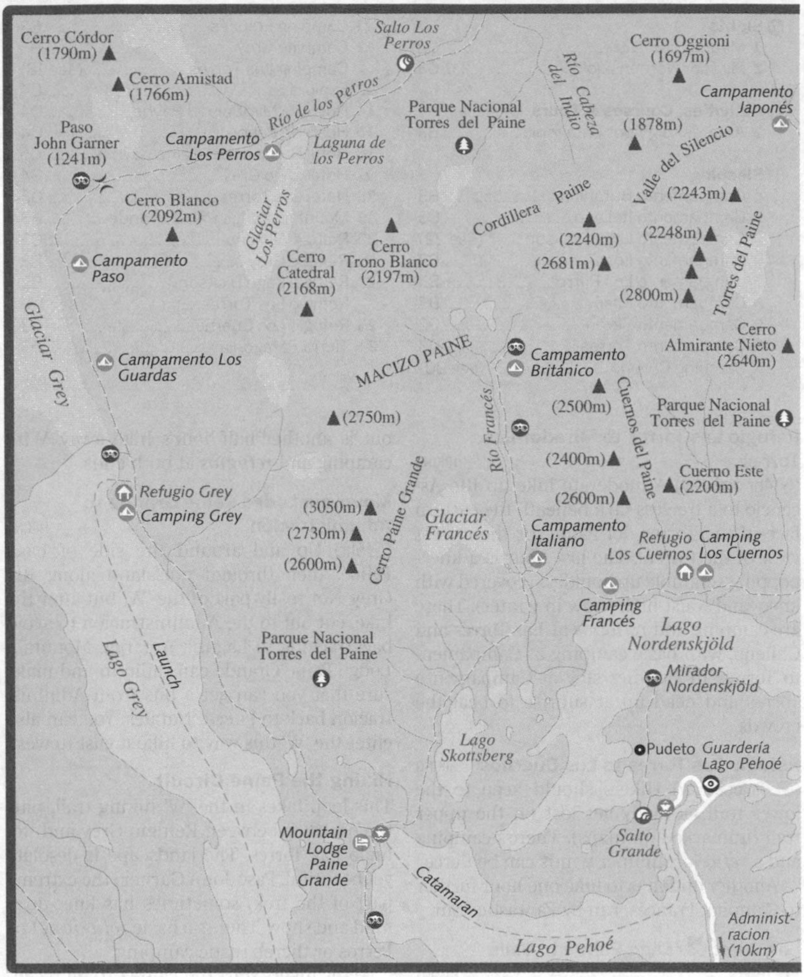

appears to be a campsite right after crossing Paso John Garner; keep going until you see a shack.

Campamento Los Perros to Campamento Lago Dickson HIKING

(Around 4½hr) A relatively easy but windy stretch.

Campamento Lago Dickson to Campamento Serón HIKING

(6hr) As the trail wraps around Lago Paine, winds can get fierce and the trails vague; stay along the trail furthest away from the lake. On the way, Campamento Coiron has been closed since the 2005 fire.

Campamento Serón to Laguna Amarga HIKING

(4-5hr) You can end the hike with a chill-out night and a decent meal at Refugio Las Torres.

Day Hikes

Walk from Guardería Lago Pehoé, on the main park highway, to **Salto Grande**, a powerful waterfall between Lago Nordenskjöld and Lago Pehoé. Another easy hour's walk leads to **Mirador Nordenskjöld**, an

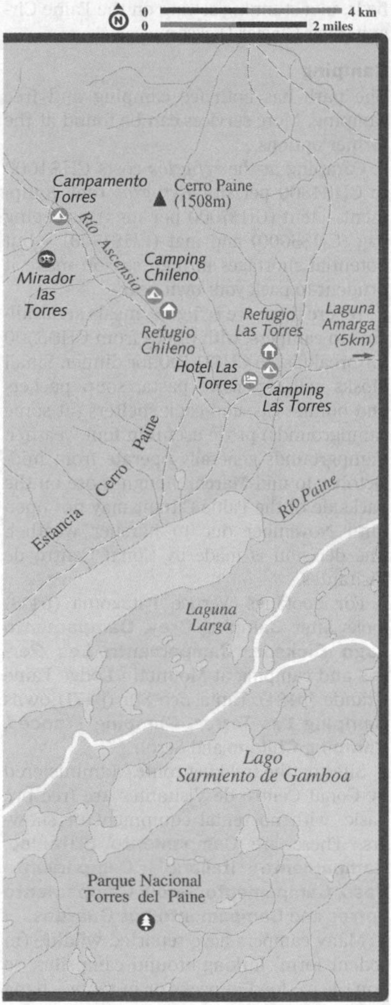

overlook with superb views. Or try the more challenging but gorgeous four-hour trek to **Lago Paine**; its northern shore is accessible only from Laguna Azul, in the park's east.

Kayaking

A great way to get up close to glaciers, Big Foot Patagonia (p474) leads three-hour tours of the iceberg-strewn Lago Grey from the former Refugio Grey (CH$55,000), several times daily in summer. It also offers multiday trips to Río Serrano.

Horseback Riding

Parque Nacional Torres del Paine is certainly a beautiful place to ride. Due to property divisions within the park, horses cannot cross between the western sections (Lagos Grey and Pehoé, Río Serrano) and the eastern part managed by Hotel Las Torres (Refugio Los Cuernos is the approximate cut-off). Baqueano Zamora (p474) runs excursions to Lagos Pingo, Paine and Azul, and Laguna Amarga (half-day CH$25,000).

Ice Trekking

A fun walk through a sculpted landscape of ice, and you don't need experience to go. Big Foot Patagonia (p474) is the sole company with a park concession for ice hikes (CH$90,000) on Glacier Grey, with trips at 8:30am and 2:30pm. Using the Conaf Centro de Visitantes house (former Refugio Grey) as a base, the excursion includes a six-hour round-trip hike and three hours on the ice, available from October to May.

Sleeping

Make reservations! Arriving without them, especially in high season, limits you to camping. Travel agencies offer reservations, but it's best to deal directly with the various management companies.

Refugios

If you are hiking the 'W' or circuit, you will be staying in *refugios* (mountain huts) or campsites along the way. It is essential to reserve your spot and specify vegetarian meals in advance if required.

Refugio rooms have four to eight bunk beds each, kitchen privileges (for lodgers and during specific hours only), hot showers and meals. Sleeping bag rentals cost CH$5000. Should a *refugio* be overbooked, staff provide all necessary camping equipment. Most *refugios* close by the end of April.

Refugios may require photo ID (ie a passport) upon check-in. Photocopy your tourist card and passport for all lodgings in advance to expedite check-in. Staff can radio ahead to confirm your next reservation.

'Most listings match the 'W' hiking description direction (see p480). Rates are basic – if you want bed linens (vs your own sleeping bag), it's extra.

Refugio Las Torres LODGE $
(dm from CH$24,500, incl full board CH$50,500; Sep-Apr; @) An ample, attractive base camp with 60 beds and the added feature

of a comfortable lounge, restaurant and bar. In high season, a nearby older building is put into use to handle the overflow, at discounted rates.

Refugio Chileno CABIN $
(dm CH$24,500, incl full board CH$50,500; ⊙Oct-Mar) Nearest to the fabled Torres del Paine, Chileno is one of the smallest *refugios*, with 32 beds and a small provisions kiosk. It's run on wind energy and toilets use composting biofilters.

Refugio Los Cuernos CABIN $
(dm CH$24,500, incl full board CH$50,500; ⊙Sep-Apr) Filling fast, this mid-W location tends to bottleneck with hikers going in either direction. But with eight beds per room, this small lodge is more than cozy. New separate showers and bathrooms for campers relieve some of the stress. For a deluxe option, eight two-person cabins with shared bathroom offer privacy, with skylights and access to a piping-hot wooden hot tub.

Mountain Lodge Paine Grande CABIN $
(☎in Puerto Natales 0612-412742; www.verticepatagonia.cl; dm CH$21,500, incl full board CH$41,000; @) Though gangly, this park installation on the W hiking circuit is nicer than most dorms, with sublime Los Cuernos views in all rooms. Its year-round presence is a godsend to cold, wet winter hikers, though meals are not available in winter (May to September). There's on-site camping, a kiosk with basic kitchen provisions and dome camping.

Between Lago Grey and Valle Francés, it's a day hike from either location and also accessible by ferry across Lago Pehoé.

Refugio Grey HUT $
(☎in Puerto Natales 0612-412742; www.verticepatagonia.cl; dm CH$14,000, incl full board CH$32,500; ⊙year-round) Relocated inland from the lake, this deluxe new trekkers' lodge features a decked-out living area with leather sofas and bar, a restaurant-grade kitchen and snug bunkrooms that house 60 people, with plenty of room for backpacks. There's also a general store, and covered cooking space for campers. Also runs in winter without meal service (May to September).

Refugio Lago Dickson CABIN $
(dm CH$14,000, incl full board CH$30,000; ⊙Nov-Mar) One of the oldest and smallest *refugios* in Parque Nacional Torres del Paine, with 30 beds, in a stunning setting on the Paine Circuit, near Glaciar Dickson.

Camping

The park has both fee camping and free camping. More services can be found at the former options.

Camping at the *refugios* costs CH$4000 to CH$4800 per site. *Refugios* rent equipment – tent (CH$7000 per night), sleeping bag (CH$5000) and mat (CH$1500) – but potential shortages in high season make it prudent to pack your own gear.

Where there are *refugios*, meals are available to campers, with prices from CH$6500 for breakfast to CH$11,500 for dinner. Small kiosks sell expensive pasta, soup packets and butane gas, and cook shelters (at some campgrounds) prove useful in foul weather. Campgrounds generally operate from mid-October to mid-March, though those on the backside of the Paine Circuit may not open until November due to harsher weather. The decision is made by Conaf Centro de Visitantes.

For bookings, Vertice Patagonia (p478) looks after **Camping Grey**, **Campamento Lago Dickson**, **Campamento Los Perros** and camping at Mountain Lodge Paine Grande (p484). Fantastico Sur (p477) owns **Camping Las Torres**, **Camping Francés**, **Camping Chileno** and Seron.

Sites on the trekking routes administered by Conaf Centro de Visitantes are free but basic, with no rental equipment or showers. These are **Campamento Británico**, **Campamento Italiano**, **Campamento Paso**, **Campamento Serón**, **Campamento Torres** and **Campamento Los Guardas**.

Many campers have reported wildlife (in rodent form) lurking around campsites, so don't leave food in packs or in tents – hang it from a tree instead.

Hotels

When choosing lodgings, pay particular attention to location. Lodgings that adjoin the 'W' circuit offer more independence and flexibility for hikers. Most offer multiday packages.

Explora HOTEL $$$
(☎in Santiago 02-206-6060; www.explora.com; d per person 4 nights incl full board & transfers US$2820; @ 🏊) Strutting with style, Torres del Paine's most sophisticated (and expensive) digs sit perched above the Salto Chico waterfall at the outlet of Lago Pehoé. Views of the entire Paine Massif pour forth from

every centimeter of the hotel. Amenities include a spa with heated lap pool, sauna, massage rooms and open-air Jacuzzi.

Rates include airport transfers, full gourmet meals and a wide variety of excursions led by young, affable, bilingual guides.

★ **Tierra Patagonia** HOTEL **$$$**
(☎ in Santiago 02-263-0606; www.tierrapatagonia.com; d per person 2 nights incl full board & transfers from US$2050; @ ⊛ ≋) Sculpted into the sprawling steppe, this sleek newcomer is an inviting option. Think luxury lodge, with a lively living and circular bar focused on a grand fire pit and a beautiful oversized artist's rendition of a park map. Large, understated rooms enjoy panoramas of the Paine Massif. All-inclusive rates include airport transfer, daily excursions, use of spa, meals and drinks.

Located on Cerro Guido *estancia,* the hotel's ranch-focused activities are a strong asset. It's on Lago Sarmiento, just outside Parque Nacional Torres del Paine about 20km from Laguna Amarga.

Hotel Las Torres HOTEL **$$$**
(☎ 617450; www.lastorres.com; booking address Magallanes 960, Punta Arenas; s/d from US$275/315; ⊙ closed Jun; ⊛) A hospitable and well-run hotel with international standards, spa with Jacuzzi and good guided excursions. Most noteworthy, the hotel donates a portion of fees to nonprofit park-based environmental group AMA. The buffet serves organic vegetables from the greenhouse and organic meat raised on nearby ranches.

Hotel Lago Grey HOTEL **$$$**
(☎ 712132; www.lagogrey.cl; booking address Lautaro Navarro 1061, Punta Arenas; s/d/tr US$261/308/358; @) Open year-round, this tasteful hotel has snug white cottages linked by raised boardwalks. The new deluxe rooms are lovely – with lake views and sleek modern style. The cafe (open to the public) overlooks the grandeur. Boat tours visit the glacier, stopping at the Conaf Centro de Visitantes office on the other side of Lago Grey to pick up and drop off passengers.

Hostería Mirador del Payne INN **$$$**
(☎ 226930; www.miradordelpayne.com; s/d/tr US$200/245/265) On the Estancia El Lazo in the seldom-seen Laguna Verde sector, this comfortable inn is known for its serenity, proximity to spectacular viewpoints and top-rate service – but not for easy Parque Nacional Torres del Paine access. Activities include bird-watching, horseback riding and sport fishing. Call to arrange a ride from the road junction.

Hotel Cabañas del Paine CABIN **$$$**
(☎ 730177; www.cabanasdelpaine.cl; s/d US$264/275) On the banks of the Río Serrano, these cabin-style rooms stand apart as tasteful and well integrated into the landscape with great views.

Hostería Pehoé HOTEL **$$$**
(☎ in Santiago 02-296-1238; www.pehoe.cl; d/superior US$215/270) On the far side of Lago Pehoé, linked to the mainland by a long footbridge. Pehoé enjoys five-star panoramas of Los Cuernos and Paine Grande, but it's poor value with dated rooms reminiscent of a roadside motel. The restaurant and bar are open to the public.

ℹ Information

Parque Nacional Torres del Paine is 112km north of Puerto Natales via a decent but sometimes bumpy gravel road. At Cerro Castillo there is a seasonal border crossing into Argentina at Cancha Carrera. From here the road continues 40km north and west to Portería Sarmiento, the main entrance where fees are collected. It's another 37km to the Administración and the **Conaf Centro de Visitantes** (⊙ 9am-8pm Dec-Feb), with good information on park ecology and trail status. A new road from Puerto Natales to the Administración provides a shorter, more direct southern approach to the park.

The park is open year-round, subject to your ability to get there. Transportation connections are less frequent in low season and winter weather adds extra challenges to hiking. The shoulder seasons of November and March are some of the best times for trekking. In both months the park is less crowded, with typically windy conditions usually abating in March. Internet resources include www.torresdelpaine.com and www.erraticrock.com, with a good backpacker equipment list. Erratic Rock (p477) also holds an excellent information session daily at 3pm; go for solid advice on everything from trail conditions to camping. Travelers can also rent equipment on-site.

The best trekking maps, by JLM and Luis Bertea Rojas, are widely available in Puerto Natales. For detailed trekking suggestions and maps, consult Lonely Planet's *Trekking in the Patagonian Andes*.

ℹ Getting There & Away

Going to El Calafate from Parque Nacional Torres del Paine on the same day requires joining a tour or careful advance planning, since there is no direct service. Your best bet is to return to Puerto Natales.

Getting Around

Shuttles (CH$2500) drop off and pick up passengers at Laguna Amarga, at the Hielos Patagónicos catamaran launch at Pudeto and at Administración.

The catamaran leaves Pudeto for Mountain Lodge Paine Grande (one way/round-trip per person CH$12,000/19,000) at 9:30am, noon and 6pm December to mid-March, at noon and 6pm in late March and November, and at noon only in September, October and April. Another launch travels Lago Grey between Hotel Lago Grey and the beach near Refugio Grey (CH$40,000, 1½ to two hours) a couple of times daily; contact the hotel for the current schedule.

THE FALKLAND ISLANDS/ISLAS MALVINAS

☎500 / POP HUMANS 2930, SHEEP 600,000

Besides their status as an unusually polemical piece of property, what do the Falklands offer the intrepid traveler? Bays, inlets, estuaries and beaches create a tortuous, attractive coastline flanked by abundant wildlife. Located 500km to the east of Argentina in the South Atlantic Ocean, these sea islands attract striated and crested caracaras, cormorants, oystercatchers, snowy sheathbills and a plethora of penguins share top billing with elephant seals, sea lions, fur seals, five dolphin species and killer whales.

Stanley (population 2000), the islands' capital on East Falkland, is an assemblage of brightly painted metal-clad houses and a good place to throw down a few pints and listen to island lore. 'Camp' – as the rest of the islands are known – hosts settlements that began as company towns (hamlets where shipping could collect wool) and now provide rustic backcountry lodging and a chance to experience pristine nature and wildlife.

When to Go

The best time to visit is from October to March, when migratory birds (including penguins) and marine mammals return to the beaches and headlands. Cruise ships to South Georgia and Antarctica run from November through March. The annual sports meetings, with horse racing, bull riding and sheepdog trials, take place in Stanley between Christmas and New Year, and on East and West Falkland at the end of the shearing season in late February. Summer never gets truly hot (the maximum high is 24°C; 75°F), but high winds bring chills.

History

The sheep boom in Tierra del Fuego and Patagonia owes its origins to the cluster of islands known as Las Islas Malvinas to the Argentines or the Falkland Islands to the British. They had been explored, but never fully captured the interest of either country until Europe's mid-19th-century wool boom. After the Falkland Islands Company (FIC) became the islands' largest landholder, a population of stranded gauchos and mariners grew rapidly with the arrival of English and Scottish immigrants.

Argentina's claim goes back to 1833, but it wasn't until 1982 that Argentine President Leopoldo Galtieri, then drowning in economic chaos and allegations of corruption, gambled that reclaiming the islands would unite his country. British Prime Minister Margaret Thatcher (also suffering in the polls) didn't hesitate in striking back, thoroughly humiliating Argentina in the Falklands War (Guerra de las Malvinas).

In 2010 Argentine President Cristina Fernández de Kirchner made statements that renewed Argentina's claim on the Falklands, diffusing the progress that had been made in the previous decade for increased cooperation between British, Falkland Islands and Argentine governments. To settle the lingering controversy, the Falklands held a referendum on its political status in March, 2013, when 99% of voters supported continuing British rule. Relations with Argentina remain cool, with most South American trade going via Chile.

Visas & Documents

Visitors from Britain and Commonwealth countries, the EU, North America, Mercosur countries and Chile don't need visas. If coming from another country, check with the British consulate in that country. All nationalities must carry a valid passport, an onward ticket and proof of sufficient funds (credit cards are fine) and pre-arranged accommodations. In practice, those who arrive on the islands without prebooked accommodations are held in the arrivals area of the airport while rooms are found for them.

Falkland Islands/Islas Malvinas

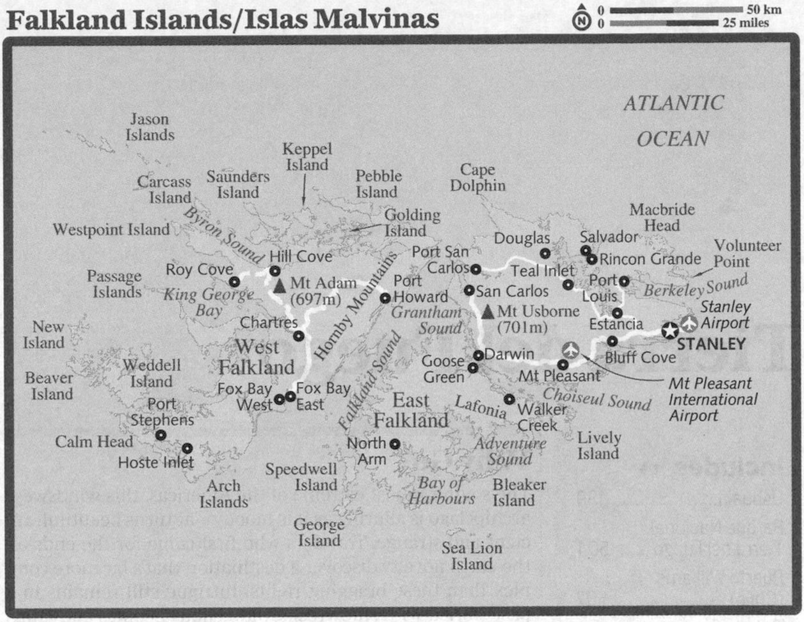

Money

There's no ATM on the Falklands and only one bank in Stanley, though credit and debit cards are widely accepted. Pounds sterling and US dollars in cash or travelers checks are readily accepted, but the exchange rate for US currency is poor. Don't bother changing to Falkland pounds (FK£). In peak season, expect to spend US$150 to US$350 per day, not including airfare; less if camping or staying in self-catering cottages.

ℹ Information

Visit Stanley's **Jetty Visitors Centre** (☎22215; info@falklandislands.com; ⏲10am-5pm Mon-Fri, 9am-5pm Sat, 10am-4pm Sun), at the public jetty on Ross Rd. The *Visitor Accommodation Guide* lists lodgings and campgrounds. For trip planning, see the essential website **Falkland Islands Tourism** (www.falklandislands.com). In the UK, contact **Falkland House** (☎020-7222-2542; www.falklands.gov.fk/self-governance/london-office; 14 Broadway, London SW1H 0BH).

ℹ Getting There & Away

From South America, **LanChile** (www.lan.com) flies to Mt Pleasant International Airport (MPA; near Stanley) every Saturday from Santiago, Chile, via Puerto Montt, Punta Arenas and – one Saturday each month – Río Gallegos, Argentina. Round-trip fares are CH$435,000 from Punta Arenas with advance booking.

From **RAF Brize Norton** (www.raf.mod.uk/rafbrizenorton), in Oxfordshire, England, there are regular Royal Air Force flights to Mt Pleasant (18 hours, including a two-hour refueling stop on tiny Ascension Island in the South Atlantic). Round-trip fares are UK£2222. Travelers continuing on to Chile can purchase one-way tickets for half the fare. Bookings from the UK can be made through the **Falkland Islands Government Office** (☎020-7222-2542; www.falklands.gov.fk; 14 Broadway, Falkland House, Westminster, London SW1H 0BH). Payment is by cash, or personal or bank check; credit cards are not accepted.

ℹ Getting Around

From Stanley, **Figas** (☎27219; reservations@figas.gov.fk) serves outlying destinations in eight-seater aircraft.

Several Stanley operators run day trips to East Falkland settlements, including **Discovery Falklands** (☎21145, 21027; discovery@horizon.co.fk). **Adventure Falklands** (☎21383; pwatts@horizon.co.fk) specializes in wildlife (featuring king, gentoo and Magellanic penguins) and historical tours.

Trekking and camping are feasible; however, there are no designated trails and getting lost is not unheard of. Always seek permission before entering private land.

Tierra del Fuego

Includes ➡

Best Places to Eat

➡ Kalma Resto (p502)
➡ Kaupé (p502)
➡ María Lola Restó (p498)
➡ Chiko (p498)
➡ Chez Manu (p502)

Best Places to Stay

➡ Galeazzi-Basily B&B (p496)
➡ Antarctica Hostel (p495)
➡ Estancia Las Hijas (p510)
➡ Hostería Yendegaia (p511)
➡ Los Cauquenes Resort & Spa (p497)

Why Go?

The southernmost extreme of the Americas, this windswept archipelago is alluring as it is moody – at turns beautiful, ancient and strange. Travelers who first came for the ends-of-the-earth novelty discover a destination that's far more complex than these bragging rights. Intrigue still remains in a past storied with shipwrecks, indigenous peoples and failed missions. In Tierra del Fuego, nature is writ bold and reckless, from the scoured plains, rusted peat bogs and mossy lenga forests to the snowy ranges above the Beagle Channel.

While distant and isolated, Tierra del Fuego is by no means cut off from the mainland, though the Argentine half is far more developed than its Chilean counterpart. Ports buzz with commerce and oil refineries prosper while adventure seekers descend in droves to fly-fish, hike and start Antarctic cruises. Shared with Chile, this archipelago features one large island, Isla Grande, Chile's Isla Navarino and many smaller uninhabited ones.

When to Go

Ushuaia

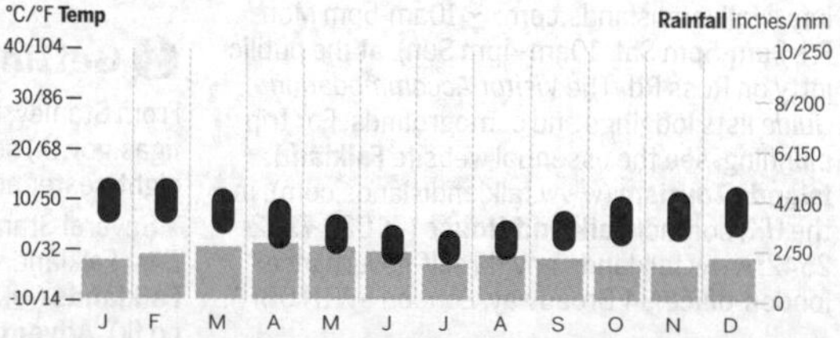

Nov–Mar Warmest months, best for hiking, penguin watching and *estancia* visits.

Mid-Nov–mid-Apr Fly-fishing season.

Jul–Sep Optimal for skiing, snowboarding or dog sledding.

Getting There & Around

The most common overland route from Patagonia is via the ferry crossing at Punta Delgada. Unlike the rest of Argentina, Tierra del Fuego has no designated provincial highways, but has secondary roads known as *rutas complementarias,* modified by a lowercase letter. References to such roads made here are given as 'RC-a,' for example.

If renting a car in mainland Argentina, be aware that you must cross in and out of Chile a couple of times to reach Tierra del Fuego, and that this requires special documents and additional international insurance coverage. Most car-rental agencies can arrange this paperwork if given advance notice.

At the time of writing, Chile was building an alternate road to the southern end of the island. It currently links with Lago Fagnano, but a 4WD vehicle is required.

Visitors can fly into Río Grande or Ushuaia. Buses take the ferry from Chile's Punta Delgada; all pass through Río Grande before arriving in Ushuaia.

USHUAIA

02901 / POP 57,000

A busy port and adventure hub, the city of Ushuaia is a sliver of steep streets and jumbled buildings below the snowcapped Martial Range. Here the Andes meet the southern ocean in a sharp skid, making way for the city before reaching a sea of lapping currents.

It's a location matched by few, and chest-beating Ushuaia takes full advantage of its end-of-the-world status, with an increasing number of Antarctica-bound vessels calling in to port. Its endless mercantile hustle knows no irony: the souvenir shop named for Jimmy Button (an indigenous man kidnapped for show in England), the ski center named for a destructive invasive species...you get the idea. That said, with a pint of the world's southernmost microbrew in hand, you can happily plot the dazzling outdoor options: hiking, sailing, skiing, kayaking and even scuba diving are all just minutes from town.

Tierra del Fuego's comparatively high wages draw Argentines from all over to resettle here, and some locals lament the loss of small-town culture. Meanwhile, expansion means that haphazard development is advancing in the few directions the mad geography allows.

History

In 1870 the British-based South American Missionary Society set its sights on the Yahgan (or Yamaná), a nomadic tribe whose members faced brutal weather conditions almost entirely naked – they didn't have any permanent shelter to keep clothing dry, and believed that the natural oil of their skin was better protection than soaking wet animal fur. Charles Darwin branded them 'the lowest form of humanity on earth.' Missionary Thomas Bridges didn't agree. After years among them, he created a Yahgan-English dictionary in the late 19th century, deeming their language complex and subtle.

The mission made Ushuaia its first permanent Fuegian outpost, but the Yahgan, who had survived 6000 years without contact, were vulnerable to foreign-brought illnesses and faced increasing infringement by sealers, settlers and gold prospectors. Four Yámana, including a teenager dubbed 'Jimmy Button,' were kidnapped by the naval captain Robert Fitz Roy and shipped back to England to be educated and paraded as examples of gentrified savages. One died of disease. After months of public criticism, Fitz Roy agreed to return the rest to their homeland.

The tribe's legacy is now reduced to shell mounds, Thomas Bridges' famous dictionary and Jimmy Button souvenirs. At the time of writing, one elderly Yamaná woman was still alive on Isla Navarino, the only native speaker of the language.

Between 1884 and 1947 the city became a penal colony, incarcerating many notorious criminals and political prisoners, both here and on remote Isla de los Estados. Since 1950 the town has been an important naval base.

Sights

Paralleling the Beagle Channel, Av Maipú becomes Malvinas Argentinas west of the cemetery, then turns into RN3, continuing 12km to Parque Nacional Tierra del Fuego. To the east, public access ends at Yaganes, which heads north to meet RN3 going north toward Lago Fagnano. Most visitor services are on or near Av San Martín, a block from the waterfront.

The tourist office distributes a free city-tour map with information on the historic houses around town. The 1894 **Legislatura Provincial** (Provincial Legislature; Av Maipú 465) was the governor's official residence. The

Tierra del Fuego Highlights

1. Explore the ancient Fuegian forests of **Parque Nacional Tierra del Fuego** (p504)
2. Speed through frozen valleys on a **dog-sledding tour** (p493) near Ushuaia
3. Land the big one while fly-fishing at an **estancia** (p510) near Río Grande
4. Relive grim times in Ushuaia's infamous prison-turned-museum, **Museo Marítimo & Museo del Presidio** (p492)
5. Ski and snowboard with sublime views at the world's southernmost resort, **Cerro Castor** (p493)
6. Browse back in time in the quiet seaside village of **Porvenir** (p510)
7. Trek around the jagged peaks and sculpted landscapes on the five-day circuit of **Dientes de Navarino** (p507) near Puerto Williams

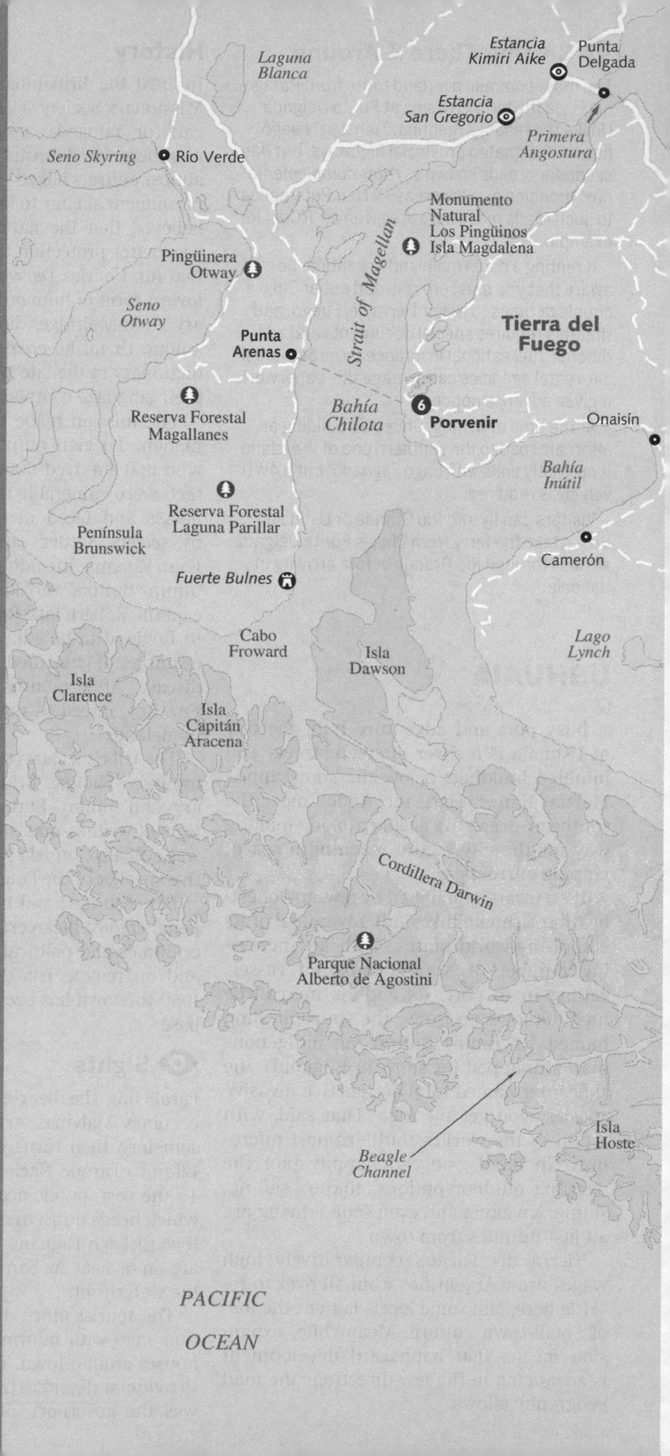

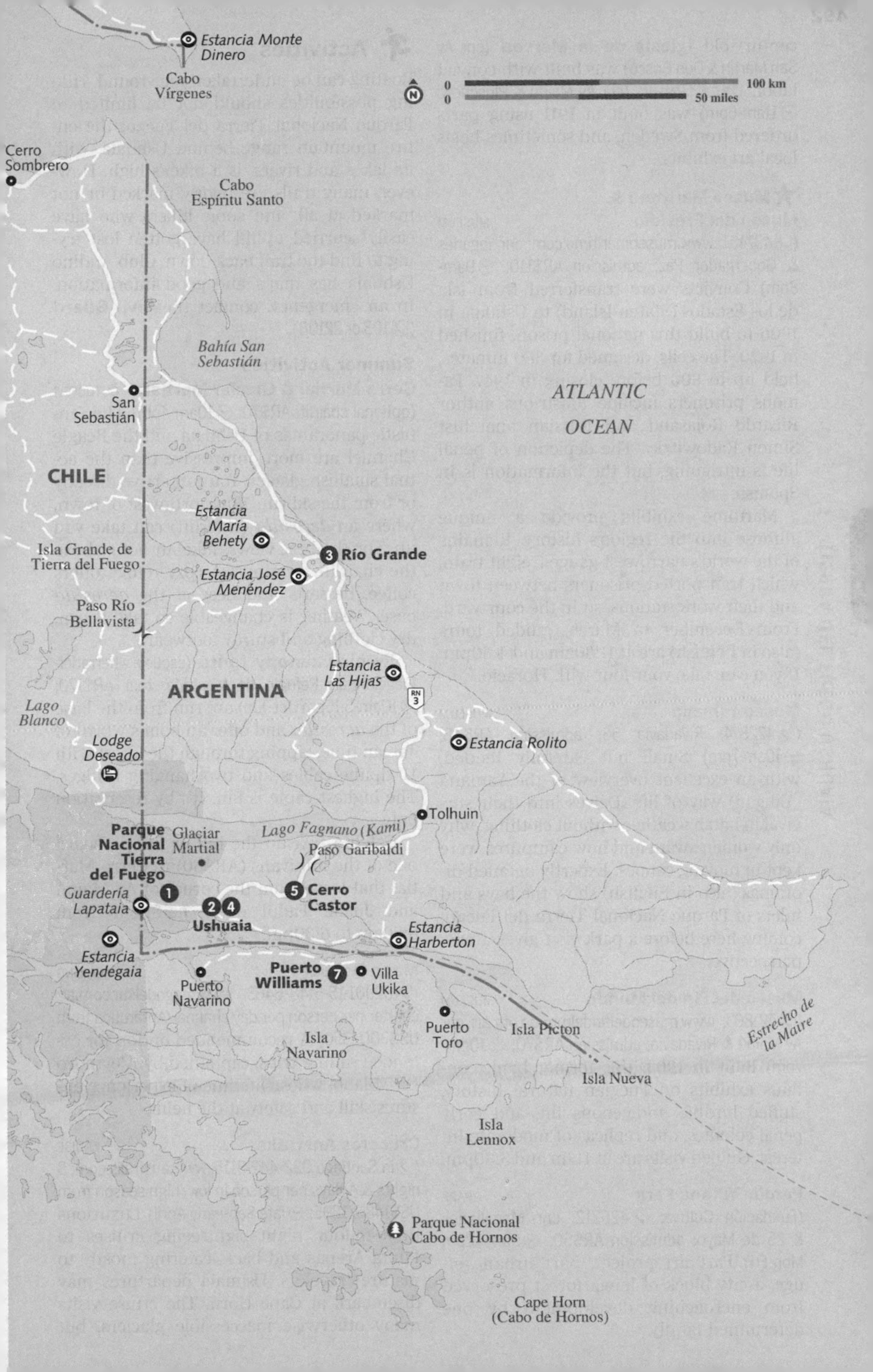

Estancia Monte Dinero
Cabo Vírgenes
0
100 km
0
50 miles
Cerro Sombrero
Cabo Espíritu Santo
Bahía San Sebastián
San Sebastián
ATLANTIC OCEAN
CHILE
Estancia María Behety
Isla Grande de Tierra del Fuego
3 Río Grande
Estancia José Menéndez
Paso Río Bellavista
Estancia Las Hijas
ARGENTINA
RN 3
Lago Blanco
Estancia Rolito
Lodge Deseado
Tolhuin
Parque Nacional Tierra del Fuego
Glaciar Martial
Lago Fagnano (Kami)
Paso Garibaldi
Guardería Lapataia
1
2
4
5 Cerro Castor
Ushuaia
Estancia Harberton
Estancia Yendegaia
Puerto Navarino
7 Puerto Williams
Villa Ukika
Puerto Toro
Isla Picton
Estrecho de la Maire
Isla Navarino
Isla Nueva
Isla Lennox
Parque Nacional Cabo de Hornos
Cape Horn (Cabo de Hornos)

century-old **Iglesia de la Merced** (cnr Av San Martín & Don Bosco) was built with convict labor. **Casa Beban** (cnr Av Maipú & Plúschow; 11am-6pm) was built in 1911 using parts ordered from Sweden, and sometimes hosts local art exhibits.

★Museo Marítimo & Museo del Presidio — MUSEUM

(437481; www.museomaritimo.com; cnr Yaganes & Gobernador Paz; admission AR$110; 9am-8pm) Convicts were transferred from Isla de los Estados (Staten Island) to Ushuaia in 1906 to build this national prison, finished in 1920. The cells, designed for 380 inmates, held up to 800 before closing in 1947. Famous prisoners include illustrious author Ricardo Rojasand and Russian anarchist Simón Radowitzky. The depiction of penal life is intriguing, but the information is in Spanish.

Maritime exhibits provide a unique glimpse into the region's history. Remains of the world's narrowest-gauge freight train, which transported prisoners between town and their work stations, sit in the courtyard. From December to March, guided tours (also in English) are at 11:30am and 4:30pm. If you can, take your tour with Horacio.

Museo Yamaná — MUSEUM

(422874; Rivadavia 56; admission AR$48; 10am-7pm) Small but carefully tended, with an excellent overview of the Yamaná (Yahgan) way of life. Delves into their survival in harsh weather without clothing, why only women swam and how campfires were kept in moving canoes. Expertly detailed dioramas (also in English) show the bays and inlets of Parque Nacional Tierra del Fuego; coming here before a park visit gives a new perspective.

Museo del Fin del Mundo — MUSEUM

(421863; www.museodelfindelmundo.org.ar; cnr Av Maipú & Rivadavia; admission AR$70; 10am-7pm) Built in 1903, this former bank contains exhibits on Fuegian natural history, stuffed birdlife, indigenous life and early penal colonies, and replicas of moderate interest. Guided visits are at 11am and 3:30pm.

Parque Yatana Park — PARK

(Fundación Cultiva; 425212; cnr Magallanes & 25 de Mayo; admission AR$50; 9am-12pm Mon-Fri) Part art project, part urban refuge, a city block of lenga forest preserved from encroaching development by one determined family.

Activities

Boating can be undertaken year-round. Hiking possibilities should not be limited to Parque Nacional Tierra del Fuego; the entire mountain range behind Ushuaia, with its lakes and rivers, is a hiker's high. However, many trails are poorly marked or not marked at all, and some hikers who have easily scurried uphill have gotten lost trying to find the trail back down. Club Andino Ushuaia has maps and good information. In an emergency, contact the **Civil Guard** (103 or 22108).

Summer Activities

Cerro Martial & Glaciar Martial — OUTDOORS

(optional chairlift AR$70; 10am-4pm) The fantastic panoramas of Ushuaia and the Beagle Channel are more impressive than the actual smallish glacier. You can arrive directly or from the ski run 7km northwest of town, where an *aerosilla* (chairlift) can take you up. For the best views, hike an hour above the chairlift terminus. A cozy refuge offers coffee, desserts and beer at the *aerosilla* base. Weather is changeable so take warm, dry clothing and sturdy footwear.

Evening **canopy tours** (escuela@tierradelfuego.org.ar; Refugio de Montaña; tour AR$170; 10am-5:15pm Oct-Jun) are run from the base of the *aerosilla* and offer an hour's worth of Tarzan time, zipping through the forest with 11 zipline cables and two hanging bridges. The highest cable is 8m. It's by reservation only.

Catch a taxi up the hill or jump aboard one of the minivans (AR$60) to Cerro Martial that leave from the corner of Av Maipú and Juana Fadul every half-hour from 8:30am to 6:30pm.

Mago Del Sur — SAILING

(02901-15-5148-6463; www.magodelsur.com.ar; charter per person per day channel/Antarctica from US$300/350) A recommended option for extended sailing trips, captained by Alejandro Da Milano, whose lifetime of experience ensures skill and safety at the helm.

Cruceros Australis — CRUISE

(in Santiago 022-442-3115; www.australis.com; 3 nights & 4 days per person in low/high season from US$1486/1895; late Sep-early April) Luxurious three-to-four night sightseeing cruises to Punta Arenas and back, catering mostly to mature travelers. Ushuaia departures may disembark at Cape Horn. The cruise visits many otherwise inaccessible glaciers, but time alone and hiking opportunities are limited; the focus is more on nature talks and group excursions.

Low season is the first and last two months of the season. The first and last departures of each season are severely discounted. Turismo Comapa handles local bookings.

Aeroclub Ushuaia SCENIC FLIGHTS
(☎421892, 421717; 5-passenger charter per person US$200) Offers scenic rides over the channel and may travel to Puerto Williams, Chile (10kg luggage allowed). Leaves before 1pm, confirm three days in advance. The departure tax is US$26 extra.

Winter Activities

With the surrounding peaks loaded with powder, winter visitors should jump at the chance to explore the local ski resorts. Accessed from RN3, the resorts offer both downhill and cross-country options. The ski season runs from June to September, with July (winter vacation) the busiest month.

Cerro Castor SKIING
(☎499301; www.cerrocastor.com; full-day lift ticket adult/child AR$400/275; ⏲mid-Jun–mid-Oct) Fun and incredibly scenic, the largest resort is 26km via RN3 from Ushuaia, with 15 runs spanning 400 hectares and a number of lodges with cafes and even a hip sushi bar. Rentals are available for skis, boards and cross-country skis. Multiday and shoulder-season tickets are discounted. Clear windbreaks are added to lifts on cold days.

Tierra Mayor SNOW SPORTS
(☎430329; http://antartur.com.ar; RN3, Km3018; guided dog sledding AR$200) Snowshoe a beautiful alpine valley or dog sled with Siberian and Alaskan huskies bumping across Tierra Mayor. For a memorable night, combine either with an evening bonfire (AR$650 to A$800). Also does guided snowcat rides. It's 19km from Ushuaia via RN3.

Centro de Deportes Invernales Glaciar Martial SNOW SPORTS
(☎421423, 423340) About 7km northwest of Ushuaia, this family-oriented area has downhill runs well suited to beginners; it also rents equipment.

Cerro Martial & Glaciar Martial SNOW SPORTS
(optional chairlift AR$100; ⏲10am-4pm) Ideal for families or a few hours of fun, this town winter sports center also rents ski equipment; ask about snowshoes to take a winter walk.

☞ Tours

Many travel agencies sell tours around the region. You can go horseback riding, hiking or canoeing, visit Lagos Escondido and Fagnano, stay at an *estancia* (ranch) or spy on birds and beavers.

Beagle Channel BOAT TOUR
(Cruise around AR$400) Navigating the Beagle Channel's gunmetal-gray waters, with glaciers and rocky isles in the distance, offers a fresh perspective and decent wildlife-watching. Operators are found on the tourist wharf Maipú between Lasserre and Roca. Harbor cruises are usually four-hour morning or afternoon excursions to sea lion and cormorant colonies. The number of passengers, extent of snacks and hiking options may vary between operators. A highlight is an island stop to hike and look at *conchales,* middens (shell mounds) left by the native Yahgan.

Canal Fun ADVENTURE TOUR
(☎435777; www.canalfun.com; Roca 136) Run by hip young guys, these popular all-day outings include hiking and kayaking in Parque Nacional Tierra del Fuego, the famous 4WD adventure around Lago Fagnano, and a multisport outing that includes kayaking around Estancia Harberton and a visit to the penguin colony.

Che Tango BOAT TOUR
(☎02901-15-517967; navegandoelfindelmundo@gmail.com; Tourist Wharf) With two 12-passenger boats, this owner-run tour includes a trek on Bridges Island and Beagle (what else?) beer on tap served for the cruise back to the harbor – very popular with the hostel crowd. No website, but has a Facebook page.

★Compañía de Guías de Patagonia ADVENTURE TOUR
(☎437753; www.companiadeguias.com.ar) A reputable outfitter organizing excursions in Parque Nacional Tierra del Fuego, full-day treks and ice-hiking on Glaciar Vinciguerra, and recommended three-day treks to Valle Andorra and Paso la Oveja. It also offers mountain biking, sea kayaking and Antarctic trips.

Patagonia Adventure Explorer BOAT TOUR
(☎02901-15-465842; www.patagoniaadvent.com.ar; Tourist Wharf) Comfortable boats with snacks and a short hike on Isla Bridges. For extra adventure, set sail in the 18ft sailboat.

Ushuaia

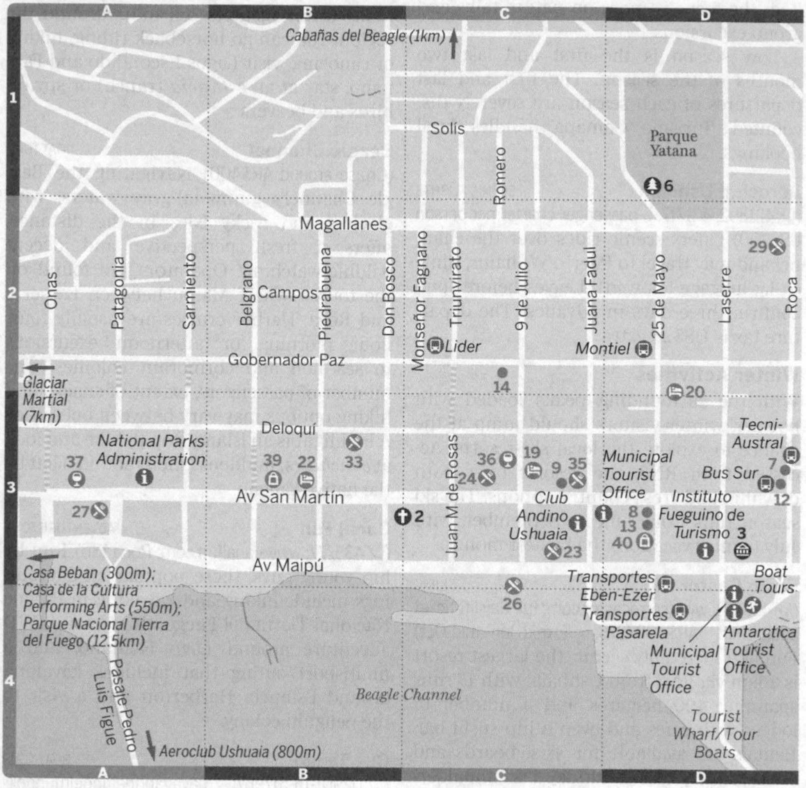

Full-day sail trips with wine and gourmet snacks or multiday trips are also available.

Piratour BOAT TOUR
(☎ 435557; www.piratour.com.ar; Av San Martín 847) Runs 20-person tours to Isla Martillo for trekking around Magellanic and Papúa penguins. There is also an office on the Tourist Wharf.

★ **Tierra** ADVENTURE TOUR
(☎ 02901-15-486886; www.tierraturismo.com; Campos 36, 5C) Doing active tours and unusual tailored trips with aplomb, this small agency was created by former guides hoping to create a more personalized experience. Partners Juan and Nacho lead some of the tours themselves. Options include a 4WD trip to Lago Fagnano with boating and hiking (AR$700), treks in Parque Nacional Tierra del Fuego (half-day AR$380) and Estancia Harberton visits.

Tierra Mayor ADVENTURE TOUR
(☎ 430329; http://antartur.com.ar) Offers competitively priced adventure tours and has its own mountain base. Many travelers have enjoyed the 4WD day trip to Lago Fagnano with canoeing and a full barbecue.

Tres Marías Excursiones BOAT TOUR
(☎ 436416; www.tresmariasweb.com; Tourist Wharf) The only outfitter with permission to land on Isla 'H' in the Isla Bridges natural reserve, which has shell mounds and a colony of rock cormorants. It takes only eight passengers.

Tolkar GUIDED TOUR
(☎ 431412, 431408; www.tolkarturismo.com.ar; Roca 157) A helpful, popular, all-round agency, affiliated with Tecni-Austral buses.

Turismo Comapa TOUR
(☎ 430727; www.comapa.com; Av San Martín 409) Confirm Navimag and Cruceros Aus-

tralis passages at this longstanding agency also selling conventional tours and boat transfer to Puerto Williams, Chile.

Turismo de Campo GUIDED TOUR
(437351; www.turismodecampo.com; Fuegia Basquet 414) This outfit organizes light trekking, Beagle Channel sailing trips and visits to Estancia Rolito near Río Grande. It also sells nine- to 12-night passages to Antarctica.

Ushuaia Turismo TOUR
(436003; www.ushuaiaturismoevt.com.ar; Gobernador Paz 865) Offers last-minute Antarctica cruise bookings.

Festivals & Events

Fin del Mundo Marathon RUNNING
(early Mar) A hugely popular international marathon on the southernmost course on the continent.

Festival Nacional de la Noche Más Larga FESTIVAL
(Longest Night; mid-Jun) This festival features two weeks of shows and music recitals (ranging from tango to jazz and popular music), with free events at locations throughout the city. For more information, contact the Municipal Tourist Office.

Marcha Blanca SNOW SPORTS
(www.marchablanca.com; mid-Aug) Running for a quarter of a century, Ushuaia's biggest ski event is the annual cross-country event which re-creates San Martín's historic August 17, 1817 crossing of the Andes. There's also a master class for ski enthusiasts, snow sculptures and a Nordic ski marathon.

Sleeping

Reserve ahead from January to early March. Check when booking for free arrival transfers. Winter rates drop a bit; some places close altogether, though winter visits are becoming popular. Most offer laundry service.

The Municipal Tourist Office has lists of B&Bs and *cabañas* (cabins), and also posts a list of available lodgings outside after closing time.

Hostels abound, all with kitchens and most with internet access. Rates typically drop 25% in low season (April to October).

★ **Antarctica Hostel** HOSTEL $
(435774; www.antarcticahostel.com; Antártida Argentina 270; dm AR$120, d/tr AR$350/380; @) This friendly backpacker hub delivers with a warm atmosphere and helpful staff. The open floor plan and beer on tap are plainly conducive to making friends. Guests lounge and play cards in the common room and cook in a cool balcony kitchen. Cement rooms are clean and ample, with radiant floor heating.

Yakush HOSTEL $
(435807; www.hostelyakush.com.ar; Piedrabuena 118; dm AR$120-130, d AR$500, without bathroom AR$380; mid-Oct–mid-Apr; @) Adorned with whimsical drawings, this colorful hostel is well kept and exceedingly friendly. Dorms have fresh sheets and good beds, and social spaces include an ample upstairs lounge with futons and slanted ceilings. Doubles with private bathroom are on the expensive side for what you get.

Hostel Cruz del Sur HOSTEL $
(434099; www.xdelsur.com.ar; Deloquí 242; dm AR$110; @) This easygoing hostel

Ushuaia

Top Sights
1 Museo Marítimo & Museo del Presidio F2

Sights
2 Iglesia de la Merced B3
3 Legislatura Provincial D3
4 Museo del Fin del Mundo E3
5 Museo Yamaná E3
6 Parque Yatana Park D1

Activities, Courses & Tours
7 Canal Fun D3
8 Compañía de Guías de Patagonia D3
9 Piratour C3
10 Tierra F2
11 Tolkar E3
12 Turismo Comapa D3
13 Turismo de Campo D3
14 Ushuaia Turismo C2

Sleeping
15 Antarctica Hostel E3
16 Galeazzi-Basily B&B E1
17 Hostel Cruz del Sur E3
18 La Casa de Tere B&B E1
19 Martín Fierro B&B C3
20 Mil 810 ..... D2
21 Posada Fin del Mundo E1
22 Yakush B3

Eating
23 Almacen Ramos Generales C3
24 Bodegón Fueguino C3
25 Chiko E3
26 Christopher C3
27 El Turco A3
28 Kalma Resto F3
29 Kaupé D2
30 La Anónima E2
31 La Estancia E3
32 Lomitos Martinica F3
33 María Lola Restó B3
34 Tante Sara E3
35 Tante Sara C3

Drinking & Nightlife
36 Dublin Irish Pub C3
37 Macario 1910 ..... A3

Entertainment
38 Cine Pakawaia F2

Shopping
39 Boutique del Libro B3
40 Boutique del Libro D3

comprises two renovated houses (1920 and 1926), painted tangerine and joined by a passageway. Dorm prices are based on room capacity; the only disadvantage is that your bathroom might be on another floor. There's a fine backyard patio, though indoor shared spaces are scant.

Camping La Pista del Andino CAMPGROUND $
(☎ 414664, 435890; Alem 2873; campsites per person AR$50; ❄ @ 📶) A steep, uphill, 3km trek leads to this pleasant campground offering grassy or forested sites with views. While it's short on showers and toilets, perks include decent cooking facilities, a bar-restaurant, good common areas and bikes for rent. It's at Club Andino Ushuaia's ski area. Call for free pickup from the airport or town center.

Camping Municipal CAMPGROUND $
(RN3) FREE About 10km west of town, en route to Parque Nacional Tierra del Fuego, this free campground boasts a lovely setting but minimal facilities.

★ **Galeazzi-Basily B&B** B&B $$
(☎ 423213; www.avesdelsur.com.ar; Valdéz 323; d withouth bathroom US$68, 2-/4-person cabin US$100/124; @ 📶) The best feature of this elegant wooded residence is its warm and hospitable family who will make you feel right at home. Rooms are small but offer a personal touch. Since beds are twin-sized, couples may prefer a modern cabin out back. It's a peaceful spot, and where else can you practice your English, French, Italian and Portuguese?

Mysten Kepen GUESTHOUSE $$
(☎ 02901-15-497391, 430156; mystenkepen@hotmail.com; Rivadavia 826; d/tr/q AR$550/660/770; 📶) If you want an authentic Argentine family experience, this is it. Hosts Roberto and Rosario still recount stories of favorite guests from years past, and their two-kid home feels busy and lived in, in a good way. Rooms have newish installations, bright corduroy duvets and handy shelving for nighttime reading. The hosts also offer airport transfers and winter discounts.

La Posta HOSTEL $$
(☎ 444650; www.laposta-ush.com.ar; Perón Sur 864; dm/d AR$145/460; @ 📶) This cozy hostel and guesthouse on the outskirts of town is hugely popular with young travelers thanks to warm service, homey decor and spotless open kitchens. The downside is that the

place is far from the town center, but public buses and taxis are plentiful.

Los Cormoranes HOSTEL **$$**
(☎423459; www.loscormoranes.com; Kamshen 788; dm AR$130-170, d/tr/q AR$500/585/660; @ 📶) This friendly, mellow HI hostel is a 10-minute (uphill) walk north of the town center. Good, warm, six-bed dorms face outdoor plank hallways, some with private bathrooms. Modern doubles have polished cement floors and bright down duvets – the best is room 10, with bay views. The abundant breakfast includes toast, coffee, DIY eggs and fresh orange juice.

La Casa de Tere B&B B&B **$$**
(☎422312; www.lacasadetere.com.ar; Rivadavia 620; d US$110, without bathroom US$80) Tere showers guests with attention, but also gives them the run of the place in this beautiful modern home with great views. Its three tidy rooms fill up fast. Guests can cook, and there's cable TV and a fireplace in the living room. It's a short but steep walk uphill from the town center.

Posada Fin del Mundo B&B **$$**
(☎437345; www.posadafindelmundo.com.ar; cnr Rivadavia & Valdéz; d/tr US$110/130, without bathroom AR$100/120) This expansive home exudes good taste and character, from the snug living room with folk art and expansive water views to the doddling chocolate Lab. Each of the nine rooms is distinct, with the best upstairs. Some are small but beds are long. Breakfast is abundant and there's also afternoon tea and cakes. Sometimes booked by entire ski teams in winter.

Familia Piatti B&B B&B **$$**
(☎437104; www.familiapiatti.com; Bahía Paraíso 812, Bosque del Faldeo; d/tr US$86/107; @ 📶) If idling in the forest sounds good, head for this friendly B&B with warm down duvets and native lenga-wood furniture. Hiking trails nearby lead up into the mountains. The friendly owners are multilingual (English, Italian, Spanish and Portuguese) and can arrange transportation and guided excursions. Check the website for location directions.

Martín Fierro B&B B&B **$$**
(☎430525; www.martinfierrobyb.com.ar; 9 de Julio 175; s/d AR$500/650, without bathroom AR$350/500 ; 🕗Sep-Apr; 📶) Spending a night at this charming inn feels like staying at the cool mountain cabin of a worldly friend who makes strong coffee and has a great book collection. The owner, Javier, personally built the interiors with local wood and stone; these days he cultivates a friendly, laid-back atmosphere in which travelers get into deep conversations at the breakfast table.

Cabañas del Beagle CABIN **$$$**
(☎432785; www.cabanasdelbeagle.com; Las Aljabas 375; 2-person cabin AR$1530, 2-night minimum) Couples in search of a romantic hideaway delight in these rustic chic cabins with heated stone floors, crackling fireplaces, and full kitchens stocked daily with fresh bread, coffee and other treats. The personable owner, Alejandro, wins high praise for his attentive service. It's 13 blocks uphill from the town center and accessed via Av Leandro Alem.

Cabañas Aldea Nevada CABIN **$$$**
(☎422851; www.aldeanevada.com.ar; Martial 1430; 2-/4-person cabins from AR$880/1150, 2-night minimum; @ 📶) You expect the elves to arrive here any minute. This beautiful patch of lenga forest is discreetly dotted with 13 log cabins with outdoor grills and rough-hewn benches contemplatively placed by the ponds. Interiors are rustic but modern, with functional kitchens, wood stoves and hardwood details.

Cumbres del Martial INN **$$$**
(☎424779; www.cumbresdelmartial.com.ar; Martial 3560; d/cabin US$332/477; @ 📶) This stylish place sits at the base of the Glaciar Martial. Standard rooms have a touch of the English cottage, while the two-story wooden cabins are simply stunners, with stone fireplaces, Jacuzzis and dazzling vaulted windows. Lush robes, optional massages (extra) and your country's newspaper delivered to your mailbox are some of the delicious details.

Los Cauquenes Resort & Spa RESORT **$$$**
(☎441300; www.loscauquenes.com; d US$360-541, ste US$663-995; @ 📶 🏊) Precious and exclusive, this sprawling wooden lodge sits directly on the Beagle Channel, in a private neighborhood with gravel-road access. Rooms are tasteful and well appointed; special features include a play room stocked with kids' games and outdoor terraces with glass windbreaks and stunning channel views. Free shuttles go downtown every few hours. It's 4km west of the airport.

It also has a spa, sauna and indoor-outdoor pool. Proof that Argentines will market anything, the spa features *yerba mate* scrubs and Andean peat masks.

Mil 810 HOTEL $$$

(☎437710; www.hotel1810.com; 25 de Mayo 245; d/tr US$180/195; @) Billed as boutique, this is more like a small upscale hotel. The design is modern, with elements of nature, like a retention wall of river stones and a rock face trickling with water. Its 38 rooms feature brocade walls, rich tones, luxuriant textures and touches of abstract art. Rooms have flat-screen TVs and safes, and halls are monitored.

Eating

Almacen Ramos Generales CAFE $

(☎427317; www.ramosgeneralesushuaia.com; Av Maipú 749; mains AR$47-78; ⌚9am-midnight) With its quirky memorabilia and postings of local environmental issues you've never heard of, this former general store is a peek inside the real Ushuaia. Locals hold their pow-wows here. Croissants and crusty baguettes are baked by the French pastry chef. But there's also local beer on tap, a wine list, and light fare such as sandwiches, soups and quiche.

El Turco CAFE $

(☎424711; Av San Martín 1410; mains AR$32-89; ⌚noon-3pm & 8pm-midnight) Nothing fancy, this classic, dated Argentine cafe nonetheless charms with reasonable prices and swift bow-tied waiters game to try out their French on tourists. Standards include *milanesa* (breaded meat), pizzas, crispy fries and roast chicken.

Lomitos Martinica ARGENTINE $

(☎432134; Av San Martín 68; mains AR$60-80; ⌚11:30am-3pm & 8:30pm-midnight Mon-Sat) Cheap and cheerful, this greasy spoon with grill-side seating serves enormous *milanesa* sandwiches and offers a cheap lunch special.

La Anónima SUPERMARKET $

(cnr Gobernador Paz & Rivadavia) A grocery store with cheap takeout.

Chiko SEAFOOD $$

(☎432036; Antartida Argentina 182; mains AR$58-135; ⌚noon-3pm & 7:30-11:30pm Mon-Sat) Great value, this popular 2nd-floor restaurant is a clear boon to seafood lovers. Crisp calamari rings, *paila marina* (shellfish stew) and fish dishes such as *abadejo a pil pil* (pollock in garlic sauce) are done so right that you might not mind the slow service. An odd assemblage of Chilean memorabilia spells homesickness for the owners from Chiloé.

María Lola Restó ARGENTINE $$

(☎421185; Deloquí 1048; mains AR$75-140; ⌚noon-midnight Mon-Sat) 'Satisfying' defines the experience at this creative cafe-style restaurant overlooking the channel. Locals pack this silver house for homemade pasta with seafood or strip steak in rich mushroom sauce. Service is good and portions tend toward humongous: desserts can easily be split. It's among the few downtown restaurants with off-street parking.

Bodegón Fueguino PATAGONIAN $$

(☎431972; Av San Martín 859; mains AR$65-140; ⌚Tue-Sun) The spot to sample hearty home-style Patagonian fare or gather for wine and appetizers. Painted peach, this century-old Fuegian home is cozied up with sheepskin-clad benches, cedar barrels and ferns. A *picada* (shared appetizer plate) for two includes eggplant, lamb brochettes, crab and bacon-wrapped plums.

La Estancia STEAKHOUSE $$

(☎431241; cnr Godoy & San Martín; mains AR$60-130; ⌚12-3pm & 8-11pm) For authentic Argentine *asado* (barbecue grill) it is hard to beat this reliable, well-priced grill. There are many others along the main drag, but this is the one that consistently delivers. At night it's packed with locals and travelers alike, feasting on whole roast lamb, juicy steaks, sizzling ribs and heaping salads.

Christopher PARRILLA $$

(☎425079; www.christopherushuaia.com.ar; Av Maipú 828; mains AR$80-130; ⌚12-3pm & 8pm-12am, until 1am Sat) This classic grill and brewpub is deservedly popular with the locals. Standouts include the tender pork loin, big salads and burgers. It's good value, with large portions that you might want to share. Grab a table by the window for great harbor views.

Küar Resto Bar PUB $$

(☎437396; www.kuar.com.ar; Av Perito Moreno 2232; mains AR$80-135; ⌚6pm-late) This chic log-cabin-style hangout offers local beer, cheese boards and tapas, as well as complete dinners with ample fresh seafood. The interior is stylish but the highlight, especially at sunset, is the jaw-dropping views over the water. Weekdays boast a AR$60 set lunch – a steal. You'll have to catch a cab.

ANTARCTICA: THE ICE

For many travelers, a journey to Antarctica represents a once-in-a-lifetime adventure. Despite its high price tag, it is much more than just a continent to tick off your list. You will witness both land and ice shelves piled with hundreds of meters of undulating, untouched snow. Glaciers drop from mountainsides and icebergs form sculptures as tall as buildings. The wildlife is thrilling, with thousands of curious penguins and an extraordinary variety of flying birds, seals and whales.

More than 90% of Antarctic-bound boats pass through Ushuaia. In the 2010–11 season, that meant more than 36,000 tourists – a stunning contrast to the continent's population of 5000 (summer) or 1200 (winter) scientists and staff. But travel here is not without its costs. On November 23, 2007, the hull of the MV *Explorer* was gashed by ice but evacuated successfully before sinking. The circumstances were highly unusual, although the incident provoked further safety measures.

So long as you've got two or three weeks to spare, hopping on board a cruise ship is not out of the question. Some voyages take in the Falkland Islands (Islas Malvinas) and South Georgia (human population 10 to 20, estimated penguin population two to three million); some go just to the Antarctic Peninsula; others focus on retracing historic expeditions. A small but growing handful of visitors reach Antarctica aboard private vessels. All are sailboats (equipped with auxiliary engines).

The season runs from mid-October to mid-March, depending on ice conditions. It used to be that peak-season voyages sold out; now most trips do. When shopping around, ask how many days you will actually spend in Antarctica, as crossing the Southern Ocean takes up to two days each way. And how many landings will there be? The smaller the ship, the more landings there are per passenger (always depending on the weather, of course). Tour companies charge anywhere from US$7000 to US$70,000, although some ships allow walk-ons, which can cost as little as US$5000 for 10 days.

Due to Ushuaia's proximity to the Antarctic Peninsula, most cruises leave from here. Last-minute bookings can be made through Ushuaia Turismo (p495). Other travel agencies and tour operators offering packages include Rumbo Sur (p503), All Patagonia (p503) and Canal Fun (p493), though there are many more.

Check that your company is a member of **IAATO** (International Association Antarctica Tour Operators; www.iaato.org), which mandates strict guidelines for responsible travel to Antarctica. The following are just a few companies that go to Antarctica:

Adventure Associates Cruise (www.adventureassociates.com) Australia's first tour company to Antarctica, with many ships and destinations.

National Geographic Expeditions (www.nationalgeographicexpeditions.com) Highly recommended, with quality naturalists and experts, aboard the 148-passenger *National Geographic Explorer*.

Peregrine Adventures (www.peregrineadventures.com) Offers unique trips that include visiting the Antarctic Circle, with kayaking and camping options.

Quark Expeditions (www.quarkexpeditions.com) Three kinds of ships, from an icebreaker to a 48-passenger ship for close-knit groups.

WildWings Travel (www.wildwings.co.uk) UK-based company that focuses on birdwatching and wildlife in Antarctica.

For more information see Lonely Planet's *Antarctica* guidebook. Also check www.70south.com for up-to-date information and articles. In Ushuaia consult the very helpful **Oficina Antártica** (☎430015; www.tierradelfuego.org/ar/antartida; Av Maipú 505) at the pier.

Tante Sara CAFE $$
(☎423912; www.tantesara.com; cnr Av San Martín & Juana Fadul; mains AR$60-130; ⏲7:30am-2am Mon-Sat, 8am-1am Sun) Popular for its ambience, this corner bistro serves the usual suspects in a bubbly atmosphere. If you want a late-night bite, this is your best bet, since it's the only kitchen open until 2am. The sister branch (☎433710; Rivadavia & Av San Martín;

1

RALPH LEE HOPKINS/GETTY IMAGES ©

2

4

1. Ushuaia (p489)
The Andes meets the Southern Ocean in this bustling end-of-the-world port town.

2. Parque Nacional Tierra del Fuego (p504)
The hillsides of this national park take on a spectacular glow of red during autumn.

3. Paso la Oveja (p493)
A three-day trek to this area is grueling, but rewarding.

4. Estancia Harberton (p502)
Founded in 1886, this *estancia* (ranch) is a bird-watcher's paradise.

mains AR$60-130; ⏲8am-8:30pm Mon-Thu, 8am-9pm Fri & Sat, closed Sun) is often packed with locals having coffee and pastries.

★**Kalma Resto** INTERNATIONAL **$$$**
(☎425786; www.kalmaresto.com.ar; Antártida Argentina 57; mains AR$130-150; ⏲8pm-midnight Tue-Sun, lunch by reservation only) This tiny chef-owned gem presents Fuegian staples such as crab and octopus in a giddy new context. Black sea bass, a rich deep-sea dweller, wears a tart tomato sauce for contrast, there's roast lamb stews with earthy pine mushrooms, and the summer greens and edible flowers come fresh from the garden.

Service is stellar, with young chef Jorge making the rounds of the few black-linen tables. For dessert, splurge with a not-too-sweet deconstructed chocolate cake.

Kaupé INTERNATIONAL **$$$**
(☎422704; www.kaupe.com.ar; Roca 470; mains AR$80-140) For an out-of-body seafood experience, head to this candlelit house overlooking the bay. Chef Ernesto Vivian employs the freshest of everything and service is impeccable. The tasting menu (AR$360 with wine and champagne) features two starters, a main dish and dessert, with standouts such as king crab and spinach chowder or black sea bass in blackened butter.

Chez Manu INTERNATIONAL **$$$**
(☎432253; www.chezmanu.com; Martial 2135; mains AR$80-170) If you are headed to Glaciar Martial, don't miss this gem on the way, 2km from town. Chef Emmanuel puts a French touch on fresh local ingredients, such as Fuegian lamb or mixed plates of cold *fruits de mer*. The three-course set lunch is the best deal. Views are a welcome bonus.

Drinking

Geographically competitive drinkers should note that the southernmost bar in the world is not here but on a Ukrainian research station in Antarctica.

Dublin Irish Pub PUB
(☎430744; www.dublinushuaia.com; 9 de Julio 168) Dublin doesn't feel so far away amid the lively banter and free-flowing drinks at this dimly lit foreigners' favorite. Look for occasional live music and be sure to try at least one of its three local Beagle beers.

OFF THE BEATEN TRACK

ESTANCIA HARBERTON

Tierra del Fuego's first *estancia*, **Harberton** (☎Skype: estanciaharberton.turismo; www.estanciaharberton.com; tour & museum adult/child AR$60/free, half-board s/d/tr US$240/390/540; ⏲10am-7pm Oct 15–Apr 15), was founded in 1886 by English missionary Thomas Bridges and his family. The location earned fame from a stirring memoir written by Bridges' son Lucas, titled *Uttermost Part of the Earth*, about his coming of age among the now-extinct Selk'nam and Yahgan people. Available in English, the book is an excellent introduction to the history of the region and the ways of indigenous peoples.

In a splendid location, the *estancia* is owned and run by Tomas Bridges' descendants. There's lodging and day visitors can join guided tours (featuring the island's oldest house and a replica Yahgan dwelling), dine at the restaurant and visit the Reserva Yecapasela penguin colony. It's also a popular destination for bird watchers.

On-site, the impressive **Museo Acatushún** (www.acatushun.com; tours adult/12yr & under AR$60/free) houses a vast collection of mammal and bird specimens compiled by biologist Natalie Prosser Goodall. Emphasizing the region's marine mammals, the museum has inventoried thousands of mammals and birds; among the rarest is a Hector's beaked whale. Many of the specimens were found at Bahía San Sebastián, north of Río Grande, where a difference of up to 11km between high and low tide leaves animals stranded. Confirm the museum's opening hours with the *estancia*.

Reserve well in advance as there are no phones at the *estancia*, though Skyping may be possible. With advance permission, free primitive camping is allowed at Río Lasifashaj, Río Varela and Río Cambaceres. Harberton is 85km east of Ushuaia via RN3 and rough RC-j, a 1½- to two-hour drive. In Ushuaia, shuttles leave from the base of 25 de Mayo at Av Maipú at 9am, returning around 3pm. Day-long catamaran tours are organized by local agencies.

Macario 1910 PUB
(☎422757; www.macario1910.com; Av San Martín 1485; ⏲6pm-late) A welcoming pub with a transatlantic style of polished wood and leather booths. The tasty locally made Beagle beer flows on tap and the above-average pub fare includes fresh tuna sandwiches on homemade bread and plates stacked with shoestring fries made from scratch. It's also good for cheap set meals (AR$25).

☆ Entertainment

Cine Pakawaia CINEMA
(☎436500; cnr Yaganes & Gobernador Paz; tickets AR$12) First-run movies are shown at the Presidio's fully restored hangar-style theater.

Casa de la Cultura Performing Arts PERFORMING ARTS
(☎422417; cnr Malvinas Argentinas & 12 de Octubre) Hidden behind a gym, this center hosts occasional live-music shows.

Shopping

Boutique del Libro BOOKS
(☎432117; 25 de Mayo 62; ⏲10am-9pm) Outstanding selection of Patagonia and Antarctica-themed material, with literature, guidebooks and pictorials (also in English); there's an Av San Martín (☎424750; Av San Martín 1120) branch.

Information

Several banks on Avs Maipú and San Martín have ATMs.

All Patagonia (☎433622; www.allpatagonia.com; Juana Fadul 48) Amex rep offering conventional and luxurious trips.

Automóvil Club Argentino (ACA; www.aca.org.ar; cnr Malvinas Argentinas & Onachaga) Argentina's auto club; good source for provincial road maps.

Cambio Thaler (Av San Martín 209; ⏲10am-1pm & 5-8pm Mon-Sat, 5-8pm Sun) Convenience equals slightly poorer exchange rates.

Club Andino Ushuaia (☎422335; www.clubandinoushuaia.com.ar; Juana Fadul 50; ⏲9am-1pm & 3-8pm Mon-Fri) Sells a map and bilingual trekking, mountaineering and mountain-biking guidebook. The club occasionally organizes hikes and can recommend guides. Unguided trekkers are strongly encouraged to register here or with the municipal tourist office before hiking and after a safe return.

Hospital Regional (☎423200, 107; cnr Fitz Roy & 12 de Octubre)

Immigration office (☎422334; Beauvoir 1536; ⏲9am-noon Mon-Fri)

Instituto Fueguino de Turismo (Infuetur; ☎421423; www.tierradelfuego.org.ar; AV Maipú 505) On the ground floor of Hotel Albatros.

Municipal Tourist Office (☎437666; Prefectura Naval 470; ⏲8am-5pm) Very helpful, with English- and French-speaking staff, a message board and multilingual brochures, as well as good lodging, activities and transport info. Also at Av San Martín (☎432000; www.turismoushuaia.com; Av San Martín 674; ⏲5-9pm) and the Airport (☎423970; ⏲during flight arrivals).

National Parks Administration (☎421315; Av San Martín 1395)

Post Office (cnr Av San Martín & Godoy)

Rumbo Sur (☎422275; www.rumbosur.com.ar; Av San Martín 350) Ushuaia's longest-running agency specializes in conventional activities, plus a catamaran harbor cruise. It also handles bookings to Antarctica.

Getting There & Away

AIR

LAN is the best bet for Buenos Aires; purchase tickets through local travel agencies. **Aerolíneas Argentinas** (☎0810-2228-6527; cnr Av Maipú & 9 de Julio) jets to Buenos Aires (one way from AR$1481, 3½ hours) several times daily, sometimes stopping in El Calafate (70 minutes).

LADE (☎421123; Av San Martín 542) flies to Buenos Aires, El Calafate and Río Grande and may serve other destinations.

BOAT

A few private yachts charter trips around the Beagle Channel, to Cape Horn and Antarctica. These trips must be organized well in advance.

For Puerto Williams, **Ushuaia Boating** (☎02901-436193; www.ushuaiaboating.com.ar; Gobernador Paz 233; one way US$115, Sat US$130) goes daily in Zodiac boats. Tickets include a 40-minute crossing plus an overland transfer from Puerto Navarino. Note: inclement weather often means cancellation. Options include a 9:30am departure and sometimes a 6pm departure (with sufficient demand). The more comfortable covered boat from **Fernandez Campbell** (☎433232; www.fernandezcampbell.com; Tourist Wharf; one way US$125; ⏲departure 10am Fri-Sun) docks directly in Puerto Williams, with fewer winter departures. Another option to Puerto Williams is offered by Piratour (p494).

The departure tax *(tasa de embarque)* is AR$10 for Beagle Channel trips or AR$30 for international trips, paid at the pier.

BUS

Ushuaia has no bus terminal. Book outgoing bus tickets as much in advance as possible; many readers have complained about getting stuck here in high season. Depending on your luck, long waits at border crossings can be expected.

Bus Sur (☎430727; Av San Martín 245) Buses to Punta Arenas and Puerto Natales, Chile, three times weekly at 5:30am, connecting with Montiel. The office is in Comapa, which also does tours and ferries in Chile.

Lider (☎442264; Gobernador Paz 921) Door-to-door minivans to Tolhuin and Río Grande six to eight times daily, with fewer departures on Sunday.

Montiel (☎421366; Gobernador Paz 605) Door-to-door minivans to Tolhuin and Río Grande six to eight times daily, with fewer departures on Sunday.

Tecni-Austral (☎431408, 431412; Roca 157;) Buses to Río Grande at 5am via Tolhuin; to Punta Arenas three times weekly; and to Río Gallegos daily at 5am.

Taqsa (☎435453; Godoy 41) Buses to Río Grande at 5am via Tolhuin; to Punta Arenas and Puerto Natales three times weekly at 5am; to Río Gallegos, El Calafate and Bariloche daily at 5am.

Transportes Pasarela (☎433712; cnr Av Maipú & 25 de Mayo) Round-trip shuttles to Lago Esmeralda (AR$100), Lago Escondido (AR$150) and Lago Fagnano (AR$150), leaving around 10am and returning at 2pm and 6:30pm. Pay one way if you're planning to stay overnight, and arrange for pickup.

Buses from Ushuaia

DESTINATION	COST (AR$)	DURATION (HR)
Bariloche	1300	36
Calafate	384	18
Punta Arenas, Chile	400	11
Río Gallegos	500	12
Río Grande	100	4
Tolhuin	60	2

Getting Around

Taxis to/from the modern airport, 4km southwest of downtown, cost AR$55. Taxis can be chartered for around AR$140 per hour. There's a local bus service along Av Maipú.

Rental rates for compact cars, including insurance, start at around AR$440 per day; try **Localiza** (☎430739; Sarmiento 81). Some agencies may not charge for drop-off in other parts of Argentine Tierra del Fuego.

Hourly ski shuttles (AR$100 round-trip) leave from the corner of Juana Fadul and Av Maipú to resorts along RN3, from 9am to 2pm daily. Each resort also provides its own transportation from downtown Ushuaia.

PARQUE NACIONAL TIERRA DEL FUEGO

Banked against the Beagle Channel, the hushed, fragrant southern forests of Tierra del Fuego are a stunning setting to explore. West of Ushuaia some 12km along RN3, **Parque Nacional Tierra del Fuego** (admission AR$110; fee collected 8am-8pm) was Argentina's first coastal national park and extends 630 sq km from the Beagle Channel in the south to beyond Lago Fagnano in the north. For information visit the **Centro de Visitantes Alakush** (9am-7pm, shorter hr Mar-Nov).

The public has access to only a couple of thousand hectares along the southern edge of the park, with short, easy trails designed more for day-tripping families than backpacking trekkers. The rest is protected as a *reserva natural estricta* (strictly off-limits zone). Despite this, a few scenic hikes along the bays and rivers, or through dense native forests of evergreen coihue, canelo and deciduous lenga, are worthwhile. For spectacular color, come in autumn when hillsides of ñire glow red.

Birdlife is prolific, especially along the coastal zone. Keep an eye out for condors, albatross, cormorants, gulls, terns, oystercatchers, grebes, kelp geese and flightless, orange-billed steamer ducks. Common invasive species include the European rabbit and the North American beaver, both wreaking ecological havoc despite their cuteness. Gray and red foxes, enjoying the abundance of rabbits, may also be seen.

Sleeping & Eating

There is one *refugio* and various, mostly free, campgrounds. Most get crowded, which means sites can get unreasonably messy. Do your part to take your trash out of the park and follow a leave-no-trace ethic. **Camping Ensenada** is 16km from the park entrance and nearest the Senda Costera trail; **Camping Río Pipo** is 6km from the entrance and easily accessed by either the road to Cañadon del Toro or the Senda Pampa Alta trail. **Camping Las Bandurrias**, **Camping Laguna Verde** and **Camping Los Cauquenes** are on the islands in Río Lapataia.

The only fee-based campground and refugio is **Camping & Refugio Lago Roca** (☎15-412649; campsites per person/dm AR$30/70), 9km from the park entrance. The *refugio* dorm is available year-round except

Parque Nacional Tierra del Fuego – Lapataia Sector

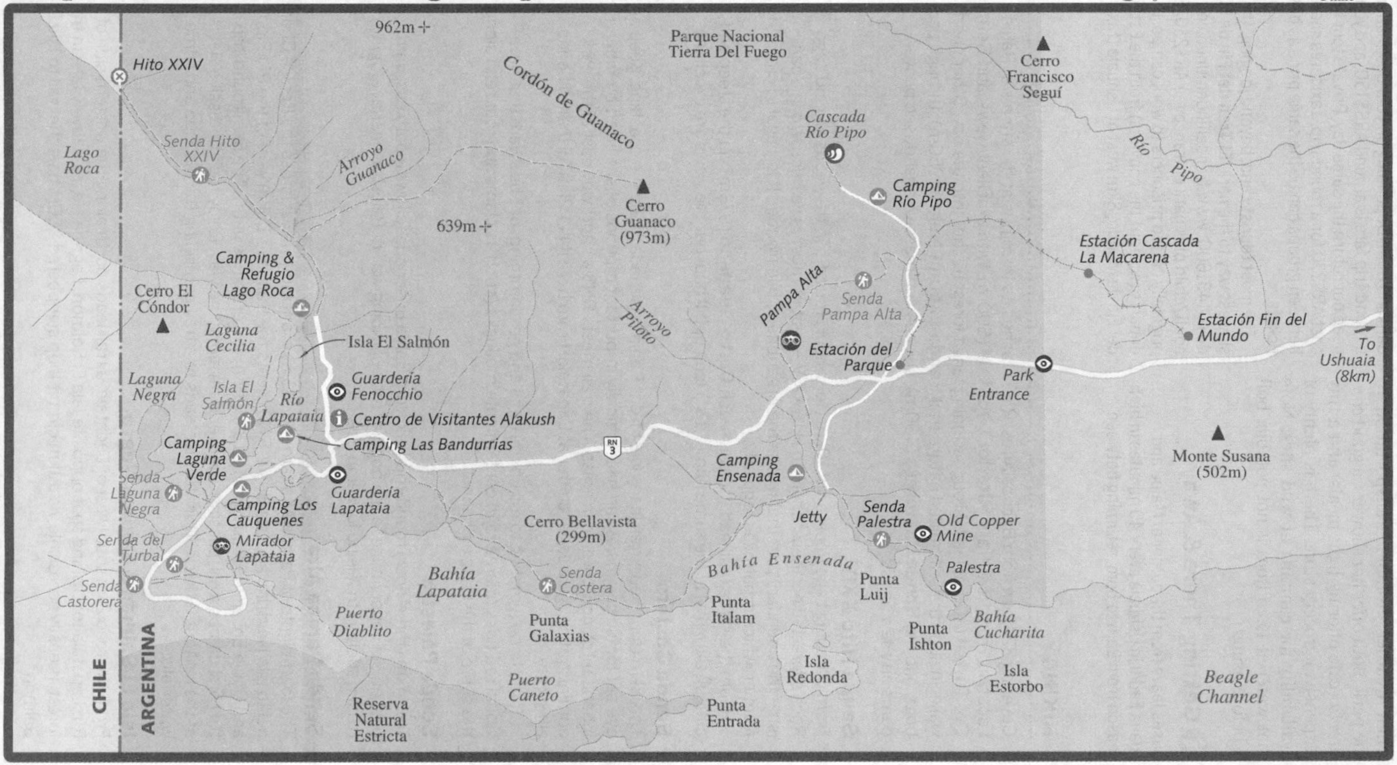

when weather prohibits transportation to the park. Both offer hot showers, a good *confitería* (cafe offering light meals) and a tiny (expensive) grocery store. There is plenty of availability for camping at wild sites. Note that water at Lago Roca is not potable; boil it before using.

Getting There & Away

Buses leave from the corner of Maipú and Juana Fadul in Ushuaia every 40 minutes in high season from 9am to 6pm, returning between 8am and 8pm. Depending on your destination, a round-trip fare is around ARS$150, and you need not return the same day. Private tour buses cost AR$270 for a round-trip. Taxi fares shared between groups can be the same price as bus tickets.

The most touristy and, beyond jogging, the slowest way to the park, **El Tren del Fin de Mundo** (☎431600; www.trendelfindemundo.com.ar; adult/child plus park entrance fee AR$230/80) originally carted prisoners to work camps. It departs (without the convicts) from the Estación del Fin de Mundo, 8km west of Ushuaia (taxis

HIKING

Covering 3242km from Buenos Aires, RN3 reaches its terminus at the shores of Bahía Lapataia. From here, trails **Mirador Lapataia** (500m), with excellent views, and **Senda Del Turbal** (400m) lead through winding lenga forest further into the bay. Other short walks include the self-guided nature trail **Senda Laguna Negra** (950m), through peat bogs, and the **Senda Castorera** (400m), showcasing massive abandoned beaver dams on a few ponds.

Senda Hito XXIV

From Camping Lago Roca, a flat 10km (four-hour) round-trip trek leads around Lago Roca's forested northeast shore to Hito XXIV – that number is *veinticuatro* in Spanish – the boundary post that marks the Argentina–Chile frontier. It is illegal to cross the frontier, which is patrolled regularly.

From the same trailhead you can reach **Cerro Guanaco** (973m) via the steep and difficult 8km trail of the same name; it's a long uphill haul but the views are excellent.

Senda Costera

This 8km (four-hour) trek leads west from Bahía Ensenada along the coastline. Keep an eye out for old *conchales* (archaeologically important mounds of shells left by Yahgan inhabitants), now covered in grass. The trail meets RN3 a short way east of the park administration *(guardería)* center at Lapataia. From here it is 1.2km further to Senda Hito XXIV.

It might be tempting to roll up the cuffs and go clamming, but be aware that occasional red tides *(marea roja)* contaminate mollusks (such as clams and mussels) along the shore of the Beagle Channel.

Senda Palestra

This 4km (three-hour) round-trip trek from Bahía Ensenada follows a path eastward past an old copper mine to the popular rock-climbing wall of Palestra, near a *refugio* (rustic shelter) that is no longer in use.

Senda Pampa Alta

The low heights of Pampa Alta (around 315m) grant long views across the Beagle Channel to Isla Navarino and Isla Hoste. RN3 meets the trailhead 1.5km west of the Río Pipo and Bahía Ensenada road turnoffs (3km from the entrance gate). The 5km round-trip trail first climbs a hill, passing a beaver dam along the way. Enjoy the impressive views at the lookout. A quick 300m further leads to a trail paralleling the Río Pipo and some waterfalls.

Isla El Salmón & Laguna Negra

From the road 2km southwest of Lapataia, a trail leads north along the western side of Río Lapataia to a fishing spot opposite Isla El Salmón. Laguna Negra, a lovely lake in the forest, is easily accessible via a 1km circuit loop signposted 200m past the trail to Isla El Salmón.

one way AR$60), three or four times daily in summer and once or twice daily in winter.

The one-hour, scenic narrow-gauge train ride comes with historical explanations in English and Spanish. Reserve in January and February, when cruise-ship tours take over. You can take it one way and return via minibus, though the train fee is the same one-way or round-trip.

Hitchhiking is feasible, but many cars are already full.

PUERTO WILLIAMS (CHILE)

☎0612 / POP 2874

Forget Ushuaia: the end of the world starts where colts roam Main St and yachts rounding Cape Horn take refuge. Naval settlement Puerto Williams is the only town on Isla Navarino, the official port of entry for vessels en route to Cape Horn and Antarctica, and home to the last living Yahgan speaker.

Just outside Puerto Williams is some of the Southern Cone's most breathtaking scenery. With more than 150km of trails, Isla Navarino is a rugged, backpackers' paradise, with slate-colored lakes, mossy lenga forests and the ragged spires of the Dientes de Navarino. Trails lead past beaver dams, bunkers and army trenches as they climb steeply into the mountains and deeper into forests. The beaver plague, introduced from Canada in the 1940s, is diminishing due to an active eradication campaign.

Mid-19th-century missionaries, followed by fortune-seekers during the 1890s gold rush, established a permanent European presence here. The remaining mixed-race descendants of the Yahgan (Yamaná) people are established in the small seaside village of Villa Ukika, a 15-minute walk east of town along the waterfront.

Sights

Museo Martín Gusinde MUSEUM
(cnr Araguay & Gusinde; donation requested; 9am-1pm & 3-6pm Mon-Fri, limited hr in low season) An attractive museum honoring the German priest and ethnographer who worked among the Yahgans from 1918 to 1923. Focuses on ethnography and natural history.

Parque Etnobotanico Omora PARK
(www.omora.org) Latin America's southernmost ethnobotanical park has trails with plant names marked in Yahgan, Latin and Spanish. Take the road to the right of the Virgin altar, 4km (an hour's walk) toward Puerto Navarino. Donations accepted.

Yelcho LANDMARK
Near the entrance to the military quarters is the original bow of the ship that rescued Ernest Shackleton's Antarctic expedition from Elephant Island in 1916.

Activities

★Dientes de Navarino HIKING
Gaining in popularity, this four- to five-day trekking circuit offers impossibly raw and windswept vistas under Navarino's toothy spires. For detailed trekking routes, refer to Lonely Planet's *Trekking in the Patagonian Andes*.

Cerro Bandera HIKING
With expansive views of the Beagle Channel, this four-hour round-trip starts at the Dientes de Navarino circuit. The trail ascends steeply through lenga to a blustery stone-littered hillside planted with a Chilean flag. Self-sufficient backpackers can continue on the Dientes de Navarino circuit.

Lago Windhond HIKING
This remote lake is a lesser known, but worthy, alternative to hiking the Dientes de Navarino circuit, with sheltered hiking through forest and peat bogs. The four-day round-trip is a better bet if there are high winds. For route details, ask at Turismo Shila or go with a guide.

Tours

Fuegia & Co GUIDED TOUR
(☎621251; fuegia@usa.net; Ortiz 049) For guided trekking or day trips to archaeological sites, Denis Chevallay offers professional guiding in French, German or English with a wealth of botanical and historical knowledge.

Sleeping & Eating

Residencial Pusaki GUESTHOUSE $
(☎621116; pattypusaki@yahoo.es; Piloto Pardo 242; s/d CH$11,500/26,000) With legendary warmth, Patty invites guest into this small home with comfortable, carpeted rooms, some without private bathrooms (there's no difference in cost, it's first come, first served).

Refugio El Padrino HOSTEL $
(☎621136; Costanera 276; dm CH$10,000) Friendly and conducive to meeting others,

this clean, self-service hostel offers small dorm rooms, located right on the Beagle Channel.

Hotel Lakutaia HOTEL $$$
(☎621733; www.lakutaia.cl; s/d/t US$200/250/300) About 3km east of town heading toward the airport, this modern full-service lodge will arrange transportation from Punta Arenas, and can organize day hikes to the Dientes de Navarino circuit and trips to Cape Horn. The library contains interesting history and nature references. Its only disadvantage is its isolation; you might leave without getting much of a feel for the quirky town.

Lunch and dinner are also available.

La Picada del Castor SANDWICHES $
(Plaza de Ancla; mains CH$4000-6000; ⏲10am-10pm Mon-Sat) A serviceable, plain restaurant serving huge sandwiches and platters of fries at low-lit booths.

★ **La Picada de los Veleros** CHILEAN $$
(☎098-333248, 621118; Piloto Pardo 260; meals CH$6000-11,000; ⏲sporadic hr) Wonderful family-style dinners are served to a menagerie of travelers, visiting workers and whoever makes a reservation. A bottle of wine is always welcome on the table.

Drinking

Club de Yates Micalvi BAR
(⏲late Sep-May) As watering holes go, this may be like no other. A grounded German cargo boat, the *Micalvi* was declared a regional naval museum in 1976 but found infinitely better use as a floating bar, frequented by navy men and yachties.

Information

Near the main roundabout, the Centro Comercial contains the post office, internet access, Aerovías DAP and call centers. ATM, money exchange (US cash only, US$100 minimum) and Visa cash advances are possible at Banco de Chile.

Sernatur (☎621011; O'Higgins 165; ⏲8am-1pm & 2-5pm Mon-Fri) Tourist information, including printouts of a hiking map for the Dientes de Navarino circuit. It's located in the Municipalidad.

Turismo Shila (☎7897-2005; www.turismoshila.cl; O'Higgins 220) With friendly service, offers local guides for trekking and fishing, camping rentals and GPS maps.

Turismo SIM (☎621150; www.simltd.com; Margaño 168) Expert sailors specializing in Cape Horn, the Cordillera Darwin, Isla Navarino, South Georgia Island and the Antarctic Peninsula.

Getting There & Away

Puerto Williams is accessible by plane or boat.

Aerovías DAP (☎621051; www.aeroviasdap.cl; Plaza de Ancla s/n) Flies to Punta Arenas Wednesday through Saturday and Monday from November to March, with fewer winter options. Often passengers are wait-listed until the company has enough bookings to run a flight; the practice can be frustrating for visitors with little extra time to spare. Note luggage restrictions when you purchase your ticket. DAP flights to Antarctica may make a brief stopover here.

Transbordador Austral Broom (☎728100; www.tabsa.cl) The ferry *Patagonia* sails between the Tres Puentes sector of Punta Arenas and Puerto Williams three or four times a month. Departs from Puerto Williams to Punta Arenas on Saturdays (reclining seat/bunk CH$93,000/130,000 including meals, 30 hours). In good weather there are good views on deck and the possibility of spotting dolphins or whales.

Turismo Internacional Onaisin Travels (Piratour; ☎mobile 963334679; www.piratour.net; one way US$130) With its main office in Ushuaia (called Piratours), this newcomer runs Zodiac boats to Ushuaia. Tickets include a 40-minute crossing plus an overland transfer from Puerto Navarino. Note: inclement weather often means cancellations.

TOLHUIN & LAGO FAGNANO

☎02901

Named for the Selk'nam word meaning 'like a heart,' Tolhuin (population 2000) is a lake town nestled in the center of Tierra del Fuego, 132km south of Río Grande and 104km northeast of Ushuaia via smooth asphalt. Muddy streets and clearcut forests mark this fast-growing frontier town on the eastern shore of Lago Fagnano, also known as Lago Kami. Lago Fagnano, with low-key horseback riding, mountain biking, boating and fishing, is worth checking out as a tranquil lake spot.

Shared with Chile, the glacial-formed Lago Fagnano offers 117km of beaches, with most of its shoreline remote and roadless. Plans to create road access from Chile and put a catamaran here are developing.

◎ Sights

Museo Historico Kami MUSEUM
(tdf@gmail.com; Lago Fagnano s/n; ⊙1-8pm Tue-Sun) **FREE** If you make one stop in Tolhuin, check out this museum, especially worthwhile for Spanish speakers. Don't be shy to ask for a tour. A former 1920s police post, the little house is now dedicated to regional history, starting with the indigenous Selknam people. One exhibit documents community members' stories of the still-recent pioneer times. It's located next to Camping Hain, on Lago Fagnano.

🛏 Sleeping & Eating

Camping Hain CAMPGROUND **$**
(☑02964-15-603606; Lago Fagnano; campsite per person AR$50, 3-/6-person refugio AR$300/600) Located on Lago Fagnano, with hot showers, grassy sites with wooden windbreaks, a huge barbecue pit and a *fogon* (sheltered fire pit and kitchen area).

Hostería Ruta Al Sur HOTEL **$$**
(☑492278; www.rutalsur.com.ar; RN3, Km2954; d AR$460; ⊙mid-Oct–Apr; @🛜) Considering it's on the side of the main road, this lovely lodge surrounded by old beech trees is a bit of a surprise. So is the uneven service. Confirm the rates in advance since you may be charged more as a foreigner (to be fair, it has rates for Tierra del Fuego residents and non-residents). Rooms are sparkling and there is a sprawling living room and restaurant serving a basic breakfast.

Panadería La Unión BAKERY **$**
(☑492202; www.panaderialaunion.com.ar; Jeujepen 450, Tolhuin; snacks AR$9; ⊙24hr) First-rate *facturas* (pastries) and second-rate Nescafé cappuccinos keep this roadside attraction hopping. You may or may not recognize the Argentine celebrities gracing the walls (hint: the men are aging rock stars, the women surgically enhanced). Buses break here to pick up passengers and hot water for *mate* (a bitter ritual tea).

ⓘ Information

Tolhuin's **tourist office** (☑492125, 492380; www.tierradelfuego.org.ar/tolhuin; Av de los Shelknam 80; ⊙8am-10pm Mon-Fri), behind the gas station, has information on hiking, horseback-riding tours and gear rentals. Those coming from Ushuaia might get more-complete info from Ushuaia's tourist office. **Banco de Tierra del Fuego** (Menkiol s/n) has an ATM.

ⓘ Getting There & Away

Throughout the day, buses and minivans passing along RN3 (often already full in high season) stop at Panadería La Union en route to Ushuaia or Río Grande (AR$100).

RÍO GRANDE

☑02964 / POP 70,042
A monster trout sculpture at the entrance to town announces the de facto fly-fishing capital of Tierra del Fuego, with world-class blue-ribbon angling for its colossal sea-run trout. But nonfishers will likely stay in wind-swept Río Grande for a few hours, before hopping on a bus to Ushuaia, 230km southwest.

As the sheep stations of wool baron José Menéndez developed, Río Grande grew as a makeshift service town. In 1893 the Salesian order, under the guidance of Monseñor Fagnano, set up a mission in an unsuccessful attempt to shelter the Selk'nam from the growing infringement. As a petroleum service center, the town has an industrial feel: even the public art looks like giant, grim tinker toys. Geared to the business traveler, it's also pricey for visitors. Duty-free status, meant to foster local development, has brought in electronics manufacturing plants and wholesale appliance stores. During the Falklands War (Guerra de las Malvinas) the military played an important role here; memorials pay tribute to fallen soldiers.

Catering to high-end anglers, **Posada de los Sauces** (☑432895; www.posadadelossauces.com.ar; Elcano 839; d $650; @🛜) fosters a lodge atmosphere, with fresh scents and woodsy accents. Opposite Casino Status, **Hotel Villa** (☑424998; hotelvillarg@hotmail.com; Av San Martín 281; d/tr AR$495/570; @🛜) has a popular restaurant, and a dozen spacious and stylish rooms. Hosting both ladies having tea and cake, and boys at the varnished bar downing beer and burgers, **Tante Sara** (Belgrano 402; mains AR$60-120) serves good cafe food, though service can be sluggish.

Most visitor services are along Avs San Martín and Belgrano. For tourist information, visit **Instituto Fueguino de Turismo** (Infuetur; ☑426805; www.tierradelfuego.org.ar; Av Belgrano 319; ⊙9am-9pm) on the south side of the plaza or the **Municipal Tourist Kiosk** (☑431324; turismo@riogrande.gob.ar; ⊙9am-8pm), a helpful kiosk on the plaza, with maps, *estancia* brochures and fishing details. **Mariani Travel** (☎426010; mariani@marianitravel.com.ar; Rosales 281) books flights and represents nearby *estancias*.

Getting There & Away

The **airport** (☎420699; off RN3) is a short taxi ride from town. **Aerolíneas Argentinas** (☎424467) flies daily to Buenos Aires (one way from AR$1877). **LADE** (☎422968; Lasserre 445) flies a couple of times weekly to Río Gallegos, El Calafate and Buenos Aires.

The following bus companies depart from **Terminal Fuegina** (Finocchio 1194):

Bus Sur (☎420997; www.bus-sur.cl; ticket office 25 de Mayo 712) Buses to Ushuaia, Punta Arenas and Puerto Natales, Chile, three times weekly at 5:30am, connecting with Montiel.

Buses Pacheco (☎421554) Buses to Punta Arenas three times weekly at 10am.

Lider (☎424-2000, 420003; www.lidertdf.com.ar; Moreno 635) Best option for Ushuaia and Tolhuin is this door-to-door minivan service, with several daily departures. Call to reserve.

Montiel (☎420997; 25 de Mayo 712) Buses to Ushuaia and Tolhuin.

Taqsa/Marga (☎434316) Buses to Ushuaia via Tolhuin.

Tecni-Austral (☎434316; ticket office Moyano 516) Buses to Ushuaia via Tolhuin three times weekly at 8:30am; to Río Gallegos and Punta Arenas three times weekly.

BUSES FROM RÍO GRANDE

DESTINATION	COST (AR$)	DURATION (HR)
Punta Arenas, Chile	280-370	9
Río Gallegos	355	8
Tolhuin	60	2
Ushuaia	100	4

ESTANCIAS AROUND RÍO GRANDE

Much of Tierra del Fuego was once the sprawling backyard of wool baron José Menéndez. His first *estancia* – La Primera Argentina (1897), now known as **Estancia José Menéndez**, 20km southwest of Río Grande via RN3 and RC-b – covered 1600 sq km, with more than 140,000 head of sheep. His second and most treasured venture was La Segunda Argentina, totaling 1500 sq km. Later renamed **Estancia María Behety** (☎in Buenos Aires 011-4331-5061; www.maribety.com.ar; 1 week per person US$7500; ⏱Dec-Apr) after his wife, it's still a working ranch, 17km west of Río Grande via RC-c. Besides boasting the world's largest shearing shed, it is a highly exclusive lodge, catering to elite anglers eager to fish some of the world's largest brown sea trout, which grow up to 16kg. Two lodges accommodate up to 18 fly-fishers, the full quota for the river.

Several *estancias* have opened to small-scale tourism, offering a unique chance to learn about the region's history and enjoy its magic. Reserve as far in advance as possible.

The lauded **Estancia Las Hijas** (☎02901-15-617022, 02901-15-554462; www.estancialashijas.com.ar; RP16; per person overnight or day trip US$85, day trip incl transport $290) offers small-scale family visits for small groups (inquire ahead since different parties can combine). They are known around these parts as 'locos divinos' (crazy but fun). After horseback riding, rounding sheep and barbecues, guests stay in basic lodgings with shared bathrooms. It's located 33km north of Tolhuin, 7km in on the dirt road RP16 (formerly 'G'). If you go with transportation included (from Ushuaia or Río Grande), there's must be a minimum of two people. A stay includes dinner, breakfast and activities.

The rustic and charismatic **Estancia Rolito** (☎02901-432419, 02901-437351; www.tierradelfuego.org.ar/rolito; RC-a, Km14; r per person half-/full board US$155/235) is very Argentine and very inviting. Guests rave about the hikes through ñire and lenga forest. Day trips from Ushuaia (with Turismo de Campo) stop by for lunch or dinner and activities. Rates are based on double occupancy. Rolito is 100km from Río Grande and 150km from Ushuaia.

PORVENIR (CHILE)

If you want a slice of home-baked Fuegian life, this is it. Most visitors come on a quick day trip from Punta Arenas tainted by seasickness. But spending a night in this rustic village of metal-clad Victorian houses affords you an opportunity to explore the nearby bays and countryside and absorb a little of the local life; bird watchers can admire the nearby king penguins and lively populations of cormorants, geese and seabirds. While known for inaccessibility (there's no bus route here), the government is investing in completing roads through the southern

THE TROUT ATLAS

You know a place takes fishing seriously when the tourism board posts a trout map online (www.tierradelfuego.org.ar/funcardio/trutamap.jpg). Hollywood stars, heads of state and former US presidents all flock to desolate stretches around Río Grande with dreams of the big one. Usually they are in luck.

Rivers around Río Grande were stocked in the 1930s with brown, rainbow and brook trout. It's now one of the world's best sea-run trout-fishing areas, with some local specimens weighing in at 15kg. Rainbow trout can reach 9kg.

Fishing excursions are mostly organized through outside agents, many in the USA. 'Public' fishing rivers, on which trips can be organized, include the Fuego, Menéndez, Candelaria, Ewan and MacLennan. Many of the more elite angling trips are lodged in *estancias* (ranches) with exclusive use of some of the best rivers.

There are two types of fishing licenses. License 1 is valid throughout the province, except in Parque Nacional Tierra del Fuego. Contact **Asociación Caza y Pesca** (☎02901-422423; cazapescaush@infovia.com.ar; Maipú 822) in Ushuaia, or **Club de Pesca John Goodall** (☎02964-15-503074; http://clubdepescatdf.blogspot.com; Ricardo Rojas 606) in Río Grande. License 2 is valid for Parque Nacional Tierra del Fuego and Patagonia. Contact the National Parks office (p503) in Ushuaia or find more information on sport fishing in Argentina through the online portal **Pesca Argentina** (www.pescaargentina.com.ar). Other useful information:

Flies Rubber legs and woolly buggers.

License fees AR$180 per day or AR$720 per season, depending on where you fish.

Limit One fish per person per day, catch and release.

Methods Spinning and fly casting; no night fishing.

Season November 1 to April 15, with catch-and-release restrictions from April 1 to April 15.

extension of Chilean Tierra del Fuego, which will open up a whole untouched wilderness to visitors.

Porvenir experienced waves of immigration, many from Croatia, when gold was discovered in 1879. Sheep *estancias* provided more reliable work, attracting droves of Chileans from the island of Chiloé, who also came for fishing work. Today's population is a unique combination of the two.

Sights

Museo de Tierra del Fuego MUSEUM
(☎581800; www.museoporvenir.cl; Zavattaro 402; admission CH$500; ⏲8am-5pm Mon-Thu, 8am-4pm Fri, 10:30am-1:30pm & 3-5pm Sat & Sun) On the Plaza de Armas, this intriguing museum has some unexpected materials, including Selk'nam skulls and mummies, musical instruments used by the mission inhabitants on Isla Dawson and an exhibit on early Chilean cinematography.

Tours

Though little-known as a wildlife-watching destination, Chilean Tierra del Fuego has abundant marine and bird life, which includes Peale's dolphins around Bahía Chilota and king penguins, found seasonally in Bahía Inútil. This new king penguin colony has created quite a stir. As of yet, there's little procedure in place to protect the penguins from over-visitation. Please make your visit with a reputable agency, give the penguins ample berth and respect the nesting season.

Gold-panning, horseback riding and 4WD tours can be arranged through the tourist office.

Far South Expeditions OUTDOORS
(www.fsexpeditions.com; 4-passenger tours CH$80,000) Offers transport to the king penguin colony or guided naturalist-run tours, with packages from Punta Arenas available.

Sleeping & Eating

★**Hostería Yendegaia** B&B $$
(☎581919; www.hosteriayendegaia.com; Croacia 702; s/d/tr CH$25,000/40,000/50,000; 📶) Everything a B&B should be, with naturalist books (some authored by the owner) to browse, abundant breakfast, views of the

OFF THE BEATEN TRACK

LAGO DESEADO & BEYOND

South of Camerón, access to Chilean Tierra del Fuego once petered out into stark, roadless wilderness and the rugged Cordillera Darwin. But the Ministry of Public Works is working hard to create access to these southern points and develop future tourism destinations.

Projects are underway to build a road to the new Parque Nacional Yendegaia, on the island's southern shore. It currently reaches Seno Almirantazgo in the Cordillera Darwin.

For now, there's at least one worthy destination on the road. **Lodge Deseado** (☎91652564; www.lodgedeseado.cl; 2-/3-person cabin CH$135,000/160,000), on the lake of the same name, marks a cozy spot to reel in wild trout, kick back in cool modern cabins and swap stories with the engaging owner, Ricardo. Transportation from Punta Arenas is available. Week-long packages visit major nature sights throughout Tierra del Fuego (including the king penguin colony).

A 4WD is required for this remote region. A road now connects to the Argentine side, with an official border crossing at mountain pass Río Bellavista (open only mid-December through March).

strait and spacious rooms with thick down duvets. This historic Magellanic home (the first lodging in Porvenir) has been lovingly restored, and its family of hosts are helpful. Its tour agency, Far South Expeditions, runs naturalist-led trips.

Hotel Rosas GUESTHOUSE $$
(☎580088; hotelrosas@chile.com; Philippi 296; s/d CH$22,000/33,000; 📶) Eleven clean and pleasant rooms offer heating and cable TV; some have wonderful views. Alberto, the owner, knows heaps about the region and arranges tours to Circuito del Loro, a historical mining site. The **restaurant** (daily special CH$5000), serves fresh seafood and more, and gets crowded at meal times.

La Chispa CAFE $
(☎580054; Señoret 202; plato del día CH$4000) Located in an old firehouse packed with locals, who come for salmon dinners, lamb and potatoes, and other home-cooked fare. It's a couple of blocks uphill from the water.

Club Croata SEAFOOD $$
(☎580053; Señoret 542; mains CH$4000-10,000; ⏲11am-4pm & 7-10:30pm Tue-Sun) Formal to the verge of stuffy, this restaurant serves good seafood at reasonable prices, in addition to Croat specialties – pork chops with *chucrut* (sauerkraut). The pub is open to 3am.

Information

Banco de Estado (cnr Philippi & Croacia) Has a 24-hour ATM.

Hospital (☎580034; Wood, btwn Señoret & Guerrero)

Post Office (Philippi 176) Faces Plaza de Armas.

Tourist Office (☎580098, 580094; www.muniporvenir.cl; Zavattaro 434; ⏲9am-5pm Mon-Fri, 11am-5pm Sat & Sun) Information is also available at the handicrafts shop on the *costanera* (seaside road) between Philippi and Schythe.

Getting There & Away

A good gravel road runs east along Bahía Inútil to the Argentine border at San Sebastián; allow about four hours. From San Sebastián (where there's gas and a motel), northbound motorists should avoid the heavily traveled and rutted truck route directly north and instead take the route from Onaisín to the petroleum company town of Cerro Sombrero, en route to the crossing of the Strait of Magellan at Punta Delgada–Puerto Espora.

Aerovías DAP (☎616100; www.aeroviasdap.cl; O'Higgins 891) Flies to Punta Arenas (CH$29,000, 15 minutes) Monday to Saturday from November to March, with fewer flights in low season. Also provides local transfer (CH$2000).

Transbordador Austral Broom (☎580089; www.tabsa.cl) Operates the car and passenger ferry *Crux Australis* to/from Punta Arenas (per person/vehicle CH$5800/37,000, 2½ to four hours). It usually leaves at 9am but has some afternoon departures; check the current online schedule. The bus to the ferry terminal (CH$500), 5km away, departs from the waterfront kiosk an hour before the ferry's departure.

Uruguay

Includes ➡

Best Places to Eat

➡ Café Picasso (p548)

➡ Estrecho (p526)

➡ Bodega y Granja Narbona (p541)

Best Places to Stay

➡ Hostel Estancia El Galope (p533)

➡ Estancia La Sirena (p541)

➡ El Diablo Tranquilo (p562)

➡ Guardia del Monte (p561)

➡ Termas San Nicanor (p545)

Why Go?

Wedged like a grape between Brazil's gargantuan thumb and Argentina's long forefinger, Uruguay has always been something of an underdog. Yet after two centuries living in the shadow of its neighbors, one of South America's smallest countries is finally getting a little well-deserved recognition. Progressive, stable, safe and culturally sophisticated, Uruguay offers visitors opportunities to experience everyday 'not-made-for-tourists' moments, whether caught in a cow-and-gaucho traffic jam on a dirt road to nowhere or strolling with *mate*-toting locals along Montevideo's beachfront.

Short-term visitors will find plenty to keep them busy in cosmopolitan Montevideo, picturesque Colonia and party-till-you-drop Punta del Este. But it pays to dig deeper. Go wildlife-watching along the Atlantic coast, hot-spring-hopping up the Río Uruguay, or horseback riding under the big sky of Uruguay's interior, where vast fields spread out like oceans.

When to Go

Montevideo

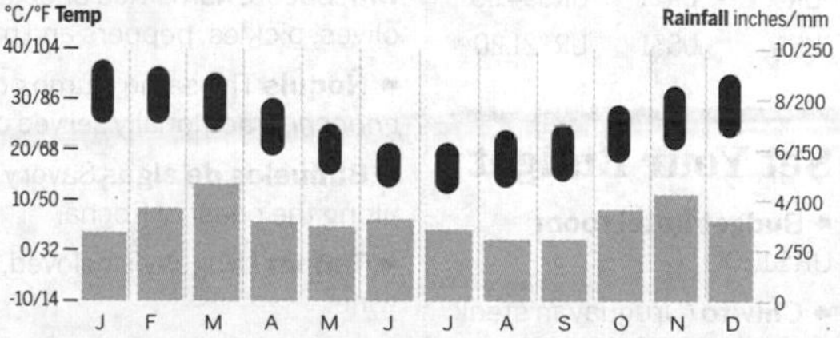

Feb Street theater and drumming consume Montevideo during Carnaval celebrations.

Mar Tacuarembó's gaucho festival, plus lower prices on the still-sunny Atlantic coast.

Oct Soak in Salto's hot springs, or channel Carlos Gardel at Montevideo's tango festival.

AT A GLANCE

- **Currency** Uruguayan peso (UR$)
- **Language** Spanish
- **Money** ATMs widespread; credit cards widely accepted
- **Visas** Not required for nationals of Western Europe, Australia, USA, Canada or New Zealand

Fast Facts

- **Area** 176,215 sq km
- **Population** 3.3 million
- **Capital** Montevideo
- **Emergency** 911
- **Telephone country code** 598

Exchange Rates

Argentina	AR$1	UR$3.28
Australia	A$1	UR$18.90
Brazil	R$1	UR$10.14
Canada	C$1	UR$19.95
Euro zone	€1	UR$29.25
Japan	¥100	UR$20.25
New Zealand	NZ$1	UR$17.35
UK	UK£1	UR$34.95
USA	US$1	UR$21.20

Set Your Budget

- **Budget hotel room** UR$1200
- **Chivito** (Uruguayan steak sandwich) UR$110-210
- **Montevideo bus ride** UR$21
- **1L bottle of local beer** UR$120
- **Coffee** UR$65

Itineraries

Just popping over from Buenos Aires for a couple of days? Don't overdo it! Focus your energy on the easygoing, picturesque historical river-port of Colonia or the urban attractions of Montevideo, both an easy ferry ride from the Argentine capital.

If you've got a week up your sleeve, continue north along the Atlantic coast and sample a few of Uruguay's best beaches: the early-20th-century resort of Piriápolis, glitzy Punta del Este, isolated Cabo Polonio, surfer-friendly La Paloma and La Pedrera, or the relaxed beach-party town of Punta del Diablo. Alternatively, follow the Río Uruguay upstream towards Iguazú Falls via the wineries of Carmelo, the quirky industrial museum at Fray Bentos and the hot springs of Salto.

With a whole two weeks to spare, get out and explore Uruguay's interior, ride horses on a tourist *estancia* (ranch) and settle into a slower-paced lifestyle under the wide open skies of Tacuarembó, Quebrada de los Cuervos or Villa Serrana.

GETTING THERE & AWAY

Most visitors cross by ferry from Buenos Aires, arriving in Colonia, Montevideo or Carmelo. A few airlines, including American and Air Europa, offer direct international flights to Montevideo; several others connect through Buenos Aires or São Paulo. Land links include three international bridges across the Río Uruguay to Argentina, and six main border crossings into Brazil.

Essential Food & Drink

- **Asado** Uruguay's national gastronomic obsession, a mixed grill cooked over a wood fire, featuring various cuts of beef and pork, chorizo, *morcilla* (blood sausage) and more.
- **Chivito** A cholesterol bomb of a steak sandwich piled high with bacon, ham, fried or boiled egg, cheese, lettuce, tomato, olives, pickles, peppers and mayonnaise.
- **Ñoquis** The same plump potato dumplings the Italians call *gnocchi*, traditionally served on the 29th of the month.
- **Buñuelos de algas** Savory seaweed fritters, a specialty along the coast of Rocha.
- **Tannat** Uruguay's beloved, internationally acclaimed red wine.
- **Grappamiel** Strong Italian-style grappa (grape brandy), sweetened and mellowed with honey.

MONTEVIDEO

POP 1.3 MILLION

The nation's capital and home to nearly half of Uruguay's population, Montevideo is a vibrant, eclectic place with a rich cultural life. Stretching 20km from east to west, the city wears many faces, from its industrial port to the exclusive beachside suburb of Carrasco near the airport. In the historic downtown business district, art deco and neoclassical buildings jostle for space alongside grimy, worn-out skyscrapers that appear airlifted from Havana or Ceauşescu's Romania, while to the southeast the shopping malls and modern high-rises of beach communities such as Punta Carretas and Pocitos bear more resemblance to Miami or Copacabana. Music, theater and the arts are alive and well here – from elegant older theaters and cozy little tango bars to modern beachfront discos – and there's a strong international flavor, thanks to the many foreign cultural centers and Montevideo's status as administrative headquarters for Mercosur, South America's leading trading bloc.

Montevideo lies almost directly across the Río de la Plata from Buenos Aires. For many visitors, the most intriguing area is the Ciudad Vieja, the formerly walled colonial grid straddling the western tip of a peninsula between the sheltered port and the wide-open river. Just east of the old town gate, the Centro (downtown) begins at Plaza Independencia, surrounded by historic buildings of the republican era. Av 18 de Julio, downtown Montevideo's commercial thoroughfare, runs east past Plaza del Entrevero, Plaza Cagancha and the Intendencia (town hall) towards Tres Cruces bus terminal. There it changes name to Av Italia and continues east towards Carrasco International Airport and the Interbalnearia highway to Punta del Este.

Westward across the harbor, 132m Cerro de Montevideo was a landmark for early navigators and still offers outstanding views of the city. Eastward, the Rambla hugs Montevideo's scenic waterfront, snaking past attractive Parque Rodó and through a series of sprawling residential beach suburbs – Punta Carretas, Pocitos, Buceo and Carrasco – that are very popular with the capital's residents in summer and on evenings and weekends.

Sights

Note that many Montevideo museums are known by their acronyms. Most exhibits are in Spanish only.

Ciudad Vieja

★Mercado del Puerto MARKET

(Pérez Castellano) No visitor should miss Montevideo's old port market building, at the Atlantic end of Pérez Castellano, whose impressive wrought-iron superstructure shelters a gaggle of bustling *parrillas* (steak restaurants). On weekend afternoons in particular, it's a lively, colorful place where the city's artists, craftspeople and street musicians hang out.

Plaza Matriz PLAZA

Also known as Plaza Constitución, this leafy plaza was the heart of colonial Montevideo. On its east side stands the **Cabildo** (finished in 1812), a neoclassical stone structure that contains the **Museo y Archivo Histórico Municipal** (Municipal Archive & Historical Museum; ☎2915-9685; www.cabildo.montevideo.gub.uy; Juan Carlos Gómez 1362; ⏲noon-5:45pm Mon-Fri, 10am-4pm Sat) FREE, a historical museum displaying 18th-century paintings of Montevideo and other artifacts from the city's early days. Opposite the Cabildo is the **Iglesia Matriz** (Plaza Matriz), Montevideo's oldest public building. It was completed in 1799.

★Teatro Solís THEATER

(☎1950-3323; www.teatrosolis.org.uy; Buenos Aires 678) Just off Plaza Independencia, elegant Teatro Solís is Montevideo's premier performance space. First opened in 1856, and completely renovated during the past decade, it has superb acoustics. Regularly scheduled tours (Tuesday through Sunday) provide an opportunity to see the actual performance space without attending a show. Spanish-language tours are free on Wednesdays, UR$20 other days; English- and Portuguese-language tours cost UR$50.

Museo del Carnaval MUSEUM

(☎2916-5493; www.museodelcarnaval.org; Rambla 25 de Agosto 218; admission UR$65; ⏲11am-5pm Wed-Mon) This museum houses a wonderful collection of costumes, drums, masks, recordings and photos documenting the 100-plus-year history of Montevideo's Carnaval. Behind the museum are bleachers where spectators can view performances during the summer months. The museum

Uruguay Highlights

1. Dance to a different drummer during Montevideo's month-long **Carnaval** (p531)
2. Catch a wave or a late-night beach party along the untamed shoreline at **Punta del Diablo** (p561)
3. Soak your weary traveling muscles in the thermal baths near **Salto** (p544)
4. Get way off the beaten track in the rural nature preserves of **Quebrada de los Cuervos** and **Valle del Lunarejo** (p562)
5. Sunbathe on the 18th-century town wall, or wander the leafy plazas and cobbled streets of picturesque **Colonia del Sacramento** (p535)
6. Lose yourself in the sand dunes and survey the sea lions from atop the lighthouse at **Cabo Polonio** (p559)
7. Tour the ghostly remains of Uruguay's most historic meat-processing factory, a 2014 Unesco World Heritage site candidate, in **Fray Bentos** (p542)
8. Hit the beaches by day and the clubs by night in glitzy **Punta del Este** (p549)

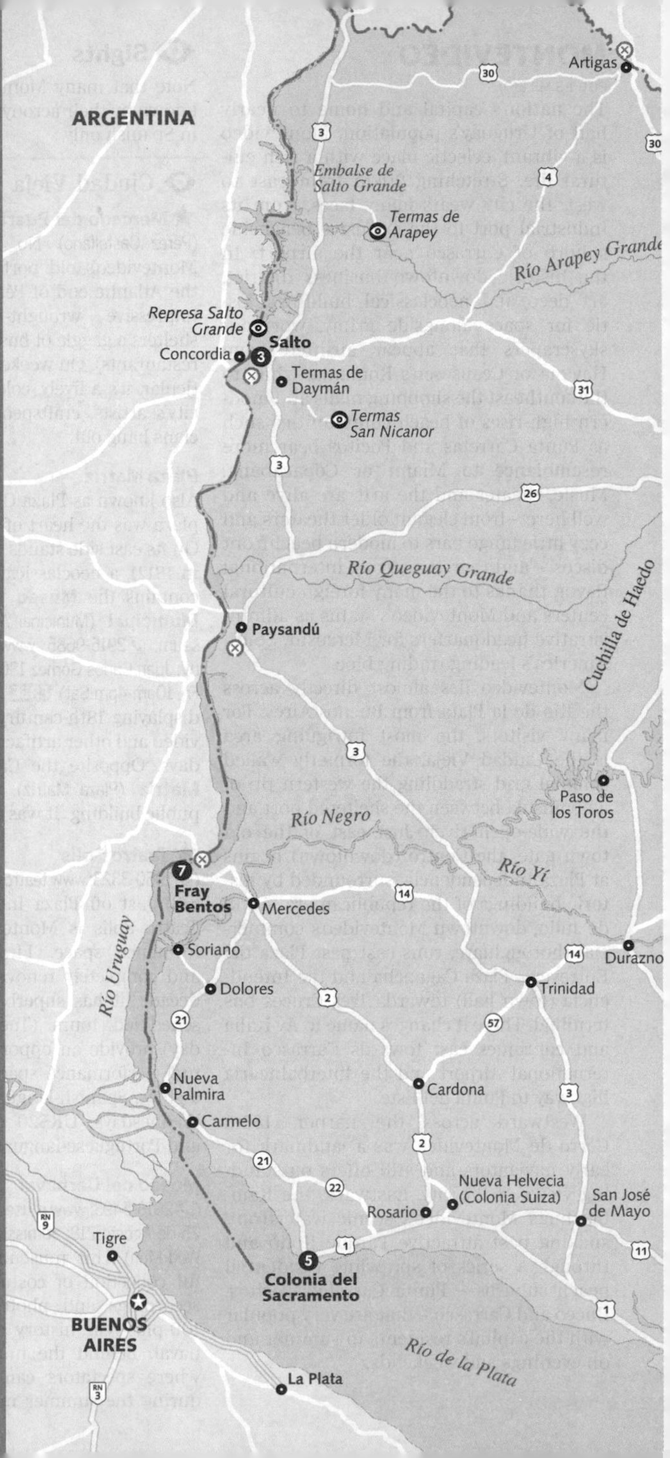

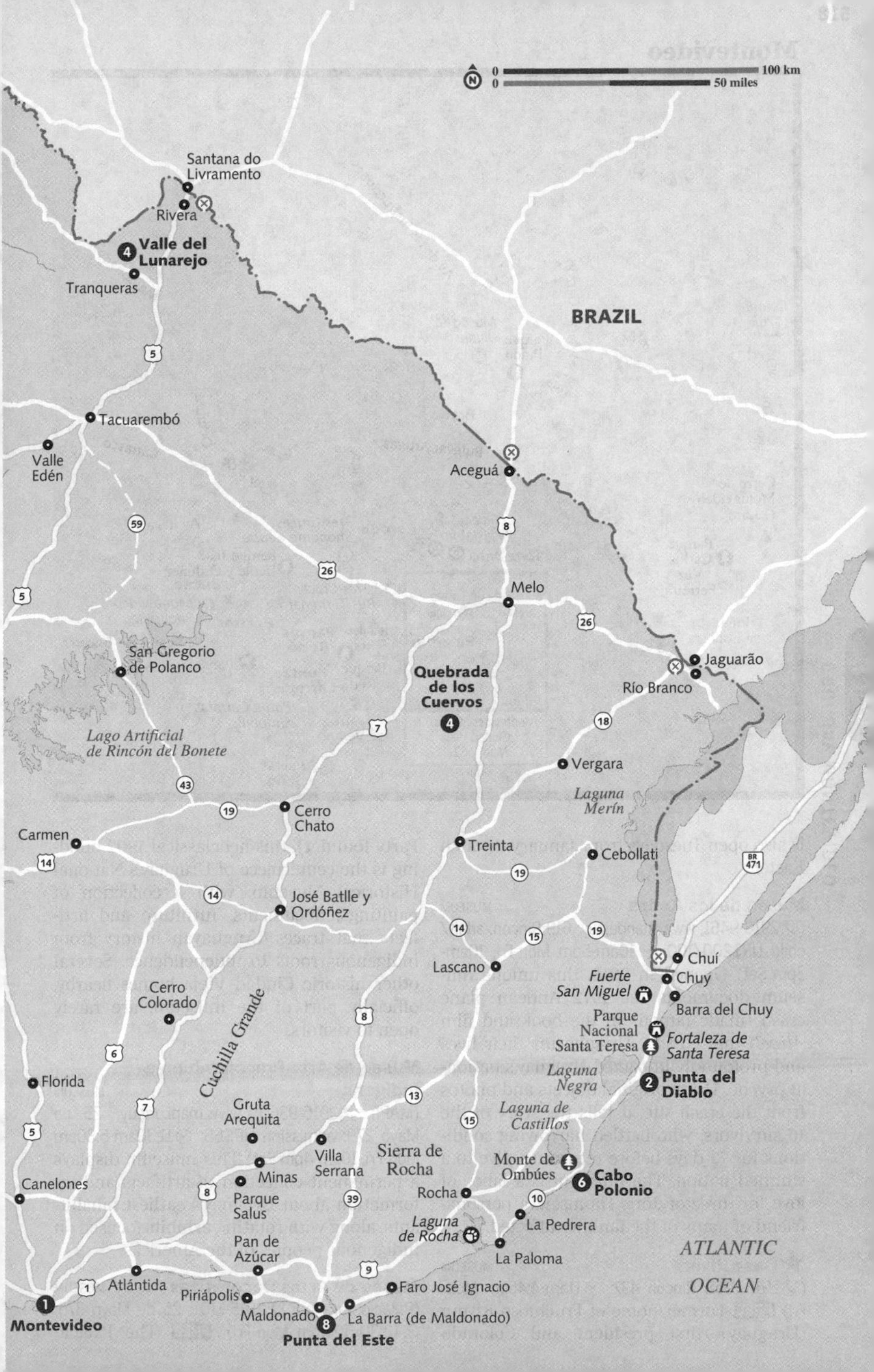
0
100 km
0
50 miles
BRAZIL
Santana do Livramento
Rivera
4 Valle del Lunarejo
Tranqueras
5
Tacuarembó
Valle Edén
59
5
26
Aceguá
8
Melo
26
Jaguarão
Río Branco
San Gregorio de Polanco
Quebrada de los Cuervos
4
Lago Artificial de Rincón del Bonete
7
18
Vergara
Laguna Merín
43
19
Cerro Chato
Carmen
14
Treinta
Cebollati
BR 471
19
14
José Batlle y Ordóñez
14
15
19
Chuí
Lascano
Chuy
Fuerte San Miguel
Barra del Chuy
Parque Nacional Santa Teresa
Fortaleza de Santa Teresa
Cerro Colorado
8
Cuchilla Grande
6
Laguna Negra
2 Punta del Diablo
Florida
7
13
Laguna de Castillos
15
Gruta Arequita
5
Villa Serrana
Sierra de Rocha
Monte de Ombúes
6 Cabo Polonio
Minas
Canelones
8
Parque Salus
39
Rocha
10
La Pedrera
Laguna de Rocha
La Paloma
ATLANTIC
Pan de Azúcar
9
OCEAN
1
Atlántida
Faro José Ignacio
Piriápolis
1 Montevideo
Maldonado
8 Punta del Este
La Barra (de Maldonado)

Montevideo

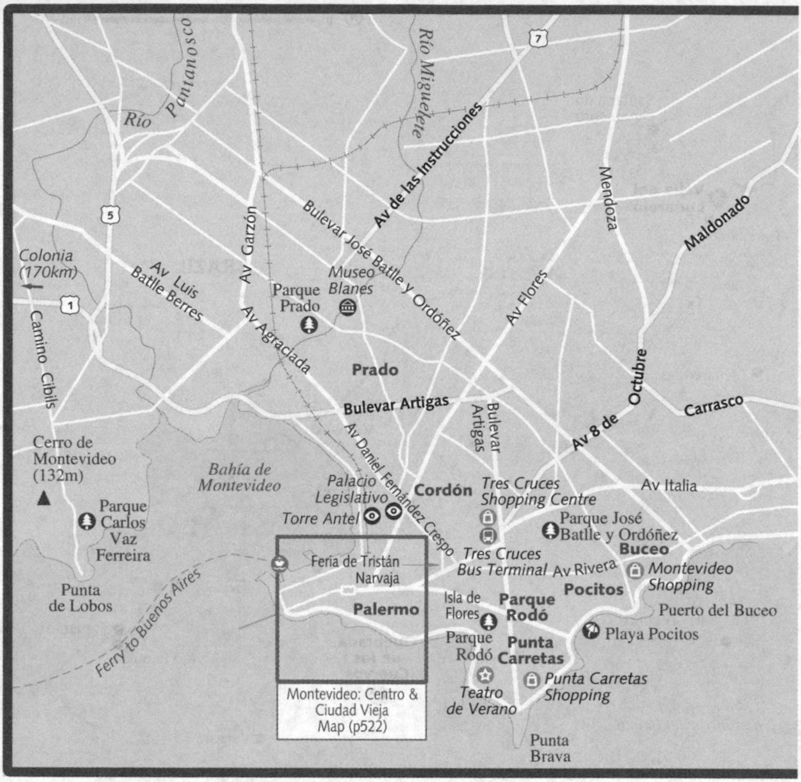

is also open Tuesdays from January through Easter.

Museo de los Andes MUSEUM
(2916-9461; www.mandes.uy; 619 Rincón; adult/child UR$200/100; 10am-5pm Mon-Fri, 10am-3pm Sat) Opened in 2013, this unique museum documents the 1972 Andean plane crash (made famous in the book and film *Alive!*) that cost 29 Uruguayans their lives and profoundly impacted Uruguay's national psyche. Using original objects and photos from the crash site, it tells the story of the 16 survivors, who battled harrowing conditions for 72 days before returning alive to a stunned nation. The museum is a labor of love for director Jörg Thomsen, a personal friend of many of the families affected.

★**Casa Rivera** MUSEUM
(2915-1051; Rincón 437; 11am-4:45pm Mon-Fri) FREE Former home of Fructuoso Rivera (Uruguay's first president and Colorado Party founder), this neoclassical 1802 building is the centerpiece of Uruguay's National Historical Museum, with a collection of paintings, documents, furniture and artifacts that traces Uruguayan history from indigenous roots to independence. Several other historic Ciudad Vieja homes nearby, officially part of the museum, are rarely open to visitors.

Museo de Arte Precolombino e Indígena MUSEUM
(MAPI; 2916-9360; www.mapi.org.uy; 25 de Mayo 279; admission UR$65; 11:30am-5:30pm Mon-Fri, 10am-4pm Sat) This museum displays a permanent collection of artifacts and information about Uruguay's earliest inhabitants, along with rotating exhibits focused on indigenous peoples of the Americas.

Museo de Artes Decorativas MUSEUM
(Palacio Taranco; 2915-1101; 25 de Mayo 376; 12:30-5:30pm Mon-Fri) FREE The Palacio

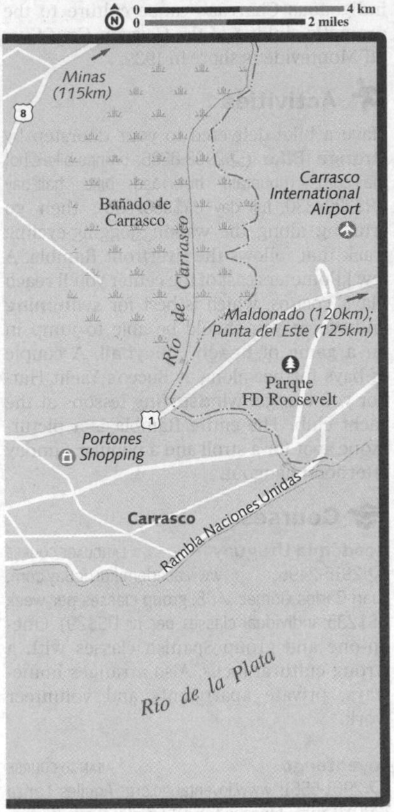

Taranco, a wealthy 1910 merchant's residence designed by famous French architects Charles Girault and Jules Chifflot, is filled with ornate period furnishings and paintings by European artists including Ghirlandaio and Goya.

Museo Figari MUSEUM

(☎2915-7065; www.museofigari.gub.uy; Juan Carlos Gómez 1427; ⏰1-6pm Tue-Fri, 10am-2pm Sat) FREE One of Ciudad Vieja's newest museums is devoted to Uruguayan painter Pedro Figari, whose landscapes and portraits masterfully convey a sense of Uruguayan life in the late 19th and early 20th centuries.

Museo Gurvich MUSEUM

(www.museogurvich.org; Ituzaingó 1377; admission UR$65; ⏰10am-6pm Mon-Fri, 11am-3pm Sat) On Ciudad Vieja's main square, this museum is devoted to Lithuanian-born Constructivist artist José Gurvich (1927–74), who lived most of his life in Uruguay.

Museo Torres García MUSEUM

(☎2916-2663; www.torresgarcia.org.uy; Sarandí 683; admission UR$70; ⏰10am-6pm Mon-Sat) This museum showcases the work of 20th-century Uruguayan painter Joaquín Torres García, and has revolving exhibitions featuring other contemporary artists.

Centro

Plaza Independencia PLAZA

Montevideo's largest downtown plaza commemorates independence hero José Artigas with a 17m, 30-ton statue and the subterranean **Mausoleo de Artigas** (⏰9am-5pm), where an honor guard keeps 24-hour vigil over Artigas' remains. Other notable structures surrounding the plaza include the stone gateway **Puerta de la Ciudadela** (Plaza Independencia) (a lonely remnant of the colonial citadel demolished in 1833); the 19th-century **Palacio Estévez**; and the 26-story **Palacio Salvo**, once the continent's tallest building when it opened in 1927; it's a classic Montevideo landmark, but not open for tourist visits.

★ **Museo del Gaucho** MUSEUM

(☎2900-8764; Av 18 de Julio 998; ⏰10am-5pm Mon-Fri) FREE Housed in the ornate Palacio Heber, this museum displays a superb collection of historical gaucho artifacts, including horse gear, silver work, and *mates* and *bombillas* (metal straws with filters, used for drinking *mate*; a bitter ritual tea) in whimsical designs.

North of Centro

Museo Blanes MUSEUM

(☎2336-2248; blanes.montevideo.gub.uy; Av Millán 4015; ⏰12:15-5:45pm Tue-Sat, 2-7:30pm Sun) FREE Housed in an old mansion in the suburb of Prado, this museum shows the work of Uruguay's most famous painter, Juan Manuel Blanes.

Torre Antel TOWER

(☎2928-4417; Guatemala 1075; ⏰tours 3:30-5pm Mon, Wed & Fri, 10:30am-noon Tue & Thu) FREE For great views out across the city, take the elevator to the top of Montevideo's most dramatic modern skyscraper.

Palacio Legislativo HISTORIC BUILDING

(☎2924-1783; www.parlamento.gub.uy; Av Libertador General Lavalleja) Dating from 1908, and still playing host to Uruguay's Asamblea General (legislative branch), the three-story neoclassical Parliament building is also open for guided tours (UR$60) at 10:30am and 3pm Monday to Friday.

East of Centro

Espacio de Arte Contemporáneo GALLERY
(☎2929-2066; www.eac.gub.uy; Arenal Grande 1930; ⏲2-8pm Wed-Sat, 11am-5pm Sun) FREE This gallery makes thought-provoking use of the cells of a 19th-century prison, creating an avant-garde exhibit space for revolving exhibitions of contemporary art.

Museo del Fútbol MUSEUM
(☎2480-1259; Estadio Centenario, Av Ricaldoni s/n, Parque José Batlle y Ordóñez; admission UR$100; ⏲10am-5pm Mon-Fri) A must-see for any *fútbol* fan, this museum displays memorabilia from Uruguay's 1930 and 1950 World Cup wins. Visitors can also tour the stands.

Museo Nacional de Artes Visuales MUSEUM
(MNAV; ☎2711-6124; www.mnav.gub.uy; Giribaldi 2283; ⏲2-6:45pm Tue-Sun) FREE Uruguay's largest collection of paintings is housed here in Parque Rodó. The large rooms are graced with works by Blanes, Cúneo, Figari and Torres García.

La Rambla & Eastern Beaches

La Rambla, Montevideo's multikilometer coastal promenade, is one of the city's defining elements, connecting downtown to the eastern beach communities of Punta Carretas, Pocitos, Buceo and Carrasco. This is Montevideo's social hub on Sunday afternoons, when the place is packed with locals cradling thermoses of *mate* and mingling with friends.

Castillo Pittamiglio HISTORIC BUILDING
(☎2710-1089; www.castillopittamiglio.com; Rambla Gandhi 633; guided tours UR$80) On the Rambla between Punta Carretas and Pocitos is this eccentric legacy of local alchemist and architect, Humberto Pittamiglio. Its quirky facade alone is worth a look. Guided Spanish-language tours of the interior are available; see website for monthly schedules.

Museo Naval MUSEUM
(☎2622-1084; cnr Rambla Costanera & Av LA de Herrera; admission UR$60; ⏲9am-noon & 2-6pm Fri-Wed) Along the eastern waterfront in Buceo, this museum traces the role of boats and ships in Uruguayan history, from the indigenous Charrúa's canoe culture to the dramatic sinking of the German *Graf Spee* off Montevideo's shore in 1939.

Activities

Have a bike delivered to your doorstep by **Orange Bike** (☎2908-8286; orange.bike@hotmail.com; mountain bike/road bike half-day UR$220/330, full day UR$330/550), then go cruising along the walking-jogging-cycling track that follows the riverfront Rambla. A few kilometers east of the center you'll reach Playa Pocitos, which is best for **swimming** and where you should be able to jump in on a game of **beach volleyball**. A couple of bays further along at Buceo's Yacht Harbor you can get **windsurfing** lessons at the yacht club. The entire Rambla is a picturesque spot for a stroll and a popular Sunday afternoon hangout.

Courses

Academia Uruguay LANGUAGE COURSE
(☎2915-2496; www.academiauruguay.com; Juan Carlos Gómez 1408; group classes per week US$235, individual classes per hr US$29) One-on-one and group Spanish classes with a strong cultural focus. Also arranges homestays, private apartments and volunteer work.

Joventango TANGO COURSE
(☎2901-5561; www.joventango.org; Aquiles Lanza 1290) Tango classes for all levels, from beginner to expert.

Tours

Bus Turístico BUS TOUR
(www.busturisticomontevideo.com.uy; 24hr/48hr ticket UR$416/640; ⏲9am-5pm summer, 9:30am-3:30pm winter) Originating at Mercado del Puerto, this hop-on, hop-off double-decker tourist bus makes a nine-stop, 2½-hour circuit through Montevideo, with audio commentary in nine languages. Buses serve each stop approximately once an hour.

Festivals & Events

Much livelier than its Buenos Aires counterpart, Montevideo's **Carnaval,** held in late-summer is the city's cultural highlight of the year.

At Parque Prado, north of downtown, Semana Criolla festivities during **Semana Santa** (Holy Week) include displays of

DON'T MISS

MONTEVIDEO WEEKEND HIGHLIGHTS

Weekends are the time to enjoy several of Montevideo's quintessential experiences. Note that Ciudad Vieja, outside of Mercado del Puerto, is a virtual ghost town on Sundays, when businesses are closed and the pulse of local life moves east to the long Rambla waterfront.

Saturday morning Browse the antiques market on Plaza Matriz.

Saturday afternoon Discover your inner carnivore over lunch at Mercado del Puerto.

Saturday night Attend a performance at Teatro Solís or Sala Zitarrosa, sip *uvitas* (sweet wine drinks) and listen to live music at Baar Fun Fun, mingle with locals dancing tango at Mercado de la Abundancia or party all night at clubs like El Pony Pisador.

Sunday morning Explore the labyrinth of market stalls at Mercado de Tristán Narvaja.

Sunday afternoon Join the parade of *mate*-toting locals strolling the 20km-long beachfront Rambla.

Sunday evening Catch a pre-Carnaval drumming rehearsal on the streets of Palermo or Parque Rodó.

gaucho skills, *asados* (barbecues) and other such events.

In the last weekend of September or first weekend of October, Montevideo's museums, churches, and historic homes all open their doors free to the public during the **Días del Patrimonio** (National Heritage Days).

For 10 days in October, tango fills Montevideo's streets and performance halls during the **Festival del Tango**, organized by Joventango (p520).

Sleeping

Montevideo offers a smattering of boutique and luxury hotels, as well as a thriving hosteling scene, and a host of dependable, if somewhat faded, midrange hotels in the Centro area.

Ciudad Vieja

★Hotel Palacio HOTEL $
(☎2916-3612; www.hotelpalacio.com.uy; Bartolomé Mitre 1364; r without/with balcony US$47/54; ❄ 📶) If you can snag one of the two 6th-floor rooms at this ancient family-run hotel one block off Plaza Matriz, do it! Both feature air-conditioning and balconies with superb views of Ciudad Vieja's rooftops. The rest of the hotel also offers great value, with wood floors, antique furniture, a vintage elevator and old-school service reminiscent of a European pension.

El Viajero Hostel – Ciudad Vieja HOSTEL $
(☎2915-6192; www.elviajeromontevideo.com; Ituzaingó 1436; dm UR$310-380, d UR$1000-1260; @ 📶) Only a few steps away from the old city's abundant nightlife, this hostel has a homey, hip atmosphere, and an appealing layout on two upper floors of an older Ciudad Vieja building. There are separate kitchens and lounging areas on each level, a DVD library, roof deck, bikes for rent, city tours and a helpful bulletin board of cultural events.

Spléndido Hotel HOTEL $
(☎2916-4900; www.splendidohotel.com.uy; Bartolomé Mitre 1314; s with shared bathroom from US$38, d with shared/private bathroom from US$45/65; @ 📶) Faded and funky, the Spléndido offers decent value for budget travelers preferring privacy over a hostel-style party vibe. The better rooms have 5m-high ceilings and French doors opening to balconies, some overlooking Teatro Solís. Others are cramped and/or reeking of cigarette smoke; ask to see the options before you commit. Bars on the street below get extremely noisy on weekends.

★Casa Sarandí GUESTHOUSE $$
(☎2400-6460; www.casasarandi.com; Buenos Aires 558, 3rd fl; d US$79-89; 📶) One block south of Plaza Matriz, three attractive guest rooms in a vintage apartment share a guest kitchen and comfortable living room adorned with local artwork and parquet wood floors. Reserve ahead to set a time to meet the Welsh-Argentine owners, who live offsite but provide a key and a helpful handout filled with eating, entertainment and transport tips.

Montevideo: Centro & Ciudad Vieja

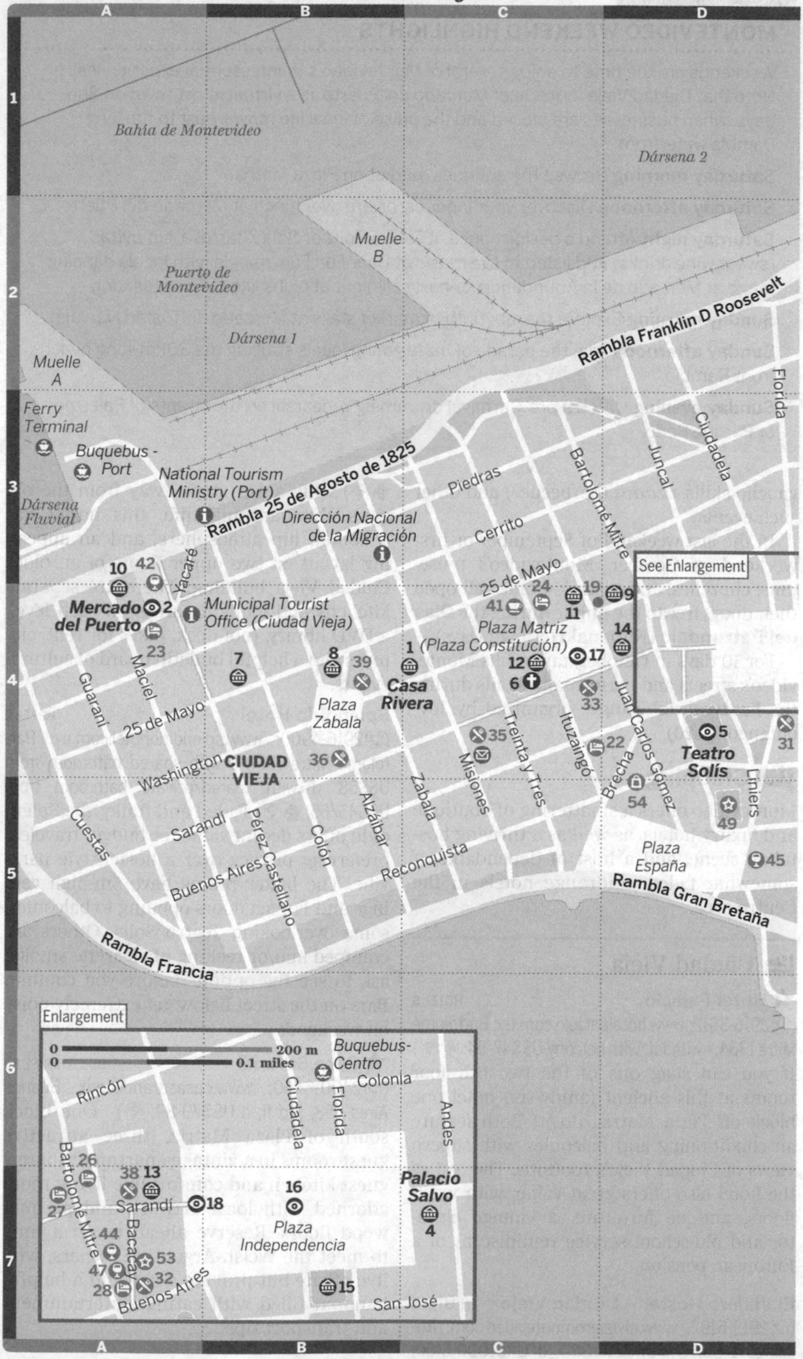

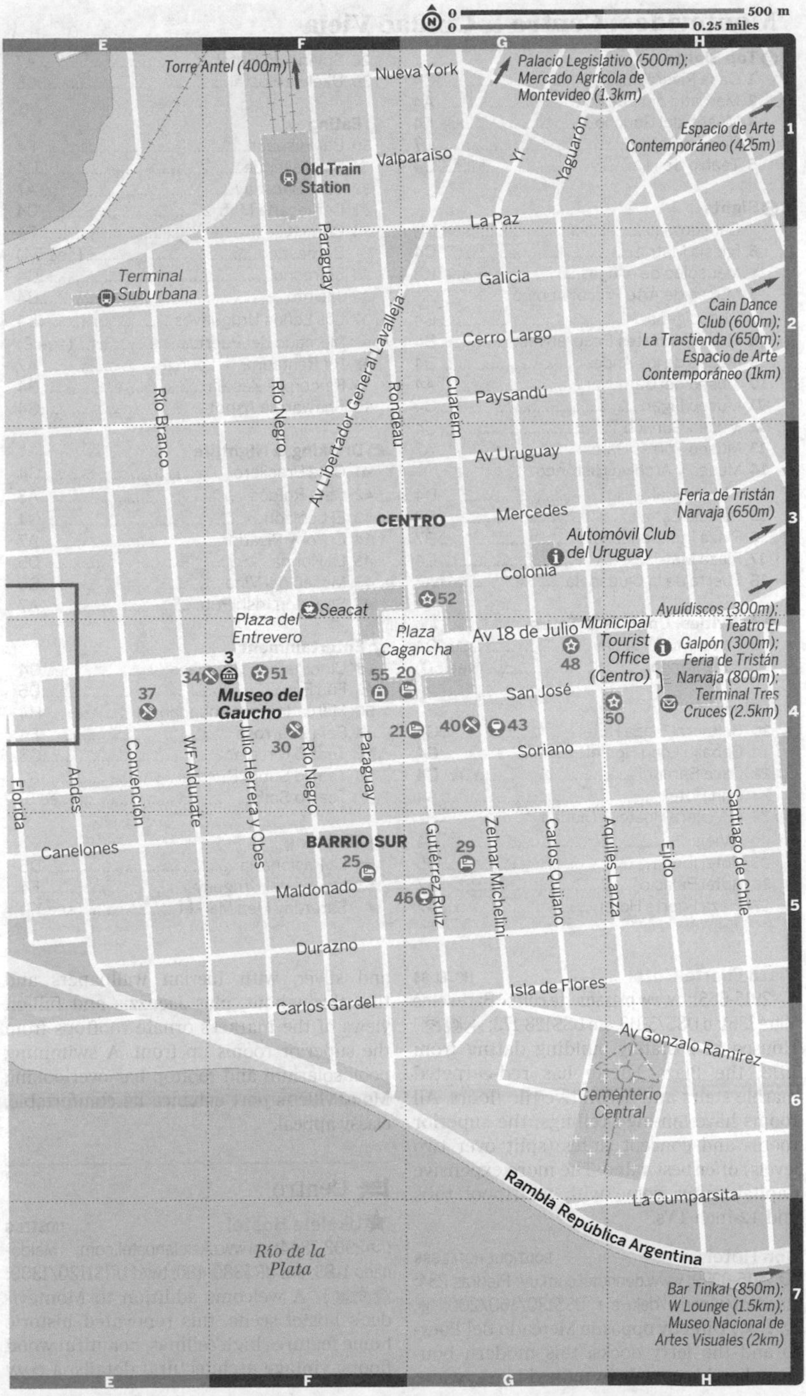
0 500 m
0 0.25 miles
E F G H
1 2 3 4 5 6 7
Torre Antel (400m)
Nueva York
Palacio Legislativo (500m); Mercado Agrícola de Montevideo (1.3km)
Espacio de Arte Contemporáneo (425m)
Old Train Station
Valparaiso
Yi
Yaguarón
La Paz
Paraguay
Terminal Suburbana
Galicia
Av Libertador General Lavalleja
Cain Dance Club (600m); La Trastienda (650m); Espacio de Arte Contemporáneo (1km)
Cerro Largo
Río Branco
Río Negro
Rondeau
Cuareim
Paysandú
Av Uruguay
Feria de Tristán Narvaja (650m)
CENTRO
Mercedes
Automóvil Club del Uruguay
Colonia
52
Seacat
Plaza del Entrevero
Plaza Cagancha
Av 18 de Julio
Municipal Tourist Office (Centro)
Ayuídiscos (300m); Teatro El Galpón (300m); Feria de Tristán Narvaja (800m); Terminal Tres Cruces (2.5km)
3
34
51
48
Museo del Gaucho
55
20
37
San José
50
21
40
43
30
Soriano
Florida
Andes
Convención
WF Aldunate
Julio Herrera y Obes
Río Negro
Paraguay
Canelones
BARRIO SUR
Gutiérrez Ruiz
Zelmar Michelini
Carlos Quijano
Aquiles Lanza
Ejido
Santiago de Chile
25
29
Maldonado
46
Durazno
Isla de Flores
Carlos Gardel
Av Gonzalo Ramírez
Cementerio Central
Rambla República Argentina
La Cumparsita
Río de la Plata
Bar Tinkal (850m); W Lounge (1.5km); Museo Nacional de Artes Visuales (2km)

Montevideo: Centro & Ciudad Vieja

Top Sights
1 Casa Rivera ... C4
2 Mercado del Puerto ... A4
3 Museo del Gaucho ... F4
4 Palacio Salvo ... C7
5 Teatro Solís ... D4

Sights
Cabildo ... (see 14)
6 Iglesia Matriz ... C4
Mausoleo de Artigas ... (see 16)
7 Museo de Arte Precolombino e Indígena ... B4
8 Museo de Artes Decorativas ... B4
9 Museo de los Andes ... D4
10 Museo del Carnaval ... A4
11 Museo Figari ... C4
12 Museo Gurvich ... C4
13 Museo Torres García ... A7
14 Museo y Archivo Histórico Municipal ... D4
15 Palacio Estévez ... B7
16 Plaza Independencia ... B7
17 Plaza Matriz ... C4
18 Puerta de la Ciudadela ... A7

Activities, Courses & Tours
19 Academia Uruguay ... C4
Joventango ... (see 50)

Sleeping
20 Balmoral Plaza Hotel ... G4
21 Caballo Loco Hostel ... G4
22 Casa Sarandí ... C4
23 Don Hotel ... A4
24 El Viajero Hostel – Ciudad Vieja ... C4
25 Hotel Iberia ... F5
26 Hotel Palacio ... A7
27 Plaza Fuerte Hotel ... A7
28 Spléndido Hotel ... A7
29 Ukelele Hostel ... G5

Eating
30 Bar Hispano ... F4
31 Bar Tasende ... D4
32 Café Bacacay ... A7
33 Cervecería Matriz ... C4
34 Comi.K ... F4
Doméstico ... (see 54)
35 Estrecho ... C4
36 Jacinto ... B4
37 Los Leños Uruguayos ... E4
Mercado del Puerto ... (see 2)
38 PV Restaurante Lounge ... A7
39 Rincón de Zabala ... B4
40 Shawarma Ashot ... G4

Drinking & Nightlife
41 Café Brasilero ... C4
42 Café Roldós ... A3
43 El Lobizón ... G4
44 El Pony Pisador ... A7
45 La Ronda ... D5
46 Museo del Vino ... G5
47 Shannon Irish Pub ... A7

Entertainment
48 Cinemateca Uruguaya ... G4
49 Fun Fun ... D5
50 Mercado de la Abundancia ... H4
51 Sala Zitarrosa ... F4
52 Teatro Circular ... G3
53 Teatro Sobre Ruedas ... A7
Teatro Solís ... (see 5)

Shopping
54 La Pasionaria ... D5
55 Manos del Uruguay ... F4
Saturday Flea Market ... (see 17)

Plaza Fuerte Hotel HOTEL $$
(2915-6651; www.plazafuerte.com; Bartolomé Mitre 1361; d US$73-113, ste US$128-173;) Housed in a stately building dating from 1913, the Plaza Fuerte has red-carpeted marble stairs and decorative tile floors. All rooms have 5m-high ceilings; the superior rooms and concept suites (split over two levels) offer best value. The more expensive Capital suites come with whirlpool tubs and 42-inch TVs.

Don Hotel BOUTIQUE HOTEL $$$
(2915-9999; www.donhotel.com.uy; Piedras 234; standard/superior/deluxe r US$130/160/200;) Directly opposite Mercado del Puerto and the ferry docks, this modern boutique hotel is a study in refined black, white and silver, with Iberian wallpapers and tiles throughout, plus Jacuzzis and full-on views of the market's ornate rooftops from the superior rooms up front. A swimming pool, solarium and rooftop bar overlooking Montevideo's port enhance its comfortable, classy appeal.

Centro

★ **Ukelele Hostel** HOSTEL $
(2902-7844; www.ukelelehostel.com; Maldonado 1183; dm UR$380-480, tw/d UR$1120/1300;) A welcome addition to Montevideo's hostel scene, this renovated historic home features high ceilings, beautiful wood floors, vintage architectural details, a cozy

music room and a grassy pool and patio area out back for lounging. Top it off with friendly staff and a good mix of dorms and private rooms and you've got the perfect midtown budget option.

Caballo Loco Hostel HOSTEL $
(☎2902-6494; www.caballolocohostel.com; Gutierrez Ruiz 1287; dm US$18-20; ❄📶) Enjoying an unbeatable location in the heart of downtown, only steps from leafy Plaza Cagancha and the bus stops for Montevideo's bus station and beaches, this new hostel in a remodeled old building is also recommended for its spic-and-span four- to 10-bed dorms and friendly owners.

Hotel Iberia HOTEL $$
(☎2901-3633; www.hoteliberia.com.uy; cnr Maldonado & Paraguay; d/tr/q from US$64/82/98; ❄📶) Located just south of the city center, the Hotel Iberia offers a range of solid midrange amenities at very reasonable rates. Superior doubles (costing US$8 extra) come with whirlpool tubs.

Balmoral Plaza Hotel HOTEL $$$
(☎2902-2393; www.balmoral.com.uy; Plaza Cagancha 1126; s/d/ste from US$126/136/181; ❄@📶) Central downtown location and bird's-eye views of leafy Plaza Cagancha are the big draws here. All rooms have minibars, safes, big TVs and double-glazed, soundproof windows. There's also a garage, gym, sauna, business center and restaurant (fixed-price lunch menu UR$265).

La Rambla & Eastern Beaches

Pocitos Hostel HOSTEL $
(☎2711-8780; www.pocitos-hostel.com; Sarmiento 2641, Pocitos; dm US$16-20, tw/d US$60/70; @📶) A few blocks from the Pocitos waterfront, this appealing hostel squeezes several four- to six-bed dorms and a couple of doubles into a converted old home with fireplace, high ceilings, guest kitchen, backyard barbecue and friendly staff.

Destino 26 HOSTEL $
(☎2707-6041; www.destino26hostel.com; 26 de Marzo 1125, Pocitos; dm US$18-20, d with shared/private bath US$60/75; @📶) On a residential street four blocks from the beach, this homey hostel beckons guests with a comfy living-dining area, large guest kitchen, grassy backyard and friendly reception. Upstairs rooms in the main house are nicest.

> **HOTEL PRICING: DOLLARS VS PESOS**
>
> Accommodations in Uruguay often quote prices in US dollars rather than Uruguayan pesos, especially in tourist destinations such as Montevideo, Colonia and the Atlantic coast. Throughout this chapter we have chosen to list prices in the currency quoted to us by each business during research. This means that some hotel and hostel prices will be listed in US dollars (US$), while others will be listed in Uruguayan pesos (UR$). So keep an attentive eye as you look through the listings!

Cala di Volpe BOUTIQUE HOTEL $$$
(☎2710-2000; www.hotelcaladivolpe.com.uy; cnr Rambla Gandhi & Parva Domus, Punta Carretas; r US$104-143, ste US$158-197; ❄@📶🏊) This classy place across from the beach abounds in boutique hotel features: comfy couches, writing desks, gleaming tile-and-marble bathrooms, and floor-to-ceiling picture windows with sweeping river views. There's a small rooftop pool and a nice restaurant.

Sofitel Montevideo Casino Carrasco & Spa LUXURY HOTEL $$$
(☎2604-6060; www.sofitel.com; Rambla Republica de Mexico 6451, Carrasco; r US$320-400, ste US$384-630) Completely renovated and reopened as a luxury hotel in 2013, Carrasco's casino is easily Montevideo's showiest lodging option. The 116 rooms in this monumental early-20th-century building, long a major waterfront landmark in this well-heeled neighborhood, include 23 distinctive suites, complemented by a casino, a spa with indoor and outdoor swimming pools, and Uruguay's most sumptuous breakfast spread.

Eating

For a break from the downtown restaurant scene, check out Montevideo's newest foodie attraction, the **Mercado Agrícola de Montevideo** (MAM; www.mam.com.uy; José Terra 2220; ⏰9am-10pm), a renovated early-20th-century market building 2.5km north of the center housing more than 100 merchants, including fruit and veggie vendors, cafes, restaurants and specialty food shops.

Ciudad Vieja

Rincón de Zabala CAFETERIA $

(www.rdz.com.uy; Rincón 387; sandwiches UR$110-145, full meals incl dessert UR$190-250; 9am-5pm Mon-Fri;) This modern corner place serves up free wi-fi along with affordable breakfasts, sandwiches and cafeteria-style daily specials.

★ **Estrecho** INTERNATIONAL $$

(Sarandí 460; mains UR$230-360; noon-4pm Mon-Fri) Grab a stove-side counter seat and watch the chefs whip up delicious daily specials at this cozy Ciudad Vieja lunch spot. French owner Bénédicte Buffard's international menu includes baguette sandwiches with beef, blue cheese and Dijon mustard; salads with toasted pecans and raspberry vinaigrette; and seafood stews with cilantro and crunchy vegetables. Save room for the divine desserts.

Jacinto INTERNATIONAL $$

(cnr Sarandí & Alzáibar; mains UR$140-350; 9am-6pm Mon-Sat) Fresh-baked bread, flavorful salads and soups (try the gazpacho with crunchy homemade croutons) and delicious savory tarts and sandwiches are served alongside more substantial main dishes at this high-ceilinged eatery with checkerboard marble floors. The homemade *aguas saborizadas* (spring water flavored with fresh fruits and herbs, such as grapefruit-thyme, orange-rosemary or lemon-ginger-mint) make a refreshing, if overpriced, accompaniment.

PV Restaurante Lounge URUGUAYAN $$

(pvloungerestaurante.com; Peatonal Sarandí 675; mains UR$270-375; 10am-8pm Mon-Fri, 10am-6pm Sat) Occupying the elegant upper floor of Más Puro Verso bookstore, this art nouveau eatery with floor-to-ceiling bookshelves and grand windows overlooking Ciudad Vieja's pedestrian zone makes a pleasant hideaway at teatime, or at lunch for the UR$330 *menú del día* (appetizer, main dish and dessert).

Café Bacacay FUSION $$

(www.bacacay.com.uy; Bacacay 1306; dishes UR$210-430; 9am-1am Mon-Fri, 10am-1am Sat) This chic little cafe across from Teatro Solís serves a variety of goodies: fish of the day with wasabi or *limoncello* (lemon liqueur) sauce; build-your-own salads with tasty ingredients such as grilled eggplant, spinach and smoked salmon; and a wide-ranging drinks menu. Desserts include pear tart and apple cake with ice cream.

Doméstico CAFE, VEGETARIAN $$

(www.domestico.com.uy; Reconquista 587; mains UR$220-290; 10am-7pm Mon-Fri, 11am-5pm Sat;) Tucked into the back of an artsy gift shop, this bright little cafe features a short menu of soups, salads and daily specials, with options for vegetarians, especially on 'meat-free Mondays.'

Cervecería Matriz BEER HALL $$

(www.matriz.com.uy; Sarandí 582; dishes UR$195-390; 8am-1am Mon-Sat) Join the crowds enjoying beer and *chivitos* (Uruguay's classic steak sandwich) under the trees at this informal eatery on Ciudad Vieja's most picturesque square.

★ **Mercado del Puerto** PARRILLA $$$

(Pérez Castellano; mains UR$200-700; 11am-6pm) This converted market on Ciudad Vieja's waterfront remains a Montevideo classic, even if the steady influx of cruise ships into the adjacent port has made it increasingly pricey. Take your pick of the densely packed *parrillas* (steakhouses displaying immense racks of grilled meat and veggies) and pull up a stool. Weekends are ideal for savoring the market's vibrant energy.

Centro

Shawarma Ashot MIDDLE EASTERN $

(Michelini 1295; sandwiches UR$80-180; 11am-5pm Mon-Fri) Delicious Middle Eastern treats such as felafel, shawarma, plus Armenian sandwiches (including cheese, tomato, cucumber and olives) fill the menu at this popular hole-in-the-wall eating spot.

Bar Tasende BAR, PIZZERIA $

(cnr Ciudadela & San José; pizza slices UR$60; 10am-1am) With brick walls, high ceilings and a 3m-tall statue of Don Quixote, this classic corner bar has been wooing patrons since 1931 with its trademark *muzzarella al tacho*, simple but tasty pizza slices laden with mozzarella, a perfect snack to accompany a beer any time of day.

Bar Hispano URUGUAYAN $

(San José 1050; meals UR$130-285; 7am-1am) Old-school neighborhood *confiterías* (cafes offering light meals) like this are disappearing fast. The black-clad, gruffly efficient waiters can take any order you throw at them – a stiff drink to start the day, a full meal at 5pm or a chocolate binge in the early hours. The plethora of ever-changing *platos del día* includes options for every taste and budget.

Los Leños Uruguayos PARRILLA **$$**
(www.parrilla.com.uy; San José 909; dishes UR$215-420; ⌚11:30am-3:30pm & 7:30-11:30pm) This favorite haunt of Montevideo's business set has a nice salad bar and a big rack of meat that's always roasting on the fire up front. The lunchtime *menú Los Leños* (fixed-price lunch menu; UR$295) is a good deal, including *cubierto* (cover charge), bread, main dish, dessert and coffee.

Comi.K BRAZILIAN **$$**
(Av 18 de Julio 994, 2nd fl; specials incl drink & dessert UR$275; ⌚8am-9:30pm Mon-Fri, 8am-4pm Sat) Inside the Brazilian cultural center, reasonably priced meals – including *feijoada* (Brazil's classic meat-and-black-bean stew) – are served in an elegant 2nd-floor salon with high ceilings and stained glass. There's live Brazilian music most Friday evenings.

La Rambla & Eastern Beaches

Bar Tinkal SANDWICHES **$**
(☎2418-4705; cnr Frugoni & La Rambla; chivitos UR$200; ⌚9am-midnight Mon-Sat) This corner bar between Centro and Parque Rodó has sunset views toward the river, but locals also rave about the *chivitos al pan* (classic Uruguayan steak sandwiches), which stand out for their simplicity and quality. Rather than piling on an absurd number of ingredients, Tinkal focuses on basics: tender meat, fresh lettuce and a good roll to hold everything together.

La Pulpería PARRILLA **$$**
(cnr Lagunillas & Nuñez, Punta Carretas; mains UR$200-310; ⌚8pm-12:30am Tue-Sat, noon-4pm Sun) The epitome of an intimate neighborhood *parrilla*, this corner place doesn't advertise its presence (drop by before 8pm and you won't even find a sign outside); instead, it focuses on grilling prime cuts of meat to perfection, and relies on word of mouth to do the rest. Grab a barstool by the blazing fire or a table on the sidewalk outside.

La Fonda del Puertito PARRILLA, SEAFOOD **$$**
(☎2628-7362; lafondadelpuertito.com.uy; Av LA de Herrera 1132, Pocitos; mains UR$210-400; ⌚noon-4pm & 8pm-late) In the thick of Pocitos' bar and restaurant row, between the waterfront and Montevideo Shopping mall, La Fonda draws a buzzing crowd every evening with its varied menu of grilled meat and fish, seafood, clay oven specialties and homemade desserts, all complemented by an extensive wine and drinks list.

Drinking & Nightlife

Montevideo offers an intriguing mix of venerable old cafes and trendy nightspots. Bars are concentrated on Bartolomé Mitre in Ciudad Vieja, south of Plaza Independencia in the Centro and along Av Luis Alberto de Herrera in Pocitos.

Ciudad Vieja

★**Café Brasilero** CAFE
(Ituzaingó 1447; ⌚9am-8pm Mon-Fri) This vintage 1877 cafe with dark-wood paneling and historic photos gracing the walls makes a delightful spot for morning coffee or afternoon tea. It's also an excellent lunch stop, with homemade bread, tasty pasta dishes and good-value *menus ejecutivos* – starter, main course, water and dessert from UR$255.

Café Roldós BAR-CAFE
(roldos.com.uy; Mercado del Puerto; ⌚9am-5pm) Since 1886, this venerable bar-cafe in Mercado del Puerto has been pouring its famous *medio y medio*, a refreshing concoction made from half wine, half sparkling wine (per bottle/glass UR$160/60). Throw in a few tasty sandwiches (UR$50 to UR$55 each), and you've got a meal! It's a perennial favorite with families on Sundays and with younger Montevideans on Saturdays.

El Pony Pisador CLUB
(☎2915-7470; www.facebook.com/pony.pisador.1; Bartolomé Mitre 1324; ⌚5pm-late Mon-Fri, 8pm-late Sat & Sun) The Ciudad Vieja branch of this thriving bar and disco features live music nightly and opens early on weekdays for 'after-office' drinks. Depending on the evening, you may find yourself dancing to anything from blues, Brazilian, flamenco, oldies, soul, Latin or rock covers in English and Spanish.

Shannon Irish Pub PUB
(www.theshannon.com.uy; Bartolomé Mitre 1318; ⌚7pm-late) A perennial favorite, the Shannon pours a good pint and features live

CHRISTOPHER GROENHOUT/GETTY IMAGES ©

1. Colonia del Sacramento (p535)
Only 50km from Buenos Aires by ferry, this picturesque town is a Unesco World Heritage site.

2. Punta del Este (p549)
One of South America's most-glamorous resorts, this seaside place positively buzzes.

3. Mercado del Puerto (p526)
Montevideo's old port market should not be missed, especially on weekends.

4. Playa El Emir (p551)
This Atlantic Ocean beach is a magnet for surfers.

GARY JOHN NORMAN/GETTY IMAGES ©

WAYNE WALTON/GETTY IMAGES ©

WALTER BIBIKOW/GETTY IMAGES ©

music every night, from rock to traditional Irish bands.

Centro

La Ronda BAR
(Ciudadela 1182; noon-late Mon-Sat, 7pm-late Sun) At this often jam-packed bar, youthful patrons straddle the windowsills between the dark interior plastered with vintage album covers and the sidewalk tables cooled by breezes off the Rambla.

El Lobizón BAR
(www.ellobizon.com; Zelmar Michelini 1264; 7pm-3am) Lobizón's cellar-bar atmosphere, free-flowing pitchers of sangría and *clericó* (white wine mixed with fruit), and tasty snacks such as its famous *gramajo* (potatoes, ham and eggs fried up with onions and parsley) make it a popular gathering place for young, artistic types.

Museo del Vino WINE BAR
(2908-3430; www.museodelvino.com.uy; Maldonado 1150) A wine store by day, this downtown venue also hosts frequent live tango performances in the evenings, accompanied by an excellent selection of Uruguayan wines.

Cain Dance Club GAY
(www.caindance.com; Cerro Largo 1833, Cordón; midnight-7am Fri & Sat) Montevideo's premier gay nightspot, Cain is a multilevel club with two dance floors playing everything from techno to Latin beats.

La Rambla & Eastern Beaches

W Lounge CLUB
(www.wlounge.com.uy; cnr Rambla Wilson & Sarmiento, Parque Rodó; midnight-7am Thu-Sat) With two dance floors accommodating 3000 people, this nightclub in Parque Rodó is *the* place to shake your thang to rock, *cumbia* and techno beats.

El Pony Pisador CLUB
(cnr Iturriaga & Av LA de Herrera, Pocitos; 8pm-late Thu-Sat) The Pocitos branch of this famous club really gets hopping on the weekends.

Philomène TEAHOUSE
(www.philomenecafe.com; Solano García 2455, Punta Carretas; 9am-8:30pm Mon-Fri, 11am-8:30pm Sat) Big pots of tea, complete with tea cozies, are served alongside cookies and light meals in this pair of super-cozy, happily wallpapered, parlor-sized rooms in Punta Carretas.

☆ Entertainment

Spanish-language websites with entertainment listings include www.cartelera.com.uy, www.vivomontevideo.com/cartelera, www.elpais.com.uy/divertite and www.socioespectacular.com.uy.

Live Music & Dance

Tango legend Carlos Gardel spent time in Montevideo, where the tango is no less popular than in Buenos Aires. Music and dance venues abound downtown.

★ **Fun Fun** LIVE MUSIC
(2915-8005; www.barfunfun.com; Ciudadela 1229, Mercado Central, Ciudad Vieja; 8:30pm-late Tue-Sat) Since 1895 this intimate, informal venue with pleasant front deck has been serving its famous *uvita* (a sweet wine drink) while hosting tango and other live music on a tiny stage.

Teatro Solís PERFORMING ARTS
(1950-3323; www.teatrosolis.org.uy; Buenos Aires 678, Ciudad Vieja; admission from UR$200) The city's top venue is home to the Montevideo Philharmonic Orchestra and hosts formal concerts of classical, jazz, tango and other music, as well as music festivals, ballet and opera.

Sala Zitarrosa PERFORMING ARTS
(2901-7303; www.salazitarrosa.com.uy; Av 18 de Julio 1012, Centro) Montevideo's best informal auditorium venue for big-name music and dance performances, including tango, rock, flamenco, reggae and *zarzuela* (traditional Spanish musical theater).

Mercado de la Abundancia LIVE MUSIC
(cnr San José & Aquiles Lanza, Centro; admission free Sat, UR$120 Sun; 10pm-late Sat, 8pm-late Sun) On Saturday evenings, locals throng the top floor of this historic market building to dance to live tango music. Join in, or watch from the sidelines at one of the adjacent restaurants. On Sundays, Montevideo's leading tango organization, Joventango (also based in the market), sponsors regular tango shows at 8pm, then opens its floor for dancing from 9:30pm onwards.

El Tartamudo Café LIVE MUSIC
(2480-4332; www.eltartamudo.com.uy; cnr 8 de Octubre & Presidente Berro, Tres Cruces; 7pm-late Tue-Sat) Performances at this place east

DON'T MISS

CARNAVAL IN MONTEVIDEO

If you thought Brazil was South America's only Carnaval capital, think again! *Montevideanos* cut loose in a big way every February, with music and dance filling the air for a solid month.

Not to be missed is the early February **Desfile de las Llamadas**, a two-night parade of *comparsas* (neighborhood Carnaval societies) through the streets of Palermo and Barrio Sur districts, just southeast of the Centro. *Comparsas* are made up of *negros* (persons of African descent) and *lubolos* (white people who paint their faces black for Carnaval, a long-standing Uruguayan tradition). Neighborhood rivalries play themselves out as wave after wave of dancers whirl to the electrifying rhythms of traditional Afro-Uruguayan *candombe* drumming, beaten on drums of three different pitches: the *chico* (soprano), *repique* (contralto) and *piano* (tenor). The heart of the parade route is Isla de Flores, between Salto and Gaboto. Spectators can pay for a chair on the sidewalk or try to snag a spot on one of the balconies overlooking the street.

Another key element of Montevideo's Carnaval are the *murgas*, organized groups of 15 to 17 gaudily dressed performers, including three percussionists, who perform original pieces of musical theater, often satirical and based on political themes. During the dictatorship in Uruguay, *murgas* were famous for their subversive commentary. All *murgas* use the same three instruments: the *bombo* (bass drum), *redoblante* (snare drum) and *platillos* (cymbals). *Murgas* play all over the city, and also compete throughout February in Parque Rodó at the **Teatro de Verano** (admission from UR$70). The competition has three rounds, with judges determining who advances and who gets eliminated.

The fascinating history of Montevideo's Carnaval is well documented in the city's Museo del Carnaval (p515). Another great way to experience Carnaval out of season is by attending one of the informal *candombe* practice sessions that erupt in neighborhood streets throughout the year. Two good places to find these are at the corner of Isla de Flores and Gaboto in Palermo, and in Parque Rodó, where the all-female group **La Melaza** (www.lamelaza.com) gathers at the corner of Blanes and Gonzalo Ramírez and continues down San Salvador. Drumming at both locations usually starts around 7pm on Sunday nights.

of Tres Cruces bus terminal run from rock to tango to *candombe* to jazz.

La Trastienda LIVE MUSIC
(☎2402-6929; www.latrastienda.com.uy; Fernández Crespo 1763, Cordón; ⊙9pm-late Wed-Sat) Hosts an eclectic mix of international music, from rock to reggae, jazz to folk, tango to electronica.

Cinema

Aside from Cinemateca Uruguaya, Montevideo's cinema scene is concentrated in the shopping malls east of downtown.

Cinemateca Uruguaya CINEMA
(☎2900-9056; www.cinemateca.org.uy; Av 18 de Julio 1280, Centro; individual film tickets for members/non-members free/UR$130) For art-house flicks, this film club charges a modest membership (UR$300 per month, plus UR$140 one-time sign-up fee) allowing unlimited viewing at its four cinemas; non-members pay a small entry fee (UR$130) per film. It hosts the Festival Cinematográfico Internacional del Uruguay in March or April.

Theater

Montevideo's active theater scene spans many worlds: from classical to commercial to avant-garde. Regular Spanish-language performances are staged at Teatro Solís (p530), **Teatro El Galpón** (☎2408-3366; www.teatroelgalpon.org.uy; Av 18 de Julio 1618, Centro) and **Teatro Circular** (☎2901-5952; www.teatrocircular.org.uy; Rondeau 1388, Centro). Alternatively, **Teatro Sobre Ruedas** (☎2900-8618; www.barronegro.com; Bacacay 1318, Ciudad Vieja) stages interactive theater on a city bus whizzing through Montevideo's streets.

Spectator Sports

Fútbol, a Uruguayan passion, inspires large and regular crowds. The main stadium, the **Estadio Centenario** (Av Ricaldoni, Parque José Batlle y Ordóñez), opened in 1930 for the first

World Cup, in which Uruguay defeated Argentina 4-2 in the final.

Fanáticos Fútbol Tours (www.futboltours.com.uy) offers personalized tours led by knowledgeable, multilingual *fútbol* aficionados; prices include tickets to a match of your choosing, plus hotel transport.

Shopping

Central Montevideo's traditional downtown shopping area is Av 18 de Julio. Locals also flock to several large shopping malls east of downtown, including Punta Carretas Shopping, Tres Cruces Shopping (above the bus terminal) and Montevideo Shopping in Pocitos/Buceo.

Feria de Tristán Narvaja MARKET
(Tristán Narvaja, Cordón; 9am-4pm Sun) This colorful Sunday-morning outdoor market is a decades-long tradition which was started by Italian immigrants. The market sprawls from Av 18 de Julio northwards along Calle Tristán Narvaja, spilling over onto several side streets. You can find used books, music, clothing, jewelry, live animals, antiques and souvenirs in its many makeshift stalls.

Saturday Flea Market MARKET
(Plaza Matriz, Ciudad Vieja; 8am-1pm Sat) Every Saturday, vendors take over Ciudad Vieja's central square, selling antique door knockers, saddles, household goods and just about anything else you can imagine.

Manos del Uruguay WOOLENS
(2900-4910; www.manos.com.uy; San José 1111, Centro; 10am-7pm Mon-Fri, 10am-2pm Sat) This national cooperative, a member of the World Fair Trade Organization, is famous for its quality woolen goods. In addition to its downtown branch, it also has shops in Montevideo Shopping and Punta Carretas Shopping east of downtown.

La Pasionaria HANDICRAFTS
(2916-6141; www.lapasionaria.com.uy; Reconquista 587, Ciudad Vieja; 10am-6pm Mon-Fri, 11am-5pm Sat) This colorful shop in Ciudad Vieja carries work by a variety of Uruguayan craftspeople.

Hecho Acá HANDICRAFTS
(2622-6683; www.hechoaca.com.uy; Montevideo Shopping, 1st fl, Local 147; 10am-10pm) Woolen goods and other handicrafts from around the country are nicely displayed here.

Ayuídiscos MUSIC
(2403-1526; www.tacuabe.com/ayui-discos; Av 18 de Julio 1618, Centro; 10am-8pm Mon-Fri, 10am-1pm Sat) This little store is an excellent source for Uruguayan music of all kinds.

Information

DANGERS & ANNOYANCES

While Montevideo is pretty sedate by Latin American standards, you should exercise caution as in any large city. The Ciudad Vieja west of Plaza Matriz should be avoided at night, as wallet- and purse-snatchings are not uncommon. Montevideo's *policía turística* (tourist police) patrol the streets throughout Ciudad Vieja and the Centro and can help if you encounter any problems.

EMERGENCY

Ambulance (105)

Fire (104) For emergencies.

Police (911)

Tourist Police (0800-8226; Calle Uruguay 1667)

INTERNET ACCESS

Most accommodations have a guest computer in the lobby, free in-room wi-fi, or both.

MEDIA

Montevideo's leading dailies are **El País** (www.elpais.com.uy), **El Observador** (www.elobservador.com.uy) and **Últimas Noticias** (www.unoticias.com.uy). The newsweekly **Búsqueda** (www.busqueda.com.uy) is also widely available at newsstands.

MEDICAL SERVICES

Hospital Británico (2487-1020; www.hospitalbritanico.com.uy; Av Italia 2420) Highly recommended private hospital with English-speaking doctors; 2.5km east of downtown.

MONEY

Banks, exchange houses and ATMs are everywhere, including the airport and bus terminal; downtown they're mainly along Av 18 de Julio.

POST

Post Office Centro (cnr Ejido & San José); Ciudad Vieja (Misiones 1328); Tres Cruces bus terminal (cnr Bulevar Artigas & Av Italia)

TELEPHONE

Antel Centro (cnr San José & Paraguay); Ciudad Vieja (Rincón 501); Tres Cruces bus terminal (cnr Bulevar Artigas & Av Italia)

TOURIST INFORMATION

Municipal Tourist Office (www.descubrimontevideo.uy) Centro (1950-1830; cnr Av 18 de Julio & Ejido; 9am-5:30pm); Ciudad

WORTH A TRIP

ESTANCIA LIVING ON A LIMITED BUDGET

What do you get when you cross a tourist *estancia* and a hostel? Find out at the unique **Hostel Estancia El Galope** (☎099-105985; www.elgalope.com.uy; Cno Concordia; dm US$25, d US$90, without bathroom US$70) in the countryside 115km from Montevideo and 60km from Colonia. Experienced world travelers Mónica and Miguel offer guests a chance to 'get away from it all' and settle into the relaxing rhythms of rural life for a few days. Horseback jaunts for riders of all levels (US$25 to US$35, 2½ hours) are expertly led by Miguel himself, and there's a sauna (US$10) to soothe those aching muscles at the end of the day. Breakfast is included; other meals, from lunches to fondue to full-fledged *asados* (barbecues) are available for US$8 to US$14. Taxi pickup from the bus stop in nearby Colonia Valdense is available upon request (US$10).

Vieja (☎2916-8434; cnr Piedras & Pérez Castellanos; ⏲9am-5pm Nov-May, 10am-4pm Jun-Oct) City maps and general Montevideo information. Downloadable visitor's guide to the city in English, Spanish and Portuguese.

National Tourism Ministry Carrasco airport (☎2604-0386; ⏲8am-8pm); Port (☎2188-5111; Rambla 25 de Agosto & Yacaré; ⏲9am-6pm Mon-Fri); Tres Cruces bus terminal (☎2409-7399; cnr Bulevar Artigas & Av Italia; ⏲9am-10pm) Info about Montevideo and destinations throughout Uruguay.

Getting There & Away

AIR

Montevideo's stylishly modern **Carrasco international airport** (☎2604-0272; www.aeropuertodecarrasco.com.uy) is served by fewer airlines than Ezeiza airport in Buenos Aires. Direct flights are available from Madrid and Miami, and one-stop service is available from several other European and North American cities via Buenos Aires or São Paulo.At the time of research, the only airline offering domestic service within Uruguay was **BQB** (www.flybqb.com), with four weekly flights from Montevideo to Salto, and onward international connections to Foz de Iguazú, Argentina.

BOAT

Buquebus (☎130; www.buquebus.com.uy) Centro (Radisson Hotel, cnr Colonia & Florida; ⏲10am-6pm Mon-Fri, 9am-1pm Sat); Port (Terminal Fluvio-Marítima, Port of Montevideo); Tres Cruces bus terminal (ticket counters 28 & 29; ⏲6:30am-2am) Runs daily high-speed ferries direct from Montevideo to Buenos Aires, including the superfast Francisco boat (2¼ hours), launched in 2013 and named after Pope Francis, which shaves 45 minutes off the traditional three-hour crossing time. Full *turista*-class fares are UR$2120. Buquebus also offers less expensive bus-boat combinations from Montevideo to Buenos Aires via Colonia (slow boat UR$935, 6½ hours; fast boat UR$1596, 4½ hours). Better fares for all services above are available with online advance purchase.

Seacat (☎2915-0202, 2900-6617; www.seacatcolonia.com.uy; Río Negro 1400; ⏲9am-7pm Mon-Fri, 9am-noon Sat) offers more economical bus-boat connections from Montevideo to Buenos Aires via Colonia (4¼ hours). One-way fares range between UR$850 and UR$1170.

Even more affordable, but less comfortable, are the bus-boat combinations offered by **Colonia Express** (☎2401-6666; www.coloniaexpress.com; ticket counter 31A, Tres Cruces bus terminal; ⏲10am-7pm Mon-Fri, to 4pm Sat, to noon Sun). Standard one-way fares for the 4¼-hour trip are UR$1040 per person; online advance-purchase rates drop as low as UR$810.

Cacciola Viajes (☎2401-9350; www.cacciolaviajes.com; ticket counter 32B, Tres Cruces bus terminal) runs a scenic twice- to thrice-daily bus-launch service from Montevideo to Buenos Aires via the riverside town of Carmelo and the Argentine Delta suburb of Tigre. The eight-hour trip costs UR$1091 one way (UR$1201 on holidays and long weekends).

BUS

Montevideo's modern **Tres Cruces bus terminal** (☎2401-8998; www.trescruces.com.uy; cnr Bulevar Artigas & Av Italia) is about 3km east of downtown. It has tourist information, clean toilets, a luggage check (UR$124 per 24 hours), public phones, ATMs and a shopping mall upstairs.

A taxi from the terminal to downtown costs between UR$100 and UR$120. To save your pesos, take city bus CA1, which leaves from directly in front of the terminal (on the eastern side), traveling to Ciudad Vieja via Av 18 de Julio (UR$14, 15 minutes).

For the beach neighborhoods of Punta Carretas and Pocitos, take city buses 174 and 183, respectively, from in front of the terminal (UR$21). A taxi to either neighborhood costs around UR$120.

All domestic destinations are served daily, and most several times a day. A small *tasa de embarque* (departure tax) is added to the ticket prices. Travel times are approximate.

EGA (☎2402-5164; www.ega.com.uy) provides the widest range of service to neighboring countries. Destinations in Argentina include Paraná, Santa Fe and Mendoza (all once weekly, on Friday), plus Córdoba and Rosario (each four times weekly). EGA also runs buses once weekly to Santiago, Chile (Monday) and São Paulo, Brazil (Sunday), twice weekly to Asunción, Paraguay (Wednesday and Saturday), four times weekly to Florianópolis, Brazil, and daily except Saturday to Porto Alegre, Brazil.

Services to BA are more frequent, with several companies offering multiple daily departures.

Buses from Montevideo

DESTINATION	COST (UR$)	DURATION (HR)
INTERNATIONAL		
Asunción (Paraguay)	3250	21
Buenos Aires (Argentina)	1090-1210	10
Córdoba (Argentina)	2215	15½
Florianópolis (Brazil)	3031	18
Porto Alegre (Brazil)	1990	12
Santiago (Chile)	4005	28
São Paulo (Brazil)	4265	28
DOMESTIC		
Carmelo	359	3¼
Colonia	258	2¾
La Paloma	344	3½
La Pedrera	358	4
Mercedes	401	4
Paysandú	559	4½
Piriápolis	143	1½
Punta del Diablo	430	5
Punta del Este	208	2¼
Salto	731	6½
Tacuarembó	558	4½

Getting Around

TO/FROM THE AIRPORT

From **Terminal Suburbana** (☎1975; cnr Río Branco & Galicia), five blocks north of Plaza del Entrevero, local Copsa buses 700, 710 and 711 and Cutcsa buses C1 and C5 run to Carrasco airport (UR$40, 45 minutes). Alternatively take COT's direct service to the airport (UR$139, 30 minutes) from the Tres Cruces bus terminal. Coming from the airport, board at the stop directly in front of the arrivals hall.

Taxis charge an official fixed rate of UR$1220 for the 30- to 45-minute taxi ride from the airport to downtown Montevideo; the return trip to the airport is cheaper (between UR$700 and UR$900, depending on time of day and place of departure).

BUS

Montevideo's city buses, operated by **Cutcsa** (☎19333; www.cutcsa.com.uy), go almost everywhere for UR$21 per ride. For a clickable map showing which buses serve any given destination, visit www.montevideobus.com.uy (in Spanish).

CAR

Most major international companies have counters at Carrasco airport. In downtown Montevideo, you can also try the following Uruguayan companies (with nationwide branches).

Multicar (☎2902-2555; www.redmulticar.com; Colonia 1227, Centro)

Punta Car (☎2900-2772; www.puntacar.com.uy; Cerro Largo 1383, Centro)

TAXI

Montevideo's black-and-yellow taxis are all metered. Cabbies carry two official price tables, one effective on weekdays, the other (20% higher) used at night between 10pm and 6am, and on Sundays and holidays. It costs UR$31 to drop the flag (UR$37 nights and Sundays) and roughly UR$1.78 per unit thereafter (UR$2.14 nights and Sundays). Even for a long ride, you'll rarely pay more than UR$200, unless you're headed to Carrasco airport.

WESTERN URUGUAY

From Colonia's tree-shaded cobblestone streets to the hot springs of Salto, the slow-paced river towns of western Uruguay have a universally relaxing appeal, with just enough urban attractions to keep things interesting. Here, the border with Argentina is defined by the Río de la Plata and the Río Uruguay, and the region is commonly referred to as *el litoral* (the shore).

Further inland you'll find the heart of what some consider the 'real' Uruguay – the gaucho country around Tacuarembó, with *estancias* sprinkled throughout the rural landscape and some beautiful, rarely visited nature preserves.

Colonia del Sacramento

POP 26,230

On the east bank of the Río de la Plata, 180km west of Montevideo, but only 50km from Buenos Aires by ferry, Colonia is an irresistibly picturesque town enshrined as a Unesco World Heritage site. Its Barrio Histórico, an irregular colonial-era nucleus of narrow cobbled streets, occupies a small peninsula jutting into the river. Pretty rows of sycamores offer protection from the summer heat, and the riverfront provides a venue for spectacular sunsets. Colonia's charm and its proximity to Buenos Aires draw thousands of Argentine visitors; on weekends, especially in summer, prices tend to rise and it can be difficult to find a room.

Colonia was founded in 1680 by Manuel Lobo, the Portuguese governor of Rio de Janeiro, and occupied a strategic position almost exactly opposite Buenos Aires across the Río de la Plata. The town grew in importance as a source of smuggled trade items, undercutting Spain's jealously defended mercantile monopoly and provoking repeated sieges and battles between Spain and Portugal.

Although the two powers agreed over the cession of Colonia to Spain around 1750, it wasn't until 1777 that Spain took final control of the city. From this time, the city's commercial importance declined as foreign goods proceeded directly to Buenos Aires.

Sights & Activities

Barrio Histórico

Colonia's Barrio Histórico is filled with visual delights. Picturesque spots for wandering include the narrow, roughly cobbled **Calle de los Suspiros** (Street of Sighs), lined with tile-and-stucco colonial houses, the **Paseo de San Gabriel**, on the western riverfront, the **Puerto Viejo** (Old Port) and the historic center's two main squares: vast **Plaza Mayor 25 de Mayo** and shady **Plaza de Armas** (the latter also known as Plaza Manuel Lobo).

A single UR$50 ticket covers admission to Colonia's eight **historical museums** (☎4523-1237; www.museoscolonia.com.uy; ⏲11:15am-4:45pm). All keep the same hours, but closing day varies by museum.

Portón de Campo GATE

(Manuel de Lobos) The most dramatic way to enter Barrio Histórico is via the reconstructed 1745 city gate. From here, a thick fortified wall runs south along the Paseo de San Miguel to the river, its grassy slopes popular with sunbathers.

Iglesia Matriz CHURCH

(Plaza de Armas) Uruguay's oldest church – begun by the Portuguese in 1680, then completely rebuilt twice under Spanish rule – is the centerpiece of pretty Plaza de Armas. The plaza also holds the foundations of a house dating from Portuguese times.

Faro LIGHTHOUSE

(admission UR$20; ⏲11am-sunset) One of the town's most prominent landmarks, Colonia's 19th-century lighthouse provides an excellent view of the old town and the Río de la Plata. It stands within the ruins of the 17th-century **Convento de San Francisco**, just off the southwest corner of Plaza Mayor 25 de Mayo.

Teatro Bastión del Carmen THEATER, GALLERY

(Rivadavia 223; ⏲10am-10pm) FREE Incorporating part of the city's ancient fortifications, this theater and gallery complex hosts rotating art exhibits and periodic concerts.

Museo Portugués MUSEUM

(Plaza Mayor 25 de Mayo 180; ⏲closed Wed & Fri) In this beautiful old house, you'll find Portuguese relics including porcelain, furniture, maps, Manuel Lobo's family tree and the old stone shield that once adorned the Portón de Campo.

Museo Municipal MUSEUM

(Plaza Mayor 25 de Mayo 77; ⏲closed Tue & Thu) Houses an eclectic collection of treasures including a whale skeleton, an enormous rudder from a shipwreck, historical timelines and a scale model of Colonia (c 1762).

Archivo Regional MUSEUM

(Misiones de los Tapes 115; ⏲closed Sat & Sun) On the northwest edge of the plaza, Archivo Regional contains historical documents along with pottery and glass excavated from the 18th-century Casa de los Gobernadores nearby.

Casa Nacarello MUSEUM

(Plaza Mayor 25 de Mayo 67; ⏲closed Tue & Fri) One of the prettiest colonial homes in town, with period furniture, thick whitewashed

Colonia del Sacramento

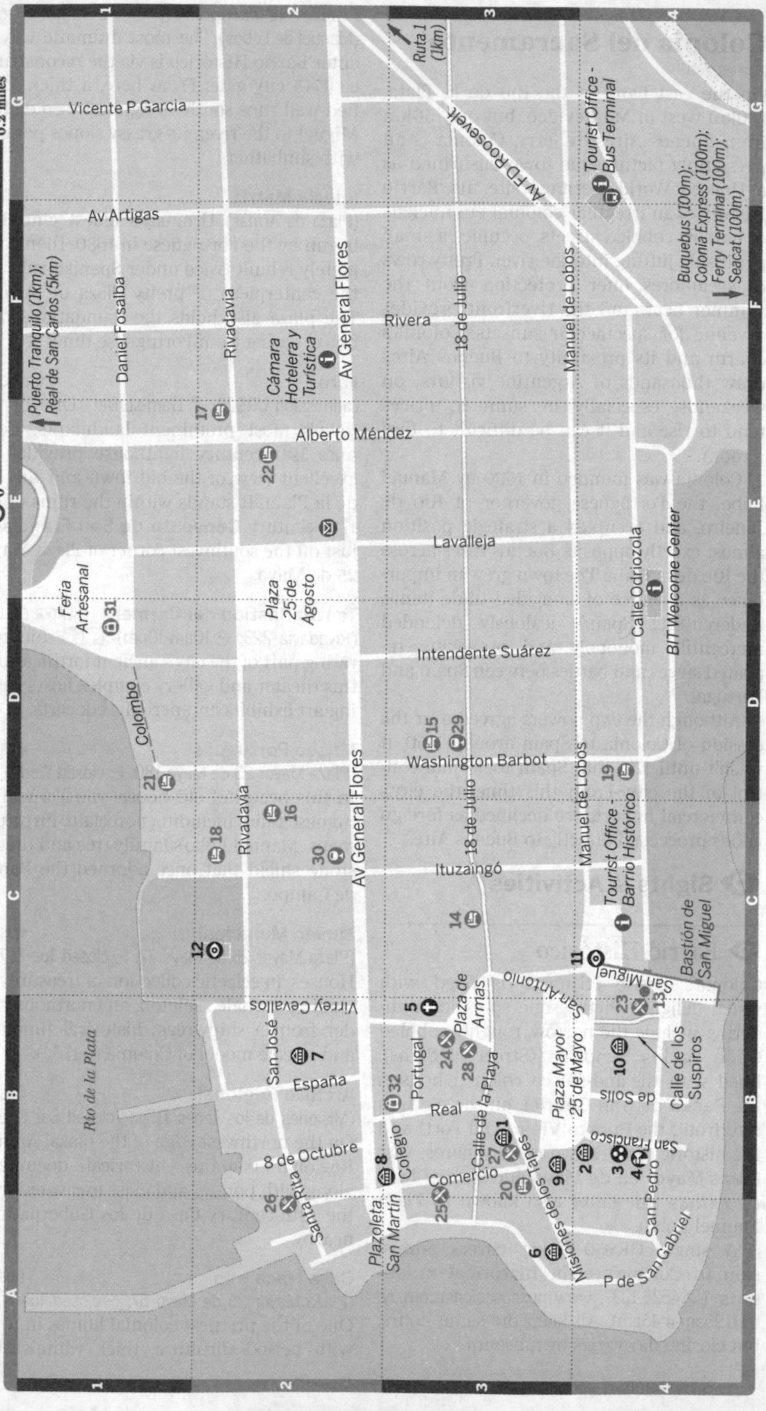
0.2 miles
400 m
Río de la Plata
Puerto Tranquilo (1km); Real de San Carlos (5km)
Ruta 1 (1km)
Buquebus (100m); Colonia Express (100m); Ferry Terminal (100m); Seacat (100m)
Vicente P Garcia
Av Artigas
Daniel Fosalba
Rivadavia
Av General Flores
18 de Julio
Manuel de Lobos
Av FD Roosevelt
Tourist Office - Bus Terminal
Rivera
Cámara Hotelera y Turística
Alberto Méndez
Lavalleja
Feria Artesanal
Plaza 25 de Agosto
Calle Odriozola
BIT Welcome Center
Intendente Suárez
Colombo
Washington Barbot
Ituzaingó
Tourist Office - Barrio Histórico
Bastión de San Miguel
San Miguel
San Antonio
Plaza de Armas
Virrey Cevallos
San José
España
Portugal
Real
Calle de la Playa
Plaza Mayor 25 de Mayo
Calle de los Suspiros
de Solís
San Francisco
San Pedro
8 de Octubre
Colegio
Comercio
Misiones de los Tapes
Santa Rita
Plazoleta San Martín
P de San Gabriel
1
2
3
4
A
B
C
D
E
F
G

Colonia del Sacramento

Sights

1 Archivo Regional	B3
2 Casa Nacarello	B4
3 Convento de San Francisco	B4
4 Faro	B4
5 Iglesia Matriz	B3
6 Museo del Azulejo	A3
7 Museo Español	B2
8 Museo Indígena	B3
9 Museo Municipal	B3
10 Museo Portugués	B4
11 Portón de Campo	C4
12 Teatro Bastión del Carmen	C2

Activities, Courses & Tours

13 Bike & Coffee	C4

Sleeping

14 El Capullo	C3
15 El Viajero Hostel	D3
16 Hostel del Río	C2
17 Nova Posada	E2
18 Posada de la Flor	C2
19 Posada del Ángel	D4
20 Posada Plaza Mayor	B3
21 Radisson Colonia Hotel	D1
22 Sur Hostel	E2

Eating

23 Buen Suspiro	B4
24 El Drugstore	B3
25 La Bodeguita	B3
26 Lentas Maravillas	A2
27 Pulpería de los Faroles	B3
28 Viejo Barrio	B3

Drinking & Nightlife

29 Barbot	D3
30 Matamala Bar	C2

Shopping

31 Feria Artesanal	D1
32 Malvón	B3

walls, wavy glass and original lintels (duck if you're tall!).

Museo Indígena MUSEUM
(Comercio s/n; closed Mon & Thu) Houses Roberto Banchero's personal collection of Charrúa stone tools, exhibits on indigenous history, and an amusing map upstairs showing how many European countries could fit inside Uruguay's borders (it's at least six!).

Museo del Azulejo MUSEUM
(cnr Misiones de los Tapes & Paseo de San Gabriel; closed Thu & Fri) This dinky 17th-century stone house has a sampling of French, Catalan and Neapolitan tilework.

Museo Español MUSEUM
(San José 164; closed Tue & Wed) This recently reopened museum has a varied collection of Spanish artifacts, including colonial pottery, engravings, clothing and maps.

Real de San Carlos

At the turn of the 20th century, Argentine entrepreneur Nicolás Mihanovich spent US$1.5 million building an immense tourist complex 5km north of Colonia at Real de San Carlos. The complex included a 10,000-seat bullring, a 3000-seat *frontón* (court) for the Basque sport of *jai alai*, a hotel-casino and a racecourse.

Only the racecourse functions today, but the ruins of the remaining buildings make an interesting excursion, and the adjacent beach is popular with locals on Sundays.

Museo Paleontológico MUSEUM
(Real de San Carlos; Thu-Sun) This two-room museum displays glyptodon shells, bones and other locally excavated finds from the private collection of self-taught palaeontologist Armando Calcaterra.

Tours

Walking Tours WALKING TOUR
(tour per person in Spanish/other languages UR$150/200) The tourist office outside Colonia's old town gate organizes good walking tours led by local guides. Spanish-language tours leave at 11am and 3pm daily year-round, with occasional sunset tours added at 7pm in January and February. Tours in other languages can also be arranged; just ask at the tourist office.

Vintage Car Tours DRIVING TOUR
(099-806106; 1929vintage@gmail.com; per 15min/hr US$20/60) Local resident Gabriel Gaidano offers spins around town for up to four people in his 1929 Model A convertible. Look for him on Plaza de Armas.

Bike & Coffee BICYCLE TOUR
(4523-2646; bikeandcoffee.com.ar; San Miguel 81; 2hr bike tour UR$400, 4hr/8hr bike rental UR$200/300; 9am-11pm Fri-Sun) This Buenos Aires–based outfit offers bicycle tours and rentals from its cafe just inside Colonia's old

town walls. The two-hour tours go from the historic district to Playa Ferrando, a pretty beach on the river east of town.

Sleeping

Some hotels charge higher rates Friday through Sunday. Summer weekends are best avoided or booked well in advance.

★ El Viajero Hostel HOSTEL $
(4523-2683; www.elviajerocolonia.com; Washington Barbot 164; dm US$18-20, d US$64-74;) With bike rental, horseback excursions, a bar for guests and air-con in all rooms, this hostel is brighter, fancier and somewhat cozier than the competition, and the location two blocks east of Plaza de Armas couldn't be better.

Hostel del Río HOSTEL $
(4523-2870; www.hosteldelrio.com; Rivadavia 288; dm UR$360-400, d UR$1800-2000) Well-placed at the edge of the historic center, this new hostel offers squeaky-clean four- to six-bed dorms and a half-dozen private rooms, along with a streetside front deck, guest kitchen and back patio. The atmosphere is a bit sterile, but the bright white rooms come with thoughtful features like individual bedside reading lights on the bunk beds.

Sur Hostel HOSTEL $
(4522-0553; www.surhostel.com; Rivadavia 448; dm US$17-20, s US$35-40, d US$50-60;) Just outside the historic center, this place has a mix of private rooms and four- to 10-bed dorms, all with private bathrooms. There's a spacious guest kitchen and an upstairs sun terrace for clothes-washing and weekly barbecues (UR$170).

Posada del Ángel HOTEL $$
(4522-4602; www.posadadelangel.net; Washington Barbot 59; d US$80-120;) Cheerfully painted in yellow and periwinkle blue, this little hotel has amenities such as down comforters and a sauna for chilly nights and a swimming pool for the summer heat. Standard interior-facing rooms are dark; it's worth splurging on one with a view.

Nova Posada HOTEL $$
(4522-2952; www.novaposada.com; Rivadavia 463; s US$50, d US$100-140;) With gleaming modernist decor, wood floors, comfy beds, cable TV and a grassy backyard, this spiffy new hotel is especially good value for solo travelers midweek, when discounted single rates are available.

Posada de la Flor HOTEL $$
(4523-0794; www.posada-delaflor.com; Ituzaingó 268; r with fan US$75, with air-con US$85-95;) Serenely situated on a sycamore-lined street that ends at a small beach, the Flor's biggest draw is its upstairs terrace with lounge chairs overlooking the river.

Posada Plaza Mayor INN $$$
(4522-3193; www.posadaplazamayor.com; Comercio 111; d US$125-160, ste US$185-250;) Near the river in the heart of historic Colonia, the Playa Mayor comprises two colonial houses. The stone-walled, high-ceilinged 19th-century Spanish rooms surround a beautiful courtyard with a fountain; the adjoining 18th-century Portuguese structure houses several lovely common areas.

El Capullo B&B $$
(4523-0135; www.elcapullo.com; 18 de Julio 219; d US$120-165;) Friendly and well-traveled English-speaking owners, a prime Barrio Histórico location, a grassy yard and a swimming pool are the big attractions at this remodeled colonial posada. It's worth paying extra for one of the rooms upstairs or adjoining the back patio.

Radisson Colonia Hotel LUXURY HOTEL $$$
(4523-0460; www.radissoncolonia.com; Washington Barbot 283; s/d weekends from US$210/265, weekdays from US$140/155;) If you value chain-hotel comforts over colonial charm, the Radisson has what you're looking for. This all-in-one facility features two pools and a spacious deck overlooking the river, plus sauna, gym, solarium, children's play area and garage. Visit during the week for much better rates.

Eating & Drinking

Buen Suspiro PICADAS $$
(4522-6160; www.buensuspiro.com; Calle de los Suspiros 90; picadas from UR$205; 11am-midnight) Duck under the wood beams into this cozy spot specializing in *picadas* (little snacks eaten with a toothpick). Sample local wines by the bottle or glass, accompanied by spinach and leek tarts, ricotta-and-sesame balls, local cheese and sausage, and more. Reserve ahead for a fireside table in winter, or while away a summer afternoon on the intimate back patio.

La Bodeguita PIZZERIA $$
(www.labodeguita.net; Comercio 167; mini pizzas UR$115, dishes UR$220-390; 8:30pm-midnight year-round, plus 12:30-3:30pm Sat & Sun Apr-Nov)

Nab a table the out back on the sunny two-level deck and soak up the sweeping river views while drinking sangría (UR$200 per liter) or munching on La Bodeguita's trademark mini pizzas, served on a cutting board.

Lentas Maravillas INTERNATIONAL **$$**
(Santa Rita 61; sandwiches & salads UR$280-300; ⌚2-8:30pm Thu-Tue) As cozy as a friend's home, this is a dreamy spot to kick back with tea and cookies or a glass of wine and a sandwich between meals. Flip through an art book from owner Maggie Molnar's personal library and enjoy the river views, either from the upstairs fireplace room or from the chairs on the grassy lawn down below.

El Drugstore INTERNATIONAL **$$**
(Portugal 174; mains UR$180-500; ⌚noon-midnight) This funky corner place on Plaza de Armas is touristy but fun, with polka-dot tablecloths, vividly colored walls, an open kitchen and two vintage cars on the cobblestones doubling as romantic dining nooks. Half of the 24-page menu is devoted to drinks; the other half to tapas and full meals, including a few vegetarian offerings. There's also frequent live guitar music.

Viejo Barrio ITALIAN **$$**
(Vasconcellos 169; dishes UR$220-320; ⌚noon-4pm & 8pm-midnight Thu-Mon, noon-4pm Tue) Whether you're amused or annoyed by the eccentric waiter and his funny hats, Viejo Barrio remains a perennial old-town favorite thanks to its excellent homemade pasta and picturesque setting on historic Plaza de Armas.

Pulpería de los Faroles SEAFOOD **$$**
(www.pulperiadelosfarolesrestaurant.com; Misiones de los Tapes 101; dishes UR$245-520; ⌚noon-midnight) Specializing in seafood and pasta, this eatery has a rainbow of colorful tablecloths in the interior dining room, plus a sea of informal outdoor seating on Plaza Mayor 25 de Mayo.

Barbot BREWPUB
(☎4522-7268; www.facebook.com/barbotcerveceria; Washington Barbot 160; ⌚7pm-late Wed-Sun) A welcome addition to Colonia's drinking scene, this upscale brewpub (Colonia's first) opened in 2013, serving a wide selection of homebrews, accompanied by pizza, *picadas* and Mexican fare.

Matamala Bar BAR
(Ituzaingó 222; ⌚9pm-late Thu-Sat) This little nightclub and bar with a fireplace makes for a chic choice if you're after tapas and drinks.

Puerto Tranquilo BAR
(Rambla de las Américas s/n; ⌚10am-midnight) For drinks and snacks on a sunny afternoon, this 'resto-bar', located 1km north of the town center makes a great getaway from historic Colonia's touristy madness. From the shaded outdoor deck, you can watch the sunset and get picture-postcard views of locals splashing in the river or playing *fútbol* and sunbathing on the sandy beach below.

Shopping

Feria Artesanal HANDICRAFTS
(cnr Intendente Suárez & Daniel Fosalba; ⌚10am-7pm or 8pm) This handicrafts market, which is open daily, is located on the northern waterfront.

Malvón WOOLENS
(☎4522-1793; Av General Flores 100; ⌚11am-7pm) Sells woolen goods sourced from the national cooperative Manos del Uruguay, as well as a variety of other Uruguayan handicrafts.

Information

Antel Barrio Histórico (Av General Flores 172); Centro (cnr Lavalleja & Rivadavia) Internet for UR$45 per hour.

BBVA (Av General Flores 299) This is one of a number of ATMs spread along Av General Flores.

BIT Welcome Center (☎4522-1072; www.bitcolonia.com; Odriozola 434; ⌚10am-7pm Dec-Apr, 9am-6pm May-Nov) Colonia's sparkling new welcome center, located just across from the port, has tourist information, as well as touch-screen information displays, a 'Welcome to Uruguay' video presentation and much more.

Cámara Hotelera y Turística (☎4522-7302; www.hotelesencolonia.com; cnr Av General Flores & Rivera; ⌚11am-6pm) Helps with hotel bookings.

Hospital Colonia (☎4522-2994; 18 de Julio 462)

Post Office (Lavalleja 226)

Tourist Office (☎4522-8506; www.coloniaturismo.com) Barrio Histórico (Manuel de Lobos 224; ⌚9am-6pm); Bus terminal (cnr Manuel Lobo & Av Roosevelt; ⌚9am-8pm)

Getting There & Away

BOAT

From the ferry terminal at the foot of Rivera, **Buquebus** (☎130; www.buquebus.com.uy) runs two slow boats (UR$935, three hours) plus three or more fast boats (UR$1330, one hour) daily to Buenos Aires.

Colonia Express (www.coloniaexpress.com.uy; Ferry terminal) and **Seacat** (www.seacatcolonia.com; Ferry terminal) run less frequent but more affordable high-speed ferry services. Each company offers two to three departures daily. Crossings take one hour, with day-of-departure fares ranging from UR$580 to UR$1023.

All three companies offer child, senior and advance-purchase discounts.

Immigration for both countries is handled at the port before boarding.

BUS

Colonia's modern **bus terminal** (cnr Manuel Lobo & Av Roosevelt) is conveniently located near the port, within easy walking distance of the Barrio Histórico. It has tourist information, luggage storage, money-changing and internet facilities.

Buses from Colonia del Sacramento

The following destinations are served at least twice daily.

DESTINATION	COST (UR$)	DURATION (HR)
Carmelo	115	1¼
Mercedes	260	3½
Montevideo	258	2¾
Paysandú	473	6
Salto	644	8

Getting Around

Walking is enjoyable in compact Colonia, but motor scooters, bicycles and gas-powered buggies are popular alternatives. **Thrifty** (☎4522-2939; Av General Flores 172; bicycle/scooter/golf cart per hr US$3/10/14, per 24hr US$10/25/50) rents out everything from beater bikes to cars. Several other agencies rent cars and motorbikes just near the bus and ferry terminals, including **Multicar/Moto Rent** (www.redmulticar.com; Manuel de Lobos 505), **Punta Car** (www.puntacar.com.uy; cnr 18 de Julio & Rivera) and **Europcar** (www.europcar.com.uy; Av Artigas 152). The latter company offers one-way car rentals between Colonia and Montevideo.

Local COTUC buses go to the beaches and bullring at Real de San Carlos (UR$17) from along Av General Flores.

Carmelo

POP 18,040

Carmelo, dating from 1816, is a laid-back town of cobblestone streets and low-set old houses, a center for yachting, fishing and exploring the Paraná Delta. It straddles the Arroyo de las Vacas, a stream that widens into a sheltered harbor just below the Río Uruguay's confluence with the Río de la Plata. The town center, north of the arroyo (creek), is Plaza Independencia. South of the arroyo lies a large park with open space, camping, swimming and a huge casino.

Launches connect Carmelo to the Buenos Aires suburb of Tigre.

Sights & Activities

The arroyo, with large, rusty boats moored along it, makes for a great ramble, as does the 30-minute stroll to the beaches across the bridge.

Local wines have an excellent reputation. Just outside town (look for the gigantic wine bottle!), **Bodega Irurtia** (☎4542-2323; www.irurtia.com.uy; Av Paraguay, Km2.3) produces award-winning tannats and pinot noirs. Visitors can take a basic 40-minute tour (UR$100) of the cellars including tastings of two wines; a two-hour tour (UR$700) followed by wine, cheese and grappa tasting; or a five-hour tour (UR$1300) including tastings and a three-course lunch amid the vineyards at well-regarded Campotinto restaurant.

Sleeping & Eating

Camping Náutico Carmelo CAMPGROUND $
(☎4542-2058; dnhcarmelo@adinet.com.uy; Arroyo de las Vacas s/n; per tent site UR$258) South of the arroyo, this pleasant tree-shaded campground with hot showers caters to yachties but accepts walk-ins too. Sites accommodate up to four people.

Hotel Rambla HOTEL $$
(☎4542-2390; www.ciudadcarmelo.com/ramblahotel; Uruguay 51; s/d US$45/75; ❄📶) The blocky Rambla won't win any design awards, but it's conveniently close to the launch docks. The upstairs doubles with balconies facing the arroyo are cheerier than the interior rooms.

Piccolino URUGUAYAN $
(☎4542-4850; cnr 19 de Abril & Roosevelt; dishes UR$150-260; ⏲noon-3:30pm & 7pm-midnight) This place has decent *chivitos* (steak sandwiches) and views of Carmelo's main square.

★ **Bodega y Granja Narbona** ITALIAN $$$
(☎4540-4778; www.narbona.com.uy; Hwy 21, Km268; dishes US$17-29; ⊙9am-11pm) A refined rural retreat set amid vineyards, orchards and verdant farmland 13km from Carmelo, this restaurant in a restored 1908 farmstead serves gourmet pasta, local organic vegetables and fabulous tannat and *grappamiel* (grape brandy with honey) from Narbona's award-winning cellars. Inside, browse shelves stacked floor to ceiling with locally produced olive oil, peach preserves and *dulce de leche* (milk caramel).

Information

Antel (Barrios 329)

Banco Comercial (Uruguay 403) On Plaza Independencia.

Casa de la Cultura (www.ciudadcarmelo.com/casacultura; cnr Barrios & 19 de Abril; ⊙10am-6pm) Three blocks south of the main square and eight blocks northeast of the launch docks.

Hospital (☎4542-2107; cnr Uruguay & Artigas)

Post Office (Uruguay 360)

Getting There & Away

Cacciola (☎4542-7551; www.cacciolaviajes.com; José de San Martin s/n; ⊙4:30-5:30am & 9am-7pm) runs twice-daily launches (thrice-daily in summer) to the Buenos Aires suburb of Tigre. The one-way 2½-hour trip costs UR$835 (UR$918 on holidays and long weekends).

All bus companies are on or near Plaza Independencia. **Berrutti** (☎4542-2504, www.berruttiturismo.com/horarios.htm; Uruguay 337) has the most frequent service to Colonia; **Chadre** (☎4542-2987; www.agenciacentral.com.uy; 18 de Julio 411) is the best bet for all other destinations.

BUSES FROM CARMELO

DESTINATION	COST (UR$)	DURATION (HR)
Colonia	115	1½
Mercedes	143	2
Montevideo	344	3½
Paysandú	344	5
Salto	516	7

Mercedes

POP 42,000

Capital of the department of Soriano, Mercedes is a livestock center with cobblestoned streets and a small pedestrian zone around the 18th-century cathedral on the central Plaza Independencia. The town's most appealing feature is its leafy waterfront along the south bank of the Río Negro.

Sights & Activities

Activities along the riverfront include boating, fishing and swimming at the sandy beaches, or simply strolling along the Rambla (especially popular on Sunday afternoons).

Museo Paleontológico Alejandro Berro MUSEUM
(☎4532-3290; Parque Castillo Mauá; ⊙11am-5pm) FREE About 6km west of town, this museum displays a substantial fossil collection and an impressively well-preserved glyptodon shell discovered in a nearby riverbank in early 2010.

Tours

Catamarán Soriano I BOAT TOUR
(☎4532-2201 ext 2503; tours per person UR$200-500) This cruise boat offers occasional excursions on the Río Negro and Río San Salvador. For schedules and tickets, inquire at Mercedes' downtown tourist office.

Sleeping & Eating

Camping Isla del Puerto CAMPGROUND $
(☎4532-2733; Isla del Puerto; sites per person/tent UR$24/78) Mercedes' spacious campground, one of the region's best, occupies half the Isla del Puerto in the Río Negro. Connected to the mainland by a bridge, it has swimming, fishing and sanitary facilities.

★ **Estancia La Sirena** ESTANCIA $$$
(☎9910-2130, 4530-2271; www.lasirena.com.uy; Ruta 14, Km4.5; s/d with half board US$135/210, full board US$160/270, all incl horseback rides & other activities) Surrounded by rolling open country 15km upriver from Mercedes, this *estancia* is one of Uruguay's oldest and most welcoming. The spacious 1830 ranch house, with its cozy parlor and fireplaces and end-of-the-road setting, makes a perfect base for relaxation, late-afternoon conversation under the eucalyptus trees, stargazing and horseback excursions to the nearby Río Negro. Homemade meals are delicious.

Martiniano Parrilla Gourmet PARRILLA $$
(☎4532-2649; Rambla Costanera s/n; dishes UR$200-350; ⊙noon-3pm & 8pm-midnight Tue-Sun) The prime riverfront setting at the foot of 18 de Julio is complemented by a varied

WORTH A TRIP

THE LITTLE BEEF CUBE THAT CIRCLED THE GLOBE

In 1865 the Liebig Extract of Meat Company located its pioneer South American plant near the river town of Fray Bentos, 35km west of Mercedes. It soon became Uruguay's most important industrial complex. British-run El Anglo took over operations in the 1920s and by WWII the factory employed 4000 people, slaughtering cattle at the astronomical rate of 2000 a day.

Looking at the abandoned factory today, you'd never guess that its signature product, the Oxo beef cube, once touched millions of lives on every continent. Oxo cubes sustained WWI soldiers in the trenches, Jules Verne sang their praises in his book *Around the Moon*, Stanley brought them on his search for Livingstone, Scott and Hillary took them to Antarctica and Everest. More than 25,000 people from more than 60 countries worked here, and at its peak the factory was exporting nearly 150 different products, using every part of the cow except its moo.

A candidate for Unesco World Heritage status in 2014, the former factory is now a museum – the **Museo de la Revolución Industrial** (☎4562-3690; museo.anglo@rionegro.gub.uy; admission UR$30, incl guided tour UR$50, free on Tue; ⏲9:30am-5:30pm). Guided tours (10am and 3pm daily) grant access to the intricate maze of passageways, corrals and abandoned slaughterhouses behind the museum. At noon on Tuesdays, Thursdays and Sundays visitors can also tour the Casa Grande, a mansion that housed the factory's manager.

Inside the museum dozens of colorful displays – ranging from the humorous to the poignant – bring the factory's history vividly to life: a giant cattle scale where school groups are invited to weigh themselves; or the old company office upstairs, left exactly as it was when the factory closed in 1979, with grooves rubbed into the floor by the foot of an accountant who sat at the same desk for decades.

The adjacent town of Fray Bentos, with its pretty riverfront promenade, is the southernmost overland crossing over the Río Uruguay from Argentina. It's 45 minutes by bus from Mercedes, four hours from Colonia or Buenos Aires, or 4½ hours from Montevideo.

menu featuring homemade pasta, grilled meat and fish.

Shopping

★Lanas de Soriano WOOLENS
(☎4532-2158; www.lanasdesoriano.com; Colón 60; ⏲9am-noon Mon-Fri, 3-6:30pm Mon & Wed-Fri) A rainbow of beautiful handmade woolens is available in this shop, hidden away in a residential neighborhood near the waterfront.

Information

Antel (WF Aldunate 681; internet per hr UR$19) Provides phone and internet service.

Banco Comercial (Giménez 719) ATM on Plaza Independencia.

Hospital Mercedes (☎4532-2177; Sánchez 204)

Municipal Tourist Office (☎4532-2201 ext 2501; turismo@soriano.gub.uy; El Rosedal, cnr Av Asencio & Artigas; ⏲8am-9pm Dec-Easter, 8am-6pm rest of year) Located in a crumbling white building near the bridge to the campground.

Post Office (cnr Rodó & 18 de Julio)

Getting There & Away

Mercedes' modern, air-conditioned **bus terminal** (Plaza General Artigas) is located about 10 blocks from Plaza Independencia, in a shopping center that also houses ATMs, a post office, free public bathrooms and luggage storage, as well as an emergency medical clinic. A local bus, costing UR$16, leaves hourly from just in front of the bus terminal, and makes a circuit around downtown.

BUSES FROM MERCEDES

The following destinations are served at least once daily.

DESTINATION	COST (UR$)	DURATION (HR)
Buenos Aires	880	3½
Carmelo	147	2
Colonia	265	3
Montevideo	401	3½-4½
Paysandú	179	2
Salto	398	4

Paysandú

POP 76,400

On the east bank of the Río Uruguay, connected to Colón, Argentina by the Puente Internacional General Artigas, Uruguay's third-largest city is just a stopover for most travelers en route to or from Argentina. The activity is on Plaza Constitución, six blocks north of the bus terminal.

Founded as a mid-18th-century outpost of cattle herders from the Jesuit mission at Yapeyú (in present-day Argentina), Paysandú gradually rose to prominence as a meat-processing center. Repeated sieges of the city during the 19th century (the last in 1864–65) earned it the local nickname 'the American Troy.'

Despite its turbulent history and its ongoing status as a major industrial center, modern-day Paysandú is surprisingly sedate. To see the city's wilder side, visit during Carnaval or the annual week-long **beer festival** (held during Semana Santa).

Sights & Activities

Museo Histórico MUSEUM
(4722-6220 ext 247; Av Zorrilla de San Martín 874; 10am-5pm Tue-Fri, 9am-2pm Sat & Sun) FREE This museum displays evocative images from the multiple 19th-century sieges of Paysandú, including of the bullet-riddled shell of the cathedral, and the women in exile watching the city's bombardment from an island.

Museo de la Tradición MUSEUM
(4722-3125; Av de los Iracundos 5; 9am-2pm) FREE In parkland near the riverfront, this museum has a small, well-displayed selection of anthropological artifacts and gaucho gear.

Sleeping

Hotel Rafaela HOTEL $
(4722-4216; 18 de Julio 1181; s/d with fan & shared bathroom UR$650/850, with air-con & private bathroom UR$900/1150;) A decent budget option just west of the main square. Rafaela's rooms are dark but large, and some have their own small patios.

Hotel Casagrande HOTEL $$
(4722-4994; www.hotelcasagrande.com.uy; Florida 1221; s/d UR$1500/2300;) Homey and conveniently located, Paysandú's nicest downtown hotel has comfy armchairs, marble tabletops, big brass beds, free parking and a gourmet restaurant on-site (mains around UR$400).

Estancia La Paz ESTANCIA $$
(4720-2272; www.estancialapaz.com.uy; Ruta 24, Km86.5; r/ste/4-person apt US$113/145/160;) The tennis courts, swimming pool and Muzak-filled common areas feel incongruous among the historic buildings and pristine natural setting at this tourist *estancia* 25km southeast of Paysandú. Equestrians will appreciate the horseback-riding excursions, lasting from one day to a full week. Access is via a long dirt road: turn off at Km 86.5 on Ruta 24 or Km 336 on Ruta 3.

Eating & Drinking

Confitería Las Familias SWEETS $
(www.postrechaja.com; 18 de Julio 1152; chajá UR$66; 9am-7:30pm) If you've got a sweet tooth (and we mean a *really* sweet tooth) pull up a stool at this ancient confectioner's shop and sample one of Uruguay's classic desserts: *chajá*, a dentist-friendly concoction of sugary meringue, fruit and cream invented here in 1927.

Pan Z URUGUAYAN $$
(4722-9551; cnr 18 de Julio & Setembrino Pereda; dishes UR$170-420; noon-3pm & 8pm-midnight) Popular 'Panceta' serves pizza, *chivitos* stacked high with every ingredient imaginable, and tasty desserts such as strawberry cake and tiramisu.

Los Tres Pinos PARRILLA $$
(www.lostrespinos.com.uy; Av España 1474; dishes UR$140-300; noon-3pm & 8:30pm-midnight) Carnivores will swoon over the excellent *parrilla* at this place five blocks east of Plaza Constitución, while budget travelers will appreciate the lunchtime *menú ejecutivo*, featuring main course, side dish, water and dessert for UR$260.

Entertainment

Along the waterfront, 4km northwest of the center, Paysandú's intimate, tree-encircled **Teatro de Verano** is just across the street from the larger **Anfiteatro del Río Uruguay**, which seats up to 20,000 people and hosts major concerts during Paysandú's annual beer festival. Check with the tourist office for details of upcoming events at both venues.

Information

Antel (Montevideo 875)
Banco Santander (18 de Julio 1137) One of several ATMs along Paysandú's main street.

Hospital Escuela del Litoral (☎4722-4836; Montecaseros 520) Southeast of bus terminal.

Post Office (cnr 18 de Julio & Montevideo)

Tourist Office Centro (☎4722-6220 ext 184; turismo@paysandu.gub.uy; 18 de Julio 1226; 9am-6pm); Riverfront (☎4722-9235; plandelacosta@paysandu.gub.uy; Av de Los Iracundos; 9am-9pm); Bus terminal (cnr Artigas & Av Zorrilla de San Martin; 7am-1pm Dec-Apr, noon-6pm May-Nov) The Centro office is on Plaza Constitución; the riverfront office is next to the Museo de la Tradición.

Getting There & Away

Paysandú's **bus terminal** (☎4722-3225; cnr Artigas & Av Zorrilla de San Martín), six blocks due south of Plaza Constitución, is a hub for travel to and from Argentina. **Flechabus** (www.flechabus.com.ar) and **COIT** (www.coit.com.uy) both go to Buenos Aires, while **EGA** (www.ega.com.uy) serves Córdoba (via Paraná and Santa Fe) and Asunción, Paraguay.

From the bus station to the main square, take a local Copay bus (UR$15) down Av Zorrilla de San Martín.

BUSES FROM PAYSANDÚ

DESTINATION	COST (UR$)	DURATION (HR)
Asunción (Paraguay)	3250-3970	17
Buenos Aires (Argentina)	662	5½
Carmelo	344	5
Colón (Argentina)	89	¾
Colonia	473	6
Córdoba (Argentina)	1495	11
Mercedes	177	2½
Montevideo	552	4½
Paraná	790	5¼
Salto	177	2
Santa Fe	830	6
Tacuarembó	352	3½

Salto

POP 104,000

Built near the falls where the Río Uruguay makes its 'big jump' (Salto Grande), Salto is Uruguay's second-largest city and the most northerly crossing point to Argentina. It's a relaxed place with some 19th-century architecture and a pretty riverfront. People come here for the nearby hot springs and the recreation area above the enormous Salto Grande hydroelectric dam.

Sights & Activities

Salto's museums all close during January.

Museo de Bellas Artes y Artes Decorativas MUSEUM
(Uruguay 1067; 3-9pm Tue-Sat, 6-9pm Sun) FREE Displays a nice collection of Uruguayan painting and sculpture in a historic two-story mansion with a grand staircase, stained glass and back garden.

Museo del Hombre y la Tecnología MUSEUM
(cnr Av Brasil & Zorrilla; 10am-5pm Mon-Fri, 2-7pm Sat & Sun) FREE Housed in a historic market building and features excellent displays on local cultural development and history upstairs, and a small archaeological section downstairs.

Represa Salto Grande DAM
(☎4732-6131; www.saltogrande.org; 8am-4pm) This massive hydroelectric dam, 14km north of town, provides more than 50% of Uruguay's electricity and is a symbol of national pride. Free 90-minute guided tours visit both the Uruguayan and Argentine sides (no minimum group size, maximum wait 30 minutes). There's no public transport; a taxi from Salto costs about UR$800 round-trip. En route, check out the stands selling freshly squeezed local orange juice for UR$20 a liter!

Sleeping

Nearby hot springs (see p545) offer some of the region's best-value accommodations.

Gran Hotel Concordia HOTEL $$
(☎4733-2735; www.granhotelconcordia.com.uy; Uruguay 749; s UR$650-750, d UR$1300-1500;) This faded 1860s relic, a national historical monument, remains Salto's most atmospheric downtown budget option. A life-size cutout of Carlos Gardel, who once stayed in room 32, beckons you down a marble corridor into a leafy courtyard filled with murals and sculptures, surrounded by tired and musty rooms with tall French-shuttered windows.

★**Art Hotel Deco** BOUTIQUE HOTEL $$$
(☎4732-8585; www.arthoteldeco.com; Sarandí 145; d/ste US$120/150;) Just paces from the city center, this classy newcomer (opened in 2013) easily outshines Salto's other down-

DON'T MISS

SALTO'S HOT SPRINGS

A whole slew of hot springs bubbles up around Salto.

★ **Termas San Nicanor** (☎4730-2209; www.sannicanor.com.uy; Ruta 3, Km475; camp site per person UR$200, dm per person US$24-40, tw US$90-100, d US$100-120, 4-person cabin US$180 ;) Surrounded by a vast pastoral landscape, this is the most tranquil option. It has two gigantic outdoor thermal pools, a restaurant, and accommodations for every budget, including a high-ceilinged *estancia* house with large fireplaces and peacocks strolling the grounds. The 12km unpaved access road leaves Ruta 3 10km south of Salto. Daily **shuttles** (☎099-411534, 099-732368) leave for the springs at 10am from the corner of Larrañaga and Artigas in Salto (UR$100, 45 minutes). There's sometimes a 6pm departure as well; call ahead to verify.

Termas de Daymán (www.termasdedayman.com; admission UR$80) About 8km south of Salto, Daymán is a heavily developed Disneyland of thermal baths complete with kids' water park. It's popular with Uruguayan and Argentine tourists who roam the town's block-long main street in bathrobes. For comfortable accommodations adjacent to the springs, try **La Posta del Daymán** (☎4736-9801; www.lapostadeldayman.com; camp site per person UR$150, r per person incl breakfast UR$750-920;). Buses to the baths (UR$17) leave Salto's port via Av Brasil at 30 minutes past every hour (6:30am to 10:30pm), returning hourly from 7am to 11pm.

Termas de Arapey (www.termasarapey.com) About 90km northeast of Salto, Arapey offers multiple pools surrounded by gardens, fountains and paths to the Río Arapey Grande. Lodging is available at **Hotel Municipal** (☎4768-2441; www.hoteltermasdelarapey.com; s/d UR$1160/1590, optional breakfast per person UR$125;). **Argentur** (☎4732-9931; minibusesargentur.blogspot.com) runs one daily bus (two on Monday, Wednesday and Friday) from Salto (UR$160, 1½ hours).

town sleeping options. The renovated historic building abounds in period details, including high ceilings, polished wood floors, art deco door and window frames, an elegant sitting room and a lush back garden. Amenities include Egyptian cotton sheets, cable TV, sauna and gym.

Eating

Casa de Lamas URUGUAYAN $$
(☎4732-9376; Chiazzaro 20; dishes UR$190-420; ⏲8pm-midnight Wed, noon-3pm & 8pm-midnight Thu-Mon) Down near the riverfront, Salto's swankest eatery is housed in a 19th-century building with pretty vaulted brickwork in the dining room. There's an excellent *menú de la casa* (set menu including appetizer, main dish, dessert and drink) for UR$385.

La Caldera PARRILLA $$
(Uruguay 221; dishes UR$140-280; ⏲11am-3pm & 8pm-midnight Tue-Sun) With fresh breezes blowing in off the river and sunny outdoor seating, this *parrilla* makes a great lunch stop; at dinnertime, the cozy interior dining room, with its view of the blazing fire, is equally atmospheric.

La Trattoria URUGUAYAN $$
(Uruguay 754; dishes UR$140-270; ⏲noon-2am) Locals flock to this high-ceilinged downtown eatery for fish, meat and pasta. Sit in the wood-paneled dining room or people-watch from a sidewalk table on busy Calle Uruguay.

Information

Antel (Grito de Asencio 33)

Banco Comercial (cnr Uruguay & Lavalleja) One of several banks at this intersection.

Hospital Regional Salto (☎4733-3333; cnr 18 de Julio & Varela)

Post Office (cnr Artigas & Treinta y Tres)

Tourist Office (☎4733-4096; turismo@salto.gub.uy) Bus terminal (Salto Shopping Center, cnr Ruta 3 & Av Bastille; ⏲8am-9pm); Centro (Uruguay 1052; ⏲8am-7pm Mon-Sat)

Getting There & Away

AIR

From Salto's Nueva Hespérides airport, 6km south of town, **BQB Lineas Aereas** (☎4733-8919; www.flybqb.com; Brasil 819, Centro) flies four times weekly to Montevideo's Carrasco airport (1¼ hours), with onward connections to Buenos Aires (2½ hours). BQB also offers

Tuesday and Saturday service to Asunción, Paraguay (1¾ hours), and Sunday and Thursday service to Foz do Iguaçu, Brazil (1¾ hours), with three-night air-plus-hotel deals starting at US$380 per person. Flights listed above operate between March and December only.

BOAT

Transporte Fluvial San Cristóbal (☎4733-2461; cnr Av Brasil & Costanera Norte) runs launches across the river to Concordia, Argentina (adult/child UR$140/70, 15 minutes) four times daily between 9:30am and 7:15pm, except Sunday.

BUS

Salto's **bus terminal** (Salto Shopping Center, cnr Ruta 3 & Av Batlle), in a spiffy modern shopping center 2km east of downtown, has a tourist info kiosk, ATMs, internet facilities, free public restrooms and a supermarket.

Buses from Salto

DESTINATION	COST (UR$)	DURATION (HR)
Buenos Aires (Argentina)	873	8
Concordia (Argentina)	110	1
Colonia	644	8
Montevideo	716	6½
Paysandú	172	2
Tacuarembó	415	4

Connect in Concordia for additional Argentine destinations.

Tacuarembó

POP 54,800

In the rolling hills along the Cuchilla de Haedo, Tacuarembó is gaucho country. Not your 'we pose for pesos' types, but your real-deal 'we tuck our baggy pants into our boots and slap on a beret just to go to the local store' crew. It's also the alleged birthplace of tango legend Carlos Gardel.

Capital of its department, Tacuarembó has sycamore-lined streets and attractive plazas that make it one of Uruguay's most agreeable interior towns. The town center is Plaza 19 de Abril, linked by the main thoroughfares 25 de Mayo and 18 de Julio.

Sights

Museo del Indio y del Gaucho MUSEUM
(cnr Flores & Artigas; ⏲10am-5pm Tue-Sat) FREE Paying romantic tribute to Uruguay's gauchos and indigenous peoples, this museum's collection includes stools made from leather and cow bones, elegantly worked silver spurs and other accessories of rural life.

Festivals & Events

Fiesta de la Patria Gaucha GAUCHO FESTIVAL
(www.patriagaucha.com.uy) In the first or second week of March, this colorful five-day festival attracts visitors from around the country to exhibitions of traditional gaucho skills, music and other activities. It takes place in Parque 25 de Agosto, north of town.

Sleeping & Eating

★ **Yvytu Itaty** ESTANCIA $$
(☎099-837555, 4630-8421; www.viviturismorural.com.uy; s incl full board, farm activities & horseback riding UR$2000, per person 2 or more people UR$1800) Pedro and Nahir Clariget's unpretentious ranch-style home, 50km southwest of Tacuarembó, offers a first-hand look at real gaucho life. Guests are invited to accompany Pedro and his friendly cattle dogs around the 636-hectare working *estancia* on horseback, participate in daily work routines and sip *mate* on the patio at sunset in anticipation of Nahir's tasty home cooking.

Call in advance for driving directions or to arrange pickup at Tacuarembó's bus station (UR$1300 round-trip for a group of any size).

Hotel Plaza HOTEL $$
(☎4632-7988; www.plazahotel.com.uy; 25 de Agosto 247; s/d UR$850/1320; ❄@📶) For a decent night's sleep without breaking the bank, this is one of downtown Tacuarembó's better options. Rooms are unexceptional, but breakfasts feature fresh-squeezed orange juice, and the central location just off Plaza Colón can't be beat.

La Rueda PARRILLA $$
(W Beltrán 251; dishes UR$130-280; ⏲noon-3pm & 8pm-midnight Mon-Sat, noon-4pm Sun) With its thatched roof and walls covered with gaucho paraphernalia, this neighborhood *parrilla* is a perennial local favorite.

Information

Antel (Sarandí 242)

Banco Santander (18 de Julio 258) One of several ATMs near Plaza Colón.

Hospital Regional (☎4632-2955; cnr Treinta y Tres & Catalogne)

Post Office (Ituzaingó 262)

Tourist Office (☎4632-7144; www.imtacuarembo.com; ⏰8am-7pm Mon-Fri, 9am-noon Sat & Sun) Just outside the bus terminal.

Getting There & Around

The **bus terminal** (cnr Ruta 5 & Av Victorino Pereira) is 1km northeast of the center. A taxi into town costs about UR$70.

BUSES FROM TACUAREMBÓ

DESTINATION	COST (UR$)	DURATION (HR)
Montevideo	558	4½
Paysandú	344	3½
Salto	415	4

Valle Edén

Valle Edén, a lush valley 24km southwest of Tacuarembó, is home to the **Museo Carlos Gardel** (☎099-107303; admission UR$25; ⏰9:30am-6:30pm Tue-Sun). Reached via a drive-through creek spanned by a wooden suspension footbridge, and housed in a former *pulpería* (the general store/bar that used to operate on many *estancias*), the museum documents Tacuarembó's claim as birthplace of the revered tango singer – a claim vigorously contested by both Argentina and France!

Accommodations in Valle Edén are available at **Camping El Mago** (☎4632-7144; campsites per tent/person UR$100/40) or at **Posada Valle Edén** (☎4630-2345; www.posadavalleeden.com.uy; d UR$1190-1960), where you can eat and stay in the lovely historic mud-and-stone main inn, or sleep in one of the modern *cabañas* across the street.

Empresa Calebus runs an 11:45am bus from Tacuarembó to Valle Edén, returning at 7:15pm (UR$50, 20 minutes).

EASTERN URUGUAY

The gorgeous 340km sweep of beaches, dunes, forests and lagoons stretching northeast from Montevideo to the Brazilian border is one of Uruguay's national treasures. Still largely unknown except to Uruguayans and their immediate neighbors, this region lies nearly dormant for 10 months of each year, then explodes with summer activity from Christmas to Carnaval, when it seems like every bus out of Montevideo is headed somewhere up the coast. For sheer fun-in-the-sun energy, there's nothing like the peak season, but if you can make it here slightly off-season (in March or the first three weeks of December), you'll experience all the same beauty for literally half the price.

Near the Brazilian border, amid the wide-open landscapes and untrammeled beaches of Rocha department, abandoned hilltop fortresses and shipwrecks offer mute testimony to the time when Spain and Portugal struggled for control of the new continent. Where lookouts once scanned the wide horizon for invading forces, a new wave of invaders has taken hold, from binocular-wielding whale watchers in Cabo Polonio to camera-toting celebrity watchers in Punta del Este.

Piriápolis

POP 8800

With its grand old hotel and beachfront promenade backed by small mountains, Piriápolis is vaguely reminiscent of a Mediterranean beach town and exudes a certain old-school coastal resort charm. It was developed for tourism in the early 20th century by Argentine entrepreneur Francisco Piria, who built the landmark Argentino Hotel and an eccentric hillside residence known as Castillo de Piria (Piria's Castle).

Almost all the action happens in the 10-block stretch of beachfront between Av Artigas (the access road from Ruta 9) and Av Piria (where the coastline makes a broad curve southwards). Streets back from the beach quickly become residential.

The surrounding countryside holds many interesting features, including two of Uruguay's highest summits.

HOSTEL-HOPPING UP THE COAST

Summer Bus (summerbus.com) is a convenient hop-on, hop-off bus offering door-to-door transport between hostels up and down Uruguay's Atlantic coast. With a single US$95 ticket, you can start your journey at the hostel of your choice and visit all 12 destinations, from Montevideo to Punta del Diablo; alternatively, buy a one-way ticket between any two destinations (US$12 to US$45, depending on distance traveled).

OFF THE BEATEN TRACK

VILLA SERRANA

Those seeking an off-the-beaten-track retreat will love the serenity of this little village nestled in hills above a small lake, 170km northeast of Montevideo. Nearby attractions include **Salto del Penitente** (☎4440-3096; www.saltodelpenitente.com; Ruta 8, Km125; admission UR$20; ⏱9:30am-7pm), a 60m waterfall.

Picturesquely perched above the valley, **La Calaguala** (☎4440-2955; www.lacalaguala.com; Ruta 8, Km145; dm/s/d UR$250/850/1700, camp site up to 4 people UR$350) is a friendly family-run posada with attached restaurant; horseback riding, cycling and hiking excursions can be arranged.

To get here, take a bus from Montevideo to Minas (UR$177, two hours), then transfer to a **COSU** (☎4442-2256) bus to Villa Serrana (UR$58, 30 minutes, 9am and 5:30pm Tuesday and Thursday). Alternatively, any bus traveling northbound from Minas along Ruta 8 can drop you at Km 145, from where it's a stiff 4km uphill walk into town.

Sights & Activities

Swimming and **sunbathing** are the most popular activities, and there's good **fishing** off the rocks at the end of the beach, where Rambla de los Argentinos becomes Rambla de los Ingleses.

For a great view of Piriápolis, take the **chairlift** (Aerosilla; adult/child UR$150/90; ⏱10am-sunset) to the summit of **Cerro San Antonio** at the east end of town.

Sleeping

Prices here are for high season. Low-season rates are up to 50% less.

Hostel Piriápolis HOSTEL $
(☎4432-0394; www.hosteluruguay.org/piriapolis.html; Simón del Pino 1106; dm/tw/d incl breakfast UR$330/780/950, non-member surcharge per person UR$100; @ 📶) This 240-bed hostel, one of South America's largest, has several four-bed dorms, dozens of doubles (the best-value budget rooms in town) and a guest kitchen. It as desolate as an airplane hangar when empty, but full of life (and often booked solid) in January and February.

Bungalows Margariteñas BUNGALOW $$
(☎4432-2245; www.margaritenias.com; cnr Zufriategui & Piedras; d/tr/q UR$1450/1600/1800; @ 📶) Near the bus terminal, this place has well-equipped, individually decorated bungalows that sleep two to four. Affable owner Corina speaks English and meets guests at the bus station upon request.

Argentino Hotel LUXURY HOTEL $$$
(☎4432-2791; www.argentinohotel.com.uy; Rambla de los Argentinos s/n; r per person incl breakfast US$108-136, incl half board US$138-166; ❄ @ 📶 🏊) Even if you don't stay here, you should visit this elegant 350-room European-style spa with two heated river-water pools, a casino, ice-skating rink and other luxuries.

Eating

Most restaurants in Piriápolis are within a block of the Rambla.

★ **Café Picasso** SEAFOOD $$
(☎4432-2597; cnr Rojas & Caseros; dishes UR$200-450; ⏱12:30-3:30pm & 8-11:30pm daily Jul-Apr, weekends only May & Jun) Hidden down a residential backstreet several blocks from the beach, septuagenarian chef-owner Carlos has converted his carport and front room into an informal, colorfully decorated restaurant with open-air grill. Locals chat astride plastic chairs and listen to tango recordings while Carlos cooks up some of the best fish anywhere on Uruguay's Atlantic coast, along with paella on Sundays.

La Corniche CAFE $$
(www.visitelacorniche.com.uy; Rambla de los Argentinos 1254; dishes UR$155-260; ⏱8am-1am daily Nov-Apr, 8am-5pm Sat & Sun May-Oct) This beachfront cafe serves good espresso and pastries at breakfast time, followed by an eclectic lunch and dinner menu featuring fresh seafood, pasta and ciabatta-bread sandwiches alongside Mexican, Asian and vegetarian offerings.

Information

Antel (cnr Barrios & Buenos Aires; internet per hr UR$19; ⏱9am-6pm Mon-Sat)

Banco de la República (Rambla de los Argentinos, btwn Sierra & Sanabria) Convenient ATM.

Centro de Hoteles y Restaurantes (☎4432-2218; www.piriapolis.org.uy; Rambla de los Argentinos; ⏱9am-midnight Dec-Mar, 10am-4pm Apr-Nov) Adjacent to the tourist office;

provides local hotel information and booking assistance.

Post Office (Av Piria s/n) Two blocks in from the beachfront.

Tourist Office (☎4432-5055; www.destinopiriapolis.com; Rambla de los Argentinos; ⏲9am-midnight Dec-Mar, 10am-6pm Apr-Nov) Helpful staff and public toilets, on the waterfront near Argentino Hotel.

Getting There & Away

The **bus terminal** (☎4432-4526; cnr Misiones & Niza) is a few blocks back from the beach. COT and COPSA run frequent buses to Montevideo (UR$153, 1½ hours) and Punta del Este (UR$96, 50 minutes).

Around Piriápolis

North of town is **Castillo de Piria** (☎4432-3268; Ruta 37, Km4; ⏲10am-3:45pm Tue-Sun Apr-Nov, to 6pm Dec-Mar) FREE, Francisco Piria's opulent former residence. At the time of research the upper floor was closed for renovations, but the ground floor, with Spanish-language displays on the history of Piriápolis, remained open to the public. About 1km further inland, hikers can climb Uruguay's fourth-highest 'peak,' **Cerro Pan de Azúcar** (389m). The trail (2½ hours round-trip) starts from the parking lot of the **Reserva de Fauna Autóctona** (Ruta 37, Km5; ⏲7am-8:30pm) FREE, narrowing from a gradual dirt road into a steep path marked with red arrows.

The privately operated **Sierra de las Ánimas** (☎094-419891; www.sierradelasanimas.com; Ruta 9, Km86; admission UR$50; ⏲9am-sunset Sat & Sun, plus Carnaval & Easter weeks) is just off the Interbalnearia (coastal highway), 25km toward Montevideo from Piriápolis. There are two good hiking trails, each three to four hours round-trip: one leads to the 501m summit (Uruguay's second-highest), the other to the **Cañadón de los Espejos**, a series of waterfalls and natural swimming holes that are especially impressive after good rainfall. Other activities include mountain biking and camping. Coming from Montevideo by bus, get off at Parador Los Cardos restaurant and cross the highway. In cold or rainy weather, call ahead to verify it's open.

SOS Rescate de Fauna Marina (☎094-330795; www.facebook.com/s.o.s.faunamarina; Punta Colorada; admission UR$100; ⏲by appointment), a few kilometers south of Piriápolis along the coastal road to pretty Punta Colorada, is Uruguay's premier marine-animal rescue and rehabilitation center. Run entirely by volunteers, its emphasis is on educating schoolchildren, who can assist with daily feedings and observe penguins, sea lions, turtles and other rescued wildlife (advance notice requested).

Punta del Este

POP 9300

OK, here's the plan: tan it, wax it, buff it at the gym, then plonk it on the beach at 'Punta.' Once you're done there, go out and shake it at one of the town's famous clubs.

Punta del Este – with its many beaches, elegant seaside homes, yacht harbor, high-rise apartment buildings, pricey hotels and glitzy restaurants – is one of South America's most glamorous resorts and easily the most expensive place in Uruguay. Extremely popular with Argentines and Brazilians, Punta suffered a period of decline during the Uruguayan and Argentine recessions, but has come back with a vengeance.

Celebrity watchers have a full-time job here. Punta is teeming with big names, and local gossipmongers keep regular tabs on who's been sighted where. Surrounding towns caught up in the whole Punta mystique include the famed club zone of La Barra to the east and Punta Ballena to the west.

Punta itself is relatively small, confined to a narrow peninsula that officially divides the Río de la Plata from the Atlantic Ocean. The town has two separate grids: north of a constricted isthmus, just east of the yacht harbor, is the high-rise hotel zone; the southern area is largely residential. Street signs bear both names and numbers, though locals refer to most streets only by their number. An

DON'T MISS

THE HAND IN THE SAND

La Mano en la Arena (Hand in the Sand), sculpted in iron and cement by Chilean artist Mario Irarrázabal, won first prize in a monumental art contest in 1982 and has been a Punta fixture ever since. The hand exerts a magnetic attraction over visitors to Punta, who climb and jump off its digits and pose for thousands of photos with it every year. Look for it along the beachfront just southeast of the bus station.

Punta del Este

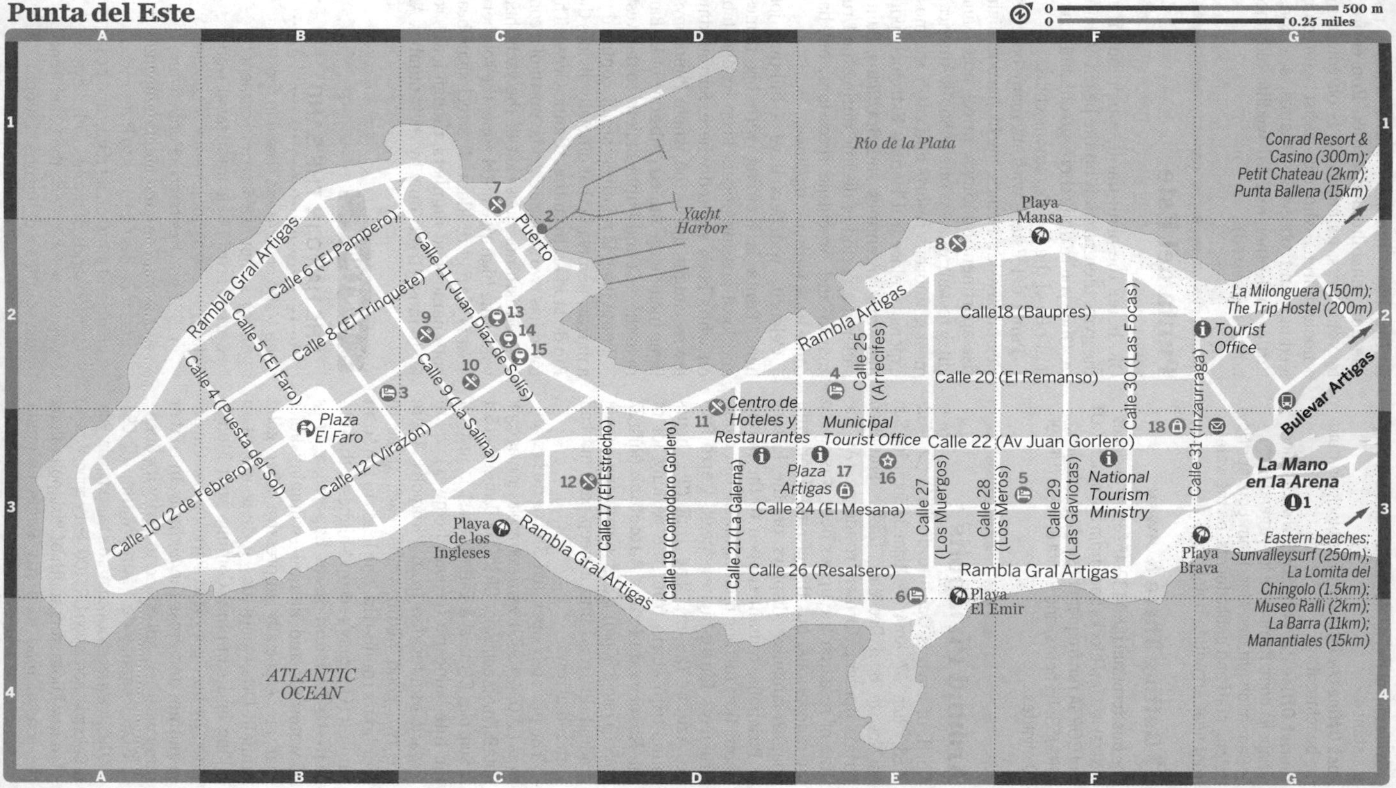
0 500 m
0 0.25 miles
Río de la Plata
Yacht Harbor
Puerto
ATLANTIC OCEAN
Rambla Gral Artigas
Rambla Artigas
Bulevar Artigas
Calle 4 (Puesta del Sol)
Calle 5 (El Faro)
Calle 6 (El Pampero)
Calle 8 (El Trinquete)
Calle 9 (La Salina)
Calle 10 (2 de Febrero)
Calle 11 (Juan Díaz de Solís)
Calle 12 (Virazón)
Calle 17 (El Estrecho)
Calle18 (Baupres)
Calle 19 (Comodoro Gorlero)
Calle 20 (El Remanso)
Calle 21 (La Galerna)
Calle 22 (Av Juan Gorlero)
Calle 24 (El Mesana)
Calle 25 (Arrecifes)
Calle 26 (Resalsero)
Calle 27 (Los Muergos)
Calle 28 (Los Meros)
Calle 29 (Las Gaviotas)
Calle 30 (Las Focas)
Calle 31 (Inzaurraga)
Plaza El Faro
Plaza Artigas
Playa de los Ingleses
Playa Mansa
Playa El Emir
Playa Brava
Centro de Hoteles y Restaurantes
Municipal Tourist Office
National Tourism Ministry
Tourist Office
La Mano en la Arena
Conrad Resort & Casino (300m); Petit Chateau (2km); Punta Ballena (15km)
La Milonguera (150m); The Trip Hostel (200m)
Eastern beaches; Sunvalleysurf (250m); La Lomita del Chingolo (1.5km); Museo Ralli (2km); La Barra (11km); Manantiales (15km)
1
2
3
4
5
6
7
8
9
10
11
12
13
14
15
16
17
18
A
B
C
D
E
F
G

Punta del Este

Top Sights
1 La Mano en la Arena G3

Activities, Courses & Tours
2 Dimar Tours C2

Sleeping
3 Atlántico Boutique Hotel B2
4 Bonne Étoile E2
5 Tas D'Viaje Hostel F3
6 Tas D'Viaje Summer Hostel E3

Eating
7 Artico C1
8 Guappa E2
9 Il Baretto C2
10 Lo de Charlie C2
11 Lo de Tere D2
12 Supermercado Disco C3

Drinking & Nightlife
13 Mambo Club C2
14 Moby Dick C2
15 Soho C2

Entertainment
16 Cine Libertador E3

Shopping
17 Feria Artesanal E3
18 Manos del Uruguay F3

exception is Av Juan Gorlero (Calle 22), the main commercial street, universally referred to as just 'Gorlero' (not to be confused with Calle 19, *Comodoro* Gorlero).

Rambla Claudio Williman and Rambla Lorenzo Batlle Pacheco are coastal thoroughfares that converge at the top of the isthmus from northwest and northeast, respectively. Locations along the Ramblas are usually identified by numbered *paradas* (bus stops, marked with signs along the waterfront).

Sights

Beaches & Islands

Beaches are the big daytime draw in sunny Punta and there are plenty to choose from. On the west side of town, Rambla Gral Artigas snakes along the calm **Playa Mansa** on the Río de la Plata, then passes the busy **yacht harbor**, overflowing with boats, restaurants, nightclubs and beautiful people, before circling around the peninsula to the open Atlantic Ocean.

On the eastern side of the peninsula the water is rougher, as reflected in the name **Playa Brava** (Fierce Beach); the waves and currents here have claimed several lives. Also on the Atlantic side, you'll find surfer-friendly beaches such as **Playa de los Ingleses** and **Playa El Emir**.

From Playa Mansa, heading west along Rambla Williman, the main beach areas are La Pastora, Marconi, Cantegril, Las Delicias, Pinares, La Gruta at Punta Ballena, and Portezuelo. Eastward, along Rambla Lorenzo Batlle Pacheco, the prime beaches are La Chiverta, San Rafael, La Draga and Punta de la Barra. In summer, all have *paradores* (small restaurants) with beach service.

Punta's most famous landmark is **La Mano en la Arena** (Hand in the Sand; Playa Brava), a monster-sized sculpted hand protruding from the sands of Playa Brava.

Boats leave every half-hour or so (daily in season, weekends in off-season) from Punta del Este's yacht harbor for the 15-minute trip to **Isla Gorriti**, which has excellent sandy beaches, a couple of restaurants and the ruins of **Baterías de Santa Ana**, an 18th-century fortification.

About 10km offshore, **Isla de Lobos** is home to the world's second-largest southern sea-lion colony (200,000 at last count), as well as South America's tallest lighthouse. The island is protected and can only be visited on an organized tour.

Other Sights

★ Casapueblo GALLERY
(☎ 4257-8041; carlospaezvilaro.com.uy/nuevo/museo-taller; admission UR$160; ⏲ 10am-sunset) Gleaming white in the sun and cascading nine stories down a cliffside, Uruguayan artist Carlos Páez Vilaró's exuberantly whimsical villa and art gallery sits atop Punta Ballena, a jutting headland 15km west of Punta del Este. Visitors can tour five rooms, view a film on the artist's life and travels, and eat up the spectacular views at the upstairs cafeteria-bar. There's a hotel and restaurant, too. It's a 2km walk from the junction where Codesa's Línea 8 bus drops you.

Museo Ralli MUSEUM
(☎ 4248-3476; www.museoralli.org; Los Arrayanes s/n; ⏲ 5-9pm Tue-Sun Jan & Feb, 2-6pm Tue-Sun Mar, 2-6pm Sat & Sun Apr, May & Oct-Dec) FREE In the suburb called Beverly Hills, this museum displays a wide-ranging collection of works by contemporary Latin American artists.

Uruguay's Beaches

Stretching from Montevideo to Brazil, 300km of beaches hug the Río de la Plata and the Atlantic Ocean. Choose the style that suits: from Punta del Este's glitz to Cabo Polonio's rusticity.

Cabo Polonio

1 Its lighthouse beckoning from a lonely point dotted with makeshift houses, Cabo Polonio (p559) is a nature-lover's dream. Getting here, on a pitching truck ride through the dunes, is half the fun.

La Paloma

2 Grab an ice cream and head for the waves. Family-friendly La Paloma (p557), tucked behind a wall of sand dunes, is the very picture of unadorned beachside fun.

Punta del Este

3 The dividing line between the wild Atlantic and the Río de la Plata, Punta del Este's (p549) tidy peninsula full of highrises and perfect beaches morphs annually from sleepy beach town to summer playground for South America's 'see-and-be-seen' party set.

Punta del Diablo

4 Punta del Diablo (p561) is the end of the line. A few steps down the beach and you're in Brazil, but most folks stay put, seduced by waves, seafood shacks, beach bonfires and the national park.

Piriápolis

5 A throwback to the 1930s, Piriápolis (p547) is about strolling the beachfront promenade past the grand hotel, or surveying the calm waters from the top of the chairlift.

La Pedrera

6 No view on Uruguay's entire Atlantic coast matches the wide-angle perspective from La Pedrera's (p558) cliffs. Join the surfers up top and contemplate your beach options for the day.

Clockwise from top left

1. Cabo Polonio (p559) **2.** La Paloma (p557)
3. *La Mano en la Arena* (p551), Playa Brava, Punta del Este

2

DANITA DELIMONT/GETTY IMAGES ©

KRZYSZTOF DYDYNSKI/GETTY IMAGES ©

Activities

In summer, **parasailing**, **waterskiing** and **jet skiing** are possible on Playa Mansa. Operators set up on the beach along Rambla Claudio Williman between Paradas 2 and 20.

Sunvalleysurf SURFING
(☎4248-1388; www.sunvalleysurf.com; Parada 3½, Playa Brava; ⏲11am-7pm) Wetsuits, surfboards, bodyboards and lessons are available from the original shop on Playa Brava, plus branches on Playa El Emir and in La Barra.

Tours

Dimar Tours BOAT TOUR
(☎4244-4750; www.isladelobos.com.uy; Puerto) Offers tours to the Isla de Lobos (adult/child US$50/30) and Isla Gorriti (UR$300 per person), leaving daily in the high season, and on weekends in the low season. Make reservations in advance. Other operators have offices along the same boardwalk – it's worth going for a wander to see who has the best prices on the day.

Sleeping

In summer Punta is jammed with people, and prices are astronomical; even hostels double their prices in January. In winter it's a ghost town, and places that stay open lower their prices considerably. During peak season, even places classified as midrange tend to charge top-end rates. Off-season visitors will find prices more in keeping with standard ranges.

The Trip Hostel HOSTEL $
(☎4248-8181; www.thetriphostel.com; Sader btwn Artigas & Francia; dm US$15-33, d US$50-80; @📶) Founded by a group of Uruguayan friends in 2012, this small hostel has plenty of *onda* (good vibes), with a full on-site bar, cozy lounge with fireplace, and great rooftop terrace. The location, one block north of the bus station, and only a couple blocks from Playas Mansa and Brava, is also very convenient.

Tas D'Viaje Hostel HOSTEL $
(☎4244-8789; www.tasdviaje.com; Calle 24 btwn Calles 28 & 29; dm US$11-45, d US$50-120; ⏲Aug-May; ❄@📶) This newish hostel in an older downtown home wins points for its friendly reception, unbeatable central location, and inviting common areas with hammocks for warm-weather lounging and a fireplace for winter nights. During the summer months, it also opens a sister **hostel** (Calle 26 btwn Calles 25 & 27; ⏲Dec-Feb), half a block from the beach at Playa El Emir. Bike and surfboard rentals are available.

Camping San Rafael CAMPGROUND $
(☎4248-6715; www.campingsanrafael.com.uy; Saravia s/n; campsites per person US$12.50; ⏲Nov-Easter) This campground, near the bridge to La Barra, has well-kept facilities on woodsy grounds, complete with store, restaurant, laundry, 24-hour hot water and other amenities.

Manantiales Hostel HOSTEL $
(☎4277-4427; www.elviajeropuntadeleste.com; Ruta 10, Km164; dm UR$380-750, d UR$1180-3000; ⏲mid-Dec–Easter; ❄@📶🏊) The scruffy backstreet location 12km east of Punta and 3km east of La Barra doesn't inspire confidence, but if you're here to surf or just chill out, this hostel with swimming pool, surfboard rentals and easy walking access to Bikini Beach makes an interesting alternative to Punta's more centrally located hostels. Private rooms and some dorms have air-con.

Bonne Étoile HOTEL $$
(☎4244-0301; www.hotelbonneetoile.com; Calle 20, btwn Calles 23 & 25; s US$125-155, d US$135-165; ❄@📶) In a 1940s beach house adjoining a more modern six-story tower, Bonne Étoile offers clean, spacious rooms, some with river views. Off-season rates are among the best in town, and the location between Gorlero and the port is hard to beat.

La Lomita del Chingolo GUESTHOUSE $$
(☎4248-6980; www.lalomitadelchingolo.com; Las Acacias btwn Los Eucaliptus & Le Mans; dm US$20-35, d US$55-140; @📶) With one six-person dorm and five private rooms, this relaxed place is in a residential neighborhood about 4km north of the center. Hospitable owners Rodrigo and Alejandra welcome guests with internet and kitchen facilities, tasty breakfasts, impromptu backyard barbecues and plenty of information about the local area.

Petit Chateau B&B $$
(☎4248-4369; www.petitchateau.com.uy; cnr Paris & Francia; r US$90-290; 📶🏊) On a quiet residential street 2km north of the center, this family-run place offers five rooms of varying size in a spacious older house, plus a dozen cookie-cutter units in the new building out back. The relaxing common areas include a vast living room with fireplace, a grassy lawn and a swimming pool.

★ Atlántico Boutique Hotel BOUTIQUE HOTEL $$$
(☎ 4244-0229; hotelatlanticopuntadeleste.com; cnr Calles 7 & 10; r US$110-352, ste US$209-462; ❄📶🏊) With gleaming white decor, wood floors and a backyard swimming pool and bar area, this boutique hotel between the port and the tip of the peninsula has been a huge hit since opening in December 2012. Amenities include 32-inch TVs in every room, an on-site pizzeria, an extensive video library and ample buffet breakfasts.

★ Las Cumbres BOUTIQUE HOTEL $$$
(☎ 4257-8689; www.cumbres.com.uy; Ruta 12, Km3.9, Laguna del Sauce; d US$215-360, ste US$420-660; ❄@📶🏊) Near Punta Ballena, this understatedly luxurious hilltop paradise is eclectically decorated with treasures from the owners' world travels. Rooms abound with special features, such as writing desks, fireplaces and outdoor whirlpool tubs. Guests have access to spa treatments, beach chairs and umbrellas, and free mountain bikes, and the tearoom terrace (open to the public) has magnificent sunset views.

La Posta del Cangrejo HOTEL $$$
(☎ 4277-0021; www.lapostadelcangrejo.com; La Barra; d US$140-460, ste US$290-650; ❄@📶🏊) This beachside hotel in the heart of La Barra has whitewashed adobe walls, an award-winning French restaurant and a poolside terrace within earshot of the ocean. The upstairs suites have fireplaces, Jacuzzis and nice sound systems.

Conrad Resort & Casino LUXURY HOTEL $$$
(☎ 4249-1111; www.conrad.com.uy; Parada 4, Playa Mansa; d US$270-700; ❄@📶🏊) A longtime downtown fixture, this high-rise five-star remains one of the focal points of Punta's summertime 'see-and-be-seen' social life. Better rooms have terraces with sea views, the pool and spa complex is fabulous, and the casino offers entertainment extravaganzas.

Eating

Supermercado Disco SUPERMARKET $
(Calle 17, btwn Gorlero & Calle 24; ⌚8am-10pm) For shelter from Punta's high prices, shop for groceries or grab a snack from the *rotisería* (delicatessen) here.

Rex Diner SANDWICHES, AMERICAN $$
(www.rexpuntadeleste.com; Ruta 10, La Barra; UR$150-300; ⌚24hr Dec & Jan, 11:30am-10pm Feb-Nov) Sporting yellow tile floors, bright red booths and a back terrace with ocean views, this American-style diner in the heart of La Barra is an atmospheric spot for *chivitos*, burgers, waffles, apple pie, milkshakes and ice-cream sundaes, especially in peak season when it's open all night long.

La Milonguera PARRILLA $$
(cnr Lenzina & Blvd Artigas; mains UR$220-450; ⌚1-5pm & 8pm-midnight) A couple of blocks north of the bus station, this friendly place serves great grilled meat in a no-frills setting.

Artico CAFETERIA $$
(Calle 8 No 1181; dishes UR$230-335; ⌚11:30am-4pm & 7:30-11pm) This port-side fish wholesaler does a brisk business in grilled seafood and paella, with lower prices that reflect its cafeteria-style service. It's one of the few places in Punta where you can eat by the water without spending a fortune; arrive early for best quality.

Lo de Charlie MEDITERRANEAN $$$
(☎ 4244-4183; www.lodecharlie.com.uy; Calle 12, No 819; dishes UR$520-735; ⌚8pm-late Dec-Mar, 8pm-midnight Thu-Sat & 11am-4pm Fri-Sun Apr-Nov) Owned by a fishing buddy of local artist Carlos Páez Vilaró and decorated with some of the latter's work, this is one of Punta's premier restaurants. The culinary delights include gazpacho, paella, risotto, homemade pasta, fish and shellfish.

Lo de Tere INTERNATIONAL $$$
(☎ 4244-0492; www.lodetere.com; Rambla Artigas & Calle 21; mains UR$580-970; ⌚noon-3pm & 8pm-midnight) Even with early-bird discounts (20% to 40% depending on time of arrival) Lo de Tere is hard on the wallet, but you won't find finer food anywhere in Punta. The wide-ranging menu includes black crab ravioli, orange-scented shrimp risotto, Uruguayan steak with rock salt and homemade chimichurri, and the famous rack of lamb, all accompanied by fine harbor views.

Guappa URUGUAYAN $$$
(☎ 4244-0951; guappa.com.uy; Rambla Artigas btwn Calles 27 & 28; mains UR$330-760; ⌚10am-midnight) For seafood, salads, pasta, panini or *chivitos* in one of Punta's prettiest waterfront settings, grab a spot on the beachside deck here, then enjoy watching the waiters try to look dignified as they cross the street with loaded trays. A popular spot to watch the sun go down.

WORTH A TRIP

FARO JOSÉ IGNACIO

The rich and famous flock to this highly fashionable little beachside town with its pretty lighthouse 30km east of Punta. Staying here is not for the faint of wallet; US$1000-a-night accommodations are the norm, such as the oceanfront **Playa Vik** (☎094-605212; playavik.com; cnr Los Cisnes & Los Horneros; r US$750-1500, house from US$1300;), launched by billionaire Scandinavian businessman and art patron Alex Vik. For *slightly* saner prices and a unique sleeping experience, head 8km north of José Ignacio and take the free ferry to the floating hotel **Laguna Garzón Lodge** (☎4480-6016; www.lagunagarzon.com.uy; Ruta 10, Km190.5, Laguna Garzón; r US$200-300), where 12 mini-houseboats bob on a vast lagoon, with meals available at the adjacent Garzuana restaurant. Back in town, a great place for day-trippers to soak up José Ignacio's rarefied atmosphere along with fine ocean views is the beachside eatery **Parador La Huella** (☎4486-2279; www.paradorlahuella.com; Playa Brava, José Ignacio; ⏲noon-5:30pm & 8pm-1am daily Dec-Mar, noon-3pm Fri-Sun & 8pm-midnight Fri & Sat Apr-Nov), which specializes in sushi, grilled fish and clay-oven-fired pizza. COT runs two buses daily from Punta to José Ignacio (UR$82, 40 minutes).

Il Baretto ITALIAN $$$
(☎4244-5565; www.ilbarettopunta.com; cnr Calles 9 & 10; pizza UR$220-390, dishes UR$395-660; ⏲11am-4pm & 8pm-midnight daily mid-Dec–Carnaval, Fri-Sun rest of year) Candlelit garden seating on plush chairs and couches provides a romantic setting for 'after-beach' drinks, or for feasting on homemade pasta, pizza and desserts.

Drinking & Nightlife

A cluster of clubs in Punta's port area stays open all year (weekends only in low season). During the super-peak season from Christmas through January, an additional slew of beach clubs with ever-changing names open along Playa Brava, on the beach road to La Barra.

Bear in mind that it's social suicide to turn up at a nightclub before 2am here. In general, Punta's bars stay open as long as there's a crowd and sometimes have live music on weekends.

Moby Dick PUB
(www.mobydick.com.uy; Calle 13, btwn Calles 10 & 12) This classic pub near the yacht harbor is where Punta's dynamic social scene kicks off every evening.

Mambo Club CLUB
(www.facebook.com/MamboClubPuntaDelEste; cnr Calle 13 & Calle 10) A popular dance spot featuring Latin grooves.

Soho CLUB
(www.facebook.com/SohoPuntaUy; Calle 13, btwn Calles 10 & 12) Another dependable year-round dance spot featuring an ever-changing cast of international DJs.

Entertainment

Medio y Medio JAZZ
(☎4257-8791; www.medioymedio.com; Camino Lussich s/n, Punta Ballena) This jazz club and restaurant near the beach in Punta Ballena brings in top-name performers from Uruguay, Argentina and Brazil.

Cine Libertador CINEMA
(Gorlero 796) Open year-round with movies on two screens.

Shopping

Manos del Uruguay WOOLENS
(www.manos.com.uy; Gorlero btwn Calles 30 & 31) The local branch of Uruguay's national cooperative, selling fine woolens.

Feria Artesanal HANDICRAFTS
(Plaza Artigas; ⏲1-7pm Apr-Nov, longer hours Dec-Mar) Artisan fair on Punta's central square.

Information

Most hotels and restaurants offer free wi-fi, and there's free municipal wi-fi on Plaza Artigas. Punta's many banks, ATMs and exchange offices are concentrated along Gorlero.

Antel (cnr Calles 25 & 24; ⏲9am-6pm Mon-Fri) A dependable option for internet (per hour UR$45) in the low season.

Centro de Hoteles y Restaurantes (☎4244-0512; www.puntadelestehoteles.com; Gorlero btwn Calles 21 & 23; ⏲10am-6pm Mon-Sat) Helps with hotel bookings.

Municipal Tourist Office (☎4244-6510; www.maldonado.gub.uy; Plaza Artigas; ⊗8am-11pm mid-Dec–Feb, 10:30am-4pm rest of year) Maintains additional branches at the bus terminal, the port and at Playa Mansa (☎4244-6519; cnr Calles 18 & 31; ⊗11am-5pm Apr-Nov, 9am-10pm Dec-Mar).

National Tourism Ministry (☎4244-1218; puntadeleste@mintur.gub.uy; Gorlero 942; ⊗10am-5pm Mon-Sat, noon-4pm Sun)

Post Office (Gorlero 1035)

Getting There & Away

AIR

Aeropuerto Internacional de Punta del Este (PDP; www.puntadeleste.aero) is at Laguna del Sauce, 20km west of Punta del Este.

Aerolíneas Argentinas (☎4244-4343; www.aerolineas.com.ar; Edificio Santos Dumont, Gorlero btwn Calles 30 & 31) Direct flights to Buenos Aires' Aeroparque.

BQB (www.flybqb.com) Direct flights to Buenos Aires' Aeroparque.

Sol (www.sol.com.ar) Direct flights to Rosario, Argentina.

BUS

From Punta's **bus terminal** (☎4249-4042; cnr Calle 32 & Bulevar Artigas), dozens of daily buses ply the coastal route to Montevideo. COT also has two daily northeast-bound buses to Rocha, the transfer point for La Paloma, La Pedrera and Cabo Polonio.

Buses from Punta del Este

DESTINATION	COST (UR$)	DURATION (HR)
Montevideo	208	2¼
Carrasco Airport (MVD)	208	1¾
Piriápolis	86	1
Punta del Diablo	286	3
Rocha	143	1½

Getting Around

TO/FROM THE AIRPORT

COT (☎4248-3558; www.cot.com.uy) runs direct minivans from the bus station to Punta del Este's airport (UR$160, 20 minutes), leaving 1½ hours before each flight.

BUS

From December through March, bus 14, operated by **Codesa** (☎4266-9129; www.codesa.com.uy), runs from Punta's bus terminal via the eastern beaches to La Barra (UR$30, 20 minutes) and José Ignacio (UR$48, 45 minutes); other Codesa buses run year-round to points west, including Punta Ballena.

CAR

Several major international car-rental companies have counters at Punta del Este's airport. Downtown along Gorlero you'll also find Uruguayan rental agencies such as **Punta Car** (www.puntacar.com.uy; Bulevar Artigas 101) and **Multicar** (www.redmulticar.com; Gorlero 860).

La Paloma

POP 3500

In the pretty rural department of Rocha, on a small peninsula 225km east of Montevideo, the seaside town of La Paloma is rather bland and sprawling, but it has attractive sandy beaches and some of Uruguay's best surfing. On summer weekends the town often hosts free concerts on the beach, making accommodations bookings essential.

Sights & Activities

El Faro del Cabo Santa María LIGHTHOUSE
(admission UR$20; ⊗10am-1pm & 3pm-sunset) The 1874 completion of this local lighthouse marked La Paloma's genesis as a summer beach resort. The unfinished first attempt collapsed in a violent storm, killing 17 French and Italian workers who are buried nearby. Outside is a solar clock using shadows cast by the lighthouse.

Laguna de Rocha RESERVE
An ecological reserve protected under Uruguay's SNAP program, this vast and beautiful wetland 10km west of La Paloma has populations of black-necked swans, storks, spoonbills and other waterfowl.

Peteco Surf Shop SURFING
(Av Nicolás Solari btwn Av El Sirio & Av del Navío) This friendly surf shop rents all the necessary equipment (shortboards, longboards, bodyboards, sandboards, wetsuits and kayaks) and can hook you up with good local instructors. The best surfing beaches are Los Botes, Solari and Anaconda southwest of town, and La Aguada and La Pedrera to the north.

Sleeping & Eating

La Balconada Hostel HOSTEL $
(☎4479-6273; www.labalconadahostel.com.uy; Centauro s/n; dm US$22-50, d US$80-120, d with shared bathroom US$50-90; 📶) This surfer-friendly hostel has an enviable location

that's a stone's throw from La Balconada beach, about 1km southwest of the center. Take a taxi from the bus station and the hostel will pick up the tab.

Hotel Bahía HOTEL $$$
(☎4479-6029; www.elbahia.com.uy; cnr Av del Navío & del Sol; d US$80-130, with air-con US$110-145; ❄📶) For its central location and overall comfort, Bahía is hard to beat. Rooms are clean and bright, with firm mattresses and bedside reading lights. The seafood restaurant downstairs (mains UR$220 to UR$480, closed Tuesday) has been in business since 1936 and regularly gets recommended by locals as La Paloma's best.

Punto Sur SEAFOOD $$
(Centauro s/n; dishes UR$250-400; ⏲11:30am-2am Christmas–Carnaval) For casual dining with an ocean view, this summer-only place on Playa La Balconada is the obvious choice, featuring tapas, paella, grilled fish and homemade pasta.

Lo de Edinson PARRILLA, PIZZERIA $$
(cnr Juno & Ceres; mains UR$150-360; ⏲noon-midnight) Best known for its grilled meats, this corner eatery in the heart of town also does decent pizzas.

☆ Entertainment

Peteco Resto-Pub LIVE MUSIC
(Av Nicolás Solari; ⏲noon-3pm & 8pm-3am late Dec–early Mar) Behind Peteco Surf Shop, this patio bar hosts live music nightly in summer. Out of season it opens only on Saturday nights.

ℹ Information

Banks, post and telephone offices are all on the main street, Av Nicolás Solari.

Tourist Office (☎4479-6088; Av Nicolás Solari; ⏲10am-10pm daily mid-Dec–Easter, 10:30am-4:30pm Tue-Sun rest of year) On the traffic circle at the heart of town. A second office in the bus terminal opens seasonally.

ℹ Getting There & Around

From La Paloma's bus terminal, 500m northwest of the center, COT, Cynsa and Rutas del Sol all run frequently to Montevideo (UR$344, four hours). There's also frequent local service to La Pedrera (UR$43, 15 minutes). Rutas del Sol runs twice daily to the Cabo Polonio turnoff (UR$86, 45 minutes) and once daily to Punta del Diablo (UR$172, two hours). For other destinations, take a bus to the departmental capital of Rocha (UR$47, 30 minutes, frequent), where hourly buses ply the coastal route in both directions.

La Pedrera

POP 230

Long a mecca for surfers, laid-back La Pedrera sits atop a bluff with magnificent sweeping views of the beaches stretching north toward Cabo Polonio and south toward La Paloma. In recent years, the town has also become famous for its Carnaval, which has grown increasingly raucous with the influx of out-of-town visitors. Even so, La Pedrera remains downright sleepy outside the summer months, with most hotels and tourist services closing between May and October.

🛏 Sleeping & Eating

As elsewhere along the coast, rates drop dramatically in the off-season.

El Viajero La Pedrera Hostel HOSTEL $
(☎4479-2252; www.elviajerolapedrera.com; cnr Benteveo & Zorzal; dm UR$400-840, d UR$1440-2880, d with shared bathroom UR$800-1680; ⏲mid-Dec–mid-Mar; @📶) Part of Uruguay's largest hostel chain, this well-located seasonal hostel is tucked down a side street, 200m from the OSE water tank (La Pedrera's most prominent landmark), a five-minute walk from the bus stop and only 500m from the beach.

Pueblo Barrancas CABAÑAS $$$
(☎4479-2236; www.pueblobarrancas.com; Ruta10, Km227.5; tents US$90-130, yurts US$90-130, cabañas US$130-200; ⏲noon-11pm daily mid-Dec–Easter, weekends only rest of year) At this low-key eco-resort 2km south of town, 30 spacious thatch-roofed cabañas, yurts and canvas-walled tents with wooden decks and hammocks are sprinkled throughout a landscape of coastal 'badlands' *(cárcavas)* leading to a windswept surfing beach. Dine beside the circular pool at the on-site restaurant, which features fresh-caught fish, organic produce from Pueblo Barrancas' own gardens, and locally foraged mushrooms.

Brisas de la Pedrera BOUTIQUE HOTEL $$$
(☎099-804656, 4479-2265; www.brisasdelapedrera.com; d US$150-280; ⏲Sep-Easter; ❄📶) La Pedrera's oldest hotel, luxuriously remodeled in 2009, woos high-end guests with sunny, spacious rooms, spectacular ocean views and plenty of comfortable amenities (but no TVs).

Costa Brava SEAFOOD $$
(dishes UR$260-450; ⏲ noon-3pm & 8pm-midnight daily Dec-Mar, weekends only rest of year) Perched atop the bluffs overlooking the Atlantic, Costa Brava is all about seafood accompanied by an unbeatable view.

La Pe SEAFOOD, ITALIAN $$
(☎ 094-408955; www.facebook.com/RestaurantLaPe; Calle Principal; mains UR$250-450; ⏲ 1-4pm & 8:30pm-12:30am Dec-Mar) 'P' is for pasta, paella and – in Spanish – *pescado* (fish). This popular place, which is smack in the heart of La Pedrera's main street, serves all three, with outdoor seating under the trees and a nice play area for kids. Look for the red, vine-covered building with the fish logo.

Perillán SEAFOOD $$$
(cnr Av Principal & Rambla; dishes UR$380-460; ⏲ noon-3pm & 8pm-midnight daily Dec-Mar, weekends only rest of year) Candlelit and cozy, with colorfully decorated wooden tables, excellent seafood, a good wine list and an outdoor deck with a front-row seat on the crashing waves across the street, Perillán is ideal for a romantic dinner. Specialties include *gambas al ajillo* (garlic shrimp) and *cazuela de mariscos* (seafood stew with shrimp, squid, octopus and potatoes in a rich tomato broth).

Information

La Pedrera's **tourist office** (⏲ Dec-Easter) is in a tiny wooden kiosk on Calle Principal, a few blocks in from the beach. The closest ATMs are in La Paloma.

Getting There & Away

Buses southbound to Montevideo (UR$358) and northbound to the Cabo Polonio turnoff (UR$53) stop at the OSE water tower (La Pedrera's tallest landmark) on the main street, a few blocks in from the waterfront. Schedules vary seasonally; a list is posted at the tourist office, opposite the bus stop. There are also frequent buses to Rocha (UR$72), where you can make connections north and south.

Cabo Polonio

POP 100

Northeast of La Paloma at Km264.5 on Ruta 10 lies the turnoff to Cabo Polonio, one of Uruguay's wildest areas and home to its second-biggest sea-lion colony, near a tiny fishing village nestled in sand dunes on a windswept point crowned by a lonely lighthouse. In 2009 the region was declared a national park, under the protective jurisdiction of Uruguay's SNAP program. Despite a growing influx of tourists (and an incongruously spiffy entrance portal erected in 2012), Cabo Polonio remains one of Uruguay's most rustic coastal villages. There are no banking services, and the town's limited electricity is derived from generators, solar and wind power.

OFF THE BEATEN TRACK

HORSING AROUND IN THE HILLS

An hour inland from La Pedrera, the Sierra de Rocha is a lovely landscape of grey rocky crags interspersed with rolling rangeland. **Caballos de Luz** (☎ 099-400446; www.caballosdeluz.com; s/d incl full board & horseback rides US$130/220), run by the multilingual Austrian-Uruguayan couple Lucie and Santiago, offers hill-country horse treks lasting from two hours to a week, complete with three delicious vegetarian meals daily and overnight accommodation in a pair of comfortable thatched guesthouses. Call for pickup at the bus station in Rocha (US$15), or drive there yourself (it's about 30 minutes off Hwy 9).

Sights

Faro Cabo Polonio LIGHTHOUSE
(admission UR$20; ⏲ 10am-1pm & 3pm-sunset) Cabo Polonio's striking lighthouse provides a fabulous perspective on the point, the sea-lion colony, and the surrounding dunes and islands.

Activities

Wildlife viewing is excellent year-round. Below the lighthouse, southern sea lions (*Otaria flavescens*) and South American fur seals (*Arctocephalus australis*) frolic on the rocks. You can also spot southern right whales from August to October, penguins on the beach between May and August, and the odd southern elephant seal (*Mirounga leonina*) between January and March on nearby Isla de la Raza.

Surfing classes are available in high season along with sandboard, skimboard and surfboard rentals. Inquire at the shop

DON'T MISS

ESTANCIA TOURISM IN URUGUAY

Estancias, the giant farms of Uruguay's interior, are a national cultural icon. The Uruguayan Ministry of Tourism has designated 'Estancia Turística' as a distinct lodging category, and dozens of such places have opened their doors to tourists, from traditional working farms to opportunistic wannabes. Typically, *estancias* organize daily activities with a heavy emphasis on horseback riding; many also provide overnight accommodations. Most are difficult to reach without a vehicle, although they'll often pick guests up with advance notice.

One of Uruguay's most impressive *estancias* is **San Pedro de Timote** (☎4310-8086; www.sanpedrodetimote.com; Ruta 7, Km142, Cerro Colorado; s/d incl all meals & activities from US$140/220 Sun-Thu, from US$205/300 Fri & Sat;), whose remarkable setting – 14km up a dirt road amid 253 hectares of rolling cattle country – is greatly enhanced by the complex of historic structures, some dating to the mid-19th century: a gracious white chapel, a courtyard with soaring palm trees, a library with gorgeous tilework and a circular stone corral. Common areas feature parquet wood floors, big fireplaces, comfy leather armchairs, two pools and a sauna. Prices include three meals, afternoon tea and two daily horseback-riding excursions, plus occasional bonfires and full-moon walks. Non-overnight guests can pay US$75 for lunch, afternoon tea and two horseback rides. The turnoff is just outside the town of Cerro Colorado, 160km northeast of Montevideo on Ruta 7.

Other favorite tourist *estancias* featured elsewhere in this guide include include La Sirena (p541) (near Mercedes), Guardia del Monte (p561) (near the northern Atlantic coast), and Yvytu Itaty (p546) (near Tacuarembó).

In Montevideo, **Lares** (☎2901-9120; www.lares.com.uy; WF Aldunate 1341) and **Cecilia Regules Viajes** (☎2916-3012; www.ceciliaregulesviajes.com; Bacacay 1334, Local C) are travel agencies specializing in *estancia* tourism.

with the crazy surfing penguin logo, in the square where trucks from Ruta 10 drop you off.

Local accommodations can arrange **horseback rides** along the beach and into the surrounding dunes. For more extensive horseback excursions, including monthly full-moon rides, try **Cabalgatas Valiceras** (☎099-574685; cabalgatasvaliceras.com.uy; Barra de Valizas), an excellent operator based in nearby Barra de Valizas.

Sleeping & Eating

Unless otherwise noted, places listed below are open year-round. Many locals also rent rooms and houses. The hardest time to find accommodation is during the first two weeks of January. Off-season, prices drop dramatically (40% to 70%).

Cabo Polonio Hostel HOSTEL $
(☎099-445943;www.cabopoloniohostel.com;dm/d US$33/120; ⊗closed Jun-Aug) Longtime resident Alfredo's rustic hostel (a two-minute walk from the bus stop) is lit by candlelight and solar power. There are hammocks overlooking the beach and a woodstove for cooking and staying cozy on stormy nights. Even in summer, its dorms and one double hold a maximum of 14, making it a tranquil alternative to some of Polonio's more jam-packed hostels.

Posada Rosada de los Corvinos HOSTEL, POSADA $
(☎098-565966; vientodobien@gmail.com; dm UR$750, d UR$2000, with shared bath UR$1600-1800) A short walk north of the bus stop, this sweet pink house with colorful murals houses one six-bed dorm, three double rooms and Cabo Polonio's town library. Solar panels provide the electricity, a woodstove provides the heat, and guests share access to a kitchen, living room and small yard with hammocks.

Pancho Hostal del Cabo HOSTEL $
(☎095-412633; www.hostaldelcabo.com; dm UR$600) Providing bare-bones dorms on two levels, Pancho's popular hostel is impossible to miss; look for the yellow corrugated roof, labeled with giant red letters, as you enter town. Nicest is the 2nd-floor dorm under the A-frame roof, with a small terrace looking straight out at the ocean.

Mariemar HOTEL $$$
(☎4470-5164, 9987-5260; posadamariemar@hotmail.com; r upstairs/downstairs US$180/160) Tucked below the lighthouse, with beach access right outside the back door and a restaurant on-site (mains UR$210 to UR$420), this hotel-restaurant is one of Polonio's oldest year-round businesses. The simple rooms all have ocean views, with downstairs units costing slightly less than those upstairs. In the off-season, singles go for as little as US$40.

La Majuga URUGUAYAN $
(snacks UR$35-140; 8:30am-11pm Nov-Apr) At this teal-green shack half a block from the bus stop, Señora Neli cooks up delicious empanadas (baked savory turnovers; UR$35) filled with *siri* (crab) and *pescado* (fish), along with *chivitos*, *milanesas* (breaded cutlets), fries and other reasonably priced Uruguayan snacks.

Getting There & Away

Rutas del Sol runs two to five buses daily from Montevideo to the Cabo Polonio turnoff (UR$395, 4½ hours), where waiting 4WD trucks offer rides across the dunes into town (UR$170 round-trip, 30 minutes each way).

Laguna de Castillos

Northwest of Cabo Polonio is the Laguna de Castillos, a vast coastal lagoon that shelters Uruguay's largest concentration of ombúes, graceful treelike plants whose anarchic growth pattern results in some rather fantastic shapes. In other parts of Uruguay the ombú is a solitary plant, but specimens here – some of them centuries old – grow in clusters, insulated by the lagoon from the bovine trampling that has spelled their doom elsewhere.

At **Monte de Ombúes** (☎099-295177), on the lagoon's western shore (near Km267 on Ruta 10), brothers Marcos and Juan Carlos Olivera, whose family received this land from the Portuguese crown in 1793, lead two- to three-hour excursions (per person UR$400, five-person minimum). Tours begin with a 20-minute boat ride through a wetland teeming with cormorants, ibis, cranes and black swans, followed by a hike through the ombú forest. Departures are frequent in summer (anytime five people show up); other times of year, reserve ahead. With advance notice, longer bird-watching tours of the lagoon can be arranged in the off-season for a flat fee of US$100 (one to five people).

★**Guardia del Monte** (☎4475-9064, 099-872588; www.guardiadelmonte.com; Ruta 9, Km261.5; r per person incl breakfast/half-board/full board US$110/150/180), overlooking the lagoon's northern shore, is a now-tranquil hideaway, originally established in the 18th century as a Spanish guard post to protect the Camino Real and the coastal frontier from pirates and Portuguese marauders. The lovely *estancia* house still oozes history, from the parlor displaying 18th-century maps and bird drawings to the kitchen's Danish woodstove salvaged from an 1884 shipwreck. Overnight rates include optional afternoon tea, plus walking and horseback excursions along the lakeshore and into the surrounding ombú forest. Meals are served on the ancient brick patio or by the fireplace in the cozy dining room. It's at the end of a 10km dead-end road, off Ruta 9, 4km south of the town of Castillos.

Punta del Diablo

POP 820

Once a sleepy fishing village, Punta del Diablo has long since become a prime summer getaway for Uruguayans and Argentines, and the epicenter of Uruguay's backpacker beach scene. Waves of seemingly uncontrolled development have pushed further inland and along the coast in recent years, but the stunning shoreline and laid-back lifestyle still exert their age-old appeal. To avoid the crowds, come outside the Christmas-to-February peak season; in particular, avoid the first half of January, when as many as 30,000 visitors inundate the town.

From the town's traditional center, a sandy 'plaza' 200m inland from the ocean, small dirt streets fan out in all directions.

Sights & Activities

During the day you can rent surfboards or horses along the town's main beach, or trek an hour north to Parque Nacional Santa Teresa. In the evening there are sunsets to watch, spontaneous bonfires and drum sessions to drop in on…you get the idea.

Sleeping

The town's hostel scene has taken off dramatically in recent years. *Cabañas* are the other accommodations of choice; this term

OFF THE BEATEN TRACK

URUGUAY'S OFF-THE-BEATEN-TRACK NATURE PRESERVES

Uruguay's interior, with its vast open spaces, is a naturalist's dream. The Uruguayan government has designated several natural areas for protection under its **SNAP** (Sistema Nacional de Áreas Protegidas; www.snap.gub.uy) program. Funding remains minimal, and tourist infrastructure rudimentary, but intrepid travelers will be richly rewarded for seeking out these little-visited spots. Below are two preserves that best capture the spirit of Uruguay's wild gaucho country. Other SNAP preserves mentioned in this book include Cabo Polonio (p559), Cerro Verde (p563) and Laguna de Rocha (p557).

Valle del Lunarejo

This gorgeous valley, 95km north of Tacuarembó, is a place of marvelous peace and isolation, with birds and rushing water providing the only soundtrack.

Visitors can spend the night at enchanting **Posada Lunarejo** (☎4650-6400; www.posadalunarejo.com; Ruta 30, Km238; r per person incl breakfast/full board UR$1200/1800), a restored 1880 building 2km off the main road, 3km from the river and a few steps from a garza (crane) colony.

CUT (www.cutcorporacion.com.uy) offers the most convenient bus schedule to Valle del Lunarejo on its daily Montevideo–Tacuarembó–Artigas bus (leaving Montevideo at noon, UR$673, six hours; leaving Tacuarembó at 4:50pm, UR$115, 1¼ hours). Posada Lunarejo can meet your bus if you call ahead.

Quebrada de los Cuervos

This hidden little canyon cuts through the rolling hill country 40km northwest of Treinta y Tres (325km northeast of Montevideo), providing an unexpectedly moist and cool habitat for a variety of plants and birds. There are a couple of self-guided hiking trails (2½ hours each), one looping through the canyon and another leading to the Cascada de Olivera waterfall.

A perfect base for exploring this region is **Cañada del Brujo** (☎099-297448, 4452-2837; www.pleka.com/delbrujo; dm/d/tr incl breakfast UR$650/1300/1950, incl half board UR$1100/2200/3000), a rustic hostel in an old schoolhouse 12km from the park. Hostel owner Pablo Rado can take you hiking (UR$220) or horseback riding (UR$450) to nearby waterfalls and introduce you to the joys of gaucho life: living by candlelight, drinking *mate*, sleeping under a wool poncho, eating simple meals cooked on the woodstove and watching spectacular sunsets under the big sky. With advance notice, he can provide transport to the hostel from Treinta y Tres (per person UR$300) or from the highway turnoff at Km306.7 on Ruta 8 (per person UR$150).

Nuñez (www.cynsa.com.uy) and **EGA** (www.ega.com.uy) run frequent buses from Montevideo to Treinta y Tres (UR$415, 4¼ hours).

applies to everything from rustic-to-a-fault shacks to custom-built designer condos with all modern conveniences. Most *cabañas* have kitchens; some require you to bring your own bedding. For help finding something, ask at Supermercado El Vasco in the heart of town, or check online at www.portaldeldiablo.com.uy. Rates skyrocket between Christmas and February.

★El Diablo Tranquilo HOSTEL $
(☎4477-2519; www.eldiablotranquilo.com; Av Central; dm US$18-40, d US$75-180, without bathroom US$52-100; @ 📶) Follow the devilish red glow into one of South America's most seductive hostels, whose endless perks include inviting chill-out areas, bike and surfboard rentals, yoga and language classes, horseback excursions and Paypal cash advances. At the beachside Playa Suites annex, upstairs rooms have full-on ocean views, while the raucous bar-restaurant offers meals, beach service, and a late-night party scene.

La Casa de las Boyas HOSTEL $
(☎4477-2074; www.lacasadelasboyas.com; Playa del Rivero; dm US$15-35, s/d/q from US$60/70/80; @ 📶 🏊) A stone's throw from the beach and a 10-minute walk north of the bus stop, this hostel offers a pool, a guest kitchen and 13 dorms of varying sizes. From April to November, the better rooms – equipped with

en suite bathrooms, kitchenettes and satellite TV – are rented out as private apartments for individuals, couples and groups.

Hostel de la Viuda HOSTEL $
(☎4477-2690; www.hosteldelaviuda.com; cnr San Luis & Nueva Granada; dm US$15-35, d US$56-90) It's a bit remote (2km southwest of the town center), but La Viuda offers good amenities, including free bus-station pickup, a backyard pool, a spacious kitchen and a comfy fireplace room perfect for enjoying games and movies or sipping hot chocolate at night. It's a six-block walk from Playa La Viuda, Punta del Diablo's southern beach.

Del Norte Vengo y En El Sur Me Quedo CABAÑA $$
(☎4477-2420, 099-878357; www.portaldeldiablo.com.uy; d US$80-130, q US$100-180) In the heart of town, these colorful two-level *cabañas* have upstairs decks, ocean views, and satiny curtains and bedspreads. Owners José and Dahiana lived in the US for several years and speak excellent English.

Eating

In high season, simply stroll the beachfront for your pick of seafood eateries and snack shacks by the dozen. Eateries listed below are among the few that remain open in winter. Another dependable year-round choice is the bar-restaurant at El Diablo Tranquilo (mains from US$10).

★Resto-Pub 70 ITALIAN $
(mains UR$200-260; noon-3pm Sat & Sun, 8pm-midnight daily mid-Dec–Easter) Run by a mother-father-son trio of recent Italian immigrants, this portside eatery decorated with Vespa paraphernalia serves divine homemade pasta, *cantucci con vino dolce* (almond biscotti dipped in sweet wine) and *limoncino* (an artisanal liqueur made with fragrant Uruguayan lemons). The *lasagne alle cipolle* (veggie lasagna with walnuts and caramelized onions) is to die for.

Cero Stress INTERNATIONAL $$
(Av de los Pescadores; mains UR$290-360; noon-4pm & 8pm-midnight) This laid-back spot features an eclectic menu, a rustic interior dining room and an open kitchen, but its greatest asset by far is the outdoor deck, which offers amazing ocean views. It's the perfect place to sip a *caipirinha* (Brazilian cocktail with sugar-cane alcohol) at sunset while contemplating your evening plans.

Lo de Olga SEAFOOD $$
(mains UR$250-430; noon-3pm & 7-11pm) For delicious home-cooked fish and puffy-as-a-cloud *buñuelos de algas* (seaweed fritters), try this simple family-run restaurant on the way down to the port.

Information

Punta del Diablo has no ATMs except for the temporary ones set up briefly each summer. Bring cash with you, as few businesses accept credit cards and the nearest banks are an hour away in Castillos (40km southwest) or Chuy (45km north).

Getting There & Away

Rutas del Sol, COT and Cynsa all offer service to Punta del Diablo's dreary new bus terminal, 2.5km west of town. Between Christmas and Carnaval, all buses terminate here, leaving you with a five- to 10-minute shuttle (UR$25) or taxi (UR$100) ride into town. During the rest of the year, buses continue from the terminal to the town plaza near the waterfront.

Several direct buses run daily to Montevideo and Chuy on the Brazilian border; for other coastal destinations, you'll usually need to change buses in Castillos or Rocha.

BUSES FROM PUNTA DEL DIABLO

DESTINATION	COST (UR$)	DURATION (HR)
Castillos	57	1
Chuy	72	1
Montevideo	430	5
Punta del Este	278	3
Rocha	143	1½

Parque Nacional Santa Teresa

This **national park** (☎4477-2101; sepae.webnode.es; 8am-8pm Dec-Mar, to 6pm Apr-Nov), 35km south of the Brazilian border, is administered by the army and attracts many Uruguayan and Brazilian visitors to its relatively uncrowded beaches. It offers 2000 dispersed campsites (per person UR$100 to UR$150) in eucalyptus and pine groves, a very small zoo and a plant conservatory. There's also a variety of four- to 10-person *cabañas* for rent; in January, prices range from UR$1500 for a basic A-frame to UR$4000 for a fancier oceanfront unit; between March and December these rates get slashed in half.

Buses from Punta del Diablo (UR$43, 15 minutes) will drop you off at Km302 on Hwy 9; from here, walk or take a shuttle 1km to the Capatacía (park headquarters), where there's a phone, post office, market, bakery and **restaurant** (dishes UR$105-260; ⏲noon-4pm & 7:30-9pm). Alternatively, walk north along the beach a couple of kilometers from Punta del Diablo to reach the park's southern edge at Playa Grande.

The park's star attraction, 4km north of park headquarters on Ruta 9, is the impressive hilltop fortress, **Fortaleza de Santa Teresa** (admission UR$20; ⏲10am-7pm daily Dec-Mar, 1-7pm Wed-Sun Apr-Nov), begun by the Portuguese in 1762 and finished by the Spaniards after its capture in 1793. At the park's northeastern corner is **Cerro Verde**, a coastal bluff protected under Uruguay's SNAP program.

Directly opposite the park entrance, on the west side of Ruta 9, a 5km dead-end dirt road leads to **Laguna Negra**, a vast lagoon where flamingos, capybaras and other wildlife can be spotted.

UNDERSTAND URUGUAY

Uruguay Today

The past decade has seen remarkable developments in Uruguayan culture and politics. After nearly two centuries of back-and-forth rule between the two traditional parties, Blancos and Colorados, Uruguayans elected the leftist Frente Amplio (Broad Front) to power in 2004 and again in 2009. Over that span, the Frente Amplio government has presided over numerous social changes, including the legalization of marijuana, abortion and same-sex marriage, and an ambitious program called Plan Ceibal that has distributed internet-ready laptops to every student in the country.

Most of these changes occurred during the five-year term of José Mujica (2009–14), a leftist and former guerrilla who famously survived 13 years of imprisonment and torture during Uruguay's period of military rule. As president, Mujica has been better known for his grandfatherly style and humility, famously donating the majority of his salary to charities, refusing to live in the presidential palace, and eschewing suits and ties in favor of sweaters.

As this book goes to press, new presidential and parliamentary elections are scheduled for October 2014, with the Frente Amplio widely expected to maintain control of the government.

Uruguay enters 2014 with a stable economy (inflation, at less than 10% annually, has been much less severe than in neighboring Argentina) and with high hopes for its national *fútbol* team, whose return to the World Cup is a source of tremendous national pride.

History

Uruguay's aboriginal inhabitants were the Charrúa along the coast and the Guaraní north of the Río Negro. The hunting-and-gathering Charrúa discouraged European settlement for more than a century by killing Spanish explorer Juan de Solís and most of his party in 1516. In any event there was little to attract the Spanish, who valued these lowlands along the Río de la Plata only as an access route to gold and other quick riches further inland.

The first Europeans to settle on the Banda Oriental (Eastern Shore) were Jesuit missionaries near present-day Soriano, on the Río Uruguay. Next came the Portuguese, who established present-day Colonia in 1680 as a beachhead for smuggling goods into Buenos Aires. Spain responded by building its own citadel at Montevideo in 1726. The following century saw an ongoing struggle between Spain and Portugal for control of these lands along the eastern bank of the Río de la Plata.

Napoleon's invasion of the Iberian peninsula in the early 19th century precipitated a weakening of Spanish and Portuguese power and the emergence of strong independence movements throughout the region. Uruguay's homegrown national hero, José Gervasio Artigas, originally sought to form an alliance with several states in present-day Argentina and southern Brazil against the European powers, but he was ultimately forced to flee to Paraguay. There he regrouped and organized the famous '33 Orientales,' a feisty band of Uruguayan patriots under General Juan Lavalleja who, with Argentine support, crossed the Río Uruguay on April 19, 1825, and launched a campaign to liberate modern-day Uruguay from Brazilian control. In 1828, after three years' struggle, a British-mediated treaty established Uruguay as a small independent buffer between the emerging continental powers.

For several decades, Uruguay's independence remained fragile. There was civil war between Uruguay's two nascent political parties, the Colorados and the Blancos (named, respectively, for the red and white bands they wore); Argentina besieged Montevideo from 1838 to 1851; and Brazil was an ever-present threat. Things finally settled down in the second half of the 19th century, with region-wide recognition of Uruguay's independence and the emergence of a strong national economy based on beef and wool production.

In the early 20th century, visionary president José Batlle y Ordóñez introduced such innovations as pensions, farm credits, unemployment compensation and the eight-hour work day. State intervention led to the nationalization of many industries, the creation of others, and a new era of general prosperity. However, Batlle's reforms were largely financed through taxing the livestock sector, and when exports faltered mid-century, the welfare state crumbled. A period of military dictatorship began in the early 1970s, during which torture became routine, and more than 60,000 citizens were arbitrarily detained before the 1980s brought a return to democratic traditions.

Culture

The one thing Uruguayans will tell you is that they're *not* anything like their *porteño* cousins across the water. Where Argentines can be brassy and sometimes arrogant, Uruguayans tend to be more humble and relaxed. Where the former have always been a regional superpower, the latter have always lived in the shadow of one. Those jokes about Punta del Este being a suburb of Buenos Aires don't go down so well on this side of the border. There are plenty of similarities, though: the near-universal appreciation for the arts, the Italian influence and the gaucho heritage.

Uruguayans like to take it easy and pride themselves on being the opposite of the hot-headed Latino type. Sunday's the day for family and friends, to throw half a cow on the *parrilla* (grill), sit back and sip some *mate*. The population is well educated. The gap between rich and poor is much less pronounced than in most other Latin American countries, although the economic crises of the early 21st century have put a strain on the middle class.

Population

With 3.3 million people, Uruguay is South America's smallest Spanish-speaking country. The population is predominately white (88%) with 8% mestizo (people with mixed Spanish and indigenous blood) and 4% black. Indigenous peoples are practically nonexistent. The average life expectancy (76.61 years) is one of Latin America's highest. The literacy rate is also high, at 98.1%, while population growth is a slow 0.25%. Population density is roughly 19 people per sq km.

Religion

Uruguay has more self-professed atheists per capita than any other Latin American country. According to a 2008 American Religious Identification Survey, only slightly more than half of Uruguayans consider themselves religious. Forty-seven percent identify themseles as Roman Catholic, with 11% claiming affiliation with other Christian denominations. There's a small Jewish minority, numbering around 18,000.

Sports

Uruguayans, like just about all Latin Americans, are crazy about *fútbol* (soccer). Uruguay has won the World Cup twice, including the first tournament played in Montevideo in 1930. The national team (known commonly as La Celeste) continues to excel at the international level, winning the 2011 Copa America and qualifying for the 2014 World Cup in Brazil.

The most notable *fútbol* teams are the Montevideo-based Nacional and Peñarol. If you go to a match between these two, make sure you sit on the sidelines, not behind the goal, unless you're up for some serious rowdiness.

The **Asociación Uruguayo de Fútbol** (☎2400-7101; www.auf.org.uy; Guayabos 1531) in Montevideo has information on matches and venues.

Arts

Despite its small population, Uruguay has an impressive literary and artistic tradition. The country's most famous philosopher and essayist is José Enrique Rodó, whose 1900 essay *Ariel,* contrasting North American and Latin American civilizations, is a classic of the country's literature. Major contemporary writers include Juan Carlos Onetti, Mario Benedetti and Eduardo Galeano.

The most famous Uruguay-related film is Costa-Gavras' engrossing *State of Siege* (1973), filmed in Allende's Chile, which deals with the Tupamaro guerrillas' kidnapping and execution of suspected American CIA officer Dan Mitrione. Among the best movies to come out of Uruguay recently are César Charlone's award-winning *El Baño del Papa* (2007), based on Pope John Paul II's 1988 visit to Uruguay, and *3 Millones* (2011), in which father-son team Jaime and Yamandú Roos document their experiences accompanying Uruguay's *fútbol* team to the 2010 South Africa World Cup.

Theater is popular and playwrights like Mauricio Rosencof are prominent. The most renowned painters are the late Juan Manuel Blanes, Pedro Figari and Joaquín Torres García. Sculptors include José Belloni.

Tango is big in Montevideo – Uruguayans claim tango legend Carlos Gardel as a native son, and one of the best-known tangos, 'La Cumparsita,' was composed by Uruguayan Gerardo Matos Rodríguez. During Carnaval, Montevideo's streets reverberate to the energetic drumbeats of *candombe,* an African-derived rhythm brought to Uruguay by slaves from 1750 onwards. On the contemporary scene, several Uruguayan rock bands have won a following on both sides of the Río de la Plata, including Buitres, La Vela Puerca and No Te Va Gustar.

Food & Drink

Uruguayan cuisine revolves around grilled meat. *Parrillas* (restaurants with big racks of meat roasting over a wood fire) are everywhere, and weekend *asados* (barbecues) are a national tradition. *Chivitos* (classic Uruguayan steak sandwiches) are hugely popular, as are *chivitos al plato* (served with fried potatoes instead of bread). Vegetarians often have to content themselves with the ubiquitous pizza and pasta, although there are a few veggie restaurants lurking about. Seafood is excellent on the coast. Desserts are a dream of meringue, *dulce de leche* (milk caramel), burnt sugar and custard.

Tap water is OK to drink in most places. Uruguayan wines (especially tannats) are excellent, and local beers (Patricia, Pilsen and Zillertal) are passable.

Uruguayans consume even more *mate* (a kind of tea-like beverage) than Argentines. If you get the chance, try to acquire the taste – there's nothing like whiling away an afternoon with new-found friends passing around the *mate*.

In major tourist destinations such as Punta del Este and Colonia, restaurants charge *cubiertos* (cover charges of UR$20 or more). Theoretically these pay for the basket of bread offered before your meal.

Environment

Though one of South America's smallest countries, Uruguay is not so small by European standards. Its area of 176,215 sq km is greater than England and Wales combined, or slightly bigger than the US state of Florida.

Uruguay's two main ranges of interior hills are the Cuchilla de Haedo, west of Tacuarembó, and the Cuchilla Grande, south of Melo; neither exceeds 500m in height. West of Montevideo the terrain is more level. The Río Negro flowing through the center of the country forms a natural dividing line between north and south. The Atlantic coast has impressive beaches, dunes, headlands and lagoons. Uruguay's grasslands and forests resemble those of Argentina's pampas or southern Brazil, and patches of palm savanna persist in the east, along the Brazilian border.

The country is rich in birdlife, especially in the coastal lagoons of Rocha department. Most large land animals have disappeared, but the occasional ñandú (rhea) still races across northwestern Uruguay's grasslands. Whales, fur seals and sea lions are common along the coast.

SURVIVAL GUIDE

Directory A-Z

ACCOMMODATIONS

Uruguay has an excellent network of hostels and campgrounds, especially along the Atlantic coast. Other low-end options include *hospedajes* (family homes) and *residenciales* (budget hotels).

Posadas (inns) are available in all price ranges and tend to be homier than hotels. Hotels are ranked from one to five stars, according to amenities.

Country *estancias turísticas* (marked with blue National Tourism Ministry signs) provide lodging on farms.

ACTIVITIES

Punta del Diablo, La Paloma, La Pedrera and Punta del Este all get excellent surfing waves, while Cabo Polonio and the coastal lagoons of Rocha department are great for whale and bird-watching, respectively. Punta del Este's beach scene is more upmarket, with activities such as parasailing, windsurfing and jet skiing.

Horseback riding is very popular in the interior and can be arranged on most tourist *estancias*.

BUSINESS HOURS

Standard opening times:

Banks 1-6pm Mon-Fri. Exchange offices usually keep longer hours.

Restaurants noon-3pm & 8pm-midnight or later. If serving breakfast, opening around 8am.

Bars, pubs & clubs 6pm-late. Things don't get seriously shaking until after midnight.

Shops 9am-1pm & 3-7pm Mon-Sat. In larger cities, department stores and supermarkets stay open at lunchtime and/or Sundays.

ELECTRICITY

Uruguay uses the same electrical plug as Argentina (see p600).

EMBASSIES & CONSULATES

All listings are in Montevideo:

Argentine Embassy Embassy (☎2902-8166; eurug.cancilleria.gov.ar; Cuareim 1470); Consulate (☎2902-8623; cmdeo.mrecic.gov.ar; WF Aldunate 1281)

Australian Consulate (☎2901-0743; www.dfat.gov.au/missions/countries/uy.html; Cerro Largo 1000)

Brazilian Embassy Embassy (☎2707-2119; montevideu.itamaraty.gov.br; Artigas 1394); Consulate (☎2901-2024; cgmontevideu.itamaraty.gov.br; Convención 1343, 6th fl)

Canadian Embassy (☎2902-2030; uruguay.gc.ca; Plaza Independencia 749, Oficina 102)

French Embassy (☎2-1705-0000; www.ambafranceuruguay.org; Av Uruguay 853)

German Embassy (☎2902-5222; www.montevideo.diplo.de; La Cumparsita 1435)

UK Embassy (☎2622-3630; ukinuruguay.fco.gov.uk; Marco Bruto 1073)

US Embassy (☎2-1770-2000; uruguay.usembassy.gov; Lauro Muller 1776)

GAY & LESBIAN TRAVELERS

Uruguay has become more LGBT-friendly in recent years. In January 2008 it became the first Latin American country to recognize same-sex civil unions, and in 2013 same-sex marriage was legalized.

In Montevideo, look for the pocket-sized **Friendly Map** (www.friendlymap.com.uy) listing LGBT-friendly businesses throughout Uruguay.

PRICE RANGES

Throughout this chapter the following price ranges within Sleeping listings refer to a double room with bathroom in high season. Breakfast is usually included in the price.

$ less than UR$1250

$$ UR$1250-2500

$$$ more than UR$2500

Within Eating listings the following price ranges refer to a standard main course.

$ less than UR$250

$$ UR$250-400

$$$ more than UR$400

HEALTH

No vaccinations are required for Uruguayan travel. Uruguay has a good public-health system, and tap water is generally safe to drink.

INSURANCE

Worldwide travel insurance is available at www.lonelyplanet.com/travel_services. You can buy, extend and claim online anytime – even if you're already on the road.

INTERNET ACCESS

Wi-fi zones and internet cafes are commonplace in cities and larger towns. Many Antel (state telephone company) offices also provide internet for UR$19 to UR$45 per hour.

LEGAL MATTERS

Uruguay has some of Latin America's most lenient drug laws. In December 2013 Uruguay became the first country in the world to legalize and regulate the sale of marijuana at the national level. Possession of small amounts of other drugs for personal use has also been decriminalized, but their sale remains illegal.

MAPS

Local tourist offices throughout Uruguay hand out excellent free city maps. **ITMB** (shop.itmb.ca) publishes a useful map depicting Montevideo on one side and Uruguay on the other, with inset maps of Colonia and Punta del Este. Other good map sources in Uruguay include Ancap service stations, the Automóvil Club del Uruguay (p570) and **Servicio Geográfico Militar** (☎2487-1810;

FESTIVALS & EVENTS

Uruguay's Carnaval lasts for more than a month and is livelier than Argentina's. Semana Santa (Holy Week) has become known as Semana Turismo – many Uruguayans travel out of town, and finding accommodations is tricky during this time. Other noteworthy events include Paysandú's beer festival, Tacuarembó's Fiesta de la Patria Gaucha and the nationwide Días del Patrimonio in early October, during which visitors are invited to tour Uruguay's most important historical and cultural monuments free of charge.

www.sgm.gub.uy; 8 de Octubre 3255, Montevideo; ⌚8am-1pm Mon-Fri).

MONEY

Prices are in *pesos uruguayos* (UR$), the official Uruguayan currency. Banknote values are 20, 50, 100, 200, 500, 1000 and 2000. There are coins of one, two, five, 10 and 50 pesos.

US dollars are commonly accepted in major tourist hubs, where top-end hotels and even some budget accommodations quote US$ prices. However, beware of poor exchange rates at hotel desks. In many cases, you'll come out ahead paying in pesos. Away from the touristed areas, dollars are of limited use.

Unlike Argentina, Uruguay has no black or 'blue' market offering higher exchange rates for US and European banknotes.

ATMs

In all but the smallest interior towns, getting cash with your ATM card is easy. Machines marked with the green Banred or blue Redbrou logo serve all major international banking networks.

ATMs dispense bills in multiples of 100 pesos. To avoid getting stuck with large bills, don't request multiples of UR$1000 (ie take out UR$900 rather than UR$1000, UR$1900 rather than UR$2000 etc).

Many ATMs dispense US dollars, designated as U$S, but only in multiples of US$100.

Credit Cards

Most upmarket hotels, restaurants and shops accept credit cards.

Moneychangers

There are *casas de cambio* in Montevideo, Colonia, the Atlantic beach resorts and border towns such as Chuy. They keep longer hours than banks but often offer lower rates.

Tipping

- In restaurants, leave 10% of the bill.
- In taxis, round up the fare a few pesos.

POST

Correo Uruguayo (www.correo.com.uy), the national postal service, has offices throughout Uruguay. Rates are reasonable, though service can be slow.

PUBLIC HOLIDAYS

Año Nuevo (New Year's Day) January 1

Día de los Reyes (Epiphany) January 6

Viernes Santo/Pascua (Good Friday/Easter) March/April (dates vary)

Desembarco de los 33 (Return of the 33 Exiles) April 19; honors the exiles who returned to Uruguay in 1825 to liberate the country from Brazil with Argentine support

Día del Trabajador (Labor Day) May 1

Batalla de Las Piedras (Battle of Las Piedras) May 18; commemorates a major battle of the fight for independence

Natalicio de Artigas (Artigas' Birthday) June 19

Jura de la Constitución (Constitution Day) July 18

Día de la Independencia (Independence Day) August 25

Día de la Raza (Columbus Day) October 12

Día de los Muertos (All Souls' Day) November 2

Navidad (Christmas Day) December 25

TELEPHONE

Uruguay's country code is 598. **Antel** (www.antel.com.uy) is the state telephone company, with offices in every town.

All Uruguayan landline numbers are eight digits long, beginning with 2 for Montevideo or 4 for elsewhere in the country. Cell (mobile) phone numbers consist of a three-digit prefix (most commonly 099) followed by a six-digit number. If dialing internationally, drop the leading zero.

Public phones require prepaid cards, sold in values of 25, 50, 100, 200 and 500 pesos, available at Antel offices or newspaper kiosks.

Most internet cafes have headphone-microphone setups and Skype installed on their computers.

Cell Phones

Three companies – **Antel** (www.antel.com.uy), **Movistar** (www.movistar.com.uy) and **Claro** (www.claro.com.uy) – provide cell-phone service in Uruguay. Rather than use expensive roaming plans, many travelers bring an unlocked cell phone (or buy a cheap one here) and simply insert a local SIM card. These are readily available at most kiosks, as are prepaid cards to recharge your credit.

TIME

Uruguay Standard Time is three hours behind GMT and one hour ahead of Argentina. Daylight-saving time, when clocks are moved forward one hour, starts on the first Sunday in October. Clocks are put back an hour on the second Sunday in March.

TOURIST INFORMATION

The **National Tourism Ministry** (Ministerio de Turismo y Deporte; www.turismo.gub.uy) operates 10 offices around the country. It distributes excellent free maps for each of Uruguay's 19 departments, along with specialized information on *estancia* tourism, Carnaval, surfing and other subjects of interest to travelers. Most towns also have a muncipal tourist office on the plaza or at the bus terminal.

TRAVELERS WITH DISABILITIES

Uruguay is slowly beginning to deliver for travelers with special needs. In Montevideo, for example, you'll find newly constructed ramps and dedicated bathrooms in high-profile destinations such as Plaza Independencia and Teatro Solís, disabled access on some bus lines, as well as a growing number of ATM machines for the visually impaired. However, there's still a long way to go. Spanish-language websites that can provide useful resources for those with disabilities include pronadis.mides.gub.uy, www.accesibilidad.gub.uy and www.discapacidaduruguay.org.

VISAS

Nationals of Western European countries, Australia, the USA, Canada and New Zealand automatically receive a 90-day tourist card, renewable for another 90 days. Other nationals may require visas. For an official list of current visa requirements by nationality, see www.dnm.minterior.gub.uy/visas.php. For extensions, visit the **Dirección Nacional de la Migración** (☎2916-0471; www.dnm.minterior.gub.uy; Misiones 1513) in Montevideo, or local offices in border towns.

VOLUNTEERING

Academia Uruguay (www.academiauruguay.com) Language school offering volunteer opportunities in Montevideo.

Karumbé (www.karumbe.org) Sea-turtle conservation.

WOMEN TRAVELERS

Women are generally treated with respect, and traveling alone in Uruguay is substantially safer here than in many other Latin American countries.

ℹ Getting There & Away

Flights and tours can be booked online at lonelyplanet.com/bookings.

URUGUAYAN BORDER CROSSINGS

FROM	TO	ROAD NUMBER/ DESCRIPTION
ARGENTINA		
Buenos Aires	Montevideo	Boat (Buquebus)
Buenos Aires	Colonia	Boat (Buquebus, Colonia Express, Seacat)
Tigre	Carmelo	Boat (Cacciola)
Gualeguaychú	Fray Bentos	Puente General San Martín (bridge)
Colón	Paysandú	Puente General Artigas (bridge)
Concordia	Salto	Represa de Salto Grande (dam)
Concordia	Salto	Boat (Transporte Fluvial San Cristóbal)
BRAZIL		
Chuí	Chuy	Hwy BR-471/UR-9
Jaguarão	Río Branco	Hwy BR-116/ UR-26
Aceguá	Aceguá	Hwy BR-153/UR-8
Santana do Livramento	Rivera	Hwy BR-293/ UR-5
Quaraí	Artigas	Hwy BR-377/ UR-30
Barra do Quaraí	Bella Unión	Hwy BR-472/ UR-3

ENTERING THE COUNTRY

Uruguay requires passports of all foreigners, except those from neighboring countries (who need only national identification cards).

AIR

Airports & Airlines

Montevideo's Carrasco International Airport (p533) is the main port of entry, although a few direct flights from neighboring countries serve **Punta del Este international airport** (Aeropuerto Laguna del Sauce; ☎4255-9777; www.puntadeleste.aero) and Nueva Hespérides airport in Salto (p545).

Pluna, the Uruguayan national airline, declared bankruptcy and ceased service in July 2012. At the time of research, a new national airline known as Alas-U was expected to begin service by mid-2014.

Airlines with direct flights to Uruguay:

Aerolíneas Argentinas (www.aerolineas.com.ar)
Air Europa (www.aireuropa.com)
American Airlines (www.aa.com)
Avianca/TACA (www.avianca.com)
BQB (www.flybqb.com)
Copa (www.copaair.com)
Gol (www.voegol.com.br)
LAN (www.lan.com)
Sol (www.sol.com.ar)
TAM (www.tam.com.br)

LAND & SEA

Uruguay shares land borders with the Argentine province of Entre Ríos and the southern Brazilian state of Rio Grande do Sul. The major highways and bus services are generally good, although buses from Montevideo to Buenos Aires are slower and less convenient than the ferries across the Río de la Plata. For Iguazú Falls, traveling via Argentina is faster, cheaper and more straightforward than traveling through Brazil.

Getting Around

BUS

Buses are comfortable, fares are reasonable and distances are short. Many companies offer free wi-fi on board. In the few cities that lack terminals, all companies are within easy walking distance of each other, usually around the main plaza.

Reservations are unnecessary except during holiday periods. On peak travel dates a single company may run multiple departures at the same hour, in which case they'll mark a bus number on your ticket; check with the driver to make sure you're boarding the right bus, or you may find yourself in the 'right' seat on the wrong bus!

Most towns with central bus terminals have a fee-based left-luggage facility.

CAR & MOTORCYCLE

Visitors to Uruguay who are staying less than 90 days need only bring a valid driver's license from their home country. Uruguayan drivers are extremely considerate, and even bustling Montevideo is quite sedate compared with Buenos Aires.

Uruguay imports all its oil. Due to government regulation, all service stations charge the same price for fuel. Unleaded gasoline cost UR$40.60 a liter at the time of research.

The **Automóvil Club del Uruguay** (☎1707; www.acu.com.uy; Colonia 1251, Montevideo) has good maps and information.

Car Hire

Economy cars rent locally for upwards of UR$1000 a day in the high season, with tax and insurance included. Advance online bookings are often cheaper than in-country rentals. Most credit-card companies' automatic LDW (loss-damage-waiver) insurance covers rentals in Uruguay.

Road Rules & Hazards

Drivers are required to turn on their headlights during the daytime on all highways. Most towns have alternating one-way streets, with an arrow marking the allowed direction of travel.

Outside Montevideo, most intersections have neither a stop sign nor a traffic light; right of way is determined by who reaches the corner first. This can be nerve-wracking for the uninitiated!

Outside the capital and coastal tourist areas, traffic is minimal and poses few problems. Roads are generally in reasonable shape, but some interior roads can be rough. Keep an eye out for livestock and wildlife. Even in Montevideo's busy downtown, horse-drawn carts still operate, hauling trash or freight.

Speed limits are clearly posted but rarely enforced. Arbitrary police stops are rare.

HITCHHIKING

It's not uncommon to see locals hitchhiking in rural areas, as gas is expensive and relatively few people own cars. Safety is not as serious a concern as in most other countries.

LOCAL TRANSPORTATION

Taxis, *remises* (radio-dispatched taxis) and local buses are similar to those in Argentina. Taxis are metered, and drivers calculate fares using meter readings and a photocopied chart. Between 10pm and 6am, and on Sundays and holidays, fares are 20% higher. There's a small additional charge for luggage, and passengers generally tip the driver by rounding fares up to the next multiple of five or 10 pesos. City bus service is excellent in Montevideo and other urban areas, while *micros* (minibuses) form the backbone of the local transit network in smaller coastal towns such as La Paloma.

Understand Argentina

Argentina Today

Argentina has two faces: it's a country that has harbored both prosperity and decline. Today inflation is rampant, the economy continues to stumble and the black market for US dollars remains robust despite government crackdowns – yet an economic comeback is always around the corner. And though president Cristina Kirchner's popularity goes up and down, she's a master of resilience – you should never count her out.

Best in Print

Kiss of the Spider Woman (Manuel Puig, 1976) Two prisoners and their developing relationship in a Buenos Aires prison; made into the Oscar-winning 1985 film.

In Patagonia (Bruce Chatwin, 1977) Evocative writing on Patagonia's history and mystique.

The Motorcycle Diaries (1993, Ernesto Che Guevara et al) Based on the travel diary of the Argentine-born revolutionist.

And the Money Kept Rolling In (and Out) (Paul Blustein, 2005) How the IMF helped bankrupt Argentina.

Best on Film

La historia oficial (The Official Story, 1985) Oscar-winning film on the Dirty War.

Pizza, birra, faso (Pizza, Beer, Cigarettes, 1998) Four Buenos Aires gangster youths try to survive on the city streets.

Nueve reinas (Nine Queens, 2000) Two con men chasing the big score.

El secreto de sus ojos (The Secret in Their Eyes, 2009) Thriller that won the 2010 Oscar for best foreign-language film.

Cristina's Reign

Since Cristina Kirchner's re-election in 2011, things haven't been so rosy. Her popularity plunged as the economy hit the brakes, inflation skyrocketed and crime kept rising. *The Economist* and international agencies such as the IMF have accused her government of cooking the books (especially inflation figures). Her health has been on the rocks. She had to have surgery to remove her thyroid in 2012, and she underwent a procedure to remove a blood clot on her brain in 2013. She lost even more political support in the October 2013 mid-term elections. This made the possibility of a Chavez-like third term – currently not allowed in the constitution, but something many thought Cristina was after – very unlikely.

But nobody can write 'la presidenta' off yet – she still maintains majorities in both chambers, her term won't be up until 2015 and she's been known to make comebacks. And despite her many detractors, Cristina has made admirable social strides. She has addressed abuses perpetrated by the military dictatorship, championed same-sex marriage laws and, above all, supported the blue-collar classes. And her people will still love her for it, just as they did Evita.

Economic Woes

Argentina's currency devaluation in 2002 caused surging demand for its suddenly cheap agricultural products. Helped along by skyrocketing government spending and strong growth in Brazil and China, this economic boom lasted through 2007 and revved up again in 2010. But high inflation, a stronger peso and lower commodity prices have reined in the economy.

In October 2011, in an effort to curb the flow of capital heading overseas, the government started requiring Argentines to substantiate their purchases of US dollars. This created a black market for US dollars, which are highly sought after as a stable currency. And the real-estate market stalled, since purchases were pretty much always transacted in US dollars.

Many economists believe that the government needs to reduce spending and stop borrowing from its central bank; control inflation; and maintain foreign-exchange reserves. Moreover, government policies need to become more transparent to encourage both domestic and foreign investment. These are tall orders and go against the traditional Argentine economic flow, but recession and even devaluation are increasing risks. Who knows – maybe another crash is just what Argentina needs to get on top again.

(Almost) Everyone Loves the Pope

After Cardinal Jorge Mario Bergoglio, the archbishop of Buenos Aires, was named pope in March 2013 he took the name Francis I. Not only was he the first pontiff to bear that moniker, he was also the first to hail from the Americas and the first to belong to the Jesuit order. It's a fair bet that he's also the first pope to have grown up drinking *mate,* tangoing at *milongas* and ardently supporting the San Lorenzo *fútbol* club.

Bergoglio was a humble man who had eschewed the archbishop's palace in Olivos, remaining in his modest apartment and getting around Buenos Aires by bus and the Subte. As pope he has continued such habits, emulating his namesake and personal hero, the saint from Assisi who once renounced all worldly possessions. This humility, coupled with the very personable humanity Francis displays, has made him an extremely popular pontiff.

Oddly enough, one person who is at odds with Pope Francis is Cristina Kirchner. She and her late husband Néstor once considered the conservative Bergoglio a political arch-rival who clashed with their liberal social views. Today, however, she's had to pull an about-face and make peace with the world's most powerful religious leader.

AREA: **2.8 MILLION SQ KM**

POPULATION: **41.8 MILLION**

GDP: **US$475 BILLION**

INFLATION: **26% (UNOFFICIAL)**

UNEMPLOYMENT RATE: **7.2%**

if Argentina were 100 people

92 would be Roman Catholics
2 would be Jewish
2 would be Protestant
4 would be other

ethnicity

(% of population)

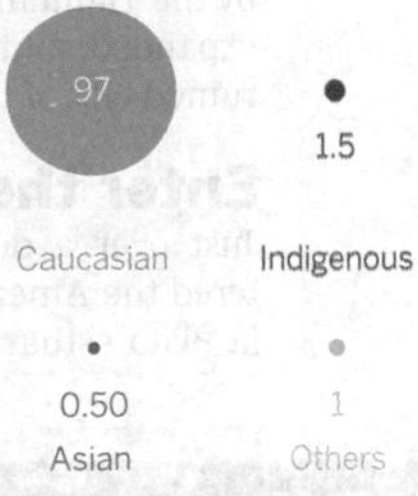

population per sq km

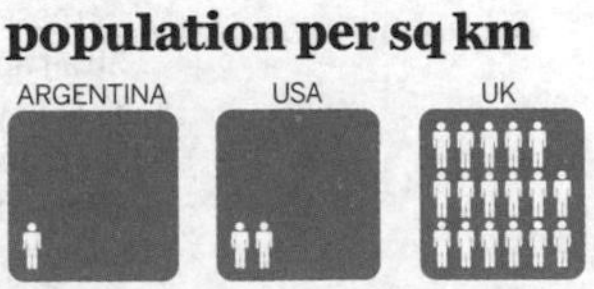

History

Like all Latin American countries, Argentina has a tumultuous history, one tainted by periods of despotic rule, corruption and hard times. But its history is also illustrious, the story of a country that fought off Spanish colonial rule and was once among the world's economic powerhouses. It's a country that gave birth to international icons such as the gaucho, Evita Perón and Che Guevara. Understanding Argentina's past is paramount to understanding its present and, most importantly, to understanding Argentines themselves.

Argentina's national beer, Quilmes, is named after the now decimated indigenous group of northwest Argentina. It's also the name of a city in the province of Buenos Aires.

Native Peoples

Many different native peoples ranged throughout what became Argentina. On the pampas lived the hunter-gatherer Querandí; in the north the Guaraní were semisedentary agriculturalists and fishermen. In the Lake District and Patagonia, the Pehuenches and Puelches gathered the pine nuts of the araucaria; while the Mapuche entered the region from the west as the Spanish pushed south. Today there are several Mapuche reservations, especially in the area around Junín de los Andes.

Until they were wiped out by Europeans, there were indigenous inhabitants as far south as Tierra del Fuego (Land of Fire), where the Selk'nam, Haush, Yahgan and Alacaluf peoples lived as mobile hunters and gatherers. Despite frequently inclement weather they wore little or no clothing, but constant fires kept them warm and gave the region its name.

Of all of Argentina, the northwest was the most developed. Several indigenous groups, notably the Diaguita, practiced irrigated agriculture in the valleys of the eastern Andean foothills. Inhabitants were influenced by the Tiahuanaco empire of Bolivia and by the great Inca empire, which expanded south from Peru from the early 1480s. In Salta province the ruined city of Quilmes is one of the best-preserved pre-Incan sites.

Enter the Spanish

Just over a decade after Christopher Columbus accidentally encountered the Americas, other European explorers began probing the Río de la Plata estuary. Most early explorations of the area were motivated by

TIMELINE

10,000 BC

Humans, having crossed the Bering Strait approximately 20,000 years earlier, finally reach the area of modern-day Argentina. The close of one of the world's greatest human migrations nears.

7370 BC

Toldense culture makes its first paintings of hands inside Patagonia's famous Cueva de las Manos. The paintings prove humans inhabited the region this far back.

4000 BC

The indigenous Yahgan, later referred to as Fuegians by the English-speaking world, begin populating the southernmost islands of Tierra del Fuego. Humans could migrate no further south.

rumors of vast quantities of silver. Spaniard Sebastian Cabot optimistically named the river the Río de la Plata (River of Silver) and, to drive the rumors home, part of the new territory was even given the Latin name for silver *(argentum)*. But the mineral riches that the Spanish found in the Inca empire of Peru never panned out in this misnamed land.

The first real attempt at establishing a permanent settlement on the estuary was made in 1536, by Spanish aristocrat Pedro de Mendoza. He landed at present-day Buenos Aires but, after the colonists tried pilfering food from the Querandí, the indigenous people turned on them violently. Within four years Mendoza fled back to Spain without a lick of silver, and the detachment of troops he left behind beat it upriver to the gentler environs of Asunción, present-day capital of Paraguay.

Northwest Supremacy

Although Spanish forces reestablished Buenos Aires by 1580, it remained a backwater in comparison to Andean settlements founded by a separate and more successful Spanish contingency moving south from Alto Perú (now Bolivia). With ties to the colonial stronghold of Lima and financed by the bonanza silver mine at Potosí, the Spanish founded some two dozen cities as far south as Mendoza (1561) during the latter half of the 16th century.

The two most important centers were Tucumán (founded in 1565) and Córdoba (1573). Tucumán lay in the heart of a rich agricultural region and supplied Alto Perú with grains, cotton and livestock. Córdoba became an important educational center, and Jesuit missionaries established *estancias* (ranches) in the sierras to supply Alto Perú with mules, foodstuffs and wine. Córdoba's Manzana Jesuítica (Jesuit Block) is now the finest preserved group of colonial buildings in the country, and several Jesuit *estancias* in the Central Sierras are also preserved. These sites, along with the central plazas of Salta (founded in 1582) and Tucumán, boast the finest colonial architecture.

The Mission (1986), starring Robert De Niro and Jeremy Irons, is an epic film about the Jesuit missions and missionaries in 18th-century South America. It's the perfect kick-off for a trip to northern Argentina's missions.

Buenos Aires: Bootlegger to Boomtown

As the northwest prospered, Buenos Aires suffered the Crown's harsh restrictions on trade for nearly 200 years. But because the port was ideal for trade, frustrated merchants turned to smuggling, and contraband trade with Portuguese Brazil and nonpeninsular European powers flourished. The wealth passing through the city fueled its initial growth.

With the decline of silver mining at Potosí in the late 18th century, the Spanish Crown was forced to recognize Buenos Aires' importance for direct transatlantic trade. Relaxing its restrictions, Spain made Buenos Aires the capital of the new viceroyalty of the Río de la Plata – which included Paraguay, Uruguay and the mines at Potosí – in 1776.

AD 1480s

The Inca empire expands into present-day Argentina's Andean Northwest. At the time, the region is inhabited by Argentina's most advanced indigenous cultures, including the Diaguita and Tafí.

1536

Pedro de Mendoza establishes Puerto Nuestra Señora Santa María del Buen Aire on the Río de la Plata. But the Spaniards anger the indigenous Querandí, who soon drive the settlers out.

1553

Francisco de Aguirre establishes Santiago del Estero, furthering Spain's expansion into present-day Argentina from Alto Perú. Today the city is the country's oldest permanent settlement.

1561

The city of Mendoza is founded by Spaniards during their push to establish access to the Río de la Plata, where Spanish ships could deliver more troops and supplies.

The new viceroyalty had internal squabbles over trade and control issues, but when the British raided the city in 1806 and again in 1807 (in an attempt to seize control of Spanish colonies during the Napoleonic Wars), the response was unified. Locals rallied against the invaders without Spanish help and chased them out of town.

The late 18th century also saw the emergence of the gauchos of the pampas. The South American counterpart to North America's cowboys, they hunted wild cattle and broke in wild horses whose numbers had multiplied after being left behind by expeditions on the Río de la Plata.

Independence & Infighting

One of the best-known contemporary accounts of postindependence Argentina is Domingo Faustino Sarmiento's *Life in the Argentine Republic in the Days of the Tyrants* (1868). Also superb is his seminal classic, *Facundo, or Civilization and Barbarism* (1845).

Toward the end of the 18th century, criollos (people of pure Spanish descent born in the New World) became increasingly dissatisfied and impatient with Spanish authority. The expulsion of British troops from Buenos Aires gave the people of the Río de la Plata new confidence in their ability to stand alone. After Napoleon invaded Spain in 1808, Buenos Aires finally declared its independence on May 25, 1810.

Independence movements throughout South America soon united to expel Spain from the continent by the 1820s. Under the leadership of General José de San Martín and others, the United Provinces of the Río de la Plata (the direct forerunner of the Argentine Republic) declared formal independence at Tucumán on July 9, 1816.

Despite achieving independence, the provinces were united in name only. With a lack of any effective central authority, regional disparities within Argentina – formerly obscured by Spanish rule – became more obvious. This resulted in the rise of the caudillos (local strongmen), who resisted Buenos Aires as strongly as Buenos Aires had resisted Spain.

Argentine politics was divided between the Federalists of the interior, who advocated provincial autonomy, and the Unitarists of Buenos Aires, who upheld the city's central authority. For almost 20 years bloody conflicts between the two factions left the country nearly exhausted.

The Reign of Rosas

In the first half of the 19th century Juan Manuel de Rosas came to prominence as a caudillo in Buenos Aires province, representing the interests of rural elites and landowners. He became governor of the province in 1829 and, while he championed the Federalist cause, he also helped centralize political power in Buenos Aires and proclaimed that all international trade be funneled through the capital. His reign lasted more than 20 years (to 1852), and he set ominous precedents in Argentine political life, creating the infamous mazorca (his ruthless political police force) and institutionalizing torture.

1565

Diego de Villarroel founds Argentina's third-oldest city, San Miguel de Tucumán (referred to today simply as Tucumán). The city was relocated further east 120 years later.

1573

The city of Córdoba is founded by Tucumán Governor Jerónimo Luis de Cabrera, establishing an important link on the trade routes between Chile and Alto Perú.

1580

Buenos Aires is re-established by Spanish forces, but the city remains a backwater for years, in comparison with the growing strongholds of Mendoza, Tucumán and Santiago del Estero.

1609

Jesuits begin building missions in Northeast Argentina, including San Ignacio Miní (1610), Loreto (1632) and Santa Ana (1633), concentrating the indigenous Guaraní into settlements known as *reducciones*.

Under Rosas, Buenos Aires continued to dominate the new country, but his extremism turned many against him, including some of his strongest allies. Finally, in 1852 a rival caudillo named Justo José de Urquiza (once a staunch supporter of Rosas) organized a powerful army and forced Rosas from power. Urquiza's first task was to draw up a constitution, which was formalized by a convention in Santa Fe on May 1, 1853.

The Fleeting Golden Age

Elected the Republic of Argentina's first official president in 1862, Bartolomé Mitre was concerned with building the nation and establishing infrastructure. His goals, however, were subsumed by the War of the Triple Alliance (Paraguayan War), which lasted from 1864 to 1870. Not until Domingo Faustino Sarmiento, an educator and journalist from San Juan, became president did progress in Argentina really kick in.

Buenos Aires' economy boomed and immigrants poured in from Spain, Italy, Germany and Eastern Europe. The new residents worked in the port area, lived tightly packed in the tenement buildings and developed Buenos Aires' famous dance – the tango – in the brothels and smoky nightclubs of the port. Elsewhere in the country, Basque and Irish refugees became the first shepherds, as both sheep numbers and wool exports increased nearly tenfold between 1850 and 1880.

Still, much of the southern pampas and Patagonia were inaccessible to settlers because of resistance from indigenous Mapuche and Tehueche. In 1878 General Julio Argentino Roca carried out an extermination campaign against the indigenous people, in what is known as the Conquista del Desierto (Conquest of the Desert). This doubled the area under state control and opened Patagonia to settlement and sheep.

By the turn of the 20th century Argentina had a highly developed rail network (financed largely by British capital), fanning out from Buenos Aires in all directions. Still, the dark cloud of a vulnerable economy loomed. Industry could not absorb all the immigration, labor unrest grew and imports surpassed exports. Finally, with the onset of the worldwide Great Depression, the military took power under conditions of considerable social unrest. An obscure but oddly visionary colonel, Juan Domingo Perón, was the first leader to try to come to grips with the country's economic crisis.

Tomás Eloy Martínez' *The Perón Novel* (1998) is a fascinating, fictionalized version of the life of ex-president Juan Perón, culminating in his return to Buenos Aires in 1973.

Juan Perón

Juan Perón emerged in the 1940s to become Argentina's most revered, as well as most despised, political figure. He first came to national prominence as head of the National Department of Labor, after a 1943 military

1767

The Spanish Crown expels the Jesuits from all of New Spain, and the mission communities decline rapidly.

1776

Spain makes Buenos Aires capital of the new viceroyalty of the Río de la Plata. The territory includes the areas of present-day Paraguay, Uruguay and the mines at Potosí (Bolivia).

1806–07

Attempting to seize control of Spanish colonies, British forces raid Buenos Aires in 1806 and in 1807. Buenos Aires militias defeat British troops without Spain's help, which kindles ideas of independence.

1810

Buenos Aires declares its independence from Spain on May 25, although actual independence is still several years off. The city names the Plaza de Mayo in honor of the event.

EVITA, LADY OF HOPE

'I will come again, and I will be millions.'

Eva Perón, 1952

From her humble origins in the pampas to her rise to power beside President Juan Perón, María Eva Duarte de Perón is one of the most revered political figures on the planet. Known affectionately to all as Evita, she is Argentina's beloved First Lady, in some ways even eclipsing the legacy of her husband, who governed Argentina from 1946 to 1955.

At the age of 15 Eva Duarte left her hometown of Junín for Buenos Aires. She was looking for work as an actor, but eventually landed a job in radio. Her big chance came in 1944, when she attended a benefit at Buenos Aires' Luna Park. Here Duarte met Colonel Juan Perón, who fell in love with her; they were married in 1945.

Shortly after Perón won the presidency in 1946, Evita went to work in the office of the Department of Labor and Welfare. During Perón's two terms, Evita empowered her husband both through her charisma and by reaching out to the nation's poor, who came to love her dearly. She built housing for the poor, created programs for children, and distributed clothing and food items to needy families. She campaigned for the aged, offered health services to the poor and advocated for a law extending suffrage to women.

Perón won his second term in 1952, but that same year Evita – at age 33 and at the height of her popularity – died of cancer. It was a blow to Argentina and her husband's presidency.

Although remembered for extending social justice to those she called the country's *descamisados* (shirtless ones), Evita and her husband ruled with an iron fist. They jailed opposition leaders and newspapers, and banned *Time* magazine when it referred to her as an 'illegitimate child.' However, there is no denying the extent to which she empowered women at all levels of Argentine society and helped the country's poor.

Today Evita enjoys near-saint status. Get to know her at Museo Evita, or visit her tomb in the Recoleta cemetery; both are in Buenos Aires. You can also read her ghostwritten autobiography *La razón de mi vida* (My Mission in Life, 1951).

coup toppled civilian rule. With the help of his second wife, Eva Duarte (Evita), he ran for and won the presidency in 1946.

During previous sojourns in fascist Italy and Nazi Germany, Perón had grasped the importance of spectacle in public life and also developed his own brand of watered-down Mussolini-style fascism. He held massive rallies from the balcony of the Casa Rosada, with the equally charismatic Evita at his side. Although they ruled by decree rather than consent, the Peróns legitimized the trade-union movement, extended political rights to working-class people, secured voting rights for women and made university education available to any capable individual. Of course, many

1816

After successful independence movements throughout South America, the United Provinces of the Río de la Plata (Argentina's forerunner) declares formal independence from Spain at Tucumán.

1829

Federalist caudillo Juan Manuel de Rosas becomes governor of Buenos Aires province and de facto ruler of the Argentine Confederation. He rules with an iron fist for more than 20 years.

1852

Federalist and former Rosas ally Justo José de Urquiza defeats Rosas at the Battle of Caseros and, in 1853, draws up Argentina's first constitution.

1862

Bartolomé Mitre is elected president of the newly titled Republic of Argentina and strives to modernize the country by expanding the railway network, creating a national army and postal system, and more.

of these social policies made him disliked by conservatives and the rich classes.

Economic hardship and inflation undermined Juan Perón's second presidency in 1952, and Evita's death the same year dealt a blow to both the country and the president's popularity. In 1955 a military coup sent him into exile in Spain. Thirty years of catastrophic military rule would follow.

During his exile, Perón plotted his return to Argentina. In the late 1960s increasing economic problems, strikes, political kidnappings and guerrilla warfare marked Argentine political life. In the midst of these events, Perón returned to Argentina and was voted president again in 1973; however, after an 18-year exile, there was no substance to his rule. Chronically ill, Perón died in mid-1974, leaving a fragmented country to his ill-qualified third wife, Isabel.

Nunca más (Never Again, 1984), the official report of the National Commission on the Disappeared, systematically details military abuses from 1976 to 1983 – during Argentina's Dirty War.

The Dirty War & the Disappeared

In the late 1960s and early '70s antigovernment feeling was rife and street protests often exploded into all-out riots. Armed guerrilla organizations emerged as radical opponents of the military, the oligarchies and US influence in Latin America. With increasing official corruption exacerbating Isabel's incompetence, Argentina found itself plunged into chaos.

On March 24, 1976, a military coup led by army general Jorge Rafael Videla took control of the Argentine state apparatus and ushered in a period of terror and brutality. Videla's sworn aim was to crush the guerrilla movements and restore social order. During what the regime euphemistically labeled the Process of National Reorganization (known as 'El Proceso'), security forces went about the country arresting, torturing and killing anyone on their hit list of suspected leftists.

During the period between 1976 and 1983, often referred to as the Guerra Sucia or Dirty War, human-rights groups estimate that anywhere from 10,000 to 30,000 people 'disappeared.' Ironically, the Dirty War ended only when the Argentine military attempted a real military operation: liberating the Falkland Islands (Islas Malvinas) from British rule.

The Falklands/Malvinas War

In late 1981 General Leopoldo Galtieri assumed the role of president. To stay in power amid a faltering economy and mass social unrest, Galtieri played the nationalist card and launched an invasion in April 1982 to dislodge the British from the Falkland Islands, which had been claimed by Argentina as its own Islas Malvinas for nearly a century and a half.

However, Galtieri underestimated the determined response of British Prime Minister Margaret Thatcher. After only 74 days Argentina's

1865

More than 150 Welsh immigrants traveling aboard the clipper *Mimosa* land in Patagonia and establish Argentina's first Welsh colony in the province of Chubut.

1865–70

The War of the Triple Alliance is fought between Paraguay and the allied countries of Argentina, Brazil and Uruguay. Paraguay is defeated and loses territory.

1868

Domingo Faustino Sarmiento, an educator and journalist from San Juan, is elected president. He encourages immigration to Argentina, ramps up public education and pushes to Europeanize the country.

1869–95

The Argentine economy booms, immigration skyrockets as Italian and Spanish immigrants flood in, and Buenos Aires' population grows from 90,000 to 670,000. The tango emerges in Buenos Aires.

LAS MADRES DE LA PLAZA DE MAYO

In 1977 after a year of brutal human-rights violations under the leadership of General Jorge Rafael Videla, 14 mothers marched into the Plaza de Mayo in Buenos Aires. They did this despite the military government's ban on public gatherings and despite its reputation for torturing and killing anyone it considered dissident. The mothers, wearing their now-iconic white head scarves, demanded information about their missing children, who had 'disappeared' as part of the government's efforts to quash political opposition.

The group, which took on the name Las Madres de la Plaza de Mayo (The Mothers of Plaza de Mayo), developed into a powerful social movement and was the only political organization that overtly challenged the military government. Las Madres were particularly effective as they carried out their struggle under the banner of motherhood, which made them relatively unassailable in Argentine culture. Their movement showed the power of women – at least in a traditional role – in Argentine culture, and they are generally credited with helping to kick-start the reestablishment of the country's civil society.

After Argentina's return to civilian rule in 1983, thousands of Argentines were still unaccounted for, and Las Madres continued their marches and their demands for information and retribution. In 1986 Las Madres split into two factions. One group, known as the Línea Fundadora (Founding Line), dedicated itself to recovering the remains of the disappeared and to bringing military perpetrators to justice. The other, known as the Asociación Madres de Plaza de Mayo held its last yearly protest in January 2006, saying it no longer had an enemy in the presidential seat. Línea Fundadora, however, still holds a silent vigil every Thursday afternoon in remembrance of the disappeared – and to protest other social causes.

ill-trained, poorly motivated and mostly teenaged forces surrendered ignominiously. The military regime collapsed, and in 1983 Argentines elected civilian Raúl Alfonsín to the presidency.

Aftermath of the Dirty War

In his successful 1983 presidential campaign, Alfonsín pledged to prosecute military officers responsible for human-rights violations during the Dirty War. High-ranking junta officials were convicted for kidnapping, torture and homicide, but when the government attempted to try junior officers they responded with uprisings in several different parts of the country. The timid administration succumbed to military demands and produced the Ley de la Obediencia Debida (Law of Due Obedience), allowing lower-ranking officers to use the defense that they were following orders, as well as the Ley de Punto Final (Full Stop Law), declaring dates beyond which no criminal or civil prosecutions could take place. At the

1926

Novelist and poet Ricardo Güiraldes publishes *Don Segundo Sombra*, a classic work of gaucho literature evoking the spirit of the gaucho and its impact on Argentine society.

1946

Juan Perón is elected president and makes changes to the Argentine political structure. Evita embarks on her social-assistance programs to help lower-class women and children.

1952

Eva Perón dies of cancer on July 26 at age 33, one year into her husband's second term as president. Her death would severely weaken the political might of her husband.

1955

After the economy slides into recession President Perón loses further political clout and is finally thrown from the presidency and exiled to Spain after another military coup.

time these measures eliminated prosecutions of notorious individuals; in 2003, however, they were repealed. Dirty War crime cases have since been reopened, and in recent years several officers have been convicted for Dirty War crimes. Despite these arrests, many of the leaders of El Proceso remain free, both in Argentina and abroad.

The Menem Years

Carlos Saúl Menem was elected president in 1989, and quickly embarked on a period of radical free-market reform. In pegging the peso to the US dollar, he effectively created a period of false economic stability, one that would create a great deal of upward mobility among Argentina's middle class. However, his policies are widely blamed for the country's economic collapse in 2002, when the overvalued peso was considerably devalued.

Menem's presidency was characterized by the privatization of state-owned companies – and a few scandals. In 2001 he was charged with illegally selling arms to Croatia and Ecuador and placed under house arrest. After five months of judicial investigation, the charges were dropped; the following day he announced he would run again for president. In 2003 he did, only to withdraw after the first round. A failed 2007 bid for governor of his home province of La Rioja has pretty much written him off politically.

'La Crisis'

Fernando de la Rua succeeded Menem in the 1999 elections, inheriting an unstable economy and US$114 billion in foreign debt. With the Argentine peso pegged to the US dollar, Argentina was unable to compete on the international market and exports slumped. A further decline in international prices of agricultural products pummeled the Argentine economy, which depended heavily on farm-product exports.

By 2001 the Argentine economy teetered on the brink of collapse, and the administration, with Minister of Economy Domingo Cavallo at the wheel, took measures to end deficit spending and slash state spending. After attempted debt swaps and talk of devaluing the peso, middle-class Argentines began emptying their bank accounts. Cavallo responded by placing a cap of US$250 per week on withdrawals, but it was the beginning of the end.

In mid-December unemployment hit 18.3% and unions began a nationwide strike. Things came to a head on December 20 when middle-class Argentines took to the streets in protest De la Rua's handling of the economic situation. Rioting spread throughout the country and President de la Rua resigned. Three interim presidents had resigned by the time Eduardo Duhalde took office in January 2002, becoming the fifth president in two weeks. Duhalde devalued the peso and announced that

The Falklands War (Guerra de las Malvinas) is still a somewhat touchy subject in Argentina. If the subject comes up, try to call them the 'Malvinas' instead of the 'Falklands,' as many Argentines have been taught from a young age that these islands have always belonged to Argentina.

Héctor Olivera's 1983 film *Funny Dirty Little War* is an unsettling but excellent black comedy set in a fictitious town just before the 1976 military coup.

1976–83
Under the leadership of General Jorge Videla, a military junta takes control of Argentina, launching the country into the Dirty War. In eight years an estimated 30,000 people 'disappear.'

1982
With the economy on the brink of collapse once again, General Leopoldo Galtieri invades the Falkland Islands/Islas Malvinas, unleashing a wave of nationalism and distracting the country from its problems.

1983
After the failure of the Falklands War (Guerra de las Malvinas) and with an economy on the skids, Raúl Alfonsín is elected the first civilian leader of the country since 1976.

1989
Peronist Carlos Menem succeeds Alfonsín as president and overcomes the hyperinflation that reached nearly 200% per month by instituting free-market reforms.

Argentina would default on US$140 billion in foreign debt, the biggest default in world history.

Enter Néstor Kirchner

A bit of trivia: Carlos Menem's Syrian ancestry earned him the nickname 'El Turco' (the Turk). And in 2001 he married Cecilia Bolocco, a former Miss Universe who was 35 years his junior; they're now separated.

Duhalde's Minister of Economy, Roberto Lavagna, negotiated a deal with the IMF in which Argentina would pay only the interest on its debts. Simultaneously, devaluation of the peso meant that Argentina's products were suddenly affordable on the world market, and by 2003 exports were booming. The surge was great for the country's GNP, but prices at home skyrocketed, plunging more of Argentina's already shaken middle class into poverty.

A presidential election was finally held in April 2003, and Santa Cruz Governor Néstor Kirchner emerged victoriously after his opponent, former president Carlos Menem, bowed out of the election.

By the end of his term in 2007, Kirchner had become one of Argentina's most popular presidents. He reversed amnesty laws that protected members of the 1976–83 junta from being charged for atrocities committed during the Dirty War. He took a heavy stance against government corruption and steered the economy away from strict alignment with the US (realigning it with that of Argentina's South American neighbors). And in 2005 he paid off Argentina's entire debt to the IMF in a single payment. By the end of Kirchner's presidency in 2007, unemployment had fallen to just under 9% – from a high of nearly 25% in 2002.

At least two terms arose from Argentina's economic crisis: *el corralito* (a small enclosure) refers to the cap placed on cash withdrawals from bank accounts during 'La Crisis'; while *cacerolazo* (from the word *cacerola*, meaning pan) is a street protest in which angry people bang pots and pans.

But not everything was bread and roses. The fact that Argentina had repaid its debt was fantastic news indeed, but economic stability didn't necessarily follow. In fact, a series of problems ensued during Kirchner's presidency: high inflation rates caused by a growing energy shortage; unequal distribution of wealth; and a rising breach between rich and poor that was slowly obliterating the middle class.

However, things were going well enough for Kirchner. When the presidential seat went up for grabs in 2007, Argentines expressed their satisfaction with Kirchner's policies by electing his wife, well-known Senator Cristina Fernández de Kirchner, as president. Cristina won the presidency with a whopping 22% margin over her nearest challenger and became Argentina's first elected female president.

The Trials & Tribulations of Cristina

When Néstor Kirchner stepped aside in favor of his wife's candidacy for the presidential race, many started wondering: would 'Queen Cristina' (as she's often called, due to her regal comportment) be just a puppet for her husband, who intended to rule behind the scenes?

Weak opposition and her husband's enduring clout were some of the reasons for Cristina's clear-cut victory, despite the lack of straightforward

1999–2000	2002	2003	2007
Fernando de la Rua succeeds Menem as president, inheriting a failing economy. Agricultural exports slump and strikes begin throughout the country. The IMF grants Argentina US$40 million in aid.	Interim president Eduardo Duhalde devalues the peso, and Argentina defaults on a US$140 billion international debt (US$800 million owed to the World Bank), the largest default in history.	Nestor Kirchner is elected president of Argentina after Carlos Menem bows out of the presidential race, despite winning more votes in the first round of elections.	Former First Lady Cristina Fernández de Kirchner is elected president.

policies during her campaign. While this was not the first time Argentina had had a female head of state (Isabel Perón held a brief presidency by inheriting her husband's term), Cristina was the first woman to be elected president by popular vote in Argentina. As a lawyer and senator she has often been compared to Hillary Clinton; as a fashion-conscious political figure with a penchant for chic dresses and designer bags, she also evokes memories of Evita.

Cristina's tumultuous presidency has been laced with scandals, unpopular decisions and roller-coaster approval ratings. In March 2008 she significantly raised the export tax on soybeans, infuriating farmers, who soon went on strike and blockaded highways. In June 2009 Kirchner's power base was shattered during the mid-term elections, when her ruling party lost its majority in both houses of Congress. Soon after, she enacted an unpopular law set to break apart Clarín, a media conglomerate that often reflected unfavorably on her presidency. All the while, Argentina has been hounded by inflation that has been unofficially estimated at up to 25%.

Unlike your typical politician, Amado Boudou – Cristina Kirchner's vice president – drives a Harley-Davidson and jams with his band on a Fender guitar. But like your typical politician, he's been accused of embezzlement and money laundering.

Her presidency has seen some positive sides. The economy grew strongly during the first part of her tenure, bolstered by high consumer spending and strong demand for the country's agricultural exports and manufactured goods. In a true Peronist vein, Cristina implemented a wide range of social programs to beef up the pension system, benefit impoverished children and help fight cases related to crimes against humanity. And in July 2010 she signed a bill that legalized same-sex marriage in Argentina, making it Latin America's first country to do so.

On October 27, 2010, Cristina's presidency was dealt a serious blow when Néstor Kirchner died suddenly of a heart attack. As Néstor was expected to run for the presidency in 2011, this was widely seen as a disaster for the Kirchner dynasty. But the country rallied around Cristina's sorrow, and her popularity in early 2011 remained high enough that she ran for office again and was easily re-elected. She had run on a platform that appealed to the populist vote, promising to raise incomes, restore industry and maintain Argentina's economic boom. Her approach worked like a charm, but her acclaim wasn't to last. For more recent news on Cristina and Argentina, see p572.

2010
Néstor Kirchner dies suddenly, dealing a serious blow to the Kirchner dynasty. Many thought he would run for president in 2011, and very likely win.

2011
Cristina Kirchner wins the presidential re-election race; a few months later she undergoes successful surgery for cancer.

2012
Inflation is running at about 25%, though the government's official figures say that it's less than 10%. Kirchner passes a law restricting the sale of US dollars, creating huge black-market demand.

2013
Argentina experiences its largest currency devaluation since 2002.

Life in Argentina

Throughout Latin America, Argentines endure a reputation for being cocky. 'How does an Argentine commit suicide?' goes the old joke. 'By jumping off his ego.' Traveling to Argentina, you'll find a nugget of truth in this stereotype. But you'll also realize that a warm and gregarious social nature more accurately defines the Argentine psyche.

Regional Identity

Argentines almost always exchange a kiss on the cheek in greeting – even among men. In formal and business situations, though, it is better to go with a handshake.

Opinionated, brash and passionate, generally speaking, Argentines are quick to engage in conversation and will talk after dinner or over coffee until the wee hours of the morning. But they also hold a subtle broodiness to their nature. This stems from a pessimism they've acquired watching their country, one of the world's economic powerhouses during the late 19th and early 20th centuries, descend into a morass of international debt. They've endured military coups and severe government repression, while witnessing their beloved Argentina being plundered by corrupt politicians. But melancholy is just a part of the picture. Add everything together and you get a people who are fun, fiery, opinionated and proud. And you'll come to love them for it.

Lifestyle

Although Buenos Aires holds more than one-third of the country's population, it's surprisingly unlike the rest of Argentina or, for that matter, much of Latin America. As is the case throughout the country, one's lifestyle in the capital depends mostly on money. A modern apartment rented by a young advertising creative in Buenos Aires' Las Cañitas neighborhood differs greatly from a family home in one of the city's impoverished *villas* (shantytowns), where electricity and clean water are luxuries.

Geography and ethnicity also play important roles. Both of these Buenos Aires homes have little in common with that of an indigenous family living in an adobe house in a desolate valley of the Andean Northwest, where life is eked out through subsistence agriculture and earth goddess Pachamama outshines Evita as a cultural icon. In regions such as the Pampas, Mendoza province and Patagonia, a provincial friendliness surrounds a robust outdoor lifestyle.

Argentina's workforce is more than 40% female, and women currently occupy over a third of Argentina's congressional seats.

Argentina has a reasonably-sized middle class, though it's been shrinking significantly in recent years, and poverty has grown. On the other side of the spectrum, wealthy city dwellers have moved into *countries* (gated communities) in surprising numbers.

One thing that most Argentines have in common is their devotion to family. The Buenos Aires advertising exec joins family for weekend dinners, and the cafe owner in San Juan meets friends out at the family *estancia* (ranch) for a Sunday *asado* (barbecue). Children commonly live with their parents until they're married, especially within poorer families.

SOCIAL DOS & DON'TS

When it comes to social etiquette in Argentina, knowing a few intricacies will keep you on the right track.

Dos

- Greet people you encounter with *buenos días* (good morning), *buenas tardes* (good afternoon) or *buenas noches* (good evening).
- In small villages, greet people on the street and when walking into a shop.
- Accept and give *besos* (kisses) on the cheek.
- Use *usted* (the formal term for 'you') when addressing elders and in formal situations.
- Dress for the occasion; only tourists and athletes wear shorts in Buenos Aires.

Don'ts

- Don't refer to the Islas Malvinas as the Falkland Islands, and don't talk to strangers about the Dirty War.
- Don't suggest that Brazil is better than Argentina at *fútbol*, or that Pelé is better than Maradona. And don't refer to *fútbol* as soccer.
- Don't show up at bars before midnight, or nightclubs before 3am, or dinner parties right on time (be fashionably late).
- Don't refer to people from the United States as Americans or *americanos*; use the term *estadounidenses* (or even *norteamericanos*) instead. Some Latin Americans consider themselves 'American' (literally from America, whether it be North, Central or South).

The Sporting Life

Fútbol (soccer) is an integral part of Argentines' lives, and on game day you'll know it by the cheers and yells emanating out of shops and cafes. The national team has been to the FIFA (Féderation Internationale de Football Association) World Cup final four times and has triumphed twice, in 1978 and 1986. The Argentine team also won Olympic gold twice, at the 2004 and 2008 games. The most popular teams are Boca Juniors and River Plate (there are around two-dozen professional teams in Buenos Aires alone) and the fanatical behavior of the country's *barra brava* (hooligans) rivals that of their European counterparts. Among the best-known *fútbol* players are Diego Maradona, Gabriel Batistuta and, of course, Lionel Messi, who has been voted FIFA's best player of the year for three years running.

Jimmy Burns' *The Hand of God* (1997) is the definitive book about football legend Diego Maradona and makes a great read – even if you're not a soccer fanatic.

Rugby's popularity has increased in Argentina ever since Los Pumas, the national team, beat France in the first game of the 2007 Rugby World Cup and *again* in the play-off for third place. As an indicator of just how popular the sport has become, the *Superclásico* (the famed soccer match between Boca and River Plate) was rescheduled so it wouldn't conflict with Los Pumas' quarter-final match.

Argentina has the top polo horses and players in the world, and the Dakar Rally has been taking place partly or mostly in Argentina since 2009. Horse racing, tennis, basketball, golf and boxing are also popular.

Pato is Argentina's traditional sport, played on horseback and mixing elements from both polo and basketball. It was originally played with a duck (a 'pato') but now, thankfully, uses a ball encased in leather handles. Despite its long history and tradition, however, relatively few people follow it.

The Sounds of Argentina

A variety of music genres are well represented in Argentina, especially when it comes to the country's most famous export, the tango. But the country also grooves to different sounds, be it *chamamé* in Corrientes, *cuarteto* in Córdoba or *cumbia villera* in the poor neighborhoods of Buenos Aires.

Carlos Gardel played an enormous role in creating the tango *canción* (song), and his crooning voice, suaveness and charisma made him a huge success during tango's golden years. Unfortunately, he died tragically in a 1935 plane crash.

Tango

There's no better place to dive into tango than through the music of the genre's most legendary performer, singer Carlos Gardel (1887–1935). Violinist Juan D'Arienzo's orchestra reigned over tango throughout the 1930s and into the 1940s. Osvaldo Pugliese and Héctor Varela are important band leaders from the 1940s, but the real giant of the era was *bandoneón* (small type of accordion) player Aníbal Troilo.

Modern tango is largely dominated by the work of Astor Piazzolla, who moved the *tango nuevo* (traditional tango music infused with modern elements) genre from the dance halls into the concert halls. Piazzolla paved the way for the tango fusion, which emerged in the 1970s and is popularized by neo-tango groups such as Gotan Project, Bajofondo Tango Club and Tanghetto.

While in Buenos Aires, keep an eye out for Orquesta Típica Fernández Fierro, musicians who put a new twist on traditional tango songs but also perform original creations (check out their award-winning documentary, *Orquesta Típica,* by Nicolas Entel). Other orchestras to watch out for are Orquesta Típica Imperial and El Afronte.

Contemporary influential tango singers include Susana Rinaldi, Daniel Melingo, Adriana Varela and the late Eladia Blásquez.

Folk Music

The folk (*folklore* or *folklórico*) music of Argentina takes much of its inspiration from the northwestern Andean region and countries to the north, especially Bolivia and Peru. It spans a variety of styles, including *chacarera, chamamé* and zamba.

The late Atahualpa Yupanqui (1908–92) was Argentina's most important *folklórico* musician of the 20th century. Yupanqui's music emerged with the *nueva canción* ('new song') movement that swept Latin America in the 1960s. *Nueva canción* was rooted in folk music and its lyrics often dealt with social and political themes. The genre's grande dame was Argentina's Mercedes Sosa (1935–2009) of Tucumán, winner of several Latin Grammy awards.

Another contemporary *folklórico* musician is accordionist Chango Spasiuk, a virtuoso of Corrientes' *chamamé* music. Singer-songwriter-guitarist Horacio Guarany's 2004 album *Cantor de Cantores* was nominated for a Latin Grammy in the Best Folk Album category.

Mariana Baraj is a singer and percussionist who experiments with Latin America's traditional folk music as well as elements of jazz, classical music and improvisation. Soledad Pastorutti's first two albums have been Sony's top sellers in Argentina – ever!

Other big names in *folklórico* are El Chaqueño Palavecino of Salta; Suna Rocha of Córdoba; Antonio Tarragó Ross; Eduardo Falú; Víctor Heredia; Los Chalchaleros; León Gieco (aka 'The Argentine Bob Dylan') and the Conjunto Pro Música de Rosario.

Rock & Pop

Musicians such as Charly García, Fito Páez and Luis Alberto Spinetta are *rock nacional* (Argentine rock) icons. Soda Stereo, Sumo, Los Pericos and Grammy winners Los Fabulosos Cadillacs rocked Argentina throughout the 1980s. Bersuit Vergarabat endures as one of Argentina's best rock bands, with a musical complexity that is arguably without peer. R&B-influenced Ratones Paranoicos opened for the Rolling Stones in 1995, while La Portuaria – who fuse Latin beats with jazz and R&B – collaborated with David Byrne in 2006.

Other big-name groups are offbeat Babasónicos, punk rockers Attaque 77, fusion rockers Los Piojos and original Les Luthiers, along with Los Redonditos de Ricota, Los Divididos, Catupecu Machu and Gazpacho. Illya Kuryaki and the Valderramas are metal-meets-hip-hop, while catchy Miranda! has an electro-pop style. Eclectic Kevin Johansen sings in both English and Spanish.

Born in Córdoba in the early 1940s, *cuarteto* is Argentina's original pop music: despised by the middle and upper classes for its arresting rhythm and offbeat musical pattern, as well as its working-class lyrics, it is definitely music from the margins. Although definitively *cordobés* (from Córdoba), it's played in working-class bars, dance halls and stadiums throughout the country.

Murga is a form of athletic musical theater composed of actors and percussionists. Primarily performed in Uruguay, *murga* in Argentina is more heavily focused on dancing than singing. You're most likely to see this exciting musical art form at Carnaval celebrations.

Electrónica & More

Electrónica exploded in Argentina in the 1990s and has taken on various forms in popular music. Hybrid electronic bands are led by the likes of Intima, Mujik and Adicta.

Argentina's heavyweights in DJ-based club and dance music include Aldo Haydar (progressive house), Bad Boy Orange (drum 'n' bass), Diego Ro-K ('the Maradona of Argentine DJs') and Gustavo Lamas (blending ambient pop and electro house). Award-winning Hernán Cattáneo has played with Paul Oakenfold and at Burning Man.

Música tropical – a lively, Afro-Latin sound of salsa, *merengue* and especially *cumbia* – has swept Argentina in recent years. Originating in Colombia, *cumbia* combines an infectious dance rhythm with lively melodies, often carried by brass.

One of Buenos Aires' most interesting music spectacles is La Bomba del Tiempo, a collective of percussionists whose explosive performances are improvisational, tribal and even simulate electronic dance music. Check them out at Ciudad Cultural Konex on Monday evenings.

Every genre of Argentine music has experienced the hybrid phenomenon of blending electronic music with more traditional sounds. Digital *folklore* is no exception.

Tonolec is a musical duo that combines folk songs of the Toba indigenous community from Argentina's north with an electronic sound. Onda Vaga's smooth harmonies add a jazzy feel to traditional *folklore*. Tremor mixes Andean flutes, the Argentine *bombo legüero* (drum), electric guitars and a synthesizer into a blend of ancient and digital sounds. Juana Molina's ambient-electronic music has been compared to Björk's. There's also Chancha via Circuito, whose 2010 album *Río Arriba* mixes melodic flutes and slow tempos, making it more meditative than dance oriented.

Cumbia villera is a relatively recent musical phenomenon: a fusion of *cumbia* and gangsta posturing with a punk edge and reggae overtones. Born of Buenos Aires' shantytowns, its aggressive lyrics deal with marginalization, poverty, drugs, sex and the Argentine economic crisis.

Literature & Cinema

Perhaps because of its history of authoritarian rule, Argentina has developed a strong literary heritage, with many contemporary writers using the country's darkest moments as inspiration for their complex and sometimes disturbing novels. Argentina also has a vibrant, evolving film industry. The country has won two Oscars for best foreign-language film (in 1985 and 2009) – the only Latin American country ever to have won the award – and continues to produce excellent directors and movies.

Literature

Victoria Ocampo (1890–1979) was a famous writer, publisher and intellectual who founded *Sur*, a renowned cultural magazine of the 1930s. You can also visit her mansion near Buenos Aires.

Journalist, poet and politician José Hernández (1831–86) gave rise to the *gauchesco* literary tradition with his epic poem *Martín Fierro* (1872), which acknowledged the role of the gauchos in Argentina's development. Argentine writing only reached an international audience during the 1960s and '70s, when the stories of Jorge Luis Borges, Julio Cortázar, Ernesto Sábato, Adolfo Bioy Casares and Silvina Ocampo, among many others, were widely translated for the first time.

Jorge Luis Borges (1899–1986), the brightest light of Argentine literature, is best known for the complex labyrinthine worlds and sophisticated mind teasers constructing his stories. His early stories, such as *Death and the Compass* and *Streetcorner Man,* offer a metaphysical twist on Argentine themes, while his later works – including *The Lottery in Babylon, The Circular Ruins* and *Garden of the Forking Paths* – are works of fantasy. *Collected Fictions* (1999) is a complete set of his stories.

Despite being discovered and influenced by Borges in the 1940s, the writing of Julio Cortázar (1914–84) was considerably different. His short stories and novels are more anthropological and concern people living seemingly normal lives in a world where the surreal becomes commonplace. Cortázar's most famous book is *Hopscotch*.

Another great writer is Ernesto Sábato (1911–2011), whose complex and uncompromising novels have been extremely influential on later Argentine literature. *The Tunnel* (1948) is Sábato's engrossing existentialist novella about an obsessed painter and his distorted personal take on reality.

Adolfo Bioy Casares' (1914–99) sci-fi novella *The Invention of Morel* (1940) not only gave Alain Resnais the plot for his classic film *Last Year at Marienbad*, but also introduced the idea of the holodeck decades before *Star Trek* existed.

The contemporary, post-boom generation of Argentine writers is more reality-based, often reflecting the influence of popular culture and directly confronting the political angles of 1970s authoritarian Argentina. One of the most famous post-boom Argentine writers is Manuel Puig (1932–90, author of *Kiss of the Spider Woman*). In the Argentine tradition, Puig did much of his writing in exile, fleeing Argentina during the Perón years and ultimately settling in Mexico.

Osvaldo Soriano (1943–97), perhaps Argentina's most popular contemporary novelist, wrote *A Funny Dirty Little War* (1986) and *Winter*

Quarters (1989). Juan José Saer (1937–2005) penned short stories and complex crime novels, while Rodrigo Fresán (1963–), the youngster of the post-boom generation, wrote the international bestseller *The History of Argentina* (1991).

Gabriela Bejerman, a multimedia artist, released an album in 2007 that incorporated some of her poetry with electro music. Other notable contemporary writers include Federico Andahazi, Ricardo Piglia, Tomás Eloy Martínez, Andrés Newman, Oliverio Coelho and Pedro Mairal.

Cinema

One of Argentina's major contributions to cinema is Luis Puenzo's *The Official Story* (1985), which deals with the Dirty War. Another well-known international movie is Héctor Babenco's *Kiss of the Spider Woman* (1985), based on Argentine-born Manuel Puig's novel. Both movies won Oscars.

New Argentine Cinema developed in the 1990s, brought about by economic and political unrest. Films that spearheaded this movement include Martín Rejtman's *Rapado* (1992) and *Pizza, birra, faso* (Pizza, Beer, Cigarettes, 1998) by Adrián Caetano and Bruno Stagnaro.

Metegol (Foosball; 2013) is a 3D film directed by Juan José Campanella; it cost US$22 million, making it the most expensive Argentine movie ever produced.

Pablo Trapero is one of Argentina's foremost filmmakers. Among his works are award-winning *Mundo grúa* (Crane World, 1999), the ensemble road movie *Familia rodante* (Rolling Family, 2004) and *Nacido y criado* (Born and Bred, 2006), a stark story about a Patagonian man's fall from grace. His 2010 film noir played at Cannes Film Festival, as did his most recent work, *Elefante blanco* (White Elephant, 2012).

Daniel Burman's films include *Esperando al mesíah* (Waiting for the Messiah, 2000), *El abrazo partido* (Lost Embrace, 2004) and *Derecho de familia* (Family Law, 2006). His most recent effort, *Dos hermanos* (Brother and Sister, 2010) is the story of aging siblings who've recently lost their mother. Burman's other claim to fame is his co-production of Walter Salles' Che Guevara–inspired *The Motorcycle Diaries* (2004).

Another director to have made a mark on Argentina cinema is the late Fabián Bielinsky. He left behind a small but powerful body of work that includes his award-winning feature *Nueve reinas* (Nine Queens, 2000). His last film, the 2005 neo-noir flick *El aura*, screened at Sundance and was the official Argentine entry for the 2006 Oscars.

Lucrecia Martel's 2001 debut *La ciénaga* (The Swamp) and *La niña santa* (The Holy Girl, 2004) deal with the themes of social decay, Argentine bourgeois and sexuality in the face of Catholic guilt. Her powerful *La mujer sin cabeza* (The Headless Woman, 2008) was showcased at Cannes. Another acclaimed director, Carlos Sorin, takes us to the deep south of Argentina in *Historias mínimas* (Minimal Stories, 2002) and *Bombón el perro* (Bombón the Dog, 2004).

Argentina's biggest film event is the Buenos Aires International Festival of Independent Film, held in April each year. Check out www.bafici.gov.ar for more information.

Juan José Campanella's *El hijo de la novia* (Son of the Bride) received an Oscar nomination for best foreign-language film in 2001. His *Luna de avellaneda* (Moon of Avellaneda, 2004) is a clever story about a social club and those who try to save it. In 2010 he won the Oscar for best foreign-language film with *El secreto de sus ojos* (The Secret in Their Eyes).

Other noteworthy films include Lucía Puenzo's *XXY* (2007), the tale of a 15-year-old hermaphrodite, and Juan Diego Solanas' *Nordeste* (Northeast, 2005), which tackles difficult social issues such as child trafficking; both were screened at Cannes. In 2013 Puenzo directed *Wakolda* (The German Doctor), a true story about the family who unknowingly lived with Josef Mengele during his exile in South America.

The Natural World

Argentina. For anyone raised on *National Geographic* and adventure stories, the name is loaded with images: the Magellanic penguins of the Atlantic coast, the windswept mysteries of Patagonia and Tierra del Fuego, the vast grasslands of the pampas, the towering Andes and raging Iguazú Falls. Spanning from the subtropics to the edge of Antarctica, the country is simply unmatched in natural wonders.

Above Glaciar Perito Moreno (p464)

The Land

With a total land area of about 2.8 million sq km, Argentina is the world's eighth-largest country. It stretches from La Quiaca on the Bolivian border, where summers can be brutally hot, to Ushuaia in Tierra del Fuego, where winters are experienced only by seasoned locals and the nuttiest of travelers. It's a distance of nearly 3500km, an expanse that encompasses a vast array of environments and terrain.

The Central & Northern Andes

In the extreme north, the Andes are basically the southern extension of the Bolivian *altiplano*, a thinly populated high plain between 3000m and 4000m in altitude, punctuated by even higher volcanic peaks. Although days can be surprisingly hot, frosts occur almost nightly. The Andean Northwest is also known as the puna.

Further south, in the arid provinces of San Juan and Mendoza, the Andes climb to their highest altitudes, with 6962m Cerro Aconcagua topping out as the highest point in the western hemisphere. Here, the highest peaks lie covered in snow through the winter. Although rainfall on the eastern slopes is inadequate for crops, perennial streams descend from the Andes and provide irrigation water, which has brought prosperity to the wine-producing provinces of Mendoza, San Juan and San Luis. Winter in San Juan province is the season of the *zonda*, a hot, dry wind descending from the Andes that causes dramatic temperature increases.

At its mouth, the Río de la Plata is an amazing 200km wide, making it the widest river in the world – though some consider it more like a river estuary.

The Chaco

East of the Andes and the Andean foothills, much of northern Argentina consists of subtropical lowlands. This arid area, known as the Argentine Chaco, is part of the much larger Gran Chaco, an extremely rugged, largely uninhabited region that extends into Bolivia, Paraguay and Brazil. The Argentine Chaco encompasses the provinces of Chaco, Formosa and Santiago del Estero, the western reaches of Jujuy, Catamarca and Salta provinces, and the northernmost parts of Santa Fe and Córdoba.

The Chaco has a well-defined winter dry season, and summer everywhere in the Chaco is brutally hot. Rainfall decreases as you move east to west. The wet Chaco, which encompasses the eastern parts of Chaco and Formosa provinces and northeast Santa Fe, receives more rain than the dry Chaco, which covers central and western Chaco and Formosa provinces, most of Santiago del Estero and parts of Salta.

Mesopotamia

Also referred to as the Litoral (as in littoral), Mesopotamia is the name for the region of Northeast Argentina between the Río Paraná and Río Uruguay. Here the climate is mild and rainfall is heavy in the provinces of Entre Ríos and Corrientes, which make up most of Mesopotamia. Hot and humid Misiones province, a politically important province surrounded on three sides by Brazil and Paraguay, contains part of Iguazú Falls, whose waters descend from southern Brazil's Paraná Plateau. Shallow summer flooding is common throughout Mesopotamia and into the eastern Chaco, but only the immediate river flood plains become inundated in the west.

Iguazú Falls consists of more than 275 individual falls that tumble from heights as great as 80m. They stretch for nearly 3km and are arguably the most amazing waterfalls on earth.

The Pampas & Atlantic Coast

Bordered by the Atlantic Ocean and Patagonia and stretching nearly to Córdoba and the Central Sierras, the pampas are Argentina's agricultural heartland. Geographically, this region covers the provinces of Buenos Aires and La Pampa, as well as southern chunks of Santa Fe and Córdoba.

This area can be subdivided into the humid pampas, along the Litoral, and the arid pampas of the western interior and the south. More than a third of the country's population lives in and around Buenos Aires. Annual rainfall exceeds 900mm, but several hundred kilometers westward it's less than half that.

The absence of nearly any rises in the land makes some parts of this area vulnerable to flooding from the relatively few, small rivers that cross

Lago Nahuel Huapi (p362)

it. Only the granitic Sierra de Tandil (484m) and the Sierra de la Ventana (1273m), in southwestern Buenos Aires province, and the Sierra de Lihué Calel disrupt the otherwise monotonous terrain.

Along the Atlantic coast, the province of Buenos Aires features the sandy, often dune-backed beaches that attracted the development of seaside resorts. South of Viedma, cliffs begin to appear but the landscape remains otherwise desolate for its entire stretch south through Patagonia.

The largest dinosaur ever discovered is *Argentinosaurus huinculensis*, uncovered in Neuquén province; the herbivore measured a massive 40m long and 18m high.

Patagonia & the Lake District

Ever-alluring Patagonia is the region of Argentina south of the Río Colorado, which flows southeast from the Andes and passes just north of the city of Neuquén. The Lake District is a subregion of Patagonia. Province-wise, Patagonia consists of Neuquén, Río Negro, Chubut and Santa Cruz. It's separated from Chilean Patagonia by the Andes.

The Andean cordillera (range) is high enough that Pacific storms drop most of their rain and snow on the Chilean side. In the extreme southern reaches of Patagonia, however, enough snow and ice still accumulates to form the largest southern-hemisphere glaciers outside of Antarctica.

East of the Andean foothills, the cool, arid Patagonian steppes support huge flocks of sheep. For such a southerly location, temperatures are relatively mild, even in winter, when more uniform atmospheric pressure moderates the strong gales that blow most of the year.

Except for urban centers such as Comodoro Rivadavia and Río Gallegos, Patagonia is thinly populated. Tidal ranges along the Atlantic coast are too great for major port facilities. In the valley of the Río Negro and at the outlet of the Río Chubut (near the town of Trelew), people farm and cultivate fruit orchards.

Ushuaia (p489) and the Martial Range

Tierra del Fuego

The world's southernmost permanently inhabited territory, Tierra del Fuego ('Land of Fire') consists of one large island (Isla Grande), unequally divided between Chile and Argentina, and many smaller ones. When Europeans first passed through the Strait of Magellan (which separates Isla Grande from the Patagonian mainland), the fires that gave this land its name stemmed from the activities of the now endangered Yaghan people.

The northern half of Isla Grande, resembling the Patagonian steppes, is devoted to sheep grazing, while its southern half is mountainous and partly covered by forests and glaciers. As in Patagonia, winter conditions are rarely extreme.

Península Valdés is one of the few places on earth where killer whales (orcas) have been seen hunting sea lions by beaching themselves. You'd be *very* lucky to witness this phenomenon, however.

Wildlife

With such variances in terrain and such great distances, it's no wonder Argentina boasts a wide range of flora and fauna. Subtropical rainforests, palm savannas, high-altitude deserts and steppes, humid-temperate grasslands, alpine and sub-Antarctic forests and rich coastal areas all support their own special life forms.

Animals

Northeast Argentina boasts the country's most diverse animal life. One of the best areas on the continent to enjoy wildlife is the swampy Esteros del Iberá, in Corrientes province, where animals such as swamp deer, capybara and caiman, along with many large migratory birds, are common. It's comparable to – arguably even better than – Brazil's more famous Pantanal.

CAPYBARAS

Treading, with its webbed feet, a very fine line between cute and ugly, the capybara is a sizable semiaquatic beast that you're bound to encounter in the Esteros del Iberá area. Weighing in at up to 75kg, the *carpincho*, as it's known in Spanish, is the world's largest rodent.

Very much at home both on land and in the water, the gentle and vaguely comical creatures eat aquatic plants and grasses in great quantity. They form small herds, with a dominant male living it up with four to six females. The male can be recognized by a protrusion on his forehead that emits a territory-marking scent. The lovably roly-poly babies are born in spring.

Though protected in the Iberá area, the capybara is farmed and hunted elsewhere for its skin, which makes a soft, flexible leather. The meat is also considered a delicacy in traditional communities.

In the drier northwest the most conspicuous animal is the domestic llama, but its wild cousins, the guanaco and vicuña, can also be seen. Your odds of seeing them are excellent if you travel by road through Parque Nacional Los Cardones to Salta. Their yellow fur is often an extraordinary puff of color against the cactus-studded backdrop. Many migratory birds, including flamingos, inhabit the high saline lakes of the Andean Northwest.

In less densely settled areas, including the arid pampas of La Pampa province, guanacos and foxes are not unusual sights. Many bodies of water, both permanent and seasonal, provide migratory-bird habitat.

Most notable in Patagonia and Tierra del Fuego is the wealth of coastal wildlife, ranging from Magellanic penguins, cormorants and gulls to sea lions, fur seals, elephant seals, orcas and whales. Several coastal reserves, from Río Negro province south to Tierra del Fuego, are home to enormous concentrations of wildlife that are one of the region's greatest visitor attractions. Inland on the Patagonian steppe, as in the northwest, the guanaco is the most conspicuous mammal, but the flightless rhea, resembling the ostrich, runs in flocks across the plains.

Plants

When it comes to plant life, the country's most diverse regions are in Northeast Argentina, the Lake District, the Patagonian Andes and the subtropical forests of northwest Argentina.

The high northern Andes are dry and often barren, and vegetation is limited to sparse bunch grasses and low, widely spaced shrubs. In Jujuy and La Rioja provinces, however, huge, vertically branched cardón cacti add a rugged beauty to an otherwise empty landscape. In the Andean precordillera, between the Chaco and the Andes proper, lies a strip of dense, subtropical montane cloud forest known as the Yungas. This area sees heavy summertime rains and is one of the most biologically diverse regions in the country.

The wet Chaco is home to grasslands and gallery forests with numerous tree species, including the quebracho colorado and caranday palm. The dry Chaco, although extremely parched, is still thick with vegetation. It hosts taller trees and a dense understory of low-growing spiny trees and shrubs.

In Mesopotamia rainfall is sufficient to support swampy lowland forests and upland savanna. Misiones' native vegetation is dense subtropical forest, though its upper elevations are studded with araucaria pines.

The once lush native grasses of the Argentine pampas have suffered under grazing pressure and the proliferation of grain farms that produce cash crops such as soybeans. Today very little native vegetation remains, except along watercourses such as the Río Paraná.

Above Fitz Roy Range, Parque Nacional Los Glaciares (North, p452)
Right Capybara

JOHANNES COMPAAN/GETTY IMAGES ©

Parque Nacional Nahuel Huapi (p362)

Most of Patagonia lies in the rain shadow of the Chilean Andes, so the vast steppes of southeastern Argentina resemble the sparse grasslands of the arid Andean highlands. Closer to the border there are pockets of dense *nothofagus* (southern beech), *Araucaria araucana* (monkey-puzzle trees) and coniferous woodlands that owe their existence to the winter storms that sneak over the cordillera. Northern Tierra del Fuego is a grassy extension of the Patagonian steppe, but the heavy rainfall of the mountainous southern half supports verdant southern-beech forests.

Argentina's National Parks

Argentina's national and provincial parks offer a huge variety of environments, from the sweltering tropics of Parque Nacional Iguazú to the crashing glaciers of Parque Nacional Los Glaciares to the animal-rich coastal waters of Reserva Faunística Península Valdés.

One of Latin America's first national park systems, Argentina's dates from the turn of the 20th century, when explorer and surveyor Francisco P Moreno donated 75 sq km near Bariloche to the state in return for guarantees that the parcel of land would be preserved for the enjoyment of all Argentines. In 1934 this area became part of Parque Nacional Nahuel Huapi, Argentina's first national park.

Since then the country has established many other parks and reserves, mostly but not exclusively in the Andean region. There are also important provincial parks and reserves, such as Reserva Faunística Península Valdés, which do not fall within the national-park system but deserve attention. Some national parks are more visitor-oriented than the provincial parks, but there are exceptions.

Visitors in Buenos Aires can stop at the national parks administration (www.parquesnacionales.gov.ar) for maps and brochures, which are sometimes in short supply in the parks.

Survival Guide

Directory A–Z

Accommodations

Accommodations in Argentina range from campgrounds to five-star luxury hotels. At the tourist-oriented hotels staff members will speak some English, though at more provincial accommodations you'll be practicing your *castellano* (what Argentina calls its Spanish).

All but the cheapest hotels have private bathrooms, and most accommodations include breakfast – usually *medialunas* (croissants) and coffee or tea. Note that many hotels offer discounted rates for extended stays, usually a week or more; negotiate this *before* you begin your stay.

Cabañas

Some tourist destinations, especially at the beach or in the country, have *cabañas* for rent. These are usually stand-alone cabin-type accommodations, and nearly always have a stocked kitchen. They are a great deal for groups or families (as they often have several rooms), though sometimes their off-the-beaten-track location means you'll need a vehicle to reach them. The destination's tourist office is a good place to find a list of local *cabañas*.

Camping & Refugios

Camping can be a splendid way to experience Argentina, particularly the Lake District and Patagonia, where there are many good campgrounds. Nearly every Argentine city or town has a fairly central municipal campground, but these are hit-and-miss – sometimes delightfully woodsy, sometimes crowded and ugly.

Private campgrounds usually have good facilities: hot showers, toilets, laundry, barbecue for grilling, restaurant or *confitería* (cafe) and small grocery store. Free campgrounds are often excellent, especially in the Lake District, although they lack facilities. Municipal campgrounds are cheap, but can become party central on weekends.

Argentine camping equipment is often more expensive than and inferior to what you may be used to. Camp stoves take locally available butane cartridges (which should *not* be taken on airplanes). There are definitely mosquitoes in Argentina, but mosquito repellent is widely available.

Backpacking and backcountry camping opportunities abound in and around national parks, especially those in the Lake District and the south. Some parks have free or cheap *refugios* (basic shelters), which have cooking facilities and rustic bunks.

Estancias

Few experiences feel more typically Argentine than staying at an *estancia* (a traditional ranch, often called *fincas* in the northwest). *Estancias* are a wonderful way to spend time in remote areas of the country – and wine, horses and *asados* (traditional barbecues) are almost always involved. *Estancias* are especially common in the area around Buenos Aires, near Esteros del Iberá and throughout the Lake District and Patagonia. In the latter, they're often geared toward anglers. They're not cheap, but rates generally include room, board and some activities.

Hospedajes, Pensiones & Residenciales

Aside from hostels, these are Argentina's cheapest accommodations, and the differences among them are sometimes ambiguous.

A *hospedaje* is usually a large family home with a few extra bedrooms (and, gener-

BOOK YOUR STAY ONLINE

For more accommodations reviews by Lonely Planet authors, check out http://lonelyplanet.com/hotels/argentina. You'll find independent reviews, as well as recommendations on the best places to stay. Best of all, you can book online.

ally, a shared bathroom). Similarly, a *pensión* offers short-term accommodations in a family home, but may also have permanent lodgers. *Residenciales* generally occupy buildings designed for short-stay accommodations, although some (known euphemistically as *albergues transitorios)* cater to clientele who intend only *very* short stays – of two hours maximum. These are mostly used by young Argentine couples.

Rooms at these accommodations are modest, often basic and usually clean; those with shared bathrooms are the cheapest.

SLEEPING PRICE RANGES

Inflation in Argentina is rampant, running (unofficially) at around 25%. To avoid getting price shock, check current prices.

Accommodations prices listed in this book include tax and are general high-season rates (although not peak seasons like Christmas or Easter). Budget and midrange hotels almost always include taxes when quoting their prices, but top-end hotels usually do not – and it's 21%.

Payment in cash (usually at mid- to top-end hotels) sometimes results in a 10% discount. Likewise, you can be charged a 'fee' for using credit cards. Paying with a foreign debit card is sometimes – but not always – possible at no extra charge.

High season is generally January and February (when Argentines take their summer breaks), Semana Santa (Easter week) and July and August (except in Patagonia). Reserve ahead during these times. Outside these times, prices can drop anywhere from 20% to 50%.

The following price ranges are typical during high season. Unless otherwise stated, double rooms include bathroom, and breakfast is included in the price.

$ less than AR$400/US$70 for a double room; AR$85 to AR$115/US$15 to US$20 for a dorm bed

$$ from AR$400 to AR$1000/US$70 to US$175 per double room

$$$ more than AR$1000/US$175 per double room

Hostels

Hostels are common in Argentina and range from basic no-frill deals to beautiful, multiperk offerings more luxurious than your basic hotel. Most fall in between, but all have common kitchens, living areas, shared bathrooms and dorm rooms. Most have a few private rooms with or without bathroom.

Hostels are a great way to meet other travelers, both Argentines and foreigners, especially if you're by yourself. Social events such as *asados* often take place, and local tours can be offered. However, remember that Argentines are night owls and hostelers tend to follow suit, so earplugs can be very handy.

Hostelling International (HI; www.hihostels.com) members get discounts at HI facilities. Other hostel networks include **minihostels** (www.minihostels.com) and **HoLa** (www.holahostels.com).

Hotels

Argentine hotels vary from depressing, utilitarian one-star places to luxurious five-star hotels with all the usual top-tier services. Oddly enough, many one- and two-star hotels can prove better value than three- and four-star lodgings. In general, hotels provide a room with private bathroom, often a telephone and usually a TV with cable. Sometimes they have a *confitería* or restaurant and rates almost always include breakfast, whether it be a few *medialunas* with coffee or full American-style buffet.

Rentals & Homestays

House and apartment rentals often save you money if you're staying in one place for an extended period. This can be an especially good deal during high season at resort locations, such as Bariloche or beach cities along the Atlantic coast (just book way ahead) – especially for groups. Tourist offices are good sources for listings.

During the tourist season, mostly in the interior, families rent rooms to visitors. Often these are excellent bargains, permitting access to cooking and laundry facilities while encouraging contact with Argentines. Homestays change regularly. Tourist offices in many smaller towns or cities often maintain lists of such accommodations, so ask.

Courses

Argentina is a hot destination in which to learn Spanish. Most opportunities for Spanish-language instruction are based in Buenos Aires, though larger cities such as Mendoza and Córdoba are also excellent.

Tango classes are hugely popular in Buenos Aires, where cooking classes – both for Argentine and international cuisine – are also available.

Asking fellow travelers for recommendations is the best way to pick a good institute or tango and cooking classes that cater to your needs.

Customs Regulations

Argentine officials are generally courteous and reasonable toward tourists. Electronic items, including laptops, cameras and cell (mobile) phones, can be brought into the country duty free, provided they are not intended for resale. If you have a lot of electronic equipment, however, it may be useful to have a typed list of the items you are carrying (including serial numbers) or a pile of purchase receipts.

If you're entering Argentina from a neighboring country, officials focus on different things. Travelers southbound from the central Andean countries may be searched for drugs, while those from bordering countries will have fruits and vegetables confiscated. Carrying illegal drugs will pretty much get you into trouble no matter which country you're coming from.

Discount Cards

The International Student Identity Card (ISIC) is available through www.isic.org; in Buenos Aires head to the student and discount travel agency **Asatej** (www.asatej.net), with several offices. It can help travelers obtain discounts on public transportation and admissions to museums. Any official-looking university identification *may* be accepted as a substitute.

An HI card, available at any **HI hostel** (www.hostels.org.ar), will get you discounts on your stay at any HI facility. The **minihostels** (www.minihostels.com) and **HoLa** (www.holahostels.com) cards work in a similar way for a different network of hostels.

Travelers over the age of 60 can sometimes obtain senior-citizen discounts on museum admissions and the like. Usually a passport with date of birth is sufficient evidence of age.

Electricity

Argentina's current operates on 220V, 50 Hertz. Adapters are available from almost any *ferretería* (hardware store).

Most electronic equipment (such as cameras, telephones and computers) are dual/multi-voltage, but if you're bringing something that's not (such as a hairdryer), use a voltage converter or you might short out your device.

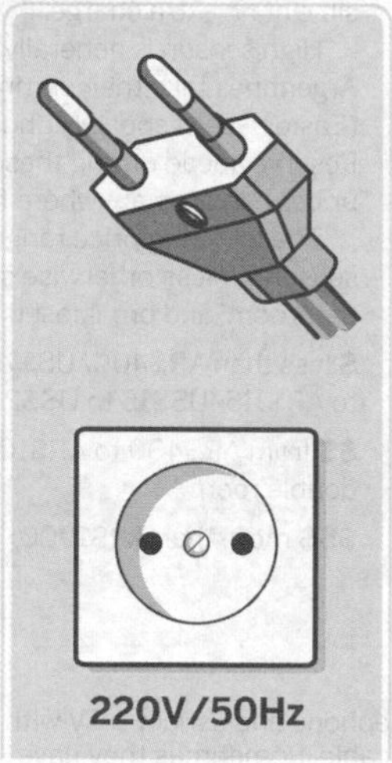

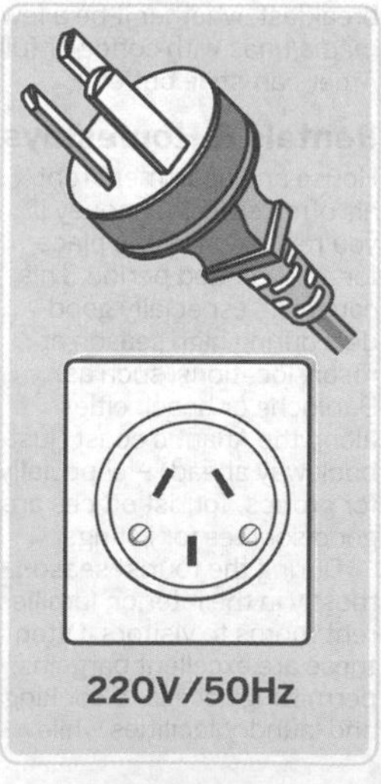

Embassies & Consulates

Following is a basic list of embassies and consulates in Buenos Aires. Some other cities around Argentina (especially near the borders) also have consulates to certain countries.

Australian Embassy (☎011-4779-3500; www.argentina.embassy.gov.au; Villanueva 1400)

Bolivian Embassy (☎011-4394-1463; www.embajadadebolivia.com.ar; Av Corrientes 545)

Brazilian Consulate (☎011-4515-2400; www.brasil.org.ar; Carlos Pellegrini 1363, 5th fl)

Canadian Embassy (☎011-4808-1000; www.canadainternational.gc.ca; Tagle 2828)

Chilean Embassy (☎011-4331-6229; www.chileabroad.gov.cl/buenos-aires; Diagonal Roque Saenz Peña 547, 2nd fl)

Dutch Embassy (☎011-4338-0050; www.embajadaholanda.int.ar; Olga Cossettini 831, 3rd fl)

French Embassy (☎011-4515-7030; www.embafrancia-argentina.org; Cerrito 1399)

German Embassy (☎011-4778-2500; www.buenosaires.diplo.de; Villanueva 1055)

Italian Consulate (☎011-4114-4800; www.consbuenosaires.esteri.it; Reconquista 572)

New Zealand Embassy (☎011-5070-0700; www.nzembassy.com/argentina; Carlos Pellegrini 1427, 5th fl)

Paraguay (☎011-4814-4803; www.consulparbaires.org; Viamonte 1851)

Peruvian Embassy (☎011-4381-6913; Av Rivadavia 1501)

Spanish Consulate (☎011-4814-9100; www.spanish-embassy.com/buenos-aires.html; Guido 1770)

UK Embassy (☎011-4808-2200; www.ukinargentina.fco.gov.uk; Dr Luis Agote 2412)

Uruguay (☎011-4807-3040; www.embajadadeluruguay.com.ar; Av General Las Heras 1907)

US Embassy (☎011-5777-4533; http://argentina.usembassy.gov; Colombia 4300)

Gay & Lesbian Travelers

Argentina has become increasingly gay-friendly over recent years. Buenos Aires is one of the world's top gay destinations – with dedicated hotels and B&Bs, bars, nightclubs and restaurants. The capital is home to South America's largest annual gay pride parade and in 2002 became the first Latin American city to legalize same-sex civil unions; in July 2010 Argentina became the first Latin American country to legalize same-sex marriage.

Although Buenos Aires (and, to a lesser extent, Argentina's other large cities) is becoming increasingly tolerant, most of the rest of Argentina still feels uncomfortable with homosexuality. Homophobia rarely takes the form of physical violence, however, and gay people regularly travel throughout the country to return home with nothing but praise.

When it comes to public affection, Argentine men are more physically demonstrative than their North American and European counterparts. Behaviors such as kissing on the cheek in greeting or a vigorous embrace are innocuous even to those who express unease with homosexuality. Lesbians walking hand in hand should attract little attention, since heterosexual Argentine women frequently do so, but this would be very conspicuous behavior for men. When in doubt, it's best to be discreet.

EATING PRICE RANGES

The following price ranges used throughout this book refer to a standard main course.

$ less than AR$70

$$ AR$70-110

$$$ more than AR$110

Health

Argentina is a modern country with good health and dental services. Sanitation and hygiene at restaurants is relatively high, and tap water is generally safe to drink throughout the country. If you want to make sure, ask '*¿Se puede tomar el agua de la canilla*?' (Is the tap water drinkable?).

Public health care in Argentina is reasonably good and free, even if you're a foreigner. Waits can be long, however, and quality inconsistent. Those who can afford it usually opt for the superior private-care system, and here most doctors and hospitals will expect payment in cash. Many medical personnel speak English.

If you develop a life-threatening medical problem you may want to be evacuated to your home country. Since this may cost thousands of dollars, be sure to have the appropriate insurance before you depart. Your embassy can also recommend medical services.

A signed and dated note from your doctor, describing your medical conditions and medications (with their generic or scientific names) is a good idea. It's also a good idea to bring medications in their clearly labeled, original containers. Most pharmacies in Argentina are well supplied.

For more specific information on vaccinations to get before traveling to Argentina, see wwwnc.cdc.gov/travel/destinations/argentina.htm.

Dengue Fever

Dengue fever is a viral infection found throughout South America. It is transmitted by Aedes mosquitoes, which prefer to bite during the day time and breed primarily in artificial water containers such as cans, cisterns, plastic containers and discarded tires. As a result, dengue is especially common in densely populated, urban environments.

In 2009 several thousand cases of dengue were reported in the northern provinces of Argentina, with Chaco and Catamarca being hit the worst. There were even a few dozen cases in Buenos Aires. Fortunately, relatively few deaths resulted. Dengue usually causes flulike symptoms, including fever, muscle aches, joint pains, headaches, nausea and vomiting, often followed by a rash. The body aches may be quite uncomfortable, but most cases resolve uneventfully in a few days.

Malaria

Malaria is transmitted by mosquitos, which usually bite between dusk and dawn. The main symptom is high spiking fevers, which may be accompanied by chills, sweats, headache, body aches, weakness, vomiting or diarrhea. Severe cases may involve the central nervous system and lead to seizures, confusion, coma and death.

Taking malaria pills is recommended for travel to rural areas along the borders with Bolivia (lowlands of Salta and Jujuy provinces) and Paraguay (lowlands of Misiones and Corrientes provinces).

PRACTICALITIES

- **Addresses** In Argentine addresses, the word *local* refers to a suite or office. If an address has 's/n' – short for *sin numero* (without number) – the address has no street number.
- **Laundry** Affordable *lavanderías* are widely available in Argentina.
- **Newspapers** Argentina's biggest papers are centrist *Clarín* (www.clarin.com), conservative *La Nación* (www.lanacion.com.ar) and lefty *Página 12* (www.pagina12.com.ar). The English-language daily is *Buenos Aires Herald* (www.buenosairesherald.com). *The Argentina Independent* (www.argentinaindependent.com) is an excellent English-language online newspaper.
- **Photography** Many photo stores can affordably transfer images from your digital camera to CD; you can also get them printed out. Old-fashioned print and slide film are available, as is developing.
- **Radio** In Buenos Aires tune in to FM 92.7 for 24-hour tango, FM 98.3 for Argentine rock and FM 98.7 for Argentine folk music.
- **Smoking** Smoking bans differ by province. In Buenos Aires smoking is banned in most enclosed public spaces, including the majority of bars, restaurants and public transportation.
- **Weights & Measures** Metric.

Yellow Fever

Yellow fever is a life-threatening viral infection transmitted by mosquitoes in forested areas. The illness begins with flulike symptoms, which may include fever, chills, headache, muscle aches, backache, loss of appetite, nausea and vomiting. These symptoms usually subside in a few days, but one person in six enters a second, toxic phase characterized by recurrent fever, vomiting, listlessness, jaundice, kidney failure and hemorrhage, leading to death in up to half of the cases. There is no treatment except for supportive care.

The yellow-fever vaccine is recommended for all travelers over the age of nine months who visit the northeastern forest areas near the border with Brazil and Paraguay.

Insurance

A travel insurance policy to cover theft, loss, medical problems and trip cancellation or delays is a good idea. Some policies specifically exclude dangerous activities such as scuba diving, skiing, rock climbing and even trekking; read the fine print. Check that the policy covers ambulances or an emergency flight home.

Keep all your paperwork in case you have to file a claim later. Paying for your flight with a credit card often provides limited travel insurance – ask your credit card company what it is prepared to cover. Worldwide travel insurance is available at www.lonelyplanet.com/travel_services. You can buy, extend cover and claim online anytime – even if you're already on the road.

Internet Access

Wi-fi is available at many (if not most) hotels and cafes, restaurants and airports, and it's generally good and free. Internet cafes and *locutorios* (small telephone officers) with very affordable internet access can be found in practically all Argentine towns and cities. To find the @ *(arroba)* symbol on keyboards, hold down the Alt key and type 64, or type AltGr-2. You can also ask the attendant *'¿Cómo se hace la arroba?'* ('How do you make the@sign?').

Legal Matters

Police can demand identification at any time and for whatever reason, though it's unlikely to happen. Always carry a photo ID or a copy of your passport, and – most importantly – *always* be courteous and cooperative.

Drugs and most other substances that are illegal in the USA and many European countries are also illegal here, though marijuana has been somewhat decriminalized in Argentina (and is legal in Uruguay). If arrested, you have the constitutional right to a lawyer, a telephone call and to remain silent (beyond giving your name, nationality, age and passport number). Don't sign anything until you talk to a lawyer. If you don't speak Spanish, a translator should be provided for you.

Maps

Tourist offices throughout the country provide free city maps that are good enough for tooling around town.

With offices in nearly every Argentine city, the **Automóvil Club Argentino** (ACA; www.aca.org.ar) publishes excellent maps of provinces and cities that are great for driving. Card-carrying members of foreign automobile clubs can get discounts.

Geography nerds will adore the topographic maps available from the **Instituto Geográfico Nacional** (☎4576-5576; www.ign.gob.ar; Av Cabildo 381) in Buenos Aires.

Money

The Argentine unit of currency is the peso (AR$).

Carrying cash and an ATM card is the way to go in Argentina.

ATMs

Cajeros automáticos (ATMs) are found in nearly every city and town in Argentina and can also be used for cash advances on major credit cards. They're the best way to get money, and nearly all have instructions in English. Depending on your home bank there are varying upper limits per withdrawal, and a small fee is charged on ATM transactions by the local bank (not including charges by your home bank). You can withdraw several times per day, but beware these charges – which are per transaction. Banelco ATMs tend to allow larger withdrawls.

Cash

Notes come in denominations of two, five, 10, 20, 50 and 100 pesos. One peso equals 100 *centavos;* coins come in denominations of five, 10, 25 and 50 *centavos*, as well as one and two pesos. At present, US dollars are accepted by many tourist-oriented businesses, but you should always carry some pesos.

Don't be dismayed if you receive dirty and hopelessly tattered banknotes; they'll be accepted everywhere. Some places refuse torn or marked foreign banknotes, however, so make sure you arrive in Argentina with pristine bills.

Counterfeiting, of both local and US bills, has become a problem in recent years, and merchants are very careful when accepting large denominations. You should be too; look for a clear watermark or running thread on the largest bills, and get familiar with the local currency *before* you arrive in Argentina. See www.landingpadba.com/ba-basics-counterfeit-money. Being aware of fake bills is especially important in dark places like nightclubs or taxis.

Getting change from large denominations can be a problem for small purchases. Large supermarkets and restaurants are your best bet. Always keep a stash of change with you, in both small bills and coins.

Credit Cards

Many (but not all!) tourist services, larger stores, hotels and restaurants – especially in the bigger cities – take credit cards such as Visa and MasterCard. The latter two are most widely accepted credit cards, though American Express and a few others are valid in some establishments. Before you leave home, warn your credit-card company that you'll be using it abroad.

Some businesses add a *recargo* (surcharge) of 5% to 10% to credit-card purchases. Also, the actual amount you'll eventually pay depends upon the exchange rate not at the time of sale, but when the purchase is posted to an overseas account, sometimes weeks later.

If you use a credit card to pay in a restaurant, be aware that tips can't usually be added to the bill. Many lower-end hotels and private tour companies will not accept credit cards. Many places will give you a small discount if you pay in cash, rather than use a credit card.

Moneychangers

US dollars are by far the preferred foreign currency, although Chilean and Uruguayan pesos can be readily exchanged at the borders. Cash dollars and euros can be changed at banks and *cambios* (exchange houses) in most larger cities, but other currencies can be difficult to change outside Buenos Aires. You'll need your passport to change money; it might be best to avoid any sort of street-tout moneychanger.

Taxes & Refunds

One of Argentina's primary state revenue-earners is the 21% value-added tax known as the Impuesto de Valor Agregado (IVA). Under limited circumstances, foreign visitors may obtain IVA refunds on purchases of Argentine products upon

TWO-TIER PRICING

Over the last decade, Argentina's popularity as a tourism destination has given birth to an annoying two-tier pricing system: some businesses in certain areas (mostly in Buenos Aires, but also in Patagonia and parts of the Lake District) charge Argentines one price and 'nonresidents' a higher price. While you won't find this everywhere, you will encounter it at some tango shows, museums, *estancias* (ranches), national parks, airlines and upmarket hotels throughout the country.

Many accommodations also quote prices in US dollars rather than pesos. This doesn't necessarily mean you're getting charged more than Argentines; the peso is just so unstable that places prefer to use a currency that isn't always fluctuating.

departing the country. A 'Tax Free' window decal (in English) identifies participants in this program, but always check that the shop is part of the tax-free program before making your purchase.

You can obtain tax refunds on purchases of AR$70 or more made at one of these participating stores. To do so, present your passport to the merchant, who will make out an invoice for you. On leaving the country keep the purchased items in your carry-on baggage. A customs official will check them and stamp your paperwork, then tell you where to obtain your refund. Be sure to leave yourself a bit of extra time at the airport to get this done.

Tipping & Bargaining

In restaurants and cafes it's customary to tip about 10% of the bill for decent service. An interesting note: when your server is taking your bill with payment away, you saying *'gracias'* usually implies that the server should keep the change as a tip. If you want change back, don't say *'gracias'* – say *'cambio, por favor'* instead.

Note that tips can't be added to credit-card bills, so carry cash for this purpose. Also note that the *cubierto* that some restaurants charge is not a tip; it's a 'cover charge' for the use of utensils and bread.

Bartenders They don't expect a tip, but it's fine to leave a small bill for a drink or particularly good cocktail.

Bus porters A small bill

Delivery persons A small bill

Hotel cleaning staff AR$10 per day (only at fine, upscale hotels)

Hotel porter a small bill

Restaurant servers 10%; 15% for fine restaurants with great service

Spas 15%

Taxi drivers no tip unless they help with luggage; many people round the fare up to nearest peso

Tour guides 10% to 15%

Unlike many other South American countries, bargaining is generally not the norm in Argentina.

Traveler's Checks

Be aware that very high commissions are levied on traveler's checks, which are difficult to cash anywhere and specifically *not* recommended for travel in Argentina. Stores will *not* accept traveler's checks, and outside Buenos Aires it's even harder to change them.

ARGENTINA'S 'BLUE MARKET'

Because many Argentines are desperate for hard currency to combat their country's high inflation, mistrust the peso's stability *and* are not allowed to easily buy them, Argentina has a robust black market for US dollars, especially in Buenos Aires (BA). This market is also called the *mercado azul* (blue market, or 'cambio blue'). The blue-market rate can be nearly twice the official exchange rate, though rates fluctuate daily. Many people think this parallel market can't last forever, and the government is constantly tinkering with laws to combat it.

In BA, some people use this market on Calle Florida, where *arbolitos* (touts; literally, 'little trees') constantly call out *'cambio, cambio, cambio'*. The *arbolito* leads the interested party to a *cueva* (unofficial exchange office) for the transaction. Unobtrusive storefront *cuevas* also exist in some tourist neighborhoods in BA; many locals use them and know where they are. Be aware that this shady activity – although commonplace (newspapers even publish the going blue rate) – is technically illegal. Scams and fake bills do exist, and unwary travelers make very good targets.

Instead of using *arbolitos*, some people change money (or pay for services) at certain stores, travel agents, restaurants and accommodations for rates close to the blue market's. Outside BA, some *cambios* might give you the unofficial rate. Hundred-dollar bills get the highest rates.

Note that ATMs in Argentina don't give out US currency, no matter what their screen says. Some ATMs in Uruguay will, however, though there are daily limits for withdrawals.

Another way travelers bypass the official exchange rate is by using international money-transfer services such as www.xoom.com (for those with US bank accounts) or Azimo (for those with UK bank accounts).

Do your research very carefully before coming to Argentina. And no matter how you end up getting your pesos, use them all before your flight home. It's unlikely you'll be able to change them back to a hard currency at a decent rate – if at all.

Opening Hours

There are always exceptions, but the following are general opening hours:

Banks 8am to 3pm or 4pm Monday to Friday; some open till 1pm Saturday

Bars 8pm or 9pm to between 4am and 6am nightly (downtown, some open and close earlier)

Cafes 6am to midnight or much later; open daily

Clubs 1am to 2am to between 6am and 8am Friday and Saturday

Office business hours 8am to 5pm

Post offices 8am to 6pm Monday to Friday, 9am to 1pm Saturday

Restaurants Noon to 3:30pm, 8pm-midnight or 1am (later on weekends)

Shops 9am or 10am to 8pm or 9pm Monday to Saturday

Post

The often unreliable **Correo Argentino** (www.correoargentino.com.ar) is the government postal service. Essential overseas mail should be sent *certificado* (registered). You can send packages less than 2kg from any post office, but anything heavier needs to go through *aduana* (a customs office). In Buenos Aires, this office is near Retiro bus terminal and is called Correo Internacional. Take your passport and keep the package open as you'll have to show its contents to a customs official.

Domestic couriers, such as **Andreani** (www.andreani.com.ar) and **OCA** (www.oca.com.ar), and international couriers such as DHL and FedEx are far more dependable than the post office. But they're also far more expensive. The last two have offices only in the largest cities, while the first two usually serve as their connections to the interior of the country.

If a package is being sent to you, expect to wait awhile before receiving notification of its arrival. Nearly all parcels sent to Buenos Aires go to the Correo Argentino office, near the bus terminal. To collect the package you'll have to wait (sometimes hours) first to get it and then to have it checked by customs. There is also a processing fee. Don't expect any valuables to make it through.

Public Holidays

Government offices and businesses are closed on Argentina's numerous public holidays. If the holiday falls on a Wednesday or weekend day, it's often bumped to the nearest Monday; if it falls on a Tuesday or Thursday, then the in-between days of Monday and Friday are taken as holidays.

Public-transportation options are more limited on holidays, when you should reserve tickets far in advance. Hotel booking should also be done ahead of time.

The following list does not include provincial holidays, which may vary considerably.

January 1 Año Nuevo, New Year's Day

February/March Carnaval. Dates vary from year to year, but celebrations always fall on a Monday and Tuesday and become holidays.

March 24 Día de la Memoria; Memorial Day. Anniversary of the day that started the 1976 dictatorship and subsequent Dirty War.

March/April Semana Santa; Easter week. Dates vary; most businesses close on 'Good Thursday' and Good Friday; major travel week.

April 2 Día de las Malvinas; honors the fallen Argentine soldiers from the Falkland Islands (Islas Malvinas) war in 1982.

May 1 Día del Trabajador; Labor Day

May 25 Revolución de Mayo; commemorates the 1810 revolution against Spain.

June 20 Día de la Bandera; Flag Day. Anniversary of death of Manuel Belgrano, creator of Argentina's flag and military leader.

July 9 Día de la Independencia; Independence Day

August (third Monday in August) Día del Libertador San Martín; marks the anniversary of José de San Martín's death (1778–1850).

October 12 (second Monday in October) Día del Respeto a la Diversidad Cultural; a day to respect cultural diversity.

November 20 (fourth Monday in November) Día de la Soberanía Nacional; Day of National Sovereignty

December 8 Día de la Concepción Inmaculada; celebrates the immaculate conception of the Virgin Mary.

December 25 Navidad; Christmas Day

Note that Christmas Eve and New Year's Day are treated as semi-holidays, and you will find some businesses closed for the latter half of those days.

Safe Travel

For tourists, Argentina is one of the safest countries in Latin America. This isn't to say you should skip down the street drunk with your money belt strapped to your head, but with a little common sense you can visit Argentina's big cities as safely as you could London, Paris or New York. That said, crime has been on the rise.

Petty Crime

The economic crisis of 1999–2001 plunged a lot of people into poverty, and street crime (pickpocketing, bag-snatching and armed robbery) has subsequently risen, especially in Buenos Aires. Here, be especially watchful for pickpockets on crowded buses, on the Subte and at busy *ferias* (street markets). Still, most people feel perfectly safe in the big cities. In the small towns of the provinces you'd have to *search* for a crook to rob you.

Bus terminals are commonly where tourists become separated from their possessions. For the most part bus terminals are safe, as they're usually full of families traveling and saying goodbyes, but they can also be prime grounds for bag-snatchers. Always keep an eagle eye on your goods. This is especially true in Buenos Aires' Retiro station.

At sidewalk cafe or restaurant tables, always keep your bag close to you, preferably touching your body. You can also place the strap around your leg or tie it around the furniture. Be careful showing off expensive electronics such as laptops, or tablets. Other places to be wary are tourist destinations and on crowded public transportation.

In Buenos Aires the **Tourist Police** (☎0800-999-5000, 011-4346-5748) provides interpreters and helps victims of robberies and rip-offs.

ELECTRONICS WARNING

Note that buying a smart phone, and especially an iPhone, is extremely expensive in Argentina due to import restrictions – and they are not widely available. If you do bring your smart phone, don't flash it around unnecessarily or leave it unprotected somewhere. This goes for tablet computers and laptop computers, too.

Pickets & Protests

Street protests have become part of daily life in Argentina, especially in Buenos Aires' Plaza de Mayo area. Generally these have little effect on tourists other than blocking traffic or making it difficult to see Plaza de Mayo and the Casa Rosada. The country has many *gremios* or *sindicatos* (trade unions), and it seems that one of them is always on strike. Transportation-union strikes can affect travelers directly by delaying domestic flights and bus services. It's always a good idea to keep your eye on the news before setting off on your travels.

Drivers

Being a pedestrian in Argentina is perhaps one of the country's more difficult ventures. Many Argentine drivers jump the gun when the traffic signal is about to change to green, drive extremely fast and change lanes unpredictably. Even though pedestrians at corners and crosswalks have the legal right of way, very few drivers respect this and will hardly slow down when you are crossing. Be especially careful of buses, which can be reckless and, because of their large size, particularly dangerous.

Police & Military

The police and military have a reputation for being corrupt or irresponsible, but both are generally helpful and courteous to tourists. If you feel you're being patted down for a bribe (most often if you're driving), you can respond by tactfully paying up or asking the officer to accompany you to the police station to take care of it. The latter will likely cause the officer to drop it – though it could also lead you into the labyrinthine bureaucracy of the Argentine police system. Pretending you don't understand Spanish may also frustrate a potential bribe.

Telephone

Two companies, Telecom and Telefónica, run the country's telephone services.

To use street phones, you'll need to pay with regular coins or *tarjetas telefónicas* (magnetic phone cards available at many kiosks). You'll only be able to speak for a limited time before you get cut off, so carry enough credit.

Toll-free numbers begin with ☎0800; these calls can only be made within Argentina. Numbers that start with ☎0810 are charged on at a local rate only, no matter where (in Argentina) you are calling from.

The cheapest way to make an international call is to use an online service (such as Skype or Google Voice) or use a phone card. International calls can be made at *locutorios* but they tend to be more expensive this way. When dialing abroad, dial ☎00, followed by the code of the country you're calling, then the area code and number.

Directory Assistance (☎110)

Fire (☎100)

Medical Emergency (☎107)

Police (☎101, in some larger cities ☎911)

Tourist Police in Buenos Aires (☎0800-999-5000, 011-4346-5748)

Cell Phones

It's best to bring your own unlocked tri- or quad-band GSM cell phone to Argentina, then buy an inexpensive SIM chip (you'll get a local number) and credits (*carga virtual*) as needed. Both SIM chips and credits can be bought at many kiosks or *locutorios;* look for the *'recarga facil'* signs. Many Argentines use this system with their cell phones. Phone unlocking services are available; ask around.

You can also buy cell phones that use SIM chips which will usually include some credits for your first batch of calls. Be careful renting phones as they're not usually a better deal than outright buying a cell phone.

If you plan to travel with an iPhone or other G3 smart phone, prepare yourself – you may need to purchase an international plan to avoid being hit by a huge bill for roaming costs. On the other hand, it's possible to call internationally for free or very cheaply, using a VoIP (Voice over Internet Protocol) system such as Skype. This is a constantly changing field, so do some research before you travel.

Cell phone numbers in Argentina are preceded by '15.' If you're calling a cell phone number from a landline, you'll have to dial 15 first. But if you're calling a cell phone from another cell phone, you don't need to dial 15.

When calling cell phones from outside Argentina, dial your country's international access code, then ☎54 9 11 and then the eight-digit number, leaving out the 15.

CALLING ARGENTINA

To call a number in Argentina from another country, dial your international exit code, then the country code for Argentina, then the area code (without the zero) and number. For example, if you're calling a Buenos Aires landline number from the United States, you'd dial:

☎011-54-11-xxxx-xxxx

☎011 is the United States' international exit code

☎54 is Argentina's country code

☎11 is Buenos Aires' city code without the beginning zero

☎xxxx-xxxx is your local Buenos Aires phone number, usually eight digits

When dialing an Argentine cell phone from another country, dial your international exit code, then 54, then 9, then the area code without the 0, then the number – leaving out the 15 (which most Argentine cell phone numbers start with). For example, if you're calling a Buenos Aires cell phone number from the United States, you'd dial:

☎011-54-9-11-xxxx-xxxx

Phonecards

Telephone calling cards are sold at nearly all kiosks and make domestic and international calls far cheaper than calling direct. They must be used from a fixed line such as a home or hotel telephone (provided you can dial outside the hotel). They cannot be used at most pay phones. Some *locutorios* will allow you to use them, and although they levy a surcharge, the call is still cheaper than dialing direct. When purchasing one, tell the clerk the country you will call so they give you the right card.

Locutorios & Internet Cafes

The easiest way to make a local phone call is to find a *locutorio* (small telephone office) that has private cabins where you make calls and then pay at the register. *Locutorios* can be found on practically every other block. They cost about the same as street phones, are much quieter and you won't run out of coins. Most *locutorios* are supplied with phone books.

When making international calls from *locutorios* ask about off-peak discount hours, which generally apply after 10pm and on weekends. Making international calls over the internet using Skype, is a cheap option.

Faxes are cheap and widely available at most *locutorios* and internet cafes.

Time

Argentina is three hours behind GMT and generally does not observe daylight saving time (though this situation can easily change). When it's noon in Argentina, it's 10am in New York, 7am in San Francisco, 3pm in London and 1pm the next day in Sydney (add one hour to these destinations during their daylight saving times). Argentina uses the 24-hour clock in written communications, but both the 12- and 24-hour clocks can be used conversationally.

Toilets

Public toilets in Argentina are better than in most of South America, but there are certainly exceptions. The better restaurants and cafes are good alternatives. Large shopping malls often have public bathrooms, as do international fast-food chains. Always carry your own toilet paper, since it often runs out in public restrooms, and don't expect luxuries such as soap, hot water and paper towels either. In smaller towns, some public toilets charge a small fee for entry. Changing facilities for babies are not always available.

Some travelers may find bidets a novelty; they are those strange shallow ceramic bowls with knobs and a drain, often accompanying toilets in hotel bathrooms. They are meant for between-shower cleanings of nether regions. Turn knobs slowly, or you may end up spraying yourself or the ceiling.

Tourist Information

Argentina's national tourist board is the Secretaría de Turismo de la Nación (www.turismo.gov.ar); its main office is in Buenos Aires. Almost every destination city or town has a tourist office, usually on or near the main plaza or at the bus terminal. Each Argentine province also has its own representation in Buenos Aires. Most of these are well organized, often offering a computerized database of tourist information, and can be worth a visit before heading for the provinces.

Travelers with Disabilities

Negotiating Argentina as a disabled traveler is not the easiest of tasks. Those in wheelchairs in particular will quickly realize that many cities' narrow, busy and uneven sidewalks are difficult to negotiate. Crossing streets is also a problem, since not every corner has ramps (which, if provided, are often in need of repair) and traffic can be ruthless when it comes to pedestrians and wheelchair-users. A few buses do have *piso bajo* – they 'kneel' and have extra-large spaces – but the Subte (subway) in Buenos Aires does not cater to the mobility-impaired.

International hotel chains often have wheelchair-accessible rooms, as do other less fancy hotels. Some restaurants, tourist sights and public buildings have ramps, but bathrooms are not always wheelchair-accessible (in bigger cities, shopping malls are a good bet for these). In Buenos Aires, **QRV Transportes Especiales** (☎011-15-6863-9555, 011-4306-6635; www.qrvtransportes.com.ar) offers private transport, and city tours in vans fully equipped for wheelchair users.

Other than the use of Braille on ATMs, little effort has been made to improving accessibility for the vision impaired. Stoplights are rarely equipped with sound alerts. The **Biblioteca Argentina Para Ciegos** (Argentine Library for the Blind, BAC; ☎011-4981-0137; www.bac.org.ar; Lezica 3909) in Buenos Aires maintains a Braille collection of books in Spanish, as well as other resources.

Also check out the following organizations:

Accessible Journeys (www.disabilitytravel.com)

Flying Wheels Travel (www.flyingwheelstravel.com)

Mobility International USA (www.miusa.org)

Society for Accessible Travel & Hospitality (www.sath.org)

Visas

Nationals of the USA, Canada, most Western European countries, Australia and New Zealand do not need a visa to visit Argentina. Upon arrival, most visitors get a 90-day stamp in their passport. Those from the USA, Canada and Australia, however, must pay a significant 'reciprocity fee' before arriving (see boxed text, p609).

Dependent children traveling without *both* parents theoretically need a notarized document certifying that both parents agree to the child's travel. Parents may also wish to bring a copy of the custody form, however, there's a good chance they won't be asked for either document.

Depending on your nationality, very short visits to neighboring countries sometimes do not require visas. For instance, you might not need a Brazilian visa to cross from the Argentine town of Puerto Iguazú to Foz do Iguaçu and/or Ciudad del Este, Paraguay, as long as you return the same day.

The same situation is true at the Bolivian border town of Villazón, near La Quiaca. Officials at Paraguayan crossings can fine crossers who don't have a Paraguayan visa.

Visa Extensions

For a 90-day extension on your tourist visa, get ready for bureaucracy and visit Buenos Aires' immigration office **Dirección Nacional de Migraciones** (☎4317-0234; www.migraciones.gov.ar/accesibleingles/?categorias; Antártida Argentina 1355; ⏰8am-2pm Mon-Fri). The fee is AR$300 – interestingly enough, the same charge as for overstaying your visa (be aware that the rules can change quickly).

Another option if you're staying for more than three months is to cross into Colonia or Montevideo (both in Uruguay; Colonia can be an easy day trip) or Chile for a day or two before your visa expires, then return with a new 90-day visa. This only works if you don't need a visa to enter the other country.

Volunteering

There are many opportunities for volunteering in Argentina, from food banks to *villas miserias* (shantytowns) to organic farms. Some ask for just your time, or a modest fee, and some charge hundreds of dollars (with likely a low percentage of money going directly to those in need). Before choosing an organization, it's a good idea to talk to other volunteers about their experiences.

Organizations include:

Aldea Luna (www.aldealuna.com.ar) Work on a farm in a nature reserve.

AMA Torres del Paine (www.patagoniavolunteer.org) Volunteer in spectacular Torres del Paine, Chile.

Anda Responsible Travel (www.andatravel.com.ar/en/volunteering) Buenos Aires travel agency supporting local communities.

Centro Conviven (www.conviven.org.ar) Helps kids in Buenos Aires' shantytowns.

Conservación Patagonica (www.patagonialandtrust.org/makeadifference_v.htm) Help to create a national park.

Eco Yoga Park (www.ecoyogavillages.org/volunteer-programs) One of a kind.

Fundación Banco de Alimentos (www.bancodealimentos.org.ar) Short-term work at a food bank.

Habitat for Humanity Argentina (www.hpha.org.ar) Building communities.

Patagonia Volunteer (www.patagoniavolunteer.org) Has opportunities in Patagonia.

Volunteer South America (www.volunteersouthamerica.net) Lists NGOs with volunteer opportunities in South America.

WWOOF Argentina (www.wwoofargentina.com) Organic farming in Argentina.

Women Travelers

Being a woman traveling in Argentina can sometimes be a challenge, especially if you are young, alone and/or maintaining an inflexible liberal attitude. In some ways Argentina is a safer place for a woman than Europe, the USA and most other Latin American countries, but dealing with its machismo culture can be a real pain.

Some males feel the need to comment on a woman's attractiveness. This often happens when the woman is alone and walking by on the street; it occasionally happens to two or more women walking together, but never to a heterosexual couple. Verbal comments include crude language, hisses, whistles and *piropos* (flirtatious comments).

The best thing to do is completely ignore the comments. After all, many Argentine women enjoy getting these 'compliments' and most men don't necessarily mean to be insulting; they're just doing what males in their culture are brought up to do.

On the plus side of machismo, expect men to hold a door open for you and let you enter first, including getting on buses; this gives you a better chance at grabbing an empty seat.

ARGENTINA'S RECIPROCITY FEE

Citizens from some countries have to pay a reciprocity fee (*tasa de reciprocidad*) before arriving in Argentina; ideally you'll be reminded of this when you buy your airplane ticket. This fee is equal to what Argentines are charged for visas to visit those countries. You'll need to pay this fee online via credit card; see www.migraciones.gov.ar/accesibleingles and click on 'Pay your Reciprocity Rate' on the left column.

These fees are US$100 for Australians (good for one year), US$160 for Americans (good for 10 years) and US$75 for Canadians (per entry – sucks, eh? Or go for the US$150, good-for-five-years option). You'll need to prepay this fee before entering Argentina via other airports, borders or ports (that means you, cruise ship passengers) too, or you might be turned around.

Work

Unless you have a special skill, business, and/or speak Spanish, it's hard to find paid work in Argentina other than teaching English – or perhaps putting time in at a hostel or expat bar. It's good to be aware that you're not likely to get rich doing these things.

Native English speakers usually work out of language institutes. Twenty hours a week of actual teaching is about enough for most people (you aren't paid for prep time or travel time, which can add another hour or two for each hour of teaching). Frustrations include dealing with unpleasant institutes, time spent cashing checks at the bank, classes being spread throughout the day and cancelled classes. Turnover is high and most people don't teach for more than a year.

A TEFL certificate can certainly help but isn't mandatory for all jobs (see www.teflbuenosaires.com). You'll make more money teaching private students, but it takes time to gain a client base. And you should take into account slow periods, such as December through February, when many locals leave town on summer vacation.

To find a job, call up the institutes or visit expat bars and start networking. March is when institutes are ramping up their courses, so it's the best time to find work. Many teachers work on tourist visas, heading over to Uruguay every three months for a new visa or visiting the immigration office for an extension.

For general job postings, check out www.landingpadba.com/jobs-and-working-in-argentina, http://buenosaires.en.craigslist.org and www.indeed.com/q-Argentina-jobs.html. You could also try posting on expat website forums, such as www.baexpats.org.

Transportation

GETTING THERE & AWAY

Flights, tours and rail tickets can be booked online at lonelyplanet.com/bookings.

Entering Argentina

Entering Argentina is straightforward; immigration officials at airports are generally quick to the point, while those at border crossings may take more time scrutinizing your passport. Once you're in the country, police can still demand identification any time. Carry at least a photocopy of your passport around at all times.

Air

Argentina has direct flights between North America, the UK, Europe, Australia and South Africa, and from nearly all South American countries. You can also fly to a neighboring country, such as Brazil or Chile, and continue overland to Argentina.

Airports & Airlines

Most international flights arrive at Buenos Aires' **Aeropuerto Internacional Ministro Pistarini** (Ezeiza; ☎011-5480-6111; www.aa2000.com.ar), which is a 40- to 60-minute shuttle bus or taxi ride out of town (35km).

Close to downtown Buenos Aires is **Aeroparque Internacional Jorge Newbery** (Aeroparque; ☎011-5480-6111; www.aa2000.com.ar), which handles mostly domestic flights but also a few international ones from neighboring countries.

There are several other international airports around Argentina. Basic information on most Argentine airports can be found online at **Aeropuertos Argentina 2000** (www.aa2000.com.ar).

Aerolíneas Argentinas (AR; www.aerolineasargentinas.com) is the national carrier and has a decent international reputation.

Land

Border Crossings

There are numerous border crossings from neighboring Chile, Bolivia, Paraguay, Brazil and Uruguay; the following lists are only the principal crossings. Generally, border formalities are straightforward as long as all your documents are in order.

BOLIVIA

La Quiaca to Villazón Many buses go from Jujuy and Salta to La Quiaca, where you must walk across a bridge to the Bolivian border.

Aguas Blancas to Bermejo From Orán, reached by bus from Salta or Jujuy, take a bus to Aguas Blancas and then Ber-

CLIMATE CHANGE & TRAVEL

Every form of transport that relies on carbon-based fuel generates CO_2, the main cause of human-induced climate change. Modern travel is dependent on airplanes, which might use less fuel per mile per person than most cars but travel much greater distances. The altitude at which aircraft emit gases (including CO_2) and particles also contributes to their climate change impact. Many websites offer 'carbon calculators' that allow people to estimate the carbon emissions generated by their journey and, for those who wish to do so, to offset the impact of the greenhouse gases emitted with contributions to portfolios of climate-friendly initiatives throughout the world. Lonely Planet offsets the carbon footprint of all staff and author travel.

ARRIVAL TIPS: AEROPUERTO INTERNACIONAL MINISTRO PISTARINI

➡ Citizens from some countries have to pay a reciprocity fee *(tasa de reciprocidad)* before flying into Argentina; this fee is equal to what Argentines are charged for visas to visit those countries. These fees are US$100 for Australians (good for one year), US$160 for Americans (good for 10 years) and US$75 for Canadians (per entry – sucks, eh? Or go for the US$150, good-for-five-years option).

Normally you need to pay this fee online via credit card; see www.migraciones.gov.ar/accesibleingles and click on 'Pay your Reciprocity Rate' on the left column. Ideally you'll be reminded of this fee when you buy your airplane ticket. At border crossings, you may or may not be able to pay on the spot – ask around ahead of time for current rules.

➡ To change money at Ezeiza, don't use the *cambios* (exchange houses) there – their rates are generally bad. Better rates are found at the local bank branch; after exiting customs, pass the rows of transport booths, go outside the doors into the reception hall and make a U-turn to the right to find Banco de la Nación's small office. Its rates are identical to downtown offices, there's an ATM and it's open 24 hours, though long lines are common. There are other ATMs at Ezeiza, too.

➡ There's a tourist information booth just beyond the city's 'Taxi Ezeiza' stand.

➡ Shuttle buses and taxis frequently run from Ezeiza to the center; see p112 for details.

➡ When flying out of Ezeiza, get there at least two to three hours before your international flight. Security and immigration lines can be long, and be aware that traffic is often bad getting to Ezeiza – it can take an hour or more to go the 35km from downtown BA. Also, even when you get past main security there may be bag checks at the gate, and neither food nor liquids may be allowed onto airplanes. Eat and drink up before boarding.

mejo, where you can catch a bus to Tarija.

Salvador Mazza (Pocitos) to Yacuiba Buses from Jujuy or Salta go to Salvador Mazza at the Bolivian border, where you cross and grab a shared taxi to Yacuiba.

BRAZIL

The most common crossing is from Puerto Iguazú to Foz do Iguaçu. Check both cities for more information on the peculiarities of this border crossing, especially if you're crossing the border into Brazil only to see the other side of Iguazú Falls. There is also a border crossing from Paso de los Libres to Uruguaiana (Brazil).

CHILE

There are numerous crossings between Argentina and Chile. Except in far southern Patagonia, every land crossing involves crossing the Andes. Due to weather, some high-altitude passes close in winter; even the busy Mendoza–Santiago route over RN7 can close for several days (sometimes longer) during a severe storm. Always check road conditions, especially if you have a flight scheduled on the other side of the mountains. The following are the most commonly used crossings:

Bariloche to Puerto Montt This border crossing over the Andes to Chile is usually no fuss; an optional 'tour' is the famous, scenic 12-hour bus-boat combination. It takes two days in winter.

El Calafate to Puerto Natales and Parque Nacional Torres del Paine Probably the most beaten route down here, heading from the Glaciar Perito Moreno (near El Calafate) to Parque Nacional Torres del Paine (near Puerto Natales). Several buses per day in summer; one to two daily in the off-season.

Los Antiguos to Chile Chico Those entering Argentina from Chile can access the rugged RN40 from here and head down to El Chaltén and El Calafate. Best in summer, when there's actually public transport available.

Mendoza to Santiago The most popular crossing between the two countries, passing 6962m Aconcagua en route.

Salta to San Pedro de Atacama (via Jujuy, Purmamarca and Susques) A 10-hour bus ride through the altiplano with stunningly beautiful scenery.

Ushuaia to Punta Arenas Daily buses in summer, fewer in winter, on this 10- to 12-hour trip (depending on weather conditions), which includes a ferry crossing at either Porvenir or Punta Delgada/Primera Angostura.

URUGUAY & PARAGUAY

There are two direct border crossings between Argentina and Paraguay: Clorinda to Asunción, and Posadas to Encarnación. From Puerto Iguazú, Argentina, you can also cross through Brazil into Ciudad del Este, Paraguay.

Border crossings from Argentine cities to Uruguayan cities include: Gualeguaychú to Fray Bentos; Colón to Paysandú; and Concordia to Salto. All involve crossing bridges. Buses from Buenos Aires to Montevideo and other waterfront cities, however, are slower and less convenient than the ferries (or ferry-bus combinations) across the Río de la Plata.

Bus

Travelers can bus to Argentina from most bordering countries. Buses are usually comfortable, modern and fairly clean. Crossing over does not involve too many hassles; just make sure that you have any proper visas beforehand.

River

There are several river crossings between Uruguay and Buenos Aires that involve ferry or hydrofoil, and often require combinations with buses.

Buenos Aires to Colonia Daily ferries (one to three hours) head to Colonia, with bus connections to Montevideo (additional three hours).

Buenos Aires to Montevideo High-speed ferries carry passengers from downtown Buenos Aires to the Uruguayan capital in only 2¼ hours.

Tigre to Carmelo Regular passenger launches speed from the Buenos Aires suburb of Tigre to Carmelo in 2½ hours (services also go to Montevideo from Tigre).

GETTING AROUND

Air

Airlines in Argentina

The national carrier, **Aerolíneas Argentinas** (AR; www.aerolineasargentinas.com), offers the most domestic flights, but it's not necessarily better than its competitors. Other airlines with domestic flights include **LAN** (www.lan.com) and **Líneas Aéreas del Estado** (LADE; www.lade.com.ar), the air force's passenger service. The latter has some of the least expensive air tickets and specializes in Patagonia, but it has very few flights and most are short hops.

Some domestic airlines operate on a two-tier system, where foreigners pay more than locals for the same ticket. If you fly to Argentina with Aerolíneas Argentinas, however, you can get discounted domestic tickets via a special 'air pass'. The catch is that you must purchase these outside Argentina, usually when you purchase your international flight.

Demand for flights around the country can be heavy, especially during some holidays (such as Christmas or Easter) and the vacation months of January, February and July. Seats are often booked out well in advance so reserve as far ahead as possible.

Nearly all domestic flights land at **Aeroparque Internacional Jorge Newbery** (Aeroparque; ☎011-5480-6111; www.aa2000.com.ar), a short distance north of downtown Buenos Aires. It's worth noting that Argentina's domestic flight system can be very unreliable – flights are often cancelled or delayed, and there can be frequent labor strikes. It might be a good idea to avoid tight itineraries; for example, leave a day's cushion in between your domestic and international flights.

Bicycle

If you dig cycling your way around a country, Argentina has potential. You'll see the landscape in greater detail, have far more freedom than you would if beholden to public transportation, and likely meet more locals.

Road bikes are suitable for many paved roads, but byways are often narrow and surfaces can be rough. A *todo terreno* (mountain bike) is often safer and more convenient, allowing you to use the unpaved shoulder and the very extensive network of gravel roads throughout the country. Argentine bicycles are improving in quality, but are still far from equal to their counterparts in Europe or the USA.

There are two major drawbacks to long-distance bicycling in Argentina. One is the wind, which in Patagonia can slow your progress to a crawl. The other is Argentine motorists: on many of the country's straight, narrow, two-lane highways, they can be a serious hazard to cyclists. Make yourself as visible as possible, and wear a helmet.

Bring an adequate repair kit and extra parts (and the know-how to use them) and stock up on good maps, which is usually easier to do once you're in Argentina. Always confirm directions and inquire about conditions locally; maps can be unreliable and conditions change regularly. In Patagonia, a windbreaker and warm clothing are essential. Don't expect much traffic on some back roads.

There are some good places around the country in which to spin your wheels, including Argentina's quintessential road trip, Ruta Nacional 40.

Rental

Bicycle rentals (mostly mountain bikes) are available in many popular tourist destinations, such as along the Atlantic Coast, Mendoza, Bariloche and other towns throughout the Lake District and Córdoba's Central Sierras. Prices are by the hour or day, and are affordable.

Purchase

Many towns have bike shops, but high-quality bikes are

expensive, and repair parts can be hard to come by. If you do decide to buy while you're here, you're best off doing so in Buenos Aires – selection in other major cities can be pretty slim. Prices for an imported bike (which you'll want if you're doing serious cycling) are much higher than in their country of origin.

Boat

Opportunities for boat or river travel in and around Argentina are limited, though there are regular international services to/from Uruguay and to/from Chile via the Lake District. Further south, from Ushuaia, operators offer boat trips on the Beagle Channel in Tierra del Fuego.

Otherwise, if you must be on the water, head to the Buenos Aires suburb of Tigre, where there are numerous boat excursions around the delta of the Río de la Plata.

Bus

If you're doing any serious traveling around Argentina, you'll become very familiar with the country's excellent bus network, which reaches almost everywhere. Long-distance buses (known as *micros*) are fast, surprisingly comfortable and can be a rather luxurious experience. It's the way most Argentines get around. Larger luggage is stowed in the hold below, security is generally good (especially on the 1st-class buses) and attendants tag your bags. If you have a long way to go – say, Buenos Aires to Mendoza – overnight buses are the way to go, saving you a night's accommodations and leaving you with the daylight hours for fun.

Most cities and towns have a central bus terminal where each company has its own ticket window. Some companies post schedules prominently, and the ticket price and departure time is always on the ticket you buy. Expect restrooms, left luggage, fast-food stalls, kiosks and newspaper vendors inside or near almost every large terminal. In tourist destination cities they'll often have a tourist information office. There are generally few if any hotel touts or other traveler-hassling types at terminals; El Calafate is one notable exception.

Two websites that sell long-distance bus ticket online (and without commission) are www.plataforma10.com and www.omnilineas.com.

Classes & Costs

Most bus lines have modern coaches with spacious, comfortable seats, large windows, air-conditioning, TVs, toilets (though don't expect luxury here – and bring toilet paper) and sometimes an attendant serving coffee and snacks.

On overnight trips it's well worth the extra pesos to go *coche cama* (sleeper class), though the cheaper *semi-cama* (semisleeper) is definitely manageable. In *coche cama* seats are wider, recline almost flat and are far more comfortable. For even more luxury there's *ejecutivo* (executive) which is available on a few popular runs. If pinching pesos, *común* (common) is the cheapest class. For trips less than about five hours, there's usually no choice and buses are *común* or *semi-cama*, which are both usually just fine.

Bus fares vary widely depending on season, class and company. Patagonia runs tend to be the most expensive. Many companies accept credit cards.

Reservations

Often you don't need to buy bus tickets beforehand unless you're traveling on a Friday between major cities, when overnight *coche cama* services sell out fast. During holiday stretches, such as late December through February, July and August, tickets sell quickly so buy ahead of time. As soon as you arrive somewhere, especially if it's a town with limited services, find out which companies go to your next destination and when, and plan your trip.

When the bus terminal is on the outskirts of a big town or city, there are often downtown agencies selling tickets without commission. Ask at your hotel.

Seasonal Services

In the Lake District and northern Patagonia, bus services are good during summer (November through March), when there are many microbus routes to campgrounds, along lake circuits, to trail heads and to other destinations popular with tourists. Outside summer, however, these services slow way down.

In Patagonia the famed stretch of RN40, or Ruta Nacional Cuarenta (Route 40), was once infrequently traveled and rough – though now much of it is paved (though it's still good to have a 4WD for side roads). However, there's still little public transport, and it's mostly via expensive, summertime microbus 'tours.'

Car & Motorcycle

Because Argentina is so large, many parts are accessible only by private vehicle, despite the country's extensive public transport system. This is especially true in Patagonia, where distances are great and buses can be infrequent.

Automobile Associations

Whenever driving in Argentina, it's worth being a member of the **Automóvil Club Argentino** (ACA; www.aca.org.ar), which has offices, gas stations and garages throughout the country and offers road service and towing in and around major destinations. ACA recognizes members of most overseas auto clubs and grants them privileges including road service and discounts on maps and accommodations. Bring your card.

Bringing Your Own Vehicle

Chile is probably the best country on the continent for shipping a vehicle from overseas, though Argentina is feasible. Getting the vehicle out of customs typically involves routine but time-consuming paperwork.

Driver's License & Documents

Technically you're supposed to have an International Driving Permit to supplement your national or state driver's license (though you can rent a car without one). If you are stopped, police will inspect your automobile registration and insurance and tax documents, all of which must be up to date.

Drivers of Argentine vehicles must carry their title document (*tarjeta verde* or 'green card'); if it's a rental, make sure it's in the glove box. For foreign vehicles, customs permission is the acceptable substitute. Liability insurance is obligatory, and police often ask to see proof of insurance at checkpoints.

Fuel

Nafta (gas) prices are more expensive than the US. Avoid *común* (regular) as it's usually low quality. Super and premium are better choices. In Patagonia gas prices are about a third less than elsewhere. *Estaciones de servicio* (gas stations) are fairly common, but outside the cities keep an eye on your gas gauge. In Patagonia it's a good idea to carry extra fuel.

Insurance

Liability insurance is obligatory in Argentina, and police ask to see proof of insurance at checkpoints. If you plan on taking the car to neighboring countries, make sure it will remain covered (you'll have to pay extra). Among the reputable insurers in Argentina are **Mapfre** (www.mapfre.com.ar) and **ACA** (www.aca.org.ar).

Rental

To rent a car, you must be at least 21 years of age and have a credit card and valid driver's license from your country. Agencies rarely ask for an International Driving Permit.

When you rent a vehicle find out how many kilometers are included. Unlimited-kilometer deals exist but are usually much more expensive, depending on the destination. Reserving a car with one of the major international agencies in your home country often gets you lower rates; you can also try online sites like www.despegar.com or www.webcarhire.com.

One of the cheapest places to rent a car is Bariloche; if you're heading to Patagonia for example, this is a good place to rent. Taking a rental car out of Argentina is not usually allowed.

For motorcycle rentals, you must be at least 25 years of age and head to **Motocare** (☎4761-2696; www.motocare.com.ar/rental; Echeverria 738, Vicente Lopez) located in Buenos Aires or Neuquén. Honda Transalps 700 are available; bring your own helmet and riding gear. For driving outside big cities only.

Purchase

Purchasing a vehicle in Argentina can be complicated for foreigners. This usually involves having a permanent local address, obtaining a CDI (a tax ID number) and paying for the vehicle in cash. To buy a used vehicle, you must transfer the title at a title transfer office, with the current owner and all his/her proper papers present. Make sure all licenses, unpaid tickets and taxes have been paid.

Speaking Spanish helps. Getting insurance without a DNI (national document) can be difficult but not impossible. As a foreigner without a DNI you may own a vehicle in Argentina; however, you theoretically cannot take it out of the country without a notarized authorization, which can be difficult to obtain.

It's wise to supplement this information with your own current research.

Road Rules & Hazards

Anyone considering driving in Argentina should know that Argentine drivers are aggressive and commonly ignore speed limits, road signs and even traffic signals. Night driving is not recommended; in many regions animals hang out on the road for warmth.

Have on hand some emergency reflectors *(balizas)* and a fire extinguisher *(matafuego)*. Headrests are required for the driver and passengers, and seatbelts are obligatory (though few wear them). Motorcycle helmets are also obligatory, although this law is rarely enforced.

A HANDY WEBSITE FOR DRIVERS

A very handy website for those driving around Argentina is www.ruta0.com. Among other things, you can punch in two destinations and get the recommended routes (and whether they're paved or not), distances (in kilometers), driving times and even how much it will cost in gas consumption. Now if it could only warn you where to avoid those crazy Argentine drivers.

You won't often see police patrolling the highways, but might meet them at major intersections and roadside checkpoints where they conduct meticulous document and equipment checks. Sometimes these checks are pretexts for graft. If you are uncertain about your rights, politely state your intention to contact your embassy or consulate. If you *do* want to pay a bribe for the sake of expediency, ask '*¿Puedo pagar la multa ahora?*' ('Can I pay the fine now?').

Hitchhiking

Hitchhiking *(hacer dedo)* is never entirely safe in any country in the world. Travelers who decide to hitch should understand that they are taking a small but potentially serious risk. People who do choose to hitch will be safer if they travel in pairs and let someone know where they are planning to go.

Along with Chile, Argentina is probably the best country for hitching in all of South America. The major drawback is that Argentine vehicles are often stuffed full with families and children, but truckers will sometimes pick up backpackers. A good place to ask is at *estaciones de servicio* at the outskirts of large Argentine cities, where truckers gas up their vehicles.

Women can and do hitchhike alone, but should exercise caution and especially avoid getting into a car with more than one man. In Patagonia, where distances are great and vehicles few, hitchers should expect long waits and carry warm, windproof clothing and refreshments.

Having a sign will improve your chances for a pickup, especially if it says something like *visitando Argentina de Canada* (visiting Argentina from Canada), rather than just a destination. Argentines are fascinated by foreigners.

For good information (in Spanish) see www.autostopargentina.com.ar, or try www.wander-argentina.com/hitchhiking-in-argentina.

Local Transportation

Bus

Local Argentine buses, called *colectivos,* are notorious for charging down the street and spewing clouds of black smoke while traveling at breakneck speeds. Riding on them is a good way to see the cities and get around, providing you can sort out the often complex bus systems. Buses are clearly numbered and usually carry a placard indicating their final destination. Sometimes, identically numbered buses serve slightly different routes (especially in big cities), so pay attention to the placards. To ask 'Does this bus go (to the town center)?' say '*¿Va este colectivo (al centro)?*'

Most city buses operate on coins; you pay as you board. In some cities, such as Mendoza or Mar del Plata, you must buy prepaid bus cards, purchased at many kiosks.

Subway

Buenos Aires is the only Argentine city with a subway system (known as the Subte), and it's the quickest and cheapest way of getting around the city center.

Taxi & Remise

The people of Buenos Aires make frequent use of taxis, which are digitally metered and cheap by US and European standards. Outside the capital, meters are common but not universal, and you'll need to agree on a fare in advance.

Where public transportation is scarce it's possible to hire a taxi or *remise* with driver for the day. This can be especially convenient and economical for a group, especially for taking an area tour. Always negotiate the fee in advance.

Remises are unmarked radio taxis, usually without meters, that have fixed fares (comparable to taxis) within a given zone. Any business will phone one for you if you ask.

Train

For many years there were major reductions in long-distance train service in Argentina, but recent years have seen some rail lines being progressively reopened. A good source for information is www.seat61.com/south-america.htm.

Trains continue to serve most of Buenos Aires and some surrounding provinces. During the holiday periods, such as Christmas or national holidays, buy tickets in advance. Train fares tend to be lower than comparable bus fares, but trains are slower and there are fewer departure times and destinations. Long-distance trains have sleepers.

Train buffs will want to take the narrow-gauge *La Trochita*, which runs 20km between Esquel and Nahuel Pan. Another legendary ride is Salta's touristy but spectacular *Tren a las Nubes* (Train to the Clouds), which at one point spans a desert canyon at the altitude of 4220m – though it's famously unreliable. And finally, the scenic *Tren Patagónico* connects Bariloche to Viedma – though it was suspended at research time (check ahead).

Language

Latin American Spanish pronunciation is easy, as most sounds have equivalents in English. Read our coloured pronunciation guides as if they were English, and you'll be understood. Note that kh is a throaty sound (like the 'ch' in the Scottish *loch*), v and b are like a soft English 'v' (between a 'v' and a 'b'), and r is strongly rolled. Also note that the letters *ll* (pronounced ly or simplified to y in most parts of Latin America) and *y* are pronounced like the 's' in 'measure' or the 'sh' in 'shut' in Argentina, which gives the language its very own local flavor. In this chapter, we've used the symbol sh to represent this sound. You'll get used to this very quickly listening to and taking your cues from the locals.

The stressed syllables are indicated with an acute accent in written Spanish (eg *días*) and with italics in our pronunciation guides.

The polite form is used in this chapter; where both polite and informal options are given, they are indicated by the abbreviations 'pol' and 'inf'. Where necessary, both masculine and feminine forms of words are included, separated by a slash and with the masculine form first, eg *perdido/a* (m/f).

BASICS

Hello.	*Hola.*	o·la
Goodbye.	*Adiós./Chau.*	a·*dyos*/chow
How are you?	*¿Qué tal?*	ke tal
Fine, thanks.	*Bien, gracias.*	byen *gra*·syas
Excuse me.	*Perdón.*	per·*don*
Sorry.	*Lo siento.*	lo *syen*·to
Please.	*Por favor.*	por fa·*vor*
Thank you.	*Gracias.*	*gra*·syas
You're welcome.	*De nada.*	de *na*·da
Yes./No.	*Sí./No.*	see/no

My name is ...
Me llamo ... — me *sha*·mo ...

What's your name?
¿Cómo se llama Usted? — *ko*·mo se *sha*·ma oo·*ste* (pol)
¿Cómo te llamas? — *ko*·mo te *sha*·mas (inf)

Do you speak English?
¿Habla inglés? — *a*·bla een·*gles* (pol)
¿Hablas inglés? — *a*·blas een·*gles* (inf)

I don't understand.
Yo no entiendo. — yo no en·*tyen*·do

> **WANT MORE?**
>
> For in-depth language information and handy phrases, check out Lonely Planet's *Latin American Spanish Phrasebook*. You'll find it at **shop.lonelyplanet.com**, or you can buy Lonely Planet's iPhone phrasebooks at the Apple App Store.

ACCOMMODATIONS

I'd like a ... room.	*Quisiera una habitación ...*	kee·*sye*·ra *oo*·na a·bee·ta·*syon* ...
single	*individual*	een·dee·vee·*dwal*
double	*doble*	*do*·ble

How much is it per night/person?
¿Cuánto cuesta por noche/persona? — *kwan*·to *kwes*·ta por *no*·che/per·*so*·na

Does it include breakfast?
¿Incluye el desayuno? — een·*kloo*·she el de·sa·*shoo*·no

campsite	*terreno de cámping*	te·*re*·no de *kam*·peeng
hotel	*hotel*	o·*tel*
guesthouse	*hostería*	os·te·*ree*·a
youth hostel	*albergue juvenil*	al·*ber*·ge khoo·ve·*neel*

air-con	*aire acondicionado*	ai·re a·kon·dee·syo·*na*·do
bathroom	*baño*	*ba*·nyo
bed	*cama*	*ka*·ma
window	*ventana*	ven·*ta*·na

DIRECTIONS

Where's ...?	
¿Dónde está ...?	*don*·de es·*ta* ...
What's the address?	
¿Cuál es la dirección?	kwal es la dee·rek·*syon*
Could you please write it down?	
¿Puede escribirlo, por favor?	*pwe*·de es·kree·*beer*·lo por fa·*vor*
Can you show me (on the map)?	
¿Me lo puede indicar (en el mapa)?	me lo *pwe*·de een·dee·*kar* (en el *ma*·pa)

at the corner	*en la esquina*	en la es·*kee*·na
at the traffic lights	*en el semáforo*	en el se·*ma*·fo·ro
behind ...	*detrás de ...*	de·*tras* de ...
in front of ...	*enfrente de ...*	en·*fren*·te de ...
left	*izquierda*	ees·*kyer*·da
next to ...	*al lado de ...*	al *la*·do de ...
opposite ...	*frente a ...*	*fren*·te a ...
right	*derecha*	de·*re*·cha
straight ahead	*todo recto*	*to*·do *rek*·to

EATING & DRINKING

Can I see the menu, please?	
¿Puedo ver el menú, por favor?	*pwe*·do ver el me·*noo* por fa·*vor*
What would you recommend?	
¿Qué me recomienda?	ke me re·ko·*myen*·da
Do you have vegetarian food?	
¿Tienen comida vegetariana?	*tye*·nen ko·*mee*·da ve·khe·ta·*rya*·na
I don't eat (red meat).	
No como (carne roja).	no *ko*·mo (*kar*·ne *ro*·kha)
That was delicious!	
¡Estaba buenísimo!	es·*ta*·ba bwe·*nee*·see·mo
Cheers!	
¡Salud!	sa·*loo*
The bill, please.	
La cuenta, por favor.	la *kwen*·ta por fa·*vor*

I'd like a table for ...	*Quisiera una mesa para ...*	kee·*sye*·ra *oo*·na *me*·sa *pa*·ra ...
(eight) o'clock	*las (ocho)*	las (*o*·cho)
(two) people	*(dos) personas*	(dos) per·*so*·nas

LUNFARDO

Below are are some of the spicier *lunfardo* (slang) terms you may hear on your travels in Argentina.

boliche – disco or nightclub

boludo – jerk, asshole, idiot; often used in a friendly fashion, but a deep insult to a stranger

bondi – bus

buena onda – good vibes

carajo – asshole, prick; bloody hell

chabón/chabona – kid, guy/girl (term of endearment)

che – hey

diez puntos – OK, cool, fine (literally '10 points')

fiaca – laziness

guita – money

laburo – job

macanudo – great, fabulous

mango – one peso

masa – a great, cool thing

mina – woman

morfar – eat

pendejo – idiot

piba/pibe – cool young guy/girl

piola – cool, clever

pucho – cigarette

re – very, eg *re interestante* (very interesting)

trucho – fake , imitation , bad quality

¡Ponete las pilas! – Get on with it! (literally 'Put in the batteries!')

Me mataste. – I don't know; I have no idea. (literally 'You've killed me')

Le faltan un par de jugadores. – He's not playing with a full deck. (literally 'He's a couple of players short')

che boludo – The most *porteño* phrase on earth. Ask a friendly local youth to explain.

Key Words

appetisers	*aperitivos*	a·pe·ree·*tee*·vos
bottle	*botella*	bo·*te*·sha
bowl	*bol*	bol
breakfast	*desayuno*	de·sa·*shoo*·no
children's menu	*menú infantil*	me·*noo* een·fan·*teel*
(too) cold	*(muy) frío*	(mooy) *free*·o
dinner	*cena*	*se*·na
food	*comida*	ko·*mee*·da

fork	*tenedor*	te·ne·*dor*
glass	*vaso*	*va*·so
hot (warm)	*caliente*	ka·*lyen*·te
knife	*cuchillo*	koo·*chee*·yo
lunch	*almuerzo*	al·*mwer*·so
main course	*plato principal*	*pla*·to preen·see·*pal*
plate	*plato*	*pla*·to
restaurant	*restaurante*	res·tow·*ran*·te
spoon	*cuchara*	koo·*cha*·ra
with/without	*con/sin*	kon/seen

Meat & Fish

beef	*carne de vaca*	*kar*·ne de *va*·ka
chicken	*pollo*	*po*·sho
duck	*pato*	*pa*·to
fish	*pescado*	pes·*ka*·do
lamb	*cordero*	kor·*de*·ro
pork	*cerdo*	*ser*·do
turkey	*pavo*	*pa*·vo
veal	*ternera*	ter·*ne*·ra

Fruit & Vegetables

apple	*manzana*	man·*sa*·na
apricot	*damasco*	da·*mas*·ko
artichoke	*alcaucil*	al·kow·*seel*
asparagus	*espárragos*	es·*pa*·ra·gos
banana	*banana*	ba·*na*·na
beans	*chauchas*	*chow*·chas
beetroot	*remolacha*	re·mo·*la*·cha
cabbage	*repollo*	re·*po*·sho
carrot	*zanahoria*	sa·na·*o*·rya
celery	*apio*	*a*·pyo
cherry	*cereza*	se·*re*·sa
corn	*choclo*	*cho*·klo
cucumber	*pepino*	pe·*pee*·no
fruit	*fruta*	*froo*·ta
grape	*uvas*	*oo*·vas
lemon	*limón*	lee·*mon*
lentils	*lentejas*	len·*te*·khas
lettuce	*lechuga*	le·*choo*·ga
mushroom	*champiñón*	cham·pee·*nyon*
nuts	*nueces*	*nwe*·ses
onion	*cebolla*	se·*bo*·sha
orange	*naranja*	na·*ran*·kha
peach	*durazno*	doo·*ras*·no
peas	*arvejas*	ar·*ve*·khas
(red/green) pepper	*pimiento (rojo/verde)*	pee·*myen*·to (*ro*·kho/*ver*·de)
pineapple	*ananá*	a·na·*na*
plum	*ciruela*	seer·*we*·la
potato	*papa*	*pa*·pa
pumpkin	*zapallo*	sa·*pa*·sho
spinach	*espinacas*	es·pee·*na*·kas
strawberry	*frutilla*	froo·*tee*·sha
tomato	*tomate*	to·*ma*·te
vegetable	*verdura*	ver·*doo*·ra
watermelon	*sandía*	san·*dee*·a

Other

bread	*pan*	pan
butter	*manteca*	man·*te*·ka
cheese	*queso*	*ke*·so

EL VOSEO

Spanish in the Río de la Plata region differs from that of Spain and the rest of the Americas, most notably in the use of the informal form of 'you'. Instead of *tuteo* (the use of *tú*), Argentines commonly speak with *voseo* (the use of *vos*), a relic from 16th-century Spanish requiring slightly different grammar. All verbs change in spelling, stress and pronunciation. Examples of verbs ending in *-ar*, *-er* and *-ir* are given below – the *tú* forms are included to illustrate the contrast. Imperative forms (commands) also differ, but negative imperatives are identical in *tuteo* and *voseo*.

The Spanish phrases in this chapter use the *vos* form. An Argentine inviting a foreigner to address him or her informally will say *Me podés tutear* (literally 'You can address me with *tú*'), even though they'll use the *vos* forms in subsequent conversation.

Verb	Tuteo	Voseo
hablar (speak): You speak./Speak!	*Tú hablas./¡Habla!*	*Vos hablás./¡Hablá!*
comer (eat): You eat./Eat!	*Tú comes./¡Come!*	*Vos comés./¡Comé!*
venir (come): You come./Come!	*Tú vienes./¡Ven!*	*Vos venís./¡Vení!*

egg	*huevo*	we·vo
honey	*miel*	myel
jam	*mermelada*	mer·me·*la*·da
oil	*aceite*	a·*sey*·te
pasta	*pasta*	*pas*·ta
pepper	*pimienta*	pee·*myen*·ta
rice	*arroz*	a·*ros*
salt	*sal*	sal
sugar	*azúcar*	a·*soo*·kar
vinegar	*vinagre*	vee·*na*·gre

Drinks

beer	*cerveza*	ser·*ve*·sa
coffee	*café*	ka·*fe*
(orange) juice	*jugo (de naranja)*	*khoo*·go (de na·*ran*·kha)
milk	*leche*	*le*·che
tea	*té*	te
(mineral) water	*agua (mineral)*	*a*·gwa (mee·ne·*ral*)
(red/white) wine	*vino (tinto/ blanco)*	*vee*·no (*teen*·to/ *blan*·ko)

EMERGENCIES

Help!	*¡Socorro!*	so·*ko*·ro
Go away!	*¡Vete!*	*ve*·te
Call ...!	*¡Llame a ...!*	*sha*·me a ...
a doctor	*un médico*	oon *me*·dee·ko
the police	*la policía*	la po·lee·*see*·a

I'm lost.
Estoy perdido/a. es·*toy* per·*dee*·do/a (m/f)

I'm ill.
Estoy enfermo/a. es·*toy* en·*fer*·mo/a (m/f)

I'm allergic to (antibiotics).
Soy alérgico/a a (los antibióticos). soy a·*ler*·khee·ko/a a (los an·tee·*byo*·tee·kos) (m/f)

Where are the toilets?
¿Dónde están los baños? *don*·de es·*tan* los *ba*·nyos

Question Words

How?	*¿Cómo?*	*ko*·mo
What?	*¿Qué?*	ke
When?	*¿Cuándo?*	*kwan*·do
Where?	*¿Dónde?*	*don*·de
Who?	*¿Quién?*	kyen
Why?	*¿Por qué?*	por ke

Signs

Abierto	Open
Cerrado	Closed
Entrada	Entrance
Hombres/Varones	Men
Mujeres/Damas	Women
Prohibido	Prohibited
Salida	Exit
Servicios/Baños	Toilets

SHOPPING & SERVICES

I'd like to buy ...
Quisiera comprar ... kee·*sye*·ra kom·*prar* ...

I'm just looking.
Sólo estoy mirando. *so*·lo es·*toy* mee·*ran*·do

Can I look at it?
¿Puedo verlo? *pwe*·do *ver*·lo

How much is it?
¿Cuánto cuesta? *kwan*·to *kwes*·ta

That's too expensive.
Es muy caro. es mooy *ka*·ro

Can you lower the price?
¿Podría bajar un poco el precio? po·*dree*·a ba·*khar* oon *po*·ko el *pre*·syo

There's a mistake in the bill.
Hay un error en la cuenta. ai oon e·*ror* en la *kwen*·ta

ATM	*cajero automático*	ka·*khe*·ro ow·to·*ma*·tee·ko
credit card	*tarjeta de crédito*	tar·*khe*·ta de *kre*·dee·to
internet cafe	*cibercafé*	see·ber·ka·*fe*
market	*mercado*	mer·*ka*·do
post office	*correos*	ko·*re*·os
tourist office	*oficina de turismo*	o·fee·*see*·na de too·*rees*·mo

TIME & DATES

What time is it?	*¿Qué hora es?*	ke *o*·ra es
It's (10) o'clock.	*Son (las diez).*	son (las dyes)
It's half past (one).	*Es (la una) y media.*	es (la *oo*·na) ee *me*·dya
morning	*mañana*	ma·*nya*·na
afternoon	*tarde*	*tar*·de
evening	*noche*	*no*·che
yesterday	*ayer*	a·*sher*
today	*hoy*	oy
tomorrow	*mañana*	ma·*nya*·na

Monday	*lunes*	*loo*·nes
Tuesday	*martes*	*mar*·tes
Wednesday	*miércoles*	*myer*·ko·les
Thursday	*jueves*	*khwe*·ves
Friday	*viernes*	*vyer*·nes
Saturday	*sábado*	*sa*·ba·do
Sunday	*domingo*	do·*meen*·go

TRANSPORTATION

boat	*barco*	*bar*·ko
bus	*colectivo/ micro*	ko·lek·*tee*·vo/ *mee*·kro
plane	*avión*	a·*vyon*
train	*tren*	tren

first	*primero*	pree·*me*·ro
last	*último*	*ool*·tee·mo
next	*próximo*	*prok*·see·mo

A ... ticket, please.	*Un boleto de ..., por favor.*	oon bo·*lee*·to de ... por fa·*vor*
1st-class	*primera clase*	pree·*me*·ra *kla*·se
2nd-class	*segunda clase*	se·*goon*·da *kla*·se
one-way	*ida*	*ee*·da
return	*ida y vuelta*	*ee*·da ee *vwel*·ta

I want to go to ...
Quisiera ir a ... kee·*sye*·ra eer a ...

Does it stop at ...?
¿Para en ...? *pa*·ra en ...

What stop is this?
¿Cuál es esta parada? kwal es *es*·ta pa·*ra*·da

What time does it arrive/leave?
¿A qué hora llega/sale? a ke *o*·ra *she*·ga/*sa*·le

Please tell me when we get to ...
¿Puede avisarme cuando lleguemos a ...? *pwe*·de a·vee·*sar*·me *kwan*·do she·*ge*·mos a ...

I want to get off here.
Quiero bajarme aquí. *kye*·ro ba·*khar*·me a·*kee*

airport	*aeropuerto*	a·e·ro·*pwer*·to
bus stop	*parada de colectivo*	pa·*ra*·da de ko·lek·*tee*·vo
platform	*plataforma*	pla·ta·*for*·ma
ticket office	*taquilla*	ta·*kee*·sha
timetable	*horario*	o·*ra*·ryo
train station	*estación de trenes*	es·ta·*syon* de *tre*·nes

Numbers

1	*uno*	*oo*·no
2	*dos*	dos
3	*tres*	tres
4	*cuatro*	*kwa*·tro
5	*cinco*	*seen*·ko
6	*seis*	seys
7	*siete*	*sye*·te
8	*ocho*	*o*·cho
9	*nueve*	*nwe*·ve
10	*diez*	dyes
20	*veinte*	*veyn*·te
30	*treinta*	*treyn*·ta
40	*cuarenta*	kwa·*ren*·ta
50	*cincuenta*	seen·*kwen*·ta
60	*sesenta*	se·*sen*·ta
70	*setenta*	se·*ten*·ta
80	*ochenta*	o·*chen*·ta
90	*noventa*	no·*ven*·ta
100	*cien*	syen
1000	*mil*	meel

I'd like to hire a ...	*Quisiera alquilar ...*	kee·*sye*·ra al·kee·*lar* ...
4WD	*un todo-terreno*	oon to·do·te·*re*·no
bicycle	*una bicicleta*	*oo*·na bee·see·*kle*·ta
car	*un coche/ auto*	oon *ko*·che/ *aw*·to
motorcycle	*una moto*	*oo*·na *mo*·to

helmet	*casco*	*kas*·ko
hitchhike	*hacer dedo*	a·*ser de*·do
mechanic	*mecánico*	me·*ka*·nee·ko
petrol/gas	*nafta*	*naf*·ta
service station	*estación de servicio*	es·ta·*syon* de ser·*vee*·syo

Is this the road to ...?
¿Se va a ... por esta carretera? se va a ... por *es*·ta ka·re·*te*·ra

Can I park here?
¿Puedo estacionar acá? *pwe*·do e·sta·syo·*nar* a·*ka*

The car has broken down.
El coche se ha averiado. el *ko*·che se a a·ve·*rya*·do

I've run out of petrol.
Me he quedado sin nafta. me e ke·*da*·do seen *naf*·ta

I have a flat tyre.
Tengo una goma pinchada. *ten*·go *oo*·na *go*·ma peen·*cha*·da

GLOSSARY

aerosilla – chairlift
alcalde – mayor
alerce – large coniferous tree, resembling a California redwood, from which Argentina's Parque Nacional Los Alerces takes its name
arbolito – literally 'little tree'; a street moneychanger and to be avoided
arroyo – creek, stream
autopista – freeway or motorway

baliza – emergency reflector
balneario – any swimming or bathing area, including beach resorts
bandoneón – an accordion-like instrument used in tango music
barrio – neighborhood or borough of the city

cabildo – colonial town council; also, the building that housed the council
cajero automático – ATM
cambio – money-exchange office; also *casa de cambio*
campo – the countryside; alternately, a field or paddock
cartelera – an office selling discount tickets
casa de cambio – money-exchange office, often shortened to *cambio*
casa de familia – family accommodations
casa de gobierno – a government building
castellano – the term used for the Spanish language spoken throughout Latin America
catarata – waterfall
cerro – hill, mountain
certificado – certified mail
chacra – small, independent farm
coche cama – sleeper class on a train
coima – a bribe; one who solicits a bribe is a *coimero*
colectivo – local bus
combi – long-distance bus
común – common class on a train
correo – post office
costanera – seaside, riverside or lakeside road or walkway
criollo – a term used for any Latin American of European descent
cruce – crossroads

dique – a dam; the resultant reservoir is often used for recreational purposes; can also refer to a drydock

edificio – a building
ejecutivo – executive class on a train
esquina – street corner
estacion de servicio – gas station
estancia – extensive ranch for cattle or sheep; some are now open to tourists
este – east

feria – a street fair or street market
fútbol – soccer

horario – schedule

locutorio – private long-distance telephone office, often with fax and internet

manzana – literally 'apple'; also used to define one square block of a city
mercado artesanal – handicraft market
mestizo – a person of mixed Indian and Spanish descent
mirador – scenic viewpoint, usually on a hill but often in a building
municipalidad – city hall

nafta – gasoline or petrol
neumático – spare tire
norte – north

oeste – west

parada – a bus stop
paseo – an outing, such as a walk in the park or downtown
peatonal – pedestrian mall, usually in the downtown area of major Argentine cities
peña – club that hosts informal folk-music gatherings
piropo – a flirtatious remark
piso – floor
primera – 1st class on a train
propina – a tip, for example, in a restaurant or cinema
pulpería – a country store or tavern

quebrada – a canyon

rambla – boardwalk
rancho – a rural house, generally of adobe, with a thatched roof
recargo – additional charge, usually 10%, that many Argentine businesses add to credit-card transactions
refugio – a usually rustic shelter in a national park or remote area
remise – taxi
ripio – gravel
rotisería – takeout shop
rotonda – traffic circle, roundabout
RN – Ruta Nacional; a national highway
RP – Ruta Provincial; a provincial highway

s/n – sin número, indicating a street address without a number
semi-cama – semisleeper class on a train
sendero – a trail in the woods
sur – south

tarjeta magnética – magnetic bus card
tarjeta telefónica – telephone card

turista – 2nd class on a train, usually not very comfortable

zona franca – duty-free zone
zonda – a hot, dry wind descending from the Andes

FOOD GLOSSARY

a punto – cooked medium well (referring to steak)

agua de canilla – tap water (drinkable in BA)

agua mineral – mineral water, usually available *con/sin gas* (still/sparkling)

ajo – garlic

alfajor – two flat, soft cookies filled with *dulce de leche* and covered in chocolate or meringue

almuerzo – lunch

amargo – bitter

asado – Argentine barbecue (both the food and the event), often a family event on Sunday

bien cocido – well done (referring to steak)

bife (de chorizo/costilla/lomo) – (sirloin strip/T-bone/tenderloin) steak

bombilla – metal straw with filter for drinking *mate*

bondiola – cured pork shoulder

budín de pan – bread pudding

café – coffee

casero – homemade

carne – meat (usually beef)

cerdo – pork

cena – dinner

cerveza – beer

chimichurri – a spicy marinade for meat, usually made of parsley, garlic, spices and olive oil

chinchulines – intestines

choclo – corn

chopp – draft beer

choripán – a spicy sausage served in a bread roll

chorizo – sausage (note the difference from *bife de chorizo*)

comedor – basic cafeteria

confitería – a shop that serves quick meals

cortado – espresso with steamed milk added

costillas – short ribs

crudo – raw

cubierto – in restaurants, the cover charge you pay for utensil use and bread

desayuno – breakfast

dulce – sweet

dulce de leche – Argentina's national sweet, found in many desserts; a type of thick, milky caramel

empanada – meat or vegetable hand pie; popular Argentine snack

entrada – appetizer

entraña – skirt steak

facturas – pastries; also receipts

frito/a – fried

fruta – fruit

frutos secos – nuts (nuts are also called *nueces*)

helado – ice cream

heladería – an ice-cream shop

hielo – ice

hígado – liver

hongo – mushroom (also called champignon)

huevos – eggs

jamón – ham

jarra – pitcher

jengibre – ginger

jugo (exprimido) – juice (freshly squeezed)

jugoso – medium rare (referring to steak); also general term for juicy

lengua – tongue

lenguado – flounder (fish)

licuado – fruit shake

locro – a traditional meat and corn stew from northern Argentina

lomito – a steak sandwich

lomo – tenderloin

manteca – butter

mariscos – seafood

matambre – a thin cut of beef, sometimes made into a stuffed roll *(matambre relleno)*

mate – a gourd used for drinking *yerba mate* or the tea itself

medialuna (de manteca/de grasa) – croissant (sweet/savory)

merienda – afternoon tea

merluza – hake (fish)

mermelada – jam or jelly

miel – honey

milanesa – breaded cutlet (usually beef)

minuta – in a restaurant or *confitería*, a short order such as spaghetti or *milanesa*

mollejas – sweetbreads

morcilla – blood sausage

ñoquis – gnocchi

ojo de bife – rib-eye steak

pancho – hot dog

papas frita – french fries

parrillada – a mixed grill of steak and other beef cuts

parrilla – a restaurant specializing in steak dishes

pescado – fish

picada – a cheese and cured meat sample plate

pollo – chicken

postre – dessert

propina – tip (gratuity)

puchero – soup combining vegetables and meats, served with rice

recargo – an additional charge (such as for use of a credit card, usually about 10%)

rotisería – takeout shop

sandwiches de miga – thin sandwiches made from crustless white bread

sorrentino – a stuffed pasta, like ravioli but large and round

submarino – hot milk served with a bar of dark chocolate

tallarines – noodles

tenedor libre – literally 'free fork'; an all-you-can-eat restaurant

tira de asada – grilled beef ribs

vacio – flank steak

verduras – vegetables

vegetariano/a – vegetarian

vinoteca – wine bar

vino (blanco/tinto) – (red/white) wine

yerba mate – 'Paraguayan tea' *(Ilex paraguariensis)*, which Argentines and Uruguayans consume in very large amounts

Behind the Scenes

SEND US YOUR FEEDBACK

We love to hear from travelers – your comments keep us on our toes and help make our books better. Our well-traveled team reads every word on what you loved or loathed about this book. Although we cannot reply individually to your submissions, we always guarantee that your feedback goes straight to the appropriate authors, in time for the next edition. Each person who sends us information is thanked in the next edition – the most useful submissions are rewarded with a selection of digital PDF chapters.

Visit **lonelyplanet.com/contact** to submit your updates and suggestions or to ask for help. Our award-winning website also features inspirational travel stories, news and discussions.

Note: We may edit, reproduce and incorporate your comments in Lonely Planet products such as guidebooks, websites and digital products, so let us know if you don't want your comments reproduced or your name acknowledged. For a copy of our privacy policy visit lonelyplanet.com/privacy.

OUR READERS

Many thanks to the travelers who used the last edition and wrote to us with helpful hints, useful advice and interesting anecdotes: Gabriela Bosak, Eduardo Brito, Enrique de Larminat, Catherine Deschoenmaeker, Marjet Docter, Angelika Fenner, Jonathan Freeman, Micha George-McFarlane, Steffie Hendrix, John Jenkins, Vanessa Jones, Wancy Lam, Lone and Ronald Larsen, Tim Laslavic, Gabriela Las Heras, Bas de Lege, Alessandra Luppi, Margaret McAspurn, Christina Mønsted, Hugh Mullan, Guy Nicholson, Michael Perrett, Jonathan Schor, Ward Servaes, Brian Short, Carina Soderlund, Bob Stanley, Michael Stuber, John Tenny, Mark Tincombe, Ellen van den Berg, Christine Wegmann, Daniëlle Wolbers, Natasha Wright

AUTHOR THANKS

Sandra Bao

I'm grateful for the support over the years from my excellent ex-commissioning editor Kathleen Munnelly – I'll miss you. My co-authors were stellar and patient with all my demands, as usual. Also many thanks to Graciela and Silvia Guzmán, Lucas Markowiecki, Sylvia Zapiola, Madi Lang, Jed Rothenburg and Dan Perlman. Gustavo and Miriam were awesome for their companionship and opinions. Cariños to Elsa, Jorge, Fung and David Bao and Daniel. Finally, lots of love to my husband, Ben Greensfelder.

Gregor Clark

Muchísimas gracias to countless Uruguayans, Argentines and resident expatriates who shared their local knowledge with me, especially Judy in Tandil, the Draghi family in Areco, María, Giuseppe and Tonino in Mar del Plata, Stefano, Emanuela and Gioele in Punta del Diablo, Miguel and Monica at El Galope, Rodney and Lucia at La Sirena, Gloria in Colonia and Alain in Montevideo. Above all, enormous thanks to Kathleen Munnelly, who ably guided this book through so many editions; we will miss her.

Carolyn McCarthy

Big and heartfelt thanks go out to Sandra Bao, Lucas Vidgen, Estefanía, the Oszust family, Estancia la Oriental, Marcelo and Cecilia, Gaston, Alejandro and Frances, Astrid and Matías. Dedicated to the memory of gaucho Manuel Pardo, without whom the steppe is even emptier.

Andy Symington

I owe thanks to many helpful people along the way: remise drivers, tourist office staff, gomeros and more. Special thanks to Sebastián Clerico, Douglas Tompkins, Carolina Morgado, Jorge Guasp, Mauricio Pagani, Laura Hoogen, Tim Laslavic and staff in several tourist offices. Huge thanks and *un abrazo fuerte* to Kathleen

Munnelly. Thanks also to Sandra Bao and my fellow authors – Carolyn McCarthy in particular and Lucas Vidgen for the author summit. Back home, thanks to my family for their support, and for various kindnesses to Álvaro Falcó Prieto, Mike Burren and Elena Vázquez.

Lucas Vidgen

Thanks first and foremost to the Argentines for making a country that's such a joy to travel and work in. In Mendoza, Charlie O'Malley and Adam Stern were a great source of information and general gossip. A huge shout out to Vicky Toledo for patient explanations and ever-welcome insights. Silvia Lareo-Vazquez and Martin Mendel helped fill in some serious blanks. And as always, thanks to Sofía and Teresa for being there, and for being there when I got back.

ACKNOWLEDGMENTS

Climate map data adapted from Peel MC, Finlayson BL & McMahon TA (2007) 'Updated World Map of the Köppen-Geiger Climate Classification', Hydrology and Earth System Sciences, 11, 1633¬44.

Cover photograph: Iguazú falls, Iguazú National Park, Nigel Pavitt/AWL.

THIS BOOK

This 9th edition of Lonely Planet's *Argentina* guidebook was researched and written by Sandra Bao, Gregor Clark, Carolyn McCarthy, Andy Symington and Lucas Vidgen. The previous edition was written and researched by the same authoring team. This guidebook was commissioned in Lonely Planet's Oakland office, and produced by the following:

Commissioning Editor Kathleen Munnelly

Coordinating Editors Katie O'Connell, Kristin Odijk

Senior Cartographer Mark Griffiths

Book Designers Virginia Moreno, Wendy Wright

Senior Editors Karyn Noble, Catherine Naghten

Assisting Editors Carolyn Bain, Judith Bamber, Janice Bird, Kate James, Jodie Martire, Stephanie Ong, Jeanette Wall

Assisting Cartographer Rachael Imeson

Cover Researcher Naomi Parker

Language Content Branislava Vladisavljevic

Thanks to Anita Banh, Elin Berglund, Ryan Evans, Larissa Frost, Anna Harris, Genesys India, Jouve India, Elizabeth Jones, Alison Lyall, Wayne Murphy, Martine Power, Angela Tinson

Index

Map Pages **000**
Photo Pages **000**

Pages **000**
Pages **000**

p Pages **000**
'o Pages **000**

ap Pages **000**
to Pages **000**

Map Legend

Sights
- Beach
- Bird Sanctuary
- Buddhist
- Castle/Palace
- Christian
- Confucian
- Hindu
- Islamic
- Jain
- Jewish
- Monument
- Museum/Gallery/Historic Building
- Ruin
- Sento Hot Baths/Onsen
- Shinto
- Sikh
- Taoist
- Winery/Vineyard
- Zoo/Wildlife Sanctuary
- Other Sight

Activities, Courses & Tours
- Bodysurfing
- Diving
- Canoeing/Kayaking
- Course/Tour
- Skiing
- Snorkeling
- Surfing
- Swimming/Pool
- Walking
- Windsurfing
- Other Activity

Sleeping
- Sleeping
- Camping

Eating
- Eating

Drinking & Nightlife
- Drinking & Nightlife
- Cafe

Entertainment
- Entertainment

Shopping
- Shopping

Information
- Bank
- Embassy/Consulate
- Hospital/Medical
- Internet
- Police
- Post Office
- Telephone
- Toilet
- Tourist Information
- Other Information

Geographic
- Beach
- Hut/Shelter
- Lighthouse
- Lookout
- Mountain/Volcano
- Oasis
- Park
- Pass
- Picnic Area
- Waterfall

Population
- Capital (National)
- Capital (State/Province)
- City/Large Town
- Town/Village

Transport
- Airport
- Border crossing
- Bus
- Cable car/Funicular
- Cycling
- Ferry
- Metro station
- Monorail
- Parking
- Petrol station
- Subway/Subte station
- Taxi
- Train station/Railway
- Tram
- Underground station
- Other Transport

Note: Not all symbols displayed above appear on the maps in this book

Routes
- Tollway
- Freeway
- Primary
- Secondary
- Tertiary
- Lane
- Unsealed road
- Road under construction
- Plaza/Mall
- Steps
- Tunnel
- Pedestrian overpass
- Walking Tour
- Walking Tour detour
- Path/Walking Trail

Boundaries
- International
- State/Province
- Disputed
- Regional/Suburb
- Marine Park
- Cliff
- Wall

Hydrography
- River, Creek
- Intermittent River
- Canal
- Water
- Dry/Salt/Intermittent Lake
- Reef

Areas
- Airport/Runway
- Beach/Desert
- Cemetery (Christian)
- Cemetery (Other)
- Glacier
- Mudflat
- Park/Forest
- Sight (Building)
- Sportsground
- Swamp/Mangrove